P9-CRO-695

The LAYMAN'S BIBLE ENCYCLOPEDIA

The LAYMAN'S BIBLE ENCYCLOPEDIA

Non-Denominational, Biblically Centered,
Scholarly in Presentation,
Written for the High and Holy Purpose
of Encouraging Laymen to Read,
Study, and Understand the Scriptures

by WILLIAM C. MARTIN, M.A., B.D.

The Southwestern Company

NASHVILLE, TENNESSEE

Copyright © 1964, The Southwestern Company, Nashville, Tennessee

All Rights Reserved

Library of Congress Catalog Card Number: 64-15419

The Lakeside Press, R. R. Donnelley & Sons Company
Chicago, Illinois; Willard, Ohio; and Crawfordsville, Indiana
Printed in the United States of America R.R.D. 3-66

Foreword

THE CHIEF PURPOSE of this work is to provide a reference book on the Bible to meet the needs of the average layman. While it is true that almost all Bibles are supplied with references, they are not in such form as to be handled with ease and intelligence by all Bible readers. Often they are arranged in such a way that none but a minister or an advanced Bible student can follow them to advantage and get from them just exactly what is desired. Still more often they are not sufficiently full to meet the requirements of the person searching the Scriptures. A third difficulty is that, in going from one reference to another, the mind of the student becomes confused and the real end of research is lost in the maze of conflicting ideas and thoughts encountered by the searcher. This obstacle to the attainment of Biblical knowledge often confronts the trained intellect of the minister or the student. How much more of a barrier is it then to the untrained person seeking further and deeper acquaintance with the vast wealth of religious treasure and thought contained in the Holy Scriptures?

To overcome this difficulty many methods have been devised at various times, but only a few of them have proved successful. It seems to the author that the most effective of these is the setting out of the references in full. By this plan the reader has before his eyes just exactly what the Bible has to say upon a subject, thus doing away with long and confusing searches from book to book, chapter to chapter, and verse to verse, a task which often results in the searcher's losing the kernel of thought in the last reference read. This method has been followed in the *Layman's Bible Encyclopedia.* An attempt has been made to arrange all topics and references in such a manner that finding a given topic and reading the various references to it throughout the Bible will be a simple matter, well within the reach of any child who has learned to use a dictionary and other simple reference books.

Insofar as is practical, each person, place, or topic included has been explained before the references to it are given. Not every character or subject mentioned in the Bible has been dealt with in this book, but an earnest attempt has been made to include those which are likely to be of interest to the average Bible student. The author has utilized the best resources and research methods available to him. He has tried to combine the results of impartial Biblical scholarship with a sincere love and respect for the Bible as a vehicle for God's word. In many instances, subjects are treated upon which there are differences of thought according to differences in denominational belief. In no instance of this character has the author permitted himself to be influenced by considerations of denominational doctrine. It has been his sole aim to set forth material of a nature that should be of interest to all persons, no matter what their shade of faith.

It has seemed best to adopt the alphabetical arrangement in the treatment of the subjects discussed. In the handling of a subject a discussion is first given, and following this, in most cases, come the references to it, quoted in full and with book, chapter, and verse attached. These references are arranged, so far as is practical, in the order in which they appear in the Bible. In the case of a person, the references give an outline of his life. In the case of a topic, they are arranged under logical subdivisions, showing the various phases, attributes, or characteristics of it.

In a single book of this size, it is impossible to give every reference to every subject in full; however, care has been taken to give the more important ones and then, in many cases, to direct the reader to additional references of less importance.

Cross references are given wherever it is possible so to do, in order that the reader may keep in complete touch with any given subject by referring to collateral and related subjects. Careful study of these cross references will be found to be quite beneficial, throwing additional light upon the subject under consideration.

The index at the rear of the book can be of special use to the serious student. In addition to giving him the location of the major discussion of a subject, it will frequently direct him to other articles related to the subject in question, thus providing him with a wider perspective for study of the topic. In many cases, a subject has not been deemed important enough to require a separate article. Yet, by consulting the index, the reader will often be able to learn what the Bible has to say on these topics.

If used correctly, this book should enable the reader to study the Bible in a much more efficient manner than ever before. This is not intended to lure him into spending less time in Bible study. On the contrary, it is intended to give him a wider knowledge of the Bible in the same amount of time he now gives to its study, and to awaken his desire to drink more deeply of the thirst-quenching stream of truth which flows from its sacred pages.

Contents

Key to Pronunciation

ā	as in	fate
ä	"	far
â	"	fare
a	"	fat
ạ	"	fall
ȧ	"	senate
ch	"	church
dū̑	"	verdure
ē	"	me
ė	"	event
e	"	met

ẽ	as in	ever
g	"	go
ī	"	ice
i	"	pin
n	"	man
ō	"	old
ô	"	orb
o	"	not
ȯ	"	obey
oi	"	oil
o͞o	"	noon

o͝o	as in	book
ou	"	sound
sh	"	ship
th	"	thing
tū̑	"	culture
ū	"	use
û	"	urn
u	"	but
u̇	"	unite
y	"	yet
zu	"	azure

Abbreviations

AV	for	Authorized Version
RV	"	Revised Version
OT	"	Old Testament
NT	"	New Testament
Gen.	"	Genesis
Ex.	"	Exodus
Lev.	"	Leviticus
Num.	"	Numbers
Deut.	"	Deuteronomy
Josh.	"	Joshua
Judg.	"	Judges
Ruth	"	Ruth
1 Sam.	"	1 Samuel
2 Sam.	"	2 Samuel
1 Kin.	"	1 Kings
2 Kin.	"	2 Kings
1 Chr.	"	1 Chronicles
2 Chr.	"	2 Chronicles
Ezra	"	Ezra
Neh.	"	Nehemiah
Esth.	"	Esther
Job	"	Job
Psa.	"	Psalms
Prov.	"	Proverbs
Eccl.	"	Ecclesiastes
Song	"	Song of Solomon
Isa.	"	Isaiah
Jer.	"	Jeremiah
Lam.	"	Lamentations
Ezek.	"	Ezekiel
Dan.	"	Daniel
Hos.	"	Hosea
Joel	"	Joel
Amos	"	Amos
Obad.	for	Obadiah
Jonah	"	Jonah
Mic.	"	Micah
Nah.	"	Nahum
Hab.	"	Habakkuk
Zeph.	"	Zephaniah
Hag.	"	Haggai
Zech.	"	Zechariah
Mal.	"	Malachi
Matt.	"	Matthew
Mark	"	Mark
Luke	"	Luke
John	"	John
Acts	"	Acts
Rom.	"	Romans
1 Cor.	"	1 Corinthians
2 Cor.	"	2 Corinthians
Gal.	"	Galatians
Eph.	"	Ephesians
Phil.	"	Philippians
Col.	"	Colossians
1 Thess.	"	1 Thessalonians
2 Thess.	"	2 Thessalonians
1 Tim.	"	1 Timothy
2 Tim.	"	2 Timothy
Tit.	"	Titus
Philem.	"	Philemon
Heb.	"	Hebrews
Jas.	"	James
1 Pet.	"	1 Peter
2 Pet.	"	2 Peter
1 John	"	1 John
2 John	"	2 John
3 John	"	3 John
Jude	"	Jude
Rev.	"	Revelation
N	"	North
E	"	East
S	"	South
W	"	West

The LAYMAN'S BIBLE ENCYCLOPEDIA

The Layman's Bible Encyclopedia

AARON

[âr′un] The eldest son of Amram and Jochebed, direct descendants of Levi, and brother of Miriam and Moses. Aaron was married to Elisheba, by whom he had four sons, Nadab, Abihu, Eleazar and Ithamar. When Moses protested that he was "slow of speech" and would therefore be unable to serve as leader for the Israelites, Aaron was appointed as his "mouth", indicating that he was an eloquent man. In this capacity he aided Moses in bringing about the Exodus, both through speeches to the Israelites and appearances at the court of the Pharaoh. Throughout the rest of his life, he served as Moses' close companion and assistant.

Aaron is first pictured in an unfavorable light in the episode of the golden calf. After Moses remained on Mt. Sinai for many days, the people urged Aaron to make an image which they could worship. Gathering the gold which they brought to him, he fashioned a molten calf. The narrative states that they credited it with having delivered them from Egypt and made it the center of an orgiastic celebration. When confronted by Moses, Aaron weakly tried to shift the blame to the people. Despite his participation in this infamous affair, Aaron and his sons were anointed priests at the erection of the tabernacle. As high priest, Aaron alone was permitted to enter the Holy of Holies on the annual Day of Atonement.

After joining with Miriam in criticizing Moses for his Cushite wife (*see* MIRIAM), Aaron himself became the object of criticism in the rebellion led by Korah, Dathan, and Abiram (*see* KORAH), in which it was charged that he and Moses had unjustifiably usurped their positions of authority. It was only through the action of Aaron that the full punishment of God was averted on this occasion. He was then confirmed in his priestly office by the budding of his rod into a yielding almond tree.

After being denied entrance to Canaan because of his unbelief at Meribah, Aaron died and was buried on Mount Hor, having turned over his robes and office to his oldest living son, Eleazar, and thus founding in his family the succession to the high-priesthood. His death was mourned by Israel for thirty days. The priestly descendants of Aaron are sometimes referred to as Aaronites.

See PRIESTHOOD, MOSES

SCRIPTURE

Chosen to Aid Moses

Ex. 4 14 And the anger of the LORD was kindled against Moses, and he said, Is not Aaron the Levite thy brother? I know that he can speak well. And also, behold, he cometh forth to meet thee: and when he seeth thee, he will be glad in his heart.
15 And thou shalt speak unto him, and put words in his mouth: and I will be with thy mouth, and with his mouth, and will teach you what ye shall do. 16 And he shall be thy

spokesman unto the people: and he shall be, even he shall be to thee instead of a mouth, and thou shalt be to him instead of God.

27And the LORD said to Aaron, Go into the wilderness to meet Moses. And he went, and met him in the mount of God, and kissed him. 28And Moses told Aaron all the words of the LORD who had sent him, and all the signs which he had commanded him.

29And Moses and Aaron went, and gathered together all the elders of the children of Israel.

Ex. 5 1And afterward Moses and Aaron went in, and told Pharaoh, Thus saith the LORD God of Israel, Let my people go, that they may hold a feast unto me in the wilderness.

Works Miracles

Ex. 7 10And they did so as the LORD had commanded: and Aaron cast down his rod before Pharaoh, and before his servants, and it became a serpent. 20And Moses and Aaron did so, as the LORD commanded; and he lifted up the rod and smote the waters that were in the river, in the sight of Pharaoh, and in the sight of his servants; and all the waters that were in the river were turned into blood.

Ex. 8 6And Aaron stretched out his hand over the waters of Egypt; and the frogs came up, and covered the land of Egypt.

17And they did so; for Aaron stretched out his hand with his rod, and smote the dust of the earth, and it became lice in man and in beast: all the dust of the land became lice throughout all the land of Egypt.

Ex. 9 8And the LORD said unto Moses and unto Aaron, Take to you handfuls of ashes of the furnace, and let Moses sprinkle it toward the heaven in the sight of Pharaoh. 10And they took ashes of the furnace, and stood before Pharaoh; and Moses sprinkled it up toward heaven: and it became a boil breaking forth with blains upon man, and upon beast.

Holds Moses' Hands

Ex. 17 8Then came Amalek, and fought with Israel in Rephidim. 9And Moses said unto Joshua, Choose us out men, and go out, fight with Amalek: to-morrow I will stand on the top of the hill with the rod of God in mine hand. 11And it came to pass, when Moses held up his hand, that Israel prevailed: and when he let down his hand, Amalek prevailed. 12But Moses' hands were heavy; and they took a stone, and put it under him, and he sat thereon: and Aaron and Hur stayed up his hands, the one on the one side, and the other on the other side; and his hands were steady until the going down of the sun.

Appointment to Priesthood

Ex. 28 1And take thou unto thee Aaron thy brother, and his sons with him, from among the children of Israel, that he may minister unto me in the priest's office, even Aaron, Nadab and Abihu, Eleazar and Ithamar, Aaron's sons.

Lev. 10 8And the LORD spake unto Aaron, saying, 9Do not drink wine nor strong drink, thou, nor thy sons with thee, when ye go into the tabernacle of the congregation, lest ye die; it shall be a statute for ever throughout your generations.

Sins

MAKES THE GOLDEN CALF

Ex. 32 3And all the people brake off the golden ear-rings which were in their ears, and brought them unto Aaron. 4And he received them at their hand, and fashioned it with a graving tool, after he had made it a molten calf: and they said, These be thy gods, O Israel, which brought thee up out of the land of Egypt.

21 And Moses said unto Aaron, What did this people unto thee, that thou hast brought so great a sin upon them? 22 And Aaron said, Let not the anger of my lord wax hot: thou knowest the people, that they are set on mischief. 23 For they said unto me, Make us gods, which shall go before us: for as for this Moses, the man that brought us up out of the land of Egypt, we wot not what is become of him. 24 And I said unto them, Whosoever hath any gold, let them break it off. So they gave it me: then I cast it into the fire, and there came out this calf.

SPEAKS AGAINST MOSES

Num. 12 1 And Miriam and Aaron spake against Moses because of the Ethiopian woman whom he had married: for he had married an Ethiopian woman. 2 And they said, Hath the LORD indeed spoken only by Moses? hath he not spoken also by us? And the LORD heard it. 9 And the anger of the LORD was kindled against them; and he departed. 10 And the cloud departed from off the tabernacle; and behold, Miriam became leprous, white as snow: and Aaron looked upon Miriam, and behold, she was leprous. 11 And Aaron said unto Moses, Alas, my lord, I beseech thee, lay not the sin upon us, wherein we have done foolishly, and wherein we have sinned.

Stays Plague after Korah's Rebellion

Num. 16 1 Now Korah, the son of Izhar, the son of Kohath, the son of Levi; and Dathan and Abiram, the sons of Eliab; and On, the son of Peleth, sons of Reuben, took men: 2 And they rose up before Moses, with certain of the children of Israel, two hundred and fifty princes of the assembly, famous in the congregation, men of renown: 3 And they gathered themselves together against Moses and against Aaron, and said unto them, Ye take too much upon you, seeing all the congregation are holy, every one of them, and the LORD is among them: wherefore then lift ye up yourselves above the congregation of the LORD?

46 And Moses said unto Aaron, Take a censer, and put fire therein from off the altar, and put on incense, and go quickly unto the congregation, and make an atonement for them: for there is wrath gone out from the LORD; the plague is begun. 47 And Aaron took as Moses commanded, and ran into the midst of the congregation; and behold, the plague was begun among the people: and he put on incense, and made an atonement for the people. 48 And he stood between the dead and the living; and the plague was stayed.

Confirmed as High-Priest

Num. 17 8 And it came to pass, that on the morrow Moses went into the tabernacle of witness; and behold, the rod of Aaron for the house of Levi was budded, and brought forth buds, and bloomed blossoms, and yielded almonds.

Num. 18 1 And the LORD said unto Aaron, Thou, and thy sons, and thy father's house with thee, shall bear the iniquity of the sanctuary: and thou and thy sons with thee shall bear the iniquity of your priesthood.

Takes Part in Moses' Sin

Num. 20 7 And the LORD spake unto Moses, saying, 8 Take the rod, and gather thou the assembly together, thou and Aaron thy brother, and speak ye unto the rock before their eyes; and it shall give forth his water, and thou shalt bring forth to them water out of the rock: so thou shalt give the con-

gregation and their beasts drink. 9And
Moses took the rod from before the LORD,
as he commanded him. 10And Moses and
Aaron gathered the congregation together
before the rock, and he said unto them,
Hear now, ye rebels; must we fetch you
water out of this rock? 11And Moses lifted
up his hand, and with his rod he smote the
rock twice: and the water came out abundantly, and the congregation drank, and
their beasts also.
12And the LORD spake unto Moses and
Aaron, Because ye believed me not, to sanctify me in the eyes of the children of Israel,
therefore ye shall not bring this congregation into the land which I have given
them.

Death of Aaron

Num. 20 27And Moses did as the LORD
commanded: and they went up into mount
Hor in the sight of all the congregation.
28And Moses stripped Aaron of his garments, and put them upon Eleazar his son;
and Aaron died there in the top of the
mount: and Moses and Eleazar came down
from the mount.

REFERENCE: *Ex. 14:1-11; Ex. 29; Lev. 8; Psa. 105:26; 1 Chr. 6:49; Heb. 5:4.*

ABADDON

[a bad'on] A Hebrew word referring to the world of the dead, in its most dismal and destructive aspects. As used in *Rev. 9:11*, it refers not to the place of the dead, but to the angel who rules over it; the Greek equivalent of his name is Apollyon.

See HELL, HADES, SHEOL, GEHENNA

SCRIPTURE

Rev. 9 1And the fifth angel sounded,
and I saw a star fall from heaven unto the
earth: and to him was given the key of the
bottomless pit. 2And he opened the bottomless pit; and there arose a smoke out of
the pit, as the smoke of a great furnace;
and the sun and the air were darkened by
reason of the smoke of the pit. 3And there
came out of the smoke locusts upon the
earth: and unto them was given power,
as the scorpions of the earth have power.
11And they had a king over them, which is
the angel of the bottomless pit, whose
name in the Hebrew tongue is Abaddon,
but in the Greek tongue hath his name
Apollyon.

ABBA

[ab'a] A transliteration of the Aramaic form of the Hebrew word *ab*, meaning "father." Jesus used this term when he addressed God in prayer.

SCRIPTURE

Mark 14 36And he said, Abba, Father,
all things are possible unto thee; take away
this cup from me: nevertheless, not what I
will, but what thou wilt.
Rom. 8 15For ye have not received the
spirit of bondage again to fear; but ye have
received the Spirit of adoption, whereby
we cry, Abba, Father.
Gal. 4 6And because ye are sons, God
hath sent forth the Spirit of his Son into
your hearts, crying, Abba, Father.

ABEL

[ā b'l] The second son of Adam and Eve, and "a keeper of sheep." When he and his brother Cain, who was a farmer, offered sacrifice, God accepted Abel's offering, but for some reason rejected that of Cain; in jealous anger, Cain slew his brother. In the New Testament Abel is referred to as a type of innocent suffering.

See CAIN, ADAM, EVE

SCRIPTURE

Gen. 4 1And Adam knew Eve his wife;
and she conceived, and bare Cain, and said,

I have gotten a man from the LORD. 2And she again bare his brother Abel: and Abel was a keeper of sheep, but Cain was a tiller of the ground. 3And in process of time it came to pass, that Cain brought of the fruit of the ground an offering unto the LORD. 4And Abel, he also brought of the firstlings of his flock, and of the fat thereof. And the LORD had respect unto Abel, and to his offering. 5But unto Cain, and to his offering, he had not respect: and Cain was very wroth, and his countenance fell. 8And Cain talked with Abel his brother: and it came to pass, when they were in the field, that Cain rose up against Abel his brother, and slew him.

Heb. 11 4By faith Abel offered unto God a more excellent sacrifice than Cain, by which he obtained witness that he was righteous, God testifying of his gifts: and by it he being dead yet speaketh.

REFERENCE: *Matt. 23:35; Luke 11:51; Heb. 12: 24; 1 John 3:12.*

ABIATHAR

[a bī'a thar, ab i ā'thar] A priest in the lineage of Eli. Abiathar was the son of the high priest Ahimelech, and escaped to David when Saul massacred the priests at Nob. David and Abiathar apparently had a warm relationship; on several occasions the king consulted the LORD through the ephod which Abiathar had brought from Nob. Abiathar was made associate high priest with Zadok after David brought the ark to Jerusalem. These remained loyal to David during the revolt of Absalom. After David's death Abiathar was banished to Anathoth when he conspired to support Adonijah instead of Solomon in the struggle for David's throne.

See SOLOMON, ZADOK, ADONIJAH

SCRIPTURE

Survives Massacre at Nob

1 Sam. 22 18And the king said to Doeg, Turn thou, and fall upon the priests. And Doeg the Edomite turned, and he fell upon the priests, and slew on that day fourscore and five persons that did wear a linen ephod. 19And Nob, the city of the priests, smote he with the edge of the sword, both men and women, children and sucklings, and oxen, and asses, and sheep, with the edge of the sword.

20And one of the sons of Ahimelech the son of Ahitub, named Abiathar, escaped, and fled after David. 21And Abiathar shewed David that Saul had slain the LORD's priests. 22And David said unto Abiathar, I knew it that day, when Doeg the Edomite was there, that he would surely tell Saul: I have occasioned the death of all the persons of thy father's house. 23Abide thou with me, fear not: for he that seeketh my life seeketh thy life: but with me thou shalt be in safeguard.

Has Charge of the Ephod

1 Sam. 23 9And David knew that Saul secretly practised mischief against him; and he said to Abiathar the priest, Bring hither the ephod.

1 Sam. 30 7And David said to Abiathar the priest, Ahimelech's son, I pray thee bring me hither the ephod. And Abiathar brought thither the ephod to David.

Co-Priest with Zadok

2 Sam. 15 24And lo, Zadok also, and all the Levites were with him, bearing the ark of the covenant of God: and they set down the ark of God; and Abiathar went up, until all the people had done passing out of the city. 25And the king said unto Zadok, Carry back the ark of God into the city: if I shall find favour in the eyes of the LORD, he will bring me again, and shew me both it, and his habitation: 26But if he thus say, I have no delight in thee; behold, here am I, let him do to me as seemeth good unto him. 27The king said also unto Zadok the priest, Art not thou a seer? return into the city in peace, and your two sons with you, Ahimaaz thy son, and Jonathan the son of Abiathar. 28See, I will tarry in the plain of the wilderness, until there come word from you to certify me. 29Zadok therefore and Abiathar carried the ark of God again to Jerusalem: and they tarried there.

35And hast thou not there with thee Zadok and Abiathar the priests? therefore it shall be, that what thing soever thou shalt hear out of the king's house, thou shalt tell it to Zadok and Abiathar the priests. 36Behold, they have there with them their two sons, Ahimaaz Zadok's son, and Jonathan Abiathar's son; and by them ye shall send unto me everything that ye can hear.

Sides with Adonijah against Solomon

1 Kin. 1 7And he conferred with Joab the Son of Zeruiah, and with Abiathar the priest: and they following Adonijah helped him.

19And he hath slain oxen and fat cattle and sheep in abundance, and hath called all the sons of the king, and Abiathar the priest, and Joab the captain of the host: but Solomon thy servant hath he not called.

Banished by Solomon

1 Kin. 2 26And unto Abiathar the priest said the king, Get thee to Anathoth, unto thine own fields; for thou art worthy of death: but I will not at this time put thee to death, because thou barest the ark of the Lord God before David my father, and because thou hast been afflicted in all wherein my father was afflicted. 27So Solomon thrust out Abiathar from being priest unto the Lord; that he might fulfil the word of the Lord, which he spake concerning the house of Eli in Shiloh.

ABIGAIL

[ab′i gāl] The beautiful wife of Nabal, a rich shepherd of southern Judea. Nabal, a "churlish and evil" man, was shearing sheep in Carmel when David, encamped nearby, sent men to ask him for provisions. Nabal insultingly refused and thus stirred up the anger of David, who determined to take vengeance on him. David was stayed from his purpose through the prudent actions of Abigail, who met him with a large present and entreated him to overlook the actions of her foolish husband. When Abigail informed Nabal of these proceedings, he suffered a stroke and died within ten days. Abigail later became the wife of David and bore him a son, Chileab (also called Daniel).

Not to be confused with the wife of Nabal is a sister of David by the same name.

See Nabal

SCRIPTURE

Saves Nabal from Ruin

1 Sam. 25 1And Samuel died: and all the Israelites were gathered together, and lamented him, and buried him in his house at Ramah. And David arose, and went down to the wilderness of Paran. 2And there was a man in Maon, whose possessions were in Carmel; and the man was very great, and he had three thousand sheep, and a thousand goats: and he was shearing his sheep in Carmel. 3Now the name of the man was Nabal; and the name of his wife Abigail: and she was a woman of good understanding, and of a beautiful countenance: but the man was churlish and evil in his doings; and he was of the house of Caleb.

4And David heard in the wilderness that Nabal did shear his sheep. 5And David sent out ten young men, and David said unto the young men, Get you up to Carmel, and go to Nabal, and greet him in my name; 9And when David's young men came, they spake to Nabal according to all those words in the name of David, and ceased.

10 And Nabal answered David's servants, and said, Who is David? and who is the son of Jesse? there be many servants nowadays that break away every man from his master. 11 Shall I then take my bread, and my water, and my flesh that I have killed for my shearers, and give it unto men, whom I know not whence they be? 12 So David's young men turned their way, and went again, and came and told him all those sayings. 13 And David said unto his men, Gird ye on every man his sword. And they girded on every man his sword; and David also girded on his sword: and there went up after David about four hundred men; and two hundred abode by the stuff.

14 But one of the young men told Abigail, Nabal's wife, saying, Behold, David sent messengers out of the wilderness to salute our master; and he railed on them.

18 Then Abigail made haste, and took two hundred loaves, and two bottles of wine, and five sheep ready dressed, and five measures of parched corn, and a hundred clusters of raisins, and two hundred cakes of figs, and laid them on asses. 19 And she said unto her servants, Go on before me; behold, I come after you. But she told not her husband Nabal. 20 And it was so, as she rode on the ass, that she came down by the covert of the hill, and, behold, David and his men came down against her; and she met them. 23 And when Abigail saw David, she hasted, and lighted off the ass, and fell before David on her face, and bowed herself to the ground. 24 And fell at his feet, and said, Upon me, my lord, upon me let this iniquity be: and let thine handmaid, I pray thee, speak in thine audience, and hear the words of thine handmaid. 25 Let not my lord, I pray thee, regard this man of Belial, even Nabal: for as his name is, so is he: Nabal is his name, and folly is with him: but I thine handmaid saw not the young men of my lord, whom thou didst send. 26 Now therefore, my lord, as the LORD liveth, and as thy soul liveth, seeing the LORD hath withholden thee from coming to shed blood, and from avenging thyself with thine own hand, now let thine enemies and they that seek evil to my lord, be as Nabal. 27 And now this blessing which thine handmaid hath brought unto my lord, let it even be given unto the young men that follow my lord. 28 I pray thee, forgive the trespass of thine handmaid: for the LORD will certainly make my lord a sure house; because my lord fighteth the battles of the LORD, and evil hath not been found in thee all thy days.

32 And David said to Abigail, Blessed be the LORD God of Israel, which sent thee this day to meet me: 33 And blessed be thy advice, and blessed be thou, which hast kept me this day from coming to shed blood, and from avenging myself with mine own hand. 35 So David received of her hand that which she had brought him, and said unto her, Go up in peace to thine house; see, I have hearkened to thy voice, and have accepted thy person.

36 And Abigail came to Nabal; and, behold, he held a feast in his house, like the feast of a king; and Nabal's heart was merry within him, for he was very drunken: wherefore she told him nothing, less or more, until the morning light. 37 But it came to pass in the morning, when the wine was gone out of Nabal, and his wife had told him these things, that his heart died within him, and he became as a stone. 38 And it came to pass about ten days after, that the LORD smote Nabal, that he died.

Becomes David's Wife

1 Sam. 25 39 And when David heard that

Nabal was dead, he said, Blessed be the LORD, that hath pleaded the cause of my reproach from the hand of Nabal, and hath kept his servant from evil: for the LORD hath returned the wickedness of Nabal upon his own head. And David sent and communed with Abigail, to take her to him to wife. 40And when the servants of David were come to Abigail to Carmel, they spake unto her, saying, David sent us unto thee, to take thee to him to wife. 41And she arose, and bowed herself on her face to the earth, and said, Behold, let thine handmaid be a servant to wash the feet of the servants of my lord. 42And Abigail hasted, and arose, and rode upon an ass, with five damsels of hers that went after her: and she went after the messengers of David, and became his wife.

REFERENCE: *1 Sam. 27:3; 30:1-18; 2 Sam. 2:2; 3:3.*

ABIHU

[å bī′hū] The son of Aaron and Elisheba. Abihu was among the select leaders of Israel who accompanied Moses when he ascended Mt. Sinai to receive the Law from God. He was later chosen to be a priest and was struck dead along with his brother, Nadab, when they used "strange fire" in offering incense.

See NADAB

SCRIPTURE

Ex. 6 23And Aaron took him Elisheba daughter of Amminadab, sister of Naashon to wife; and she bare him Nadab and Abihu, Eleazar and Ithamar.

Ex. 24 9Then went up Moses, and Aaron, Nadab, and Abihu, and seventy of the elders of Israel.

Ex. 28 1And take thou unto thee Aaron thy brother, and his sons with him, from among the children of Israel, that he may minister unto me in the priest's office, even Aaron, Nadab and Abihu, Eleazar and Ithamar, Aaron's sons.

Lev. 10 1And Nadab and Abihu, the sons of Aaron, took either of them his censer, and put fire therein, and put incense thereon, and offered strange fire before the LORD, which he commanded them not. 2And there went out fire from the LORD, and devoured them, and they died before the LORD.

See Num. 3:2

ABIJAH

[a bī′jä] The son of Rehoboam and second king of Judah (915-913 BC). The only event of real interest in Abijah's short reign is a decisive victory which he gained over Northern Israel. (*See 2 Chr. 13*)

See KINGS

REFERENCE: *1 Chr. 3:10; 2 Chr. 11:20-14.*

ABIMELECH

[a bim′e lek] 1. The name, or perhaps the royal title, of the king of Philistia. Abraham and Isaac are both said to have deceived a Philistine king by this name by pretending that their wives were their sisters. In each case, the Philistine learned of the deception and was understandably vexed at the patriarchs. The similarity between the two stories is continued as both Abraham and Isaac made a covenant with Abimelech at Beersheba. It has been suggested that Abraham and Isaac dealt with two different kings, probably father and son. Other scholars have asserted a single occurrence was ascribed to both Abraham and Isaac.

2. The son of Gideon by his concubine. Abimelech aspired to the leadership of Shechem and, with the aid of his mother's relatives, gathered considerable support. He then murdered all of the seventy sons of Gideon except Jotham, who, after proclaiming the famous parable of the bramble from atop Mt. Gerizim, fled for his life. (*See* JOTHAM) With all of the legitimate successors to Gideon out of the way, the people of Shechem proclaimed Abimelech king. He reigned for three years, during which time he ruthlessly put

down a revolt engineered by Gaal, the son of Ebed. Abimelech met his death while attacking the city of Thebez; standing near the wall of the city he was struck by a millstone which a woman had thrown down. To avoid the shame of death at the hands of a woman, he commanded his armor-bearer to kill him with his sword. His death is referred to as fulfilling the "curse of Jotham."

SCRIPTURE

Abimelech King of Gerar

Gen. 20 [1]And Abraham journeyed from
thence toward the south country, and dwelt
between Kadesh and Shur, and sojourned
in Gerar. [2]And Abraham said of Sarah his
wife, She is my sister: and Abimelech king
of Gerar sent, and took Sarah. [3]But God
came to Abimelech in a dream by night,
and said to him, Behold, thou art but a
dead man, for the woman which thou hast
taken; for she is a man's wife. [4]But Abimelech had not come near her: and he said,
LORD, wilt thou slay also a righteous nation? [5]Said he not unto me, She is my sister? and she, even she herself said, He is
my brother: in the integrity of my heart
and innocency of my hands have I done
this. [6]And God said unto him in a dream,
Yea, I know that thou didst this in the integrity of thy heart; for I also withheld
thee from sinning against me: therefore
suffered I thee not to touch her. [7]Now
therefore restore the man his wife; for he
is a prophet, and he shall pray for thee, and
thou shalt live: and if thou restore her not,
know thou that thou shalt surely die, thou,
and all that are thine. [8]Therefore Abimelech rose early in the morning, and called
all his servants, and told all these things in
their ears: and the men were sore afraid.
[9]Then Abimelech called Abraham, and
said unto him, What hast thou done unto
us? and what have I offended thee, that
thou hast brought on me and on my kingdom a great sin? thou hast done deeds unto
me that ought not to be done. [14]And Abimelech took sheep, and oxen, and menservants, and womenservants, and gave them
unto Abraham, and restored him Sarah
his wife. [15]And Abimelech said, Behold,
my land is before thee: dwell where it
pleaseth thee. [16]And unto Sarah he said,
Behold, I have given thy brother a thousand pieces of silver: behold, he is to thee
a covering of the eyes, unto all that are
with thee, and with all other: thus she was
reproved.
[17]So Abraham prayed unto God: and
God healed Abimelech, and his wife, and
his maidservants; and they bare children.
[18]For the LORD had fast closed up all the
wombs of the house of Abimelech, because
of Sarah, Abraham's wife.

REFERENCE: *Gen. 21:22-34; 26:6-33.*

Abimelech King of Shechem

BECOMES KING

Judg. 9 [1]And Abimelech the son of Jerubbaal went to Shechem unto his mother's brethren, and communed with them,
and with all the family of the house of his
mother's father, saying, [2]Speak, I pray
you, in the ears of all the men of Shechem,
Whether is better for you, either that all
the sons of Jerubbaal, which are threescore
and ten persons, reign over you, or that
one reign over you? remember also that I
am your bone and your flesh. [3]And his
mother's brethren spake of him in the ears
of all the men of Shechem all these words:
and their hearts inclined to follow Abimelech; for they said, He is our brother.
[4]And they gave him threescore and ten
pieces of silver out of the house of Baal-
berith, wherewith Abimelech hired vain
and light persons, which followed him.

[5]And he went unto his father's house at Ophrah, and slew his brethren the sons of Jerubbaal, being threescore and ten persons, upon one stone: notwithstanding, yet Jotham the youngest son of Jerubbaal was left; for he hid himself. [6]And all the men of Shechem gathered together, and all the house of Millo, and went and made Abimelech king, by the plain of the pillar that was in Shechem.

QUELLS A REVOLT

Judg. 9 [22]When Abimelech had reigned three years over Israel, [23]Then God sent an evil spirit between Abimelech and the men of Shechem; and the men of Shechem dealt treacherously with Abimelech:

[39]And Gaal went out before the men of Shechem, and fought with Abimelech. [40]And Abimelech chased him, and he fled before him, and many were overthrown and wounded, even unto the entering of the gate. [44]And Abimelech, and the company that was with him, rushed forward, and stood in the entering of the gate of the city: and the two other companies ran upon all the people that were in the fields, and slew them. [45]And Abimelech fought against the city all that day; and he took the city, and slew the people that was therein, and beat down the city, and sowed it with salt.

DEATH OF ABIMELECH

Judg. 9 [50]Then went Abimelech to Thebez, and encamped against Thebez, and took it. [51]But there was a strong tower within the city, and thither fled all the men and women, and all they of the city, and shut it to them, and gat them up to the top of the tower. [52]And Abimelech came unto the tower, and fought against it, and went hard unto the door of the tower to burn it with fire. [53]And a certain woman cast a piece of a millstone upon Abimelech's head, and all to brake his skull. [54]Then he called hastily unto the young man his armourbearer, and said unto him, Draw thy sword, and slay me, that men say not of me, A woman slew him. And his young man thrust him through, and he died.

ABINADAB

[a bin'a dab] This name is given to several Bible characters, the chief of them being the Levite of Kirjath-jearim, in whose house the Ark of the Covenant rested for twenty years after its return from the land of the Philistines.

See Ark of the Covenant

SCRIPTURE

1 Sam. 7 [1]And the men of Kirjath-jearim came, and fetched up the ark of the Lord, and brought it into the house of Abinadab in the hill, and sanctified Eleazar his son to keep the ark of the Lord.

2 Sam. 6 [3]And they set the ark of God upon a new cart, and brought it out of the house of Abinadab that was in Gibeah: and Uzzah and Ahio, the sons of Abinadab, drave the new cart.

ABISHAG

[ab'i shag, a bī'shag] The name of a beautiful young Shunammite woman who became the personal attendant and nurse of David in his old age. After David's death, Adonijah, his eldest son, wanted Abishag for his wife; when Solomon learned of this he used it as a pretext for securing the execution of his brother, who had been a threat to his accession to the throne of David.

See Adonijah, Solomon

SCRIPTURE

1 Kin. 1 [1]Now king David was old and stricken in years; and they covered him with clothes, but he gat no heat. [2]Where-

fore his servants said unto him, Let there
be sought for my lord the king a young virgin: and let her stand before the king, and
let her cherish him, and let her lie in thy
bosom, that my lord the king may get heat.
3So they sought for a fair damsel throughout all the coasts of Israel, and found Abishag a Shunammite, and brought her to
the king. 4And the damsel was very fair,
and cherished the king, and ministered to
him: but the king knew her not.

1 Kin. 2 13And Adonijah the son of Haggith came to Bathsheba the mother of Solomon. And she said, Comest thou peaceably? And he said, Peaceably. 17And he
said, Speak, I pray thee, unto Solomon the
king, (for he will not say thee nay,) that
he give me Abishag the Shunammite to
wife. 18And Bathsheba said, Well; I will
speak for thee unto the king.

19Bathsheba therefore went unto king
Solomon, to speak unto him for Adonijah.
And the king rose up to meet her, and
bowed himself unto her, and sat down on
his throne, and caused a seat to be set for
the king's mother; and she sat on his right
hand. 20Then she said, I desire one small
petition of thee; I pray thee, say me not
nay. And the king said unto her, Ask on,
my mother; for I will not say thee nay.
21And she said, Let Abishag the Shunammite be given to Adonijah thy brother to
wife. 22And king Solomon answered and
said unto his mother, And why dost thou
ask Abishag the Shunammite for Adonijah? ask for him the kingdom also; for he is
mine elder brother; even for him, and for
Abiathar the priest, and for Joab the son
of Zeruiah. 23Then king Solomon sware
by the LORD, saying, God do so to me, and
more also, if Adonijah have not spoken this
word against his own life. 24Now therefore, as the LORD liveth, which hath established me, and set me on the throne of David my father, and who hath made me a
house, as he promised, Adonijah shall be
put to death this day. 25And king Solomon
sent by the hand of Benaiah the son of Jehoiada; and he fell upon him that he died.

ABNER

[ab′nēr] A cousin of King Saul and commander of his army. In the struggle for the throne that ensued after the death of Saul, Abner supported Saul's son Ishbosheth, in opposition to David. During the internecine strife which followed, Abner slew Asahel, the brother of Joab, David's chief commander, and incurred that warrior's enmity. Later, Abner abandoned Ishbosheth's cause and went over to David, who received him with great honor. When Joab learned of Abner's presence, he siezed the first opportunity which presented itself and slew him "for the blood of Asahel his brother." David followed the funeral procession personally and wept at the grave of Abner.

See ISHBOSHETH, JOAB, SAUL

SCRIPTURE

Captain of Saul's Army

1 Sam. 14 50And the name of Saul's wife
was Ahinoam, the daughter of Ahimaaz:
and the name of the captain of his host
was Abner, the son of Ner, Saul's uncle.

Supports Ishbosheth, against David

2 Sam. 2 8But Abner the son of Ner,
captain of Saul's host, took Ishbosheth the
son of Saul, and brought him over to Mahanaim; 9And he made him king over Gilead, and over the Ashurites, and over Jezreel, and over Ephraim, and over Benjamin,
and over all Israel. 10Ishbosheth Saul's son
was forty years old when he began to reign
over Israel, and reigned two years: but the
house of Judah followed David. 11And the
time that David was king in Hebron, over
the house of Judah, was seven years and
six months.

12 And Abner the son of Ner, and the servants of Ishbosheth the son of Saul, went out from Mahanaim to Gibeon. 13 And Joab the son of Zeruiah, and the servants of David went out, and met together by the pool of Gibeon: and they sat down, the one on the one side of the pool and the other on the other side of the pool. 14 And Abner said to Joab, Let the young men now arise, and play before us. And Joab said, Let them arise. 15 Then there arose, and went over by number, twelve of Benjamin, which pertained to Ishbosheth the son of Saul, and twelve of the servants of David. 16 And they caught every one his fellow by the head, and thrust his sword in his fellow's side; so they fell down together: wherefore that place was called Helkathhazzurim, which is in Gibeon. 17 And there was a very sore battle that day; and Abner was beaten, and the men of Israel, before the servants of David.

18 And there were three sons of Zeruiah there, Joab, and Abishai, and Asahel: and Asahel was as light of foot as a wild roe. 19 And Asahel pursued after Abner; and in going he turned not to the right hand nor to the left from following Abner. 20 Then Abner looked behind him, and said, Art thou Asahel? And he answered, I am. 21 And Abner said to him, Turn thee aside to thy right hand or to thy left, and lay thee hold on one of the young men, and take thee his armour. But Asahel would not turn aside from following of him. 22 And Abner said again to Asahel, Turn thee aside from following me: wherefore should I smite thee to the ground? how then should I hold up my face to Joab thy brother? 23 Howbeit he refused to turn aside: wherefore Abner with the hinder end of the spear smote him under the fifth rib, that the spear came out behind him; and he fell down there, and died in the same place: and it came to pass, that as many as came to the place where Asahel fell down and died stood still. 24 Joab also and Abishai pursued after Abner: and the sun went down when they were come to the hill of Ammah, that lieth before Giah by the way of the wilderness of Gibeon.

25 And the children of Benjamin gathered themselves together after Abner, and became one troop, and stood on the top of a hill. 26 Then Abner called to Joab, and said, Shall the sword devour for ever? knowest thou not that it will be bitterness in the latter end? how long shall it be then, ere thou bid the people return from following their brethren? 27 And Joab said, As God liveth, unless thou hadst spoken, surely then in the morning the people had gone up every one from following his brother. 28 So Joab blew a trumpet, and all the people stood still, and pursued after Israel no more, neither fought they any more. 29 And Abner and his men walked all that night through the plain, and passed over Jordan, and went through all Bithron, and they came to Mahanaim. 30 And Joab returned from following Abner: and when he had gathered all the people together, there lacked of David's servants nineteen men and Asahel. 31 But the servants of David had smitten of Benjamin, and of Abner's men, so that three hundred and threescore men died.

32 And they took up Asahel, and buried him in the sepulchre of his father, which was in Bethlehem. And Joab and his men went all night, and they came to Hebron at break of day.

Abner Deserts to David

2 Sam. 3 6 And it came to pass, while there was war between the house of Saul and the house of David, that Abner made himself strong for the house of Saul. 7And Saul had a concubine, whose name was Rizpah, the daughter of Aiah: and Ishbosheth said to Abner, Wherefore hast thou gone in unto my father's concubine? 8Then was Abner very wroth for the words of Ishbosheth, and said, Am I a dog's head, which against Judah do shew kindness this day unto the house of Saul thy father, to his brethren, and to his friends, and have not delivered thee into the hand of David, that thou chargest me to-day with a fault concerning this woman? 9So do God to Abner, and more also, except, as the LORD hath sworn to David, even so I do to him; 10To translate the kingdom from the house of Saul, and to set up the throne of David over Israel and over Judah, from Dan even to Beersheba. 11And he could not answer Abner a word again, because he feared him.

12And Abner sent messengers to David on his behalf, saying, Whose is the land? saying also, Make thy league with me, and, behold, my hand shall be with thee, to bring about all Israel unto thee.

13And he said, Well; I will make a league with thee: but one thing I require of thee, that is, Thou shalt not see my face, except thou first bring Michal Saul's daughter, when thou comest to see my face. 14And David sent messengers to Ishbosheth Saul's son, saying, Deliver me my wife Michal, which I espoused to me for a hundred foreskins of the Philistines. 15And Ishbosheth sent, and took her from her husband, even from Phaltiel the son of Laish. 16And her husband went with her along weeping behind her to Bahurim. Then said Abner unto him, Go, return. And he returned.

17And Abner had communication with the elders of Israel, saying, Ye sought for David in times past to be king over you: 18Now then do it: for the LORD hath spoken of David, saying, By the hand of my servant David I will save my people Israel out of the hand of the Philistines, and out of the hand of all their enemies. 19And Abner also spake in the ears of Benjamin: and Abner went also to speak in the ears of David in Hebron all that seemed good to Israel, and that seemed good to the whole house of Benjamin. 20So Abner came to David to Hebron, and twenty men with him. And David made Abner and the men that were with him a feast. 21And Abner said unto David, I will arise and go, and will gather all Israel unto my lord the king, that they may make a league with thee, and that thou mayest reign over all that thine heart desireth. And David sent Abner away; and he went in peace.

Joab Murders Abner

2 Sam. 3 22And, behold, the servants of David and Joab came from pursuing a troop, and brought in a great spoil with them: but Abner was not with David in Hebron; for he had sent him away, and he was gone in peace. 23When Joab and all the host that was with him were come, they told Joab, saying, Abner the son of Ner came to the king, and he hath sent him away, and he is gone in peace. 24Then Joab came to the king, and said, What hast thou done? behold, Abner came unto thee; why is it that thou hast sent him away, and he is quite gone? 25Thou knowest Abner the son of Ner, that he came to deceive thee, and to know thy going out and thy coming in, and to know all that thou doest. 26And when Joab was come out from David, he sent messengers after Abner, which brought him again from the well of Sirah:

but David knew it not. 27And when Abner was returned to Hebron, Joab took him aside in the gate to speak with him quietly, and smote him there under the fifth rib, that he died, for the blood of Asahel his brother.

28And afterward when David heard it, he said, I and my kingdom are guiltless before the LORD for ever from the blood of Abner the son of Ner: 29Let it rest on the head of Joab, and on all his father's house; and let there not fail from the house of Joab one that hath an issue, or that is a leper, or that leaneth on a staff, or that falleth on the sword, or that lacketh bread. 30So Joab and Abishai his brother slew Abner, because he had slain their brother Asahel at Gibeon in the battle.

31And David said to Joab, and to all the people that were with him, Rend your clothes, and gird you with sackcloth, and mourn before Abner. And king David himself followed the bier. 32And they buried Abner in Hebron: and the king lifted up his voice and wept at the grave of Abner; and all the people wept. 33And the king lamented over Abner, and said, Died Abner as a fool dieth? 34Thy hands were not bound, nor thy feet put into fetters: as a man falleth before wicked men, so fellest thou. And all the people wept again over him. 35And when all the people came to cause David to eat meat while it was yet day, David sware, saying, So do God to me, and more also, if I taste bread or aught else, till the sun be down. 36And all the people took notice of it, and it pleased them: as whatsoever the king did pleased all the people. 37For all the people and all Israel understood that day that it was not of the king to slay Abner the son of Ner. 38And the king said unto his servants, Know ye not that there is a prince and a great man fallen this day in Israel? 39And I am this day weak, though anointed king; and these men the sons of Zeruiah be too hard for me: the LORD shall reward the doer of evil according to his wickedness.

REFERENCE: *1 Sam. 17:55; 26:5, 14-16.*

ABOMINATION

[a bom i nā'shun] The feeling of extreme disgust and abhorrence; that which causes disgust and loathing; that which is considered to be a reversal of the natural. It is used in the Bible to refer to those things which are abhorrent to God and opposed to the requirements of his religion. The term is applied to heathen gods and anything connected with their worship, including the animals which were offered in sacrifice to these gods. It is also used of sexual transgressions, especially of incest and homosexuality, which are regarded as gross perversions of the true nature of a man. The "abomination of desolation," mentioned in the book of Daniel and alluded to by Jesus, has reference to some act of the most outrageous sort. The phrase has usually been interpreted to refer to various desecrations of the Temple by conquerors of Jerusalem, including the setting up of an altar to Zeus on the altar of burnt offerings and the threatened erection of a statue of Caligula in the Temple.

SCRIPTURE

Ex. 8 26And Moses said, it is not meet so to do; for we shall sacrifice the abomination of the Egyptians to the LORD our God: lo, shall we sacrifice the abomination of the Egyptians before their eyes, and will they not stone us?

Deut. 18 9When thou art come into the land which the LORD thy God giveth thee, thou shalt not learn to do after the abominations of those nations. 12For all that do these things are an abomination unto the LORD: and because of these abominations the LORD thy God doth drive them out from before thee.

Prov. 16 [12]It is an abomination to kings to commit wickedness: for the throne is established by righteousness.

Ezek. 5 [11]Wherefore, as I live, saith the LORD God; Surely, because thou hast defiled my sanctuary with all thy detestable things, and with all thine abominations, therefore will I also diminish thee: neither shall mine eye spare, neither will I have any pity.

Ezek. 8 [6]He said furthermore unto me, Son of man, seest thou what they do? even the great abominations that the house of Israel committeth here, that I should go far off from my sanctuary? but turn thee yet again, and thou shalt see greater abominations.

Abomination of Idolatry

Deut. 7 [25]The graven images of their gods shall ye burn with fire: thou shalt not desire the silver or gold that is on them, nor take it unto thee, lest thou be snared therein: for it is an abomination to the LORD thy God. [26]Neither shalt thou bring an abomination into thine house, lest thou be a cursed thing like it: but thou shalt utterly detest it, and thou shalt utterly abhor it: for it is a cursed thing.

Deut. 27 [15]Cursed be the man that maketh any graven or molten image, an abomination unto the LORD, the work of the hands of the craftsman, and putteth it in a secret place: and all the people shall answer and say, Amen.

Jer. 2 [7]And I brought you into a plentiful country, to eat the fruit thereof and the goodness thereof; but when ye entered, ye defiled my land, and made mine heritage an abomination.

Ezek. 18 [12]Hath oppressed the poor and needy, hath spoiled by violence, hath not restored the pledge, and hath lifted up his eyes to the idols, hath committed abomination.

Luke 16 [15]And he said unto them, Ye are they which justify yourselves before men, but God knoweth your hearts: for that which is highly esteemed amongst men, is abomination in the sight of God.

Abomination of Defilement

Deut. 24 [4]Her former husband which sent her away, may not take her again to be his wife, after that she is defiled; for that is abomination before the LORD: and thou shalt not cause the land to sin, which the LORD thy God giveth thee for an inheritance.

Isa. 66 [17]They that sanctify themselves, and purify themselves in the gardens behind one tree in the midst, eating swine's flesh, and the abomination, and the mouse, shall be consumed together, saith the LORD.

Rev. 21 [27]And there shall in no wise enter into it any thing that defileth, neither whatsoever worketh abomination, or maketh a lie: but they which are written in the Lamb's book of life.

Falsity an Abomination

Prov. 11 [1]A false balance is abomination to the LORD: but a just weight is his delight.

Prov. 17 [15]He that justifieth the wicked, and he that condemneth the just, even they both are abomination to the LORD.

Prov. 20 [10]Divers weights, and divers measures, both of them are alike abomination to the LORD. [23]Divers weights are an abomination unto the LORD; and a false balance is not good.

Sorcery and Necromancy an Abomination

Deut. 18 [10]There shall not be found

among you any one that maketh his son or his daughter to pass through the fire, or that useth divination, or an observer of times, or an enchanter, or a witch, [11]Or a charmer, or a consulter with familiar spirits, or a wizard, or a necromancer.

Sexual Abomination

Deut. 22 [5]The woman shall not wear that which pertaineth unto a man, neither shall a man put on a woman's garment, for all that do so are abomination unto the LORD thy God.

Lev. 18 [6]None of you shall approach to any that is near of kin to him, to uncover their nakedness: I am the LORD.

Lev. 18 [18]Neither shalt thou take a wife to her sister, to vex her, to uncover her nakedness, besides the other in her life time. [19]Also thou shalt not approach unto a woman to uncover her nakedness, as long as she is put apart for her uncleanness. [20]Moreover thou shalt not lie carnally with thy neighbor's wife, to defile thyself with her.

Insincere Worship an Abomination

Deut. 17 [1]Thou shalt not sacrifice unto the LORD thy God any bullock, or sheep, wherein is blemish, or any evil favouredness, for that is an abomination unto the LORD thy God.

Prov. 15 [8]The sacrifice of the wicked is an abomination to the LORD; but the prayer of the upright is his delight. [9]The way of the wicked is an abomination unto the LORD; but he loveth him that followeth after righteousness.

Prov. 28 [9]He that turneth away his ear from hearing the law, even his prayer shall be abomination.

Isa. 1 [13]Bring no more vain oblations: incense is an abomination unto me; the new-moons and sabbaths, the calling of assemblies, I cannot away with; it is iniquity, even the solemn meeting.

Abomination of Desolation

Dan. 9 [27]And he shall confirm the covenant with many for one week: and in the midst of the week he shall cause the sacrifice and the oblation to cease, and for the overspreading of abominations, he shall make it desolate, even until the consummation, and that determined shall be poured upon the desolate.

Dan. 12 [11]And from the time that the daily sacrifice shall be taken away, and the abomination that maketh desolate set up, there shall be a thousand two hundred and ninety days.

Dan. 11 [31]And arms shall stand on his part, and they shall pollute the sanctuary of strength, and shall take away the daily sacrifice, and they shall place the abomination that maketh desolate.

Mark 13 [14]But when ye shall see the abomination of desolation spoken of by Daniel the Prophet, standing where it ought not (let him that readeth understand), then let them that be in Judea flee to the mountains.

ABRAHAM

[ā′bra ham] The son of Terah and the ultimate ancestor of Israel's faith, called Abram until *Gen. 17:5*. It is impossible to determine precisely when Abraham lived, as there is neither Biblical reference to datable historical events nor extra-Biblical reference to Abraham. Archaeology has found parallels to the type of life described in the patriarchal narratives which indicate that his time probably falls in the first half of the second millenium BC, or about 2000-1550 BC. While a resident in Haran, Abraham received the call of the LORD promising him the two things most meaningful to a nomad—land and progeny. Abraham, together with his nephew Lot, his wife Sarah (called Sarai until *Gen. 17:15*), and a considerable retinue, set out for the land of Canaan.

After a sojourn of unspecified length, a severe famine forced him to travel to Egypt. He was well-received by the Pharaoh, but displayed weakness in allowing Sarah to be taken into the royal harem in order to save his life. When Pharaoh learned that she was Abraham's wife and not merely his sister, as he had claimed, he expelled him and his party from the land.

Back in Canaan, Abraham and Lot parted company after their respective possessions became so great that they could not travel together harmoniously. Abraham's magnanimity is seen in his offering to his nephew the best portion of available land, while he set up his own tent at the oaks of Mamre near Hebron. Shortly thereafter, Lot was taken captive by a coalition of Elamite and Babylonian chieftains who raided Sodom and Gomorrah. Abraham joined forces with his Amorite neighbors and defeated these chieftains, securing the release of Lot and his family. It was on the return from this battle that Abraham was met by Melchizedek, "king of Salem" and "priest of the most high God," to whom he paid a tithe.

Although the covenant between God and Abraham had been renewed after the meeting with Melchizedek, Sarah despaired of bearing children of her own and gave her handmaid Hagar to Abraham, the arrangement being that all children born of this union would be reckoned as Sarah's. Ancient writings have been found which confirm the existence of such a custom. The child Ishmael was born and received circumcision as a sign of the covenant which God had made with Abraham, but he was not the child of promise.

Following the destruction of Sodom and Gomorrah, there came a brief sojourn in Gerar, during which Abraham deceived its king with respect to Sarah, in much the same manner as he had the Egyptian Pharaoh. Shortly thereafter, though well past the normal age of childbearing, Sarah conceived and bore a son, Isaac. The greatest test of Abraham's faith came when he was commanded to take this long-awaited child and sacrifice him on Mount Moriah. According to the narrative, only divine intervention stopped Abraham from dutifully carrying out this dreaded order.

The stature which Abraham had among his Canaanite neighbors is reflected in the reluctance of Ephron the Hittite to accept payment for the plot of land which Abraham purchased as a burial ground for Sarah. After Sarah's death, Abraham married Keturah, who bore him other children.

See SARAH, HAGAR, ISHMAEL, LOT, ISAAC, etc.

SCRIPTURE

Abraham's Family

Gen. 11 [27]Now these are the generations of Terah: Terah begat Abram, Nahor, and Haran: and Haran begat Lot.
[28]And Haran died before his father Terah
in the land of his nativity, in Ur of the
Chaldees. [29]And Abram and Nahor took
them wives: the name of Abram's wife was
Sarai; and the name of Nahor's wife Milcah, the daughter of Haran, the father of
Milcah, and the father of Iscah.

First Promise

Gen. 12 [1]Now the LORD had said unto
Abram, Get thee out of thy country, and
from thy kindred, and from thy father's
house, unto a land that I will shew thee:
[2]And I will make of thee a great nation,
and I will bless thee, and make thy name
great; and thou shalt be a blessing: [3]And
I will bless them that bless thee, and curse
him that curseth thee: and in thee shall all
families of the earth be blessed.

Departure from Haran

Gen. 12 [5]And Abram took Sarai his
wife, and Lot his brother's son, and all
their substance that they had gathered,
and the souls that they had gotten in
Haran; and they went forth to go into the
land of Canaan; and into the land of Canaan they came.

Abraham Deceives Pharaoh

Gen. 12 [10]And there was a famine in
the land: and Abram went down into
Egypt to sojourn there; for the famine was

grievous in the land. [11]And it came to pass, when he was come near to enter into Egypt, that he said unto Sarai his wife, Behold now, I know that thou art a fair woman to look upon: [12]Therefore it shall come to pass, when the Egyptians shall see thee, that they shall say, This is his wife: and they will kill me, but they will save thee alive. [13]Say, I pray thee, thou art my sister: that it may be well with me for thy sake; and my soul shall live because of thee.

[18]And Pharaoh called Abram, and said, What is this that thou hast done unto me? why didst thou not tell me that she was thy wife? [19]Why saidst thou, She is my sister? so I might have taken her to me to wife: now therefore behold thy wife, take her, and go thy way. [20]And Pharaoh commanded his men concerning him: and they sent him away, and his wife, and all that he had.

Separation of Abraham and Lot

Gen. 13 [1]And Abram went up out of Egypt, he, and his wife, and all that he had, and Lot with him, into the south. [2]And Abram was very rich in cattle, in silver, and in gold.

[8]And Abram said unto Lot, Let there be no strife, I pray thee, between me and thee, and between my herdmen and thy herdmen; for we be brethren. [11]Then Lot chose him all the plain of Jordan; and Lot journeyed east: and they separated themselves the one from the other. [12]Abram dwelt in the land of Canaan, and Lot dwelt in the cities of the plain, and pitched his tent toward Sodom. [13]But the men of Sodom were wicked and sinners before the LORD exceedingly.

Promise of a Son

Gen. 15 [1]After these things the word of the LORD came unto Abram in a vision, saying, Fear not, Abram, I am thy shield, and thy exceeding great reward. [2]And Abram said, Lord GOD, what wilt thou give me, seeing I go childless, and the steward of my house is this Eliezer of Damascus? [3]And Abram said, Behold, to me thou hast given no seed: and lo, one born in my house is mine heir. [4]And behold, the word of the LORD came unto him, saying, This shall not be thine heir; but he that shall come forth out of thine own bowels shall be thine heir. [18]In that same day the LORD made a covenant with Abram, saying, Unto thy seed have I given this land, from the river of Egypt unto the great river, the river Euphrates.

Birth of Ishmael

Gen. 16 [1]Now Sarai, Abram's wife, bare him no children: and she had an handmaid, an Egyptian, whose name was Hagar.

[15]And Hagar bare Abram a son; and Abram called his son's name, which Hagar bare, Ishmael.

Covenant and Change of Name

Gen. 17 [3]And Abram fell on his face: and God talked with him, saying, [4]As for me, behold, my covenant is with thee, and thou shalt be a father of many nations. [5]Neither shall thy name any more be called Abram; but thy name shall be Abraham: for a father of many nations have I made thee. [6]And I will make thee exceedingly fruitful, and I will make nations of thee; and kings shall come out of thee. [7]And I will establish my covenant between me and thee, and thy seed after thee, in their generations, for an everlasting covenant; to be a God unto thee, and to thy seed after thee.

[19]And God said, Sarah thy wife shall

bear thee a son indeed; and thou shalt call
his name Isaac: and I will establish my
covenant with him for an everlasting covenant, and with his seed after him.

Birth of Isaac

Gen. 21 3And Abraham called the name
of his son that was born unto him, whom
Sarah bare to him, Isaac.

Abraham's Temptation

Gen. 22 1And it came to pass after these
things, that God did tempt Abraham, and
said unto him, Abraham: and he said,
Behold, here I am. 2And he said, Take
now thy son, thine only son Isaac, whom
thou lovest, and get thee into the land of
Moriah; and offer him there for a burnt-
offering upon one of the mountains which
I will tell thee of.
10And Abraham stretched forth his hand,
and took the knife to slay his son. 13And
Abraham lifted up his eyes, and looked,
and behold behind him a ram caught in a
thicket by his horns: and Abraham went
and took the ram, and offered him up for a
burnt-offering in the stead of his son.

Abraham's Death

Gen. 25 7And these are the days of the
years of Abraham's life which he lived,
an hundred threescore and fifteen years.
8Then Abraham gave up the ghost, and
died in a good old age, an old man, and
full of years; and was gathered to his people. 9And his sons Isaac and Ishmael buried him in the cave of Machpelah, in the
field of Ephron the son of Zohar the Hittite, which is before Mamre.

REFERENCE: *Isa. 41:8; Jer. 33:26; Mic. 7:20; Luke 1:55, 73; John 8:39; Acts 7:2-5; Rom. 4:1-13; Gal. 3:6, 16; Heb. 11:8-10; Jas. 2:21; Matt. 3:9; 8:11; Luke 3:8; 16:22; Rom. 9:7; John 8:56.*

ABSALOM

[ab'sa lom] The third son of David, by his wife Maacah. Born about the middle of the eleventh century BC, Absalom was reputed to be the handsomest man in the kingdom, noted particularly for the remarkable beauty of his hair. There is little mention of him until he arranged the murder of Amnon, David's oldest son, for the wrong he had committed against Tamar, Absalom's sister and Amnon's half-sister. At the great furor raised over the killing, Absalom fled to his maternal grandfather at Geshur, where he remained three years. Shortly after his return, Absalom began plotting to succeed his father on the throne. His beauty, his aristocratic bearing, and his diplomacy soon rallied around him a strong party, and he is said to have "stolen the hearts of the men of Israel." A revolt was organized and David was forced to flee from his capital; David still retained a number of friends in the capital, however, who functioned as spies and protected his interests as much as possible. Especially valuable in this capacity was Hushai, who thwarted the plan for immediate attack which had been suggested by Ahithophel, formerly one of David's most trusted counsellors. The delay of the attack provided David's forces enough time to gather strength and enabled them to rout completely the armies of Absalom in the encounter in the forests of Ephraim. It was in this battle that Absalom's hair became entangled in the branches of a tree and "he was taken up between heaven and earth; and the mule that was under him went away." David's powerful general, Joab, then thrust three darts into Absalom's heart and the soldiers who were with him "compassed about and smote Absalom, and slew him." When the news of Absalom's death reached David, he uttered the words which have become a classical expression of a father's mourning for his children.

See DAVID, JOAB

SCRIPTURE

Birth and Early History

2 Sam. 3 2And unto David were sons
born in Hebron: and his first-born was
Amnon, of Ahinoam the Jezreelitess;

[3]And his second, Chileab, of Abigail the wife of Nabal the Carmelite; and the third, Absalom the son of Maacah, the daughter of Talmai king of Geshur.

2 Sam. 13 [1]And it came to pass after this, that Absalom the son of David had a fair sister, whose name was Tamar; and Amnon the son of David loved her.

[22]And Absalom spake unto his brother Amnon neither good nor bad: for Absalom hated Amnon, because he had forced his sister Tamar.

[23]And it came to pass after two full years, that Absalom had sheep-shearers in Baal-hazor, which is beside Ephraim: and Absalom invited all the king's sons.

[28]Now Absalom had commanded his servants, saying, Mark ye now when Amnon's heart is merry with wine, and when I say unto you, Smite Amnon; then kill him, fear not; have not I commanded you? be courageous, and be valiant. [29]And the servants of Absalom did unto Amnon as Absalom had commanded. Then all the king's sons arose, and every man gat him up upon his mule, and fled.

[37]But Absalom fled, and went to Talmai, the son of Ammihud, king of Geshur. And David mourned for his son every day. [38]So Absalom fled, and went to Geshur, and was there three years. [39]And the soul of King David longed to go forth unto Absalom: for he was comforted concerning Amnon, seeing he was dead.

2 Sam. 14 [1]Now Joab the son of Zeruiah perceived that the king's heart was toward Absalom.

[23]So Joab arose and went to Geshur, and brought Absalom to Jerusalem. [24]And the king said, Let him turn to his own house, and let him not see my face. So Absalom returned to his own house, and saw not the king's face.

[25]But in all Israel there was none to be so much praised as Absalom for his beauty: from the sole of his foot even to the crown of his head there was no blemish in him. [26]And when he polled his head, (for it was at every year's end that he polled it; because the hair was heavy on him, therefore he polled it;) he weighed the hair of his head at two hundred shekels after the king's weight.

Plots against David

2 Sam. 15 [4]Absalom said moreover, Oh that I were made judge in the land, that every man which hath any suit or cause might come unto me, and I would do him justice! [5]And it was so, that when any man came nigh to him to do him obeisance, he put forth his hand, and took him, and kissed him. [6]And on this manner did Absalom to all Israel that came to the king for judgment: so Absalom stole the hearts of the men of Israel.

[10]But Absalom sent spies throughout all the tribes of Israel, saying, As soon as ye hear the sound of the trumpet, then ye shall say, Absalom reigneth in Hebron.

[14]And David said unto all his servants that were with him at Jerusalem, Arise, and let us flee; for we shall not else escape from Absalom: make speed to depart, lest he overtake us suddenly, and bring evil upon us, and smite the city with the edge of the sword.

Revolt and Death

2 Sam. 17 [1]Moreover, Ahithophel said unto Absalom, Let me now choose out twelve thousand men, and I will arise and pursue after David this night: [2]And I will come upon him while he is weary and weak-handed, and will make him afraid: and all the people that are with him shall flee; and I will smite the king only. [14]And Absalom and all the men of Israel said, The counsel of Hushai the Archite is better than the counsel of Ahithophel. For the LORD had appointed to defeat the good counsel of Ahithophel, to the intent that the LORD might bring evil upon Absalom.

2 Sam. 18 5And the king commanded Joab and Abishai and Ittai, saying, Deal gently for my sake with the young man, even with Absalom. And all the people heard when the king gave all the captains charge concerning Absalom.

6So the people went out into the field against Israel; and the battle was in the wood of Ephraim.

9And Absalom met the servants of David. And Absalom rode upon a mule, and the mule went under the thick boughs of a great oak, and his head caught hold of the oak, and he was taken up between the heaven and the earth; and the mule that was under him went away. 14Then said Joab, I may not tarry thus with thee. And he took three darts in his hand, and thrust them through the heart of Absalom, while he was yet alive in the midst of the oak.

33And the king was much moved, and went up to the chamber over the gate, and wept: and as he wept, thus he said, O my son Absalom! my son, my son Absalom! would God I had died for thee, O Absalom, my son, my son.

ABSTINENCE

[ab′sti nence] Refraining from the use of certain things, such as forbidden luxuries, foods, drinks, or acts. It is distinguished from temperance, which is a moderate use of things, and from fasting, which is abstinence for a time only from a religious motive.

See ASCETICISM, FASTING, TEMPERANCE

SCRIPTURE

Jewish Abstinence

Gen. 9 4But flesh with the life thereof, which is the blood thereof, shall ye not eat.

Gen. 32 32Therefore the children of Israel eat not of the sinew which shrank, which is upon the hollow of the thigh, unto this day; because he touched the hollow of Jacob's thigh in the sinew that shrank.

Ex. 22 31And ye shall be holy men unto me: neither shall ye eat any flesh that is torn of beasts in the field; ye shall cast it to the dogs.

Deut. 14 21Ye shall not eat of any thing that dieth of itself: thou shalt give it unto the stranger that is in thy gates, that he may eat it; or thou mayest sell it unto an alien: for thou art an holy people unto the LORD thy God. Thou shalt not seethe a kid in his mother's milk.

REFERENCE: For flesh and meat forbidden to the Jews, *Lev. 11*.

Christian Abstinence

1 Cor. 8 13Wherefore, if meat make my brother to offend, I will eat no flesh while the world standeth, lest I make my brother to offend.

Acts 15 29That ye abstain from meats offered to idols, and from blood, and from things strangled, and from fornication: from which if ye keep yourselves, ye shall do well. Fare ye well.

1 Thess. 5 22Abstain from all appearance of evil.

1 Tim. 4 3Forbidding to marry, and commanding to abstain from meats, which God hath created to be received with thanksgiving of them which believe and know the truth. 4For every creature of God is good, and nothing to be refused, if it be received with thanksgiving.

1 Pet. 2 11Dearly beloved, I beseech you, as strangers and pilgrims, abstain from fleshly lusts, which war against the soul.

ACCESS

[ak′ses] A coming to, a near approach, admission. Used in the Bible chiefly with reference to the approach by faith of one of God's children to Him.

SCRIPTURE

Rom. 5 [2]By whom also we have access by faith into this grace wherein we stand, and rejoice in hope of the glory of God.

Eph. 2 [18]For through him we both have an access by one Spirit unto the Father.

Eph. 3 [12]In whom we have boldness and access, with confidence, by the faith of him.

ACCURSED (Anathema)

[a kûrs′ed, a kûrst′] This word, as used in the King James Version of the Bible, usually refers to something which belongs wholly to God and must not be touched or used by men. (*See* HOLINESS, CLEANNESS and UNCLEANNESS) In the wars of Israel, the enemies of God were "accursed" in this sense; therefore, the Israelites utterly destroyed their opposition—men, women, children, and goods. (*See Josh. 6* and *7; 1 Sam. 15* and article on WAR) Most revised versions translate this word "devoted."

In the New Testament "accursed" is the King James rendering of "anathema", which, in addition to the meaning given above, came to connote moral worthlessness.

SCRIPTURE

Deut. 21 [23]His body shall not remain all night upon the tree, but thou shalt in any wise bury him that day; (for he that is hanged is accursed of God); that thy land be not defiled, which the LORD thy God giveth thee for an inheritance.

Josh. 6 [17]And the city shall be accursed, even it, and all that are therein, to the LORD: only Rahab the harlot shall live, she and all that are with her in the house, because she hid the messengers that we sent. [18]And ye, in any wise keep yourselves from the accursed thing, lest ye make yourselves accursed, when ye take of the accursed thing, and make the camp of Israel a curse, and trouble it.

Josh. 7 [1]But the children of Israel committed a trespass in the accursed thing: for Achan, the son of Carmi, the son of Zabdi, the son of Zerah, of the tribe of Judah, took of the accursed thing: and the anger of the LORD was kindled against the children of Israel.

[11]Israel hath sinned, and they have also transgressed my covenant which I commanded them: for they have even taken of the accursed thing, and have also stolen, and dissembled also, and they have put it even among their own stuff. [12]Therefore the children of Israel could not stand before their enemies, but turned their backs before their enemies, because they were accursed: neither will I be with you any more, except ye destroy the accursed from among you. [15]And it shall be, that he that is taken with the accursed thing shall be burnt with fire, he and all that he hath: because he hath transgressed the covenant of the LORD, and because he hath wrought folly in Israel.

Rom. 9 [3]For I could wish that myself were accursed from Christ, for my brethren, my kinsmen according to the flesh.

1 Cor. 12 [3]Wherefore I give you to understand, that no man speaking by the Spirit of God, calleth Jesus accursed: and that no man can say that Jesus is the LORD, but by the Holy Ghost.

Gal. 1 [8]But though we, or an angel from heaven, preach any other gospel unto you than that which we have preached unto you, let him be accursed.

ACELDAMA (AKELDAMA)

[a sel′da ma, a kel′da ma] "The field of blood,"

the name given to the field purchased with the money for which Judas betrayed Christ. It was used as a potter's field, or burying place for strangers.

See JUDAS

SCRIPTURE

Matt. 27 [6]And the chief priests took the silver pieces, and said, It is not lawful for to put them into the treasury, because it is the price of blood. [7]And they took counsel, and bought with them the potter's field, to bury strangers in. [8]Wherefore that field was called, The field of blood, unto this day.

Acts 1 [19]And it was known unto all the dwellers at Jerusalem; insomuch as that field is called in their proper tongue, Aceldama, that is to say, The field of blood.

ACHAN

[ā'kan] An individual who, in violation of the rules of Holy Warfare, could not resist the temptation to take certain valuable items from the loot of the conquered city of Jericho. The subsequent defeat of the Israelites at Ai was traced to this sin. Achan confessed and was executed by stoning.

See WAR

SCRIPTURE

Josh. 7 [1]But the children of Israel committed a trespass in the accursed thing: for Achan, the son of Carmi, the son of Zabdi, the son of Zerah, of the tribe of Judah, took of the accursed thing: and the anger of the LORD was kindled against the children of Israel.

[18]And he brought his household man by man; and Achan, the son of Carmi, the son of Zabdi, the son of Zerah, of the tribe of Judah, was taken. [19]And Joshua said unto Achan, My son, give, I pray thee, glory to the LORD God of Israel, and make confession unto him; and tell me now what thou hast done; hide it not from me. [20]And Achan answered Joshua, and said, Indeed I have sinned against the LORD God of Israel, and thus and thus have I done: [21]When I saw among the spoils a goodly Babylonish garment, and two hundred shekels of silver, and a wedge of gold of fifty shekels weight, then I coveted them, and took them; and, behold, they are hid in the earth in the midst of my tent, and the silver under it.

[22]So Joshua sent messengers, and they ran unto the tent; and, behold, it was hid in his tent, and the silver under it. [23]And they took them out of the midst of the tent, and brought them unto Joshua, and unto all the children of Israel, and laid them out before the LORD. [24]And Joshua, and all Israel with him, took Achan the son of Zerah, and the silver, and the garment, and the wedge of gold, and his sons, and his daughters, and his oxen, and his asses, and his sheep, and his tent, and all that he had: and they brought them unto the valley of Achor. [25]And Joshua said, Why hast thou troubled us? the LORD shall trouble thee this day. And all Israel stoned him with stones, and burned them with fire, after they had stoned them with stones.

Josh. 22 [20]Did not Achan the son of Zerah commit a trespass in the accursed thing, and wrath fell on all the congregation of Israel? and that man perished not alone in his iniquity.

ADAM

[ad'am] The Hebrew word meaning "man" or "mankind." Employed as a proper name, it refers to the man in the account of the creation in *Gen. 1-5*. According to the Bible Adam was created by God "in his own image" out "of the dust of the ground." He was given dominion over the animals and was put in the garden of Eden to care for it and to eat of its produce. Adam was led by his wife Eve, who had been created as companion and helper, to eat of the forbidden fruit; they were expelled from the garden and condemned to a moral life of suffering and toil. The pair is credited with three named sons—Cain, Abel and Seth—and other "sons and daughters." (*Gen. 5:4*) According to *Gen. 5:5*, Adam lived 930 years.

See EVE, FALL, EDEN, CAIN, ABEL

SCRIPTURE

Adam as Mankind

Gen. 1 [26]And God said, Let us make man in our image, after our likeness: and let them have dominion over the fish of the sea, and over the fowl of the air, and over the cattle, and over all the earth, and over every creeping thing that creepeth upon the earth. [27]So God created man in his own image, in the image of God created he him; male and female created he them.

Gen. 5 [1]This is the book of the generations of Adam: In the day that God created man, in the likeness of God made he him: [2]Male and female created he them; and blessed them, and called their name Adam, in the day when they were created.

Adam the First Man

Gen. 2 [7]And the LORD God formed man of the dust of the ground, and breathed into his nostrils the breath of life; and man became a living soul.

[8]And the LORD God planted a garden eastward in Eden; and there he put the man whom he had formed.

[19]And out of the ground the LORD God formed every beast of the field, and every fowl of the air, and brought them unto Adam to see what he would call them; and whatsoever Adam called every living creature, that was the name thereof. [20]And Adam gave names to all cattle, and to the fowl of the air, and to every beast of the field: but for Adam there was not found an help meet for him. [21]And the LORD God caused a deep sleep to fall upon Adam, and he slept; and he took one of his ribs, and closed up the flesh instead thereof.

Gen. 3 [20]And Adam called his wife's name Eve, because she was the mother of all living.

Gen. 5 [3]And Adam lived an hundred and thirty years, and begat a son in his own likeness, after his image; and called his name Seth: [4]And the days of Adam after he had begotten Seth were eight hundred years: and he begat sons and daughters. [5]And all the days that Adam lived were nine hundred and thirty years: and he died.

Adam's Transgression

Gen. 3 [17]And unto Adam he said, Because thou hast hearkened unto the voice of thy wife, and hast eaten of the tree of which I commanded thee, saying, Thou shalt not eat of it: cursed is the ground for thy sake; in sorrow shalt thou eat of it all the days of thy life.

Job 31 [33]If I covered my transgressions as Adam, hiding mine iniquity in my bosom.

Rom. 5 [14]Nevertheless, death reigned from Adam to Moses, even over them that had not sinned after the similitude of Adam's transgression, who is the figure of him that was to come.

Relation to Second Adam

1 Cor. 15 [22]For as in Adam all die, even so in Christ shall all be made alive. [45]And so it is written, The first man Adam was made a living soul, the last Adam was made a quickening spirit.

ADONIJAH

[ad on nī'jä] The son of David and Haggith, the

fourth of David's sons. Adonijah is pictured as a handsome man of aristocratic manner, as evidenced in his practice of having fifty men run before his chariot. He came to prominence in the waning days of David's reign as he sought to gather the necessary strength to assure him of succession to the throne. Among his supporters in this campaign were Joab and Abiathar. The movement reached its climax at a feast to which Adonijah invited all of the royal officials of Judah, except those who favored Solomon. His plan was thwarted, however, by the efforts of Nathan, who instructed Bath-sheba to appear before the aged king and remind him of his intention to name Solomon as his successor. While she was speaking with David, Nathan dramatically entered into the room and announced that Adonijah was being proclaimed king at the feast. This moved David to carry out the action which he had contemplated; he quickly dispatched Zadok to anoint Solomon king. When word of this reached the feast, "all the guests that were with Adonijah were afraid, and rose up, and went every man his way," indicating that his hold on them was something less than absolute. Adonijah himself ran in fear to the altar, where he plead for his life. Solomon spared him for the moment but when he later requested David's nurse, Abishag the Shunnamite, for his wife, Solomon used this as a pretext for having him slain.

See SOLOMON, NATHAN, JOAB, DAVID, ABISHAG

SCRIPTURE

Adonijah Plots to Gain Kingdom

1 Kin. 1 5 Then Adonijah the son of Haggith exalted himself, saying, I will be king: and he prepared him chariots and horsemen, and fifty men to run before him. 6 And his father had not displeased him at any time in saying, Why hast thou done so? and he also was a very goodly man; and his mother bare him after Absalom. 7 And he conferred with Joab the son of Zeruiah, and with Abiathar the priest: and they, following Adonijah, helped him. 8 But Zadok the priest, and Benaiah the son of Jehoiada, and Nathan the prophet, and Shimei, and Rei, and the mighty men which belonged to David, were not with Adonijah. 9 And Adonijah slew sheep, and oxen, and fat cattle, by the stone of Zoheleth, which is by Enrogel, and called all his brethren the king's sons, and all the men of Judah the king's servants: 10 But Nathan the prophet, and Benaiah and the mighty men, and Solomon his brother, he called not.

His Plot Fails

1 Kin. 1 39 And Zadok the priest took a horn of oil out of the tabernacle, and anointed Solomon. And they blew the trumpet; and all the people said, God save king Solomon. 40 And all the people came up after him, and the people piped with pipes, and rejoiced with great joy, so that the earth rent with the sound of them.

41 And Adonijah and all the guests that were with him heard it as they had made an end of eating. And when Joab heard the sound of the trumpet, he said, Wherefore is this noise of the city being in an uproar? 42 And while he yet spake, behold, Jonathan the son of Abiathar the priest came: and Adonijah said unto him, Come in; for thou art a valiant man, and bringest good tidings. 43 And Jonathan answered and said to Adonijah, Verily our lord king David hath made Solomon king. 49 And all the guests that were with Adonijah were afraid, and rose up, and went every man his way.

50 And Adonijah feared because of Solomon, and arose, and went, and caught hold on the horns of the altar. 51 And it was told Solomon, saying, Behold, Adonijah feareth king Solomon: for, lo, he hath caught hold on the horns of the altar, saying, Let king Solomon swear unto me today that he will not slay his servant with the sword.

See 1 Kin. 1-2

His Request for Abishag Results in His Death

1 Kin. 2 [13]And Adonijah the son of Haggith came to Bathsheba the mother of Solomon. And she said, Comest thou peaceably? And he said, Peaceably. [14]He said moreover, I have somewhat to say unto thee. And she said, Say on. [15]And he said, Thou knowest that the kingdom was mine, and that all Israel set their faces on me, that I should reign: howbeit the kingdom is turned about, and is become my brother's: for it was his from the LORD. [16]And now I ask one petition of thee, deny me not. And she said unto him, Say on. [17]And he said, Speak, I pray thee, unto Solomon the king, (for he will not say thee nay,) that he give me Abishag the Shunammite to wife. [18]And Bathsheba said, Well; I will speak for thee unto the king.

[21]And she said, Let Abishag the Shunammite be given to Adonijah thy brother to wife. [22]And king Solomon answered and said unto his mother, And why dost thou ask Abishag the Shunammite for Adonijah? ask for him the kingdom also; for he is mine elder brother; even for him, and for Abiathar the priest, and for Joab the son of Zeruiah. [23]Then king Solomon sware by the LORD, saying, God do so to me, and more also, if Adonijah have not spoken this word against his own life. [24]Now therefore, as the LORD liveth, which hath established me, and set me on the throne of David my father, and who hath made me a house, as he promised, Adonijah shall be put to death this day. [25]And king Solomon sent by the hand of Benaiah the son of Jehoiada; and he fell upon him that he died.

ADOPTION

[a dop'shun] The act of taking the child of other parents to be one's own child. Paul used the term to show the privilege of sonship bestowed by God upon those who accept Jesus as LORD.

SCRIPTURE

Adoption by God the Father

John 1 [12]But as many as received him, to them gave he power to become the sons of God, even to them that believe on his name.

John 20 [17]Jesus saith unto her, Touch me not: for I am not yet ascended to my Father: but go to my brethren, and say unto them, I ascend unto my Father and your Father, and to my God and your God.

Rom. 8 [14]For as many as are led by the Spirit of God, they are the sons of God.

2 Cor. 6 [18]And will be a Father unto you, and ye shall be my sons and daughters, saith the LORD Almighty.

Eph. 1 [5]Having predestinated us unto the adoption of children by Jesus Christ to himself, according to the good pleasure of his will.

Gal. 4 [5]To redeem them that were under the law, that we might receive the adoption of sons.

Jas. 1 [18]Of his own will begat he us with the word of truth, that we should be a kind of first-fruits of his creatures.

1 John 3 [1]Behold what manner of love the Father hath bestowed upon us, that we should be called the sons of God! therefore the world knoweth us not, because it knew him not.

Adoption of the Gentiles

Isa. 66 [19]And I will set a sign among them, and I will send those that escape of them unto the nations, to Tarshish, Pul, and Lud, that draw the bow, to Tubal, and Javan, to the isles afar off, that have not heard my fame, neither have seen my glory; and they shall declare my glory among the Gentiles.

Hos. 2 [23]And I will sow her unto me in the earth; and I will have mercy upon her that had not obtained mercy; and I will say to them which were not my people, Thou art my people; and they shall say, Thou art my God.

Rom. 8 [23]And not only they, but ourselves also, which have the first-fruits of the Spirit, even we ourselves groan within ourselves, waiting for the adoption, to wit, the redemption of our body.

ADULLAM

[a dul'am] 1. A lowland city of Judah, mentioned several times in the Bible, always in connection with a number of other cities.

REFERENCE: *Josh. 12:15; 15:35; 2 Chr. 11:7; Neh. 11:30; Mic. 1:15.*

2. A cave, probably located near the city of Adullam, in which David made his headquarters part of the time that he was a fugitive from Saul. The Hebrew language will allow the interpretation that this was not a single cave, but a group of caves—a theory which renders more plausible the statements that David kept a band of four hundred men in the cave.

REFERENCE: *1 Sam. 22:1; 2 Sam. 23:13; 1 Chr. 11:15.*

ADULTERY

[a dul'tĕr i] In the Old Testament, this term refers to voluntary sexual intercourse of a man, either single or married, with a married woman not his wife; under the Law, adultery was punishable by death. The seventh commandment was primarily a safeguard for the home and the marriage bond rather than a general commandment of moral purity. A married man who has intercourse with an unmarried woman is not regarded by the Old Testament as an adulterer, although every sort of sexual unchastity is viewed as displeasing to God. The demand for sexual purity reaches its highest level in the Bible in Jesus' declaration that "every one that looketh on a woman to lust after her hath committed adultery with her already in his heart." Jesus also made the following connections between adultery and divorce: (1) a man who divorces his wife, except for fornication, makes her an adulteress and commits adultery himself if he marries another woman; (2) a man who marries a divorced woman commits adultery; and (3) a woman who divorces her husband commits adultery if she marries another.

See Fornication, Divorce

SCRIPTURE

Forbidden

Ex. 20 [14]Thou shalt not commit adultery.

Lev. 18 [20]Moreover thou shalt not lie carnally with thy neighbor's wife, to defile thyself with her.

Matt. 5 [28]But I say unto you, That whosoever looketh on a woman to lust after her hath committed adultery with her already in his heart.

Penalties

Lev. 20 [10]And the man that committeth adultery with another man's wife, even he that committeth adultery with his neighbor's wife, the adulterer and the adulteress shall surely be put to death.

John 8 [4]They say unto him, Master, this woman was taken in adultery, in the very act. [5]Now Moses in the law commanded us, that such should be stoned: but what sayest thou?

1 Cor. 6 [9]Know ye not that the unrighteous shall not inherit the kingdom of God? Be not deceived: neither fornicators, nor idolaters, nor adulterers, nor effeminate, nor abusers of themselves with mankind.

Gal. 5 [19]Now the works of the flesh are manifest, which are these, Adultery, fornication, uncleanness, lasciviousness.

Heb. 13 [4]Marriage is honorable in all,

and the bed undefiled: but whoremongers and adulterers God will judge.

See Num. 5:11-30

Adultery and Divorce

Matt. 5 [32]But I say unto you, That whosoever shall put away his wife, saving for the cause of fornication, causeth her to commit adultery: and whosoever shall marry her that is divorced committeth adultery.

Matt. 19 [9]And I say unto you, Whosoever shall put away his wife, except it be for fornication, and shall marry another, committeth adultery: and whoso marrieth her which is put away doth commit adultery.

Rom. 7 [3]So then if, while her husband liveth, she be married to another man, she shall be called an adulteress: but if her husband be dead, she is free from the law; so that she is no adulteress, though she be married to another man.

See Luke 16:18; Mark 10:11

ADVERSARY

[ad'vẽr sa ri] This word is used in the Bible to translate Hebrew and Greek words which have the meaning of one who distresses someone, one who strives against another, or one who lies in wait against another. The general connotation is that of an enemy or antagonist. It is also used as a designation of Satan.

See Satan

SCRIPTURE

Ex. 23 [22]But if thou shalt indeed obey his voice, and do all that I speak; then I will be an enemy unto thine enemies, and an adversary unto thine adversaries.

Esth. 7 [6]And Esther said, The adversary and enemy is this wicked Haman. Then Haman was afraid before the king and the queen.

Isa. 1 [24]Therefore saith the Lord, the Lord of hosts, the mighty One of Israel, Ah, I will ease me of mine adversaries, and avenge me of mine enemies.

Zech. 3 [1]And he shewed me Joshua the high priest standing before the angel of the Lord, and Satan standing at his right hand to resist him.

1 Pet. 5 [8]Be sober, be vigilant; because your adversary the devil, as a roaring lion, walketh about, seeking whom he may devour.

Reference: *Num. 22:22; 1 Sam. 1:6; 1 Sam. 29:4; 1 Kin. 5:4; 1 Kin. 11:14; Job 31:35; Psa. 74:10; Isa. 50:8; Lam. 1:10; Luke 18:3; 1 Tim. 5:14; Heb. 10:27; Phil. 1:28; 1 Cor. 16:9; Luke 3:17; 21:15; Lam. 2:17; Psa. 109:20, 29.*

ADVOCATE (Comforter)

[ad'vo kåt] The Greek word of which this is a translation may mean: (1) a legal advocate; (2) an intercessor; or (3) a helper of any sort. The word is used to refer to Jesus, who is our advocate in the first two senses particularly, making intercession on the basis of his atoning work while on earth. It is also used in reference to the Holy Spirit, although in the King James Version, the Greek word is translated "Comforter"; other scriptures, however, amply attest to the fact that the Spirit's help is of a much wider range than the mere giving of comfort.

See Holy Spirit, Paraclete

SCRIPTURE

As Applied to Jesus

1 John 2 [1]My little children, these things write I unto you, that ye sin not. And if any man sin, we have an advocate with the Father, Jesus Christ the righteous.

The Holy Spirit

John 14 [16]And I will pray the Father, and he shall give you another Comforter, that he may abide with you for ever. [26]But the Comforter, which is the Holy Ghost, whom the Father will send in my name, he shall teach you all things, and bring all things to your remembrance, whatsoever I have said unto you.

John 15 [26]But when the Comforter is come, whom I will send unto you from the Father, even the Spirit of truth, which proceedeth from the Father, he shall testify of me.

John 16 [7]Nevertheless I tell you the truth; It is expedient for you that I go away: for if I go not away, the Comforter will not come unto you; but if I depart, I will send him unto you.

AFFLICTION

[a flik'shun] The cause of continued pain of body or mind; the state of being in continuous pain of body or mind; all manner of distress, persecution, pain, or sorrow.

SCRIPTURE

Affliction as the Result of Sin

Lev. 26 [28]Then I will walk contrary unto you also in fury; and I, even I, will chastise you seven times for your sins.

Deut. 28 [20]The LORD shall send upon thee cursing, vexation, and rebuke, in all that thou settest thine hand unto for to do, until thou be destroyed, and until thou perish quickly; because of the wickedness of thy doings, whereby thou hast forsaken me.

2 Sam. 7 [14]I will be his father, and he shall be my son. If he commit iniquity, I will chasten him with the rod of men, and with the stripes of the children of men.

Job 5 [6]Although affliction cometh not forth of the dust, neither doth trouble spring out of the ground; [7]Yet man is born unto trouble, as the sparks fly upward.

Psa. 89 [32]Then will I visit their transgression with the rod, and their iniquity with stripes.

Psa. 107 [17]Fools, because of their transgression, and because of their iniquities, are afflicted.

Lam. 1 [5]Her adversaries are the chief, her enemies prosper; for the LORD hath afflicted her for the multitude of her transgressions; her children are gone into captivity before the enemy.

Affliction Comes from God

Gen. 15 [13]And he said unto Abram, Know of a surety that thy seed shall be a stranger in a land that is not theirs, and shall serve them; and they shall afflict them four hundred years.

Ex. 4 [11]And the LORD said unto him, Who hath made man's mouth? or who maketh the dumb, or deaf, or the seeing, or the blind? have not I the LORD?

Job 6 [4]For the arrows of the Almighty are within me, the poison whereof drinketh up my spirit: the terrors of God do set themselves in array against me.

Psa. 66 [11]Thou broughtest us into the net; thou laidest affliction upon our loins.

Jer. 45 [3]Thou didst say, Woe is me now! for the LORD hath added grief to my sorrow; I fainted in my sighing, and I find no rest.

Afflictions Sent in Love and Mercy

Gen. 50 [20]But as for you, ye thought evil against me; but God meant it unto good, to bring to pass, as it is this day, to save much people alive.

Deut. 8 [16]Who fed thee in the wilderness with manna, which thy fathers knew not, that he might humble thee, and that he might prove thee, to do thee good at thy latter end.

Psa. 119 [75]I know, O LORD, that thy

judgments are right, and that thou in faithfulness hast afflicted me.

Prov. 3 [11]My son, despise not the chastening of the LORD; neither be weary of his correction. [12]For whom the LORD loveth he correcteth; even as the father the son in whom he delighteth.

Ezek. 20 [37]And I will cause you to pass under the rod, and I will bring you into the bond of the covenant.

Matt. 24 [9]Then shall they deliver you up to be afflicted, and shall kill you: and ye shall be hated of all nations for my name's sake.

Acts 20 [23]Save that the Holy Ghost witnesseth in every city, saying, that bonds and afflictions abide me.

Rom. 8 [18]For I reckon, that the sufferings of this present time are not worthy to be compared with the glory which shall be revealed in us.

Heb. 12 [6]For whom the LORD loveth he chasteneth, and scourgeth every son whom he receiveth.

Jas. 5 [10]Take, my brethren, the prophets, who have spoken in the name of the LORD, for an example of suffering affliction, and of patience.

Support under Affliction

Isa. 43 [2]When thou passest through the waters, I will be with thee; and through the rivers, they shall not overflow thee: when thou walkest through the fire, thou shalt not be burned; neither shall the flame kindle upon thee.

Jer. 16 [19]O LORD, my strength and my fortress, and my refuge in the day of affliction, the Gentiles shall come unto thee from the ends of the earth, and shall say, Surely our fathers have inherited lies, vanity, and things wherein there is no profit.

Jer. 39 [17]But I will deliver thee in that day, saith the LORD: and thou shalt not be given into the hand of the men of whom thou art afraid.

Nah. 1 [7]The LORD is good, a strong hold in the day of trouble; and he knoweth them that trust in him.

Matt. 11 [28]Come unto me, all ye that labour, and are heavy laden, and I will give you rest.

John 14 [27]Peace I leave with you, my peace I give unto you: not as the world giveth, give I unto you. Let not your heart be troubled, neither let it be afraid.

Heb. 2 [18]For in that he himself hath suffered, being tempted, he is able to succour them that are tempted.

Comfort under Affliction

Psa. 27 [5]For in the time of trouble he shall hide me in his pavilion: in the secret of his tabernacle shall he hide me; he shall set me up upon a rock.

Isa. 49 [13]Sing, O heavens; and be joyful, O earth; and break forth into singing, O mountains: for the LORD hath comforted his people, and will have mercy upon his afflicted.

Jer. 31 [13]Then shall the virgin rejoice in the dance, both young men and old together: for I will turn their mourning into joy, and will comfort them, and make them rejoice from their sorrow.

Matt. 5 [4]Blessed are they that mourn: for they shall be comforted.

John 16 [20]Verily, verily, I say unto you, that ye shall weep and lament, but the world shall rejoice: and ye shall be sorrowful, but your sorrow shall be turned into joy. [33]These things I have spoken unto you, that in me ye might have peace. In the world ye shall have tribulation, but be of good cheer: I have overcome the world.

2 Cor. 1 [4]Who comforteth us in all our

tribulation, that we may be able to comfort them which are in any trouble by the comfort wherewith we ourselves are comforted of God.

Endurance of Affliction

Job 1 [21]The LORD gave, and the LORD hath taken away; blessed be the name of the LORD.

Job 5 [17]Behold, happy is the man whom God correcteth: therefore despise not thou the chastening of the Almighty.

Job 13 [15]Though he slay me, yet will I trust in him: but I will maintain mine own ways before him.

Psa. 39 [9]I was dumb, I opened not my mouth; because thou didst it.

Luke 21 [19]In your patience possess ye your souls.

Rom. 12 [12]Rejoicing in hope; patient in tribulation; continuing instant in prayer.

2 Thess. 1 [4]So that we ourselves glory in you in the churches of God, for your patience and faith in all your persecutions and tribulations that ye endure.

Supplication under Affliction

2 Kin. 20 [1]In those days was Hezekiah sick unto death. And the prophet Isaiah the son of Amoz came to him, and said unto him, Thus saith the LORD, Set thine house in order; for thou shalt die, and not live. [2]Then he turned his face to the wall, and prayed unto the LORD.

2 Chr. 14 [11]And Asa cried unto the LORD his God, and said, LORD, it is nothing with thee to help, whether with many, or with them that have no power: help us, O LORD our God; for we rest on thee, and in thy name we go against this multitude. O LORD, thou art our God; let not man prevail against thee.

Psa. 40 [13]Be pleased, O LORD, to deliver me: O LORD, make haste to help me. [17]But I am poor and needy; yet the LORD thinketh upon me: thou art my help and my deliverer; make no tarrying, O my God.

Psa. 55 [1]Give ear to my prayer, O God; and hide not thyself from my supplication.

Psa. 102 [2]Hide not thy face from me in the day when I am in trouble; incline thine ear unto me: in the day when I call answer me speedily.

Jer. 31 [18]I have surely heard Ephraim bemoaning himself thus; Thou hast chastised me, and I was chastised, as a bullock unaccustomed to the yoke: turn thou me, and I shall be turned; for thou art the LORD my God.

Lam. 5 [1]Remember, O LORD, what is come upon us: consider, and behold our reproach.

Dan. 9 [3]And I set my face unto the LORD God, to seek by prayer and supplications, with fasting, and sackcloth, and ashes.

Matt. 26 [39]And he went a little further, and fell on his face, and prayed, saying, O my Father, if it be possible, let this cup pass from me: nevertheless, not as I will, but as thou wilt.

2 Cor. 12 [7]And lest I should be exalted above measure through the abundance of the revelations, there was given to me a thorn in the flesh, the messenger of Satan to buffet me, lest I should be exalted above measure. [8]For this thing I besought the LORD thrice, that it might depart from me.

Jas. 5 [13]Is any among you afflicted? let him pray. Is any merry? let him sing psalms.

Brings Confession and Repentance

Num. 21 [7]Therefore the people came to Moses, and said, We have sinned, for we have spoken against the LORD, and against thee; pray unto the LORD, that he take away the serpents from us. And Moses prayed for the people.

Job 7 [20]I have sinned; what shall I do unto thee, O thou preserver of men? why hast thou set me as a mark against thee, so that I am a burden to myself?

Psa. 32 [5]I acknowledged my sin unto thee, and mine iniquity have I not hid. I said, I will confess my transgressions unto the LORD; and thou forgavest the iniquity of my sin. Selah.

Hos. 6 [1]Come, and let us return unto the LORD: for he hath torn, and he will heal us; he hath smitten, and he will bind us up.

Mic. 7 [9]I will bear the indignation of the LORD, because I have sinned against him, until he plead my cause, and execute judgment for me: he will bring me forth to the light, and I shall behold his righteousness.

Luke 15 [18]I will arise and go to my father, and will say unto him, Father, I have sinned against heaven and before thee.

Deliverances from Affliction

Psa. 34 [4]I sought the LORD, and he heard me, and delivered me from all my fears. [19]Many are the afflictions of the righteous: but the LORD delivereth him out of them all.

Psa. 40 [2]He brought me up also out of an horrible pit, out of the miry clay, and set my feet upon a rock, and established my goings.

Isa. 63 [9]In all their affliction he was afflicted, and the angel of his presence saved them: in his love and in his pity he redeemed them; and he bare them, and carried them all the days of old.

Jonah 2 [1]Then Jonah prayed unto the LORD his God out of the fish's belly, [2]And said, I cried by reason of mine affliction unto the LORD, and he heard me; out of the belly of hell cried I, and thou heardest my voice.

2 Tim. 3 [11]Persecutions, afflictions, which came unto me at Antioch, at Iconium, at Lystra; what persecutions I endured: but out of them all the LORD delivered me.

2 Tim. 4 [17]Notwithstanding, the LORD stood with me, and strengthened me; that by me the preaching might be fully known, and that all the Gentiles might hear; and I was delivered out of the mouth of the lion. [18]And the LORD shall deliver me from every evil work, and will preserve me unto his heavenly kingdom; to whom be glory for ever and ever. Amen.

Benefits of Affliction

Job. 23 [10]But he knoweth the way that I take: when he hath tried me, I shall come forth as gold.

Job 36 [8]And if they be bound in fetters, and be holden in cords of affliction, [9]Then he sheweth them their work, and their transgressions that they have exceeded.

Psa. 119 [67]Before I was afflicted I went astray: but now have I kept thy word. [71]It is good for me that I have been afflicted; that I might learn thy statutes.

Eccl. 7 [2]It is better to go to the house of mourning, than to go to the house of feasting: for that is the end of all men; and the living will lay it to his heart.

Isa. 48 [10]Behold, I have refined thee, but not with silver; I have chosen thee in the furnace of affliction.

Hos. 5 [15]I will go and return to my place, till they acknowledge their offense, and seek my face: in their affliction they will seek me early.

Rom. 5 [3]And not only so, but we glory in tribulations also; knowing that tribulation worketh patience.

1 Cor. 11 [32]But when we are judged, we

are chastened of the LORD, that we should not be condemned with the world.

2 Cor. 4 17For our light affliction, which is but for a moment, worketh for us a far more exceeding and eternal weight of glory.

1 Pet. 5 10But the God of all grace, who hath called us unto his eternal glory by Christ Jesus, after that ye have suffered a while, make you perfect, stablish, strengthen, settle you.

AGABUS

[ag′a bus] A Christian prophet. Agabus first appears in Antioch, where he had come to announce a great famine which was approaching. His visit became the occasion of encouraging the disciples at Antioch "to send relief to the brethren which dwelt in Judea: which also they did, and sent it to the elders by the hands of Barnabas and Saul" (*Acts 11:29-30*). Apparently, it was this same prophet who met Paul at Caesarea on his return from his third missionary journey. Binding himself with Paul's girdle, he uttered this prediction: "So shall the Jews at Jerusalem bind the man that owneth this girdle, and shall deliver him into the hands of the Gentiles" (*Acts 21:10-11*). According to the writer of *Acts*, both of these prophecies were fulfilled.

See PAUL

AGAG

[ā′gag] The king of the Amalekites, longstanding opponents of Israel. After defeating the Amalekites in a battle in the Negeb, King Saul spared Agag, in direct disobedience to the laws for Holy Warfare which had been given by Samuel. It was this incident which caused the breach in the relationship between Saul and Samuel. After Samuel bitterly rebuked Saul for his disobedience, he summoned the Amalekite king before him and "hewed Agag in pieces before the LORD in Gilgal."

See SAUL, SAMUEL, WAR

SCRIPTURE

1 Sam. 15 8And he took Agag the king of the Amalekites alive, and utterly destroyed all the people with the edge of the sword. 9But Saul and the people spared Agag . . . .

32Then said Samuel, Bring ye hither to me Agag the king of the Amalekites. And Agag came unto him delicately. And Agag said, Surely the bitterness of death is past.
33And Samuel said, As thy sword hath made women childless, so shall thy mother be childless among women. And Samuel hewed Agag in pieces before the LORD in Gilgal.

AGRICULTURE

[ag′ri kul tûr] The art or science of cultivating the ground; the production of crops or livestock on a farm; farming. Though prominent in the narratives concerning Adam, Cain, and Noah, agriculture was apparently little practiced by the patriarchs. When Israel settled in Palestine and became a nation, the people took up farming which they learned from the Canaanites and agriculture became the basis of the league of the twelve tribes. The family heritage of land was deemed so important that even when sold, it was to revert to the original owner in the year of Jubilee; according to the law, therefore, land could only be "leased"—that is, only so many years of occupancy of the land could be sold (*Lev. 25:8-16, 23-35*). Three types of agriculture were most common: the growing of grain, the care of vineyards, and the raising of flocks. The grain crops which are most often mentioned in the Bible are wheat, barley, rye, and millet. These were sown by hand, after which the ground was plowed. The plow was probably very light, one yoke of oxen usually sufficing to draw it. Mountains, steep places, and corners of fields were hoed by hand. When ready for harvesting, the grains were reaped by the sickle or pulled up by the roots. They were bound in sheaves or gathered in piles for transporting to the threshing-floor. This "floor" was a hard circular spot of ground on which the grain was placed and threshed by tramping by animals or humans or by dragging various types of threshing instruments over it. After the trampling process was completed the mixture of chaff and grain was "winnowed", or tossed in the air so that the wind would blow away the chaff. The grain was then shaken in a sieve or wooden tray to separate it from the dirt and refuse not removed by the winnowing process. The care of vineyards, with the duties of pruning and hoeing fitted well into the schedule of the average householder, since this could be done at times when the other crops demanded little attention. (*See Isa. 5:1-6* and article on VINE) The keeping of flocks was usually reserved for the more wealthy. Flocks furnished their owners with both food (milk, cheese and less frequently, meat) and clothing (sheepskin or woven garments made from wool or mohair). Many of the ancient agricultural processes described above have been retained into the twentieth century.

AHAB

[ā′hab] The son of Omri and the seventh king of Israel (849-850 BC). Ahab was efficient and strong in manipulative and administrative powers, but weak and vascillating in the face of his powerful wife, Jezebel. Despite great odds Ahab continued the work of Omri in strengthening the northern kingdom. He cemented the bond with Tyre by marrying Jezebel, the daughter of the king, and made peace with the kingdom of Judah. This latter alliance was strengthened by the marriage of his daughter Athaliah to the crown prince of Judah. Ahab's marriage to Jezebel proved to be a major factor in the eventual fall of the Omride dynasty. Jezebel was a clever and determined woman, devoted to the worship of Baal and Ahserah and determined to substitute their worship for that of the true God. (*See* JEZEBEL) It was she, being devoid of the egalitarian principles which characterized the religion of the Hebrews, who secured the vineyard of Naboth for her pouting husband. (*See* NABOTH) This egregious offence became a battle cry of the revolution to overthrow the house of Omri. (*See* JEHU)

One of Ahab's constant enemies was the fiery prophet Elijah. Elijah appeared before Ahab and predicted a three-year drought as a punishment for the sins of Ahab. At the end of the three years, Elijah blamed the drought on the religious policy of Ahab and sought to illustrate his point by the famous contest with the prophets of Baal on Mount Carmel. (*See* ELIJAH) After the Naboth incident, Elijah announced that Ahab's house would be destroyed and that dogs would eat the flesh of Jezebel, both of which came to pass.

Ahab evidently excelled as a military leader. Despite great odds, he defeated Ben-Hadad of Syria twice and later joined with him in a coalition against Shalmaneser II, king of Assyria. His last battle again involved Ben-Hadad. When this king threatened the land of Palestine, Ahab, in disregard for the warnings of the prophet Micaiah (*see* MICAIAH), joined with Jehoshaphat king of Judah to resist him. Although he entered the battle in disguise, he was struck by a random arrow and died before the day was ended. A strange mixture of strength and weakness, Ahab had sown the seeds of a violent revolution which would ultimately undo the great work begun by Omri. (*See* JEHU)

See KINGS

SCRIPTURE

Idolatrous King of Israel

1 Kin. 16 29 And in the thirty and eighth
year of Asa king of Judah began Ahab the
son of Omri to reign over Israel: and Ahab
the son of Omri reigned over Israel in
Samaria twenty and two years. 30 And
Ahab the son of Omri did evil in the sight
of the LORD above all that were before
him. 31 And it came to pass, as if it had
been a light thing for him to walk in the
sins of Jeroboam the son of Nebat, that he
took to wife Jezebel the daughter of Ethbaal king of the Zidonians, and went and
served Baal, and worshiped him. 32 And
he reared up an altar for Baal in the house
of Baal, which he had built in Samaria.
33 And Ahab made a grove; and Ahab did
more to provoke the LORD God of Israel
to anger than all the kings of Israel that
were before him.

A Foe of Elijah

1 Kin. 17 1 And Elijah the Tishbite, who

was of the inhabitants of Gilead, said unto Ahab, As the LORD God of Israel liveth, before whom I stand, there shall not be dew nor rain these years, but according to my word.

1 Kin. 18 [17]And it came to pass when Ahab saw Elijah, that Ahab said unto him, Art thou he that troubleth Israel?

1 Kin. 19 [1]And Ahab told Jezebel all that Elijah had done, and withal how he had slain all the prophets with the sword.

Cursed by Elijah for Taking Naboth's Vineyard

1 Kin. 21 [2]And Ahab spake unto Naboth, saying, Give me thy vineyard, that I may have it for a garden of herbs, because it is near unto my house: and I will give thee for it a better vineyard than it; or if it seem good to thee, I will give thee the worth of it in money. [3]And Naboth said to Ahab, The LORD forbid it me, that I should give the inheritance of my fathers unto thee. [4]And Ahab came into his house heavy and displeased, because of the word which Naboth the Jezreelite had spoken to him: for he had said, I will not give thee the inheritance of my fathers. And he laid him down upon his bed, and turned away his face, and would eat no bread.

[15]And it came to pass, when Jezebel heard that Naboth was stoned, and was dead, that Jezebel said to Ahab, Arise, take possession of the vineyard of Naboth the Jezreelite, which he refused to give thee for money: for Naboth is not alive, but dead. [16]And it came to pass, when Ahab heard that Naboth was dead, that Ahab rose up to go down to the vineyard of Naboth the Jezreelite, to take possession of it.

[17]And the word of the LORD came to Elijah the Tishbite, saying, [18]Arise, go down to meet Ahab king of Israel, which is in Samaria: behold, he is in the vineyard of Naboth, whither he is gone down to possess it. [19]And thou shalt speak unto him, saying, Thus saith the LORD, Hast thou killed, and also taken possession? And thou shalt speak unto him, saying, Thus saith the LORD, In the place where dogs licked the blood of Naboth shall dogs lick thy blood, even thine. [20]And Ahab said to Elijah, Hast thou found me, O mine enemy? And he answered, I have found thee: because thou hast sold thyself to work evil in the sight of the LORD.

[27]And it came to pass, when Ahab heard those words, that he rent his clothes, and put sackcloth upon his flesh, and fasted, and lay in sackcloth, and went softly. [28]And the word of the LORD came to Elijah the Tishbite, saying, [29]Seest thou how Ahab humbleth himself before me? because he humbleth himself before me, I will not bring the evil in his days: but in his son's days will I bring the evil upon his house.

Death of Ahab

1 Kin. 22 [34]And a certain man drew a bow at a venture, and smote the king of Israel between the joints of the harness: wherefore he said unto the driver of his chariot, Turn thine hand, and carry me out of the host: for I am wounded.

[37]So the king died, and was brought to Samaria; and they buried the king in Samaria. [38]And one washed the chariot in the pool of Samaria; and the dogs licked up his blood; and they washed his armour; according unto the word of the LORD which he spake.

2 Kin. 9 [7]And thou shalt smite the house of Ahab thy master, that I may avenge the blood of my servants the prophets, and the blood of all the servants of the LORD, at the hand of Jezebel.

2 Kin. 10 [11]So Jehu slew all that remained of the house of Ahab in Jezreel, and all his great men, and his kinsfolks, and his priests, until he left him none remaining.

AHASUERUS

[a haz ū ē'rus] The Persian king in the book of *Esther*. In all probability, this individual is to be identified with Xerxes, who ruled over the Persian empire from 485-465 BC, having inherited from his father, Darius I, a vast empire which stretched "from India to Ethiopia." The major difficulty with this identification is that *Esther* states that the wife of Ahasuerus was Vashti; the wife of Xerxes is known to have been Amnestris. Some scholars have identified Amnestris with Esther, but there is as yet no final solution to this problem. (See article on ESTHER for Ahasuerus' role in this fascinating story)

See HAMAN, MORDECAI, VASHTI

REFERENCE: The Book of *Esther*.

AHAZ

[ā'haz] The son of Jotham and king of Judah (734-715 BC). Ahaz was a man of syncretistic tendencies, introducing various aspects of idolatrous religion into Judah, even offering his own son to the god Molech. Ahaz refused to join with Rezin king of Syria and Pekah king of Israel in a coalition against Tiglath-Pileser and was attacked by the forces of these two kings. Jerusalem held, but the southern kingdom sustained heavy losses of men and territory. Against the advice of the prophet Isaiah, Ahaz appealed to Tiglath-Pileser for aid. The Assyrian king leveled Syria and raided Israel, thus relieving the pressure on Judah, but leaving Ahaz as a vassal of Assyria. It appears certain that Tiglath-Pileser would have invaded Damascus and Israel anyway and was doubtless delighted to be paid for it and to pick up Judah as a tributary in the bargain. In his remaining years as king, Ahaz introduced a whole series of impieties, including the construction of a replica of a heathen altar which he had seen while on a visit to the court of Assyria. Judah suffered even further reverses and was able to avoid the captivity which had been Israel's fate only by a vassalage alliance with Assyria which involved the worship of Assyrian gods.

See PEKAH, TIGLATH-PILESER, etc.

REFERENCE: *2 Kin. 16; 2 Chr. 28; Isa. 7.*

AHAZIAH (King of Israel)

[ā ha zī'a] The son of Ahab and Jezebel and the eighth king of Israel, reigning only two years (850-849 BC). During his reign Moab rebelled against Israel, apparently without significant resistance. There is some confusion in the Biblical narratives of Ahaziah's attempts to revive a shipping cartel in league with Judah (*see 1 Kin. 22: 48, 49* and *2 Chr. 20:35-37*), but they both agree that no benefit was received from the effort. Like his notorious parents, Ahaziah was a worshipper of Baal. When he lay severely injured from a fall, he sent to Baalzebub, the god of Ekron, to learn of his chances for recovery. On the way, the messengers were met by Elijah who rebuked them for their dependence on Baalzebub and prophesied the death of Ahaziah. The king summoned the prophet to his bedside where the judgment was repeated; Ahaziah died shortly thereafter.

See AHAB, BAAL, ELIJAH, JEZEBEL, KINGS

REFERENCE: *1 Kin. 22:48-52; 2 Kin. 1:1-18; 2 Chr. 20:35-37.*

AHAZIAH (King of Judah)

[ā ha zī'a] The youngest son of Jehoram and sixth king of Judah (842 BC), also written Jehoahaz. His mother was Athaliah, the daughter of Ahab and Jezebel. Ahaziah joined with his uncle, Jehoram, king of Israel, in an expedition against Ben-Hadad of Syria and succeeded in capturing Ramoth-Gilead. Jehoram, however, was wounded and retired to Jezreel to recover. While Ahaziah visited him, Jehu stormed down from Ramoth-Gilead to begin his violent revolution against the house of Ahab and slew both kings.

See ATHALIAH, JEHORAM, JEHU, KINGS

REFERENCE: 2 Kin. 8; 25-29; *9:14-29; 2 Chr. 20:35-22:9.*

AHIJAH

[a hī′ja] The prophet of Shiloh who lived in the time of Jeroboam I, ruler of the northern kingdom of Israel (c. 922-901). While Solomon was still alive, Ahijah put on a new garment and led Jeroboam out of Jerusalem into the open country. When they were alone, Ahijah tore the garment into twelve pieces, giving ten of them to Jeroboam. This signified that Jeroboam would become ruler over ten of the twelve tribes of Israel, leaving only Judah and Benjamin for the descendants of Solomon. Ahijah states that this is a judgment of God brought upon Solomon because of his participation in the idolatrous worship of his heathen wives. Later, when Jeroboam had broken with the ancient religion of Israel by establishing the bull cultus, his son became ill and he sent his wife to ask assistance of Ahijah. The prophet received her harshly, foretold the death of the son, and prophesied the complete destruction of the house of Jeroboam.

See JEROBOAM

REFERENCE: *1 Kin. 11:29-40; 14:1-20.*

AI

[ā′ī] A town of central Palestine, just east of Bethel. In the Biblical narrative of the conquest, Ai was the first city of the hill country of Palestine to be taken by Joshua. As a result of Achan's sin in connection with the destruction of Jericho (*see* ACHAN), the first attack on Ai resulted in a rout of the Israelites; after Achan's sin was discovered and his entire family slain, another assault was made and the city was taken and burned, being left a heap of ruins. Based on archaeological findings which indicate that Ai was only very sparsely inhabited - if at all - during the time of Joshua's conquest of Canaan, some scholars have advanced the theory that it was actually Bethel which was destroyed, but, since it was quickly occupied by the invading Israelites, the story was transferred to a large heap of ruins nearby. This receives some support from the fact that the word Ai means "ruin", and from evidence that Bethel was burned about this time, although the book of *Joshua* contains no reference to its conquest, but there is as yet no way to be absolutely certain concerning this matter.

REFERENCE: *Josh. 7, 8.*

ALABASTER

[al′a bas tẽr] Crystalline gypsum or sulphate of lime, a fine, light-colored, marble-like stone used in the manufacture of vessels to hold pomades, ointments, and perfumes. Such vessels were themselves called alabasters. In the gospel accounts of two occasions on which Jesus was anointed with precious ointment, the ointment is said to have been contained in alabaster boxes.

REFERENCE: *Matt. 26:6-13; Mark 14:3-9; Luke 7:37; John 12:1-8.*

ALMS

[ämz] Alms may refer to anything given gratuitously to relieve the poor. The giving of alms in a humane and unbegrudging spirit was enjoined upon the Israelites by the Law of Moses and eventually came to be regarded as among the most important of religious duties. There is some evidence that the practice was viewed as having the power to atone for sins. In Jesus' time, almsgiving was often accompanied by ostentatious publicity; he urged his disciples to shun this self-righteous attention-seeking and to rest content with the knowledge that God is aware of their benevolence.

See GIVING, BENEVOLENCE

SCRIPTURE

General

Prov. 28 27He that giveth unto the poor shall not lack: but he that hideth his eyes shall have many a curse.

Acts 10 4And when he looked on him, he was afraid, and said, What is it, Lord? And he said unto him, Thy prayers and thine alms are come up for a memorial before God.

Almsgiving Enjoined

Deut. 15 7If there be among you a poor

man of one of thy brethren within any of thy gates in thy land which the LORD thy God giveth thee, thou shalt not harden thine heart, nor shut thine hand from thy poor brother: [8]But thou shalt open thine hand wide unto him, and shalt surely lend him sufficient for his need, in that which he wanteth. [9]Beware that there be not a thought in thy wicked heart, saying, The seventh year, the year of release, is at hand; and thine eye be evil against thy poor brother, and thou givest him nought; and he cry unto the LORD against thee, and it be sin unto thee. [10]Thou shalt surely give him, and thine heart shall not be grieved when thou givest unto him: because that for this thing the LORD thy God shall bless thee in all thy works, and in all that thou puttest thine hand unto. [11]For the poor shall never cease out of the land: therefore I command thee, saying, Thou shalt open thine hand wide unto thy brother, to thy poor, and to thy needy, in thy land.

Matt. 5 [42]Give to him that asketh thee, and from him that would borrow of thee turn not thou away.

Matt. 19 [21]Jesus said unto him, If thou wilt be perfect, go and sell that thou hast, and give to the poor, and thou shalt have treasure in heaven: and come and follow me.

Luke 11 [41]But rather give alms of such things as ye have; and, behold, all things are clean unto you.

Luke 12 [33]Sell that ye have, and give alms; provide yourselves bags which wax not old, a treasure in the heavens that faileth not, where no thief approacheth, neither moth corrupteth.

1 John 3 [17]But whoso hath this world's good, and seeth his brother have need, and shutteth up his bowels of compassion from him, how dwelleth the love of God in him?

Almsgiving Viewed as Atoning for Sin

Job 29 [12]Because I delivered the poor that cried, and the fatherless, and him that had none to help him. [13]The blessing of him that was ready to perish came upon me: . . . .

Psa. 112 [9]He hath dispersed, he hath given to the poor; his righteousness endureth for ever; his horn shall be exalted with honor.

Prov. 11 [4]Riches profit not in the day of wrath: but righteousness delivereth from death.

Prov. 14 [21]He that despiseth his neighbor sinneth: but he that hath mercy on the poor, happy is he.

Prov. 19 [17]He that hath pity upon the poor lendeth unto the LORD; and that which he hath given will he pay him again.

Prov. 21 [3]To do justice and judgment is more acceptable to the LORD than sacrifice.

Proper Manner and Spirit of Almsgiving

Matt. 6 [1]Take heed that ye do not your alms before men, to be seen of them: otherwise ye have no reward of your Father which is in heaven. [2]Therefore when thou doest thine alms, do not sound a trumpet before thee, as the hypocrites do in the synagogues and in the streets, that they may have glory of men. Verily I say unto you, They have their reward. [3]But when thou doest alms, let not thy left hand know what thy right hand doeth: [4]That thine alms may be in secret: and thy Father which seeth in secret himself shall reward thee openly.

1 Cor. 13 [3]And though I bestow all my goods to feed the poor, and though I give my body to be burned, and have not charity, it profiteth me nothing.

2 Cor. 9 [5]Therefore I thought it neces-

sary to exhort the brethren, that they would go before unto you, and make up beforehand your bounty, whereof ye had notice before, that the same might be ready, as a matter of bounty, and not as of covetousness.
[6]But this I say, He which soweth sparingly shall reap also sparingly; and he which soweth bountifully shall reap also bountifully.
[7]Every man according as he purposeth in his heart, so let him give; not grudgingly, or of necessity: for God loveth a cheerful giver.

ALPHA AND OMEGA

[al′fa, o mē′ga] The first and last letters of the Greek alphabet. As a figure of speech it meant "from beginning to end," like our "from A to Z." It is used in the Bible in reference to the eternity of God and Christ.

SCRIPTURE

Rev. 1
[8]I am Alpha and Omega, the beginning and the ending, saith the Lord, which is, and which was, and which is to come, the Almighty.
[11]Saying, I am Alpha and Omega, the first and the last: and, What thou seest write in a book, and send it unto the seven churches which are in Asia; unto Ephesus, and unto Smyrna, and unto Pergamos, and unto Thyatira, and unto Sardis, and unto Philadelphia, and unto Laodicea.

Rev. 21
[6]And he said unto me, It is done. I am Alpha and Omega, the beginning and the end. I will give unto him that is athirst of the fountain of the water of life freely.

ALTAR

[ôl′tẽr] A structure or place on which sacrifices are offered or incense is burned in worship of a deity. The Bible mentions a number of altars, the most important of which are the altars of burnt-offerings and the altars of incense which stood in the tabernacle and the temple. In the tabernacle the altar of burnt-offerings was square, five cubits in length and breadth, and three cubits high. It was made of planks of acacia (shittim) wood, overlaid with brass. (*See Ex. 27*) In Solomon's Temple the length and breadth were near twenty cubits, and the height was ten cubits. It is referred to as the "brazen altar", which some take to mean it was overlaid with brass, as was the altar in the tabernacle, and others, that it was made entirely of brass. The altar of incense was called the "golden altar", to distinguish it from the altar of burnt-offerings. That in the tabernacle was made of acacia wood overlaid with pure gold. Its shape was square, being a cubit in length and breadth, and two cubits in height. It had horns at the four corners and stood just before the veil which separated the Holy Place from the Holy of Holies. In Solomon's temple, it was made of cedar wood overlaid with gold and was two cubits square with a height of three cubits.

See Tabernacle; Temple; on the Cubit, *see* Weights and Measures (Appendix)

REFERENCE: *Gen. 8:20; 12:7, 8; 26:25; 33:20; Ex. 17:15; 1 Sam. 7:17; Ezra 3:1-6; Ezek. 43:13-27.*

AMASA

[a mā′sa] A nephew of David and commander of the rebel army of Absalom. When the revolt of Absalom had been put down, David forgave Amasa for his part in it and appointed him as commander of the royal forces, in place of Joab, who had fallen from honor. His first major assignment was a campaign against the rebel forces led by Sheba. Amasa did not carry out his orders quickly enough to satisfy David and a force led by Abishai and Joab was sent out to hasten matters. When Joab met Amasa, he assassinated him while pretending to salute him and regained his old position at the head of the army.

See Joab

REFERENCE: *2 Sam. 17:25; 19:11-13; 20:8-12; 1 Kin. 2:5.*

AMAZIAH

[am a zī′a] The son of Jehoash and tenth king

of Judah (797-769 BC). As a result of the crushing defeat which his father had suffered at the hands of Hazael king of Syria and the ruinous tribute which had been increased, Amaziah became ruler over a severely depressed people. In an effort to strengthen the state, Amaziah conceived of a plan to regain the territory of Edom which had been lost under Jehoram. To effect this he gathered a large army from Judah and hired mercenaries from the northern kingdom. When a prophet convinced him not to use these mercenaries they were sent home unemployed; enraged, they plundered the towns of Judah on their return northward. When Amaziah returned from his eminently successful campaign in Edom and learned of the actions of these soldiers, he angrily declared war on Jehoash king of Israel. Jehoash attempted to dissuade him but was finally forced to fight and inflicted extensive damage on Judah, taking Amaziah captive. He was returned to his throne but shortly thereafter was assassinated in a palace revolt and succeeded by his son Uzziah.

See JEHOASH, JEHORAM, KINGS

REFERENCE: *2 Kin. 14:1-20; 2 Chr. 25.*

AMBITION

[am bi'shun] An eager, often inordinate, desire for position, wealth, power, superiority, etc.; the desire to attain something.

See PRIDE, LUST

SCRIPTURE

General

Psa. 49 11Their inward thought is, that their houses shall continue forever, and their dwelling places to all generations; they call their lands after their own names. 12Nevertheless man being in honour abideth not; he is like the beasts that perish.

1 John 2 16For all that is in the world, the lust of the flesh, and the lust of the eyes, and the pride of life, is not of the Father, but is of the world.

Reproof of Ambition

Isa. 14 12How art thou fallen from heaven, O Lucifer, son of the morning! how art thou cut down to the ground, which didst weaken the nations!

Matt. 18 1At the same time came the disciples unto Jesus, saying, Who is the greatest in the kingdom of heaven? 2And Jesus called a little child unto him, and set him in the midst of them, 3And said, Verily I say unto you, Except ye be converted, and become as little children, ye shall not enter into the kingdom of heaven.

Matt. 20 25But Jesus called them unto him, and said, Ye know that the princes of the Gentiles exercise dominion over them, and they that are great exercise authority upon them. 26But it shall not be so among you: but whosoever will be great among you, let him be your minister.

Matt. 23 8But be not ye called Rabbi: for one is your Master, even Christ; and all ye are brethren.

Luke 22 24And there was also a strife among them, which of them should be accounted the greatest.

AMEN

[ā men', sometimes pronounced ä men'] This word originally comes from the Hebrew. Ordinarily it is used in a liturgical sense, expressing solemn assent by an individual or the entire assembly to a prayer or to the words of another. In the gospels, however, it is used to mean "truly" or "verily," giving a special emphasis. The word is also found at the end of several New Testament epistles.

SCRIPTURE

Deut. 27 15Cursed be the man that maketh any graven or molten image, an abomination unto the LORD, the work of the hand of the craftsman, and putteth it in a secret place: and all the people shall answer and say, Amen.

1 Chr. 16 36Blessed be the LORD God of

Israel for ever and ever. And all the people said, Amen, and praised the LORD.

Psa. 41 [13]Blessed be the LORD God of Israel from everlasting, and to everlasting. Amen, and Amen.

Psa. 72 [19]And blessed be his glorious name for ever: and let the whole earth be filled with his glory; Amen, and Amen.

Psa. 89 [52]Blessed be the LORD for evermore. Amen, and Amen.

Jer. 28 [6]Even the prophet Jeremiah said, Amen: the LORD do so: the LORD perform thy words which thou hast prophesied, to bring again the vessels of the LORD's house, and all that is carried away captive from Babylon into this place.

Matt. 6 [13]And lead us not into temptation, but deliver us from evil. For thine is the kingdom, and the power, and the glory for ever. Amen.

John 3 [3]Jesus answered and said unto him, Verily, verily, I say unto thee, Except a man be born again, he cannot see the kingdom of God.

2 Cor. 1 [20]For all the promises of God in him are yea, and in him Amen, unto the glory of God by us.

Rev. 1 [18]I am he that liveth, and was dead; and behold, I am alive for evermore, Amen; and have the keys of hell and of death.

Rev. 5 [14]And the four beasts said, Amen. And the four and twenty elders fell down and worshiped him that liveth for ever and ever.

Rev. 22 [20]He which testifieth these things saith, Surely I come quickly: Amen. Even so, come, Lord Jesus.

REFERENCE: *Deut. 11:26.*

AMMONITES

[am'on īts] According to the Biblical tradition, the Ammonites were descended from Ben-Ammi, the son of Lot by his younger daughter (*Gen. 19:39*), and were therefore related to the Israelites. They dwelt east of the Dead Sea and the Jordan River. Throughout the history of Israel, there was enmity between the Ammonites and the Israelites, said to have arisen after the refusal of the Ammonites to give assistance to the Israelites on their approach to Canaan (*Deut. 23:4*). During the judgeship of Jephthah, the Ammonites oppressed the Israelites east of the Jordan, falsely claiming that they had been deprived of part of their land when the Israelites came from Egypt. The hostility continued into the reigns of Saul and David, when the Ammonites became the subjects of Israel. Upon the split of the kingdom of Israel, Ammon came under the control of Jeroboam, king of Northern Israel. When Ben-hadad deprived Israel of her transjordanic possessions, Ammon became a tributary of Syria and sent troops to assist Ben-Hadad in his battle with the Assyrians at Qarqar in 854 BC. After the rise of Tiglath-Pileser, they were generally subject to Assyria. The Ammonites aided the Chaldeans in the final subjugation of Judah in 587 BC (*2 Kin. 24:2*) and then conspired to obtain the death of Gedeliah, the capable governor appointed by the Babylonians to rule over those who were not exiled to Babylon. (*See* GEDELIAH) At the return of the Jews from exile, one of those who took the lead in attempting to thwart the efforts of Nehemiah to rebuild the wall of Jerusalem was Tobiah the Ammonite. We learn from sources outside the Bible that the Ammonites joined with the Syrians in their wars against Judea during the period of the Maccabees.

The chief deity of the Ammonites was Molech, part of whose worship included the offering of human sacrifices.

See MOLECH

REFERENCE: *Gen. 19:38; Deut. 2:19; 23:3; Judg. 11:4, 33; 1 Sam. 11:11; 2 Sam. 12:26; Jer. 25:21; Jer. 49:1; Ezek. 21:28; Ezek. 25:2, 3; Amos 1:13; Zeph. 2:8.*

AMON

[ā'mon] The son of Manasseh and king of Judah (642-640 BC). Amon is characterized as having engaged in all the idolatrous practices which marked the evil reign of his father. Like his father, he was apparently content to remain a vassal of Assyria. After a short reign of two years

Amon was assassinated, perhaps by an anti-Assyrian party. After further machinations, his young son Josiah was set up as king in his stead.

See MANASSEH, JOSIAH, KINGS

REFERENCE: *2 Kin. 21:19-26; 2 Chr. 33:21-25.*

AMORITES

[am′o rīts] This name is used in the Old Testament to designate: (1) the inhabitants of Palestine generally; (2) people who live in the hill country of Palestine, as opposed to those who live in the plains; and (3) a specific people under a king, Sihon. After the Israelites defeated Sihon, the Amorites are never again referred to as a people under a single king.

See SIHON

SCRIPTURE

Amorites as Inhabitants of Palestine

Gen. 14 [7]And they returned, and came to Enmishpat, which is Kadesh, and smote all the country of the Amalekites, and also the Amorites, that dwelt in Hazezontamar.
[13]And there came one that had escaped, and told Abram the Hebrew; for he dwelt in the plain of Mamre the Amorite, brother of Eshcol, and brother of Aner: and these were confederate with Abram.

Gen. 48 [22]Moreover I have given to thee one portion above thy brethren, which I took out of the hand of the Amorite with my sword and with my bow.

Deut. 3 [8]And we took at that time out of the hand of the two kings of the Amorites the land that was on this side Jordan, from the river of Arnon unto mount Hermon;

Deut. 4 [47]And they possessed his land, and the land of Og king of Bashan, two kings of the Amorites, which were on this side Jordan toward the sunrising;

Deut. 20 [17]But thou shalt utterly destroy them; namely, the Hittites, and the Amorites, the Hivites, and the Jebusites; as the LORD thy God hath commanded thee:

Judg. 6 [10]And I said unto you, I am the LORD your God; fear not the gods of the Amorites, in whose land ye dwell: but ye have not obeyed my voice.

As Hill-dwellers

Num. 13 [29]The Amalekites dwell in the land of the south: and the Hittites, and the Jebusites, and the Amorites, dwell in the mountains: and the Canaanites dwell by the sea, and by the coast of Jordan.

As a Specific Kingdom

Num. 21 [21]And Israel sent messengers unto Sihon king of the Amorites, saying,
[22]Let me pass through thy land: we will not turn into the fields, or into the vineyards; we will not drink of the waters of the well: but we will go along by the king's high way, until we be past thy borders.
[23]And Sihon would not suffer Israel to pass through his border: but Sihon gathered all his people together, and went out against Israel into the wilderness: and he came to Jahaz, and fought against Israel.
[24]And Israel smote him with the edge of the sword, and possessed his land from Arnon unto Jabbok, even unto the children of Ammon: for the border of the children of Ammon was strong.
[25]And Israel took all these cities: and Israel dwelt in all the cities of the Amorites, in Heshbon, and in all the villages thereof.

[31]Thus Israel dwelt in the land of the Amorites.

Deut. 2 [26]And I sent messengers out of the wilderness of Kedemoth unto Sihon king of Heshbon with words of peace, saying,
[27]Let me pass through thy land: I will go along by the high way, I will neither turn unto the right hand nor to the left.
[28]Thou shalt sell me meat for money, that

I may eat; and give me water for money, that I may drink: only I will pass through on my feet; [29](As the children of Esau which dwell in Seir, and the Moabites, which dwell in Ar, did unto me;) until I shall pass over Jordan into the land which the LORD our God giveth us. [30]But Sihon king of Heshbon would not let us pass by him: for the LORD thy God hardened his spirit, and made his heart obstinate, that he might deliver him into thy hand, as appeareth this day. [31]And the LORD said unto me, Behold, I have begun to give Sihon and his land before thee: begin to possess, that thou mayest inherit his land. [32]Then Sihon came out against us, he and all his people, to fight at Jahaz. [33]And the LORD our God delivered him before us; and we smote him, and his sons, and all his people. [34]And we took all his cities at that time, and utterly destroyed the men, and the women, and the little ones, of every city, we left none to remain: [35]Only the cattle we took for a prey unto ourselves, and the spoil of the cities which we took.

AMOS

[ā'mos] A prophet of the northern kingdom, active about the middle of the eighth century BC and a contemporary of Hosea. Amos was a native of the tiny village of Tehoa, on the edge of the wilderness of Judah. The village itself has never been found, but tomb groups in the area indicate that it easily could have existed. Amos was not of the professional class of prophets nor was he a son of a prophet; he was a herdsman and a dresser of sycamore trees when he received his summons from God—"The LORD took me as I followed the flock, and the LORD said unto me, 'Go, prophesy to my people Israel'" (*Amos 7:15*). Although this type of life was austere and simple, Amos had evidently come in contact with the commercial centers of Palestine, as he displays considerable knowledge of the habits and attitudes of the people to whom his message is directed. His oracles are not those of a primitive rustic but are literary masterpieces, full of vivid figures and allusions. At the beginning of Amos' prophetic ministry, Israel was enjoying the prosperous reign of Jeroboam II.

Samaria had established herself as a great commercial center. A rich merchant class had grown up and, as a result of robbery, violence and a general absence of scruples, was enjoying all manner of luxuries, as seen in the sumptuous character of their houses (*Amos 3:15*). The merchants were encouraged to follow this course by their avaricious wives whom Amos describes as "cows of Bashan" (*Amos 4:1*). The whole picture is one of complete lack of justice, mercy, and normal regard for human life.

The one condition of religion in Israel was on a level which matched the low moral and social standard. Although the shrines of God were well attended, they were subjected to the grossest sort of immorality and abuse, fornication and drunkenness being practiced in the very presence of the altar. The worship which was carried on was strictly a formal affair, devoid of any spiritual content; its effect on the conduct of the worshippers was negligible. Amos inveighed against this situation in a manner which demonstrated unflagging conviction that sin will not go unpunished and that the righteousness of God will ultimately triumph.

See JEROBOAM II, HOSES

REFERENCE: The Book of *Amos*.

ANANIAS

[an a nī'as] Three individuals in the book of *Acts* bear this name.

1. A covetous member of the church in Jerusalem. After selling a plot of land, this Ananias and his wife Sapphira pretended to donate the entire proceeds to the church, while in reality they kept back a portion of it. For their hypocrisy, they were punished with death.

2. A Christian in Damascus who was dispatched to "the street which is called Straight" to lay hands on Saul of Tarsus, to restore his sight, to charge him with his apostolic mission, and to baptize him.

3. The high priest before whom Paul was tried in Jerusalem.

SCRIPTURE

Ananias of Jerusalem

Acts 5 1But a certain man named Ananias, with Sapphira his wife, sold a possession, 2And kept back part of the price, his wife also being privy to it, and brought a certain part, and laid it at the apostles' feet. 3But Peter said, Ananias, why hath Satan filled thine heart to lie to the Holy Ghost, and to keep back part of the price of the land? 4Whiles it remained, was it not thine own? and after it was sold, was it not in thine own power? why hast thou conceived this thing in thine heart? thou hast not lied unto men, but unto God. 5And Ananias hearing these words fell down, and gave up the ghost: and great fear came on all them that heard these things. 6And the young men arose, wound him up, and carried him out, and buried him. 7And it was about the space of three hours after, when his wife, not knowing what was done, came in. 8And Peter answered unto her, Tell me whether ye sold the land for so much? And she said, Yea, for so much. 9Then Peter said unto her, How is it that ye have agreed together to tempt the Spirit of the Lord? behold, the feet of them which have buried thy husband are at the door, and shall carry thee out. 10Then fell she down straightway at his feet, and yielded up the ghost: and the young men came in, and found her dead, and, carrying her forth, buried her by her husband. 11And great fear came upon all the church, and upon as many as heard these things.

Ananias of Damascus

Acts 9 10And there was a certain disciple at Damascus, named Ananias; and to him said the Lord in a vision, Ananias. And he said, Behold, I am here, Lord. 11And the Lord said unto him, Arise, and go into the street which is called Straight, and enquire in the house of Judas for one called Saul, of Tarsus: for, behold, he prayeth, 12And hath seen in a vision a man named Ananias coming in, and putting his hand on him, that he might receive his sight. 13Then Ananias answered, Lord, I have heard by many of this man, how much evil he hath done to thy saints at Jerusalem: 14And here he hath authority from the chief priests to bind all that call on thy name. 15But the Lord said unto him, Go thy way: for he is a chosen vessel unto me, to bear my name before the Gentiles, and kings, and the children of Israel. 16For I will shew him how great things he must suffer for my name's sake. 17And Ananias went his way, and entered into the house; and putting his hands on him said, Brother Saul, the Lord, even Jesus, that appeared unto thee in the way as thou camest, hath sent me, that thou mightest receive thy sight, and be filled with the Holy Ghost. 18And immediately there fell from his eyes as it had been scales: and he received sight forthwith, and arose, and was baptized.

Ananias the High Priest

Acts 23 1And Paul, earnestly beholding the council, said, Men and brethren, I have lived in all good conscience before God until this day. 2And the high priest Ananias commanded them that stood by him to smite him on the mouth. 3Then said Paul unto him, God shall smite thee, thou whited wall: for sittest thou to judge me after the law, and commandest me to be smitten contrary to the law? 4And they that stood by said, Revilest thou God's high priest? [5]Then said Paul, I wist not, brethren, that he was the high priest: for it is written, Thou shalt not speak evil of the ruler of thy people.

Acts 24 [1]And after five days Ananias the high priest descended with the elders, and with a certain orator named Tertullus, who informed the governor against Paul.

Acts 25 [2]Then the high priest and the chief of the Jews informed him against Paul, and besought him, [3]And desired favour against him, that he would send for him to Jerusalem, laying wait in the way to kill him.

ANAT

[an′at] A female consort of the pagan deity Baal. (*See* Baal) Anat's name does not appear in the Bible except in names of places, for example, Beth-anath ("House of Anat").

ANDREW

[an′drōō] A Galilean fisherman from the city of Bethsaida. Andrew was a disciple of John who was chosen by Jesus to be an apostle. It was he who introduced his more famous brother, Peter, to Jesus. Although he is less well known than some of the other apostles, the gospels clearly indicate that Andrew was a regular companion of Jesus. He is also listed among the disciples who met together after the Lord's ascension.

See Apostles

SCRIPTURE

First Contacts with Jesus

John 1 [35]Again the next day after, John stood, and two of his disciples. [36]And looking upon Jesus as he walked, he saith, Behold the Lamb of God! [37]And the two disciples heard him speak, and they followed Jesus. [40]One of the two which heard John speak, and followed him, was Andrew, Simon Peter's brother. [41]He first findeth his own brother Simon, and saith unto him, We have found the Messias, which is, being interpreted, the Christ. [42]And he brought him to Jesus. . . .

[43]The day following Jesus would go forth into Galilee, and findeth Philip, and saith unto him, Follow me. [44]Now Philip was of Bethsaida, the city of Andrew and Peter.

His Call to be an Apostle

Matt. 4 [18]And Jesus, walking by the sea of Galilee, saw two brethren, Simon called Peter, and Andrew his brother, casting a net into the sea: for they were fishers. [19]And he saith unto them, Follow me, and I will make you fishers of men.

See Mark 1:16-17

Listed Among the Twelve

Matt. 10 [2]Now the names of the twelve apostles are these; The first, Simon, who is called Peter, and Andrew his brother; James the son of Zebedee, and John his brother;

See Mark 3:18; Luke 6:14

REFERENCE: *John 1:44; Mark 13:3-4; John 6:8; 12:20-22; Acts 1:13.*

ANGEL

[ān′jel] This word is used in the Bible to translate the Hebrew and Greek words for "messengers" and usually refers to an order of supernatural or heavenly beings who act as God's messengers. In the early writings of the Old Testament, "the angel of the Lord" denoted an appearance of God in human form. The scriptures picture God as being attended by a heavenly host of angels who serve as intermediaries between God and man, bringing God's revelation and assistance and acting as intercessors for men.

See Gabriel, Michael

SCRIPTURE

Angels as an Appearance of God in Human Form

Gen. 16 [7]And the angel of the LORD found her by a fountain of water in the wilderness, by the fountain in the way to Shur. [8]And he said, Hagar, Sarai's maid, whence camest thou? and whither wilt thou go? And she said, I flee from the face of my mistress Sarai. [9]And the angel of the LORD said unto her, Return to thy mistress, and submit thyself under her hands. [13]And she called the name of the LORD that spake unto her, Thou God seest me: for she said, Have I also here looked after him that seeth me?

Gen. 22 [10]And Abraham stretched forth his hand, and took the knife to slay his son. [11]And the angel of the LORD called unto him out of heaven, and said, Abraham, Abraham: and he said, Here am I.

[15]And the angel of the LORD called unto Abraham out of heaven the second time, [16]And said, By myself have I sworn, saith the LORD, for because thou hast done this thing, and hast not withheld thy son, thine only son, [17]That in blessing I will bless thee, and in multiplying I will multiply thy seed as the stars of the heaven, and as the sand which is upon the seashore; and thy seed shall possess the gate of his enemies; [18]And in thy seed shall all the nations of the earth be blessed; because thou hast obeyed my voice.

Ex. 3 [2]And the angel of the LORD appeared unto him in a flame of fire out of the midst of a bush: and he looked, and, behold, the bush burned with fire, and the bush was not consumed. [4]And when the LORD saw that he turned aside to see, God called unto him out of the midst of the bush, and said, Moses, Moses. And he said, Here am I.

See Judg. 2:1ff; 5:23; 6:11-24; 13:3ff

The Heavenly Host

Gen. 28 [12]And he dreamed, and behold a ladder set up on the earth, and the top of it reached to heaven: and behold the angels of God ascending and descending on it.

1 Kin. 22 [19]And he said, Hear thou therefore the word of the LORD: I saw the LORD sitting on his throne, and all the host of heaven standing by him on his right hand and on his left.

Neh. 9 [6]Thou, even thou, art LORD alone: thou hast made heaven, the heaven of heavens, with all their host, the earth, and all things that are therein, the seas, and all that is therein, and thou preservest them all; and the host of heaven worshippeth thee.

Psa. 68 [17]The chariots of God are twenty thousand, even thousands of angels: the LORD is among them, as in Sinai, in the holy place.

Psa. 103 [20]Bless the LORD, ye his angels, that excel in strength, that do his commandments, hearkening unto the voice of his word. [21]Bless ye the LORD, all ye his hosts; ye ministers of his, that do his pleasure.

Heb. 12 [22]But ye are come unto mount Sion, and unto the city of the living God, the heavenly Jerusalem, and to an innumerable company of angels,

Nature, Office, Duties, etc., of Angels

2 Sam. 24 [16]And when the angel stretched out his hand upon Jerusalem to destroy it, the LORD repented him of the evil, and said to the angel that destroyed the people, It is enough: stay now thine hand. And the angel of the LORD was by the threshingplace of Araunah the Jebusite.

1 Kin. 19 [5]And as he lay and slept under a juniper-tree, behold, then an angel touched him, and said unto him, Arise and eat.

Psa. 91 [11]For he shall give his angels charge over thee, to keep thee in all thy ways.

Matt. 13 [39]The enemy that sowed them is the devil; the harvest is the end of the world; and the reapers are the angels.

Matt. 16 [27]For the son of man shall come in the glory of his Father, with his angels; and then he shall reward every man according to his works.

Matt. 24 [31]And he shall send his Angels with a great sound of a trumpet, and they shall gather together his Elect from the four winds, from one end of heaven to the other.

Matt. 25 [31]When the Son of man shall come in his glory, and all the holy angels with him, then shall he sit upon the throne of his glory.

2 Thess. 1 [7]And to you, who are troubled, rest with us, when the Lord Jesus shall be revealed from heaven with his mighty angels, [8]In flaming fire taking vengeance on them that know not God, and that obey not the gospel of our Lord Jesus Christ.

Heb. 1 [4]Being made so much better than the angels, as he hath by inheritance obtained a more excellent name than they. [5]For unto which of the angels said he at any time, Thou art my Son, this day have I begotten thee? And again, I will be to him a Father, and he shall be to me a Son? [6]And again, when he bringeth in the first-begotten into the world, he saith, And let all the angels of God worship him. [7]And of the angels he saith, Who maketh his angels spirits, and his ministers a flame of fire.

Visitations of Angels

TO HAGAR

Gen. 16 [7]And the angel of the LORD found her by a fountain of water in the wilderness, by the fountain in the way to Shur.

Gen. 21 [17]And God heard the voice of the lad; and the angel of God called to Hagar out of heaven, and said unto her, What aileth thee, Hagar? Fear not; for God hath heard the voice of the lad where he is.

TO ABRAHAM

Gen. 18 [1]And the LORD appeared unto him in the plains of Mamre: and he sat in the tent door in the heat of the day; [2]And he lift up his eyes and looked, and, lo, three men stood by him: and when he saw them, he ran to meet them from the tent door, and bowed himself toward the ground.

Gen. 22 [11]And the angel of the LORD called unto him out of heaven, and said, Abraham, Abraham: and he said, Here am I.

TO LOT

Gen. 19 [1]And there came two angels to Sodom at even; and Lot sat in the gate of Sodom; and Lot, seeing them, rose up to meet them; and he bowed himself with his face toward the ground.

TO BALAAM

Num. 22 [31]Then the LORD opened the

eyes of Balaam, and he saw the angel of the LORD standing in the way, and his sword drawn in his hand: and he bowed down his head, and fell flat on his face.

TO THE ISRAELITES

Judg. 2 [1]And an angel of the LORD came up from Gilgal to Bochim, and said, I made you to go up out of Egypt, and have brought you unto the land which I sware unto your fathers; and I said, I will never break my covenant with you.

TO GIDEON

Judg. 6 [11]And there came an angel of the LORD, and sat under an oak which was in Ophrah, that pertained unto Joash the Abi-ezrite: and his son Gideon threshed wheat by the wine-press, to hide it from the Midianites. [12]And the angel of the LORD appeared unto him, and said unto him, The LORD is with thee, thou mighty man of valour.

TO MANOAH'S WIFE

Judg. 13 [2]And there was a certain man of Zorah, of the family of the Danites, whose name was Manoah; and his wife was barren, and bare not. [3]And the angel of the LORD appeared unto the woman, and said unto her, Behold, now, thou art barren, and bearest not: but thou shalt conceive, and bear a son.

TO DAVID

1 Chr. 21 [15]And God sent an angel unto Jerusalem to destroy it: and as he was destroying, the LORD beheld, and he repented him of the evil, and said to the angel that destroyed, It is enough, stay now thine hand. And the angel of the LORD stood by the threshingfloor of Ornan the Jebusite. [16]And David lifted up his eyes, and saw the angel of the LORD stand between the earth and the heaven, having a drawn sword in his hand stretched out over Jerusalem. Then David and the elders of Israel, who were clothed in sackcloth, fell upon their faces.

TO ELIJAH

1 Kin. 19 [5]And as he lay and slept under a juniper-tree, behold, then an angel touched him, and said unto him, Arise and eat. [6]And he looked, and behold, there was a cake baken on the coals, and a cruse of water at his head: and he did eat and drink, and laid him down again. [7]And the angel of the LORD came again the second time, and touched him, and said, Arise and eat, because the journey is too great for thee.

TO DANIEL

Dan. 8 [16]And I heard a man's voice between the banks of Ulai, which called, and said, Gabriel, make this man to understand the vision. [17]So he came near where I stood: and when he came, I was afraid, and fell upon my face: but he said unto me, Understand, O son of man: for at the time of the end shall be the vision.

Dan. 9 [21]Yea, while I was speaking in prayer, even the man Gabriel, whom I had seen in the vision at the beginning, being caused to fly swiftly, touched me about the time of the evening oblation.

Dan. 10 [16]And behold, one like the similitude of the sons of men touched my lips: then I opened my mouth, and spake, and said unto him that stood before me, O my lord, by the vision my sorrows are turned upon me, and I have retained no strength.

TO NEBUCHADNEZZAR

Dan. 3 [24]Then Nebuchadnezzar the king was astonied, and rose up in haste, and spake, and said unto his counsellors, Did not we cast three men bound into the midst of the fire? They answered and said unto the king, True, O king. [25]He answered and said, Lo, I see four men loose, walking in the midst of the fire, and they have no hurt: and the form of the fourth is like the Son of God.

TO JESUS

Matt. 4 [11]Then the devil leaveth him, and behold, angels came and ministered unto him.

Luke 22 [43]And there appeared an angel unto him from heaven, strengthening him.

TO JOSEPH

Matt. 1 [20]But while he thought on these things, behold, the angel of the Lord appeared unto him in a dream, saying, Joseph, thou son of David, fear not to take unto thee Mary thy wife; for that which is conceived in her is of the Holy Ghost.

TO MARY MAGDALENE

Matt. 28 [1]In the end of the sabbath, as it began to dawn toward the first day of the week, came Mary Magdalene and the other Mary to see the sepulchre. [2]And behold, there was a great earthquake: for the angel of the Lord descended from heaven, and came and rolled back the stone from the door, and sat upon it.

TO ZACHARIAS

Luke 1 [11]And there appeared unto him an angel of the Lord, standing on the right side of the altar of incense. [12]And when Zacharias saw him, he was troubled, and fear fell upon him.

TO THE VIRGIN MARY

Luke 1 [26]And in the sixth month the angel Gabriel was sent from God unto a city of Galilee, named Nazareth, [27]To a virgin espoused to a man whose name was Joseph, of the house of David; and the virgin's name was Mary.

TO THE SHEPHERDS

Luke 2 [8]And there were in the same country shepherds abiding in the field, keeping watch over their flock by night. [9]And lo, the angel of the Lord came upon them, and the glory of the Lord shone round about them; and they were sore afraid. [13]And suddenly there was with the angel a multitude of the heavenly host praising God, and saying, [14]Glory to God in the highest, and on earth peace, good will toward men.

TO PETER AND OTHERS

Acts 5 [19]But the angel of the Lord by night opened the prison-doors, and brought them forth, and said, [20]Go, stand and speak in the temple to the people all the words of this life.

Acts 12 [7]And behold, the angel of the Lord came upon him, and a light shined in the prison; and he smote Peter on the side, and raised him up, saying, Arise up quickly. And his chains fell off from his hands.

TO PHILIP

Acts 8 [26]And the angel of the Lord spake unto Philip, saying, Arise, and go toward the south, unto the way that goeth down from Jerusalem unto Gaza, which is desert.

TO CORNELIUS

Acts 10 [3]He saw in a vision evidently, about the ninth hour of the day, an angel of God coming in to him, and saying unto him, Cornelius.

TO PAUL

Acts 27 [23]For there stood by me this night the Angel of God, whose I am, and whom I serve, [24]Saying, Fear not, Paul, thou must be brought before Caesar, and lo, God hath given thee all them that sail with thee.

Basis of the Doctrine of Guardian Angels

Matt. 18 [10]Take heed that ye despise not one of these little ones; for I say unto you, That in heaven their angels do always behold the face of my Father which is in heaven.

Acts 12 [15]And they said unto her, Thou art mad. But she constantly affirmed that it was even so. Then said they, It is his angel.

ANGER

[an′gẽr] A strong passion or emotion of displeasure, and usually antagonism, excited by real or supposed injury, insult, or wrong. It may be sinful or wise, according to its motive; displeasure at sin may be entirely righteous. When ascribed to God, anger is not to be understood as a tumultous human passion, but a righteous aversion to sin and wrongdoing. Sinful anger often exists in man, as a work of the flesh or as a result of pride; it may often lead to the commission of even greater sins.

SCRIPTURE

Human Anger: Nature and Effects

Gen. 4 [5]But unto Cain and to his offering he had not respect. And Cain was very wroth, and his countenance fell. [8]And Cain talked with Abel his brother: and it came to pass, when they were in the field, that Cain rose up against Abel his brother, and slew him.

Gen. 44 [18]Then Judah came near unto him, and said, O my lord, let thy servant, I pray thee, speak a word in my lord's ears, and let not thine anger burn against thy servant: for thou art even as Pharaoh.

Gen. 49 [7]Cursed be their anger, for it was fierce: and their wrath, for it was cruel: I will divide them in Jacob, and scatter them in Israel.

Ex. 32 [19]And it came to pass as soon as he came nigh unto the camp, that he saw the calf, and the dancing: and Moses' anger waxed hot, and he cast the tables out of his hands, and brake them beneath the mount.

Prov. 15 [18]A wrathful man stirreth up strife: but he that is slow to anger appeaseth strife.

Prov. 16 [32]He that is slow to anger is better than the mighty; and he that ruleth his spirit, than he that taketh a city.

Prov. 19 [11]The discretion of a man deferreth his anger; and it is his glory to pass over a transgression.

Prov. 21 [19]It is better to dwell in the wilderness, than with a contentious and an angry woman.

Prov. 29 [22]An angry man stirreth up strife, and a furious man aboundeth in transgression.

Eccl. 7 [9]Be not hasty in thy spirit to be angry: for anger resteth in the bosom of fools.

Matt. 5 [22]But I say unto you, That whosoever is angry with his brother without a cause, shall be in danger of the judgment: and whosoever shall say to his brother, Raca, shall be in danger of the council: but whosoever shall say, Thou fool, shall be in danger of hell-fire.

Human Anger: Remedies and Warnings

Psa. 37 [8]Cease from anger, and forsake wrath: fret not thyself in any wise to do evil.

Prov. 15 [1]A soft answer turneth away wrath: but grievous words stir up anger.

Prov. 21 [14]A gift in secret pacifieth anger: and a reward in the bosom, strong wrath.

Eph. 4 [26]Be ye angry, and sin not: let not the sun go down upon your wrath. [31]Let all bitterness, and wrath, and anger, and clamour, and evil-speaking, be put away from you, with all malice.

Col. 3 [8]But now ye also put off all these; anger, wrath, malice, blasphemy, filthy communication out of your mouth.

Divine Anger: Existence, Manifestation, etc.

Gen. 3 [14]And the LORD God said unto the serpent, Because thou hast done this, thou art cursed above all cattle, and above every beast of the field: upon thy belly shalt thou go, and dust shalt thou eat all the days of thy life. [16]Unto the woman he said, I will greatly multiply thy sorrow and thy conception; in sorrow thou shalt bring forth children; and thy desire shall be to thy husband, and he shall rule over thee. [17]And unto Adam he said, Because thou hast hearkened unto the voice of thy wife, and hast eaten of the tree, of which I commanded thee, saying, Thou shalt not eat of it: cursed is the ground for thy sake; in sorrow shalt thou eat of it all the days of thy life.

Gen. 4 [10]And he said, What hast thou done? the voice of thy brother's blood crieth unto me from the ground. [11]And now art thou cursed from the earth, which hath opened her mouth to receive thy brother's blood from thy hand.

Deut. 29 [20]The LORD will not spare him, but then the anger of the LORD and his jealousy shall smoke against that man, and all the curses that are written in this book shall lie upon him, and the LORD shall blot out his name from under heaven.

Deut. 32 [16]They provoked him to jealousy with strange gods, with abominations provoked they him to anger.

Josh. 23 [16]When ye have transgressed the covenant of the LORD your God, which he commanded you, and have gone and served other gods, and bowed yourselves to them; then shall the anger of the LORD be kindled against you, and ye shall perish quickly from off the good land which he hath given unto you.

Job 9 [13]If God will not withdraw his anger, the proud helpers do stoop under him.

Psa. 7 [11]God judgeth the righteous, and God is angry with the wicked every day.

Psa. 21 [9]Thou shalt make them as a fiery oven in the time of thine anger: the LORD shall swallow them up in his wrath, and the fire shall devour them.

Psa. 69 [24]Pour out thine indignation upon them, and let thy wrathful anger take hold of them.

Psa. 78 [21]Therefore the LORD heard this, and was wroth: so a fire was kindled against Jacob, and anger also came up against Israel. [58]For they provoked him to anger with their high places, and moved him to jealousy with their graven images.

Psa. 90 [11]Who knoweth the power of thine anger? even according to thy fear so is thy wrath.

Isa. 30 [27]Behold, the name of the LORD cometh from far, burning with his anger, and the burden thereof is heavy: his lips are full of indignation, and his tongue as a devouring fire.

Jer. 3 [5]Will he reserve his anger for ever? will he keep it to the end? Behold, thou hast spoken and done evil things as thou couldest.

Jer. 7 [19]Do they provoke me to anger? saith the LORD: do they not provoke themselves to the confusion of their own faces?

Jer. 44 [3]Because of their wickedness which they have committed to provoke me to anger, in that they went to burn incense, and to serve other gods, whom they knew not, neither they, ye, nor your fathers.

Mark 3 [5]And when he had looked round about on them with anger, being grieved for the hardness of their hearts, he saith unto the man, Stretch forth thine hand. And he stretched it out: and his hand was restored whole as the other.

Divine Anger: Kindled

Num. 11 [1]And when the people complained, it displeased the LORD: and the LORD heard it: and his anger was kindled; and the fire of the LORD burnt among them, and consumed them that were in the uttermost parts of the camp.

Josh. 7 [1]But the children of Israel committed a trespass in the accursed thing: for Achan, the son of Carmi, the son of Zabdi, the son of Zerah, of the tribe of Judah, took of the accursed thing: and the anger of the LORD was kindled against the children of Israel.

2 Sam. 6 [7]And the anger of the LORD was kindled against Uzzah, and God smote him there for his error; and there he died by the ark of God.

2 Sam. 24 [1]And again the anger of the LORD was kindled against Israel, and he moved David against them to say, Go, number Israel and Judah.

Psa. 2 [12]Kiss the Son, lest he be angry, and ye perish from the way, when his wrath is kindled but a little. Blessed are all they that put their trust in him.

Jer. 17 [4]And thou, even thyself, shalt discontinue from thine heritage that I gave thee; and I will cause thee to serve thine enemies in the land which thou knowest not: for ye have kindled a fire in mine anger, which shall burn forever.

Hos. 8 [5]Thy calf, O Samaria, hath cast thee off; mine anger is kindled against them: how long will it be ere they attain to innocency?

Zech. 10 [3]Mine anger was kindled against the shepherds, and I punished the goats: for the LORD of hosts hath visited his flock the house of Judah, and hath made them as his goodly horse in the battle.

Divine Anger: Slow or Deferred

Psa. 103 [8]The LORD is merciful and gracious, slow to anger, and plenteous in mercy. [9]He will not always chide; neither will he keep his anger for ever.

Isa. 48 [9]For my name's sake will I defer mine anger, and for my praise will I refrain for thee, that I cut thee not off.

Hos. 14 [4]I will heal their backsliding, I will love them freely: for mine anger is turned away from him.

Divine Anger: Laid up for Wicked

Rom. 2 [5]But after thy hardness and impenitent heart, treasurest up unto thyself wrath against the day of wrath, and revelation of the righteous judgment of God; [6]Who will render to every man according to his deeds.

2 Pet. 3 [7]But the heavens and the earth, which are now, by the same word are kept in store, reserved unto fire against the day of judgment and perdition of ungodly men.

Divine Anger: Prayer against

Ex. 32 [11]And Moses besought the LORD, his God, and said, LORD, why doth thy wrath wax hot against thy people, which thou hast brought forth out of the land of Egypt, with great power, and with a mighty hand?

2 Sam. 24 [17]And David spake unto the LORD when he saw the angel that smote the people, and said, Lo, I have sinned, and I have done wickedly: but these sheep, what have they done? Let thine hand, I pray thee, be against me, and against my father's house.

Psa. 6 [1]O LORD, rebuke me not in thine anger, neither chasten me in thy hot displeasure.

Psa. 27 [9]Hide not thy face far from me; put not thy servant away in anger: thou hast been my help; leave me not, neither forsake me, O God of my salvation.

Psa. 39 [10]Remove thy stroke away from me: I am consumed by the blow of thine hand.

Psa. 74 [1]O God, why hast thou cast us off for ever? why doth thine anger smoke against the sheep of thy pasture?

Psa. 79 [5]How long, LORD? wilt thou be angry for ever? shall thy jealousy burn like fire? [6]Pour out thy wrath upon the heathen that have not known thee, and upon the kingdoms that have not called upon thy name.

Psa. 80 [4]O LORD God of hosts, how long wilt thou be angry against the prayer of thy people?

Psa. 85 [4]Turn us, O God of our salvation, and cause thine anger toward us to cease. [5]Wilt thou be angry with us for ever? wilt thou draw out thine anger to all generations?

Isa. 64 [9]Be not wroth very sore, O LORD, neither remember iniquity for ever: behold, see, we beseech thee, we are all thy people.

Dan. 9 [16]O LORD, according to all thy righteousness, I beseech thee, let thine anger and thy fury be turned away from thy city Jerusalem, thy holy mountain: because for our sins, and for the iniquities of our fathers, Jerusalem and thy people are become a reproach to all that are about us.

Hab. 3 [2]O LORD, I have heard thy speech and was afraid: O LORD, revive thy work in the midst of the years, in the midst of the years make known; in wrath remember mercy.

Luke 18 [13]And the publican, standing afar off, would not lift up so much as his eyes unto heaven, but smote upon his breast, saying, God be merciful to me a sinner.

Divine Anger: Christ's Propitiation

Rom. 3 [25]Whom God hath set forth to be a propitiation, through faith in his blood, to declare his righteousness for the remission of sins that are past, through the forbearance of God.

Rom. 5 [9]Much more then, being now justified by his blood, we shall be saved from wrath through him.

2 Cor. 5 [18]And all things are of God, who hath reconciled us to himself by Jesus Christ, and hath given to us the ministry of reconciliation.

Col. 1 [20]And, having made peace through the blood of his cross, by him to reconcile all things unto himself; by him, I say, whether they be things in earth, or things in heaven.

1 Thess. 1 [10]And to wait for his Son from heaven, whom he raised from the dead, even Jesus, which delivered us from the wrath to come.

1 John 2 [2]And he is the propitiation for our sins: and not for ours only, but also for the sins of the whole world.

Divine Anger: Turned by Repentance

1 Kin. 21 [29]Seest thou how Ahab humbleth himself before me? because he humbleth himself before me, I will not bring the evil in his days: but in his son's days will I bring the evil upon his house.

Jer. 3 [12]Go and proclaim these words toward the north, and say, Return, thou backsliding Israel, saith the LORD; and I will not cause mine anger to fall upon you: for I am merciful, saith the LORD, and I will not keep anger for ever.

ANNAS

[an′as] A high priest of the Jews from AD 7 to AD 15, at which time he was deposed by Valerius Gratus. Ordinarily the high-priesthood was for life, but under Roman rule a priest was retained in office only so long as his policy was pleasing to the Roman officials. Jesus was brought before Annas in the early stage of his trial (*John 18:13, 19, 24*). Annas was also present, and referred to as high priest, when Peter and John were brought before the chief priests and rulers of the Jews (*Acts 4:6*). These references to Annas seem to indicate that, despite his deposition, he remained an influential leader in the priestly party, being regarded as the real high priest, although officially the office was filled by another. That he obviously had a controlling interest in the high priesthood is demonstrated by the fact that five of his sons and his son-in-law Caiaphas all held the office of high priest in almost unbroken succession.

See CAIAPHAS

REFERENCE: *Luke 3:2; John 18:13, 19, 24; Acts 4:6.*

ANOINTING

[a noint′ing] The application of unguents or oils to the body and head. Among the ancient Hebrews, those who could afford it anointed their bodies daily with olive oil, plain or mixed with perfumes, as a regular part of their everyday toilet. The poor, of course, were forced to reserve its use for special occasions. During periods of mourning, this practice was suspended; its resumption signalled the end of mourning. Anointing the head or feet of a guest was counted as a mark of esteem.

Anointing as a religious rite was found in application both to persons and things. Kings and priests were set apart for their office by the pouring of consecrated oil on their heads. This was believed to impart to them a special measure of the spirit of the LORD; persons receiving this anointing are sometimes referred to as "the LORD's anointed," translated in the Bible as Messiah or Christ. It was also a custom among the Hebrews to anoint sacred stones and various articles used in worship.

SCRIPTURE

Anointing in Everyday Life

Ruth 3 [3]Wash thyself therefore, and anoint thee, and put thy raiment upon thee, and get thee down to the floor: but make not thyself known unto the man, until he shall have done eating and drinking.

2 Sam. 12 [20]Then David arose from the earth, and washed, and anointed himself, and changed his apparel, and came to his own house; and when he required, they set bread before him, and he did eat.

2 Sam. 14 [2]And Joab sent to Tekoah, and fetched thence a wise woman, and said unto her, I pray thee, feign thyself to be a mourner, and put on now mourning apparel, and anoint not thyself with oil, but be as a woman that had a long time mourned for the dead.

A Sign of Honor to Guests

Psa. 23 [5]Thou preparest a table before me in the presence of mine enemies: thou anointest my head with oil; my cup runneth over.

Luke 7 [38]And stood at his feet behind him weeping, and began to wash his feet with tears, and did wipe them with the hairs of her head, and kissed his feet, and anointed them with the ointment. [46]My head with oil thou didst not anoint: but this woman hath anointed my feet with ointment.

Anointing of Persons

AARON

Lev. 8 [12]And he poured of the anointing oil upon Aaron's head, and anointed him, to sanctify him.

SAUL

1 Sam. 10 [1]Then Samuel took a vial of oil, and poured it upon his head, and kissed him, and said, Is it not because the LORD hath anointed thee to be captain over his inheritance?

DAVID

1 Sam. 16 [13]Then Samuel took the horn of oil, and anointed him in the midst of his brethren: and the Spirit of the LORD came upon David from that day forward. So Samuel rose up, and went to Ramah.

SOLOMON

1 Kin. 1 [39]And Zadok the priest took an horn of oil out of the tabernacle, and anointed Solomon. And they blew the trumpet; and all the people said, God save king Solomon.

ELISHA AND JEHU

1 Kin. 19 [16]And Jehu the son of Nimshi shalt thou anoint to be king over Israel: and Elisha the son of Shaphat of Abelmeholah shalt thou anoint to be prophet in thy room.

JEHU

2 Kin. 9 [6]And he arose, and went into the house; and he poured the oil on his head, and said unto him, Thus saith the LORD God of Israel, I have anointed thee king over the people of the LORD, even over Israel.

JOASH

2 Kin. 11 [12]And he brought forth the king's son, and put the crown upon him, and gave him the testimony; and they made him king, and anointed him; and they clapped their hands, and said, God save the king.

JESUS

Matt. 26 [7]There came unto him a woman having an alabaster-box of very precious ointment, and poured it on his head as he sat at meat.

Mark 14 [3]And being in Bethany, in the house of Simon the leper, as he sat at meat, there came a woman having an alabaster-box of ointment of spikenard, very precious; and she brake the box, and poured it on his head.

John 12 [3]Then took Mary a pound of ointment of spikenard, very costly, and anointed the feet of Jesus, and wiped his feet with her hair: and the house was filled with the odour of the ointment.

Luke 7 [37]And behold, a woman in the city, which was a sinner, when she knew that Jesus sat at meat in the Pharisee's house, brought an alabaster-box of ointment, [38]And stood at his feet behind him weeping, and began to wash his feet with tears, and did wipe them with the hairs of her head, and kissed his feet, and anointed them with the ointment.

Anointing of Things

Gen. 28 [18]And Jacob rose up early in the morning, and took the stone that he had put for his pillows, and set it up for a pillar, and poured oil upon the top of it.

Ex. 30 [29]And thou shalt sanctify them, that they may be most holy: whatsoever toucheth them shall be holy.

Ex. 40 [9]And thou shalt take the anointing oil, and anoint the tabernacle, and all that is therein, and shalt hallow it, and all the vessels thereof: and it shall be holy.

ANTICHRIST

[an'ti krīst] This term refers to the force or forces of evil which, according to scripture, will arise in a final effort shortly before the return of the LORD. In the epistles of John, the Antichrist is identified as he who "denieth that Jesus is the Christ," "that denieth the Father and the Son," and "confesseth not that Jesus Christ is come in the flesh" (*1 John 2:22; 4:2-3*). John speaks of "many Antichrists" (*1 John 2:18*), in contrast to Paul, who seems to view the Man of Sin as a single individual. In every age, Christians have discerned the Antichrist, and surely the spirit of Antichrist has been evident. The most that Christians can say, however, is that in their own day more complete embodiments of Antichrist appear than have ever appeared before. In the face of the forces of evil which threaten us, it is heartening to recognize that the work of Antichrist or the Man of Sin is always discussed against the background of the ultimate triumph of the LORD and his Kingdom.

SCRIPTURE

1 John 2 [18]Little children, it is the last time: and as ye have heard that antichrist shall come, even now are there many antichrists; whereby we know that it is the last time. [22]Who is a liar but he that denieth that Jesus is the Christ? He is antichrist, that denieth the Father and the Son.

1 John 4 [3]And every spirit that confesseth not that Jesus Christ is come in the flesh, is not of God. And this is that spirit of antichrist, whereof ye have heard that it should come; and even now already is it in the world.

2 John 1 [7]For many deceivers are entered into the world, who confess not that Jesus Christ is come in the flesh. This is a deceiver and an antichrist.

The Man of Sin

2 Thess. 2 [2]That ye be not soon shaken in mind, or be troubled, neither by spirit, nor by word, nor by letter as from us, as that the day of Christ is at hand. [3]Let no man deceive you by any means: for that day shall not come, except there come a falling away first, and that man of sin be revealed, the son of perdition.

ANTIOCH

[an'ti ok] The Bible mentions two cities by this name, Antioch in Pisidia and Antioch in Syria, both of which were founded by Seleucus Nicator, ruler of Syria from 301-380 BC, and named for his father Antiochus.

1. *Antioch in Pisidia.* This city was strategically important, having been built on a plateau commanding one of the roads leading from the East to the Maeander river and Ephesus. It is mentioned in the Bible in connection with the visits of the apostle Paul on his various missionary journies. On his first visit Paul preached the gospel in the synagogue and incurred the wrath of a number of the Jews of that city. So opposed were they to his preaching that they continued their persecution of him when he journeyed to Lystra. On the backswing of the first journey, he passed through Antioch again. It is to be assumed that he also visited the city on his second and third tours.

2. *Antioch in Syria.* Seleucus Nicator founded this Antioch on the banks of the Orontes river, about fifteen miles inland. Through fortunate political circumstances, Antioch was favored by Roman rulers when Rome became mistress of the world and was made into a city even more splendid than under her Syrian masters. She was the third city of the empire, ranking behind only Rome and Alexandria. Antioch is best known to Christians as the cradle of Gentile Christianity and as the headquarters for Paul's missionary efforts. It was largely because of the church at

Antioch that the council at Jerusalem declared that gentile Christians were not subject to the Jewish law. It was here, during the early labors of Paul and Barnabas, that the followers of Jesus were first called Christians. Long after the Apostolid era closed, Antioch continued to be a center of Christianity and Christian scholarship.

REFERENCE: *Acts 11:19-30; Acts 13:1-3; 14:26-27; 15:22; Gal. 2:11-15.*

APOLLOS

[a pol'os] A Jew of Alexandria, "an eloquent man, and mighty in the scriptures," "Instructed in the way of the Lord" according to the imperfect view of the disciples of John the Baptist. On his coming to Ephesus during a temporary absence of Paul, Aquila, and Priscilla, two disciples in that city, "expounded unto him the way of God more perfectly." After that he preached the gospel in Greece; the essence of his work and message is contained in the following words: "he mightily convinced the Jews, and that publicly, shewing by the scriptures that Jesus was Christ." In *1 Cor.*, he is spoken of as having "watered," or nourished, those Christians which Paul had "planted." Apollos is thought by many to have been the author of the Epistle to the Hebrews.

SCRIPTURE

Acts 18 [24]And a certain Jew named Apollos, born at Alexandria, an eloquent man, and mighty in the scriptures, came to Ephesus. [25]This man was instructed in the way of the Lord; and being fervent in the spirit, he spake and taught diligently the things of the Lord, knowing only the baptism of John. [26]And he began to speak boldly in the synagogue: whom when Aquila and Priscilla had heard, they took him unto them, and expounded unto him the way of God more perfectly. [27]And when he was disposed to pass into Achaia, the brethren wrote, exhorting the disciples to receive him: who, when he was come, helped them much which had believed through grace: [28]For he mightily convinced the Jews and that publickly, shewing by the scriptures that Jesus was Christ.

1 Cor. 3 [4]For while one saith, I am of Paul; and another, I am of Apollos; are ye not carnal? [5]Who then is Paul, and who is Apollos, but ministers by whom ye believed, even as the Lord gave to every man? [6]I have planted, Apollos watered; but God gave the increase.

APOSTASY

[a pos'ta si] A falling away, a withdrawal, a defection from the faith. Apostasy, or forsaking the LORD, was the characteristic sin of Israel and is repeatedly cited as the cause of her misfortunes. In the New Testament Paul was accused of preaching apostasy from Moses and he himself predicted that apostasy would be common in "the latter days."

See BACKSLIDING

SCRIPTURE

Apostasy Foretold

Matt. 24 [10]And then shall many be offended, and shall betray one another, and shall hate one another. [11]And many false prophets shall rise, and shall deceive many. [12]And because iniquity shall abound, the love of many shall wax cold.

2 Thess. 2 [3]Let no man deceive you by any means: for that day shall not come, except there come a falling away first, and that man of sin be revealed, the son of perdition;

1 Tim. 4 [1]Now the Spirit speaketh expressly, that in the latter times some shall depart from the faith, giving heed to seducing spirits, and doctrines of devils; [2]Speaking lies in hypocrisy; having their conscience seared with a hot iron. [3]Forbidding to marry, and commanding to abstain from meats, which God hath created to be received with thanksgiving of them which believe and know the truth.

2 Pet. 3 [17]Ye therefore, beloved, seeing

ye know these things before, beware lest ye also, being led away with the error of the wicked, fall from your own stedfastness.

Causes of Apostasy

PERSECUTION

Matt. 24 [9]Then shall they deliver you up to be afflicted, and shall kill you: and ye shall be hated of all nations for my name's sake. [10]And then shall many be offended, and shall betray one another, and shall hate one another.

FALSE TEACHERS

Matt. 24 [11]And many false prophets shall rise, and shall deceive many.

TEMPTATION

Luke 8 [13]They on the rock are they, which, when they hear, receive the word with joy; and these have no root, which for a while believe, and in time of temptation fall away.

MORAL LAPSE

Heb. 6 [4]For it is impossible for those who were once enlightened, and have tasted of the heavenly gift, and were made partakers of the Holy Ghost, [5]And have tasted the good word of God, and the powers of the world to come, [6]If they shall fall away, to renew them again unto repentance; seeing they crucify to themselves the Son of God afresh, and put him to an open shame.

FORSAKING WORSHIP AND SPIRITUAL LIVING

Heb. 10 [25]Not forsaking the assembling of ourselves together, as the manner of some is; but exhorting one another; and so much the more, as ye see the day approaching. [26]For if we sin wilfully after that we have received the knowledge of the truth, there remaineth no more sacrifice for sins, [27]But a certain fearful looking for of judgment and fiery indignation, which shall devour the adversaries. [28]He that despised Moses' law died without mercy under two or three witnesses: [29]Of how much sorer punishment, suppose ye, shall he be thought worthy, who hath trodden under foot the Son of God, and hath counted the blood of the covenant, wherewith he was sanctified, an unholy thing, and hath done despite unto the Spirit of grace?

UNBELIEF

Heb. 3 [12]Take heed, brethren, lest there be in any of you an evil heart of unbelief, in departing from the living God.

REFERENCE: Saul, *1 Sam 15:11;* Amaziah, *2 Chr. 25:14, 27*; Disciples, *John 6:66*; Hymenaeus and Alexander, *1 Tim. 1:19-20;* Demas, *2 Tim. 4:10.*

APOSTLE

[a pos'l] In the New Testament, this word means "one sent forth," a delegate, envoy, or messenger, especially God's messengers. The term is first used in connection with the Twelve, a group of highly honored believers chosen by Jesus to assist him in his evangelical mission in Palestine. In addition to those, it is used of Matthias, Barnabas, Paul, and Jesus. On the basis of *2 Cor. 8:23, Phil. 2:35* and early extra-Biblical references, some scholars feel that there was a much wider circle of Christian messengers and teachers who were called by the name "apostle."

SCRIPTURE

Those Designated as Apostles

THE TWELVE

Matt. 10 [1]And when he had called unto him his twelve disciples, he gave them the power against unclean spirits, to cast them out, and to heal all manner of sickness and all manner of disease. [2]Now the names of the twelve apostles are these; The first, Simon, who is called Peter, and Andrew his brother; James the son of Zebedee, and John his brother; [3]Philip, and Bartholomew; Thomas, and Matthew the publican; James the son of Alpheus, and Lebbeus, whose surname was Thaddeus; [4]Simon the Canaanite, and Judas Iscariot, who also betrayed him.

See *Mark 3:14; 6:30; Luke 6:13; 9:1; Acts 1:2, 26* and individual articles on these apostles

MATTHIAS

Acts 1 [26]And they gave forth their lots; and the lost fell upon Matthias; and he was numbered with the eleven apostles.

BARNABAS

1 Cor. 9 [5]Have we not power to lead about a sister, a wife, as well as other apostles, and as the brethren of the Lord and Cephas? [6]Or I only and Barnabas, have not we power to forbear working?

Gal. 2 [9]And when James, Cephas, and John, who seemed to be pillars, perceived the grace that was given unto me, they gave to me and Barnabas the right hands of fellowship; that we should go unto the heathen, and they unto the circumcision.

PAUL

Rom. 1 [1]Paul, a servant of Jesus Christ, called to be an apostle, separated unto the gospel of God,

Gal. 1 [1]Paul, an apostle, (not of men, neither by man, but by Jesus Christ, and God the Father, who raised him from the dead;)

JESUS

Heb. 3 [1]Wherefore, holy brethren, partakers of the heavenly calling, consider the Apostle and High Priest of our profession, Christ Jesus;

A POSSIBLE "CLASS" OF APOSTLES

2 Cor. 8 [23]Whether any do inquire of Titus, he is my partner and fellow helper concerning you: or our brethren be inquired of, they are the messengers of the churches, and the glory of Christ.

Phil. 2 [25]Yet I supposed it necessary to send to you Epaphroditus, my brother, and companion in labor, and fellow soldier, but your messenger, and he that ministered to my wants.

AQUILA AND PRISCILLA (Prisca)

[ak′wi la, pri sil′a] Jews whom Paul met in Corinth, possibly through their mutual trade of tentmaking. They were refugees from Rome, having been expelled by order of the emperor Claudius in AD 52. While in Corinth, Paul lived with Aquila and Priscilla for a year and a half; when he finally departed for Ephesus, they accompanied him. It was in Ephesus that Aquila and Priscilla contacted Apollos and "expounded unto him the way of God more perfectly." We are told in *1 Cor. 16:9* that the church in Ephesus met in their house. By the time of Paul's writing of the Roman epistle, however, they seem to have returned to their home in Italy, the edict of Claudius having been only temporarily enforced. (*See Rom. 16:3*) They are a splendid example of a first-century Christian couple.

See APOLLOS

SCRIPTURE

Acts 18 [1]After these things Paul departed from Athens, and came to Corinth; [2]And found a certain Jew named Aquila, born in Pontus, lately come from Italy, with his wife Priscilla; (because that Claudius had commanded all Jews to depart from Rome:) and came unto them. [3]And because he was of the same craft, he abode

with them, and wrought: for by their occupation they were tentmakers.
[18]And Paul after this tarried there yet a
good while, and then took his leave of the
brethren, and sailed thence into Syria, and
with him Priscilla and Aquila; having
shorn his head in Cenchrea: for he had a
vow.
[24]And a certain Jew named Apollos,
born at Alexandria, an eloquent man, and
mighty in the scriptures, came to Ephesus.
[25]This man was instructed in the way of
the Lord; and being fervent in the spirit,
he spake and taught diligently the things
of the Lord, knowing only the baptism of
John. [26]And he began to speak boldly in
the synagogue: whom when Aquila and
Priscilla had heard, they took him unto
them, and expounded unto him the way
of God more perfectly.
Rom. 16 [3]Greet Priscilla and Aquila my
helpers in Christ Jesus: [4]Who have for
my life laid down their own necks: unto
whom not only I give thanks, but also all
the churches of the Gentiles.

ARAM

[a'ram] The Aramaean states were located in Upper Mesopotamia and Syria. References in the English Old Testament to Syria and Syrians are to these states and their inhabitants. Aram figures prominently in the history of the Israelite monarchy. King Saul is said to have defeated the kings of Zobah, a division of Aram (*2 Sam. 14:47*). One of David's wives and the mother of Absalom was the daughter of Talmai king of the state of Geshur. Later in his reign, David fought with Hadadezer the powerful ruler of Aram-Zobah. David's conquests made him ruler over all of Syria. Solomon was able to maintain lordship over most of Aram, but he was constantly opposed by Rezon, who gathered a band of marauders and made himself king of Damascus. At Rezon's death about 920 BC, Hezion arose and established a dynasty that lasted almost a century. The most famous member of this dynasty was Ben-Hadad I, who enjoyed an extremely long reign (c. 900-843 BC) and who was a foe of Ahab king of Israel. (*See* BEN-HADAD, AHAB) Ben-Hadad was assassinated and succeeded by Hazael, fulfilling the words of the prophet Elisha (*2 Kin. 8:7-15*). Shortly thereafter Hazael clashed with Joram king of Israel (*2 Kin. 8:28, 29; 9:15*), at which time Jehu arose and became ruler of Israel. Jehu quickly became a vassal of Assyria, leaving Hazael as the lone major opponent to the powerful Assyrians. After surviving encounters with Assyria in 841 and 837 BC, Hazael attacked Israel, seizing the territory east of the Jordan (*2 Kin. 10:32-33*).

Hazael was succeeded by his son Ben-Hadad II, during whose reign Jehoash was able to recover the Transjordan territory which had been lost to Hazael (*2 Kin. 8:14-19, 22-25*). Under Jeroboam II Israel gained domination of the chief Aramaean city of Damascus (*2 Kin. 14:28*). Under King Rezin, Damascus reasserted itself and appears as an ally of Israel in a coalition against Assyria. When Ahaz king of Judah refused to join this alliance, Rezin and Pekah king of Israel marched on Judah, threatening to destroy Jerusalem. Against the warnings of Isaiah, Ahaz appealed to Tiglath-Pileser III of Assyria for help. Tiglath-Pileser gladly responded, for it was doubtless a part of his plan to conquer Israel and Syria, as well as Judah. In 732 BC, Rezin was slain, the Aramaeans defeated, and large numbers of them were transported to Qir in Assyria (*2 Kin. 16:5-9*), thus concluding the history of Aram as a world power.

Perhaps the greatest contribution left by the Aramaeans was their language, which we call Aramaic. From the 9th century BC until New Testament times, Aramaic was used as the common language of international commerce and diplomacy. It is referred to in *2 Kin. 18:26*. Jesus himself doubtlessly spoke Aramaic. In fact, New Testament references to the Hebrew language probably refer not to Hebrew as we know it, but to the closely related Aramaic.

ARARAT

[ar'a rat] A mountainous region in western Asia mentioned in the Bible as: (1) the resting place of the ark after the flood (*Gen. 8:4*); (2) the asylum of the sons of Sennacherib (*2 Kin. 19:37;*

Isa. 37:38); and (3) as the ally of Minni and Ashchenez in Jeremiah's judgment on Babylon (*Jer. 51:27*).

SCRIPTURE

Gen. 8 [4]And the ark rested in the seventh month, on the seventeenth day of the month, upon the mountains of Ararat.

2 Kin. 19 [37]And it came to pass, as he was worshipping in the house of Nisroch his god, that Adrammelech and Sharezer his sons smote him with the sword: and they escaped into the land of Armenia. And Esar-haddon his son reigned in his stead.

Jer. 51 [27]Set ye up a standard in the land, blow the trumpet among the nations, prepare the nations against her, call together against her the kingdoms of Ararat, Minni, and Ashchenaz; appoint a captain against her; cause the horses to come up as the rough caterpillars.

See Isa. 37:38

AREOPAGUS (Mars' Hill)

[ar ē op′a gus, marz hil] A small hill or spur jutting out from the western end of the Acropolis, a larger hill which was the civic center of Athens. "Areopagus" is a Greek word meaning "hill of Ares," the Greek war-god. In the King James Version, it is translated "Mars' Hill," Mars being another name for Ares. The name Areopagus was also applied to a court which in ancient times met at that place. While in Athens on his second missionary journey, the apostle Paul was brought before this court to speak to those who desired to learn more of the things which he was preaching. When Paul "stood in the midst of the Areopagus" in the first century AD, however, it had long since transferred its meeting-place from the hill down into the city itself.

REFERENCE: *Acts 17:16-34.*

ARK OF THE BULRUSHES

[ärk, bŏŏl′rush iz] A name sometimes given to the reed basket into which Moses was placed and allowed to float near the place where Pharaoh's daughter was accustomed to bathe.

See MOSES, MIRIAM

SCRIPTURE

Ex. 2 [3]And when she could not longer hide him, she took for him an ark of bulrushes, and daubed it with slime and with pitch, and put the child therein; and she laid it in the flags by the river's brink.

ARK OF THE COVENANT

[ärk, kuv′e nant] A piece of furniture in the Tabernacle. (*See* TABERNACLE) It appears to have been an oblong chest of acacia (shittim) wood, fitted with rings, one at each of the four corners, through which were passed staves by which it was carried. It served as a container for the tables of the Law, the rod of Aaron which budded, and a pot of manna. It was also the support of the "mercy-seat," which served as a throne or pedestal on which the LORD appeared and from which he spoke. The ark often accompanied the Israelites into battle and was thought to insure the presence and assistance of the LORD. The ark was captured by the Philistines during the time of Eli and sojourned at various places until it was finally brought to Jerusalem after David had made that city his capital. For the remainder of David's reign it resided in a tent which he had erected for it. Upon the completion of the great temple of Solomon, the ark was placed beneath the wings of two gigantic cherubim. (*See* CHERUBIM) It is assumed that it remained there until the destruction of Jerusalem in 587 BC.

SCRIPTURE

Directions for Making Ark

Ex. 25 [10]And they shall make an ark of shittim wood: two cubits and a half shall be the length thereof, and a cubit and a half the breadth thereof, and a cubit and a half the height thereof. [11]And thou shalt overlay it with pure gold, within and without shalt thou overlay it, and shalt make upon it a crown of gold round about. [12]And thou shalt cast four rings of gold for it, and put them in the four corners thereof; and two rings shall be in the one side of it, and two rings in the other side of it. [13]And thou shalt make staves of shittim wood, and overlay them with gold. [14]And thou shalt put the staves into the rings by the sides of the ark, that the ark may be borne with them. [15]The staves shall be in the rings of the ark: they shall not be taken from it.

Contents of Ark

Heb. 9 [4]Which had the golden censer, and the ark of the covenant overlaid round about with gold, wherein was the golden pot that had manna, and Aaron's rod that budded, and the tables of the covenant;

Place of the Ark

Ex. 40 [21]And he brought the ark into the tabernacle, and set up the veil of the covering, and covered the ark of the testimony; as the LORD commanded Moses.

REFERENCE: *Num. 3:30-31; 4:4-6; Josh. 6:6-20; 18:1; 1 Sam. 4:10-11; 6; 7:1-2; 2 Sam. 6:4, 9-11.*

ARK OF NOAH

[ärk, nō′a] A large boat built by Noah at the command of God; its purpose was to preserve Noah's family and representatives of the various kinds of animals from the flood which God sent upon the earth. The flood narratives describe the ark as having been 300 cubits long, 50 cubits broad, and 30 cubits high, three stories high, and "pitched within and without with pitch" or asphalt. The wood to be used in its construction was "gopher-wood."

See FLOOD, NOAH

SCRIPTURE

Gen. 6 [14]Make thee an ark of gopher wood; rooms shalt thou make in the ark, and shalt pitch it within and without with pitch. [15]And this is the fashion which thou shalt make it of: The length of the ark shall be three hundred cubits, the breadth of it fifty cubits, and the height of it thirty cubits. [16]A window shalt thou make to the ark, and in a cubit shalt thou finish it above; and the door of the ark shalt thou set in the side thereof: with lower, second, and third stories shalt thou make it.

ARM OF GOD

There are numerous references in the Bible to the "Arm" of God. This figure is used to refer both to God's power and to his grace, or salvation. It is especially common in the book of *Isaiah.*

SCRIPTURE

Ex. 15 [16]Fear and dread shall fall upon them; by the greatness of thine arm they shall be as still as a stone; till thy people pass over, O LORD, till the people pass over, which thou hast purchased.

Psa. 77 [15]Thou hast with thine arm redeemed thy people, the sons of Jacob and Joseph. Selah.

Psa. 89 [13]Thou hast a mighty arm: strong is thy hand, and high is thy right hand.

Psa. 98 [1]O sing unto the LORD a new song: for he hath done marvelous things: his right hand, and his holy arm, hath gotten him the victory.

Isa. 33 [2]O LORD, be gracious unto us; we have waited for thee: be thou their arm every morning, our salvation also in the time of trouble.

Isa. 40 [10]Behold, the Lord GOD will come with strong hand, and his arm shall rule for him: behold, his reward is with him, and his work before him.

Isa. 51 [5]My righteousness is near; my

salvation is gone forth, and mine arms shall judge the people; the isles shall wait upon me, and on mine arm shall they trust.

[9]Awake, awake, put on strength, O arm of the LORD; awake, as in the ancient days, in the generations of old. Art thou not it that hath cut Rahab, and wounded the dragon?

Isa. 52 [10]The LORD hath made bare his holy arm in the eyes of all the nations; and all the ends of the earth shall see the salvation of our God.

Isa. 53 [1]Who hath believed our report? and to whom is the arm of the LORD revealed?

Jer. 27 [5]I have made the earth, the man and the beast that are upon the ground, by my great power and by my outstretched arm, and have given it unto whom it seemed meet unto me.

Luke 1 [51]He hath shewed strength with his arm; he hath scattered the proud in the imagination of their hearts.

Acts 13 [17]The God of this people of Israel chose our fathers, and exalted the people when they dwelt as strangers in the land of Egypt, and with an high arm brought he them out of it.

ARMOR

[är′mẽr] From the earliest times mankind wore and used devices for the protection of the body in battle. These devices were of different types and made of different material, from heavy leather to hardened steel. Usually they consisted of a shield carried on one arm, a coat or breastplate, leather or iron casings for the legs and feet, and a helmet for the head. Paul spoke of armor in a figurative sense, with reference to righteousness as a protection to the follower of God against the assaults of evil or temptation.

SCRIPTURE

Rom. 13 [12]The night is far spent, the day is at hand: let us therefore cast off the works of darkness, and let us put on the armour of light.

2 Cor. 6 [7]By the word of truth, by the power of God, by the armour of righteousness on the right hand and on the left.

Eph. 6 [13]Wherefore take unto you the whole armour of God, that ye may be able to withstand in the evil day, and having done all, to stand. [14]Stand therefore, having your loins girt about with truth, and having on the breast-plate of righteousness; [15]And your feet shod with the preparation of the gospel of peace. [16]Above all, taking the shield of faith, wherewith ye shall be able to quench all the fiery darts of the wicked. [17]And take the helmet of salvation, and the sword of the Spirit, which is the word of God.

1 Thess. 5 [8]But let us, who are of the day, be sober, putting on the breast-plate of faith and love; and for an helmet, the hope of salvation.

ARTAXERXES I

[är ta zurk′sēz] Ruler of the Persian empire, reigning 465-424 BC. In secular history, he is commonly referred to as Longimanus. It was Artaxerxes who granted permission to Ezra and Nehemiah to return to Jerusalem for the purpose of instituting widespread social and religious reforms.

See EZRA, NEHEMIAH

REFERENCE: *Ezra 4, 7; Neh. 2; 13:6.*

ASA

[ā′sa] The son of Abijah, grandson of Rehoboam, and the third king of Judah (913-873 BC). A zealous reformer, Asa broke down many of the images, altars, and pillars of idolatry and banished the male cult prostitutes. Urged on by the prophet Azariah, he complemented these measures by encouraging a positive revival of the true religion of the LORD, calling for great sacrifices and a covenant-renewal ceremony. Early in his long reign, Asa thoroughly routed the attacking troops of Zerah, the ruler of Ethiopia. In later years, when Judah was threatened by Baasha, King of Israel, Asa enlisted the aid of Ben-hadad of Syria and thus preserved his kingdom. (*See* BAASHA) Asa was offended by the criticism of the prophet Hanani for this dependence on a foreign power and had Hanani cast into prison. Shortly thereafter, Asa was attacked by a disease of the feet and died.

See BAASHA, BEN-HADAD, KINGS

REFERENCE: *1 Kin. 15:9-24; 2 Chr. 14:1-16:14.*

ASAPH

[ā'saf] One of the chief musicians in the service of David, working in cooperation with Heman and Jeduthun. When the ark of the covenant was brought into the city of David, Asaph was appointed "to sound the cymbals" and to direct a chorus. *Psa. 50* and *73-83* are ascribed to Asaph.

REFERENCE: *1 Chr. 6:39; 2 Chr. 5:12; 29:30; 33:15; Neh. 12:46.*

ASCENSION

[a sen'shun] The taking up into heaven of Jesus. The ascension of exaltation of Jesus was a regular theme in the preaching of the early church. It attested to the Christian belief that Jesus was "at the right hand of God," that is, that he now acts in a manner which completely transcends the limitations of space. The ascended Christ is King, all things coming under his sovereignty; he is also Priests and Forerunner, having entered the "Holy of Holies" in our behalf and making intercession for us as one in whom human nature has been perfected and whose death constituted the perfect and abiding sacrifice. The Church depends for its existence on the assistance of the ascended and exalted Christ.

See JESUS

SCRIPTURE

The Ascension

Mark 16 [19]So then after the Lord had spoken unto them, he was received up into heaven, and sat on the right hand of God.

Luke 24 [50]And he led them out as far as to Bethany: and he lifted up his hands, and blessed them. [51]And it came to pass, while he blessed them, he was parted from them, and carried up into heaven.

John 14 [2]In my Father's house are many mansions: if it were not so, I would have told you. I go to prepare a place for you.

John 16 [7]Nevertheless, I tell you the truth, it is expedient for you that I go away: for if I go not away, the Comforter will not come unto you: but if I depart, I will send him unto you.

Acts 1 [9]And when he had spoken these things, while they beheld, he was taken up; and a cloud received him out of their sight. [10]And while they looked steadfastly toward heaven as he went up, behold, two men stood by them in white apparel; [11]Which also said, Ye men of Galilee, why stand ye gazing up into heaven? this same Jesus which is taken up from you into heaven, shall so come in like manner as ye have seen him go into heaven.

1 Pet. 3 [22]Who is gone into heaven, and is on the right hand of God; angels and authorities and powers being made subject unto him.

The Ascended Christ

AS KING

Eph. 1 [20]Which he wrought in Christ, when he raised him from the dead, and set him at his own right hand in the heavenly places,

Phil. 2 [9]Wherefore God also hath highly exalted him, and given him a name which is above every name: [10]That at the name of Jesus every knee should bow, of things in heaven, and things in earth, and things under the earth; [11]And that every tongue should confess that Jesus Christ is Lord, to the glory of God the Father.

Heb. 1 [3]Who being the brightness of his glory, and the express image of his person, and upholding all things by the word of his power, when he had by himself purged our sins, sat down on the right hand of the Majesty on high;

1 Pet. 3 [22]Who is gone into heaven, and is on the right hand of God; angels and authorities and powers being made subject unto him.

AS FORERUNNER

John 14 [3]And if I go and prepare a place for you, I will come again, and receive you unto myself; that where I am, there ye may be also.

Eph. 2 [6]And hath raised us up together, and made us sit together in heavenly places in Christ Jesus:

Heb. 6 [20]Whither the forerunner is for us entered, even Jesus, made a high priest for ever after the order of Melchisedec.

Heb. 10 [19]Having therefore, brethren, boldness to enter into the holiest by the blood of Jesus, [20]By a new and living way, which he hath consecrated for us, through the vail, that is to say, his flesh; [21]And having an high priest over the house of God; [22]Let us draw near with a true heart in full assurance of faith, having our hearts sprinkled from an evil conscience, and our bodies washed with pure water.

AS PRIEST

Rom. 8 [34]Who is he that condemneth? It is Christ that died, yea rather, that is risen again, who is even at the right hand of God, who also maketh intercession for us.

Heb. 4 [14]Seeing then that we have a great high priest, that is passed into the heavens, Jesus the Son of God, let us hold fast our profession. [15]For we have not an high priest which cannot be touched with the feeling of our infirmities; but was in all points tempted like as we are, yet without sin. [16]Let us therefore come boldly unto the throne of grace, that we may obtain mercy, and find grace to help in time of need.

Heb. 7 [25]Wherefore he is able also to save them to the uttermost that come unto God by him, seeing he ever liveth to make intercession for them. [26]For such an high priest became us, who is holy, harmless, undefiled, separate from sinners, and made higher than the heavens;

ASCETICISM

[a set'i siz'm] The practice of austere self-denial for the purpose of achieving complete subordination of the body to the mind; a disciplinary course of conduct pursued as a means of drawing closer to God. Virtually every religion which has appeared in history has had in its ranks those who devoted themselves to ascetic practices. These practices vary widely and include such things as fasting, vegetarianism, total abstinence from wine or strong drink, hermitism, extreme poverty, flagellation, and self-mutilation. Jesus himself did not follow an ascetic pattern of life; in fact, his manner of life was in such contrast with that of John the Baptist that his critics accused him of being "a winebibber and a glutton." Nevertheless, throughout Jesus' teaching there runs a thread of teaching which urges the disciple to deny himself of any activity or pleasure which might hinder his "seeking first the kingdom of God." On occasion Jesus made reference to fasting in such a way as to indicate that he looked upon moderate asceticism as an altogether proper aid to devotion.

See ABSTINENCE, NAZIRITE, RECHABITE

SCRIPTURE

Jesus' Views on Asceticism

HIS PRACTICE

Matt. 11 [19]The Son of man came eating

and drinking, and they say, Behold a man gluttonous, and a winebibber, a friend of publicans and sinners. But wisdom is justified of her children.

See Luke 7:34

HIS TEACHING

Matt. 6 [16]Moreover when ye fast, be not, as the hypocrites, of a sad countenance: for they disfigure their faces, that they may appear unto men to fast. Verily I say unto you, They have their reward. [17]But thou, when thou fastest, anoint thine head, and wash thy face; [18]That thou appear not unto men to fast, but unto thy Father which is in secret: and thy Father, which seeth in secret, shall reward thee openly.

Matt. 9 [14]Then came to him the disciples of John, saying, Why do we and the Pharisees fast oft, but thy disciples fast not? [15]And Jesus said unto them, Can the children of the bridechamber mourn, as long as the bridegroom is with them? but the days will come, when the bridegroom shall be taken from them, and then shall they fast. [16]No man putteth a piece of new cloth unto an old garment, for that which is put in to fill it up taketh from the garment, and the rent is made worse. [17]Neither do men put new wine into old bottles: else the bottles break, and the wine runneth out, and the bottles perish: but they put new wine into new bottles, and both are preserved.

See Mark 2:18-22; Luke 5:33-39

Paul's Teaching on Asceticism

Col. 2 [20]Wherefore if ye be dead with Christ from the rudiments of the world, why, as though living in the world, are ye subject to ordinances, [21](Touch not; taste not; handle not; [22]Which all are to perish with the using;) after the commandments and doctrines of men? [23]Which things have indeed a shew of wisdom in will worship, and humility, and neglecting of the body; not in any honour to the satisfying of the flesh.

1 Tim. 4 [1]Now the Spirit speaketh expressly, that in the latter times some shall depart from the faith, giving heed to seducing spirits, and doctrines of devils; [2]Speaking lies in hypocrisy; having their conscience seared with a hot iron; [3]Forbidding to marry, and commanding to abstain from meats, which God hath created to be received with thanksgiving of them which believe and know the truth. [4]For every creature of God is good, and nothing to be refused, if it be received with thanksgiving: [8]For bodily exercise profiteth little: but godliness is profitable unto all things, having promise of the life that now is, and of that which is to come.

ASHDOD

[ash′dod] A strong city on the southeast coast of the Mediterranean Sea, about twenty-five miles north of Gaza, and thirty-four west of Jerusalem. It was within the territory of the tribe of Judah (*Josh. 15:47*), but the Philistines either retained or retook it. Here stood the famous temple of Dagon, into which the ark of the covenant was brought, causing the idol of the temple to fall and bringing a plague on the inhabitants of Ashdod (*1 Sam. 5*). Another name for Ashdod is Azotus; after preaching to the Ethiopian eunuch, Philip the evangelist came to Azotus to preach the gospel.

ASHERAH

[a shē′ra] The name of a goddess whose worship was widely spread in Canaan and Syria. The plural form of this name is Asherim. Like so many other elements in Canaanite religion, the cult of Asherah was imported from Assyria. She was represented by the trunk of a tree or a pillar of wood. Because of this association with trees, the King James Version mistranslates Asherah as "grove." In most other versions, however, the proper name is used.

See ASHTORETH, BAAL

REFERENCE: *Deut. 16:21; 1 Kin. 15:13; 18:19; 2 Kin. 23:4.*

ASHES

[ash'iz] Among the ancient Hebrews and other Orientals, ashes were a customary token of mourning or humiliation and were usually put on the head. The penitent or afflicted were sometimes known to sit or wallow in ashes. When used figuratively, ashes signified frailty, insignificance, and worthlessness.

See REPENTANCE

SCRIPTURE

A Mark of Sorrow or Humiliation

Neh. 9 [1]Now in the twenty and fourth day of this month the children of Israel were assembled with fasting, and with sackclothes, and earth upon them.

Esth. 4 [1]When Mordecai perceived all that was done, Mordecai rent his clothes, and put on sackcloth with ashes, and went out into the midst of the city, and cried with a loud and a bitter cry.

Job 42 [6]Wherefore I abhor myself, and repent in dust and ashes.

Psa. 102 [9]For I have eaten ashes like bread, and mingled my drink with weeping.

2 Sam. 13 [19]And Tamar put ashes on her head, and rent her garment of divers colours that was on her, and laid her hand on her head, and went on crying.

Isa. 58 [5]Is it such a fast that I have chosen? a day for a man to afflict his soul? is it to bow down his head as a bulrush, and to spread sackcloth and ashes under him? wilt thou call this a fast, and an acceptable day to the LORD?

Jer. 6 [26]O daughter of my people, gird thee with sackcloth, and wallow thyself in ashes: make thee mourning, as for an only son, most bitter lamentation: for the spoiler shall suddenly come upon us.

Jonah 3 [6]For word came unto the king of Nineveh, and he arose from his throne, and he laid his robe from him, and covered him with sackcloth, and sat in ashes.

Luke 10 [13]Woe unto thee, Chorazin! woe unto thee, Bethsaida! for if the mighty works had been done in Tyre and Sidon, which have been done in you, they had a great while ago repented, sitting in sackcloth and ashes.

A Symbol of Worthlessness

Gen. 18 [27]And Abraham answered and said, Behold now, I have taken upon me to speak unto the LORD, which am but dust and ashes.

Job 30 [19]He hath cast me into the mire, and I am become like dust and ashes.

Isa. 44 [20]He feedeth on ashes: a deceived heart hath turned him aside, that he cannot deliver his soul, nor say, Is there not a lie in my right hand?

ASHTORETH

[ash'to reth] The supreme goddess of Canaan and the female consort of Baal. The cult of this deity originated in Babylonia, where she was worshipped with prostitution and other immoral rites. The name is often found in its plural form, Ashtaroth.

See BAAL, ASHERAH

SCRIPTURE

Judg. 2 [13]And they forsook the LORD, and served Baal and Ashtaroth.

1 Sam. 7 [3]And Samuel spake unto all the house of Israel, saying, If ye do return unto the LORD with all your hearts, then put away the strange gods and Ashtaroth from among you, and prepare your hearts unto the LORD, and serve him only: and he will deliver you out of the hand of the Philistines. [4]Then the children of Israel did put away Baalim and Ashtaroth, and served the LORD only.

1 Kin. 11 [5]For Solomon went after Ashtoreth the goddess of the Zidonians, and after Milcom the abomination of the Ammonites.

REFERENCE: *Judg. 10:6; 1 Sam. 12:10; 31:10; 1 Kin. 11:33; 2 Kin. 23:13.*

ASSYRIA

[a sir'i a] An ancient country of the Upper Mesopotamian plain, bounded by Babylonia on the South, the Syrian desert on the West, and the Armenian and Persian hills on the North and East. The principle cities of Assyria were Nineveh, Assur, and Calah. The origins of the people who came to be called Assyrians is uncertain, but it is known that Sumerians were present in Assur at least as early as 2900 BC.

Assyria was long a prosperous agricultural community, but its appearance in the Bible is largely related to its rise as a world military power. Soon after the division of the kingdom of Solomon, Asshurnasirpal II (883-859 BC) extended the Assyrian empire into Lebanon and Philistia and posed a definite threat to Israel. His son Shalmaneser III (859-824 BC) continued this policy of expansion. He was at first resisted by a coalition of anti-Assyrian kings to which, according to Assyrian annals, "Ahab the Israelite" contributed 2,000 chariots and 14,000 men. By 841 BC, however, this coalition split up, enabling Shalmaneser to confine the Aramaean (Syrian) forces and to subject Tyre, Sidon, and Israel (under King Jehu) to a vassalage relationship.

During the period from 783 to 745 BC, the struggle with Syria and growing internecine strife allowed Israel considerable freedom. Jeroboam II (c. 783-748 BC) took advantage of this and raised Israel to heights it had not known since the days of Solomon. The rise of Tiglath-Pileser III (745-727 BC), sometimes referred to in the Bible as Pul, was to mark the end to this brief freedom from Assyrian oppression. Tiglath-Pileser set out to regain the territory which Assyria had lost. In 732 BC, Damascus fell before his awesome might. The Assyrian was resisted by a coalition led by Rezin of Damascus and Pekah of Israel. These rulers tried to force Ahaz king of Judah to join them and, when he refused, marched into Judah intent on destroying Jerusalem. Against the counsel of Isaiah, Ahaz enlisted the aid of Tiglath-Pileser. Israel was attacked and a large number carried into Assyrian captivity. Judah was saved but at a cost rather too dear. The southern kingdom was placed under a ruinous tribute and, in addition, was forced to accept a number of Assyrian religious practices. (*See* AHAZ)

Tiglath-Pileser was succeeded by his son Shalmaneser V (727-722 BC). When Hoshea king of Israel, who had been placed on the throne by Tiglath-Pileser, refused to pay the annual tribute, Shalmaneser laid siege to the capital city of Samaria. In 722 BC, Samaria fell either to Shalmaneser or, more likely, to his successor Sargon II (722-705 BC). Sargon deported over 27,000 Israelites to the area of the Upper Euphrates and Media and the kingdom of Israel passed from history.

Sargon was succeeded by the well-known figure, Sennacharib (705-681 BC). In the early years of his reign he was engaged in suppressing revolts which had broken out shortly before his father's death. There is difficulty in unraveling the Biblical accounts of the relations between Sennacharib and Hezekiah, but it appears to this writer that in 701 BC Sennacharib forced Hezekiah to come to terms at Lachish. The temporary respite cost Judah considerable territory and high tribute, but Sennacharib seems to have returned to Assyria, according to the agreement. After about a decade, revolt flared in the West once again. Eastern troubles prevented immediate action, but by 688 BC, Sennacharib was free to move westward to crush the opposition. It was apparently in this campaign that the army of Sennacharib was decimated by a terrible plague, forcing him to return home without destroying Jerusalem. Although Assyrian records break off after about 689 BC, *2 Kin. 19:37* informs us that Sennacharib met his death at the hands of two of his sons and was replaced by a third son, Esarhaddon.

Although he was faced with some revolts, Esarhaddon was able to maintain his power and even managed to push into the Upper Delta region of Egypt, setting up Assyrian governors at Thebes and Memphis. Near the end of his life the Egyptians, led by Tirhakah, revolted; Esarhaddon died before he was able to take decisive action, but his son Asshurbanapal (669-c. 633 BC) finally managed to regain control after three arduous campaigns, culminating in the sack of Thebes (the "No" of Nahum's prophecy) in 663 BC. Then revolts in Babylon and the threat of the rising Median power gave Egypt and Judah their freedom by default. It was this freedom which enabled Josiah to carry out his program of reform. (*See* JOSIAH)

Asshurbanapal was followed by his sons Assur-etil-ilani (632-628 BC) and Sin-sar-iskun (628-612 BC). During the reign of the latter, the Assyrians were driven out of Babylon, which had served as the Southern capital of the Empire. In 614 BC the Babylonians and Medes joined to destroy Assur and in 612 BC Nineveh was overrun, an event noted in the prophecies of Nahum and Zephaniah. By 609 BC Assyria had passed into the hands of the Babylonians.

In later years the term "Assyria" was used as a general designation for the original territory in Upper Mesopotamia.

ATHALIAH

[ath a lī'a] The daughter of Ahab and Jezebel, wife of Jehoram, mother of Ahaziah, and the only queen of Judah (852-836 BC). Athaliah had been married to Jehoram, son of Jehoshaphat, to cement an alliance between Judah and Israel. When her son, Ahaziah, was slain in the revolution of Jehu, she secured the throne by the murder of all other legitimate successors with the exception of Jehoash (Joash), the infant son of Ahaziah, who was hidden and secretly reared by the priest Jehoida. In the seventh year of her reign this child was brought forth by Jehoida and proclaimed king. Hearing the shouts that accompanied the proclamation of the new king, Athaliah ran to the temple to assess the situation. Recognizing that her position was hopeless, she ran through the temple with cries of "Treason! Treason!" and was slain by the captains of the army at the horse gate of the king's house.

See JEHOASH, JEHOIDA, JEHORAM, KINGS

REFERENCE: *2 Kin. 11; 2 Chr. 22:10-23:15.*

ATONEMENT

[a tōn'ment] A theological term denoting the restoration of man to a right relationship with God through: (1) the sacrificial system of the religion of Israel and (2) the obedience and death of Jesus Christ. The Hebrew word translated "atonement" in the Old Testament has a double meaning. In some passages, atonement for sin seems to involve "propitiation," or the appeasing of the wrath of God by some action directed toward him—in this case, the offering of sacrifice—that he might be reconciled to man. The other idea contained in the word is "expiation," that is, that the sacrifice has a direct effect on the sin itself, covering it or blotting it out. Scholars are divided as to which of these meanings is primary, since both receive support from scripture.

In a similar fashion, the atoning work of Jesus Christ has been the subject of a wide range of interpretations. Some have viewed the death of Christ as a ransom paid to Satan for the release of souls held captive by sin. Others conceive of the atonement as the means by which God's honor and justice were satisfied. The predominant theory emerging out of the Protestant reformation was that Christ had made expiation for sin by taking upon himself the punishment which would otherwise have been borne by men. Another prominent strain of thought has viewed the atonement as a cosmic victory over sin, death, the world, and the powers of evil. Still another interpretation is that which sees in the cross primarily the tremendous moral influence of an unparallelled example of sacrificial love. That each of these theories has received wide support witnesses to the fact that the richness of the doctrine of the atonement cannot be contained under any single rubric or captured in any single precise formulation. The entire Bible is a story of God's bearing the sin of man in an effort to reconcile him to his creator, to his neighbor, and to himself. This story reaches its culmination in the life and death of the one who lived in freedom from man's universal subjection to the powers of sin, death, and the world. The meaning of the cross is expressed in the New Testament in various metaphorical terms. It is impossible to grasp one facet, forget the others, and hope to reach an adequate understanding of the atonement. The atonement is not a theory; it is an event, an act of God in history, a sacrifice by which God's justice is satisfied, man's sins covered, perfect love fulfilled and set forth as a goal, and victory over sin and death proclaimed and achieved, once and for all time. It is the heart of the confession and testimony which the church must make to the world, "To wit, that God was in Christ, reconciling the world unto himself, not imputing their trespasses unto them: and hath committed unto us the word of reconciliation."

SCRIPTURE

Atonement made by Animal Sacrifice

Lev. 4 20 And he shall do with the bullock as he did with the bullock for a sin offering, so shall he do with this: and the priest shall make an atonement for them, and it shall be forgiven them.

31 And he shall take away all the fat thereof, as the fat is taken away from off the sacrifice of peace offerings; and the priest shall burn it upon the altar for a sweet savour unto the LORD; and the priest shall make an atonement for him, and it shall be forgiven him.

Lev. 5 6 And he shall bring his trespass offering unto the LORD for his sin which he hath sinned, a female from the flock, a lamb or a kid of the goats, for a sin offering; and the priest shall make an atonement for him concerning his sin.

Lev. 6 7 And the priest shall make an atonement for him before the LORD: and it shall be forgiven him for any thing of all that he hath done in trespassing therein.

Lev. 9 7 And Moses said unto Aaron, Go unto the altar, and offer thy sin offering, and thy burnt offering, and make an atonement for thyself, and for the people: and offer the offering of the people, and make an atonement for them; as the LORD commanded.

Lev. 16 6 And Aaron shall offer his bullock of the sin offering, which is for himself, and make an atonement for himself, and for his house. 10 But the goat, on which the lot fell to be the scapegoat, shall be presented alive before the LORD, to make an atonement with him, and to let him go for a scapegoat into the wilderness.

16 And he shall make an atonement for the holy place, because of the uncleanness of the children of Israel, and because of their transgressions in all their sins: and so shall he do for the tabernacle of the congregation, that remaineth among them in the midst of their uncleanness. 17 And there shall be no man in the tabernacle of the congregation when he goeth in to make an atonement in the holy place, until he come out, and have made an atonement for himself, and for his household, and for all the congregation of Israel. 18 And he shall go out unto the altar that is before the LORD, and make an atonement for it; and shall take of the blood of the bullock, and of the blood of the goat, and put it upon the horns of the altar round about.

29 And this shall be a statute for ever unto you: that in the seventh month, on the tenth day of the month, ye shall afflict your souls, and do no work at all, whether it be one of your own country, or a stranger that sojourneth among you: 30 For on that day shall the priest make an atonement for you, to cleanse you, that ye may be clean from all your sins before the LORD. 33 And he shall make an atonement for the holy sanctuary, and he shall make an atonement for the tabernacle of the congregation, and for the altar, and he shall make an atonement for the priests, and for all the people of the congregation. 34 And this shall be an everlasting statute unto you, to make an atonement for the children of Israel for all their sins once a year. And he did as the LORD commanded Moses.

Lev. 17 11 For the life of the flesh is in

the blood: and I have given it to you upon the altar to make an atonement for your souls: for it is the blood that maketh an atonement for the soul.

Lev. 19 [22]And the priest shall make an atonement for him with the ram of the trespass offering before the LORD for his sin which he hath done: and the sin which he hath done shall be forgiven him.

Heb. 9 [22]And almost all things are by the law purged with blood: and without shedding of blood is no remission.

Atonement through Christ

Matt. 1 [21]And she shall bring forth a son, and thou shalt call his name Jesus: for he shall save his people from their sins.

Matt. 20 [28]Even as the Son of man came not to be ministered unto, but to minister, and to give his life a ransom for many.

John 1 [29]The next day John seeth Jesus coming unto him, and saith, Behold the Lamb of God, which taketh away the sin of the world.

[35]Again the next day after John stood, and two of his disciples; [36]And looking upon Jesus as he walked, he saith, Behold the Lamb of God!

John 3 [16]For God so loved the world, that he gave his only begotten Son, that whosoever believeth in him should not perish, but have everlasting life. [17]For God sent not his Son into the world to condemn the world; but that the world through him might be saved.

John 6 [51]The bread that I will give is my flesh, which I will give for the life of the world.

John 11 [49]And one of them, named Caiaphas, being the high priest that same year, said unto them, Ye know nothing at all, [50]Nor consider that it is expedient for us, that one man should die for the people, and that the whole nation perish not. [51]And this spake he not of himself: but being high priest that year, he prophesied that Jesus should die for that nation;

Acts 5 [31]Him hath God exalted with his right hand to be a Prince and a Saviour, for to give repentance to Israel, and forgiveness of sins.

Acts 20 [28]Take heed therefore unto yourselves, and to all the flock, over the which the Holy Ghost hath made you overseers, to feed the church of God, which he hath purchased with his own blood.

Rom. 3 [24]Being justified freely by his grace through the redemption that is in Christ Jesus: [25]Whom God hath set forth to be a propitiation through faith in his blood, to declare his righteousness for the remission of sins that are past, through the forbearance of God;

Rom. 5 [6]For when we were yet without strength, in due time Christ died for the ungodly. [8]But God commendeth his love toward us, in that, while we were yet sinners, Christ died for us. [18]Therefore as by the offence of one judgment came upon all men to condemnation; even so by the righteousness of one the free gift came upon all men unto justification of life. [19]For as by one man's disobedience many were made sinners, so by the obedience of one shall many be made righteous.

2 Cor. 5 [18]And all things are of God, who hath reconciled us to himself by Jesus Christ, and hath given to us the ministry of reconciliation; [19]To wit, that God was in Christ, reconciling the world unto himself, not imputing their trespasses unto them; and hath committed unto us the word of reconciliation. [20]Now then we are ambassadors for Christ, as though God did beseech you by us: we pray you in Christ's stead, be ye reconciled to God. [21]For he hath made him to be sin for us, who knew no sin; that we might be made the righteousness of God in him.

Gal. 3 [13]Christ hath redeemed us from the curse of the law, being made a curse for us: for it is written, Cursed is every one that hangeth on a tree: [14]That the blessing of Abraham might come on the Gentiles through Jesus Christ; that we might receive the promise of the Spirit through faith.

Heb. 1 [3]Who being the brightness of his glory, and the express image of his person, and upholding all things by the word of his power, when he had by himself purged our sins, sat down on the right hand of the Majesty on high;

Heb. 2 [14]Forasmuch then as the children are partakers of flesh and blood, he also himself likewise took part of the same; that through death he might destroy him that had the power of death, that is, the devil; [15]And deliver them who through fear of death were all their lifetime subject to bondage.

Heb. 9 [12]Neither by the blood of goats and calves, but by his own blood he entered in once into the holy place, having obtained eternal redemption for us. [13]For if the blood of bulls and of goats, and the ashes of an heifer sprinkling the unclean, sanctifieth to the purifying of the flesh: [14]How much more shall the blood of Christ, who through the eternal Spirit offered himself without spot to God, purge your conscience from dead works to serve the living God?

1 John 2 [2]He is the propitiation for our sins: and not for ours only, but also for the sins of the whole world.

1 John 3 [5]Ye know that he was manifested to take away our sins; and in him is no sin.

1 John 4 [10]Herein is love, not that we loved God, but that he loved us, and sent his Son to be a propitiation for our sins.

REFERENCE: *Mark 10:45; 1 Cor. 2:8.*

BAAL, BAALIM

[bā'al, bā'a lim] The singular and plural forms of the Hebrew word meaning "lord," "master," or "possessor." This word is often applied as a title or proper name to various Babylonian, Canaanite, and Phoenician sun and storm deities. Baal was loved for the vegetation-producing light and warmth which he brought, and feared for the scorching heat and storms which destroyed this vegetation. An important theme in Canaanite mythology was the death and resurrection of Baal, corresponding to the annual cycles of nature. Each locality had its own Baal, or Lord; quite frequently, the name of the deity was drawn from the land of which he was "possessor," such as Baal-hermon (*Judg. 3:3*) and Baal-Peor (*Num. 25:1-3*). In other instances, the title "Baal" was attached to the proper name of a deity, as in the case of Baal-Merodach of Babylon and Baal-Melqart of Tyre. Occasionally, the word was simply part of a title by which the deity worshipped was known, as Baal-Shemaim ("Lord of Heaven"), Baal-Berith ("Lord of the Covenant", *Judg. 8:33; 9:4*), and Baal-zebub ("King of the Flies", *2 Kin. 1:2;* called Beelzebub in the New Testament, *Matt. 10:25*). In the case of the chief active deity in Canaan at the time of the Israelite conquest, the proper name had fallen into disuse and he was known as Baal. It is now virtually certain that this deity was the Semitic storm-god Hadad, who was said to reign as king of the gods on a high mountain far to the north. Ordinarily, the worship of these Baalim was carried on in conjunction with that of a female consort, such as Astarte (in the Bible, Ashtaroth or Ashtoreth), Asherah, or Anat (*see* index for further information on these). These represented the female principle in the fertility cult and were usually portrayed as sacred courtesans or pregnant mothers, although they sometimes took the form of bloodthirsty goddesses of war. The worship of these deities varied with the shrine and the occasion. It might consist of the burning of incense, animal sacrifices, or even human sacrifices. It often included such debasing practices as sacred prostitution, homosexuality, self-mutilation, and other orgiastic rites.

In the early history of the nation of Israel, the title Baal was applied to Yahweh. (*See* YAHWEH) This is made clear by the occurrence of names utilizing the word Baal, such as Meribbaal, Ishbaal, and Beeliada; these are children of David and Jonathan, two known worshippers of the true God of Israel (*1 Chr. 8:34; 9:40; 14:7*). In later years, however, Israel's idolatry caused the name to fall into disrepute and Hosea admonishes his hearers to refrain from referring to the LORD as Baali ("My Baal" or "My Lord" *Hos. 2:16*).

The period in which the worship of Baal offered the greatest threat to that of the true God was during the reign of Ahab and Jezebel, king and queen of Northern Israel in the middle of the ninth century BC. Jezebel was the daughter of the Phoenician king Ethbaal and a worshipper of Baal-Melqart and Asherah. When she married Ahab, sealing a political alliance between the two nations, she imported the worship of her deities into Samaria. With great missionary zeal, Jezebel sought to make the cult of Baal-Melqart the official state religion—and very nearly succeeded. The royal court and the entire national structure were thoroughly paganized. A temple was built in Samaria (*1 Kin. 16:32-33*); a huge number of priests and prophets of Baal were given official status at court (*see 1 Kin. 18:19; 2 Kin. 10:19*); many who remained faithful to God were executed. Rising to stem this tide of paganism were the fiery prophet Elijah and his successor Elisha. These two men declared Holy War on Jezebel and the worship of Baal and finally, in 842 BC, the cult of Baal-Melqart was extirpated in the brutal revolution led by Jehu. (*See* JEHU)

In the Southern Kingdom, Athaliah, daughter of Ahab and Jezebel, and queen of Judah, introduced Baal-Melqart to Jerusalem. The conservative folk of Judah were never as prone to idolatry as their northern kinsmen and when Joash (Jehoash) was made king Athaliah was slain and the temple of Baal demolished (*2 Kin. 11:18*).

See AHAB, JEZEBEL, ELIJAH, ELISHA, JEHU, ATHALIAH, JOASH

BAASHA

[bā'a sha] The son of Ahijah and a member of the tribe of Issachar, Baasha became the third king of Israel by slaying Nadab and usurping the throne. His first recorded act was to exterminate the house of Jeroboam, fulfilling the prophecy of Ahijah. (*See* AHIJAH, JEROBOAM) Baasha attempted to fortify Ramah, only five miles north of Jerusalem, planning to use it as a base of operations against the Southern Kingdom. To counteract this move, Asa, king of Judah, persuaded Ben-hadad of Syria to break an alliance which he had made with Baasha and to attack him. Ben-hadad complied, forcing Baasha to abandon his project at Ramah, removing this threat from the Southern capital. Because of his wickedness, Baasha was told by the prophet Jehu that the fate of his house would be like that of Jeroboam. Although Baasha enjoyed a relatively long reign (900-877 BC), his house was completely destroyed by the usurper Zimri in 876 BC.

See KINGS

REFERENCE: *1 Kin. 15:16ff; 16:1ff; 2 Chr. 16:1ff; 1 Kin. 21:22; 2 Kin. 9:9.*

BABEL, TOWER OF

[bā'bel] The phrase "tower of Babel" does not occur in the Old Testament, but is popularly used to refer to the tower described in *Gen. 11* as having been erected in a plain of Shinar by wandering peoples. In all probability, the type of edifice to which this refers is the Babylonian *ziggurat*, a structure built in terraced stages with a rectangular temple serving as a platform for a tower, at the top of which was a small chapel. This story provides another account of the displeasure of God at the efforts of men to overcome his creatureliness and to ascend to a position like that of God. It also provides an explanation for the various nations and their languages.

SCRIPTURE

Gen. 11 [1]And the whole earth was of
one language, and of one speech. [2]And it
came to pass, as they journeyed from the
east, that they found a plain in the land of
Shinar; and they dwelt there. [3]And they
said one to another, Go to, let us make
brick, and burn them thoroughly. And
they had brick for stone, and slime had
they for mortar. [4]And they said, Go to, let

us build us a city, and a tower, whose top
may reach unto heaven; and let us make us
a name, lest we be scattered abroad upon
the face of the whole earth. 5And the
LORD came down to see the city and the
tower, which the children of men builded.
6And the LORD said, Behold, the people is
one, and they have all one language; and
this they begin to do: and now nothing will
be restrained from them, which they have
imagined to do. 7Go to, let us go down,
and there confound their language, that
they may not understand one another's
speech. 8So the LORD scattered them
abroad from thence upon the face of all
the earth: and they left off to build the city.
9Therefore is the name of it called Babel:
because the LORD did there confound the
language of all the earth: and from thence
did the LORD scatter them abroad upon
the face of all the earth.

BABYLONIA

[bab i lō'ni a] A territory in Southwest Asia, now Southern Iraq, which derived its name from the capital city of Babylon. It is sometimes referred to in the Bible as Shinar (*Gen. 10:10; 11:2; Isa. 11:11*), the land of the Chaldeans (*Jer. 24:5; Ezek. 12:13*), and Akkad (*Gen. 10:10*). In the Old Testament, Babylonia first assumes a role of importance during the period of the divided kingdom. In 745 BC Tiglath-Pileser III of Assyria (*see* TIGLATH-PILESER, ASSYRIA) claimed the throne of Babylonia for himself; in the reference to this in *1 Chr. 5:26*, Tiglath-Pileser is called by his given name Pul. During the period in which Assyria was engaged in the final defeat of the Israelite capital of Samaria (726-722 BC), Babylonia asserted its freedom and, ruled by Merodach-Baladan, remained independent of Assyrian rule until 710 BC, at which time the forces of Sargon occupied Babylonia. Merodach-Baladan was, however, retained as a local ruler and, after the death of Sargon in 705 BC, he sought to enlist the aid of Hezekiah king of Judah in a rebellion against Assyria. Sargon's successor Sennacharib was able to crush Merodach-Baladan's revolt and to establish Assyrian control once more.

In 681 BC Sennacharib was succeeded by his son Esarhaddon, who made arrangements before his death for his twin sons, Asshurbanapal and Samas-sum-ukin, to succeed to the thrones of Assyria and Babylon, respectively. By 652, however, Samas-sum-ukin was in open revolt against his brother's government; in 648, Asshurbanapal sacked Babylon and replaced his brother with a loyal viceroy.

After Asshurbanapal's death, the various tribes which constituted Babylonia banded together to support the Chaldean Nabopolassar against the Assyrian Sin-sar-iskun. Nabopolassar became king of Babylonia in 626 BC and began an offensive war against Assyria. With the aid of the Medes he captured the major Assyrian cities, taking Assur in 614 BC and Nineveh in 612. In 605 BC Nabopolassar turned his power over to Nebuchadrezzar (Nebuchadnezzar) who launched campaigns against the Egyptians. It was during this westward push that the first captives from Judah, including Daniel, were deported to Babylonia. In 601 BC the Babylonians again fought the Egyptians, both sides sustaining heavy losses. During the lull which followed Jehoiakim king of Judah switched his allegiance from Nebuchadrezzar to Necho II king of Egypt (*2 Kin. 24:1; Jer. 27:9-11*). As a result, Nebuchadnezzar marched on Jerusalem and sacked it in March of 597 BC. King Jehoiachin, who had replaced Jehoiakim, was captured and Zedekiah (Mattaniah) was placed on the throne as a vassal of Babylonia. In 587 BC, Zedekiah rebelled, precipitating the final destruction of Jerusalem and the second great deportation of captives into Babylonia.

For our purposes, we may pass to the time of Cyrus the Great. In 539 BC Cyrus' general Gobryas took control of Babylon, killing the ruler Nabonidus and his son Belshazzar, who had served as co-regent. It was during Cyrus' reign (539-530 BC) that the Jews were allowed to return to Jerusalem to reestablish the cult and society of Israel. Cyrus and his successors established what is known to us as the Persian Empire.

See PERSIA

BACKBITE

[bak'bīt] To slander or speak evil of an absent

person. The Bible, in several places, cautions against this practice.

See GOSSIP, SLANDER, etc.

SCRIPTURE

Psa. 15 [1]LORD, who shall abide in thy tabernacle? who shall dwell in thy holy hill? [2]He that walketh uprightly, and worketh righteousness, and speaketh the truth in his heart. [3]He that backbiteth not with his tongue, nor doeth evil to his neighbour, nor taketh up a reproach against his neighbour.

Prov. 25 [23]The north wind driveth away rain: so doth an angry countenance a backbiting tongue.

Rom. 1 [28]And even as they did not like to retain God in their knowledge, God gave them over to a reprobate mind, to do those things which are not convenient; [30]Backbiters, haters of God, despiteful.

2 Cor. 12 [20]For I fear, lest, when I come, I shall not find you such as I would, and that I shall be found unto you such as ye would not: lest there be debates, envyings, wraths, strifes, backbitings, whisperings, swellings, tumults:

BACKSLIDING

[bak′slid ing] Turning gradually, voluntarily, or insensibly from the knowledge, faith, love, and profession of God, after having once entered into a covenant relationship with Him.

SCRIPTURE

Examples of Backsliding

ISRAEL

Psa. 78 [10]They kept not the covenant of God, and refused to walk in his law; [11]And forgat his works, and his wonders that he had shewed them. [40]How oft did they provoke him in the wilderness, and grieve him in the desert! [41]Yea, they turned back and tempted God, and limited the Holy One of Israel. [42]They remembered not his hand, nor the day when he delivered them from the enemy. [43]How he had wrought his signs in Egypt, and his wonders in the field of Zoan: [56]Yet they tempted and provoked the most high God, and kept not his testimonies: [57]But turned back, and dealt unfaithfully like their fathers: they were turned aside like a deceitful bow.

Jer. 2 [19]Thine own wickedness shall correct thee, and thy backslidings shall reprove thee: know therefore and see that it is an evil thing and bitter, that thou hast forsaken the LORD thy God, and that my fear is not in thee, saith the Lord GOD of hosts.

Jer. 3 [6]The LORD said also unto me in the days of Josiah the king, Hast thou seen that which backsliding Israel hath done?

Hos. 4 [16]For Israel slideth back as a backsliding heifer: now the LORD will feed them as a lamb in a large place.

Hos. 11 [7]And my people are bent to backsliding from me: though they called them to the Most High, none at all would exalt him.

REFERENCE: Backsliding at Meribah, *Ex. 17:1-7;* when Aaron made the Golden calf, *Ex. 32;* after Joshua's death, *Judg. 2:11ff;* during Asa's reign, *2 Chr. 15;* during Hezekiah's reign, *2 Chr. 30:2-12.*

SAUL

1 Sam. 15 [11]It repenteth me that I have set up Saul to be king: for he is turned back from following me, and hath not performed my commandments. And it grieved Samuel; and he cried unto the LORD all night.

SOLOMON

1 Kin. 11 [3]And he had seven hundred

wives, princesses, and three hundred concubines: and his wives turned away his heart. [4]For it came to pass, when Solomon was old, that his wives turned away his heart after other gods: and his heart was not perfect with the LORD his God, as was the heart of David his father.

PETER

Matt. 26 [69]Now Peter sat without in the palace: and a damsel came unto him, saying, Thou also wast with Jesus of Galilee. [70]But he denied before them all, saying, I know not what thou sayest. [71]And when he was gone out into the porch, another maid saw him, and said unto them that were there, This fellow was also with Jesus of Nazareth. [72]And again he denied with an oath, I do not know the man. [73]And after a while came unto him they that stood by, and said to Peter, Surely thou also art one of them; for thy speech bewrayeth thee. [74]Then began he to curse and to swear, saying, I know not the man. And immediately the cock crew.

GALATIAN CHURCHES

Gal. 1 [6]I marvel that ye are so soon removed from him that called you into the grace of Christ unto another gospel:

Gal. 4 [9]But now, after that ye have known God, or rather are known of God, how turn ye again to the weak and beggarly elements, whereunto ye desire again to be in bondage? [10]Ye observe days, and months, and times, and years. [11]I am afraid of you, lest I have bestowed upon you labour in vain.

Warnings against Backsliding

Deut. 8 [11]Beware that thou forget not the LORD thy God, in not keeping his commandments, and his judgments, and his statutes, which I command thee this day: [12]Lest when thou hast eaten and art full, and hast built goodly houses, and dwelt therein; [13]And when thy herds and thy flocks multiply, and thy silver and thy gold is multiplied, [14]Then thine heart be lifted up, and thou forget the LORD thy God, which brought thee forth out of the land of Egypt, from the house of bondage;

Luke 9 [62]No man, having put his hand to the plough, and looking back, is fit for the kingdom of God.

Luke 17 [32]Remember Lot's wife.

God's Displeasure at Backsliding

Psa. 78 [56]Yet they tempted and provoked the most high God, and kept not his testimonies: [57]But turned back, and dealt unfaithfully like their fathers: they were turned aside like a deceitful bow. [58]For they provoked him to anger with their high places, and moved him to jealousy with their graven images. [59]When God heard this, he was wroth, and greatly abhorred Israel.

Pardon of Backsliders

Deut. 4 [29]But if from thence thou shalt seek the LORD thy God, thou shalt find him, if thou seek him with all thy heart and with all thy soul. [30]When thou art in tribulation, and all these things are come upon thee, even in the latter days, if thou turn to the LORD thy God, and shalt be obedient unto his voice;

2 Chr. 7 [14]If my people, which are called by my name, shall humble themselves, and pray, and seek my face, and turn from their wicked ways; then will I hear from heaven, and will forgive their sin, and will heal their land.

Jer. 3 [12]Go and proclaim these words toward the north, and say, Return, thou backsliding Israel, saith the LORD; and I will not cause mine anger to fall upon you:

for I am merciful, saith the LORD, and I will not keep anger for ever.

[22]Return, ye backsliding children, and I will heal your backslidings. Behold, we come unto thee; for thou art the LORD our God.

Return from Backsliding

Isa. 17 [7]At that day shall a man look to his Maker, and his eyes shall have respect to the Holy One of Israel.

Isa. 29 [24]They also that erred in spirit shall come to understanding, and they that murmured shall learn doctrine.

Isa. 31 [6]Turn ye unto him from whom the children of Israel have deeply revolted.
[7]For in that day every man shall cast away his idols of silver, and his idols of gold, which your own hands have made unto you for a sin.

Jer. 50 [4]In those days, and in that time, saith the LORD, the children of Israel shall come, they and the children of Judah together, going and weeping: they shall go, and seek the LORD their God. [5]They shall
ask the way to Zion with their faces thitherward, saying, Come, and let us join ourselves to the LORD in a perpetual covenant that shall not be forgotten.

REFERENCE: Return of Jews, *Ezra 6:16-21;* David, *Psa. 51*; Jonah, *Jonah 2, 3*; Peter, *Matt. 27:75; Mark 14:72; Luke 22:62.*

BALAAM

[bā'lam] A man of Pethor in Mesopotania who was endowed with the gift of divining. When the Israelites were encamped in the plains of Moab, Balak, king of Moab, sent for Balaam to curse them. We are told that Balaam was at first forbidden by God to go, but was eventually permitted to accompany those who came for him, on the condition that he would speak nothing except what was given him by the LORD. While on the way, the strange behavior of his ass further impressed upon him the necessity of obeying the will of God. On three occasions, Balak prepared sacrifices according to Balaam's instructions and the diviner set about to curse Israel; in each case, however, he could not but bless the people of God. This so upset Balak that he discharged Balaam from his service and sent him away without the promised pay. Nothing further is said of Balaam until *Num. 31*, in which we are told that he died a violent death at the hands of the Israelites. That his death was merited is borne out by verse 16 of this chapter, in which it is stated that Balaam had given the counsel which had brought about the plague which attacked the ranks of Israel.

The story of Balaam harmonizes well with what archaeologists have discovered concerning the Mesopotamian diviner, or *baru*. The Babylonians developed elaborate means of divination, relying heavily on every sort of omen. Ordinarily, the divination was carried out early in the morning, as the best results were thought to be obtained before sunrise. Even the three attempts which Balaam made fit the pattern, as the number three played an important role in Babylonian magic.

See BALAK

SCRIPTURE

Balak Sends for Balaam

Num. 22 [4]And Moab said unto the elders of Midian, Now shall this company lick up all that are round about us, as the ox licketh up the grass of the field. And Balak the son of Zippor was king of the Moabites at that time. [5]He sent messengers therefore unto Balaam the son of Beor to Pethor, which is by the river of the land of the children of his people, to call him, saying, Behold, there is a people come out from Egypt: behold, they cover the face of the earth, and they abide over against me:
[6]Come now therefore, I pray thee, curse me this people; for they are too mighty for me: peradventure I shall prevail, that we may smite them, and that I may drive them out of the land: for I wot that he whom

thou blessest is blessed, and he whom thou cursest is cursed.

20And God came unto Balaam at night, and said unto him, If the men come to call thee, rise up, and go with them; but yet the word which I shall say unto thee, that shalt thou do. 21And Balaam rose up in the morning, and saddled his ass, and went with the princes of Moab.

Balaam's Ass

Num. 22 22And God's anger was kindled because he went: and the angel of the LORD stood in the way for an adversary against him. Now he was riding upon his ass, and his two servants were with him. 23And the ass saw the angel of the LORD standing in the way, and his sword drawn in his hand: and the ass turned aside out of the way, and went into the field: and Balaam smote the ass, to turn her into the way. 24But the angel of the LORD stood in a path of the vineyards, a wall being on this side, and a wall on that side. 25And when the ass saw the angel of the LORD, she thrust herself unto the wall, and crushed Balaam's foot against the wall: and he smote her again. 26And the angel of the LORD went further, and stood in a narrow place, where was no way to turn either to the right hand or to the left. 27And when the ass saw the angel of the LORD, she fell down under Balaam: and Balaam's anger was kindled, and he smote the ass with a staff. 28And the LORD opened the mouth of the ass, and she said unto Balaam, What have I done unto thee, that thou hast smitten me these three times? 29And Balaam said unto the ass, Because thou hast mocked me: I would there were a sword in mine hand, for now would I kill thee. 30And the ass said unto Balaam, Am not I thine ass, upon which thou hast ridden ever since I was thine unto this day? was I ever wont to do so unto thee? And he said, Nay. 31Then the LORD opened the eyes of Balaam, and he saw the angel of the LORD standing in the way, and his sword drawn in his hand: and he bowed down his head, and fell flat on his face.

Balaam Prophesies

Num. 22 41And it came to pass on the morrow, that Balak took Balaam, and brought him up into the high places of Baal, that thence he might see the utmost part of the people.

Num. 23 1And Balaam said unto Balak, Build me here seven altars and prepare me here seven oxen and seven rams. 2And Balak did as Balaam had spoken; and Balak and Balaam offered on every altar a bullock and a ram. 3And Balaam said unto Balak, Stand by thy burnt offering, and I will go; peradventure the LORD will come to meet me; and whatsoever he sheweth me I will tell thee. And he went to a high place. 4And God met Balaam: and he said unto him, I have prepared seven altars, and I have offered upon every altar a bullock and a ram. 5And the LORD put a word in Balaam's mouth, and said, Return unto Balak, and thus thou shalt speak. 6And he returned unto him, and, lo, he stood by his burnt sacrifice, he, and all the princes of Moab. 7And he took up his parable, and said, Balak the king of Moab hath brought me from Aram, out of the mountains of the east, saying, Come, curse me Jacob, and come, defy Israel. 8How shall I curse, whom God hath not cursed? or how shall I defy, whom the LORD hath not defied? 9For from the top of the rocks I see him, and from the hills I behold him: lo, the people shall dwell alone, and shall not be reckoned among the nations. 10Who can count the dust of Jacob, and the number of the fourth part of Israel? Let me die the death of the righteous, and let my last end be like his!

Balak Displeased After Balaam Blesses Israel

Num. 23 [11]And Balak said unto Balaam, What hast thou done unto me? I took thee to curse mine enemies, and, behold, thou hast blessed them altogether.

[25]And Balak said unto Balaam, Neither curse them at all, nor bless them at all.

Num. 24 [10]And Balak's anger was kindled against Balaam, and he smote his hands together: and Balak said unto Balaam, I called thee to curse mine enemies, and, behold, thou hast altogether blessed them these three times. [11]Therefore now flee thou to thy place: I thought to promote thee unto great honour; but, lo, the LORD hath kept thee back from honour.

Death of Balaam

Num. 31 [8]And they slew the kings of Midian, besides the rest of them that were slain; namely, Evi, and Rekem, and Zur, and Hur, and Reba, five kings of Midian: Balaam also the son of Beor they slew with the sword.

Reason for His Death

Num. 31 [16]Behold, these caused the children of Israel, through the counsel of Balaam, to commit trespass against the LORD in the matter of Peor, and there was a plague among the congregation of the LORD.

Rev. 2 [14]But I have a few things against thee, because thou hast there them that hold the doctrine of Balaam, who taught Balac to cast a stumbling-block before the children of Israel, to eat things sacrificed unto idols, and to commit fornication.

REFERENCE: *Num. 22-24; Deut. 23:4; Josh. 13:22; 24:9; 2 Pet. 2:15-16; Jude 11.*

BALAK

[bā'lak] The king of Moab who hired Balaam to pronounce a curse on the Israelites.

See BALAAM

REFERENCE: *Num. 22-24.*

BAPTISM, BAPTIZE

[bap'tizm, bap tīz'] Both these words have their root in the Greek "bapto," meaning to immerse, dip, or plunge under water; to wash; the words are sometimes used metaphorically, as a baptism of blood, of fire, of the Holy Spirit. Baptism was not an invention of Christianity; both Judaism and the pagan mystery religions recognized the natural symbolism of ceremonial washings and utilized baptism as a rite of initiation into their circle. Baptism first appears in the New Testament in the narratives concerning John the Baptist. John's preaching ushered in the Messianic Age; as he spoke of the imminent breaking in of the Kingdom of God, urging his hearers to "flee from the wrath to come," crowds were "baptized of him in the river of Jordan, confessing their sins" (*Mark 1:5*). His baptism was symbolic of and accompanied by repentance. Jesus himself was baptized of John, making clear the continuity between their ministries. The effect of John's preaching was so widespread that his baptism was still being administered thirty years later in Alexandria and Ephesus (*Acts 18:25; 19:1-7*).

In the development of Christian theology, the rite of baptism has been viewed in many different lights with regard to its nature and efficacy. Although it is not possible in this article to treat each of these views fully, they may be summarized as follows: (1) that baptism is for the remission of sins and therefore essential to salvation; (2) that it is a public avowal of fealty to God; (3) that it is a sign and seal of the ingrafting into Christ and the accompanying spiritual benefits, that is, an outward sign of an inward spiritual grace; (4) that it is an ordinance for admitting men into discipleship, a sign of initiation, leading to final deliverance from all evil; (5) that it is a symbol of regeneration given only to those who exhibit signs of the new life in Christ; and (6) that it is a symbol of purification.

In *Acts of the Apostles* and the epistles of

Paul, baptism is frequently mentioned in connection with conversion, as a natural step in the acceptance of the gospel message. Baptism is into Christ or his name, signifying union with him; this union involves sharing in his death, burial, and resurrection, of which baptism is an obvious symbol. Two of the verses which emphasize the significance of baptism are *Acts 2:38* and *22:16*. Baptism is also closely connected with the gift of the Holy Spirit (*John 3:5, Acts 2:38*, (*1 Cor. 12:13*). Many think the phrase "born of water and of the Spirit" (*John 3:5*) is a description of baptism as understood in the early church, while others tend to emphasize either water or Spirit as having priority over the other. Another classic passage dealing with baptism is *Matt. 28:19*, "Go ye therefore, and teach all nations, baptizing them in the name of the Father, and of the Son, and of the Holy Ghost."

The mode of baptism varies in different religious groups. Immersion was the original form of the rite. Affusion, or the pouring of large amounts of water over the subject, was introduced rather early as an alternative method of administration. Aspersion, or sprinkling, was first introduced to accommodate the sick and infirm, but was not generally accepted until the thirteenth century. There is also a division of opinion on the matter of infant baptism. Some contend that repentance and faith are a necessary precondition of baptism, thus eliminating infants as fit candidates. Others justify the practice on the basis of Original Sin and the contention that children of believing parents are born within the church.

See BAPTISM FOR THE DEAD, BAPTISM OF FIRE, BAPTISM OF THE HOLY SPIRIT

SCRIPTURE

John's Baptism

Matt. 3 [5]Then went out to him Jerusalem, and all Judaea, and all the region
round about Jordan, [6]And were baptized
of him in Jordan, confessing their sins.
[7]But when he saw many of the Pharisees
and Sadducees come to his baptism, he
said unto them, O generation of vipers,
who hath warned you to flee from the
wrath to come? [8]Bring forth therefore
fruits meet for repentance: [11]I indeed
baptize you with water unto repentance:
but he that cometh after me is mightier
than I, whose shoes I am not worthy to
bear: he shall baptize you with the Holy
Ghost, and with fire:
[13]Then cometh Jesus from Galilee to
Jordan unto John, to be baptized of him.
[14]But John forbad him, saying, I have need
to be baptized of thee, and comest thou to
me? [15]And Jesus answering said unto him,
Suffer it to be so now: for thus it becometh
us to fulfil all righteousness. Then he suffered him. [16]And Jesus, when he was baptized, went up straightway out of the water: and, lo, the heavens were opened unto
him, and he saw the Spirit of God descending like a dove, and lighting upon him:

Matt. 21 [25]The baptism of John, whence
was it? from heaven, or of men?

Mark 1 [4]John did baptize in the wilderness, and preach the baptism of repentance for the remission of sins. [5]And there
went out unto him all the land of Judaea,
and they of Jerusalem, and were all baptized of him in the river of Jordan, confessing their sins.

Luke 3 [12]Then came also publicans to
be baptized, and said unto him, Master,
what shall we do? [21]When all the people
were baptized, it came to pass, that Jesus
also being baptized, and praying, the
heaven was opened.

Luke 7 [29]All the people that heard him,
and the publicans, justified God, being
baptized with the baptism of John. [30]But
the Pharisees and lawyers rejected the
counsel of God against themselves, being
not baptized of him.

John 1 [25]And they asked him, and said
unto him, Why baptizest thou then, if thou
be not that Christ, nor Elias, neither that
prophet? [26]John answered them, saying,
I baptize with water: but there standeth

one among you, whom ye know not; [28]These things were done in Bethabara beyond Jordan, where John was baptizing.

[31]I knew him not: but that he should be made manifest to Israel, therefore am I come baptizing with water. [33]He that sent me to baptize with water, the same said unto me, Upon whom thou shalt see the Spirit descending, and remaining on him, the same is he which baptizeth with the Holy Ghost.

John 3 [23]And John also was baptizing in Aenon, near to Salim, because there was much water there: and they came, and were baptized.

Acts 1 [5]John truly baptized with water; but ye shall be baptized with the Holy Ghost not many days hence.

[22]Beginning from the baptism of John, unto that same day that he was taken up from us, must one be ordained to be a witness with us of his resurrection.

Acts 10 [37]That word, I say, ye know, which was published throughout all Judaea, and began from Galilee, after the baptism which John preached;

Acts 11 [16]Then remembered I the word of the Lord, how that he said, John indeed baptized with water; but ye shall be baptized with the Holy Ghost.

Acts 19 [3]And he said unto them, Unto what then were ye baptized? And they said, Unto John's baptism. [4]Then said Paul, John verily baptized with the baptism of repentance, saying unto the people, that they should believe on him which should come after him, that is, on Christ Jesus.

REFERENCE: *Mark 1:8-10; Luke 3:7, 8; John 10:40; Mark 11:30; Luke 20:4; Acts 18:25.*

Christian Baptism

Matt. 28 [19]Go ye therefore, and teach all nations, baptizing them in the name of the Father, and of the Son, and of the Holy Ghost:

Mark 16 [16]He that believeth and is baptized shall be saved;

John 3 [5]Jesus answered, Verily, verily, I say unto thee, Except a man be born of water and of the Spirit, he cannot enter into the kingdom of God.

[22]After these things came Jesus and his disciples into the land of Judaea; and there he tarried with them, and baptized.

John 4 [1]The Lord knew how the Pharisees had heard that Jesus made and baptized more disciples than John, [2](Though Jesus himself baptized not, but his disciples,)

Acts 2 [38]Peter said unto them, Repent, and be baptized every one of you in the name of Jesus Christ for the remission of sins, and ye shall receive the gift of the Holy Ghost.

[41]Then they that gladly received his word were baptized: and the same day there were added unto them about three thousand souls.

Acts 8 [12]When they believed Philip preaching the things concerning the kingdom of God, and the name of Jesus Christ, they were baptized, both men and women. [13]Then Simon himself believed also: and when he was baptized, he continued with Philip, ... [36]And as they went on their way, they came unto a certain water: and the eunuch said, See, here is water; what doth hinder me to be baptized? [37]Philip said, If thou believest with all thine heart, thou mayest. And he answered and said, I believe that Jesus Christ is the Son of God. [38]And he commanded the chariot to stand still: and they went down both into the water, both Philip and the eunuch; and he baptized him.

Acts 9 [18]And immediately there fell from his eyes as it had been scales: and he

received sight forthwith, and arose, and
was baptized.

Acts 10 [46]Then answered Peter, [47]Can
any man forbid water, that these should
not be baptized, which have received the
Holy Ghost as well as we? [48]And he commanded them to be baptized in the name
of the Lord.

Acts 16 [14]And a certain woman named
Lydia, a seller of purple, of the city of Thyatira, which worshipped God, heard us:
whose heart the Lord opened, that she attended unto the things which were spoken
of Paul. [15]And when she was baptized,
and her household, she besought us, saying, If ye have judged me to be faithful to
the Lord, come into my house, and abide
there.

[33]He took them the same hour of the
night, and washed their stripes; and was
baptized, he and all his, straightway.

Acts 18 [8]Many of the Corinthians hearing believed, and were baptized.

[25]This man was instructed in the way of
the Lord; and being fervent in the spirit,
he spake and taught diligently the things
of the Lord, knowing only the baptism of
John.

Acts 19 [4]Then said Paul, John verily
baptized with the baptism of repentance,
saying unto the people, that they should
believe on him which should come after
him, that is, on Christ Jesus. [5]When they
heard this, they were baptized in the name
of the Lord Jesus.

Acts 22 [16]And now why tarriest thou?
arise, and be baptized, and wash away thy
sins, calling on the name of the Lord.

Rom. 6 [3]Know ye not, that so many of
us as were baptized into Jesus Christ were
baptized into his death? [4]Therefore we
are buried with him by baptism into death:
that like as Christ was raised up from the
dead by the glory of the Father, even so
we also should walk in newness of life.

1 Cor. 1 [13]Were ye baptized in the name
of Paul? [14]I thank God that I baptized
none of you, but Crispus and Gaius;
[15]Lest any should say that I had baptized
in mine own name. [16]And I baptized also
the household of Stephanas: besides, I
know not whether I baptized any other.
[17]For Christ sent me not to baptize, but to
preach the gospel:

1 Cor. 10 [1]Moreover, brethren, I would
not that ye should be ignorant, how that all
our fathers were under the cloud, and all
passed through the sea; [2]And were all
baptized unto Moses in the cloud and in
the sea;

1 Cor. 12 [13]By one Spirit are we all baptized into one body, whether we be Jews
or Gentiles, whether we be bond or free;
and have been all made to drink into one
Spirit.

1 Cor. 15 [29]What shall they do which
are baptized for the dead, if the dead rise
not at all? why are they then baptized for
the dead?

Gal. 3 [27]As many of you as have been
baptized into Christ have put on Christ.

Eph. 4 [5]One Lord, one faith, one baptism,

Eph. 5 [26]That he might sanctify and
cleanse it with the washing of water by the
word,

Col. 2 [12]Buried with him in baptism,
wherein also ye are risen with him through
the faith of the operation of God, who hath
raised him from the dead.

Heb. 6 [2]Of the doctrine of baptisms,
and of laying on of hands, and of resurrection of the dead, and of eternal judgment.

1 Pet. 3 [18]Christ also hath once suffered
for sins, the just for the unjust, that he

might bring us to God, being put to death in the flesh, but quickened by the Spirit: 21The like figure whereunto even baptism doth also now save us (not the putting away of the filth of the flesh, but the answer of a good conscience toward God,) by the resurrection of Jesus Christ:

BAPTISM FOR THE DEAD

In *1 Cor. 15:29*, Paul presents an argument in support of the resurrection in the following words: "Else what shall they do which are baptized for the dead, if the dead rise not at all? Why are they then baptized for the dead?" Despite the fact that the practice receives no mention elsewhere in scripture, the most obvious interpretation of this statement is that some Christians in Corinth, and perhaps elsewhere, were being vicariously baptized on behalf of friends or relatives who had died in an unsaved condition. Many other interpretations of this problematic phrase have been given and it is impossible to be certain as to exactly what the apostle meant. It is well-known, however, that belief in the efficacy of vicarious symbolic acts was widespread and it does not seem unlikely that such was the case in Corinth.

BAPTISM OF FIRE

In *Matt. 3:11*, it is said of Jesus that "he shall baptize you with the Holy Ghost, and with fire." This has usually been interpreted as referring either to the judgment of fire or to the work of the Holy Spirit, which is likened to a refining fire.

BAPTISM OF THE HOLY SPIRIT

In the gospels (*Matt. 3:11; Mark 1:8; Luke 3:16; John 1:33*) and in *Acts 1:5*, the baptism of the Holy Spirit is viewed as still to come. The first occurrence of the phenomenon is recorded in *Acts 2*. The outpouring of the Spirit upon the disciples at Pentecost was accompanied by the physical manifestations of "a sound from heaven as of a rushing mighty wind" (*Acts 2:2*), "cloven tongues like as of fire" which "sat upon each of them" (*Acts 2:3*), and the speaking in tongues by the disciples (*Acts 2:4*). The conversion of the centurian Cornelius was also accompanied by this baptism of promise (*Acts 10:44-48; 11:15-16*). It is clear from this and the other cases of conversion in the book of *Acts* that the baptism of the Holy Spirit was a special outpouring of God's Spirit and was never intended to supersede water baptism.

See BAPTISM

SCRIPTURE

Joel 2 28And it shall come to pass afterward, that I will pour out my spirit upon all flesh; and your sons and your daughters shall prophesy, your old men shall dream dreams, your young men shall see visions: 29And also upon the servants and upon the handmaids in those days will I pour out my spirit.

Matt. 3 11I indeed baptize you with water unto repentance: but he that cometh after me is mightier than I, whose shoes I am not worthy to bear: he shall baptize you with the Holy Ghost, and with fire:

16And Jesus, when he was baptized, went up straightway out of the water: and, lo, the heavens were opened unto him, and he saw the Spirit of God descending like a dove, and lighting upon him:

Luke 24 49And, behold, I send the promise of my Father upon you: but tarry ye in the city of Jerusalem, until ye be endued with power from on high.

Acts 1 5John truly baptized with water; but ye shall be baptized with the Holy Ghost not many days hence.

Acts 2 1And when the day of Pentecost was fully come, they were all with one accord in one place. 2And suddenly there came a sound from heaven as of a rushing mighty wind, and it filled all the house where they were sitting. 3And there appeared unto them cloven tongues like as of fire, and it sat upon each of them. [4]And they were all filled with the Holy Ghost, and began to speak with other tongues, as the Spirit gave them utterance.

[38]Peter said unto them, Repent, and be baptized every one of you in the name of Jesus Christ for the remission of sins, and ye shall receive the gift of the Holy Ghost.

[41]Then they that gladly received his word were baptized: and the same day there were added unto them about three thousand souls.

Acts 8 [15]Who (Peter and John), when they were come down, prayed for them, that they might receive the Holy Ghost: [16](For as yet he was fallen upon none of them: only they were baptized in the name of the Lord Jesus.) [17]Then laid they their hands on them, and they received the Holy Ghost.

Acts 10 [38]How God anointed Jesus of Nazareth with the Holy Ghost and with power:

[44]While Peter yet spake these words, the Holy Ghost fell on all them which heard the word. [45]And they of the circumcision which believed were astonished, as many as came with Peter, because that on the Gentiles also was poured out the gift of the Holy Ghost. [47]Can any man forbid water, that these should not be baptized, which have received the Holy Ghost as well as we?

Acts 11 [15]And as I began to speak, the Holy Ghost fell on them, as on us at the beginning. [16]Then remembered I the word of the Lord, how that he said, John indeed baptized with water; but ye shall be baptized with the Holy Ghost.

Acts 19 [2]He said unto them, Have ye received the Holy Ghost since ye believed? And they said unto him, We have not so much as heard whether there be any Holy Ghost. [6]And when Paul had laid his hands upon them, the Holy Ghost came on them;

REFERENCE: *Luke 3:22; John 1:32, 33.*

BAR-

[bär] The Aramaic equivalent for the Hebrew prefix "ben-" (*see* BEN), meaning "son" or "son of." It is frequently used as a proper name, such as Simon Bar-Jonah, or Simon, Son of Jonah. Other New Testament names containing this prefix are Barabbas, Bar-Jesus, Barnabas, Barsabas, Bartholomew, Bartimaeus.

BARABBAS

[ba rab'as] A robber who had committed murder in an insurrection, and who was in prison in Jerusalem under the sentence of death at the time of the trial of Jesus. It was an annual custom for the governor to release one prisoner at the feast of Passover. Pilate, recognizing that Jesus had done nothing guilty of punishment, sought to free him by offering the crowd the choice between Jesus and the notorious criminal Barabbas. The perverse crowd, at the instigation of the chief priests, chose Barabbas.

SCRIPTURE

Matt. 27 [15]Now at that feast the governor was wont to release unto the people a prisoner, whom they would. [16]And they had then a notable prisoner, called Barabbas. [17]Therefore when they were gathered together, Pilate said unto them, Whom will ye that I release unto you? Barabbas, or Jesus which is called Christ? [18]For he knew that for envy they had delivered him.

[19]When he was set down on the judgment seat, his wife sent unto him, saying, Have thou nothing to do with that just man: for I have suffered many things this day in a dream because of him. [20]But the chief priests and elders persuaded the multitude that they should ask Barabbas, and destroy Jesus. [21]The governor an-

swered and said unto them, Whether of
the twain will ye that I release unto you?
They said, Barabbas. 22Pilate saith unto
them, What shall I do then with Jesus
which is called Christ? They all say unto
him, Let him be crucified. 23And the governor said, Why, what evil hath he done?
But they cried out the more, saying, Let
him be crucified.

24When Pilate saw that he could prevail nothing, but that rather a tumult was
made, he took water, and washed his
hands before the multitude, saying, I am
innocent of the blood of this just person:
see ye to it. 25Then answered all the people, and said, His blood be on us, and on
our children.

26Then released he Barabbas unto them:
and when he had scourged Jesus, he delivered him to be crucified.

REFERENCE: *Mark 15:6-15; Luke 23:18-25; John 18:40.*

BARAK

[bā′rak] A military leader of Israel who was ordered by Deborah to lead an army against Sisera, the general of the armies of the Canaanite king of Hazor. Barak was reluctant but agreed to go when assured that Deborah would accompany him. With an army of 10,000 Barak defeated the forces of Sisera. The Canaanite general himself escaped but Barak, pursuing him, found him slain at the hands of a woman in whose tent he had sought refuge.

See DEBORAH

SCRIPTURE

Judg. 4 4And Deborah, a prophetess,
the wife of Lapidoth, she judged Israel at
that time. 5And she dwelt under the palm
tree of Deborah, between Ramah and
Bethel in mount Ephraim: and the children of Israel came up to her for judgment.
6And she sent and called Barak the son of
Abinoam out of Kedeshnaphtali, and said
unto him, Hath not the LORD God of Israel commanded, saying, Go and draw
toward mount Tabor, and take with thee
ten thousand men of the children of Naphtali and of the children of Zebulun?
7And I will draw unto thee, to the river
Kishon, Sisera, the captain of Jabin's army,
with his chariots and his multitude; and I
will deliver him into thine hand. 8And
Barak said unto her, If thou wilt go with
me, then I will go: but if thou wilt not go
with me, then I will not go. 9And she said,
I will surely go with thee: notwithstanding
the journey that thou takest shall not be
for thine honour; for the LORD shall sell
Sisera into the hand of a woman. And Deborah arose, and went with Barak to Kedesh.

10And Barak called Zebulun and Naphtali to Kedesh; and he went up with ten
thousand men at his feet: and Deborah
went up with him. 11Now Heber the Kenite, which was of the children of Hobab the
father in law of Moses, had severed himself from the Kenites, and pitched his tent
unto the plain of Zaanaim, which is by
Kedesh. 12And they shewed Sisera that
Barak the son of Abinoam was gone up to
mount Tabor. 13And Sisera gathered together all his chariots, even nine hundred
chariots of iron, and all the people that
were with him, from Harosheth of the
Gentiles unto the river of Kishon. 14And
Deborah said unto Barak, Up; for this is
the day in which the LORD hath delivered
Sisera into thine hand: is not the LORD
gone out before thee? So Barak went down
from mount Tabor, and ten thousand men
after him. 15And the LORD discomfited
Sisera, and all his chariots, and all his host,
with the edge of the sword before Barak;
so that Sisera lighted down off his chariot,

and fled away on his feet. [16]But Barak pursued after the chariots, and after the host, unto Harosheth of the Gentiles: and all the host of Sisera fell upon the edge of the sword; and there was not a man left.

BARNABAS

[bär′na bas] Variously translated "son of consolation" or "son of exhortation", this is the name given by the apostles to Joses, or Joseph, a Levite of the island of Cyprus who sold a field and donated the money to the common fund of the church in Jerusalem. He is described as "a good man, and full of the Holy Ghost and of faith:" (*Acts 11:24*), and is designated as our apostle in *Acts 14:14.* After Saul's marvelous conversion on the road to Damascus, it was Barnabas who interceded on his behalf and persuaded the disciples in Jerusalem to accept their former persecutor as a fellow-worker in Christ. When the Jerusalem church learned of the presence of a group of disciples in Antioch, Barnabas was dispatched to that city to encourage the work in whatever way he could. After a short visit with them, he departed for Tarsus to enlist Saul's aid in this promising work. It was during the period of their work with the church in Antioch that the disciples were first called Christians. Following a brief mission to Jerusalem to deliver relief funds during a time of famine, Barnabas and Saul returned to Antioch and set out on what is usually referred to as the First Missionary Journey. After returning from this trip among the Gentiles, Barnabas accompanied Paul (Saul), who had now become the chief spokesman, to Jerusalem, where they discussed the problems of the relationship of Gentile Christians to the Law of Moses. Shortly thereafter, a rift began to appear between these two zealous co-workers, at first over Barnabas' inconsistency with regard to matters discussed at Jerusalem (*see Gal. 2:13*) and then over Paul's refusal to allow John Mark to accompany them on a second tour. Unable to reach agreement over the latter, Paul chose Silas to accompany him and Barnabas and Mark set out for Cyprus. Many feel that *1 Cor. 9:6* implies that Paul and Barnabas were later reconciled.

See MARK, PAUL

REFERENCE: *Acts 4:36, 37; 9:25-27; 11:22-30; 13:15; Gal. 2:1-13; 1 Cor. 9:6.*

BARTHOLOMEW

[bär thol′ô mū] One of the twelve apostles. It has been conjectured that he is identical with the Nathanael mentioned in *John 1:45ff.* Tradition has it that Bartholomew preached the gospel in India, but there is no means by which this may be verified.

See APOSTLES

REFERENCE: *Matt. 10:3; Mark 3:18; Luke 6:14; Acts 1:13.*

BARTIMAEUS

[bär ti me′us] Name means son of Timaeus. A blind beggar of Jericho whose sight was restored by Jesus.

SCRIPTURE

Mark 10 [46]And they came to Jericho:
and as he went out of Jericho with his disciples and a great number of people, blind Bartimaeus, the son of Timaeus, sat by the
highway side begging. [47]And when he
heard that it was Jesus of Nazareth, he began to cry out, and say, Jesus, thou son
of David, have mercy on me. [48]And many
charged him that he should hold his peace: but he cried the more a great deal, Thou
son of David, have mercy on me. [49]And
Jesus stood still, and commanded him to be called. And they call the blind man, saying unto him, Be of good comfort, rise;
he calleth thee. [50]And he, casting away his
garment, rose, and came to Jesus. [51]And
Jesus answered and said unto him, What wilt thou that I should do unto thee? The blind man said unto him, Lord, that I might receive my sight. And Jesus said unto him, Go thy way; thy faith hath made thee whole. And immediately he received his sight, and followed Jesus in the way.

BARUCH

[bā′ruk] The friend and secretary of the prophet Jeremiah. Baruch wrote down the prophecies of Jeremiah and read them in the hearing of the people in the temple. He was then summoned before the princes of Judah, to whom also he read the prophecies. The roll was then delivered to King Jehoiakim, who burned it in his fireplace, but Baruch escaped harm, having hidden himself at the suggestion of the princes. In the days that followed, he rewrote and enlarged the scroll. Despite the trials which Jeremiah underwent in the last days of Judah, Baruch is seen to have remained a faithful companion. After their forced exile to Egypt, nothing definite is known of Baruch.

See Jeremiah

SCRIPTURE

Jer. 36 1 And it came to pass in the fourth year of Jehoiakim the son of Josiah king of Judah, that this word came unto Jeremiah from the Lord, saying, 2 Take thee a roll of a book, and write therein all the words that I have spoken unto thee against Israel, and against Judah, and against all the nations, from the day I spake unto thee, from the days of Josiah, even unto this day. 3 It may be that the house of Judah will hear all the evil which I purpose to do unto them; that they may return every man from his evil way; that I may forgive their iniquity and their sin. 4 Then Jeremiah called Baruch the son of Neriah: and Baruch wrote from the mouth of Jeremiah all the words of the Lord, which he had spoken unto him, upon a roll of a book. 5 And Jeremiah commanded Baruch, saying, I am shut up; I cannot go into the house of the Lord: 6 Therefore go thou, and read in the roll, which thou hast written from my mouth, the words of the Lord in the ears of the people in the Lord's house upon the fasting day: and also thou shalt read them in the ears of all Judah that come out of their cities. 7 It may be they will present their supplication before the Lord, and will return every one from his evil way: for great is the anger and the fury that the Lord hath pronounced against this people. 8 And Baruch the son of Neriah did according to all that Jeremiah the prophet commanded him, reading in the book the words of the Lord in the Lord's house. 9 And it came to pass in the fifth year of Jehoiakim the son of Josiah king of Judah, in the ninth month, that they proclaimed a fast before the Lord to all the people in Jerusalem, and to all the people that came from the cities of Judah unto Jerusalem. 10 Then read Baruch in the book the words of Jeremiah in the house of the Lord, in the chamber of Gemariah the son of Shaphan the scribe, in the higher court, at the entry of the new gate of the Lord's house, in the ears of all the people.

11 When Michaiah the son of Gemariah, the son of Shaphan, had heard out of the book all the words of the Lord, 12 Then he went down into the king's house, into the scribe's chamber: and, lo, all the princes sat there, even Elishama the scribe, and Delaiah the son of Shemaiah, and Elnathan the son of Achbor, and Gemariah the son of Shaphan, and Zedekiah the son of Hananiah, and all the princes. 13 Then Michaiah declared unto them all the words that he had heard, when Baruch read the book in the ears of the people. 14 Therefore all the princes sent Jehudi the son of Nethaniah, the son of Shelemiah, the son of Cushi, unto Baruch, saying, Take in thine hand the roll wherein thou hast read in the ears of the people, and come. So Baruch the son of Neriah took the roll in his hand, and came unto them. 15 And they said unto him, Sit down now, and read it in our ears. So Baruch read it in their ears. 16 Now it came to pass, when they had heard all the words, they were afraid both one and other, and said unto Baruch, We will surely tell the king of all these words.

[17]And they asked Baruch, saying, Tell us now, How didst thou write all these words at his mouth? [18]Then Baruch answered them, He pronounced all these words unto me with his mouth, and I wrote them with ink in the book. [19]Then said the princes unto Baruch, Go, hide thee, thou and Jeremiah; and let no man know where ye be.

[20]And they went in to the king into the court, but they laid up the roll in the chamber of Elishama the scribe, and told all the words in the ears of the king. [21]So the king sent Jehudi to fetch the roll: and he took it out of Elishama the scribe's chamber. And Jehudi read it in the ears of the king, and in the ears of all the princes which stood beside the king. [22]Now the king sat in the winter house in the ninth month; and there was a fire on the hearth burning before him. [23]And it came to pass, that when Jehudi had read three or four leaves, he cut it with the penknife, and cast it into the fire that was on the hearth, until all the roll was consumed in the fire that was on the hearth. [24]Yet they were not afraid, nor rent their garments, neither the king, nor any of his servants that heard all these words. [25]Nevertheless Elnathan and Delaiah and Gemariah had made intercession to the king that he would not burn the roll; but he would not hear them. [26]But the king commanded Jerahmeel the son of Hammelech, and Seraiah the son of Azriel, and Shelemiah the son of Abdeel, to take Baruch the scribe and Jeremiah the prophet: but the LORD hid them.

[27]Then the word of the LORD came to Jeremiah, after that the king had burned the roll, and the words which Baruch wrote at the mouth of Jeremiah, saying, [28]Take thee again another roll, and write in it all the former words that were in the first roll, which Jehoiakim the king of Judah hath burned. [29]And thou shalt say to Jehoiakim king of Judah, Thus saith the LORD; Thou hast burned this roll, saying, Why hast thou written therein, saying, The king of Babylon shall certainly come and destroy this land, and shall cause to cease from thence man and beast? [30]Therefore thus saith the LORD, of Jehoiakim king of Judah; He shall have none to sit upon the throne of David: and his dead body shall be cast out in the day to the heat, and in the night to the frost. [31]And I will punish him and his seed and his servants for their iniquity; and I will bring upon them, and upon the inhabitants of Jerusalem, and upon the men of Judah, all the evil that I have pronounced against them; but they hearkened not.

[32]Then took Jeremiah another roll, and gave it to Baruch the scribe, the son of Neriah; who wrote therein from the mouth of Jeremiah all the words of the book which Jehoiakim king of Judah had burned in the fire: and there were added besides unto them many like words.

Jer. 43 [6]Even men, and women, and children, and the king's daughters, and every person that Nebuzaradan the captain of the guard had left with Gedaliah the son of Ahikam the son of Shaphan, and Jeremiah the prophet, and Baruch the son of Neriah.

REFERENCE: *Jer. 32:12-16; 45:1-5.*

BATH-

[bath] A Hebrew prefix meaning "daughter", employed in compound names such as Bath-sheba.

See BEN-, BAR-

BATH-SHEBA

[bath-shē'ba] The beautiful wife of Uriah the Hittite with whom David committed adultery after having seen her bathing on her rooftop. When David learned that she was pregnant, he recalled her husband from battle, expecting to induce him to go home to Bath-sheba and thus to remove the blame from the king. When he refused, David had him sent into the front line of battle, where he met his death. He then summoned Bath-sheba to his house and she bore him a son. After the severe rebuke which David received from the prophet Nathan, the child died. Bath-sheba bore David four other sons, including Solomon, whom she assisted in the struggle for the throne after David's death.

See DAVID, JOAB, URIAH

SCRIPTURE

Becomes David's Wife

2 Sam. 11 [1]And it came to pass, after the year was expired, at the time when kings go forth to battle, that David sent Joab, and his servants with him, and all Israel; and they destroyed the children of Ammon, and besieged Rabbah. But David tarried still at Jerusalem.

[2]And it came to pass in an eveningtide, that David arose from off his bed, and walked upon the roof of the king's house: and from the roof he saw a woman washing herself; and the woman was very beautiful to look upon. [3]And David sent and inquired after the woman. And one said, Is not this Bath-sheba, the daughter of Eliam, the wife of Uriah the Hittite? [4]And David sent messengers, and took her; and she came in unto him, and he lay with her; for she was purified from her uncleanness: and she returned unto her house. [5]And the woman conceived, and sent and told David, and said, I am with child.

[26]And when the wife of Uriah heard that Uriah her husband was dead, she mourned for her husband. [27]And when the mourning was past, David sent and fetched her to his house, and she became his wife, and bare him a son. But the thing that David had done displeased the LORD.

Their Marriage Brings Rebuke by Nathan the Prophet

2 Sam. 12 [1]And the LORD sent Nathan unto David. And he came unto him, and said unto him, There were two men in one city; the one rich, and the other poor. [2]The rich man had exceeding many flocks and herds: [3]But the poor man had nothing, save one little ewe lamb, which he had bought and nourished up: and it grew up together with him, and with his children; it did eat of his own meat, and drank of his own cup, and lay in his bosom, and was unto him as a daughter. [4]And there came a traveller unto the rich man, and he spared to take of his own flock and of his own herd, to dress for the wayfaring man that was come unto him; but took the poor man's lamb, and dressed it for the man that was come to him. [5]And David's anger was greatly kindled against the man; and he said to Nathan, As the LORD liveth, the man that hath done this thing shall surely die. [6]And he shall restore the lamb fourfold, because he did this thing, and because he had no pity.

[7]And Nathan said to David, Thou art the man. Thus saith the LORD God of Israel, I anointed thee king over Israel, and I delivered thee out of the hand of Saul: [8]And I gave thee thy master's house, and thy master's wives into thy bosom, and gave thee the house of Israel and of Judah; and if that had been too little, I would moreover have given unto thee such and such things. [9]Wherefore hast thou despised the commandment of the LORD, to do evil in his sight? thou hast killed Uriah the Hittite with the sword, and hast taken his wife to be thy wife, and hast slain him with the sword of the children of Ammon. [10]Now therefore the sword shall never depart from thine house; because thou hast

despised me, and hast taken the wife of Uriah the Hittite to be thy wife. [11]Thus saith the LORD, Behold, I will raise up evil against thee out of thine own house, and I will take thy wives before thine eyes, and give them unto thy neighbour, and he shall lie with thy wives in the sight of this sun. [12]For thou didst it secretly: but I will do this thing before all Israel, and before the sun. [13]And David said unto Nathan, I have sinned against the LORD. And Nathan said unto David, The LORD also hath put away thy sin; thou shalt not die. [14]Howbeit, because by this deed thou hast given great occasion to the enemies of the LORD to blaspheme, the child also that is born unto thee shall surely die.

[15]And Nathan departed unto his house. And the LORD struck the child that Uriah's wife bare unto David, and it was very sick. [16]David therefore besought God for the child; and David fasted, and went in, and lay all night upon the earth. [17]And the elders of his house arose, and went to him, to raise him up from the earth: but he would not, neither did he eat bread with them. [18]And it came to pass on the seventh day, that the child died. And the servants of David feared to tell him that the child was dead: for they said, Behold, while the child was yet alive, we spake unto him, and he would not hearken unto our voice: how will he then vex himself, if we tell him that the child is dead? [19]But when David saw that his servants whispered, David perceived that the child was dead: therefore David said unto his servants, Is the child dead? And they said, He is dead. [20]Then David arose from the earth, and washed, and anointed himself, and changed his apparel, and came into the house of the LORD, and worshipped: then he came to his own house; and when he required, they set bread before him, and he did eat. [21]Then said his servants unto him, What thing is this that thou hast done? thou didst fast and weep for the child while it was alive; but when the child was dead, thou didst rise and eat bread. [22]And he said, While the child was yet alive, I fasted and wept: for I said, Who can tell whether God will be gracious to me, that the child may live? [23]But now he is dead, wherefore should I fast? can I bring him back again? I shall go to him, but he shall not return to me.

[24]And David comforted Bath-sheba his wife, and went in unto her, and lay with her: and she bare a son, and he called his name Solomon: and the LORD loved him. [25]And he sent by the hand of Nathan the prophet; and he called his name Jedidiah, because of the LORD.

Bath-sheba Intercedes for Adonijah

See ADONIJAH and ABISHAG

BEATITUDES

[bē at′i tūdz] This word is not found in the Bible, but is derived from a Latin word meaning blessedness. Since the time of Ambrose, it has been used to refer to the sayings which form the introduction to the Sermon on the Mount and which serve as a description of the qualities to be found in Christ's true disciples. They are as follows:

SCRIPTURE

Matt. 5 [3]Blessed are the poor in spirit: for theirs is the kingdom of heaven. [4]Blessed are they that mourn: for they shall be comforted. [5]Blessed are the meek: for they shall inherit the earth. [6]Blessed are they which do hunger and thirst after righteousness: for they shall be filled. [7]Blessed are the merciful: for they shall obtain mercy. [8]Blessed are the pure in heart: for they shall see God. [9]Blessed are the peacemakers: for they shall be called

the children of God. [10]Blessed are they
which are persecuted for righteousness'
sake: for theirs is the kingdom of heaven.
[11]Blessed are ye, when men shall revile
you, and persecute you, and shall say all
manner of evil against you falsely for my
sake.

BEAUTY

[bū'ti] That quality or aggregate of qualities in a thing which gives pleasure to the sense or pleasurably exalts the mind or spirit; physical, moral, or spiritual loveliness. The Bible is replete with references to various sorts of beauties, pointing out the vanity, danger, and temporary quality of mere personal attractions and calling attention to the higher and more permanent quality of the beauties of mind, character, and temperament.

SCRIPTURE

Vanity of Beauty

Psa. 39 [11]When thou with rebukes dost correct man for iniquity, thou makest his beauty to consume away like a moth: surely every man is vanity. Selah.

Prov. 6 [25]Lust not after her beauty in thine heart; neither let her take thee with her eye-lids.

Prov. 31 [30]Favour is deceitful, and beauty is vain: but a woman that feareth the LORD, she shall be praised.

Psa. 49 [14]Like sheep they are laid in the grave; death shall feed on them; and the upright shall have dominion over them in the morning; and their beauty shall consume in the grave from their dwelling.

BEELZEBUB

[bē el'zē bub] Originally, a Philistine deity. The name means "lord of the flies." In the New Testament, Beelzebub is referred to as the prince of demons. Jesus was called Beelzebub by his enemies and his exorcisms of demons were charged to the help of Beelzebub.

SCRIPTURE

Matt. 10 [25]It is enough for the disciple that he be as his master, and the servant as his lord. If they have called the master of the house Beelzebub, how much more shall they call them of his household?

Matt. 12 [24]But when the Pharisees heard it, they said, This fellow doth not cast out devils, but by Beelzebub the prince of the devils.

Mark 3 [22]And the scribes which came down from Jerusalem said, He hath Beelzebub, and by the prince of the devils casteth he out devils.

Luke 11 [15]But some of them said, He
casteth out devils through Beelzebub the
chief of the devils. [18]If Satan also be divided against himself, how shall his kingdom stand? because ye say that I cast out
devils through Beelzebub. [19]And if I by
Beelzebub cast out devils, by whom do
your sons cast them out? therefore shall
they be your judges.

BEER

[bē'er] A Hebrew word, usually found in compound names of places, meaning "well," "spring," or "fountain."

BEERSHEBA

[bē ĕr shē'ba] One of the old places in Palestine which formed the southern limit of the cultivated land of the country. There are two accounts of the origin of the name. According to the first, a well was dug by Abraham, and the name given because there he and Abimelech, king of the Philistines, made a covenant and sealed it with an oath (*Gen. 21:31*). Here the name is ascribed to the Hebrew root, "to swear." This would make the word Beersheba mean "well of the oath." Since seven sacrificial victims were often associated with oaths, there is also support for the idea that the word means "well of seven." A second account concerns an oath made by Isaac, after which his servants informed him of their having found a well, "and he called it Shibah; therefore the name of the city is Beer-sheba unto this day" (*Gen. 26:23-33*). Beersheba was a sacred shrine and appears in the narratives concerning Hagar (*Gen. 21:17*), Jacob (*Gen. 46:2*), and Elijah (*1 Kin. 19:5*). In later years it was denounced by Amos as a seat of idolatrous worship.

BELSHAZZAR

[bel shaz′ar] According to *Dan. 5* he was the Chaldean king when Babylon was taken by Darius the Mede. There is some difficulty in reconciling the Biblical account with Babylonian records, since the Bible states that Belshazzar was the son of Nebuchadnezzar and was reigning in his father's stead. In Babylonian records, however, Belshazzar (Bel-shar-usur) is said to have been the son of Nabonidus (Nabunaid), not Nebuchadnezzar. This fits well with other data, since Nabonidus is known to have left the rule of the kingdom to his son in order to spend long periods of time in Teima; on the other hand, there is no record of Nebuchadnezzar's ever having surrendered his throne. In attempting to solve this difficulty, many scholars feel that the name of the more famous Nebuchadnezzar was merely substituted for the lesser known Nabonidus.

See BABYLON, NEBUCHADNEZZAR

SCRIPTURE

Belshazzar's Great Feast

Dan. 5 [1]Belshazzar the king made a great feast to a thousand of his lords, and drank wine before the thousand. [2]Belshazzar, while he tasted the wine, commanded to bring the golden and silver vessels which his father Nebuchadnezzar had taken out of the temple which was in Jerusalem; that the king and his princes, his wives and his concubines, might drink therein.

The Handwriting on the Wall

Dan. 5 [5]In the same hour came forth fingers of a man's hand, and wrote over against the candlestick upon the plaster of the wall of the king's palace: and the king saw the part of the hand that wrote. [6]Then the king's countenance was changed, and his thoughts troubled him, so that the joints of his loins were loosed, and his knees smote one against another.

[25]And this is the writing that was written, MENE, MENE, TEKEL, UPHARSIN. [26]This is the interpretation of the thing: MENE; God hath numbered thy kingdom, and finished it. [27]TEKEL; Thou art weighed in the balances, and art found wanting. [28]PERES; Thy kingdom is divided, and given to the Medes and Persians.

Belshazzar's Death

Dan. 5 [30]In that night was Belshazzar the king of the Chaldeans slain. [31]And Darius the Median took the kingdom, being about threescore and two years old.

BEN-

[ben] A Hebrew prefix meaning "son" or "son of." It is found as part of many compound names like Benjamin, Ben-hadad, etc. It is also used to express many other relationships besides sonship: a resident of the city of Jabesh might be referred to as a "son of Jabesh," or a man prone to trouble might be called a "son (or child) of trouble." The plural form of this prefix is used in such phrases as "children of Israel."

See BAR

BENEDICTION

[be ne dik′shun] A blessing, or an expression of a blessing; a calling down upon the people of God's goodness. In *Num. 6:24-26* the following form of the priestly benediction is given: "The LORD bless and keep thee: the LORD make his face shine upon thee and be gracious unto thee; the LORD lift up his countenance upon thee and give thee peace." This blessing was pronounced with uplifted hands, and the people responded by saying "Amen."

In *Mark 10:16* and *Luke 24:50* Jesus is spoken of as having blessed little children, and in *Matt. 26:26* He delivered a blessing on the occasion of the institution of the Lord's Supper.

The apostolic benediction is the universal Christian benediction. It is found in *2 Cor. 13:14*: "The grace of our Lord Jesus Christ, and the love of God, and the communion of the Holy Ghost, be with you all. Amen."

BENEFICENCE

[bē nef'i sens] Active goodness, kindness, charity. The Bible contains many statements which make it plain that no man can be a true servant of God who is not beneficent toward his fellowman.

See GIVING, ALMS, LIBERALITY

SCRIPTURE

Deut. 15 7If there be among you a poor
man of one of thy brethren within any of
thy gates in thy land which the LORD thy
God giveth thee, thou shalt not harden
thine heart, nor shut thine hand from thy
poor brother: 8But thou shalt open thine
hand wide unto him, and shalt surely lend
him sufficient for his need, in that which
he wanteth.

Psa. 41 1Blessed is he that considereth
the poor: The LORD will deliver him in
time of trouble.

Prov. 22 9He that hath a bountiful eye
shall be blessed; for he giveth of his bread
to the poor.

Prov. 25 21If thine enemy be hungry,
give him bread to eat; and if he be thirsty,
give him water to drink: 22For thou shalt
heap coals of fire upon his head, and the
LORD shall reward thee.

Matt. 5 42Give to him that asketh thee,
and from him that would borrow of thee
turn not thou away.

Matt. 25 35For I was an hungred, and ye
gave me meat: I was thirsty, and ye gave
me drink: I was a stranger, and ye took me
in: 36Naked, and ye clothed me: I was
sick, and ye visited me: I was in prison,
and ye came unto me. 37Then shall the
righteous answer him, saying, Lord, when
saw we thee an hungred, and fed thee?
or thirsty, and gave thee drink? 38When
saw we thee a stranger, and took thee in?
or naked, and clothed thee? 39Or when
saw we thee sick, or in prison, and came
unto thee? 40And the King shall answer
and say them, Verily, I say unto you, inasmuch as ye have done it unto one of the
least of these my brethren, ye have done
it unto me.

Luke 3 11He that hath two coats, let him
impart to him that hath none; and he that
hath meat, let him do likewise.

Acts 11 29Then the disciples, every man
according to his ability, determined to
send relief unto the brethren which dwelt
in Judaea: 30Which also they did, and
sent it to the elders by the hands of Barnabas and Saul.

Rom. 15 25But now I go unto Jerusalem
to minister unto the saints. 26For it hath
pleased them of Macedonia and Achaia
to make a certain contribution for the poor
saints which are at Jerusalem. 27It hath
pleased them verily; and their debtors
they are. For if the Gentiles have been
made partakers of their spiritual things,
their duty is also to minister unto them in
carnal things.

Gal. 2 10Only they would that we
should remember the poor; the same
which I also was forward to do.

Phil. 4 15Now ye Philippians know also,
that in the beginning of the gospel, when I
departed from Macedonia, no church communicated with me as concerning giving
and receiving, but ye only.

1 Tim. 6 18That they do good, that they

be rich in good works, ready to distribute, willing to communicate;

Jas. 2 [15]If a brother or sister be naked, and destitute of daily food, [16]And one of you say unto them, Depart in peace, be ye warmed and filled; notwithstanding ye give them not those things which are needful to the body; what doth it profit?

BEN-HADAD

[ben-hā′dad] Hadad was the Syrian storm god; the name Ben-Hadad means "son of Hadad" and was applied to several Syrian kings, in accord with the custom of referring to a king as a son of God.

1. Ben-Hadad I, "the son of Hezion, king of Syria, that dwelt at Damascus" (*1 Kin. 15:18*), reigning about 880-842 BC. Ben-Hadad I came to his throne at a time when Syria was a strong power in Western Asia. His reign is closely interwoven with the history of the kingdoms of Judah and Israel. In about 877 BC Asa king of Judah persuaded Ben-Hadad, with an enormous gift of treasure, to break his alliance with Baasha king of Israel and to force that king to withdraw his forces from the borders of Judah. Asa's immediate purpose was achieved, but at the cost of the royal treasures and, probably, some of his political independence.

During the reign of Ahab king of Israel (869-850 BC), Ben-Hadad's forces were engaged east of the Jordan and decisively defeated. Ben-Hadad himself was taken prisoner, but received lenient treatment and, after signing a treaty, was allowed to return to his kingdom. The threat of the rise of Assyria forced these two kings to enter into a coalition which met Shalmaneser III at Qarqar in 853 BC. Shalmaneser's records boast of a victory, but his advance was nevertheless effectively checked for several years. In 842 BC, Ben-Hadad I was treacherously assassinated by Hazael, one of his officers. (*See* HAZAEL) Many commentaries and Bible dictionaries have assigned the events discussed above to two Syrian kings whom they designated as Ben-Hadad I and Ben-Hadad II. The best evidence, however, indicates that this all transpired during the long reign of one king, Ben-Hadad I.

See ASA, BAASHA, AHAB, SHALMANESER, etc.

2. Ben-Hadad II. The son and successor of Hazael, reigning from 806 BC. In 802 BC Damascus was finally crushed by Shalmaneser III and Ben-Hadad II was placed under a ruinous tribute. The prostrate condition of Syria under his reign allowed Jehoash king of Judah to recover territory which had been lost to Hazael and provided an atmosphere in which Israel could rise to prosperity under the capable leadership of Jeroboam II.

See SHALMANESER, JEHOASH, JEROBOAM II

REFERENCE: *2 Kin. 13:3, 24, 25; Amos 1:4.*

BENJAMIN

[ben′ja min] The son of Jacob and Rachel, and the youngest of Jacob's twelve sons. After Joseph was sold into Egypt by his brethren, Benjamin, the remaining son of Jacob's favorite wife, and a full brother of Joseph, became the object of his father's special affection. When the brothers traveled to Egypt during the famine to secure corn, Benjamin remained behind in Canaan. Joseph, desirous of seeing his younger brother, kept Simeon as a hostage until Benjamin should be brought to him. When this was done, against the wishes of Jacob, Joseph arranged to have a silver cup secreted in the grain sack of Benjamin, making it appear as if he had stolen it. In the scene which followed, Judah so earnestly pleaded for his brother's life that Joseph was overcome and revealed himself to his brethren. At the time of the settlement of Jacob's family in Egypt, Benjamin is said to have had ten sons. One of the Israelite tribes later traced its origin to him.

See JOSEPH

REFERENCE: *Gen. 35:18, 24; 42-45; 46:19-21; 49:27.*

BEREA

[be rē′a] A populous city of southwest Macedonia, visited by Paul, Silas and Timothy on the second missionary journey. The Jews of the synagogue at Berea are characterized as having been "more noble than those in Thessalonica, in that they received the word with all readiness of mind, and searched the scriptures daily, whether those things were so" (*Acts 17:11*). A number of both Jews and Greeks believed Paul's preaching; this prompted a contingent of Jews from nearby Thessalonica, from which Paul had been forced to leave, to come to Berea to stir up trouble. To avoid further disturbance, Paul left the city, leaving Silas and Timothy to continue their work a few days longer.

SCRIPTURE

Acts 17 [10]And the brethren immediately sent away Paul and Silas by night
unto Berea: who coming thither went into
the synagogue of the Jews. [11]These were
more noble than those in Thessalonica, in
that they received the word with all readiness of mind, and searched the scriptures daily, whether those things were so.
[12]Therefore many of them believed; also
of honourable women which were Greeks,
and of men, not a few. [13]But when the
Jews of Thessalonica had knowledge that
the word of God was preached of Paul at
Berea, they came thither also, and stirred
up the people. [14]And then immediately
the brethren sent away Paul to go as it
were to the sea: but Silas and Timotheus
abode there still. [15]And they that conducted Paul brought him unto Athens:
and receiving a commandment unto Silas
and Timotheus for to come to him with all
speed, they departed.

BETH

[beth, bāth] A Hebrew word meaning house or habitation. It is frequently employed in compound names of places, such as Bethel, meaning "house of God."

BETHANY

[beth'a ni] A village about two miles from Jerusalem, on the road to Jericho, at the Mount of Olives. It was the home of Simon the leper, Martha, Mary, and Lazarus. When in Judea, Jesus appears to have preferred Bethany to Jerusalem as a place of residence. This little town was the site of one of Jesus' most famous miracles, the raising of Lazarus (*John 11*). It was there, at the house of Simon, that he allowed the woman to anoint him with the expensive ointment (*Matt. 26:1-13; Mark 14:3-9; John 12:1-18*). The Ascension itself is said to have taken place "over against Bethany" (*Luke 24:50-51*).

BETHEL

[beth'el] A well-known city and holy place of central Palestine, west of Ai, and at the top of the ascent from the Jordan valley. The Bible asserts that this city was originally called Luz and gives two accounts of the changing of its name to Bethel. According to the first, the name was bestowed on the spot where Jacob received the vision of the heavenly ladder while on his way to Haran to seek a wife. In the morning after the dream, he set up the stone which had served as his pillow, consecrated it by pouring oil on it, and called the place Bethel, or "house of God" (*Gen. 28:10-22*). According to the other account, however, Bethel received its name on the occasion of a blessing bestowed by God upon Jacob after his return from Padan-aram, at which time also, according to the narrative, the patriarch received the name Israel. Probably, the name Bethel was applied only to the sacred spot, but eventually became associated with the adjoining town. When Israel came from Egypt to Canaan, Bethel was a royal city of the Canaanites. Although the book of *Joshua* does not include an account of the capture of Bethel, *Judg. 1:22ff* records that it was taken in the first wave of conquest. This fits in well with archaeological information which indicates that Bethel suffered a severe conflagration in the thirteenth century.

The ark was brought from Gilgal to Bethel and hither the people came to ask the counsel of God (*Judg. 20:18, 26, 31; 21:2*). During the judgeship of Samuel, Bethel was a regular place on his circuit (*1 Sam. 7:16*). Bethel's greatest significance came when it was made the religious center of the Northern Kingdom during the reign of Jeroboam. At that time a shrine was built and one of the golden bulls which Jeroboam had made was placed within it. A priesthood was appointed and Bethel became the royal sanctuary of Israel. By the era of Amos and Hosea, the rites at Bethel had become grossly immoral and licentious and received the unsparing condemnation of these prophets (*Amos 3:14; 4:4; 5:11; 9:1; Hos. 4:15; 5:8; 10:5, 8, 13*). After the fall of Israel at the hands of Assyria, Bethel still remained an abode of priests (*2 Kin. 17:28*) and receives some brief notices in the remaining historical sections of the Old Testament.

BETHESDA

[bê thez′da] A pool in Bethesda about which nothing certain is known apart from the following statement in *John 5:2-4:* "Now there is at Jerusalem by the sheep market a pool, which is called in the Hebrew tongue Bethesda, having five porches. In these lay a great multitude of impotent folk, of blind, halt, withered, waiting for the moving of the water. For an angel went down at a certain season into the pool, and troubled the water: whosoever then first after the troubling of the water stepped in was made whole of whatsoever disease he had."

BETHLEHEM

[beth′lê hem] One of the oldest towns in Palestine, already in existence at the time of Jacob's return to the area (*Gen. 35:16, 19; 48:7*); also called Ephrath, Ephrathah, and Bethlehem-Judah. It is located about five miles south of Jerusalem. Bethlehem was the home of Ruth and Boaz and of David. It is most famous, of course, as the birthplace of Jesus.

SCRIPTURE

Ruth and Bethlehem

Ruth 1 19So they two went until they
came to Bethlehem. And it came to pass,
when they were come to Bethlehem, that
all the city was moved about them, and
they said, Is this Naomi?

David and Bethlehem

1 Sam. 16 1And the LORD said unto
Samuel, How long wilt thou mourn for
Saul, seeing I have rejected him from
reigning over Israel? fill thy horn with oil,
and go, I will send thee to Jesse the Bethlehemite: for I have provided me a king
among his sons. 4And Samuel did that
which the LORD spake, and came to Bethlehem. And the elders of the town trembled at his coming, and said, Comest thou
peaceably?

2 Sam. 23 15And David longed, and
said, Oh that one would give me drink
of the water of the well of Beth-lehem,
which is by the gate!

Jesus' Birth at Bethlehem

Matt. 2 1Now when Jesus was born in
Bethlehem of Judea in the days of Herod
the king, behold, there came wise men
from the east to Jerusalem.

Luke 2 4And Joseph also went up from
Galilee, out of the city of Nazareth, into
Judea, unto the city of David, which is
called Bethlehem, (because he was of the
house and lineage of David.)

John 7 42Hath not the scripture said,
That Christ cometh of the seed of David,
and out of the town of Bethlehem, where
David was?

Jesus' Birth There Foretold

Mic. 5 2But thou, Beth-lehem Ephratah, though thou be little among the thousands of Judah, yet out of thee shall he
come forth unto me that is to be Ruler in
Israel; whose goings forth have been from
of old, from everlasting.

BETHPHAGE

[beth′fā ge, beth′fāj] A village near Jerusalem, mentioned in connection with Bethany. It was apparently located near the Mount of Olives and the road from Jerusalem to Jericho.

See BETHANY, MOUNT OF OLIVES

REFERENCE: *Matt. 21:1; Mark 11:1; Luke 19:29.*

BETHSAIDA

[beth sā′i da] "House of fishing." In the time of Jesus there were apparently two different cities by this name:

1. A city east of the Jordan to which Jesus retired to rest, but was followed by a multitude whom he fed with five loaves and two fishes (*Mark 6:30-44; Luke 9:10-17*). It was here also that he healed a blind man (*Mark 8:22-26*).

2. A Galilean city which was the home of Philip, Andrew, Peter, and perhaps James and John (*John 1:44; 12:21*). Based on the fact that the home of Andrew and Peter seems to have been close to the synagogue at Capernaum (*Matt. 8:14; Mark 1:29*), it is conjectured that Bethsaida lay closely by Capernaum. It is quite possible that it was the fishing village attached to the larger city.

BEZALEEL AND AHOLIAB

[bez′a lēl, a ho lī′ab] The two master workmen to whom was given the major responsibility in the construction of the tabernacle and its furnishings. Their names are sometimes written Bezalel and Oholiab.

SCRIPTURE

Ex. 31 [1]And the LORD spake unto Moses, saying, [2]See, I have called by name Bezaleel the son of Ori, the son of Hur, of the tribe of Judah: [3]And I have filled him with the spirit of God, in wisdom, and in understanding, and in knowledge, and in all manner of workmanship, [4]To devise cunning works, to work in gold, and in silver, and in brass, [5]And in cutting of stones, to set them, and in carving of timber, to work in all manner of workmanship. [6]And I, behold, I have given with him Aholiab the son of Ahisamach, of the tribe of Dan: and in the hearts of all that are wise hearted I have put wisdom, that they may make all that I have commanded thee;

REFERENCE: *Ex. 35:30-35; 36:1-2.*

BIRTHRIGHT

[bûrth′rīt] The right which normally belonged to the firstborn son. Among the ancient Hebrews this seems to have consisted of (1) a double portion of the property that was to be divided among the heirs, (2) the succession to the head of the family and the responsibility for the remaining members of the family, and (3) the receipt of the special blessing of the father, usually given shortly before his death. Under certain circumstances these could be given to another member of the family, the most famous example of this being the purchase of Esau's birthright by Jacob. Reuben, the eldest son of Jacob, was deprived of his birthright because of his sin. *Deuteronomy* contains a law which forbids transfer of the birthright from the firstborn to the son of a favored wife.

See REUBEN, ESAU, JACOB, EPHRAIM, MANASSEH, FIRSTBORN

SCRIPTURE

Jacob Obtains Esau's Birthright

Gen. 25 [31]And Jacob said, Sell me this day thy birthright. [32]And Esau said, Behold, I am at the point to die: and what profit shall this birthright do to me? [33]And Jacob said, Swear to me this day; and he sware unto him: and he sold his birthright unto Jacob. [34]Then Jacob gave Esau bread and pottage of lentiles; and he did eat and drink, and rose up, and went his way: thus Esau despised his birthright.

Jacob Fraudulently Obtains the Paternal Blessing

Gen. 27 [18]And he came unto his father, and said, My father; and he said, Here am I; who art thou, my son? [19]And Jacob said unto his father, I am Esau thy firstborn; I have done according as thou badest me: arise, I pray thee, sit and eat of my venison, that thy soul may bless me. [20]And Isaac said unto his son, How is it that thou hast found it so quickly, my son? And he said, Because the LORD thy God brought it to me. [21]And Isaac said unto Jacob, Come near, I pray thee, that I may feel thee, my son, whether thou be my very son

Esau or not. [22]And Jacob went near unto Isaac his father; and he felt him, and said, The voice is Jacob's voice, but the hands are the hands of Esau. [23]And he discerned him not, because his hands were hairy, as his brother Esau's hands: so he blessed him.

Reuben Deprived of His Birthright

Gen. 49 [3]Reuben, thou art my firstborn, my might, and the beginning of my strength, the excellency of dignity, and the excellency of power: [4]Unstable as water, thou shalt not excel; because thou wentest up to thy father's bed; then defiledst thou it: he went up to my couch.

Special Law Concerning the Birthright

Deut. 21 [15]If a man have two wives, one beloved, and another hated, and they have borne him children, both the beloved and the hated; and if the firstborn son be hers that was hated; [16]Then it shall be, when he maketh his sons to inherit that which he hath, that he may not make the son of the beloved firstborn before the son of the hated, which is indeed the firstborn. [17]But he shall acknowledge the son of the hated for the firstborn, by giving him a double portion of all that he hath: for he is the beginning of his strength; the right of the firstborn is his.

BLASPHEMY

[blas'fê mi] Indignity offered to God in words, writing, signs, or acts; also, an act of claiming the attributes or prerogatives of deity; any act or word detracting from the honor of God. Among the Jews the sin of blasphemy was punishable by death; the claims of Jesus to be the son of God were regarded as blasphemy and, therefore, worthy of death. The scriptures at various places speak of the magnitude of the act, and blasphemy against the Holy Spirit is mentioned as a sin forever unpardonable. The specific nature of this phase of blasphemy has been the subject of considerable dispute, the two most prominent views being (1) that it is attributing the miracles of Jesus to Satan, and (2) that it is constant and unalterable opposition to the benign workings of the Holy Spirit.

SCRIPTURE

General

Lev. 24 [16]And he that blasphemeth the name of the LORD, he shall surely be put to death, and all the congregation shall certainly stone him: as well the stranger, as he that is born in the land, when he blasphemeth the name of the LORD, shall be put to death.

Psa. 74 [18]Remember this, that the enemy hath reproached, O LORD, and that the foolish people have blasphemed thy name.

Isa. 65 [7]Your iniquities, and the iniquities of your fathers together, saith the LORD, which have burned incense upon the mountains, and blasphemed me upon the hills: therefore will I measure their former work into their bosom.

Ezek. 35 [12]And thou shalt know that I am the LORD, and that I have heard all thy blasphemies which thou hast spoken against the mountains of Israel, saying, they are laid desolate, they are given us to consume. [13]Thus with your mouth ye have boasted against me: I have heard them.

Matt. 15 [19]For out of the heart proceed evil thoughts, murders, adulteries, fornications, thefts, false witness, blasphemies.

Col. 3 [8]But now you also put off all these, anger, wrath, malice, blasphemy, filthy communication out of your mouth.

1 Tim. 1 [13]Who was before a blasphemer, and a persecutor, and injurious: but I obtained mercy, because I did it ignorantly in unbelief.

Jas. 2 [7]Do not they blaspheme that worthy name by the which ye are called?

False Accusations of Blasphemy

1 Kin. 21 [13]And there came in two men, children of Belial, and sat before him: and the men of Belial witnessed against him, even against Naboth, in the presence of the people, saying, Naboth did blaspheme God and the king. Then they carried him forth out of the city, and stoned him with stones, that he died.

Matt. 9 [2]And behold, they brought to him a man sick of the palsy, lying on a bed: and Jesus, seeing their faith, said unto the sick of the palsy, Son, be of good cheer; thy sins be forgiven thee. [3]And behold, certain of the scribes said within themselves, This man blasphemeth.

Matt. 26 [65]Then the high priest rent his clothes, saying, He hath spoken blasphemy; what further need have we of witnesses? behold, now ye have heard his blasphemy.

John 10 [33]The Jews answered him, saying, For a good work we stone thee not; but for blasphemy, and because that thou, being a man, makest thyself God. [34]Jesus answered them, Is it not written in your law, I said, Ye are gods? [35]If he called them gods, unto whom the word of God came, and the scripture cannot be broken; [36]Say ye of him whom the Father hath sanctified, and sent into the world, Thou blasphemest; because I said, I am the Son of God?

Acts 6 [8]And Stephen, full of faith and power, did great wonders and miracles among the people. [9]Then there arose certain of the synagogue, which is called the synagogue of the Libertines, and Cyrenians, and Alexandrians, and of them of Cilicia, and of Asia, disputing with Stephen. [10]And they were not able to resist the wisdom and the spirit by which he spake. [11]Then they suborned men, which said, We have heard him speak blasphemous words against Moses, and against God.

Blasphemy against the Holy Ghost

Matt. 12 [31]Wherefore I say unto you, All manner of sin and blasphemy shall be forgiven unto men: but the blasphemy against the Holy Ghost shall not be forgiven unto men.

Mark 3 [28]Verily I say unto you, All sins shall be forgiven unto the sons of men, and blasphemies wherewith soever they shall blaspheme: [29]But he that shall blaspheme against the Holy Ghost hath never forgiveness, but is in danger of eternal damnation.

Luke 12 [10]And whosoever shall speak a word against the Son of man, it shall be forgiven him: but unto him that blasphemeth against the Holy Ghost, it shall not be forgiven.

BLESS, BLESSED

[bles, bles'ed] 1. *Bless.* A word used in the Bible a great number of times and with many different meanings. The more important of them are: (1) to set apart and hallow, or make holy; (2) to confer happiness upon; (3) to bestow good or grant favor to; (4) to express a wish for happiness for some other person; (5) to invoke special attributes upon; (6) to praise or glorify.

2. *Blessed.* Hallowed, consecrated, or holy; highly favored; blissful or joyful; enjoying spiritual happiness.

See BEATITUDES, CURSE

SCRIPTURE

General

Gen. 12 [3]And I will bless them that bless thee, and curse him that curseth thee: and in thee shall all families of the earth be blessed.

Isa. 30 [18]And therefore will the LORD wait, that he may be gracious unto you, and therefore will he be exalted, that he may have mercy upon you: for the LORD is a God of judgment: blessed are all they that wait for him.

Matt. 25 [34]Then shall the King say unto them on his right hand, Come, ye blessed of my Father, inherit the kingdom prepared for you from the foundation of the world.

Luke 14 [14]And thou shalt be blessed: for they cannot recompense thee: for thou shalt be recompensed at the resurrection
of the just. [15]And when one of them that sat at meat with him, heard these things, he said unto him, Blessed is he that shall eat bread in the kingdom of God.

Rom. 4 [6]Even as David also describeth the blessedness of the man unto whom God imputeth righteousness without
works, [7]Saying, Blessed are they whose iniquities are forgiven, and whose sins are
covered. [8]Blessed is the man to whom the
Lord will not impute sin. [9]Cometh this blessedness then upon the circumcision only, or upon the uncircumcision also? For we say that faith was reckoned to Abraham for righteousness.

Those Chosen, Called, or Chastened by God

Psa. 65 [4]Blessed is the man whom thou choosest, and causest to approach unto thee, that he may dwell in thy courts: we shall be satisfied with the goodness of thy house, even of thy holy temple.

Eph. 1 [3]Blessed be the God and Father of our Lord Jesus Christ, who hath blessed us with all spiritual blessings in heavenly
places in Christ: [4]According as he hath chosen us in him, before the foundation of the world, that we should be holy and without blame before him in love.

Isa. 51 [2]Look unto Abraham your father, and unto Sarah that bare you: for I called him alone, and blessed him, and increased him.

Rev. 19 [9]And he saith unto me, Write, Blessed are they which are called unto the marriage-supper of the Lamb. And he saith unto me, These are the true sayings of God.

Psa. 94 [12]Blessed is the man whom thou chastenest, O LORD, and teachest him out of thy law.

Those Who Trust, Fear, and Delight in the Lord

Psa. 2 [12]Kiss the Son, lest he be angry, and ye perish from the way, when his wrath is kindled but a little. Blessed are all they that put their trust in him.

Psa. 34 [8]O taste and see that the LORD is good: blessed is the man that trusteth in him.

Psa. 40 [4]Blessed is that man that maketh the LORD his trust, and respecteth not the proud, nor such as turn aside to lies.

Psa. 84 [12]O LORD of hosts, blessed is the man that trusteth in thee.

Jer. 17 [7]Blessed is the man that trusteth in the LORD, and whose hope the LORD is.

Psa. 128 [4]Behold, that thus shall the man be blessed that feareth the LORD.

Psa. 112 [1]Praise ye the LORD. Blessed is the man that feareth the LORD, that delighteth greatly in his commandments.

Those Who Hear and Obey

Psa. 119 [2]Blessed are they that keep his testimonies, and that seek him with the whole heart.

Matt. 13 [16]But blessed are your eyes, for they see: and your ears, for they hear.

Luke 11 [28]But he said, Yea, rather blessed are they that hear the word of God, and keep it.

Jas. 1 [25]But whoso looketh into the perfect law of liberty, and continueth therein, he being not a forgetful hearer, but a doer of the work, this man shall be blessed in his deed.

Rev. 1 [3]Blessed is he that readeth, and they that hear the words of this prophecy, and keep those things which are written therein: for the time is at hand.

Rev. 22 [14]Blessed are they that do his commandments, that they may have right to the tree of life, and may enter in through the gates into the city.

Those Who Know, Believe in, and Suffer for Christ

Matt. 16 [17]And Jesus answered and said unto him, Blessed art thou, Simon Bar-jona: for flesh and blood hath not revealed it unto thee, but my Father which is in heaven.

Luke 1 [45]And blessed is she that believed: for there shall be a performance of those things which were told her from the Lord.

Gal. 3 [9]So then they which be of faith are blessed with faithful Abraham.

Luke 6 [22]Blessed are ye when men shall hate you, and when they shall separate you from their company, and shall reproach you, and cast out your name as evil, for the Son of man's sake.

Matt. 5 [10]Blessed are they which are persecuted for righteousness' sake: for theirs is the kingdom of heaven. [11]Blessed are ye, when men shall revile you, and persecute you, and shall say all manner of evil against you falsely, for my sake.

Other Special Blessings

Psa. 1 [1]Blessed is the man that walketh not in the counsel of the ungodly, nor standeth in the way of sinners, nor sitteth in the seat of the scornful.

Psa. 84 [4]Blessed are they that dwell in thy house: they will be still praising thee. Selah. [5]Blessed is the man whose strength is in thee; in whose heart are the ways of them.

Jas. 1 [12]Blessed is the man that endureth temptation: for when he is tried, he shall receive the crown of life, which the Lord hath promised to them that love him.

Psa. 119 [1]Blessed are the undefiled in the way, who walk in the law of the LORD.

Psa. 106 [3]Blessed are they that keep judgment, and he that doeth righteousness at all times.

Prov. 10 [6]Blessings are upon the head of the just: but violence covereth the mouth of the wicked.

Prov. 20 [7]The just man walketh in his integrity: his children are blessed after him.

Psa. 5 [12]For thou, LORD, wilt bless the righteous; with favour wilt thou compass him as with a shield.

Psa. 112 [2]His seed shall be mighty upon earth: the generation of the upright shall be blessed.

Prov. 28 [20]A faithful man shall abound with blessings: but he that maketh haste to be rich shall not be innocent.

Deut. 15 [10]Thou shalt surely give him, and thine heart shall not be grieved when thou givest unto him: because that for this thing the LORD thy God shall bless thee in all thy works, and in all that thou puttest thine hand unto.

Psa. 41 [1]Blessed is he that considereth the poor: the LORD will deliver him in time of trouble. [2]The LORD will preserve him, and keep him alive; and he shall be blessed upon the earth: and thou wilt not deliver him unto the will of his enemies.

Prov. 22 [9]He that hath a bountiful eye shall be blessed; for he giveth of his bread to the poor.

Matt. 5 [6]Blessed are they which do

hunger and thirst after righteousness: for they shall be filled.

Luke 6 [20]And he lifted up his eyes on his disciples, and said, Blessed be ye poor; for yours is the kingdom of God.

[21]Blessed are ye that hunger now: for ye shall be filled. Blessed are ye that weep now: for ye shall laugh.

Psa. 32 [1]Blessed is he whose transgression is forgiven, whose sin is covered. [2]Blessed is the man unto whom the LORD imputeth not iniquity, and in whose spirit there is no guile.

Rev. 14 [13]And I heard a voice from heaven, saying unto me, Write, Blessed are the dead which die in the Lord from henceforth: Yea, saith the Spirit, that they may rest from their labours; and their works do follow them.

See BEATITUDES

BLINDNESS

[blīnd′ness] The state of being without sight. Blindness was and is a common malady in Palestine and neighboring lands. The most common form of blindness among these people is called ophthalmia, it is a highly infectious disease, transmitted chiefly by flies and aggravated by sand, sun-glare, and filth. The Law barred a blind man from the priesthood, yet it taught that persons suffering from loss of sight should be treated with great kindness. Blindness is used in a metaphorical sense to indicate lack of discernment and intelligent spiritual vision.

SCRIPTURE

Physical Blindness

BLIND DISQUALIFIED FROM PRIESTHOOD

Lev. 21 [18]For whatsoever man he be that hath a blemish, he shall not approach: a blind man, or a lame, or he that hath a flat nose, or any thing superfluous.

Care for the Blind

Lev. 19 [14]Thou shalt not curse the deaf, nor put a stumbling-block before the blind, but shalt fear thy God: I am the LORD.

Deut. 28 [18]Cursed be he that maketh the blind to wander out of the way: and all the people shall say, Amen.

Blindness Inflicted

UPON SYRIANS

2 Kin. 6 [18]And when they came down to him, Elisha prayed unto the LORD, and said, Smite this people, I pray thee, with blindness. And he smote them with blindness, according to the word of Elisha.

UPON PAUL

Acts 9 [8]And Saul arose from the earth; and when his eyes were opened, he saw no man: but they led him by the hand, and brought him into Damascus. [9]And he was three days without sight, and neither did eat nor drink.

UPON ELYMAS

Acts 13 [11]And now behold, the hand of the Lord is upon thee, and thou shalt be blind, not seeing the sun for a season. And immediately there fell on him a mist and a darkness, and he went about, seeking some to lead him by the hand.

Healed by Christ

Matt. 9 [27]And when Jesus departed thence, two blind men followed him, crying, and saying, Thou son of David, have mercy on us. [28]And when he was come into the house, the blind men came to him: and Jesus saith unto them, Believe ye that I am able to do this? They said unto him,

Yea, Lord. [29]Then touched he their eyes, saying, According to your faith, be it unto you.

Matt. 12 [22]Then was brought unto him one possessed with a devil, blind, and dumb: and he healed him, insomuch that the blind and dumb both spake and saw.

Matt. 20 [34]So Jesus had compassion on them, and touched their eyes: and immediately their eyes received sight, and they followed him.

Mark 8 [22]And he cometh to Bethsaida; and they bring a blind man unto him, and besought him to touch him. [23]And he took the blind man by the hand, and led him out of the town; and when he had spit on his eyes, and put his hands upon him, he asked him if he saw aught.

Mark 10 [46]And they came to Jericho: and as he went out of Jericho with his disciples, and a great number of people, blind Bartimeus, the son of Timeus, sat by the highway side begging. [52]And Jesus said unto him, Go thy way; thy faith hath made thee whole. And immediately he received his sight, and followed Jesus in the way.

Luke 7 [21]And in that same hour he cured many of their infirmities, and plagues, and of evil spirits; and unto many that were blind he gave sight.

John 9 [11]He answered and said, A man that is called Jesus, made clay, and anointed mine eyes, and said unto me, Go to the pool of Siloam, and wash: and I went and washed, and I received sight.

Spiritual Blindness

Psa. 82 [5]They know not, neither will they understand: they walk on in darkness: all the foundations of the earth are out of course.

Isa. 56 [10]His watchmen are blind: they are all ignorant, they are all dumb dogs, they cannot bark; sleeping, lying down, loving to slumber.

Isa. 59 [9]Therefore is judgment far from us, neither doth justice overtake us: we wait for light, but behold obscurity; for brightness, but we walk in darkness. [10]We grope for the wall like the blind, and we grope as if we had no eyes: we stumble at noon-day.

Matt. 15 [14]Let them alone: they be blind leaders of the blind. And if the blind lead the blind, both shall fall into the ditch.

Matt. 23 [19]Ye fools and blind: for whether is greater, the gift, or the altar that sanctifieth the gift? [24]Ye blind guides, which strain at a gnat, and swallow a camel. [26]Thou blind Pharisee, cleanse first that which is within the cup and platter, but within they are full of extortion and excess.

John 9 [39]And Jesus said, For judgment I am come into this world, that they which see not might see; and that they which see might be made blind.

BLOOD

[blud] Literally, the fluid which circulates in the heart, arteries, and veins of animals, carrying nourishment and oxygen to all parts of the body, and bringing away waste products. In the Bible, it has the additional meaning of the end of life, or death (usually violent death). One who murders is said to have blood on his hands or head (*2 Sam. 1:16; 1 Kin. 2:36; Josh. 2:19*, etc.) and murder is referred to as a sin against innocent blood (*1 Sam. 19:5*). Judas confessed that he had betrayed innocent blood (*Matt. 27:4*) and Pilate declared his innocence of the blood of Jesus, thereby repudiating responsibility for Jesus' death. This meaning was clearly understood by the mob to whom he spoke, as evidenced by their cry, "his blood be on us and on our children" (*Matt. 27:24-25*).

The phrase most commonly used in the New

Testament to refer to the atoning death of Jesus is "the blood of Christ." Just as the blood sprinkled on the doorpost was a sign that the participants in the Passover feast were being sheltered from death by the death of the sacrificial lamb (*Ex. 12:1-20*), the shed blood of Christ was the visible sign of a life given in sacrifice that men might be released from death and reconciled to God. (*See* ATONEMENT)

The prohibition against the drinking of blood (*Lev. 17:3-7, 10-14*, cf. *Acts 15:29*) was given to remind men that God alone has control over the source of life and that man has no right to appropriate it.

SCRIPTURE

Human Bloodshedding Forbidden

Gen. 9 [5]And surely your blood of your lives will I require: at the hand of every beast will I require it, and at the hand of man; at the hand of every man's brother will I require the life of man. [6]Whoso sheddeth man's blood, by man shall his blood be shed: for in the image of God made he man.

Prov. 6 [16]These six things doth the LORD hate; yea, seven are an abomination unto him: [17]A proud look, a lying tongue, and hands that shed innocent blood.

Matt. 27 [6]And the chief Priests took the silver pieces, and said, It is not lawful for to put them into the treasury, because it is the price of blood.

Sacrifice of Blood

Ex. 29 [12]And thou shalt take of the blood of the bullock, and put it upon the horns of the altar with thy finger, and pour all the blood beside the bottom of the altar.

Lev. 17 [11]For the life of the flesh is in the blood; and I have given it to you upon the altar, to make an atonement for your souls: for it is the blood that maketh an atonement for the soul.

Heb. 9 [13]For if the blood of bulls and of goats, and the ashes of an heifer sprinkling the unclean, sanctifieth to the purifying of the flesh: [14]How much more shall the blood of Christ, who through the eternal Spirit offered himself without spot to God, purge your conscience from dead works to serve the living God?

Christ's Sacrifice of Blood

1 Cor. 10 [16]The cup of blessing which we bless, is it not the communion of the blood of Christ? The bread which we break, is it not the communion of the body of Christ?

Eph. 2 [13]But now in Christ Jesus, ye who sometimes were far off are made nigh by the blood of Christ.

Heb. 9 [13]For if the blood of bulls and of goats, and the ashes of a heifer sprinkling the unclean, sanctifieth to the purifying of the flesh; [14]How much more shall the blood of Christ, who through the eternal Spirit offered himself without spot to God, purge your conscience from dead works to serve the living God?

1 Pet. 1 [19]But with the precious blood of Christ, as of a Lamb without blemish and without spot.

1 John 1 [7]But if we walk in the light, as he is in the light, we have fellowship one with another, and the blood of Jesus Christ his Son cleanseth us from all sin.

Salvation by Blood

Heb. 9 [12]Neither by the blood of goats and calves, but by his own blood he entered in once into the Holy place, having obtained eternal redemption for us.

Heb. 13 [12]Wherefore Jesus also, that he might sanctify the people with his own blood, suffered without the gate.

Heb. 9 [22]And almost all things are by

the law purged with blood: and without shedding of blood is no remission.

Rev. 1 [5]And from Jesus Christ, who is the faithful witness, and the first begotten of the dead, and the Prince of the kings of the earth: unto him that loved us, and washed us from our sins in his own blood.

Blood and the Lord's Supper

Matt. 26 [28]For this is my blood of the new testament, which is shed for many for the remission of sins.

Mark 14 [24]And he said unto them, This is my blood of the new testament, which is shed for many.

Luke 22 [20]Likewise also the cup after supper, saying, This cup is the new testament in my blood, which is shed for you.

1 Cor. 11 [25]After the same manner also he took the cup when he had supped, saying, This cup is the new testament in my blood: this do ye, as oft as ye drink it, in remembrance of me.

Redemption by Blood

Eph. 1 [7]In whom we have redemption through his blood, the forgiveness of sins, according to the riches of his grace.

Col. 1 [20]And, having made peace through the blood of his cross, by him to reconcile all things unto himself; by him, I say, whether they be things in earth, or things in heaven.

Heb. 12 [24]And to Jesus the mediator of the new covenant, and to the blood of sprinkling, that speaketh better things than that of Abel.

1 John 1 [7]But if we walk in the light, as he is in the light, we have fellowship one with another, and the blood of Jesus Christ his Son cleanseth us from all sin.

Rev. 5 [9]And they sung a new song, saying, Thou art worthy to take the book, and to open the seals thereof: for thou wast slain, and hast redeemed us to God by thy blood out of every kindred, and tongue, and people, and nation.

Redemption by Blood Typified

Ex. 12 [13]And the blood shall be to you for a token upon the houses where ye are: and when I see the blood, I will pass over you, and the plague shall not be upon you to destroy you, when I smite the land of Egypt.

Blood as Food Forbidden

Gen. 9 [4]But flesh with the life thereof, which is the blood thereof, shall ye not eat.

Lev. 3 [17]It shall be a perpetual statute for your generations throughout all your dwellings, that ye eat neither fat nor blood.

Deut. 12 [16]Only ye shall not eat the blood; ye shall pour it upon the earth as water.

BOASTING

[bōst′ing] To vaunt oneself or one's possessions; to brag; saying or telling things calculated to give others a high opinion of one's self. The Bible, in a number of places, teaches that boasting is to be shunned.

SCRIPTURE

Psa. 49 [6]They that trust in their wealth, and boast themselves in the multitude of their riches; [7]None of them can by any means redeem his brother, nor give to God a ransom for him.

Psa. 52 [1]Why boastest thou thyself in mischief, O mighty man? the goodness of God endureth continually.

Psa. 94 [4]How long shall they utter and speak hard things? and all the workers of iniquity boast themselves?

Prov. 20 [14]It is naught, it is naught, saith

the buyer: but when he is gone his way, then he boasteth.

Prov. 27 [1]Boast not thyself of to-morrow; for thou knowest not what a day may bring forth.

Isa. 10 [15]Shall the axe boast itself against him that heweth therewith? or shall the saw magnify itself against him that shaketh it? as if the rod should shake itself against them that lift it up, or as if the staff should lift up itself, as if it were no wood.

Jer. 9 [23]Thus saith the LORD, Let not the wise man glory in his wisdom, neither let the mighty man glory in his might, let not the rich man glory in his riches: [24]But let him that glorieth glory in this, that he understandeth and knoweth me, that I am the LORD which exercise loving-kindness, judgment, and righteousness, in the earth: for in these things I delight, saith the LORD.

Rom. 3 [27]Where is boasting then? It is excluded by what law? of works? Nay; but by the law of faith.

Jas. 3 [5]Even so the tongue is a little member, and boasteth great things. Behold, how great a matter a little fire kindleth!

Jas. 4 [10]But now ye rejoice in your boastings: all such rejoicing is evil.

Eph. 2 [8]For by grace are ye saved, through faith; and that not of yourselves: it is the gift of God: [9]Not of works, lest any man should boast.

BODY

[bod'i] This term is used in the Bible to refer to several different realities: (1) the natural body of man, created by God and adapted to life on earth. (2) The spiritual body which men will receive at the resurrection. This does not mean that the fleshly atoms of the deceased will be reassembled, but that a body of another order than flesh and blood, adapted for life in the eternal realm, will be bestowed on each individual. This is in direct contrast to the Greek idea of immortality as absorption into the infinite. (3) The body of Christ is a figurative term referring to the whole community of Christians. Men are baptized into this body and take their appropriate places, each fulfilling a function without which the body cannot attain full life.

SCRIPTURE

Human Body

TO BE KEPT PURE AND HOLY:

Rom. 12 [1]I beseech you therefore, brethren, by the mercies of God, that ye present your bodies a living sacrifice, holy, acceptable unto God, which is your reasonable service.

1 *Thess.* 4 [4]That every one of you should know how to possess his vessel in sanctification and honour.

Temple of Holy Spirit

1 *Cor.* 3 [16]Know ye not that ye are the temple of God, and that the Spirit of God dwelleth in you? [17]If any man defile the temple of God, him shall God destroy: for the temple of God is holy, which temple ye are.

1 *Cor.* 6 [19]What! know ye not that your body is the temple of the Holy Ghost which is in you, which ye have of God, and ye are not your own? [20]For ye are bought with a price; therefore glorify God in your body, and in your spirit, which are God's.

2 *Cor.* 6 [16]And what agreement hath the temple of God with idols? for ye are the temple of the living God; as God hath said, I will dwell in them, and walk in them; and I will be their God, and they shall be my people.

The Spiritual Body of the Resurrection

1 *Cor.* 15 [12]Now if Christ be preached

that he rose from the dead, how say some among you that there is no resurrection of the dead? [13]But if there be no resurrection of the dead, then is Christ not risen: [35]But some man will say, How are the dead raised up? and with what body do they come? [36]Thou fool, that which thou sowest is not quickened, except it die: [37]And that which thou sowest, thou sowest not that body that shall be, but bare grain, it may chance of wheat, or of some other grain: [38]But God giveth it a body as it hath pleased him, and to every seed his own body. [42]So also is the resurrection of the dead. It is sown in corruption; it is raised in incorruption: [43]It is sown in dishonour; it is raised in glory; it is sown in weakness; it is raised in power: [44]It is sown a natural body; it is raised a spiritual body. There is a natural body, and there is a spiritual body. [47]The first man is of the earth, earthy: the second man is the Lord from heaven. [48]As is the earthy, such are they also that are earthy: and as is the heavenly, such are they also that are heavenly. [49]And as we have borne the image of the earthy, we shall also bear the image of the heavenly. [50]Now this I say, brethren, that flesh and blood cannot inherit the kingdom of God; neither doth corruption inherit incorruption.

Phil. 3 [21]Who shall change our vile body, that it may be fashioned like unto his glorious body, according to the working whereby he is able even to subdue all things unto himself.

The Body of Christ

Rom. 12 [4]For as we have many members in one body, and all members have not the same office: [5]So we, being many, are one body in Christ, and every one members one of another.

1 Cor. 10 [16]The cup of blessing which we bless, is it not the communion of the blood of Christ? The bread which we break, is it not the communion of the body of Christ? [17]For we being many are one bread, and one body: for we are all partakers of that one bread.

1 Cor. 12 [12]For as the body is one, and hath many members, and all the members of that one body, being many, are one body: so also is Christ.

Eph. 1 [22]And hath put all things under his feet, and gave him to be the head over all things to the church, [23]Which is his body, the fulness of him that filleth all in all.

Eph. 4 [12]For the perfecting of the saints, for the work of the ministry, for the edifying of the body of Christ.

Eph. 5 [23]For the husband is the head of the wife, even as Christ is the head of the church: and he is the Saviour of the body.

Col. 1 [18]And he is the head of the body, the church: who is the beginning, the firstborn from the dead; that in all things he might have the pre-eminence.

BOLDNESS

[bōld′nes] Confidence, fearlessness, venturesomeness; sometimes, lacking proper modesty or restraint.

See Courage

SCRIPTURE

Boldness through Faith

Prov. 28 [1]The wicked flee when no man pursueth: but the righteous are bold as a lion.

Isa. 50 [7]For the Lord God will help me: therefore shall I not be confounded: therefore have I set my face like a flint, and I know that I shall not be ashamed.

Eph. 3 [11]According to the eternal purpose which he purposed in Christ Jesus our Lord: [12]In whom we have boldness and access with confidence by the faith of him.

1 John 4 [17]Herein is our love made perfect, that we may have boldness in the day of judgment: because as he is, so are we in this world. [18]There is no fear in love; but perfect love casteth out fear: because fear hath torment. He that feareth, is not made perfect in love.

Acts 4 [13]Now when they saw the boldness of Peter and John, and perceived that they were unlearned and ignorant men, they marvelled; and they took knowledge of them, that they had been with Jesus.

BONDAGE

[bon′dåj] The condition of slavery or servitude, a common feature of ancient life. When used in a literal sense in the Bible, the word ordinarily refers to the condition of the Hebrews during the original bondage, or during the later captivity under Babylonia and Persia. It is used in the New Testament in a metaphorical sense to signify the power of sin on a man's life, and to contrast life under the law of Moses with freedom in Christ.

See CAPTIVITY

SCRIPTURE

Israel's Bondage in Egypt

Ex. 1 [13]And the Egyptians made the children of Israel to serve with rigour. [14]And they made their lives bitter with hard bondage, in mortar, and in brick, and in all manner of service in the field: all their service wherein they made them serve was with rigour.

Ex. 3 [7]And the LORD said, I have surely seen the affliction of my people which are in Egypt, and have heard their cry by reason of their taskmasters; for I know their sorrows.

Acts 7 [6]And God spake on this wise, That his seed should sojourn in a strange land; and that they should bring them into bondage, and entreat them evil four hundred years.

Israel's Bondage to Babylon

2 Kin. 25 [11]Now the rest of the people that were left in the city, and the fugitives that fell away to the king of Babylon, with the remnant of the multitude, did Nebuzar-adan the captain of the guard carry away.

Ezra 9 [7]Since the days of our fathers have we been in a great trespass unto this day; and for our iniquities have we, our kings, and our priests, been delivered into the hand of the kings of the lands, to the sword, to captivity, and to a spoil, and to confusion of face, as it is this day.

Spiritual Bondage

John 8 [34]Jesus answered them, Verily, verily, I say unto you, Whosoever committeth sin is the servant of sin.

Acts 8 [23]For I perceive that thou art in the gall of bitterness, and in the bond of iniquity.

Rom. 6 [16]Know ye not, that to whom ye yield yourselves servants to obey, his servants ye are to whom ye obey; whether of sin unto death, or of obedience unto righteousness?

Rom. 7 [23]But I see another law in my members, warring against the law of my mind, and bringing me into captivity to the law of sin which is in my members.

Gal. 2 [4]And that because of false brethren unawares brought in, who came in privily to spy out our liberty which we have in Christ Jesus, that they might bring us into bondage.

Gal. 4 [3]Even so we, when we were children, were in bondage under the elements of the world.

2 Pet. 2 [19]While they promise them liberty, they themselves are the servants of corruption: for of whom a man is overcome, of the same is he brought in bondage.

Deliverance by Christ

Isa. 61 [1]The Spirit of the Lord GOD is upon me; because the LORD hath anointed me to preach good tidings unto the meek; he hath sent me to bind up the brokenhearted, to proclaim liberty to the captives, and the opening of the prison to them that are bound.

Luke 4 [18]The Spirit of the Lord is upon me, because he hath anointed me to preach the gospel to the poor; he hath sent me to heal the broken-hearted, to preach deliverance to the captives, and recovering of sight to the blind, to set at liberty them that are bruised.

BOOK

[bŏŏk] A written or printed narrative or record, or series of them; especially, a literary composition; any record of thought in words. In Biblical times, books were written on stone, clay, vellum, or papyrus. Vellum was simply a fine quality of animal skin prepared for writing on both sides. Papyrus was produced by taking strips of pith from the papyrus reed and gluing them together in a horizontal and vertical pattern to form a mat. This was then pounded or pressed and allowed to dry, producing a suitable surface for writing. The width of these pieces might be anywhere from five inches to a foot, depending on their quality. These pieces of papyrus were then pasted into scrolls, usually about thirty feet long, and occasionally reaching over 100 feet in length. In the second century AD the papyrus "codex" came into being. The codex is that form used in our own books; that is, pages were fastened together to form a volume. These could contain a larger amount of writing than a scroll and therefore facilitated the collection of books into groups, in the manner of the Bible.

God is represented as having a record of all those who are under his special care. To be blotted out of his Book of Life is to be cut off from his favor. In the New Testament, the Book of Life refers to the record of the righteous who are to gain eternal life.

SCRIPTURE

Book of the Law

Deut. 28 [61]Also every sickness, and every plague which is not written in the book of this law, them will the LORD bring upon thee, until thou be destroyed.

2 Kin. 22 [8]And Hilkiah the high priest said unto Shaphan the scribe, I have found the book of the law in the house of the LORD. And Hilkiah gave the book to Shaphan, and he read it.

Gal. 3 [10]For as many as are of the works of the law, are under the curse: for it is written, Cursed is every one that continueth not in all things which are written in the book of the law to do them.

Book of Life

Ex. 32 [33]And the LORD said unto Moses, Whosoever hath sinned against me, him will I blot out of my book.

Psa. 69 [28]Let them be blotted out of the book of the living, and not be written with the righteous.

Phil. 4 [3]And I entreat thee also, true yokefellow, help those women which laboured with me in the gospel, with Clement also, and with other my fellowlabourers, whose names are in the book of life.

Rev. 3 [5]He that overcometh, the same shall be clothed in white raiment, and I will not blot out his name out of the book of life, but I will confess his name before my Father, and before his angels.

Rev. 13 [8]And all that dwell upon the earth, shall worship him, whose names are not written in the book of life of the Lamb slain from the foundation of the world.

Rev. 21 [27]And there shall in no wise enter into it any thing that defileth, neither whatsoever worketh abomination, or maketh a lie; but they which are written in the Lamb's book of life.

Rev. 22 [19]And if any man shall take away from the words of the book of this prophecy, God shall take away his part out of the book of life, and out of the holy city, and from the things which are written in this book.

BORROWING

[bor'ō ing] To receive with the implied or expressed intention of returning the same or giving an equivalent. The Old Testament references to borrowing deal with loans made in time of poverty or extreme distress and are to be differentiated from our common practice of borrowing for commercial purposes. It is for this reason that Israelites were forbidden to take interest from one another.

See Lending

SCRIPTURE

Ex. 22 [14]And if a man borrow ought of his neighbour, and it be hurt, or die, the owner thereof being not with it, he shall surely make it good. [15]But if the owner thereof be with it, he shall not make it good: if it be an hired thing, it came for his hire.

Psa. 37 [21]The wicked borroweth, and payeth not again: but the righteous sheweth mercy, and giveth.

BRAZEN SERPENT

[brā'zen sẽr'pent] An image of polished metal, in the form of one of the fiery serpents which were sent to chastise the murmuring Israelites in the wilderness, and whose bite caused violent heat, thirst, and inflammation. By divine command "Moses made a serpent of brass," or copper, and "put it upon a pole; and it came to pass, that if a serpent had bitten any man, when he beheld the serpent of brass, he lived" (*Num. 21:6-9*). *2 Kin. 18:4* tells us that this serpent, preserved as a monument of the divine mercy, eventually became an instrument of idolatry.

BREAD

[bred] The Hebrew and Greek words which are translated "bread" in the Bible may refer not only to bread specifically, but to food in general. They are often used to refer to the basic necessities of life. Although bread is spoken of as a gift of God, man is expected to do his part in earning it. Bread is used in a figurative sense in such phrases as "bread of affliction" (*1 Kin. 22:27*) and "bread of tears" (*Psa. 80:5*). It is also used of Jesus, when he is spoken of as "the true bread out of heaven," implying that just as Israel ate the manna in the wilderness to avoid starvation, it is necessary to accept Jesus to make possible full spiritual life. The phrase "to eat bread" is significant; to eat bread with someone established a mutual obligation (*Psa. 41:9*); "to eat bread in the kingdom of God" (*Luke 14:15*) means to enjoy the privileges of the kingdom. Bread played an important role in Hebrew worship, various kinds being offered with the sacrifices. Ordinarily, the bread offered was unleavened, leaven being regarded as a form of corruption. Both the tabernacle and the temple contained the table of shewbread. (*See* Shewbread) In Christian worship, the use of bread is found in the Lord's Supper, or Eucharist.

See Manna

SCRIPTURE

The Staff of Life

Ezek. 4 [16]Moreover he said unto me, Son of man, behold, I will break the staff of bread in Jerusalem: and they shall eat bread by weight, and with care; and they shall drink water by measure, and with astonishment.

See Ezek. 5:16, 14:13

Obligation to Earn One's Own Bread

Gen. 3 [19]In the sweat of thy face shalt thou eat bread, till thou return unto the ground; for out of it wast thou taken: for dust thou art, and unto dust shalt thou return.

2 Thess. 3 [8]Neither did we eat any man's bread for nought; but wrought with labor and travail night and day, that we might not be chargeable to any of you: [12]Now them that are such we command and exhort by our Lord Jesus Christ, that with quietness they work, and eat their own bread.

Nevertheless, Bread a Gift of God

Ruth 1 [6]Then she arose with her daughters-in-law, that she might return from the country of Moab: for she had heard in the country of Moab how that the LORD had visited his people in giving them bread.

Psa. 104 [15]And wine that maketh glad the heart of man, and oil to make his face to shine, and bread which strengtheneth man's heart.

Matt. 6 [11]Give us this day our daily bread.

Bread Not Everything

Deut. 8 [3]And he humbled thee, and suffered thee to hunger, and fed thee with manna, which thou knewest not, neither did thy fathers know; that he might make thee know that man doth not live by bread only, but by every word that proceedeth out of the mouth of the LORD doth man live.

Matt. 4 [3]And when the tempter came to him, he said, If thou be the Son of God, command that these stones be made bread. [4]But he answered and said, It is written, Man shall not live by bread alone, but by every word that proceedeth out of the mouth of God.

Jesus, the True Bread

John 6 [31]Our fathers did eat manna in the desert; as it is written, He gave them bread from heaven to eat. [32]Then Jesus said unto them, Verily, verily, I say unto you, Moses gave you not that bread from heaven; but my Father giveth you the true bread from heaven. [33]For the bread of God is he which cometh down from heaven, and giveth life unto the world. [34]Then said they unto him, Lord, evermore give us this bread. [35]And Jesus said unto them, I am the bread of life: he that cometh to me shall never hunger; and he that believeth on me shall never thirst.

Bread in the Lord's Supper

Matt. 26 [26]And as they were eating, Jesus took bread, and blessed it, and brake it, and gave it to the disciples, and said, Take, eat; this is my body.

1 Cor. 10 [16]And the cup of blessing which we bless, is it not the communion of the blood of Christ: The bread which we break, is it not the communion of the body of Christ? [17]For we being many are one bread, and one body: for we are all partakers of that one bread.

1 Cor. 11 [23]For I have received of the Lord that which also I delivered unto you, That the Lord Jesus, the same night in which he was betrayed, took bread: [24]And when he had given thanks, he brake it, and said, Take, eat; this is my body, which is broken for you: this do in remembrance of me.

Other Figurative Uses of Bread

1 Kin. 22 [27]And say, Thus saith the king, Put this fellow in the prison, and feed him with bread of affliction and with water of affliction, until I come in peace.

Psa. 80 [5]Thou feedest them with the bread of tears; and givest them tears to drink in great measure.

Psa. 127 [2]It is vain for you to rise up early, to sit up late, to eat the bread of sorrows: for so he giveth his beloved sleep.

Isa. 55 [2]Wherefore do ye spend money for that which is not bread? and your labor for that which satisfieth not? hearken diligently unto me, and eat ye that which is good, and let your soul delight itself in fatness.

BRETHREN

[breth′ren] Literally, brothers. This word is used in many places in the Bible, referring not only to children of the same parents, but to national kinsmen as well. In the New Testament it is often employed to express the family unity that should exist between Christians.

SCRIPTURE

Duties of Brethren

Gen. 13 [8]And Abram said unto Lot, Let there be no strife, I pray thee, between me and thee, and between my herdmen and thy herdmen; for we be brethren.

Deut. 15 [7]If there be among you a poor man of one of thy brethren within any of thy gates in thy land which the LORD thy God giveth thee, thou shalt not harden thy heart, nor shut thine hand from thy poor brother.

Deut. 24 [14]Thou shalt not oppress an hired servant that is poor and needy, whether he be of thy brethren, or of thy strangers that are in thy land within thy gates.

Psa. 133 [1]Behold, how good and how pleasant it is for brethren to dwell together in unity!

Matt. 5 [22]But I say unto you, that whosoever is angry with his brother without a cause, shall be in danger of the Judgment: and whosoever shall say to his brother, Raca, shall be in danger of the council: but whosoever shall say, Thou fool, shall be in danger of hell fire.

Matt. 18 [15]Moreover, if thy brother shall trespass against thee, go and tell him his fault between thee and him alone: if he shall hear thee, thou hast gained thy brother.

[21]Then came Peter to him, and said, Lord, how oft shall my brother sin against me, and I forgive him? till seven times? [22]Jesus saith unto him, I say not unto thee, Until seven times: but, Until seventy times seven.

Matt. 25 [40]And the King shall answer and say unto them, Verily I say unto you, Inasmuch as ye have done it unto one of the least of these my brethren, ye have done it unto me.

John 13 [34]A new commandment I give unto you, That ye love one another; as I have loved you, that ye also love one another.

Rom. 12 [10]Be kindly affectioned one to another with brotherly love; in honour preferring one another.

1 Cor. 6 [5]I speak to your shame. Is it so, that there is not a wise man among you? no, not one that shall be able to judge between his brethren? [6]But brother goeth to law with brother, and that before the unbelievers. [7]Now therefore there is utterly a fault among you, because ye go to law one with another. Why do ye not rather take wrong? why do ye not rather suffer yourselves to be defrauded? [8]Nay, ye do wrong, and defraud, and that your brethren.

1 Cor. 8 [13]Wherefore if meat make my brother to offend, I will eat no flesh while the world standeth, lest I make my brother to offend.

Gal. 6 [1]Brethren, if a man be overtaken in a fault, ye which are spiritual, restore such an one in the spirit of meekness; considering thyself, lest thou also be tempted.

1 Thess. 4 [9]But as touching brotherly love ye need not that I write unto you: for ye yourselves are taught of God to love one another.

Heb. 13 [1]Let brotherly love continue.

1 John 2 [9]He that saith he is in the light, and hateth his brother, is in darkness even until now.

1 John 3 [17]But whoso hath this world's good, and seeth his brother have need, and shutteth up his bowels of compassion from him, how dwelleth the love of God in him?

BRIBERY

[brĭb'ẽr i] The act of giving or taking rewards or favors with a view to pervert the judgment or corrupt the conduct of a person in a position of trust.

SCRIPTURE

Ex. 23 [8]And thou shalt take no gift; for the gift blindeth the wise, and perverteth the words of the righteous.

Deut. 16 [18]Judges and officers shalt thou make thee in all thy gates, which the LORD thy God giveth thee, throughout thy tribes: and they shall judge the people with just judgment. [19]Thou shalt not wrest judgment; thou shalt not respect persons, neither take a gift: for a gift doth blind the eyes of the wise, and pervert the words of the righteous.

1 Sam. 8 [1]And it came to pass, when Samuel was old, that he made his sons judges over Israel. [2]Now the name of his firstborn was Joel; and the name of his second, Abiah: they were judges in Beer-sheba. [3]And his sons walked not in his ways, but turned aside after lucre, and took bribes, and perverted judgment.

Prov. 17 [23]A wicked man taketh a gift out of the bosom to pervert the ways of judgment.

Prov. 29 [4]The king by judgment establisheth the land: but he that receiveth gifts overthroweth it.

Job 15 [34]For the congregation of hypocrites shall be desolate, and fire shall consume the tabernacles of bribery.

Eccl. 7 [7]Surely oppression maketh a wise man mad; and a gift destroyeth the heart.

Amos 5 [12]For I know your manifold transgressions and your mighty sins: they afflict the just, they take a bribe, and they turn aside the poor in the gate from their right.

REFERENCE: Delilah, *Judg. 16:5*; Samuel's sons, *1 Sam. 8:1-3;* The false prophet, Shemaiah, *Neh. 6:10-13*; Chief priests bribe Judas, *Matt. 26:15; 27:3-9; Mark 14:11*; Soldiers bribed to declare that the disciples stole the body of Jesus, *Matt. 28:12-15;* Felix seeks a bribe from Paul, *Acts 24:26.*

BRIMSTONE

[brim'stōn] Another name for sulphur, one of the chemical elements. Sulphur springs are found on the shores or brim of the Dead Sea and doubtless figured in the destruction of Sodom and Gomorrah. Brimstone is a favorite symbol for torment and punishment, particularly in the future state.

SCRIPTURE

Isa. 30 [33]For Tophet is ordained of old; yea, for the king it is prepared; he hath made it deep and large: the pile thereof is fire and much wood; the breath of the LORD, like a stream of brimstone, doth kindle it.

Rev. 9 [18]By these three was the third part of men killed, by the fire, and by the smoke, and by the brimstone, which issued out of their mouths.

Rev. 14 [10]The same shall drink of the wine of the wrath of God, which is poured out without mixture into the cup of his indignation; and he shall be tormented with fire and brimstone in the presence of the holy angels, and in the presence of the Lamb.

Rev. 19 [10]And the beast was taken, and with him the false prophet, that wrought miracles before him, with which he deceived them that had received the mark of the beast, and them that worshipped his image. These both were cast alive into a lake of fire burning with brimstone.

Rev. 21 [8]But the fearful, and unbelieving, and the abominable, and murderers, and whoremongers, and sorcerers, and idolaters, and all liars, shall have their part in the lake which burneth with fire and brimstone: which is the second death.

BURIAL

[ber'i al] The act of interment of a corpse. In Palestine during Biblical times, it was customary to carry out the burial as soon after death as was expedient, sometimes within a matter of two or three hours. Usually, however, enough time was taken to wash the body, anoint it with spices and other preparations to retard decomposition, and swathe it in grave-wrappings. The Jews made great lamentation over the dead. Tearing the hair, uttering cries, striking the breast, wearing sackcloth, sprinkling dust on the head, and fasting were common. The procession to the grave or tomb was often led by professional mourners, paid for their ability to shriek and wail in a convincing fashion thus exciting the sympathy of spectators and assuring all that a proper amount of sorrow was being exhibited. The body was carried on a bier or litter and placed either in a grave dug in the earth or in a cave or tomb which had been cut in the rock.

SCRIPTURE

Deut. 21 [23]His body shall not remain all night upon the tree, but thou shalt in any wise bury him that day; (for he that is hanged is accursed of God;) that thy land be not defiled, which the LORD thy God giveth thee for an inheritance.

Eccl. 12 [5]Also when they shall be afraid of that which is high, and fears shall be in the way, and the almond tree shall flourish, and the grasshopper shall be a burden, and desire shall fail: because man goeth to his long home, and the mourners go about the streets:

Jer. 9 [17]Thus saith the LORD of hosts, Consider ye, and call for the mourning women, that they may come; and send for cunning women, that they may come.

Amos 5 [16]Therefore the LORD, the God of hosts, the LORD, saith thus; Wailing shall be in all streets; and they shall say in all highways, Alas! alas! and they shall call the husbandman to mourning, and such as are skilful of lamentation to wailing.

Mark 16 [1]And when the sabbath was past, Mary Magdalene, and Mary the mother of James, and Salome, had bought sweet spices, that they might come and anoint him.

Luke 24 [1]Now upon the first day of the week, very early in the morning, they came unto the sepulchre, bringing the spices which they had prepared, and certain others with them.

John 11 [44]And he that was dead came forth, bound hand and foot with graveclothes; and his face was bound about with a napkin.

John 12 [7]Then said Jesus, Let her alone: against the day of my burying hath she kept this.

John 19 [39]And there came also Nicodemus, which at the first came to Jesus by night, and brought a mixture of myrrh and aloes, about a hundred pound weight.

Acts 9 [37]And it came to pass in those

days, that she was sick, and died: whom when they had washed, they laid her in an upper chamber.

BUSYBODY

[biz'i bo'di] One who meddles in the affairs of others. The Bible contains several passages which censure such persons.

SCRIPTURE

Prov. 20 [3]It is an honour for a man to cease from strife: but every fool will be meddling.

Prov. 26 [17]He that passeth by, and meddleth with strife belonging not to him, is like one that taketh a dog by the ears.

1 Thess. 4 [11]And that ye study to be quiet, and to do your own business, and to work with your own hands, as we commanded you.

2 Thess. 3 [11]For we hear that there are some which walk among you disorderly, working not at all, but are busybodies. [12]Now them that are such, we command, and exhort by our Lord Jesus Christ, that with quietness they work, and eat their own bread.

1 Tim. 5 [13]And withal they learn to be idle, wandering about from house to house; and not only idle, but tattlers also, and busybodies, speaking things which they ought not.

1 Pet. 4 [15]But let none of you suffer as a murderer, or as a thief, or as an evil-doer, or as a busybody in other men's matters.

CAESAREA

[ses a rē'a] 1. *Caesarea in Palestine.* This city, located on the Mediterranean coast of Palestine, was built by Herod the Great and named in honor of Augustus. Herod outfitted the city in a sumptuous manner, including a magnificent harbor and a grand sewer system. It later became the official residence of the Roman procurators. The apostle Peter was sent to Caesarea to bring the gospel message to the Roman centurion Cornelius (*Acts 10*). Paul passed through Caesarea several times on his missionary tours (*Acts 9:30; 18:22; 21:8*). After his arrest in Jerusalem, he was taken to Caesarea, where he remained until his departure for Rome (*Acts 23:12-27:2*).

2. *Caesarea Philippi.* Located at the base of Mount Hermon, this city bore the name Paneas until the reign of the tetrarch Philip, who renamed it after Caesar Augustus and himself. It was near Caesarea Philippi that Simon Peter made his well-known confession of faith in Jesus as the Son of God (*Matt. 16:13-18; Mark 8:27-33*).

CAIAPHAS

[kā'a fas, kī'a fas] Son-in-law of Annas and high priest in Jerusalem "in that year", that is, the fateful year in which Jesus met his death. Caiaphas played a key role in the machinations which led to Jesus' crucifixion. When the Sanhedrin met to decide how to deal with the threat which Jesus posed for their personal and national security, it was Caiaphas who suggested "that it is expedient for us, that one man should die for the people, and that the whole nation perish not" (*John 11:50*). After Jesus was arrested, he was led for a preliminary investigation to Annas and then brought before Caiaphas for formal interrogation. Many false witnesses offered testimony, but Jesus answered nothing; finally, Caiaphas spoke, "I adjure thee by the living God, that thou tell us whether thou be the Christ, the Son of God." When Jesus answered, "Thou hast said", Caiaphas rent his clothes, saying, "He hath spoken blasphemy; what further need have we of witnesses? Behold, now ye have heard his blasphemy" (*Matt. 26:63-66*). Despite the illegality of the trial of Jesus, the Master was found "guilty of death" and delivered up to be crucified.

Caiaphas is also found among those who were present at the trial of Peter and John recorded in *Acts 4*. From extra-Biblical sources, we know that Caiaphas was deposed by Vitellius about AD 36.

See ANNAS, JESUS, SANHEDRIN

REFERENCE: *Matt. 26:3-5, 57-68; Mark 14:53-65; Luke 22:66-71; John 11:47-53; 18:13-14, 19-24.*

CAIN

[kān] The son of Adam and Eve and a "tiller of the ground", or farmer. When God rejected Cain's sacrificial offering, but accepted that of Abel, Cain murdered his brother in a jealous rage. For his sin, he was made to be a fugitive for the rest of his life. The Bible tells us that Cain found a wife in the land of Nod (wandering) and that she bore him a son named Enoch.

See ABEL

SCRIPTURE

Gen. 4 [1]And Adam knew Eve his wife; and she conceived, and bare Cain, and said, I have gotten a man from the LORD. [2]And she again bare his brother Abel. And Abel was a keeper of sheep, but Cain was a tiller of the ground. [3]And in process of time it came to pass, that Cain brought of the fruit of the ground an offering unto the LORD. [4]And Abel, he also brought of the firstlings of his flock and of the fat thereof. And the LORD had respect unto Abel and to his offering: [5]But unto Cain and to his offering he had not respect and Cain was very wroth, and his countenance fell. [6]And the LORD said unto Cain, Why art thou wroth? and why is thy countenance fallen? [7]If thou doest well, shalt thou not be accepted? and if thou doest not well, sin lieth at the door: and unto thee shall be his desire, and thou shalt rule over him. [8]And Cain talked with Abel his brother: and it came to pass, when they were in the field, that Cain rose up against Abel his brother, and slew him.

[9]And the LORD said unto Cain, Where is Abel thy brother? And he said, I know not: Am I my brother's keeper? [10]And he said, What hast thou done? the voice of thy brother's blood crieth unto me from the ground. [11]And now art thou cursed from the earth, which hath opened her mouth to receive thy brother's blood from thy hand. [12]When thou tillest the ground, it shall not henceforth yield unto thee her strength; a fugitive and a vagabond shalt thou be in the earth. [13]And Cain said unto the LORD, My punishment is greater than I can bear. [14]Behold, thou hast driven me out this day from the face of the earth; and from thy face shall I be hid; and I shall be a fugitive and a vagabond in the earth; and it shall come to pass, that every one that findeth me shall slay me. [15]And the LORD said unto him, Therefore whosoever slayeth Cain, vengeance shall be taken on him sevenfold. And the LORD set a mark upon Cain, lest any finding him should kill him.

[16]And Cain went out from the presence of the LORD, and dwelt in the land of Nod, on the east of Eden. [17]And Cain knew his wife; and she conceived, and bare Enoch: and he builded a city, and called the name of the city, after the name of his son, Enoch.

CALEB

[kā′leb] The son of Jephunneh, and one of the twelve sent by Moses to spy out the land of Canaan. Joshua and he alone brought back a favorable report and, because of this, are said to be the only adults of the first census (*see Num. 1*) who entered the promised land. As a further reward, Caleb received the city of Hebron, after driving out the inhabitants. He is also mentioned as the father of Achsah, whom Othniel received as his wife when he conquered Kiriath-sepher.

REFERENCE: *Num. 13:30; 14:6; 26:65; 32:12; Deut. 1:36; Josh. 14:6; 15:13; Judg. 1:12-15.*

CALF, GOLDEN

[kaf, gol′den] In *Ex. 32:4* we are told that Aaron, urged by the people in the continued absence of Moses, made a molten calf of the golden earrings of the people, to represent the deity which brought Israel out of Egypt. Probably it was a wooden figure laminated with gold—a process which is known to have existed in Egypt. There has been considerable dispute respecting this figure—as well as those of Jeroboam (*see* JEROBOAM)—as to whether the Israelites intended them to represent some Egyptian deity, or to serve merely as a symbol for the true God.

SCRIPTURE

Made by Aaron

Ex. 32 3And all the people brake off the golden earrings which were in their ears, and brought them unto Aaron. 4And he received them at their hand, and fashioned it with a graven tool, after he had made it a molten calf: and they said, These be thy gods, O Israel, which brought thee up out of the land of Egypt.

Set Up by Jeroboam

1 Kin. 12 28Whereupon the king took counsel, and made two calves of gold, and said unto them, It is too much for you to go up to Jerusalem: behold thy gods, O Israel, which brought thee up out of the land of Egypt. 29And he set the one in Bethel, and the other put he in Dan. 30And this thing became a sin: for the people went to worship before the one, even unto Dan. 31And he made a house of high places, and made priests of the lowest of the people, which were not of the sons of Levi. 32And Jeroboam ordained a feast in the eighth month, on the fifteenth day of the month, like unto the feast that is in Judah, and he offered upon the altar. So did he in Bethel, sacrificing unto the calves that he had made: and he placed in Bethel the priests of the high places which he had made. 33So he offered upon the altar which he had made in Bethel the fifteenth day of the eighth month, even in the month which he had devised of his own heart; and ordained a feast unto the children of Israel: and he offered upon the altar, and burnt incense.

CALL, Called, Calling

[kôl] Literally, "to give a name to" or "to summon." As used in the Bible, it often means to appoint for a particular office or destiny. In the New Testament, it has a technical sense referring to the invitation given to men by God to accept salvation in Jesus Christ.

SCRIPTURE

Call to Repentance and Salvation

Isa. 45 22Look unto me, and be ye saved, all the ends of the earth: for I am God, and there is none else.

Isa. 55 1Ho, every one that thirsteth, come ye to the waters, and he that hath no money; come ye, buy, and eat; yea, come, buy wine and milk without money and without price. 2Wherefore do ye spend money for that which is not bread? and your labour for that which satisfieth not? hearken diligently unto me, and eat ye that which is good, and let your soul delight itself in fatness. 3Incline your ear, and come unto me: hear, and your soul shall live; and I will make an everlasting covenant with you, even the sure mercies of David.

Joel 2 12Therefore also now, saith the LORD, Turn ye even to me with all your heart, and with fasting, and with weeping, and with mourning: 13And rend your heart, and not your garments, and turn unto the LORD your God: for he is gracious and merciful, slow to anger, and of great kindness, and repenteth him of the evil.

Matt. 3 2And saying, Repent ye; for the kingdom of heaven is at hand.

Matt. 11 28Come unto me, all ye that labour and are heavy laden, and I will give you rest. 29Take my yoke upon you, and learn of me; for I am meek and lowly in heart: and ye shall find rest unto your souls. 30For my yoke is easy, and my burden is light.

John 7 [37]In the last day, that great day of the feast, Jesus stood, and cried, saying, If any man thirst, let him come unto me, and drink. [38]He that believeth on me, as the Scripture hath said, out of his belly shall flow rivers of living water.

John 12 [44]Jesus cried, and said, He that believeth on me, believeth not on me, but on him that sent me. [45]And he that seeth me, seeth him that sent me. [46]I am come a light into the world, that whosoever believeth on me, should not abide in darkness. [47]And if any man hear my words, and believe not, I judge him not; For I came not to judge the world, but to save the world.

Rom. 8 [28]And we know that all things work together for good, to them that love God, to them who are the called according to his purpose. [29]For whom he did foreknow, he also did predestinate to be conformed to the image of his son, that he might be the firstborn amongst many brethren. [30]Moreover, whom he did predestinate, them he also called: and whom he called, them he also justified: and whom he justified, them he also glorified.

2 Cor. 5 [20]Now then we are ambassadors for Christ, as though God did beseech you by us: we pray you in Christ's stead, be ye reconciled to God.

Rev. 22 [17]And the Spirit and the Bride say, Come. And let him that heareth say, Come. And let him that is athirst come. And whosoever will, let him take the water of life freely.

Danger of Declining Call

Prov. 1 [28]Then shall they call upon me, but I will not answer; they shall seek me early, but they shall not find me.

Prov. 29 [1]He that, being often reproved, hardeneth his neck, shall suddenly be destroyed, and that without remedy.

Isa. 66 [4]I also will choose their delusions, and will bring their fears upon them; because when I called, none did answer; when I spake, they did not hear; but they did evil before mine eyes, and chose that in which I delighted not.

Jer. 6 [19]Hear, O earth: Behold, I will bring evil upon this people, even the fruit of their thoughts, because they have not hearkened unto my words, nor to my law, but rejected it.

Jer. 35 [17]Therefore thus saith the LORD God of hosts, the God of Israel; Behold, I will bring upon Judah and upon all the inhabitants of Jerusalem all the evil that I have pronounced against them; because I have spoken unto them, but they have not heard; and I have called unto them, but they have not answered.

Matt. 22 [8]Then saith he to his servants, The wedding is ready, but they which were bidden, were not worthy [9]Go ye therefore into the highways, and as many as ye shall find, bid to the marriage.

John 12 [48]He that rejecteth me, and receiveth not my words, hath one that judgeth him: the word that I have spoken, the same shall judge him in the last day.

Acts 13 [46]Then Paul and Barnabas waxed bold, and said, It was necessary that the word of God should first have been spoken to you: but seeing you put it from you, and judge yourselves unworthy of everlasting life, lo, we turn to the Gentiles.

2 Thess. 2 [10]And with all deceivableness of unrighteousness in them that perish; because they received not the love of the truth, that they might be saved.

The Christian's Calling

2 Cor. 1 [21]Now he which stablisheth us

with you in Christ, and hath anointed us, is God.

2 Cor. 2 [15]For we are unto God a sweet savour of Christ, in them that are saved, and in them that perish. [16]To the one we are the savour of death unto death; and to the other the savour of life unto life. And who is sufficient for these things? [17]For we are not as many, which corrupt the word of God: but as of sincerity, but as of God, in the sight of God speak we in Christ.

2 Cor. 5 [20]Now then we are ambassadors for Christ, as though God did beseech you by us: we pray you in Christ's stead, be ye reconciled to God.

Eph. 1 [18]The eyes of your understanding being enlightened; that ye may know what is the hope of his calling, and what the riches of the glory of his inheritance in the saints.

Eph. 4 [1]I therefore, the prisoner of the Lord, beseech you that ye walk worthy of the vocation wherewith ye are called.

Phil. 3 [14]I press toward the mark for the prize of the high calling of God in Christ Jesus.

2 Thess. 1 [11]Wherefore also we pray always for you, that our God would count you worthy of this calling, and fulfil all the good pleasure of his goodness, and the work of faith with power; [12]That the name of our Lord Jesus Christ may be glorified in you, and ye in him, according to the grace of our God, and the Lord Jesus Christ.

2 Tim. 1 [9]Who hath saved us, and called us with an holy calling, not according to our works, but according to his own purpose and grace, which was given us in Christ Jesus, before the world began.

Heb. 12 [25]See that ye refuse not him that speaketh. For if they escaped not who refused him that spake on earth, much more shall not we escape, if we turn away from him that speaketh from heaven.

1 Pet. 2 [9]But ye are a chosen generation, a royal priesthood, an holy nation, a peculiar people; that ye should shew forth the praises of him who hath called you out of darkness into his marvellous light.

1 John 2 [27]But the anointing which ye have received of him abideth in you, and ye need not that any man teach you: but as the same anointing teacheth you of all things, and is truth, and is no lie, and even as it hath taught you, ye shall abide in him.

1 John 4 [6]We are of God: he that knoweth God heareth us; he that is not of God heareth not us. Hereby know we the spirit of truth, and the spirit of error.

Special Calls to Individuals

TO ABRAHAM

Gen. 12 [1]Now the LORD had said unto Abram, Get thee out of thy country and from thy kindred, and from thy father's house, unto a land that I will shew thee: [2]And I will make of thee a great nation, and I will bless thee, and make thy name great; and thou shalt be a blessing: [3]And I will bless them that bless thee, and curse him that curseth thee: and in thee shall all families of the earth be blessed.

TO JACOB

Gen. 28 [13]And, behold, the LORD stood above it, and said, I am the LORD God of Abraham thy father, and the God of Isaac: the land whereon thou liest, to thee will I give it, and to thy seed.

TO MOSES

Ex. 3 [10]Come now therefore, and I will send thee unto Pharaoh, that thou mayest bring forth my people, the children of Israel, out of Egypt.

TO GIDEON

Judg. 6 11And there came an angel of the LORD, and sat under an oak which was in Ophrah, that pertained unto Joash the Abi-ezrite: and his son Gideon threshed wheat by the wine-press, to hide it from the Midianites. 12And the angel of the LORD appeared unto him, and said unto him, The LORD is with thee, thou mighty man of valour.

TO SAMUEL

1 Sam. 3 10And the LORD came, and stood and called as at other times, Samuel, Samuel. Then Samuel answered, Speak; for thy servant heareth.

TO ELIJAH

1 Kin. 17 2And the word of the LORD came unto him, saying, 3Get thee hence, and turn thee eastward, and hide thyself by the brook Cherith, that is before Jordan. 4And it shall be, that thou shalt drink of the brook; and I have commanded the ravens to feed thee there.

TO ELISHA

1 Kin. 19 19So he departed thence, and found Elisha the son of Shaphat, who was ploughing with twelve yoke of oxen before him, and he with the twelfth: and Elijah passed by him, and cast his mantle upon him.

TO ISAIAH

Isa. 6 8Also I heard the voice of the LORD, saying, Whom shall I send, and who will go for us? Then said I, Here am I; send me.

TO JONAH

Jonah 1 1Now the word of the LORD came unto Jonah the son of Amittai, saying, 2Arise, go to Nineveh, that great city, and cry against it; for their wickedness is come up before me.

TO PETER AND ANDREW

Matt. 4 18And Jesus, walking by the sea of Galilee, saw two brethren, Simon called Peter, and Andrew his brother, casting a net into the sea: for they were fishers. 19And he saith unto them, Follow me, and I will make you fishers of men.

TO PAUL

Acts 9 6And he trembling and astonished, said, Lord, what wilt thou have me to do? And the Lord said unto him, Arise, and go into the city, and it shall be told thee what thou must do.

Rom. 1 1Paul, a servant of Jesus Christ, called to be an apostle, separated unto the gospel of God.

Gal. 1 1Paul, an apostle, (not of men, neither by man, but by Jesus Christ, and God the Father, who raised him from the dead;)

CANA OF GALILEE

[kā'na] A village or town not far from Capernaum, memorable as the scene of Christ's first miracle (*John 2:1-11*). It was also the home of Nathanael (*John 21:2*). The exact site on which Cana stood has never been identified.

CANAAN

[kā'nan] This term is usually employed to refer to the "promised land" of Palestine which began to be occupied by the Israelites in the thirteenth century BC. At the time of the Israelite immigration, the population of this land was composed mostly of Canaanites and Amorites. In the Bible these two terms are often used synonymously but, technically, these were different peoples. The Canaanites were a northwest-semitic people who had occupied Palestine and Syria throughout historic times. They were most thickly settled along the coast of Palestine. The Amorites, another northwest-semitic people, infiltrated Palestine in the early second millenium BC, settling mainly in the mountainous interior. By the time of the Exodus, the cultures of these two peoples had mixed and it was not improper to speak of them simply as Canaanites. Palestine also contained Indo-Aryans and Hurrians, together with such non-semitic elements as Hittites, Hivites, Horites, Jebusites, Girgashites, Perizzites, etc., but these were all essentially Canaanite in culture at the time of the Conquest of Joshua. (*See* CONQUEST)

At the time of the influx of the Israelites, Canaanites culture had declined somewhat, but it was not without its impressive features. Well-built cities, consisting of fine patrician houses surrounded by the meanest of hovels, attest to the feudal character of the society. The major commercial ventures of the Canaanites included the exporting of timber, textiles, and purple-dye. Because of their involvement in international trade, the Canaanites were able to absorb features of other cultures; considerable quantities of pottery and other imports from the Mycenaean and Minoan civilizations indicate wide contact with the known world. Perhaps the major achievement of the Canaanites was the invention of the linear alphabet, an ancestor of our own alphabet. For a discussion of the religion of the Canaanites, the reader is invited to consult the article on BAAL.

Politically, Canaan was a conglomeration of city-states under the feudal oversight of Egypt. Notoriously corrupt Egyptian administration drained the country of much of its resources and left it solely dependent on Egypt for its military protection. In a period when Egypt was weak, as in the time of the Israelite conquest, the Canaanites were virtually powerless to defend themselves. It was this situation which, humanly speaking, made the conquests of Joshua possible. These various elements of Canaanites culture should be kept in mind if the Biblical narratives are to be understood in their proper context.

CAPERNAUM

[ka pĕr′na um] A city in or near the plain of Gennesaret (archaeologists have as yet been unable to settle on its exact location) which served as a center of Jesus' activity during a large part of his public ministry. Capernaum was apparently of considerable significance during the time of Jesus. We know that it was a customs station, for it was here that Jesus found Matthew collecting taxes, and summoned him to be a disciple (*Matt. 9:9ff*). That it was also the base of a detachment of Roman soldiers is indicated by the fact that the local synagogue is said to have been built by a centurion (*Luke 7:1-5*). Although Jesus was reared in Nazareth, the gospels refer to Capernaum as his "home" (*Matt. 4:13; Mark 2:1*). Despite the fact that Capernaum had ample opportunity to witness the mighty acts of Jesus, there was apparently insufficient response on the part of the residents, drawing forth the severe rebuke of the master—"And thou, Capernaum, which are exalted unto heaven, shalt be brought down to hell: for if the mighty works, which have been done in thee, had been done in Sodom, it would have remained until this day. But I say unto you, that it shall be more tolerable for the land of Sodom in the day of judgment, than for thee" (*Matt. 11:23, 24;* cf. *Luke 10:15*).

CAPTIVITY

[kap tiv′i ti] The state of being held in bondage or confinement. This word is used by Bible students to denote the periods which marked the end of the kingdoms of Israel and Judah. The northern position of the kingdom of Israel left it vulnerable to repeated attacks of Syria and Assyria. By 733 BC Tiglath-Pileser of Assyria had taken all but the territory of Ephraim and Western Manasseh. In an effort to break down nationalistic lines, Tiglath-Pileser transported a considerable number of Israelites to Assyria, replacing them with Assyrian subjects. Hoshea was appointed king over the remaining Israelites. After a few years of subservience Hoshea revolted, precipitating the final downfall of the Northern Kingdom. In 722 BC Sargon II of Assyria captured the capital city of Samaria and carried more than 27,000 Israelites into Assyrian captivity. The subsequent fortunes of the ten tribes which constituted the kingdom of Israel are lost to history.

The southern kingdom of Judah was able to elude a similar fate for over a century; in 597 BC, however, Nebuchadnezzar of Babylon overran

Judah and deported much of the better element of Judaean population. Ten years later (587 BC), after a siege of a year and a half, Jerusalem itself fell and a second wave of captives was taken to Babylon. Of those that remained behind, some were killed, others fled to Egypt, and many died of starvation or disease. The population of Judah was reduced from over 250,000 to less than 20,000. Another once-great nation had ceased to be.

The lot of those who were carried into Babylon and Southern Mesopotamia seems not to have been too severe. They were dispersed throughout the land, but were allowed to live in separate settlements (*Ezek. 3:15; Ezra 2:59; 8:17*). There they were permitted to build houses, to earn their living by farming and other pursuits and to assemble for worship (*Jer. 29:5; Ezek. 8:1; 14:1; 33:30-31*). Some, however, still clung to the dream of returning to Jerusalem. The agent who was to bring that dream to fruition was Cyrus the Persian. By 550 BC he had siezed control of the vast Median Empire. In 539 he was received as king of Babylon and the world was his. A year later, Cyrus decreed the restoration of the Jewish community and cult in Palestine (*Ezra 1:2-4*). For an account of the rebuilding of Israel and Judaism, *see* the articles on ZERUBBABEL, EZRA, NEHEMIAH, TEMPLE, CYRUS, etc.

REFERENCE: Captivity of the kingdom of Israel, *2 Kin. 16:6, 23, 24; 18:9-12;* Captivity of Judah in Babylon, *2 Kin. 24:11-16; 25; 2 Chr. 36; Jer. 52:28-30;* Return from Captivity, *Ezra 2, 3, 8.*

CARE

[kâr] The basic idea of this word is concern. This concern may be entirely proper, as solicitude for the welfare of another, or it may become a burdensome anxiety with regard to oneself or one's possessions, an anxious striving after unworthy goals. The New Testament teaches that dependence on Christ frees one from improper concern and anxiety, enabling him to direct his full attention to the kingdom of God.

SCRIPTURE

Matt. 6 25Therefore I say unto you, Take no thought for your life, what ye shall eat, or what ye shall drink, nor yet for your body, what ye shall put on: Is not the life more than meat? and the body than raiment? 34Take therefore no thought for the morrow: for the morrow shall take thought for the things of itself: sufficient unto the day is the evil thereof.

Luke 8 14And that which fell among thorns, are they, which, when they have heard, go forth, and are choked with cares, and riches, and pleasures of this life, and bring no fruit to perfection.

Luke 21 34Take heed to yourselves, lest at any time your hearts be overcharged with surfeiting, and drunkenness, and cares of this life, and so that day come upon you unawares,

John 6 27Labour not for the meat which perisheth, but for that meat which endureth unto everlasting life, which the Son of man shall give unto you: for him hath God the Father sealed.

1 Cor. 7 32But I would have you without carefulness. He that is unmarried careth for the things that belong to the Lord, how he may please the Lord: 33But he that is married careth for the things that are of the world, how he may please his wife.

Phil. 4 6Be careful for nothing; but in every thing by prayer and supplication with thanksgiving let your requests be made known unto God.

2 Tim. 2 4No man that warreth entangleth himself with the affairs of this life; that he may please him who hath chosen him to be a soldier.

Heb. 13 5Let your conversation be without covetousness; and be content with such things as ye have: for he hath said, I will never leave thee, nor forsake thee.

1 Pet. 5 6Humble yourselves therefore

under the mighty hand of God, that he may exalt you in due time, [7]Casting all your care upon him, for he careth for you.

CELIBACY

[sel′i ba si] The state of being unmarried; single life, especially that of one who has vowed not to marry. Although the celibate condition enables one to give his full attention to the work of the Lord, Jesus recognized that "not all men can receive this saying" (*Matt. 19:11*) and did not urge his followers to refrain from marriage. Paul's teaching on the matter is similar. He recognized that marriage often causes a man to be more concerned with things of this world than with the things of the Kingdom, but he conceded that "nevertheless, to avoid fornication, let every man have his own wife, and let every woman have her own husband . . . for it is better to marry than to burn" (*1 Cor. 7:2, 9*). In *1 Tim. 4:3*, those who forbid marriage on religious grounds are condemned.

See MARRIAGE

SCRIPTURE

Matt. 19 [10]His disciples say unto him, If the case of the man be so with his wife, it is not good to marry. [11]But he said unto them, All men cannot receive this saying, save they to whom it is given. [12]For there are some eunuchs, which were so born from their mother's womb: and there are some eunuchs which were made eunuchs of men: and there be eunuchs, which have made themselves eunuchs for the kingdom of heaven's sake. He that is able to receive it, let him receive it.

1 Cor. 7 [1]Now concerning the things whereof ye wrote unto me: It is good for a man not to touch a woman. [2]Nevertheless, to avoid fornication, let every man have his own wife, and let every woman have her own husband. [7]For I would that all men were even as I myself. But every man hath his proper gift of God, one after this manner, and another after that. [8]I say therefore to the unmarried and widows, It is good for them if they abide even as I. [9]But if they cannot contain, let them marry: for it is better to marry than to burn. [25]Now concerning virgins I have no commandment of the Lord: yet I give my judgment, as one that hath obtained mercy of the Lord to be faithful. [26]I suppose therefore that this is good for the present distress, I say, that it is good for a man so to be. [32]But I would have you without carefulness. He that is unmarried careth for the things that belong to the Lord, how he may please the Lord: [33]But he that is married careth for the things that are of the world, how he may please his wife. [34]There is difference also between a wife and a virgin. The unmarried woman careth for the things of the Lord, that she may be holy both in body and in spirit: but she that is married careth for the things of the world, how she may please her husband. [35]And this I speak for your own profit; not that I may cast a snare upon you, but for that which is comely, and that ye may attend upon the Lord without distraction. [36]But if any man think that he behaveth himself uncomely toward his virgin, if she pass the flower of her age, and need so require, let him do what he will, he sinneth not: let them marry. [37]Nevertheless he that standeth stedfast in his heart, having no necessity, but hath power over his own will, and hath so decreed in his heart that he will keep his virgin, doeth well. [38]So then he that giveth her in marriage doeth well; but he that giveth her not in marriage doeth better. [39]The wife is bound by the law as long as her husband liveth; but if her husband be dead, she is at liberty to be married to whom she will; only in the Lord. [40]But she is happier if she so abide, after my judgment: and I think also that I have the Spirit of God.

1 Cor. 9 5Have we not power to lead about a sister, a wife, as well as other apostles, and as the brethren of the Lord, and Cephas?

1 Tim. 4 1Now the Spirit speaketh expressly, that in the latter times some shall depart from the faith, giving heed to seducing spirits, and doctrines of devils; 2Speaking lies in hypocrisy; having their conscience seared with a hot iron; 3Forbidding to marry, and commanding to abstain from meats, which God hath created to be received with thanksgiving of them which believe and know the truth.

CHALDEA

[kal dē′a] The name of a territory in Southern Babylonia, sometimes used to denote Babylonia as a whole. The Bible sometimes refers to the whole of Babylonia as Chaldea or "The land of the Chaldeans." For discussion of major historical matters, see BABYLONIA.

REFERENCE: *Gen. 11:28, 31; 15:7; Isa. 23:13; Hab. 1:6.*

CHARACTER

[kar′ak tēr] The aggregate of distinctive qualities belonging to an individual or group of individuals. The scriptures contain many references which describe and contrast the characters of children of God and children of Satan.

SCRIPTURE

Character of Saints

Rom. 8 14For as many as are led by the Spirit of God, they are the sons of God.

Phil. 2 15That ye may be blameless and harmless, the sons of God, without rebuke, in the midst of a crooked and perverse nation, among whom ye shine as lights in the world;

Col. 3 12Put on therefore, as the elect of God, holy and beloved, bowels of mercies, kindness, humbleness of mind, meekness, long-suffering; 13Forbearing one another, and forgiving one another, if any man have a quarrel against any: even as Christ forgave you, so also do ye.

1 Pet. 5 5Likewise, ye younger, submit yourselves unto the elder. Yea, all of you be subject one to another, and be clothed with humility: for God resisteth the proud, and giveth grace to the humble.

See PURITY, HONESTY, etc.

Character of the Wicked

Psa. 10 3For the wicked boasteth of his heart's desire, and blesseth the covetous, whom the LORD abhorreth.

Mic. 2 2And they covet fields, and take them by violence; and houses, and take them away: so they oppress a man and his house, even a man and his heritage.

John 3 20For every one that doeth evil hateth the light, neither cometh to the light, lest his deeds should be reproved.

Rom. 1 29Being filled with all unrighteousness, fornication, wickedness, covetousness, maliciousness, full of envy, murder, debate, deceit, malignity; whisperers. 30Backbiters, haters of God, despiteful, proud, boasters, inventors of evil things, disobedient to parents, 31Without understanding, covenant-breakers, without natural affection, implacable, unmerciful: 32Who knowing the judgment of God, that they which commit such things are worthy of death, not only do the same, but have pleasure in them that do them.

Phil. 3 19Whose end is destruction, whose God is their belly, and whose glory is in their shame, who mind earthly things.)

2 Tim. 3 2For men shall belovers of

their own selves, covetous, boasters, proud, blasphemers, disobedient to parents, unthankful, unholy, [3]Without natural affection, truce-breakers, false accusers, incontinent, fierce, despisers of those that are good, [4]Traitors, heady, highminded, lovers of pleasures more than lovers of God; [5]Having a form of godliness, but denying the power thereof: from such turn away.

Tit. 3 [3]For we ourselves also were sometime foolish, disobedient, deceived, serving divers lusts and pleasures, living in malice and envy, hateful, and hating one another.

CHARITY

[char′i ti] This word has come to mean liberality and generosity to the poor and suffering, otherwise known as almsgiving. In the King James Version of the Bible, it often appears as the translation for the word *agape*, which is elsewhere rendered "love." It may also refer to lenience in judging men and their actions.

See LOVE

SCRIPTURE

Charity as Love to Neighbors

Mark 12 [33]And to love him with all the heart, and with all the understanding, and with all the soul, and with all the strength, and to love his neighbour as himself, is more than all whole burnt offerings and sacrifices.

1 Cor. 13 [13]And now abideth faith, hope, charity, these three; but the greatest of these is charity.

1 Thess. 3 [6]But now when Timotheus came from you unto us, and brought us good tidings of your faith and charity, and that ye have good remembrance of us always, desiring greatly to see us, as we also to see you.

1 Thess. 4 [9]But as touching brotherly love, ye need not that I write unto you: for ye yourselves are taught of God to love one another.

1 Tim. 1 [5]Now the end of the commandment is charity out of a pure heart, and of a good conscience, and of faith unfeigned.

1 Tim. 4 [12]Let no man despise thy youth, but be thou an example of the believers, in word, in conversation, in charity, in spirit, in faith, in purity.

2 Tim. 3 [10]But thou hast fully known my doctrine, manner of life, purpose, faith, long-suffering, charity, patience.

Heb. 6 [10]For God is not unrighteous to forget your work and labour of love, which ye have shewed toward his name, in that ye have ministered to the saints, and do minister.

Jas. 2 [8]If ye fulfil the royal law according to the scripture, Thou shalt love thy neighbour as thyself, ye do well.

1 John 4 [20]If a man say, I love God, and hateth his brother, he is a liar. For he that loveth not his brother whom he hath seen, how can he love God whom he hath not seen? [21]And this commandment have we from him, that he who loveth God, love his brother also.

Rev. 2 [19]I know thy works, and charity, and service, and faith, and thy patience, and thy works; and the last to be more than the first.

Charity as Almsgiving

Lev. 25 [35]And if thy brother be waxen poor, and fallen in decay with thee; then thou shalt relieve him: yea, though he be a stranger, or a sojourner; that he may live with thee.

Prov. 19 [17]He that hath pity upon the poor, lendeth unto the LORD; and that which he hath given will he pay him again.

Matt. 19 [21]Jesus said unto him, If thou wilt be perfect, go and sell that thou hast, and give to the poor, and thou shalt have treasure in heaven: and come and follow me.

Luke 11 [41]But rather give alms of such things as ye have; and behold, all things are clean unto you.

Luke 12 [33]Sell that ye have, and give alms; provide yourselves bags which wax not old, a treasure in the heavens that faileth not, where no thief approacheth, neither moth corrupteth.

Acts 10 [4]And when he looked on him, he was afraid, and said, What is it, Lord? And he said unto him, Thy prayers and thine alms are come up for a memorial before God.

2 Cor. 9 [7]Every man according as he purposeth in his heart, so let him give; not grudgingly, or of necessity: for God loveth a cheerful giver. [8]And God is able to make all grace abound toward you; that ye, always having all sufficiency in all things, may abound to every good work.

Charity Commanded

Lev. 19 [18]Thou shalt not avenge, nor bear any grudge against the children of thy people, but thou shalt love thy neighbour as thyself: I am the LORD.

Matt. 5 [44]But I say unto you, Love your enemies, bless them that curse you, do good to them that hate you, and pray for them which despitefully use you, and persecute you.

Matt. 22 [39]And the second is like unto it, Thou shalt love thy neighbour as thyself.

John 13 [34]A new commandment I give unto you, That ye love one another, as I have loved you, that ye also love one another.

Signs and Effects of Charity or Love

1 Cor. 8 [1]Now as touching things offered unto idols, we know that we all have knowledge. Knowledge puffeth up: but Charity edifieth.

1 Cor. 13 [1]Though I speak with the tongues of men and of angels, and have not charity, I am become as sounding brass or a tinkling cymbal. [2]And though I have the gift of prophecy, and understand all mysteries and all knowledge: and though I have all faith, so that I could remove mountains, and have not charity, I am nothing. [3]And though I bestow all my goods to feed the poor, and though I give my body to be burned, and have not charity, it profiteth me nothing. [4]Charity suffereth long, and is kind: charity envieth not: charity vaunteth not itself, is not puffed up, [5]Doth not behave itself unseemly, seeketh not her own, is not easily provoked, thinketh no evil, [6]Rejoiceth not in iniquity, but rejoiceth in the truth: [7]Beareth all things, believeth all things, hopeth all things, endureth all things. [8]Charity never faileth: but whether there be prophecies, they shall fail; whether there be tongues, they shall cease; whether there be knowledge, it shall vanish away.

Col. 3 [14]And above all these things put on charity, which is the bond of perfectness.

1 Pet. 4 [8]And above all things have fervent charity among yourselves: for charity shall cover the multitude of sins.

Evidences of Charity

Isa. 58 [7]Is it not to deal thy bread to the hungry, and that thou bring the poor that are cast out to thy house? when thou seest the naked, that thou cover him; and that thou hide not thyself from thine own flesh?

Matt. 25 [35]For I was an hungred, and ye
gave me meat: I was thirsty, and ye gave
me drink: I was a stranger, and ye took
me in: [36]Naked, and ye clothed me: I was
sick, and ye visited me: I was in prison,
and ye came unto me.

John 13 [35]By this shall all men know that ye are my disciples, if ye have love one to another.

CHERUBIM

[cher'ŭ bim] The plural form of cherub. Although subject to some variation (*see Ezek. 10*), the basic form of the cherub was that of a winged sphinx or winged lion with a human head. In the art and religious symbolism of Syria and Palestine during the Biblical period, it is quite common to find kings or deities enthroned on winged sphinxes, or cherubim. Likewise, in Israelite religion God is designated as "He who sitteth on the cherubim" (*1 Sam. 4:4*). The cherubim on the "mercy-seat" in the Holy of Holies of the tabernacle, constituted a throne on which the glory of the LORD appeared and from which he spoke. A pair of cherubim of colossal size overshadowed the ark in Solomon's temple. The modern concept of a cherub as a tiny winged boy stems from the tradition of Renaissance artists.

See SERAPHIM

SCRIPTURE

At the Garden of Eden

Gen. 3 [24]So he drove out the man: and he placed at the east of the garden of Eden cherubim, and a flaming sword which turned every way, to keep the way of the tree of life.

In the Tabernacle

Ex. 25 [18]And thou shalt make two cherubim of gold, of beaten work shalt thou
make them, in the two ends of the mercy
seat. [19]And make one cherub on the one
end, and the other cherub on the other
end: even of the mercy seat shall ye make
the cherubim on the two ends thereof.
[20]And the cherubim shall stretch forth
their wings on high, covering the mercy
seat with their wings, and their faces shall
look one to another; toward the mercy seat
shall the faces of the cherubim be.

Ex. 26 [1]Moreover thou shalt make the tabernacle with ten curtains of fine twined linen, and blue, and purple, and scarlet: with cherubim of cunning work shalt thou make them.

[31]And thou shalt make a veil of blue, and purple, and scarlet, and fine twined linen of cunning work: with cherubim shall it be made.

See Ex. 36:35; Ex. 37:7-9; Ex. 36:8

In the Temple

1 Kin. 6 [23]And within the oracle he
made two cherubim of olive tree, each ten
cubits high. [24]And five cubits was the one
wing of the cherub, and five cubits the
other wing of the cherub: from the uttermost part of the one wing unto the uttermost part of the other were ten cubits.
[25]And the other cherub was ten cubits:
both the cherubim were of one measure
and one size. [26]The height of the one
cherub was ten cubits, and so was it of the
other cherub. [27]And he set the cherubim
within the inner house: and they stretched
forth the wings of the cherubim, so that the
wing of the one touched the one wall, and
the wing of the other cherub touched the
other wall; and their wings touched one
another in the midst of the house. [28]And
he overlaid the cherubim with gold. [29]And
he carved all the walls of the house round
about with carved figures of cherubim and
palm trees and open flowers, within and
without. [30]And the floor of the house he
overlaid with gold, within and without.

31 And for the entering of the oracle he made doors of olive tree: the lintel and side posts were a fifth part of the wall. 32 The two doors also were of olive tree; and he carved upon them carvings of cherubim and palm trees and open flowers, and overlaid them with gold, and spread gold upon the cherubim, and upon the palm trees. 33 So also made he for the door of the temple posts of olive tree, a fourth part of the wall. 34 And the two doors were of fir tree: the two leaves of the one door were folding, and the two leaves of the other door were folding. 35 And he carved thereon cherubim and palm trees and open flowers: and covered them with gold fitted upon the carved work.

1 Kin. 7 29 And on the borders that were between the ledges were lions, oxen, and cherubim: and upon the ledges there was a base above: and beneath the lions and oxen were certain additions made of thin work. 36 For on the plates of the ledges thereof, and on the borders thereof, he graved cherubim, lions, and palm trees, according to the proportion of every one, and additions round about.

See 2 Chr. 3:7, 10-14

In Ezekiel's Visions

Ezek. 10 1 Then I looked, and, behold, in the firmament that was above the head of the cherubim there appeared over them as it were a sapphire stone, as the appearance of the likeness of a throne. 2 And he spake unto the man clothed with linen, and said, Go in between the wheels, even under the cherub, and fill thine hand with coals of fire from between the cherubim, and scatter them over the city. And he went in in my sight. 3 Now the cherubim stood on the right side of the house, when the man went in; and the cloud filled the inner court. 4 Then the glory of the LORD went up from the cherub, and stood over the threshold of the house; and the house was filled with the cloud, and the court was full of the brightness of the LORD's glory. 5 And the sound of the cherubim's wings was heard even to the outer court, as the voice of the Almighty God when he speaketh. 6 And it came to pass, that when he had commanded the man clothed with linen, saying, Take fire from between the wheels, from between the cherubim; then he went in, and stood beside the wheels. 7 And one cherub stretched forth his hand from between the cherubim unto the fire that was between the cherubim, and took thereof, and put it into the hands of him that was clothed with linen; who took it, and went out.

8 And there appeared in the cherubim the form of a man's hand under their wings. 9 And when I looked, behold the four wheels by the cherubim, one wheel by one cherub, and another wheel by another cherub: and the appearance of the wheels was as the colour of a beryl stone. 10 And as for their appearances, they four had one likeness, as if a wheel had been in the midst of a wheel. 11 When they went, they went upon their four sides; they turned not as they went, but to the place whither the head looked they followed it; they turned not as they went. 12 And their whole body, and their backs, and their hands, and their wings, and the wheels, were full of eyes round about, even the wheels that they four had. 13 As for the wheels, it was cried unto them in my hearing, O wheel. 14 And every one had four faces: the first face was the face of a cherub, and the second face was the face of a man, and the third the face of a lion, and the fourth the face of an eagle. 15 And

the cherubim were lifted up. This is the living creature that I saw by the river of Chebar. [16]And when the cherubim went, the wheels went by them: and when the cherubim lifted up their wings to mount up from the earth, the same wheels also turned not from beside them. [17]When they stood, these stood; and when they were lifted up, these lifted up themselves also: for the spirit of the living creature was in them. [18]Then the glory of the LORD departed from off the threshold of the house, and stood over the cherubim. [19]And the cherubim lifted up their wings, and mounted up from the earth in my sight: when they went out, the wheels also were beside them, and every one stood at the door of the east gate of the LORD's house; and the glory of the God of Israel was over them above. [20]This is the living creature that I saw under the God of Israel by the river of Chebar; and I knew that they were the cherubim. [21]Every one had four faces apiece, and every one four wings; and the likeness of the hands of a man was under their wings. [22]And the likeness of their faces was the same faces which I saw by the river of Chebar, their appearances and themselves: they went every one straight forward.

Ezek. 41 [18]And it was made with cherubim and palm trees, so that a palm tree was between a cherub and a cherub; and every cherub had two faces; [19]So that the face of a man was toward the palm tree on the one side, and the face of a young lion toward the palm tree on the other side: it was made through all the house round about. [20]From the ground unto above the door were cherubim and palm trees made, and on the wall of the temple. [25]And there were made on them, on the doors of the temple, cherubim and palm trees, like as were made upon the walls; and there were thick planks upon the face of the porch without.

CHILD, CHILDREN

[child, chil'dren] Children are mentioned in the Bible in a number of ways, both literal and figurative. Scripture teaches that they are the gift of God and that parents are blessed with them. They, on their part, are required to be obedient, and their duties to parents are plainly taught. All men, especially those who are obedient to Him, are spoken of as children of God. Jesus and Paul sometimes referred to their disciples or followers as children, as a term of affection. Children are also regarded as a symbol of innocence.

SCRIPTURE

Children the Gift of God

Gen. 33 [5]And he lifted up his eyes, and saw the women and the children; and said, Who are those with thee? And he said, The children which God hath graciously given thy servant.

Psa. 127 [3]Lo, children are an heritage of the LORD.

Psa. 128 [3]Thy wife shall be as a fruitful vine by the sides of thine house: thy children like olive-plants round about thy table.

Children a Blessing

Prov. 10 [1]The proverbs of Solomon. A wise son maketh a glad father; but a foolish son is the heaviness of his mother.

Prov. 17 [6]Children's children are the crown of old men; and the glory of children are their fathers.

Prov. 23 [24]The father of the righteous shall greatly rejoice: and he that begetteth a wise child shall have joy of him.

Prov. 27 [11]My son, be wise, and make my heart glad, that I may answer him that reproacheth me.

Children of the Righteous, Blessed

Prov. 11 [21]Though hand join in hand, the wicked shall not be unpunished: but the seed of the righteous shall be delivered.

Prov. 12 [7]The wicked are overthrown, and are not: but the house of the righteous shall stand.

Prov. 13 [22]A good man leaveth an inheritance to his children's children: and the wealth of the sinner is laid up for the just.

Prov. 20 [7]The just man walketh in his integrity: his children are blessed after him.

Duty of Children

Ex. 20 [12]Honour thy father and thy mother; that thy days may be long upon the land which the LORD thy God giveth thee.

Lev. 19 [3]Ye shall fear every man his mother and his father, and keep my sabbaths: I am the LORD your God.

Deut. 5 [16]Honour thy father and thy mother, as the LORD thy God hath commanded thee; that thy days may be prolonged, and that it may go well with thee, in the land which the LORD thy God giveth thee.

Prov. 1 [8]My son, hear the instruction of thy father, and forsake not the law of thy mother.

Prov. 13 [1]A wise son heareth his father's instruction: but a scorner heareth not rebuke.

Prov. 15 [5]A fool despiseth his father's instruction: but he that regardeth reproof is prudent.

Prov. 24 [21]My son, fear thou the LORD and the king: and meddle not with them that are given to change.

Eccl. 12 [1]Remember now thy Creator in the days of thy youth, while the evil days come not, nor the years draw nigh, when thou shalt say, I have no pleasure in them.

Eph. 6 [1]Children, obey your parents in the Lord: for this is right. [2]Honour thy father and mother, (which is the first commandment with promise,) [3]That it may be well with thee, and thou mayest live long on the earth.

Col. 3 [20]Children, obey your parents in all things: for this is well-pleasing unto the LORD.

1 Tim. 5 [4]But if any widow have children or nephews, let them learn first to shew piety at home, and to requite their parents: for that is good and acceptable before God.

Correction of Children

Prov. 13 [24]He that spareth his rod hateth his son: but he that loveth him chasteneth him betimes.

Prov. 19 [18]Chasten thy son while there is hope, and let not thy soul spare for his crying.

Prov. 22 [15]Foolishness is bound in the heart of a child; but the rod of correction shall drive it far from him.

Prov. 23 [13]Withhold not correction from the child: for if thou beatest him with the rod, he shall not die. [14]Thou shalt beat him with the rod, and shalt deliver his soul from hell.

Prov. 29 [15]The rod and reproof give wisdom: but a child left to himself bringeth his mother to shame. [17]Correct thy son, and he shall give thee rest; yea, he shall give delight unto thy soul.

Eph. 6 [4]And, ye fathers, provoke not your children to wrath: but bring them up in the nurture and admonition of the Lord.

Col. 3 [21]Fathers, provoke not your children to anger, lest they be discouraged.

Children of God

Heb. 12 [5]And ye have forgotten the exhortation which speaketh unto you as unto children, My son, despise not thou the chastening of the Lord, nor faint when thou art rebuked of him.

Eph. 5 [1]Be ye therefore followers of God, as dear children.

Luke 16 [8]And the Lord commended the unjust Steward, because he had done wisely: for the children of this world are in their generation wiser than the children of light.

John 12 [36]While ye have light, believe in the light, that ye may be the children of light. These things spake Jesus, and departed, and did hide himself from them.

Eph. 5 [8]For ye were sometimes darkness, but now are ye light in the Lord: walk as children of light.

1 Thess. 5 [5]Ye are all the children of light, and the children of the day: we are not of the night, nor of darkness.

Wicked Children

Prov. 19 [26]He that wasteth his father, and chaseth away his mother, is a son that causeth shame, and bringeth reproach.

Prov. 20 [20]Whoso curseth his father or his mother, his lamp shall be put out in obscure darkness.

Prov. 28 [7]Whoso keepeth the law is a wise son: but he that is a companion of riotous men shameth his father. [24]Whoso robbeth his father or his mother, and saith, It is no transgression; the same is the companion of a destroyer.

Prov. 30 [11]There is a generation that curseth their father, and doth not bless their mother. [17]The eye that mocketh at his father, and despiseth to obey his mother, the ravens of the valley shall pick it out, and the young eagles shall eat it.

Punishment of Wicked Children

Ex. 21 [15]And he that smiteth his father, or his mother, shall be surely put to death.

Deut. 21 [18]If a man have a stubborn and rebellious son, which will not obey the voice of his father, or the voice of his mother, and that, when they have chastened him, will not hearken unto them: [19]Then shall his father and his mother lay hold on him, and bring him out unto the elders of his city, and unto the gate of his place; [20]And they shall say unto the elders of his city, This our son is stubborn and rebellious, he will not obey our voice; he is a glutton, and a drunkard. [21]And all the men of his city shall stone him with stones, that he die: so shalt thou put evil away from among you, and all Israel shall hear, and fear.

Deut. 27 [16]Cursed be he that setteth light by his father or his mother. And all the people shall say, Amen.

2 Kin. 2 [23]And he went up from thence unto Beth-el: and as he was going up by the way, there came forth little children out of the city, and mocked him, and said unto him, Go up, thou bald-head; go up, thou bald-head. [24]And he turned back, and looked on them, and cursed them in the name of the LORD. And there came forth two she-bears out of the wood, and tare forty and two children of them.

Children a Symbol of the Regenerated

Matt. 18 [2]And Jesus called a little child unto him, and set him in the midst of them, [3]And said, Verily I say unto you, Except ye be converted, and become as little children, ye shall not enter into the kingdom of heaven. [4]Whosoever therefore shall humble himself as this little child, the same is greatest in the kingdom of heaven. [5]And whoso shall receive one such little child in my name receiveth me. [6]But whoso shall offend one of these little ones which believe in me, it were better for him that a millstone were hanged about his neck, and that he were drowned in the depth of the sea.

Mark 10 [15]Verily I say unto you, whosoever shall not receive the kingdom of God as a little child, he shall not enter therein.

Figurative

1 Cor. 13 [11]When I was a child, I spake as a child, I understood as a child, I thought as a child: but when I became a man, I put away childish things.

1 Cor. 14 [20]Brethren, be not children in understanding: howbeit in malice be ye children, but in understanding be men.

1 Pet. 2 [2]As newborn babes, desire the sincere milk of the word, that ye may grow thereby:

CHRIST

[krīst] The English form of the Greek word *Christos*, meaning "Anointed One"; its equivalent in Hebrew, the language of the Old Testament, is *mashiach*, from which the word "Messiah" is drawn. In the early days of Israel, kings and priests were anointed with oil as a sign of their consecration (*Ex. 29:7*); hence, the title "anointed one" signifies one who is chosen by God for a special office. During the period between the writing of the Old and New Testaments, the term "Messiah" or "Christ" came to be applied to a hoped-for ruler who would deliver Israel from her enemies and restore the former glory of the kingdom of David. The messiahship of Jesus of Nazareth was unlike that which the Jews had expected, and throughout his ministry the exact nature of his mission was understood, even by his disciples, only obscurely. The frequent appellation, "Son of Man" is normally regarded as a messianic title. (*See* SON OF MAN)

In the first three of our gospels, Christ is seen as the bringer of a new age, the herald of the kingdom of God (*Mark 1:14-15; 2:19-22*). He calls and instructs his disciples with absolute authority, authority that can come only from his intimate relationship with God (*Mark 1:16-20; 2:14; 3:35; 11:33*). In his ministry he demonstrates not only mastery over the forces of nature (*Mark 4:35-41; 6:34-52*), but the power to forgive sins (*Mark 2:10*).

In the writings of Paul, the term "Christ" is applied to Jesus either as a surname (Jesus Christ), a prefix (Christ Jesus), or simply as a substitute for his proper name. Paul views Christ as the one who has made possible man's justification and reconciliation to God (*Rom. 3:24; 2 Cor. 5:18-20*), who has caused the debt of sin to be canceled and remembered no more (*Rom. 3:25; Col. 2:14-15*), and who has enabled those who believe on him to receive adoption as sons of God (*Rom. 8:15-16*). These believers constitute the church, which, with its several members, is thought of as the body of Christ (*1 Cor. 12:13-31; Eph. 1:22-23; Col. 1:24*).

According to *Phil. 2:5-11*, Christ was originally in the form of God, but "emptied" himself and took on human form in order to execute his mission of salvation. This humanity of Christ is emphasized in *Hebrews*, in which he is said to have "tasted death for every man" (*Heb. 2:9*). He is pictured as the perfect high priest, offering up the perfect sacrifice of his own unblemished life (*Heb. 9:11-12*). Thus his priesthood is superior to the Aaronic priesthood and is compared to that of Melchizedek (*Heb. 5:6-10; 6:13-7:17*). As our high priest he is also the perfect mediator, since he has undergone the same temptations as we, though he did not sin (*Heb. 4:15*).

The doctrine of Christ's nature and mission, called Christology, reaches its highest point in the gospel according to John. Here it is made clear that Christ is of divine origin, in fact, that he is the word of God, and that everything which has come into being has done so through him. In Paul's writings Christ is in some sense subordinate to God, but in the fourth gospel it is made quite clear that he may properly be identified with the Father (*John 3:35; 5:18; 10:18-36; 16:32; 17:10*). In this gospel and in *Revelation*, also ascribed to John, Christ is frequently spoken of as the Lamb of God (*John 1:29; Rev. 6:16*).

For material relating to the earthly life of the Christ, *see* JESUS, ATONEMENT, CHURCH, GOD, HOLY SPIRIT, MELCHIZEDEK, SALVATION, SON OF MAN, TRINITY, etc.

SCRIPTURE

The Lord Jesus Christ

Luke 2 [11]For unto you is born this day, in the city of David, a Saviour, which is Christ the Lord.

John 1 [41]He first findeth his own brother Simon, and saith unto him, We have found the Messias, which is, being interpreted, the Christ.

John 4 [42]And said unto the woman, Now we believe, not because of thy saying: for we have heard him ourselves, and know that this is indeed the Christ, the Saviour of the world.

Acts 11 [17]Forasmuch then as God gave them the like gift as he did unto us, who believed on the Lord Jesus Christ, what was I, that I could withstand God?

Acts 15 [11]But we believe that through the grace of the Lord Jesus Christ we shall be saved even as they.

Acts 16 [31]And they said, Believe on the Lord Jesus Christ, and thou shalt be saved, and thy house.

Acts 20 [21]Testifying both to the Jews, and also to the Greeks, repentance toward God, and faith toward our Lord Jesus Christ.

Rom. 5 [1]Therefore being justified by faith, we have peace with God, through our Lord Jesus Christ. [11]And not only so, but we also joy in God, through our Lord Jesus Christ, by whom we have now received the atonement.

Rom. 6 [23]For the wages of sin is death: but the gift of God is eternal life, through Jesus Christ our Lord.

Rom. 7 [25]I thank God through Jesus Christ our Lord. So then, with the mind I myself serve the law of God: but with the flesh the law of sin.

Rom. 13 [14]But put ye on the Lord Jesus Christ, and make not provision for the flesh, to fulfil the lusts thereof.

Rom. 15 [6]That ye may with one mind and one mouth glorify God, even the Father of our Lord Jesus Christ. [30]Now I beseech you, brethren, for the Lord Jesus Christ's sake, and for the love of the Spirit, that ye strive together with me in your prayers to God for me.

1 Cor. 1 [3]Grace be unto you, and peace from God our Father, and from the Lord Jesus Christ. [4]I thank my God always on your behalf, for the grace of God which is given you by Jesus Christ; [5]That in every thing ye are enriched by him, in all utterance, and in all knowledge; [6]Even as the testimony of Christ was confirmed in you: [7]So that ye come behind in no gift; waiting for the coming of our Lord Jesus Christ: [8]Who shall also confirm you unto the end, that ye may be blameless in the day of our Lord Jesus Christ. [9]God is faithful, by whom ye were called unto the fellowship of his Son Jesus Christ our Lord.

Eph. 5 [20]Giving thanks always for all things unto God, and the Father, in the Name of our Lord Jesus Christ.

Phil. 3 [20]For our conversation is in heaven, from whence also we look for the Saviour, the Lord Jesus Christ.

1 Tim. 5 [21]I charge thee before God, and the Lord Jesus Christ, and the elect Angels, that thou observe these things without preferring one before another, doing nothing by partiality.

2 Tim. 1 [10]But is now made manifest by

the appearing of our Saviour Jesus Christ, who hath abolished death, and hath brought life and immortality to light, through the Gospel.

Philem. 1 [3]Grace to you, and peace from God our Father, and the Lord Jesus Christ.

Heb. 13 [8]Jesus Christ the same yesterday, and to-day, and for ever. [20]Now the God of peace, that brought again from the dead our Lord Jesus, that great Shepherd of the sheep, through the blood of the everlasting covenant, [21]Make you perfect in every good work, to do his will, working in you that which is well-pleasing in his sight, through Jesus Christ; to whom be glory for ever and ever. Amen.

1 Pet. 1 [3]Blessed be the God and Father of our Lord Jesus Christ, which, according to his abundant mercy, hath begotten us again unto a lively hope by the resurrection of Jesus Christ from the dead.

2 Pet. 1 [11]For so an entrance shall be ministered unto you abundantly into the everlasting kingdom of our Lord and Saviour Jesus Christ.

Jude 1 [21]Keep yourselves in the love of God, looking for the mercy of our Lord Jesus Christ unto eternal life.

Jesus Christ, the Son of God

Matt. 2 [15]And was there until the death of Herod, that it might be fulfilled which was spoken of the Lord by the Prophet, saying, Out of Egypt have I called my son.

Matt. 3 [17]And lo, a voice from heaven, saying, This is my beloved Son, in whom I am well pleased.

Matt. 26 [63]But Jesus held his peace. And the high priest answered and said unto him, I adjure thee by the living God, that thou tell us whether thou be the Christ, the Son of God. [64]Jesus saith unto him, Thou hast said: nevertheless, I say unto you, Hereafter shall ye see the Son of man sitting on the right hand of power, and coming in the clouds of heaven.

Luke 1 [32]He shall be great, and shall be called the Son of the Highest; and the Lord God shall give unto him the throne of his father David. [35]And the angel answered and said unto her, The Holy Ghost shall come upon thee, and the power of the Highest shall overshadow thee: therefore also that holy thing which shall be born of thee, shall be called the Son of God.

Luke 3 [22]And the Holy Ghost descended in a bodily shape like a dove upon him, and a voice came from heaven, which said, Thou art my beloved Son; in thee I am well pleased.

Luke 4 [41]And devils also came out of many, crying out, and saying, Thou art Christ the Son of God. And he rebuking them, suffered them not to speak: for they knew that he was Christ.

John 1 [34]And I saw and bare record, that this is the Son of God.

[49]Nathanael answered and saith unto him, Rabbi, thou art the Son of God; thou art the King of Israel.

John 3 [16]For God so loved the world, that he gave his only begotten Son, that whosoever believeth in him should not perish, but have everlasting life. [17]For God sent not his Son into the world to condemn the world, but that the world through him might be saved.

[18]He that believeth on him, is not condemned: but he that believeth not, is condemned already, because he hath not believed in the name of the only begotten Son of God.

[35]The Father loveth the Son, and hath given all things into his hand. [36]He that believeth on the Son hath everlasting life: and he that believeth not the Son, shall

not see life; but the wrath of God abideth on him.

John 5 22For the Father judgeth no man: but hath committed all judgment unto the Son: 23That all men should honour the Son, even as they honour the Father. He that honoureth not the Son, honoureth not the Father which hath sent him. 25Verily, verily, I say unto you, The hour is coming, and now is, when the dead shall hear the voice of the Son of God: and they that hear shall live. 26For as the Father hath life in himself so hath he given to the Son to have life in himself.

John 6 40And this is the will of him that sent me, that every one which seeth the Son, and believeth on him, may have everlasting life: and I will raise him up at the last day.

69 And we believe and are sure that thou art that Christ, the Son of the living God.

John 12 26If any man serve me, let him follow me; and where I am, there shall also my servant be: if any man serve me, him will my Father honour.

John 14 13And whatsoever ye shall ask in my name, that will I do, that the Father may be glorified in the Son.

John 15 23He that hateth me, hateth my Father also.

John 16 28I came forth from the Father, and am come into the world: again, I leave the world, and go to the Father.

John 17 1These words spake Jesus, and lifted up his eyes to heaven, and said, Father, the hour is come; glorify thy Son, that thy Son also may glorify thee.

Rom. 5 10For if when we were enemies, we were reconciled to God, by the death of his Son, much more, being reconciled, we shall be saved by his life.

Rom. 8 3For what the law could not do, in that it was weak through the flesh, God sending his own Son in the likeness of sinful flesh, and for sin, condemned sin in the flesh. 29For whom he did foreknow, he also did predestinate to be conformed to the image of his Son, that he might be the first-born among many brethren. 32He that spared not his own Son, but delivered him up for us all, how shall he not with him also freely give us all things?

1 Cor. 1 9God is faithful by whom ye were called unto the fellowship of his Son Jesus Christ our Lord.

Gal. 4 4But when the fulness of the time was come, God sent forth his Son made of a woman, made under the law, 5To redeem them that were under the law, that we might receive the adoption of sons. 6And because ye are sons, God hath sent forth the spirit of his Son into your hearts, crying, Abba, Father.

1 Thess. 1 10And to wait for his Son from heaven, whom he raised from the dead, even Jesus which delivered us from the wrath to come.

Heb. 1 1God who at sundry times, and in divers manners, spake in time past unto the Fathers by the Prophets, 2Hath in these last days spoken unto us by his Son, whom he hath appointed heir of all things, by whom also he made the worlds, 3Who being the brightness of his glory, and the express image of his person, and upholding all things by the word of his power, when he had by himself purged our sins, sat down on the right hand of the Majesty on high, 4Being made so much better than the Angels, as he hath by inheritance obtained a more excellent Name than they. 5For unto which of the Angels said he at any time, Thou art my son, this day have I begotten thee?

Heb. 4 14Seeing then that we have a great High Priest, that is passed into the heavens, Jesus the Son of God, let us hold fast our profession.

Heb. 5 [8]Though he were a Son, yet learned he obedience by the things which he suffered.

1 John 1 [3]That which we have seen and heard, declare we unto you, that ye also may have fellowship with us; and truly our fellowship is with the Father, and with his Son Jesus Christ. [7]But if we walk in the light, as he is in the light, we have fellowship one with another, and the blood of Jesus Christ his Son cleanseth us from all sin.

1 John 4 [9]In this was manifested the love of God towards us, because that God sent his only begotten Son into the world, that we might live through him. [10]Herein is love, not that we loved God, but that he loved us, and sent his Son to be the propitiation for our sins.

1 John 5 [20]And we know that the Son of God is come, and hath given us an understanding that we may know him that is true: and we are in him that is true, even in his Son Jesus Christ. This is the true God, and eternal life.

Jesus Christ as Son of Man

Matt. 8 [20]And Jesus saith unto him, The foxes have holes, and the birds of the air have nests: but the Son of man hath not where to lay his head.

Matt. 9 [6]But that ye may know that the Son of man hath power on earth to forgive sins, (then saith he to the sick of the palsy,) Arise, take up thy bed, and go unto thine house.

Matt. 10 [23]But when they persecute you in this city, flee ye into another: for verily I say unto you, Ye shall not have gone over the cities of Israel till the Son of man be come.

Matt. 11 [19]The Son of man came eating and drinking, and they say, Behold, a man gluttonous, and a winebibber, a friend of publicans and sinners. But wisdom is justified of her children.

Matt. 12 [8]For the Son of man is Lord even of the sabbath-day.

[32]And whosoever speaketh a word against the Son of man, it shall be forgiven him: but whosoever speaketh against the Holy Ghost, it shall not be forgiven him, neither in this world, neither in the world to come.

[40]For as Jonas was three days and three nights in the whale's belly: so shall the Son of man be three days and three nights in the heart of the earth.

Matt. 13 [41]The Son of man shall send forth his angels, and they shall gather out of his kingdom all things that offend, and them which do iniquity.

Matt. 16 [13]When Jesus came unto the coasts of Cesarea Philippi, he asked his disciples, saying, Whom do men say that I, the Son of man, am?

Matt. 17 [9]And as they came down from the mountain, Jesus charged them, saying, Tell the vision to no man, until the Son of man be risen again from the dead.

[22]And while they abode in Galilee, Jesus said unto them, The Son of man shall be betrayed into the hands of men.

Matt. 24 [27]For as the lightning cometh out of the east, and shineth even unto the west: so shall also the coming of the Son of man be.

[30]And then shall appear the sign of the Son of man in heaven: and then shall all the tribes of the earth mourn, and they shall see the Son of man coming in the clouds of heaven, with power and great glory.

[44]Therefore be ye also ready: for in such an hour as ye think not, the Son of man cometh.

Matt. 25 [31]When the Son of man shall

come in his glory, and all the holy angels with him, then shall he sit upon the throne of his glory.

Matt. 26 [24]The Son of man goeth, as it is written of him: but woe unto that man by whom the Son of man is betrayed! it had been good for that man if he had not been born.

[45]Then cometh he to his disciples, and saith unto them, Sleep on now, and take your rest: behold, the hour is at hand, and the Son of man is betrayed into the hands of sinners.

Mark 8 [38]Whosoever therefore shall be ashamed of me, and of my words, in this adulterous and sinful generation, of him also shall the Son of man be ashamed, when he cometh in the glory of his Father, with the holy angels.

Mark 9 [12]And he answered and told them, Elias verily cometh first, and restoreth all things; and how it is written of the Son of man, that he must suffer many things, and be set at nought.

Luke 6 [22]Blessed are ye when men shall hate you, and when they shall separate you from their company, and shall reproach you, and cast out your name as evil, for the Son of man's sake.

Luke 9 [22]Saying, The Son of man must suffer many things, and be rejected of the elders, and chief priests, and scribes, and be slain, and be raised the third day.

[56]For the Son of man is not come to destroy men's lives, but to save them.

Luke 12 [8]Also I say unto you, Whosoever shall confess me before men, him shall the Son of man also confess before the angels of God.

Luke 19 [10]For the Son of man is come to seek and to save that which was lost.

Luke 21 [36]Watch ye therefore, and pray always, that ye may be accounted worthy to escape all these things that shall come to pass, and to stand before the Son of man.

Luke 22 [48]But Jesus said unto him, Judas, betrayest thou the Son of man with a kiss?

John 1 [51]And he saith unto him, Verily, verily, I say unto you, Hereafter ye shall see heaven open, and the angels of God ascending and descending upon the Son of man.

John 5 [27]And hath given him authority to execute judgment also, because he is the Son of man.

John 6 [27]Labour not for the meat which perisheth, but for that meat which endureth unto everlasting life, which the Son of man shall give unto you: for him hath God the Father sealed. [53]Then Jesus said unto them, Verily, verily I say unto you, Except ye eat the flesh of the Son of man, and drink his blood, ye have no life in you. [62]What and if ye shall see the Son of man ascend up where he was before?

John 8 [28]Then said Jesus unto them, When ye have lifted up the Son of man, then shall ye know that I am he, and that I do nothing of myself; but as my Father hath taught me, I speak these things.

John 13 [31]Therefore, when he was gone out, Jesus said, Now is the Son of man glorified, and God is glorified in him.

Acts 7 [56]And said, Behold, I see the heavens opened, and the Son of man standing on the right hand of God.

Rev. 1 [13]And in the midst of the seven candlesticks, one like unto the Son of man, clothed with a garment down to the foot, and girt about the paps with a golden girdle.

Christ as Emmanuel

Isa. 7 [14]Therefore the LORD himself

shall give you a sign; Behold, a virgin shall conceive, and bear a son, and shall call his name Immanuel.

Isa. 8 [8]And he shall pass through Judah; he shall overflow and go over, he shall reach even to the neck; and the stretching out of his wings shall fill the breadth of thy land, O Immanuel.

Matt. 1 [29]Behold, a virgin shall be with child, and shall bring forth a son, and they shall call his name Emmanuel, which being interpreted is, God with us.

Christ as the Word

John 1 [1]In the beginning was the Word, and the Word was with God, and the Word was God.

[14]And the Word was made flesh, and dwelt among us (and we beheld his glory, the glory as of the only begotten of the Father,) full of grace and truth.

1 John 5 [7]For there are three that bear record in heaven, the Father, the Word, and the Holy Ghost: and these three are one.

Rev. 19 [13]And he was clothed with a vesture dipped in blood: and his name is called The Word of God.

Christ as the Lamb

John 1 [29]The next day, John seeth Jesus coming unto him, and saith, Behold the Lamb of God, which taketh away the sin of the world.

Rev. 5 [13]And every creature which is in heaven, and on the earth, and under the earth, and such as are in the sea, and all that are in them, heard I, saying, Blessing, honour, glory, and power be unto him that sitteth upon the throne, and unto the Lamb for ever and ever.

Rev. 6 [1]And I saw when the Lamb opened one of the seals, and I heard as it were the noise of thunder, one of the four beasts, saying, Come and see. [16]And said to the mountains and rocks, Fall on us, and hide us from the face of him that sitteth on the throne, and from the wrath of the Lamb.

Rev. 12 [11]And they overcame him by the blood of the Lamb, and by the word of their testimony; and they loved not their lives unto the death.

Rev. 13 [8]And all that dwell upon the earth shall worship him, whose names are not written in the book of life of the Lamb slain from the foundation of the world.

Rev. 19 [7]Let us be glad and rejoice, and give honour to him: for the marriage of the Lamb is come, and his wife hath made herself ready.

Rev. 21 [22]And I saw no temple therein: For the Lord God Almighty, and the Lamb, are the temple of it. [23]And the city had no need of the sun, neither of the moon to shine in it: for the glory of God did lighten it, and the Lamb is the light thereof.

Rev. 22 [1]And he shewed me a pure river of water of life, clear as crystal, proceeding out of the throne of God, and of the Lamb.

Christ the Mediator

1 Tim. 2 [5]For there is one God, and one mediator between God and men, the man Christ Jesus.

Heb. 7 [25]Wherefore he is able also to save them to the uttermost, that come unto God by him, seeing he ever liveth to make intercession for them.

Heb. 8 [6]But now hath he obtained a more excellent ministry, by how much also he is the mediator of a better covenant, which was established upon better promises.

Heb. 9 [15]And for this cause he is the mediator of the new testament, that by means of death, for the redemption of the transgressions that were under the first testament, they which are called might receive the promise of eternal inheritance.

Heb. 12 [24]And to Jesus the mediator of the new covenant, and to the blood of sprinkling, that speaketh better things than that of Abel.

Heb. 13 [15]By him therefore let us offer the sacrifice of praise to God continually, that is, the fruit of our lips, giving thanks to his name.

Christ Our Righteousness

Rom. 5 [17]For if by one man's offence death reigned by one; much more they which receive abundance of grace, and of the gift of righteousness, shall reign in life by one, Jesus Christ. [18]Therefore, as by the offence of one judgment came upon all men to condemnation, even so by the righteousness of one the free gift came upon all men unto justification of life.

Christ as Prophet

Acts 3 [22]For Moses truly said unto the fathers, A prophet shall the Lord your God raise up unto you of your brethren, like unto me; him shall ye hear in all things whatsoever he shall say unto you. [23]And it shall come to pass, that every soul, which will not hear that prophet, shall be destroyed from among the people.

Christ as Priest

Heb. 5 [5]So also Christ glorified not himself to be made an high priest; but he that said unto him, Thou art my Son, to day have I begotten thee. [6]As he saith also in another place, Thou art a priest for ever after the order of Melchisedec.

Christ as Lord and King

Matt. 2 [2]Saying, Where is he that is born King of the Jews? for we have seen his star in the east, and are come to worship him.

Matt. 25 [34]Then shall the King say unto them on his right hand, Come ye blessed of my Father, inherit the kingdom prepared for you from the foundation of the world.

John 19 [14]And it was the preparation of the passover, and about the sixth hour: and he saith unto the Jews, Behold your King!

[19]And Pilate wrote a title, and put it on the cross. And the writing was, JESUS OF NAZARETH, THE KING OF THE JEWS.

Acts 10 [36]The word which God sent unto the children of Israel, preaching peace by Jesus Christ: (he is Lord of all).

1 Cor. 2 [8]Which none of the princes of this world knew: for had they known it, they would not have crucified the Lord of glory.

Jas. 2 [1]My brethren, have not the faith of our Lord Jesus Christ, the Lord of glory, with respect of persons.

Rev. 19 [16]And he hath on his vesture and on his thigh a name written, KING OF KINGS, AND LORD OF LORDS.

Christ as Head of the Church

Eph. 1 [22]And hath put all things under his feet, and gave him to be the head over all things to the church, [23]Which is his body, the fulness of him that filleth all in all.

Col. 1 [18]And he is the head of the body, the church:

Christ's Glory Manifested

AS DIVINE

John 1 [1]In the beginning was the Word, and the Word was with God, and the

Word was God. [2]The same was in the beginning with God. [3]All things were made by him; and without him was not any thing made that was made. [4]In him was life; and the life was the light of men. [5]And the light shineth in darkness; and the darkness comprehended it not.

Phil. 2 [9]Wherefore God also hath highly exalted him, and given him a name which is above every name: [10]That at the name of Jesus every knee should bow, of things in heaven, and things in earth, and things under the earth: [11]And that every tongue should confess, that Jesus Christ is Lord, to the glory of God the Father.

AS GOD THE SON

Mark 1 [11]And there came a voice from heaven, saying, Thou art my beloved Son, in whom I am well pleased.

Col. 1 [15]Who is the image of the invisible God, the firstborn of every creature.

Heb. 1 [6]And again, when he bringeth in the firstbegotten into the world, he saith, And let all the angels of God worship him.

AS EQUAL TO THE FATHER

John 10 [30]I and my Father are one. [38]But if I do, though ye believe not me, believe the works: that ye may know, and believe, that the Father is in me, and I in him.

AS AGENT OF CREATION

Col. 1 [16]For by him were all things created that are in heaven, and that are in earth, visible and invisible, whether they be thrones, or dominions, or principalities, or powers: all things were created by him, and for him.

AS MEDIATOR

1 Tim. 2 [5]For there is one God, and one mediator between God and men, the man Christ Jesus.

AS PROPHET

Deut. 18 [15]The LORD thy God will raise up unto thee a Prophet from the midst of thee, of thy brethren, like unto me; unto him ye shall hearken.

Acts 3 [22]For Moses truly said unto the fathers, A prophet shall the Lord your God raise up unto you, of your brethren, like unto me; him shall ye hear in all things, whatsoever he shall say unto you.

AS PERFECT HIGH PRIEST

Heb. 4 [15]For we have not an high priest which cannot be touched with the feeling of our infirmities: but was in all points tempted like as we are, yet without sin.

Heb. 7 [26]For such an high priest became us, who is holy, harmless, undefiled, separate from sinners, and made higher than the heavens; [27]Who needeth not daily, as those high priests, to offer up sacrifice, first for his own sins, and then for the people's: for this he did once, when he offered up himself. [28]For the law maketh men high priests which have infirmity; but the word of the oath, which was since the law, maketh the Son, who is consecrated for evermore.

AS KING

Rev. 17 [14]These shall make war with the Lamb, and the Lamb shall overcome them: For he is Lord of lords, and King of kings, and they that are with him, are called, and chosen, and faithful.

AS JUDGE

Matt. 16 [27]For the Son of man shall come in the glory of his Father, with his angels: and then he shall reward every man according to his works.

AS SHEPHERD

John 10 [14]I am the good shepherd, and know my sheep, and am known of mine. [15]As the Father knoweth me, even so know I the Father: and I lay down my life for the sheep.

AS CORNERSTONE AND HEAD OF THE CHURCH

Eph. 1 [22]And hath put all things under his feet, and gave him to be the head over all things to the church.

Eph. 2 [20]And are built upon the foundation of the apostles and prophets, Jesus Christ himself being the chief corner stone.

AS THE TRUE LIGHT

Luke 1 [78]Through the tender mercy of our God; whereby the day-spring from on high hath visited us, [79]To give light to them that sit in darkness and in the shadow of death, to guide our feet into the way of peace.

John 1 [4]In him was life; and the life was the light of men. [5]And the light shineth in darkness; and the darkness comprehended it not.

[9]That was the true Light, which lighteth every man that cometh into the world.

John 8 [12]Then spake Jesus again unto them, saying, I am the light of the world: he that followeth me shall not walk in darkness, but shall have the light of life.

AS THE WAY, TRUTH, AND LIFE

John 14 [6]Jesus saith unto him, I am the way, the truth, and the life: no man cometh unto the Father but by me.

1 John 5 [20]And we know that the Son of God is come, and hath given us an understanding, that we may know him that is true; and we are in him that is true, even in his Son Jesus Christ. This is the true God, and eternal life.

Rev. 3 [7]And to the angel of the church in Philadelphia write; These things saith he that is holy, he that is true, he that hath the key of David, he that openeth, and no man shutteth; and shutteth, and no man openeth.

John 11 [25]Jesus said unto her, I am the resurrection, and the life: he that believeth in me, though he were dead, yet shall he live.

Col. 3 [4]When Christ, who is our life, shall appear, then shall ye also appear with him in glory.

1 John 5 [11]And this is the record, that God hath given to us eternal life: and this life is in his Son.

IN CHRIST'S WORDS AND WORKS

Luke 4 [22]And all bare him witness, and wondered at the gracious words which proceeded out of his mouth. And they said, Is not this Joseph's son?

Matt. 13 [54]And when he was come into his own country, he taught them in their synagogue, insomuch that they were astonished, and said, Whence hath this man this wisdom, and these mighty works?

John 2 [11]This beginning of miracles did Jesus in Cana of Galilee, and manifested forth his glory, and his disciples believed on him.

IN TRANSFIGURATION AND EXALTATION

Matt. 17 [2]And was transfigured before them: and his face did shine as the sun, and his raiment was white as the light.

Acts 7 [56]And said, Behold, I see the heavens opened, and the Son of man standing on the right hand of God.

Eph. 1 [20]Which he wrought in Christ when he raised him from the dead, and set him at his own right hand in the heavenly places, [21]Far above all principality, and power, and might, and dominion, and every name that is named, not only in this world, but also in that which is to come.

Divinity of Christ

JUDGE

Eccl. 12 [14]For God shall bring every work into judgment, with every secret thing, whether it be good, or whether it be evil.

1 Cor. 4 [4]For I know nothing by myself, yet am I not hereby justified: but he that judgeth me is the Lord. [5]Therefore judge nothing before the time, until the Lord come, who both will bring to light the hidden things of darkness, and will make manifest the counsels of the hearts: and then shall every man have praise of God.

2 Tim. 4 [1]I charge thee therefore before God, and the Lord Jesus Christ, who shall judge the quick and the dead at his appearing, and his kingdom.

EQUAL WITH GOD

John 5 [23]That all men should honour the Son, even as they honour the Father. He that honoureth not the Son honoureth not the Father which hath sent him.

John 16 [15]All things that the Father hath, are mine: therefore said I that he shall take of mine, and shall shew it unto you.

Phil. 2 [5]Let this mind be in you, which was also in Christ Jesus: [6]Who, being in the form of God, thought it not robbery to be equal with God.

SON OF GOD

Matt. 26 [63]But Jesus held his peace. And the high Priest answered, and said unto him, I adjure thee by the living God, that thou tell us, whether thou be the Christ the Son of God [64]Jesus saith unto him, Thou hast said: Nevertheless I say unto you, Hereafter shall ye see the Son of man sitting on the right hand of power, and coming in the clouds of heaven.

John 3 [16]For God so loved the world, that he gave his only begotten Son: that whosoever believeth in him, should not perish, but have everlasting life.

ONE WITH THE FATHER

John 10 [30]I and my Father are one. [38]But if I do, though ye believe not me, believe the works: that ye may know and believe that the Father is in me, and I in him.

John 12 [45]And he that seeth me seeth him that sent me.

John 14 [7]If ye had known me, ye should have known my Father also: and from henceforth ye know him, and have seen him. [8]Philip saith unto him, Lord, shew us the Father, and it sufficeth us. [9]Jesus saith unto him, Have I been so long time with you, and yet hast thou not known me, Philip? he that hath seen me hath seen the Father, and how sayest thou then, Shew us the Father? [10]Believest thou not that I am in the Father, and the Father in me? The words that I speak unto you, I speak not of myself: but the Father that dwelleth in me, he doeth the works. [11]Believe me that I am in the Father, and the Father in me: or else believe me for the very works' sake.

IN RAISING THE DEAD

John 2 [19]Jesus answered, and said unto them, Destroy this temple, and in three days I will raise it up. [20]Then said the Jews, Forty and six years was this Temple in building, and wilt thou rear it up in three days? [21]But he spake of the temple of his body.

John 10 [17]Therefore doth my Father love me, because I lay down my life that I might take it again. [18]No man taketh it from me, but I lay it down of myself: I have power to lay it down, and I have power to take it again. This commandment have I received of my Father.

RECOGNIZED BY DEMONS

Matt. 8 [29]And, behold, they cried out, saying, What have we to do with thee, Jesus, thou Son of God? art thou come hither to torment us before the time?

Mark 5 [6]But when he saw Jesus afar off, he ran and worshipped him, [7]And cried with a loud voice, and said, What have I to do with thee, Jesus, thou Son of the most high God? I adjure thee by God, that thou torment me not.

See Luke 8:28

OTHER DIVINE ATTRIBUTES

John 28 [20]Teaching them to observe all things whatsoever I have commanded you: and, lo, I am with you alway, even unto the end of the world. Amen.

John 16 [30]Now are we sure that thou knowest all things, and needest not that any man should ask thee: by this we believe that thou camest forth from God.

Phil. 3 [21]Who shall change our vile body, that it may be fashioned like unto his glorious body, according to the working whereby he is able even to subdue all things unto himself.

Humanity of Christ

BIRTH

Matt. 1 [16]And Jacob begat Joseph the husband of Mary, of whom was born Jesus, who is called Christ.

Luke 2 [7]And she brought forth her firstborn son, and wrapped him in swaddling clothes, and laid him in a manger, because there was no room for them in the Inn.

HUMAN SOUL

Matt. 26 [38]Then saith he unto them, My soul is exceeding sorrowful, even unto death: tarry ye here, and watch with me. [39]And he went a little further, and fell on his face, and prayed, saying, O my Father, if it be possible, let this cup pass from me: nevertheless, not as I will, but as thou wilt.

Luke 23 [46]And when Jesus had cried with a loud voice, he said, Father, into thy hands I commend my spirit: And having said thus, he gave up the ghost.

BODILY GROWTH

Luke 2 [52]And Jesus increased in wisdom and stature, and in favor with God and man.

HUMAN NEEDS

Matt. 4 [1]Then was Jesus led up of the spirit into the wilderness, to be tempted of the devil. [2]And when he had fasted forty days and forty nights, he was afterward an hungred.

John 4 [7]There cometh a woman of Samaria to draw water: Jesus saith unto her, Give me to drink.

Matt. 8 [24]And behold, there arose a great tempest in the sea, insomuch that the ship was covered with the waves: but he was asleep.

BY SUFFERING AND DEATH

Luke 24 [46]Thus it is written, and thus it behoved Christ to suffer, and to rise from the dead the third day.

John 19 [30]When Jesus therefore had received the vinegar, he said, It is finished, and he bowed his head, and gave up the ghost.

Acts 3 [18]But those things, which God before had shewed by the mouth of all his prophets, that Christ should suffer, he hath so fulfilled.

1 Pet. 4 [1]Forasmuch then as Christ hath suffered for us in the flesh, arm yourselves likewise with the same mind: for he that hath suffered in the flesh hath ceased from sin.

BY LIKENESS TO HUMANITY

Phil 2 [7]But made himself of no reputation, and took upon him the form of a servant, and was made in the likeness of men: [8]And being found in fashion as a man, he humbled himself, and became obedient unto death, even the death of the cross.

Heb. 2 [17]Wherefore in all things it behoved him to be made like unto his brethren, that he might be a merciful and faithful high priest, in things pertaining to God, to make reconciliation for the sins of the people.

Effect of Christ's Work

ATONEMENT

1 Pet. 2 [24]Who his own self bare our sins in his own body on the tree, that we, being dead to sins, should live unto righteousness: by whose stripes ye were healed.

1 Pet. 3 [18]For Christ also hath once suffered for sins, the just for the unjust, that he might bring us to God, being put to death in the flesh, but quickened by the Spirit:

See ATONEMENT

JUSTIFICATION

Rom. 3 [24]Being justified freely by his grace through the redemption that is in Christ Jesus.

See JUSTIFICATION

RECONCILIATION

2 Cor. 5 [18]And all things are of God, who hath reconciled us to himself by Jesus Christ, and hath given to us the ministry of reconciliation; [19]To wit, that God was in Christ, reconciling the world unto himself, not imputing their trespasses unto them; and hath committed unto us the word of reconciliation. [20]Now then we are ambassadors for Christ, as though God did beseech you by us: we pray you in Christ's stead, be ye reconciled to God.

See RECONCILIATION

CANCELS BOND OF SIN

Rom. 3 [25]Whom God hath set forth to be a propitiation through faith in his blood, to declare his righteousness for the remission of sins that are past, through the forbearance of God.

Col. 2 [14]Blotting out the handwriting of ordinances that was against us, which was contrary to us, and took it out of the way, nailing it to his cross; [15]And having spoiled principalities and powers, he made a shew of them openly, triumphing over them in it.

MAKES POSSIBLE OUR ADOPTION

Rom. 8 [15]For ye have not received the spirit of bondage again to fear; but ye have received the Spirit of adoption, whereby we cry, Abba, Father. [16]The Spirit itself beareth witness with our spirit, that we are the children of God.

Christ's Titles

1 Cor. 15 [45]And so it is written: The first man Adam was made a living soul, the last Adam was made a quickening spirit.

1 John 2 [1]My little children, these things write I unto you, that ye sin not.

And if any man sin, we have an advocate with the Father, Jesus Christ the righteous.

Rev. 1 [8]I am Alpha and Omega, the beginning and the ending, saith the Lord, which is, and which was, and which is to come, the Almighty.

Rev. 3 [14]And unto the angel of the church of the Laodiceans, write, These things saith the Amen, the faithful and true witness, the beginning of the creation of God.

Heb. 3 [1]Wherefore holy brethren, partakers of the heavenly calling, consider the Apostle and High Priest of our profession Christ Jesus.

Heb. 12 [2]Looking unto Jesus the author and finisher of our faith, who for the joy that was set before him, endured the cross, despising the shame, and is set down at the right hand of the throne of God.

1 Tim. 6 [15]Which in his times he shall shew, who is the blessed, and only Potentate, the King of kings, and Lord of lords.

Heb. 2 [10]For it became him, for whom are all things, and by whom are all things, in bringing many sons unto glory, to make the captain of their salvation perfect through sufferings.

Eph. 2 [20]And are built upon the foundation of the apostles and prophets, Jesus Christ himself being the chief corner stone.

1 Pet. 5 [4]And when the chief shepherd shall appear, ye shall receive a crown of glory that fadeth not away.

Luke 1 [78]Through the tender mercy of our God, whereby the dayspring from on high hath visited us.

Hag. 2 [7]And I will shake all nations, and the desire of all nations shall come: and I will fill this house with glory, saith the LORD of hosts.

Matt. 1 [23]Behold, a virgin shall be with child, and shall bring forth a son, and they shall call his name Emmanual, which, being interpreted is, God with us.

Col. 1 [18]And he is the head of the body, the church: who is the beginning, the firstborn from the dead; that in all things he might have the preeminence.

Heb. 1 [2]Hath in these last days spoken unto us by his Son, whom he hath appointed heir of all things, by whom also he made the worlds.

Mark 1 [24]Saying, Let us alone, what have we to do with thee, thou Jesus of Nazareth? Art thou come to destroy us? I know thee who thou art, the holy One of God.

Luke 1 [69]And hath raised up an horn of salvation for us, in the house of his servant David.

John 8 [58]Jesus said unto them, Verily, verily, I say unto you, Before Abraham was, I am.

Matt. 1 [21]And she shall bring forth a son, and thou shalt call his name Jesus: for he shall save his people from their sins.

Acts 7 [52]Which of the prophets have not your fathers persecuted? And they have slain them which shewed before of the coming of the Just One, of whom ye have been now the betrayers and murderers.

Matt. 2 [2]Saying, Where is he that is born King of the Jews? for we have seen his star in the east, and are come to worship him.

John 1 [29]The next day John seeth Jesus coming unto him, and saith, Behold the Lamb of God, which taketh away the sin of the world!

Rev. 5 [5]And one of the elders saith unto me, Weep not: behold, the Lion of the tribe of Juda, the Root of David, hath prevailed to open the book, and to loose the seven seals thereof.

1 Cor. 2 [8]Which none of the princes of this world knew: for had they known it, they would not have crucified the Lord of glory.

Rev. 15 [3]And they sing the song of Moses the servant of God, and the song of the Lamb, saying, Great and marvellous are thy works, Lord God Almighty; just and true are thy ways, thou King of saints.

Jer. 23 [6]In his days Judah shall be saved, and Israel shall dwell safely: and this is his name whereby he shall be called, THE LORD OUR RIGHTEOUSNESS.

1 Tim. 2 [5]For there is one God, and one mediator between God and man, the man Christ Jesus.

John 1 [41]He first findeth his own brother Simon, and saith unto him, We have found the Messias, which is, being interpreted, the Christ.

Isa. 60 [16]Thou shalt also suck the milk of the Gentiles, and shalt suck the breast of kings: and thou shalt know that I the LORD am thy Saviour and thy Redeemer, the mighty One of Jacob.

Rev. 22 [16]I Jesus have sent mine angel, to testify unto you these things in the churches. I am the root and the offspring of David, and the bright and morning star.

Matt. 2 [23]And he came and dwelt in a city called Nazareth, that it might be fulfilled which was spoken by the prophets, He shall be called a Nazarene.

Acts 3 [15]And killed the Prince of life, whom God hath raised from the dead, whereof we are witnesses.

Luke 24 [19]And he said unto them, What things? And they said unto him, Concerning Jesus of Nazareth, which was a prophet, mighty in deed and word before God, and all the people.

John 11 [25]Jesus said unto her, I am the resurrection, and the life: he that believeth in me, though he were dead, yet shall he live.

2 Pet. 2 [20]For if after they have escaped the pollutions of the world through the knowledge of the Lord and Saviour Jesus Christ, they are again entangled therein, and overcome, the latter end is worse with them than the beginning.

John 14 [6]Jesus saith unto him, I am the way, the truth, and the life: no man cometh unto the Father, but by me.

John 1 [1]In the beginning was the Word, and the Word was with God, and the Word was God.

False Christs

Matt. 24 [4]And Jesus answered, and said unto them, Take heed that no man deceive you. [5]For many shall come in my name, saying, I am Christ: and shall deceive many. [24]For there shall arise false Christs, and false prophets, and shall shew great signs and wonders: insomuch that (if it were possible), they shall deceive the very elect.

2 Thess. 2 [8]And then shall that Wicked be revealed, whom the Lord shall consume with the spirit of his mouth, and shall destroy with the brightness of his coming: [9]Even him, whose coming is after the working of Satan with all power and signs and lying wonders.

CHRISTIAN

[kris′chan, kris′ti an] The name given to the followers of Christ. It is found only three times in the New Testament. The only information we have of its origin is the statement in *Acts 11:26* which tells us that "the disciples were called Christians first in Antioch." It appears that the name was not widely used by Christians themselves until the middle of the second century AD, and then chiefly by writers who were trying to convince pagan readers of the truth of Christianity. According to an early Roman historian, however, the disciples were called Christians by the populace of Rome as early as the time of Nero. It is quite probable that the name was originally given by non-Christian Gentiles.

SCRIPTURE

Acts 11 [26]And the disciples were called Christians first in Antioch.

Acts 26 [28]Then Agrippa said unto Paul, Almost thou persuadest me to be a Christian.

1 Pet. 4 [16]Yet if any man suffer as a Christian, let him not be ashamed; but let him glorify God on this behalf.

CHRISTMAS

[krist'mas] A religious holiday, celebrated on December 25, commemorating the birth of Jesus. The word is derived from the medieval *Christes Masse*, the mass of Christ. The birth of Christ was not an object of celebration until the fourth century. As it was impossible to fix the date of the nativity, it was celebrated on the same day as the pagan Mithraic rites of the birth of the Sun and at the close of the Roman festival called the Saturnalia, held in mid-December. As is the case with the date, most of the customs associated with Christmas were not originally Christian. The merry-making, the feasting, the candles, and the giving of gifts have their origin in the Roman Saturnalia. The Yule log and the wassail bowl may be traced to the German and Celtic tribes' celebration of the return of the sun at the time of the winter solstice in the festival of Yule. The Christmas tree did not come into wide usage until the 18th century, and there is considerable uncertainty as to its origin.

CHURCH

[chûrch] The English word "church" is derived from the Greek *kuriakon*, meaning "the lord's house" and referring to a building. This Greek word, however, does not occur in the Bible and in the New Testament the word "church" translates the Greek term *ecclesia*, which always refers to an assembly of people and not to a building. The term was first applied to the Christian community which had been gathered at Jerusalem by the preaching of the apostles, the acceptance of Jesus as the Christ, baptism, and the gift of the Holy Spirit (*Acts 2:37-41*). As the gospel spread out from Jerusalem the word was used to signify both the local Christian community (*Acts 11:26, 13:1; 1 Cor. 11:18*, etc.) and the whole people of God (*1 Cor. 12:12; Eph. 1: 22; Col. 1:18*, etc). The church originates in the redemptive act of God in Christ and lives as a community in which the Spirit of Christ is truly active.

Of the numerous designations the church receives in the New Testament, the most suggestive is the "Body of Christ" (*Eph. 1:22-23; Col. 1:18; 1 Cor. 12*). This suggests the intimate relationship between members of the church with one another and with Christ their Head. They are unified in the one Baptism, one Supper, and one Spirit which furnishes the whole body with power, peace, hope, and love. As the head of the body, Christ rules over it, cares for it, and sanctifies it. As members in this spiritual body, Christians share in the power of the resurrection and the promised redemption and utilize their several gifts in an interdependent manner to nourish the whole.

See ELDER, DEACON, MINISTER, etc.

SCRIPTURE

The Body of Christ

Eph. 1 [22]And hath put all things under his feet, and gave him to be the head over all things to the church, [23]Which is his body, the fulness of him that filleth all in all.

Col. 1 [24]Who now rejoice in my sufferings for you, and fill up that which is behind of the afflictions of Christ in my flesh for his body's sake, which is the church:

Christ the Head of the Church

John 15 [4]Abide in me, and I in you. As the branch cannot bear fruit of itself, except it abide in the vine; no more can ye, except ye abide in me. 5I am the vine, ye are the branches: He that abideth in me, and I in him, the same bringeth forth much fruit: for without me ye can do nothing. 6If a man abide not in me, he is cast forth as a branch, and is withered; and men gather them, and cast them into the fire, and they are burned. 7If ye abide in me, and my words abide in you, ye shall ask what ye will, and it shall be done unto you. 8Herein is my Father glorified, that ye bear much fruit; so shall ye be my disciples.

Eph. 1 22Hath put all things under his feet, and gave him to be the head over all things to the church, 23Which is his body, the fulness of him that filleth all in all.

Eph. 2 20Are built upon the foundation of the apostles and prophets, Jesus Christ himself being the chief corner stone; 21In whom all the building fitly framed together groweth unto an holy temple in the Lord: 22In whom ye also are builded together for an habitation of God through the Spirit.

Eph. 4 15Speaking the truth in love, may grow up into him in all things, which is the head, even Christ:

Eph. 5 23For the husband is the head of the wife, even as Christ is the head of the church: and he is the saviour of the body. 24Therefore as the church is subject unto Christ, so let the wives be to their own husbands in every thing. 25Husbands, love your wives, even as Christ also loved the church, and gave himself for it; 26That he might sanctify and cleanse it with the washing of water by the word, 27That he might present it to himself a glorious church, not having spot, or wrinkle, or any such thing; but that it should be holy and without blemish. 28So ought men to love their wives as their own bodies. He that loveth his wife loveth himself. 29For no man ever yet hated his own flesh, but nourisheth and cherisheth it, even as the Lord the church: 30For we are members of his body, of his flesh, and of his bones. 31For this cause shall a man leave his father and mother, and shall be joined unto his wife, and they two shall be one flesh. 32This is a great mystery: but I speak concerning Christ and the church.

Col. 1 13Hath translated us into the kingdom of his dear Son: 18He is the head of the body, the church: who is the beginning, the firstborn from the dead; that in all things he might have the preeminence.

Col. 2 10And ye are complete in him, which is the head of all principality and power: 19The Head, from which all the body by joints and bands having nourishment ministered, and knit together, increaseth with the increase of God.

Divinely Established

Matt. 16 18And I say also unto thee, That thou art Peter, and upon this rock I will build my church; and the gates of hell shall not prevail against it.

Eph. 2 20And are built upon the foundation of the apostles and prophets, Jesus Christ himself being the chief corner stone; 21In whom all the building fitly framed together groweth unto an holy temple in the Lord: 22In whom ye also are builded together for an habitation of God through the Spirit.

Government of the Church

Acts 11 22Tidings of these things came unto the ears of the church which was in Jerusalem: and they sent forth Barnabas, that he should go as far as Antioch.

29The disciples, every man according to his ability, determined to send relief unto the brethren which dwelt in Judaea: 30Which also they did, and sent it to the elders by the hands of Barnabas and Saul.

Acts 13 [1]There were in the church that was at Antioch certain prophets and teachers; as Barnabas, and Simeon, . . . [3]When they had fasted and prayed, and laid their hands on them, they sent them away.

[5]They had also John to their minister.

Acts 14 [23]When they had ordained them elders in every church, and had prayed with fasting, they commended them to the Lord,

Acts 15 [1]And certain men which came down from Judaea taught the brethren, and said, Except ye be circumcised after the manner of Moses, ye cannot be saved. [2]When therefore Paul and Barnabas had no small dissension and disputation with them, they determined that Paul and Barnabas, and certain other of them, should go up to Jerusalem unto the apostles and elders about this question.

Acts 20 [17]From Miletus he sent to Ephesus, and called the elders of the church.

[28]Take heed therefore unto yourselves, and to all the flock, over the which the Holy Ghost hath made you overseers, to feed the church of God, which he hath purchased with his own blood.

1 Cor. 12 [5]There are differences of administrations, but the same Lord. [28]God hath set some in the church, first apostles, secondarily prophets, thirdly teachers, after that miracles, then gifts of healings, helps, governments, diversities of tongues.

1 Cor. 14 [26]How is it then, brethren? when ye come together, every one of you hath a psalm, hath a doctrine, hath a tongue, hath a revelation, hath an interpretation. Let all things be done unto edifying. [33]God is not the author of confusion, but of peace, as in all churches of the saints. [40]Let all things be done decently and in order.

1 Tim. 3 [1]If a man desire the office of a bishop, he desireth a good work. [2]A bishop then must be blameless, . . . [13]For they that have used the office of a deacon will purchase to themselves a good degree, and great boldness in the faith which is in Christ Jesus.

1 Tim. 4 [14]Neglect not the gift that is in thee, which was given thee by prophecy, with the laying on of the hands of the presbytery.

1 Tim. 5 [1]Rebuke not an elder, but entreat him as a father; and the younger men as brethren; [17]Let the elders that rule well be counted worthy of double honour, especially they who labour in the word and doctrine. [22]Lay hands suddenly on no man, neither be partaker of other men's sins:

Tit. 1 [5]For this cause left I thee in Crete, that thou shouldest set in order the things that are wanting, and ordain elders in every city, as I had appointed thee:

Heb. 13 [17]Obey them that have the rule over you, and submit yourselves: [24]Salute all them that have the rule over you, and all the saints.

Jas. 5 [14]Is any sick among you? let him call for the elders of the church; and let them pray over him, anointing him with oil in the name of the Lord: [15]And the prayer of faith shall save the sick,

1 Pet. 5 [1]The elders which are among you I exhort, who am also an elder, . . . [2]Feed the flock of God which is among you, taking the oversight thereof, not by constraint, but willingly; not for filthy lucre, but of a ready mind; [3]Neither as being lords over God's heritage, but being ensamples to the flock.

Discipline in the Church

Matt. 18 [15]Moreover if thy brother shall trespass against thee, go and tell him his fault between thee and him alone: if he shall hear thee, thou hast gained thy brother. [16]But if he will not hear thee, then take with thee one or two more, that in the mouth of two or three witnesses every word may be established. [17]And if he shall neglect to hear them, tell it unto the church: but if he neglect to hear the church, let him be unto thee as an heathen man and a publican. [18]Verily I say unto you, Whatsoever ye shall bind on earth shall be bound in heaven: and whatsoever ye shall loose on earth shall be loosed in heaven.

1 Cor. 5 [1]It is reported commonly that there is fornication among you, and such fornication as is not so much as named among the Gentiles, that one should have his father's wife. [2]Ye are puffed up, and have not rather mourned, that he that hath done this deed might be taken away from among you. [4]In the name of our Lord Jesus Christ, when ye are gathered together, and my spirit, with the power of our Lord Jesus Christ, [5]To deliver such an one unto Satan for the destruction of the flesh, that the spirit may be saved in the day of the Lord Jesus. [6]Your glorying is not good. Know ye not that a little leaven leaveneth the whole lump? [7]Purge out therefore the old leaven, that ye may be a new lump, as ye are unleavened. [11]I have written unto you not to keep company, if any man that is called a brother be a fornicator, or covetous, or an idolater, or a railer, or a drunkard, or an extortioner; with such an one no not to eat. [12]What have I to do to judge them also that are without? do not ye judge them that are within? [13]Therefore put away from among yourselves that wicked person.

2 Cor. 2 [6]Sufficient to such a man is this punishment, which was inflicted of many. [7]Ye ought rather to forgive him, and comfort him, lest perhaps such a one should be swallowed up with overmuch sorrow. [8]Wherefore I beseech you that ye would confirm your love toward him. [10]To whom ye forgive any thing, I forgive also: for if I forgave any thing, to whom I forgave it, for your sakes forgave I it in the person of Christ; [11]Lest Satan should get an advantage of us: for we are not ignorant of his devices.

1 Thess. 5 [14]Now we exhort you, brethren, warn them that are unruly, comfort the feebleminded, support the weak, be patient toward all men.

2 Thess. 3 [6]We command you, brethren, in the name of our Lord Jesus Christ, that ye withdraw yourselves from every brother that walketh disorderly, and not after the tradition which he received of us. [14]If any man obey not our word by this epistle, note that man, and have no company with him, that he may be ashamed. [15]Yet count him not as an enemy, but admonish him as a brother.

1 Tim. 5 [1]Rebuke not an elder, but entreat him as a father; and the younger men as brethren; [2]The elder women as mothers; the younger as sisters, with all purity. [19]Against an elder receive not an accusation, but before two or three witnesses. [20]Them that sin rebuke before all, that others also may fear.

Membership in the Church

Acts 2 [41]Then they that gladly received his word were baptized: and the same day there were added unto them about three thousand souls. [47]Praising God, and having favour with all the people. And the Lord added to the church daily such as should be saved.

Acts 4 [4]Howbeit many of them which heard the word believed; and the number of the men was about five thousand.

Acts 5 [14]And believers were the more

added to the Lord, multitudes both of men and women.

Members of Church Interdependent

1 Cor. 12 [12]For as the body is one, and hath many members, and all the members of that one body, being many, are one body: so also is Christ. [13]For by one Spirit are we all baptized into one body, whether we be Jews or Gentiles, whether we be bond or free; and have been all made to drink into one Spirit. [14]For the body is not one member, but many. [15]If the foot shall say, Because I am not the hand, I am not of the body; is it therefore not of the body? [16]And if the ear shall say, Because I am not the eye, I am not of the body; is it therefore not of the body? [17]If the whole body were an eye, where were the hearing? If the whole were hearing, where were the smelling? [18]But now hath God set the members every one of them in the body, as it hath pleased him. [19]And if they were all one member, where were the body? [20]But now are they many members, yet but one body. [21]And the eye cannot say unto the hand, I have no need of thee: nor again the head to the feet, I have no need of you. [22]Nay, much more those members of the body, which seem to be more feeble, are necessary: [23]And those members of the body, which we think to be less honourable, upon these we bestow more abundant honour; and our uncomely parts have more abundant comeliness. [24]For our comely parts have no need; but God hath tempered the body together, having given more abundant honour to that part which lacked: [25]That there should be no schism in the body; but that the members should have the same care one for another. [26]And whether one member suffer, all the members suffer with it; or one member be honoured, all the members rejoice with it. [27]Now ye are the body of Christ, and members in particular. [28]And God hath set some in the church, first apostles, secondarily prophets, thirdly teachers, after that miracles, then gifts of healings, helps, governments, diversities of tongues.

Eph. 4 [25]We are members one of another.

Eph. 5 [30]We are members of his body, of his flesh, and of his bones.

Unity of the Church

John 10 [16]Other sheep I have, which are not of this fold: them also I must bring, and they shall hear my voice; and there shall be one fold, and one shepherd.

John 17 [11]Holy Father, keep through thine own name those whom thou hast given me, that they may be one, as we are. [21]That they all may be one; as thou, Father, art in me, and I in thee, that they also may be one in us: that the world may believe that thou hast sent me. [22]And the glory which thou gavest me I have given them; that they may be one, even as we are one: [23]I in them, and thou in me, that they may be made perfect in one; and that the world may know that thou hast sent me, and hast loved them, as thou hast loved me.

Rom. 12 [4]As we have many members in one body, and all members have not the same office: [5]So we, being many, are one body in Christ, and every one members one of another.

1 Cor. 10 [17]We being many are one bread, and one body: for we are all partakers of that one bread.

1 Cor. 12 [5]There are differences of administrations, but the same Lord. [12]As the body is one, and hath many members, and all the members of that one body, being many, are one body: so also is Christ. [13]For by one Spirit are we all baptized into one body, whether we be Jews or Gentiles, whether we be bond or free; and have been all made to drink into one Spirit. [26]And whether one member suffer, all the members suffer with it; or one member be honoured, all the members rejoice with it. [27]Now ye are the body of Christ, and members in particular.

Gal. 3 [26]Ye are all the children of God by faith in Christ Jesus. [27]For as many of you as have been baptized into Christ have put on Christ. [28]There is neither Jew nor Greek, there is neither bond nor free, there is neither male nor female: for ye are all one in Christ Jesus.

Eph. 1 [10]That in the dispensation of the fulness of times he might gather together in one all things in Christ, both which are in heaven, and which are on earth; even in him:

Eph. 2 [14]For he is our peace, who hath made both one, and hath broken down the middle wall of partition between us; [15]Having abolished in his flesh the enmity, even the law of commandments contained in ordinances; for to make in himself of twain one new man, so making peace; [16]And that he might reconcile both unto God in one body by the cross, having slain the enmity thereby: [17]And came and preached peace to you which were afar off, and to them that were nigh. [18]For through him we both have access by one Spirit unto the Father. [19]Ye are no more strangers and foreigners, but fellowcitizens with the saints, and of the household of God; [21]In whom all the building fitly framed together groweth unto an holy temple in the Lord:

Eph. 3 [6]The Gentiles should be fellow heirs, and of the same body, and partakers of his promise in Christ by the gospel: [15]Of whom the whole family in heaven and earth is named,

Eph. 4 [4]There is one body, and one Spirit, even as ye are called in one hope of your calling; [5]One Lord, one faith, one baptism, [6]One God and Father of all, who is above all, and through all, and in you all. [12]For the perfecting of the saints, for the work of the ministry, for the edifying of the body of Christ: [13]Till we all come in the unity of the faith, and of the knowledge of the Son of God, unto a perfect man, unto the measure of the stature of the fulness of Christ: [16]From whom the whole body fitly joined together and compacted by that which every joint supplieth, according to the effectual working in the measure of every part, maketh increase of the body unto the edifying of itself in love. [25]We are members one of another.

Col. 3 [11]There is neither Greek nor Jew, circumcision nor uncircumcision, Barbarian, Scythian, bond nor free: but Christ is all, and in all. [15]Let the peace of God rule in your hearts, to the which also ye are called in one body;

CIRCUMCISION

[sûr kum sizh′un] The removal of the prepuce, or foreskin, a custom of ancient and unknown origin. It first appears in the Bible in the account of the ratification of the covenant between God and Abraham. In order to be included in the blessings of the covenant, every male child was to be circumcised, preferably on the eighth day after his birth. Slaves, whether homeborn or purchased, were circumcised (*Gen. 17:12-13*), and foreigners were required to be circumcised before they could participate in the passover celebration. The question of circumcision was the occasion of a long struggle in the early days of the Christian church. Some Jewish Christians felt that men could become Christians only by first becoming Jews; that is, by being circumcised. These so-called "Judaizers" caused the apostle Paul much difficulty in his Gentile missions and received his attention in several epistles. Circumcision is spoken of figuratively in several passages. Moses humbly assessed his abilities in describing himself as a man of "uncircumcised lips" (*Ex. 6:30*). Jeremiah charged his hearers with having uncircumcised ears and hearts, signifying the spiritual dross which acted as a hindrance to their reception and execution of God's will (*Jer. 6:10; 9:26*).

SCRIPTURE

Institution of Circumcision

Gen. 17 [10]This is my covenant, which ye shall keep, between me and you and thy seed after thee; Every man child among you shall be circumcised. [11]And ye shall circumcise the flesh of your foreskin; and it shall be a token of the covenant betwixt me and you. [12]And he that is eight days old shall be circumcised among you, every man child in your generations, he that is born in the house, or bought with money of any stranger, which is not of thy seed. [13]He that is born in thy house, and he that is bought with thy money, must needs be circumcised: and my covenant shall be in your flesh for an everlasting covenant. [14]And the uncircumcised man child whose flesh of his foreskin is not circumcised, that soul shall be cut off from his people; he hath broken my covenant.

Required for Observance of Passover

Ex. 12 [48]And when a stranger shall sojourn with thee, and will keep the passover to the LORD, let all his males be circumcised, and then let him come near and keep it; and he shall be as one that is born in the land: for no uncircumcised person shall eat thereof.

A Seal of Righteousness

Rom. 2 [25]For circumcision verily profiteth, if thou keep the law: but if thou be a breaker of the law, thy circumcision is made uncircumcision. [26]Therefore, if the uncircumcision keep the righteousness of the law, shall not his uncircumcision be counted for circumcision? [27]And shall not uncircumcision which is by nature, if it fulfil the law, judge thee, who by the letter and circumcision dost transgress the law? [28]For he is not a Jew, which is one outwardly; neither is that circumcision, which is outward in the flesh: [29]But he is a Jew, which is one inwardly; and circumcision is that of the heart, in the spirit, and not in the letter; whose praise is not of men, but of God.

Benefits and Obligations of Circumcision

Rom. 3 [1]What advantage then hath the Jew? or what profit is there of circumcision? [2]Much every way: chiefly, because that unto them were committed the oracles of God.

Rom. 4 [11]And he hath received the sign of circumcision, a seal of the righteousness of the faith which he had yet being uncircumcised: that he might be the father of all them that believe, though they be not circumcised; that righteousness might be imputed unto them also:

Gal. 5 [3]For I testify again to every man that is circumcised, that he is a debtor to do the whole law.

No Longer Necessary

Acts 15 [5]But there rose up certain of the sect of the Pharisees which believed, saying, That it was needful to circumcise them, and to command them to keep the law of Moses.

[6]And the apostles and elders came together for to consider of this matter. [7]And when there had been much disputing, Peter rose up, and said unto them, Men and brethren, ye know how that a good while ago God made choice among us, that the Gentiles by my mouth should hear the

word of the gospel, and believe. [8]And God, which knoweth the hearts, bare them witness, giving them the Holy Ghost, even as he did unto us; [9]And put no difference between us and them, purifying their hearts by faith. [10]Now therefore why tempt ye God, to put a yoke upon the neck of the disciples, which neither our fathers nor we were able to bear? [11]But we believe that through the grace of the Lord Jesus Christ we shall be saved, even as they.

Rom. 2 [25]For circumcision verily profiteth, if thou keep the law: but if thou be a breaker of the law, thy circumcision is made uncircumcision. [28]For he is not a Jew, which is one outwardly; neither is that circumcision, which is outward in the flesh:

Rom. 3 [30]Seeing it is one God, which shall justify the circumcision by faith, and uncircumcision through faith.

Rom. 4 [9]Cometh this blessedness then upon the circumcision only, or upon the uncircumcision also? for we say that faith was reckoned to Abraham for righteousness. [10]How was it then reckoned? when he was in circumcision, or in uncircumcision? Not in circumcision, but in uncircumcision. [11]And he received the sign of circumcision, a seal of the righteousness of the faith which he had yet being uncircumcised: that he might be the father of all them that believe, though they be not circumcised; that righteousness might be imputed unto them also:

1 Cor. 7 [18]Is any man called being circumcised? let him not become uncircumcised. Is any called in uncircumcision? let him not be circumcised. [19]Circumcision is nothing, and uncircumcision is nothing, but the keeping of the commandments of God.

Gal. 5 [2]Behold, I Paul say unto you, that if ye be circumcised, Christ shall profit you nothing. [3]For I testify again to every man that is circumcised, that he is a debtor to do the whole law. [4]Christ is become of no effect unto you, whosoever of you are justified by the law; ye are fallen from grace. [5]For we through the Spirit wait for the hope of righteousness by faith. [6]For in Jesus Christ neither circumcision availeth any thing, nor uncircumcision; but faith which worketh by love. [7]Ye did run well; who did hinder you that ye should not obey the truth? [8]This persuasion cometh not of him that calleth you. [9]A little leaven leaveneth the whole lump. [10]I have confidence in you through the Lord, that ye will be none otherwise minded: but he that troubleth you shall bear his judgment, whosoever he be. [11]And I, brethren, if I yet preach circumcision, why do I yet suffer persecution? then is the offence of the cross ceased.

Gal. 6 [13]For neither they themselves who are circumcised keep the law; but desire to have you circumcised, that they may glory in your flesh.

Eph. 2 [11]Wherefore remember, that ye being in time past Gentiles in the flesh, who are called Uncircumcision by that which is called the Circumcision in the flesh made by hands; [15]Having abolished in his flesh the enmity, even the law of commandments contained in ordinances; for to make in himself of twain one new man, so making peace;

Col. 3 [11]Where there is neither Greek nor Jew, circumcision nor uncircumcision, Barbarian, Scythian, bond nor free: but Christ is all, and in all.

CLAUDIUS I

[klôd′i us] Successor to Caius Caligula as Emperor of Rome, ruling AD 41-54. Claudius began his reign by issuing edicts restoring to the Jews rights which had originally been granted by Augustus and Tiberius, but which Caligula had revoked or altered. These edicts came partly as a result of his friendship with Herod Agrippa I, who had in some measure been responsible for his succession to the throne and whom he subsequently made king of Palestine. (*See* HEROD) In later years, probably about AD 50, Claudius expelled a number of Jews from Rome, among whom were Aquila and Priscilla (*Acts 18:2*), the faithful associates of the apostle Paul. (*See* AQUILA AND PRISCILLA) Claudius' reign was marked by a series of economic difficulties. Among these was the famine predicted by the prophet Agabus in *Acts 11:28*. Claudius died in AD 54 of poison administered by his fourth wife, Agrippina, mother of Nero. As a result of her machinations, Nero succeeded Claudius to the throne, despite the claims of the rightful heir, Britannicus.

CLEANNESS, UNCLEANNESS

[klēn′nes; un′klēn′nes] In the Old Testament "uncleanness" refers to people, animals, and objects, association with which renders a man unfit to approach God in worship until certain procedures of cleansing have been fulfilled. A similarity may be seen between this and the ideas of *tabu* which are found in other religions. The Old Testament lists four main types of uncleanness: (1) uncleanness connected with functions of reproductions, especially menstruation; (2) uncleanness connected with food; (3) uncleanness connected with leprosy; and (4) uncleanness connected with death.

"Cleanness" is simply the opposite of uncleanness. It does not imply any special dedication to God in the sense of "holiness", but simply indicates that the individual or object in question has no infectious quality. The clean person may freely approach God in worship.

See HOLINESS

REFERENCE: *Lev. 5:2, 3; 7:19-21; 17:15; 22:2-8.*

COLOSSAE

[kō los′ē] A city of Phrygia on the Lycus River, one of the tributaries of the Maeander River, in the neighborhood of Hierapolis and Laodicea. It was situated close to the great road which led from Ephesus to the Euphrates. Many of the Colossians apparently engaged in angel-worship. The most important of these angels and the protector of the city was Michael. This city was the home of Philemon, to whom Paul wrote the short epistle concerning the runaway slave Onesimus. The church at Colossae was apparently founded by Epaphras (*Col. 1:7*), and was the recipient of a letter from the apostle Paul, although he seems not to have visited there himself (*Col. 2: 1*).

See EPAPHRAS, ONESIMUS, PHILEMON

REFERENCE: The Epistle to the *Colossians.*

COMPASSION

[kom pash′un] Sorrow, pity, or feeling of sympathy elicited by the distress or misfortunes of another. The Bible enjoins Christians to cultivate compassion and mercy in emulation of God and Jesus.

SCRIPTURE

General

Job 6 14To him that is afflicted pity should be shewed from his friend; but he forsaketh the fear of the Almighty.

Psa. 35 13But as for me, when they were sick, my clothing was sackcloth: I humbled my soul with fasting; and my prayer returned into mine own bosom.

Zech. 7 9Thus speaketh the LORD of hosts, saying, Execute true judgment, and shew mercy and compassions every man to his brother.

Compassion of God

Ex. 22 27It shall come to pass, when he crieth unto me, that I will hear; for I am gracious.

Ex. 34 6The LORD, the LORD God, merciful and gracious, longsuffering, and abundant in goodness and truth, 7Keeping mercy for thousands, forgiving iniquity and transgression and sin.

Num. 14 [18]The LORD is longsuffering, and of great mercy, forgiving iniquity and transgression.

Judg. 10 [16]His soul was grieved for the misery of Israel.

2 Kin. 13 [23]The LORD was gracious unto them, and had compassion on them . . . and would not destroy them, neither cast he them from his presence as yet.

2 Kin. 14 [26]The LORD saw the affliction of Israel, that it was very bitter: for there was not any shut up, nor any left, nor any helper for Israel. [27]And the LORD said not that he would blot out the name of Israel from under heaven: but he saved them by the hand of Jeroboam.

Psa. 78 [38]But he, being full of compassion, forgave their iniquity, and destroyed them not; yea, many a time turned he his anger away, and did not stir up all his wrath.

Psa. 86 [15]Thou, O LORD, art a God full of compassion, and gracious, longsuffering, and plenteous in mercy and truth.

Compassion of Jesus

Matt. 15 [32]I have compassion on the multitude, because they continue with me now three days, and have nothing to eat: and I will not send them away fasting, lest they faint in the way.

Matt. 20 [34]So Jesus had compassion on them, and touched their eyes: and immediately their eyes received sight, and they followed him.

Mark 6 [34]And Jesus, when he came out, saw much people, and was moved with compassion toward them, because they were as sheep not having a shepherd: and he began to teach them many things.

Luke 7 [13]When the Lord saw her, he had compassion on her, and said unto her, Weep not.

Heb. 4 [15]We have not an high priest which cannot be touched with the feeling of our infirmities; but was in all points tempted like as we are, yet without sin.

Compassion Enjoined on Christians

Rom. 12 [15]Rejoice with them that do rejoice, and weep with them that weep.

Col. 3 [12]Put on therefore (as the elect of God, holy and beloved) bowels of mercies, kindness, humbleness of mind, meekness, longsuffering.

1 Pet. 3 [8]Finally be ye all of one mind, having compassion one of another, love as brethren, be pitiful, be courteous.

CONCEIT

[kon sēt′] Improper pride; an overweening estimate of one's self; excessive vanity. The Bible strongly warns against this attitude.

See HYPOCRISY, PRIDE

SCRIPTURE

Prov. 26 [5]Answer a fool according to his folly, lest he be wise in his own conceit. [12]Seest thou a man wise in his own conceit? there is more hope of a fool than of him. [16]The sluggard is wiser in his own conceit than seven men that can render a reason.

Prov. 28 [11]The rich man is wise in his own conceit; but the poor that hath understanding searcheth him out.

Isa. 5 [21]Woe unto them that are wise in their own eyes, and prudent in their own sight!

Jer. 9 [23]Thus saith the LORD, Let not the wise man glory in his wisdom, neither let the mighty man glory in his might, let not the rich man glory in his riches:

Rom. 12 [16]Be of the same mind one towards another. Mind not high things, but condescend to men of low estate. Be not wise in your own conceits.

CONCUBINAGE, CONCUBINE

[kon kū′bi nij, kon′kū bīn] Concubinage is the

act or practice of cohabiting without a legal marriage, as with a concubine, a woman retained by a man primarily for purposes of sexual gratification. Concubinage was not particularly frowned upon by the ancient Hebrews. King Solomon is said to have had seven hundred wives and three hundred concubines. Although the Greeks and Romans viewed concubinage as neither unlawful nor disgraceful, concubines were looked upon as inferior to legal wives and their children were not granted the same rights as the children born of a man's legal wives. Christianity brought an end to widespread concubinage in the western world.

CONDEMN, CONDEMNATION

[kon dem′] To pronounce to be wrong; to disapprove of; to declare the guilt of; to sentence; to doom.
[kon dem nā′shun] Act of condemning; censure; reprobation; also, the state of being condemned. In the Bible the chief use of these words is in reference to the sentence of sinners and unbelievers.

SCRIPTURE

Condemnation for Sin

Rom. 5 [12]Wherefore, as by one man sin entered into the world, and death by sin: and so death passed upon all men, for that all have sinned.

Rom. 6 [23]For the wages of sin is death; but the gift of God is eternal life through Jesus Christ our Lord.

John 3 [18]He that believeth on him, is not condemned: but he that believeth not, is condemned already, because he hath not believed in the name of the only begotten Son of God.

Matt. 23 [14]Woe unto you, scribes and Pharisees, hypocrites; for ye devour widows' houses, and for a pretence make long prayer; therefore ye shall receive the greater damnation.

Matt. 25 [46]And these shall go away into everlasting punishment: but the righteous into life eternal.

Deliverance from Condemnation

John 5 [24]Verily, verily, I say unto you, He that heareth my word, and believeth on him that sent me, hath everlasting life; and shall not come into condemnation; but is passed from death unto life.

Rom. 8 [1]There is therefore now no condemnation to them which are in Christ Jesus, who walk not after the flesh, but after the Spirit.

Self-condemnation

2 Sam. 24 [17]And David spake unto the LORD when he saw the angel that smote the people, and said, Lo, I have sinned, and I have done wickedly: but these sheep, what have they done? let thine hand, I pray thee, be against me, and against my father's house.

Job 9 [20]If I justify myself, mine own mouth shall condemn me: if I say, I am perfect, it shall also prove me perverse.

CONFESS

[kon fes′] In the Old Testament, to confess ordinarily meant to acknowledge one's sin. This involved acknowledgment of God as the true object of worship and service. This meaning is also found in the New Testament, but more often the word means to declare or admit that something is true, especially that Jesus is Lord and that he is the Son of God.

SCRIPTURE

Confession of Sin

Lev. 5 [5]And it shall be, when he shall be guilty in one of these things, that he shall confess that he hath sinned in that thing:

Lev. 16 [21]And Aaron shall lay both his hands upon the head of the live goat, and confess over him all the iniquities of the children of Israel, and all their transgressions in all their sins, putting them upon the head of the goat, and shall send him away by the hand of a fit man into the wilderness:

Jas. 5 [16]Confess your faults one to another, and pray one for another, that ye may be healed. The effectual fervent prayer of a righteous man availeth much.

1 John 1 [9]If we confess our sins, he is faithful and just to forgive us our sins, and to cleanse us from all unrighteousness.

Num. 21 [7]Therefore the people came to Moses, and said, We have sinned, for we have spoken against the LORD, and against thee; pray unto the LORD, that he take away the serpents from us. And Moses prayed for the people.

Josh. 7 [20]And Achan answered Joshua, and said, Indeed I have sinned against the LORD God of Israel, and thus and thus have I done.

1 Sam. 15 [24]And Saul said unto Samuel, I have sinned: for I have transgressed the commandment of the LORD, and thy words: because I feared the people, and obeyed their voice.

Ezra 9 [6]And said, O my God, I am ashamed and blush to lift up my face to thee, my God: for our iniquities are increased over our head, and our trespass is grown up unto the heavens.

Confession of Christ

Matt. 10 [32]Whosoever therefore shall confess me before men, him will I confess also before my Father which is heaven.

John 12 [42]Nevertheless, among the chief rulers also, many believed on him; but because of the Pharisees they did not confess him, lest they should be put out of the synagogue.

Rom. 10 [9]That if thou shalt confess with thy mouth the Lord Jesus, and shalt believe in thine heart that God hath raised him from the dead, thou shalt be saved.

1 John 2 [23]Whosoever denieth the Son, the same hath not the Father: (but) he that acknowledgeth the Son hath the Father also.

1 John 4 [2]Hereby know ye the Spirit of God: Every spirit that confesseth that Jesus Christ is come in the flesh is of God:
[3]And every spirit that confesseth not that Jesus Christ is come in the flesh is not of God: and this is that spirit of antichrist, whereof ye have heard that it should come; and even now already is it in the world.

Matt. 14 [33]Then they that were in the ship came and worshipped him, saying, Of a truth thou art the Son of God.

Matt. 16 [16]And Simon Peter answered and said, Thou art the Christ, the Son of the living God.

John 20 [28]And Thomas answered and said unto him, My Lord and my God.

1 Tim. 6 [12]Fight the good fight of faith, lay hold on eternal life, whereunto thou art also called, and hast professed a good profession before many witnesses.

CONQUEST

[kon′kwest] The act of conquering; gaining or acquiring by force of arms mastery over a people or a territory. As used in Biblical scholarship, the term refers to the taking of the land of Canaan by the Israelites after the exodus from Egypt. Archaeological evidence indicates the conquest took place in the last half of the thirteenth century BC. (*See* EXODUS for explanation of the determination of this date.) After being thrown back in their attempt to enter Canaan from the south (*Num. 13-14*), the Israelites spent about forty years wandering in the wilderness around Kadesh-Barnea. Finally, they decided to enter Canaan from the Transjordan area. When they were denied direct passage by Edom, they went around it and Moab to the Arnon River. The kingdom of Sihon stood between them and the

Jordan River, and this king also refused them passage; this time, however, the Israelites attacked and defeated Sihon and Og, a neighboring king. It was at this juncture that Balak king of Moab summoned Balaam to pronounce a curse on the Israelites. (*See* BALAAM) Upon crossing the Jordan, the Israelites, under the command of Joshua, first attacked Jericho (*Josh. 6*), and then Ai (*Josh. 8*). The territory of the Gibeonites would likely have been next had they not deceived the Israelites into an alliance by a clever stratagem (*Josh. 9*).

These preliminary victories enabled the Israelites to get a foothold in Gilead and Western Palestine; they used this as a base for a southern campaign which saw the defeat of the city-states of Lachish, Eglon, and Hebron (*Josh. 11*)— a campaign amply confirmed by archaeology. The southern campaign was followed by a foray into Galilee in which the fortified city of Hazor was destroyed and considerable territory gained for Israel (*Josh. 11*).

The common impression one receives from reading the Biblical account of the conquest is that the whole of Palestine was devastated in one magnificent campaign, but this was clearly not the case. There is practically no mention of the conquest of central Palestine, apart from Jericho and Ai; Jerusalem itself was completely avoided on the southern campaign; furthermore, in *Josh. 13*, we have a list of areas which remained to be conquered when Joshua was an old man. Archaeological evidence indicates that after the great campaign of the thirteenth century BC, the next two centuries witnessed a period of gradual but continued reduction of the power of the Canaanite city-states until Israel finally gained complete ascendancy.

See CANAAN, EXODUS

SCRIPTURE

Defeat at Kadesh-Barnea

Num. 14 [40]And they rose up early in the morning, and gat them up into the top of the mountain, saying, Lo, we be here, and will go up unto the place which the LORD hath promised: for we have sinned. [41]And Moses said, Wherefore now do ye transgress the commandment of the LORD? but it shall not prosper. [42]Go not up, for the LORD is not among you; that ye be not smitten before your enemies. [43]For the Amalekites and the Canaanites are there before you, and ye shall fall by the sword: because ye are turned away from the LORD, therefore the LORD will not be with you. [44]But they presumed to go up unto the hill top: nevertheless the ark of the covenant of the LORD, and Moses, departed not out of the camp. [45]Then the Amalekites came down, and the Canaanites which dwelt in that hill, and smote them, and discomfited them, even unto Hormah.

Passage Refused by Edom

Num. 20 [14]And Moses sent messengers from Kadesh unto the king of Edom, Thus saith thy brother Israel, Thou knowest all the travail that hath befallen us: [17]Let us pass, I pray thee, through thy country: we will not pass through the fields, or through the vineyards, neither will we drink of the water of the wells: we will go by the king's high way, we will not turn to the right hand nor to the left, until we have passed thy borders. [18]And Edom said unto him, Thou shalt not pass by me, lest I come out against thee with the sword. [19]And the children of Israel said unto him, We will go by the high way: and if I and my cattle drink of thy water, then I will pay for it: I will only, without doing any thing else, go through on my feet. [20]And he said, Thou shalt not go through. And Edom came out against him with much people, and with a strong hand. [21]Thus Edom refused to give Israel passage through his border: wherefore Israel turned away from him.

Defeat of Sihon and Og

Num. 21 [23]And Sihon would not suffer

Israel to pass through his border: but Sihon gathered all his people together, and went out against Israel into the wilderness: and he came to Jahaz, and fought against Israel. [24]And Israel smote him with the edge of the sword, and possessed his land from Arnon unto Jabbok, even unto the children of Ammon: for the border of the children of Ammon was strong.

[33]And they turned and went up by the way of Bashan: and Og the king of Bashan went out against them, he, and all his people, to the battle at Edrei. [34]And the LORD said unto Moses, Fear him not: for I have delivered him into thy hand, and all his people, and his land; and thou shalt do to him as thou didst unto Sihon king of the Amorites, which dwelt at Heshbon. [35]So they smote him, and his sons, and all his people, until there was none left him alive: and they possessed his land.

The Fall of Jericho

Josh. 6 [12]And Joshua rose early in the morning, and the priests took up the ark of the LORD. [13]And seven priests bearing seven trumpets of rams horns before the ark of the LORD went on continually, and blew with the trumpets: and the armed men went before them; but the rearward came after the ark of the LORD, the priests going on, and blowing with the trumpets. [14]And the second day they compassed the city once, and returned into the camp. So they did six days. [15]And it came to pass on the seventh day, that they rose early about the dawning of the day, and compassed the city after the same manner seven times: only on that day they compassed the city seven times. [16]And it came to pass at the seventh time, when the priests blew with the trumpets, Joshua said unto the people, Shout; for the LORD hath given you the city.

[17]And the city shall be accursed, even it, and all that are therein, to the LORD: only Rahab the harlot shall live, she and all that are with her in the house, because she hid the messengers that we sent. [18]And ye, in any wise keep yourselves from the accursed thing, lest ye make yourselves accursed, when ye take of the accursed thing, and make the camp of Israel a curse, and trouble it. [19]But all the silver, and gold, and vessels of brass and iron, are consecrated unto the LORD: they shall come into the treasury of the LORD. [20]So the people shouted when the priests blew with the trumpets: and it came to pass, when the people heard the sound of the trumpet, and the people shouted with a great shout, that the wall fell down flat, so that the people went up into the city, every man straight before him, and they took the city. [21]And they utterly destroyed all that was in the city, both man and woman, young and old, and ox, and sheep, and ass, with the edge of the sword.

Defeat of Ai

Josh. 8 [9]Joshua therefore sent them forth: and they went to lie in ambush, and abode between Bethel and Ai, on the west side of Ai: but Joshua lodged that night among the people. [10]And Joshua rose up early in the morning, and numbered the people, and went up, he and the elders of Israel, before the people to Ai. [11]And all the people, even the people of war that were with him, went up, and drew nigh, and came before the city, and pitched on the north side of Ai: now there was a valley between them and Ai. [12]And he took about five thousand men, and set them to lie in ambush between Bethel and Ai, on the west side of the city. [13]And when they had set the people, even all the host that was on the north of the city, and their liers

in wait on the west of the city, Joshua went
that night into the midst of the valley.
14 And it came to pass, when the king of
Ai saw it, that they hasted and rose up
early, and the men of the city went out
against Israel to battle, he and all his people, at a time appointed, before the plain;
but he wist not that there were liers in ambush against him behind the city. 15 And
Joshua and all Israel made as if they were
beaten before them, and fled by the way
of the wilderness. 16 And all the people
that were in Ai were called together to
pursue after them: and they pursued after
Joshua, and were drawn away from the
city. 17 And there was not a man left in Ai
or Bethel, that went not out after Israel:
and they left the city open, and pursued
after Israel. 18 And the LORD said unto
Joshua, Stretch out the spear that is in thy
hand toward Ai: for I will give it into thine
hand. And Joshua stretched out the spear
that he had in his hand toward the city.
19 And the ambush arose quickly out of
their place, and they ran as soon as he had
stretched out his hand: and they entered
into the city, and took it, and hasted and
set the city on fire. 25 And so it was, that
all that fell that day, both of men and
women, were twelve thousand, even all
the men of Ai. 28 And Joshua burnt Ai, and
made it a heap for ever, even a desolation
unto this day.

The Southern Campaign

Josh. 10 28 And that day Joshua took
Makkedah, and smote it with the edge of
the sword, and the king thereof he utterly
destroyed, them, and all the souls that
were therein; he let none remain: and he
did to the king of Makkedah as he did unto
the king of Jericho. 29 Then Joshua passed
from Makkedah, and all Israel with him,
unto Libnah, and fought against Libnah:
30 And the LORD delivered it also, and the
king thereof, into the hand of Israel; and
he smote it with the edge of the sword,
and all the souls that were therein; he let
none remain in it; but did unto the king
thereof as he did unto the king of Jericho.
31 And Joshua passed from Libnah, and
all Israel with him, unto Lachish, and encamped against it, and fought against it:
32 And the LORD delivered Lachish into the
hand of Israel, which took it on the second
day, and smote it with the edge of the
sword, and all the souls that were therein,
according to all that he had done to Libnah.
33 Then Horam king of Gezer came up to
help Lachish; and Joshua smote him and
his people, until he had left him none remaining.
34 And from Lachish Joshua passed unto
Eglon, and all Israel with him; and they
encamped against it, and fought against it:
35 And they took it on that day, and smote
it with the edge of the sword, and all the
souls that were therein he utterly destroyed that day, according to all that he
had done to Lachish. 36 And Joshua went
up from Eglon, and all Israel with him,
unto Hebron; and they fought against it:
37 And they took it, and smote it with the
edge of the sword, and the king thereof,
and all the cities thereof, and all the souls
that were therein; he left none remaining,
according to all that he had done to Eglon;
but destroyed it utterly, and all the souls
that were therein.
38 And Joshua returned, and all Israel
with him, to Debir; and fought against it:
39 And he took it, and the king thereof, and
all the cities thereof; and they smote them
with the edge of the sword, and utterly destroyed all the souls that were therein; he
left none remaining: as he had done to Hebron, so he did to Debir, and to the king

thereof; as he had done also to Libnah, and to her king.

[40]So Joshua smote all the country of the hills, and of the south, and of the vale, and of the springs, and all their kings: he left none remaining, but utterly destroyed all that breathed, as the LORD God of Israel commanded. [41]And Joshua smote them from Kadesh-barnea even unto Gaza, and all the country of Goshen, even unto Gibeon.

Defeat of Hazor in Galilee

Josh. 11 [10]And Joshua at that time turned back, and took Hazor, and smote the king thereof with the sword: for Hazor beforetime was the head of all those kingdoms. [11]And they smote all the souls that were therein with the edge of the sword, utterly destroying them: there was not any left to breathe: and he burnt Hazor with fire.

CONSCIENCE

[kon′shens] The basic meaning of this word is "co-knowledge" It refers to the faculty in man which serves as a second consciousness alongside the primary or original consciousness of an act or thought. The conscience judges the moral character of one's actions, approving or censuring according to what it considers an absolute standard of good and evil. It is possible for the conscience to be imperfectly informed or, even through persistent sinfulness, to become "seared with a hot iron." For this reason, the final court of appeals for one's actions is not the conscience, but the Word of God.

SCRIPTURE

Conscience Convicts of Sin

Gen. 3 [10]And he said, I heard thy voice in the garden: and I was afraid, because I was naked; and I hid myself.

Gen. 42 [21]And they said one to another, We are verily guilty concerning our brother, in that we saw the anguish of his soul, when he besought us, and we would not hear; therefore is this distress come upon us.

1 Sam. 24 [5]And it came to pass afterward, that David's heart smote him, because he had cut off Saul's skirt.

Prov. 20 [27]The spirit of man is the candle of the LORD, searching all the inward parts.

Matt. 27 [3]Then Judas, which had betrayed him, when he saw that he was condemned, repented himself, and brought again the thirty pieces of silver to the chief priests and elders.

John 8 [9]And they which heard it, being convicted by their own conscience, went out one by one, beginning at the eldest, even unto the last: and Jesus was left alone, and the woman standing in the midst.

Rom. 2 [15]Which shew the work of the law written in their hearts, their conscience also bearing witness, and their thoughts the mean while accusing or else excusing one another.

Conscience Purified

Heb. 9 [14]How much more shall the blood of Christ, who through the eternal Spirit offered himself without spot to God, purge your conscience from dead works, to serve the living God?

Heb. 10 [2]For then would they not have ceased to be offered, because that the worshippers once purged should have had no more conscience of sins?

Heb. 2 [22]Let us draw near with a true heart in full assurance of faith, having our hearts sprinkled from an evil conscience, and our bodies washed with pure water.

A Good Conscience

1 Tim. 1 [19]Holding faith, and a good

conscience, which some having put away concerning faith, have made shipwreck.

1 Tim. 3 [9]Holding the mystery of the faith in a pure conscience.

2 Tim. 1 [3]I thank God, whom I serve from my forefathers with pure conscience, that without ceasing I have remembrance of thee in my prayers night and day.

Heb. 13 [18]Pray for us: for we trust we have a good conscience in all things, willing to live honestly.

1 Pet. 3 [16]Having a good conscience, that whereas they speak evil of you, as of evildoers, they may be ashamed that falsely accuse your good conversation in Christ.

Effects of Good Conscience

Acts 24 [16]And herein do I exercise myself to have always a conscience void of offence toward God, and toward men.

2 Cor. 1 [12]For our rejoicing is this, the testimony of our conscience, that in simplicity and godly sincerity, not with fleshly wisdom, but by the grace of God, we have had our conversation in the world, and more abundantly to you-ward.

2 Pet. 2 [19]For this is thankworthy, if a man for conscience toward God endure grief, suffering wrongfully.

Deformed or Dead Conscience

Prov. 16 [25]There is a way that seemeth right unto a man, but the end thereof are the ways of death.

Jer. 6 [15]Were they ashamed when they had committed abomination? nay, they were not at all ashamed, neither could they blush: therefore they shall fall among them that fall: at the time that I visit them they shall be cast down, saith the LORD.

Eph. 4 [17]This I say therefore, and testify in the Lord, that ye henceforth walk not as other Gentiles walk, in the vanity of their mind.

1 Tim. 4 [2]Speaking lies in hypocrisy; having their conscience seared with a hot iron;

Tit. 1 [15]Unto the pure all things are pure: but unto them that are defiled and unbelieving is nothing pure; but even their mind and conscience is defiled.

Respect for Another's Conscience

1 Cor. 10 [27]If any of them that believe not bid you to a feast, and ye be disposed to go, whatsoever is set before you, eat, asking no question for conscience sake.
[28]But if any man say unto you, This is offered in sacrifice unto idols, eat not for his sake that shewed it, and for conscience sake. The earth is the Lord's and the fulness thereof. [29]Conscience I say, not thine own, but of the other's: for why is my liberty judged of another man's conscience?

CONSOLATION

[kon sō lā′shun] Comfort and refreshment of spirit in time of distress of mind or body; the alleviation of misery. No other book contains as much consolation for the afflicted, in either mind, body, or estate, as the Bible.

SCRIPTURE

Deut. 33 [27]The eternal God is thy refuge, and underneath are the everlasting arms: and he shall thrust out the enemy from before thee; and shall say, Destroy them.

Psa. 9 [9]The LORD also will be a refuge for the oppressed, a refuge in times of trouble. [10]And they that know thy name will put their trust in thee: for thou, LORD, hast not forsaken them that seek thee.

Psa. 23 [4]Yea, though I walk through the valley of the shadow of death, I will fear no evil: for thou art with me; thy rod and thy staff they comfort me.

Psa. 30 [5]For his anger endureth but a moment; in his favour is life: weeping may endure for a night, but joy cometh in the morning.

Psa. 34 [19]Many are the afflictions of the righteous; but the LORD delivereth him out of them all.

Psa. 46 [1]God is our refuge and strength, a very present help in trouble.

Psa. 55 [22]Cast thy burden upon the LORD, and he shall sustain thee; he shall never suffer the righteous to be moved.

Psa. 62 [8]Trust in him at all times; ye people, pour out your heart before him; God is a refuge for us.

Psa. 147 [3]He healeth the broken in heart, and bindeth up their wounds.

Isa. 25 [4]For thou hast been a strength to the poor, a strength to the needy in his distress, a refuge from the storm, a shadow from the heat, when the blast of the terrible ones is as a storm against the wall.

Nah. 1 [7]The LORD is good, a strong hold in the day of trouble; and he knoweth them that trust in him.

Matt. 5 [4]Blessed are they that mourn: for they shall be comforted. [10]Blessed are they which are persecuted for righteousness' sake: for theirs is the kingdom of heaven. [11]Blessed are ye, when men shall revile you, and persecute you, and shall say all manner of evil against you falsely, for my sake. [12]Rejoice, and be exceeding glad: for great is your reward in heaven: for so persecuted they the prophets which were before you.

John 14 [1]Let not your heart be troubled: ye believe in God, believe also in me. [2]In my Father's house are many mansions; if it were not so, I would have told you: I go to prepare a place for you. [3]And if I go and prepare a place for you, I will come again, and receive you unto myself, that where I am, there ye may be also.

Rom. 8 [28]And we know that all things work together for good to them that love God, to them who are the called according to his purpose. [38]For I am persuaded, that neither death, nor life, nor angels, nor principalities, nor powers, nor things present, nor things to come, [39]Nor height, nor depth, nor any other creature, shall be able to separate us from the love of God, which is in Christ Jesus our Lord.

2 Cor. 1 [5]For as the sufferings of Christ abound in us, so our consolation also aboundeth by Christ.

2 Cor. 12 [9]And he said unto me, My grace is sufficient for thee: for my strength is made perfect in weakness. Most gladly therefore will I rather glory in my infirmities, that the power of Christ may rest upon me.

2 Thess. 2 [16]Now our Lord Jesus Christ himself, and God even our Father, which hath loved us, and hath given us everlasting consolation, and good hope through grace, [17]Comfort your hearts, and stablish you in every good word and work.

Heb. 4 [15]For we have not an high priest which cannot be touched with the feeling of our infirmities: but was in all points tempted like as we are, yet without sin. [16]Let us therefore come boldly unto the throne of grace, that we may obtain mercy, and find grace to help in time of need.

1 Pet. 4 [13]But rejoice, inasmuch as ye are partakers of Christ's sufferings, that when his glory shall be revealed, ye may be glad also with exceeding joy. [14]If ye be reproached for the name of Christ, happy are ye; for the Spirit of glory and of God resteth upon you: . . . .

CONTENTMENT

[kon tent′ment] The state of being free from care because of satisfaction with what is already one's own; a disposition of mind undisturbed by anxiety or envy.

SCRIPTURE

General

Psa. 37 [7]Rest in the LORD, and wait patiently for him: fret not thyself because of him who prospereth in his way, ... [16]A little that a righteous man hath is better than the riches of many wicked.

Prov. 17 [1]Better is a dry morsel, and quietness therewith, than an house full of sacrifices with strife.

Eccl. 4 [6]Better is an handful with quietness, than both the hands full with travail and vexation of spirit.

Phil. 4 [11]Not that I speak in respect of want: for I have learned, in whatsoever state I am, therewith to be content. [12]I know both how to be abased, and I know how to abound: every where and in all things I am instructed both to be full and to be hungry, both to abound and to suffer need.

Exhortation to Contentment

Luke 3 [14]And the soldiers likewise demanded of him, saying, And what shall we do? And he said unto them, Do violence to no man, neither accuse any falsely, and be content with your wages.

1 Cor. 7 [20]Let every man abide in the same calling wherein he was called.

1 Tim. 6 [8]And having food and raiment let us be therewith content.

Heb. 13 [5]Let your conversation be without covetousness: and be content with such things as ye have. For he hath said, I will never leave thee, nor forsake thee.

CONVERSATION

[kon ver sā′shun] In present usage this word refers to speech between two or more parties. In the King James Version of the Bible, however, it always refers to behavior or conduct. Most later revisions give a more up-to-date translation of the original Hebrew and Greek words.

SCRIPTURE

Psa. 37 [14]The wicked have drawn out the sword, and have bent their bow, to cast down the poor and needy, and to slay such as be of upright conversation.

Psa. 50 [23]Whoso offereth praise glorifieth me: and to him that ordereth his conversation aright will I shew the salvation of God.

1 Tim. 4 [12]Let no man despise thy youth; but be thou an example of the believers, in word, in conversation, in charity, in spirit, in faith, in purity.

Jas. 3 [13]Who is a wise man and endued with knowledge amongst you? let him shew out of a good conversation his works with meekness of wisdom.

Phil. 1 [27]Only let your conversation be as it becometh the gospel of Christ, that whether I come and see you, or else be absent, I may hear of your affairs, that ye stand fast in one spirit, with one mind, striving together for the faith of the gospel.

1 Pet. 1 [15]But as he which hath called you is holy, so be ye holy in all manner of conversation.

1 Pet. 2 [12]Having your conversation honest among the Gentiles, that whereas they speak against you as evildoers, they may by your good works which they shall behold, glorify God in the day of visitation.

CONVERSION

[kon vûr′shun] A turning, or returning, to God. In the Old Testament, conversion simply means turning from false gods to Yahweh, or Jehovah, the God of Israel. This "conversion" was often marked by the making of a covenant, by which one expressed his allegiance to the true God. (*See* COVENANT) In the New Testament, conversion refers to turning to God and acceptance of the salvation which has been offered in Christ.

It involves faith which expresses itself in obedience, and repentance, in which a man turns from a life of sinfulness to live in accordance with God's commands. Christian conversion is well summed up in *Acts 26:18* as the process by which men may turn "from darkness to light, and from the power of Satan unto God, that they may receive forgiveness of sins, and inheritance among them which are sanctified by faith that is in me."

See REPENTANCE, REGENERATION, BAPTISM, etc.

CORINTH

[cor'inth] The city of Corinth was a great commercial center located on the narrow isthmus between the mainland of Greece and the peninsula of Peloponnesus. Because sailors preferred to carry their cargo overland at this narrow section of land instead of risking the dangerous voyage around the cape of Malea that lay at the tip of the Peloponnesus, Corinth became a great commercial center. At the time of Paul's contact with it, Corinth was a bustling city with an extremely cosmopolitan atmosphere, containing tradesmen, merchants, seamen, slaves, and colonists from all over the empire. As might be expected in such a city, morality was at a low level. To "live like a Corinthian" was to live the basest sort of life. The religious complexion of the city reflected the variegated composition of the population. All the leading pagan deities were worshipped, some with rites of extreme immorality. Mystery religions and philosophical schools also drew large followings. Many of the Corinthians considered Christianity a religion for the unsophisticated and unlearned. One can easily imagine the difficulties with which Paul was faced in presenting the story of Jesus to the Corinthians.

Paul founded the church at Corinth on his second missionary tour (*Acts 18:1-8*). In Paul's absence, Apollos preached to the church there (*Acts 18:24-19:1*). Judging from Paul's statements in *1 Cor. 1:26-31*, the church had drawn most of its members from the lower, uneducated class of people. These people found it difficult to shake off the influences of their environment and to commit themselves wholly to the religion of Jesus. The letters to the Corinthians, universally acknowledged to have come from Paul, witness to the problems encountered by the Corinthian church in its adjustment to the new life in Christ.

CORNELIUS

[kor nē'li us] A Roman centurion, or commander of approximately one hundred men in the Roman cohort stationed in Caesarea. He is described as "a devout man, and one that feared God with all his house, which gave much alms to the people, and prayed to God always" (*Acts 10:2*), and "of good report among the Jews" (*Acts 10:22*). Because of Cornelius' sincere desire for religious truth, he was instructed in a vision to send servants to bring Peter from Joppa to Caesarea. When the men reached Joppa, Peter himself had received a vision, the significance of which was that the Christian religion no distinction between Jew and Gentile. When Peter came to Caesarea, the centurion rehearsed the vision which he had received, moving Peter to speak the famous words, "Of a truth I perceive that God is no respecter of persons: But in every nation he that feareth him, and worketh righteousness, is accepted with him" (*Acts 10:34-35*). Then, after the Holy Spirit had fallen "on all them which heard the word," Peter baptized Cornelius and his household.

In later years, this event was cited as having set a precedent for the admission of Gentiles to full Christian fellowship.

SCRIPTURE

Acts 10 [1]There was a certain man in
Caesarea called Cornelius, a centurion of
the band called the Italian band, [2]A devout man, and one that feared God with
all his house, which gave much alms to the
people, and prayed to God alway. [3]He
saw in a vision evidently about the ninth
hour of the day an angel of God coming in
to him, and saying unto him, Cornelius.
[4]And when he looked on him, he was
afraid, and said, What is it, Lord? And he
said unto him, Thy prayers and thine alms
are come up for a memorial before God.
[5]And now send men to Joppa, and call for

one Simon, whose surname is Peter: [6]He lodgeth with one Simon a tanner, whose house is by the sea side: he shall tell thee what thou oughtest to do. [7]And when the angel which spake unto Cornelius was departed, he called two of his household servants, and a devout soldier of them that waited on him continually; [8]And when he had declared all these things unto them, he sent them to Joppa.

[9]On the morrow, as they went on their journey, and drew nigh unto the city, Peter went up upon the house top to pray about the sixth hour: [10]And he became very hungry, and would have eaten: but while they made ready, he fell into a trance, [11]And saw heaven opened, and a certain vessel descending unto him, as it had been a great sheet knit at the four corners, and let down to the earth: [12]Wherein were all manner of fourfooted beasts of the earth, and wild beasts, and creeping things, and fowls of the air. [13]And there came a voice to him, Rise, Peter; kill, and eat. [14]But Peter said, Not so, Lord; for I have never eaten any thing that is common or unclean. [15]And the voice spake unto him again the second time, What God hath cleansed, that call not thou common. [16]This was done thrice: and the vessel was received up again into heaven. [17]Now while Peter doubted in himself what this vision which he had seen should mean, behold, the men which were sent from Cornelius had made enquiry for Simon's house, and stood before the gate, [18]And called, and asked whether Simon, which was surnamed Peter, were lodged there.

[19]While Peter thought on the vision, the Spirit said unto him, Behold, three men seek thee. [20]Arise therefore, and get thee down, and go with them, doubting nothing: for I have sent them. [21]Then Peter went down to the men which were sent unto him from Cornelius; and said, Behold, I am he whom ye seek; what is the cause wherefore ye are come? [22]And they said, Cornelius the centurion, a just man, and one that feareth God, and of good report among all the nation of the Jews, was warned from God by an holy angel to send for thee into his house, and to hear words of thee. [23]Then called he them in, and lodged them. And on the morrow Peter went away with them, and certain brethren from Joppa accompanied him. [24]And the morrow after they entered into Caesarea. And Cornelius waited for them, and had called together his kinsmen and near friends. [25]And as Peter was coming in, Cornelius met him, and fell down at his feet, and worshipped him. [26]But Peter took him up, saying, Stand up; I myself also am a man. [27]And as he talked with him, he went in, and found many that were come together. [28]And he said unto them, Ye know how that it is an unlawful thing for a man that is a Jew to keep company, or come unto one of another nation; but God hath shewed me that I should not call any man common or unclean. [29]Therefore came I unto you without gainsaying, as soon as I was sent for: I ask therefore for what intent ye have sent for me? [30]And Cornelius said, Four days ago I was fasting until this hour; and at the ninth hour I prayed in my house, and, behold, a man stood before me in bright clothing, [31]And said, Cornelius, thy prayer is heard, and thine alms are had in remembrance in the sight of God. [32]Send therefore to Joppa, and call hither Simon, whose surname is Peter; he is lodged in the house of one Simon a tanner by the sea side: who, when he cometh, shall speak unto thee. [33]Immediately therefore I sent to thee; and thou hast well done that thou art come.

Now therefore are we all here present before God, to hear all things that are commanded thee of God.

[34]Then Peter opened his mouth, and
said, Of a truth I perceive that God is no
respecter of persons: [35]But in every nation he that feareth him, and worketh
righteousness, is accepted with him. [36]The
word which God sent unto the children of
Israel, preaching peace by Jesus Christ:
(he is Lord of all:) [37]That word, I say, ye
know, which was published throughout all
Judaea, and began from Galilee, after the
baptism which John preached; [38]How
God anointed Jesus of Nazareth with the
Holy Ghost and with power: who went
about doing good, and healing all that
were oppressed of the devil; for God was
with him. [39]And we are witnesses of all
things which he did both in the land of the
Jews, and in Jerusalem; whom they slew
and hanged on a tree: [40]Him God raised
up the third day, and shewed him openly;
[41]Not to all the people, but unto witnesses
chosen before of God, even to us, who did
eat and drink with him after he rose from
the dead. [42]And he commanded us to
preach unto the people, and to testify that
it is he which was ordained of God to be
the Judge of quick and dead. [43]To him
give all the prophets witness, that through
his name whosoever believeth in him shall
receive remission of sins.

[44]While Peter yet spake these words, the
Holy Ghost fell on all them which heard
the word. [45]And they of the circumcision
which believed were astonished, as many
as came with Peter, because that on the
Gentiles also was poured out the gift of the
Holy Ghost. [46]For they heard them speak
with tongues, and magnify God. Then answered Peter, [47]Can any man forbid water, that these should not be baptized,
which have received the Holy Ghost as
well as we? [48]And he commanded them
to be baptized in the name of the Lord.
Then prayed they him to tarry certain
days.

COURAGE

[kur'ȧj] That quality of mind which enables one to meet danger and difficulties with firmness; valor. Courage may manifest itself in many ways, including boldness, endurance, bravery, and gallantry. It has been viewed by men everywhere as a cardinal virtue. The Bible contains numerous examples of men and women whose natural courage was reinforced by their faith in God.

SCRIPTURE

Exhortations to Courage

Deut. 31 [6]Be strong and of a good courage, fear not, nor be afraid of them: for the LORD thy God, he it is that doth go with thee, he will not fail thee, nor forsake thee.

Josh. 1 [7]Only be thou strong and very courageous, that thou mayest observe to do according to all the law which Moses my servant commanded thee: turn not from it to the right hand or to the left, that thou mayest prosper whithersoever thou goest.

Psa. 27 [14]Wait on the LORD: be of good courage, and he shall strengthen thine heart: wait, I say, on the LORD.

Phil. 1 [28]And in nothing terrified by your adversaries: which is to them an evident token of perdition, but to you of salvation, and that of God.

Courage through Faith

ABRAHAM

Heb. 11 [8]By faith Abraham when he
was called to go out into a place which he
should after receive for an inheritance,
obeyed, and he went out, not knowing
whither he went. [17]By faith Abraham

when he was tried, offered up Isaac: and he that had received the promises, offered up his only begotten son.

MOSES

Heb. 11 [24]By faith Moses when he was come to years, refused to be called the son of Pharaoh's daughter, [25]Choosing rather to suffer affliction with the people of God, than to enjoy the pleasures of sin for a season: [26]Esteeming the reproach of Christ greater riches than the treasures in Egypt: for he had respect unto the recompense of the reward. [27]By faith he forsook Egypt, not fearing the wrath of the king: for he endured, as seeing him who is invisible.

DANIEL

Dan. 6 [10]Now when Daniel knew that the writing was signed, he went into his house; and, his windows being open in his chamber toward Jerusalem, he kneeled upon his knees three times a day, and prayed, and gave thanks before his God, as he did aforetime.

PETER AND JOHN

Acts 4 [19]But Peter and John answered and said unto them, Whether it be right in the sight of God to hearken unto you more than unto God, judge ye.

COVENANT

[kuv′e nant] A formal agreement between two parties. A covenant may be between two individuals of equal status (*Gen. 21:27; 1 Sam. 18:3*), between tribes (*1 Sam. 11:1; Judg. 2:2*), between monarchs (*1 Kin. 20:34*), between a conqueror and his subjects (*1 Kin. 20:34*), and between God and men. In a Biblical sense, the covenant is most frequently thought of as the promises of God conditioned on certain terms on the part of man. The idea of covenant is fundamental to Biblical thought, a fact made abundantly clear when it is realized that *testament* is a synonym for covenant. The key event of the Old Testament is the institution of the covenant between God and Israel at Mt. Sinai. After delivering the Israelites from Egyptian bondage, God entered into an agreement with them which is summed up by Jeremiah: "I will be your God and ye shall be my people" (*Jer. 7:23; 31:33*). The basic document of this covenant was the Decalogue, or Ten Commandments. (*See* DECALOGUE) On condition of Israel's faithfulness to these commandments and to the more detailed ordinances based upon them, God promised to lead Israel into Palestine and to sustain her life there. Also connected with the covenant were the consequences of disobedience. The history of Israel is one of repeated infidelity to the covenant, with its attendant disasters, culminating in the Assyrian and Babylonian captivities. The primary aim of the classical prophets was to convict Israel of her unfaithfulness and to persuade her to reestablish the covenant relationship with God, who stood ready to forgive her infidelity.

At the Last Supper, Jesus referred to the cup as "the new covenant in my blood" (*1 Cor. 11: 25*). He thought of himself as establishing a new covenant between God and man through his sacrificial death on the cross. In the Pauline writings, and in *Hebrews*, this covenant is viewed as an ordinance of salvation from God. It is a covenant of the spirit, not the letter, mediated through the blood of Jesus, once for all offered on the cross for the sins of all mankind. It is new in the sense that it fulfills and supersedes the old covenant made with Moses.

COVETOUSNESS

[kuv′et us nes] An inordinate, ungoverned, selfish desire for the possession of money or wealth of any sort, or for the possession of something of real or supposed value belonging to some other person. The Bible views covetousness as a great sin, and contains numerous warnings against it. In the Ten Commandments it is grouped right alongside murder, adultery, theft, and false testimony. It may, in fact, be viewed as the condition from which these sins frequently arise.

SCRIPTURE

Covetousness Described

Eccl. 4 [8]There is one alone, and there is

not a second; yea, he hath neither child nor brother: yet is there no end of all his labour; neither is his eye satisfied with riches: neither saith he, For whom do I labour, and bereave my soul of good? This is also vanity, yea, it is a sore travail.

Eccl. 5 10He that loveth silver shall not be satisfied with silver; nor he that loveth abundance with increase: this is also vanity. 11When goods increase, they are increased that eat them: and what good is there to the owners thereof, saving the beholding of them with their eyes?

1 Tim. 6 10For the love of money is the root of all evil, which while some coveted after, they have erred from the faith, and pierced themselves through with many sorrows.

Covetousness Forbidden

Ex. 20 17Thou shalt not covet thy neighbour's house, thou shalt not covet thy neighbour's wife, nor his manservant, nor his maidservant, nor his ox, nor his ass, nor any thing that is thy neighbour's.

Luke 12 15And he said unto them, Take heed and beware of covetousness: for a man's life consisteth not in the abundance of the things which he possesseth.

Heb. 13 5Let your conversation be without covetousness; and be content with such things as ye have: . . . .

See Rom. 1:29; 1 Cor. 5:11; Eph. 5:3

Its Evil Consequences

Prov. 1 18And they lay wait for their own blood; they lurk privily for their own lives. 19So are the ways of every one that is greedy of gain; which taketh away the life of the owners thereof.

Prov. 15 27He that is greedy of gain troubleth his own house; but he that hateth gifts shall live.

Prov. 28 20A faithful man shall abound with blessings: but he that maketh haste to be rich shall not be innocent.

Punishment of Covetousness

Hab. 2 9Woe to him that coveteth an evil covetousness to his house, that he may set his nest on high, that he may be delivered from the power of evil!

1 Cor. 6 10Nor thieves, nor covetous, nor drunkards, nor revilers, nor extortioners, shall inherit the kingdom of God.

REFERENCE: Eve, *Gen. 3:5*; Lot, *Gen. 13:10-13*; Achan, *Josh. 7:21*; David, *2 Sam. 11:2-5;* Ahab, *1 Kin. 21:2-16;* Gehazi, *2 Kin. 5:20-27;* Simon Magus, *Acts 8:18-23;* Demetrius, *Acts 19:24, 27;* Demas, *2 Tim. 4:10.*

CREATION

[krē a'shun] The Biblical account of creation must be understood as religious and not scientific. Its purpose is not to sketch in detail every aspect of God's bringing the universe to its present state. It is intended primarily to impress upon us the notion that God is prior to and distinct from his creation, that he is directly responsible for its having come into being, through the agency of his Word, that its continued existence is dependent upon him, and that man has been given the highest position of honor and responsibility in the universe.

SCRIPTURE

God as Creator

Isa. 40 12Who hath measured the waters in the hollow of his hand, and meted out heaven with the span, and comprehended the dust of the earth in a measure, and weighed the mountains in scales, and the hills in a balance?

26Lift up your eyes on high, and behold who hath created these things, that bringeth out their host by number: he calleth them all by names by the greatness of his might, for that he is strong in power; not one faileth.

[28]Hast thou not known? hast thou not heard, that the everlasting God, the LORD, the Creator of the ends of the earth, fainteth not, neither is weary? there is no searching of his understanding.

Isa. 42 [5]Thus saith God the LORD, he that created the heavens, and stretched them out; he that spread forth the earth, and that which cometh out of it; . . . .

Isa. 44 [24] . . . I am the LORD that maketh all things; that stretcheth forth the heavens alone; that spreadeth abroad the earth by myself;

Isa. 45 [7]I form the light, and create darkness: I make peace, and create evil: I the LORD do all these things. [12]I have made the earth, and created man upon it: I, even my hands, have stretched out the heavens, and all their host have I commanded. [18]Thus saith the LORD that created the heavens; God himself that formed the earth and made it; he hath established it, he created it not in vain, he formed it to be inhabited: . . . .

Gen. 1 [1]In the beginning God created the heaven and the earth. [2]And the earth was without form, and void; and darkness was upon the face of the deep. And the Spirit of God moved upon the face of the waters.

Creation Is by the Word

Gen. 1 [3]And God said, Let there be light; and there was light.

Psa. 33 [9]For he spake, and it was done; he commanded, and it stood fast.

Psa. 148 [5]Let them praise the name of the LORD: for he commanded, and they were created.

John 1 [1]In the beginning was the Word, and the Word was with God, and the Word was God. [2]The same was in the beginning with God. [3]All things were made by him; and without him was not anything made that was made.

Heb. 11 [3]Through faith we understand that the worlds were framed by the word of God, so that things which are seen were not made of things which do appear.

2 Pet. 3 [5]For this they willingly are ignorant of, that by the word of God the heavens were of old, and the earth standing out of the water and in the water:

CROSS, CRUCIFIXION

[kros; kroo si fik'shun] The chief symbol of Christian religion. In the time of Christ there were three types of crosses: (1) the type usually pictured in Christian art; (2) a cross shaped like a T; and (3) a cross shaped like an X.

As an instrument of death, the cross was abhorred by both Jews and Romans; although the Romans administered execution by crucifixion, no Roman citizen could be crucified. Among the Romans, crucifixion was preceded by scourging, probably to hasten death. The victim was then either tied to the cross beams or fastened with nails or stakes. If he was tied to the cross, nothing further was done and he was left to die of starvation. If he was nailed, a potion was sometimes given to deaden the pain. The combination of inflamed wounds, heat, exposure, hunger, thirst, and possible tetanus made crucifixion a truly horrible means of death. Although the time required to kill a man by crucifixion varied with the stamina of the individual, death rarely came before thirty-six hours had elapsed. This explains the astonishment of Pilate when he received word that Jesus was already dead after only a few hours on the cross. Death was sometimes hastened, as in the case of the two malefactors who died with Christ, by breaking the legs of the victims.

During the reign of the first Christian emperor, Constantine, crucifixion was abolished as an insult to Christianity.

SCRIPTURE

Christ's Death on the Cross

Luke 23 [33]And when they were come

to the place which is called Calvary, there they crucified him, and the malefactors, one on the right hand, and the other on the left.

Phil. 2 [8]And being found in fashion as a man, he humbled himself, and became obedient unto death, even the death of the cross.

Heb. 12 [2]Looking unto Jesus the author and finisher of our faith; who for the joy that was set before him endured the cross, despising the shame, and is set down at the right hand of the throne of God.

Power of Christ's Cross

1 Cor. 1 [17]For Christ sent me not to baptize, but to preach the Gospel; not with wisdom of words, lest the cross of Christ should be made of none effect. [18]For the preaching of the cross is to them that perish foolishness: but unto us which are saved it is the power of God.

The Christian's Cross

Matt. 10 [38]And he that taketh not his cross, and followeth after me, is not worthy of me.

Matt. 16 [24]Then said Jesus unto his disciples, If any man will come after me, let him deny himself, and take up his cross, and follow me. [25]For whosoever will save his life, shall lose it: and whosoever will lose his life for my sake, shall find it.

CROWN

[kroun] An adornment for the head, varying widely in materials, ornamentation, and cost. Crowns were used as decoration; as a sign of consecration or coronation, as in the case of the high priest or king and as a symbol of exaltation or reward, expressing recognition of victory in war, games, races, etc. The Bible contains many references to crowns, both literal and figurative, the most famous of which is probably the crown of thorns which was placed on Jesus' head as a mockery at his trial.

SCRIPTURE

Worn by the High Priest

Ex. 29 [6]And thou shalt put the mitre upon his head, and put the holy crown upon the mitre.

Worn by the King

2 Kin. 11 [12]And he brought forth the king's son, and put the crown upon him, and gave him the testimony; and they made him king, and anointed him; and they clapped their hands, and said, God save the king.

A Sign of Victory

2 Tim. 2 [5]And if a man also strive for masteries, yet is he not crowned, except he strive lawfully.

Jesus' Crown of Thorns

Matt. 27 [29]And when they had platted a crown of thorns, they put it upon his head, and a reed in his right hand: and they bowed the knee before him, and mocked him, saying, Hail, King of the Jews.

Figurative

1 Cor. 9 [25]And every man that striveth for the mastery is temperate in all things. Now they do it to obtain a corruptible crown; but we an incorruptible.

2 Tim. 4 [8]Henceforth there is laid up for me a crown of righteousness, which the Lord, the righteous judge, shall give me at that day: and not to me only, but unto all them also that love his appearing.

Jas. 1 [12]Blessed is the man that endureth temptation: for when he is tried, he shall receive the crown of life, which the

Lord hath promised to them that love him.

1 Pet. 5 [4]And when the chief Shepherd shall appear, ye shall receive a crown of glory that fadeth not away.

Rev. 2 [10]Fear none of those things which thou shalt suffer: behold, ...

Rev. 3 [11]Behold, I come quickly: hold that fast which thou hast, that no man take thy crown.

CRUELTY

[kroo͞′el ti] The willful infliction of injury, either physical or otherwise, upon others; inhumanity. In the Bible cruelty is contrasted with the kindness and mercy which characterizes true children of God.

SCRIPTURE

Prov. 11 [17]The merciful man doeth good to his own soul; but he that is cruel troubleth his own flesh.

Prov. 12 [10]A righteous man regardeth the life of his beast: but the tender mercies of the wicked are cruel.

Ezek. 18 [18]As for his father, because he cruelly oppressed, spoiled his brother by violence, and did that which is not good among his people, lo, even he shall die in his iniquity.

REFERENCE: Of Sarah to Hagar, *Gen. 16:6; 21:9-14;* Egyptians to the Israelites, *Ex. 5:6-18;* Peninnah to Hannah, *1 Sam. 1:4-7; 2:3;* Of the Jews to Jesus, *Matt. 26:67; 27:28-31.*

CUPBEARER

[kup′bâr ẽr] A high office of ancient courts, whose formal task it was to serve the wine at the king's table. Because of frequent plots against the lives of monarchs, it was necessary for the cupbearer to be a person of unquestionable integrity and trustworthiness. He was sometimes required to taste the wine before serving it to the king to prove that it contained nothing of a poisonous nature. Such a position of intimacy with the king naturally gave the cupbearer wide influence. Nehemiah was cupbearer to Artaxerxes I ruler of Persia and used this position to secure permission to lead a contingent of exiled Jews to Jerusalem to rebuild the great wall.

See NEHEMIAH

CURSE

[kûrs] 1. A prayer or invocation for injury, disease, ill-success, desolation, death, etc., to come upon one; the opposite of "blessing." In ancient times, when a curse was pronounced, it was not considered simply as a wish for misfortune to befall an individual or a group, but was thought to have the inherent power of conveying itself into effect.

2. The term is also used in reference to the penalty for disobedience of God's law. The classical expression of this usage is in the "curses and blessings" ceremony depicted in *Deut. 27-28.*

3. Based on the statement in *Deut. 21:22-23,* "he that hangeth on a tree is accursed of God," death by crucifixion was regarded as a sign of God's opposition to the victim. (*See* CRUCIFIXION) The decision by the Jews to crucify Jesus doubtless had as a partial motive the desire to discredit him by association with this curse. In *Gal. 3:8-14,* Paul deals with Christ's "having become a curse for us."

See CRUCIFIXION

SCRIPTURE

The Divine Curse

Gen. 3 [17]And unto Adam he said, Because thou hast hearkened unto the voice of thy wife, and hast eaten of the tree of which I commanded thee, saying, Thou shalt not eat of it: cursed is the ground for thy sake; in sorrow shalt thou eat of it all the days of thy life.

Gen. 4 [11]And now art thou cursed from the earth, which hath opened her mouth to receive thy brother's blood from thy hand.

Deut. 11 [26]Behold, I set before you this day a blessing and a curse: [27]A blessing, if ye obey the commandments of the LORD your God which I command you this day; [28]And a curse, if ye will not obey the commandments of the LORD your God.

See Deut. 27-28

Human Cursing Forbidden

Ex. 21 [17]And he that curseth his father or his mother, shall surely be put to death.

Psa. 109 [17]As he loved cursing, so let it come unto him: as he delighted not in blessing, so let it be far from him.

Jas. 3 [10]Out of the same mouth proceedeth blessing and cursing: my brethren, these things ought not so to be.

Matt. 5 [44]But I say unto you, Love your enemies, bless them that curse you, do good to them that hate you, and pray for them which despitefully use you, and persecute you.

Rom. 12 [14]Bless them which persecute you, bless, and curse not.

REFERENCE: Against Canaan, Noah's son, *Gen. 9:24-27*; against Gehazi, *2 Kin. 5:27*; Balak commands Balaam to curse Israel, *Num. 22:6; 23:11.*

The Curse of the Cross

Deut. 21 [22]And if a man have committed a sin worthy of death, and he be to be put to death, and thou hang him on a tree: [23]His body shall not remain all night upon the tree, but thou shalt in any wise bury him that day; (for he that is hanged is accursed of God;) that thy land be not defiled, which the LORD thy God giveth thee for an inheritance.

Gal. 3 [13]Christ hath redeemed us from the curse of the law, being made a curse for us: for it is written, Cursed is every one that hangeth on a tree:

CYRUS THE PERSIAN

[sī′rus] As vassal king of Anshan in southern Iran, Cyrus engineered a revolt which made him head of the vast Median empire by 550 BC. By 547 he had removed all opposition between himself and the control of the Babylonian empire. In 539 his armies marched into Babylon itself, taking control without a fight. In the first year of his reign Cyrus, fulfilling the Biblical prophecies which had been made concerning him, issued a decree which made possible the return to Jerusalem of the Jews who had been captive in Babylon and the restoration of Jewish life and worship, including the rebuilding of the Jerusalem Temple with imperial funds. After proving himself one of history's truly enlightened rulers, Cyrus met his death in a campaign beyond the Jaxartes River in 530 BC and was succeeded by his eldest son Cambyses.

REFERENCE: *2 Chr. 36:22, 23; Ezra 1; 3:7; 4:3; 5:13, 14; 6:3.*

DAGON

[dā′gon] A god of the Philistines, associated particularly with Gaza and Ashdod. Many scholars feel that the image of Dagon was half fish and half man. It was the temple of Dagon in Gaza which Samson pulled down, killing himself and a large number of Philistines (*Judg. 16: 21-30*). When the ark of the covenant was captured by the Philistines in the time of Eli, it was placed in the temple of Dagon at Ashdod. The next morning the image of the god lay on the floor before the ark. It was restored to its position, but on the following day was again found on the floor, this time with its head and hands severed from the body and lying on the threshold of the temple. The writer adds the footnote that "therefore neither the priests of Dagon, nor any that come into Dagon's house, tread on the threshold of Dagon in Ashdod unto this day" (*1 Sam. 5:1-5*). At the death of King Saul, his head was hung in the temple of Dagon (*1 Chr. 10:10*).

DAMASCUS

[da mas′kus] The ancient capital city of Syria. The region of Damascus is an oasis situated on the Nahr Barada (the Biblical Abana) and just north of the Nahr el A'waj (the Biblical Pharpar); these two rivers are mentioned in the account of the healing of Naaman's leprosy. There is evidence of Damascus' having been inhabited from earliest historical times. Abraham's servant Eliezer is said to have been a native of Damascus (*Gen. 15:2*). In the time of David's reign, Damascus came under the control of Israel. Later, under Rezon of Hobah, Damascus became the capital of the city-state of Aram (Syria). His successors Hezion and Tabrimmon increased Damascus' strength and influence until, at the time of Ben-Hadad I, it is seen as a leading power in the Near East.

In accord with the words of Elijah (*1 Kin. 19:15*) and Elisha (*2 Kin. 8:7-13*), Hazael assassinated Ben-Hadad and succeeded to the throne of Damascus in c. 842 BC. In 841 BC he was attacked by Shalmaneser III of Assyria and, after heavy losses in the Lebanon mountains, was forced to retreat into Damascus itself, which he held with great difficulty. By the beginning of the 8th century BC, Assyrian attacks had so weakened Damascus that Jehoash king of Israel was able to recover several northern cities which Hazael had previously seized.

Damascus' next real revival of power came under Rezin (c. 740-732 BC). Rezin revolted against Tiglath-Pileser III of Assyria and oppressed Judah, taking many inhabitants of the southern kingdom into Syrian captivity (*2 Kin. 16:6; 2 Chr. 28:5*). Against the warnings of Isaiah, Ahaz king of Judah appealed to Tiglath-Pileser for aid. This resulted in the death of Rezin and in the capture and sack of Damascus (*Isa. 8:4; 2 Kin. 16:9*), but Judah was placed under heavy tribute as a vassal of Assyria. As a result of his visits to the Assyrian headquarters in Damascus, Ahaz introduced the worship of Syrian deities into the temple at Jerusalem (*2 Kin. 16:10-12; 2 Chr. 28:23*). Under the Assyrians Damascus lost its political influence, but continued to be a center of economic importance.

Saul of Tarsus (the apostle Paul) was confronted with a vision of Jesus while on the road to this ancient and historic city. Having been temporarily blinded, he was led to the house of one Judas who lived on the "Street called Straight" (*Acts 9:10-12*). After a visit from Ananias, who baptized him, Saul began to preach the Christian gospel until opposition in the city forced him to flee over the wall in a fish basket (*Acts 9:19-27*). At this time, Damascus was a subsidiary of Antioch, a position which it retained until the Arab conquests of AD 634.

See BEN-HADAD, HAZAEL, TIGLATH-PILESER, ETC.

DAMNATION

[dam nā'shun] This word ordinarily conveys to our minds the idea of eternal punishment in hell as penalty for sin; it may, however, also be used to refer to punishment of a lesser sort, or to judgment.

SCRIPTURE

Matt. 23 [14]Woe unto you, scribes and Pharisees, hypocrites! For ye devour widows' houses, and for a pretense make long prayer: therefore ye shall receive the greater damnation.

Mark 16 [16]He that believeth and is baptized, shall be saved, but he that believeth not, shall be damned.

John 5 [29]And shall come forth, they that have done good, unto the resurrection of life, and they that have done evil, unto the resurrection of damnation.

Rom. 3 [8]And not rather as we be slanderously reported, and as some affirm that we say, Let us do evil, that good may come? whose damnation is just.

Rom. 13 [2]Whosoever therefore resisteth the power, resisteth the ordinance of God: and they that resist, shall receive to themselves damnation.

2 Thess. 2 [12]That they all might be damned who believe not the truth, but had pleasure in unrighteousness.

1 Tim. 5 [12]Having damnation, because they have cast off their first faith.

2 Pet. 2 [3]And through covetousness shall they with feigned words make merchandise of you, whose judgment now of a long time lingereth not, and their damnation slumbereth not.

DAN

[dan] The northernmost city of the land of Israel, most famous perhaps for its occurrence in the common phrase "from Dan even to Beer-sheba," indicating the entire sweep of the land. (*See* BEER-SHEBA) The ancient name of Dan seems to have been Laish or Leshem (*Judg. 18:7*). When Jeroboam king of Israel set up the cult of the golden bulls (*see* JEROBOAM), Dan was chosen as one of the sites for a sanctuary (*1 Kin. 12:28-39*). Jewish tradition has it that the image of the bull was captured and taken to Assyria by Tiglath-Pileser.

SCRIPTURE

"From Dan to Beer-sheba"

Judg. 20 [1]Then all the children of Israel went out, and the congregation was gathered together as one man, from Dan even to Beer-sheba, with the land of Gilead, unto the LORD in Mizpeh.

1 Sam. 3 [20]And all Israel from Dan even to Beer-sheba knew that Samuel was established to be a prophet of the LORD.

Jeroboam Sets Up the Golden Bull

1 Kin. 12 [28]Whereupon the king took counsel, and made two calves of gold, and said unto them, It is too much for you to go up to Jerusalem: behold thy gods, O Israel, which brought thee up out of the land of Egypt. [29]And he set the one in Bethel, and the other put he in Dan.

REFERENCE: *Judg. 18; 1 Kin. 15:20; 2 Chr. 16:4; 2 Kin. 14:25; 15:29.*

DANIEL

[dan′yel] The main character of the book which bears his name. Daniel, also called Belteshazzar, was a youth of Jerusalem, possibly of aristocratic background, who had been carried to Babylon by Nebuchadnezzar in the first wave of captives. Among his companions were Shadrach, Meshach, and Abednego. Daniel quickly distinguished himself in Babylon by refusing to eat the "dainties" which the king had set before him and by exercising his unusual ability to interpret dreams. In time, he was brought before Nebuchadnezzar to offer an interpretation of a puzzling dream which the king had dreamt; his explanation so impressed Nebuchadnezzar that Daniel was allowed to rise to a place of great prominence in the kingdom. He afterwards interpreted the "handwriting on the wall." The famous delivery from the lion's den came after he had become the victim of a plot to cause him to lose favor in the eyes of Darius the Mede, the conqueror of Babylon who had also honored Daniel.

SCRIPTURE

A Captive in Babylon

Dan. 1 [3]And the king spake unto Ashpenaz the master of his eunuchs, that he should bring certain of the children of Israel, and of the king's seed, and of the princes; [4]Children in whom was no blemish, but well favoured, and skilful in all wisdom, and cunning in knowledge, and understanding science, and such as had ability in them to stand in the king's palace, and whom they might teach the learning and the tongue of the Chaldeans. [5]And the king appointed them a daily provision of the king's meat, and of the wine which he drank: so nourishing them three years, that at the end thereof they might stand before the king. [6]Now, among these were of the children of Judah, Daniel, Hananiah, Mishael, and Azariah:

[17]As for these four children, God gave them knowledge and skill in all learning and wisdom: and Daniel had understanding in all visions and dreams.

Interprets the King's Dream

Dan. 2 [31]Thou, O king, sawest, and behold a great image. This great image, whose brightness was excellent, stood before thee; and the form thereof was terrible. 32This image's head was of fine gold, his breast and his arms of silver, his belly and his thighs of brass. 33His legs of iron, his feet part of iron and part of clay. 34Thou sawest till that a stone was cut out without hands, which smote the image upon his feet that were of iron and clay, and brake them to pieces. 35Then was the iron, the clay, the brass, the silver, and the gold, broken to pieces together, and became like the chaff of the summer threshingfloors; and the wind carried them away, that no place was found for them: and the stone that smote the image became a great mountain, and filled the whole earth.

36This is the dream; and we will tell the interpretation thereof before the king. 37Thou, O king, art a king of kings: for the God of heaven hath given thee a kingdom, power, and strength, and glory. 38And wheresoever the children of men dwell, the beasts of the field and the fowls of the heaven hath he given into thine hand, and hath made thee ruler over them all. Thou art this head of gold. 39And after thee shall arise another kingdom inferior to thee, and another third kingdom of brass, which shall bear rule over all the earth. 40And the fourth kingdom shall be strong as iron: forasmuch as iron breaketh in pieces and subdueth all things: and as iron that breaketh all these, shall it break in pieces and bruise. 41And whereas thou sawest the feet and toes, part of potters' clay, and part of iron, the kingdom shall be divided; but there shall be in it of the strength of the iron, forasmuch as thou sawest the iron mixed with miry clay. 42And as the toes of the feet were part of iron, and part of clay, so the kingdom shall be partly strong, and partly broken. 43And whereas thou sawest iron mixed with miry clay, they shall mingle themselves with the seed of men: but they shall not cleave one to another, even as iron is not mixed with clay. 44And in the days of these kings shall the God of heaven set up a kingdom, which shall never be destroyed: and the kingdom shall not be left to other people, but it shall break in pieces and consume all these kingdoms, and it shall stand for ever. 45Forasmuch as thou sawest that the stone was cut out of the mountain without hands, and that it brake in pieces the iron, the brass, the clay, the silver, and the gold; the great God hath made known to the king what shall come to pass hereafter: and the dream is certain, and the interpretation thereof sure.

Interprets Handwriting on Wall

Dan. 5 17Then Daniel answered and said before the king, Let thy gifts be to thyself, and give thy rewards to another; yet I will read the writing unto the king, and make known to him the interpretation.

25And this is the writing that was written, MENE, MENE, TEKEL, UPHARSIN. 26This is the interpretation of the thing: MENE; God hath numbered thy kingdom, and finished it. 27TEKEL; Thou art weighed in the balances, and art found wanting. 28PERES; Thy kingdom is divided and given to the Medes and Persians. 29Then commanded Belshazzar, and they clothed Daniel with scarlet, and put a chain of gold about his neck, and made a proclamation concerning him, that he should be the third ruler in the kingdom.

30In that night was Belshazzar the king of the Chaldeans slain.

Rises to High Place Under Darius the Mede

Dan. 5 31And Darius the Median took the kingdom, being about threescore and two years old.

Dan. 6 [1]It pleased Darius to set over the kingdom an hundred and twenty princes, which should be over the whole kingdom; [2]And over these three presidents; of whom Daniel was first: that the princes might give accounts unto them, and the king should have no damage. [3]Then this Daniel was preferred above the presidents and princes, because an excellent spirit was in him; and the king thought to set him over the whole realm.

In the Lions' Den

Dan. 6 [11]Then these men assembled, and found Daniel praying and making supplication before his God. [12]Then they came near, and spake before the king concerning the king's decree; Hast thou not signed a decree, that every man that shall ask a petition of any god or man within thirty days, save of thee, O king, shall be cast into the den of lions? The king answered and said, The thing is true, according to the law of the Medes and Persians, which altereth not. [16]Then the king commanded, and they brought Daniel, and cast him into the den of lions. Now the king spake and said unto Daniel, Thy God whom thou servest continually, he will deliver thee. [23]Then was the king exceeding glad for him, and commanded that they should take Daniel up out of the den. So Daniel was taken up out of the den, and no manner of hurt was found upon him, because he believed in his God.

[24]And the king commanded, and they brought those men which had accused Daniel, and they cast them into the den of lions, them, their children, and their wives; and the lions had the mastery of them, and brake all their bones in pieces or ever they came at the bottom of the den.

DARIUS

[da rī'us] 1. Darius the Mede. This individual is not mentioned in history outside the book of *Daniel*, in which he is designated as the son of Ahasuerus who was made ruler over the Chaldean kingdom after the death of Belshazzar and with whom Daniel was closely associated.

2. Darius I, also called Hystaspes. During a period of great upheaval in the Persian empire, Cambyses, son of Cyrus, took his own life and was succeeded by Darius, a member of his staff. The upheaval grew worse and it seemed for a time the vast empire would disintegrate. This crisis is reflected in the writings of Haggai and Zechariah. Darius is remembered in Biblical history as the individual who enabled the Jews to resume work on the Temple after it had been stopped through the influence of local politicians. His fame does not end here, however, as he was one of the ablest rulers known to history. It was he who gave the Persian empire its system of satrapies, dividing the empire into twenty provinces under the control of governors, or satraps, who were in turn closely controlled by the central government. This system proved so durable that it was still in use during the time of Alexander the Great. In various other areas Darius proved himself an administrator of remarkable ability. Under him, the fortunes of the Persian empire reached their zenith. His only major defeat was in the famous battle of Marathan in which his armies were hurled back by the Greeks. Darius was succeeded by his son Xerxes.

REFERENCE: *Hag. 1:1; Zech. 1:1; Ezra 4:5; 5, 6.*

DARKNESS

[dark'nes] Literally, the absence of light. Darkness in the physical sense is mentioned in the Bible as having been existent at the time of the creation, as having been one of the plagues sent upon Egypt before and during the Exodus, and as having been a part of the convulsions of nature attending the crucifixion. The presence of God is sometimes described as accompanied by darkness. Figuratively, the word is used as a symbol of mysterious or inexplicable things, moral depravity, human ignorance, absence of the true religion, trouble, affliction, punishment, and death.

See LIGHT

SCRIPTURE

Physical Darkness

AT CREATION

Gen. 1 [2]And the earth was without form, and void; and darkness was upon the face of the deep: and the Spirit of God moved upon the face of the waters. [3]And God said, Let there be light: and there was light. [4]And God saw the light, that it was good: and God divided the light from the darkness.

AT THE EXODUS

Ex. 10 [21]And the LORD said unto Moses, Stretch out thine hand toward heaven, that there may be darkness over the land of Egypt, even darkness which may be felt. [22]And Moses stretched forth his hand toward heaven: and there was a thick darkness in all the land of Egypt three days.

Ex. 14 [19]And the angel of God which went before the camp of Israel, removed, and went behind them; and the pillar of the cloud went from before their face, and stood behind them: [20]And it came between the camp of the Egyptians and the camp of Israel; and it was a cloud and darkness to them, but it gave light by night to these: so that the one came not near the other all the night.

AT THE CRUCIFIXION

Matt. 27 [45]Now from the sixth hour there was darkness over all the land unto the ninth hour.

ATTENDING GOD'S PRESENCE

Ex. 19 [16]And it came to pass on the third day in the morning, that there were thunders and lightnings, and a thick cloud upon the mount, and the voice of the trumpet exceeding loud; so that all the people that was in the camp trembled.

2 Sam. 22 [10]He bowed the heavens also, and came down; and darkness was under his feet. [11]And he rode upon a cherub, and did fly: and he was seen upon the wings of the wind. [12]And he made darkness pavilions round about him, dark waters, and thick clouds of the sky.

2 Chr. 6 [1]Then said Solomon, the LORD hath said that he would dwell in the thick darkness.

Psa. 18 [11]He made darkness his secret place; his pavilion round about him were dark waters and thick clouds of the skies.

Psa. 97 [2]Clouds and darkness are round about him: righteousness and judgment are the habitation of his throne.

Figurative Darkness

DARKNESS OF THE MIND AND SOUL

Job 37 [19]Teach us what we shall say unto him; for we cannot order our speech by reason of darkness.

Prov. 2 [13]Who leave the paths of uprightness, to walk in the ways of darkness.

Eccl. 2 [14]The wise man's eyes are in his head; but the fool walketh in darkness: and I myself perceived also that one event happeneth to them all.

Isa. 9 [2]The people that walked in darkness have seen a great light: they that dwell in the land of the shadow of death, upon them hath the light shined.

Isa. 42 [7]To open the blind eyes, to bring out the prisoners from the prison, and them that sit in darkness out of the prison house.

John 1 [5]And the light shineth in darkness, and the darkness comprehended it not.

John 3 [19]And this is the condemnation, that light is come into the world, and men loved darkness rather than light, because their deeds were evil.

John 8 [12]Then spake Jesus again unto them, saying, I am the light of the world: he that followeth me, shall not walk in darkness, but shall have the light of life.

John 12 [35]Then Jesus said unto them, Yet a little while is the light with you: walk while ye have the light, lest darkness come upon you: For he that walketh in darkness, knoweth not whither he goeth.

Rom. 13 [12]The night is far spent, the day is at hand: let us therefore cast off the works of darkness, and let us put on the armour of light.

1 Cor. 4 [6]For God, who commanded the light to shine out of darkness, hath shined in our hearts, to give the light of the knowledge of the glory of God in the face of Jesus Christ.

2 Cor. 6 [14]Be ye not unequally yoked together with unbelievers: for what fellowship hath righteousness with unrighteousness? and what communion hath light with darkness?

THE "POWERS OF DARKNESS"

Luke 22 [53]When I was daily with you in the Temple, ye stretched forth no hands against me: but this is your hour, and the power of darkness.

Eph. 6 [12]For we wrestle not against flesh and blood, but against principalities, against powers, against the rulers of the darkness of this world, against spiritual wickedness in high places.

Col. 1 [13]Who hath delivered us from the power of darkness, and hath translated us into the kingdom of his dear Son.

A SYMBOL OF PUNISHMENT

Matt. 8 [12]But the children of the kingdom shall be cast out into outer darkness: there shall be weeping and gnashing of teeth.

Matt. 22 [13]Then said the King to the servants, Bind him hand and foot, and take him away, and cast him into outer darkness, there shall be weeping and gnashing of teeth.

2 Pet. 2 [4]For if God spared not the angels that sinned, but cast them down to hell, and delivered them into chains of darkness, to be reserved unto judgment.

Jude 1 [6]And the angels which kept not their first estate, but left their own habitation, he hath reserved in everlasting chains under darkness, unto the judgment of the great day.

DAVID

[dā'vid] The son of Jesse the Bethlehemite, and successor to Saul as king of Israel and Judah, reigning about 1000-960 BC. In his early life David tended his father's flocks and was anointed by Samuel to succeed Saul as king of Israel. Because of the widespread popularity and acclaim which David received as a result of his slaying of Goliath, Saul grew jealous of David and he was compelled to flee for his life, becoming the leader of a band of discontented Israelites. For a considerable period he was treated as an outlaw and hunted by the king, against whom he refused to retaliate. At Saul's death, David was made king of Judah, but Ishbosheth, the only son of Saul to survive the debacle at Gilboa, was proclaimed king of the northern area of Israel. Ishbosheth was himself a weak character and had little real following. After Abner, the commander of his army, went over to David, his power was completely broken; he was soon assassinated, and David became sovereign over both Israel and Judah. David's first move was to reverse the losses suffered at Gilboa at the hands of the Philistines. His sweeping victory finally ended the struggle which had persisted between these two nations for generations. David's next task was to choose a capital city without giving offense either to Israel or Judah. He took Jerusalem from the Jebusites and it became "the city of David," the new center of Israelite life. The transfer of the ark of the covenant from Kiriath-jearim, where it had been for more than a generation, made Jerusalem the religious as well as the governmental center and doubtlessly served as a major factor in consolidating the popular support of the new regime. With his position now secure, David set about to enlarge the borders of the kingdom. He subdued the Ammonites, Moab, Edom, and the Syrian centers of Zobah and Damascus. In a short time Israel, almost prostrate at the death of Saul, became an empire of great power and wealth.

The last years of David's reign were disturbed by rebellion and court intrigues connected with succession to the throne. The best known of these crises was the usurpation attempt of Absalom (for details see ABSALOM). Then followed the brief uprising led by Sheba, which was more easily put down. Having overcome these difficulties, David's own position was once again secure, but the problem of succession was still unsettled. David had evidently assured Bathsheba that their son Solomon would be his successor, but another son, Adonijah, declared himself king at a feast at En-rogel. At the urging of Bathsheba and the prophet Nathan, David quickly had Solomon anointed king, and the support of Adonijah disintegrated. Israel's previous leaders, during the period of the Judges and in the case of Saul and David, had been chosen for their charismatic gifts of leadership. With the announcement that his son Solomon should reign after him, David instituted dynastic succession, constituting yet another break with the old order of Israel. After a reign of forty years, "David slept with his fathers, and was buried in the city of David."

David's character was a most remarkable one. Few men have succeeded in doing well even one of the many different things that he did. He was a shepherd, a soldier, a poet, prophet, priest, king, administrator, a statesman, a heroic leader, a staunch friend, and a devoted father. Into all of these roles he threw his immense energy. He had great faults, as seen especially in his sin with Bathsheba and his subsequent crime against her husband Uriah the Hittite. But at the same time his soul had qualities of unmatched nobility. When he sinned, his remorse and repentance were of the deepest sort. From the *Psalms* that he wrote, baring his whole soul to his Creator, millions of people have received comfort. David appears to us, in all that we can learn of him, as one of the grandest and most romantic characters in the Bible.

See JONATHAN, NATHAN, SAUL

SCRIPTURE

Son of Jesse

1 Chr. 2 [13]And Jesse begat his first-born
Eliab, and Abinadab the second, and
Shimma the third, [14]Nethaneel the fourth,
Raddai the fifth, [15]Ozem the sixth, David
the seventh.

Anointed by Samuel

1 Sam. 16 [13]Then Samuel took the horn of oil, and anointed him in the midst of his brethren: and the Spirit of the LORD came upon David from that day forward. So Samuel rose up, and went to Ramah.

Slays Goliath

1 Sam. 17 [50]So David prevailed over the
Philistine with a sling and with a stone,
and smote the Philistine, and slew him;
but there was no sword in the hand of David. [51]Therefore David ran, and stood
upon the Philistine, and took his sword, and drew it out of the sheath thereof, and slew him, and cut off his head therewith. And when the Philistines saw their champion was dead, they fled.

Friendship with Jonathan

1 Sam. 18 [3]Then Jonathan and David made a covenant, because he loved him as his own soul.

Saul's Jealousy and Pursuit of David

1 Sam. 18 [8]And Saul was very wroth, and the saying displeased him; and he said, They have ascribed unto David ten thousands, and to me they have ascribed but thousands: and what can he have more but the kingdom?

1 Sam. 19 [10]And Saul sought to smite David even to the wall with the javelin; but he slipped away out of Saul's presence, and he smote the javelin into the wall: and David fled, and escaped that night.

1 Sam. 22 [1]David therefore departed thence, and escaped to the cave Adullam: and when his brethren and all his father's house heard it, they went down thither to him. [2]And every one that was in distress, and every one that was in debt, and every one that was discontented, gathered themselves unto him; and he became a captain over them: and there were with him about four hundred men.

1 Sam. 24 [4]And the men of David said unto him, Behold the day of which the LORD said unto thee, Behold, I will deliver thine enemy into thine hand, that thou mayest do to him as it shall seem good unto thee. Then David arose, and cut off the skirt of Saul's robe privily.

1 Sam. 26 [12]So David took the spear and the cruse of water from Saul's bolster; and they gat them away, and no man saw it, nor knew it, neither awaked: for they were all asleep; because a deep sleep from the LORD was fallen upon them.

David Becomes King

2 Sam. 2 [4]And the men of Judah came, and there they anointed David king over the house of Judah. And they told David, saying, That the men of Jabesh-gilead were they that buried Saul.

[5]And David sent messengers unto the men of Jabesh-gilead, and said unto them, Blessed be ye of the LORD, that ye have shewed this kindness unto your lord, even unto Saul, and have buried him.

2 Sam. 3 [1]Now there was long war between the house of Saul and the house of David: but David waxed stronger and stronger, and the house of Saul waxed weaker and weaker.

2 Sam. 4 [8]And they brought the head of Ishbosheth unto David to Hebron, and said to the king, Behold the head of Ishbosheth the son of Saul thine enemy, which sought thy life; and the LORD hath avenged my lord the king this day of Saul, and of his seed.

2 Sam. 5 [3]So all the elders of Israel came to the king of Hebron; and king David made a league with them in Hebron before the LORD: and they anointed David king over Israel.

[4]David was thirty years old when he began to reign, and he reigned forty years. [5]In Hebron he reigned over Judah seven years and six months: and in Jerusalem he reigned thirty and three years over all Israel and Judah.

Forbidden to Build a Temple

2 Sam. 7 [1]And it came to pass, when the king sat in his house, and the LORD had given him rest round about from all his enemies, [2]That the king said unto Nathan the prophet, See now, I dwell in an house of cedar, but the ark of God dwelleth within curtains.

1 Chr. 17 [3]And it came to pass the same night, that the word of God came to Nathan, saying, [4]Go and tell David my servant, Thus saith the LORD, Thou shalt not build me an house to dwell in.

1 Chr. 17 [11]And it shall come to pass, when thy days be expired that thou must go to be with thy fathers, that I will raise up thy seed after thee, which shall be of thy sons; and I will establish his kingdom. [12]He shall build me an house, and I will establish his throne for ever.

Sin with Bath-sheba

2 Sam. 11 [2]And it came to pass in an eveningtide, that David arose from off his bed, and walked upon the roof of the king's house: and from the roof he saw a woman washing herself; and the woman was very beautiful to look upon. [3]And David sent and inquired after the woman. And one said, Is not this Bath-sheba the daughter of Eliam, the wife of Uriah the Hittite? [4]And David sent messengers, and took her; and she came in unto him, and he lay with her; . . . .

Rebuked by Nathan

2 Sam. 12 [7]And Nathan said to David, Thou art the man. Thus saith the LORD God of Israel, I anointed thee king over Israel, and I delivered thee out of the hand of Saul; [8]And I gave thee thy master's house, and thy master's wives into thy bosom, and gave thee the house of Israel and of Judah; and if that had been too little, I would moreover have given unto thee such and such things. [9]Wherefore hast thou despised the commandment of the LORD, to do evil in his sight? thou hast killed Uriah the Hittite with the sword, and hast taken his wife to be thy wife, and hast slain him with the sword of the children of Ammon. [10]Now therefore the sword shall never depart from thine house; because thou hast despised me, and hast taken the wife of Uriah the Hittite to be thy wife. [13]And David said unto Nathan, I have sinned against the LORD. And Nathan said unto David, The LORD also hath put away thy sin; thou shalt not die. [14]Howbeit, because by this deed thou hast given great occasion to the enemies of the LORD to blaspheme, the child also that is born unto thee shall surely die.

Revolt of Absalom

2 Sam. 15 [6]And on this manner did Absalom to all Israel that came to the king for judgment: so Absalom stole the hearts of the men of Israel.

[10]But Absalom sent spies throughout all the tribes of Israel, saying, As soon as ye hear the sound of the trumpet, then ye shall say, Absalom reigneth in Hebron. [12]And Absalom sent for Ahithophel the Gilonite, David's counsellor, from his city, even from Giloh, while he offered sacrifices. And the conspiracy was strong; for the people increased continually with Absalom.

[13]And there came a messenger to David, saying, The hearts of the men of Israel are after Absalom. [14]And David said unto all his servants that were with him at Jerusalem, Arise, and let us flee; for we shall not else escape from Absalom: make speed to depart, lest he overtake us suddenly, and bring evil upon us, and smite the city with the edge of the sword. [17]And the king went forth, and all the people after him, and tarried in a place that was far off.

2 Sam. 18 [1]And David numbered the people that were with him, and set captains of thousands and captains of hundreds over them. [2]And David sent forth a third part of the people under the hand of Joab, and a third part under the hand of Abishai the son of Zeruiah, Joab's brother, and a third part under the hand of Ittai the Gittite. And the king said unto the people, I will surely go forth with you myself also. [3]But the people answered, Thou shalt not go forth: for if we flee away, they will not care for us; neither if half of us die, will they care for us: but now thou art worth ten thousand of us: therefore now it is better that thou succour us out of the city. [4]And the king said unto them, What seemeth you best I will do. And the king stood by the gate side, and all the people came out by hundreds and by thousands. [5]And the king commanded Joab and Abishai and Ittai, saying, Deal gently for my sake with the young man, even with Absalom. And all the people heard when the king gave all the captains charge concerning Absalom.

[6]So the people went out into the field against Israel: and the battle was in the wood of Ephraim; [7]Where the people of Israel were slain before the servants of David, and there was there a great slaughter that day of twenty thousand men.

[10]And a certain man saw it, and told Joab, and said, Behold, I saw Absalom hanged in an oak. [14]Then said Joab, I may not tarry thus with thee. And he took three darts in his hand, and thrust them through the heart of Absalom, while he was yet alive in the midst of the oak. [15]And ten young men that bare Joab's armour compassed about and smote Absalom, and slew him.

[33]And the king was much moved, and went up to the chamber over the gate, and wept: and as he went, thus he said, O my son Absalom! my son, my son Absalom! would God I had died for thee, O Absalom, my son, my son!

Adonijah Proclaims Himself

1 Kin. 1 [5]Then Adonijah the son of Haggith exalted himself, saying, I will be king: and he prepared him chariots and horsemen, and fifty men to run before him. [6]And his father had not displeased him at any time in saying, Why hast thou done so? and he also was a very goodly man; and his mother bare him after Absalom.

Solomon Is Anointed King

1 Kin. 1 [28]Then king David answered and said, Call me Bath-sheba. And she came into the king's presence, and stood before the king. [29]And the king sware, and said, As the LORD liveth, that hath redeemed my soul out of all distress, [30]Even as I sware unto thee by the LORD God of Israel, saying, Assuredly Solomon thy son shall reign after me, and he shall sit upon my throne in my stead; even so will I certainly do this day. [31]Then Bath-sheba bowed with her face to the earth, and did reverence to the king, and said, Let my lord king David live for ever.

[39]And Zadok the priest took a horn of oil out of the tabernacle, and anointed Solomon. And they blew the trumpet; and all the people said, God save king Solomon.

1 Kin. 2 [1]Now the days of David drew nigh that he should die; and he charged Solomon his son, saying, [2]I go the way of all the earth: be thou strong therefore, and shew thyself a man; [3]And keep the charge of the LORD thy God, to walk in his ways, to keep his statutes, and his commandments, and his judgments, and his testimonies, as it is written in the law of Moses, that thou mayest prosper in all that thou doest, and whithersoever thou turnest thyself.

Death and Burial

1 Kin. 2 [10]So David slept with his fathers, and was buried in the city of David. [11]And the days that David reigned over Israel were forty years: seven years reigned he in Hebron, and thirty and three years reigned he in Jerusalem.

REFERENCE: *1 Sam. 16-31; 2 Sam. 1-24; 1 Kin. 1:1-2:12; 1 Chr. 11:1-23:1; 25:1; 28:1-29:30.*

DAY OF THE LORD

A frequent biblical designation of an impending decisive intervention of God in history, commonly found in the prophetic writings. It is implied in *Amos 5:18-20* that Israel had looked forward to the Day of the LORD as a day of salvation; Amos, however, warns that it will be a day of affliction and misfortune for Israel. These two views are easily reconciled: the Day of the LORD was to be a cosmic victory over all His enemies; in view of her apostasy, Israel was numbered among those enemies (*see Amos 1-2*). The events of this Day are most graphically described in the writings of the prophet Zephaniah, who is sometimes called "the prophet of the Day of the LORD." During the period of the Babylonian captivity of Israel, the Day of the LORD once more assumes the character of a day of salvation for Israel. The threats of judgment are directed not against Israel but against the "nations." The godless will be destroyed but those who fear God and worship him only will receive purification and salvation.

In the New Testament, the "day of the LORD" and similar terms refer to the second coming of Christ, at which time the final judgment upon the sins of the world will be pronounced and the salvation of the righteous consummated.

See ESCHATOLOGY

SCRIPTURE

The Day of the Lord as a Day of Affliction

Amos 5 [18]Woe unto you that desire the day of the LORD! to what end is it for you? the day of the LORD is darkness, and not light. [19]As if a man did flee from a lion, and a bear met him; or went into the house, and leaned his hand on the wall, and a serpent bit him. [20]Shall not the day of the LORD be darkness, and not light? even very dark, and no brightness in it?

Amos 8 [9]And it shall come to pass in that day, saith the Lord GOD, that I will cause the sun to go down at noon, and I will darken the earth in the clear day:

Isa. 2 [12]For the day of the LORD of hosts shall be upon every one that is proud and lofty, and upon every one that is lifted up; and he shall be brought low: [17]And the loftiness of man shall be bowed down, and the haughtiness of men shall be made low: and the LORD alone shall be exalted in that day. [19]And they shall go into the holes of the rocks, and into the caves of the earth, for fear of the LORD, and for the glory of his majesty, when he ariseth to shake terribly the earth.

Zeph. 1 [14]The great day of the LORD is near, it is near, and hasteth greatly, even the voice of the day of the LORD: the mighty man shall cry there bitterly. [15]That day is a day of wrath, a day of trouble and distress, a day of wasteness and desolation, a day of darkness and gloominess, a day of clouds and thick darkness, [16]A day of the trumpet and alarm against the fenced cities, and against the high towers.

See Zeph. 1:7ff, 14ff; 2:2-5; 3:8

A Day of Judgment Against the Nations

AGAINST BABYLON

Isa. 13 [6]Howl ye; for the day of the LORD is at hand; it shall come as a destruction from the Almighty. [9]Behold, the day of the LORD cometh, cruel both with wrath and fierce anger, to lay the land desolate: and he shall destroy the sinners thereof out of it. [13]Therefore I will shake the heavens, and the earth shall remove out of her place, in the wrath of the LORD of hosts, and in the day of his fierce anger.

AGAINST EDOM

Isa. 34 [8]For it is the day of the LORD's vengeance, and the year of recompenses for the controversy of Zion.

Isa. 63 [4]For the day of vengeance is in

mine heart, and the year of my redeemed is come.

Obad. 1 15 For the day of the LORD is near upon all the heathen: as thou hast done, it shall be done unto thee: thy reward shall return upon thine own head.

AGAINST EGYPT

Jer. 46 10 For this is the day of the Lord GOD of hosts, a day of vengeance, that he may avenge him of his adversaries: and the sword shall devour, and it shall be satiate and made drunk with their blood: for the Lord GOD of hosts hath a sacrifice in the north country by the river Euphrates.

Ezek. 30 3 For the day is near, even the day of the LORD is near, a cloudy day; it shall be the time of the heathen.

AGAINST THE PHILISTINES

Jer. 47 4 Because of the day that cometh to spoil all the Philistines, and to cut off from Tyrus and Zidon every helper that remaineth: for the LORD will spoil the Philistines, the remnant of the country of Caphtor.

A Day of Salvation, Calling for Repentance

Isa. 61 2 To proclaim the acceptable year of the LORD, and the day of vengeance of our God; to comfort all that mourn;

Joel 1 15 Alas for the day! for the day of the LORD is at hand, and as a destruction from the Almighty shall come.

Joel 2 1 Blow ye the trumpet in Zion, and sound an alarm in my holy mountain: let all the inhabitants of the land tremble: for the day of the LORD cometh, for it is nigh at hand; 2 A day of darkness and of gloominess, a day of clouds and of thick darkness, as the morning spread upon the mountains: a great people and a strong; there hath not been ever the like, neither shall be any more after it, even to the years of many generations. 11 And the LORD shall utter his voice before his army: for his camp is very great: for he is strong that executeth his word: for the day of the LORD is great and very terrible; and who can abide it?

32 And it shall come to pass, that whosoever shall call on the name of the LORD shall be delivered: for in mount Zion and in Jerusalem shall be deliverance, as the LORD hath said, and in the remnant whom the LORD shall call.

Joel 3 14 Multitudes, multitudes in the valley of decision: for the day of the LORD is near in the valley of decision. 15 The sun and the moon shall be darkened, and the stars shall withdraw their shining.

Zech. 14 1 Behold, the day of the LORD cometh, and thy spoil shall be divided in the midst of thee. 2 For I will gather all nations against Jerusalem to battle; and the city shall be taken, and the houses rifled, and the women ravished; and half of the city shall go forth into captivity, and the residue of the people shall not be cut off from the city. 3 Then shall the LORD go forth, and fight against those nations, as when he fought in the day of battle.

4 And his feet shall stand in that day upon the mount of Olives, which is before Jerusalem on the east, and the mount of Olives shall cleave in the midst thereof toward the east and toward the west, and there shall be a very great valley; and half of the mountain shall remove toward the north, and half of it toward the south. 5 And ye shall flee to the valley of the mountains; for the valley of the mountains shall reach unto Azal: yea, ye shall flee, like as ye fled from before the earthquake in the days of Uzziah king of Judah: and the LORD my God shall come, and all the saints with thee. 6 And it shall come to

pass in that day, that the light shall not be clear, nor dark: [7]But it shall be one day which shall be known to the LORD, not day, nor night: but it shall come to pass, that at evening time it shall be light. [8]And it shall be in that day, that living waters shall go out from Jerusalem; half of them toward the former sea, and half of them toward the hinder sea: in summer and in winter shall it be. [9]And the LORD shall be King over all the earth: in that day shall there be one LORD, and his name one.

[16]And it shall come to pass, that every one that is left of all the nations which came against Jerusalem, shall even go up from year to year to worship the King, the LORD of hosts, and to keep the feast of tabernacles. [17]And it shall be, that whoso will not come up of all the families of the earth unto Jerusalem to worship the King, the LORD of hosts, even upon them shall be no rain. [18]And if the family of Egypt go not up, and come not, that have no rain; there shall be the plague, wherewith the LORD will smite the heathen that come not up to keep the feast of tabernacles. [19]This shall be the punishment of Egypt, and the punishment of all nations that come not up to keep the feast of tabernacles.

[20]In that day shall there be upon the bells of the horses, HOLINESS UNTO THE LORD; and the pots in the LORD's house shall be like the bowls before the altar. [21]Yea, every pot in Jerusalem and in Judah shall be holiness unto the LORD of hosts: and all they that sacrifice shall come and take of them, and seethe therein: and in that day there shall be no more the Canaanite in the house of the LORD of hosts.

Mal. 3 [2]But who may abide the day of the coming? and who shall stand when he appeareth? for he is like a refiner's fire, and like fullers' sope:

Mal. 4 [5]Behold, I will send you Elijah the prophet before the coming of the great and dreadful day of the LORD:

The Day of the Lord in the New Testament

Luke 17 [24]For as the lightning, that lighteneth out of the one part under heaven, shineth unto the other part under heaven; so shall also the Son of man be in his day.

1 Cor. 1 [8]Who shall also confirm you unto the end, that ye may be blameless in the day of our Lord Jesus Christ:

1 Cor. 5 [5]To deliver such an one unto Satan for the destruction of the flesh, that the spirit may be saved in the day of the Lord Jesus.

2 Cor. 1 [14]As also ye have acknowledged us in part, that we are your rejoicing, even as ye also are ours in the day of the Lord Jesus.

Phil. 1 [6]Being confident of this very thing, that he which hath begun a good work in you will perform it until the day of Jesus Christ: [10]That ye may approve things that are excellent; that ye may be sincere and without offence till the day of Christ;

Phil. 2 [16]Holding forth the word of life; that I may rejoice in the day of Christ, that I have not run in vain, neither laboured in vain.

1 Thess. 5 [2]For yourselves know perfectly that the day of the Lord so cometh as a thief in the night.

2 Thess. 2 [2]That ye be not soon shaken in mind, or be troubled, neither by spirit, nor by word, nor by letter as from us, as that the day of Christ is at hand.

DEACON, DEACONESS

[dē'k'n, dē'k'n es] This word is derived from the Greek noun *diakonos,* meaning servant, minister, or attendant. Since the early days of the church it has been used to denote a special order of Christian ministers. Traditionally, the first deacons are said to have been the seven men selected to assist the apostles in the distribution of provisions to the Greek widows in Jerusalem. (*See Acts 6:1-6*) The author of *Acts* does not, however, refer to them specifically as deacons. In *Phil. 1:1* Paul uses the word in an apparently technical sense ("bishops and deacons"); in several other passages, however, *diakonos* is used of his fellow workers Timothy (*1 Thess. 3:2*), Tychicus (*Col. 4:7*), Epaphras (*Col. 1:7*), and of his own ministry (*1 Cor. 3:5*). In his classic discussion of civil government, Paul even uses the term of non-Christian rulers (*Rom. 13:4*). In most English translations of the Bible, *diakonos* is rendered "servant" in these passages, to avoid confusion.

In *Rom. 16:1*, Paul describes Phoebe, a Christian woman of Cenchreae, as a deaconess. Although the New Testament makes no reference to an order of deaconesses, many have supposed that this term did, in fact, refer to such an institution. There is some mention of such an order in early Christian literature, but it is impossible to determine whether Paul was using the term in anything more than a general sense.

From the New Testament and other early Christian writings, we learn that the particular duties of those ordained as deacons included assisting at the Lord's Table and making certain that the needs of the poor and infirm were adequately met. The qualifications for deacons, outlined in *1 Tim. 3:8-13*, are seen to be especially fitting in the light of these duties.

DEAD SEA

[ded sē] The name given by Greek and Latin writers to the remarkable lake in Southern Palestine into which the Jordan River empties. In Scripture it is referred to as the Salt Sea (*Gen. 14:3; Deut. 3:17*), the Sea of the Plain (*Josh. 3:16*), and the Eastern Sea (*Ezek. 47:18; Joel 2:20*). The length of the sea is forty-seven miles; its width varies from two to ten miles. It is approximately 1300 feet below the level of the Mediterranean Sea. Since it has no outlets, the Dead Sea retains its minerals and salts when its waters evaporate. As a result, while ordinary sea water contains about six per cent salt, that of the Dead Sea contains more than twenty-five per cent salt. No animal life can survive in waters of such high salinity, from which fact comes the name Dead. Another interesting aspect of the sea is that the salt gives to the water such a buoyancy that it is virtually impossible for an individual to sink while swimming. Although it has often been written that birds refuse to fly over the Salt Sea, this is without foundation, since, in fact, birds are known to light on its waters.

See JORDAN RIVER

DEATH

[deth] The cessation or absence of life, viewed in the Scriptures as an evil brought on by sin. Just as the Bible has to do with two kinds of life—natural and spiritual—it deals with two kinds of death—natural and spiritual. Natural dead are those from whom the breath of life has passed; spiritual dead are those from whom the breath of the spirit has passed—those steeped in wickedness and sin. The final state of the spiritually dead is spoken of as the "second death." Christ triumphed over death in that he arose from the dead and is able to raise mankind from the same state to life everlasting. The Bible contains many references both the natural and spiritual types of death.

See RESURRECTION

SCRIPTURE

General

Job 3 17There the wicked cease from troubling; and there the weary be at rest.

Job 14 12So man lieth down, and riseth not: till the heavens be no more, they shall not awake, nor be raised out of their sleep.

Psa. 6 5For in death there is no remembrance of thee; in the grave who shall give thee thanks?

Eccl. 12 7Then shall the dust return to the earth as it was: and the spirit shall return unto God who gave it.

Isa. 38 18For the grave cannot praise thee, death cannot celebrate thee: they that go down into the pit cannot hope for thy truth.

1 Pet. 1 24For all flesh is as grass, and all

the glory of man as the flower of grass. The grass withereth, and the flower thereof falleth away.

Death Consequence of the Fall

Gen. 2 [17]But of the tree of the knowledge of good and evil, thou shalt not eat of it: for in the day that thou eatest thereof thou shalt surely die.

Gen. 3 [19]In the sweat of thy face shalt thou eat bread, till thou return unto the ground; for out of it wast thou taken: for dust thou art, and unto dust shalt thou return.

Rom. 5 [12]Wherefore, as by one man sin entered into the world, and death by sin; and so death passed upon all men, for that all have sinned.

Rom. 6 [23]For the wages of sin is death; but the gift of God is eternal life through Jesus Christ our Lord.

1 Cor. 15 [21]For since by man came death, by man came also the resurrection of the dead. [22]For as in Adam all die, even so in Christ shall all be made alive.

Death Universal

Job 14 [1]Man that is born of a woman is of few days, and full of trouble. [2]He cometh forth like a flower, and is cut down: he fleeth also as a shadow, and continueth not.

Psa. 89 [48]What man is he that liveth, and shall not see death? shall he deliver his soul from the hand of the grave? Selah.

Eccl. 8 [8]There is no man that hath power over the spirit to retain the spirit: neither hath he power in the day of death: and there is no discharge in that war; neither shall wickedness deliver those that are given to it.

Death Characterized

Job 10 [21]Before I go whence I shall not return, even to the land of darkness, and the shadow of death; [22]A land of darkness, as darkness itself; and of the shadow of death, without any order, and where the light is as darkness.

Job 16 [22]When a few years are come, then I shall go the way whence I shall not return.

Psa. 23 [4]Yea, though I walk through the valley of the shadow of death, I will fear no evil: for thou art with me; thy rod and thy staff they comfort me.

Eccl. 9 [10]Whatsoever thy hand findeth to do, do it with thy might; for there is no work, nor device, nor knowledge, nor wisdom, in the grave, whither thou goest.

Preparation for Death

Psa. 90 [12]So teach us to number our days, that we may apply our hearts unto wisdom.

John 9 [4]I must work the works of him that sent me, while it is day: the night cometh, when no man can work.

Rom. 14 [8]For whether we live, we live unto the Lord; and whether we die, we die unto the Lord: whether we live therefore, or die, we are the Lord's.

1 Pet. 1 [17]And if ye call on the Father, who without respect of persons judgeth according to every man's work, pass the time of your sojourning here in fear.

Persons Exempted from Death

ENOCH

Gen. 5 [24]And Enoch walked with God: and he was not; for God took him.

Heb. 11 [5]By faith Enoch was translated, that he should not see death, and was not found, because God had translated him: For before his translation he had this testimony, that he pleased God:

ELIJAH

2 Kin. 2 [11]And it came to pass, as they still went on, and talked, that behold, there appeared a chariot of fire, and horses of fire, and parted them both asunder; and Elijah went up by a whirlwind into heaven.

Resurrection of the Dead

Job 19 [26]And though after my skin worms destroy this body, yet in my flesh shall I see God.

Psa. 49 [15]But God will redeem my soul from the power of the grave: for he shall receive me. Selah.

Isa. 26 [19]Thy dead men shall live, together with my dead body shall they arise. Awake and sing, ye that dwell in dust: for thy dew is as the dew of herbs, and the earth shall cast out the dead.

Persons Raised from the Dead

BY ELIJAH

1 Kin. 17 [22]And the LORD heard the voice of Elijah; and the soul of the child came into him again, and he revived.

BY ELISHA

2 Kin. 4 [34]And he went up, and lay upon the child, and put his mouth upon his mouth, and his eyes upon his eyes, and his hands upon his hands: and he stretched himself upon the child; and the flesh of the child waxed warm.

2 Kin. 13 [21]And it came to pass, as they were burying a man, that behold, they spied a band of men; and they cast the man into the sepulchre of Elisha: and when the man was let down, and touched the bones of Elisha, he revived, and stood up on his feet.

BY CHRIST

Matt. 9 [24]He said unto them, Give place, for the maid is not dead, but sleepeth. And they laughed him to scorn. [25]But when the people were put forth, he went in, and took her by the hand: and the maid arose.

Luke 7 [14]And he came and touched the bier: and they that bare him stood still. And he said, Young man, I say unto thee, Arise. [15]And he that was dead sat up, and began to speak. And he delivered him to his mother.

John 11 [43]And when he thus had spoken, he cried with a loud voice, Lazarus, come forth. [44]And he that was dead came forth, bound hand and foot with graveclothes: and his face was bound about with a napkin. Jesus saith unto them, Loose him, and let him go.

BY PETER

Acts 9 [40]But Peter put them all forth, and kneeled down, and prayed, and turning him to the body, said, Tabitha, arise. And she opened her eyes, and when she saw Peter, she sat up. [41]And he gave her his hand, and lift her up: and when he had called the saints and widows, presented her alive.

BY PAUL

Acts 20 [9]And there sat in a window a certain young man named Eutychus, being fallen into a deep sleep: and as Paul was long preaching, he sunk down with sleep, and fell down from the third loft, and was taken up dead. [10]And Paul went down, and fell on him, and embracing him, said, Trouble not yourselves, for his life is in him. [11]When he therefore was come up again, and had broken bread, and eaten, and talked a long while, even till break of day, so he departed. [12]And they brought the young man alive, and were not a little comforted.

Death Vanquished by Christ

Rom. 6 [9]Knowing that Christ being raised from the dead dieth no more, death hath no more dominion over him.

2 Tim. 1 [10]But is now made manifest by the appearing of our Saviour Jesus Christ, who hath abolished death, and hath brought life and immortality to light through the gospel.

Spiritual Death and Deliverance Therefrom

Matt. 8 [22]But Jesus said unto him, Follow me, and let the dead bury their dead.

Luke 1 [79]To give light to them that sit in darkness, and in the shadow of death, to guide our feet into the way of peace.

John 6 [53]Then Jesus said unto them, Verily, verily, I say unto you, Except ye eat the flesh of the Son of man, and drink his blood, ye have no life in you.

Rom. 5 [17]For if by one man's offence death reigned by one, much more they which receive abundance of grace and of the gift of righteousness, shall reign in life by one, Jesus Christ.

Rom. 6 [16]Know ye not, that to whom ye yield yourselves servants to obey, his servants ye are to whom ye obey; whether of sin unto death, or of obedience unto righteousness?

Rom. 8 [6]For to be carnally minded, is death: but to be spiritually minded, is life and peace.

Eph. 2 [1]And you hath he quickened who were dead in trespasses and sins.

Col. 2 [13]And you being dead in your sins, and the uncircumcision of your flesh, hath he quickened together with him, having forgiven you all trespasses.

John 5 [24]Verily, verily I say unto you, He that heareth my word, and believeth on him that sent me, hath everlasting life, and shall not come into condemnation: but is passed from death unto life.

Rom. 6 [10]For in that he died, he died unto sin once: but in that he liveth, he liveth unto God. [11]Likewise reckon ye also yourselves to be dead indeed unto sin, but alive unto God, through Jesus Christ our Lord.

Eph. 5 [14]Wherefore he saith: Awake thou that sleepest, and arise from the dead, and Christ shall give thee light.

Eternal Death

Dan. 12 [2]And many of them that sleep in the dust of the earth shall awake, some to everlasting life, and some to shame and everlasting contempt.

Matt. 10 [28]And fear not them which kill the body, but are not able to kill the soul: but rather fear him which is able to destroy both soul and body in hell.

Matt. 25 [41]Then shall he say also unto them on the left hand, Depart from me, ye cursed, into everlasting fire, prepared for the devil and his angels.

Rev. 20 [14]And death and hell were cast into the lake of fire. This is the second death.

Rev. 21 [8]But the fearful, and unbelieving, and the abominable, and murderers, and whoremongers, and sorcerers, and idolaters, and all liars, shall have their part in the lake which burneth with fire and brimstone; which is the second death.

Salvation from Eternal Death

1 Cor. 15 [52]In a moment, in the twinkling of an eye, at the last trump, (for the trumpet shall sound, and the dead shall be raised incorruptible, and we shall be changed.) [53]For this corruptible must put on incorruption, and this mortal must put on immortality. [54]So when this corruptible shall have put on incorruption, and this mortal shall have put on immortality, then shall be brought to pass the saying that is written, Death is swallowed up in victory. [55]O death, where is thy sting? O grave, where is thy victory? [56]The sting of death is sin; and the strength of sin is the law. [57]But thanks be to God, which giveth us the victory through our Lord Jesus Christ.

Figurative of Regeneration

Rom. 6 [1]What shall we say then? Shall we continue in sin, that grace may abound? [2]God forbid. How shall we, that are dead to sin, live any longer therein? [3]Know ye not, that so many of us as were baptized into Jesus Christ were baptized into his death? [4]Therefore we are buried with him by baptism into death: that like as Christ was raised up from the dead by the glory of the Father, even so we also should walk in newness of life. [5]For if we have been planted together in the likeness of his death, we shall be also in the likeness of his resurrection: [6]Knowing this, that our old man is crucified with him, that the body of sin might be destroyed, that henceforth we should not serve sin. [7]For he that is dead is freed from sin. [8]Now if we be dead with Christ, we believe that we shall also live with him: [9]Knowing that Christ being raised from the dead dieth no more; death hath no more dominion over him. [10]For in that he died, he died unto sin once: but in that he liveth, he liveth unto God. [11]Likewise reckon ye also yourselves to be dead indeed unto sin, but alive unto God through Jesus Christ our Lord.

Rom. 8 [11]But if the Spirit of him that raised up Jesus from the dead dwell in you, he that raised up Christ from the dead shall also quicken your mortal bodies by his Spirit that dwelleth in you.

DEBORAH

[deb′ô ra] A prophetess and judge of Israel at a time when Israel was oppressed by Jabin, king of Hazor, and Sisera, the general of his powerful army. Deborah commanded Barak to gather men to engage Sisera in battle. Although reluctant, Barak carried out his mission with Deborah at his side and routed the army of Sisera. Sisera himself escaped but was slain by Jael, the wife of Jeber the Kenite, who put him to sleep with a glass of milk and then drove a tent peg into his temple. The beautiful poem in *Judg. 5* celebrating this victory is called "The Song of Deborah."

See JUDGES, BARAK

DECALOGUE

[dek′a log] The Ten Commandments, or Ten Words, found in *Ex. 20:2-17* and *Deut. 5:6-21.* There is probably no document in the history of mankind which has had greater influence on moral and religious life. Doubtless, part of its exalted status is derived from the Hebrew idea that these "Words" were the only thing written by God himself (*Ex. 31:18; 32:16; 34:1; Deut. 4: 13; 5:22; 10:1-4*). The Decalogue serves as a summary statement of the basic duties of the Israelites toward God and toward their fellowmen, an expression of the minimum moral and spiritual requirements without which there could be no religious community; indeed, part of their genius stems from their placing morality in intimate connection with religion. This attitude has been carried over into the Christian church, although there is apt to be less emphasis on the religious prescriptions with which the list begins than on the strictly moral precepts, and greater emphasis on the motivation behind obedience to these than upon simple obedience itself. It has become a rather common practice for Christians to discover all sorts of ethical nuances and refinements in the Ten Commandments, some of which are without foundation in fact. The brief exposition given below is designed to provide the reader with an understanding of what the Commandments probably meant to the ancient Israelites.

1. *Thou shalt have no other gods before me.*

The insistence on monotheism in the first commandment constitutes one of the unique features of the religion of Israel. It is to be clearly understood that God alone is LORD. There is no other power in the universe who rules the destinies of the earth; all power in other beings, heavenly or earthly, is derived from God. He rules without consort, progeny, or pantheon; it is true that he is surrounded by a heavenly host (*Deut. 33:2; Psa. 29:9*), but the temptation to worship these was always censured (*Deut. 4:19; 2 Kin. 23:4; Jer. 8:2*).

2. *Thou shalt not make unto thee any graven image.*

The prohibitions against images is perhaps even more in conflict with Israel's environment than monotheism. A chief characteristic of pagan worship was that only what could be seen or represented materially was an object of reverence. The religion of Israel, however, tolerated no images of its deity; despite the fact that Israel is known to have engaged in idolatrous practices, not a single figure of Yahweh, the name by which the Israelites referred to God, has ever been recovered. All this attests to the idea that Yahweh is a spiritual being who resists spatial representation; he is the LORD of History and not a being whose personality can be reflected adequately in a power of nature, or captured in the figure of a beast or a bird.

3. *Thou shalt not take the name of the Lord thy God in vain.*

The Hebrew term translated "in vain" in the third commandment carries with it the idea of "without result." Since there is no evidence that profanity was a serious evil in this period, it is quite likely that the prohibition here is against speaking the name of Yahweh without result—without doing what is vowed. The fundamental idea of this commandment, then, was probably an injunction against breaking an oath.

4. *Remember the sabbath day, to keep it holy.*

This commandment may be regarded as part of the structure of life provided by the Mosaic covenant, in which the rule of God in temporal affairs is affirmed.

5. *Honor thy father and thy mother.*

Here there is a shift from the service of God to the service of mankind. This commandment provides for the preservation of the basic unit of society, the family. It is possible that it was designed to prevent the common practice of abandonment of parents and to insure the possession of land, which was dependent on the maintenance of family solidarity.

6. *Thou shalt not kill.*

The Hebrew verb in this commandment is best translated "murder," and does not refer to killing to avenge a murder, to capital punishment, or to killing in war. The concern here is with the protection of human life within the community of Israel and the prevention of the weakening of society brought about by murder.

7. *Thou shalt not commit adultery.*

The interest of the seventh commandment is probably not on moral purity, except by implication. The verb always refers to sexual relations with the wife of another man, and not to fornication. This commandment, then, may also be seen as an effort to preserve the family unity by rendering the marriage relationship sacred and inviolable.

8. *Thou shalt not steal.*

This commandment is a simple attestation to the necessity of private property rights to a unified society.

9. *Thou shalt not bear false witness against thy neighbor.*

The primary concern of the ninth commandment is the preservation of the judicial system. The verb in this prohibition means "to answer"; that is, at court, whether as plaintiff, defendant, or witness, the individual is bound to speak the truth in a charge involving his fellowman. This does not necessarily rule out the more general notions of character assassination which are ordinarily connected with the commandment, but the central concern is probably with the integrity of the judicial system.

10. *Thou shalt not covet.*

The basic purpose of the tenth commandment is to warn against the danger of the condition of covetousness (desire in the bad sense of inordinate, ungoverned, selfish desire), from which the four preceding commandments arise.

SCRIPTURE

Ex. 20 [1]And God spake all these words,
saying, [2]I am the LORD thy God, which

have brought thee out of the land of Egypt, out of the house of bondage. [3]Thou shalt have no other gods before me. [4]Thou shalt not make unto thee any graven image, or any likeness of any thing that is in heaven above, or that is in the earth beneath, or that is in the water under the earth: [5]Thou shalt not bow down thyself to them, nor serve them: For I the LORD thy God am a jealous God, visiting the iniquity of the fathers upon the children unto the third and fourth generation of them that hate me; [6]And showing mercy unto thousands of them that love me, and keep my commandments. [7]Thou shalt not take the name of the LORD thy God in vain: for the LORD will not hold him guiltless that taketh his name in vain. [8]Remember the sabbath-day to keep it holy. [6]Six days shalt thou labour, and do all thy work: [10]But the seventh day is the sabbath of the LORD thy God: in it thou shalt not do any work, thou, nor thy son, nor thy daughter, thy man-servant, nor thy maid-servant, nor thy cattle, nor thy stranger that is within thy gates: [11]For in six days the LORD made heaven and earth, the sea and all that in them is, and rested the seventh day: wherefore the LORD blessed the sabbath-day and hallowed it.

[12]Honour thy father and thy mother; that thy days may be long upon the land which the LORD thy God giveth thee. [13]Thou shalt not kill. [14]Thou shalt not commit adultery. [15]Thou shalt not steal. [16]Thou shalt not bear false witness against thy neighbour. [17]Thou shalt not covet thy neighbour's house, thou shalt not covet thy neighbour's wife, nor his man-servant, nor his maid-servant, nor his ox, nor his ass, nor any thing that is thy neighbour's.

Ex. 31 [18]And he gave unto Moses, when he had made an end of communing with him upon mount Sinai, two tables of testimony, tables of stone, written with the finger of God.

Ex. 33 [19]And it came to pass as soon as he came nigh unto the camp, that he saw the calf, and the dancing: and Moses' anger waxed hot, and he cast the tables out of his hands, and brake them beneath the mount.

Ex. 34 [1]And the LORD said unto Moses, Hew thee two tables of stone like unto the first: and I will write upon these tables the words that were in the first tables, which thou brakest.

Matt. 5 [19]Whosoever therefore shall break one of these least commandments, and shall teach men so, he shall be called the least in the kingdom of heaven: but whosoever shall do, and teach them, the same shall be called great in the kingdom of heaven.

Matt. 19 [17]And he said unto him, Why callest thou me good? there is none good but one, that is God: but if thou wilt enter into life, keep the commandments.

Matt. 22 [37]Jesus said unto him, Thou shalt love the Lord thy God with all thy heart, and with all thy soul, and with all thy mind. [38]This is the first and great Commandment. [39]And the second is like unto it, Thou shalt love thy neighbour as thyself. [40]On these two Commandments hang all the Law and the Prophets.

DECEIT

[dē sēt′] The intentional misleading of another; any underhand practice or act intended to mislead.

SCRIPTURE

General

Psa. 5 [6]Thou shalt destroy them that

speak leasing: the LORD will abhor the bloody and deceitful man.

Jer. 17 [9]The heart is deceitful above all things, and desperately wicked: who can know it?

Mark 7 [22]Thefts, covetousness, wickedness, deceit, lasciviousness, an evil eye, blasphemy, pride, foolishness: [23]All these things come from within, and defile the man.

REFERENCE: The serpent in beguiling Eve, *Gen. 2*; Abraham in stating that Sarah was his sister, *Gen. 12:13; 20:2;* Jacob in gaining the paternal blessing, *Gen. 27:6-23*; Delilah in betraying Samson, *Judg. 16:4-20;* Gehazi in obtaining money, *2 Kin. 5*; Herod in asking of the birth of Christ, *Matt. 2:8*; Ananias and Sapphira, *Acts 5*.

DELILAH

[dē lī'la] A woman of the valley of Sorek who was loved by Samson. She was paid a tremendously high price to entice from Samson the secret of his great strength. After deceiving her several times, he revealed to her that his strength lay in his great mass of hair. When he went to sleep she had his hair shorn and turned him over to the Philistines, who gouged out his eyes and put him in prison.

See SAMSON

DELUGE

[del'ūj] Another term for the Flood, used by many writers and speakers in preference to that term. See discussion under FLOOD.

DEMAS

[dē'mas] A contracted form of the common name Demetrius. Demas was a companion of Paul during his first imprisonment at Rome. In *2 Timothy,* however, written shortly before Paul's death, the apostle makes the sad notation that "Demas hath forsaken me, having loved this present world, and is departed unto Thessalonica."

SCRIPTURE

Col. 4 [14]Luke, the beloved physician, and Demas, greet you.

Philem. 1 [24]Marcus, Aristarchus, Demas, Lucas, my fellow laborers.

2 Tim. 4 [10]For Demas hath forsaken me, having loved this present world, and is departed unto Thessalonica; . . . .

DEMETRIUS

[dē mē'tri us] 1. A silversmith of Ephesus who was engaged in the making of shrines and images of Diana. When he felt that Paul's preaching was detracting from the worship of Diana and effecting the image-making business, he incited the other silversmiths to riot, producing a gigantic stir which lasted for over two hours. (*See Acts 19*)

2. A Christian praised by Paul in *3 John 12.*

See DEMAS

DEMONS

[dē'munz] The modern definition of a demon as an evil spirit is the result of a long development; the word frequently meant something entirely different to ancient writers. Originally, it referred to a sort of anonymous god, operating alongside of, but somewhat less identifiable than, the major deities of the ancient world. Ancient writers speak of both good and bad demons or "daimones." The Hebrew word *elohim,* commonly translated "god," is sometimes used in the Old Testament to express this ancient concept. Often, when one is described as "a man of god," the meaning is that he possesses the ability to interpret omens, or some such similar power, and that this ability is attributable to a divine power, or demon. (*See 1 Sam. 2:27; 9:6; 1 Kin. 13:1; 2 Kin. 4:7*) The Old Testament also refers to the objects of pagan worship and to malign spirits, in the more familiar sense, as demons.

In the New Testament the existence of demons, as responsible for all kinds of disorder, is taken for granted. They are regarded as ministers of Satan, or Belial, or Beelzebub. They are expelled by the invoking of the name of God and by the preaching of his redemptive power and are destined to final defeat by the forces of righteousness, to be followed by consignment to everlasting fire. As in the Old Testament, the objects of pagan worship are occasionally referred to as demons.

See SATAN, BEELZEBUB

SCRIPTURE

Objects of Pagan Worship

Lev. 17 7And they shall no more offer their sacrifices unto devils, after whom they have gone a whoring. This shall be a statute for ever unto them throughout their generations.

Deut. 32 17They sacrificed unto devils, not to God; to gods whom they knew not, to new gods that came newly up, whom your fathers feared not.

2 Chr. 11 15And he ordained for him priests for the high places, and for the devils, and for the calves which he had made.

Psa. 106 37Yea, they sacrificed their sons and their daughters unto devils,

1 Cor. 10 20But I say, that the things which the Gentiles sacrifice, they sacrifice to devils, and not to God: and I would not that ye should have fellowship with devils. 21Ye cannot drink the cup of the Lord, and the cup of devils: ye cannot be partakers of the Lord's table, and of the table of devils.

1 Tim. 4 1Now the Spirit speaketh expressly, that in the latter times some shall depart from the faith, giving heed to seducing spirits, and doctrines of devils;

Rev. 9 20And the rest of the men which were not killed by these plagues yet repented not of the works of their hands, that they should not worship devils, and idols of gold, and silver, and brass, and stone, and of wood: which neither can see, nor hear, nor walk:

Disorders Pronounced by Demon Possession

Matt. 8 16When the even was come, they brought unto him many that were possessed with devils: and he cast out the spirits with his word, and healed all that were sick:

28And when he was come to the other side into the country of the Gergesenes, there met him two possessed with devils, coming out of the tombs, exceeding fierce, so that no man might pass by that way.

Matt. 9 32As they went out, behold, they brought to him a dumb man possessed with a devil.

Matt. 11 18For John came neither eating nor drinking, and they say, He hath a devil.

Matt. 12 22Then was brought unto him one possessed with a devil, blind, and dumb: and he healed him, insomuch that the blind and dumb both spake and saw.

Mark 9 18And wheresoever he taketh him, he teareth him: and he foameth, and gnasheth with his teeth, and pineth away: and I spake to thy disciples that they should cast him out; and they could not.

Luke 4 33And in the synagogue there was a man, which had a spirit of an unclean devil, and cried out with a loud voice,

Luke 13 11And, behold, there was a woman which had a spirit of infirmity eighteen years, and was bowed together, and could in no wise lift up herself.

Power Over Demons Given to Disciples

Matt. 10 1And when he had called unto him his twelve disciples, he gave them power against unclean spirits, to cast them out, and to heal all manner of sickness and all manner of disease.

Mark 16 17And these signs shall follow

them that believe; In my name shall they cast out devils; they shall speak with new tongues;

Demons Cast Out

BY JESUS

Mark 3 [22]And the scribes which came down from Jerusalem said, He hath Beelzebub, and by the prince of the devils casteth he out devils.

Luke 4 [41]And the devils came out of many, crying out, and saying, Thou art Christ the Son of God. And he rebuking them suffered them not to speak: for they knew that he was Christ.

BY THE DISCIPLES

Luke 10 [17]And the seventy returned again with joy, saying, Lord, even the devils are subject unto us through thy name.

BY PETER

Acts 5 [16]There came also a multitude out of the cities round about unto Jerusalem, bringing sick folks, and them which were vexed with unclean spirits: and they were healed every one.

BY PAUL

Acts 16 [16]And it came to pass, as we went to prayer, a certain damsel possessed with a spirit of divination met us, which brought her masters much gain by soothsaying: [17]The same followed Paul and us, and cried, saying, These men are the servants of the most high God, which shew unto us the way of salvation. [18]And this did she many days, But Paul, being grieved, turned and said to the spirit, I command thee in the name of Jesus Christ to come out of her. And he came out the same hour.

BY PHILIP

Acts 8 [7]For unclean spirits, crying with loud voice, came out of many that were possessed with them: and many taken with palsies, and that were lame, were healed.

Jesus Falsely Accused of Being Possessed by Demons

Mark 3 [22]And the scribes which came down from Jerusalem said, He hath Beelzebub, and by the prince of the devils casteth he out devils. [23]And he called them unto him, and said unto them in parables, How can Satan cast out Satan? [24]And if a kingdom be divided against itself, that kingdom can not stand. [25]And if a house be divided against itself, that house can not stand. [26]And if Satan rise up against himself, and be divided, he can not stand, but hath an end. [27]No man can enter into a strong man's house, and spoil his goods, except he will first bind the strong man; and then he will spoil his house. [28]Verily I say unto you, All sins shall be forgiven unto the sons of men, and blasphemies wherewith soever they shall blaspheme: [29]But he that shall blaspheme against the Holy Ghost hath never forgiveness, but is in danger of eternal damnation: [30]Because they said, He hath an unclean spirit.

John 7 [20]The people answered and said, Thou hast a devil: who goeth about to kill thee?

John 8 [48]Then answered the Jews, and said unto him, Say we not well that thou art a Samaritan, and hast a devil?

John 10 [20]And many of them said, He hath a devil, and is mad: why hear ye him?

Demons Believe and Tremble

Jas. 2 [19]Thou believest that there is one

God; thou doest well: the devils also believe, and tremble.

Judgment and Punishment of Demons

Matt. 8 [29]And, behold, they cried out, saying, What have we to do with thee, Jesus, thou Son of God? art thou come hither to torment us before the time?

2 Pet. 2 [4]For if God spared not the angels that sinned, but cast them down to hell, and delivered them into chains of darkness, to be reserved unto judgment;

Jude 1 [6]And the angels which kept not their first estate, but left their own habitation, he hath reserved in everlasting chains under darkness unto the judgment of the great day.

Rev. 12 [7]And there was war in heaven: Michael and his angels fought against the dragon; and the dragon fought and his angels, [8]And prevailed not; neither was their place found any more in heaven. [9]And the great dragon was cast out, that old serpent, called the Devil, and Satan, which deceiveth the whole world: he was cast out into the earth, and his angels were cast out with him.

DENIAL

[dê nī'al] The act of rejecting a person by disclaiming connection with or responsibility for him; also, refusal of assent to a proposition. The word is used in the Bible in both ways, but the more important of the references belong to the former meaning and have to do chiefly with denial of Christ.

SCRIPTURE

Warnings against Denial

2 Tim. 1 [8]Be not thou therefore ashamed of the testimony of our Lord, nor of me his prisoner, but be thou partaker of the afflictions of the Gospel according to the power of God.

Tit. 1 [16]They profess that they know God; but in works they deny him, being abominable, and disobedient, and unto every good work reprobate.

2 Pet. 2 [1]But there were false prophets also among the people, even as there shall be false teachers among you, who privily shall bring in damnable heresies, even denying the Lord that brought them, and bring upon themselves swift destruction.

Jude 1 [4]For there are certain men crept in unawares, who were before of old ordained to this condemnation, ungodly men, turning the grace of our God into lasciviousness, and denying the only Lord God, and our Lord Jesus Christ.

Punishment of Denial

Matt. 10 [33]But whosoever shall deny me before men, him will I also deny before my Father which is in heaven.

Mark 8 [38]Whosoever therefore shall be ashamed of me and of my words in this adulterous and sinful generation; of him also shall the Son of man be ashamed, when he cometh in the glory of his Father with the holy angels.

2 Tim. 2 [12]If we suffer, we shall also reign with him: if we deny him, he also will deny us.

Peter's Denial

Matt. 26 [69]Now Peter sat without in the palace: and a damsel came unto him, saying, Thou also wast with Jesus in Galilee. [70]But he denied before them all, saying, I know not what thou sayest. [71]And when he was gone out into the porch, another maid saw him, and said unto them that were there, This fellow was also with Jesus of Nazareth. [72]And again he denied with an oath, I do not know the man. [73]And after a while came unto him they that stood by, and said to Peter, Surely

thou also art one of them, for thy speech
bewrayeth thee. [74]Then began he to curse
and to swear, saying, I know not the man.
And immediately the cock crew. [75]And
Peter remembered the words of Jesus,
which said unto him, Before the cock crow,
thou shalt deny me thrice. And he went
out, and wept bitterly.

Denial by the Jews

John 18 [40]Then cried they all again, saying, Not this man, but Barabbas. Now Barabbas was a robber.

John 19 [15]But they cried out, Away with him, away with him, crucify him. Pilate saith unto them, Shall I crucify your King? The chief Priests answered, We have no king but Caesar.

Acts 3 [13]The God of Abraham, and of Isaac, and of Jacob, the God of our fathers, hath glorified his son Jesus, whom ye delivered up, and denied him in the presence of Pilate, when he was determined to let him go.

DESPAIR

[dê spâr′] To be without hope; a state of complete despondency. Many passages in the Bible warn against abandoning one's self to such moods, while others contain comfort and uplift for those who find themselves in such a condition.

SCRIPTURE

Expressions of Despair

Gen. 4 [13]And Cain said unto the Lord,
My punishment is greater than I can bear.
[14]Behold, thou hast driven me out this day
from the face of the earth; and from thy face shall I be hid; and I shall be a fugitive and a vagabond in the earth; and it shall come to pass, that everyone that findeth me shall slay me.

Ex. 6 [9]And Moses spake so unto the children of Israel: but they hearkened not unto Moses for anguish of spirit, and for cruel bondage.

Jer. 8 [20]The harvest is past, the summer is ended, and we are not saved.

Mic. 7 [1]Woe is me! for I am as when
they have gathered the summer fruits, as
the grape gleanings of the vintage: there
is no cluster to eat: my soul desired the
first ripe fruit. [2]The good man is perished
out of the earth; and there is none upright
among men: they all lie in wait for blood;
they hunt every man his brother with a
net.

Comfort and Hope in Despair

Psa. 31 [22]For I said in my haste, I am
cut off from before thine eyes: nevertheless thou heardest the voice of my supplications when I cried unto thee. [24]Be of
good courage, and he shall strengthen
your heart, all ye that hope in the Lord.

Psa. 42 [11]Why art thou cast down, O my soul: and why art thou disquieted within me? hope thou in God: for I shall yet praise him, who is the health of my countenance, and my God.

Isa. 40 [31]But they that wait upon the Lord shall renew their strength; they shall mount up with wings as eagles; they shall run, and not be weary; and they shall walk, and not faint.

2 Cor. 4 [8]We are troubled on every side,
yet not distressed; we are perplexed, but
not in despair; [9]Persecuted, but not forsaken; cast down, but not destroyed;

Exhortation to Avoid Despair

Luke 18 [1]And he spake a parable unto them to this end, that men ought always to pray, and not to faint.

John 14 [1]Let not your heart be troubled: ye believe in God, believe also in me.

Heb. 12 [5]And ye have forgotten the exhortation which speaketh unto you as unto children, My son, despise not thou the chastening of the Lord, nor faint when thou art rebuked of him: [6]For whom the Lord loveth he chasteneth, and scourgeth every son whom he receiveth.

DIANA (Artemis)

[dī an′a] In classical Greek and Roman religion Diana, or Artemis, as she is also called, was a widely worshipped female deity represented as a virgin huntress, the patroness of women, hunters, and fishermen. The "Diana of the Ephesians" mentioned in *Acts 19* bears little relation to the classical Diana; rather, she was a form of the Asian mother-goddess who had been worshipped in Ephesus since the second millenium BC. She was worshipped as a goddess of fertility in man, beast, and vegetation, and was pictured not as a virgin, but was a fecund mother. While on his third missionary tour, Paul remained in Ephesus for more than two years. His preaching proved so effective as to pose an economic threat to those engaged in making silver replicas of the temple of Diana. Led by one of their number, whose name was Demetrius, the silversmiths precipitated a riot which nearly cost the life of Gaius and Aristarchus, two of Paul's traveling companions. The account of this riot and its outcome is contained in *Acts 19:23-41*.

DILIGENCE

[dil′i jens] Constancy, earnestness, application; devoted painstaking and effort to achieve an end. Diligence is one of the many virtues upheld in the Bible.

See SLOTHFULNESS

SCRIPTURE

Diligence in Service to God

Ex. 15 [26]And said, If thou wilt diligently hearken to the voice of the LORD thy God, and wilt do that which is right in his sight, and wilt give ear to his commandments, and keep all his statutes, I will put none of these diseases upon thee, which I have brought upon the Egyptians: for I am the LORD that healeth thee.

Deut. 4 [9]Only take heed to thyself, and keep thy soul diligently, lest thou forget the things which thine eyes have seen, and lest they depart from thy heart all the days of thy life: but teach them thy sons, and thy sons' sons.

Ezra 7 [23]Whatsoever is commanded by the God of heaven, let it be diligently done for the house of the God of heaven: for why should there be wrath against the realm of the king and his sons?

Rom. 12 [8]Or he that exhorteth, on exhortation: he that giveth, let him do it with simplicity: he that ruleth, with diligence.

1 Cor. 15 [58]Therefore, my beloved brethren, be ye steadfast, unmovable, always abounding in the work of the Lord, forasmuch as ye know that your labor is not in vain in the Lord.

Gal. 6 [9]And let us not be weary in well doing: for in due season we shall reap, if we faint not.

Heb. 11 [6]But without faith it is impossible to please him: for he that cometh to God must believe that he is, and that he is a rewarder of them that diligently seek him.

2 Pet. 3 [14]Wherefore, beloved, seeing that ye look for such things, be diligent that ye may be found of him in peace, without spot, and blameless.

Diligence in Worldly Affairs

Prov. 10 [4]He becometh poor that dealeth with a slack hand; but the hand of the diligent maketh rich.

Prov. 12 [24]The hand of the diligent shall bear rule: but the slothful shall be under tribute.

Prov. 13 [4]The soul of the sluggard desireth, and hath nothing: but the soul of the diligent shall be made fat.

Prov. 22 [29]Seest thou a man diligent in his business? he shall stand before kings; he shall not stand before mean men.

DINAH

[dī′na] The daughter of Jacob and Leah. The ravishment of Dinah by the prince of the city of Shechem brought treacherous vengeance on that city at the hands of her brothers, Simeon and Levi. Many scholars feel that various elements in the narrative indicate that the significance of the story was primarily tribal rather than personal.

See SIMEON, LEVI

REFERENCE: *Gen. 30:21; 34.*

DIOTREPHES

[dī ot′re fēz] The third epistle of John was occasioned by the approaching visit of travelling missionaries to the church where Gaius was a member. These men were dependent on the hospitality of fellow-Christians for their livelihood. In the congregation was an influential man named Diotrephes. On previous occasions, he had arrogantly boycotted and excluded certain individuals from the fellowship of the church. John had previously written a letter on this matter but it had been suppressed or ignored as a result of Diotrephes' refusal to recognize the authority of the writer. This epistle was written to inform Gaius as to the proper course of action.

See GAIUS

SCRIPTURE

3 John 1 [9]I wrote unto the church: but Diotrephes, who loveth to have the preeminence among them, receiveth us not.
[10]Wherefore, if I come, I will remember his deeds which he doeth, prating against us with malicious words: and not content therewith, neither doth he himself receive the brethren, and forbiddeth them that would, and casteth them out of the church.

DISCIPLE

[di sī′p'l] A learner; a pupil, as contrasted to the teacher or master; one who accepts not only the views of the teacher, but one who attempts to put them into practice. Although used of the followers of John the Baptist, the Pharisees, and Moses, this term ordinarily refers to the adherents of Jesus; it is, in fact, the only name given to them in the gospels. After the establishment of the church in Antioch of Syria, the disciples came to be called Christians.

See CHRISTIAN

SCRIPTURE

Disciples

OF JOHN THE BAPTIST

Matt. 9 [14]Then came to him the disciples of John, saying, Why do we and the Pharisees fast oft, but thy disciples fast not?

See Luke 7:18; John 3:25

OF THE PHARISEES

Matt. 22 [16]And they sent out unto him their disciples with the Herodians, saying, Master, we know that thou art true, and teachest the way of God in truth, neither carest thou for any man: for thou regardest not the person of men.

See Mark 2:18; Luke 5:33

OF MOSES

John 9 [28]Then they reviled him, and said, Thou art his disciple; but we are Moses' disciples.

Jesus' Disciples

ALL WHO FOLLOW HIM

Matt. 10 [42]And whosoever shall give to drink unto one of these little ones a cup of cold water only in the name of a disciple, verily I say unto you, he shall in no wise lose his reward.

Luke 6 [17]And he came down with them,

and stood in the plain, and the company of his disciples, and a great multitude of people out of all Judea and Jerusalem, and from the seacoast of Tyre and Sidon, which came to hear him, and to be healed of their diseases;

John 6 [66]From that time many of his disciples went back, and walked no more with him.

THE APOSTLES

Matt. 10 [1]And when he had called unto him his twelve disciples, he gave them power against unclean spirits, to cast them out, and to heal all manner of sickness and all manner of disease.

Matt. 11 [1]And it came to pass, when Jesus had made an end of commanding his twelve disciples, he departed thence to teach and to preach in their cities.

Matt. 12 [1]At that time Jesus went on the sabbath day through the corn; and his disciples were ahungered, and began to pluck the ears of corn, and to eat.

Disciples Called Christians

Acts 11 [26]And when he had found him, he brought him unto Antioch. And it came to pass, that a whole year they assembled themselves with the church, and taught much people. And the disciples were called Christians first in Antioch.

Command to Make Disciples

Matt. 28 [19]Go ye therefore, and teach all nations, baptizing them in the name of the Father, and of the Son, and of the Holy Ghost:

DISHONESTY

[dis on′es ti] Lack of honesty, integrity; unworthy of trust or belief.

See Deceit, Honesty, Hypocrisy

SCRIPTURE

General

Psa. 37 [21]The wicked borroweth, and payeth not again: but the righteous showeth mercy, and giveth.

Amos 8 [5]When will the new moon be gone, that we may sell corn? and the sabbath, that we may set forth wheat, making the ephah small, and the shekel great, and falsifying the balances by deceit?

Dishonesty Condemned

Lev. 19 [13]Thou shalt not defraud thy neighbour, neither rob him: the wages of him that is hired shall not abide with thee all night until the morning.

[35]Ye shall do no unrighteousness in judgment, in meteyard, in weight, or in measure. [36]Just balances, just weights, a just ephah, and a just hin, shall ye have: I am the Lord your God, ...

Deut. 25 [13]Thou shalt not have in thy bag divers weights, a great and a small. [14]Thou shalt not have in thine house divers measures, a great and a small. [15]But thou shalt have a perfect and just weight, a perfect and just measure shalt thou have: . . . . [16]For all that do such things, and all that do unrighteously, are an abomination unto the Lord thy God.

Prov. 11 [1]A false balance is abomination to the Lord.

DISOBEDIENCE

[dis ō bē′di ens] Failure, through refusal or neglect, to conform to a command of a duly empowered superior. In the Bible it has the primary meaning of failure to respond in loving acquiescence to God's gracious commands. Israel's disobedience in her repeated failure to keep the covenant is cited as the source of virtually all of her misery. In both testaments, the Scriptures are insistent that those who are disobedient shall be punished.

See OBEDIENCE

SCRIPTURE

General

Deut. 28 [15]But it shall come to pass, if thou wilt not hearken unto the voice of the LORD thy God, to observe to do all his commandments and his statutes which I command thee this day: that all these curses shall come upon thee, and overtake thee.

Josh. 5 [6]For the children of Israel walked forty years in the wilderness, till all the people that were men of war which came out of Egypt were consumed, because they obeyed not the voice of the LORD: unto whom the LORD sware that he would not shew them the land which the LORD sware unto their fathers that he would give us, a land that floweth with milk and honey.

Isa. 42 [24]Who gave Jacob for a spoil, and Israel to the robbers? did not the LORD, he against whom we have sinned? for they would not walk in his ways, neither were they obedient unto his law.

Eph. 5 [6]Let no man deceive you with vain words: for because of these things cometh the wrath of God upon the children of disobedience.

Tit. 1 [16]They profess that they know God; but in works they deny him, being abominable, and disobedient, and unto every good work reprobate.

Tit. 3 [3]For we ourselves also were sometimes foolish, disobedient, deceived, serving divers lusts and pleasures, living in malice and envy, hateful, and hating one another.

Heb. 2 [2]For if the word spoken by angels was stedfast, and every transgression and disobedience received a just recompense of reward: [3]How shall we escape, if we neglect so great salvation, which at the first began to be spoken by the Lord, and was confirmed unto us by them that heard him?

REFERENCE: Adam and Eve eating the forbidden fruit, *Gen. 3:6-11;* Lot's wife in looking back at Sodom, *Gen. 19:26;* Moses in smiting the rock, *Num. 20:11, 23, 24;* Achan in keeping the spoil of Jericho for himself, *Josh. 7:15-26*; Saul in offering sacrifice, *1 Sam. 13:13*; and Saul in sparing Agag and the Amaelkites, *1 Sam. 15*.

DISPENSATION

[dis pen sā′shun] Literally, the act of dispensing, or dealing out; in a theological sense, the word is often used to designate a system of principles, promises and rules ordained and administered as "the Christian dispensation."

DISPERSION

[dis pûr′shun] Also called the Diaspora, this was the designation applied to Jews living outside of Palestine who still maintained the Jewish religious observances and manner of life among the Gentiles. The Assyrian and Babylonian captivities were the initial, but by no means the only, cause of the Dispersion. There were captivities under Syria, Egypt, and Roman rulers which scattered Jews to Phrygia, Lydia, Alexandria, and Rome. In addition, many Jews emigrated of their own volition to various commercial centers of the world. The great monument of the Dispersion was the Septuagint, the Greek translation of the Hebrew Old Testament. This was produced in Alexandria, in the third century, for the use of Jews among whom the Hebrew tongue had fallen into disuse. The Septuagint was the Bible used by Jesus, the Apostles, and the early Christians. Its name means "seventy" and is derived from the old tradition that the work of translation was performed by either seventy or seventy-two scholars. In commentaries, etc., it is often designated by the Roman numerals LXX.

SCRIPTURE

Jer. 16 [15]But, the LORD liveth, that
brought up the children of Israel from the
land of the north, and from all the lands
whither he had driven them: and I will
bring them again into their land that I gave
unto their fathers.

John 7 [35]Then said the Jews among
themselves, Whither will he go, that we
shall not find him? will he go unto the dispersed among the Gentiles, and teach the
Gentiles?

DIVISION

[di vizh'un] The separation of a thing into parts; also, discord or disunion. In the Old Testament the word is sometimes used to designate a particular body of people, such as the subgroupings within a tribe. In the New Testament it appears primarily in passages warning against schisms within the body of Christ.

See UNITY

SCRIPTURE

Admonitions against Division

Rom. 16 [17]Now I beseech you, brethren,
mark them which cause divisions and offenses contrary to the doctrine which ye
have learned; and avoid them. [18]For they
that are such serve not our Lord Jesus
Christ, but their own belly; and by good
words and fair speeches deceive the hearts
of the simple.

1 Cor. 1 [10]Now I beseech you, brethren,
by the name of our Lord Jesus Christ, that
ye all speak the same thing, and that there
be no divisions among you; but that ye be
perfectly joined together in the same mind
and in the same judgment. [12]Now this I
say, that every one of you saith, I am of
Paul; and I of Apollos; and I of Cephas;
and I of Christ. [13]Is Christ divided? was
Paul crucified for you? or were ye baptized in the name of Paul?

1 Cor. 3 [3]For ye are yet carnal: for
whereas there is among you envying, and
strife, and divisions, are ye not carnal, and
walk as men? [4]For while one saith, I am
of Paul; and another, I am of Apollos; are
ye not carnal?

1 Cor. 11 [18]For first of all, when ye come
together in the church, I hear that there
be divisions among you; and I partly believe it. [19]For there must be also heresies
among you, that they which are approved
may be manifest among you.

1 Tim. 6 [3]If any man teach otherwise,
and consent not to wholesome words, even
the words of our Lord Jesus Christ, and to
the doctrine which is according to godliness; [4]He is proud, knowing nothing, but
doting about questions and strifes of
words, whereof cometh envy, strife, railings, evil surmisings,

DIVORCE

[di vōrs'] Legal dissolution of a marriage relation. In Old Testament times, divorce was generally permitted if the husband desired it. The most common grounds for divorce seem to have been barrenness and "indecency" (*Deut. 23:14*), a term whose exact meaning has been widely disputed. When a man divorced his wife he gave her a "bill of divorcement" and sent her away from him. There were two situations in which Israelite law prohibited divorce: when a man had falsely accused his wife of unchastity (*Deut. 22:13-19*), and when a man had had sexual relations with a girl and had been compelled by her father to marry her (*Deut. 22:28-29*).

Jesus viewed the laxity of the Law with regard to divorce as a concession to the weakness of the Israelites and cited sexual infidelity as the only permissible grounds for divorce (*Matt. 5:32; 19:3-12; Mark 10:2-13; Luke 16:18*).

In dealing with the difficult problem of maintaining Christian marriage in a pagan society, Paul asserts that the unmarried state leaves an individual free to devote himself wholly to things spiritual, yet he counsels against divorce except in such cases in which an unbelieving partner wishes to divorce his Christian spouse.

See MARRIAGE, ADULTERY, FORNICATION

SCRIPTURE

Mosaic Divorce

Deut. 24 [1]When a man hath taken a wife, and married her, and it come to pass that she find no favour in his eyes, because he hath found some uncleanness in her: then let him write her a bill of divorcement, and give it in her hand, and send her out of his house. [2]And when she is departed out of his house, she may go and be another man's wife. [3]And if the latter husband hate her, and write her a bill of divorcement, and giveth it in her hand, and sendeth her out of his house; or if the latter husband die, which took her to be his wife; [4]Her former husband, which sent her away, may not take her again to be his wife, after that she is defiled; for that is abomination before the LORD: and thou shalt not cause the land to sin, which the LORD thy God giveth thee for an inheritance.

Christ's Law

Matt. 5 [31]It hath been said, Whosoever shall put away his wife, let him give her a writing of divorcement: [32]But I say unto you, That whosoever shall put away his wife, saving for the cause of fornication, causeth her to commit adultery: and whosoever shall marry her that is divorced committeth adultery.

Matt. 19 [3]The Pharisees also came unto him, tempting him, and saying unto him, Is it lawful for a man to put away his wife for every cause? [4]And he answered and said unto them, Have ye not read, that he which made them at the beginning made them male and female, [5]And said, For this cause shall a man leave father and mother, and shall cleave to his wife: and they twain shall be one flesh? [6]Wherefore they are no more twain, but one flesh. What therefore God hath joined together, let not man put asunder. [7]They say unto him, Why did Moses then command to give a writing of divorcement, and to put her away? [8]He saith unto them, Moses because of the hardness of your hearts suffered you to put away your wives: but from the beginning it was not so. [9]And I say unto you, Whosoever shall put away his wife, except it be for fornication, and shall marry another, committeth adultery: and whoso marrieth her which is put away doth commit adultery.

Mark 10 [2]And the Pharisees came to him, and asked him, Is it lawful for a man to put away his wife? tempting him. [3]And he answered and said unto them, What did Moses command you? [4]And they said, Moses suffered to write a bill of divorcement, and to put her away. [5]And Jesus answered and said unto them, For the hardness of your heart he wrote you this precept. [6]But from the beginning of the creation God made them male and female. [7]For this cause shall a man leave his father and mother, and cleave to his wife; [8]And they twain shall be one flesh: so then they are no more twain, but one flesh. [9]What therefore God hath joined together, let not man put asunder. [10]And in the house his disciples asked him again of the same matter. [11]And he saith unto them, Whosoever shall put away his wife, and marry another, committeth adultery against her. [12]And if a woman shall put away her husband, and be married to another, she committeth adultery.

Paul's Teaching

1 Cor. 7 [10]And unto the married I com-

mand, yet not I, but the Lord, Let not the
wife depart from her husband: 11But and
if she depart, let her remain unmarried, or
be reconciled to her husband: and let not
the husband put away his wife. 12But to
the rest speak I, not the Lord: If any
brother hath a wife that believeth not, and
she be pleased to dwell with him, let him
not put her away. 13And the woman which
hath an husband that believeth not, and if
he be pleased to dwell with her, let her not
leave him. 14For the unbelieving husband
is sanctified by the wife, and the unbelieving wife is sanctified by the husband: else
were your children unclean; but now are
they holy. 15But if the unbelieving depart,
let him depart. A brother or a sister is not
under bondage in such cases: but God hath
called us to peace. 16For what knowest
thou, O wife, whether thou shalt save thy
husband? or how knowest thou, O man,
whether thou shalt save thy wife? 17But
as God hath distributed to every man, as
the Lord hath called every one, so let him
walk. And so ordain I in all churches.

DOCTRINE

[dok'trin] Literally, that which is taught. The term may refer to any special code or system of religion, morals, ethics, or principles taught or delivered; such as, Catholic doctrine, Presbyterian doctrine, Baptist doctrine, etc. The Christian doctrine is based on the preaching and writing of Jesus and his apostles. The New Testament contains numerous warnings against false doctrine.

See TEACH, HERESY

SCRIPTURE

The Doctrine of Christ

Matt. 7 28And it came to pass, when Jesus had ended these sayings, the people
were astonished at his doctrine. 29For he
taught them as one having authority, and
not as the Scribes.

John 7 16Jesus answered them, My doctrine is not mine, but his that sent me. 17If
any man will do his will, he shall know of
the doctrine, whether it be of God, or
whether I speak of myself.

Acts 2 42And they continued stedfastly
in the Apostles' doctrine and fellowship,
and in breaking of bread, and in prayers.

1 Tim. 4 16Take heed unto thyself, and
unto the doctrine: continue in them: for
in doing this, thou shalt both save thyself,
and them that hear thee.

1 Tim. 6 3If any man teach otherwise,
and consent not to wholesome words, even
the words of our Lord Jesus Christ, and to
the doctrine which is according to godliness; 4He is proud, knowing nothing, but
doting about questions, and strifes of
words, whereof cometh envy, strife, railings, evil surmisings.

2 Tim. 3 16All Scripture is given by inspiration of God, and is profitable for doctrine, for reproof, for correction, for instruction in righteousness, 17That the man
of God may be perfect, throughly furnished unto all good works.

2 John 1 9Whosoever transgresseth and
abideth not in the doctrine of Christ, hath
not God: he that abideth in the doctrine of
Christ, he hath both the Father and the
Son. 10If there come any unto you, and
bring not this doctrine, receive him not
into your house, neither bid him God
speed.

False Doctrine

Matt. 5 19Whosoever therefore shall
break one of these least commandments,
and shall teach men so, he shall be called
the least in the kingdom of heaven: but
whosoever shall do and teach them, the
same shall be called great in the kingdom
of heaven.

Matt. 15 9But in vain they do worship

me, teaching for doctrines the commandments of men.

Rom. 16 [17]Now I beseech you, brethren, mark them which cause divisions and offenses contrary to the doctrine which ye have learned; and avoid them.

Gal. 1 [6]I marvel that ye are so soon removed from him that called you into the grace of Christ unto another gospel:

Eph. 4 [14]That we henceforth be no more children, tossed to and fro, and carried about with every wind of doctrine, by the sleight of men, and cunning craftiness, whereby they lie in wait to deceive;

1 Tim. 4 [1]Now the Spirit speaketh expressly, that in the latter times some shall depart from the faith, giving heed to seducing spirits, and doctrines of devils; [2]Speaking lies in hypocrisy; having their conscience seared with a hot iron; [3]Forbidding to marry, and commanding to abstain from meats, which God hath created to be received with thanksgiving of them which believe and know the truth.

Tit. 3 [10]A man that is a heretic, after the first and second admonition, reject; [11]Knowing that he that is such is subverted, and sinneth, being condemned of himself.

2 Pet. 2 [1]But there were false prophets also among the people, even as there shall be false teachers among you, who privily shall bring in damnable heresies, even denying the Lord that bought them, and bring upon themselves swift destruction. [2]And many shall follow their pernicious ways; by reason of whom the way of truth shall be evil spoken of.

DORCAS

[dôr′kas] This name is the Greek equivalent for the Aramaic Tabitha, meaning Gazelle. It was the name of a disciple at Joppa who was "full of good works and almsdeeds which she did." At her death the disciples, having heard that Peter was in nearby Lydda and had healed Eneas of the palsy, summoned him to Joppa. When he arrived, a number of widows stood around weeping and holding up garments which Dorcas had made for them while she was alive. Then Peter went into the room where she had been laid, commanded her to rise, and "presented her alive. And it was known throughout all Joppa; and many believed in the Lord."

REFERENCE: *Acts 9:36-42.*

DOVE

[duv] A well-known bird of the family *Columbidae*, closely related to the pigeon. The first mention of the dove occurs in the story of Noah, in which a dove was sent out to determine whether the flood waters had abated (*Gen. 8:8-12*). Passages dealing with the sacrificial system of the religion of Israel inform us that doves were a common sacrifice. The dove is referred to in the Bible as a figure for beauty, tenderness, harmlessness, purity, and gentleness. To Christians, the dove has been remembered as a symbol of the Holy Spirit, based on the gospel accounts of Jesus' baptism, in which the Spirit is said to have descended upon Jesus "in a bodily shape like a dove."

REFERENCE: *Gen. 8:8-12; Lev. 1:14-17; 5:7-10; Num. 6:10; Matt. 3:16; 10:16; Luke 3:22; John 1:32.*

DREAM

[drēm] A series of thoughts, images, or emotions, occurring during sleep; any seeming of reality occurring to one sleeping. The Bible contains numerous references to dreams as a means of God's communication with men.

See VISION

REFERENCE: *Gen. 20:3; 28:12; 31:10, 24; 37:5; 40:5; Judg. 7:13; 1 Kin. 3:5; Dan. 2 and 4; Matt. 2:12; 27:19; Acts 10.*

DRINK, DRUNKARD, DRUNKENNESS

[drink, drunk′ẽrd, drunk″n nes] The Hebrew word translated in the Old Testament as "strong drink" refers to every sort of intoxicating beverage except wine; there was a separate word for wine, but the two are almost always coupled together as exhaustive of all types of intoxicants. That the drinking of these intoxicants to excess was a common practice among the ancient Hebrews, is made quite clear by numerous accounts of individual drunkenness and by references to drunkenness as a social evil. Although the Bible contains no prescription of total abstinence as a universal rule, it is consistent in its condemnation of intemperance in the use of intoxicants. Drunkenness is sometimes used as a figure for intellectual, moral, or spiritual confusion.

See TEMPERANCE, ABSTINENCE

SCRIPTURE

Drink Forbidden

Num. 6 [3]He shall separate himself from wine and strong drink, and shall drink no vinegar of wine, or vinegar of strong drink, neither shall he drink any liquor of grapes, nor eat moist grapes, or dried.

Prov. 31 [4]It is not for kings, O Lemuel, it is not for kings to drink wine; nor for princes strong drink: [5]Lest they drink, and forget the law, and pervert the judgment of any of the afflicted.

Prov. 20 [1]Wine is a mocker, strong drink is raging: and whosoever is deceived thereby is not wise.

Prov. 23 [31]Look not thou upon the wine when it is red, when it giveth his color in the cup, when it moveth itself aright, [32]At the last it biteth like a serpent, and stingeth like an adder.

Drunkards

Prov. 23 [20]Be not among winebibbers; among riotous eaters of flesh: [21]For the drunkard and the glutton shall come to poverty: and drowsiness shall clothe a man with rags.

Joel 1 [5]Awake, ye drunkards, and weep: and howl, all ye drinkers of wine, because of the new wine; for it is cut off from your mouth.

1 Cor. 5 [11]But now I have written unto you not to keep company, if any man that is called a brother be a fornicator, or covetous, or an idolater, or a railer, or a drunkard, or an extortioner; with such an one no not to eat.

See 1 Cor. 6:9-10

Drunkenness

Prov. 21 [17]He that loveth wine . . . shall not be rich.

Hab. 2 [15]Woe unto him that giveth his neighbour drink, that puttest thy bottle to him, and makest him drunken also, that thou mayest look on their nakedness!

Luke 21 [34]Take heed to yourselves, lest at any time your hearts be overcharged with surfeiting, and drunkenness, and cares of this life, and so that day come upon you unawares.

Eph. 5 [18]Be not drunk with wine, wherein is excess; . . . .

1 Thess. 5 [7] . . . They that be drunken are drunken in the night. [8]But let us, who are of the day, be sober, ...

REFERENCE: Noah, *Gen. 9:21;* Lot, *Gen. 19:33, 35;* Nabal, *1 Sam. 25:36;* Benhadad, *1 Kin. 20:16.*

DUST

[dust] Fine dry pulverized particles of earth or other matter. In the Bible, dust is used as a figure for things that are low, humble, impure, and contemptuous. Since man is said to have been formed of the dust of the earth, it is used as a symbol of human frailty. As an expression of execration, dust was sometimes cast into the air. Closely related to this is the shaking of dust from one's feet, indicating renunciation of a person or a group of persons.

SCRIPTURE

General

Gen. 2 [7]And the LORD God formed man of the dust of the ground, and breathed into his nostrils the breath of life; and man became a living soul.

Gen. 3 [19]In the sweat of thy face shalt thou eat bread, till thou return unto the ground; for out of it wast thou taken: for dust thou art, and unto dust shalt thou return.

Gen. 18 [27]And Abraham answered and said, Behold now, I have taken upon me to speak unto the LORD, which am but dust and ashes.

Job 10 [9]Remember, I beseech thee, that thou hast made me as the clay; and wilt thou bring me into dust again?

Job 34 [15]All flesh shall perish together, and man shall turn again unto dust.

As a Sign of Disgust or Renunciation

2 Sam. 16 [13]And as David and his men went by the way, Shimei went along on the hillside over against him, and cursed as he went, and threw stones at him, and cast dust.

Matt. 10 [14]And whosoever shall not receive you, nor hear your words, when ye depart out of that house or city, shake off the dust of your feet.

Luke 10 [11]Even the very dust of your city which cleaveth on us, we do wipe off against you: notwithstanding, be ye sure of this, that the kingdom of God is come nigh unto you.

Acts 22 [23]And as they cried out, and cast off their clothes, and threw dust into the air.

See Mark 6:11; Luke 9:5

EASTER

[ēs′tẽr] An annual celebration observed by much of the Christian church, commemorating Christ's resurrection. Modern observance of Easter represents a convergence of three traditions: (1) The Hebrew Passover, celebrated during Nisan, the first month of the Hebrew lunar calendar (*see* FEASTS); (2) The Christian commemoration of the crucifixion and resurrection of Jesus, which took place at the feast of the Passover; and (3) The Norse *Ostara* or *Eostra* (from which the name "Easter" is derived), a pagan festival of spring which fell at the vernal equinox, March 21. Prominent symbols in this celebration of the resurrection of nature after the winter were rabbits, signifying fecundity, and eggs, colored like the rays of the returning sun and the northern lights, or aurora borealis.

The fixing of the date of the celebration of Jesus' resurrection was the occasion of much controversy in the early church. One group insisted that the festival fall on a Sunday, since the Lord rose on the first day of the week; the opposition insisted that it be coordinated with the Jewish passover, which might fall on any day of the week. In AD 325 the council of Nicaea decreed that the resurrection would ordinarily be celebrated on the first Sunday after the full moon following the vernal equinox; if, however, the full moon fell on a Sunday, the celebration was to be postponed a week, to avoid coincidence with the Jewish Passover. This method of reckoning the date of Easter, which is still in use, means that Easter may fall at any time within the 35-day period between March 22 and April 25.

EBAL

[e′bal] A mountain which rises north of the valley of Shechem, opposite mount Gerizim. (*See* GERIZIM) On this mountain Joshua erected an altar of unhewn stones and wrote upon it a copy of the Law of Moses. In what must have been an impressive ceremony, the ancient Hebrews gathered on the lower slopes of these two mountains, with the ark, the priests, and the Levites in the valley between them. Then the Curses and Blessings of the law were read by the Levites; at the reading of the Curses, the tribes gathered on Mount Ebal would shout "Amen" in chorus. The congregation on Gerizim gave a similar response at the reading of the Blessings of the law. The acoustics of this area have been tested a number of times, proving conclusively the possibility of such a ceremony.

SCRIPTURE

Deut. 11 [29]And it shall come to pass,

when the LORD thy God hath brought thee in unto the land whither thou goest to possess it, that thou shalt put the blessing upon mount Gerizim, and the curse upon mount Ebal.

Deut. 27 [12]These shall stand upon mount Gerizim to bless the people, when ye are come over Jordan; Simeon, and Levi, and Judah, and Issachar, and Joseph, and Benjamin: [13]And these shall stand upon mount Ebal to curse; Reuben, Gad, and Asher, and Zebulun, Dan, and Naphtali.

Josh. 8 [30]Then Joshua built an altar unto the LORD God of Israel in mount Ebal:

[33]And all Israel, and their elders, and officers, and their judges, stood on this side the ark and on that side before the priests the Levites, which bare the ark of the covenant of the LORD, as well the stranger, as he that was born among them; half of them over against mount Gerizim, and half of them over against mount Ebal; as Moses the servant of the LORD had commanded before, that they should bless the people of Israel.

EBED-MELECH

[eb ed-mel′lek] An Ethiopian eunuch, the servant of Zedekiah king of Judah. It was he who rescued the prophet Jeremiah from the cistern into which he had been cast, for which act Jeremiah promised that his life would be spared in the fall of Jerusalem.

See EUNUCH

SCRIPTURE

Jer. 38 [7]Now when Ebed-melech the Ethiopian, one of the eunuchs which was in the king's house, heard that they had put Jeremiah in the dungeon; the king then sitting in the gate of Benjamin; [8]Ebed-melech went forth out of the king's house, and spake to the king, saying, [9]My lord the king, these men have done evil in all that they have done to Jeremiah the prophet, whom they have cast into the dungeon; and he is like to die for hunger in the place where he is: for there is no more bread in the city. [10]Then the king commanded Ebed-melech the Ethiopian, saying, Take from hence thirty men with thee, and take up Jeremiah the prophet out of the dungeon, before he die. [11]So Ebed-melech took the men with him, and went into the house of the king under the treasury, and took thence old cast clouts and old rotten rags, and let them down by cords into the dungeon to Jeremiah. [12]And Ebed-melech the Ethiopian said unto Jeremiah, Put now these old cast clouts and rotten rags under thine armholes under the cords. And Jeremiah did so. [13]So they drew up Jeremiah with cords, and took him up out of the dungeon; and Jeremiah remained in the court of the prison.

Jer. 39 [15]Now the word of the LORD came unto Jeremiah, while he was shut up in the court of the prison, saying, [16]Go and speak to Ebed-melech the Ethiopian, saying, Thus saith the LORD of hosts, the God of Israel; Behold, I will bring my words upon this city for evil, and not for good; and they shall be accomplished in that day before thee. [17]But I will deliver thee in that day, saith the LORD: and thou shalt not be given into the hand of the men of whom thou art afraid. [18]For I will surely deliver thee, and thou shalt not fall by the sword, but thy life shall be for a prey unto thee; because thou hast put thy trust in me, saith the LORD.

EBENEZER

[eb en ē′zẽr] A Hebrew word meaning "stone of help." It was the name given to the stone set up by Samuel in commemoration of the help which Israel had obtained from God in gaining a victory over the Philistines.

SCRIPTURE

1 Sam. 7 [12]Then Samuel took a stone, and set it between Mizpeh and Shen, and called the name of it Ebenezer, saying, Hitherto hath the LORD helped us.

See 1 Sam. 4:1-5:1

EDEN

[ē'd'n] Probably derived from a word meaning "plain," this is the name given to the land in which "God planted a garden" and in which "he put the man whom he had formed." The word has come to be used as a synonym for "paradise." The Garden of Eden is said to have contained animal life of every kind and abundant vegetation, including the "tree of life" and the "tree of knowledge of good and evil." The uncertain geographical allusions in the *Genesis* account have resulted in various attempts to place the location of the Garden, ranging all the way from Babylonia to the North Pole. It is impossible to determine what area the original author had in mind.

See ADAM, EVE, CREATION, FALL

SCRIPTURE

Gen. 2 [8]And the LORD God planted a garden eastward in Eden; and there he put the man whom he had formed. [9]And out of the ground made the LORD God to grow every tree that is pleasant to the sight, and good for food; the tree of life also in the midst of the garden, and the tree of knowledge of good and evil. [10]And a river went out of Eden to water the garden; and from thence it was parted, and became into four heads. [15]And the LORD God took the man, and put him into the garden of Eden to dress it and to keep it.

REFERENCE: *Isa. 51:3; Ezek. 28:13; 31:9, 16, 18; 36:35; Joel 2:3.*

EDIFICATION

[ed i fi kā'shun] Literally, a building up. When applied to spiritual things the word means advancing, improving, instructing, adorning, or comforting the mind and spiritual nature. Men receive edification through prayer, hearing the gospel, attending to the Lord's business, reading the Scriptures, good works, and meditation.

SCRIPTURE

Rom. 14 [19]Let us therefore follow after the things which make for peace, and things wherewith one may edify another.

Rom. 15 [2]Let every one of us please his neighbour for his good to edification.

1 Cor. 8 [1]Now as touching things offered unto idols, we know that we all have knowledge. Knowledge puffeth up, but charity edifieth.

1 Cor. 14 [4]He that speaketh in an unknown tongue, edifieth himself: but he that prophesieth, edifieth the Church. [5]I would that ye all spake with tongues, but rather that ye prophesied: for greater is he that prophesieth than he that speaketh with tongues, except he interpret, that the Church may receive edifying.

Eph. 4 [29]Let no corrupt communication proceed out of your mouth, but that which is good to the use of edifying, that it may minister grace unto the hearers.

EDOM, EDOMITES

[ē'dum, ē'dum īts] The Edomites were regarded as the descendants of Esau and were thus related to the Hebrews, but there was a longstanding enmity between them. Throughout the Old Testament prophecies, there is a denunciation of Edom. The Edomites lived in the rocky range south of the Dead Sea and built almost impregnable fortresses in the canyons and gorges of these mountains. The magnificent ruins at Petra attest to the greatness which Edom once knew. In 582 BC, only four years after the destruction of Jerusalem, the Edomites were overcome by the Babylonians. Until the time of Christ they enjoyed several revivals of power (the Herods, for instance, were an Edomite family), but after the destruction of Jerusalem in AD 70, the Edomites disappeared from history.

EGLON

[eg'lon] 1. A Canaanite city which fell to Israel in the Judean campaign led by Joshua during the period of the Conquest, in about 1200 BC. Its king had joined with other kings in the area in an alliance which was overwhelmingly defeated by Joshua's army.

REFERENCE: *Josh. 10:1-35.*

2. A king of Moab in the period of the Judges who, in alliance with Ammon and Amalek, put Israel under subjection for a period of eighteen years. At the end of this period this king was assassinated in a daring plot executed by Ehud, one of the judges of Israel, thus ending the Moabite rule.

See EHUD

REFERENCE: *Judg. 3:12-20.*

EGYPT

[ē'jipt] The territory in the northeast corner of Africa, linked with Asia by the Sinai peninsula. The scope of this article is limited to salient features in the history of Egypt which have a direct bearing on the Biblical narrative. Recorded history of Egypt goes back to about 3000 BC. It was in the period from about 2650-2200 that Egyptian culture first achieved full flower, culminating in the Great Pyramid of Cheops. In the eighteenth century BC there came to power a dynasty of Semitic Pharaohs called Hyksos. Joseph is probably to be placed within this period. The Hyksos were expelled from Egypt in the sixteenth century BC by Amosis, one of the founders of the strong eighteenth century dynasty. By the beginning of the fifteenth century BC, the armies of this dynasty had extended the borders of Egypt to the banks of the Euphrates river. After two and a half centuries, this powerful dynasty began to crumble under Amenophis IV (c. 1370-1353 BC). This rather weak king aroused widespread dissention and opposition by embracing the worship of Aten, the solar disk, as the one true God. He went so far as to change his name from Amenophis to Akhen-aten. At his death, he was succeeded by his son-in-law, Tutankhamun, the famous King Tut whose magnificent tomb was discovered in 1922.

After a thirty year period (1340-1310 BC) in which the powerful general Haremhab kept Egypt from utter chaos, Ramses I, who traced his ancestry back to the Hyksos, established the nineteenth dynasty. In 1290 BC, Ramses II, the grandson of Ramses I, came to the throne of Egypt. The early part of his reign was spent in conflict with the Hittites, in the course of which Egypt lost her holdings in Syria. After the resolution of this conflict by treaty, Ramses II directed his attention to an ambitious building program in which he rebuilt the old Hyksos capital of Avaris and founded the new capital of Rameses. Egyptian annals of this period contain references to a group of people known as "Hapiru," who worked as slaves on these royal projects. The similarity of this word to "Hebrew," and the fact that a number of Semitic words passed into the Egyptian language at this time makes it quite likely that the events described in the early chapters of *Exodus* are to be placed within the reign of Ramses II. This theory is further enhanced by the fact that, in 1220 BC, Merneptah, the successor of Ramses II, set up a stele (a pillar of stone bearing an inscription), which tells of his defeat of the Israelites shortly after their arrival in Palestine. This would mean the Exodus and Conquest are probably to be dated in the thirteenth century BC. (*See* EXODUS, CONQUEST) During Merneptah's reign (1224-1216 BC), a group of invaders called the Peoples of the Sea overran the Hittite Empire and flooded into Egypt. Merneptah was able to beat them back temporarily, but in the reign of the 20th Dynasty (1180-1065 BC), certain of these Peoples of the Sea were allowed to settle in territory which had been held by the Egyptians. Among them were the Philistines, who gave their name to the land in which they settled—Palestine.

The 21st Dynasty, also called the Tanite Dynasty (c. 1065-935 BC), was generally impotent, making it fairly clear that Egypt's great days of empire-building were over. This dynasty was overthrown by Shishak, who founded the 22nd, or Bubastite, Dynasty (935-725 BC). It was Shishak who gave asylum to Jeroboam during the reign of Solomon and who, during the reign of Rehoboam, devastated Jerusalem and many other towns and cities in Palestine.

Egypt's importance to the Biblical narrative is next seen in connection with the fall of the northern kingdom of Israel. In about 724 BC Hoshea king of Israel withheld tribute from Shalmaneser V, king of Assyria. When Assyrian attack was imminent, Hoshea appealed to Egypt for help, but the turmoil in that state, evidenced by the fact that the 22nd, 23rd, and 24th dynasties all claimed authority, precluded the possibility of any effective help, and in 722 BC, the kingdom of Israel passed into oblivion.

In 713 Ashdod led a rebellion against Sennacharib king of Assyria, in which Judah and Egypt were expected to join. The prophet Isaiah persuaded Hezekiah king of Judah not to join the coalition and thus apparently saved Judah from destruction. Still in a state of confusion, Egypt likewise failed to provide resistance and the rebellion was crushed. Neither Egypt nor Judah, however, was content to remain subservient to Assyria. In the reign of Shabako, a representative of the 25th, or Ethiopian, Dynasty, a sizable coalition was formed to resist Sennacharib, in which Hezekiah took a leading part. Sennacharib's forces proved irresistible and both states were placed in a vassalage relationship.

In 663 BC, Psammetichus I began to consolidate his power in Egypt and founded the 26th, or Saite, Dynasty. In about 655 BC, he announced himself independent of Assyrian rule. The current Assyrian king, Ashurbanipal (c. 669-633 BC), was in no position to repudiate his claims, and Egypt regained a measure of stature. In 609 BC, Psammetichus' son and successor, Necoh II (609-593 BC), set out for Carchemish to retake Haran from the Babylonians. Josiah king of Judah foolishly tried to stop him and was killed. Necoh proceeded to Carchemish and was defeated; he then turned back to consolidate his holdings in the West. He deposed Jehoahaz, who had succeeded his father on the throne of Judah, and deported him to Egypt (*2 Kin. 23:31-35*); he then replaced him with another of Josiah's sons, Eliakim, whose name he changed to Jehoiakim. It was this petty tyrant Jehoiakim who was king of Judah during much of the ministry of the prophet Jeremiah. In 605 BC, the Egyptians were twice defeated by the Babylonians under the command of Nebuchadnezzar, first at Carchemish, then at Hamath. They met again in 601 BC, at which time both sides suffered heavy losses. By 568, Nebuchadnezzar had reduced Egypt to an obedient, if not willing, vassal. In 539 BC, Cyrus the Persian took control of Babylon and thus made himself master of the world. Egypt was officially annexed to the Persian empire in 525 BC, the date of its conquest by Cambyses, Cyrus' son and successor. Shortly thereafter, Egypt became one of the satrapies of the Persian empire (*see* PERSIA), a status it retained until it passed under the rule of Alexander the Great in 332 BC.

After the fall of Jerusalem in 587 BC, Egypt became a leading center for exiled Jews. Among the first groups of Jewish refugees was the band which became a leading Jewish population center; it was here that the Septuagint, the Greek version of the Hebrew Old Testament, was produced, thus providing a copy of the scriptures for those Jews who had forgotten their native tongue and opening a new avenue of communication between Jew and Gentile.

See index for articles on various individuals mentioned in this article.

EHUD

[ē'hud] The son of Gera and a Benjaminite, Ehud delivered Israel from Moabite oppression. While on a mission to pay Israel's tribute to Moab, Ehud gained a private audience with Eglon, the king of Moab, and assassinated him. Spurred on by this daring deed, the Israelites rallied to the call of Ehud and overthrew the Moabites, gaining rest for the land of Israel.

See JUDGES, EGLON, MOAB

SCRIPTURE

Judg. 3 [15]But when the children of Israel cried unto the LORD, the LORD raised them up a deliverer, Ehud the son of Gera, a Benjamite, a man lefthanded: and by him the children of Israel sent a present unto Eglon the king of Moab. [16]But Ehud made him a dagger which had two edges, of a cubit length; and he did gird it under his raiment upon his right thigh. [17]And he brought the present unto Eglon king of

Moab: and Eglon was a very fat man.
18And when he had made an end to offer
the present, he sent away the people that
bare the present. 19But he himself turned
again from the quarries that were by Gilgal, and said, I have a secret errand unto
thee, O king: who said, Keep silence. And
all that stood by him went out from him.
20And Ehud came unto him; and he was
sitting in a summer parlour, which he had
for himself alone: and Ehud said, I have a
message from God unto thee. And he arose
out of his seat. 21And Ehud put forth his
left hand, and took the dagger from his
right thigh, and thrust it into his belly:
22And the haft also went in after the blade;
and the fat closed upon the blade, so that
he could not draw the dagger out of his
belly; and the dirt came out. 23Then Ehud
went forth through the porch, and shut the
doors of the parlour upon him, and locked
them. 24When he was gone out, his servants came; and when they saw that, behold, the doors of the parlour were locked,
they said, Surely he covereth his feet in
his summer chamber. 25And they tarried
till they were ashamed: and, behold,
he opened not the doors of the parlour;
therefore they took a key, and opened
them: and, behold, their lord was fallen
down dead on the earth. 26And Ehud escaped while they tarried, and passed beyond the quarries, and escaped into Seirath. 27And it came to pass, when he was
come, that he blew a trumpet in the mountain of Ephraim, and the children of Israel
went down with him from the mount, and
he before them. 28And he said unto them,
Follow after me: for the LORD hath delivered your enemies the Moabites into your
hand. And they went down after him, and
took the fords of Jordan toward Moab, and
suffered not a man to pass over. 29And
they slew of Moab at that time about ten
thousand men, all lusty, and all men of
valour: and there escaped not a man. 30So
Moab was subdued that day under the
hand of Israel. And the land had rest fourscore years.

ELAH

[ē′la] The son of Baasha who succeeded his father as the fourth king of Israel, reigning only two years (877-876). While engaged in a drinking party, he was assassinated by Zimri, one of his military commanders, who then usurped the throne and wiped out the entire house of Baasha, according to the word of the prophet Jehu.

See KINGS

REFERENCE: *1 Kin. 16:6-14.*

ELDER

[el′dẽr] Literally, an older man. Among virtually all peoples, it is a natural thing to associate age with wisdom. Among the ancient Hebrews, the elders served as local magistrates, whose duty it was to enforce the Law of Moses. The elders often carried out their duties at the gates of the city over which they had jurisdiction. (*See* GATES) In the New Testament, the word is used in a technical sense of Jewish elders of the synagogue and of officials in the local Christian churches. The latter, who seem to have been identical with bishops, were appointed to exercise spiritual oversight over the congregations of which they were members.

SCRIPTURE

Elders Among the Israelites

Deut. 1 13Take you wise men, and understanding, and known among your
tribes, and I will make them rulers over
you. 14And ye answered me, and said, The
thing which thou hast spoken is good for
us to do. 15So I took the chief of your
tribes, wise men, and known, and made
them heads over you, captains over thousands, and captains over hundreds, and

captains over fifties, and captains over tens, and officers among your tribes.

1 Sam. 15 [30]Then he said, I have sinned: yet honor me now, I pray thee, before the elders of my people, and before Israel, and turn again with me, that I may worship the LORD thy God.

Deut. 19 [12]Then the elders of his city shall send and fetch him thence, and deliver him into the hand of the avenger of blood, that he may die.

Deut. 22 [15]Then shall the father of the damsel, and her mother, take and bring forth the tokens of the damsel's virginity unto the elders of the city in the gate.

Deut. 27 [1]And Moses with the elders of Israel commanded the people, saying, Keep all the commandments which I command you this day.

Elders in the Christian Church

Acts 14 [23]And when they had ordained them elders in every church, and had prayed with fasting, they commended them to the Lord, on whom they believed.

Acts 20 [17]And from Miletus he sent to Ephesus, and called the elders of the church.

1 Tim. 3 [1]This is a true saying, If a man desire the office of a bishop, he desireth a good work. [2]A bishop then must be blameless, the husband of one wife, vigilant, sober, of good behaviour, given to hospitality, apt to teach; [3]Not given to wine, no striker, not greedy of filthy lucre; but patient, not a brawler, not covetous; [4]One that ruleth well his own house, having his children in subjection with all gravity; [5](For if a man know not how to rule his own house, how shall he take care of the church of God?) [6]Not a novice, lest being lifted up with pride he fall into the condemnation of the devil. [7]Moreover he must have a good report of them which are without; lest he fall into reproach and the snare of the devil.

Tit. 1 [5]For this cause left I thee in Crete, that thou shouldest set in order the things that are wanting, and ordain elders in every city, as I had appointed thee: [6]If any be blameless, the husband of one wife, having faithful children not accused of riot or unruly. [7]For a bishop must be blameless, as the steward of God; not self-willed, not soon angry, not given to wine, no striker, not given to filthy lucre; [8]But a lover of hospitality, a lover of good men, sober, just, holy, temperate; [9]Holding fast the faithful word as he hath been taught, that he may be able by sound doctrine both to exhort and to convince the gainsayers.

ELEAZAR

[el ē ā′zar] The son of Aaron and Elisheba and the father of Phinehas. After the death of Nadab and Abihu, Eleazar became chief of the Levites and had charge of the tabernacle. He became high priest at the death of Aaron and is found at the side of Moses in the numbering of Israel after the plague in the wilderness and with Joshua at the division of the land of Canaan. At his death he was succeeded by his son Phinehas.

REFERENCE: *Ex. 6:23, 25; Num. 3:32; 4:16; 20:26, 28; 26:63; 34:17; Josh. 24:33.*

ELECTION

[ē lek′shun] The conviction that God has chosen one of a group of individuals or communities and established a particular relationship with it, imposing certain demands and promising certain rewards. In the Old Testament this concept is applied mainly to the notion of Israel; in the New Testament, to the Christian community. Throughout the Bible, it is made clear that at bottom the choice rests not with man, but with God. This raises the problem of man's freedom, a problem on which theologians of the Christian church have never been in complete agreement.

In one's own Christian experience there is usually a consciousness of "electing" for Christ, especially at the beginning, but as one progresses in his spiritual growth it is not uncommon for him to develop a growing sense of having been somehow chosen by God prior to his own personal response. In the thinking of this writer; the tension inherent in the doctrine of election is probably unresolvable and must be left among the mysteries impenetrable to our sinful intellects.

SCRIPTURE

Elect: God's Chosen

Isa. 42 [1]Behold my servant, whom I uphold; mine elect, in whom my soul delighteth; I have put my Spirit upon him: he shall bring forth judgment to the Gentiles.

Isa. 65 [9]And I will bring forth a seed out of Jacob, and out of Judah an inheritor of my mountains: and mine elect shall inherit it, and my servants shall dwell there.

1 Pet. 2 [6]Wherefore it is contained in the Scripture, Behold, I lay in Sion a chief corner stone, elect, precious, and he that believeth on him shall not be confounded.

Elect Under the Gospel

Matt. 24 [22]And except those days should be shortened, there should no flesh be saved: but for the elect's sake those days shall be shortened.

Luke 18 [7]And shall not God avenge his own elect, which cry day and night unto him, though he bear long with them?

Rom. 8 [33]Who shall lay any thing to the charge of God's elect? It is God that justifieth.

Rom. 11 [5]Even so then at this present time also there is a remnant according to the election of grace. [6]And if by grace, then is it no more of works: otherwise grace is no more grace. But if it be of works, then is it no more grace, otherwise work is no more work. [7]What then? Israel hath not obtained that which he seeketh for, but the election hath obtained it, and the rest were blinded.

Col. 3 [12]Put on therefore, as the elect of God, holy and beloved, bowels of mercies, kindness, humbleness of mind, meekness, longsuffering.

2 Tim. 2 [10]Therefore I endure all things for the elect's sake, that they may also obtain the salvation which is in Christ Jesus, with eternal glory.

Election

1 Cor. 1 [26]For ye see your calling, brethren, how that not many wise men after the flesh, not many mighty, not many noble are called. [27]But God hath chosen the foolish things of the world, to confound the wise: and God hath chosen the weak things of the world, to confound the things which are mighty: [28]And base things of the world, and things which are despised, hath God chosen, yea and things which are not, to bring to nought things that are:

1 Thess. 1 [4]Knowing, brethren beloved, your election of God.

2 Pet. 1 [10]Wherefore, the rather, brethren, give diligence to make your calling and election sure: for if ye do these things, ye shall never fall. [11]For so an entrance shall be ministered unto you abundantly into the everlasting kingdom of our Lord and Saviour Jesus Christ.

ELI

[ē'lī] Judge of Israel and Priest at the sanctuary at Shiloh, and a descendant of Ithamar, son of Aaron.

The first mention of Eli is in connection with the prayer of Hannah for a son. When he saw the woman moving her lips but speaking no words aloud, he thought her to be drunken. Learning the truth, he assured her that her petition would be answered. In due time the child Samuel was born and, when he was weaned, Hannah consecrated him to the service of the LORD, under the tutelage of Eli. Although Eli seems to have been a devout man himself, he lacked the ability to control his two worthless sons, who were guilty of serious abuse of the priesthood. (*See* HOPHNI AND PHINEHAS) He was twice warned of the disaster which would result, once by an unnamed prophet, and once by the young Samuel. The curse was fulfilled at Aphek in a battle with the Philistines in which both sons were slain and the Ark of the Covenant captured. When the news reached Eli it upset him so "that he fell from off the seat backward by the side of the gate, and his neck broke, and he died, for he was an old man, and heavy."

REFERENCE: *1 Sam. 1-4.*

SCRIPTURE

Assures Hannah of a Son

1 Sam. 1 9So Hannah rose up after they had eaten in Shiloh, and after they had drunk. Now Eli the priest sat upon a seat by a post of the temple of the LORD. 10And she was in bitterness of soul, and prayed unto the LORD, and wept sore. 11And she vowed a vow, and said, O LORD of hosts, if thou wilt indeed look on the affliction of thine handmaid, and remember me, and not forget thine handmaid, but wilt give unto thine handmaid a man child, then I will give him unto the LORD all the days of his life, and there shall no razor come upon his head. 12And it came to pass, as she continued praying before the LORD, that Eli marked her mouth. 13Now Hannah, she spake in her heart; only her lips moved, but her voice was not heard: therefore Eli thought she had been drunken. 14And Eli said unto her, How long wilt thou be drunken? put away thy wine from thee. 15And Hannah answered and said, No, my lord, I am a woman of a sorrowful spirit: I have drunk neither wine nor strong drink, but have poured out my soul before the LORD. 16Count not thine handmaid for a daughter of Belial: for out of the abundance of my complaint and grief have I spoken hitherto. 17Then Eli answered and said, Go in peace: and the God of Israel grant thee thy petition that thou hast asked of him. 18And she said, Let thine handmaid find grace in thy sight. So the woman went her way, and did eat, and her countenance was no more sad.

His Evil Sons

1 Sam. 2 12Now the sons of Eli were sons of Belial; they knew not the LORD. 13And the priest's custom with the people was, that, when any man offered sacrifice, the priest's servant came, while the flesh was in seething, with a fleshhook of three teeth in his hand; 14And he struck it into the pan, or kettle, or caldron, or pot; all that the fleshhook brought up the priest took for himself. So they did in Shiloh unto all the Israelites that came thither. 15Also before they burnt the fat, the priest's servant came, and said to the man that sacrificed, Give flesh to roast for the priest; for he will not have sodden flesh of thee, but raw. 16And if any man said unto him, Let them not fail to burn the fat presently, and then take as much as thy soul desireth; then he would answer him, Nay; but thou shalt give it me now: and if not, I will take it by force. 17Wherefore the sin of the young men was very great before the LORD: for men abhorred the offering of the LORD.

22Now Eli was very old, and heard all that his sons did unto all Israel; and how they lay with the women that assembled at the door of the tabernacle of the congregation. 23And he said unto them, Why do ye such things? for I hear of your evil dealings by all this people. 24Nay, my sons; for it is no good report that I hear: ye make the LORD's people to transgress. 25If one man sin against another, the judge shall judge him: but if a man sin against

the LORD, who shall entreat for him? Notwithstanding, they hearkened not unto the
voice of their father, because the LORD
would slay them.

Death of Eli

1 Sam. 4 11And the ark of God was
taken; and the two sons of Eli, Hophni
and Phinehas, were slain.
12And there ran a man of Benjamin out
of the army, and came to Shiloh the same
day with his clothes rent, and with earth
upon his head. 13And when he came, lo,
Eli sat upon a seat by the way side watching: for his heart trembled for the ark of
God. And when the man came into the
city, and told it, all the city cried out.
14And when Eli heard the noise of the crying, he said, What meaneth the noise of
this tumult? And the man came in hastily,
and told Eli. 15Now Eli was ninety and
eight years old; and his eyes were dim,
that he could not see. 16And the man said
unto Eli, I am he that came out of the
army, and I fled to-day out of the army.
And he said, What is there done, my son?
17And the messenger answered and said,
Israel is fled before the Philistines, and
there hath been also a great slaughter
among the people, and thy two sons also,
Hophni and Phinehas, are dead, and the
ark of God is taken. 18And it came to pass,
when he made mention of the ark of God,
that he fell from off the seat backward by
the side of the gate, and his neck brake,
and he died: for he was an old man, and
heavy. And he had judged Israel forty
years.

ELIEZER

[el i ē′zẽr] The chief servant of Abraham, usually referred to as Eliezer of Damascus. Before the birth of either Ishmael or Isaac, Abraham despaired of having any children and sought to make Eliezer his heir; he was assured, however, that this would not be necessary, that Sarah would bear him a son. When the child of promise, Isaac, grew to maturity, it was perhaps this same servant who was sent to Abraham's relatives to secure Rebekah as a wife for him.

SCRIPTURE

Gen. 15 1After these things the word of
the LORD came unto Abram in a vision,
saying, Fear not, Abram: I am thy shield,
and thy exceeding great reward. 2And
Abram said, Lord GOD, what wilt thou
give me, seeing I go childless, and the
steward of my house is this Eliezer of Damascus? 3And Abram said, Behold, to me
thou hast given no seed: and, lo, one born
in my house is mine heir. 4And behold,
the word of the LORD came unto him, saying, This shall not be thine heir; but he
that shall come forth out of thine own
bowels shall be thine heir. 5And he
brought him forth abroad, and said, Look
now toward heaven, and tell the stars, if
thou be able to number them: and he said
unto him, So shall thy seed be. 6And he
believed in the LORD; and he counted it
to him for righteousness.

See Gen. 24

ELIJAH

[ē lī′ja] The great prophet of the time of Ahab, king of Israel. Virtually nothing is known of Elijah's background and parentage. In his first recorded act, he appeared before the evil king Ahab and predicted a severe drought. He then went to the brook Cherith where he was sustained by the LORD in a most remarkable manner. Later he went to Zarephath, where he dwelt with a widow whose son he had restored to life after apparent death. The drought continued, and famine caused by the failure of the crops descended on Samaria. After more than three years, the prophet showed himself once more to Ahab and placed the blame for the famine on the king's sinful policies. The issue of this meeting was the famous contest on Mount Carmel with the prophets of Baal (*1 Kin. 18:19ff*). Following the contest, Elijah fled, fearing the vengeance of Jezebel for his having slain the prophets of Baal. He journeyed to the wilderness around Horeb; there the LORD appeared to him in "a still small voice" and instructed him to make Elisha his successor.

Elijah's next confrontation with Ahab came in the vineyard of Naboth after that king had secured the land through the wickedness of his wife Jezebel; Elijah placed a terrible curse on the king and his descendants, promising that the entire house of Ahab would be exterminated. This prophecy was to be brutally fulfilled by Jehu.

Several years pass when nothing is heard of Elijah. Then, after a severe accident, King Ahaziah sent to an oracle of Baal in the Philistine town of Ekron to learn if he would recover. Elijah met the messenger on the road and issued a pronouncement of the king's death. He later went before the king and repeated the judgment of doom.

The last episode of Elijah's colorful career concerns the transfer of his mantle to his companion Elisha. Setting out from Gilgal, Elijah tried to persuade Elisha to remain behind, but the younger prophet would not so easily give up his master. Finally, after they crossed the Jordan River together, "there appeared a chariot of fire and horses of fire, and parted them both asunder, and Elijah went up by a whirlwind into heaven" (*2 Kin. 2:11*). Taking up the mantle which had fallen from his master's shoulders, Elisha set out to prove himself a worthy successor to the fiery man of God.

See AHAB, NABOTH, JEZEBEL, ELISHA, JEHU, etc.

REFERENCE: *1 Kin. 17-19; 21; 2 Kin. 1:1-2:12.*

SCRIPTURE

Announces a Drought

1 Kin. 17 [1]And Elijah the Tishbite, who was of the inhabitants of Gilead, said unto Ahab, As the LORD God of Israel liveth, before whom I stand, there shall not be dew nor rain these years, but according to my word. [5]So he went and did according unto the word of the LORD: for he went and dwelt by the brook Cherith, that is before Jordan. [6]And the ravens brought him bread and flesh in the morning, and bread and flesh in the evening; and he drank of the brook.

Dwells with a Widow of Zarephath

1 Kin. 17 [8]And the word of the LORD came unto him, saying, [9]Arise, get thee to Zarephath, which belongeth to Zidon, and dwell there: behold, I have commanded a widow woman there to sustain thee.

[17]And it came to pass after these things, that the son of the woman, the mistress of the house, fell sick; and his sickness was so sore, that there was no breath left in him. [18]And she said unto Elijah, What have I to do with thee, O thou man of God? art thou come unto me to call my sin of remembrance, and to slay my son? [19]And he said unto her, Give me thy son. And he took him out of her bosom, and carried him up into a loft, where he abode, and laid him upon his own bed. [20]And he cried unto the LORD, and said, O LORD my God, hast thou also brought evil upon the widow with whom I sojourn, by slaying her son? [21]And he stretched himself upon the child three times, and cried unto the LORD, and said, O LORD my God, I pray thee, let this child's soul come into him again. [22]And the LORD heard the voice of Elijah; and the soul of the child came into him again, and he revived.

Contest with the Prophets of Baal

1 Kin. 18 [17]And it came to pass, when Ahab saw Elijah, that Ahab said unto him, Art thou he that troubleth Israel? [18]And he answered, I have not troubled Israel; but thou, and thy father's house, in that ye have forsaken the commandments of the LORD, and thou hast followed Baalim. [19]Now therefore send, and gather to me all Israel unto mount Carmel, and the prophets of Baal four hundred and fifty, and the prophets of the groves four hundred, which eat at Jezebel's table. [20]So Ahab sent unto all the children of Israel, and gathered the prophets together unto mount Carmel. [21]And Elijah came unto all the people and said, How long halt ye between two opinions? if the Lord be God, follow him: but if Baal, then follow him. And the people answered him not a word. [22]Then said Elijah unto the people, I, even I only, remain a prophet of the Lord; but Baal's prophets are four hundred and fifty men. [23]Let them therefore give us two bullocks; and let them choose one bullock for themselves, and cut it in pieces, and lay it on wood, and put no fire under: and I will dress the other bullock, and lay it on wood, and put no fire under: [24]And call ye on the name of your gods, and I will call on the name of the Lord: and the God that answereth by fire, let him be God. And all the people answered and said, It is well spoken. [25]And Elijah said unto the prophets of Baal, Choose you one bullock for yourselves, and dress it first; for ye are many; and call on the name of your gods, but put no fire under. [26]And they took the bullock which was given them, and they dressed it, and called on the name of Baal from morning even until noon, saying, O Baal, hear us. But there was no voice, nor any that answered. And they leaped upon the altar which was made. [27]And it came to pass at noon, that Elijah mocked them, and said, Cry aloud: for he is a god; either he is talking, or he is pursuing, or he is in a journey, or peradventure he sleepeth, and must be awaked. [28]And they cried aloud, and cut themselves after their manner with knives and lancets, till the blood gushed out upon them. [29]And it came to pass, when midday was past, and they prophesied until the time of the offering of the evening sacrifice, that there was neither voice, nor any to answer, nor any that regarded. [30]And Elijah said unto all the people, Come near unto me. And all the people came near unto him. And he repaired the altar of the Lord that was broken down. [31]And Elijah took twelve stones, according to the number of the tribes of the sons of Jacob, unto whom the word of the Lord came, saying, Israel shall be thy name: [32]And with the stones he built an altar in the name of the Lord: and he made a trench about the altar, as great as would contain two measures of seed. [33]And he put the wood in order, and cut the bullock in pieces, and laid him on the wood, and said, Fill four barrels with water, and pour it on the burnt sacrifice, and on the wood. [34]And he said, Do it the second time. And they did it the second time. And he said, Do it the third time. And they did it the third time. [35]And the water ran round about the altar; and he filled the trench also with water. [36]And it came to pass at the time of the offering of the evening sacrifice, that Elijah the prophet came near and said, Lord God of Abraham, Isaac, and of Israel, let it be known this day that thou art God in Israel, and that I am thy servant, and that I have done all these things at thy word. [37]Hear me, O Lord, hear me, that this people may know that thou art the Lord God, and that thou hast turned their heart back again. [38]Then the fire of the Lord fell, and consumed the burnt sacrifice, and the wood, and the stones, and the dust, and licked up the water that was in the trench. [39]And when all the people saw it, they fell on their faces: and they said, The Lord, he is the God; the Lord, he is the God. [40]And Elijah said unto them, Take the prophets of Baal; let not one of them escape. And they took them; and Elijah brought them down to the brook Kishon, and slew them there.

A Fugitive from Jezebel

1 Kin. 19 [1]And Ahab told Jezebel all that Elijah had done, and withal how he had slain all the prophets with the sword. [2]Then Jezebel sent a messenger unto Elijah, saying, So let the gods do to me, and more also, if I make not thy life as the life of one of them by to-morrow about this time. [3]And when he saw that, he arose, and went for his life, and came to Beer-sheba, which belongeth to Judah, and left his servant there.

[4]But he himself went a day's journey into the wilderness, and came and sat down under a juniper tree: and he requested for himself that he might die; and said, It is enough; now, O LORD, take away my life; for I am not better than my fathers. [5]And as he lay and slept under a juniper tree, behold, then an angel touched him, and said unto him, Arise and eat. [6]And he looked, and, behold, there was a cake baken on the coals, and a cruse of water at his head. And he did eat and drink, and laid him down again. [7]And the angel of the LORD came again the second time, and touched him, and said, Arise and eat; because the journey is too great for thee. [8]And he arose, and did eat and drink, and went in the strength of that meat forty days and forty nights unto Horeb the mount of God.

Confronted by God

1 Kin. 19 [9]And he came thither unto a cave, and lodged there; and, behold, the word of the LORD came to him, and he said unto him, What doest thou here, Elijah? [10]And he said, I have been very jealous for the LORD God of hosts: for the children of Israel have forsaken thy covenant, thrown down thine altars, and slain thy prophets with the sword; and I, even I only, am left; and they seek my life, to take it away. [11]And he said, Go forth, and stand upon the mount before the LORD. And, behold, the LORD passed by, and a great and strong wind rent the mountains, and brake in pieces the rocks before the LORD; but the LORD was not in the wind: and after the wind an earthquake; but the LORD was not in the earthquake: [12]And after the earthquake a fire; but the LORD was not in the fire: and after the fire a still small voice. [13]And it was so, when Elijah heard it, that he wrapped his face in his mantle, and went out, and stood in the entering in of the cave. And, behold, there came a voice unto him, and said, What doest thou here, Elijah? [14]And he said, I have been very jealous for the LORD God of hosts: because the children of Israel have forsaken thy covenant, thrown down thine altars, and slain thy prophets with the sword; and I, even I only, am left; and they seek my life, to take it away. [15]And the LORD said unto him, Go, return on thy way to the wilderness of Damascus: and when thou comest, anoint Hazael to be king over Syria: [16]And Jehu the son of Nimshi shalt thou anoint to be king over Israel: and Elisha the son of Shaphat of Abel-meholah shalt thou anoint to be prophet in thy room.

Confronts Ahab after Naboth's Death

1 Kin. 21 [17]And the word of the LORD came to Elijah the Tishbite, saying, [18]Arise, go down to meet Ahab king of Israel, which is in Samaria: behold, he is in the vineyard of Naboth, whither he is gone down to possess it. [19]And thou shalt speak unto him, saying, Thus saith the LORD, Hast thou killed, and also taken possession? And thou shalt speak unto him, saying, Thus saith the LORD, In the place where dogs licked the blood of Naboth shall dogs lick thy blood, even thine. [20]And Ahab said to Elijah, Hast thou found me, O mine enemy? And he answered, I have found thee: because thou hast sold thyself to work evil in the sight of the LORD. [21]Behold, I will bring evil upon thee, and will take away thy posterity, and will cut off from Ahab him that pisseth against the wall, and him that is shut up and left in Israel. [22]And will make thine house like the house of Jeroboam the son of Nebat, and like the house of Baasha the son of Ahijah, for the provocation wherewith thou hast provoked me to anger, and made Israel to sin. [23]And of Jezebel also spake the LORD, saying, The dogs shall eat Jezebel by the wall of Jezreel. [24]Him that dieth of Ahab in the city the dogs shall eat; and him that dieth in the field shall the fowls of the air eat.

[25]But there was none like unto Ahab, which did sell himself to work wickedness in the sight of the LORD, whom Jezebel his wife stirred up. [26]And he did very abominably in following idols, according to all things as did the Amorites, whom the LORD cast out before the children of Israel. [27]And it came to pass, when Ahab heard those words, that he rent his clothes, and put sackcloth upon his flesh, and fasted, and lay in sackcloth, and went softly. [28]And the word of the LORD came to Elijah the Tishbite, saying, [29]Seest thou how Ahab humbleth himself before me? because he humbleth himself before me, I will not bring the evil in his days: but in his son's days will I bring the evil upon his house.

Confers Mantle on Elisha

2 Kin. 2 [9]And it came to pass, when they were gone over, that Elijah said unto Elisha, Ask what I shall do for thee, before I be taken away from thee. And Elisha said, I pray thee, let a double portion of thy spirit be upon me. [10]And he said, Thou hast asked a hard thing: nevertheless, if thou see me when I am taken from thee, it shall be so unto thee; but if not, it shall not be so. [11]And it came to pass, as they still went on, and talked, that, behold, there appeared a chariot of fire, and horses of fire, and parted them both asunder; and Elijah went up by a whirlwind into heaven.

[12]And Elisha saw it, and he cried, My father, my father, the chariot of Israel, and the horsemen thereof. And he saw him no more: and he took hold of his own clothes, and rent them in two pieces. [13]He took up also the mantle of Elijah that fell from him, and went back, and stood by the bank of Jordan.

Elijah at Transfiguration

Matt. 17 [3]And behold, there appeared unto them Moses, and Elias, talking with him. [4]Then answered Peter, and said unto Jesus, Lord, it is good for us to be here: If thou wilt, let us make here three tabernacles: one for thee, and one for Moses, and one for Elias.

Forerunner of John the Baptist

Mal. 4 [5]Behold, I will send you Elijah the prophet before the coming of the great and dreadful day of the LORD: [6]And he shall turn the heart of the fathers to the children, and the heart of the children to their fathers, lest I come and smite the earth with a curse.

Matt. 11 [13]For all the Prophets and the Law prophesied until John. [14]And if ye will receive it, this is Elias which was for to come.

Luke 1 [17]And he shall go before him in

the spirit and power of Elias, to turn the hearts of the fathers to the children, and the disobedient to the wisdom of the just, to make ready a people prepared for the Lord.

ELISABETH

[ē liz′a beth] A member of the priestly lineage, the wife of Zacharias, the mother of John the Baptist, and the cousin of Mary the mother of Jesus.

See Mary, John the Baptist, Zacharias

reference: *Luke 1.*

ELISHA

[ē lī′sha] A prophet, the disciple and successor of Elijah. He is first mentioned in the appearance of the Lord to Elijah at Horeb, where the great prophet was told that Elisha would be his successor as "chief prophet" in Israel. After the departure of his master and the assumption of his mantle, Elisha returned to dwell at Jericho. While there, he purified a noxious spring by throwing salt into it in the name of the Lord. He then passed to Bethel where he was harassed by some boys of the town. Elisha assumed the sternness of Elijah and cursed the boys, whereupon two bears attacked them. The narrative of his life contains the record of a number of miracles, including the cure of Naaman's leprosy and the restoration of life to the son of the Shunnamite woman. The action of the prophet which had the most widespread consequences was his instigation of the revolution of Jehu which led to the complete annihilation of the house of Ahab and the death of the kings both of Judah and Israel. The last episode of the prophet's life took place during the time of the illness which ended in his death. Elisha was visited by Jehoash, king of Israel, with whom he apparently had a good relationship, at which time he predicted great victory over Syria.

See Elijah, Naaman, Jehu, Jehoash

reference: *2 Kin. 2-10.*

SCRIPTURE

Succeeds Elijah As Chief Prophet of Israel

1 Kin. 19 16And Jehu the son of Nimshi shalt thou anoint to be king over Israel: and Elisha the son of Shaphat of Abel-meholah shalt thou anoint to be prophet in thy room. 17And it shall come to pass, that him that escapeth the sword of Hazael shall Jehu slay: and him that escapeth from the sword of Jehu shall Elisha slay. 18Yet I have left me seven thousand in Israel, all the knees which have not bowed unto Baal, and every mouth which hath not kissed him.

19So he departed thence and found Elisha the son of Shaphat, who was ploughing with twelve yoke of oxen before him, and he with the twelfth: and Elijah passed by him, and cast his mantle upon him. 20And he left the oxen, and ran after Elijah, and said, Let me, I pray thee, kiss my father and my mother, and then I will follow thee. And he said unto him, Go back again: for what have I done to thee? 21And he returned back from him, and took a yoke of oxen, and slew them, and boiled their flesh with the instruments of the oxen, and gave unto the people, and they did eat. Then he arose, and went after Elijah, and ministered unto him.

2 Kin. 2 9And it came to pass, when they were gone over, that Elijah said unto Elisha, Ask what I shall do for thee, before I be taken away from thee. And Elisha said, I pray thee, let a double portion of thy spirit be upon me. 10And he said, Thou hast asked a hard thing: nevertheless, if thou see me when I am taken from thee, it shall be so unto thee; but if not, it shall not be so. 11And it came to pass, as they still went on, and talked, that, behold, there appeared a chariot of fire, and horses of fire, and parted them both asunder; and Elijah went up by a whirlwind into heaven.

12And Elisha saw it, and he cried, My father, my father, the chariot of Israel, and the horsemen thereof! And he saw him no more: and he took hold of his own clothes, and rent them in two pieces. 13He took up also the mantle of Elijah that fell from him, and went back, and stood by the bank of Jordan; 14And he took the mantle of Elijah that fell from him, and smote the waters, and said, Where is the LORD God of Elijah? And when he also had smitten the waters, they parted hither and thither: and Elisha went over.

Miracles Performed by Elisha

2 Kin. 2 19And the men of the city said unto Elisha, Behold, I pray thee, the situation of this city is pleasant, as my lord seeth: but the water is naught, and the ground barren. 20And he said, Bring me a new cruse, and put salt therein. And they brought it to him. 21And he went forth unto the spring of the waters, and cast the salt in there, and said, Thus saith the LORD, I have healed these waters; there shall not be from thence any more death or barren land. 22So the waters were healed unto this day, according to the saying of Elisha which he spake.

2 Kin. 4 1Now there cried a certain woman of the wives of the sons of the prophets unto Elisha, saying, Thy servant my husband is dead; and thou knowest that thy servant did fear the LORD: and the creditor is come to take unto him my two sons to be bondmen. 2And Elisha said unto her, What shall I do for thee? tell me, what hast thou in the house? And she said, Thine handmaid hath not any thing in the house, save a pot of oil. 3Then he said, Go, borrow thee vessels abroad of all thy neighbours, even empty vessels; borrow not a few. 4And when thou art come in, thou shalt shut the door upon thee and upon thy sons, and shalt pour out into all those vessels, and thou shalt set aside that which is full. 5So she went from him, and shut the door upon her and upon her sons, who brought the vessels to her; and she poured out. 6And it came to pass, when the vessels were full, that she said unto her son, Bring me yet a vessel. And he said unto her, There is not a vessel more. And the oil stayed. 7Then she came and told the man of God. And he said, Go, sell the oil, and pay thy debt, and live thou and thy children of the rest.

8And it fell on a day, that Elisha passed to Shunem, where was a great woman; and she constrained him to eat bread. And so it was, that as oft as he passed by, he turned in thither to eat bread. 9And she said unto her husband, Behold, now, I perceive that this is a holy man of God, which passeth by us continually. 10Let us make a little chamber, I pray thee, on the wall; and let us set for him there a bed, and a table, and a stool, and a candlestick: and it shall be, when he cometh to us, that he shall turn in thither. 11And it fell on a day, that he came thither, and he turned into the chamber, and lay there. 12And he said to Gehazi his servant, Call this Shunammite. And when he had called her, she stood before him. 13And he said unto him, Say now unto her, Behold, thou hast been careful for us with all this care; what is to be done for thee? wouldest thou be spoken for to the king, or to the captain of the host? And she answered, I dwell among mine own people. 14And he said, What then is to be done for her? And Gehazi answered, Verily she hath no child, and her husband is old. 15And he said, Call her. And when he had called her, she stood in the door. 16And he said, About this season, according to the time of life, thou shalt embrace a son. And she said, Nay, my lord, thou man of God, do not lie unto thine handmaid. 17And the woman conceived, and bare a son at that season that Elisha had said unto her, according to the time of life.

[32]And when Elisha was come into the house, behold, the child was dead, and laid upon his bed. [33]He went in therefore, and shut the door upon them twain, and prayed unto the LORD. [34]And he went up, and lay upon the child, and put his mouth upon his mouth, and his eyes upon his eyes, and his hands upon his hands: and he stretched himself upon the child; and the flesh of the child waxed warm. [35]Then he returned, and walked in the house to and fro; and went up, and stretched himself upon him: and the child sneezed seven times, and the child opened his eyes.

[40]So they poured out for the men to eat. And it came to pass, as they were eating of the pottage, that they cried out, and said, O thou man of God, there is death in the pot. And they could not eat thereof. [41]But he said, Then bring meal. And he cast it into the pot; and he said, Pour out for the people, that they may eat. And there was no harm in the pot.

2 Kin. 5 [9]So Naaman came with his horses and with his chariot, and stood at the door of the house of Elisha. [10]And Elisha sent a messenger unto him, saying, Go and wash in Jordan seven times, and thy flesh shall come again to thee, and thou shalt be clean. [11]But Naaman was wroth, and went away, and said, Behold, I thought he will surely come out to me, and stand, and call on the name of the LORD his God, and strike his hand over the place, and recover the leper. [12]Are not Abana and Pharpar, rivers of Damascus, better than all the waters of Israel? may I not wash in them, and be clean? So he turned and went away in a rage. [13]And his servants came near, and spake unto him, and said, My father, if the prophet had bid thee do some great thing, wouldest thou not have done it? how much rather then, when he saith to thee, Wash, and be clean? [14]Then went he down, and dipped himself seven times in Jordan, according to the saying of the man of God: and his flesh came again like unto the flesh of a little child, and he was clean.

Prophesies Concerning Ben-hadad of Syria

2 Kin. 8 [7]And Elisha came to Damascus; and Ben-hadad the king of Syria was sick; and it was told him, saying, The man of God is come hither. [8]And the king said unto Hazael, Take a present in thine hand, and go, meet the man of God, and inquire of the LORD by him, saying, Shall I recover of this disease? [9]So Hazael went to meet him, and took a present with him, even of every good thing of Damascus, forty camels' burden, and came and stood before him, and said, Thy son Ben-hadad king of Syria hath sent me to thee, saying, Shall I recover of this disease? [10]And Elisha said unto him, Go, say unto him, Thou mayest certainly recover: howbeit the LORD hath shewed me that he shall surely die. [11]And he settled his countenance steadfastly, until he was ashamed: and the man of God wept. [12]And Hazael said, Why weepeth my lord? And he answered, Because I know the evil that thou wilt do unto the children of Israel: their strong holds wilt thou set on fire, and their young men wilt thou slay with the sword, and wilt dash their children, and rip up their women with child.

Names Jehu King of Israel

2 Kin. 9 [1]And Elisha the prophet called one of the children of the prophets, and said unto him, Gird up thy loins, and take this box of oil in thine hand, and go to Ramoth-gilead: [2]And when thou comest thither, look out there Jehu the son of Jehoshaphat, the son of Nimshi, and go in, and make him arise up from among his brethren, and carry him to an inner chamber; [3]Then take the box of oil, and pour it on his head, and say, Thus saith the LORD, I have anointed thee king over Israel. Then open the door, and flee, and tarry not.

[4]So the young man, even the young man the prophet, went to Ramoth-gilead.

Death of Elisha

2 Kin. 13 [14]Now Elisha was fallen sick of his sickness whereof he died. And Joash the king of Israel came down unto him, and wept over his face, and said, O my father, my father! the chariot of Israel, and the horsemen thereof! [15]And Elisha said unto him, Take bow and arrows. And he took unto him bow and arrows. [16]And he said to the king of Israel, Put thine hand upon the bow. And he put his hand upon it: and Elisha put his hands upon the king's hands. [17]And he said, Open the window eastward. And he opened it. Then Elisha said, Shoot. And he shot. And he said, The arrow of the LORD's deliverance, and the arrow of deliverance from Syria: for thou shalt smite the Syrians in Aphek, till thou have consumed them. [18]And he said, Take the arrows. And he took them. And he said unto the king of Israel, Smite upon the ground. And he smote thrice, and stayed. [19]And the man of God was wroth with him, and said, Thou shouldest have smitten five or six times; then hadst thou smitten Syria till thou hadst consumed it: whereas now thou shalt smite Syria but thrice.

[20]And Elisha died, and they buried him. And the bands of the Moabites invaded the land at the coming in of the year. [21]And it came to pass, as they were burying a man, that, behold, they spied a band of men; and they cast the man into the sepulchre of Elisha: and when the man was let down, and touched the bones of Elisha, he revived, and stood up on his feet.

ENEMY

[en'e mi] Those who are unfriendly or hostile to us; those who wish us evil or do evil to us. The Bible, particularly the New Testament, is explicit as to the way in which we should treat enemies, this being one of the surest tests of the Christian character.

See LOVE

SCRIPTURE

Treatment of Enemies

Ex. 23 [4]If thou meet thine enemy's ox or his ass going astray, thou shalt surely bring it back to him again. [5]If thou see the ass of him that hateth thee lying under his burden, and wouldest forbear to help him, thou shalt surely help with him.

1 Sam. 24 [9]And David said to Saul, Wherefore hearest thou men's words, saying, Behold, David seeketh thy hurt? [10]Behold, this day thine eyes have seen how that the LORD had delivered thee today into mine hand in the cave: and some bade me kill thee; but mine eye spared thee; and I said, I will not put forth mine hand against my lord; for he is the LORD's anointed.

Prov. 24 [17]Rejoice not when thine enemy falleth, and let not thine heart be glad when he stumbleth.

Prov. 25 [21]If thine enemy be hungry, give him bread to eat; and if he be thirsty, give him water to drink: [22]For thou shalt heap coals of fire upon his head, and the LORD shall reward thee.

Matt. 5 [43]Ye have heard that it hath been said, Thou shalt love thy neighbour, and hate thine enemy. [44]But I say unto you, Love your enemies, bless them that curse you, do good to them that hate you, and pray for them which despitefully use you, and persecute you.

Luke 6 [35]But love ye your enemies, and do good, and lend, hoping for nothing again: and your reward shall be great, and ye shall be the children of the Highest: for he is kind unto the unthankful, and to the evil.

God Delivers from Enemies

Psa. 18 [48]He delivereth me from mine enemies: yea, thou liftest me up above those that rise up against me: thou hast delivered me from the violent man.

Psa. 61 [3]For thou hast been a shelter for me, and a strong tower from the enemy.

God's Enemies Punished

Ex. 15 [6]Thy right hand, O LORD, is become glorious in power: thy right hand, O LORD, hath dashed in pieces the enemy.

Psa. 68 [1]Let God arise, let his enemies be scattered: let them also that hate him flee before him.

Psa. 92 [9]For lo, thine enemies, O LORD, for lo, thine enemies shall perish; all the workers of iniquity shall be scattered.

Isa. 1 [24]Therefore saith the LORD, the LORD of hosts, the mighty One of Israel, Ah, I will ease me of mine adversaries, and avenge me of mine enemies.

2 Thess. 1 [7]And to you who are troubled, rest with us, when the Lord Jesus shall be revealed from heaven, with his mighty angels, [8]In flaming fire, taking vengeance on them that know not God, and that obey not the Gospel of our Lord Jesus Christ.

Enmity between God and Man

Rom. 8 [6]For to be carnally minded is death; but to be spiritually minded is life and peace. [7]Because the carnal mind is enmity against God: for it is not subject to the law of God, neither indeed can be.

Eph. 2 [14]For he is our peace, who hath made both one, and hath broken down the middle wall of partition between us: [15]Having abolished in his flesh the enmity, even the law of commandments contained in ordinances, for to make in himself of twain one new man, so making peace.

Col. 1 [20]And (having made peace through the blood of his cross) by him to reconcile all things unto himself, by him, I say, whether they be things in earth, or things in heaven. [21]And you that were sometimes alienated, and enemies in your mind by wicked works, yet now hath he reconciled.

ENOCH

[ē′nok] Although little is contained in the Bible concerning Enoch, he is remembered as the man who "walked with God: and he was not; for God took him." He is thus numbered among the select few biblical characters represented as having escaped death—"By faith Enoch was translated that he should not see death and was not found, because God had translated him: for before his translation, he had this testimony, that he pleased God" (*Heb. 11:5*). We are also told that he was the father of Methuselah.

REFERENCE: *Gen. 5:21-24; Heb. 11:5.*

ENVY

[en′vi] Discontent at the excellence, good fortunes, or possessions of another; resentful begrudging. The Bible regards envy as a sin and a stumblingblock to the person who seeks to pursue the religious life.

SCRIPTURE

General

Prov. 14 [30]A sound heart is the life of

the flesh: but envy the rottenness of the bones.

Prov. 27 [4]Wrath is cruel, and anger is outrageous; but who is able to stand before envy?

Eccl. 4 [4]Again, I considered all travail, and every right work, that for this a man is envied of his neighbour. This is also vanity and vexation of spirit.

Matt. 27 [17]Therefore when they were gathered together, Pilate said unto them, Whom will ye that I release unto you? Barabbas, or Jesus, which is called Christ? [18]For he knew that for envy they had delivered him.

Acts 7 [9]And the Patriarchs, moved with envy, sold Joseph into Egypt: but God was with him.

Rom. 1 [28]And even as they did not like to retain God in their knowledge, God gave them over to a reprobate mind, to do those things which are not convenient: [29]Being filled with all unrighteousness, fornication, wickedness, covetousness, maliciousness, full of envy, murder, debate, deceit, malignity, whisperers.

1 Cor. 3 [3]For ye are yet carnal: for whereas there is among you envying, and strife, and divisions, are ye not carnal, and walk as men?

2 Cor. 12 [20]For I fear lest when I come, I shall not find you such as I would, and that I shall be found unto you such as ye would not, lest there be debates, envyings, wraths, strifes, backbitings, whisperings, swellings, tumults.

1 Tim. 6 [4]He is proud, knowing nothing, but doting about questions and strifes of words, whereof cometh envy, strife, railings, evil surmisings.

Envy Forbidden

Psa. 37 [1]Fret not thyself because of evil doers, neither be thou envious against the workers of iniquity.

Prov. 3 [31]Envy thou not the oppressor, and choose none of his ways.

Rom. 13 [13]Let us walk honestly, as in the day; not in rioting and drunkenness, not in chambering and wantonness, not in strife and envying.

1 Pet. 2 [1]Wherefore laying aside all malice, and all guile, and hypocrisies, and envies, and evil speakings.

Consequences of Envy

Job 5 [2]For wrath killeth the foolish man, and envy slayeth the silly one.

Isa. 26 [11]LORD, when thy hand is lifted up, they will not see: but they shall see, and be ashamed for their envy at the people; yea, the fire of thine enemies shall devour them.

Jas. 3 [16]For where envying and strife is, there is confusion, and every evil work.

REFERENCE: Envy: Cain of Abel, *Gen. 4:4-8*; Sarah of Hagar, *Gen. 16:5-6; 21:9-10*; Joseph's Brethren of Joseph, *Gen. 37:4-11, 19, 20*; Miriam and Aaron of Moses, *Num. 12:1-10;* Korah, Dothan, and Abiram of Moses, *Num. 16:3*; Saul of David, *1 Sam. 18:8, 9, 29.*

EPAPHRAS

[ep'a fras] A "faithful minister of Christ" and a beloved fellow-servant of Paul during the first Roman imprisonment. Paul identifies Epaphras as the founder of the church in Colossae and a diligent worker for those in Laodicea and Hierapolis, who had brought him a report of the progress of the church in the area of Colossae.

SCRIPTURE

Col. 1 [4]Since we heard of your faith in Christ Jesus, and of the love which ye have to all the saints, [5]For the hope which is laid up for you in heaven, whereof ye heard before in the word of the truth of the gospel; [6]Which is come unto you, as it is in all the world: and bringeth forth fruit, as it doth also in you, since the day ye heard of it, and knew the grace of God in truth: [7]As ye also learned of Epaphras our dear fellowservant, who is for you a faithful minister of Christ;

Col. 4 [12]Epaphras, who is one of you, a servant of Christ, saluteth you, always labouring fervently for you in prayers, that ye may stand perfect and complete in all the will of God. [13]For I bear him record, that he hath a great zeal for you, and them that are in Laodicea, and them in Hierapolis,

Philem. 1 [23]There salute thee Epaphras, my fellowprisoner in Christ Jesus;

EPAPHRODITUS

[ê paf rô dī'tus] A companion of Paul during the first Roman imprisonment. Epaphroditus was sent by the Philippian church to carry a gift to the imprisoned apostle and to minister to him in whatever way possible. In discharging his duties, he became dangerously ill and was at the point of death. At his recovery Paul sent him back to Philippi with the epistle to that church, commending him highly and instructing the church to receive him with joy and honor.

SCRIPTURE

Phil. 2 [25]Yet I supposed it necessary to send to you Epaphroditus, my brother, and companion in labour, and fellowsoldier, but your messenger, and he that ministered to my wants. [26]For he longed after you all, and was full of heaviness, because that ye had heard that he had been sick.
[27]For indeed he was sick nigh unto death: but God had mercy on him; and not on him only, but on me also, lest I should have sorrow upon sorrow. [28]I sent him therefore the more carefully, that, when ye see him again, ye may rejoice, and that I may be the less sorrowful. [29]Receive him therefore in the Lord with all gladness; and hold such in reputation: [30]Because for the work of Christ he was nigh unto death, not regarding his life, to supply your lack of service toward me.

Phil. 4 [18]But I have all, and abound: I am full, having received of Epaphroditus the things which were sent from you, an odour of a sweet smell, a sacrifice acceptable, wellpleasing to God.

EPHESUS

[ef'e sus] A major city of the Roman province of Asia, situated nearly opposite the island of Samos. Ephesus possessed an artificial harbor capable of handling the largest of merchant ships, this, coupled with the coast roads which lead northward to Smyrna and southward to Miletus, made Ephesus the most easily accessible city in Asia, both by land and sea. A great deal of the prominence which belonged to Ephesus was due to the presence of the great temple of Diana, which employed great hosts of people engaged in the making of images and shrines. (*See* DIANA) Paul visited Ephesus on his second journey, staying but a short while (*Acts 18:19-21*). On his third journey, however, he remained in Ephesus for two years, teaching daily in the school of Tyrannus. His work there was so effective that a great number of the citizenry believed, burning their magic books. An even greater attestation is seen in the riot stirred up by Demetrius and the other silversmiths, who felt that "The Way" constituted a real threat to the worship of Diana and the attendant silversmith trade. A strong church was established at Ephesus, and was the addressee of one of seven letters in *Revelation.* The apostle John is said to have been a leader in this church.

See PAUL

SCRIPTURE

Paul Visits on Second Journey

Acts 18 [19]And he came to Ephesus, and

left them there: but he himself entered
into the synagogue, and reasoned with the
Jews. [20]When they desired him to tarry
longer time with them, he consented not;
[21]But bade them farewell, saying, I must
by all means keep this feast that cometh in
Jerusalem: but I will return again unto
you, if God will. And he sailed from Ephesus.

The Third Journey

PAUL PREACHES

Acts 19 [1]And it came to pass, that, while
Apollos was at Corinth, Paul having
passed through the upper coasts came to
Ephesus: and finding certain disciples.
[8]And he went into the synagogue, and
spake boldly for the space of three months,
disputing and persuading the things concerning the kingdom of God. [9]But when
divers were hardened, and believed not,
but spake evil of that way before the multitude, he departed from them, and separated the disciples, disputing daily in the
school of one Tyrannus. [10]And this continued by the space of two years; so that
all they which dwelt in Asia heard the
word of the Lord Jesus, both Jews and
Greeks.

WORKS MIRACLES

Acts 19 [11]And God wrought special
miracles by the hands of Paul: [12]So that
from his body were brought unto the sick
handkerchiefs or aprons, and the diseases
departed from them, and the evil spirits
went out of them.

THE BURNING OF THE BOOKS

Acts 19 [17]And this was known to all the
Jews and Greeks also dwelling at Ephesus;
and fear fell on them all, and the name
of the Lord Jesus was magnified. [18]And
many that believed came, and confessed,
and shewed their deeds. [19]Many of them
also which used curious arts brought their
books together, and burned them before
all men: and they counted the price of
them, and found it fifty thousand pieces
of silver. [20]So mightily grew the word of
God and prevailed.

THE RIOT

Acts 19 [23]And the same time there arose
no small stir about that way. [24]For a certain man named Demetrius, a silversmith,
which made silver shrines for Diana,
brought no small gain unto the craftsmen;
[25]Whom he called together with the workmen of like occupation, and said, Sirs, ye
know that by this craft we have our
wealth. [26]Moreover ye see and hear, that
not alone at Ephesus, but almost throughout all Asia, this Paul hath persuaded and
turned away much people, saying that
they be no gods, which are made with
hands: [27]So that not only this our craft
is in danger to be set at nought; but also
that the temple of the great goddess Diana
should be despised, and her magnificence
should be destroyed, whom all Asia and
the world worshippeth. [28]And when they
heard these sayings, they were full of
wrath, and cried out, saying, Great is Diana of the Ephesians. [29]And the whole
city was filled with confusion: and having caught Gaius and Aristarchus, men of
Macedonia, Paul's companions in travel,
they rushed with one accord into the theatre. [30]And when Paul would have entered
in unto the people, the disciples suffered
him not. [31]And certain of the chief of Asia,
which were his friends, sent unto him, desiring him that he would not adventure
himself into the theatre. [32]Some therefore
cried one thing, and some another: for the
assembly was confused; and the more part

knew not wherefore they were come together. 33And they drew Alexander out of the multitude, the Jews putting him forward. And Alexander beckoned with the hand, and would have made his defence unto the people. 34But when they knew that he was a Jew, all with one voice about the space of two hours cried out, Great is Diana of the Ephesians. 35And when the townclerk had appeased the people, he said, Ye men of Ephesus, what man is there that knoweth not how that the city of the Ephesians is a worshipper of the great goddess Diana, and of the image which fell down from Jupiter? 36Seeing then that these things cannot be spoken against, ye ought to be quiet, and to do nothing rashly. 37For ye have brought hither these men, which are neither robbers of churches, nor yet blasphemers of your goddess. 38Wherefore if Demetrius, and the craftsmen which are with him, have a matter against any man, the law is open, and there are deputies: let them implead one another. 39But if ye enquire any thing concerning other matters, it shall be determined in a lawful assembly. 40For we are in danger to be called in question for this day's uproar, there being no cause whereby we may give an account of this concourse. 41And when he had thus spoken, he dismissed the assembly.

Character of the Ephesian Church

Rev. 2 1Unto the angel of the church of Ephesus write; These things saith he that holdeth the seven stars in his right hand, who walketh in the midst of the seven golden candlesticks; 2I know thy works, and thy labour, and thy patience, and how thou canst not bear them which are evil: and thou hast tried them which say they are apostles, and are not, and hast found them liars: 3And hast borne, and hast patience, and for my name's sake hast laboured, and hast not fainted. 4Nevertheless I have somewhat against thee, because thou hast left thy first love. 5Remember therefore from whence thou art fallen, and repent, and do the first works; or else I will come unto thee quickly, and will remove thy candlestick out of his place, except thou repent. 6But this thou hast, that thou hatest the deeds of the Nicolaitanes, which I also hate.

See EPHESIANS

EPHOD

[ef'od] A sacred vestment designed originally for the high priest. The high priest's ephod was made "of gold, blue, and purple, and scarlet, and fine twined linen"; it was held together by two shoulderpieces on which were two onyx stones bearing the names of the twelve tribes of Israel. Attached to the ephod by golden chains was a breastplate containing twelve precious stones in four rows. In a later period, the ephod was worn by ordinary priests (*1 Sam. 22:18*) and was deemed characteristic of the priestly office (*1 Sam. 2:18, 28*). When David danced in the procession accompanying the bringing of the ark of the covenant into Jerusalem, he wore a linen ephod (*2 Sam. 6:14*). There is also mention of an ephod in connection with idolatrous images, but it is impossible to determine the shape, size, or purpose of the ephods mentioned here, although it is not unlikely that they too were priestly garments.

See THUMMIM, URIM

REFERENCE: The High Priest's Ephod, *Ex. 28:3-35.*

SCRIPTURE

Samuel's Ephod

1 Sam. 2 18But Samuel ministered before the LORD, being a child, girded with a linen ephod.

28And did I choose him out of all the tribes of Israel to be my priest, to offer upon mine altar, to burn incense, to wear an ephod before me? and did I give unto the house of thy father all the offerings made by fire of the children of Israel?

Ephod a Garment of Ordinary Priests

1 Sam. 22 18And the king said to Doeg, Turn thou, and fall upon the priests. And Doeg the Edomite turned, and he fell upon the priests, and slew on that day fourscore and five persons that did wear a linen ephod.

David Wears an Ephod

2 Sam. 6 14And David danced before the LORD with all his might; and David was girded with a linen ephod.

Connection with Idolatry

Judg. 17 5And the man Micah had an house of gods, and made an ephod, and teraphim, and consecrated one of his sons, who became his priest.

Judg. 18 14Then answered the five men that went to spy out the country of Laish, and said unto their brethren, Do ye know that there is in these houses an ephod, and teraphim, and a graven image, and a molten image? now therefore consider what ye have to do.

Hos. 3 4For the children shall abide many days without a king, and without a prince, and without a sacrifice, and without an image, and without an ephod, and without teraphim:

EPHRAIM

[ē′fra im, ē′frå im] The son of Joseph and his wife Asenath, the daughter of Potiphera, Priest of On. Two Israelite tribes traced their lineage to Joseph, calling themselves by the names of his two sons, Manasseh and Ephraim. The relative importance of these two tribes is traced to the giving of the paternal blessing by Jacob, in which Ephraim was favored, although younger than Manasseh.

REFERENCE: *Gen. 41:50-52; 48:8-22.*

EPICUREANS

[ep i cū rē′anz] A school of thought based on the teachings of Epicurus, a Greek philosopher who lived in Athens about 342-271 BC. Epicurus taught that the natural aim and the highest good of man was pleasure; this is not to be confused with the "pleasure of the profligates", or the sensual, carnal indulgence implied in the phrase, "Eat, drink, and be merry", so often associated with the Epicureans. On the contrary, the pleasure which Epicurus sought was largely negative, meaning freedom from pain, trouble, and perturbation. It was to be found in the joy of pure and simple existence. To achieve this simplicity of life, Epicurus urged his followers to withdraw from public life, to abstain from marriage and the begetting of children, and to live a quiet, hidden life. Through this pattern of life, man could be freed from the fear of death, the gods, and the "powers" which surround and threaten his happiness. Epicureans are mentioned as having been present at Paul's speech on the Areopagus, or Mar's Hill.

See STOICS, AREOPAGUS

SCRIPTURE

Acts 17 18Then certain philosophers of the Epicureans, and of the Stoics, encountered him. And some said, What will this babbler say? other some, He seemeth to be a setter forth of strange gods: because he preached unto them Jesus, and the resurrection.

EPISTLES

[ĕ pis′l] A letter to a person or group of persons; especially a didactic, or elegant letter, used particularly of the twenty-one letters contained in the New Testament. The epistles appear to be the work of five or six men. Thirteen bear Paul's name, three are attributed to John, two to Peter, and one each to James and Jude; the epistles to the *Hebrews* is anonymous. The Pauline epistles contain the sub-groups of the Prison or Captivity epistles (*Ephesians, Philippians, Colossians,* and *Philemon*) and Pastoral epistles (*1 and 2 Timothy* and *Titus*). The epistles possess a vitality and charm which set them apart from the sacred literature of other Near Eastern and Eastern religions.

ESAU

[ē'sô] The son of Isaac and Rebekah and twin brother of Jacob. A rugged outdoorsman, Esau was favored by his father but was deprived of the blessings which would have fallen to him as the eldest son by the famous sale of his birthright to Jacob for a mess of pottage (*Gen. 5:29-34*), by the deception of Jacob and Rebekah at the reception of the paternal blessing from Isaac (*Gen. 27*). Esau angrily vowed to kill his brother at the death of their father, but Rebekah sent Jacob to Haran until Esau's wrath subsided. When they met again after many years, Jacob still greatly feared his brother and sought to propitiate him with elaborate gifts; apparently, Esau had forgiven Jacob and received him graciously. The only other recorded meeting between the two was at the death of their father, about twenty years later. Esau is regarded in the Old Testament as the ancestor of the Edomites.

See JACOB, ISAAC, REBEKAH

SCRIPTURE

Birth of Esau

Gen. 25 21 And Isaac entreated the LORD
for his wife, because she was barren: and
the LORD was entreated of him, and Rebekah his wife conceived. 22 And the children struggled together within her; and
she said, If it be so, why am I thus? And
she went to inquire of the LORD. 23 And
the LORD said unto her, Two nations are in
thy womb, and two manner of people shall
be separated from thy bowels; and the one
people shall be stronger than the other
people; and the elder shall serve the
younger.
24 And when her days to be delivered
were fulfilled, behold, there were twins in
her womb. 25 And the first came out red,
all over like a hairy garment; and they
called his name Esau. 26 And after that
came his brother out, and his hand took
hold on Esau's heel; and his name was
called Jacob: and Isaac was threescore
years old when she bare them.

Deprived of His Birthright

Gen. 25 27 And the boys grew: and Esau
was a cunning hunter, a man of the field;
and Jacob was a plain man, dwelling in
tents. 28 And Isaac loved Esau, because he
did eat of his venison: but Rebekah loved
Jacob.
29 And Jacob sod pottage: and Esau
came from the field, and he was faint:
30 And Esau said to Jacob, Feed me, I pray
thee, with that same red pottage; for I am
faint: therefore was his name called Edom.
31 And Jacob said, Sell me this day thy
birthright. 32 And Esau said, Behold, I
am at the point to die: and what profit shall
this birthright do to me? 33 And Jacob said,
Swear to me this day; and he sware unto
him: and he sold his birthright unto Jacob.
34 Then Jacob gave Esau bread and pottage
of lentiles; and he did eat and drink, and
rose up, and went his way. Thus Esau despised his birthright.

Deprived of Isaac's Blessing

Gen. 27 15 And Rebekah took goodly raiment of her eldest son Esau, which were
with her in the house, and put them upon
Jacob her younger son: 16 And she put the
skins of the kids of the goats upon his
hands, and upon the smooth of his neck:
17 And she gave the savoury meat and the
bread, which she had prepared, into the
hand of her son Jacob.
18 And he came unto his father, and said,
My father: and he said, Here am I; who art

thou, my son? [19]And Jacob said unto his
father, I am Esau thy firstborn; I have
done according as thou badest me: arise,
I pray thee, sit and eat of my venison, that
thy soul may bless me. [20]And Isaac said
unto his son, How is it that thou hast found
it so quickly, my son? And he said, Because the LORD thy God brought it to me.
[21]And Isaac said unto Jacob, Come near, I
pray thee, that I may feel thee, my son,
whether thou be my very son Esau or not.
[22]And Jacob went near unto Isaac his father; and he felt him, and said, The voice
is Jacob's voice, but the hands are the
hands of Esau. [23]And he discerned him
not, because his hands were hairy, as his
brother Esau's hands: so he blessed him.

[41]And Esau hated Jacob because of the
blessing wherewith his father blessed him:
and Esau said in his heart, The days of
mourning for my father are at hand; then
will I slay my brother Jacob.

REFERENCE: *Gen. 33, 36.*

ESTHER

[es'ter] The Persian name of Hadassah, a Jewish orphan girl who had been reared by her cousin Mordecai, who had an office in the household of Ahasuerus—to be identified with the Persian ruler Xerxes (*see* AHASUERUS)—and who dwelt in the capital city of Shushan, or Susa. According to the book of *Esther*, when Vashti was dismissed from being queen (*see* VASHTI), all the fairest virgins of the kingdom were collected at Shushan, from which Ahasuerus was to choose the successor to the deposed queen. Unaware of her race and parentage, Ahasuerus chose Esther to be his queen. Later, because of the refusal of Mordecai to pay homage to Haman, a man "above all the princes" in the Persian government, the latter influenced the King to issue a decree calling for the extermination of the Jews. Mordecai persuaded Esther to intervene, at the risk of her life, on the Jews' behalf. Finding favor with Ahasuerus, Esther revealed the heinous plot of Haman. The result was that Haman was hanged and Mordecai was elevated to a place of high honor. Although, according to Persian law, the decree of the King concerning the Jews could not be rescinded, it was counteracted by this issuing of another decree which allowed the Jews to defend themselves. To celebrate the deliverance of the Jews, the feast of Purim was instituted.

See PURIM, MORDECAI, VASHTI, HAMAN

SCRIPTURE

Esther Becomes Queen

Esth. 2 [8]So it came to pass, when the
king's commandment and his decree was
heard, and when many maidens were gathered together unto Shushan the palace,
to the custody of Hegai, that Esther was
brought also unto the king's house, to the
custody of Hegai, keeper of the women.
[9]And the maiden pleased him, and she obtained kindness of him; and he speedily
gave her her things for purification, with
such things as belonged to her, and seven
maidens which were meet to be given her,
out of the king's house: and he preferred
her and her maids unto the best place of
the house of the women.

Urged to Intervene on Behalf of Jews

Esth. 4 [12]And they told to Mordecai
Esther's words. [13]Then Mordecai commanded to answer Esther, Think not with
thyself that thou shalt escape in the king's
house, more than all the Jews. [14]For if
thou altogether holdest thy peace at this
time, then shall there enlargement and deliverance arise to the Jews from another
place; but thou and thy father's house shall
be destroyed: and who knoweth, whether
thou art come to the kingdom for such a
time as this?

[15]Then Esther bade them return Mordecai this answer, [16]Go, gather together all
the Jews that are present in Shushan, and

fast ye for me, and neither eat nor drink three days, night or day: I also and my maidens will fast likewise; and so will I go in unto the king, which is not according to the law: and if I perish, I perish. [17]So Mordecai went his way, and did according to all that Esther had commanded him.

Esth. 5 [1]Now it came to pass on the third day, that Esther put on her royal apparel, and stood in the inner court of the king's house, over against the king's house: and the king sat upon his royal throne in the royal house, over against the gate of the house. [2]And it was so, when the king saw Esther the queen standing in the court, that she obtained favour in his sight: and the king held out to Esther the golden sceptre that was in his hand. So Esther drew near, and touched the top of the sceptre. [3]Then said the king unto her, What wilt thou, queen Esther? and what is thy request? it shall be even given thee to the half of the kingdom.

Counteracts Haman's Plot

Esth. 8 [1]On that day did the king Ahasuerus give the house of Haman, the Jews' enemy, unto Esther the queen. And Mordecai came before the king; for Esther had told what he was unto her. [2]And the king took off his ring which he had taken from Haman, and gave it unto Mordecai. And Esther set Mordecai over the house of Haman.

[7]Then the king Ahasuerus said unto Esther the queen, and to Mordecai the Jew, Behold, I have given Esther the house of Haman, and him they have hanged upon the gallows, because he laid his hand upon the Jews. [8]Write ye also for the Jews, as it liketh you, in the king's name, and seal it with the king's ring: for the writing which is written in the king's name and sealed with the king's ring, may no man reverse. [11]Wherein the king granted the Jews which were in every city to gather themselves together, and to stand for their life, to destroy, to slay, and to cause to perish, all the power of the people and province that would assault them, both little ones and women, and to take the spoil of them for a prey, [12]Upon one day in all the provinces of king Ahasuerus, namely, upon the thirteenth day of the twelfth month, which is the month Adar.

Sanctions the Feast of Purim

Esth. 9 [32]And the decree of Esther confirmed these matters of Purim; and it was written in the book.

REFERENCE: The Book of *Esther*.

ETERNITY, ETERNAL LIFE

[ē tĕr′ni ti, ē tĕr′nal līf] In Greek thought, eternity indicates timelessness, a state qualitatively different from time; if we are to be true to Biblical thought, however, it is probably more accurate to conceive of eternity as an endless span of time. The fourth gospel teaches us that "whoso eateth my flesh, and drinketh my blood, hath eternal life;" (*John 6:54*). Obviously this does not mean that Christians are exempted from physical death, but that the new relationship to Christ is such that it is not affected by the temporal boundaries of life.

God is spoken of as eternal, in that he is absolute LORD over time and is in no way bound by it (*see*, for example, *Psa. 90:4*). Frequently, the Hebrew and Greek words which are translated "eternal" simply indicate the unknown length of a lifetime (*1 Sam. 1:22, 28; 1 Cor. 8:13; Luke 1:70; Mark 11:4*) or any indefinite span of time.

SCRIPTURE

Eternal Life

John 6 [27]Labour not for the meat which perisheth, but for that meat which endureth unto everlasting life, which the Son of man shall give unto you: for him hath God

the Father sealed. [40]And this is the will of
him that sent me, that every one which
seeth the Son, and believeth on him, may
have everlasting life: and I will raise him
up at the last day. [47]Verily, verily, I say
unto you, He that believeth on me hath
everlasting life.

Rom. 2 [7]To them who by patient continuance in well doing seek for glory and honour and immortality, eternal life:

Rom. 5 [21]That as sin hath reigned unto death, even so might grace reign through righteousness unto eternal life by Jesus Christ our Lord.

Rom. 6 [22]But now being made free from
sin, and become servants to God, ye have
your fruit unto holiness, and the end everlasting life. [23]For the wages of sin is death;
but the gift of God is eternal life through
Jesus Christ our Lord.

Tit. 1 [2]In hope of eternal life, which God, that cannot lie, promised before the world began;

Tit. 3 [7]Being justified by his grace, we should be made heirs according to the hope of eternal life.

1 John 2 [25]And this is the promise that he hath promised us, even eternal life.

ETHIOPIAN EUNUCH

[ē thi ō′pi an ū′nuk] 1. The royal treasurer for Candace queen of the Ethiopians. His name is not given in scripture. This man was converted to Christ by Philip the evangelist, whom he met while riding home from Jerusalem. He was apparently a very religious man, for when Philip joined him in his chariot, he was reading from the prophet Isaiah. Beginning at the scripture where he read, Philip "preached unto him Jesus," and shortly thereafter baptized him into Christ.

2. For information on a lesser known Ethiopian eunuch, see the article on EBED-MELECH.

See PHILIP, EUNUCH

REFERENCE: *Acts 8:26-40.*

EUNUCH

[ū′nuk] An emasculated man. Eunuchs were commonly found in the service of ancient rulers usually serving as harem guards or military and administrative officers. Self-mutilation was a common practice in a number of oriental religions and was thought to honor the gods; in contrast to this, the law of Moses originally prohibited eunuchs from participating in public worship, although this was eventually modified.

Jesus spoke of several classes of eunuchs, including those "which have made themselves eunuchs for the kingdom of heaven's sake." There has been considerable dispute as to the meaning of this phrase, but most scholars have felt that Jesus referred to those who had gained complete control of the sex instinct, rather than to those who resorted to literal self-mutilation.

See ETHIOPIAN EUNUCH, EBED-MELECH

REFERENCE: *Deut. 23:1; Isa. 56:3-5; Jer. 38:7-13; 52:25; Dan. 1:3; Matt. 19:12; Acts 8:26-29.*

EUPHRATES

[ū frā′tēz] "The Good and Abounding River." Because of its fame this waterway is frequently denoted in the Bible simply as "the river." The Euphrates is the largest, the longest, and by far the most important of the rivers of Western Asia. It rises in the Armenian mountains and flows into the Persian Gulf. The entire course is 1780 miles, and of this distance more than two thirds (1200 miles) is navigable for boats.

SCRIPTURE

In the Garden

Gen. 2 [14]And the name of the third river is Hiddekel: that is it which goeth toward the east of Assyria. And the fourth river is Euphrates.

The Eastern Limit of the Promised Land

Gen. 15 [18]In that same day the LORD made a covenant with Abram, saying, Unto thy seed have I given this land, from the river of Egypt unto the great river, the river Euphrates:

Ex. 23 [31]And I will set thy bounds from the Red sea even unto the sea of the Philistines, and from the desert unto the river: for I will deliver the inhabitants of the land into your hand; and thou shalt drive them out before thee.

Deut. 1 [7]Turn you, and take your journey, and go to the mount of the Amorites, and unto all the places nigh thereunto, in the plain, in the hills, and in the vale, and in the south, and by the sea side, to the land of the Canaanites, and unto Lebanon, unto the great river, the river Euphrates.

"The River"

Deut. 11 [24]Every place whereon the soles of your feet shall tread shall be yours: from the wilderness and Lebanon, from the river, the river Euphrates, even unto the uttermost sea shall your coast be.

See Ex. 23:31

EVE

[ēv] The name given to the woman in the *Genesis* account of creation. She was created as a companion and helper for Adam. The entrance of sin into humanity is attributed to Eve's being seduced by the serpent to eat fruit which had been prohibited by God. After she persuaded Adam to eat of it, they were expelled from the garden of Eden and condemned to a life of toil and suffering. Further brief mention is made of Eve, as the mother of Cain, Abel, and Seth.

See Adam, Fall

SCRIPTURE

Gen. 1 [27]So God created man in his own image, in the image of God created he him; male and female created he them.

Gen. 2 [21]And the Lord God caused a deep sleep to fall upon Adam, and he slept: and he took one of his ribs, and closed up the flesh instead thereof; [22]And the rib, which the Lord God had taken from man, made he a woman, and brought her unto the man. [23]And Adam said, This is now bone of my bones, and flesh of my flesh: she shall be called Woman, because she was taken out of Man.

Gen. 3 [20]And Adam called his wife's name Eve; because she was the mother of all living.

Gen. 3 [1]Now the serpent was more subtil than any beast of the field which the Lord God had made. And he said unto the woman, Yea, hath God said, Ye shall not eat of every tree of the garden? [2]And the woman said unto the serpent, We may eat of the fruit of the trees of the garden: [3]But of the fruit of the tree which is in the midst of the garden, God hath said, Ye shall not eat of it, neither shall ye touch it, lest ye die. [4]And the serpent said unto the woman, Ye shall not surely die: [5]For God doth know that in the day ye eat thereof, then your eyes shall be opened, and ye shall be as gods, knowing good and evil. [6]And when the woman saw that the tree was good for food, and that it was pleasant to the eyes, and a tree to be desired to make one wise, she took of the fruit thereof, and did eat, and gave also unto her husband with her; and he did eat. [13]And the Lord God said unto the woman, What is this that thou hast done? And the woman said, The serpent beguiled me, and I did eat. [16]Unto the woman he said, I will greatly multiply thy sorrow and thy conception; in sorrow thou shalt bring forth children: and thy desire shall be to thy husband, and he shall rule over thee.

EVIL

[ēv'l, ē'vil] The Greek and Hebrew words

which are translated "evil" in the Bible may refer either to "physical" or "moral" evil—that is, to anything that causes pain, suffering, or unhappiness, including discipline or punishment sent by God; the precise meaning of the word must be determined by its context. In the sense that God sometimes sends adversity on mankind, he may properly be spoken of as the creator of evil; this is not, however, to be understood as moral evil, for "God cannot be tempted with evil, and he himself tempteth no man" (*Jas. 1:13*). It is quite natural that the word should have developed a moral connotation, since men tend to view any action which is harmful to them as wicked.

See Sin

SCRIPTURE

Isa. 45 [7]I form the light, and create darkness; I make peace, and create evil: I the Lord do all these things.

Amos 5 [14]See good, and not evil, that ye may live: and so the Lord, the God of hosts, shall be with you, as ye have spoken.

Mic. 3 [2]Who hate the good, and love the evil; who pluck off their skin from off them, and their flesh from off their bones;

1 Thess. 5 [22]Abstain from all appearance of evil.

EXODUS

[ex′o dus] Literally, a going out. This term is applied to the journey of the Israelites from Egypt to Canaan, under the leadership of Moses. This journey, carried out under the direction of God, was the fundamental event in the religion of Israel. The Exodus is probably to be dated around 1275 BC. At approximately this period, Pharaoh Ramses II was engaged in a royal building program in which he employed as slave labor a group of people known in Egyptian annals as Hapiru; the similarity to Hebrew is apparent. One of the cities which Ramses built was Raamses (House of Ramses), mentioned in *Ex. 1:11* as one of the cities on which the Hebrews worked. If the Hebrews left Egypt somewhere near this time and spent approximately forty years in the wilderness, that would mean they arrived in Canaan toward the end of the thirteenth century BC. Several archaeological discoveries confirm this theory. Numerous towns sprang up east of the Jordan river between the thirteenth and eleventh centuries. Several cities mentioned in the account of the conquest in *Joshua,* including Lachish, Hebron, and Hazor, are known to have been destroyed between 1225 and 1200 BC. Further, the discovery of a stele (a pillar of stone bearing an inscription) set up by Pharaoh Merneptah in 1220 BC tells of the defeat of a people called Israel, who had been in Palestine only a short time. This date also fits nicely with the statement in *Ex. 12:40* that "the sojourning of the children of Israel, who dwelt in Egypt, was four hundred and thirty years"; that is, that the Exodus fell 430 years after the arrival of the first settlers in the time of Joseph. This would place the activity of Joseph about 1705 BC, during the period of the Hyksos rulers. (*See* Egypt) The era of the Hyksos is known to have been a period of great prosperity for Egypt, not unlike that described in the book of *Genesis.* (*See Gen. 39-50*) Also pertinent is the fact that the land of Goshen, in which the family of Joseph settled, is near the Hyksos capital of Avaris, but not the traditional capital of Thebes, used by most other dynasties. This accumulation of evidence can make us reasonably confident that the date suggested above is correct.

When the oppression of the Hebrews became almost unbearable, God appointed Moses to lead them to the land that had been promised to the descendants of Abraham. Moses was unable to persuade Pharaoh to allow the Hebrews to depart until God visited the ten plagues on the Egyptians (*see* Plagues), culminating in the death of all the firstborn of Egypt (*Ex. 7-11*). Shortly thereafter, the Hebrews departed from Egypt, avoiding major Egyptian fortifications by taking a route which brought them to a body of water commonly thought to be the Red Sea; the Hebrew text of the Old Testament, however, states it was the sea of Reeds, not the Red Sea. (*See* Red Sea)

In *Ex. 14,* we read of the miraculous opening of this sea, enabling the Hebrews to cross, and the subsequent drowning of the pursuing Egyptians. God's further providential care is seen in the provision of manna (*Ex. 16:14-36*), quails (*Ex. 16:13*), and water (*Num. 20:9-11*) to sustain the great host on their journey.

Eventually the Hebrews made their way to Mount Sinai, at the south end of the Sinai peninsula, at which place they entered into the sacred covenant with God (*Ex. 19-20*). It was here also that instructions were given concerning the erection and furnishing of the tabernacle (*Ex. 25-31* and *see* TABERNACLE). After leaving Sinai, they made their way across the wilderness of Paran into the wilderness of Zin, in which Kadesh was located. From Kadesh twelve spies were sent to spy out the land of Canaan; when the majority of the spies returned with a discouraging report, the people despaired of the possibility of entering the land. On witnessing this manifestation of faithlessness, God announced that none of the adults among the Hebrews would be permitted to enter the promised land except Joshua and Caleb, the two spies who brought back a favorable report. The Hebrews were overwhelmed by this judgment, and resolved to enter the land; without the help of the LORD, however, they were defeated by the Amalekites and fell back upon Kadesh. They spent the greater part of the next forty years wandering about in this area. Finally, in the latter part of the thirteenth century, they sought once more to enter Canaan, this time through the land of the Edomites. The Edomites refused passage and they were forced to circle to the east and enter through the transjordanic kingdoms of Sihon and Og. For a further discussion of their entry into Canaan, see CONQUEST.

REFERENCE: *See Exodus, Numbers, Joshua.*

EZEKIEL

[ē zē'ki el] The great prophet of the Babylonian exile whose dated prophecies range from about 593-571 BC. Ezekiel was taken captive in the first deportation from Jerusalem in 597 BC. He was a member of a community of Hebrew exiles who settled on the banks of the Chebar, a river of Babylon. It was by this river "in the land of the Chaldeans" that he received his call to the prophetic office, in the fourth month of "the fifth year of King Jehoiachin's captivity." He was married and had a house in his place of exile; he lost his wife by a sudden and unforeseen stroke on the very day that the siege of Jerusalem began. The last date mentioned in his prophecy is the twenty-seventh year of the captivity, so it is certain that his ministry lasted over twenty years. Tradition asserts that he was murdered in Babylon by some Hebrew prince whom he had convicted of idolatry, and was buried on the banks of the Euphrates. Ezekiel's prophecy is characterized by the frequency of visions and fantastic symbolical acts which were witnessed or performed by the prophet.

See EXILE

REFERENCE: The Book of *Ezekiel.*

EZRA

[ez'ra] Priest and scribe of Israel after the return from Babylonian captivity. Although Nehemiah had made great strides in restoring Jewish faith and life in Palestine, much remained to be done. The individual chosen to do it was Ezra. On order of the king, he set out from Babylon with a copy of the law and the authority to enforce it on all who chose to call themselves Jews. Arriving probably about the year 428 BC (although there is wide diversity of opinion as to the proper date), Ezra and his assistants soon presented the law publicly at the time of the Feast of the Tabernacles. The major problem with which Ezra had to deal seems to have been the widespread practice of mixed marriages with the non-Jewish elements in the land. Recalling the idolatrous abuses to which this had led in Israel's history, Ezra succeeded in effecting the dissolution of all mixed marriages. Having removed this obstacle to a successful restoration, Ezra set about to reconstitute the community on the basis of the law which he brought from Babylon. Ezra seems to have brought his reforming work to completion within a year of his arrival in Jerusalem, and after this nothing more is heard of him. Because of his great contribution to normative Judaism, Ezra is often regarded as second in importance only to Moses.

See NEHEMIAH

REFERENCE: The Book of *Ezra.*

FAITH, FAITHFULNESS

[fāth; fāth'ful nes] In the Old Testament, faith is more accurately rendered "faithfulness," indicating firmness, reliability, or steadfastness; the faithful individual holds on confidently to his own integrity and to the precepts of the Law, strengthened by his confidence in the object believed, the God of Israel. In the New Testament, faith is thought of as an act by which the individual avails himself of the gifts of God, submits himself in obedience to God's commands, and abandons all thought of self, trusting only in God. Here the emphasis shifts from the reliance on self which is found in the Old Testament to complete reliance on God. The writer of *Hebrews* introduced the concept of faith as being in opposition to "sight"; to him faith is confident trust in the *unseen* power of God. In some instances, faith refers simply to the Christian Religion.

SCRIPTURE

The Nature of Faith

Heb. 11 [1]Now faith is the substance of things hoped for, the evidence of things not seen. [2]For by it the elders obtained a good report. [3]Through faith we understand that the worlds were framed by the word of God, so that things which are seen were not made of things which do appear.

Its Power to Justify, Purify, Sanctify

Rom. 3 [28]Therefore we conclude that a man is justified by faith without the deeds of the law.

Rom. 5 [1]Therefore being justified by faith, we have peace with God through our Lord Jesus Christ: [2]By whom also we have access by faith into this grace wherein we stand, and rejoice in hope of the glory of God.

Gal. 2 [16]Knowing that a man is not justified by the works of the law, but by the faith of Jesus Christ, even we have believed in Jesus Christ, that we might be justified by the faith of Christ, and not by the works of the law: for by the works of the law shall no flesh be justified.

Acts 15 [9]And put no difference between us and them, purifying their hearts by faith.

Acts 26 [18]To open their eyes, and to turn them from darkness to light, and from the power of Satan unto God, that they may receive forgiveness of sins, and inheritance among them which are sanctified by faith that is in me.

Godhead Object of Faith

Mark 11 [22]And Jesus answering, saith unto them, Have faith in God. [23]For verily I say unto you, that whosoever shall say unto this mountain, Be thou removed, and be thou cast into the sea, and shall not doubt in his heart, but shall believe that those things which he saith shall come to pass: he shall have whatsoever he saith.

John 14 [1]Let not your heart be troubled: ye believe in God, believe also in me.

John 20 [31]But these are written, that ye might believe that Jesus is the Christ the Son of God, and that believing ye might have life through his Name.

Faith Given by the Spirit

1 Cor. 2 [4]And my speech and my preaching was not with enticing words of man's wisdom, but in demonstration of the Spirit and of power: [5]That your faith should not stand in the wisdom of men, but in the power of God.

1 Cor. 12 [9]To another faith, by the same spirit: to another the gifts of healing, by the same spirit.

Unity of Faith

Eph. 4 [5]One Lord, one Faith, one Baptism. [13]Till we all come in the unity of the faith, and of the knowledge of the Son of God, unto a perfect man, unto the measure of the stature of the fulness of Christ.

Jude 1 [3]Beloved, when I gave all diligence to write unto you of the common salvation: it was needful for me to write unto you, and exhort you that ye should earnestly contend for the faith which was once delivered unto the Saints.

Faith and Salvation

Mark 16 16He that believeth and is baptized shall be saved; but he that believeth not shall be damned.

John 1 12But as many as received him, to them gave he power to become the sons of God, even to them that believe on his Name.

John 3 16For God so loved the world, that he gave his only begotten Son, that whosoever believeth in him should not perish, but have everlasting life.

36He that believeth on the Son hath everlasting life: and he that believeth not the Son shall not see life: but the wrath of God abideth on him.

Gal. 3 11But that no man is justified by the law in the sight of God, it is evident: for, The just shall live by faith.

Eph. 2 8For by grace are ye saved, through faith, and that not of yourselves: it is the gift of God.

2 Tim. 3 15And that from a child thou hast known the holy Scriptures, which are able to make thee wise unto salvation through faith which is in Christ Jesus.

Heb. 11 6But without faith it is impossible to please him: for he that cometh to God must believe that he is, and that he is a rewarder of them that diligently seek him.

Faith Works by Love

1 Cor. 13 2And though I have the gift of prophecy, and understand all mysteries, and all knowledge; and though I have all faith, so that I could remove mountains, and have not charity, I am nothing. 13And now abideth faith, hope, charity, these three; but the greatest of these is charity.

Gal. 5 6For in Jesus Christ neither circumcision availeth any thing, nor uncircumcision, but faith which worketh by love.

1 Tim. 1 5Now the end of the commandment is charity, out of a pure heart, and of a good conscience, and of faith unfeigned.

1 Pet. 1 22Seeing ye have purified your souls in obeying the truth through the Spirit unto unfeigned love of the brethren, see that ye love one another with a pure heart fervently.

Faith without Works

Jas. 2 17Even so faith, if it hath not works, is dead being alone. 18Yea, a man may say, Thou hast faith, and I have works: shew me thy faith without thy works, and I will shew thee my faith by my works. 19Thou believest that there is one God, thou doest well: the devils also believe, and tremble. 20But wilt thou know, O vain man, that faith without works is dead?

Brings Peace and Joy

Rom. 5 1Therefore being justified by faith, we have peace with God, through our Lord Jesus Christ.

Rom. 15 13Now the God of hope fill you with all joy and peace in believing, that ye may abound in hope through the power of the Holy Ghost.

1 Pet. 1 7That the trial of your faith, being much more precious than of gold that perisheth, though it be tried with fire, might be found unto praise, and honour, and glory, at the appearing of Jesus Christ: 8Whom having not seen, ye love, in whom though now ye see him not, yet believing, ye rejoice with joy unspeakable, and full of glory.

Blessings from Faith

John 6 40And this is the will of him that

sent me, that every one which seeth the Son, and believeth on him, may have everlasting life: and I will raise him up at the last day.

Rom. 4 [16]Therefore it is of faith, that it might be by grace; to the end the promise might be sure to all the seed; not to that only which is of the law, but to that also which is of the faith of Abraham; who is the father of us all.

Eph. 3 [11]According to the eternal purpose which he purposed in Christ Jesus our Lord: [12]In whom we have boldness and access with confidence by the faith of him.

1 Tim. 1 [4]Neither give heed to fables and endless genealogies, which minister questions, rather than godly edifying which is in faith.

Miracles through Faith

Matt. 9 [22]But Jesus turned him about, and when he saw her, he said, Daughter, be of good comfort, thy faith hath made thee whole. And the woman was made whole from that hour.

Luke 8 [50]But when Jesus heard it, he answered him, saying, Fear not, believe only, and she shall be made whole.

Acts 3 [16]And his name through faith in his name hath made this man strong, whom ye see and know: yea, the faith which is by him hath given him this perfect soundness in the presence of you all.

Power of Faith

Matt. 17 [20]And Jesus said unto them, Because of your unbelief: for verily I say unto you, If ye have faith as a grain of mustard seed, ye shall say unto this mountain, Remove hence to yonder place; and it shall remove; and nothing shall be impossible unto you.

Mark 9 [23]Jesus said unto him, If thou canst believe, all things are possible to him that believeth.

1 John 5 [4]For whatsoever is born of God, overcometh the world, and this is the victory that overcometh the world, even our faith.

Faith's Trials

2 Thess. 1 [4]So that we ourselves glory in you in the churches of God for your patience and faith in all your persecutions and tribulations that ye endure.

Heb. 11 [17]By faith Abraham, when he was tried, offered up Isaac: and he that had received the promises offered up his only begotten son.

Jas. 1 [3]Knowing this, that the trying of your faith worketh patience.

1 Pet. 1 [7]That the trial of your faith, being much more precious than of gold that perisheth, though it be tried with fire, might be found unto praise and honour and glory at the appearing of Jesus Christ.

In Christian's Armor

Eph. 6 [16]Above all, taking the shield of faith, wherewith ye shall be able to quench all the fiery darts of the wicked.

1 Thess. 5 [8]But let us, who are of the day, be sober, putting on the breastplate of faith and love, and for an helmet, the hope of salvation.

Constancy in Faith

1 Cor. 16 [13]Watch ye, stand fast in the faith, quit you like men: be strong.

2 Cor. 13 [5]Examine yourselves, whether ye be in the faith: prove your own selves. Know ye not your own selves, how that Jesus Christ is in you, except ye be reprobates?

Phil. 1 [27]Only let your conversation be as it becometh the gospel of Christ: that whether I come and see you, or else be absent, I may hear of your affairs, that ye stand fast in one spirit, with one mind striving together for the faith of the gospel.

Col. 2 [6]As ye have therefore received Christ Jesus the Lord, so walk ye in him: [7]Rooted and built up in him, and stablished in the faith, as ye have been taught, abounding therein with thanksgiving.

1 Tim. 1 [18]This charge I commit unto thee, son Timothy, according to the prophecies which went before on thee, that thou by them mightest war a good warfare; [19]Holding faith, and a good conscience; which some having put away concerning faith have made shipwreck.

Faithfulness in God's Service

Matt. 24 [45]Who then is a faithful and wise servant, whom his Lord hath made ruler over his household, to give them meat in due season?

2 Cor. 4 [2]But have renounced the hidden things of dishonesty, not walking in craftiness, nor handling the word of God deceitfully, but by manifestation of the truth commending ourselves to every man's conscience in the sight of God.

3 John 1 [5]Beloved, thou doest faithfully whatsoever thou doest to the Brethren, and to strangers: [6]Which have borne witness of thy charity before the Church: whom if thou bring forward on their journey after a godly sort, thou shalt do well.

Faithfulness toward Men

Prov. 11 [13]A tale-bearer revealeth secrets: but he that is of a faithful spirit concealeth the matter.

Prov. 13 [17]A wicked messenger falleth into mischief: but a faithful ambassador is health.

Prov. 14 [5]A faithful witness will not lie: but a false witness will utter lies.

Luke 16 [10]He that is faithful in that which is least, is faithful also in much: and he that is unjust in the least, is unjust also in much. [11]If therefore ye have not been faithful in the unrighteous Mammon, who will commit to your trust the true riches? [12]And if ye have not been faithful in that which is another man's, who shall give you that which is your own?

1 Cor. 4 [1]Let a man so account of us, as of the ministers of Christ, and stewards of the mysteries of God. [2]Moreover, it is required in stewards, that a man be found faithful.

1 Tim. 6 [2]And they that have believing masters, let them not despise them, because they are brethren; but rather do them service, because they are faithful and beloved, partakers of the benefit. These things teach and exhort.

REFERENCE: Faith of Noah in building the ark, *Gen. 6:14-22*; Abraham in leaving his homeland at the command of God, *Gen. 12:1-4*, and in offering Isaac, *Gen. 22:1-10; Heb. 11:8-19*; Moses in leading his people, *Heb. 11:24-28*; the widow of Zarephath in feeding Elijah, *1 Kin. 17:13-15*; Daniel in the lions' den, *Dan. 6*; the woman with the issue of blood, *Matt. 9:21-22*; those who brought the paralytic to Jesus, *Luke 5:18-20*; the Syrophenician woman, *Mark 7:26*.

FALL

[fa̤l] The Fall of Man is a theological term referring to man's loss of primitive innocence and his subsequent subjection to sin and death. The *Genesis* story of the Fall is a simple one. After placing Adam and Eve in the Garden of Eden, God issued a single command, prohibiting their eating from "the tree of knowledge of good and evil." Being tempted by the serpent, Eve ate of the fruit of this tree and persuaded Adam to do likewise. As a result of their transgression, they were expelled from the garden and sentenced to a mortal life of toil and suffering. The theological insights to be gained from this narrative are profound indeed. It is made clear that human evil has its basis in the will of man and cannot be blamed on God. The whole of society —the descendants of Adam and Eve—is involved in the fall and comes under the judgment of God. The basic attitude underlying the Fall is mans refusal to accept creatureliness, his desire to be "as the gods." This same attitude is reflected again in the story of the tower of Babel (*Gen. 11*).

See ADAM, EVE, CREATION, EDEN, SIN

SCRIPTURE

The Command

Gen. 2 16 And the LORD God commanded the man, saying, Of every tree of the garden thou mayest freely eat: 17 But of the tree of the knowledge of good and evil, thou shalt not eat of it: for in the day that thou eatest thereof thou shalt surely die.

The Fall and Judgment

Gen. 3 1 Now the serpent was more subtile than any beast of the field which the LORD God had made. And he said unto the woman, Yea, hath God said, Ye shall not eat of every tree of the garden? 2 And the woman said unto the serpent, We may eat of the fruit of the trees of the garden: 3 But of the fruit of the tree which is in the midst of the garden, God hath said, Ye shall not eat of it, neither shall ye touch it, lest ye die. 4 And the serpent said unto the woman, Ye shall not surely die: 5 For God doth know that in the day ye eat thereof, then your eyes shall be opened, and ye shall be as gods, knowing good and evil. 6 And when the woman saw that the tree was good for food, and that it was pleasant to the eyes, and a tree to be desired to make one wise, she took of the fruit thereof, and did eat, and gave also unto her husband with her; and he did eat. 7 And the eyes of them both were opened, and they knew that they were naked; and they sewed fig leaves together, and made themselves aprons. 8 And they heard the voice of the LORD God walking in the garden in the cool of the day: and Adam and his wife hid themselves from the presence of the LORD God amongst the trees of the garden. 9 And the LORD God called unto Adam, and said unto him, Where art thou? 10 And he said, I heard thy voice in the garden, and I was afraid, because I was naked; and I hid myself. 11 And he said, Who told thee that thou wast naked? Hast thou eaten of the tree, whereof I commanded thee that thou shouldest not eat? 12 And the man said. The woman whom thou gavest to be with me, she gave me of the tree, and I did eat. 13 And the LORD God said unto the woman, What is this that thou hast done? And the woman said, The serpent beguiled me, and I did eat. 14 And the LORD God said unto the serpent, Because thou hast done this, thou art cursed above all cattle, and above every beast of the field: upon thy belly shalt thou go, and dust shalt thou eat all the days of thy life: 15 And I will put enmity between thee and the woman, and between thy seed and her seed: it shall bruise thy head, and thou shalt bruise his heel. 16 Unto the woman he said, I will greatly multiply thy sorrow and thy conception; in sorrow thou shalt bring forth children: and thy desire shall be to thy husband, and he shall rule over thee. 17 And unto Adam he said, Because thou hast hearkened unto the voice of thy wife, and hast eaten of the tree of which I commanded thee, saying, Thou shalt not eat of it: cursed is the ground for thy sake; in sorrow shalt thou eat of it all the days of thy life; 18 Thorns also and thistles shall it bring forth to thee; and thou shalt eat the herb of the field: 19 In the sweat of thy face shalt thou eat bread, till thou return unto the ground; for out of it wast thou taken: for dust thou art, and unto dust shalt thou return.

[22]And the LORD God said, Behold, the man is become as one of us, to know good and evil: and now, lest he put forth his hand, and take also of the tree of life, and eat, and live for ever: [23]Therefore the LORD God sent him forth from the garden of Eden, to till the ground from whence he was taken. [24]So he drove out the man: and he placed at the east of the garden of Eden Cherubims, and a flaming sword which turned every way, to keep the way of the tree of life.

Rom. 5 [12]Wherefore, as by one man sin entered into the world, and death by sin; and so death passed upon all men, for that all have sinned.

1 Cor. 15 [21]For since by man came death, by man came also the resurrection of the dead. [22]For as in Adam all die, even so in Christ shall all be made alive.

FAMILY

[fam'i li] In Biblical times the family was composed of all who claimed kin to the father of a household. This included the wife (or wives), children, unmarried brothers and sisters, parents, and other relatives, as well as servants and concubines. The father's position in the family was that of possessor and master. His will was binding upon the community which attached itself to him. A man's strength and authority were carried on in his sons; thus there was an emphasis on the bearing of many children. Although her primary duty was to bear children, the mother also possessed considerable authority over the family and was due the respect and honor of her husband and children. (*See* MARRIAGE, WOMAN)

The family was the central unit of Hebrew society and the concept of the family was often extended to refer to tribes, to the kingdoms of Israel and Judah, and to the Israelites as a whole. Man's relation to God and his fellow-covenanters is also described in the language of family relations, in such terms as "Father," "sons," "children," "brethren," the "household of God," and "household of faith."

FASTING

[fast'ing] To practice self-denial or abstinence, particularly from foods. Since loss of appetite commonly accompanies grief, it was natural that abstinence from food or drink should be regarded as an expression of sorrow. This explains the association of fasting with ancient mourning customs (*1 Sam. 31:13; 2 Sam. 1:12; 3:35*). It was also felt that fasting might aid one in gaining the favor of God; a good example of this attitude is seen in David's defense of his fasting before and not after the death of the child which Bath-sheba had borne him. He reasoned that his fasting might make his petitions for the life of the child effectual; after the child was dead, such prayer would be futile. Occasionally, fasting was proclaimed on a large scale, especially in times of war or pestilence (*Judg. 20:26; Joel 1:13-14*). The length of the fast and the items abstained from could vary widely. Sometimes there was complete abstinence from all foods; on other occasions there appears to have been only a restriction to a very plain diet (*Dan. 10:3*).

One fast only was appointed by the law, that on the day of Atonement (*Lev. 16:29, 31; 23:27-32; Num. 29:7*). There is no mention of any other periodical fast in the Old Testament, except in *Zech. 7:1-7; 8:19*, from which it appears that the Jews during their captivity observed four annual fasts, in the fourth, fifth, seventh, and tenth months. (*See* FEASTS, FASTS, AND FESTIVALS) Those who fasted frequently dressed in sackcloth or rent their clothes, put ashes on their head and went barefoot (*1 Kin. 21:27; Neh. 9:1*). Jesus condemned this outward display, implying that the purpose of fasting was to discipline one's soul and body for greater service, and not for an ostentatious show of piety (*Matt. 6:16-18*).

SCRIPTURE

Fasting Associated with Mourning

1 Sam. 31 [13]And they took their bones,

and buried them under a tree at Jabesh, and fasted seven days.

2 Sam. 1 [12]And they mourned, and wept, and fasted until even, for Saul, and for Jonathan his son, and for the people of the Lord, and for the house of Israel; because they were fallen by the sword.

2 Sam. 3 [35]And when all the people came to cause David to eat meat while it was yet day, David sware, saying, So do God to me, and more also, if I taste bread, or aught else, till the sun be down.

National Observance of Fasts

Judg. 20 [26]Then all the children of Israel, and all the people, went up, and came unto the house of God, and wept, and sat there before the Lord, and fasted that day until even, and offered burnt offerings and peace offerings before the Lord.

Joel 1 [13]Gird yourselves, and lament, ye priests: howl, ye ministers of the altar: come, lie all night in sackcloth, ye ministers of my God: for the meat offering and the drink offering is withholden from the house of your God.

[14]Sanctify ye a fast, call a solemn assembly, gather the elders and all the inhabitants of the land into the house of the Lord your God, and cry unto the Lord,

The Day of Atonement a Fast Day

Lev. 16 [29]And this shall be a statute for ever unto you: that in the seventh month, on the tenth day of the month, ye shall afflict your souls, and do no work at all, whether it be one of your own country, or a stranger that sojourneth among you:

Other Possible Fast Days

Zech. 8 [19]Thus saith the Lord of hosts; The fast of the fourth month, and the fast of the fifth, and the fast of the seventh, and the fast of the tenth, shall be to the house of Judah joy and gladness, and cheerful feasts; therefore love the truth and peace.

Outward Show of Fasting

1 Kin. 21 [27]And it came to pass, when Ahab heard those words, that he rent his clothes, and put sackcloth upon his flesh, and fasted, and lay in sackcloth, and went softly.

Neh. 9 [1]And in the twenty and fourth day of this month the children of Israel were assembled with fasting, and with sackclothes, and earth upon them.

Jesus' Attitude toward Fasting

Matt. 4 [2]And when he had fasted forty days and forty nights, he was afterward ahungered.

Matt. 6 [16]Moreover when ye fast, be not, as the hypocrites, of a sad countenance: for they disfigure their faces, that they may appear unto men to fast. Verily I say unto you, They have their reward. [17]But thou, when thou fastest, anoint thine head, and wash thy face; [18]That thou appear not unto men to fast, but unto thy Father which is in secret: and thy Father which seeth in secret shall reward thee openly.

FATHER

[fä'thẽr] This word is used in the Bible in several senses, the most important of which are with reference: (1) to God as the Father of Christ and of all men; (2) to a male parent; (3) to an ancestor; (4) to a chief or ruler; (5) to the author or source of anything. With relation to the second meaning the Bible is quite explicit, enjoining love, veneration, obedience, and respect for one's father. It is equally clear as to the duty of fathers toward their children, setting forth the needs of love, care, and guidance in the family and religious relations. The absence of a father in a home is considered a serious misfortune and we are taught that God is especially watchful for the fatherless.

See CHILDREN

REFERENCE: On the Fatherhood of God, see article on GOD.

SCRIPTURE

The Duty of Fathers

Prov. 3 [12]For whom the LORD loveth he correcteth; even as a father the son in whom he delighteth.

Prov. 13 [24]He that spareth his rod hateth his son: but he that loveth him chasteneth him betimes.

Prov. 19 [18]Chasten thy son while there is hope, and let not thy soul spare for his crying.

Prov. 22 [15]Foolishness is bound in the heart of a child; but the rod of correction shall drive it far from him.

Prov. 23 [13]Withhold not correction from the child: for if thou beatest him with the rod, he shall not die.

Prov. 29 [17]Correct thy son, and he shall give thee rest; yea, he shall give delight unto thy soul.

Eph. 6 [4]And, ye fathers, provoke not your children to wrath: but bring them up in the nurture and admonition of the Lord.

Col. 3 [21]Fathers, provoke not your children to anger, lest they be discouraged.

Duty to Fathers

Deut. 5 [16]Honour thy father and thy mother, as the LORD thy God hath commanded thee; that thy days may be prolonged, and that it may go well with thee, in the land which the LORD thy God giveth thee.

Deut. 27 [16]Cursed be he that setteth light by his father or his mother: and all the people shall say, Amen.

Lev. 19 [3]Ye shall fear every man his mother, and his father, and keep my sabbaths: I am the LORD your God.

Prov. 1 [8]My son, hear the instruction of thy father, and forsake not the law of thy mother;

Prov. 23 [22]Hearken unto thy father that begat thee, and despise not thy mother when she is old.

The Fatherless

Ex. 22 [22]Ye shall not afflict any widow, or fatherless child. [23]If thou afflict them in any wise, and they cry at all unto me, I will surely hear their cry; [24]And my wrath shall wax hot, and I will kill you with the sword; and your wives shall be widows, and your children fatherless.

Deut. 10 [18]He doth execute the judgment of the fatherless and widow, and loveth the stranger, in giving him food and raiment.

Deut. 27 [19]Cursed be he that perverteth the judgment of the stranger, fatherless, and widow: and all the people shall say, Amen.

Job 22 [9]Thou hast sent widows away empty, and the arms of the fatherless have been broken. [10]Therefore snares are round about thee, and sudden fear troubleth thee.

Psa. 68 [5]A father of the fatherless, and a judge of the widows, is God in his holy habitation.

FAULT

[fôlt] A failing, flaw, blemish; a deviation from the right or a neglect of duty through carelessness or a lack of knowledge rather than through purpose; some error not necessarily a sin. Christians are given instruction in the proper handling of their own faults and those of their fellowmen.

SCRIPTURE

Matt. 18 [15]Moreover, if thy brother shall trespass against thee, go and tell him his fault between thee and him alone: if he shall hear thee, thou hast gained thy brother.

Gal. 6 [1]Brethren, if a man be overtaken in a fault, ye which are spiritual, restore such a one in the spirit of meekness, considering thyself lest thou also be tempted. [2]Bear ye one another's burdens, and so fulfill the law of Christ.

Jas. 5 [16]Confess your faults one to another, and pray one for another, that ye may be healed. The effectual fervent prayer of a righteous man availeth much.

FEAR, FEAR OF GOD

[fēr] Apprehension or dread of impending danger or trouble; also, awe, profound reverence, especially for the Supreme Being. Great stress is laid upon the fear of God as a necessary adjunct to the relations between humanity and Deity. In the Old Testament, this often takes the form of dread or sheer terror, but in the New Testament the emphasis falls more upon reverence and deep respect for His greatness and mercy.

SCRIPTURE

Fear of God—General References

Job 28 [28]And unto man he said, Behold, the fear of the LORD, that is wisdom; and to depart from evil is understanding.

Psa. 111 [10]The fear of the LORD is the beginning of wisdom: a good understanding have all they that do his commandments: his praise endureth for ever.

Prov. 1 [7]The fear of the LORD is the beginning of knowledge: but fools despise wisdom and instruction.

Prov. 9 [10]The fear of the LORD is the beginning of wisdom: and the knowledge of the Holy is understanding.

Fear of God Commanded

Deut. 6 [13]Thou shalt fear the LORD thy God, and serve him, and shalt swear by his name.

Deut. 8 [6]Therefore thou shalt keep the commandments of the LORD thy God, to walk in his ways, and to fear him.

Deut. 10 [12]And now, Israel, what doth the LORD thy God require of thee, but to fear the LORD thy God, to walk in all his ways, and to love him, and to serve the LORD thy God with all thy heart and with all thy soul.

1 Sam. 12 [24]Only fear the LORD, and serve him in truth with all your heart: for consider how great things he hath done for you.

2 Kin. 17 [36]But the LORD, who brought you up out of the land of Egypt with great power and a stretched out arm, him shall ye fear, and him shall ye worship, and to him shall ye do sacrifice. [39]But the LORD your God ye shall fear; and he shall deliver you out of the hand of all your enemies.

Psa. 33 [8]Let all the earth fear the LORD: let all the inhabitants of the world stand in awe of him.

Luke 12 [4]And I say unto you my friends, Be not afraid of them that kill the body, and after that have no more that they can do. [5]But I will forewarn you whom ye shall fear: Fear him, which after he hath killed hath power to cast into hell: yea, I say unto you, Fear him.

Heb. 12 [28]Wherefore we receiving a kingdom which cannot be moved, let us have grace, whereby we may serve God acceptably with reverence and godly fear.

Blessedness of Fearing God

Ex. 20 [20]And Moses said unto the people, Fear not: for God is come to prove you, and that his fear may be before your faces, that ye sin not.

Deut. 6 [2]That thou mightest fear the LORD thy God, to keep all his statutes and his commandments, which I command thee, thou, and thy son, and thy son's son, all the days of thy life; and that thy days may be prolonged.

Psa. 25 [12]What man is he that feareth the LORD? him shall he teach in the way that he shall choose. [13]His soul shall dwell at ease; and his seed shall inherit the earth. [14]The secret of the LORD is with them that fear him; and he will shew them his covenant.

Psa. 33 [18]Behold, the eye of the LORD is upon them that fear him, upon them that hope in his mercy; [19]To deliver their soul from death, and to keep them alive in famine.

Psa. 34 [9]O fear the LORD, ye his saints: for there is no want to them that fear him.

FEASTS, FASTS, FESTIVALS

[fēsts, fasts, fes'ti v'ls]

I. The Hebrew Calendar

The Hebrew calendar contained a large number of feast and fast days; these were connected with agriculture, months and seasons, and events in the history of the nation. To avoid confusion in the material presented below, it is in order to explain some peculiar features of the Hebrew calendar. The Hebrew New Year came not at the beginning of the first month, but on the first day of the seventh month. This oddity is explained by the fact that the Hebrew lived by two different years, a civil and a ritual. The beginning and end of the civil year coincided naturally with the harvest season, when the work of one year's agricultural production was finished and preparation for another was begun. The months of which we read in the Bible are those of the ritual year. The months of the Hebrew calendar, with their approximate equivalents in our Gregorian calendar, are here given:

1. Abib (March-April). This was the first month in the ritual year, *Ex. 12:2; 13:4; Deut. 16:1.* After the captivity, the first month was known as Nisan, *Neh. 2:1; Esth. 3:7.*
2. Zif or Ziv (April-May), *1 Kin. 6:1, 37.*
3. Sivan (May-June), *Esth. 8:9.*
4. Tammuz (June-July), *Jer. 39:2; 52:6, 7.*
5. Ab (July-August), *Num. 33:38.*
6. Elul (August-September), *Neh. 6:15; Hag. 1:14, 15.*
7. Ethanim (September-October), *1 Kin. 8: 2.* This was the beginning of the civil year and contained several of the most notable of the Hebrew days of observance.
8. Bul (October-November), *1 Kin. 6:38; 12:32, 33.*
9. Chisleu or Chislev (November-December), *Ezra 10:9; Jer. 36:9, 22; Zech. 7:1.*
10. Tebeth (December-January), *Esth. 2:16; 2 Kin. 25:1.*
11. Sebat (January-February), *Zech. 1:7.*
12. Adar (February-March), *Esth. 3:7.*
13. Because of the length of the months an extra month had to be inserted about every three years; therefore, a year might contain either twelve or thirteen months. The insertion came after the twelfth month and was called "Second Adar."

II. The Festivals

Three of the great annual festivals included a pilgrimage to the central sanctuary and were connected both with agricultural processes and with historical events. These were Passover, Pentecost, and the Feast of Booths or Tabernacles.

PASSOVER (pas'ōvẽr) was celebrated on the evening of the fourteenth day of Abib (Nisan), at the time of the barley harvest. The Passover lamb was eaten in imitation of the last meal eaten by the Israelites before they took their departure from Egypt. On the following day, a sheaf was cut from the field and waved before the LORD as a peace-offering. This marked the beginning of the DAYS OF UNLEAVENED BREAD, which lasted for seven days, and in which no leaven was eaten. The name Passover has come to refer to both the evening memorial meal and the week following (*Ex. 12:6; Lev. 23:5, 8; Num. 28:16-25; Deut. 16:1-8*).

Pentecost (pen′tê kost) fell seven weeks or, to be exact, fifty days (hence the name Pentecost) following Passover, at the time of the wheat harvest. In the Old Testament it is referred to as the Feast of Weeks. It was observed as a Sabbath; all labor was suspended and the people expressed their gratitude to the Lord, symbolized in the offering of two loaves of leavened, salted bread, baked according to precise directions. In later years, the Rabbis connected Pentecost with the giving of the Law on Mount Sinai and it came to be a day of reconsecration (*Lev. 23:10-15; Num. 28:26-31*).

The Feast of Tabernacles or, more properly, Booths, fell at the end of the general autumn harvest, on the fifteenth day of the seventh month. In a spirit of rejoicing for the blessings of the previous year and in memory of the period of wanderings in the wilderness, the Israelites dwelt for seven days in leafy booths which they constructed (*Ex. 23:16; Lev. 23:33ff; Deut. 16: 13-15*). Immediately after the Feast of Booths came the Eighth Day of Assembly, which was a last great day of rejoicing before returning to their homes (*Lev. 23:26; Num. 29:35ff; John 7: 37*).

The Day of Atonement must surely be grouped with these festivals as among the most important in the Hebrew calendar. It was held on the tenth day of the seventh month, only a few days before the Feast of Booths began. On this day special sacrifices and rituals were performed to atone for all unforgiven sins committed in that year, including those of the high priest himself. On this day the high priest, clad in a simple white linen robe instead of the decorative festal garments, entered the Holy of Holies—the only day of the year in which he was permitted to do so as a matter of worship—and sprinkled the mercy seat with the blood of the sin-offering. It was also on this day that the ritual of Azazel, or the scapegoat, was performed. (*See* Scapegoat and *Lev. 16; 23:26-32; Num. 29:7-11*)

As noted above, New Year's Day fell on the first day of the seventh month; it was ushered in with a blast of trumpets and observed as a sabbath. It is sometimes called the Feast of Trumpets (*Lev. 23:24-5; Num. 29:1-6*).

The Feast of Purim was celebrated on the fourteenth and fifteenth days of the month of Adar. The book of *Esther* contains an account of the origin of this feast. (*See* Purim)

In the New Testament, reference is made to the Feast of Dedication (*John 10:22*). This is a post-exilic feast commemorating the cleansing of the temple and dedication of the altar by Judas Maccabaeus after its desecration by Antiochus Epiphanes. It was an eight day celebration beginning on the twenty-fifth day of Chisleu, and is sometimes called the Feast of Lights.

See Sabbath, Sabbatical Year, Jubilee

FELIX

[fē liks] A Roman procurator of Judaea, before whom Paul appeared at Caesarea. After his return from the third missionary journey, Paul became the center of a riot in Jerusalem, stirred up by Asian Jews who accused him of seeking to overthrow the Law of Moses and profaning the temple of the Lord; the anger of the Jews was so great that Paul was saved from death only by the quick action of the Roman tribune, Claudius Lysias. Because of its nature, the case was transferred to the jurisdiction of Felix, and Paul was taken to Caesarea. When Felix heard the accusations made by Tertullus, the spokesman for the Jews who opposed Paul, and the reply which Paul made to them, he postponed making a decision on the grounds that he wanted to hear what Lysias, the tribune, had to say. According to the writer of *Acts*, Felix had a rather accurate knowledge of the Christian movement and recognized the probable inaccuracy of the charges which had been made against Paul; in addition, he was hoping that Paul might offer him some money as a bribe for his release. For the next two years, therefore, he let the case drag on; during that time, Paul often appeared before Felix and his wife Drusilla, speaking to them "of righteousness, temperance, and judgment to come." Paul's preaching apparently disturbed Felix's conscience, but there is no evidence of any positive response. After two years, Felix was succeeded by Porcius Festus; to avoid any disturbance by the Jews, he simply left Paul in prison, rather than handing down the decision which he knew to be just.

See Festus, Lysias, Paul

SCRIPTURE

Acts 24 [24]And after certain days, when Felix came with his wife Drusilla, which was a Jewess, he sent for Paul, and heard him concerning the faith in Christ. [25]And as he reasoned of righteousness, temperance, and judgment to come, Felix trembled, and answered, Go thy way for this time; when I have a convenient season, I will call for thee. [26]He hoped also that money should have been given him of Paul, that he might loose him: wherefore he sent for him the oftener, and communed with him. [27]But after two years Porcius Festus came into Felix' room: and Felix, willing to shew the Jews a pleasure, left Paul bound.

FELLOWSHIP

[fel'ô ship] Sharing; having or giving a share in something with someone; the association together of persons with mutual aims and interests. Christian fellowship consists of a twofold relationship—with the Godhead and with fellow-Christians. With regard to the former, the saints, out of the benign grace of God and through the sufferings of Christ for them, are permitted the joy of companionship and association with the Father, Son, and Holy Spirit. With this relationship as a basis, Christians share with one another in a fellowship of mutual sympathy, love, unity, and service.

See LOVE, UNITY, etc.

SCRIPTURE

Fellowship with God

Gen. 5 [24]And Enoch walked with God: and he was not; for God took him.

Lev. 26 [12]And I will walk among you, and will be your God, and ye shall be my people.

John 14 [23]Jesus answered and said unto him, If a man love me, he will keep my words: and my Father will love him, and we will come unto him, and make our abode with him.

1 John 1 [3]Truly our fellowship is with the Father, and with his Son Jesus Christ.

Fellowship with Christ

Matt. 18 [20]For where two or three are gathered together in my name, there am I in the midst of them.

John 15 [4]Abide in me, and I in you. As the branch cannot bear fruit of itself, except it abide in the vine; no more can ye, except ye abide in me. [5]I am the vine, ye are the branches: He that abideth in me, and I in him, the same bringeth forth much fruit: for without me ye can do nothing.

1 Cor. 1 [9]God is faithful, by whom ye were called unto the fellowship of his Son Jesus Christ our Lord.

Eph. 5 [30]We are members of his body, of his flesh, and of his bones.

1 John 4 [13]Hereby know we that we dwell in him, and he in us, because he hath given us of his Spirit.

Fellowship of the Holy Spirit

Rom. 8 [9]But ye are not in the flesh, but in the Spirit, if so be that the Spirit of God dwell in you. Now if any man have not the Spirit of Christ, he is none of his.

2 Cor. 13 [14]The grace of the Lord Jesus Christ, and the love of God, and the communion of the Holy Ghost, be with you all. Amen.

Phil. 2 [1]If there be therefore any consolation in Christ, if any comfort of love, if any fellowship of the Spirit, if any bowels and mercies, [2]Fulfil ye my joy, that ye be likeminded, having the same love, being of one accord, of one mind.

Fellowship of the Righteous

Psa. 55 [14]We took sweet counsel together, and walked unto the house of God in company.

Acts 2 [42]And they continued stedfastly in the apostles' doctrine and fellowship, and in breaking of bread, and in prayers.

Rom. 1 [12]That is, that I may be comforted together with you by the mutual faith both of you and me.

1 Cor. 10 [17]For we being many are one bread, and one body: for we are all partakers of that one bread.

1 Cor. 12 [13]For by one Spirit are we all baptized into one body, whether we be Jews or Gentiles, whether we be bond or free; and have been all made to drink into one Spirit.

2 Cor. 8 [4]Praying us with much entreaty that we would receive the gift, and take upon us the fellowship of the ministering to the saints.

Gal. 2 [9]And when James, Cephas, and John, who seemed to be pillars, perceived the grace that was given unto me, they gave to me and Barnabas the right hands of fellowship; that we should go unto the heathen, and they unto the circumcision.

1 Pet. 2 [17]Love the brotherhood.

1 John 1 [3]That which we have seen and heard declare we unto you, that ye also may have fellowship with us: . . . . [7]If we walk in the light, as he is in the light, we have fellowship one with another, ...

Fellowship with the Wicked Forbidden

Num. 16 [26]And he spake unto the congregation, saying, Depart, I pray you, from the tents of these wicked men, and touch nothing of theirs, lest ye be consumed in all their sins.

Deut. 7 [2]And when the LORD thy God shall deliver them before thee; thou shalt smite them, and utterly destroy them; thou shalt make no covenant with them, nor shew mercy unto them: [3]Neither shalt thou make marriages with them; thy daughter thou shalt not give unto his son, nor his daughter shalt thou take unto thy son. [4]For they will turn away thy son from following me, that they may serve other gods: so will the anger of the LORD be kindled against you, and destroy thee suddenly.

Josh. 23 [13]Know for a certainty that the LORD your God will no more drive out any of these nations from before you; but they shall be snares and traps unto you, and scourges in your sides, and thorns in your eyes, until ye perish from off this good land which the LORD your God hath given you.

Psa. 1 [1]Blessed is the man that walketh not in the counsel of the ungodly, nor standeth in the way of sinners, nor sitteth in the seat of the scornful.

Prov. 4 [14]Enter not into the path of the wicked, and go not in the way of evil men.

1 Cor. 10 [20]But I say, that the things which the Gentiles sacrifice, they sacrifice to devils, and not to God: and I would not that ye should have fellowship with devils.

1 Cor. 15 [33]Be not deceived: evil communications corrupt good manners.

2 Cor. 6 [14]Be ye not unequally yoked together with unbelievers: for what fellowship hath righteousness with unrighteousness? and what communion hath light with darkness?

Eph. 5 [11]And have no fellowship with the unfruitful works of darkness, but rather reprove them.

2 Thess. 3 [6]Now we command you brethren, in the name of our Lord Jesus Christ, that ye withdraw yourselves from every brother that walketh disorderly, and not after the tradition which he received of us.

FESTUS, PORCIUS

[fes′tus, pôr′shi us] Successor of Felix as procurator or governor of the province of Judaea. During the last two years of Felix' term in office, a case which the Jews had brought against Paul had been allowed to drag along without a decision and the apostle was still in prison when Festus became governor. On his first trip to Jerusalem after entering the province, Festus was confronted by a group of Jews who urged him to have Paul sent to Jerusalem, planning an ambush to kill him on the way. Being somewhat unfamiliar with the case, and in accordance with Roman law (*see Acts 25:16*), Festus decided that a better course of action would be to have a rehearsal of the charges against Paul, to be held in Caesarea. The accusations which were subsequently brought against the apostle were of a religious nature and Festus was at a loss as to how to investigate them. Wishing to do the Jews a favor, he asked Paul if he would like to go to Jerusalem and be tried on these charges. It was at this point that Paul made the famous appeal to Caesar which was to take him to Rome. Paul's Roman citizenship left Festus with no choice but to grant his appeal. Before Paul's transfer to Rome could be arranged, King Agrippa and his sister Bernice appeared in Caesarea and, learning of the case, asked to have Paul appear before them. Festus was happy to arrange this, as he desired to obtain more definite information to include in the report which would accompany Paul to Rome. In the midst of Paul's defense before the dignitaries, Festus interrupted him and charged him with madness; despite this opinion, however, he and Agrippa agreed that Paul had done nothing worthy of death or imprisonment. As Paul represented a threat to order in his province, Festus probably had little use for him or his teachings; nevertheless, his concern for Roman law and impartial justice mark him as a capable ruler and deserves our admiration.

See FELIX, PAUL, HEROD, AGRIPPA II

REFERENCE: *Acts 25-26.*

FILTH, FILTHINESS

[filth, fil′thi nes] In the original texts, the words rendered in English as "filth" or "filthiness" meant "foul matter" or anything that soils, defiles, or pollutes.

SCRIPTURE

Filthiness of Sin

Job 15 16 How much more abominable and filthy is man, which drinketh iniquity like water?

Psa. 14 3 They are all gone aside, they are all together become filthy: there is none that doeth good, no, not one.

Isa. 64 6 But we are all as an unclean thing, and all our righteousnesses are as filthy rags; and we all do fade as a leaf; and our iniquities, like the wind, have taken us away.

Ezek. 24 13 In thy filthiness is lewdness: because I have purged thee, and thou wast not purged, thou shalt not be purged from thy filthiness any more till I have caused my fury to rest upon thee.

Purification from Filthiness

Isa. 4 4 When the LORD shall have washed away the filth of the daughters of Zion, and shall have purged the blood of Jerusalem from the midst thereof by the spirit of judgment, and by the spirit of burning.

Ezek. 22 15 And I will scatter thee among the heathen, and disperse thee in the countries, and will consume thy filthiness out of thee.

Ezek. 36 25 Then will I sprinkle clean water upon you, and ye shall be clean: from all your filthiness, and from all your idols, will I cleanse you.

1 Cor. 6 11 And such were some of you: but ye are washed, but ye are sanctified, but ye are justified in the Name of the Lord Jesus, and by the Spirit of our God.

2 Cor. 7 1 Having therefore these promises (dearly beloved) let us cleanse ourselves from all filthiness of the flesh and spirit, perfecting holiness in the fear of God.

FIRE

[fīr] Fire is mentioned in many ways in the Bible, since the Hebrews used it for various domestic purposes, for warmth, and in their worship of God. Fire was not to be kindled on the Sabbath, and for burnt offerings none could be used except that taken from the altar fire. There are a number of instances in which fire accompanied divine appearances. The Bible is particularly explicit regarding the use of fire as an instrument of God's judgment and as the means of everlasting punishment.

SCRIPTURE

God Appears by Fire

TO MOSES

Ex. 3 [2]And the angel of the LORD appeared unto him in a flame of fire out of the midst of a bush; and he looked, and, behold, the bush burned with fire, and the bush was not consumed.

TO ISRAELITES

Ex. 13 [21]And the LORD went before them by day in a pillar of a cloud, to lead them the way; and by night in a pillar of fire, to give them light: to go by day and night.

Ex. 19 [18]And mount Sinai was altogether on a smoke, because the LORD descended upon it in fire: and the smoke thereof ascended as the smoke of a furnace, and the whole mount quaked greatly.

TO EZEKIEL

Ezek. 1 [4]And I looked, and behold, a whirlwind came out of the north, a great cloud, and a fire infolding itself, and a brightness was about it, and out of the midst thereof as the colour of amber, out of the midst of the fire.

TO DANIEL

Dan. 7 [9]I beheld till the thrones were cast down, and the Ancient of days did sit, whose garment was white as snow, and the hair of his head like the pure wool: his throne was like the fiery flame, and his wheels as burning fire.

CHRIST TO JOHN

Rev. 1 [14]His head and his hairs were white like wool, as white as snow, and his eyes were as a flame of fire, [15]And his feet like unto fine brass, as if they burned in a furnace: and his voice as the sound of many waters.

HOLY GHOST AT PENTECOST

Acts 2 [3]And there appeared unto them cloven tongues, like as of fire, and it sat upon each of them. [4]And they were all filled with the Holy Ghost, and began to speak with other tongues, as the spirit gave them utterance.

Miracles Connected with Fire

CONSUMES ABRAHAM'S SACRIFICE

Gen. 15 [17]And it came to pass, that, when the sun went down, and it was dark, behold a smoking furnace, and a burning lamp that passed between those pieces.

CONSUMES ELIJAH'S SACRIFICE

1 Kin. 18 [38]Then the fire of the LORD fell, and consumed the burnt sacrifice, and the wood, and the stones, and the dust, and licked up the water that was in the trench.

ELIJAH'S TRANSLATION

2 Kin. 2 [11]And it came to pass, as they

still went on, and talked, that, behold, there appeared a chariot of fire, and horses of fire, and parted them both asunder; and Elijah went up by a whirlwind into heaven.

Fire as Instrument of Judgment

Gen. 19 [24]Then the LORD rained upon Sodom and upon Gomorrah brimstone and fire from the LORD out of heaven.

Ex. 9 [23]And Moses stretched forth his rod toward heaven, and the LORD sent thunder and hail, and the fire ran along upon the ground: and the LORD rained hail upon the land of Egypt.

Lev. 10 [1]And Nadab and Abihu, the sons of Aaron, took either of them his censer, and put fire therein, and put incense thereon, and offered strange fire before the LORD, which he commanded them not.
[2]And there went out fire from the LORD, and devoured them, and they died before the LORD.

Num. 11 [1]And when the people complained, it displeased the LORD: and the LORD heard it: and his anger was kindled; and the fire of the LORD burnt among them, and consumed them that were in the uttermost parts of the camp.

Num. 16 [35]And there came out a fire from the LORD, and consumed the two hundred and fifty men that offered incense.

2 Kin. 1 [10]And Elijah answered and said to the captain of fifty, If I be a man of God, then let fire come down from heaven, and consume thee and thy fifty. And there came down fire from heaven, and consumed him and his fifty.

2 Thess. 1 [7]And to you who are troubled, rest with us, when the Lord Jesus shall be revealed from heaven, with his mighty angels, [8]In flaming fire, taking vengeance on them that know not God, and that obey not the Gospel of our Lord Jesus Christ.

Everlasting Fire

Deut. 32 [22]For a fire is kindled in mine anger, and shall burn unto the lowest hell, and shall consume the earth with her increase, and set on fire the foundations of the mountains.

Isa. 33 [14]The sinners in Zion are afraid; fearfulness hath surprised the hypocrites. Who among us shall dwell with the devouring fire? Who among us shall dwell with everlasting burnings?

Mark 9 [45]And if thy foot offend thee, cut it off: it is better for thee to enter halt into life, than having two feet, to be cast into hell, into the fire that never shall be quenched.

FIRSTBORN

[fûrst′bôrn] In the Old Testament the firstborn male, whether of human beings or animals, was regarded as belonging to the LORD. Firstborn animals were usually sacrificed; firstborn sons were dedicated to the service of the LORD. Since the Levites had been appointed to serve in the tabernacle and temple, the firstborn was exempted from his obligation by the payment of a small ransom to the priest. The firstborn normally possessed the birthright, with all its attendant privileges, including a double share of the inheritance and the father as head of the estate. (*See* BIRTHRIGHT) The word "firstborn" is also used of Israel, indicating her privileged positions among the nations of the world, and of Christ, indicating his preeminence over the creation.

SCRIPTURE

Redemption of Firstborn

Ex. 13 [11]And it shall be when the LORD shall bring thee into the land of the Canaanites, as he sware unto thee and to thy fathers, and shall give it thee, [12]That thou shalt set apart unto the LORD all that openeth the matrix, and every firstling that cometh of a beast which thou hast; the male shall be the LORD's. [13]And every firstling of an ass thou shalt redeem with a lamb; and if thou wilt not redeem it, then thou shalt break his neck: and all the firstborn of man among thy children shalt thou redeem.

[14]And it shall be when thy son asketh thee in time to come, saying, What is this? that thou shalt say unto him, By strength of hand the LORD brought us out from Egypt, from the house of bondage: [15]And it came to pass, when Pharaoh would hardly let us go, that the LORD slew all the firstborn in the land of Egypt, both the firstborn of man, and the firstborn of beast: therefore I sacrifice to the LORD all that openeth the matrix, being males; but all the firstborn of my children I redeem. [16]And it shall be for a token upon thine hand, and for frontlets between thine eyes: for by strength of hand the LORD brought us forth out of Egypt.

Ex. 34 [19]All that openeth the matrix is mine; and every firstling among thy cattle, whether ox or sheep, that is male. [20]But the firstling of an ass thou shalt redeem with a lamb: and if thou redeem him not, then shalt thou break his neck. All the firstborn of thy sons thou shalt redeem. And none shall appear before me empty.

See Deut. 15:19-23

Israel as the Firstborn

Ex. 4 [22]And thou shalt say unto Pharaoh, Thus saith the LORD, Israel is my son, even my firstborn:

Jer. 31 [9]They shall come with weeping, and with supplications will I lead them: I will cause them to walk by the rivers of waters in a straight way, wherein they shall not stumble; for I am a father to Israel, and Ephraim is my firstborn.

Christ as Firstborn

Rom. 8 [29]For whom he did foreknow, he also did predestinate to be conformed to the image of his Son, that he might be the firstborn among many brethren.

Col. 1 [15]Who is the image of the invisible God, the firstborn of every creature: [18]And he is the head of the body, the church: who is the beginning, the firstborn from the dead; that in all things he might have the preeminence.

Heb. 1 [6]And again, when he bringeth in the first-begotten into the world, he saith, And let all the angels of God worship him.

Rev. 1 [5]And from Jesus Christ, who is the faithful witness, and the first-begotten of the dead, and the prince of the kings of the earth. Unto him that loved us, and washed us from our sins in his own blood.

FLATTERY

[flat′ẽr i] False, insincere, or excessive praise, usually given to gratify the recipient's vanity or to ingratiate oneself. The Bible speaks of flattery as a dangerous practice, as it encourages insincerity and may lead to lying.

SCRIPTURE

Job 17 [5]He that speaketh flattery to his friends, even the eyes of his children shall fail.

Job 32 [21]Let me not, I pray you, accept any man's person; neither let me give flattering titles unto man. [22]For I know not to give flattering titles; in so doing my Maker would soon take me away.

Psa. 12 [2]They speak vanity every one with his neighbour: with flattering lips and with a double heart do they speak. [3]The LORD shall cut off all flattering lips, and the tongue that speaketh proud things.

Psa. 36 [2]For he flattereth himself in his own eyes, until his iniquity be found to be hateful.

Psa. 78 [36]Nevertheless they did flatter him with their mouth, and they lied unto him with their tongues.

Prov. 24 [24]He that saith unto the wicked, Thou art righteous; him shall the people curse, nations shall abhor him.

Prov. 26 [28]A lying tongue hateth those that are afflicted by it; and a flattering mouth worketh ruin.

Prov. 28 [23]He that rebuketh a man, afterwards shall find more favour than he that flattereth with the tongue.

Prov. 29 [5]A man that flattereth his neighbour spreadeth a net for his feet.

FLESH

[flesh] This word is used many times in the Bible, with a variety of meanings. Frequently it refers simply to the chief substance of the body of animals and men. As an extension of this, it is sometimes used to designate the whole of the animal creation, whether man or beast, in such expressions as "all flesh."

It is also commonly found in the sense of relationship, as one's own "flesh and blood" that is, one's own relatives, whether familial, tribal, or national. Paul often designates man's carnal nature as flesh, contrasting it with "spirit." This does not imply that flesh is inherently sinful; rather, it suggests the frailty and ignorance which characterizes human nature, as contrasted with the higher possibilities of the spiritual nature, especially as the latter is informed by God's Holy Spirit. In itself, flesh is morally neutral but it is subject to deterioration and dissolution and is inevitably associated with death; it is therefore naturally contrasted with the spirit, which has the capacity for eternal life and we are urged to subdue the flesh in order to preserve the spirit. Despite its weakness, flesh is the ideal mode for human existence and, as such, was chosen to be the vessel of God's supreme manifestation of himself in Jesus Christ.

See INCARNATION, SPIRIT, SOUL

SCRIPTURE

General

Gen. 2 [21]And the LORD God caused a deep sleep to fall upon Adam, and he slept; and he took one of his ribs, and closed up the flesh instead thereof.

Gen. 37 [27]Come and let us sell him to the Ishmaelites, and let not our hand be upon him; for he is our brother and our flesh: and his brethren were content.

Num. 16 [22]And they fell upon their faces, and said, O God, the God of the spirits of all flesh, shall one man sin, and wilt thou be wroth with all the congregation?

Psa. 65 [2]O thou that hearest prayer, unto thee shall all flesh come.

Isa. 31 [3]Now the Egyptians are men and not God; and their horses flesh, and not spirit.

Flesh Contrasted with Spirit

Rom. 7 [5]For when we were in the flesh, the motions of sins which were by the law did work in our members, to bring forth fruit unto death.

Rom. 8 [1]There is therefore now no condemnation to them which are in Christ Jesus, who walk not after the flesh, but after the spirit.

Gal. 3 [3]Are ye so foolish? having begun in the Spirit, are ye now made perfect by the flesh?

Gal. 5 [17]For the flesh lusteth against the Spirit, and the spirit against the flesh: and these are contrary the one to the other: so that ye cannot do the things that ye would.

Gal. 6 [8]For he that soweth to his flesh, shall of the flesh reap corruption: but he that soweth to the spirit, shall of the spirit reap life everlasting.

Flesh to Be Subdued

1 Cor. 5 [5]To deliver such a one unto

Satan for the destruction of the flesh, that the spirit may be saved in the day of the Lord Jesus.

2 Cor. 7 [1]Having therefore these promises (dearly beloved) let us cleanse ourselves from all filthiness of the flesh and spirit, perfecting holiness in the fear of God.

Gal. 5 [16]This I say then, Walk in the spirit, and ye shall not fulfil the lust of the flesh.

Col. 2 [11]In whom also ye are circumcised with the circumcision made without hands, in putting off the body of the sins of the flesh, by the circumcision of Christ.

1 Pet. 4 [1]Forasmuch then as Christ hath suffered for us in the flesh, arm yourselves likewise with the same mind: for he that hath suffered in the flesh, hath ceased from sin: [2]That he no longer should live the rest of his time in the flesh, to the lusts of men, but to the will of God.

1 John 2 [16]For all that is in the world, the lust of the flesh, the lust of the eyes, and the pride of life, is not of the Father, but is of the world.

God Manifest in Flesh

John 1 [14]And the Word was made flesh, and dwelt among us (and we beheld his glory, the glory as of the only begotten of the Father,) full of grace and truth.

2 Cor. 5 [16]Wherefore henceforth know we no man after the flesh: yea, though we have known Christ after the flesh, yet now henceforth know we him no more.

1 Tim. 3 [16]And without controversy, great is the mystery of godliness: God was manifest in the flesh, justified in the Spirit, seen of angels, preached unto the Gentiles, believed on in the world, received up into glory.

1 Pet. 3 [18]For Christ also hath once suffered for sins, the just for the unjust, that he might bring us to God, being put to death in the flesh, but quickened by the Spirit.

1 John 4 [2]Hereby know ye the Spirit of God: Every spirit that confesseth that Jesus Christ is come in the flesh is of God.

FLOOD

[flud] The Flood is the term commonly used to refer to the great cataclysm described in *Gen.* 7 and 8, in which all earthly animal life except that on the ark of Noah is said to have been destroyed. Despite claims to the contrary in popular handbooks and articles on the subject, archaeology has not provided conclusive proof of the veracity of the *Genesis* narrative; consequently, it is pointless to speculate as to its exact nature and scope. Archaeologists and anthropologists have, however, performed a valuable service in bringing to light numerous ancient traditions of such a deluge in which a select few were preserved from destruction, usually in some kind of ship. Most striking in its similarity to the Biblical account is the "Gilgamesh epic" of ancient Babylon. Other peoples which possess such a tradition include Chinese, Indian, Egyptian, Greek, British Druid, and the Indians of North and South America. Thus, despite the absence of archaeological proof, it is difficult to discount the idea that these stem from a common tradition of a great flood far back in the history of mankind. The *Genesis* account makes it clear that this deluge was a means of God's moral judgment on a wicked generation, drawing more sharply than any of the above-mentioned legends the relation between the Flood and the moral order of our world.

See Ark, Noah, Ham, Shem, Japheth

SCRIPTURE

Gen. 7 [11]In the six hundredth year of Noah's life, in the second month, the seventeenth day of the month, the same day were all the fountains of the great deep broken up, and the windows of heaven were opened. [12]And the rain was upon the earth forty days and forty nights. [13]In the selfsame day entered Noah, and Shem,

and Ham, and Japheth, the sons of Noah,
and Noah's wife, and the three wives of
his sons with them, into the ark; 14They,
and every beast after his kind, and all the
cattle after their kind, and every creeping
thing that creepeth upon the earth after
his kind, and every fowl after his kind, every bird of every sort. 15And they went in
unto Noah into the ark, two and two of all
flesh, wherein is the breath of life. 16And
they that went in, went in male and female
of all flesh, as God had commanded him:
and the LORD shut him in. 17And the flood
was forty days upon the earth; and the
waters increased, and bare up the ark, and
it was lifted up above the earth. 18And the
waters prevailed, and were increased
greatly upon the earth; and the ark went
upon the face of the waters. 19And the
waters prevailed exceedingly upon the
earth; and all the high hills, that were
under the whole heaven, were covered.
20Fifteen cubits upward did the waters
prevail; and the mountains were covered.
21And all flesh died that moved upon the
earth, both of fowl, and of cattle, and of
beast, and of every creeping thing that
creepeth upon the earth, and every man:
22All in whose nostrils was the breath of
life, of all that was in the dry land, died.
23And every living substance was destroyed which was upon the face of the
ground, both man, and cattle, and the
creeping things, and the fowl of the
heaven; and they were destroyed from
the earth: and Noah only remained alive,
and they that were with him in the ark.
24And the waters prevailed upon the earth
a hundred and fifty days.

See Gen. 6-8

FOOLS

[fo͞ol] The Bible ordinarily used the word "fool" to describe a person lacking in religious or ethical qualities rather than intellectual ones; in other words, the Biblical fool is not insane or a person of weak mind, but an individual whose life is guided by principles which may be regarded as the opposite of wisdom, a person who through perverseness of will does and says foolish things. To the Hebrew mind, it was worse to be called a fool than to be called stupid or mad, since the fool was usually regarded as disobedient to the law of God. This enables us better to understand Jesus' statement in *Matt. 5:22*, prohibiting his disciples to address a man as a fool.

SCRIPTURE

Fools Described

Psa. 14 1The fool hath said in his heart,
There is no God. They are corrupt, they
have done abominable works, there is
none that doeth good.

Prov. 10 23It is as sport to a fool to do
mischief: but a man of understanding hath
wisdom.

Prov. 12 23A prudent man concealeth
knowledge: but the heart of fools proclaimeth foolishness.

Prov. 13 19The desire accomplished is
sweet to the soul: but it is abomination to
fools to depart from evil.

Prov. 14 8The wisdom of the prudent
is to understand his way: but the folly of
fools is deceit. 9Fools make a mock at sin:
but among the righteous there is favour.
16A wise man feareth, and departeth from
evil: but the fool rageth, and is confident.
33Wisdom resteth in the heart of him that
hath understanding: but that which is in
the midst of fools is made known.

Prov. 15 2The tongue of the wise useth
knowledge aright: but the mouth of fools
poureth out foolishness. 7The lips of the
wise disperse knowledge: but the heart of
the foolish doeth not so. 14The heart of
him that hath understanding seeketh
knowledge: but the mouth of fools feedeth on foolishness.

Prov. 16 [22]Understanding is a well-spring of life unto him that hath it: but the instruction of fools is folly.

Prov. 17 [16]Wherefore is there a price in the hand of a fool to get wisdom, seeing he hath no heart to it? [24]Wisdom is before him that hath understanding; but the eyes of a fool are in the ends of the earth.

Eccl. 4 [5]The fool foldeth his hands together, and eateth his own flesh.

Eccl. 9 [17]The words of wise men are heard in quiet more than the cry of him that ruleth among fools.

Eccl. 10 [3]Yea also, when he that is a fool walketh by the way, his wisdom faileth him, and he saith to every one that he is a fool.

Treatment and Punishment

Prov. 23 [9]Speak not in the ears of a fool: for he will despise the wisdom of thy words.

Prov. 26 [3]A whip for the horse, a bridle for the ass, and a rod for the fool's back. [4]Answer not a fool according to his folly, lest thou also be like unto him. [5]Answer a fool according to his folly, lest he be wise in his own conceit.

Prov. 27 [22]Though thou shouldest bray a fool in a mortar among wheat with a pestle, yet will not his foolishness depart from him.

Prov. 1 [32]For the turning away of the simple shall slay them, and the prosperity of fools shall destroy them.

Prov. 10 [8]The wise in heart will receive commandments: but a prating fool shall fall.

Prov. 11 [29]He that troubleth his own house shall inherit the wind: and the fool shall be servant to the wise of heart.

Prov. 13 [20]He that walketh with wise men shall be wise: but a companion of fools shall be destroyed.

Eccl. 10 [12]The words of a wise man's mouth are gracious; but the lips of a fool will swallow up himself.

FOOTWASHING

[foot′wash ing] An act of hospitality extended to guests during Biblical times in Palestine. The combination of dusty roads and open sandals made this a refreshing and highly desirable service. It was usually performed by a servant of the host, either upon the arrival of guests at the home or while they sat at table. At the Last Supper Jesus washed his disciples' feet as a sign of the humble service which his followers were to render to one another. The practice of footwashing is still observed in some churches, especially in connection with the celebration of Easter.

SCRIPTURE

Mark 1 [7]And preached, saying, There cometh one mightier than I after me, the latchet of whose shoes I am not worthy to stoop down and unloose.

Luke 7 [44]And he turned to the woman, and said unto Simon, Seest thou this woman? I entered into thine house, thou gavest me no water for my feet: but she hath washed my feet with tears, and wiped them with the hairs of her head.

John 13 [4]He riseth from supper, and laid aside his garments; and took a towel, and girded himself. [5]After that he poureth water into a basin, and began to wash the disciples' feet, and to wipe them with the towel wherewith he was girded. [8]Peter saith unto him, Thou shalt never wash my feet. Jesus answered him, If I wash thee not, thou hast no part with me. [9]Simon Peter saith unto him, Lord, not my feet only, but also my hands and my head. [12]So after he had washed their feet, and had taken his garments, and was set down again, he said unto them, Know ye what I have done to you? [13]Ye call me Master and Lord: and ye say well; for so I am.

[14]If I then, your Lord and Master, have washed your feet; ye also ought to wash one another's feet. [15]For I have given you an example, that ye should do as I have done to you.

1 Tim. 5 [9]Let not a widow be taken into the number under threescore years old, having been the wife of one man, [10]Well reported of for good works; if she have brought up children, if she have lodged strangers, if she have washed the saints' feet, if she have relieved the afflicted, if she have diligently followed every good work.

FORBEARANCE

[for bâr′ans] Patience with another under trying circumstances. As used in the New Testament, it is virtually synonymous with "longsuffering", referring primarily to God's delay in bringing punishment for our sins, thereby enabling us to repent. As God is forbearing, Christians are required to be forbearing, exhibiting a readiness to forgive and an unwillingness to insist upon one's rights, especially when to do so might cause another to suffer.

SCRIPTURE

Forbearance Commended

Eph. 4 [1]I therefore the prisoner of the Lord, beseech you that ye walk worthy of the vocation wherewith ye are called, [2]With all lowliness and meekness, with longsuffering, forbearing one another in love.

Eph. 6 [9]And ye masters, do the same things unto them, forbearing threatening: knowing that your master also is in heaven, neither is there respect of persons with him.

Col. 3 [12]Put on therefore (as the elect of God, holy and beloved) bowels of mercies, kindness, humbleness of mind, meekness, longsuffering, [13]Forbearing one another, and forgiving one another, if any man have a quarrel against any: even as Christ forgave you, so also do ye.

Forbearance of God

Rom. 2 [4]Or despisest thou the riches of his goodness, and forbearance, and longsuffering, not knowing that the goodness of God leadeth thee to repentance?

Rom. 3 [24]Being justified freely by his grace, through the redemption that is in Jesus Christ: [25]Whom God hath set forth to be a propitiation, through faith in his blood, to declare his righteousness for the remission of sins that are past, through the forbearance of God.

FOREKNOWLEDGE

[fōr nol′ej] This term is used in the Bible in two senses: (1) to refer to the foresight of God, that is, to his knowledge of human events before they happen; and (2) as a near synonym for "foreordination" or "predestination."

SCRIPTURE

Isa. 42 [9]Behold, the former things are come to pass, and new things do I declare: before they spring forth I tell you of them.

Isa. 46 [9]Remember the former things of old: for I am God, and there is none else; I am God, and there is none like me, [10]Declaring the end from the beginning, and from ancient times the things that are not yet done, saying, My counsel shall stand, and I will do all my pleasure:

Matt. 6 [8]Be not ye therefore like unto them: for your Father knoweth what things ye have need of, before ye ask him.

Acts 2 [23]Him, being delivered by the determinate counsel and foreknowledge of God, ye have taken, and by wicked hands have crucified and slain:

Acts 15 [18]Known unto God are all his works from the beginning of the world.

Rom. 8 [29]For whom he did foreknow, he also did predestinate to be conformed to the image of his Son, that he might be the firstborn among many brethren.

Rom. 11 [2]God hath not cast away his people which he foreknew.

FORGIVENESS

[for giv′nes] The various Hebrew words which are translated "forgiveness" in the Old Testament all carry with them the sense of removal of sin and restoration of the relationship which was damaged by sin. In all cases, this forgiveness is conditional upon repentance, a changing of the mind and will.

In the New Testament, a proper relationship with God is also contingent upon forgiveness of sins. Jesus instructed his disciples to practice forgiveness without limitation—"until seventy times seven"—for without this willingness to forgive, there could be no forgiveness of their own sins.

SCRIPTURE

Mutual Forgiveness Commanded

Matt. 6 [14]For, if ye forgive men their trespasses, your heavenly Father will also forgive you. [15]But, if ye forgive not men their trespasses, neither will your Father forgive your trespasses.

Matt. 18 [21]Then came Peter to him, and said, Lord, how oft shall my brother sin against me, and I forgive him? till seven times? [22]Jesus saith unto him, I say not unto thee, Until seven times: but, Until seventy times seven.

[35]So likewise shall my heavenly Father do also unto you, if ye from your hearts forgive not every one his brother their trespasses.

Luke 11 [4]And forgive us our sins: for we also forgive every one that is indebted to us. And lead us not into temptation, but deliver us from evil.

2 Cor. 2 [7]So that contrariwise, ye ought rather to forgive him, and comfort him, lest perhaps such a one should be swallowed up with overmuch sorrow.

Eph. 4 [32]And be ye kind one to another, tender-hearted, forgiving one another, even as God for Christ's sake hath forgiven you.

Col. 3 [13]Forbearing one another, and forgiving one another, if any man have a quarrel against any: even as Christ forgave you, so also do ye.

Forgiveness Prayed for

Ex. 32 [31]And Moses returned unto the LORD, and said, Oh, this people have sinned a great sin, and have made them gods of gold. [32]Yet now, if thou wilt forgive their sin: and if not, blot me, I pray thee, out of thy book which thou hast written.

1 Kin. 8 [30]And hearken thou to the supplication of thy servant, and of thy people Israel, when they shall pray toward this place: and hear thou in heaven thy dwelling place: and when thou hearest, forgive.

Psa. 25 [18]Look upon mine affliction and my pain; and forgive all my sins.

Psa. 32 [5]I acknowledged my sin unto thee, and mine iniquity have I not hid. I said, I will confess my transgressions unto the LORD; and thou forgavest the iniquity of my sin. Selah.

Psa. 51 [1]Have mercy upon me, O God, according to thy loving-kindness: according unto the multitude of thy tender mercies blot out my transgressions. [2]Wash me thoroughly from mine iniquity, and cleanse me from my sin. [3]For I acknowledge my transgressions: and my sin is ever before me.

Psa. 79 [9]Help us, O God of our salvation, for the glory of thy name: and deliver us, and purge away our sins, for thy name's sake.

Psa. 130 [3]If thou, LORD, shouldest mark iniquities, O LORD, who shall stand? [4]But there is forgiveness with thee, that thou mayest be feared.

Matt. 6 [12]And forgive us our debts, as we forgive our debtors.

Forgiveness Promised

2 Chr. 7 [14]If my people, which are called by my name, shall humble themselves, and pray, and seek my face, and turn from their wicked ways; then will I hear from heaven, and will forgive their sin, and will heal their land.

Isa. 55 [7]Let the wicked forsake his way, and the unrighteous man his thoughts: and let him return unto the LORD, and he will have mercy upon him; and to our God, for he will abundantly pardon.

Mic. 7 [18]Who is a God like unto thee, that pardoneth iniquity, and passeth by the transgression of the remnant of his heritage? he retaineth not his anger for ever, because he delighteth in mercy.

Luke 24 [47]And that repentance and remission of sins should be preached in his Name, among all nations, beginning at Jerusalem.

Acts 5 [31]Him hath God exalted with his right hand to be a Prince and a Saviour, for to give repentance to Israel, and forgiveness of sins.

Acts 26 [18]To open their eyes, and to turn them from darkness to light, and from the power of Satan unto God, that they may receive forgiveness of sins, and inheritance among them which are sanctified by faith that is in me.

Col. 1 [14]In whom we have redemption through his blood, even the forgiveness of sins.

Jas. 5 [15]And the prayer of Faith shall save the sick, and the Lord shall raise him up: and if he have committed sins, they shall be forgiven him.

1 John 1 [9]If we confess our sins, he is faithful and just to forgive us our sins, and to cleanse us from all unrighteousness.

FORNICATION

[for ni kā'shun] Sexual intercourse outside of marriage. It may also refer to adultery, as in *Matt. 5:22* and *19:9*, or to an incestuous relationship such as that described in *1 Cor. 5*. We are told that fornicators shall not inherit the kingdom of God.

See ADULTERY

SCRIPTURE

Matt. 5 [32]But I say unto you, That whosoever shall put away his wife, saving for the cause of fornication, causeth her to commit adultery: and whosoever shall marry her that is divorced committeth adultery.

Acts 15 [20]But that we write unto them, that they abstain from pollutions of idols, and from fornication, and from things strangled, and from blood.

1 Cor. 5 [1]It is reported commonly that there is fornication among you, and such fornication as is not so much as named among the Gentiles, that one should have his father's wife. [9]I wrote unto you in an epistle not to company with fornicators:

1 Cor. 6 [9]Know ye not that the unrighteous shall not inherit the kingdom of God? Be not deceived: neither fornicators, nor idolaters, nor adulterers, nor effeminate, nor abusers of themselves with mankind, [10]Nor thieves, nor covetous, nor drunkards, nor revilers, nor extortioners, shall inherit the kingdom of God. [13]Meats for the belly, and the belly for meats: but God shall destroy both it and them. Now the body is not for fornication, but for the Lord; and the Lord for the body. [18]Flee fornication. Every sin that a man doeth is without the body; but he that committeth fornication sinneth against his own body.

1 Cor. 7 [1]Now concerning the things whereof ye wrote unto me: It is good for a man not to touch a woman. [2]Nevertheless, to avoid fornication, let every man have his own wife, and let every woman have her own husband.

See Matt. 19:9

FRANKINCENSE

[frank′in sens] A fragrant gum resin obtained from trees of the genus *Boswellia*, which grow on the limestone rocks of south Arabia and Somaliland. It has a bitter taste and is used in the preparation of incense. In the Bible, it is associated with myrrh and was one of the gifts brought by the Magi to the infant Jesus.

See MYRRH

SCRIPTURE

Ex. 30 [34]And the LORD said unto Moses, Take unto thee sweet spices, stacte, and onycha, and galbanum; these sweet spices with pure frankincense: of each shall there be a like weight:

Lev. 24 [7]And thou shalt put pure frankincense upon each row, that it may be on the bread for a memorial, even an offering made by fire unto the LORD.

Song 3 [6]Who is this that cometh out of the wilderness like pillars of smoke, perfumed with myrrh and frankincense, with all powders of the merchant?

Matt. 2 [11]And when they were come into the house, they saw the young child with Mary his mother, and fell down, and worshipped him: and when they had opened their treasures, they presented unto him gifts; gold, and frankincense, and myrrh.

FRIEND, FRIENDSHIP

[frend, frend′ship] Friends and friendship are often mentioned in the Bible, which teaches the beauty and value of good and true friends. The friendship of David and Jonathan is among the best known in all literature. The influence which friends have over one another is also noted in the warnings against friendship with evil persons.

See FELLOWSHIP

SCRIPTURE

Value of Friends

Prov. 18 [24]A man that hath friends must shew himself friendly: and there is a friend that sticketh closer than a brother.

Prov. 27 [19]As in water face answereth to face, so the heart of man to man.

Amos 3 [3]Can two walk together, except they be agreed?

Prov. 17 [17]A friend loveth at all times, and a brother is born for adversity.

Prov. 27 [6]Faithful are the wounds of a friend; but the kisses of an enemy are deceitful. [10]Thine own friend, and thy father's friend, forsake not; neither go into thy brother's house in the day of thy calamity: for better is a neighbour that is near than a brother far off.

Eccl. 4 [9]Two are better than one; because they have a good reward for their labour. [10]For if they fall, the one will lift up his fellow: but woe to him that is alone when he falleth; for he hath not another to help him up. [11]Again, if two lie together, then they have heat: but how can one be warm alone? [12]And if one prevail against him, two shall withstand him; and a threefold cord is not quickly broken.

Evil Friends

Prov. 21 [10]The soul of the wicked desireth evil: his neighbour findeth no favour in his eyes.

Prov. 22 [24]Make no friendship with an angry man; and with a furious man thou shalt not go; [25]Lest thou learn his ways, and get a snare to thy soul.

Prov. 25 [19]Confidence in an unfaithful man in time of trouble is like a broken tooth, and a foot out of joint.

Friendship of David and Jonathan

1 Sam. 18 [1]And it came to pass, when he had made an end of speaking unto Saul, that the soul of Jonathan was knit with the soul of David, and Jonathan loved him as his own soul. [2]And Saul took him that day, and would let him go no more home to his father's house. [3]Then Jonathan and David made a covenant, because he loved him as his own soul.

1 Sam. 20 [4]Then said Jonathan unto David, Whatsoever thy soul desireth, I will even do it for thee.

2 Sam. 1 [26]I am distressed for thee, my brother Jonathan: very pleasant hast thou been unto me: thy love to me was wonderful, passing the love of women.

GABRIEL

[gā′bri el] The name by which an angel prominent in several Biblical narratives is called. He is mentioned as assisting Daniel in the interpretation of visions and in the making of predictions. He is better known, however, as the agent of God in announcing the birth of Jesus to Mary and the birth of John the Baptist to Zacharias. Jewish and Christian writers have assigned a high rank to Gabriel, often referring to him as archangel, but the Scripture makes no such designation.

SCRIPTURE

Dan. 8 [16]And I heard a man's voice between the banks of Ulai, which called, and said, Gabriel, make this man to understand the vision.

Dan. 9 [21]Yea, while I was speaking in prayer, even the man Gabriel, whom I had seen in the vision at the beginning, being caused to fly swiftly, touched me about the time of the evening oblation.

Luke 1 [19]And the angel answering said unto him, I am Gabriel, that stand in the presence of God; and am sent to speak unto thee, and to show thee these glad tidings. [26]And in the sixth month the angel Gabriel was sent from God unto a city of Galilee, named Nazareth,

GADARA

[gad′a ra] A strong city situated east of the Sea of Galilee. Gadara itself is not mentioned in the Bible, but it is evidently identical with the "Country of the Gadarenes" (*Matt. 8:28; Mark 5:1; Luke 8:26, 37*). The King James Version of the Bible incorrectly translates all three of these passages. In *Matt. 8:28*, it reads "country of the Gergesenes", which simply cannot be supported by the Greek text. In the passages from *Mark* and *Luke*, the Greek text reads "country of the Gerasenes" but is translated "country of the Gadarenes." It is probable that Gerasa was a nearby town, subordinate to Gadara, which could properly be described as belonging either to the Gadarenes or the Gerasenes. Most modern speech versions of the Bible correctly translate these passages.

The region designated by these two terms is known to the Bible students as the scene of Jesus' healing of the demoniac "whose name was Legion." The demons which were cast out of him went into a herd of swine, who raced over the edge of a steep incline and plunged into the sea. The news of this occurrence so frightened the natives of the area that they pleaded with Jesus to leave their country.

See DEMONS

REFERENCE: *Matt. 8:28-34; Mark 5:1-20; Luke 8:26-39.*

GAIUS

[gā′yus] This name, one of the most common in the Greek-speaking world, was worn by several characters in the New Testament:

1. Gaius of Macedonia, a companion of Paul who was siezed by Demetrius and the silversmiths at the riot in Ephesus (*Acts 19:29*).

2. Gaius of Derbe, a companion of Paul on the third missionary journey (*Acts 20:4*).

3. Gaius, whom Paul baptized at Corinth (*1 Cor. 1:14*).

4. Gaius, Paul's host at the time he wrote the epistle to the *Rom. 16:23.* It is quite possible that this is the same individual as (3) above.

5. "Beloved" Gaius, to whom 3 John is addressed (*3 John 1:1, 2, 5, 11*).

GALATIA, GALATIANS

[ga lā'shi a, ga lā'shi anz] In the heart of the peninsula which is now Asia Minor swelt Celtic people who, on coming from Gaul, preserved the name, "Galatians." When the Roman territory spread in the early years of the second century BC, these heathens retained the status of a dependent kingdom. About a century and a half later the land passed into various hands, and ultimately into the Roman provincial system. At the time of Paul, the province of Galatia included the old kingdom of Galatia to the north, and also parts of Lycaonia, Pisidia, and Phrygia which adjoined it to the south. The term "Galatia" may be either provincial or ethnic in meaning; that is, it may refer either to old Galatia proper (North Galatia) or to the entire Roman province, which would include Southern Galatia, namely, the cities of Lystra, Derbe, Iconium, and Antioch. It is probable that the epistle to the *Galatians* was addressed to churches in the southern area.

GALILEE

[gal'i lē] A word meaning "circuit" or "district", referring to the northern area of Palestine. Galilean territory was first won for Israel by the northern conquests under Joshua. (*See* CONQUEST) Later, King Solomon gave Hiram of Tyre twenty towns situated in this region (*1 Kin. 9:11*).

Galilee apparently always contained a large non-Jewish element and is referred to by Isaiah as "Galilee of the Gentiles" (*Isa. 9:1*). In the time of Jesus, Palestine west of the Jordan was divided into three provinces, Judea, Samaria, and Galilee. Galilee was the scene of the greater part of Christ's private life and public acts. His early years were spent at Nazareth; when he entered on his public work, he made Capernaum his home (*Matt. 4:13; 9:1*). The first three Gospels are chiefly concerned with Christ's ministrations in this province, while the Gospel of John dwells more upon those in Judaea. The apostles were all either Galileans by birth or residence (*Acts 1:11*).

See SEA OF GALILEE, CAPERNAUM

GALLIO

[gal'i ō] Proconsul of Achaia. While in Corinth on his second missionary journey, Paul was brought before Gallio and charged with persuading men "to worship God contrary to the law." The proconsul declared that he had no interest in the quibblings of the Jews over points of their law and had them driven from the tribunal. In anger, they siezed Sosthenes, the ruler of the synagogue, and beat him in front of the tribunal, but Gallio paid no attention, displaying complete indifference to matters outside the realm of Roman law or common morality. Gallio's real importance for New Testament study rests on an inscription which has been found at Delphi and which serves as one of the few possibilities of dating Paul's work. The inscription states that Gallio became proconsul in Corinth in either AD 51 or 52; this would date Paul's coming to Corinth in about AD 50.

See SOSTHENES

SCRIPTURE

Acts 18 [12]And when Gallio was the deputy of Achaia, the Jews made insurrection with one accord against Paul, and brought him to the judgment seat, [13]Saying, This fellow persuadeth men to worship God contrary to the law. [14]And when Paul was now about to open his mouth, Gallio said unto the Jews, If it were a matter of wrong or wicked lewdness, O ye Jews, reason would that I should bear with you: [15]But if it be a question of words and names, and of your law, look ye to it; for I will be no judge of such matters; [16]And he drave them from the judgment seat. [17]Then all the Greeks took Sosthenes, the chief ruler of the synagogue, and beat him before the judgment seat. And Gallio cared for none of these things.

GAMALIEL

[ga mā'li el] A member of the Sanhedrin who advised the use of reason and moderation in the treatment of the apostles, whom the Jews sought to kill. A pharisee, a "doctor of the law" and a man of great reputation among the Jews, Gamaliel reminded the enraged mob of recent uprisings led by men named Theudas and Judas and noted that these had quickly disappeared. If the disturbance led by these men were of this nature, it would suffer the same fate. On the other hand, he assented, "if it be of God, ye cannot overthrow it; lest haply ye be found even to fight against God." Out of respect for the great wisdom of Gamaliel, the crowd took his advice, resting content to beat the apostles and charge them not to speak further of Jesus. When Paul delivered his speech from the steps of the barracks of the Roman tribunal in Jerusalem, he referred to Gamaliel as the teacher who had instructed him in the Law.

SCRIPTURE

Acts 5 33When they heard that, they were cut to the heart, and took counsel to slay them. 34Then stood there up one in the council, a Pharisee, named Gamaliel, a doctor of the law, had in reputation among all the people, and commanded to put the apostles forth a little space; 35And said unto them, Ye men of Israel, take heed to yourselves what ye intend to do as touching these men. 36For before these days rose up Theudas, boasting himself to be somebody; to whom a number of men, about four hundred, joined themselves: who was slain; and all, as many as obeyed him, were scattered, and brought to nought. 37After this man rose up Judas of Galilee in the days of the taxing, and drew away much people after him: he also perished; and all, even as many as obeyed him, were dispersed. 38And now I say unto you, Refrain from these men, and let them alone: for if this counsel or this work be of men, it will come to nought: 39But if it be of God, ye cannot overthrow it; lest haply ye be found even to fight against God. 40And to him they agreed: and when they had called the apostles, and beaten them, they commanded that they should not speak in the name of Jesus, and let them go.

Acts 22 3I am verily a man which am a Jew, born in Tarsus, a city in Cilicia, yet brought up in this city at the feet of Gamaliel, and taught according to the perfect manner of the law of the fathers, and was zealous toward God, as ye all are this day.

GATES

[gāts] In the ancient Near East, many of the cities were walled and had large gates at the entrances. Ordinarily these gates were made of wood strengthened with metal plating (*Psa. 107:16, Isa. 45:2*), although some were of solid metal. When closed, the gates were fastened with a huge bar of wood or metal. Since everyone entering or leaving the city had to pass through the gates, they were a common place of meeting and transacting business. The elders sat at the gates, counselling and acting as local magistrates. Because of the crowds there, it was to the gates that prophets and teachers commonly went with their messages. "Gates" is sometimes used in a figurative sense to denote the city itself.

SCRIPTURE

General

Deut. 16 18Judges and officers shalt thou make thee in all thy gates, which the Lord thy God giveth thee, throughout thy tribes: and they shall judge the people with just judgment.

2 Sam. 15 2And Absalom rose up early, and stood beside the way of the gate: and it was so, that when any man that had a controversy came to the king for judgment, then Absalom called unto him, and said, Of what city art thou? And he said, Thy servant is of one of the tribes of Israel.

2 Sam. 19 [8]Then the king arose, and sat in the gate. And they told unto all the people, saying, Behold, the king doth sit in the gate. And all the people came before the king: for Israel had fled every man to his tent.

1 Kin. 22 [10]And the king of Israel and Jehoshaphat and king of Judah sat each on his throne, having put on their robes, in a void place in the entrance of the gate of Samaria; and all the prophets prophesied before them.

2 Kin. 7 [1]Then Elisha said, Hear ye the word of the LORD; Thus saith the LORD, Tomorrow about this time shall a measure of fine flour be sold for a shekel, and two measures of barley for a shekel, in the gate of Samaria.

Neh. 2 [3]And said unto the king, Let the king live for ever: why should not my countenance be sad, when the city, the place of my fathers' sepulchres, lieth waste, and the gates thereof are consumed with fire?

Psa. 69 [12]They that sit in the gate speak against me; and I was the song of the drunkards.

Isa. 45 [2]I will go before thee, and make the crooked places straight: I will break in pieces the gates of brass, and cut in sunder the bars of iron:

Jer. 17 [19]Thus said the LORD unto me; Go and stand in the gate of the children of the people, whereby the kings of Judah come in, and by the which they go out, and in all the gates of Jerusalem;

Nah. 3 [13]Behold, thy people in the midst of thee are women: the gates of thy land shall be set wide open unto thine enemies: the fire shall devour thy bars.

Figurative

Isa. 3 [26]And her gates shall lament and mourn; and she being desolate shall sit upon the ground.

Isa. 14 [31]Howl, O gate; cry, O city; thou, whole Palestina, art dissolved: for there shall come from the north a smoke, and none shall be alone in his appointed times.

Jer. 14 [2]Judah mourneth, and the gates thereof languish; they are black unto the ground; and the cry of Jerusalem is gone up.

Matt. 16 [18]And I say also unto thee, That thou art Peter, and upon this rock I will build my church; and the gates of hell shall not prevail against it.

GATH

[gath] One of the five chief cities of the Philistines (*Josh. 13:3, 1 Sam. 6:17*). It was not taken by Joshua in the first wave of Israelite conquest; in fact, it seems not to have fallen until the time of David (*1 Chr. 18:1*). Gath figures in several well-known Biblical incidents. It was the home of the giant Goliath, whom David slew with the slingshot (*1 Sam. 17:4*). When the Philistines captured the ark of the covenant, the Ashdodites, having been stricken with a plague, conveyed it to Gath, whose people were also subsequently stricken (*1 Sam. 5:8-9*). After several destructions and rebuildings, the city finally disappeared from history and it has been impossible to determine exactly where it stood.

GAZA

[gā'za] Also called Azzah, this is one of the five chief cities of the Philistines, and probably the oldest. It is situated about forty miles south of Joppa and is the last town in the southwest of Palestine, on the frontier toward Egypt. In the account of the conquest of Joshua, the territory of Gaza is mentioned as one which the Israelites were not able to subjugate (*Josh. 10:41; 11:22; 13:3*). It was the gates of this city which Samson is said to have deposited on a nearby hill-top when the inhabitants tried to trap him with the city walls (*Judg. 16:1-3*). The occasion of his death, at which time he pulled down the temple of Dagon, also took place at Gaza (*Judg. 16:21-*

30). Gaza is mentioned only once in the New Testament, in the account of the conversion of the Ethiopian eunuch.

GEDALIAH

[ged a lī'a] The individual appointed by Nebuchadnezzar to govern the remnant left in Judah after the fall of Jerusalem and the subsequent deportation of captives to Babylon. With his headquarters at Mizpah, Gedaliah's able rule drew to him a considerable body of refugees, including the prophet Jeremiah; he assured these individuals of peace and security if they were willing to accede to the moderate requirements of the Babylonian rule. Baalis king of the Ammonites viewed Gedaliah's stable government as a threat to his plans and arranged with Ishmael, a Jewish soldier, to have him assassinated. News of the plot reached Gedaliah through Johanan, a loyal Jewish soldier, but he refused to believe such a thing of Ishmael. Nevertheless, in the seventh month of that year, Ishmael and ten companions successfully executed their plot, slaying Gedaliah and his staff, and escaping to the Ammonites. Johanan and the other Jewish soldiers feared they would be punished by the Babylonians for Gedaliah's death and forced the remaining inhabitants of the land to flee with them to Egypt. Among those making the enforced emigration were Baruch and Jeremiah, who had fervently implored the people to remain in the land.

See JEREMIAH

SCRIPTURE

Jer. 40 11 Likewise when all the Jews that were in Moab, and among the Ammonites, and in Edom, and that were in all the countries, heard that the king of Babylon had left a remnant of Judah, and that he had set over them Gedaliah the son of Ahikam the son of Shaphan; 12 Even all the Jews returned out of all places whither they were driven, and came to the land of Judah, to Gedaliah, unto Mizpah, and gathered wine and summer fruits very much.

13 Moreover Johanan the son of Kareah, and all the captains of the forces that were in the fields, came to Gedaliah to Mizpah, 14 And said unto him, Dost thou certainly know that Baalis the king of the Ammonites hath sent Ishmael the son of Nethaniah to slay thee? But Gedaliah the son of Ahikam believed them not. 15 Then Johanan the son of Kareah spake to Gedaliah in Mizpah secretly, saying, Let me go, I pray thee, and I will slay Ishmael the son of Nethaniah, and no man shall know it: wherefore should he slay thee, that all the Jews which are gathered unto thee should be scattered, and the remnant in Judah perish? 16 But Gedaliah the son of Ahikam said unto Johanan the son of Kareah, Thou shalt not do this thing: for thou speakest falsely of Ishmael.

Jer. 41 1 Now it came to pass in the seventh month, that Ishmael the son of Nethaniah the son of Elishama, of the seed royal, and the princes of the king, even ten men with him, came unto Gedaliah the son of Ahikam to Mizpah; and there they did eat bread together in Mizpah. 2 Then rose Ishmael the son of Nethaniah, and the ten men that were with him, and smote Gedaliah the son of Ahikam the son of Shaphan with the sword, and slew him, whom the king of Babylon had made governor over the land.

GEHAZI

[gē hā'zī] The servant of Elisha. Gehazi first appears in connection with the Shunnamite woman who had befriended his master. When Elisha was unable to persuade the woman to name some favor which he might obtain for her, it was Gehazi who suggested that she would be most pleased with the gift of a son, for she and her husband had no children. The following year, the Shunnamite woman bore a son. After a few years, the boy died and the Shunnamite sought out the man of God for help, prostrating herself before him and catching hold of his feet. This bold action offended Gehazi and he moved as if to thrust her away. Elisha, however, stopped him and sent him ahead to the woman's house to see what could be done. When Gehazi returned with word that the child had "not awaked", Elisha himself went and restored life to the child.

The next episode involving Gehazi was the healing of Naaman's leprosy. The Syrian general had offered Elisha rich gifts for the cure which he had wrought, but the prophet had refused them. Gehazi, however, could not let such an opportunity pass. He ran to Naaman and obtained a considerable gift, deceiving him with a story that Elisha had changed his mind as a result of the unexpected arrival of guests. When Elisha learned of Gehazi's duplicity he called down on him the disease which Naaman had been cured, "and he went out from his presence a leper as white as snow."

The last mention of Gehazi is in connection with his appearance before King Joram to recount the wondrous deeds of Elisha. As he spoke of the restoration of life to the Shunnamite woman's son, the woman herself appeared before the king to ask that the lands which she had lost be returned to her. On the basis of Gehazi's identification of the woman and her son, the king made complete restitution for all she had lost. On the basis of this incident, it is often surmised that Gehazi somehow regained the favor of his master.

See ELISHA

REFERENCE: *2 Kin. 4, 5, 8:1-6.*

SCRIPTURE

Gehazi's Sin and Punishment

2 Kin. 5 20 But Gehazi, the servant of
Elisha the man of God, said, Behold, my
master hath spared Naaman this Syrian, in
not receiving at his hands that which he
brought: but, as the LORD liveth, I will
run after him, and take somewhat of him.
21 So Gehazi followed after Naaman. And
when Naaman saw him running after him,
he lighted down from the chariot to meet
him, and said, Is all well? 22 And he said,
All is well. My master hath sent me, saying,
Behold, even now there be come to me
from mount Ephraim two young men of
the sons of the prophets: give them, I pray
thee, a talent of silver, and two changes of
garments. 23 And Naaman said, Be content,
take two talents. And he urged him,
and bound two talents of silver in two bags,
with two changes of garments, and laid
them upon two of his servants; and they
bare them before him. 24 And when he
came to the tower, he took them from their
hand, and bestowed them in the house:
and he let the men go, and they departed.
25 But he went in, and stood before his master.
And Elisha said unto him, Whence
comest thou, Gehazi? And he said, Thy
servant went no whither. 26 And he said
unto him, Went not mine heart with thee,
when the man turned again from his chariot
to meet thee? Is it a time to receive
money, and to receive garments, and
oliveyards, and vineyards, and sheep, and
oxen, and menservants, and maidservants?
27 The leprosy therefore of Naaman shall
cleave unto thee, and unto thy seed for
ever. And he went out from his presence
a leper as white as snow.

GEHENNA

[gē hen′a] The place of torment of the wicked, translated in the King James Version as "hell." The word is derived from the Valley of Hinnom, near Jerusalem; this valley was once the scene of the idolatrous worship of Molech, to whom children were sacrificed by fire (*2 Chr. 28:3; 33:6*). It later became the city dump where rubbish was burnt. These associations with fire and defilement made it a fitting symbol of eternal punishment.

See PARADISE, HELL, HADES, SHEOL

REFERENCE: The Greek word for Gehenna occurs in the following verses: *Matt. 5:22, 29, 30; 10:28; 18:9; 23:15, 33; Mark 9:43, 45, 47; Luke 12:5; Jas. 3:6.*

GENTILES

[jen′tīlz] In the Old Testament the Hebrew word *goy* signified foreigners, as opposed to Israel; it is also translated "heathen" and "nation." In the early years of Israel's religion, Gentiles were kindly treated and received almost as equals (*Deut. 10:19, 24:15; Ex. 23:9; Num. 35:15*). By the time of Christ, however, there was a sharp differentiation between Jew and Gentile; Gentiles were regarded as unclean persons, contact with whom was contaminating. This attitude engendered considerable antipathy on the part of non-Jews, as reflected in the writings of such men as Cicero, Seneca, and Tacitus. A major problem in the early Christian church was the matter of admittance of Gentiles to full fellowship. Many Jews felt that salvation was given only to the Jews and that before a man could become a Christian, he must first become a Jew through the rite of circumcision. This problem is reflected in much of the writings of the apostle Paul.

GENTLENESS

[jen′t'l nes] Kindness and softness in manner, considerateness, readiness to look humanely and reasonably at the facts of a situation. Gentleness is viewed in the Bible as a beautiful virtue, and righteous persons are urged to cultivate it.

See KINDNESS

SCRIPTURE

Gal. 5 [22]But the fruit of the Spirit is love, joy, peace, longsuffering, gentleness.

2 Tim. 2 [24]And the servant of the Lord must not strive; but be gentle unto all men, apt to teach, patient.

Tit. 3 [1]Put them in mind . . . [2]To speak evil of no man, to be no brawlers, but gentle, shewing all meekness unto all men.

Jas. 3 [17]But the wisdom that is from above is first pure, then peaceable, gentle, and easy to be intreated, full of mercy and good fruits, without partiality, and without hypocrisy.

GERAR

[ge′rar] An ancient city in the Philistine plain south of Gaza (*Gen. 10:19*). According to *Gen. 20* and *26*, both Abraham and Isaac deceived Abimelech king of Gerar concerning their wives.

See ABIMELECH

GERIZIM

[ger′i zim] A mountain standing opposite Mount Ebal north of the valley of Shechem. Gerizim was the mountain of the Blessings in the ceremony described in the article on EBAL, in which the law was read to the assembled congregation of Israel, to the accompaniment of appropriate responses. It was from a spur of Gerizim that Jotham spoke his taunting parable of the bramble to the men of Shechem (*Judg. 9*); doubtless he chose this position for its acoustics, demonstrated in the above-mentioned ceremony. In the period after the exile, the Samaritans erected a temple on Mount Gerizim to rival that in Jerusalem, thus beginning a schism in Judaism which has never been healed.

See EBAL

GETHSEMANE

[geth sem′a nē] A small, enclosed piece of ground, described as a "garden" or simply a "place" (*Matt. 26:36; Mark 14:32*), situated across the brook Kedron (*John 18:1*), probably at the foot of Mount Olivet (*Luke 22:39*), and about one half to three-quarters of a mile northwest from the walls of Jerusalem. It was to this garden or orchard that Jesus and the inner circle of his disciples retired after the last supper and in which he was betrayed by Judas Iscariot (*Matt. 26:36-50; Mark 14:32-46; Luke 22:32-48; John 18:1-5*).

GIBEONITES

[gib ē un īts] Inhabitants of Gibeon, a royal city of the Hivites. After the conquering Israelites had overrun the first cities which they attacked, the Gibeonites duped them into making a treaty with them by pretending they were residents of a far country. When the Israelites learned of the deception, they were quite angry, as they had been instructed not to make treaties with any resident of the land of Canaan. Joshua spared the lives of the Gibeonites but he sentenced them to a role of slave-labor. A coalition of kings in southern Palestine considered the stratagem of the Gibeonites as traitorous and banded together to attack them. According to the terms of the treaty, Joshua was obliged to defend them; he did so, routing the forces of the coalition and moving on to further conquests in the area.

During the reign of David, the Gibeonites demanded blood vengeance for a slaughter of their number which had taken place under Saul. David sought to satisfy them by a payment of money, but finally turned over to them seven of Saul's sons and grandsons to be slaughtered. After Rizpah, the mother of two of the hanged men, watched over their bodies for a considerable time, David had them buried in the tomb of Kish, Saul's father.

See GIBEON

REFERENCE: *Josh. 9-10; 2 Sam. 21:1-9.*

GIDEON

[gid'ê un] Also called Jerubbaal, he was the youngest son of Joash, a member of the tribe of Manasseh, and the fifth named of the Judges of Israel. In the time of Gideon, Israel was under severe pressure from the invading Midianites. These marauding tribes had continually harassed Israel for seven years, destroying the produce and animals of the land and forcing the Israelites to flee to dens and caves in the mountains. It is interesting to note that the Midianites are the first people known to have domesticated camels in such raids. Finally, Gideon received a divine commission to assume the leadership of his tribe. His first act was to cut down the altar of Baal and the Asherah and to build an altar to the true God. This was done under cover of darkness and when the townspeople arose the next morning, they were incensed at Gideon's actions. Joash, Gideon's father, protected his son from the angry crowd by pointing out that, if Baal were truly a god, he could avenge himself.

Gideon's most famous exploit was his defeat of the Midianites with a small band of Israelites. *Judg. 6* tells us that he set out against the hordes of Midian with a force of 32,000 men. After the episode of the dry and wet fleece, in which Gideon became convinced of the aid of the LORD, all but 300 of his men were sent home. Then, with trumpets and lights concealed in pitchers, Gideon's army surrounded the camp of the Midianites. Breaking the pitchers to reveal the lights, sounding the trumpets loudly and shouting, the Israelites threw their enemies into a panic and were able to rout them completely. The two greatest chiefs of Midian, Zebah and Zalmunna, escaped into the land east of the Jordan. Gideon and his men pursued them and finally caught and slew them. On his return he punished the people of Penuel and Succoth who had refused aid to his army, out of fear for the Midianites. Gideon had seventy-one sons, the most famous of whom were Jotham and Abimelech.

See JUDGES, MIDIANITES

REFERENCE: *Judg. 6, 7, 8.*

SCRIPTURE

Chosen to Deliver Israel

Judg. 6 [11]And there came an angel of
the LORD, and sat under an oak which was
in Ophrah, that pertained unto Joash the
Abiezrite: and his son Gideon threshed
wheat by the winepress, to hide it from the
Midianites. [12]And the angel of the LORD
appeared unto him, and said unto him,
The LORD is with thee, thou mighty man
of valour. [13]And Gideon said unto him, O
my Lord, if the LORD be with us, why then
is all this befallen us? and where be all his
miracles which our fathers told us of, saying, Did not the LORD bring us up from
Egypt? but now the LORD hath forsaken
us, and delivered us into the hands of the
Midianites. [14]And the LORD looked upon
him, and said, Go in this thy might, and
thou shalt save Israel from the hand of the
Midianites: have not I sent thee? [15]And
he said unto him, O my Lord, wherewith
shall I save Israel? behold, my family is
poor in Manasseh, and I am the least in my

father's house. [16]And the LORD said unto him, Surely I will be with thee, and thou shalt smite the Midianites as one man. [17]And he said unto him, If now I have found grace in thy sight, then shew me a sign that thou talkest with me. [18]Depart not hence, I pray thee, until I come unto thee, and bring forth my present, and set it before thee. And he said, I will tarry until thou come again.

[19]And Gideon went in, and made ready a kid, and unleavened cakes of an ephah of flour: the flesh he put in a basket, and he put the broth in a pot, and brought it out unto him under the oak, and presented it. [20]And the angel of God said unto him, Take the flesh and the unleavened cakes, and lay them upon this rock, and pour out the broth. And he did so.

[21]Then the angel of the LORD put forth the end of the staff that was in his hand, and touched the flesh and the unleavened cakes; and there rose up fire out of the rock, and consumed the flesh and the unleavened cakes. Then the angel of the LORD departed out of his sight. [22]And when Gideon perceived that he was an angel of the LORD, Gideon said, Alas, O Lord GOD! for because I have seen an angel of the LORD face to face. [23]And the LORD said unto him, Peace be unto thee; fear not: thou shalt not die. [24]Then Gideon built an altar there unto the LORD, and called it Jehovah-shalom: unto this day it is yet in Ophrah of the Abiezrites.

Destroys the Altar of Baal

Judg. 6 [25]And it came to pass the same night, that the LORD said unto him, Take thy father's young bullock, even the second bullock of seven years old, and throw down the altar of Baal that thy father hath, and cut down the grove that is by it: [26]And build an altar unto the LORD thy God upon the top of this rock, in the ordered place, and take the second bullock, and offer a burnt sacrifice with the wood of the grove which thou shalt cut down. [27]Then Gideon took ten men of his servants, and did as the LORD had said unto him: and so it was, because he feared his father's household, and the men of the city, that he could not do it by day, that he did it by night.

Receives a Sign

Judg. 6 [36]And Gideon said unto God, If thou wilt save Israel by my hand, as thou hast said, [37]Behold, I will put a fleece of wool in the floor: and if the dew be on the fleece only, and it be dry upon all the earth besides, then shall I know that thou wilt save Israel by my hand, as thou hast said. [38]And it was so: for he rose up early on the morrow, and thrust the fleece together, and wringed the dew out of the fleece, a bowl full of water. [39]And Gideon said unto God, Let not thine anger be hot against me, and I will speak but this once: let me prove, I pray thee, but this once with the fleece; let it now be dry only upon the fleece, and upon all the ground let there be dew. [40]And God did so that night: for it was dry upon the fleece only, and there was dew on all the ground.

Defeats the Midianites

Judg. 7 [7]And the LORD said unto Gideon, By the three hundred men that lapped will I save you, and deliver the Midianites into thine hand: and let all the other people go every man unto his place. [8]So the people took victuals in their hand, and their trumpets: and he sent all the rest of Israel every man unto his tent, and retained those three hundred men: and the host of Midian was beneath him in the valley.

[16]And he divided the three hundred men into three companies, and he put a trumpet in every man's hand, with empty pitchers, and lamps within the pitchers. [17]And he said unto them, Look on me, and do likewise: and, behold, when I come to the outside of the camp, it shall be that, as I do, so shall ye do. [18]When I blow with a trumpet, I and all that are with me, then blow ye the trumpets also on every side of all the camp, and say, The sword of the LORD, and of Gideon.

[19]So Gideon, and the hundred men that were with him came unto the outside of the camp in the beginning of the middle watch; and they had but newly set the watch: and they blew the trumpets, and brake the pitchers that were in their hands. [20]And the three companies blew the trumpets, and brake the pitchers, and held the lamps in their left hands, and the trumpets in their right hands to blow withal: and they cried, The sword of the LORD, and of Gideon. [21]And they stood every man in his place round about the camp: and all the host ran, and cried, and fled.

Death of Gideon

Judg. 8 [29]And Jerubbaal the son of Joash went and dwelt in his own house. [30]And Gideon had threescore and ten sons of his body begotten: for he had many wives. [31]And his concubine that was in Shechem, she also bare him a son, whose name he called Abimelech.

[32]And Gideon the son of Joash died in a good old age, and was buried in the sepulchre of Joash his father, in Ophrah of the Abiezrites. [33]And it came to pass, as soon as Gideon was dead, that the children of Israel turned again, and went a whoring after Baalim, and made Baalberith their god. [34]And the children of Israel remembered not the LORD their God, who had delivered them out of the hands of all their enemies on every side: [35]Neither shewed they kindness to the house of Jerubbaal, namely, Gideon, according to all the goodness which he had shewed unto Israel.

GILBOA

[gil bō′a] A mountain on the eastern side of the plain of Esdraelon on which Saul and his sons met their death at the hands of the Philistines.

See SAUL

REFERENCE: *1 Sam. 28:4; 31: 1, 8; 2 Sam. 1:6, 21.*

GILEAD

[gil′ē ad] 1. A mountain mass west of the Jordan, lying between the River Yarmuk on the north and the Wady Hesban on the south. Its eastern boundary was the desert. The name is sometimes used to denote the entire country east of the Jordan (*Josh. 22:9; 2 Sam. 2:9*). For accounts of events connected with the cities and men of this region, see articles on JEPHTHAH, JABESH-GILEAD, and RAMOTH-GILEAD. In the Assyrian conquests under Tiglath-Pileser, Gilead was overrun and its inhabitants carried into captivity.

2. A city named in *Hos. 6:8; 12:11.*

3. A mountain named in *Judg. 7:3.*

GILGAL

[gil′gal] The first camp of Israel after the crossing of the Jordan River (*Josh. 4:19*). It was located north of the valley of Achor, which formed the border between Judah and Benjamin. After the setting up of memorial stones to commemorate the crossing of the river, the people of Israel were circumcised (the practice not having been observed in the wilderness), the Passover was celebrated, and the manna ceased (*Josh. 5*). Gilgal served as Israel's main headquarters during the conquest under Joshua. When the major campaigns were ended, the headquarters were transferred to Shiloh. Gilgal later appears as one of the places of judgment on Samuel's circuit (*1 Sam. 7:16*), as the site of Samuel's execution of Agag (*1 Sam. 15:33*), and as the spot at which Saul was crowned king of Israel (*1 Sam. 11:14, 15*). Gilgal seems ever to have been a special spot for sacrifices (*1 Sam. 10:8; 13:8, 10; 15:21*) and is represented by Hosea and Amos as a center of idolatry in their day (*Hos. 4:15; 9:15; 12: 11; Amos 4:4; 5:5*).

GIVING

[giv'ing] The verb "to give" is used in countless ways in the Bible. The scriptures contained below refer to the contribution of the church and to the giving of alms to the poor. For fuller treatment the reader is invited to consult the articles on ALMS, BENEFICENCE, and LIBERALITY.

SCRIPTURE

Rules for Giving

Psa. 76 [11]Vow, and pay unto the LORD your God: let all that be round about him bring presents unto him that ought to be feared.

Matt. 6 [1]Take heed that ye do not your alms before men, to be seen of them: otherwise ye have no reward of your Father which is in heaven. [2]Therefore when thou doest thine alms, do not sound a trumpet before thee, as the hypocrites do in the synagogues and in the streets, that they may have glory of men. Verily I say unto you, They have their reward. [3]But when thou doest alms, let not thy left hand know what thy right hand doeth: [4]That thine alms may be in secret: and thy Father which seeth in secret himself shall reward thee openly.

Luke 6 [38]Give, and it shall be given unto you; good measure, pressed down, and shaken together, and running over, shall men give into your bosom. For with the same measure that ye mete withal it shall be measured to you again.

1 Cor. 16 [2]Upon the first day of the week let every one of you lay be him in store, as God hath prospered him, that there be no gatherings when I come.

2 Cor. 8 [11]Now therefore perform the doing of it; that as there was a readiness to will, so there may be a performance also out of that which ye have. [12]For if there be first a willing mind, it is accepted according to that a man hath, and not according to that he hath not. [14]But by an equality, that now at this time your abundance may be a supply for their want, that their abundance also may be a supply for your want; that there may be equality.

2 Cor. 9 [6]But this I say, He which soweth sparingly shall reap also sparingly; and he which soweth bountifully shall reap also bountifully. [7]Every man according as he purposeth in his heart, so let him give; not grudgingly, or of necessity: for God loveth a cheerful giver.

General

Acts 20 [35]I have showed you all things, how that so laboring ye ought to support the weak, and to remember the words of the Lord Jesus, how he said, It is more blessed to give than to receive.

Eph. 4 [28]Let him that stole steal no more: but rather let him labor, working with his hands the thing which is good, that he may have to give to him that needeth.

GLUTTONY

[glut' 'n i] Excess in eating and drinking. In several passages the Bible declares gluttony to be a practice not to be indulged in by the righteous. Jesus was called a glutton because of his freedom from the asceticism which characterized John the Baptist.

SCRIPTURE

Prov. 23 [1]When thou sittest to eat with a ruler, consider diligently what is before thee: [2]And put a knife to thy throat, if thou be a man given to appetite. [20]Be not among wine-bibbers; among riotous eaters of flesh: [21]For the drunkard and the glutton shall come to poverty: and drowsiness shall clothe a man with rags.

Prov. 25 [16]Hast thou found honey? eat so much as is sufficient for thee, lest thou be filled therewith, and vomit it.

1 Pet. 4 [3]For the time past of our life may suffice us to have wrought the will of the Gentiles, when we walked in lasciviousness, lusts, excess of wine, revellings, banquetings, and abominable idolatries. [7]But the end of all things is at hand: be ye therefore sober, and watch unto prayer.

Matt. 11 [19]The Son of man came eating and drinking, and they say, Behold a man gluttonous, and a winebibber, a friend of publicans and sinners.

GOD

[god] In the Bible God is viewed not as some abstract, impersonal principle, but as the living, active LORD of history. As men encountered this LORD of history, they developed a fuller picture of his nature and purposes. From their experience of him as the deliverer of his people and the controller of the rise and fall of nations, there arose the notion that he possesses absolute power over all that is. This power over the universe is traceable to his being its creator and sustainer. In the New Testament this understanding is deepened as God the Creator is seen also to be God the Redeemer. Just as the physical creation was effected through his word, so that Word, incarnate in Jesus Christ, becomes the agency of a new, spiritual creation—Reconciled Man.

Our finite minds can never attain to perfect knowledge of God in this life, but certain qualities or characteristics may be attributed to him on the basis of our reflection upon his revelation of himself in history and Holy Scripture. God may be spoken of as Spirit, in that he is not material and transcends all that is physical and spatial. This is not to say, however, that he is something vague and impersonal. If God is living it is normal to assume he is also personal, since to be a person is the most adequate way of being alive which our finite minds can comprehend. The attribute of Holiness suggests the infinite distance between God and his creatures. Although it originally implied no necessary ethical content, this separateness eventually came to be looked upon as one of moral purity. (*See* HOLINESS) The boundlessness of God is expressed in the three related attributes of Omnipotence, Omniscience, and Omnipresence. God is omnipotent in that he is able to do everything which is consistent with his nature and will. His omniscience means that he knows all things instantaneously and eternally, that his knowledge is all-comprehensive and certain, entirely devoid of darkness or lack of knowledge. God's omnipresence means he is in some way present in all points of space and time. Another of the primary attributes of God is Righteousness. This includes his faithfulness to the covenants he has made, his zeal for the social rights of the poor and helpless, his compassion for all those who are in misery, his patience in dealing with those deserving of punishment, and the impartiality of his justice. God's wrath is also to be understood as an expression of his righteous aversion to sin.

If any one attribute can be singled out as peculiarly descriptive of God, surely it is Love. This love is not something accidental or incidental, but such a vital part of his being that we are told in *1 John 4:8* that "God is Love." God's long-suffering attitude toward the sinfulness of the Israelites is compared to the unself-seeking love of a man for his adulterous wife. (*See* HOSEA) His love desires to possess its objects. It is this characteristic which causes God to call himself a "jealous" God. This does not mean he is a petty tyrant; rather, it is an intense assertion of his moral claim and right to exclusive possession of his people. The love of God is manifested in the Incarnation and Atonement, for it was in sending his son to die for our sins that God revealed the full measure of his concern for his creation. It is also God's love that leads us to conceive of him as a Father. God's fatherhood is two-fold. In the broadest sense, he is the father of the whole creation. He shows mercy to all his works, shedding his blessings on the evil and good alike. In a special sense, he is the father of those who have received adoption through his son Jesus Christ and have entered into a covenant relationship with him.

As men recognized Christ was in a very real sense a manifestation of God's love and power and that God continued to be present among his people through his Holy Spirit, there arose the Doctrine of the Trinity. The essence of this doctrine is that the unity of God is not simple and undifferentiated, but that there exists within the Godhead three "persons"—Father, Son, and Holy Spirit—united in essence, will, action, purpose, and nature, and that these three persons are coeternal, none having preceded the others in coming into existence. Although the New Testament does not provide us with a developed doctrine of the Trinity, the beginnings of a trinitarian understanding of God are certainly present, as may be seen from the references below.

See CHRIST, HOLY SPIRIT, JEHOVAH, JESUS

SCRIPTURE

God Described

AS THE LORD GOD ALMIGHTY

Gen. 17 [1]And when Abram was ninety years old and nine, the LORD appeared to Abram, and said unto him, I am the Almighty God; walk before me, and be thou perfect.

Ex. 6 [3]And I appeared unto Abraham, unto Isaac, and unto Jacob by the name of God Almighty, but by my name JEHOVAH was I not known to them.

Rev. 1 [8]I am Alpha and Omega, the beginning and the ending, saith the Lord, which is, and which was, and which is to come, the Almighty.

AS THE CREATOR

Gen. 1 [1]In the beginning God created the heaven and the earth.

[27]So God created man in his own image, in the image of God created he him; male and female created he them.

Neh. 9 [6]Thou, even thou, art LORD alone; thou hast made heaven, the heaven of heavens, with all their host, the earth, and all things that are therein, the seas, and all that is therein, and thou preservest them all; and the host of heaven worshippeth thee.

Psa. 19 [1]The heavens declare the glory of God; and the firmament sheweth his handy work.

Psa. 89 [11]The heavens are thine, the earth also is thine: as for the world, and the fulness thereof, thou hast founded them.

Isa. 37 [16]O LORD of hosts, God of Israel, that dwellest between the cherubims, thou art the God, even thou alone, of all the kingdoms of the earth; thou hast made heaven and earth.

Isa. 45 [8]Drop down, ye heavens, from above, and let the skies pour down righteousness: let the earth open, and let them bring forth salvation, and let righteousness spring up together; I the LORD have created it.

John 1 [3]All things were made by him, and without him was not anything made that was made.

Col. 1 [16]For by him were all things created that are in heaven, and that are in earth, visible and invisible, whether they be thrones, or dominions, or principalities, or powers: all things were created by him, and for him.

AS THE FATHER

Matt. 11 [25]At that time Jesus answered, and said, I thank thee, O Father, Lord of heaven and earth, because thou hast hid these things from the wise and prudent, and hast revealed them unto babes.

Matt. 28 [19]Go ye therefore, and teach all nations, baptizing them in the Name of the Father, and of the Son, and of the holy Ghost.

Mark 14 [36]And he said, Abba, Father, all things are possible unto thee, take away this cup from me: Nevertheless, not that I will, but what thou wilt.

Luke 23 [34]Then said Jesus, Father, forgive them, for they know not what they do: And they parted his raiment, and cast lots.

[46]And when Jesus had cried with a loud voice, he said, Father, into thy hands I commend my spirit: And having said thus, he gave up the ghost.

John 1 [14]And the Word was made flesh, and dwelt among us, (and we beheld his glory, the glory as of the only begotten of the Father,) full of grace and truth.

Acts 15 [6]That ye may with one mind and one mouth glorify God, even the Father of our Lord Jesus Christ.

1 Cor. 8 [6]But to us there is but one God, the Father, of whom are all things, and we in him, and one Lord Jesus Christ, by whom are all things, and we by him.

1 Cor. 15 [24]Then cometh the end, when he shall have delivered up the kingdom to God even the Father, when he shall have put down all rule, and all authority and power.

2 Cor. 1 [3]Blessed be God, even the Father of our Lord Jesus Christ, the Father of mercies, and the God of all comfort.

1 Pet. 1 [17]And if ye call on the Father, who without respect of persons judgeth according to every man's work, pass the time of your sojourning here in fear.

SEARCHER OF HEARTS

1 Chr. 28 [9]And thou, Solomon my son, know thou the God of thy father, and serve him with a perfect heart, and with a willing mind: for the LORD searcheth all hearts, and understandeth all the imaginations of the thoughts: if thou seek him, he will be found of thee; but if thou forsake him, he will cast thee off for ever.

Psa. 44 [21]Shall not God search this out? for he knoweth the secrets of the heart.

Jer. 17 [10]I the LORD search the heart, I try the reins, even to give every man according to his ways, and according to the fruit of his doings.

Acts 1 [24]And they prayed, and said, Thou, Lord, which knowest the hearts of all men, shew whether of these two thou hast chosen.

Rom. 8 [27]And he that searcheth the hearts knoweth what is the mind of the Spirit, because he maketh intercession for the saints according to the will of God.

DISPOSER OF EVENTS

Gen. 31 [29]It is in the power of my hand to do you hurt: but the God of your father spake unto me yesternight, saying, Take thou heed that thou speak not to Jacob either good or bad.

Gen. 45 [7]And God sent me before you to preserve you a posterity in the earth, and to save your lives by a great deliverance. [8]So now it was not you that sent me hither, but God: and he hath made me a father to Pharaoh, and lord of all his house, and a ruler throughout all the land of Egypt.

Gen. 50 [19]And Joseph said unto them, Fear not: for am I in the place of God? [20]But as for you, ye thought evil against me; but God meant it unto good, to bring to pass, as it is this day, to save much people alive.

Prov. 16 [9]A man's heart deviseth his way: but the LORD directeth his steps.

Prov. 19 [21]There are many devices in a man's heart; nevertheless the counsel of the LORD, that shall stand.

Prov. 20 [24]Man's goings are of the LORD; how can a man then understand his own way?

Prov. 21 [30] There is no wisdom nor understanding nor counsel against the LORD.

John 7 [30]Then they sought to take him:

but no man laid hands on him, because his hour was not yet come.

SUPREME JUDGE

1 Chr. 16 [14]He is the LORD our God; his judgments are in all the earth.

Job 21 [22]Shall any teach God knowledge? seeing he judgeth those that are high.

Job 23 [7]There the righteous might dispute with him; so should I be delivered forever from my judge.

Psa. 7 [8]The LORD shall judge the people: judge me, O LORD, according to my righteousness, and according to mine integrity that is in me.

Psa. 9 [8]And he shall judge the world in righteousness, he shall minister judgment to the people in uprightness.

Psa. 50 [4]He shall call to the heavens from above, and to the earth, that he may judge his people.

Psa. 75 [7]But God is the judge: he putteth down one, and setteth up another.

Psa. 96 [13]Before the LORD: for he cometh, for he cometh to judge the earth: he shall judge the world with righteousness, and the people with his truth.

1 Cor. 4 [4]For I know nothing by myself; yet am I not hereby justified: but he that judgeth me is the Lord. [5]Therefore judge nothing before the time, until the Lord come, who both will bring to light the hidden things of darkness, and will make manifest the counsels of the hearts: and then shall every man have praise of God.

God's Attributes

ETERNAL

Gen. 21 [33]And Abraham planted a grove in Beer-sheba, and called there on the name of the LORD, the everlasting God.

Deut. 32 [40]For I lift up my hand to heaven, and say, I live for ever.

Deut. 33 [27]The eternal God is thy refuge, and underneath are the everlasting arms: and he shall thrust out the enemy from before thee; and shall say, Destroy them.

Psa. 9 [7]But the LORD shall endure for ever: he hath prepared his throne for judgment.

Psa. 90 [2]Before the mountains were brought forth, or ever thou hadst formed the earth and the world, even from everlasting to everlasting, thou art God.

Psa. 93 [2]Thy throne is established of old: thou art from everlasting.

Psa. 102 [12]But thou, O LORD, shalt endure for ever; and thy remembrance unto all generations.

Psa. 135 [13]Thy name, O LORD, endureth for ever; and thy memorial, O LORD, throughout all generations.

Psa. 146 [10]The LORD shall reign for ever, even thy God, O Zion, unto all generations. Praise ye the LORD.

Isa. 57 [15]For thus saith the high and lofty One that inhabiteth eternity, whose name is Holy; I dwell in the high and holy place, with him also that is of a contrite and humble spirit, to revive the spirit of the humble, and to revive the heart of the contrite ones.

Isa. 63 [16]Doubtless thou art our Father, though Abraham be ignorant of us, and Israel acknowledge us not: thou, O LORD, art our Father, our Redeemer: thy name is from everlasting.

Jer. 10 [10]But the LORD is the true God, he is the living God; and an everlasting King: at his wrath the earth shall tremble, and the nations shall not be able to abide his indignation.

1 Tim. 6 [15]Which in his times he shall

shew, who is the blessed and only Potentate, the Kings of kings, and the Lord of lords; [16]Who only hath immortality, dwelling in the light which no man can approach unto; whom no man hath seen, nor can see: to whom be honour and power everlasting. Amen.

2 Pet. 3 [8]But, beloved, be not ignorant of this one thing, that one day is with the Lord as a thousand years, and a thousand years as one day.

Rev. 1 [4]John to the seven churches which are in Asia: Grace be unto you, and peace, from him which is, and which was, and which is to come; and from the seven Spirits which are before his throne.

Rev. 1 [8]I am Alpha and Omega, the beginning and the ending, saith the Lord, which is, and which was, and which is to come, the Almighty.

IMMUTABLE

Num. 23 [19]God is not a man, that he should lie; neither the son of man, that he should repent: hath he said, and shall he not do it? or hath he spoken, and shall he not make it good?

1 Sam. 15 [29]And also the Strength of Israel will not lie nor repent: for he is not a man, that he should repent.

Job 23 [13]But he is in one mind, and who can turn him? and what his soul desireth, even that he doeth.

Psa. 33 [11]The counsel of the LORD standeth for ever, the thoughts of his heart to all generations.

Psa. 119 [89]For ever, O LORD, thy word is settled in heaven.

Mic. 3 [6]For I am the LORD, I change not; therefore ye sons of Jacob are not consumed.

Jas. 1 [7]Every good gift and every perfect gift is from above, and cometh down from the Father of lights, with whom is no variableness, neither shadow of turning.

OMNISCIENT

Job 12 [22]He discovereth deep things out of darkness, and bringeth out to light the shadow of death.

Job 36 [6]Hell is naked before him, and destruction hath no covering.

Psa. 33 [13]The LORD looketh from heaven; he beholdeth all the sons of men. [14]From the place of his habitation he looketh upon all the inhabitants of the earth.

Psa. 139 [11]If I say, Surely the darkness shall cover me; even the night shall be light about me. [12]Yea, the darkness hideth not from thee; but the night shineth as the day: the darkness and the light are both alike to thee.

Psa. 147 [5]Great is our LORD, and of great power: his understanding is infinite.

Prov. 15 [3]The eyes of the LORD are in every place, beholding the evil and the good.

Amos 9 [2]Though they dig into hell, thence shall mine hand take them; though they climb to heaven, thence will I bring them down. [3]And though they hide themselves in the top of Carmel, I will search and take them out thence; and though they be hid from my sight in the bottom of the sea, thence will I command the serpent, and he shall bite them.

Acts 15 [18]Known unto God are all his works from the beginning of the world.

1 John 3 [20]For if our heart condemn us, God is greater than our heart, and knoweth all things.

OMNIPRESENT

1 Kin. 8 [27]But will God indeed dwell on the earth? behold, the heaven and heaven of heavens cannot contain thee; how much less this house that I have builded?

2 Chr. 2 [6]But who is able to build him a house, seeing the heaven and heaven of heavens cannot contain him? who am I then, I should build him a house, save only to burn sacrifice before him?

Psa. 139 [7]Whither shall I go from thy Spirit? or whither shall I flee from thy presence? [8]If I ascend up into heaven, thou art there: if I make my bed in hell, behold, thou art there. [9]If I take the wings of the morning, and dwell in the uttermost parts of the sea; [10]Even there shall thy hand lead me, and thy right hand shall hold me.

Isa. 66 [1]Thus saith the LORD, The heaven is my throne, and the earth is my footstool: where is the house that ye build unto me? and where is the place of my rest?

Jer. 23 [23]Am I a God at hand, saith the LORD, and not a God afar off?

Acts 17 [27]That they should seek the Lord, if haply they might feel after him, and find him, though he be not far from every one of us.

OMNIPOTENT

Gen. 17 [1]And when Abram was ninety years old and nine, the LORD appeared to Abram, and said unto him, I am the Almighty God; walk before me, and be thou perfect.

Ex. 6 [3]And I appeared unto Abraham, unto Isaac, and unto Jacob, by the name of God Almighty; but by my name JEHOVAH was I not known to them.

Job 5 [17]Behold, happy is the man whom God correcteth: therefore despise not thou the chastening of the Almighty.

Psa. 68 [14]When the Almighty scattered kings in it, it was white as snow in Salmon.

Matt. 19 [26]But Jesus beheld them, and said unto them, With men this is impossible; but with God all things are possible.

Mark 10 [27]And Jesus looking upon them saith, With men it is impossible, but not with God: for with God all things are possible.

Rev. 1 [8]I am Alpha and Omega, the beginning and the ending, saith the Lord, which is, and which was, and which is to come, the Almighty.

Rev. 19 [6]And I heard as it were the voice of a great multitude, and as the voice of many waters, and as the voice of mighty thunderings, saying, Alleluia: for the Lord God omnipotent reigneth.

INVISIBLE

Ex. 33 [20]And he said, Thou canst not see my face: for there shall no man see me, and live.

John 1 [18]No man hath seen God at any time; the only begotten Son, which is in the bosom of the Father, he hath declared him.

John 5 [37]And the Father himself, which hath sent me, hath borne witness of me. Ye have neither heard his voice at any time, nor seen his shape.

1 Tim. 1 [17]Now unto the King eternal, immortal, invisible, the only wise God, be honour and glory for ever and ever. Amen.

1 Tim. 6 [16]Who only hath immortality, dwelling in the light which no man can approach unto; whom no man hath seen, nor can see: to whom be honour and power everlasting. Amen.

UNSEARCHABLE

Job 11 [7]Canst thou by searching find out God? canst thou find out the Almighty unto perfection?

Job 26 [14]Lo, these are parts of his ways; but how little a portion is heard of him? but the thunder of his power who can understand?

Psa. 145 [3]Great is the LORD, and greatly to be praised; and his greatness is unsearchable.

Eccl. 8 [17]Then I beheld all the work of God, that a man cannot find out the work that is done under the sun: because though a man labour to seek it out, yet he shall not find it; yea, further; though a wise man think to know it, yet shall he not be able to find it.

Rom. 11 [33]O the depth of the riches both of the wisdom and knowledge of God! how unsearchable are his judgments, and his ways past finding out!

UNKNOWN

Job 36 [26]Behold, God is great, and we know him not, neither can the number of his years be searched out.

Job 37 [5]God thundereth marvellously with his voice; great things doeth he, which we cannot comprehend.

Psa. 40 [5]Many, O LORD my God, are thy wonderful works which thou hast done, and thy thoughts which are to us-ward: they cannot be reckoned up in order unto thee: if I would declare and speak of them, they are more than can be numbered.

Eccl. 3 [11]He hath made every thing beautiful in his time: also he hath set the world in their heart, so that no man can find out the work that God maketh from the beginning to the end.

Isa. 45 [15]Verily thou art a God that hidest thyself, O God of Israel, the Saviour.

YET REVEALED

Matt. 11 [27]All things are delivered unto me of my Father: and no man knoweth the Son, but the Father; neither knoweth any man the Father, save the Son, and he to whomsoever the Son will reveal him.

Rom. 1 [19]Because that which may be known of God is manifest in them, for God hath shewed it unto them. [20]For the invisible things of him from the Creation of the world are clearly seen, being understood by the things that are made, even his eternal Power and Godhead, so that they are without excuse.

1 Cor. 2 [10]But God hath revealed them unto us by his Spirit: for the Spirit searcheth all things, yea, the deep things of God. [11]For what man knoweth the things of a man, save the spirit of man which is in him? even so the things of God knoweth no man, but the Spirit of God. [12]Now we have received, not the spirit of the world, but the Spirit which is of God; that we might know the things that are freely given to us of God. [14]But the natural man receiveth not the things of the Spirit of God: for they are foolishness unto him: neither can he know them, because they are spiritually discerned. [15]But he that is spiritual judgeth all things, yet he himself is judged of no man. [16]For who hath known the mind of the Lord, that he may instruct him? But we have the mind of Christ.

1 John 5 [20]And we know that the Son of God is come, and hath given us an understanding, that we may know him that is true; and we are in him that is true, even in his Son Jesus Christ. This is the true God, and eternal life.

HOLY

Lev. 11 [45]For I am the LORD that bringeth you up out of the land of Egypt, to be your God: ye shall therefore be holy, for I am holy.

Lev. 19 [2]Speak unto all the congregation of the children of Israel, and say unto them, Ye shall be holy: for I the LORD your God am holy.

1 Sam. 2 [2]There is none holy as the LORD: for there is none besides thee: neither is there any rock like our God.

Psa. 5 [4]For thou art not a God that hath

pleasure in wickedness: neither shall evil dwell with thee.

Psa. 22 [3]But thou art holy, O thou that inhabitest the praises of Israel.

Psa. 97 [12]Rejoice in the LORD, ye righteous; and give thanks at the remembrance of his holiness.

Isa. 5 [16]But the LORD of hosts shall be exalted in judgment, and God that is holy shall be sanctified in righteousness.

Isa. 6 [3]And one cried unto another, and said, Holy, holy, holy, is the LORD of hosts: the whole earth is full of his glory.

Isa. 43 [15]I am the LORD, your Holy One, the Creator of Israel, your King.

Jas. 1 [13]Let no man say when he is tempted, I am tempted of God: for God cannot be tempted with evil, neither tempteth he any man.

1 Pet. 1 [15]But as he which hath called you is holy, so be ye holy in all manner of conversation; [16]Because it is written, Be ye holy; for I am holy.

Rev. 4 [8]And the four beasts had each of them six wings about him; and they were full of eyes within: and they rest not day and night, saying, Holy, holy, holy, Lord God Almighty, which was, and is, and is to come.

JUST

Deut. 32 [4]He is the Rock, his work is perfect: for all his ways are judgment: a God of truth and without iniquity, just and right is he.

Job 8 [3]Doth God pervert judgment? or doth the Almighty pervert justice?

Psa. 9 [4]For thou hast maintained my right and my cause; thou satest in the throne judging right.

Psa. 11 [7]For the righteous LORD loveth righteousness; his countenance doth behold the upright.

Psa. 33 [5]He loveth righteousness and judgment: the earth is full of the goodness of the LORD.

Psa. 71 [19]Thy righteousness also, O God, is very high, who hast done great things: O God, who is like unto thee!

Psa. 89 [14]Justice and judgment are the habitation of thy throne: mercy and truth shall go before thy face.

Psa. 97 [2]Clouds and darkness are round about him: righteousness and judgment are the habitation of his throne.

Psa. 99 [4]The king's strength also loveth judgment; thou dost establish equity, thou executest judgment and righteousness in Jacob.

Psa. 119 [137]Righteous art thou, O LORD, and upright are thy judgments.

Psa. 145 [17]The LORD is righteous in all his ways, and holy in all his works.

Ezek. 18 [29]Yet saith the house of Israel, The way of the LORD is not equal. O house of Israel, are not my ways equal? are not your ways unequal?

Zeph. 3 [5]The just LORD is in the midst thereof; he will not do iniquity: every morning doth he bring his judgment to light, he faileth not; but the unjust knoweth no shame.

Rom. 2 [2]But we are sure that the judgment of God is according to truth against them which commit such things. [3]And thinkest thou this, O man, that judgest them which do such things, and doest the same, that thou shalt escape the judgment of God?

Rom. 3 [5]But if our unrighteousness commend the righteousness of God, what shall we say? Is God unrighteous who taketh vengeance? (I speak as a man,) [6]God forbid: for then how shall God judge the world?

Rev. 16 [7]And I heard another out of the altar say, Even so, Lord God Almighty, true and righteous are thy judgments.

IMPARTIAL, FAITHFUL, TRUE

Deut. 10 [17]For the LORD your God is God of gods, and LORD of lords, a great God, a mighty, and a terrible, which regardeth not persons, nor taketh reward.

Acts 10 [34]Then Peter opened his mouth, and said, Of a truth I perceive God is no respecter of persons.

Rom. 2 [11]For there is no respect of persons with God.

Gal. 2 [6]But of those who seemed to be somewhat, whatsoever they were, it maketh no matter to me: God accepteth no man's person: for they who seemed to be somewhat in conference added nothing to me.

Eph. 6 [8]Knowing that whatsoever good thing any man doeth, the same shall he receive of the Lord, whether he be bond or free.

Col. 3 [25]But he that doeth wrong shall receive for the wrong which he hath done: and there is no respect of persons.

Deut. 7 [9]Know therefore that the LORD thy God, he is God, the faithful God, which keepeth covenant and mercy with them that love him and keep his commandments to a thousand generations.

1 Kin. 8 [24]Who hast kept with thy servant David my father that thou promisedst him: thou spakest also with thy mouth, and hast fulfilled it with thine hand, as it is this day.

LOVING, GOOD, MERCIFUL

John 3 [16]For God so loved the world, that he gave his only begotten Son, that whosoever believeth in him should not perish, but have everlasting life.

2 Cor. 13 [11]Finally, brethren, farewell. Be perfect, be of good comfort, be of one mind, live in peace; and the God of love and peace shall be with you. [14]The grace of the Lord Jesus Christ, and the love of God, and the communion of the Holy Ghost, be with you all. Amen.

1 John 4 [8]He that loveth not, knoweth not God; for God is love. [16]And we have known and believed the love that God hath to us. God is love; and he that dwelleth in love dwelleth in God, and God in him.

1 Chr. 16 [34]O give thanks unto the LORD; for he is good; for his mercy endureth for ever.

Psa. 34 [8]O taste and see that the LORD is good: blessed is the man that trusteth in him.

Psa. 86 [5]For thou, LORD, art good, and ready to forgive; and plenteous in mercy unto all them that call upon thee.

Psa. 118 [29]O give thanks unto the LORD; for he is good: for his mercy endureth for ever.

Psa. 136 [1]O give thanks unto the LORD; for he is good: for his mercy endureth for ever.

Psa. 145 [7]They shall abundantly utter the memory of thy great goodness, and shall sing of thy righteousness.

Matt. 5 [45]That ye may be the children of your Father which is in heaven: for he maketh his sun to rise on the evil and on the good, and sendeth rain on the just and on the unjust.

Mark 10 [18]And Jesus said unto him, Why callest thou me good? there is none good but one, that is, God.

Neh. 9 [31]Nevertheless for thy great mercies' sake thou didst not utterly consume them, nor forsake them; for thou art a gracious and merciful God.

Psa. 62 [12]Also unto thee, O LORD, belongeth mercy: for thou renderest to every man according to his work.

Psa. 103 [8]The LORD is merciful and gracious, slow to anger, and plenteous in mercy. [9]He will not always chide: neither will he keep his anger for ever.

Lam. 3 [22]It is of the LORD's mercies that we are not consumed, because his compassions fail not.

Dan. 9 [9]To the LORD our God belong mercies and forgiveness, though we have rebelled against him.

JEALOUS

Ex. 20 [5]Thou shalt not bow down thyself to them, nor serve them: for I the LORD thy God am a jealous God, visiting the iniquity of the fathers upon the children unto the third and fourth generation of them that hate me.

Ex. 34 [14]For thou shalt worship no other god: for the LORD, whose name is Jealous, is a jealous God.

Deut. 4 [24]For the LORD thy God is a consuming fire, even a jealous God.

Deut. 32 [21]They have moved me to jealousy with that which is not God; they have provoked me to anger with their vanities: and I will move them to jealousy with those which are not a people; I will provoke them to anger with a foolish nation.

Psa. 78 [58]For they provoked him to anger with their high places, and moved him to jealousy with their graven images.

Psa. 79 [5]How long, LORD? wilt thou be angry for ever? shall thy jealousy burn like fire?

God's Glory

EXHIBITED IN POWER, HOLINESS, MAJESTY, ETC.

Deut. 32 [3]Because I will publish the name of the LORD: ascribe ye greatness unto our God.

1 Chr. 16 [27]Glory and honour are in his presence; strength and gladness are in his place.

Psa. 92 [8]But thou, LORD, art most high for evermore.

Psa. 93 [1]The LORD reigneth, he is clothed with majesty; the LORD is clothed with strength, wherewith he hath girded himself: the world also is stablished, that it cannot be moved.

Psa. 99 [2]The LORD is great in Zion; and he is high above all the people.

Psa. 104 [1]Bless the LORD, O my soul. O LORD my God, thou art very great; thou art clothed with honour and majesty.

Isa. 12 [6]Cry out and shout, thou inhabitant of Zion: for great is the Holy One of Israel in the midst of thee.

Isa. 40 [15]Behold, the nations are as a drop of a bucket, and are counted as the small dust of the balance: behold, he taketh up the isles as a very little thing.

Matt. 19 [26]But Jesus beheld them, and said unto them, With men this is impossible; but with God all things are possible.

Mark 10 [27]And Jesus looking upon them saith, With men it is impossible, but not with God: for with God all things are possible.

Luke 1 [37]For with God nothing shall be impossible.

Luke 18 [27]And he said, The things which are impossible with men are possible with God.

EXHIBITED IN CHRIST

John 1 [14]And the Word was made flesh, and dwelt among us, (and we beheld his glory, the glory as of the only begotten of the Father,) full of grace and truth.

2 Cor. 4 [6]For God, who commanded the light to shine out of darkness, hath shined in our hearts, to give the light of the knowledge of the glory of God in the face of Jesus Christ.

Heb. 1 [2]Hath in these last days spoken unto us by his Son, whom he hath appointed heir of all things, by whom also he made the worlds; [3]Who being the brightness of his glory, and the express image of his person, and upholding all things by the word of his power, when he had by himself purged our sins, sat down on the right hand of the Majesty on high.

EXHIBITED IN HIS GOODNESS

2 Chr. 30 [18]For a multitude of the people, even many of Ephraim, and Manasseh, Issachar and Zebulun, had not cleansed themselves, yet did they eat the passover otherwise than it was written. But Hezekiah prayed for them, saying, The good LORD pardon every one [19]That prepareth his heart to seek God, the LORD God of his fathers, though he be not cleansed according to the purification of the sanctuary.

Psa. 25 [8]Good and upright is the LORD: therefore will he teach sinners in the way.

Psa. 31 [19]Oh how great is thy goodness, which thou hast laid up for them that fear thee; which thou hast wrought for them that trust in thee before the sons of men!

Psa. 33 [5]He loveth righteousness and judgment: the earth is full of the goodness of the LORD.

Psa. 68 [10]Thy congregation hath dwelt therein: thou, O God, hast prepared of thy goodness for the poor.

Psa. 119 [68]Thou art good, and doest good; teach me thy statutes.

Matt. 19 [17]And he said unto him, Why callest thou me good? there is none good but one, that is, God: but if thou wilt enter into life, keep the commandments.

Acts 14 [17]Nevertheless, he left not himself without witness, in that he did good, and gave us rain from heaven, and fruitful seasons, filling our hearts with food and gladness.

Rom. 2 [4]Or despisest thou the riches of his goodness, and forbearance, and longsuffering, not knowing that the goodness of God leadeth thee to repentance?

God's Gifts

GENERAL

Num. 14 [8]If the LORD delight in us, then he will bring us into this land, and give it us; a land which floweth with milk and honey.

Eccl. 2 [26]For God giveth to a man that is good in his sight, wisdom, and knowledge, and joy: but to the sinner he giveth travail, to gather and to heap up, that he may give to him that is good before God.

Rom. 8 [32]He that spared not his own Son, but delivered him up for us all, how shall he not with him also freely give us all things?

1 Cor. 7 [7]For I would that all men were even as I myself. But every man hath his proper gift of God, one after this manner, and another after that.

Jas. 1 [17]Every good gift, and every perfect gift is from above, and cometh down from the Father of lights, with whom is no variableness, neither shadow of turning.

SPIRITUAL

Psa. 29 [11]The LORD will give strength unto his people; the LORD will bless his people with peace.

Psa. 68 [18]Thou hast ascended on high, thou hast led captivity captive: thou hast received gifts for men; yea, for the rebellious also, that the LORD God might dwell among them.

Isa. 42 [6]I the LORD have called thee in righteousness, and will hold thine hand, and will keep thee, and give thee for a covenant of the people, for a light of the Gentiles.

Ezek. 11 [19]And I will give them one

heart, and I will put a new spirit within you; and I will take the stony heart out of their flesh, and will give them an heart of flesh.

Matt. 7 [11]If ye then, being evil, know how to give good gifts unto your children, how much more shall your Father which is in heaven give good things to them that ask him?

Matt. 11 [28]Come unto me, all ye that labour and are heavy laden, and I will give you rest.

John 3 [16]For God so loved the world, that he gave his only begotten Son: that whosoever believeth in him, should not perish, but have everlasting life.

John 4 [10]Jesus answered, and said unto her, If thou knewest the gift of God, and who it is that saith to thee, Give me to drink; thou wouldest have asked of him, and he would have given thee living water.

John 17 [22]And the glory which thou gavest me I have given them; that they may be one, even as we are one.

Acts 8 [20]But Peter said unto him, Thy money perish with thee, because thou hast thought that the gift of God may be purchased with money.

Acts 11 [18]When they heard these things, they held their peace, and glorified God, saying, Then hath God also to the Gentiles granted repentance unto life.

Rom. 5 [16]And not as it was by one that sinned, so is the gift: for the judgment was by one to condemnation: but the free gift is of many offences unto justification.
[17]For if by one man's offence death reigned by one, much more they which receive abundance of grace and of the gift of righteousness, shall reign in life by one, Jesus Christ.

Rom. 6 [23]For the wages of sin is death; but the gift of God is eternal life through Jesus Christ our Lord.

Eph. 2 [8]For by grace are ye saved through faith; and that not of yourselves: it is the gift of God: [9]Not of works, lest any man should boast.

Jas. 4 [6]But he giveth more grace, wherefore he saith, God resisteth the proud, but giveth grace unto the humble.

TEMPORAL

Lev. 26 [6]And I will give peace in the land, and ye shall lie down, and none shall make you afraid: and I will rid evil beasts out of the land, neither shall the sword go through your land.

Isa. 42 [5]Thus saith God the LORD, he that created the heavens, and stretched them out; he that spread forth the earth, and that which cometh out of it; he that giveth breath unto the people upon it, and spirit to them that walk therein.

Acts 14 [17]Nevertheless, he left not himself without witness, in that he did good, and gave us rain from heaven, and fruitful seasons, filling our hearts with food and gladness.

1 Tim. 4 [4]For every creature of God is good, and nothing to be refused, if it be received with thanksgiving: [5]For it is sanctified by the word of God, and prayer.

1 Tim. 6 [17]Charge them that are rich in this world, that they be not high-minded, nor trust in uncertain riches, but in the living God, who giveth us richly all things to enjoy.

God as Triune

Matt. 28 [19]Go ye therefore, and teach all nations, baptizing them in the name of the Father, and of the Son, and of the Holy Ghost:

Luke 1 [35]The angel answered and said unto her, The Holy Ghost shall come upon thee, and the power of the Highest shall overshadow thee: therefore also that holy thing which shall be born of thee shall be called the Son of God.

Luke 3 [22]The Holy Ghost descended in a bodily shape like a dove upon him, and a voice came from heaven, which said, Thou art my beloved Son; in thee I am well pleased.

John 3 [34]For he whom God hath sent speaketh the words of God: for God giveth not the Spirit by measure unto him. [35]The Father loveth the Son, and hath given all things into his hand.

John 14 [16]And I will pray the Father, and he shall give you another Comforter, that he may abide with you for ever; [17]Even the Spirit of truth; whom the world cannot receive, because it seeth him not, neither knoweth him: but ye know him; for he dwelleth with you, and shall be in you. [26]But the Comforter, which is the Holy Ghost, whom the Father will send in my name, he shall teach you all things, and bring all things to your remembrance, whatsoever I have said unto you.

John 15 [26]When the Comforter is come, whom I will send unto you from the Father, even the Spirit of truth, which proceedeth from the Father, he shall testify of me:

2 Cor. 13 [14]The grace of the Lord Jesus Christ, and the love of God, and the communion of the Holy Ghost, be with you all.

1 Pet. 1 [2]Elect according to the foreknowledge of God the Father, through sanctification of the Spirit, unto obedience and sprinkling of the blood of Jesus Christ:

God's Names

Gen. 14 [18]And Melchizedek king of Salem brought forth bread and wine: and he was the priest of the most high God.

Ex. 3 [14]And God said unto Moses, I AM THAT I AM: And he said, Thus shalt thou say unto the children of Israel, I AM hath sent me unto you.

Ex. 6 [3]And I appeared unto Abraham, unto Isaac, and unto Jacob by the name of God Almighty, but by my name JEHOVAH was I not known to them.

Ex. 34 [14]For thou shalt worship no other god: for the LORD, whose name is Jealous, is a jealous God.

Deut. 5 [26]For who is there of all flesh that hath heard the voice of the living God speaking out of the midst of the fire, as we have, and lived? [27]Go thou near, and hear all that the LORD our God shall say: and speak thou unto us all that the LORD our God shall speak unto thee; and we will hear it, and do it.

2 Kin. 19 [22]Whom hast thou reproached and blasphemed? and against whom hast thou exalted thy voice, and lifted up thine eyes on high? even against the Holy One of Israel.

Neh. 1 [5]And said, I beseech thee, O LORD God of heaven, the great and terrible God, that keepeth covenant and mercy for them that love him and observe his commandments.

Job 6 [10]Then should I yet have comfort; yea, I would harden myself in sorrow: let him not spare; for I have not concealed the words of the Holy One.

Psa. 50 [1]The mighty God, even the LORD, hath spoken, and called the earth from the rising of the sun unto the going down thereof.

Psa. 80 [4]O LORD God of hosts, how long wilt thou be angry against the prayer of thy people?

Psa. 81 [1]Sing aloud unto God our strength: make a joyful noise unto the God of Jacob.

Eccl. 12 [1]Remember now thy Creator in the days of thy youth, while the evil days come not, nor the years draw nigh, when thou shalt say, I have no pleasure in them.

Isa. 1 [24]Therefore saith the LORD, the LORD of hosts, the mighty One of Israel, Ah, I will ease me of mine adversaries, and avenge me of mine enemies.

Matt. 5 [16]Let your light so shine before men, that they may see your good works, and glorify your Father which is in heaven.

Rom. 9 [29]And as Esaias said before, Except the Lord of Sabaoth had left us a seed, we had been as Sodoma, and been made like unto Gomorrah.

Jas. 1 [17]Every good gift, and every perfect gift is from above, and cometh down from the Father of lights, with whom is no variableness, neither shadow of turning.

Rev. 19 [16]And he hath on his vesture and on his thigh a name written, KING OF KINGS, AND LORD OF LORDS.

False Gods

Ex. 20 [3]Thou shalt have no other gods before me.

Deut. 8 [19]And it shall be, if thou do at all forget the LORD thy God, and walk after other gods, and serve them, and worship them, I testify against you this day that ye shall surely perish.

Deut. 18 [20]But the prophet, which shall presume to speak a word in my name, which I have not commanded him to speak, or that shall speak in the name of other gods, even that prophet shall die.

GODLINESS

[god'li nes] Piety caused by knowledge and love and God, leading to complete, constant, and cheerful obedience to His commands; the summing up of genuine religion.

SCRIPTURE

1 Tim. 2 [1]I exhort therefore, that, first of all, supplications, prayers, intercessions, and giving of thanks, be made for all men; [2]For kings, and for all that are in authority; that we may lead a quiet and peaceable life in all godliness and honesty. [3]For this is good and acceptable in the sight of God our Saviour.

1 Tim. 4 [7]But refuse profane and old wives' fables, and exercise thyself rather unto godliness. [8]For bodily exercise profiteth little, but godliness is profitable unto all things, having promise of the life that now is, and of that which is to come.

1 Tim. 6 [3]If any man teach otherwise, and consent not to wholesome words, even the words of our Lord Jesus Christ, and to the doctrine which is according to godliness; [4]He is proud, knowing nothing, but doting about questions and strifes of words, whereof cometh envy, strife, railings, evil surmisings, [5]Perverse disputings of men of corrupt minds, and destitute of the truth, supposing that gain is godliness: from such withdraw thyself. [6]But godliness with contentment is great gain. [11]But thou, O man of God, flee these things; and follow after righteousness, godliness, faith, love, patience, meekness.

2 Pet. 1 [3]According as his divine power hath given unto us all things that pertain unto life and godliness, through the knowledge of him that hath called us to glory and virtue.

2 Pet. 3 [11]Seeing then that all these things shall be dissolved, what manner of persons ought ye to be in all holy conversation and godliness.

GOLGOTHA

[gol'gȯ tha] "The place of the skull", a designation for the hill outside Jerusalem on which Jesus was crucified. The two major theories concerning the origin of its name are: (1) that it was shaped like a skull, and (2) that human skulls were to be found lying about, indicating that it was a place of public execution. There is no way of being certain on this matter, neither has it been possible to discover the exact location of the crucifixion site. Another and perhaps better known name of this hill is Mount Calvary.

SCRIPTURE

Matt. 27 33And when they were come
unto a place called Golgotha, that is to
say, a place of a skull,

See Mark 15:22; Luke 23:33; John 19:17

GOLIATH

[gȯ lī'ath] A giant of Gath and the champion of the Philistine army. When the armies of Israel and Philistia were encamped against one another at Ephesdammim, this enormous individual hurled a challenge to the Israelites to send out a man to engage him in hand-to-hand combat; this individual contest was to decide the issue between the two armies. Goliath was then slain with a simple slingshot wielded by the youth David. Goliath's height was "six cubits and a span." According to various estimates, this would make him between nine and eleven feet tall.

See SLINGSHOT

SCRIPTURE

1 Sam. 17 1Now the Philistines gathered together their armies to battle, and
were gathered together at Shochoh, which
belongeth to Judah, and pitched between
Shochoh and Azekah, in Ephesdammim.
2And Saul and the men of Israel were
gathered together, and pitched by the
valley of Elah, and set the battle in array
against the Philistines. 3And the Philistines stood on a mountain on the one side,
and Israel stood on a mountain on the
other side: and there was a valley between
them.

4And there went out a champion out of
the camp of the Philistines, named Goliath, of Gath, whose height was six cubits
and a span. 5And he had a helmet of brass
upon his head, and he was armed with a
coat of mail; and the weight of the coat
was five thousand shekels of brass. 6And
he had greaves of brass upon his legs, and
a target of brass between his shoulders.
7And the staff of his spear was like a weaver's beam; and his spear's head weighed
six hundred shekels of iron: and one bearing a shield went before him. 8And he
stood and cried unto the armies of Israel,
and said unto them, Why are ye come out
to set your battle in array? am not I a Philistine, and ye servants to Saul? choose ye
a man for you, and let him come down to
me. 9If he be able to fight with me, and to
kill me, then will we be your servants: but
if I prevail against him, and kill him, then
shall ye be our servants, and serve us.
10And the Philistine said, I defy the armies
of Israel this day; give me a man, that we
may fight together. 11When Saul and all
Israel heard those words of the Philistine,
they were dismayed, and greatly afraid.

12Now David was the son of that Ephrathite of Bethlehem-judah, whose name
was Jesse; and he had eight sons: and the
man went among men for an old man in
the days of Saul.

32And David said to Saul, Let no man's
heart fail because of him; thy servant will
go and fight with this Philistine.

40And he took his staff in his hand, and
chose him five smooth stones out of the
brook, and put them in a shepherd's bag
which he had, even in a scrip; and his sling
was in his hand: and he drew near to the
Philistine. 41And the Philistine came on,
and drew near unto David; and the man
that bare the shield went before him.
42And when the Philistine looked about,
and saw David, he disdained him: for he
was but a youth, and ruddy, and of a fair
countenance. 43And the Philistine said

unto David, Am I a dog, that thou comest to me with staves? And the Philistine cursed David by his gods. 44And the Philistine said to David, Come to me, and I will give thy flesh unto the fowls of the air, and to the beasts of the field. 45Then said David to the Philistine, Thou comest to me with a sword, and with a spear, and with a shield: but I come to thee in the name of the LORD of hosts, the God of the armies of Israel, whom thou hast defied. 46This day will the LORD deliver thee into mine hand; and I will smite thee, and take thine head from thee; and I will give the carcasses of the host of the Philistines this day unto the fowls of the air, and to the wild beasts of the earth; that all the earth may know that there is a God in Israel. 47And all this assembly shall know that the LORD saveth not with sword and spear: for the battle is the LORD's and he will give you into our hands. 48And it came to pass, when the Philistine arose, and came and drew nigh to meet David, that David hasted, and ran toward the army to meet the Philistine. 49And David put his hand in his bag, and took thence a stone, and slang it, and smote the Philistine in his forehead, that the stone sunk into his forehead; and he fell upon his face to the earth. 50So David prevailed over the Philistine with a sling and with a stone, and smote the Philistine and slew him; but there was no sword in the hand of David. 51Therefore David ran and stood upon the Philistine, and took his sword, and drew it out of the sheath thereof, and slew him, and cut off his head therewith. And when the Philistines saw their champion was dead, they fled.

GOMORRAH

[gô mor'a] One of the cities destroyed by fire in the time of Abraham and Lot. It is thought to have been located in the plain south of the Dead Sea, now covered with water.

See LOT, SODOM

SCRIPTURE

Gen. 19 23The sun was risen upon the earth when Lot entered into Zoar. 24Then the LORD rained upon Sodom and upon Gomorrah brimstone and fire from the LORD out of heaven; 25And he overthrew those cities, and all the plain, and all the inhabitants of the cities, and that which grew upon the ground.

26But his wife looked back from behind him, and she became a pillar of salt.

27And Abraham gat up early in the morning to the place where he stood before the LORD: 28And he looked toward Sodom and Gomorrah, and toward all the land of the plain, and beheld, and, lo, the smoke of the country went up as the smoke of a furnace.

29And it came to pass, when God destroyed the cities of the plain, that God remembered Abraham, and sent Lot out of the midst of the overthrow, when he overthrew the cities in the which Lot dwelt.

GOSHEN

[gō'shen] The region in which the Hebrews dwelt while in Egypt, apparently also called "the land of Rameses" (*Gen. 47:11*) and "the field of Zoan" (*Psa. 78:12, 43*). According to the *Genesis* narrative, it was a region fit for flocks which was given by the Pharaoh to the descendants of Jacob as a favor to Joseph, a high official in the Egyptian government.

See JOSEPH

REFERENCE: *Gen. 45:9-11; 46:34; 47:1, 4, 6, 27; 50:8.*

GOSPEL

[gos'pel] The word "gospel" comes to us from

the old Anglo-Saxon word, "godspell", meaning "God story" or "narrative of God." It is used in the New Testament to translate the Greek word for "good tidings" or "good news." In the Bible, "gospel" never refers to a book but to the message which Jesus and his apostles preached. Before Jesus' death and resurrection, the content of this gospel was that the kingdom of God was at hand; afterward, the content was Christ himself and the gospel was referred to as "the Gospel of Jesus Christ, the Son of God" (*Mark 1:1*). Because they contain the record of the life and teachings of Christ, the four books written by Matthew, Mark, Luke, and John are commonly referred to as the Four Gospels; actually, it would be more accurate to think of them as four accounts of the one true gospel.

SCRIPTURE

Its Scope and Power

Matt. 4 [23]And Jesus went about all Galilee, teaching in their synagogues, and preaching the gospel of the kingdom, and healing all manner of sickness and all manner of disease among the people.

Matt. 24 [14]And this Gospel of the kingdom shall be preached in all the world, for a witness unto all nations, and then shall the end come.

Mark 1 [14]Now after that John was put in prison, Jesus came into Galilee, preaching the gospel of the kingdom of God, [15]And saying, The time is fulfilled, and the kingdom of God is at hand: repent ye, and believe the gospel.

Luke 2 [10]And the angel said unto them, Fear not: for, behold, I bring you good tidings of great joy, which shall be to all people. [11]For unto you is born this day in the city of David a Saviour, which is Christ the Lord.

Acts 13 [26]Men and brethren, children of the stock of Abraham, and whosoever among you feareth God, to you is the word of this salvation sent.

Acts 14 [3]Long time therefore abode they speaking boldly in the Lord, which gave testimony unto the word of his grace, and granted signs and wonders to be done by their hands.

Rom. 1 [1]Paul, a servant of Jesus Christ, called to be an apostle, separated unto the gospel of God, [2](Which he had promised afore by his prophets in the holy scriptures,) [3]Concerning his Son Jesus Christ our Lord, which was made of the seed of David according to the flesh. [9]For God is my witness, whom I serve with my spirit in the gospel of his Son, that without ceasing I make mention of you always in my prayers. [16]For I am not ashamed of the gospel of Christ: for it is the power of God unto salvation to every one that believeth; to the Jew first, and also to the Greek.

1 Cor. 1 [18]For the preaching of the cross is to them that perish foolishness; but unto us which are saved it is the power of God.

1 Cor. 2 [12]Now we have received, not the spirit of the world, but the spirit which is of God; that we might know the things that are freely given to us of God. [13]Which things also we speak, not in the words which man's wisdom teacheth, but which the Holy Ghost teacheth; comparing spiritual things with spiritual.

1 Cor. 15 [1]Moreover, brethren, I declare unto you the gospel which I preached unto you, which also ye have received, and wherein ye stand; [2]By which also ye are saved, if ye keep in memory what I preached unto you, unless ye have believed in vain.

2 Cor. 4 [3]But if our gospel be hid, it is hid to them that are lost: [4]In whom the god of this world hath blinded the minds of them which believe not, lest the light of the glorious gospel of Christ, who is the image of God, should shine unto them.

[5]For we preach not ourselves, but Christ Jesus the Lord; and ourselves your servants for Jesus' sake.

Eph. 1 [13]In whom ye also trusted, after that ye heard the word of truth, the gospel of your salvation: in whom also after that ye believed, ye were sealed with that holy Spirit of promise.

Eph. 6 [15]And your feet shod with the preparation of the gospel of peace.

Phil. 2 [16]Holding forth the word of life; that I may rejoice in the day of Christ, that I have not run in vain, neither laboured in vain.

Col. 1 [5]For the hope which is laid up for you in heaven, whereof ye heard before in the word of the truth of the gospel;
[6]Which is come unto you, as it is in all the world; and bringeth forth fruit, as it doth also in you, since the day ye heard of it, and knew the grace of God in truth.

Col. 3 [16]Let the word of Christ dwell in you richly in all wisdom; teaching and admonishing one another in psalms and hymns and spiritual songs, singing with grace in your hearts to the Lord.

1 Thess. 1 [5]For our gospel came not unto you in word only, but also in power, and in the Holy Ghost, and in much assurance; as ye know what manner of men we were among you for your sake.

1 Thess. 2 [8]So being affectionately desirous of you, we were willing to have imparted unto you, not the gospel of God only, but also our own souls, because ye were dear unto us.

Heb. 4 [2]For unto us was the gospel preached, as well as unto them: but the word preached did not profit them, not being mixed with faith in them that heard it.

1 Pet. 1 [12]Unto whom it was revealed, that not unto themselves, but unto us they did minister the things, which are now reported unto you by them that have preached the gospel unto you with the Holy Ghost sent down from heaven; which things the angels desire to look into.
[25]But the word of the Lord endureth for ever. And this is the word which by the gospel is preached unto you.

1 Pet. 4 [17]For the time is come that judgment must begin at the house of God: and if it first begin at us, what shall the end be of them that obey not the gospel of God?

To Whom Preached

Gal. 3 [8]And the scripture, foreseeing that God would justify the heathen through faith, preached before the gospel unto Abraham, saying, In thee shall all nations be blessed.

Matt. 11 [5]The blind receive their sight, and the lame walk, the lepers are cleansed, and the deaf hear, the dead are raised up, and the poor have the gospel preached to them.

Mark 13 [10]And the gospel must first be published among all nations.

Mark 16 [15]And he said unto them, Go ye into all the world, and preach the gospel to every creature.

Luke 4 [18]The Spirit of the Lord is upon me, because he hath anointed me to preach the gospel to the poor; he hath sent me to heal the broken-hearted, to preach deliverance to the captives, and recovering of sight to the blind, to set at liberty them that are bruised.

1 Cor. 1 [17]For Christ sent me not to baptize, but to preach the gospel: not with wisdom of words, lest the cross of Christ should be made of none effect.

1 Cor. 9 [16]For though I preach the gospel, I have nothing to glory of: for necessity is laid upon me; yea, woe is unto me, if I preach not the gospel!

Gal. 2 [2]And I went up by revelation,

and communicated unto them that gospel which I preach among the Gentiles, but privately to them which were of reputation, lest by any means I should run, or had run, in vain.

Rev. 14 [6]And I saw another angel fly in the midst of heaven, having the everlasting gospel to preach unto them that dwell on the earth, and to every nation, and kindred, and tongue, and people.

Admonition to Christians Concerning the Gospel

Mark 8 [35]For whosoever will save his life shall lose it; but whosoever shall lose his life for my sake and the gospel's, the same shall save it.

Rom. 15 [29]And I am sure that, when I come unto you, I shall come in the fulness of the blessing of the gospel of Christ.

Phil. 1 [27]Only let your conversation be as it becometh the gospel of Christ: that whether I come and see you, or else be absent, I may hear of your affairs, that ye stand fast in one spirit, with one mind striving together for the faith of the gospel.

Col. 1 [23]If ye continue in the faith grounded and settled, and be not moved away from the hope of the gospel, which ye have heard, and which was preached to every creature which is under heaven; whereof I Paul am made a minister.

Rejected by Jews

Acts 28 [25]And when they agreed not among themselves, they departed, after that Paul had spoken one word, Well spake the Holy Ghost by Esaias the prophet unto our fathers, [26]Saying, Go unto this people, and say, Hearing ye shall hear, and shall not understand; and seeing ye shall see, and not perceive.

Rom. 11 [27]For this is my covenant unto them, when I shall take away their sins. [28]As concerning the gospel, they are enemies for your sakes: but as touching the election, they are beloved for the fathers' sakes. [29]For the gifts and calling of God are without repentance. [30]For as ye in times past have not believed God, yet have now obtained mercy through their unbelief: [31]Even so have these also now not believed, that through your mercy they also may obtain mercy. [32]For God hath concluded them all in unbelief, that he might have mercy upon all.

GOSSIP

[gos'ip] A groundless rumor, idle chatter; also, one who gossips. The evil effects of this malicious practice are well-known, and the Bible clearly warns against it.

See Backbiting, Slander

SCRIPTURE

Lev. 19 [16]Thou shalt not go up and down as a talebearer among thy people.

Psa. 50 [20]Thou sittest and speakest against thy brother; thou slanderest thine own mother's son.

Prov. 11 [13]A talebearer revealeth secrets: but he that is of a faithful spirit concealeth the matter.

Prov. 20 [19]He that goeth about as a talebearer revealeth secrets: therefore meddle not with him that flattereth with his lips.

Ezek. 22 [9]In thee are men that carry tales to shed blood.

GRACE

[grās] In the Old Testament, grace usually means kindness or graciousness shown by a superior to an inferior; the same word is elsewhere translated "favor." In the New Testament, it is used in reference to God's redemptive love which acts to draw men to him and to preserve them in covenant relationship with him. This idea is also quite prominent in the Old Testament, but is usually translated there by "lovingkindness." The scarlet thread running throughout the Bible is the story of God's unmerited love and redemptive action on behalf of his children. The New Testament makes it clear that salvation is from first to last by grace, yet it also clearly states that men may abuse or refuse the grace which is offered.

SCRIPTURE

Grace of God and Christ

Psa. 84 11 For the LORD God is a sun and shield: the LORD will give grace and glory; no good thing will he withhold from them that walk uprightly.

Luke 2 40 And the child grew, and waxed strong in spirit, filled with wisdom, and the grace of God was upon him.

John 1 16 And of his fulness have all we received, and grace for grace. 17 For the Law was given by Moses, but grace and truth came by Jesus Christ.

Acts 20 24 But none of these things move me, neither count I my life dear unto myself, so that I might finish my course with joy, and the ministry which I have received of the Lord Jesus, to testify the Gospel of the grace of God.

Rom. 11 5 Even so then at this present time also there is a remnant according to the election of grace. 6 And if by grace, then is it no more of works: otherwise grace is no more grace. But if it be of works, then is it no more grace: otherwise work is no more work.

1 Cor. 15 10 But by the grace of God I am what I am: and his grace which was bestowed upon me, was not in vain: But I laboured more abundantly than they all, yet not I, but the grace of God which was with me.

2 Cor. 8 9 For ye know the grace of our Lord Jesus Christ, that though he was rich, yet for your sakes he became poor, that ye through his poverty might be rich.

2 Tim. 1 9 Who hath saved us, and called us with an holy calling, not according to our works, but according to his own purpose and grace, which was given us in Christ Jesus before the world began.

1 Pet. 5 5 Likewise, ye younger, submit yourselves unto the elder. Yea, all of you be subject one to another, and be clothed with humility: for God resisteth the proud, and giveth grace to the humble.

Grace and Salvation

Acts 15 11 But we believe that through the grace of the Lord Jesus Christ we shall be saved, even as they.

Rom. 3 24 Being justified freely by his grace through the redemption that is in Christ Jesus.

Rom. 4 4 Now to him that worketh, is the reward not reckoned of grace, but of debt.

Eph. 2 4 But God, who is rich in mercy, for his great love wherewith he loved us, 5 Even when we were dead in sins, hath quickened us together with Christ, (by grace ye are saved;) 6 And hath raised us up together, and made us sit together in heavenly places in Christ Jesus: 7 That in the ages to come he might shew the exceeding riches of his grace in his kindness toward us through Christ Jesus.

Grace's Effects

2 Cor. 1 12 For our rejoicing is this, the testimony of our conscience, that in simplicity and godly sincerity, not with fleshly wisdom, but by the grace of God, we have had our conversation in the world, and more abundantly to you-ward.

2 Cor. 12 9 And he said unto me, My grace is sufficient for thee: for my strength is made perfect in weakness. Most gladly therefore will I rather glory in my infirmities, that the power of Christ may rest upon me.

Tit. 2 [11]For the grace of God that bringeth salvation hath appeared to all men, [12]Teaching us that, denying ungodliness and worldly lusts, we should live soberly, righteously, and godly, in this present world.

1 Pet. 4 [10]As every man hath received the gift, even so minister the same one to another, as good stewards of the manifold grace of God.

Abusing Grace

Rom. 6 [1]What shall we say then? Shall we continue in sin, that grace may abound? [2]God forbid. How shall we, that are dead to sin, live any longer therein?

Rom. 6 [14]For sin shall not have dominion over you: for ye are not under the law, but under grace. [15]What then? shall we sin, because we are not under the law, but under grace? God forbid.

Jude 1 [4]For there are certain men crept in unawares, who were before of old ordained to this condemnation, ungodly men, turning the grace of our God into lasciviousness, and denying the only Lord God, and our Lord Jesus Christ.

Gal. 5 [4]Christ is become of no effect unto you, whosoever of you are justified by the law; ye are fallen from grace.

Exhortations to Grace

Heb. 12 [14]Follow peace with all men, and holiness, without which no man shall see the Lord: [15]Looking diligently lest any man fail of the grace of God; lest any root of bitterness springing up trouble you, and thereby many be defiled. [28]Wherefore we receiving a kingdom which cannot be moved, let us have grace, whereby we may serve God acceptably with reverence and godly fear.

2 Pet. 3 [10]But the God of all grace, who hath called us unto his eternal glory by Christ Jesus, after that ye have suffered a while, make you perfect, stablish, strengthen, settle you.

HABAKKUK

[ha bak′uk, hab′a kuk] A prophet of Judah. Little can be said with any degree of certainty concerning the prophet Habakkuk. He was probably a contemporary of Jeremiah, prophesying near the end of the seventh century BC. The prophecies of Habakkuk take the form of an harangue against God and the answers which God gives to his complaints. The theme of his book is "the just shall live by faith."

See PROPHETS

REFERENCE: The Book of *Habakkuk*.

HADES

[hā′dēs] The Greek term referring to the unseen state of the dead; the underworld; the region of shadows, silence, and forgetting in which the dead reside. In Biblical thought, Hades is essentially identical with Sheol, the Hebrew term used in the Old Testament to denote this region.

See HELL, GEHENNA, PARADISE, SHEOL

SCRIPTURE

Gen. 42 [38]And he said, My son shall not go down with you; for his brother is dead, and he is left alone: if mischief befall him by the way in the which ye go, then shall ye bring down my gray hairs with sorrow to the grave.

Deut. 32 [22]For a fire is kindled in mine anger, and shall burn unto the lowest hell.

2 Sam. 22 [6]The sorrows of hell compassed me about; the snares of death prevented me.

Psa. 49 [14]Like sheep they are laid in the grave; death shall feed on them; and the upright shall have dominion over them in the morning; and their beauty shall consume in the grave from their dwelling.

Isa. 14 11Thy pomp is brought down to the grave, and the noise of thy viols.

Matt. 11 23And thou, Capernaum, which art exalted unto heaven, shalt be brought down to hell.

Acts 2 31He, seeing this before, spake of the resurrection of Christ, that his soul was not left in hell, neither his flesh did see corruption.

1 Cor. 15 55O death, where is thy sting? O grave, where is thy victory?

Rev. 20 13And the sea gave up the dead which were in it; and death and hell delivered up the dead which were in them: and they were judged every man according to their works. 14And death and hell were cast into the lake of fire. This is the second death.

HAGAR

[hā′gar] The Egyptian handmaid of Sarai, the wife of Abram. Despairing at the possibility of bearing a child, Sarai gave Hagar to Abram as a concubine; in such an arrangement, all children born to Hagar would be reckoned as Sarai's. When she became pregnant, Hagar acted contemptuously toward her mistress; Sarai reacted harshly at this treatment and Hagar fled from the camp. She was met by an angel of the LORD and instructed to return, receiving the promise that the son she was to bear would be the ancestor of a great multitude. After her return, the child Ishmael was born. At a party celebrating the weaning of Isaac, the true child of Sarah and Abraham (their former names having been changed), Sarah persuaded Abraham to send Hagar and her son away. He complied and the two set out with a loaf of bread and a skin of water. Near death, she prepared to abandon her son in the wilderness, but was again confronted by an angel of the LORD who enabled her to discover a well of water. The narrative states that the child grew up, becoming an expert with the bow, that he lived in the wilderness of Paran, and that Hagar secured for him a wife from the land of Egypt.

See ISHMAEL, SARAH, ABRAHAM

SCRIPTURE

Gen. 16 1Now Sarai, Abram's wife, bare him no children: and she had a handmaid, an Egyptian, whose name was Hagar. 2And Sarai said unto Abram, Behold now, the LORD hath restrained me from bearing: I pray thee, go in unto my maid; it may be that I may obtain children by her. And Abram hearkened to the voice of Sarai. 3And Sarai, Abram's wife, took Hagar her maid the Egyptian, after Abram had dwelt ten years in the land of Canaan, and gave her to her husband Abram to be his wife.

4And he went in unto Hagar, and she conceived: and when she saw that she had conceived, her mistress was despised in her eyes. 5And Sarai said unto Abram, My wrong be upon thee: I have given my maid into thy bosom; and when she saw that she had conceived, I was despised in her eyes: the LORD judge between me and thee. 6But Abram said unto Sarai, Behold, thy maid is in thy hand; do to her as it pleaseth thee. And when Sarai dealt hardly with her, she fled from her face.

7And the angel of the LORD found her by a fountain of water in the wilderness, by the fountain in the way to Shur. 8And he said, Hagar, Sarai's maid, whence camest thou? and whither wilt thou go? And she said, I flee from the face of my mistress Sarai. 9And the angel of the LORD said unto her, Return to thy mistress, and submit thyself under her hands. 10And the angel of the LORD said unto her, I will multiply thy seed exceedingly, that it shall not be numbered for multitude. 11And the angel of the LORD said unto her, Behold, thou art with child, and shalt bear a son, and shalt call his name Ishmael; because the LORD hath heard thy affliction. 12And he will be a wild man; his hand will be against every man, and every man's hand against him: and he shall dwell in the presence of all his brethren. [13]And she called the name of the LORD that spake unto her, Thou God seest me: for she said, Have I also here looked after him that seeth me? [14]Wherefore the well was called Beerlahairoi; behold, it is between Kadesh and Bered.

[15]And Hagar bare Abram a son: and Abram called his son's name, which Hagar bare, Ishmael. [16]And Abram was fourscore and six years old, when Hagar bare Ishmael to Abram.

Gen. 21 [9]And Sarah saw the son of Hagar the Egyptian, which she had borne unto Abraham, mocking. [10]Wherefore she said unto Abraham, Cast out this bondwoman and her son: for the son of this bondwoman shall not be heir with my son, even with Isaac.

[14]And Abraham rose up early in the morning, and took bread, and a bottle of water, and gave it unto Hagar, putting it on her shoulder, and the child, and sent her away: and she departed, and wandered in the wilderness of Beersheba. [15]And the water was spent in the bottle, and she cast the child under one of the shrubs. [16]And she went, and sat her down over against him a good way off, as it were a bowshot: for she said, Let me not see the death of the child. And she sat over against him, and lifted up her voice, and wept. [17]And God heard the voice of the lad; and the angel of God called to Hagar out of heaven, and said unto her, What aileth thee, Hagar? fear not; for God hath heard the voice of the lad where he is.

HAGGAI

[hag'a ī] A prophet of the early post-exilic period. Haggai was probably born in Babylon during the captivity. He was the first prophet after the captivity and was mentioned by Ezra as having been a co-worker with Zechariah in encouraging the people to complete the building of the second temple (*Ezra 6:14*). Although it cannot be determined what span the life of Haggai covered, the prophecies contained in his book were delivered in a four-month period in 520 BC, "the second year of Darius the King" (*Hag. 1:1*).

In 536 BC, the first group of exiles returned to Judah by permission of Cyrus. They were led by Zerubbabel the governor and Jeshua the high priest. Shortly after their return, they began the task of rebuilding the temple, the foundation stone being laid in the second month of the second year after the return (*Ezra 3:8-10*). Opposition to the building program arose from the half-caste Samaritans, descendants of the foreign colonists who were introduced into Samaria in 722 BC (*2 Kin. 17:24-41*), and the work was brought to a halt. A feeling of indifference had arisen; at the time of Haggai's ministry, the people had built "ceiled houses" for themselves, but they had allowed the LORD's temple to go unfinished for sixteen years. The purpose of Haggai's preaching was to renew interest in the rebuilding of the temple. Through his efforts the work was picked up again and was finally brought to completion.

See TEMPLE, ZECHARIAH

REFERENCE: The Books of *Haggai*, *Ezra*, and *Zechariah*.

HALLELUJAH

[hal e lo͞o'ya] A Hebrew word meaning "praise ye the Lord." It is found in a number of the *Psalms*, notably *104-6, 111-13, 146-150*. In the New Testament, it appears in the song of the heavenly host of *Rev. 19:1-9*.

HAM

[hăm] The youngest son of Noah, regarded as the progenitor of the western and southwestern nations which were known to the Hebrews, including Ethiopia, Egypt, and Canaan. As a result of Ham's disrespect for his father, his descendants were cursed by Noah to the effect that they would be slaves and servants of the descendants of Shem and Japheth, Ham's two brothers.

SCRIPTURE

The Sons of Noah

Gen. 6 [10]And Noah begat three sons, Shem, Ham, and Japheth.

Ham's Disrespect toward His Father

Gen. 9 [20]And Noah began to be a husbandman, and he planted a vineyard: [21]And he drank of the wine, and was drunken; and he was uncovered within his tent. [22]And Ham, the father of Canaan, saw the nakedness of his father, and told his two brethren without. [23]And Shem and Japheth took a garment, and laid it upon both their shoulders, and went backward, and covered the nakedness of their father; and their faces were backward, and they saw not their father's nakedness.

Noah's Curse on Ham

Gen. 9 [24]And Noah awoke from his wine, and knew what his younger son had done unto him. [25]And he said, Cursed be Canaan; a servant of servants shall he be unto his brethren. [26]And he said, Blessed be the LORD God of Shem; and Canaan shall be his servant. [27]God shall enlarge Japheth, and he shall dwell in the tents of Shem; and Canaan shall be his servant.

Descendants of Ham

See Gen. 10:6-20

HAMAN

[hā'man] The chief minister or vizier under Ahasuerus king of Persia. (*See* AHASUERUS) Haman was a man of such vanity that when Mordecai refused to pay homage to him, he sought vengeance on the whole Jewish nation and persuaded the king to issue a decree calling for the extermination of all Jews in the empire on a certain day. Through the efforts of Esther on the Jews' behalf, Haman's plot was thwarted and he was hanged on the gallows which he had erected for Mordecai.

See ESTHER, MORDECAI, PURIM

SCRIPTURE

A Vain Ruler

Esth. 3 [1]After these things did king Ahasuerus promote Haman the son of Hammedatha the Agagite, and advanced him, and set his seat above all the princes that were with him. [2]And all the king's servants, that were in the king's gate, bowed, and reverence Haman: for the king had so commanded concerning him. But Mordecai bowed not, nor did him reverence. [3]Then the king's servants, which were in the king's gate, said unto Mordecai, Why transgressest thou the king's commandment? [4]Now it came to pass, when they spake daily unto him, and he hearkened not unto them, that they told Haman, to see whether Mordecai's matters would stand: for he had told them that he was a Jew. [5]And when Haman saw that Mordecai bowed not, nor did him reverence, then was Haman full of wrath.

Esth. 5 [12]Haman said moreover, Yea, Esther the queen did let no man come in with the king unto the banquet that she had prepared but myself; and tomorrow am I invited unto her also with the king. [13]Yet all this availeth me nothing, so long as I see Mordecai the Jew sitting at the king's gate.

Plots against the Jews

Esth. 3 [6]And he thought scorn to lay hands on Mordecai alone; for they had shewed him the people of Mordecai: wherefore Haman sought to destroy all the Jews that were throughout the whole kingdom of Ahasuerus, even the people of Mordecai.

[7]In the first month, that is, the month Nisan, in the twelfth year of king Ahasuerus, they cast Pur, that is, the lot, before Haman from day to day, and from month to month, to the twelfth month, that is, the month Adar.

[8]And Haman said unto king Ahasuerus, There is a certain people scattered abroad and dispersed among the people in all the provinces of thy kingdom; and their laws are diverse from all people; neither keep they the king's laws: therefore it is not for the king's profit to suffer them. [9]If it please the king, let it be written that they may be destroyed: . . . .

Plots to Have Mordecai Hanged

Esth. 5 [14]Then said Zeresh his wife and all his friends unto him, Let a gallows be made of fifty cubits high, and tomorrow speak thou unto the king that Mordecai may be hanged thereon: then go thou in merrily with the king unto the banquet. And the thing pleased Haman; and he caused the gallows to be made.

Forced to Honor Mordecai

Esth. 6 [11]Then took Haman the apparel and the horse, and arrayed Mordecai, and brought him on horseback through the street of the city, and proclaimed before him, Thus shall it be done unto the man whom the king delighteth to honour.

Esther Reveals Haman's Plot

Esth. 7 [3]Then Esther the queen answered and said, If I have found favour in thy sight, O king, and if it please the king, let my life be given me at my petition, and my people at my request: [4]For we are sold, I and my people, to be destroyed, to be slain, and to perish. But if we had been sold for bondmen and bondwomen, I had held my tongue, although the enemy could not countervail the king's damage.

[5]Then the king Ahasuerus answered and said unto Esther the queen, Who is he, and where is he, that durst presume in his heart to do so? [6]And Esther said, The adversary and enemy is this wicked Haman. Then Haman was afraid before the king and the queen.

Execution of Haman

Esth. 7 [10]So they hanged Haman on the gallows that he had prepared for Mordecai. Then was the king's wrath pacified.

HANANIAH

[han a nī′a] A false prophet of Gibeon. During the reign of Zedekiah king of Judah, Jeremiah wore a wooden yoke, symbolizing the yoke of bondage to Babylon. Hananiah predicted that the yoke would be broken within two years. He was reminded by Jeremiah that, unfortunately, those prophets who had foretold evil for the Israelites were correct more often than those who prophesied good. Hananiah then tore the yoke from Jeremiah's shoulders and broke it, stating that the LORD had informed him that the yoke of Nebuchadnezzar would be broken in the same way. Jeremiah retired for the present, but soon sent word to Hananiah that the wooden yoke would be replaced by an iron yoke of servitude which could not be broken. He also informed Hananiah that his death would fall within the year, a prophecy which is said to have been fulfilled.

See JEREMIAH

SCRIPTURE

Jer. 28 [5]Then the prophet Jeremiah said unto the prophet Hananiah in the presence of the priests, and in the presence of all the people that stood in the house of the LORD,

[10]Then Hananiah the prophet took the yoke from off the prophet Jeremiah's neck,

and brake it. 11 And Hananiah spake in the presence of all the people, saying, Thus saith the LORD; Even so will I break the yoke of Nebuchadnezzar king of Babylon from the neck of all nations within the space of two full years. And the prophet Jeremiah went his way.

12 Then the word of the LORD came unto Jeremiah the prophet, after that Hananiah the prophet had broken the yoke from off the neck of the prophet Jeremiah, saying, 13 Go and tell Hananiah, saying, Thus saith the LORD; Thou hast broken the yokes of wood; but thou shalt make for them yokes of iron. 14 For thus saith the LORD of hosts, the God of Israel: I have put a yoke of iron upon the neck of all these nations, that they may serve Nebuchadnezzar king of Babylon; and they shall serve him: and I have given him the beasts of the field also.

15 Then said the prophet Jeremiah unto Hananiah the prophet, Hear now, Hananiah; The LORD hath not sent thee; but thou makest this people to trust in a lie. 16 Therefore thus saith the LORD; Behold, I will cast thee from off the face of the earth: this year thou shalt die, because thou hast taught rebellion against the LORD. 17 So Hananiah the prophet died the same year in the seventh month.

HAND, HANDS

[hand] The hand figures to a considerable extent in the Bible, especially in idiomatic expressions and symbolic actions. It is often referred to as an indication or symbol of the power and authority of both God and men. The laying-on of hands is shown by the Scripture to have been in use as a means of setting apart men to particular offices or ministries. A ceremonial washing of the hands was an ancient declaration of innocence, especially of blood-guiltiness. The right hand was considered to be more honorable than the left; therefore, the position of honor was at the right hand. Likewise, it was the right hand which was given in confirmation of a contract or as an attestation of fellowship.

SCRIPTURE

The Hand of God—A Blessing

2 Chr. 30 12 Also in Judah the hand of God was to give them one heart to do the commandment of the king and of the princes, by the word of the LORD.

Ezra 7 9 For upon the first day of the first month began he to go up from Babylon, and on the first day of the fifth month came he to Jerusalem, according to the good hand of his God upon him.

Neh. 2 18 Then I told them of the hand of my God which was good upon me; as also the king's words that he had spoken unto me. And they said, Let us rise up and build. So they strengthened their hands for this good work.

The Hand of God—Chastisement

Deut. 2 15 For indeed the hand of the LORD was against them, to destroy them from among the host, until they were consumed.

Ruth 1 13 Would ye tarry for them till they were grown? would ye stay for them from having husbands? nay, my daughters; for it grieveth me much for your sakes, that the hand of the LORD is gone out against me.

Job 2 10 But he said unto her, Thou speakest as one of the foolish women speaketh. What! shall we receive good at the hand of God, and shall we not receive evil? In all this did not Job sin with his lips.

Job 19 21 Have pity upon me, have pity upon me, O ye my friends; for the hand of God hath touched me.

1 Pet. 5 [6]Humble yourselves therefore under the mighty hand of God, that he may exalt you in due time.

The Hand of Man—Chastisement

Judg. 1 [35]But the Amorites would dwell in mount Heres in Aijalon, and in Shaalbim: yet the hand of the house of Joseph prevailed, so that they became tributaries.

1 Sam. 22 [17]And the king said unto the footmen that stood about him, Turn, and slay the priests of the LORD; because their hand also is with David, and because they knew when we fled, and did not show it to me. But the servants of the king would not put forth their hand to fall upon the priests of the LORD.

1 Sam. 23 [16]And Jonathan Saul's son arose, and went to David into the wood, and strengthened his hand in God.

Laying-on of Hands

Num. 8 [10]And thou shalt bring the Levites before the LORD: and the children of Israel shall put their hands upon the Levites: [11]And Aaron shall offer the Levites before the LORD for an offering of the children of Israel, that they may execute the service of the LORD.

Num. 27 [18]And the Lord said unto Moses, Take thee Joshua the son of Nun, a man in whom is the spirit, and lay thine hand upon him; [19]And set him before Eleazar the priest, and before all the congregation: and give him a charge in their sight. [20]And thou shalt put some of thine honour upon him, that all the congregation of the children of Israel may be obedient.

Acts 6 [5]And the saying pleased the whole multitude: and they chose Stephen, a man full of faith and of the Holy Ghost, and Philip, and Prochorus, and Nicanor, and Timon, and Parmenas, and Nicolas a proselyte of Antioch: [6]Whom they set before the apostles: and when they had prayed, they laid their hands on them.

1 Tim. 4 [14]Neglect not the gift that is in thee, which was given thee by prophecy, with the laying on of the hands of the Presbytery.

2 Tim. 1 [6]Wherefore I put thee in remembrance that thou stir up the gift of God, which is in thee by the putting on of my hands.

Washing of Hands

Deut. 21 [6]And all the elders of that city that are next unto the slain man, shall wash their hands over the heifer that is beheaded in the valley: [7]And they shall answer and say, Our hands have not shed this blood, neither have our eyes seen it.

Psa. 26 [6]I will wash mine hands in innocency: so will I compass thine altar, O LORD.

Matt. 27 [24]When Pilate saw that he could prevail nothing, but that rather a tumult was made, he took water, and washed his hands before the multitude, saying, I am innocent of the blood of this just person: see ye to it.

The Right Hand

Eccl. 10 [2]A wise man's heart is at his right hand; but a fool's heart at his left.

Matt. 25 [33]And he shall set the sheep on his right hand, but the goats on the left.

Gal. 2 [9]And when James, Cephas, and John, who seemed to be pillars, perceived the grace that was given unto me, they gave to me and Barnabas the right hands of fellowship; that we should go unto the heathen, and they unto the circumcision.

Hands Lifted up in Prayer

Psa. 28 [2]Hear the voice of my supplications, when I cry unto thee, when I lift up my hands toward thy holy oracle.

Psa. 63 [4]Thus will I bless thee while I live: I will lift up my hands in thy name.

Psa. 141 [2]Let my prayer be set forth before thee as incense; and the lifting up of my hands as the evening sacrifice.

Psa. 143 [6]I stretch forth my hands unto thee: my soul thirsteth after thee, as a thirsty land. Selah.

1 Tim. 2 [8]I will therefore that men pray every where, lifting up holy hands without wrath and doubting.

HANNAH

[han'a] The wife of Elkanah and mother of Samuel. Before the birth of Samuel, Hannah had been barren for many years, a fact which was impressed on her at the yearly sacrifices by Elkanah's other wife, Peninnah, who had borne several children. Overhearing her fervent prayer for a son Eli, the high priest at the central sanctuary at Shiloh, assured Hannah that her desire would be fulfilled. When Samuel was born and weaned, Hannah presented the child to Eli to be trained in the service of the LORD. The narrative states that she visited her son yearly, bringing him a little coat which she had made. After the birth of Samuel, Hannah also bore other children.

See SAMUEL

SCRIPTURE

1 Sam. 1 [4]And when the time was that Elkanah offered, he gave to Peninnah his wife, and to all her sons and her daughters, portions: [5]But unto Hannah he gave a worthy portion; for he loved Hannah: but the LORD had shut up her womb. [6]And her adversary also provoked her sore, for to make her fret, because the LORD had shut up her womb. [7]And as he did so year by year, when she went up to the house of the LORD, so she provoked her; therefore she wept, and did not eat. [8]Then said Elkanah her husband to her, Hannah, why weepest thou? and why eatest thou not? and why is thy heart grieved? am not I better to thee than ten sons?

[9]So Hannah rose up after they had eaten in Shiloh, and after they had drunk. Now Eli the priest sat upon a seat by a post of the temple of the LORD. [10]And she was in bitterness of soul, and prayed unto the LORD, and wept sore. [11]And she vowed a vow, and said, O LORD of hosts, if thou wilt indeed look on the affliction of thine handmaid, and remember me, and not forget thine handmaid, but wilt give unto thine handmaid a man child, then I will give him unto the LORD all the days of his life, and there shall no razor come upon his head. [12]And it came to pass, as she continued praying before the LORD, that Eli marked her mouth. [13]Now Hannah, she spake in her heart; only her lips moved, but her voice was not heard: therefore Eli thought she had been drunken. [14]And Eli said unto her, How long wilt thou be drunken? put away thy wine from thee. [15]And Hannah answered and said, No, my lord, I am a woman of a sorrowful spirit: I have drunk neither wine nor strong drink, but have poured out my soul before the LORD. [16]Count not thine handmaid for a daughter of Belial: for out of the abundance of my complaint and grief have I spoken hitherto. [17]Then Eli answered and said, Go in peace: and the God of Israel grant thee thy petition that thou hast asked of him. [18]And she said, Let thine handmaid find grace in thy sight. So the woman went her way, and did eat, and her countenance was no more sad.

[19]And they rose up in the morning early, and worshipped before the LORD, and returned, and came to their house to Ramah: and Elkanah knew Hannah his wife; and the LORD remembered her. [20]Wherefore it came to pass, when the time was come about after Hannah had conceived,

that she bare a son, and called his name Samuel, saying, Because I have asked him of the LORD.

1 Sam. 2 [18]But Samuel ministered before the LORD, being a child, girded with a linen ephod. [19]Moreover his mother made him a little coat, and brought it to him from year to year, when she came up with her husband to offer the yearly sacrifice.

[20]And Eli blessed Elkanah and his wife, and said, The LORD give thee seed of this woman for the loan which is lent to the LORD. And they went unto their own home. [21]And the LORD visited Hannah, so that she conceived, and bare three sons and two daughters. And the child Samuel grew before the LORD.

HAPPINESS

[hap′i nes] A state of well-being and pleasurable satisfaction; bliss; blessedness. The Bible frequently reminds the child of God of his many reasons for happiness.

See JOY, BEATITUDE

SCRIPTURE

Deut. 33 [29]Happy art thou, O Israel: who is like unto thee, O people saved by the LORD, the shield of thy help, and who is the sword of thy excellency! and thine enemies shall be found liars unto thee; and thou shalt tread upon their high places.

Job 5 [17]Behold, happy is the man whom God correcteth: therefore despise not thou the chastening of the Almighty.

Psa. 40 [8]I delight to do thy will, O my God: yea, thy law is within my heart.

Psa. 144 [15]Happy is that people, that is in such a case: yea, happy is that people, whose God is the LORD.

Psa. 146 [5]Happy is he that hath the God of Jacob for his help, whose hope is in the LORD his God:

Prov. 3 [13]Happy is the man that findeth wisdom, and the man that getteth understanding:

Prov. 16 [20]Whoso trusteth in the LORD, happy is he.

Prov. 29 [18]He that keepeth the law, happy is he.

Rom. 5 [2]By whom also we have access by faith into this grace wherein we stand, and rejoice in hope of the glory of God.

Phil. 4 [7]And the peace of God, which passeth all understanding, shall keep your hearts and minds through Christ Jesus.

HARAN

[hā′ran] 1. The third son of Terah, and therefore a brother of Abraham and Nahor, and the father of Lot (*Gen. 11:26-31*).

2. The place where Terah settled after emigrating from Ur of the Chaldees, and the area in which the descendants of his brother Nahor established themselves. It was located southeast of Edessa, on the river Belias, where the trade routes from Damascus joined that from Nineveh to Carchemish. It was the land of Haran to which Abraham's servant came to seek a wife for Isaac (*Gen. 24:10ff*) and in which Jacob served for his wives Leah and Rachel (*Gen. 29*). In later Biblical history, Haran is mentioned by the Rabshakeh as one of the cities which was destroyed by the king of Assyria (*2 Kin. 19:12*). In *Acts 7:2, 4*, it is referred to under the name Charran.

HARLOT (Harlotry)

[här′lot, här′lot ri] An unchaste woman; one who engages in sexual intercourse or other promiscuous lewdness for hire; a prostitute or whore. As a result of sexual and social conditions which are universal, the harlot has found her place among all the nations of the world. Several of the heathen religions which appeared in Israel during the period of the monarchy were devoted to the worship of the reproductive forces of nature. Cults of male and female prostitutes figured prominently in their worship; the temples of these pagan deities were little more than brothels, operated in the name of religion. A similar situation existed in Greece and Asia Minor during the early years of the Christian Church.

Harlotry is often used in a figurative sense to refer to Israel's unfaithfulness to the covenant with God. The classic example of this usage is found in the book of *Hosea.*

SCRIPTURE

Lev. 19 29Do not prostitute thy daughter, to cause her to be a whore; lest the land fall to whoredom, and the land become full of wickedness.

Lev. 21 9And the daughter of any priest, if she profane herself by playing the whore, she profaneth her father: she shall be burnt with fire.

Deut. 23 17There shall be no whore of the daughters of Israel, nor a sodomite of the sons of Israel. 18Thou shalt not bring the hire of a whore, or the price of a dog, into the house of the LORD thy God for any vow: for even both these are abomination unto the LORD thy God.

Isa. 23 15And it shall come to pass in that day, that Tyre shall be forgotten seventy years, according to the days of one king: after the end of seventy years shall Tyre sing as an harlot.

Hos. 3 3And I said unto her, Thou shalt abide for me many days; thou shalt not play the harlot, and thou shalt not be for another man: so will I also be for thee.

HATRED

[hā'tred] Strong aversion, ill will, intense dislike; an opposite of love. The term is used in the Bible of hatred of men toward one another, hatred of the righteous by the ungodly, hatred of ungodliness by the righteous, and hatred of evil by God.

SCRIPTURE

Hatred of Men for One Another

Ex. 23 5If thou see the ass of him that hateth thee lying under his burden, and wouldest forbear to help him, thou shalt surely help with him.

Lev. 19 17Thou shalt not hate thy brother in thine heart: thou shalt in any wise rebuke thy neighbour, and not suffer sin upon him.

Prov. 10 12Hatred stirreth up strifes: but love covereth all sins. 18He that hideth hatred with lying lips, and he that uttereth a slander, is a fool.

Prov. 15 17Better is a dinner of herbs where love is, than a stalled ox and hatred therewith.

Prov. 26 24He that hateth dissembleth with his lips, and layeth up deceit within him; 25When he speaketh fair, believe him not; for there are seven abominations in his heart. 26Whose hatred is covered by deceit, his wickedness shall be showed before the whole congregation.

Matt. 5 43Ye have heard that it hath been said, Thou shalt love thy neighbour, and hate thine enemy. 44But I say unto you, Love your enemies, bless them that curse you, do good to them that hate you, and pray for them which despitefully use you, and persecute you.

Gal. 5 20Idolatry, witchcraft, hatred, variance, emulations, wrath, strife, seditions, heresies, 21Envyings, murders, drunkenness, revellings, and such like: of the which I tell you before, as I have also told you in time past, that they which do such things shall not inherit the kingdom of God.

Tit. 3 3For we ourselves also were sometimes foolish, disobedient, deceived, serving divers lusts and pleasures, living in malice and envy, hateful, and hating one another.

1 John 2 9He that saith he is in the light; and hateth his brother, is in darkness even until now.

1 John 3 [15]Whosoever hateth his brother is a murderer: and ye know that no murderer hath eternal life abiding in him.

Hatred of Righteous by the Ungodly

Psa. 34 [21]For our heart shall rejoice in him, because we have trusted in his holy name.

Matt. 10 [22]And ye shall be hated of all men for my name's sake: but he that endureth to the end shall be saved.

John 15 [18]If the world hate you, ye know that it hated me before it hated you.
[19]If ye were of the world, the world would love his own; but because ye are not of the world, but I have chosen you out of the world, therefore the world hateth you.
[23]He that hateth me hateth my Father also.

John 17 [14]I have given them thy word; and the world hath hated them, because they are not of the world, even as I am not of the world.

Hatred of Ungodliness by the Righteous

Psa. 97 [10]Ye that love the LORD, hate evil: he preserveth the souls of his saints; he delivereth them out of the hand of the wicked.

Psa. 101 [3]I will set no wicked thing before mine eyes: I hate the work of them that turn aside; it shall not cleave to me.

Psa. 119 [104]Through thy precepts I get understanding: therefore I hate every false way.

Psa. 139 [21]Do not I hate them, O LORD, that hate thee? and am not I grieved with those that rise up against thee? [22]I hate them with perfect hatred: I count them mine enemies.

Hatred of Evil by God

Psa. 5 [5]The foolish shall not stand in thy sight: thou hatest all workers of iniquity.

Psa. 45 [7]Thou lovest righteousness, and hatest wickedness: therefore God, thy God, hath anointed thee with the oil of gladness above thy fellows.

Mal. 2 [16]For the LORD, the God of Israel, saith that he hateth putting away: for one covereth violence with his garment, saith the LORD of hosts: therefore take heed to your spirit, that ye deal not treacherously.

HAUGHTINESS

[hô′ti nes] Disdainful and contemptuous pride; arrogance due to excessive pride. The Bible views haughtiness as unrighteous and unbecoming to a child of God.

SCRIPTURE

2 Sam. 22 [28]And the afflicted people thou wilt save: but thine eyes are upon the haughty, that thou mayest bring them down.

Prov. 16 [18]Pride goeth before destruction, and an haughty spirit before a fall.

Isa. 2 [11]The lofty looks of man shall be humbled, and the haughtiness of men shall be bowed down, and the LORD alone shall be exalted in that day.

Isa. 13 [11]And I will punish the world for their evil, and the wicked for their iniquity; and I will cause the arrogancy of the proud to cease, and will lay low the haughtiness of the terrible.

HAZAEL

[ha zā′el, hā′za el, haz′a el] King of Syria from 842-806 BC. As a ranking officer in the service of Ben-hadad I, Hazael was sent to the prophet Elisha to learn if his sovereign would recover from a current illness. Elisha told his incredulous listener that the illness would not prove fatal, but that he, Hazael, would assassinate Ben-hadad and become the perpetrator of terrible cruelties upon the people of Israel: "their strongholds wilt thou set on fire, and their young men wilt thou slay with the sword, and wilt dash their children, and rip up their women with child" (*2 Kin. 8:12*). Despite Hazael's protests, *2 Kin. 8:15* tells us that "it came to pass on the morrow, that he took a thick cloth, and dipped it in water, and spread it on his face, so that he died: and Hazael reigned in his stead."

Shalmaneser III of Assyria, who had been checked by the Syrian-led coalition at Qarqar in 853 BC (*see* BEN-HADAD I), had begun to move again in the last years of Ben-hadad's reign. He conducted several campaigns against the Syrian forces, the most serious of which occurred in 841, a short time after Hazael came to power. Shalmaneser attacked and was victorious; he was, however, unable to force Hazael to surrender Damascus. In the years immediately following, the Assyrians were occupied with campaigns on other fronts and rebellion at home, leaving Hazael free to menace Israel. At Ramoth-Gilead, he engaged the combined forces of Joram king of Israel and Ahaziah king of Judah. The outcome of the battle is uncertain, but Joram received wounds which forced him to retire to Jezreel, leaving the army in command of one Jehu. Spurred on by Elisha, Jehu siezed the throne of Israel in a fantastic revolt that saw the death of Joram, Ahaziah, Jezebel, virtually all of the descendants of Omri, and hundreds of worshippers of Baal. (*See* JEHU) Jehu's brutal extirpation of the royal family cost him the support of Judah and Phoenicia and left him powerless to withstand the might of Hazael. The Syrian easily took the whole of the territory east of the Jordan and by the time of Jehu's successor Jehoahaz (814-798 BC), Israel had been reduced to a state of pitiful helplessness, having for an army "but fifty horsemen, and ten chariots, and ten thousand footmen: for the king of Syria had destroyed them, and had made them like the dust by threshing" (*2 Kin. 13:7*). Judah was spared from widespread destruction, but only at the cost of a great tribute payment. Hazael died in 806 BC and was succeeded by his son, Ben-hadad II.

See BEN-HADAD

SCRIPTURE

His Reign Foretold by Elisha

2 Kin. 8 8And the king said unto Hazael,
Take a present in thine hand, and go, meet
the man of God, and inquire of the LORD
by him, saying, Shall I recover of this disease? 9So Hazael went to meet him, and
took a present with him, even of every
good thing of Damascus, forty camels' burden, and came and stood before him, and
said, Thy son Ben-hadad king of Syria
hath sent me to thee, saying, Shall I recover of this disease? 10And Elisha said
unto him, Go, say unto him, Thou mayest
certainly recover: howbeit the LORD hath
shewed me that he shall surely die. 11And
he settled his countenance steadfastly, until he was ashamed: and the man of God
wept. 12And Hazael said, Why weepeth
my lord? And he answered, Because I
know the evil that thou wilt do unto the
children of Israel: their strong holds wilt
thou set on fire, and their young men wilt
thou slay with the sword, and wilt dash
their children, and rip up their women
with child. 13And Hazael said, But what,
is thy servant a dog, that he should do this
great thing? And Elisha answered, The
LORD hath shewed me that thou shalt be
king over Syria. 14So he departed from Elisha, and came to his master; who said to
him, What said Elisha to thee? And he answered, He told me that thou shouldest
surely recover. 15And it came to pass on
the morrow, that he took a thick cloth, and
dipped it in water, and spread it on his
face, so that he died: and Hazael reigned
in his stead.

Defeats Joram King of Israel

2 Kin. 9 14. . . (Now Joram had kept
Ramoth-gilead, he and all Israel, because
of Hazael king of Syria. 15But king Joram
was returned to be healed in Jezreel of the
wounds which the Syrians had given him,
when he fought with Hazael king of Syria.)
And Jehu said, If it be your minds, then let

none go forth nor escape out of the city to go to tell it in Jezreel.

Reduces Territory of Israel

2 Kin. 10 [32]In those days the LORD began to cut Israel short: and Hazael smote them in all the coasts of Israel; [33]From Jordan eastward, all the land of Gilead, the Gadites, and the Reubenites, and the Manassites, from Aroer, which is by the river Arnon, even Gilead and Bashan.

Receives Tribute from Jehoash King of Judah

2 Kin. 12 [17]Then Hazael king of Syria went up, and fought against Gath, and took it: and Hazael set his face to go up to Jerusalem. [18]And Jehoash king of Judah took all the hallowed things that Jehoshaphat, and Jehoram, and Ahaziah, his fathers, kings of Judah, had dedicated, and his own hallowed things, and all the gold that was found in the treasures of the house of the LORD, and in the king's house, and sent it to Hazael king of Syria: and he went away from Jerusalem.

An Instrument of the Lord's Wrath

2 Kin. 13 [3]And the anger of the LORD was kindled against Israel, and he delivered them into the hand of Hazael king of Syria, and into the hand of Ben-hadad the son of Hazael, all their days.

[22]But Hazael king of Syria oppressed Israel all the days of Jehoahaz.

Death

2 Kin. 13 [24]So Hazael king of Syria died; and Ben-hadad his son reigned in his stead.

HAZOR

[hā'zor] A city of northern Palestine, about four miles west of the southern end of Lake Huleh. This was a city of power and influence at the time it was razed by Joshua on the northern campaign of his conquests. (*See* CONQUEST) A second crushing blow was apparently dealt the city by the armies of Deborah and Barak. During the reign of Solomon, Hazor was fortified as a major defense post against the Aramean territories (*1 Kin. 9:15*). In *2 Kin. 15:29*, however, we learn that, along with other cities of Galilee, it fell to Tiglath-Pileser. In about 730 BC, Hazor was lost to the Assyrians under Tiglath-Pileser III (*2 Kin. 15:29*).

In the twentieth century, archaeologists have discovered the ancient site of Hazor and have been able to confirm the Biblical account of its history.

SCRIPTURE

Destroyed by Joshua

Josh. 11 [10]And Joshua at that time turned back, and took Hazor, and smote the king thereof with the sword: for Hazor beforetime was the head of all those kingdoms. [11]And they smote all the souls that were therein with the edge of the sword, utterly destroying them: there was not any left to breathe: and he burnt Hazor with fire. [12]And all the cities of those kings, and all the kings of them, did Joshua take, and smote them with the edge of the sword, and he utterly destroyed them, as Moses the servant of the LORD commanded. [13]But as for the cities that stood still in their strength, Israel burnt none of them, save Hazor only; that did Joshua burn.

Oppresses Israel in the Time of Deborah

Judg. 4 [1]And the children of Israel again did evil in the sight of the LORD, when Ehud was dead. [2]And the LORD sold them into the hand of Jabin king of Canaan, that reigned in Hazor; the captain of whose host was Sisera, which dwelt in Harosheth of the Gentiles. [3]And the chil-

dren of Israel cried unto the LORD: for he
had nine hundred chariots of iron; and
twenty years he mightily oppressed the
children of Israel.

Conquered by Deborah's Forces

Judg. 4 23So God subdued on that day
Jabin the king of Canaan before the children of Israel. 24And the hand of the children of Israel prospered, and prevailed
against Jabin the king of Canaan, until
they had destroyed Jabin king of Canaan.

HEALING

[hēl'ing] Curing or restoring to a sound and healthy condition. It is noteworthy that the Greek word for Saviour may also be rendered Healer. That Jesus saw himself in both these roles is seen in his assertions that his power over disease is evidence of his power to forgive sins, (for example, *see Mark 2:1-12*). Throughout the book of *Acts* the apostles are credited with the power to perform miracles of healing (*Acts 2:43; 5:12; 8:7; 9:12, 17; 28:8*). There seems to have been a special order of persons in the early church who possessed the "gift of healing" (*1 Cor. 12:9, 28*), and in *Jas. 5:13-16*, elders are instructed to anoint the sick with oil and to pray in order to promote healing. Apart from these brief notices we have no further information regarding this phenomenon.

SCRIPTURE

Jesus as Healer

Mark 1 29And forthwith, when they
were come out of the synagogue, they
entered into the house of Simon and Andrew, with James and John. 30But Simon's
wife's mother lay sick of a fever, and anon
they tell him of her. 31And he came and
took her by the hand, and lifted her
up; and immediately the fever left her,
and she ministered unto them. 32And at
even, when the sun did set, they brought
unto him all that were diseased, and them
that were possessed with devils. 40And
there came a leper to him, beseeching him,
and kneeling down to him, and saying
unto him, If thou wilt, thou canst make me
clean. 41And Jesus, moved with compassion, put forth his hand, and touched him,
and saith unto him, I will; be thou clean.
42And as soon as he had spoken, immediately the leprosy departed from him, and
he was cleansed.

See JESUS

Disciples Given Power to Heal

Matt. 10 1And when he had called unto
him his twelve disciples, he gave them
power against unclean spirits, to cast them
out, and to heal all manner of sickness and
all manner of diseases.

Mark 6 13And they cast out many devils,
and anointed with oil many that were sick,
and healed them.

Luke 10 9And heal the sick that are
therein, and say unto them, The kingdom
of God is come nigh unto you.

Healing in the Early Church

Acts 2 43And fear came upon every soul:
and many wonders and signs were done by
the apostles.

Acts 5 12And by the hands of the
apostles were many signs and wonders
wrought among the people;

Acts 8 7For unclean spirits, crying with
loud voice, came out of many that were
possessed with them: and many taken with
palsies, and that were lame were healed.

Acts 28 8And it came to pass, that the
father of Publius lay sick of a fever and of
a bloody flux: to whom Paul entered in,
and prayed, and layed his hands on him,
and healed him.

1 Cor. 12 9. . . to another the gifts of
healing by the same Spirit; 28And God
hath set some in the church, first apostles,

secondarily prophets, thirdly teachers, after that miracles, then gifts of healings, helps, governments, diversities of tongues.

Jas. 5 [14]Is any sick among you? let him call for the elders of the church; and let them pray over him, anointing him with oil in the name of the Lord.

HEART

[härt] The organ in the human body which by its action keeps the blood in circulation, consequently, the seat of physical life. As the central organ of the body, the heart has come to stand for the center of moral, intellectual, and spiritual life. Most Biblical references to the heart have this latter sense.

SCRIPTURE

Heart of Man, Seat of Affections

Gen. 6 [5]And God saw that the wickedness of man was great in the earth, and that every imagination of the thoughts of his heart was only evil continually.

Gen. 8 [21]And the LORD smelled a sweet savour; and the LORD said in his heart, I will not again curse the ground any more for man's sake; for the imagination of man's heart is evil from his youth: neither will I again smite any more every thing living, as I have done.

Eccl. 8 [11]Because sentence against an evil work is not executed speedily, therefore the heart of the sons of men is fully set in them to do evil.

Eccl. 9 [3]This is an evil among all things that are done under the sun, that there is one event unto all: yea, also the heart of the sons of men is full of evil, and madness is in their heart while they live, and after that they go to the dead.

Jer. 17 [9]The heart is deceitful above all things, and desperately wicked: who can know it?

Matt. 12 [34]O generation of vipers, how can ye, being evil, speak good things? for out of the abundance of the heart the mouth speaketh.

Matt. 15 [18]But those things which proceed out of the mouth come forth from the heart; and they defile the man. [19]For out of the heart proceed evil thoughts, murders, adulteries, fornications, thefts, false witness, blasphemies.

Luke 6 [45]A good man out of the good treasure of his heart bringeth forth that which is good; and an evil man out of the evil treasure of his heart bringeth forth that which is evil: for of the abundance of the heart his mouth speaketh.

Rom. 2 [5]But after thy hardness, and impenitent heart, treasurest up unto thyself wrath, against the day of wrath, and revelation of the righteous judgment of God.

Searched and Tried by God

1 Chr. 28 [9]And thou, Solomon my son, know thou the God of thy father, and serve him with a perfect heart and with a willing mind: for the LORD searcheth all hearts, and understandeth all the imaginations of the thoughts: if thou seek him, he will be found of thee; but if thou forsake him, he will cast thee off for ever.

1 Chr. 29 [17]I know also, my God, that thou triest the heart, and hast pleasure in uprightness. As for me, in the uprightness of mine heart I have willingly offered all these things: and now have I seen with joy thy people, which are present here, to offer willingly unto thee.

Psa. 44 [21]Shall not God search this out? for he knoweth the secrets of the heart.

Psa. 129 [23]Search me, O God, and know my heart: try me, and know my thoughts.

Prov. 21 [2]Every way of a man is right in his own eyes: but the LORD pondereth the hearts.

Prov. 24 [12]If thou sayest, Behold, we knew it not; doth not he that pondereth the heart consider it? and he that keepeth thy soul, doth not he know it? and shall not he render to every man according to his works?

Made Better by God

2 Cor. 4 [6]For God who commanded the light to shine out of darkness, hath shined in our hearts, to give the light of the knowledge of the glory of God in the face of Jesus Christ.

Psa. 27 [14]Wait on the LORD: be of good courage, and he shall strengthen thine heart: wait, I say, on the LORD.

Prov. 16 [1]The preparations of the heart in man, and the answer of the tongue, is from the LORD.

1 Thess. 3 [13]To the end he may stablish your hearts unblameable in holiness before God even our Father, at the coming of our Lord Jesus Christ with all his Saints.

Promise of a New Heart

Jer. 24 [7]And I will give them an heart to know me, that I am the LORD: and they shall be my people, and I will be their God: for they shall return unto me with their whole heart.

Jer. 32 [39]And I will give them one heart and one way, that they may fear me for ever, for the good of them, and of their children after them.

Ezek. 36 [26]A new heart also will I give you, and a new spirit will I put within you: and I will take away the stony heart out of your flesh, and I will give you an heart of flesh.

HEAVEN

[hev″n] A word used in the Bible to indicate several different things and conditions, the more important of which are: (1) the sky, or firmament above the earth; (2) the permanent dwelling place of God and the heavenly host; (3) the abode of the blessed after the Judgment; (4) any place or condition of supreme happiness or comfort.

See HELL

SCRIPTURE

The Firmament as Heaven

Gen. 1 [1]In the beginning God created the heaven and the earth.

[8]And God called the firmament Heaven. And the evening and the morning were the second day.

Psa. 8 [1]O LORD our LORD, how excellent is thy name in all the earth! who hast set thy glory above the heavens.

Isa. 40 [22]It is he that sitteth upon the circle of the earth, and the inhabitants thereof are as grasshoppers; that stretcheth out the heavens as a curtain, and spreadeth them out as a tent to dwell in.

God's Dwelling-Place

1 Kin. 8 [30]And hearken thou to the supplication of thy servant, and of thy people Israel, when they shall pray toward this place: and hear thou in heaven thy dwelling-place: and when thou hearest, forgive.

Psa. 2 [4]He that sitteth in the heavens shall laugh: the LORD shall have them in derision.

Psa. 115 [3]But our God is in the heavens; he hath done whatsoever he hath pleased.

Psa. 123 [1]Unto thee lift I up mine eyes, O thou that dwellest in the heavens.

Isa. 66 [1]Thus saith the LORD, The heaven is my throne, and the earth is my footstool: where is the house that ye build unto me? and where is the place of my rest?

Matt. 6 [9]After this manner therefore pray ye: Our Father which art in heaven,

Hallowed be thy name. [10]Thy kingdom come. Thy will be done in earth, as it is in heaven.

Acts 7 [49]Heaven is my throne, and earth is my footstool: What house will ye build me, saith the Lord? Or what is the place of my rest?

Heb. 8 [1]Now of the things which we have spoken, this is the sum: we have such an high Priest, who is set on the right hand of the throne of the Majesty in the heavens.

Happiness in Heaven

Psa. 16 [11]Thou wilt shew me the path of life: in thy presence is fulness of joy; at thy right hand there are pleasures for evermore.

Isa. 49 [10]They shall not hunger nor thirst, neither shall the heat nor sun smite them: for he that hath mercy on them shall lead them, even by the springs of water shall he guide them.

Matt. 5 [12]Rejoice, and be exceeding glad: for great is your reward in heaven: for so persecuted they the prophets, which were before you.

Matt. 13 [43]Then shall the righteous shine forth as the sun in the kingdom of their Father. Who hath ears to hear, let him hear.

John 14 [2]In my Father's house are many mansions: if it were not so, I would have told you. I go to prepare a place for you.

1 Cor. 2 [9]But as it is written, Eye hath not seen, nor ear heard, neither have entered into the heart of man, the things which God hath prepared for them that love him.

1 Pet. 1 [4]To an inheritance incorruptible, and undefiled, and that fadeth not away, reserved in heaven for you.

Rev. 7 [16]They shall hunger no more, neither thirst any more, neither shall the Sun light on them, nor any heat. [17]For the Lamb, which is in the midst of the throne, shall feed them, and shall lead them unto living fountains of waters: and God shall wipe away all tears from their eyes.

Rev. 14 [13]And I heard a voice from heaven, saying unto me, Write, Blessed are the dead which die in the Lord, from henceforth, yea, saith the Spirit, that they may rest from their labours, and their works do follow them.

Rev. 21 [4]And God shall wipe away all tears from their eyes: and there shall be no more death, neither sorrow, nor crying, neither shall there be any more pain: for the former things are passed away.

Those Who Enter Heaven

Matt. 5 [3]Blessed are the poor in spirit: for theirs is the kingdom of heaven.

Matt. 7 [21]Not every one that saith unto me, Lord, Lord, shall enter into the kingdom of heaven; but he that doeth the will of my Father which is in heaven.

Matt. 25 [34]Then shall the King say unto them on his right hand, Come, ye blessed of my Father, inherit the kingdom prepared for you from the foundation of the world.

Rom. 8 [17]And if children, then heirs, heirs of God, and joint-heirs with Christ: if so be that we suffer with him, that we may be also glorified together.

Heb. 12 [22]But ye are come unto mount Sion, and unto the city of the living God the heavenly Jerusalem, and to an innumerable company of angels: [23]To the general assembly, and Church of the firstborn which are written in heaven, and to God the Judge of all, and to the spirits of just men made perfect.

Rev. 7 [9]After this I beheld, and lo, a great multitude which no man could number, of all nations, and kindreds, and people, and tongues, stood before the throne, and before the Lamb, clothed with white robes, and palms in their hands. [14]And I said unto him, Sir, thou knowest. And he said to me, These are they which came out of great tribulation, and have washed their robes, and made them white in the blood of the Lamb.

Those Who Enter Not

Matt. 7 [22]Many will say to me in that day, Lord, Lord, have we not prophesied in thy name? and in thy name have cast out devils? and in thy name done many wonderful works? [23]And then will I profess unto them, I never knew you: depart from me, ye that work iniquity.

Matt. 25 [41]Then shall he say also unto them on the left hand, Depart from me, ye cursed, into everlasting fire, prepared for the devil and his angels: [42]For I was an hungered, and ye gave me no meat: I was thirsty, and ye gave me no drink: [43] I was a stranger, and ye took me not in: naked, and ye clothed me not: sick, and in prison, and ye visited me not.

Luke 13 [26]Then shall ye begin to say, We have eaten and drunk in thy presence, and thou hast taught in our streets. [27]But he shall say, I tell you, I know you not whence ye are; depart from me, all ye workers of iniquity.

Rev. 21 [8]But the fearful, and unbelieving, and the abominable, and murderers, and whoremongers, and sorcerers, and idolaters, and all liars, shall have their part in the lake which burneth with fire and brimstone: which is the second death.

Heaven a Secure Abode

Matt. 16 [20]But lay up for yourselves treasures in heaven, where neither moth nor rust doth corrupt, and where thieves do not break through nor steal.

Heb. 11 [16]But now they desire a better country, that is, a heavenly: wherefore God is not ashamed to be called their God: for he hath prepared for them a city.

HEBREW

[hē′brōō] A name by which the Israelites are sometimes called in the Bible, first used in *Gen. 14:13*, with reference to Abraham. It is impossible to determine the original source of this word. Some authorities feel that it is derived from *Habiru*, or *Hapiru*, an ancient ethnic group or social class referred to in a number of early Near Eastern texts. Others maintain that its origin is to be found in the name Eber, who, according to the genealogical table in *Gen. 1:21-11:32*, was the ancestor of Abraham and therefore of the Hebrews. The language of the Israelites, a semitic dialect related to Canaanite and Amorite, is also called Hebrew.

SCRIPTURE

General

Gen. 10 [24]And Arphaxad begat Salah; and Salah begat Eber.

Gen. 14 [13]And there came one that had escaped, and told Abram the Hebrew; for he dwelt in the plain of Mamre the Amorite, brother of Eshcol, and brother of Aner: and these were confederate with Abram.

Gen. 39 [14]That she called unto the men of her house, and spake unto them, saying, See, he hath brought in a Hebrew unto us to mock us; he came in unto me to lie with me, and I cried with a loud voice:

Ex. 1 [16]And he said, When you do the office of a midwife to the Hebrew women, and see them upon the stools, if it be a son, then ye shall kill him; but if it be a daughter, then she shall live.

Acts 6 [1]And in those days, when the number of the disciples was multiplied, there arose a murmuring of the Grecians against the Hebrews, because their widows were neglected in the daily ministration.

The Language of the Jews

John 5 [2]Now there is at Jerusalem by the sheep market a pool, which is called in the Hebrew tongue Bethesda, having five porches.

John 19 [20]This title then read many of the Jews; for the place where Jesus was crucified was nigh to the city: and it was written in Hebrew, and Greek, and Latin.

Acts 21 [40]And when he had given him license, Paul stood on the stairs, and beckoned with the hand unto the people. And when there was made a great silence, he spake unto them in the Hebrew tongue, saying,

HEBRON

[hē′brun] Also called Kirjath-Arba (*Gen. 23:2; Josh. 14:15*), this is one of the most ancient cities of ancient Palestine, and one of the most important in Old Testament history. It is located midway between Jerusalem and Beer-Sheba in Southern Palestine. After several years of wandering, Abram "came and dwelt in the plain of Mamre, which is in Hebron" (*Gen. 13:18*). A number of the familiar incidents of his life took place there, including the changing of his name to Abraham (*Gen. 17:5*), the promise of a son (*Gen. 18:1-2*), and the death of Sarah (*Gen. 23:2*). On the latter occasion, Abraham purchased from Ephron the Hittite a tract of land containing the cave of Machpelah, which became the burying-ground of the patriarchs. (*See* MACHPELAH) A Muslim mosque has stood for centuries on the traditional site of this sepulcher.

Among those listed as defeated by Joshua in the conquest of Canaan is Homah king of Hebron. Subsequently, Hebron was set aside as a Levitical city and a city of refuge (*Josh. 20:7; 21:10-11*). After the death of Saul, David was anointed in Hebron and made it his capital for over seven years before the transfer to Jerusalem (*2 Sam. 5:3, 5*).

SCRIPTURE

Date of Founding

Num. 13 [22]. . . (Now Hebron was built seven years before Zoan in Egypt.)

Dwelling Place of Abraham

Gen. 23 [2]And Sarah died in Kirjath-arba; the same is Hebron in the land of Canaan: and Abraham came to mourn for Sarah, and to weep for her.

Destroyed by Joshua

Josh. 10 [36]And Joshua went up from Eglon, and all Israel with him, unto Hebron; and they fought against it: [37]And they took it, and smote it with the edge of the sword, and the king thereof, and all the cities thereof, and all the souls that were therein; he left none remaining, according to all that he had done to Eglon; but destroyed it utterly, and all the souls that were therein.

Granted to Caleb as an Inheritance

Josh. 14 [13]And Joshua blessed him, and gave unto Caleb the son of Jephunneh Hebron for an inheritance. [14]Hebron therefore became the inheritance of Caleb the son of Jephunneh the Kenezite unto this day; because that he wholly followed the LORD God of Israel. [15]And the name of Hebron before was Kirjath-arba; which Arba was a great man among the Anakim. And the land had rest from war.

Judg. 1 [20]And they gave Hebron unto Caleb, as Moses said: and he expelled thence the three sons of Anak.

A City of Refuge

Josh. 21 [13]Thus they gave to the children of Aaron the priest Hebron with her suburbs, to be a city of refuge for the slayer; and Libnah with her suburbs,

David Rules in Hebron

AS KING OF JUDAH

2 Sam. 2 1And it came to pass after this, that David inquired of the LORD, saying, Shall I go up into any of the cities of Judah? And the LORD said unto him, Go up. And David said, Whither shall I go up? And he said, Unto Hebron. 2So David went up thither, and his two wives also, Ahinoam the Jezreelitess, and Abigail Nabal's wife the Carmelite. 3And his men that were with him did David bring up, every man with his household: and they dwelt in the cities of Hebron. 4And the men of Judah came, and there they anointed David king over the house of Judah. And they told David, saying, That the men of Jabesh-gilead were they that buried Saul.

11And the time that David was king in Hebron over the house of Judah was seven years and six months.

2 Sam. 3 2And unto David were sons born in Hebron: and his firstborn was Amnon, of Ahinoam the Jezreelitess; 3And his second, Chileab, of Abigail the wife of Nabal the Carmelite; and the third, Absalom the son of Maacah, the daughter of Talmai king of Geshur; 4And the fourth, Adonijah the son of Haggith; and the fifth, Shephatiah the son of Abital; 5And the sixth, Ithream, by Eglah David's wife. These were born to David in Hebron.

AS KING OF ALL ISRAEL

2 Sam. 5 1Then came all the tribes of Israel to David unto Hebron, and spake, saying, Behold, we are thy bone and thy flesh. 2Also in time past, when Saul was king over us, thou wast he that leddest out and broughtest in Israel: and the LORD said to thee, Thou shalt feed my people Israel, and thou shalt be a captain over Israel. 3So all the elders of Israel came to the king to Hebron; and king David made a league with them in Hebron before the LORD: and they anointed David king over Israel.

4David was thirty years old when he began to reign, and he reigned forty years. 5In Hebron he reigned over Judah seven years and six months: and in Jerusalem he reigned thirty and three years over all Israel and Judah.

Absalom Proclaimed King at Hebron

2 Sam. 15 7And it came to pass after forty years, that Absalom said unto the king, I pray thee, let me go and pay my vow, which I have vowed unto the LORD, in Hebron. 8For thy servant vowed a vow while I abode in Geshur in Syria, saying, If the LORD shall bring me again indeed to Jerusalem, then I will serve the LORD. 9And the king said unto him, Go in peace. So he arose, and went to Hebron.

10But Absalom sent spies throughout all the tribes of Israel, saying, As soon as ye hear the sound of the trumpet, then ye shall say, Absalom reigneth in Hebron. 11And with Absalom went two hundred men out of Jerusalem, that were called; and they went in their simplicity, and they knew not any thing. 12And Absalom sent for Ahithophel the Gilonite, David's counsellor, from his city, even from Giloh, while he offered sacrifices. And the conspiracy was strong; for the people increased continually with Absalom.

HELL

[hel] This word, deriving from the Anglo-Saxon, was originally used to designate the world

of the dead generally, or the place of departed spirits. In modern English it has come to mean the place of punishment for the damned. It is often used in the King James Version of the Bible to translate the Hebrew word Sheol and the Greek word Hades, both of which refer to the unseen world of the dead. (*See* SHEOL, HADES) More in accordance with the modern usage of the term, "hell" is used in the New Testament as the equivalent of Gehenna, which refers to the place of torment of the wicked (*see* GEHENNA), and of Tartarus, the place of punishment of fallen angels (*2 Pet. 2:4*).

SCRIPTURE

Hell as the Grave

Acts 2 31He seeing this before, spake of the resurrection of Christ, that his soul was not left in hell, neither his flesh did see corruption.

Rev. 20 13And the sea gave up the dead which were in it: and death and hell delivered up the dead which were in them: and they were judged every man according to their works. 14And death and hell were cast into the lake of fire: this is the second death.

Hell as Place of Punishment

Matt. 11 23And thou, Capernaum, which art exalted unto heaven, shalt be brought down to hell: for if the mighty works, which have been done in thee, had been done in Sodom, it would have remained until this day.

Matt. 13 42And shall cast them into a furnace of fire: there shall be wailing and gnashing of teeth.

Luke 16 23And in hell he lifted up his eyes, being in torments, and seeth Abraham afar off, and Lazarus in his bosom.

2 Pet. 2 4For if God spared not the angels that sinned, but cast them down to hell, and delivered them into chains of darkness, to be reserved unto judgment.

Rev.14 10The same shall drink of the wine of the wrath of God, which is poured out without mixture into the cup of his indignation, and he shall be tormented with fire and brimstone, in the presence of the holy angels, and in the presence of the Lamb: 11And the smoke of their torment ascendeth up for ever and ever. And they have no rest day nor night, who worship the beast and his image, and whosoever receiveth the mark of his name.

Rev. 20 10And the devil that deceived them, was cast into the lake of fire and brimstone, where the beast and the false prophet are, and shall be tormented day and night, for ever and ever. 15And whosoever was not found written in the book of life, was cast into the lake of fire.

Those Sent to Hell

Psa. 9 17The wicked shall be turned into hell, and all the nations that forget God.

Matt. 5 22But I say unto you, That whosoever is angry with his brother without a cause shall be in danger of the judgment: and whosoever shall say to his brother, Raca, shall be in danger of the council: but whosoever shall say, Thou fool, shall be in danger of hell fire.

Matt. 23 15Woe unto you, scribes and Pharisees, hypocrites! for ye compass sea and land to make one proselyte, and when he is made, ye make him twofold more the child of hell than yourselves.

HERESY

[her′e si] An opinion held in opposition to the established or authorized doctrine of a church or sect or denomination, especially when it is of a nature likely to cause a division or separation; a lack of orthodox or sound belief. Scripture teaches the serious and dangerous nature of heresy and warns against it, showing that it tends to subvert true religion.

SCRIPTURE

1 Cor. 11 [18]For first of all, when ye come together in the church, I hear that there be divisions among you; and I partly believe it. [19]For there must be also heresies among you, that they which are approved may be made manifest among you.

Gal. 5 [19]Now the works of the flesh are manifest, which are these, adultery, fornication, uncleanness, lasciviousness, [20]Idolatry, witchcraft, hatred, variance, emulations, wrath, strife, seditions, heresies.

2 Pet. 2 [1]But there were false prophets also among the people, even as there shall be false teachers among you, who privily shall bring in damnable heresies, even denying the Lord that bought them, and bring upon themselves swift destruction.

Rom. 16 [17]Now I beseech you, brethren, mark them which cause divisions and offences contrary to the doctrine which ye have learned; and avoid them.

HEROD

[her′ud] The family name of a line of infamous rulers of Palestine, under the authority of Rome, during the lifetime of Christ and in the early years of the Christian church. Only those of prominence in the New Testament are discussed below:

1. *Herod the Great.* Through friendship with Mark Antony and Augustus, Herod the Great was able to obtain and hold the rule over Judea from 37 BC until 4 BC. In order to win favor with the Jews, he rebuilt the temple, making its splendor rival the great temple of Solomon. He is remembered by students of the Bible as the king to whom the wise men came to learn of the birth of the "king of the Jews"; sending a threat to his power, he ordered the massacre of all infant males in the region around Bethlehem. At his death, his territory was divided between his sons Archaelaus, Antipas, and Philip (*Matt. 2:22; Luke 3:1*). Herod's death came in 4 BC, indicating that the true date for the birth of Christ was actually a short time before this, instead of AD 1, as is sometimes supposed.

2. *Herod Antipas.* [an′ti pas] The son of Herod the Great by his Samaritan wife Malthace, and tetrarch of Galilee and Paraea. Antipas' first wife was the daughter of the king of Arabia, but he sent her back home after having met and seduced Herodias, the wife of his brother Philip. Because of his severe criticism of this immoral union, John the Baptist was executed at the behest of Herodias. It was this Herod who was reigning at the time of the death of Christ and who allowed the Master to be subjected to contempt and mockery. When Caius Caligula became emperor of Rome, Herod Antipas became the victim of a plot engineered by his nephew Herod Agrippa I and was banished to Lyon where he died. (*See* HERODIAS, JOHN THE BAPTIST)

3. *Herod Agrippa I.* [a grip′pa] A close friend to Emperor Caius Caligula, Agrippa I had managed to obtain the rule, with the title of King, over much of Palestine by AD 40. In *Acts 12,* we are told that he persecuted the young Christian church, counting the apostle James among his victims. His loathsome death is attributed by the writer of *Acts* to God's punishment of his overweaning egotism. Three of his children are mentioned elsewhere in *Acts*: Herod Agrippa II, Bernice, and Drusilla.

4. *Herod Agrippa II.* The son of Herod Agrippa I. Under the reigns of the emperors Claudius and Nero, Herod Agrippa II—the Agrippa of *Acts*—ruled as king over a large portion of Palestine. Paul appeared before him and his consort Bernice, a sister with whom he lived in incest and addressed him as one who had some knowledge of the scriptures. After having heard the thrilling story of Paul's conversion on the road to Damascus, Agrippa observed that Paul had done nothing worthy of imprisonment and would be allowed to go free had he not made appeal to appear before Caesar. Agrippa reigned until the destruction of the Jewish nation, after which he returned to Rome, dying in AD 100. (*See* PAUL, BERNICE)

SCRIPTURE

Herod the Great

Matt. 2 [1]Now when Jesus was born in

Bethlehem of Judea in the days of Herod
the king, behold, there came wise men from
the east to Jerusalem, [2]Saying, Where is
he that is born King of the Jews? for we
have seen his star in the east, and are come
to worship him. [3]When Herod the king
had heard these things, he was troubled,
and all Jerusalem with him. [4]And when
he had gathered all the chief priests and
scribes of the people together, he demanded of them where Christ should be
born. [5]And they said unto him, In Bethlehem of Judea: for thus it is written by the
prophet, [6]And thou Bethlehem, in the
land of Juda, art not the least among the
princes of Juda: for out of thee shall come
a Governor, that shall rule my people Israel. [7]Then Herod, when he had privily
called the wise men, inquired of them diligently what time the star appeared. [8]And
he sent them to Bethlehem, and said, Go
and search diligently for the young child;
and when ye have found him, bring me
word again, that I may come and worship
him also.

[12]And being warned of God in a dream
that they should not return to Herod, they
departed into their own country another
way. [13]And when they were departed, behold, the angel of the Lord appeareth to
Joseph in a dream, saying, Arise, and take
the young child and his mother, and flee
into Egypt, and be thou there until I bring
thee word: for Herod will seek the young
child to destroy him. [14]When he arose, he
took the young child and his mother by
night, and departed into Egypt: [15]And
was there until the death of Herod: that it
might be fulfilled which was spoken of the
Lord by the prophet, saying, Out of Egypt
have I called my son.

[16]Then Herod, when he saw that he was
mocked of the wise men, was exceeding
wroth, and sent forth, and slew all the children that were in Bethlehem, and in all the
coasts thereof, from two years old and under, according to the time which he had
diligently inquired of the wise men.

Herod Antipas

EXECUTES JOHN THE BAPTIST

Matt. 14 [1]At that time Herod the tetrarch heard of the fame of Jesus, [2]And
said unto his servants, This is John the
Baptist; he is risen from the dead; and
therefore mighty works do shew forth
themselves in him.

[3]For Herod had laid hold on John, and
bound him, and put him in prison for Herodias' sake, his brother Philip's wife. [4]For
John said unto him, It is not lawful for thee
to have her. [5]And when he would have put
him to death, he feared the multitude, because they counted him as a prophet. [6]But
when Herod's birthday was kept, the
daughter of Herodias danced before them,
and pleased Herod. [7]Whereupon he promised with an oath to give her whatsoever
she would ask. [8]And she, being before instructed of her mother, said, Give me here
John the Baptist's head in a charger. [9]And
the king was sorry: nevertheless for the
oath's sake, and them that sat with him at
meat, he commanded it to be given her.
[10]And he sent, and beheaded John in the
prison. [11]And his head was brought in a
charger, and given to the damsel: and she
brought it to her mother. [12]And his disciples came, and took up the body, and
buried it, and went and told Jesus.

SCORNED BY JESUS

Luke 13 [31]The same day there came
certain of the Pharisees, saying unto him,
Get thee out, and depart hence; for Herod
will kill thee. [32]And he said unto them, Go
ye, and tell that fox, Behold, I cast out dev-

ils, and I do cures to-day and to-morrow, and the third day I shall be perfected.

AT THE TRIAL OF JESUS

Luke 23 7And as soon as he knew that he belonged unto Herod's jurisdiction, he sent him to Herod, who himself also was at Jerusalem at that time.

8And when Herod saw Jesus, he was exceeding glad: for he was desirous to see him of a long season, because he had heard many things of him; and he hoped to have seen some miracle done by him. 9Then he questioned with him in many words; but he answered him nothing. 10And the chief priests and scribes stood and vehemently accused him. 11And Herod with his men of war set him at nought, and mocked him, and arrayed him in a gorgeous robe, and sent him again to Pilate.

12And the same day Pilate and Herod were made friends together; for before they were at enmity between themselves.

Herod Agrippa I

Acts 12 1Now about that time Herod the king stretched forth his hands to vex certain of the church. 2And he killed James the brother of John with the sword. 3And because he saw it pleased the Jews, he proceeded further to take Peter also. (Then were the days of unleavened bread.)

20And Herod was highly displeased with them of Tyre and Sidon: but they came with one accord to him, and, having made Blastus the king's chamberlain their friend, desired peace; because their country was nourished by the king's country. 21And upon a set day Herod, arrayed in royal apparel, sat upon his throne, and made an oration unto them. 22And the people gave a shout, saying, It is the voice of a god, and not of a man. 23And immediately the angel of the Lord smote him, because he gave not God the glory: and he was eaten of worms, and gave up the ghost.

Herod Agrippa II

Acts 25 23And on the morrow, when Agrippa was come, and Bernice, with great pomp, and was entered into the place of hearing, with the chief captains, and principal men of the city, at Festus' commandment Paul was brought forth. 24And Festus said, King Agrippa, and all men which are here present with us, ye see this man, about whom all the multitude of the Jews have dealt with me, both at Jerusalem, and also here, crying that he ought not to live any longer. 25But when I found that he had committed nothing worthy of death, and that he himself hath appealed to Augustus, I have determined to send him. 26Of whom I have no certain thing to write unto my lord. Wherefore I have brought him forth before you, and especially before thee, O king Agrippa, that, after examination had, I might have somewhat to write. 27For it seemeth to me unreasonable to send a prisoner, and not withal to signify the crimes laid against him.

Acts 26 1Then Agrippa said unto Paul, Thou art permitted to speak for thyself. Then Paul stretched forth the hand, and answered for himself: 27King Agrippa, believest thou the prophets? I know that thou believest. 28Then Agrippa said unto Paul, Almost thou persuadest me to be a Christian. 29And Paul said, I would to God, that not only thou, but also all that hear me this day, were both almost, and altogether such as I am, except these bonds. 30And when he had thus spoken, the king rose up, and the governor, and Bernice, and they that sat with them: 31And when they were gone aside, they talked between themselves, saying, This man doeth nothing worthy of death or of bonds. 32Then said Agrippa unto Festus, This man might have been set at liberty, if he had not appealed unto Caesar.

HERODIANS

[he rō'di anz] A political party, perhaps with some religious aspects, which arose in the time of Herod the Great. The Herodians are mentioned in the gospels as having allied themselves with the Pharisees and Sadducees in an effort to thwart the teaching and work of Jesus.

SCRIPTURE

Matt. 22 16And they sent out unto him their disciples with the Herodians, saying, Master we know that thou art true, and teachest the way of God in truth, neither carest thou for any man: for thou regardest not the person of men.

Mark 3 6And the Pharisees went forth, and straightway took counsel with the Herodians against him, how they might destroy him.

Mark 12 13And they send unto him certain of the Pharisees and of the Herodians, to catch him in his words.

HERODIAS

[hē rō'di as] The woman responsible for the death of John the Baptist. Herodias had previously been married to Herod Philip, but Herod Antipas had seduced her while in Rome and she had become his consort. John condemned this adulterous union and Herod had him imprisoned; he did not wish to execute him, however, because of his great popularity with the masses. At a great feast, the daughter of Herodias performed a sensuous dance which pleased the king so that he promised her any gift she might ask, "unto the half of my kingdom." Prompted by her wicked mother, the girl asked for and received the head of John the Baptist, delivered on a platter.

See HEROD ANTIPAS, JOHN

SCRIPTURE

Matt. 14 1At that time Herod the tetrarch heard of the fame of Jesus, 2And said unto his servants, This is John the Baptist; he is risen from the dead; and therefore mighty works do shew forth themselves in him.

3For Herod had laid hold on John, and bound him, and put him in prison for Herodias' sake, his brother Philip's wife. 4For John said unto him, It is not lawful for thee to have her. 5And when he would have put him to death, he feared the multitude, because they counted him as a prophet. 6But when Herod's birthday was kept, the daughter of Herodias danced before them, and pleased Herod. 7Whereupon he promised with an oath to give her whatsoever she would ask. 8And she, being before instructed of her mother, said, Give me here John Baptist's head in a charger. 9And the king was sorry; nevertheless for the oath's sake, and them which sat with him at meat, he commanded it to be given her. 10And he sent, and beheaded John in the prison. 11And his head was brought in a charger, and given to the damsel: and she brought it to her mother. 12And his disciples came, and took up the body, and buried it, and went and told Jesus.

See Mark 6:14-29

HEZEKIAH

[hez ē kī'a] The son of Ahaz and one of the best kings of Judah (715-687 BC). Hezekiah inherited from his idolatrous father a kingdom discontent with both the religious and political situation into which Ahaz had led them. Early in his reign Hezekiah reopened and cleansed the temple of the Assyrian cult matter which his father had introduced, thus breaking the vassalage alliance. Then, with some aplomb, he began a movement for revolt which came to a head in 705 BC with the death of Sargon and the accession of Sennacharib to the Assyrian throne. In a coalition with Moab, Edom, Philistia, Ethiopia and others, Judah prepared to fight for her independence. Sennacharib then began a devastating campaign of division and conquest which saw the retreat or defeat of the allies. Hezekiah came to terms with Sennacharib at Lachish, surrendering considerable territory and promising even further tribute. At this point there is considerable difficulty in reconciling the scriptures and the Assyrian records; the solution here suggested seems to this writer to be preferable but must be regarded as tentative. It appears that at this time (701 BC) Sennacharib returned eastward to put down a Babylonian rebellion, leaving Judah alone according to the agreement made at Lachish. In 689 BC, Hezekiah was ready to revolt again and Sennacharib, having finally overcome Babylon, was free to come west. It was on this campaign that the troops of Sennacharib, threatening to destroy Jerusalem, were decimated by a plague and the Assyrian returned home without attacking. Hezekiah died two years later and was succeeded by his son Manasseh.

See ISAIAH, KINGS, MICAH

REFERENCE: *2 Kin. 18-20; 2 Chr. 29-32.*

SCRIPTURE

A Good King

2 Kin. 18 [1]Now it came to pass in the
third year of Hoshea son of Elah king of
Israel, that Hezekiah the son of Ahaz king
of Judah began to reign. [2]Twenty and five
years old was he when he began to reign;
and he reigned twenty and nine years in
Jerusalem. His mother's name also was
Abi, the daughter of Zachariah. [3]And he
did that which was right in the sight of
the LORD, according to all that David his
father did.

[4]He removed the high places, and brake
the images, and cut down the groves, and
brake in pieces the brazen serpent that
Moses had made: for unto those days the
children of Israel did burn incense to it:
and he called it Nehushtan. [5]He trusted
in the LORD God of Israel; so that after him
was none like him among all the kings of
Judah, nor any that were before him.
[6]For he clave to the LORD, and departed
not from following him, but kept his commandments, which the LORD commanded
Moses.

Becomes Vassal of Assyria

2 Kin. 18 [13]Now in the fourteenth year
of king Hezekiah did Sennacherib king of
Assyria come up against all the fenced
cities of Judah, and took them. [14]And Hezekiah king of Judah sent to the king of Assyria to Lachish, saying, I have offended;
return from me: that which thou puttest
on me will I bear. And the king of Assyria appointed unto Hezekiah king of Judah three hundred talents of silver and
thirty talents of gold. [15]And Hezekiah
gave him all the silver that was found in
the house of the LORD, and in the treasures
of the king's house. [16]At that time did
Hezekiah cut off the gold from the doors
of the temple of the LORD, and from the
pillars which Hezekiah king of Judah had
overlaid, and gave it to the king of Assyria.

Miraculous Destruction of Sennacharib's Troops

2 Kin. 19 [35]And it came to pass that
night, that the angel of the LORD went out,
and smote in the camp of the Assyrians a
hundred fourscore and five thousand: and
when they arose early in the morning, behold, they were all dead corpses. [36]So Sennacherib king of Assyria departed, and
went and returned, and dwelt at Nineveh.

Hezekiah's Life Prolonged

2 Kin. 20 [1]In those days was Hezekiah
sick unto death. And the prophet Isaiah
the son of Amoz came to him, and said

unto him, Thus saith the LORD, Set thine house in order; for thou shalt die, and not live. [2]Then he turned his face to the wall, and prayed unto the LORD, saying, [3]I beseech thee, O LORD, remember now how I have walked before thee in truth and with a perfect heart, and have done that which is good in thy sight. And Hezekiah wept sore. [4]And it came to pass, afore Isaiah was gone out into the middle court, that the word of the LORD came to him, saying, [5]Turn again, and tell Hezekiah the captain of my people, Thus saith the LORD, the God of David thy father, I have heard thy prayer, I have seen thy tears: behold, I will heal thee: on the third day thou shalt go up unto the house of the LORD. [6]And I will add unto thy days fifteen years; and I will deliver thee and this city out of the hand of the king of Assyria; and I will defend this city for mine own sake, and for my servant David's sake. [7]And Isaiah said, Take a lump of figs. And they took and laid it on the boil, and he recovered.

[8]And Hezekiah said unto Isaiah, What shall be the sign that the LORD will heal me, and that I shall go up into the house of the LORD the third day? [9]And Isaiah said, This sign shalt thou have of the LORD, that the LORD will do the thing that he hath spoken: shall the shadow go forward ten degrees, or go back ten degrees? [10]And Hezekiah answered, It is a light thing for the shadow to go down ten degrees: nay, but let the shadow return backward ten degrees. [11]And Isaiah the prophet cried unto the LORD: and he brought the shadow ten degrees backward, by which it had gone down in the dial of Ahaz.

HITTITES

[hit′īts] A people of highly advanced culture who controlled much of the Anatolian peninsula in the second millenium BC. It is doubtful that the Biblical Hittites, who were settled mainly around Hebron, are to be identified with the classical Hittites, as the Hittite empire never extended that far to the south. The term is probably used in the Bible with reference to people who emigrated from areas of Northern Syria under Hittite control. Doubtless the Biblical Hittites were essentially Canaanite in culture.

See CANAAN

SCRIPTURE

Sell a Burying-Ground to Abraham

Gen. 23 [1]And Sarah was a hundred and seven and twenty years old: these were the years of the life of Sarah. [2]And Sarah died in Kirjath-arba: the same is Hebron in the land of Canaan: and Abraham came to mourn for Sarah, and to weep for her.

[3]And Abraham stood up from before his dead, and spake unto the sons of Heth, saying, [4]I am a stranger and a sojourner with you: give me a possession of a buryingplace with you, that I may bury my dead out of my sight. [5]And the children of Heth answered Abraham, saying unto him, [6]Hear us, my lord: thou art a mighty prince among us: in the choice of our sepulchres bury thy dead; none of us shall withhold from thee his sepulchre, but that thou mayest bury thy dead. [7]And Abraham stood up, and bowed himself to the people of the land, even to the children of Heth. [8]And he communed with them, saying, If it be your mind that I should bury my dead out of my sight, hear me, and entreat for me to Ephron the son of Zohar, [9]That he may give me the cave of Machpelah, which he hath, which is in the end of his field; for as much money as it is worth he shall give it me for a possession of a buryingplace amongst you. [10]And Ephron dwelt among the children of Heth: and Ephron the Hittite answered Abra-

ham in the audience of the children of Heth, even of all that went in at the gate of his city, saying, [11]Nay, my lord, hear me: the field give I thee, and the cave that is therein, I give it thee; in the presence of the sons of my people give I it thee: bury thy dead. [12]And Abraham bowed down himself before the people of the land. [13]And he spake unto Ephron in the audience of the people of the land, saying, But if thou wilt give it, I pray thee, hear me: I will give thee money for the field; take it of me, and I will bury my dead there. [14]And Ephron answered Abraham, saying unto him, [15]My lord, hearken unto me: the land is worth four hundred shekels of silver; what is that betwixt me and thee? bury therefore thy dead. [16]And Abraham hearkened unto Ephron; and Abraham weighed to Ephron the silver, which he had named in the audience of the sons of Heth, four hundred shekels of silver, current money with the merchant.

[20]And the field, and the cave that is therein, were made sure unto Abraham for a possession of a buryingplace by the sons of Heth.

Esau Intermarries with Hittites

Gen. 26 [34]And Esau was forty years old when he took to wife Judith the daughter of Beeri the Hittite, and Bashemath the daughter of Elon the Hittite: [35]Which were a grief of mind unto Isaac and to Rebekah.

Territory Given to the Israelites

Josh. 1 [4]From the wilderness and this Lebanon even unto the great river, the river Euphrates, all the land of the Hittites, and unto the great sea toward the going down of the sun, shall be your coast.

Josh. 24 [11]And ye went over Jordan, and came unto Jericho: and the men of Jericho fought against you, the Amorites, and the Perizzites, and the Canaanites, and the Hittites, and the Girgashites, the Hivites, and the Jebusites; and I delivered them into your hand.

Intermarry with Israelites

Judg. 3 [5]And the children of Israel dwelt among the Canaanites, Hittites, and Amorites, and Perizzites, and Hivites, and Jebusites: [6]And they took their daughters to be their wives, and gave their daughters to their sons, and served their gods.

Enslaved by Solomon

1 Kin. 9 [20]And all the people that were left of the Amorites, Hittites, Perizzites, Hivites, and Jebusites, which were not of the children of Israel, [21]Their children that were left after them in the land, whom the children of Israel also were not able utterly to destroy, upon those did Solomon levy a tribute of bondservice unto this day.

HOLINESS

[hō'li nes] OLD TESTAMENT. The original meaning of this word is uncertain, but its usage in the Old Testament indicates that the idea of separation most nearly approximates its meaning. In its early usage, it seems quite close to the concept of *tabu* which is found in primitive religions. In the Old Testament the term is applied to God in two senses. Primarily, it indicates his separation from all that is created. It is also found in reference to the holiness of his character in a distinct ethical sense. It is from the former of these two usages that the concept of ceremonial holiness so prominent in the Old Testament is derived. In general, things are counted holy because of their connection with God. A place where he shows himself is holy ground; the tabernacle or temple is a holy building. The sacrifices, the ceremonial materials, the utensils used in the worship and the days or seasons of worship are holy because they have been appropriated or set aside for the service of God. The Priests and the Levites are holy men because they have been hallowed by certain acts of consecration.

New Testament. In the New Testament this ceremonial aspect of holiness has almost disappeared. Jesus presented a view of religion in which the issues of a man's heart and mind render him clean or unclean, rather than contact with external things (*Matt. 15:17-20*). The term frequently denotes the appropriate quality of life and character which is set before Christians as an ideal and an obligation.

See Cleanness, Uncleanness

SCRIPTURE

The Holiness of God

Lev. 11 [44]For I am the Lord your God:
ye shall therefore sanctify yourselves, and
ye shall be holy; for I am holy: neither shall
ye defile yourselves with any manner of
creeping thing that creepeth upon the
earth. [45]For I am the Lord that bringeth
you up out of the land of Egypt, to be your
God: ye shall therefore be holy, for I am
holy. [47]To make a difference between the
unclean and the clean, and between . . . .

Lev. 20 [7]Sanctify yourselves therefore,
and be ye holy: for I am holy: for I am
the Lord your God.

Jesus' View of Holiness

Matt. 15 [17]Do not ye yet understand,
that whatsoever entereth in at the mouth
goeth into the belly, and is cast out into
the draught? [18]But those things which
proceed out of the mouth come forth from
the heart; and they defile the man. [19]For
out of the heart proceed evil thoughts,
murders, adulteries, fornications, thefts,
false witness, blasphemies: [20]These are
the things which defile a man: but to eat
with unwashen hands defileth not a man.

The Holiness of Christians

Rom. 12 [1]I beseech you therefore,
brethren, by the mercies of God, that ye
present your bodies a living sacrifice, holy,
acceptable unto God, which is your reasonable service.

2 Cor. 7 [1]Having therefore these promises, dearly beloved, let us cleanse ourselves from all filthiness of the flesh and spirit, perfecting holiness in the fear of God.

Eph. 1 [4]According as he hath chosen us in him, before the foundation of the world, that we should be holy, and without blame before him in love.

Eph. 4 [24]And that ye put on that new man, which after God is created in righteousness, and true holiness.

Heb. 12 [14]Follow peace with all men, and holiness, without which no man shall see the Lord.

1 Pet. 1 [15]But as he which hath called
you is holy, so be ye holy in all manner of
conversation; [16]Because it is written, Be
ye holy, for I am holy.

2 Pet. 3 [11]Seeing then that all these things shall be dissolved, What manner of persons ought ye to be in all holy conversation, and godliness?

Rev. 22 [11]He that is unjust, let him be unjust still: and he which is filthy, let him be filthy still: and he that is righteous, let him be righteous still: and he that is holy, let him be holy still.

HONESTY

[on′es ti] Integrity, truthfulness, freedom from fraud, genuineness, straightforwardness of speech or conduct. The Scriptures plainly teach that no man can be a disciple of Christ unless he is honest.

See Dishonest

SCRIPTURE

Prov. 3 [27]Withhold not good from them to whom it is due, when it is in the power of thine hand to do it. [28]Say not unto thy neighbour, Go, and come again, and tomorrow I will give; when thou hast it by thee.

Prov. 16 [8]Better is a little with righteousness, than great revenues without right.

Prov. 22 [29]Seest thou a man diligent in his business? he shall stand before kings; he shall not stand before mean men.

Psa. 37 [21]The wicked borroweth and payeth not again: but the righteous sheweth mercy, and giveth.

Rom. 12 [17]Recompense to no man evil for evil. Provide things honest in the sight of all men.

Rom. 13 [13]Let us walk honestly as in the day, not in rioting and drunkenness, not in chambering and wantonness, not in strife and envying.

2 Cor. 8 [21]Providing for honest things, not only in the sight of the Lord, but in the sight of men.

2 Cor. 13 [7]Now I pray to God that ye do no evil, not that we should appear approved, but that ye should do that which is honest, though we be as reprobates.

Phil. 4 [8]Finally, brethren, whatsoever things are true, whatsoever things are honest, whatsoever things are just, whatsoever things are pure, whatsoever things are lovely, whatsoever things are of good report: if there be any virtue, and if there be any praise, think on these things.

1 Thess. 4 [12]That ye may walk honestly toward them that are without, and that ye may have lack of nothing.

1 Tim. 2 [1]I exhort therefore, that first of all, supplications, prayers, intercessions, and giving of thanks be made for all men: [2]For Kings, and for all that are in authority, that we may lead a quiet and peaceable life in all godliness and honesty.

Heb. 13 [18]Pray for us: for we trust we have a good conscience in all things, willing to live honestly.

HONOR (HONOUR)

[on′ẽr] Used chiefly in the Bible to mean respect, esteem, reverence, deference. The Scriptures teach that honor should be paid to God, that parents should be honored, that the ruler or rulers of a country should receive honor, and that all persons in authority should receive the honor due their rank and position.

SCRIPTURE

Honor Due to God

Psa. 29 [2]Give unto the LORD the glory due unto his name; worship the LORD in the beauty of holiness.

Psa. 71 [8]Let my mouth be filled with thy praise and with thy honour all the day.

Psa. 145 [5]I will speak of the glorious honour of thy majesty, and of thy wondrous works.

Mal. 1 [6]A son honoureth his father, and a servant his master: if then I be a father, where is mine honour? and if I be a master, where is my fear? saith the LORD of hosts unto you, O priests, that despise my name. And ye say, Wherein have we despised thy name?

1 Tim. 1 [17]Now unto the king eternal, immortal, invisible, the only wise God, be honour and glory for ever and ever. Amen.

Rev. 4 [11]Thou art worthy, O Lord, to receive glory, and honour, and power: for thou hast created all things, and for thy pleasure they are, and were created.

Rev. 5 [13]And every creature which is in heaven, and on the earth, and under the earth, and such as are in the sea, and all that are in them, heard I, saying, Blessing, honour, glory, and power be unto him that sitteth upon the Throne, and unto the Lamb for ever and ever.

Honor Granted by God

1 Kin. 3 13And I have also given thee that which thou hast not asked, both riches, and honour: so that there shall not be any among the kings like unto thee all thy days.

Esth. 8 16The Jews had light, and gladness, and joy, and honour.

Prov. 3 16Length of days is in her right hand; and in her left hand riches and honour.

Prov. 4 8Exalt her, and she shall promote thee: she shall bring thee to honour, when thou dost embrace her.

Prov. 8 18Riches and honour are with me; yea, durable riches and righteousness.

Prov. 22 4By humility and the fear of the LORD are riches, and honour, and life.

Prov. 29 23A man's pride shall bring him low: but honour shall uphold the humble in spirit.

Dan. 5 18O thou king, the most high God gave Nebuchadnezzar thy father a kingdom, and majesty, and glory, and honour.

John 12 26If any man serve me, let him follow me; and where I am, there shall also my servant be: if any man serve me, him will my Father honour.

Honor Due to Parents

Ex. 20 12Honour thy father and thy mother; that thy days may be long upon the land which the LORD thy God giveth thee.

Matt. 15 4For God commanded, saying, Honour thy father and mother: and, He that curseth father or mother, let him die the death. 5But ye say, Whosoever shall say to his father or his mother, It is a gift, by whatsoever thou mightest be profited by me; 6And honour not his father or his mother, he shall be free. Thus have ye made the commandment of God of none effect by your tradition.

Honor to the Aged

Lev. 19 32Thou shalt rise up before the hoary head, and honour the face of the old man, and fear thy God: I am the LORD.

Rom. 13 1Let every soul be subject unto the higher powers. For there is no power but of God; the powers that be are ordained of God. 7Render therefore to all their dues: tribute to whom tribute is due; custom to whom custom; fear to whom fear; honor to whom honor.

1 Pet. 2 17Honour all men. Love the brotherhood. Fear God. Honour the king.

HOPE

[hōp] Desire with expectation of obtaining what is desired, or belief that it is obtainable; trust; reliance. In the New Testament, Christian hope is almost always connected with the return of Jesus Christ at the end of the age and the resurrection of the dead. This hope is "an anchor of the soul, both sure and steadfast" which enables the faithful Christian better to bear his burden and infuses strength into him when he is weak or worn.

SCRIPTURE

Good Hope

Psa. 16 9Therefore my heart is glad, and my glory rejoiceth: my flesh also shall rest in hope.

Psa. 31 24Be of good courage, and he shall strengthen your heart, all ye that hope in the LORD.

Prov. 10 28The hope of the righteous shall be gladness: but the expectation of the wicked shall perish.

Prov. 14 32The wicked is driven away in his wickedness: but the righteous hath hope in his death.

Acts 24 15And have hope towards God, which they themselves also allow, that there shall be a resurrection of the dead, both of the just and unjust.

Rom. 15 [13]Now the God of hope fill you with all joy and peace in believing, that ye may abound in hope, through the power of the Holy Ghost.

2 Thess. 2 [16]Now our Lord Jesus Christ himself, and God, even our Father, which hath loved us, and hath given us everlasting consolation and good hope through grace.

Hopes of Wicked Perish

Job 8 [13]So are the paths of all that forget God; and the hypocrite's hope shall perish.

Job 11 [20]But the eyes of the wicked shall fail, and they shall not escape, and their hope shall be as the giving up of the ghost.

Eph. 2 [12]That at that time ye were without Christ, being aliens from the commonwealth of Israel, and strangers from the covenants of promise, having no hope, and without God in the world.

Hope's Comfort

Job 11 [18]And thou shalt be secure, because there is hope; yea, thou shalt dig about thee, and thou shalt take thy rest in safety.

Psa. 146 [5]Happy is he that hath the God of Jacob for his help, whose hope is in the LORD his God.

Jer. 17 [7]Blessed is the man that trusteth in the LORD, and whose hope the LORD is.

Rom. 12 [12]Rejoicing in hope, patient in tribulation, continuing instant in prayer.

Rom. 15 [4]For whatsoever things were written aforetime, were written for our learning, that we through patience and comfort of the Scriptures might have hope.

1 Cor. 13 [13]And now abideth faith, hope, charity, these three, but the greatest of these is charity.

Eph. 4 [4]There is one body, and one spirit, even as ye are called in one hope of your calling.

Col. 1 [5]For the hope which is laid up for you in heaven, whereof ye heard before in the word of the truth of the Gospel.

Heb. 3 [6]But Christ as a Son over his own house, whose house are we, if we hold fast the confidence, and the rejoicing of the hope firm unto the end.

Hope's Encouragement

Psa. 42 [5]Why art thou cast down, O my soul? and why art thou disquieted in me? hope thou in God: for I shall yet praise him for the help of his countenance.

Psa. 130 [7]Let Israel hope in the LORD: for with the LORD there is mercy, and with him is plenteous redemption.

Lam. 3 [26]It is good that a man should both hope and quietly wait for the salvation of the LORD.

Zech. 9 [12]Turn you to the strong hold, ye prisoners of hope: even to-day do I declare that I will render double unto thee.

Col. 1 [23]If ye continue in the faith grounded and settled, and be not moved away from the hope of the gospel, which ye have heard, and which was preached to every creature which is under heaven, whereof I Paul am made a Minister.

Tit. 2 [13]Looking for that blessed hope, and the glorious appearing of the great God, and our Saviour Jesus Christ.

Heb. 6 [11]And we desire, that every one of you do shew the same diligence, to the full assurance of hope unto the end.

1 Pet. 1 [13]Wherefore gird up the loins of your mind, be sober, and hope to the end, for the grace that is to be brought unto you at the revelation of Jesus Christ.

Hope's Effects

Rom. 5 [5]And hope maketh not ashamed; because the love of God is shed abroad in

our hearts by the Holy Ghost which is
given unto us.

Rom. 8 [24]For we are saved by hope: but
hope that is seen is not hope: for what a
man seeth, why doth he yet hope for?
[25]But if we hope for that we see not, then
do we with patience wait for it.

Hope God's Gift

Gal. 5 [5]For we through the Spirit wait
for the hope of righteousness by faith.

2 Thess. 2 [16]Now our Lord Jesus Christ
himself, and God even our Father, which
hath loved us, and hath given us everlasting consolation, and good hope through
grace.

Tit. 1 [2]In hope of eternal life, which
God that cannot lie, promised before the
world began.

1 Pet. 1 [3]Blessed be the God and Father of our Lord Jesus Christ, which according to his abundant mercy hath begotten us again unto a lively hope, by the
resurrection of Jesus Christ from the dead.

HOPHNI AND PHINEHAS

[hof'nī, fin'ê as] Sons of Eli and priests of the sanctuary at Shiloh. These worthless men showed disrespect for the offerings which were brought before the LORD, using their positions as priests for personal gain; in addition to this, they committed fornication with the women who served at the entrance of the sanctuary. An unnamed prophet informed Eli of the misdeeds of his sons and prophesied their death; this warning was repeated by the boy Samuel. The curse upon the house of Eli was fulfilled at the battle with the Philistines at Aphek in which Hophni and Phinehas were killed and the Ark of the Covenant captured. When news of the catastrophe reached Eli, he fainted, breaking his neck as he fell from his seat.

See ELI

SCRIPTURE

1 Sam. 2 [12]Now the sons of Eli were
sons of Belial; they knew not the LORD.
[13]And the priest's custom with the people
was, that, when any man offered sacrifice,
the priest's servant came, while the flesh
was in seething, with a fleshhook of three
teeth in his hand; [14]And he struck it into
the pan, or kettle, or caldron, or pot; all
that the fleshhook brought up the priest
took for himself. So they did in Shiloh unto
all the Israelites that came thither. [15]Also
before they burnt the fat, the priest's servant came, and said to the man that sacrificed, Give flesh to roast for the priest; for
he will not have sodden flesh of thee, but
raw. [16]And if any man said unto him, Let
them not fail to burn the fat presently, and
then take as much as thy soul desireth;
then he would answer him, Nay; but thou
shalt give it me now: and if not, I will take
it by force. [17]Wherefore the sin of the
young men was very great before the
LORD: for men abhorred the offering of
the LORD.

[22]Now Eli was very old, and heard all
that his sons did unto all Israel; and how
they lay with the women that assembled at
the door of the tabernacle of the congregation. [23]And he said unto them, Why do ye
such things? for I hear of your evil dealings
by all this people. [24]Nay, my sons; for it is
no good report that I hear: ye make the
LORD's people to transgress. [25]If one man
sin against another, the judge shall judge
him: but if a man sin against the LORD,
who shall entreat for him? Notwithstanding, they hearkened not unto the voice of
their father, because the LORD would slay
them.

1 Sam. 4 [18]And it came to pass, when he
made mention of the ark of God, that he
fell from off the seat backward by the side
of the gate, and his neck brake, and he
died: for he was an old man, and heavy.
And he had judged Israel forty years.

HOSANNA

[hō zan′a] A Hebrew exclamation with the approximate meaning of "Save now!" It was used by the Jews as an appeal for deliverance and by Jews and Christians as an ascription of praise to God.

SCRIPTURE

Psa. 118 25Save now, I beseech thee, O LORD: O LORD, I beseech thee, send now prosperity.

Matt. 21 9And the multitudes that went before, and that followed, cried, saying, Hosanna to the Son of David: Blessed is he that cometh in the name of the Lord; Hosanna in the highest.

HOSEA

[hȯ zē′a] A prophet of the northern kingdom, active from about the middle of the eighth century and a contemporary of Amos. At the beginning of Hosea's prophetic ministry, Israel was enjoying the prosperous reign of Jeroboam II. Hosea saw disaster, however, in Israel's efforts to preserve her position by political machinations instead of reliance on God. Her past and future troubles are attributed by Hosea to her persistent practice of idolatry. The people were offering sacrifices on heathen altars; adultery and cult prostitution were prevalent. The faithless actions of Israel toward God are illustrated by the relationship between Hosea and his worthless marriage partner, Gomer. The names of his children indicate the attitude of God toward Israel. The first is name Jezreel after the city which was the scene of Jehu's brutality and which signified that God would punish his people. Lo-Ruhamah (Not pitied) and Lo-Ammi (Not my People) are the names given to the two other children, signifying the estrangement which was the inevitable result of the actions of Israel. God's love is illustrated in Hosea's willingness to take his wife back from the practice of harlotry—though not without some measure of discipline. The figure which Hosea often uses to describe the spiritual condition of the Israelites is lack of knowledge. He is not speaking simply of intellectual knowledge, but of a relationship of the most intimate sort between man and God.

See JEROBOAM II, AMOS

REFERENCE: The Book of *Hosea.*

SCRIPTURE

Hosea's Domestic Tragedy

THE HARLOT AND HER CHILDREN

Hos. 1 2The beginning of the word of the LORD by Hosea. And the LORD said to Hosea, Go, take unto thee a wife of whoredoms and children of whoredoms: for the land hath committed great whoredom, departing from the LORD. 3So he went and took Gomer the daughter of Diblaim; which conceived, and bare him a son. 4And the LORD said unto him, Call his name Jezreel; for yet a little while, and I will avenge the blood of Jezreel upon the house of Jehu, and will cause to cease the kingdom of the house of Israel. 5And it shall come to pass at that day, that I will break the bow of Israel in the valley of Jezreel.

6And she conceived again, and bare a daughter. And God said unto him, Call her name Lo-ruhamah: for I will no more have mercy upon the house of Israel; but I will utterly take them away. 7But I will have mercy upon the house of Judah, and will save them by the LORD their God, and will not save them by bow, nor by sword, nor by battle, by horses, nor by horsemen.

8Now when she had weaned Lo-ruhamah, she conceived, and bare a son.

HOSEA'S WARNING TO GOMER

Hos. 2 2Plead with your mother, plead; for she is not my wife, neither am I her husband: let her therefore put away her whoredoms out of her sight, and her adulteries from between her breasts; 3Lest I strip her naked, and set her as in the day that she was born, and make her as a wilderness, and set her like a dry land, and slay her with thirst. 4And I will not have mercy upon her children; for they be the children of whoredoms. 5For their mother hath played the harlot: she that conceived them hath done shamefully; for she said, I will go after my lovers, that give me my bread and my water, my wool and my flax, mine oil and my drink.

6Therefore, behold, I will hedge up thy way with thorns, and make a wall, that she shall not find her paths. 7And she shall follow after her lovers, but she shall not overtake them; and she shall seek them, but shall not find them: then shall she say, I will go and return to my first husband; for then was it better with me than now. 8For she did not know that I gave her corn, and wine, and oil, and multiplied her silver and gold, which they prepared for Baal. 9Therefore will I return, and take away my corn in the time thereof, and my wine in the season thereof, and will recover my wool and my flax given to cover her nakedness. 10And now will I discover her lewdness in the sight of her lovers, and none shall deliver her out of mine hand. 11I will also cause all her mirth to cease, her feast days, her new moons, and her sabbaths, and all her solemn feasts. 12And I will destroy her vines and her fig trees, whereof she hath said, These are my rewards that my lovers have given me: and I will make them a forest, and the beasts of the field shall eat them. 13And I will visit upon her the days of Baalim, wherein she burned incense to them, and she decked herself with her earrings and her jewels, and she went after her lovers, and forgat me, saith the LORD.

REWARDS FOR HER REPENTANCE

Hos. 2 14Therefore, behold, I will allure her, and bring her into the wilderness, and speak comfortably unto her. 15And I will give her her vineyards from thence, and the valley of Achor for a door of hope: and she shall sing there, as in the days of her youth, and as in the day when she came up out of the land of Egypt. 16And it shall be at that day, saith the LORD, that thou shalt call me Ishi; and shalt call me no more Baali. 17For I will take away the names of Baalim out of her mouth, and they shall no more be remembered by their name. 18And in that day will I make a covenant for them with the beasts of the field, and with the fowls of heaven, and with the creeping things of the ground: and I will break the bow and the sword and the battle out of the earth, and will make them to lie down safely. 19And I will betroth thee unto me for ever; yea, I will betroth thee unto me in righteousness, and in judgment, and in lovingkindness, and in mercies. 20I will even betroth thee unto me in faithfulness: and thou shalt know the LORD. 21And it shall come to pass in that day, I will hear, saith the LORD, I will hear the heavens, and they shall hear the earth; 22And the earth shall hear the corn, and the wine, and the oil; and they shall hear Jezreel. 23And I will sow her unto me in the earth; and I will have mercy upon her that had not obtained mercy; and I will say to them which were not my people, Thou art my people; and they shall say, Thou art my God.

Representative Prophecies

ON THE LACK OF KNOWLEDGE

Hos. 4 1Hear the word of the LORD, ye

children of Israel: for the Lord hath a controversy with the inhabitants of the land, because there is no truth, nor mercy, nor knowledge of God in the land. 2By swearing, and lying, and killing, and stealing, and committing adultery, they break out, and blood toucheth blood. 3Therefore shall the land mourn, and every one that dwelleth therein shall languish, with the beasts of the field, and with the fowls of heaven; yea, the fishes of the sea also shall be taken away. 4Yet let no man strive, nor reprove another: for thy people are as they that strive with the priest. 5Therefore shalt thou fall in the day, and the prophet also shall fall with thee in the night, and I will destroy thy mother.

6My people are destroyed for lack of knowledge: because thou hast rejected knowledge, I will also reject thee, that thou shalt be no priest to me: seeing thou hast forgotten the law of thy God, I will also forget thy children.

ON IDOLATRY

Hos. 8 5Thy calf, O Samaria, hath cast thee off; mine anger is kindled against them: how long will it be ere they attain to innocency? 6For from Israel was it also: the workman made it; therefore it is not God: but the calf of Samaria shall be broken in pieces.

Hos. 13 2And now they sin more and more, and have made them molten images of their silver, and idols according to their own understanding, all of it the work of the craftsmen: they say of them, Let the men that sacrifice kiss the calves. 3Therefore they shall be as the morning cloud, and as the early dew that passeth away, as the chaff that is driven with the whirlwind out of the floor, and as the smoke out of the chimney.

HOSHEA

[hō shē′a] The nineteenth and last king of Israel (732/1-723/2 BC). Apparently at the instigation of Tiglath-Pileser of Assyria, Hoshea gained the throne of Israel by the assassination of his predecessor, Pekah. He was, in reality, not an independent king but an Assyrian vassal; his efforts to break this relationship ended in the final disaster for the nation of Israel. Shortly after the death of Tiglath-Pileser, Hoshea sought an alliance with Egypt, but this disorganized land was in no position to help anyone. This treasonous gesture, however, raised the ire of Shalmaneser V, the new ruler of Assyria, and when Hoshea appeared at the Assyrian court to pay the annual tribute, he was taken captive and disappeared from history. Shalmaneser then marched on Samaria and after a long struggle, the once-great capital of Israel fell either to him or, more probably, to his successor, Sargon II. According to the annals of Sargon, over 27,000 captives were deported to Upper Mesopotamia and Media, where their identity was ultimately forever lost, and the land of Israel became an Assyrian province.

See Tiglath-Pileser, Kings, Pekah, Shalmaneser, Sargon

SCRIPTURE

Assassinates Pekah and Usurps Throne of Israel

2 Kin. 15 30And Hoshea the son of Elah made a conspiracy against Pekah the son of Remaliah, and smote him, and slew him, and reigned in his stead, in the twentieth year of Jotham the son of Uzziah.

An Evil King

2 Kin. 17 1In the twelfth year of Ahaz king of Judah began Hoshea the son of Elah to reign in Samaria over Israel nine years. 2And he did that which was evil in the sight of the Lord, but not as the kings of Israel that were before him.

Pays Tribute to Assyria

2 Kin. 17 [3]Against him came up Shalmaneser king of Assyria; and Hoshea became his servant, and gave him presents.

Conspires against Assyria and Is Imprisoned

2 Kin. 17 [4]And the king of Assyria found conspiracy in Hoshea: for he had sent messengers to So king of Egypt, and brought no present to the king of Assyria, as he had done year by year: therefore the king of Assyria shut him up, and bound him in prison.

Last King of Israel

2 Kin. 17 [5]Then the king of Assyria came up throughout all the land, and went up to Samaria, and besieged it three years. [6]In the ninth year of Hoshea the king of Assyria took Samaria, and carried Israel away into Assyria, and placed them in Halah and in Habor by the river of Gozan, and in the cities of the Medes.

HOSPITALITY

[hos pi tal′i ti] The act of receiving and entertaining guests—either friends or strangers—generously and kindly. The practice of hospitality to a degree that seems extreme to us was quite common in Biblical times and presents a fascinating study for the interested student. Jesus' directions to the apostles and the seventy to take nothing on their journey presupposes that they were to rely on the hospitality of the people to whom they preached. The conditions which made the hospitality of the Near East a vital aspect of life—chiefly, the absence of any other means of sustaining oneself on a journey of any distance—no longer exist in Western civilization; nevertheless, the precepts given in scripture concerning hospitality can easily be adapted to the contemporary social situation.

SCRIPTURE

Heb. 13 [2]Be not forgetful to entertain strangers: for thereby some have entertained angels unawares.

1 Pet. 4 [9]Use hospitality one to another without grudging. [10]As every man hath received the gift, even so minister the same one to another, as good stewards of the manifold grace of God.

3 John 1 [5]Beloved, thou doest faithfully whatsoever thou doest to the brethren, and to strangers; [6]Which have borne witness of thy charity before the church: whom if thou bring forward on their journey after a godly sort, thou shalt do well: [7]Because that for his name's sake they went forth, taking nothing of the Gentiles, [8]We therefore ought to receive such, that we might be fellow helpers to the truth.

2 John 1 [10]If there come any unto you, and bring not this doctrine, receive him not into your house, neither bid him God speed: [11]For he that biddeth him God speed is partaker of his evil deeds.

3 John 1 [9]I wrote unto the church: but Diotrephes, who loveth to have the preeminence among them, receiveth us not. [10]Wherefore, if I come, I will remember his deeds which he doeth, prating against us with malicious words: and not content therewith, neither doth he himself receive the brethren, and forbiddeth them that would, and casteth them out of the church.

Mark 9 [41]For whosoever shall give you a cup of water to drink in my name, because ye belong to Christ, verily I say unto you, he shall not lose his reward.

HUMILITY

[hū mil i ti] The state of being humble; freedom from pride and arrogance; a modest estimate of one's worth, or a sense of unworthiness through imperfection or sinfulness; lowliness; meekness; an opposite of pride, which may be regarded as the root and essence of sin. Humility is not to be regarded as the root and essence of sin. Humility is not to be regarded as meanness or baseness, but it is a medium between foolish and ignominious self-effacement and vainglorying. The humble man does not attribute to himself any goodness or virtue that he does not possess, he does not overrate himself, he does not take immoderate delight in himself, he realizes his imperfections, and he ascribes all his goodness and good words to God's grace. The supreme example of humility is found in the incarnation and death of the Son of God.

See MEEKNESS, PRIDE

SCRIPTURE

Humility Commanded

Matt. 18 [1]At the same time came the disciples unto Jesus, saying, Who is the greatest in the kingdom of heaven? [2]And Jesus called a little child unto him, and set him in the midst of them, [3]And said, Verily I say unto you, Except ye be converted, and become as little children, ye shall not enter into the kingdom of heaven. [4]Whosoever therefore shall humble himself as this little child, the same is greatest in the kingdom of heaven.

Matt. 20 [25]But Jesus called them unto him, and said, Ye know that the princes of the Gentiles exercise dominion over them, and they that are great exercise authority upon them. [26]But it shall not be so among you: but whosoever will be great among you, let him be your minister; [27]And whosoever will be chief among you, let him be your servant.

Matt. 23 [11]But he that is greatest among you shall be your servant. [12]And whosoever shall exalt himself shall be abased; and he that shall humble himself shall be exalted.

Luke 14 [7]And he put forth a parable to those which were bidden, when he marked how they chose out the chief rooms; saying unto them, [8]When thou art bidden of any man to a wedding, sit not down in the highest room; lest a more honourable man than thou be bidden of him; [9]And he that bade thee and him come and say to thee, Give this man place; and thou begin with shame to take the lowest room. [10]But when thou art bidden, go and sit thou in the lowest room; that when he that bade thee cometh, he may say unto thee, Friend, go up higher: then shalt thou have worship in the presence of them that sit at meat with thee. [11]For whosoever exalteth himself shall be abased; and he that humbleth himself shall be exalted.

Rom. 12 [3]For I say, through the grace given unto me, to every man that is among you, not to think of himself more highly than he ought to think; but to think soberly, according as God hath dealt to every man the measure of faith.

1 Cor. 8 [2]And if any man think that he knoweth any thing, he knoweth nothing yet as he ought to know.

Phil. 2 [3]Let nothing be done through strife or vainglory; but in lowliness of mind let each esteem other better than themselves.

Jas. 3 [1]My brethren, be not many masters, knowing that we shall receive the greater condemnation.

Jas. 4 [10]Humble yourselves in the sight of the Lord, and he shall lift you up.

1 Pet. 5 [6]Humble yourselves therefore under the mighty hand of God, that he may exalt you in due time.

Humility Rewarded

1 Kin. 21 [29]Seest thou how Ahab humbleth himself before me? because he humbleth himself before me, I will not bring the evil in his days: but in his son's days will I bring the evil upon his house.

2 Chr. 34 [27]Because thine heart was tender, and thou didst humble thyself before God, when thou heardest his words against this place, and against the inhabitants thereof, and humbledst thyself before me, and didst rend thy clothes, and weep before me; I have even heard thee also, saith the LORD.

Psa. 138 [6]Though the LORD be high, yet hath he respect unto the lowly: but the proud he knoweth afar off.

Prov. 11 [2]When pride cometh, then cometh shame: but with the lowly is wisdom.

Prov. 15 [33]The fear of the LORD is the instruction of wisdom; and before honour is humility.

Prov. 16 [19]Better it is to be of an humble spirit with the lowly, than to divide the spoil with the proud.

Prov. 18 [12]Before destruction the heart of man is haughty; and before honour is humility.

Prov. 22 [4]By humility and the fear of the LORD are riches, and honour, and life.

Jas. 4 [6]But he giveth more grace. Wherefore he saith, God resisteth the proud, but giveth grace unto the humble.

1 Pet. 5 [5]Likewise, ye younger, submit yourselves unto the elder. Yea, all of you be subject one to another, and be clothed with humility: for God resisteth the proud, and giveth grace to the humble.

Luke 18 [9]And he spake this parable unto certain which trusted in themselves that they were righteous, and despised others: [10]Two men went up into the temple to pray; the one a Pharisee, and the other a publican. [11]The Pharisee stood and prayed thus with himself, God, I thank thee, that I am not as other men are, extortioners, unjust, adulterers, or even as this publican. [12]I fast twice in the week, I give tithes of all that I possess. [13]And the publican, standing afar off, would not lift up so much as his eyes unto heaven, but smote upon his breast, saying, God be merciful to me a sinner. [14]I tell you, this man went down to his house justified rather than the other: for every one that exalteth himself shall be abased; and he that humbleth himself shall be exalted.

REFERENCE: On Humility of Jesus, *see* JESUS.

HUNGER

[hun'gẽr] A craving or need for food; any strong or eager desire; craving. The absence of hunger is spoken of as one of the characteristics of the future state of the blessed. In the prosperity of American civilization, it is difficult to appreciate this fully, but it must be remembered that hunger and famine were an ever present threat in Biblical times. Hunger is used metaphorically to refer to the striving for righteousness which mark true disciples of Christ.

SCRIPTURE

Physical Hunger

Ex. 16 [3]And the children of Israel said unto them, Would to God we had died by the hand of the LORD in the land of Egypt, when we sat by the fleshpots, and when we did eat bread to the full; for ye have brought us forth into this wilderness, to kill this whole assembly with hunger.

Deut. 8 [3]And he humbled thee, and suffered thee to hunger, and fed thee with manna, which thou knewest not, neither did thy fathers know; that he might make thee know that man doth not live by bread only, but by every word that proceedeth out of the mouth of the LORD doth man live.

Isa. 49 [10]They shall not hunger nor thirst; neither shall the heat nor sun smite them: for he that hath mercy on them shall lead them, even by the springs of water shall he guide them.

Jer. 38 [9]My lord the king, these men have done evil in all that they have done to Jeremiah the prophet, whom they have cast into the dungeon; and he is like to die for hunger in the place where he is: for there is no more bread in the city.

Matt. 21 [18]Now in the morning, as he returned into the city, he hungered.

Luke 4 [2]. . . And in those days he did eat nothing: and when they were ended, he afterward hungered.

No Hunger in Heaven

Rev. 7 [16]They shall hunger no more, neither thirst any more; neither shall the sun light on them, nor any heat. [17]For the Lamb which is in the midst of the throne shall feed them, and shall lead them unto living fountains of waters: and God shall wipe away all tears from their eyes.

Spiritual Hunger

Isa. 55 [1]Ho, every one that thirsteth, come ye to the waters, and he that hath no money; come ye, buy, and eat; yea, come, buy wine and milk without money and without price. [2]Wherefore do ye spend money for that which is not bread? and your labor for that which satisfieth not? hearken diligently unto me, and eat ye that which is good, and let your soul delight itself in fatness.

Amos 8 [11]Behold, the days come, saith the Lord GOD, that I will send a famine in the land, not a famine of bread, nor a thirst for water, but of hearing the words of the LORD: [12]And they shall wander from sea to sea, and from the north even to the east, they shall run to and fro to seek the word of the LORD, and shall not find it. [13]In that day shall the fair virgins and young men faint for thirst.

Matt. 5 [6]Blessed are they which do hunger and thirst after righteousness; for they shall be filled.

Luke 6 [21]Blessed are ye that hunger now: for ye shall be filled.

1 Pet. 2 [2]As newborn babes, desire the sincere milk of the word, that ye may grow thereby.

HUSBAND

[huz′band] Literally, a man who has a wife. In Hebrew society, the husband was possessor and master of his wife, his children, his servants, his animals, and his property. In this circle, his rule was virtually absolute. It appears that the husband had the right to divorce his wife with little reason, although she had little or no redress if she were wronged by him. Absolute faithfulness was required of the wife, but not of the husband, so long as he did not violate the rights of another husband (see discussion of seventh commandment in article on TEN COMMANDMENTS). With this power and freedom, however, came the responsibility of the husband to instruct his household in the religious and social traditions of the family, the tribe, and the nation.

The husband is used as a figure of the relation between God and Israel and between Christ and his church.

See FAMILY, WIFE, CHILDREN, MARRIAGE

SCRIPTURE

Gen. 2 [23]And Adam said, This is now bone of my bones, and flesh of my flesh: she shall be called Woman, because she was taken out of man. [24]Therefore shall a man leave his father and his mother, and shall cleave unto his wife: and they shall be one flesh.

1 Cor. 7 [3]Let the husband render unto the wife due benevolence: and likewise also the wife unto the husband. [5]Defraud ye not one the other, except it be with consent for a time, that ye may give yourselves to fasting and prayer; and come together again, that Satan tempt you not for your incontinency. [14]For the unbelieving husband is sanctified by the wife, and the unbelieving wife is sanctified by the husband: else were your children unclean; but now are they holy. [16]For what knowest thou, O wife, whether thou shalt save thy husband? or how knowest thou, O man, whether thou shalt save thy wife?

1 Cor. 11 [3]But I would have you know, that the head of every man is Christ; and the head of the woman is the man; and the head of Christ is God.

Eph. 5 [22]Wives, submit yourselves unto your own husbands, as unto the Lord. [23]For the husband is the head of the wife, even as Christ is the head of the church: and he is the saviour of the body. [24]Therefore as the church is subject unto Christ, so let the wives be to their own husbands in every thing. [25]Husbands, love your wives, even as Christ also loved the church, and gave himself for it; [26]That he might sanctify and cleanse it with the washing of water by the word, [27]That he might present it to himself a glorious church, not having spot, or wrinkle, or any such thing; but that it should be holy and without blemish. [28]So ought men to love their wives as their own bodies. He that loveth his wife loveth himself. [29]For no man ever yet hated his own flesh; but nourisheth and cherisheth it, even as the Lord the church: [30]For we are members of his body, of his flesh, and of his bones. [31]For this cause shall a man leave his father and mother, and shall be joined unto his wife, and they two shall be one flesh. [32]This is a great mystery: but I speak concerning Christ and the church. [33]Nevertheless let every one of you in particular so love his wife even as himself; and the wife see that she reverence her husband.

Col. 3 [18]Wives, submit yourselves unto your own husbands, as it is fit in the Lord. [19]Husbands, love your wives, and be not bitter against them.

1 Tim. 5 [8]But if any provide not for his own, and specially for those of his own house, he hath denied the faith, and is worse than an infidel.

1 Pet. 3 [7]Likewise, ye husbands, dwell with them according to knowledge, giving honor unto the wife, as unto the weaker vessel, and as being heirs together of the grace of life; that your prayers be not hindered.

See Matt. 19:5; Mark 10:7

HYPOCRISY, HYPOCRITE

[hi pok′ri si, hip′ô krit] A hypocrite is one who professes to be what he is not, especially in the matter of religion. Hypocrisy is the act or practice of being a hypocrite, the professing of religion where none exists. As used in the Bible these terms usually refer to impiety or unprincipled action on the part of those who have the reputation for being religious; they do not, however, always imply that those accused are consciously playing a role, but simply that their religion is empty and worthless.

See DECEIT

SCRIPTURE

Hypocrisy Condemned

Job 17 [8]Upright men shall be astonied at this, and the innocent shall stir up himself against the hypocrite.

Psa. 5 [9]For there is no faithfulness in their mouth; their inward part is very wickedness; their throat is an open sepulchre; they flatter with their tongue.

Isa. 29 [13]Wherefore the LORD said, Forasmuch as this people draw near me with their mouth, and with their lips do honour me, but have removed their heart far from me, and their fear toward me is taught by the precept of men: [14]Therefore, behold, I will proceed to do a marvellous work among this people, even a marvellous work and a wonder: for the wisdom of their wise men shall perish, and the understanding of their prudent men shall be hid.

Isa. 32 [5]The vile person shall be no more called liberal, nor the churl said to be bountiful. [6]For the vile person will speak villany, and his heart will work iniquity, to practise hypocrisy, and to utter error against the LORD, to make empty the soul of the hungry; and he will cause the drink of the thirsty to fail.

Ezek. 33 [31]And they come unto thee as the people cometh, and they sit before thee as my people, and they hear thy words, but they will not do them: for with their mouth they shew much love, but their heart goeth after their covetousness.

Matt. 15 [7]Ye hypocrites, well did Esaias prophesy of you, saying, [8]This people draweth nigh unto me with their mouth, and honoureth me with their lips; but their heart is far from me. [9]But in vain they do worship me, teaching for doctrines the commandments of men.

Matt. 23 [13]But woe unto you, scribes and Pharisees, hypocrites! for ye shut up the kingdom of heaven against men: for ye neither go in yourselves, neither suffer ye them that are entering to go in. [14]Woe unto you, scribes and Pharisees, hypocrites! for ye devour widows' houses, and for a pretence make long prayer: therefore ye shall receive the greater damnation.

Matt. 23 [23]Woe unto you, scribes and Pharisees, hypocrites! for ye pay tithe of mint and anise and cummin, and have omitted the weightier matters of the law, judgment, mercy and faith: these ought ye to have done, and not to leave the other undone. [24]Ye blind guides, which strain at a gnat, and swallow a camel. [25]Woe unto you, scribes and Pharisees, hypocrites! for ye make clean the outside of the cup and of the platter, but within they are full of extortion and excess. [26]Thou blind Pharisee, cleanse first that which is within the cup and platter, that the outside of them may be clean also. [27]Woe unto you, scribes and Pharisees, hypocrites! for ye are like unto whited sepulchres, which indeed appear beautiful outward, but are within full of dead men's bones, and of all uncleanness. [28]Even so ye also outwardly appear righteous unto men, but within ye are full of hypocrisy and iniquity. [29]Woe unto you, scribes and Pharisees, hypocrites! because ye build the tombs of the prophets, and garnish the sepulchres of the righteous, [30]And say, If we had been in the days of our fathers, we would not have been partakers with them in the blood of the prophets. [31]Wherefore ye be witnesses unto yourselves, that ye are the children of them which killed the prophets.

Rom. 2 [20]An instructor of the foolish, a teacher of babes, which hast the form of knowledge and of the truth in the law. [21]Thou therefore which teachest another, teachest thou not thyself? thou that preachest a man should not steal, dost thou steal? [22]Thou that sayest a man should not commit adultery, dost thou commit adultery? thou that abhorrest idols, dost thou commit sacrilege? [23]Thou that makest thy boast of the law, through breaking the law dishonourest thou God?

Tit. 1 [16]They profess that they know God; but in works they deny him, being abominable, and disobedient, and unto every good work reprobate.

Hypocrisy's Punishment

Job 8 [13]So are the paths of all that forget God; and the hypocrite's hope shall perish: [14]Whose hope shall be cut off, and whose trust shall be a spider's web.

Job 20 [4]Knowest thou not this of old,

since man was placed upon earth, [5]That the triumphing of the wicked is short, and the joy of the hypocrite but for a moment? [6]Though his excellency mount up to the heavens, and his head reach unto the clouds; [7]Yet he shall perish for ever like his own dung: they which have seen him shall say, Where is he? [8]He shall fly away as a dream, and shall not be found: yea, he shall be chased away as a vision of the night. [9]The eye also which saw him shall see him no more; neither shall his place any more behold him. [10]His children shall seek to please the poor, and his hands shall restore their goods. [11]His bones are full of the sin of his youth, which shall lie down with him in the dust.

Job 27 [8]For what is the hope of the hypocrite, though he hath gained, when God taketh away his soul?

Job 36 [13]But the hypocrites in heart heap up wrath: they cry not when he bindeth them. [14]They die in youth, and their life is among the unclean.

Psa. 50 [16]But unto the wicked God saith, What hast thou to do to declare my statutes, or that thou shouldest take my covenant in thy mouth? [17]Seeing thou hatest instruction, and castest my words behind thee.

HYSSOP

[his′up] An insignificant plant, common in Bible lands, used to sprinkle blood on the doorposts of the Israelites in Egypt and in certain purification ceremonies. A hyssop branch was used to support the sponge soaked with vinegar which was offered to Jesus as he hung upon the cross.

SCRIPTURE

Ex. 12 [22]And ye shall take a bunch of hyssop, and dip it in the blood that is in the basin, and strike the lintel and the two side posts with the blood that is in the basin;

Lev. 14 [4]Then shall the priest command to take for him that is to be cleansed two birds alive and clean, and cedar woods, and scarlet, and hyssop:

1 Kin. 4 [33]And he spake of trees, from the cedar tree that is in Lebanon even unto the hyssop that springeth out of the wall: he spake also of beasts, and of fowl, and of creeping things, and of fishes.

John 19 [29]Now there was set a vessel full of vinegar: and they filled a sponge with vinegar, and put it upon hyssop, and put it to his mouth.

See Num. 19:6

IDLE, IDLENESS

[ī′d'l] Unemployed; not turned to appropriate or good use; thoughtless, unprofitable; slothful or sluggish. The Bible contains many warnings against falling into such a useless state.

SCRIPTURE

Idleness Reproved

Prov. 6 [6]Go to the ant, thou sluggard; consider her ways, and be wise: [7]Which having no guide, overseer, or ruler, [8]Provideth her meat in the summer, and gathereth her food in the harvest. [9]How long wilt thou sleep, O sluggard? when wilt thou arise out of thy sleep? [10]Yet a little sleep, a little slumber, a little folding of the hands to sleep: [11]So shall thy poverty come as one that travelleth, and thy want as an armed man.

Prov. 18 [9]He also that is slothful in his work is brother to him that is a great waster.

Prov. 24 [30]I went by the field of the slothful, and by the vineyard of the man void of understanding; [31]And lo, it was all grown over with thorns, and nettles had covered the face thereof, and the stone wall thereof was broken down.

Rom. 12 [11]Not slothful in business: fervent in spirit, serving the Lord.

1 Thess. 4 [11]And that ye study to be quiet, and to do your own business, and to work with your own hands, (as we commanded you).

2 Thess. 3 [10]For even when we were with you, this we commanded you, that if any would not work, neither should he eat. [11]For we hear that there are some which walk among you disorderly, working not at all, but are busybodies.

Heb. 6 [12]That ye be not slothful, but followers of them who through faith and patience inherit the promises.

Idleness Produces Poverty

Prov. 10 [4]He becometh poor that dealeth with a slack hand; but the hand of the diligent maketh rich. [5]He that gathereth in summer is a wise son: but he that sleepeth in harvest is a son that causeth shame.

Prov. 12 [24]The hand of the diligent shall bear rule: but the slothful shall be under tribute.

Prov. 13 [4]The soul of the sluggard desireth, and hath nothing: but the soul of the diligent shall be made fat.

Prov. 19 [15]Slothfulness casteth into a deep sleep; and an idle soul shall suffer hunger.

Prov. 20 [4]The sluggard will not plough by reason of the cold; therefore shall he beg in harvest, and have nothing. [13]Love not sleep, lest thou come to poverty; open thine eyes, and thou shalt be satisfied with bread.

Eccl. 10 [18]By much slothfulness the building decayeth; and through idleness of the hands the house droppeth through.

Idleness a Source of Evil-Speaking

1 Tim. 4 [13]And withal they learn to be idle, wandering about from house to house; and not only idle, but tattlers also, and busybodies, speaking things which they ought not.

IDOL, IDOLATRY

[ī′d'l, ī dol′a tri] An idol may be defined as the image of a god, or any other material symbol which is the object of worship. In ancient times, the worship of idols including the offering of various types of sacrifices and libations, and other acts of devotion such as kissing an image, or kneeling or dancing before it. On occasion, the worshippers inflicted wounds in themselves as a special act of homage.

The second commandment of the Decalogue prohibited the making of any image of the God of Israel. Despite the fact that arks and ephods and teraphim found their place in the religion of Israel, not a single figure of God has ever been recovered by archaeologists. This feature of Israel's religion sharply distinguishes it from that of her neighbors and contemporaries, and profoundly attests to the fact that the true God is not a being whose personality can be adequately reflected in the products of human handicraft. Nevertheless, idolatry is seen to have been a constant problem in ancient Israel. Early in their occupation of Canaan, the Israelites were attracted to the worship of local deities including Baal, Asherah, and the Ashtoreth. (See individual articles on these deities.) A number of foreign deities were introduced by Solomon's many wives, but this does not seem to have posed too serious a threat to the worship of God among the general populace. A more serious development arose at the time of the division of the kingdom in 922 BC. (*See* REHOBOAM) In an effort to build up a nationalistic spirit in the Northern Kingdom, Jeroboam set up a bull cultus in Bethel in Dan to rival the temple worship in Jerusalem. There is good reason for believing that Jeroboam intended for the bulls to serve, not as objects of worship, but as pedestals for the invisible God, much in the same manner as the cherubim on the ark of the covenant. It is known from archaeological discoveries that the Semitic storm god was sometimes pictured standing on the back of a bull. If true, this hypothesis might explain the repeated failure of reformers to destroy the Bull cultus. At any rate, when the cult was left to the unsophisticated masses, it apparently degenerated into simple idolatry and, as such, received the severe condemnation of the prophets. During the reign of Ahab and Jezebel, the worship of the true God was almost replaced by the worship of the Phoenician Ball Melqart and Asherah. (*See* BAAL, ELIJAH, JEZEBEL)

The southern kingdom of Judah, while not as seriously troubled with idolatry as Israel, was not by any means free from its taint. The reforms of Hezekiah (*2 Kin. 18:4*) and Josiah (*2 Kin. 23*) dealt not only with the traditional forms of Baal-worship, but with worship of the various heavenly bodies. After the death of Josiah, the political decay in Judah was accompanied by religious decay, and the worship of various Mesopotamian and Babylonian deities was introduced into Jerusalem.

Throughout Israel's history the prophets of God inveighed against the idolatrous practices in which the people engaged. Their oracles ranged in tone from blunt denunciation to sorrowful pleading to biting satire, but it seemed that nothing could stay the Israelites from their headlong flight to disaster. Finally, when thrown back upon themselves in Babylonian exile, the Israelites developed the conviction to abandon idolatry and thereafter it seems never to have been a real threat to the worship of God.

As the Christian religion spread outside of Palestine, special problems arose in connection with the teachings of Christianity and the idolatrous practices current in Asia-Minor and Greece. In *1 Cor. 8* and *10*, Paul deals with the matter of eating meat which had been part of an animal sacrificed to an idol. He recognized that these gods had no existence apart from their images and that the meat was harmless; nevertheless, he urged enlightened Christians to for go their legitimate rights if their actions would endanger the faith of less enlightened brethren, so recently removed from the confusions of paganism.

The New Testament also designates as idolatry devotion to any created thing or human pursuit which might detract from wholehearted service to God.

SCRIPTURE

Practice of Idolatry

1 Kin. 18 [26]And they took the bullock which was given them, and they dressed it, and called on the name of Baal from morning even until noon, saying, O Baal, hear us. But there was no voice, nor any that answered. And they leaped upon the altar which was made. [28]And they cried aloud, and cut themselves after their manner with knives and lancets, till the blood gushed out upon them.

1 Kin. 19 [18]Yet I have left me seven thousand in Israel, all the knees of which have not bowed unto Baal, and every mouth which hath not kissed him.

Isa. 57 [5]Inflaming yourselves with idols under every green tree, slaying the children in the valleys under the clefts of the rocks? [6]Among the smooth stones of the stream is thy portion; they, they are thy lot: even to them hast thou poured a drink offering, thou hast offered a meat offering. Should I receive comfort in these?

Jer. 7 [18]The children gather wood, and the fathers kindle the fire, and the women knead their dough, to make cakes to the queen of heaven, and to pour out drink offerings unto other gods, that they may provoke me to anger.

Hos. 4 [13]They sacrifice upon the tops of the mountains, and burn incense upon the hills, under oaks and poplars and elms, because the shadow thereof is good: therefore your daughters shall commit whoredom, and your spouses shall commit adultery.

Hos. 13 [2]And now they sin more and more, and have made them molten images of their silver, and idols according to their own understanding, all of it the work of the craftsmen: they say of them, Let the men that sacrifice kiss the calves.

Denunciation of Idolatry

Ex. 20 [3]Thou shalt have no other gods before me. [4]Thou shalt not make unto thee any graven image, or any likeness of any thing that is in heaven above, or that is in the earth beneath, or that is in the water under the earth: [5]Thou shalt not bow down thyself to them, nor serve them: for I the LORD thy God am a jealous God, visiting the iniquity of the fathers upon the children unto the third and fourth generation of them that hate me; [6]And shewing mercy unto thousands of them that love me, and keep my commandments.

[23]Ye shall not make with me gods of silver, neither shall ye make unto you gods of gold.

Deut. 4 [15]Take ye therefore good heed unto yourselves; for ye saw no manner of similitude on the day that the LORD spake unto you in Horeb out of the midst of the fire: [16]Lest ye corrupt yourselves, and make you a graven image, the similitude of any figure, the likeness of male or female, [19]Lest thou . . . when thou seest the sun, and the moon, and the stars, even all the host of heaven, shouldest be driven to worship them, and serve them, which the LORD thy God hath divided unto all nations under the whole heaven.

Deut. 12 [31]Thou shalt not do so unto the LORD thy God: for every abomination to the LORD, which he hateth, have they done unto their gods; for even their sons and their daughters they have burnt in the fire to their gods.

Deut. 27 [15]Cursed be the man that maketh any graven or molten image, an abomination unto the LORD, the work of the hands of the craftsman, and putteth it in a secret place.

Acts 15 [29]That ye abstain from meats offered to idols,

Acts 17 [16]Now while Paul waited for them at Athens, his spirit was stirred in him, when he saw the city wholly given to idolatry.

1 Cor. 6 [9]Be not deceived: neither fornicators, nor idolaters, . . . [10] . . . shall inherit the kingdom of God.

1 Cor. 10 [14]My dearly beloved, flee from idolatry. [20]But I say, that the things which the Gentiles sacrifice, they sacrifice to devils, and not to God: and I would not that ye should have fellowship with devils.

1 John 5 [21]Little children, keep yourselves from idols.

Rev. 21 [8]Idolaters . . . shall have their part in the lake which burneth with fire and brimstone: which is the second death.

See Ex. 34:17; Rev. 22:15

Folly of Idolatry

1 Kin. 18 [27]Elijah mocked them, and said, Cry aloud: for he is a god; either he is talking, or he is pursuing, or he is in a journey, or peradventure he sleepeth, and must be awaked.

2 Chr. 25 [15]Wherefore the anger of the LORD was kindled against Amaziah, and he sent unto him a prophet, which said unto him, Why hast thou sought after the gods of the people, which could not deliver their own people out of thine hand?

Isa. 44 [9]They that make a graven image are all of them vanity; and their delectable things shall not profit; and they are their own witnesses; they see not, nor know; that they may be ashamed. [10]Who hath formed a god, or molten a graven image that is profitable for nothing? [11]Behold, all his fellows shall be ashamed; and the workmen, they are of men: let them all be gathered together, let them stand up; yet they shall fear, and they shall be ashamed together. [12]The smith with the tongs both worketh in the coals, and fashioneth it with hammers, and worketh it with the strength of his arms: yea, he is hungry, and his strength faileth: he drinketh no water, and is faint. [13]The carpenter stretcheth out his rule; he marketh it out with the line; he fitteth it with planes, and he marketh it out with the compass, and maketh it after the figure of a man, according to the beauty of a man; that it may remain in the house. [14]He heweth him down cedars, and taketh the cypress and the oak, which he strengtheneth for himself among the trees of the forest: he planteth an ash, and the rain doth nourish it. [15]Then shall it be for a man to burn: for he will take thereof, and warm himself; yea, he kindleth it, and baketh bread; yea, he maketh a god, and worshippeth it; he maketh it a graven image, and falleth down thereto. [16]He burneth part thereof in the fire; with part thereof he eateth flesh; he roasteth roast, and is satisfied: yea, he warmeth himself, and saith, Aha, I am warm, I have seen the fire: [17]And the residue thereof he maketh a god, even his graven image: he falleth down unto it, and worshippeth it, and prayeth unto it, and saith, Deliver me; for thou art my god.

See Judg. 6:31; 1 Sam. 5:3, 4

IGNORANCE

[ig'nô rans] The condition of being without knowledge, either in general or as to a particular object or for a particular reason. Ignorance may be willful or obstinate or it may exist through no fault of one's own, in which condition there seems to be less guilt attached to sins. (*See 1 Tim. 1:13* below) In either case, ignorance enslaves man to error and precludes the possibility of a rich life of service to God. That Jesus recognized this is seen in his famous commendation of genuine knowledge: "Ye shall know the truth and the truth shall make you free" (*John 8:32*). There are numerous passages in the Bible which indicate the undesirability of ignorance.

See KNOWLEDGE

SCRIPTURE

Acts 17 [23]For as I passed by, and beheld your devotions, I found an altar with this inscription, TO THE UNKNOWN GOD. Whom therefore ye ignorantly worship, him declare I unto you. [30]And the times of this ignorance God winked at; but now commandeth all men every where to repent:

Rom. 10 [2]For I bear them record, that they have a zeal of God, but not according to knowledge. [3]For they being ignorant of God's righteousness, and going about to establish their own righteousness, have not submitted themselves unto the righteousness of God.

Eph. 4 [18]Having the understanding darkened, being alienated from the life of God through the ignorance that is in them, because of the blindness of their heart: [19]Who being past feeling have given themselves over unto lasciviousness, to work all uncleanness with greediness.

2 Pet. 3 [5]For this they willingly are ignorant of, that by the word of God the heavens were of old, and the earth standing out of the water, and in the water, [6]Whereby the world that then was, being overflowed with water, perished.

1 Cor. 12 [1]Now concerning spiritual gifts, brethren I would not have you ignorant.

1 Thess. 4 [13]But I would not have you to be ignorant, brethren, concerning them which are asleep, that ye sorrow not, even as others which have no hope.

1 Tim. 1 [13]Who was before a blasphemer, and a persecutor, and injurious: but I obtained mercy, because I did it ignorantly in unbelief.

2 Pet. 3 [8]But (beloved) be not ignorant of this one thing, that one day is with the Lord as a thousand years, and a thousand years as one day.

IMMANUEL (EMMANUEL)

[i man′û el] In about 733 BC the kingdoms of Syria and Israel combined to resist the oppression of Assyria. In order to coerce Ahaz king of Judah to join with them, they marched through Judah and threatened to overrun Jerusalem. Ahaz' first impulse was to appeal to Tiglath-Pileser of Assyria for aid. At this time, however, God sent the prophet Isaiah to assure him that the attack of the coalition would not succeed and to persuade him to avoid an alliance with the Assyrians. To confirm his word, Isaiah offered Ahaz a sign: a young woman would soon bear a child whose name would be Immanuel, meaning "God with us"; before this child was old enough to tell good from bad, the nations of Syria and Israel would be left desolate (*Isa. 7: 14-16*). In *Matt. 1:23* this prophecy is quoted in connection with the birth of Jesus. Although there is no record of our Lord's ever having been called "Immanuel," it is a fitting appellation, attesting to the belief of the church that Jesus was truly "God with us." In the passage from *Isaiah*, the King James Version mistakenly translates the Hebrew term for "young women" as "virgin." Although there is difficulty in determining just who the child was, we may be fairly certain that Jesus was not the sign given to Ahaz and that the birth to which Isaiah referred was in no way supernatural. When Matthew applies the prophecy to Jesus, however, the term used clearly means "virgin." Thus, the same statement, with only slight alteration, is made to refer both to the Old Testament "child of prophecy" and to Jesus Christ.

See Virgin Birth

SCRIPTURE

Isa. 7 [14]Therefore the Lord himself shall give you a sign; Behold, a virgin shall conceive, and bear a son, and shall call his name Immanuel. [15]Butter and honey shall he eat, that he may know to refuse the evil, and choose the good. [16]For before the child shall know to refuse the evil, and choose the good, the land that thou abhorrest shall be forsaken of both her kings.

Matt. 1 [21]And she shall bring forth a son, and thou shalt call his name Jesus: for he shall save his people from their sins. [22]Now all this was done, that it might be fulfilled which was spoken of the Lord by the prophet, saying, [23]Behold, a virgin shall be with child, and shall bring forth a son, and they shall call his name Emmanuel, which being interpreted is, God with us.

INCARNATION

[in kär nā′shun] A clothing, or state of being clothed, with flesh. This is the term applied to the appearance of the second person of the Godhead in a human form; in other words, God the Son's coming to earth as a man.

See Jesus, Christ

SCRIPTURE

Luke 1 [30]And the angel said unto her, Fear not, Mary: for thou hast found favour with God. [31]And, behold, thou shalt conceive in thy womb, and bring forth a son, and shalt call his name Jesus. [32]He shall be great, and shall be called the Son of the Highest: and the Lord God shall give unto him the throne of his father David:

Luke 2 [7]And she brought forth her firstborn son, and wrapped him in swaddling clothes, and laid him in a manger; because there was no room for them in the inn. [8]And there were in the same country shepherds abiding in the field, keeping watch over their flock by night.

Luke 24 [39]Behold my hands and my

feet, that it is I myself: handle me, and see; for a spirit hath not flesh and bones, as ye see me have.

John 1 [14]The Word was made flesh, and dwelt among us, (and we beheld his glory, the glory as of the only begotten of the Father,) full of grace and truth.

Acts 2 [30]Knowing that God had sworn with an oath to him, that of the fruit of his loins, according to the flesh, he would raise up Christ to sit on his throne:

Rom. 1 [3]His Son Jesus Christ our Lord, which was made of the seed of David according to the flesh;

Rom. 8 [3]For what the law could not do, in that it was weak through the flesh, God sending his own Son in the likeness of sinful flesh, and for sin, condemned sin in the flesh.

Gal. 4 [4]When the fulness of the time was come, God sent forth his Son, made of a woman, made under the law.

1 Tim. 3 [16]Great is the mystery of godliness: God was manifest in the flesh.

1 John 4 [2]Hereby know ye the Spirit of God: Every spirit that confesseth that Jesus Christ is come in the flesh is of God:
[3]And every spirit that confesseth not that Jesus Christ is come in the flesh is not of God: and this is that spirit of antichrist, whereof ye have heard that it should come; and even now already is it in the world.

2 John 1 [7]For many deceivers are entered into the world, who confess not that Jesus Christ is come in the flesh. This is a deceiver and an antichrist.

INDUSTRY

[in′dus tri] Habitual diligence in any employment or pursuit, either mental or physical; steady attention to one's business. The Bible contains many references to industry, implying that man has a responsibility to use what God has given him to the best of his abilities.

SCRIPTURE

General

Prov. 13 [23]Much food is in the tillage of the poor: but there is that is destroyed for want of judgment.

Rom. 12 [11]Not slothful in business; fervent in spirit; serving the Lord.

Eph. 4 [28]Let him that stole steal no more: but rather let him labour, working with his hands the thing which is good, that he may have to give to him that needeth.

1 Thess. 4 [11]And that ye study to be quiet, and to do your own business, and to work with your own hands, as we commanded you; [12]That ye may walk honestly toward them that are without, and that ye may have lack of nothing.

2 Thess. 3 [10]For even when we were with you, this we commanded you, that if any would not work, neither should he eat.
[11]For we hear that there are some which walk among you disorderly, working not at all, but are busybodies. [12]Now them that are such we command and exhort by our Lord Jesus Christ, that with quietness they work, and eat their own bread.

2 Tim. 2 [6]The husbandman that laboureth must be first partaker of the fruits.

The Blessings and Rewards of Industry

1 Kin. 11 [28]And the man Jeroboam was a mighty man of valour: and Solomon seeing the young man that he was industrious, he made him ruler over all the charge of the house of Joseph.

Prov. 13 [11]Wealth gotten by vanity shall be diminished: but he that gathereth by labour shall increase.

Prov. 14 [23]In all labour there is profit: but the talk of the lips tendeth only to penury.

Prov. 16 [26]He that laboureth, laboureth for himself; for his mouth craveth it of him.

Prov. 20 [13]Love not sleep, lest thou come to poverty: open thine eyes, and thou shalt be satisfied with bread.

Prov. 21 [5]The thoughts of the diligent tend only to plenteousness; but of every one that is hasty only to want.

Prov. 27 [23]Be thou diligent to know the state of thy flocks, and look well to thy herds: [24]For riches are not for ever: and doth the crown endure to every generation? [25]The hay appeareth, and the tender grass sheweth itself, and herbs of the mountains are gathered. [26]The lambs are for thy clothing, and the goats are the price of the field. [27]And thou shalt have goats' milk enough for thy food, for the food of thy household, and for the maintenance for thy maidens.

Eccl. 5 [18]Behold that which I have seen: it is good and comely for one to eat and to drink, and to enjoy the good of all his labour that he taketh under the sun all the days of his life, which God giveth him: for it is his portion.

INJUSTICE

[in'jus tis] Lack of justice and equity; violation of the right of another or others; wrong; unfairness. The Bible demands of us that we be careful of the rights of others and deal fairly in all our activities.

See DISHONESTY

SCRIPTURE

Warnings against Injustice

Ex. 22 [21]Thou shalt neither vex a stranger, nor oppress him: for ye were strangers in the land of Egypt.

Ex. 23 [6]Thou shalt not wrest the judgment of thy poor in his cause.

Lev. 19 [15]Ye shall do no unrighteousness in judgment; thou shalt not respect the person of the poor, nor honour the person of the mighty: but in righteousness shalt thou judge thy neighbour.

Deut. 16 [19]Thou shalt not wrest judgment; thou shalt not respect persons, neither take a gift: for a gift doth blind the eyes of the wise, and pervert the words of the righteous. [20]That which is altogether just shalt thou follow, that thou mayest live, and inherit the land which the LORD thy God giveth thee.

Deut. 24 [17]Thou shalt not pervert the judgment of the stranger, nor of the fatherless, nor take a widow's raiment to pledge.

Job 31 [13]If I did despise the cause of my manservant or of my maidservant, when they contended with me; [14]What then shall I do when God riseth up? and when he visiteth, what shall I answer him?

Jer. 22 [3]Thus saith the LORD; Execute ye judgment and righteousness, and deliver the spoiled out of the hand of the oppressor: and do no wrong, do no violence to the stranger, the fatherless, nor the widow, neither shed innocent blood in this place.

Luke 16 [10]He that is faithful in that which is least is faithful also in much: and he that is unjust in the least is unjust also in much.

Results of Injustice

Prov. 11 [7]When a wicked man dieth, his expectation shall perish: and the hope of unjust men perisheth.

Prov. 28 [8]He that by usury and unjust gain increaseth his substance, he shall gather it for him that will pity the poor.

1 Thess. 4 [6]That no man go beyond and defraud his brother in any manner, because that the Lord is the avenger of all such; as we also have forewarned you, and testified.

2 Pet. 2 [9]The Lord knoweth how to deliver the godly out of temptations, and to reserve the unjust unto the day of judgment to be punished.

INSPIRATION

[in spi rā'shun] The Greek term for "inspired" (*theopneustos,* "Godbreathed") occurs only in 2 *Tim. 3:16* and there with reference to the Old Testament scriptures: "All scripture is inspired by God and profitable for teaching, for reproof, for correction, and for training in righteousness." This passage indicates to us that God's Spirit is in some way active in the production of Scripture. It does not, however, provide us with complete information as to the nature and degree of that activity and it is probably unwise to base an elaborate doctrine of Biblical inspiration on this one verse. It is certainly a mistake to view the Biblical writers as mere tools of the Holy Spirit, with no freedom or creativity; rather, they spoke and wrote as men in whom the Spirit of God held sway—as, for example, the Old Testament prophets and the Apostles of Christ—and it is thus that their writings are to be regarded both as the literary creations of their authors and as the word of God.

INTEGRITY

[in teg'ri ti] The state of being morally sound or whole; freedom from corrupting influence or motive; honesty; uprightness; genuineness; purity. The scriptures clearly assert that integrity is a necessary aspect of the godly life.

See Honesty, Purity, etc.

SCRIPTURE

Ex. 18 [21]Moreover thou shalt provide out of all the people able men, such as fear God, men of truth, hating covetousness; and place such over them, to be rulers of thousands, and rulers of hundreds, rulers of fifties, and rulers of tens.

Deut. 16 [19]Thou shalt not wrest judgment; thou shalt not respect persons, neither take a gift: for a gift doth blind the eyes of the wise, and pervert the words of the righteous.

1 Sam. 12 [3]Behold, here I am: witness against me before the Lord, and before his anointed; whose ox have I taken? or whose ass have I taken? or whom have I defrauded? whom have I oppressed? or of whose hand have I received any bribe to blind mine eyes therewith? and I will restore it you.

2 Kin. 12 [15]Moreover, they reckoned not with the men, into whose hand they delivered the money to be bestowed on workmen: for they dealt faithfully.

2 Kin. 22 [7]Howbeit, there was no reckoning made with them of the money that was delivered into their hand, because they dealt faithfully.

Job 2 [3]And the Lord said unto Satan, Hast thou considered my servant Job, that there is none like him in the earth, a perfect and an upright man, one that feareth God, and escheweth evil? and still he holdeth fast his integrity, although thou movedst me against him, to destroy him without cause.

Job 13 [15]Though he slay me, yet will I trust in him: but I will maintain mine own ways before him.

Job 31 [6]Let me be weighed in an even balance, that God may know mine integrity.

Psa. 7 [8]The Lord shall judge the people: judge me, O Lord, according to my righteousness, and according to mine integrity that is in me.

Psa. 26 [1]Judge me, O Lord; for I have walked in mine integrity: I have trusted also in the Lord; therefore I shall not slide.

Psa. 41 [12]And as for me, thou upholdest me in mine integrity, and settest me before thy face for ever.

INTERCESSION

[in ter sesh′un] Prayer, petition, or entreaty in behalf of another; the act of mediating between two parties for the purpose of effecting a reconciliation. One of the offices of Christ is that of intercession; in his capacity of mediator he intercedes with God the Father on behalf of mankind. The Bible teaches us that the Holy Spirit also makes intercession for us. In the epistles of Paul there is considerable emphasis on the duty of Christians to intercede for one another.

SCRIPTURE

Intercession of Christ

Luke 23 [34]Then said Jesus, Father, forgive them; for they know not what they do. And they parted his raiment, and cast lots.

Rom. 8 [34]Who is he that condemneth? It is Christ that died, yea rather that is risen again, who is even at the right hand of God, who also maketh intercession for us.

Heb. 2 [17]Wherefore in all things it behooved him to be made like unto his brethren, that he might be a merciful and faithful high priest in things pertaining to God, to make reconciliation for the sins of the people.

Heb. 4 [15]For we have not a high priest which cannot be touched with the feeling of our infirmities; but was in all points tempted like as we are, yet without sin.

Heb. 7 [25]Wherefore he is able also to save them to the uttermost, that come unto God by him, seeing he ever liveth to make intercession for them.

1 John 2 [1]My little children, these things write I unto you, that ye sin not. And if any man sin, we have an Advocate with the Father, Jesus Christ the righteous.

Intercession by the Holy Spirit

Rom. 8 [26]Likewise the Spirit also helpeth our infirmities: for we know not what we should pray for as we ought: but the Spirit itself maketh intercession for us with groanings which cannot be uttered.

Intercession for All Men

1 Tim. 2 [1]I exhort therefore, that, first of all, supplications, prayers, intercessions, and giving of thanks, be made for all men; [2]For kings, and for all that are in authority; that we may lead a quiet and peaceable life in all godliness and honesty. [3]For this is good and acceptable in the sight of God our Saviour; [4]Who will have all men to be saved, and to come unto the knowledge of the truth.

Eph. 6 [18]Praying always with all prayer and supplication in the Spirit, and watching thereunto with all perseverance and supplication for all saints.

Requests for Intercession

Acts 8 [24]Then answered Simon, and said, Pray ye to the Lord for me, that none of these things which ye have spoken come upon me.

Rom. 15 [30]Now I beseech you, brethren, for the Lord Jesus Christ's sake, and for the love of the Spirit, that ye strive together with me in your prayers to God for me.

2 Cor. 1 [11]You also helping together by prayer for us, that for the gift bestowed upon us by the means of many persons, thanks may be given by many on our behalf.

Col. 4 [3]Withal, praying also for us, that God would open unto us a door of utterance, to speak the mystery of Christ, for which I am also in bonds.

1 Thess. 5 [25]Brethren, pray for us.

2 Thess. 3 [1]Finally, brethren, pray for us, that the word of the Lord may have free course, and be glorified, even as it is with you.

Heb. 13 [18]Pray for us: for we trust we have a good conscience, in all things willing to live honestly. [19]But I beseech you the rather to do this, that I may be restored to you the sooner.

Intercession Exemplified

Ex. 32 [31]And Moses returned unto the LORD, and said, Oh, this people have sinned a great sin, and have made them gods of gold. [32]Yet now, if thou wilt forgive their sin—; and if not, blot me, I pray thee, out of thy book which thou hast written.

Psa. 125 [4]Do good, O LORD, unto those that be good, and to them that are upright in their hearts.

Matt. 5 [44]But I say unto you, Love your enemies, bless them that curse you, do good to them that hate you, and pray for them which despitefully use you, and persecute you;

Acts 7 [60]And he kneeled down, and cried with a loud voice, Lord, lay not this sin to their charge. And when he had said this, he fell asleep.

Rom. 1 [9]For God is my witness, whom I serve with my spirit in the gospel of his Son, that without ceasing I make mention of you always in my prayers;

2 Thess. 1 [11]Wherefore also we pray always for you, that our God would count you worthy of this calling, and fulfill all the good pleasure of his goodness, and the work of faith with power:

REFERENCE: Intercession of Jonathan for David, *1 Sam. 19:1-7;* Abigail for Nabal, *1 Sam. 25: 23-35*; Paul for Onesimus, *Philem. 1:10-21.*

ISAAC

[ī'zak] The only son of Abraham and Sarah, born to them in their old age. For some time Abraham had felt that Ishmael, his son by Hagar the handmaid of Sarah, was the child which God had promised him; finally, however, Isaac was born and, at the feast celebrating the time of his weaning, Ishmael was disinherited. In the early part of his life, Isaac almost became a human sacrifice in the famous episode of Abraham's great test of faith. Upon reaching adulthood, he married Rebekah the daughter of Bethuel and sister of Laban. There is an account of his deceiving Abimelech king of Gerar concerning Rebekah which is quite similar to the narratives of Abraham's deceiving both the Egyptian Pharaoh and another king of Gerar concerning Sarah. Rebekah bore Isaac two sons, Jacob and Esau. Isaac preferred Esau and was greatly upset when Jacob and his mother successfully conspired to deprive him of the paternal blessing which belonged to him as the elder son. Although Isaac is pictured as being quite old at the time of the giving of the blessing, his death apparently did not take place for a considerable number of years. He was buried in the ancestral burial plot at Machpelah.

See ABRAHAM, HAGAR, SARAH, etc.

SCRIPTURE

The Promise to Abraham

Gen. 17 [15]And God said unto Abraham, As for Sarai thy wife, thou shalt not call her name Sarai, but Sarah shall her name be. [16]And I will bless her, and give thee a son also of her: yea, I will bless her, and she shall be a mother of nations; kings of people shall be of her. [17]Then Abraham fell upon his face, and laughed, and said in his heart, Shall a child be born unto him that is an hundred years old? and shall Sarah, that is ninety years old, bear?

Birth of Isaac

Gen. 21 [3]And Abraham called the name

of his son that was born unto him, whom Sarah bare to him, Isaac.

Abraham Offers Isaac

Gen. 22 [1]And it came to pass after these things, that God did tempt Abraham, and said unto him, Abraham: and he said, Behold, here I am. [2]And he said, Take now thy son, thine only son Isaac, whom thou lovest, and get thee into the land of Moriah; and offer him there for a burnt-offering upon one of the mountains which I will tell thee of.

[9]And they came to the place which God had told him of; and Abraham built an altar there, and laid the wood in order, and bound Isaac his son, and laid him on the altar upon the wood. [10]And Abraham stretched forth his hand, and took the knife to slay his son. [11]And the angel of the LORD called unto him out of heaven, and said, Abraham, Abraham: and he said, Here am I. [12]And he said, Lay not thine hand upon the lad, neither do thou any thing unto him: for now I know that thou fearest God, seeing thou hast not withheld thy son, thine only son from me. [13]And Abraham lifted up his eyes, and looked, and behold behind him a ram caught in a thicket by his horns: and Abraham went and took the ram, and offered him up for a burnt-offering in the stead of his son.

Isaac Marries Rebekah

Gen. 24 [67]And Isaac brought her into his mother Sarah's tent, and took Rebekah, and she became his wife; and he loved her: and Isaac was comforted after his mother's death.

Jacob Deceives Isaac

Gen. 27 [22]And Jacob went near unto Isaac his father; and he felt him, and said, The voice is Jacob's voice, but the hands are the hands of Esau. [23]And he discerned him not, because his hands were hairy, as his brother Esau's hands: so he blessed him. [24]And he said, Art thou my very son Esau? And he said, I am. [25]And he said, Bring it near to me, and I will eat of my son's venison, that my soul may bless thee. And he brought it near to him, and he did eat: and he brought him wine, and he drank. [26]And his father Isaac said unto him, Come near now, and kiss me, my son. [27]And he came near, and kissed him: and he smelled the smell of his raiment, and blessed him, and said, See, the smell of my son is as the smell of a field which the LORD hath blessed: [28]Therefore God give thee of the dew of heaven, and the fatness of the earth, and plenty of corn and wine: [29]Let people serve thee, and nations bow down to thee: be lord over thy brethren, and let thy mother's sons bow down to thee: cursed be every one that curseth thee, and blessed be he that blesseth thee.

[30]And it came to pass, as soon as Isaac had made an end of blessing Jacob, and Jacob was yet scarce gone out from the presence of Isaac his father, that Esau his brother came in from his hunting.

Death and Burial

Gen. 35 [28]And the days of Isaac were an hundred and fourscore years. [29]And Isaac gave up the ghost and died, and was gathered unto his people, being old and full of days; and his sons Esau and Jacob buried him.

REFERENCE: *Gen. 21-28; 35:28, 29; 49:31.*

ISAIAH

[ī zā'ya, ī zī'a] One of the foremost of the Hebrew prophets. Aside from the fact that he was married to a woman called the "prophetess", little is known of the personal history of Isaiah. He began his ministry as a chief prophet in Judah in "the year that king Uzziah died" (734 BC), and continued through the reigns of Ahaz and Hezekiah and possibly into that of Manasseh, a period of almost fifty years. Tradition has it that he was placed in the trunk of a carob tree and sawn asunder during the evil reign of this latter king. Under Ahaz, Isaiah was primarily concerned to keep Judah out of entangling alliances with Assyria. It was in this connection that he uttered the famous prophecies of Immanual and the Royal Son. Despite his warnings, Ahaz appealed to Tiglath-Pileser for aid against Syria and Israel and thereby became a vassal of Assyria. This vassalage alliance saved Judah from the captivity which was the fate of Northern Israel, but it had disastrous results for the religion of Judah, as every sort of Assyrian idolatry was introduced. The period of Hezekiah's reign was somewhat brighter as this admirable and patriotic ruler broke the alliance with Assyria and cleansed the temple of the foreign cult-matter. Isaiah seems to have enjoyed wide popularity and to have exerted considerable influence on Hezekiah. The prophecies of Isaiah are lofty and dignified, stamping his work with a high mark of literary excellence.

See PROPHETS AND PROPHECY, AHAZ, HEZEKIAH, MANASSEH

REFERENCE: The Book of *Isaiah.*

SCRIPTURE

The Call to Be a Prophet

Isa. 6 [1]In the year that king Uzziah died I saw also the Lord sitting upon a throne, high and lifted up, and his train filled the temple. [2]Above it stood the seraphim: each one had six wings; with twain he covered his face, and with twain he covered his feet, and with twain he did fly. [3]And one cried unto another, and said, Holy, holy, holy, is the LORD of hosts: the whole earth is full of his glory. [4]And the posts of the door moved at the voice of him that cried, and the house was filled with smoke.

[5]Then said I, Woe is me! for I am undone; because I am a man of unclean lips, and I dwell in the midst of a people of unclean lips: for mine eyes have seen the King, the LORD of hosts. [6]Then flew one of the seraphim unto me, having a live coal in his hand, which he had taken with the tongs from off the altar: [7]And he laid it upon my mouth, and said, Lo, this hath touched thy lips; and thine iniquity is taken away, and thy sin purged. [8]Also I heard the voice of the Lord, saying, Whom shall I send, and who will go for us? Then said I, Here am I; send me.

[9]And he said, Go, and tell this people, Hear ye indeed, but understand not; and see ye indeed, but perceive not. [10]Make the heart of this people fat, and make their ears heavy, and shut their eyes; lest they see with their eyes, and hear with their ears, and understand with their heart, and convert, and be healed. [11]Then said I, Lord, how long? And he answered, Until the cities be wasted without inhabitant, and the houses without man, and the land be utterly desolate, [12]And the LORD have removed men far away, and there be a great forsaking in the midst of the land.

[13]But yet in it shall be a tenth, and it shall return, and shall be eaten: as a teil tree, and as an oak, whose substance is in them, when they cast their leaves: so the holy seed shall be the substance thereof.

Councils Ahaz against Alliance with Israel and Syria

Isa. 7 [1]And it came to pass in the days of Ahaz the son of Jotham, the son of Uzziah, king of Judah, that Rezin the king of Syria, and Pekah the son of Remaliah, king of Israel, went up toward Jerusalem to war against it, but could not prevail against it. [2]And it was told the house of David, saying, Syria is confederate with Ephraim. And his heart was moved, and the heart of

his people, as the trees of the wood are
moved with the wind. [3]Then said the
LORD unto Isaiah, Go forth now to meet
Ahaz, thou, and Shear-jashub thy son, at
the end of the conduit of the upper pool,
in the highway of the fuller's field; [4]And
say unto him, Take heed, and be quiet;
fear not, neither be fainthearted for the
two tails of these smoking firebrands, for
the fierce anger of Rezin with Syria, and of
the son of Remaliah. [5]Because Syria,
Ephraim, and the son of Remaliah, have
taken evil counsel against thee, saying,
[6]Let us go up against Judah, and vex it,
and let us make a breach therein for us,
and set a king in the midst of it, even the
son of Tabeal: [7]Thus saith the Lord GOD,
It shall not stand, neither shall it come to
pass. [8]For the head of Syria is Damascus,
and the head of Damascus is Rezin; and
within threescore and five years shall
Ephraim be broken, that it be not a people. [9]And the head of Ephraim is Samaria,
and the head of Samaria is Remaliah's son.
If ye will not believe, surely ye shall not be
established.

Warns Hezekiah of Death

Isa. 38 [1]In those days was Hezekiah
sick unto death. And Isaiah the prophet
the son of Amoz came unto him, and said
unto him, Thus saith the LORD, Set thine
house in order: for thou shalt die, and not
live. [2]Then Hezekiah turned his face toward the wall, and prayed unto the LORD,
[3]And said, Remember now, O LORD, I beseech thee, how I have walked before thee
in truth and with a perfect heart, and have
done that which is good in thy sight. And
Hezekiah wept sore.

Announces God's Mercy to Hezekiah

Isa. 38 [4]Then came the word of the
LORD to Isaiah, saying, [5]Go, and say to
Hezekiah, Thus saith the LORD, the God of
David thy father, I have heard thy prayer,
I have seen thy tears: behold, I will add
unto thy days fifteen years. [6]And I will deliver thee and this city out of the hand of
the king of Assyria: and I will defend this
city. [7]And this shall be a sign unto thee
from the LORD, that the LORD will do this
thing that he hath spoken; [8]Behold, I will
bring again the shadow of the degrees,
which is gone down in the sun dial of
Ahaz, ten degrees backward. So the sun
returned ten degrees, by which degrees it
was gone down.

Representative Prophecies from the Book of Isaiah

IMMANUEL

Isa. 7 [14]Therefore the Lord himself shall
give you a sign; Behold, a virgin shall conceive, and bear a son, and shall call his
name Immanuel. [15]Butter and honey shall
he eat, that he may know to refuse the evil,
and choose the good. [16]For before the
child shall know to refuse the evil, and
choose the good, the land that thou abhorrest shall be forsaken of both her kings.

[17]The LORD shall bring upon thee, and
upon thy people, and upon thy father's
house, days that have not come, from the
day that Ephraim departed from Judah;
even the king of Assyria.

BIRTH AND REIGN OF THE PRINCE OF PEACE

Isa. 9 [6]For unto us a child is born, unto
us a son is given: and the government shall
be upon his shoulder: and his name shall
be called Wonderful, Counsellor, The
mighty God, The everlasting Father, The
Prince of Peace. [7]Of the increase of his
government and peace there shall be no
end, upon the throne of David, and upon
his kingdom, to order it, and to establish

it with judgment and with justice from henceforth even for ever. The zeal of the LORD of hosts will perform this.

THE FUTURE HOPE OF ISRAEL

Isa. 11 [1]And there shall come forth a rod out of the stem of Jesse, and a Branch shall grow out of his roots: [2]And the Spirit of the LORD shall rest upon him, the spirit of wisdom and understanding, the spirit of counsel and might, the spirit of knowledge and of the fear of the LORD; [3]And shall make him of quick understanding in the fear of the LORD: and he shall not judge after the sight of his eyes, neither reprove after the hearing of his ears: [4]But with righteousness shall he judge the poor, and reprove with equity for the meek of the earth: and he shall smite the earth with the rod of his mouth, and with the breath of his lips shall he slay the wicked. [5]And righteousness shall be the girdle of his loins, and faithfulness the girdle of his reins. [6]The wolf also shall dwell with the lamb, and the leopard shall lie down with the kid; and the calf and the young lion and the fatling together; and a little child shall lead them. [7]And the cow and the bear shall feed; their young ones shall lie down together: and the lion shall eat straw like the ox. [8]And the sucking child shall play on the hole of the asp, and the weaned child shall put his hand on the cockatrice' den. [9]They shall not hurt nor destroy in all my holy mountain: for the earth shall be full of the knowledge of the LORD, as the waters cover the sea.

[10]And in that day there shall be a root of Jesse, which shall stand for an ensign of the people; to it shall the Gentiles seek: and his rest shall be glorious.

THE SUFFERING SERVANT

Isa. 53 [1]Who hath believed our report? and to whom is the arm of the LORD revealed? [2]For he shall grow up before him as a tender plant, and as a root out of a dry ground: he hath no form nor comeliness; and when we shall see him, there is no beauty that we should desire him. [3]He is despised and rejected of men; a man of sorrows, and acquainted with grief: and we hid as it were our faces from him; he was despised, and we esteemed him not.

[4]Surely he hath borne our griefs, and carried our sorrows: yet we did esteem him stricken, smitten of God, and afflicted. [5]But he was wounded for our transgressions, he was bruised for our iniquities: the chastisement of our peace was upon him; and with his stripes we are healed. [6]All we like sheep have gone astray; we have turned every one to his own way; and the LORD hath laid on him the iniquity of us all. [7]He was oppressed, and he was afflicted, yet he opened not his mouth: he is brought as a lamb to the slaughter, and as a sheep before her shearers is dumb, so he openeth not his mouth. [8]He was taken from prison and from judgment: and who shall declare his generation? for he was cut off out of the land of the living: for the transgression of my people was he stricken. [9]And he made his grave with the wicked, and with the rich in his death; because he had done no violence, neither was any deceit in his mouth.

[10]Yet it pleased the LORD to bruise him; he hath put him to grief: when thou shalt make his soul an offering for sin, he shall see his seed, he shall prolong his days, and the pleasure of the LORD shall prosper in his hand. [11]He shall see of the travail of his soul, and shall be satisfied: by his knowledge shall my righteous servant justify many; for he shall bear their iniquities. [12]Therefore will I divide him a portion with the great, and he shall divide the spoil

with the strong; because he hath poured out his soul unto death: and he was numbered with the transgressors; and he bare the sin of many, and made intercession for the transgressors.

THE SINS OF JUDAH

Isa. 59 [1]Behold, the LORD's hand is not shortened, that it can not save; neither his ear heavy, that it can not hear: [2]But your iniquities have separated between you and your God, and your sins have hid his face from you, that he will not hear. [3]For your hands are defiled with blood, and your fingers with iniquity; your lips have spoken lies, your tongue hath muttered perverseness. [4]None calleth for justice, nor any pleadeth for truth: they trust in vanity, and speak lies; they conceive mischief, and bring forth iniquity. [5]They hatch cockatrice' eggs, and weave the spider's web: he that eateth of their eggs dieth, and that which is crushed breaketh out into a viper. [6]Their webs shall not become garments, neither shall they cover themselves with their works: their works are works of iniquity, and the act of violence is in their hands. [7]Their feet run to evil, and they make haste to shed innocent blood: their thoughts are thoughts of iniquity; wasting and destruction are in their paths. [8]The way of peace they know not; and there is no judgment in their goings: they have made them crooked paths; whosoever goeth therein shall not know peace.

ISHBOSHETH

[ish bō′sheth] A son of Saul, called Esh-Baal in *1 Chr. 8:33, 9:39.* After the death of his father Ishbosheth was made king at Mananaim by Abner, the commander of Saul's armies. Judah, however, proclaimed David as king; war ensued, with David getting the upper hand. Ishbosheth's power was broken when Abner went over to David after an argument concerning Saul's concubine, Tizpah. Ishbosheth was treacherously murdered by two of his captains, Rechab and Baanah, who were then executed by David, from whom they had expected to receive a reward.

See ABNER, DAVID

SCRIPTURE

Succeeds Saul as King

2 Sam. 2 [8]But Abner the son of Ner, captain of Saul's host, took Ishbosheth the son of Saul, and brought him over to Mahanaim; [9]And he made him king over Gilead, and over the Ashurites, and over Jezreel, and over Ephraim, and over Benjamin, and over all Israel. [10]Ishbosheth Saul's son was forty years old when he began to reign over Israel, and reigned two years: but the house of Judah followed David.

Restores Michal to David

2 Sam. 3 [6]And it came to pass, while there was war between the house of Saul and the house of David, that Abner made himself strong for the house of Saul. [7]And Saul had a concubine, whose name was Rizpah, the daughter of Aiah: and Ishbosheth said to Abner, Wherefore hast thou gone in unto my father's concubine? [8]Then was Abner very wroth for the words of Ishbosheth, and said, Am I a dog's head, which against Judah do shew kindness this day unto the house of Saul thy father, to his brethren, and to his friends, and have not delivered thee into the hand of David, that thou chargest me to-day with a fault concerning this woman?

His Assassination

2 Sam. 4 [5]And the sons of Rimmon the Beerothite, Rechab and Baanah, went, and came about the heat of the day to the house of Ishbosheth, who lay on a bed at noon. 6And they came thither into the midst of the house, as though they would have fetched wheat; and they smote him under the fifth rib: and Rechab and Baanah his brother escaped. 7For when they came into the house, he lay on his bed in his bedchamber, and they smote him, and slew him and beheaded him, and took his head, and gat them away through the plain all night. 8And they brought the head of Ishbosheth unto David to Hebron, and said to the king, Behold the head of Ishbosheth the son of Saul thine enemy, which sought thy life; and the LORD hath avenged my lord the king this day of Saul, and of his seed.

12And David commanded his young men, and they slew them, and cut off their hands and their feet, and hanged them up over the pool in Hebron. But they took the head of Ishbosheth, and buried it in the sepulchre of Abner in Hebron.

ISHMAEL

[ish'mā el] 1. The son of Abraham by Hagar, the Egyptian handmaid of his wife Sarah. Having abandoned hope that she would bear children, Sarah gave her handmaid to Abraham; in such an arrangement, all children born to Hagar would be reckoned as Sarah's. When Hagar conceived, however, Sarah became jealous and the handmaid fled. In the wilderness she was confronted by an angel of the LORD who instructed her to return, telling her that her son would be "a wild ass of a man" and the father of a great multitude of people. She obeyed and shortly thereafter the child Ishmael was born. Subsequently, Sarah bore Isaac and, at a party celebrating the weaning of the child, she persuaded Abraham to send Hagar and Ishmael out of the camp. He acquiesced and the two set out with but small provisions. When these were exhausted, Hagar prepared to abandon Ishmael but was again met by an angel, who showed her a well of water. The promise concerning Ishmael was repeated and the narrative states that "God was with the lad; and he grew, and dwelt in the wilderness, and became an archer. And he dwelt in the wilderness of Paran: and his mother took him a wife out of the land of Egypt" (*Gen. 21:20-21*). The Arabian nomads or Bedouins are spoken of as the descendants of Ishmael. (*See* HAGAR, SARAH, ABRAHAM, ISAAC)

2. A treacherous Jewish soldier who allied himself with Baalis king of the Ammonites and assassinated Gedeliah, the able and just man appointed by Nebuchadnezzar to govern those who remained in Judah after the fall of Jerusalem. (*See* GEDELIAH)

SCRIPTURE

Ishmael, the Son of Abraham and Hagar

BIRTH

Gen. 16 1Now Sarai, Abram's wife, bare him no children: and she had a handmaid, an Egyptian, whose name was Hagar. 2And Sarai said unto Abram, Behold now, the LORD hath restrained me from bearing: I pray thee, go in unto my maid; it may be that I may obtain children by her. And Abram hearkened to the voice of Sarai.

11And the angel of the LORD said unto her, Behold, thou art with child, and shalt bear a son, and shalt call his name Ishmael; because the LORD hath heard thy affliction. 12And he will be a wild man; his hand will be against every man, and every man's hand against him: and he shall dwell in the presence of all his brethren.

15And Hagar bare Abram a son: and Abram called his son's name, which Hagar bare, Ishmael.

CIRCUMCISION

Gen. 17 20And as for Ishmael, I have heard thee: Behold, I have blessed him, and will make him fruitful, and will multiply him exceedingly; twelve princes shall he beget, and I will make him a great nation. 21But my covenant will I establish with Isaac, which Sarah shall bear unto thee at this set time in the next year.

[23]And Abraham took Ishmael his son, and all that were born in his house, and all that were bought with his money, every male among the men of Abraham's house; and circumcised the flesh of their foreskin in the self-same day, as God had said unto him. [25]And Ishmael his son was thirteen years old, when he was circumcised in the flesh of his foreskin.

SENT AWAY BY ABRAHAM

Gen. 21 [3]And Abraham called the name of his son that was born unto him, whom Sarah bare to him, Isaac.

[9]And Sarah saw the son of Hagar the Egyptian, which she had borne unto Abraham, mocking. [10]Wherefore she said unto Abraham, Cast out this bondwoman and her son: for the son of this bondwoman shall not be heir with my son, even with Isaac.

[14]And Abraham rose up early in the morning, and took bread, and a bottle of water, and gave it unto Hagar, putting it on her shoulder, and the child, and sent her away: and she departed, and wandered in the wilderness of Beersheba. [15]And the water was spent in the bottle, and she cast the child under one of the shrubs. [16]And she went, and sat her down over against him a good way off, as it were a bowshot: for she said, Let me not see the death of the child. And she sat over against him, and lifted up her voice, and wept. [18]Arise, lift up the lad, and hold him in thine hand; for I will make him a great nation. [19]And God opened her eyes, and she saw a well of water; and she went, and filled the bottle with water, and gave the lad drink. [20]And God was with the lad; and he grew, and dwelt in the wilderness, and became an archer. [21]And he dwelt in the wilderness of Paran: and his mother took him a wife out of the land of Egypt.

Ishmael, the Traitor

Jer. 40 [8]Then they came to Gedaliah to Mizpah, even Ishmael the son of Nethaniah, and Johanan and Jonathan the sons of Kareah, and Seraiah the son of Tanhumeth, and the sons of Ephai the Netophathite, and Jezaniah the son of a Maachathite, they and their men.

[13]Moreover, Johanan the son of Kareah, and all the captains of the forces that were in the fields, came to Gedaliah to Mizpah, [14]And said unto him, Dost thou certainly know that Baalis the king of the Ammonites hath sent Ishmael the son of Nethaniah to slay thee? But Gedaliah the son of Ahikam believed them not. [15]Then Johanan the son of Kareah spake to Gedaliah in Mizpah secretly, saying, Let me go, I pray thee, and I will slay Ishmael the son of Nethaniah, and no man shall know it: wherefore should he slay thee, that all the Jews which are gathered unto thee should be scattered, and the remnant in Judah perish? [16]But Gedaliah the son of Ahikam said unto Johanan the son of Kareah, Thou shalt not do this thing: for thou speakest falsely of Ishmael.

Jer. 41 [1]Now it came to pass in the seventh month, that Ishmael the son of Nethaniah the son of Elishama, of the seed royal, and the princes of the king, even ten men with him, came unto Gedaliah the son of Ahikam to Mizpah: and there they did eat bread together in Mizpah. [2]Then rose Ishmael the son of Nethaniah, and the ten men that were with him, and smote Gedaliah the son of Ahikam the son of Shaphan with the sword, and slew him, whom the king of Babylon had made governor over the land. [3]Ishmael also slew all the Jews that were with him, even with Gedaliah, at

Mizpah, and the Chaldeans that were found there, and the men of war. 4 And it came to pass the second day after he had slain Gedaliah, and no man knew it, 5 That there came certain from Shechem, from Shiloh, and from Samaria, even fourscore men, having their beards shaven, and their clothes rent, and having cut themselves, with offerings and incense in their hand, to bring them to the house of the LORD. 6 And Ishmael the son of Nethaniah went forth from Mizpah to meet them, weeping all along as he went: and it came to pass as he met them, he said unto them, Come to Gedaliah the son of Ahikam. 7 And it was so, when they came into the midst of the city, that Ishmael the son of Nethaniah slew them, and cast them into the midst of the pit, he, and the men that were with him. 8 But ten men were found among them that said unto Ishmael, Slay us not: for we have treasures in the field, of wheat, and of barley, and of oil, and of honey. So he forbare, and slew them not among their brethren. 9 Now the pit wherein Ishmael had cast all the dead bodies of the men, whom he had slain because of Gedaliah, was it which Asa the king had made for fear of Baasha king of Israel: and Ishmael the son of Nethaniah filled it with them that were slain. 10 Then Ishmael carried away captive all the residue of the people that were in Mizpah, even the king's daughters, and all the people that remained in Mizpah, whom Nebuzaradan the captain of the guard had committed to Gedaliah the son of Ahikam: and Ishmael the son of Nethaniah carried them away captive, and departed to go over to the Ammonites.

11 But when Johanan the son of Kareah, and all the captains of the forces that were with him, heard of all the evil that Ishmael the son of Nethaniah had done, 12 Then they took all the men, and went to fight with Ishmael the son of Nethaniah, and found him by the great waters that are in Gibeon. 13 Now it came to pass, that when all the people which were with Ishmael saw Johanan the son of Kareah, and all the captains of the forces that were with him, then they were glad. 14 So all the people that Ishmael had carried away captive from Mizpah cast about and returned, and went unto Johanan the son of Kareah. 15 But Ishmael the son of Nethaniah escaped from Johanan with eight men, and went to the Ammonites.

ISRAEL

[iz′râ el] A name given to Jacob (*Gen. 32: 28*) and applied to his descendants. It is the purpose of this article to present the reader with an overall picture of the history of the people of Israel, rather than a detailed discussion of each major event and personality. Fuller information may be obtained by consulting the index.

In the Biblical narrative, the history of the nation of Israel begins with Abraham and God's promises to him concerning the possession of the land of Canaan by his descendants. Although he and his wife Sarah were old, God granted to them a son, Isaac. Isaac became the father of Jacob, whose wives and concubines bore him twelve sons, the progenitors of the Twelve Tribes. One of the sons, Joseph, was sold by his brothers to a caravan of travelers, who carried him to Egypt. There he rose to a position of great power, second only to the Pharaoh. In time of famine, the brothers came to Egypt for food. Joseph revealed his identity to them and arranged to have the entire family moved into a region of Egypt called Goshen (*Gen. 46: 8-27*). This took place probably near the end of the eighteenth century BC.

The Israelites remained in Egypt for a period of 430 years during which time the favored treatment they had received in the time of Joseph gave way to oppression and slavery. In the first half of the thirteenth century BC God raised up Moses to lead the Exodus from Egypt to the promised land of Canaan. (*See* EXODUS) The escape from bondage, made possible by the various plagues, culminating in the death of the firstborn of the Egyptians, and the miraculous crossing of the Sea is of central importance to the religion of Israel. Henceforth the Exodus is regarded as that even in which God revealed himself as redeemer of Israel. The implications of this revelation were twofold, as is seen in the covenant made at Mt. Sinai shortly after the departure from Egypt. On the one hand God obligated himself to continue as sovereign LORD and Protector of this people; in turn, they pledged to abide by the ritual and moral demands of the Law, epitomized in the Decalogue, or Ten Commandments. (*See* COVENANT)

The Israelites wandered in the Wilderness south of Canaan for a period of forty years, during which time the tabernacle was constructed and the heavenly manna was given as an article of their diet. (*See* TABERNACLE, MANNA) At the close of this period, they moved to the east of Edom and Moab, entering the promised land from east of the Jordan River, at a point about five miles north of the Dead Sea.

Moses died shortly before the entering into Canaan and the leadership of the Israelites fell to Joshua, a capable military strategist. With Joshua at their head, the people soon gained a firm foothold in Canaan. (*See* CONQUEST) Once the major period of conquest was over, Israel settled into a loosely-knit tribal league, centered around the ark of the covenant at Shiloh. During this period the military, legal, and spiritual leadership lay in the hands of individuals known as judges. (*See* JUDGES OF ISRAEL) The loose organization under the judges made effective resistance against attack and oppression almost impossible. They began to clamor for a king to unite them and, in about 1020 BC, Saul was anointed by Samuel to be the first king of Israel. Saul's leadership was mainly military, but his successors, David (1000-960 BC) and Solomon (960-922 BC), welded the people into a true national unit looking to Jerusalem as its political and religious capital.

At Solomon's death in 922 BC, he was succeeded by his son Rehoboam. His refusal to lessen the heavy tax burden his father had imposed caused the ten northern tribes to renounce their allegiance to Rehoboam and Jerusalem. These ten tribes continued to wear the name Israel, while the two southern tribes, Judah and Benjamin, came to be called the Kingdom of Judah. The northern kingdom, Israel, stood for 200 years after the schism. In 722 BC, the inhabitants of the capital city of Samaria were carried off into Assyrian captivity, completing a program of conquest and deportation which saw the kingdom of Israel disappear from Palestine and from history.

It is not improper, however, to refer to the Southern kingdom as Israel; in fact, it is so designated in *Chronicles.* This kingdom outlived her northern sister by several generations, hanging on stubbornly until 587 BC, at which time Jerusalem was finally destroyed by the armies of Nebuchadnezzar and thousands of the inhabitants of Judah were taken captive to Babylonia. For the history of the kingdoms of Israel and Judah the reader is urged to consult the chart of kings in the appendix and the articles on the individual kings and other subjects related to this period.

The history of Israel does not end with the Babylonian exile. In 538 BC, only one year after the Persians siezed control of the empire that had been Babylon's, Cyrus king of Persia gave permission to the Jews to return to Jerusalem and reestablish Jewish life and worship. The restoration was slow and discouraging, but under such leaders as Zerubbabel, Ezra, Nehemiah, Haggai, and Zechariah, Jerusalem was repaired, the temple was rebuilt, and the covenant with God was renewed. The restoration was virtually complete by about 400 BC. We know little of the subsequent history of Israel until the activity of Alexander the Great (336-323 BC), at which time Palestine, with the rest of the world, fell under his power. After Alexander's early death, Palestine was claimed by both the Egyptian and Seleucid kings, heirs to the eastern portion of Alexander's empire. Finally, in 198 BC, following the battle of Paneion, the Seleucid's gained clear control. About a decade later, Antiochus Epiphanes gained the Seleucid throne. Palestine was in a state of turmoil. Religion and politics were hopelessly intermingled. Antiochus set out to remove opposition to himself by destroying the religion of Judaism and replacing it with Greek religion and culture. The temple was defiled and made into a shrine of Zeus; all practice of the Jewish faith was condemned; and Jews were forced to offer sacrifice to idols and to eat unclean foods. It was this which led to the Jewish revolt under the Hasmoneans, sometimes called the Maccabees, although this term is properly applied only to the earliest members of this ruling family. Led by Judas Maccabeus and his brothers, the Seleucid rule was overthrown in the middle of the second century BC and the Hasmoneans assumed the dual role of king and high priest. The parties known in the New Testament as Pharisees and Sadducees had their origin in this period.

In the middle of the first century BC, Palestine was invaded by the armies of Pompey and thus came under Roman control. Under the Romans the rule of the kingdom of Palestine lay in the hands of the Herod family. (*See* HEROD) The Roman period was a time of much hostility and bitterness. In AD 66 the Jews once again broke out in revolt. Despite their bravery they were, of course, no match for the Roman legions. Finally the armies of Titus, later emperor of Rome, overran Jerusalem and destroyed the temple in AD 70. For practical purposes we may take this date as the end of the history of Israel, but this is not entirely satisfactory. For it was Israel who gave us faith in one God; it was the religion of Israel which served as a seedbed for the religion of Christ; the new community in Christ is a spiritual Israel. Thus, in a sense, the history of Israel can never really end; it can only be brought to fulfillment.

JABAL

[jā'bal] The son of Lamech, said to be "the father of such as dwell in tents, and of such as have cattle" (*Gen. 4:20*).

JABESH-GILEAD

[jā'besh-gil'ē ad] A city east of the Jordan. Jabesh-gilead first appears in Biblical history when its men failed to take part in the vengeance upon the tribe of Benjamin, at which time the city was subjected to a terrible punishment. (*See Judg. 21*) Saul's first demonstration of his ability after being anointed king was his deliverance of Jabesh-gilead from the Ammonites (*1 Sam. 11:1-11*). This earned him the undying loyalty of the inhabitants of that city. After the disastrous defeat of Saul on Gilboa, his body and those of his sons were hung on the walls of Bethshan.

SCRIPTURE

1 Sam. 31 [11]And when the inhabitants
of Jabesh-Gilead heard of that which the
Philistines had done to Saul; [12]All the valiant men arose, and went all night, and
took the body of Saul and the bodies of
his sons from the wall of Bethshan, and
came to Jabesh, and burnt them there.
[13]And they took their bones, and buried
them under a tree at Jabesh, and fasted
seven days."

JACOB

[jā'kub] Son of Isaac and Rebekah, twin brother of Esau, and father of the twelve patriarchs of Israel. Through his mother's favoritism and his own shrewdness, Jacob was able to obtain the birthright and the paternal blessing which should have gone to his elder brother Esau. When Esau sought to kill him for his deception, Jacob was sent by Rebekah to her relatives in Haran for the ostensible purpose of choosing a wife. On the long journey he saw the vision of the heavenly ladder, and the covenant which God had made with his grandfather Abraham was reaffirmed. In Haran, Jacob was immediately attracted to Laban's beautiful daughter Rachel. He worked seven years for her but received her homely sister Leah instead, through a deception of Laban. After a week he also received Rachel to be his wife, but was compelled to work an additional seven years. When these fourteen years were completed, Jacob continued to work for Laban six more years. This period is characterized by the efforts of two cunning men to gain the advantage over the other. Although Jacob became a wealthy man, he was dissatisfied with his situation and sought to return to Canaan. On the way, he had to pass through the territory of Esau; fearing that his brother was still harboring his grudge against him, Jacob sought to appease him with elaborate gifts. The two were reunited without incident and Jacob passed through safely. It was during the night before the reconciliation with Esau that Jacob wrestled with an angel and had his name changed to Israel. Not long afterward, Rachel died in giving birth to Benjamin, the last of Jacob's twelve sons. After a sojourn in Canaan, Jacob and the surviving members of his family migrated to Egypt at the urging of Joseph, a son who had become powerful in the Egyptian government. At his death, Jacob was embalmed and his body carried back to the family burial place at Machpelah.

See Esau, Leah, Rachel, Rebekah, Joseph, etc.

SCRIPTURE

Jacob's Youth

Gen. 25 [27]And the boys grew: and Esau was a cunning hunter, a man of the field; and Jacob was a plain man, dwelling in tents. [28]And Isaac loved Esau, because he did eat of his venison: but Rebekah loved Jacob.

Obtains Birthright

Gen. 25 [30]And Esau said to Jacob, Feed me, I pray thee, with that same red pottage; for I am faint: therefore was his name called Edom. [31]And Jacob said, Sell me this day thy birthright. [32]And Esau said, Behold, I am at the point to die: and what profit shall this birthright do to me? [33]And Jacob said, Swear to me this day; and he sware unto him: and he sold his birthright unto Jacob.

Obtains Blessing

Gen. 27 [18]And he came unto his father, and said, My father: and he said, Here am I; who art thou, my son? [19]And Jacob said unto his father, I am Esau thy firstborn; I have done according as thou badest me: arise, I pray thee, sit and eat of my venison, that thy soul may bless me. [20]And Isaac said unto his son, How is it that thou hast found it so quickly, my son? And he said, Because the Lord thy God brought it to me. [21]And Isaac said unto Jacob, Come near, I pray thee, that I may feel thee, my son, whether thou be my very son Esau or not. [22]And Jacob went near unto Isaac his father; and he felt him, and said, The voice is Jacob's voice, but the hands are the hands of Esau. [23]And he discerned him not, because his hands were hairy, as his brother Esau's hands: so he blessed him.

The Dream and Promise

Gen. 28 [12]And he dreamed, and behold a ladder set up on the earth, and the top of it reached to heaven: and behold the angels of God ascending and descending on it. [13]And, behold, the Lord stood above it, and said, I am the Lord God of Abraham thy father, and the God of Isaac: the land whereon thou liest, to thee will I give it, and to thy seed; [14]And thy seed shall be as the dust of the earth: and thou shalt spread abroad to the west, and to the east, and to the north, and to the south: and in thee and in thy seed shall all the families of the earth be blessed. [15]And, behold, I am with thee, and will keep thee in all places whither thou goest, and will bring thee again into this land; for I will not leave thee, until I have done that which I have spoken to thee of.

Jacob's Name Changed to Israel

Gen. 32 [24]And Jacob was left alone; and there wrestled a man with him until the breaking of the day. [25]And when he saw that he prevailed not against him, he touched the hollow of his thigh; and the hollow of Jacob's thigh was out of joint, as he wrestled with him. [26]And he said, Let me go, for the day breaketh. And he said,

I will not let thee go, except thou bless me. [27]And he said unto him, What is thy name? And he said, Jacob. [28]And he said, Thy name shall be called no more Jacob, but Israel: for as a prince hast thou power with God and with men, and hast prevailed.

The Twelve Sons of Jacob

Gen. 35 [23]The sons of Leah; Reuben, Jacob's firstborn, and Simeon, and Levi, and Judah, and Issachar, and Zebulun: [24]The sons of Rachel; Joseph, and Benjamin: [25]And the sons of Bilhah, Rachel's handmaid; Dan, and Naphtali: [26]And the sons of Zilpah, Leah's handmaid; Gad, and Asher. These are the sons of Jacob, which were born to him in Padanaram.

Blesses His Sons and Dies

Gen. 49 [1]And Jacob called unto his sons, and said, Gather yourselves together, that I may tell you that which shall befall you in the last days. [2]Gather yourselves together, and hear, ye sons of Jacob; and hearken unto Israel your father.

[28]All these are the twelve tribes of Israel: and this is it that their father spake unto them, and blessed them; every one according to his blessing he blessed them. [33]And when Jacob had made an end of commanding his sons, he gathered up his feet into the bed, and yielded up the ghost, and was gathered unto his people.

JAIRUS

[jā'i rus] A ruler in a synagogue near Capernaum whose daughter was raised from the dead by Jesus. It was while on his way to the house of Jairus that Jesus healed the woman with the issue of blood. When Jesus reached the house, he was informed that the girl was dead; his assertion that she was only sleeping brought derision from those who had gathered to mourn. Heedless of their scorn, Jesus took the child by the hand and bade her to rise, "and her spirit came again, and she arose straightway: and he commanded to give her meat" (*Luke 8:55*).

SCRIPTURE

Mark 5 [22]And, behold, there cometh one of the rulers of the synagogue, Jairus by name; and when he saw him, he fell at his feet, [23]And besought him greatly, saying, My little daughter lieth at the point of death: I pray thee, come and lay thy hands on her, that she may be healed; and she shall live. [24]And Jesus went with him; and much people followed him, and thronged him. [35]While he yet spake, there came from the ruler of the synagogue's house certain which said, Thy daughter is dead; why troublest thou the Master any further? [36]As soon as Jesus heard the word that was spoken, he saith unto the ruler of the synagogue, Be not afraid, only believe. [37]And he suffered no man to follow him, save Peter, and James, and John the brother of James. [38]And he cometh to the house of the ruler of the synagogue, and seeth the tumult, and them that wept and wailed greatly. [39]And when he was come in, he saith unto them, Why make ye this ado, and weep? the damsel is not dead, but sleepeth. [40]And they laughed him to scorn. But when he had put them all out, he taketh the father and the mother of the damsel, and them that were with him, and entereth in where the damsel was lying. [41]And he took the damsel by the hand, and said unto her, Talithacumi; which is, being interpreted, Damsel, (I say unto thee,) arise. [42]And straightway the damsel arose, and walked; for she was of the age of twelve years. And they were astonished with a great astonishment. [43]And he charged them straitly that no man should know it; and commanded that something should be given her to eat.

JAMES

[jāmz] A variant of the name Jacob. Several New Testament characters bear this name:

1. James, the Son of Zebedee, a fisherman on the sea of Galilee who, with his brother John, was one of the original twelve apostles (*Matt. 10:2*). He and John, along with Simon Peter, formed what has been termed the "inner circle" of Jesus' disciples. These three alone were chosen to accompany the Master on such occasions as the raising of Jairus' daughter (*Mark 5:37*), the transfiguration (*Matt. 17:1*), and the agony in the Garden of Gethsemane (*Matt. 26:37*). These two brothers are characterized as "sons of thunder" (*Mark 3:17*), indicating perhaps that they were of a fiery temperament. This is borne out in *Luke 9:51-56* by Jesus' rebuke of them for their desire to call down fire on a Samaritan town that rejected the preaching of Jesus. On another occasion, the two brothers, prompted perhaps by their favored position, asked Jesus for places of favor at his right and left hand when he came into his glory. Jesus used this opportunity to teach his disciples on the nature of true greatness and to warn them that they could expect little more than tribulation as an earthly reward for their labors. This great apostle met his death in the persecution ordered by Herod Agrippa I, king of Palestine in 42-44 AD.

2. James the son of Alphaeus, also one of the twelve apostles (*Matt. 10:3*).

3. James the Less. He is mentioned only as the son of Mary and the brother of Joses (*Mark 15:40*). It is quite possible that he is to be identified with James the son of Alphaeus.

4. James, the father of Judas not Iscariot (*Luke 6:16*; *Acts 1:13*).

5. James, the brother of the Lord, a pillar in the church at Jerusalem (*Acts 15:12-21*; *Gal. 2:1-10*), often referred to simply as James (*Acts 12:17*; *15:13*; etc.). Based on *John 7:5*, James apparently was not a disciple during part or all of the ministry of Jesus, but in *Gal. 1:19* he is called an apostle. Although there is much disagreement over the matter, he is probably the author of the epistle of *James*.

SCRIPTURE

James, the Son of Zebedee

AN APOSTLE OF CHRIST

Matt. 10 [2]Now the names of the twelve
apostles are these; The first, Simon, who is
called Peter, and Andrew his brother;
James the son of Zebedee, and John his
brother;

ONE OF THE "INNER CIRCLE"

Mark 5 [37]And he suffered no man to follow him, save Peter, and James, and John
the brother of James.

Matt. 17 [1]And after six days Jesus taketh Peter, James, and John his brother, and
bringeth them up into a high mountain
apart.

Matt. 26 [37]And he took with him Peter
and the two sons of Zebedee, and began to
be sorrowful and very heavy.

A "SON OF THUNDER"

Mark 3 [17]And James the son of Zebedee, and John the brother of James; and he
surnamed them Boanerges, which is, The
sons of thunder:

Luke 9 [51]And it came to pass, when the
time was come that he should be received
up, he steadfastly set his face to go to Jerusalem, [52]And sent messengers before his
face: and they went, and entered into a
village of the Samaritans, to make ready
for him. [53]And they did not receive him,
because his face was as though he would
go to Jerusalem. [54]And when his disciples
James and John saw this, they said, Lord,
wilt thou that we command fire to come
down from heaven, and consume them,
even as Elias did? [55]But he turned, and rebuked them, and said, Ye know not what
manner of spirit ye are of. [56]For the Son of

man is not come to destroy men's lives, but to save them. And they went to another village.

AMBITION OF JAMES AND JOHN

Mark 10 [35]And James and John, the sons of Zebedee, come unto him, saying, Master, we would that thou shouldest do for us whatsoever we shall desire. [36]And he said unto them, What would ye that I should do for you? [37]They said unto him, Grant unto us that we may sit, one on thy right hand, and the other on thy left hand, in thy glory. [38]But Jesus said unto them, Ye know not what ye ask: can ye drink of the cup that I drink of? and be baptized with the baptism that I am baptized with? [39]And they said unto him, We can. And Jesus said unto them, Ye shall indeed drink of the cup that I drink of; and with the baptism that I am baptized withal shall ye be baptized: [40]But to sit on my right hand and on my left hand is not mine to give; but it shall be given to them for whom it is prepared. [41]And when the ten heard it, they began to be much displeased with James and John.

A MARTYR UNDER HEROD AGRIPPA I

Acts 12 [1]Now about that time Herod the king stretched forth his hands to vex certain of the church. [2]And he killed James the brother of John with the sword.

James, the Son of Alpheus

Matt. 10 [3]Philip, and Bartholomew; Thomas, and Matthew the publican; James the son of Alpheus, and Lebbeus, whose surname was Thaddeus;

James the Less

Mark 15 [40]There were also women looking on afar off: among whom was Mary Magdalene, and Mary the mother of James the less and of Joses, and Salome;

James, the Brother of Judas

Luke 6 [16]And Judas the brother of James, and Judas Iscariot, which also was the traitor.

James, the Brother of the Lord

AS JESUS' BROTHER

Mark 6 [3]Is not this the carpenter, the son of Mary, the brother of James, and Joses, and of Juda, and Simon? and are not his sisters here with us? And they were offended at him.

A LEADER IN THE JERUSALEM CHURCH

Acts 15 [12]Then all the multitude kept silence, and gave audience to Barnabas and Paul, declaring what miracles and wonders God had wrought among the Gentiles by them.

[13]And after they had held their peace, James answered, saying, Men and brethren, hearken unto me: [14]Simeon hath declared how God at the first did visit the Gentiles, to take out of them a people for his name. [15]And to this agree the words of the prophets; as it is written, [16]After this I will return, and will build again the tabernacle of David, which is fallen down; and I will build again the ruins thereof, and I will set it up: [17]That the residue of men might seek after the Lord, and all the Gentiles, upon whom my name is called, saith the Lord, who doeth all these things. [18]Known unto God are all his works from the beginning of the world. [19]Wherefore my sentence is, that we trouble not them, which from among the Gentiles are turned to God: [20]But that we write unto them, that they abstain from pollutions of idols,

and from fornication, and from things strangled, and from blood. [21]For Moses of old time hath in every city them that preach him, being read in the synagogues every sabbath day.

JAPHETH

[jā'feth] A son of Noah, regarded as the progenitor of races in Europe and Western Asia.

SCRIPTURE

Enters the Ark

Gen. 7 [13]In the selfsame day entered Noah, and Shem, and Ham, and Japheth, the sons of Noah, and Noah's wife, and the three wives of his sons with them, into the ark;

Shows Respect for Noah

Gen. 9 [20]And Noah began to be a husbandman, and he planted a vineyard: [21]And he drank of the wine, and was drunken; and he was uncovered within his tent. [22]And Ham, the father of Canaan, saw the nakedness of his father, and told his two brethren without. [23]And Shem and Japheth took a garment, and laid it upon both their shoulders, and went backward, and covered the nakedness of their father; and their faces were backward, and they saw not their father's nakedness.

JEALOUS, JEALOUSY

[jel'us, jel'us i] The root meaning of the Hebrew word translated "jealous" in the Old Testament originally meant "to be dyed dark red or black"; it was used of emotions which show themselves in bright "colors." In neither Hebrew nor Greek is it always possible to determine whether the word is being used to denote the ignoble emotion of envy or the admirable and noble passion of enthusiastic zeal. It is frequently used of a righteous man's jealousy *for* God and of God's jealousy for his people.

See ENVY, ZEAL

SCRIPTURE

God's Jealousy

Ex. 20 [5]Thou shalt not bow down thyself to them, nor serve them: For I the LORD thy God am a jealous God, visiting the iniquity of the fathers upon the children unto the third and fourth generation of them that hate me.

Deut. 29 [20]The LORD will not spare him, but then the anger of the LORD and his jealousy shall smoke against that man, and all the curses that are written in this book shall lie upon him, and the LORD shall blot out his name from under heaven.

Psa. 78 [58]For they provoked him to anger with their high places, and moved him to jealousy with their graven images.

Zeph. 1 [18]Neither their silver nor their gold shall be able to deliver them in the day of the LORD's wrath; but the whole land shall be devoured by the fire of his jealousy: for he shall make even a speedy riddance of all them that dwell in the land.

1 Cor. 10 [22]Do we provoke the Lord to jealousy? are we stronger than he?

Human Jealousy as Zeal for God

Num. 25 [11]Phinehas, the son of Eleazar, the son of Aaron the priest, hath turned my wrath away from the children of Israel, while he was zealous for my sake among them, that I consumed not the children of Israel in my jealousy. [12]Wherefore say, Behold, I give unto him my covenant of peace: [13]And he shall have it, and his seed after him, even the covenant of an everlasting priesthood; because he was zealous for his God, and made an atonement for the children of Israel.

1 Kin. 19 [10]And he said, I have been very jealous for the LORD God of hosts: for the children of Israel have forsaken thy covenant, thrown down thine altars, and slain thy prophets with the sword; and I, even I only, am left; and they seek my life, to take it away.

2 Kin. 10 [16]And he said, Come with me, and see my zeal for the LORD. So they made him ride in his chariot.

2 Cor. 11 [2]For I am jealous over you with godly jealousy: for I have espoused you to one husband, that I may present you as a chaste virgin to Christ.

See 1 Kin. 19:14

Human Jealousy as Envy

Prov. 6 [34]For jealousy is the rage of a man: therefore he will not spare in the day of vengeance. [35]He will not regard any ransom; neither will he rest content, though thou givest many gifts.

Song 8 [6]Set me as a seal upon thine heart, as a seal upon thine arm: for love is strong as death; jealousy is cruel as the grave: the coals thereof are coals of fire, which hath a most vehement flame.

Ezek. 16 [38]And I will judge thee, as women that break wedlock and shed blood are judged; and I will give thee blood in fury and jealousy.

JEBUSITES

[jeb ŭ zīts] The inhabitants of Jebus, an old name for Jerusalem. At the time of the Israelite conquest of Canaan, the Jebusites were part of the coalition defeated by Joshua in the battle of the long day. After the death of Joshua the men of Judah conquered Jerusalem, but apparently the Jebusites were able to regain control. Israel gained final possession of the city of the Jebusites when David took it for the new capital of his kingdom; its inhabitants were allowed to remain in it, however, and were eventually absorbed into the Israelite population.

SCRIPTURE

Their Land to Be Given to Israel

Deut. 7 [1]When the LORD thy God shall bring thee into the land whither thou goest to possess it, and hath cast out many nations before thee, the Hittites, and the Girgashites, and the Amorites, and the Canaanites, and the Perizzites, and the Hivites, and the Jebusites, seven nations greater and mightier than thou; [2]And when the LORD thy God shall deliver them before thee; thou shalt smite them, and utterly destroy them; thou shalt make no covenant with them, nor shew mercy unto them:

Josh. 24 [11]And ye went over Jordan, and came unto Jericho: and the men of Jericho fought against you, the Amorites, and the Perizzites, and the Canaanites, and the Hittites, and the Girgashites, the Hivites, and the Jebusites; and I delivered them into your hand.

Defeated by David at Jerusalem

2 Sam. 5 [6]And the king and his men went to Jerusalem unto the Jebusites, the inhabitants of the land: which spake unto David, saying, Except thou take away the blind and the lame, thou shalt not come in hither: thinking, David can not come in hither. [7]Nevertheless, David took the strong hold of Zion: the same is the city of David. [8]And David said on that day, Whosoever getteth up to the gutter, and smiteth the Jebusites, and the lame and the blind, that are hated of David's soul, he shall be chief and captain. Wherefore they said, The blind and the lame shall not come into the house. [9]So David dwelt in the fort, and called it the city of David. And David built round about from Millo and inward. [10]And David went on, and grew great, and the LORD God of hosts was with him.

JEHOAHAZ

[jē hō'a haz] The son of Jehu and the eleventh ruler of the northern kingdom (814-798 BC). Jehoahaz reigned in a period of great darkness for Israel. Virtually all of the land of Transjordan had been lost to the Syrian king, Hazael (cf. *2 Kin. 10:32, 33*) and Israel was still a tributary of Assyria, dating from the early days of the reign of Jehu. Civil war in Assyria, while relieving pressure from that source, gave Hazael more freedom to harass Palestine. The depths to which Israel had sunk are illustrated by the statement in *2 Kin. 13:7* that Jehu's army contained only ten chariots; during Ahab's reign (869-850 BC) Israel contributed 2,000 chariots to a coalition against Assyria.

SCRIPTURE

2 Kin. 13 [1]In the three and twentieth
year of Joash the son of Ahaziah king of Judah, Jehoahaz the son of Jehu began to
reign over Israel in Samaria, and reigned
seventeen years. [2]And he did that which
was evil in the sight of the LORD, and followed the sins of Jeroboam the son of Nebat, which made Israel to sin; he departed
not therefrom.

[3]And the anger of the LORD was kindled
against Israel, and he delivered them into
the hand of Hazael king of Syria, and into
the hand of Ben-hadad the son of Hazael,
all their days. [4]And Jehoahaz besought
the LORD, and the LORD hearkened unto
him: for he saw the oppression of Israel,
because the king of Syria oppressed them.
[5](And the LORD gave Israel a saviour, so
that they went out from under the hand of
the Syrians: and the children of Israel
dwelt in their tents, as beforetime. [6]Nev-
ertheless they departed not from the sins
of the house of Jeroboam, who made Israel
sin, but walked therein: and there remained the grove also in Samaria.) [7]Nei-
ther did he leave of the people to Jehoahaz but fifty horsemen, and ten chariots,
and ten thousand footmen; for the king of
Syria had destroyed them, and had made
them like the dust by threshing.

[8]Now the rest of the acts of Jehoahaz,
and all that he did, and his might, are they
not written in the book of the Chronicles of
the kings of Israel? [9]And Jehoahaz slept
with his fathers; and they buried him in
Samaria: and Joash his son reigned in his
stead.

JEHOAHAZ II

[jē hō'a haz] The son of Josiah and king of Judah (609/8 BC), called Shallum in *Jer. 22:11*. Jehoahaz was put on the throne by "the people of the land." Although we cannot be sure as to the identity of this group, they are also credited with securing the kingship for his worthy father, Josiah, after the assassination of Amon. After the encounter with Josiah which cost the life of the king, Pharaoh Necho II of Egypt continued his sally northward. Apparently feeling that Judah must be kept under close control, Necho deposed Jehoahaz and appointed his brother Jehoiakim to take his place as a vassal of Egypt.

See JOSIAH, JEHOIAKIM

SCRIPTURE

2 Kin. 23 [29]In his days Pharaoh-nechoh
king of Egypt went up against the king of
Assyria to the river Euphrates: and king
Josiah went against him; and he slew him
at Megiddo, when he had seen him. [30]And
his servants carried him in a chariot dead
from Megiddo, and brought him to Jerusalem, and buried him in his own sepulchre.
And the people of the land took Jehoahaz
the son of Josiah, and anointed him, and
made him king in his father's stead.

[31]Jehoahaz was twenty and three years
old when he began to reign; and he
reigned three months in Jerusalem. And
his mother's name was Hamutal, the
daughter of Jeremiah of Libnah. [32]And
he did that which was evil in the sight of

the LORD, according to all that his fathers
had done. 33And Pharaoh-nechoh put him
in bands at Riblah in the hand of Hamath,
that he might not reign in Jerusalem; and
put the land to a tribute of a hundred talents of silver, and a talent of gold. 34And
Pharaoh-nechoh made Eliakim the son of
Josiah king in the room of Josiah his father,
and turned his name to Jehoiakim, and
took Jehoahaz away: and he came to
Egypt, and died there.

JEHOASH (JOASH)

[jê hō′ash] The son of Ahaziah and king of Judah (836-797 BC), also called Joash. After the death of Ahaziah at the hands of Jehu, the queen-mother Athaliah had secured the throne by the murder of all legitimate royal successors with the exception of Jehoash, the infant son of Ahaziah who was hidden and reared in secret by the righteous priest Jehoida. In the seventh year of Athaliah's reign, Jehoash was proclaimed king and the queen was slain. Under the influence of Jehoida, the young king called for the repair and purification of the temple, a step doubtlessly made necessary by the idolatrous practices of Athaliah. Finances for this venture were raised by setting up a collection box in the temple. After the death of Jehoida, Jehoash acquiesced to the demands of a more tolerant element and allowed the reintroduction of idolatrous worship. When criticized for this by Zechariah the son of Jehoida, Jehoash put him to death. These events of the last years of his long reign indicate that the credit for the good which was done in former years goes not to the king himself, but to the worthy priest, Jehoida. In the end, after a period in which he suffered a crushing defeat at the hands of Hazael king of Syria and thereby incurred a ruinous payment of tribute, Jehoash was assassinated, to be succeeded by his son Amaziah.

See JEHU, ATHALIAH, AMAZIAH, KINGS

SCRIPTURE

2 Kin. 11 21Seven years old was Jehoash
when he began to reign.

2 Kin. 12 1In the seventh year of Jehu,
Jehoash began to reign; and forty years
reigned he in Jerusalem. And his mother's
name was Zibiah of Beersheba. 2And Jehoash did that which was right in the sight
of the LORD all his days wherein Jehoiada
the priest instructed him. 3But the high
places were not taken away: the people
still sacrificed and burnt incense in the
high places.

4And Jehoash said to the priests, All the
money of the dedicated things that is
brought into the house of the LORD, even
the money of every one that passeth the
account, the money that every man is set
at, and all the money that cometh into any
man's heart to bring into the house of the
LORD, 5Let the priests take it to them, every man of his acquaintance: and let them
repair the breaches of the house, wheresoever any breach shall be found. 6But it
was so, that in the three and twentieth year
of king Jehoash the priests had not repaired the breaches of the house. 7Then
king Jehoash called for Jehoiada the priest,
and the other priests, and said unto them,
Why repair ye not the breaches of the
house? now therefore receive no more
money of your acquaintance, but deliver
it for the breaches of the house. 8And the
priests consented to receive no more
money of the people, neither to repair the
breaches of the house. 9But Jehoiada the
priest took a chest, and bored a hole in the
lid of it, and set it beside the altar, on the
right side as one cometh into the house of
the LORD: and the priests that kept the
door put therein all the money that was
brought into the house of the LORD. 10And
it was so, when they saw that there was
much money in the chest, that the king's
scribe and the high priest came up, and
they put up in bags, and told the money

that was found in the house of the LORD.
[11]And they gave the money, being told,
into the hands of them that did the work,
that had the oversight of the house of the
LORD: and they laid it out to the carpenters
and builders, that wrought upon the house
of the LORD,

[18]And Jehoash king of Judah took all the
hallowed things that Jehoshaphat, and Jehoram, and Ahaziah, his fathers, kings of
Judah, had dedicated, and his own hallowed things, and all the gold that was
found in the treasures of the house of the
LORD, and in the king's house, and sent it
to Hazael king of Syria: and he went away
from Jerusalem.

[19]And the rest of the acts of Joash, and
all that he did, are they not written in the
book of the Chronicles of the kings of Judah? [20]And his servants arose, and made a
conspiracy, and slew Joash in the house of
Millo, which goeth down to Silla. [21]For
Jozachar the son of Shimeath, and Jehoza-
bad the son of Shomer, his servants, smote
him, and he died; and they buried him
with his fathers in the city of David: and
Amaziah his son reigned in his stead.

See 2 Chr. 24

JEHOASH (JOASH)

[jē hō'ash] The son of Jehoahaz and the twelfth king of Israel (798-782 BC). Although he did not discourage the bull cult of Jeroboam, Jehoash is seen in a more favorable light than most of his predecessors and apparently had a good relationship with the prophet Elisha (*2 Kin. 13:14ff*). During the reign of Jehoash the Assyrian nation was recovering from internecine strife and subdued Syria. In its prostrate condition, Syria was unable to resist Jehoash and under his leadership Israel regained the territory which had been taken from his father Jehoahaz. An interesting account of Elisha's prediction of victory over Syria is found in *2 Kin. 13:14ff*. Another of Jehoash's military achievements was the defeat of Amaziah, king of Judah, and the plundering of the city of Jerusalem. These accomplishments left to his son and successor, Jeroboam II, were the foundation for a strong and prosperous state.

See KINGS, JEROBOAM II, AMAZIAH, ELISHA

SCRIPTURE

Counsels with Elisha

2 Kin. 13 [14]Now Elisha was fallen sick
of his sickness whereof he died. And Joash
the king of Israel came down unto him,
and wept over his face, and said, O my father, my father! the chariot of Israel, and
the horsemen thereof. [15]And Elisha said
unto him, Take bow and arrows. And he
took unto him bow and arrows. [16]And he
said to the king of Israel, Put thine hand
upon the bow. And he put his hand upon
it: and Elisha put his hands upon the king's
hands. [17]And he said, Open the window
eastward. And he opened it. Then Elisha
said, Shoot. And he shot. And he said, The
arrow of the LORD's deliverance, and the
arrow of deliverance from Syria: for thou
shalt smite the Syrians in Aphek, till thou
have consumed them. [18]And he said, Take
the arrows. And he took them. And he said
unto the king of Israel, Smite upon the
ground. And he smote thrice, and stayed.
[19]And the man of God was wroth with him,
and said, Thou shouldest have smitten five
or six times; then hadst thou smitten Syria
till thou hadst consumed it: whereas now
thou shalt smite Syria but thrice.

Defeats Syria

2 Kin. 13 [24]So Hazael king of Syria died;
and Ben-hadad his son reigned in his
stead. [25]And Jehoash the son of Jehoahaz
took again out of the hand of Ben-hadad
the son of Hazael the cities, which he had
taken out of the hand of Jehoahaz his fa-

ther by war. Three times did Joash beat him, and recovered the cities of Israel.

Defeats Amaziah King of Judah

2 Chr. 25 [17]Then Amaziah king of Judah took advice, and sent to Joash, the son of Jehoahaz, the son of Jehu, king of Israel, saying, Come, let us see one another in the face. [18]And Joash king of Israel sent to Amaziah king of Judah, saying, The thistle that was in Lebanon sent to the cedar that was in Lebanon, saying, Give thy daughter to my son to wife: and there passed by a wild beast that was in Lebanon, and trode down the thistle. [19]Thou sayest, Lo, thou hast smitten the Edomites; and thine heart lifted thee up to boast: abide now at home; why shouldest thou meddle to thine hurt, that thou shouldest fall, even thou, and Judah with thee? [20]But Amaziah would not hear; for it came of God, that he might deliver them into the hand of their enemies, because they sought after the gods of Edom. [21]So Joash the king of Israel went up; and they saw one another in the face, both he and Amaziah king of Judah, at Beth-shemesh, which belongeth to Judah. [22]And Judah was put to the worse before Israel, and they fled every man to his tent. [23]And Joash the king of Israel took Amaziah king of Judah, the son of Joash, the son of Jehoahaz, at Beth-shemesh, and brought him to Jerusalem, and brake down the wall of Jerusalem from the gate of Ephraim to the corner gate, four hundred cubits. [24]And he took all the gold and silver, and all the vessels that were found in the house of God with Obed-edom, and the treasures of the king's house, the hostages also, and returned to Samaria.

Death

2 Kin. 14 [16]And Jehoash slept with his fathers, and was buried in Samaria with the kings of Israel; and Jeroboam his son reigned in his stead.

JEHOIACHIN

[je hoi′a kin] The son of Jehoiakim and his successor as king of Judah; also called Coniah (*Jer. 22:24, 28*). Jehoiachin's father died while Nebuchadnezzar was marching on Judah. Recognizing the hopelessness of the situation, the young king surrendered the city to Nebuchadnezzar and was carried to Babylon in the first great deportation of captives, having held his throne only three months. This first wave stripped Jerusalem not only of the better elements among the people, but also of the most valuable treasures of the temple and the palace. Jehoiachin remained in Babylon for the remainder of his life, dying there thirty-seven years later. Towards the end of his life, however, he was released from prison and given favored treatment in the royal court.

See KINGS

SCRIPTURE

2 Kin. 24 [8]Jehoiachin was eighteen years old when he began to reign, and he reigned in Jerusalem three months. And his mother's name was Nehushta, the daughter of Elnathan of Jerusalem. [9]And he did that which was evil in the sight of the LORD, according to all that his father had done.

[10]At that time the servants of Nebuchadnezzar king of Babylon came up against Jerusalem, and the city was besieged. [11]And Nebuchadnezzar king of Babylon came against the city, and his servants did besiege it. [15]And he carried away Jehoiachin to Babylon, and the king's mother, and the king's wives, and his officers, and the mighty of the land, those carried he into captivity from Jerusalem to Babylon.

2 Kin. 25 [27]And it came to pass in the seven and thirtieth year of the captivity of Jehoiachin king of Judah, in the twelfth month, on the seven and twentieth day of the month, that Evil-merodach king of

Babylon in the year that he began to reign did lift up the head of Jehoiachin king of Judah out of prison; [28]And he spake kindly to him, and set his throne above the throne of the kings that were with him in Babylon; [29]And changed his prison garments: and he did eat bread continually before him all the days of his life. [30]And his allowance was a continual allowance given him of the king, a daily rate for every day, all the days of his life.

JEHOIAKIM

[jē hoi'a kim] Brother of Jehoahaz II and king of Judah (609/8-597 BC), also called Eliakim. Pharaoh Necho II of Egypt deposed Jehoahaz II and set Jehoiakim on the throne as a vassal of Egypt. Jehoiakim proved himself an unworthy ruler. Using forced and unpaid labor he squandered what little money the treasury held to build himself a more luxurious palace. He had little interest in religion and allowed idolatries of every sort to creep back into the worship of Judah. His cutting up and burning of the scroll of Jeremiah demonstrates the cavalier attitude which he had toward the word of the LORD and provoked Jeremiah's fiercest opposition. Jehoiakim remained a vassal of Egypt until about 603, when he transferred his allegiance to the conquering Nebuchadnezzar. In about 601, after a battle between Babylon and Egypt in which both sides suffered heavily, Jehoiakim rebelled. Although Nebuchadnezzar was in no position to crush this rebellion completely, he harassed Judah with raiding parties until 598 when he began his major campaign. In the same month Jehoiakim met his death and was replaced by his son Jehoiachin.

See JEHOIACHIN, KINGS

SCRIPTURE

2 Kin. 23 [34]And Pharaoh-nechoch made Eliakim the son of Josiah king in the room of Josiah his father, and turned his name to Jehoiakim, and took Jehoahaz away: and he came to Egypt, and died there. [35]And Jehoiakim gave the silver and the gold to Pharaoh; but he taxed the land to give the money according to the commandment of Pharaoh: he exacted the silver and the gold of the people of the land, of every one according to his taxation, to give it unto Pharaoh-nechoh.

[36]Jehoiakim was twenty and five years old when he began to reign; and he reigned eleven years in Jerusalem. And his mother's name was Zebudah, the daughter of Pedaiah of Rumah. [37]And he did that which was evil in the sight of the LORD, according to all that his fathers had done.

Jer. 36 [21]So the king sent Jehudi to fetch the roll; and he took it out of Elishama the scribe's chamber. And Jehudi read it in the ears of the king, and in the ears of all the princes which stood beside the king. [22]Now the king sat in the winter house in the ninth month: and there was a fire on the hearth burning before him. [23]And it came to pass, that when Jehudi had read three or four leaves, he cut it with the penknife, and cast it into the fire that was on the hearth, until all the roll was consumed in the fire that was on the hearth.

JEHORAM

[je hō'ram] The son of Jehoshaphat and fifth king of Judah (849-842 BC). To cement an alliance between Judah and Israel, Jehoram was married by his father to Athaliah, the daughter of Ahab and Jezebel. The influence which his idolatrous wife had on him is summed up by the statement, "He walked in the ways of the kings of Israel, as did the house of Ahab" (*2 Kin. 8: 18*). When Jehoram acceeded to the throne at the death of his father, he consolidated his power by the murder of his brothers and other men of influence who might prove a threat to his reign. Militarily, Judah was weak during Jehoram's reign, losing the territories of Edom and Libnah by revolt and being overrun by an invasion of Philistines and Arabians, the latter of which cost

Jehoram all his possessions and family except his youngest son, Ahaziah (sometimes called Jehoahaz), who succeeded him on the throne. Jehoram died of a repugnant disease of the bowels and was buried without honor or sorrow.

See AHAB, ATHALIAH, KINGS

SCRIPTURE

2 Chr. 21 1 Now Jehoshaphat slept with
his fathers, and was buried with his fathers in the city of David. And Jehoram
his son reigned in his stead. 4 Now when
Jehoram was risen up to the kingdom of his
father, he strengthened himself, and slew
all his brethren with the sword, and divers
also of the princes of Israel.
5 Jehoram was thirty and two years old
when he began to reign, and he reigned
eight years in Jerusalem. 6 And he walked
in the way of the kings of Israel, like as
did the house of Ahab: for he had the
daughter of Ahab to wife: and he wrought
that which was evil in the eyes of the
LORD. 7 Howbeit the LORD would not destroy the house of David, because of the
covenant that he had made with David,
and as he promised to give a light to him
and to his sons for ever.
8 In his days the Edomites revolted from
under the dominion of Judah, and made
themselves a king. 9 Then Jehoram went
forth with his princes, and all his chariots
with him: and he rose up by night, and
smote the Edomites which compassed him
in, and the captains of the chariots. 10 So
the Edomites revolted from under the
hand of Judah unto this day. The same
time also did Libnah revolt from under
his hand; because he had forsaken the
LORD God of his fathers. 11 Moreover he
made high places in the mountains of Judah, and caused the inhabitants of Jerusalem to commit fornication, and compelled Judah thereto.
12 And there came a writing to him from
Elijah the prophet, saying, Thus saith the
LORD God of David thy father, Because
thou hast not walked in the ways of Jehoshaphat thy father, nor in the ways of
Asa king of Judah, 13 But hast walked in
the way of the kings of Israel, and hast
made Judah and the inhabitants of Jerusalem to go a whoring, like to the whoredoms of the house of Ahab, and also hast
slain thy brethren of thy father's house,
which were better than thyself: 14 Behold,
with a great plague will the LORD smite
thy people, and thy children, and thy
wives, and all thy goods: 15 And thou shalt
have great sickness by disease of thy
bowels, until thy bowels fall out by reason
of the sickness day by day.
16 Moreover, the LORD stirred up against
Jehoram the spirit of the Philistines, and
of the Arabians, that were near the Ethiopians: 17 And they came up into Judah,
and brake into it, and carried away all the
substance that was found in the king's
house, and his sons also, and his wives; so
that there was never a son left him, save
Jehoahaz the youngest of his sons.
18 And after all this the LORD smote him
in his bowels with an incurable disease.
19 And it came to pass, that in process of
time, after the end of two years, his bowels
fell out by reason of his sickness: so he
died of sore diseases. And his people made
no burning for him, like the burning of his
fathers. 20 Thirty and two years old was he
when he began to reign, and he reigned
in Jerusalem eight years, and departed
without being desired: howbeit they buried him in the city of David, but not in the
sepulchres of the kings.

See 2 Kin. 8:16-24

JEHOSHAPHAT

[jē hosh′a fat] The son of Asa and fourth king

of Judah (873-849 BC). Jehoshaphat was reasonably faithful to the worship of the true God and purged the southern kingdom of idolatrous abuses which had arisen. He arranged for the common people to receive instruction in the law of the LORD and established a system of common courts and courts of appeal. His rule was one of considerable prosperity for Judah. He apparently kept the nations to the south and west of Judah—Philisita, Arabia, and Edom—in a vassalage relationship. One of his most notable efforts at peace and security was the establishment of an alliance with the kingdom of Northern Israel. The alliance was secured by the marriage of his son, Jehoram, to Athaliah, daughter of Ahab and Jezebel. This unfortunate introduction of the Omride blood into the royal family of Judah was to result in its ruthless extermination during the revolution of Jehu some years later. (*See* OMRI, JEHU) Shortly after the union was made, Jehoshaphat joined with Ahab against Syria in the battle at Ramoth-Gilead which cost the life of the northern king. Later, he accompanied Ahab's son on an expedition against the Moabites. (*See* JORAM) There is some confusion in scripture about a joint project of Jehoshaphat and Ahaziah king of Israel to build and operate a fleet of ships, but it is clear that the project came to nothing, whatever the details (*1 Kin. 22:48-49; 2 Chr. 20:35-37*).

See AHAB, AHAZIAH, JORAM, KINGS, etc.

SCRIPTURE

Brief Life

1 Kin. 22 [41]And Jehoshaphat the son of Asa began to reign over Judah in the fourth year of Ahab king of Israel. [42]Jehoshaphat was thirty and five years old when he began to reign; and he reigned twenty and five years in Jerusalem. And his mother's name was Azubah the daughter of Shilhi. [43]And he walked in all the ways of Asa his father; he turned not aside from it, doing that which was right in the eyes of the LORD: nevertheless the high places were not taken away; for the people offered and burnt incense yet in the high places. [44]And Jehoshaphat made peace with the king of Israel. [45]Now the rest of the acts of Jehoshaphat, and his might that he shewed, and how he warred, are they not written in the book of the Chronicles of the kings of Judah? [46]And the remnant of the sodomites, which remained in the days of his father Asa, he took out of the land. [47]There was then no king in Edom: a deputy was king. [48]Jehoshaphat made ships of Tharshish to go to Ophir for gold: but they went not; for the ships were broken at Ezion-geber. [49]Then said Ahaziah the son of Ahab unto Jehoshaphat, Let my servants go with thy servants in the ships. But Jehoshaphat would not.

[50]And Jehoshaphat slept with his fathers, and was buried with his fathers in the city of David his father: and Jehoram his son reigned in his stead.

Strengthens His Nation

2 Chr. 17 [1]And Jehoshaphat his son reigned in his stead, and strengthened himself against Israel. [2]And he placed forces in all the fenced cities of Judah, and set garrisons in the land of Judah, and in the cities of Ephraim, which Asa his father had taken.

Religious Reforms

2 Chr. 17 [3]And the LORD was with Jehoshaphat, because he walked in the first ways of his father David, and sought not unto Baalim; [4]But sought to the LORD God of his father, and walked in his commandments, and not after the doings of Israel. [5]Therefore the LORD stablished the kingdom in his hand; and all Judah brought to Jehoshaphat presents; and he had riches and honour in abundance. [6]And his heart was lifted up in the ways of the LORD: moreover he took away the high places and groves out of Judah.

Inaugurates System of Public Instruction in Law

2 Chr. 17 7 Also in the third year of his reign he sent to his princes, even to Benhail, and to Obadiah, and to Zechariah, and to Nathaneel, and to Michaiah, to teach in the cities of Judah. 8 And with them he sent Levites, even Shemaiah, and Nethaniah, and Zebadiah, and Asahel, and Shemiramoth, and Jehonathan, and Adonijah, and Tobijah, and Tob-adonijah, Levites; and with them Elishama and Jehoram, priests. 9 And they taught in Judah, and had the book of the law of the LORD with them, and went about throughout all the cities of Judah, and taught the people.

The Measure of His Strength

2 Chr. 17 10 And the fear of the LORD fell upon all the kingdoms of the lands that were round about Judah, so that they made no war against Jehoshaphat. 11 Also some of the Philistines brought Jehoshaphat presents, and tribute silver; and the Arabians brought him flocks, seven thousand and seven hundred rams, and seven thousand and seven hundred he-goats.

12 And Jehoshaphat waxed great exceedingly; and he built in Judah castles, and cities of store. 13 And he had much business in the cities of Judah: and the men of war, mighty men of valour, were in Jerusalem.

Forms Alliance with Ahab Against Ramoth-Gilead

2 Chr. 18 1 Now Jehoshaphat had riches and honour in abundance, and joined affinity with Ahab. 2 And after certain years he went down to Ahab to Samaria. And Ahab killed sheep and oxen for him in abundance, and for the people that he had with him, and persuaded him to go up with him to Ramoth-gilead. 3 And Ahab king of Israel said unto Jehoshaphat king of Judah, Wilt thou go with me to Ramoth-gilead? And he answered him, I am as thou art, and my people as thy people; and we will be with thee in the war.

Rebuked by God for This Alliance

2 Chr. 19 1 And Jehoshaphat the king of Judah returned to his house in peace to Jerusalem. 2 And Jehu the son of Hanani the seer went out to meet him, and said to king Jehoshaphat, Shouldest thou help the ungodly, and love them that hate the LORD? therefore is wrath upon thee from before the LORD. 3 Nevertheless, there are good things found in thee, in that thou hast taken away the groves out of the land, and hast prepared thine heart to seek God.

Institutes Court System

2 Chr. 19 4 And Jehoshaphat dwelt at Jerusalem: and he went out again through the people from Beer-sheba to mount Ephraim, and brought them back unto the LORD God of their fathers.

5 And he set judges in the land throughout all the fenced cities of Judah, city by city, 6 And said to the judges, Take heed what ye do: for ye judge not for man, but for the LORD, who is with you in the judgment. 7 Wherefore now let the fear of the LORD be upon you; take heed and do it: for there is no iniquity with the LORD our God, nor respect of persons, nor taking of gifts.

8 Moreover in Jerusalem did Jehoshaphat set of the Levites, and of the priests, and of the chief of the fathers of Israel, for the judgment of the LORD, and for controversies, when they returned to Jerusalem. 9 And he charged them, saying, Thus shall ye do in the fear of the LORD, faithfully, and with a perfect heart. 10 And what cause soever shall come to you of your

brethren that dwell in their cities, between blood and blood, between law and commandment, statutes and judgments, ye shall even warn them that they trespass not against the LORD, and so wrath come upon you, and upon your brethren: this do, and ye shall not trespass.

Delivered by God from the Invading Moab and Ammon

2 Chr. 20 [22]And when they began to sing and to praise, the LORD set ambushments against the children of Ammon, Moab, and mount Seir, which were come against Judah; and they were smitten. [23]For the children of Ammon and Moab stood up against the inhabitants of mount Seir, utterly to slay and destroy them: and when they had made an end of the inhabitants of Seir, every one helped to destroy another. [24]And when Judah came toward the watchtower in the wilderness, they looked unto the multitude, and, behold, they were dead bodies fallen to the earth, and none escaped. [25]And when Jehoshaphat and his people came to take away the spoil of them, they found among them in abundance both riches with the dead bodies, and precious jewels, which they stripped off for themselves, more than they could carry away: and they were three days in gathering of the spoil, it was so much.

[26]And on the fourth day they assembled themselves in the valley of Berachah; for there they blessed the LORD: therefore the name of the same place was called, The valley of Berachah, unto this day. [27]Then they returned, every man of Judah and Jerusalem, and Jehoshaphat in the forefront of them, to go again to Jerusalem with joy; for the LORD had made them to rejoice over their enemies. [28]And they came to Jerusalem with psalteries and harps and trumpets unto the house of the LORD. [29]And the fear of God was on all the kingdoms of those countries, when they had heard that the LORD fought against the enemies of Israel. [30]So the realm of Jehoshaphat was quiet: for his God gave him rest round about.

Shipping Venture Fails

2 Chr. 20 [35]And after this did Jehoshaphat king of Judah join himself with Ahaziah king of Israel, who did very wickedly: [36]And he joined himself with him to make ships to go to Tarshish: and they made the ships in Ezion-gaber. [37]Then Eliezer the son of Dodavah of Mareshah prophesied against Jehoshaphat, saying, Because thou hast joined thyself with Ahaziah, the LORD hath broken thy works. And the ships were broken, that they were not able to go to Tarshish.

Death

2 Chr. 21 [1]Now Jehoshaphat slept with his fathers, and was buried with his fathers in the city of David. And Jehoram his son reigned in his stead.

JEHOVAH

[jê hō′va] The original Hebrew text of the Old Testament was written without vowels. The name of God was represented by the consonants JHWH. After the exile, no one except the temple priests pronounced this name; in its place was read or spoken the word *Adhonai* (Lord). When vowels were eventually added to the Hebrew text in the sixth and seventh centuries AD, the vowels of *Adhonai* were combined with the consonants of JHWH. The result was that the real pronunciation of JHWH was practically lost. In the sixteenth century the form Jehovah was produced; this has been hallowed by centuries of use, but is a pure invention and almost certainly bears little resemblance to the original form. Most scholars agree that the true pronunciation of the name of God should be Jahweh, or Yahweh.

JEHU

[jē'hū] The tenth king of Israel (842-814 BC) and founder of the fourth dynasty. Jehu was one of the personal bodyguards of Ahab and was present when Elijah confronted that king with his condemnation of the injustice done to Naboth. (*See* NABOTH) Shortly after Joram, the ninth king of Israel, had been wounded at Ramoth-Gilead and lay recovering in Jezreel, Elisha sent a young prophet to Jehu to anoint him as king and to charge him to exterminate the house of Ahab and Jezebel as a consequence for the enormous sins of that infamous pair. With a small body of horsemen, Jehu set out for Jezreel where he slew Joram and Ahaziah, king of Judah, who was visiting his wounded uncle. His next act was to induce several palace eunuchs to cast the wicked queen mother Jezebel from a high window. According to the prophecy of Elijah, the dogs of Jezreel ate her flesh to such an extent that there was nothing left to bury.

In thorough obedience to the charge issued by Elisha, Jehu achieved the slaughter of the entire royal house of Israel by threatening to destroy Samaria if the heads of the "seventy sons of Ahab" and their friends and partisans were not delivered to him in baskets. The residents of Samaria complied with this grisly demand and the heads were piled up at the gates of Jezreel as a warning to any who might hesitate to give their allegiance to Jehu.

The remaining features of Jehu's revolution seem cruel and excessive and cost him the friendship of Judah and Phoenicia. On the road to Samaria he came across a sizable group of princes of Judah; he and his men slaughtered these princes and cast their bodies in a nearby cistern. Proceeding to Samaria, he pretended to be a worshipper of Baal and proclaimed a great festival in that god's honor. When the worshippers were in the temple, Jehu and his soldiers slew everyone of them and tore down the temple, making it into a latrine.

Although Jehu's reign was a long one, most of what is known about him from the Bible has to do with this revolution. We are told that he did not destroy the cult of Jeroboam; some have contended that this is evidence that the bull cultus was not purely idolatrous, but was a form of worship of the true god (for further discussion, *see* JEROBOAM). His reign is marked by great loss of territory to Hazael, king of Syria, which was not regained until the time of Jeroboam II (783-748 BC). From Assyrian sources it is known that Jehu also suffered defeat at the hands of Shalmaneser II, in 842 BC. The Black Obelisk of Shalmaneser depicts Jehu bringing tribute to the Assyrian king.

Jehu's character was that of a bold, determined man who carried out the charge delivered him with awesome thoroughness. He seems, however, to have been entirely without the magnanimity and wisdom which are requisites for a truly great king.

SCRIPTURE

2 Kin. 9 [14]So Jehu the son of Jehoshaphat the son of Nimshi conspired against
Joram. (Now Joram had kept Ramoth-
gilead, he and all Israel, because of Hazael king of Syria. [15]But king Joram was
returned to be healed in Jezreel of the
wounds which the Syrians had given him,
when he fought with Hazael king of
Syria.) And Jehu said, If it be your minds,
then let none go forth nor escape out of the
city to go to tell it in Jezreel. [16]So Jehu
rode in a chariot, and went to Jezreel; for
Joram lay there. And Ahaziah king of Judah was come down to see Joram. [17]And
there stood a watchman on the tower in
Jezreel, and he spied the company of Jehu
as he came, and said, I see a company. And
Joram said, Take a horseman, and send to
meet them, and let him say, Is it peace?
[18]So there went one on horseback to meet
him, and said, Thus saith the king, Is it
peace? And Jehu said, What hast thou to
do with peace? turn thee behind me. And
the watchman told, saying, The messenger
came to them, but he cometh not again.
[19]Then he sent out a second on horseback,
which came to them, and said, Thus saith
the king, Is it peace? And Jehu answered,

What hast thou to do with peace? turn thee behind me. [20]And the watchman told, saying, He came even unto them, and cometh not again: and the driving is like the driving of Jehu the son of Nimshi; for he driveth furiously. [21]And Joram said, Make ready. And his chariot was made ready. And Joram king of Israel and Ahaziah king of Judah went out, each in his chariot, and they went out against Jehu, and met him in the portion of Naboth the Jezreelite. [22]And it came to pass, when Joram saw Jehu, that he said, Is it peace, Jehu? And he answered, What peace, so long as the whoredoms of thy mother Jezebel and her witchcrafts are so many? [23]And Joram turned his hands, and fled, and said to Ahaziah, There is treachery, O Ahaziah. [24]And Jehu drew a bow with his full strength, and smote Jehoram between his arms, and the arrow went out at his heart, and he sunk down in his chariot. [25]Then said Jehu to Bidkar his captain, Take up, and cast him in the portion of the field of Naboth the Jezreelite: for remember how that, when I and thou rode together after Ahab his father, the LORD laid this burden upon him; [26]Surely I have seen yesterday the blood of Naboth, and the blood of his sons, saith the LORD; and I will requite thee in this plat, saith the LORD. Now therefore take and cast him into the plat of ground, according to the word of the LORD.

[27]But when Ahaziah the king of Judah saw this, he fled by the way of the garden house. And Jehu followed after him, and said, Smite him also in the chariot. And they did so at the going up to Gur, which is by Ibleam. And he fled to Megiddo, and died there. [28]And his servants carried him in a chariot to Jerusalem, and buried him in his sepulchre with his fathers in the city of David. [29]And in the eleventh year of Joram the son of Ahab began Ahaziah to reign over Judah.

[30]And when Jehu was come to Jezreel, Jezebel heard of it; and she painted her face, and tired her head, and looked out at a window. [31]And as Jehu entered in at the gate, she said, Had Zimri peace, who slew his master? [32]And he lifted up his face to the window, and said, Who is on my side? who? And there looked out to him two or three eunuchs. [33]And he said, Throw her down. So they threw her down: and some of her blood was sprinkled on the wall, and on the horses: and he trode her under foot.

2 Kin. 10 [11]So Jehu slew all that remained of the house of Ahab in Jezreel, and all his great men, and his kinsfolks, and his priests, until he left him none remaining.

[13]Jehu met with the brethren of Ahaziah king of Judah, and said, Who are ye? And they answered, We are the brethren of Ahaziah; and we go down to salute the children of the king and the children of the queen. [14]And he said, Take them alive. And they took them alive, and slew them at the pit of the shearing house, even two and forty men; neither left he any of them.

[18]And Jehu gathered all the people together, and said unto them, Ahab served Baal a little; but Jehu shall serve him much. [19]Now therefore call unto me all the prophets of Baal, all his servants, and all his priests; let none be wanting: for I have a great sacrifice to do to Baal; whosoever shall be wanting, he shall not live. But Jehu did it in subtilty, to the intent that he might destroy the worshippers of Baal. [20]And Jehu said, Proclaim a solemn assembly for Baal. And they proclaimed it. [21]And Jehu sent through all Israel: and

all the worshippers of Baal came, so that there was not a man left that came not. And they came into the house of Baal; and the house of Baal was full from one end to another. [25]And it came to pass, as soon as he had made an end of offering the burnt offering, that Jehu said to the guard and to the captains, Go in, and slay them; let none come forth. And they smote them with the edge of the sword; and the guard and the captains cast them out, and went to the city of the house of Baal. [26]And they brought forth the images out of the house of Baal, and burned them. [27]And they brake down the image of Baal, and brake down the house of Baal, and made it a draught house unto this day.

JEPHTHAH

[jef'tha] The son of Gilead by a harlot, Jephthah was thrust out of his home because of his illegitimacy; he then went to the land of Tob where he gathered a band of "worthless fellows" and engaged in looting raids. At a time when the Ammonites were making war against Israel, the Israelites asked Jephthah to be their military leader. He accepted on the condition that, if successful, he should be their permanent leader and judge. After an unsuccessful effort to persuade the Ammonites that their grievance against Israel was unjustified, Jephthah prepared for battle against them. Before going into battle, he made a vow to sacrifice as a burnt offering the first thing which came out of his house if he returned from battle victorious. This foolish vow brought him great sorrow; although he was victorious, he was met on his return by his only child, a virgin daughter. Despite the sorrow which it brought to him, Jephthah apparently carried out the terms of the vow.

The Ephraimites, disgruntled at having no part in the victory over the Ammonites, instigated war against Jephthah's forces and were defeated. It was in this incident that the famous password "Shibboleth" was used. The men of Jephthah were able to identify the fugitives of Ephraim because of their inability to pronounce this word properly, and thereby prevented their escape.

See JUDGES

SCRIPTURE

Judg. 11 [1]Now Jephthah the Gileadite was a mighty man of valour, and he was the son of a harlot: and Gilead begat Jephthah. [2]And Gilead's wife bare him sons; and his wife's sons grew up, and they thrust out Jephthah, and said unto him, Thou shalt not inherit in our father's house; for thou art the son of a strange woman. [3]Then Jephthah fled from his brethren, and dwelt in the land of Tob: and there were gathered vain men to Jephthah, and went out with him.

[4]And it came to pass in process of time, that the children of Ammon made war against Israel. [5]And it was so, that when the children of Ammon made war against Israel, the elders of Gilead went to fetch Jephthah out of the land of Tob: [6]And they said unto Jephthah, Come, and be our captain, that we may fight with the children of Ammon. [9]And Jephthah said unto the elders of Gilead, If ye bring me home again to fight against the children of Ammon, and the LORD deliver them before me, shall I be your head? [10]And the elders of Gilead said unto Jephthah, The LORD be witness between us, if we do not so according to thy words.

Judg. 11 [29]Then the Spirit of the LORD came upon Jephthah, and he passed over Gilead, and Manasseh, and passed over Mizpeh of Gilead, and from Mizpeh of Gilead he passed over unto the children of Ammon. [30]And Jephthah vowed a vow unto the LORD, and said, If thou shalt without fail deliver the children of Ammon into mine hands, [31]Then it shall be, that whatsoever cometh forth of the doors of my house to meet me, when I return in peace from the children of Ammon, shall surely be the LORD's, and I will offer it up for a burnt offering.

[32]So Jephthah passed over unto the children of Ammon to fight against them; and the LORD delivered them into his hands. [33]And he smote them from Aroer, even till thou come to Minnith, even twenty cities, and unto the plain of the vineyards, with a very great slaughter. Thus the children of Ammon were subdued before the children of Israel.

[34]And Jephthah came to Mizpeh unto his house, and, behold, his daughter came out to meet him with timbrels and with dances: and she was his only child; besides her he had neither son nor daughter. [35]And it came to pass, when he saw her, that he rent his clothes, and said, Alas, my daughter! thou hast brought me very low, and thou art one of them that trouble me: for I have opened my mouth unto the LORD, and I can not go back. [36]And she said unto him, My father, if thou hast opened thy mouth unto the LORD, do to me according to that which hath proceeded out of thy mouth; forasmuch as the LORD hath taken vengeance for thee of thine enemies, even of the children of Ammon. [37]And she said unto her father, Let this thing be done for me: let me alone two months, that I may go up and down upon the mountains, and bewail by virginity, I and my fellows. [38]And he said, Go. And he sent her away for two months: and she went with her companions, and bewailed her virginity upon the mountains. [39]And it came to pass at the end of two months, that she returned unto her father, who did with her according to his vow which he had vowed: and she knew no man. And it was a custom in Israel, [40]That the daughters of Israel went yearly to lament the daughter of Jephthah the Gileadite four days in a year.

JEREMIAH

[jer ê mī'a] One of the foremost of the Hebrew prophets. Jeremiah's long career began in the thirteenth year of Josiah (c. 627 BC) and continued through the end of the Southern Kingdom. He died in Egypt about 580 BC or slightly later, after a prophetic ministry of almost half a century. Called to be a prophet while still a young man (*Jer. 1:6*), Jeremiah's condemnation of the sins of the people aroused much hostility against him, both in his home town of Anathoth and in Jerusalem (*Jer. 11:18-23*). He spoke out fearlessly and drew upon himself the anger of the court by predicting the capture and ultimate destruction of Jerusalem. He was forced into hiding during the reign of the tyrannical Jehoiakim (609/8-597 BC), who showed his contempt for Jeremiah and the word of the LORD by cutting up and burning the roll of Jeremiah's prophecies. When the puppet king Zedekiah conspired to throw off the Babylonian yoke, Jeremiah warned him that the safest course was to remain subservient. After the prophecies of Jeremiah were vindicated by the destruction of Jerusalem at the hands of Nebuchadnezzar in 587 BC, the prophet remained for a long time in the city, but was finally forced to go to Egypt along with his companion and secretary, Baruch. There, in the city of Tahpanhes, we have the last clear glimpses of his life; after this, nothing is certain. Jeremiah emerges more as a real person than does any other prophet of the Old Testament.

See JOSIAH, JEHOIAKIM, ZEDEKIAH, KINGS, PROPHETS, PROPHECY, etc.

SCRIPTURE

The Call of Jeremiah

Jer. 1 [4]Then the word of the LORD came unto me, saying, [5]Before I formed thee in the belly, I knew thee; and before thou camest forth out of the womb I sanctified thee, and I ordained thee a prophet unto the nations. [6]Then said I, Ah, Lord GOD! behold, I can not speak: for I am a child.

[7]But the LORD said unto me, Say not, I am a child: for thou shalt go to all that I shall send thee, and whatsoever I command thee thou shalt speak. [8]Be not afraid of their faces: for I am with thee to deliver thee, saith the LORD. [9]Then the LORD put forth his hand, and touched my mouth. And the LORD said unto me, Behold, I have put my words in thy mouth. [10]See, I have this day set thee over the nations and over the kingdoms, to root out, and to pull down, and to destroy, and to throw down, to build, and to plant.

[11]Moreover the word of the LORD came unto me, saying, Jeremiah, what seest thou? And I said, I see a rod of an almond tree. [12]Then said the LORD unto me, Thou hast well seen: for I will hasten my word to perform it. [13]And the word of the LORD came unto me the second time, saying, What seest thou? And I said, I see a seething pot; and the face thereof is toward the north. [14]Then the LORD said unto me, Out of the north an evil shall break forth upon all the inhabitants of the land. [15]For, lo, I will call all the families of the kingdoms of the north, saith the LORD; and they shall come, and they shall set every one his throne at the entering of the gates of Jerusalem, and against all the walls thereof round about, and against all the cities of Judah. [16]And I will utter my judgments against them touching all their wickedness, who have forsaken me, and have burned incense unto other gods, and worshipped the works of their own hands.

[17]Thou therefore gird up thy loins, and arise, and speak unto them all that I command thee: be not dismayed at their faces, lest I confound thee before them. [18]For, behold, I have made thee this day a defenced city, and an iron pillar, and brazen walls against the whole land, against the kings of Judah, against the princes thereof, against the priests thereof, and against the people of the land. [19]And they shall fight against thee; but they shall not prevail against thee; for I am with thee, saith the LORD, to deliver thee.

The Sign of the Linen Waistcloth

Jer. 13 [1]Thus saith the LORD unto me, Go and get thee a linen girdle, and put it upon thy loins, and put it not in water. [2]So I got a girdle according to the word of the LORD, and put it on my loins. [3]And the word of the LORD came unto me the second time, saying, [4]Take the girdle that thou hast got, which is upon thy loins, and arise, go to Euphrates, and hide it there in a hole of the rock. [5]So I went, and hid it by Euphrates, as the LORD commanded me. [6]And it came to pass after many days, that the LORD said unto me, Arise, go to Euphrates, and take the girdle from thence, which I commanded thee to hide there. [7]Then I went to Euphrates, and digged, and took the girdle from the place where I had hid it: and, behold, the girdle was marred, it was profitable for nothing. [8]Then the word of the LORD came unto me, saying, [9]Thus saith the LORD, After this manner will I mar the pride of Judah, and the great pride of Jerusalem. [10]This evil people, which refuse to hear my words, which walk in the imagination of their heart, and walk after other gods, to serve them, and to worship them, shall even be as this girdle, which is good for nothing. [11]For as the girdle cleaveth to the loins of a man, so have I caused to cleave unto me the whole house of Israel and the whole house of Judah, saith the LORD; that they might be unto me for a people, and for a name, and for a praise, and for a glory: but they would not hear.

The Sign of the Potter

Jer. 18 1The word which came to Jeremiah from the LORD, saying, 2Arise, and go down to the potter's house, and there I will cause thee to hear my words. 3Then I went down to the potter's house, and, behold, he wrought a work on the wheels. 4And the vessel that he made of clay was marred in the hand of the potter: so he made it again another vessel, as seemed good to the potter to make it. 5Then the word of the LORD came to me, saying, 6O house of Israel, can not I do with you as this potter? saith the LORD. Behold, as the clay is in the potter's hand, so are ye in mine hand, O house of Israel. 7At what instant I shall speak concerning a nation, and concerning a kingdom, to pluck up, and to pull down, and to destroy it; 8If that nation, against whom I have pronounced, turn from their evil, I will repent of the evil that I thought to do unto them. 9And at what instant I shall speak concerning a nation, and concerning a kingdom, to build and to plant it; 10If it do evil in my sight, that it obey not my voice, then I will repent of the good, wherewith I said I would benefit them.

11Now therefore go to, speak to the men of Judah, and to the inhabitants of Jerusalem, saying, Thus saith the LORD; Behold, I frame evil against you, and devise a device against you: return ye now every one from his evil way, and make your ways and your doings good.

Jeremiah Beaten and Put in Stocks

Jer. 20 1Now Pashur the son of Immer the priest, who was also chief governor in the house of the LORD, heard that Jeremiah prophesied these things. 2Then Pashur smote Jeremiah the prophet, and put him in the stocks that were in the high gate of Benjamin, which was by the house of the LORD. 3And it came to pass on the morrow, that Pashur brought forth Jeremiah out of the stocks. Then said Jeremiah unto him, The LORD hath not called thy name Pashur, but Magor-missabib. 4For thus saith the LORD, Behold, I will make thee a terror to thyself, and to all thy friends: and they shall fall by the sword of their enemies, and thine eyes shall behold it: and I will give all Judah into the hand of the king of Babylon, and he shall carry them captive into Babylon, and shall slay them with the sword. 5Moreover I will deliver all the strength of this city, and all the labours thereof, and all the precious things thereof, and all the treasures of the kings of Judah will I give into the hand of their enemies, which shall spoil them, and take them, and carry them to Babylon. 6And thou, Pashur, and all that dwell in thine house, shall go into captivity: and thou shalt come to Babylon, and there thou shalt die, and shalt be buried there, thou, and all thy friends, to whom thou hast prophesied lies.

The Vision of the Figs

Jer. 24 1The LORD shewed me, and, behold, two baskets of figs were set before the temple of the LORD, after that Nebuchadrezzar king of Babylon had carried away captive Jeconiah the son of Jehoiakim king of Judah, and the princes of Judah, with the carpenters and smiths, from Jerusalem, and had brought them to Babylon. 2One basket had very good figs, even like the figs that are first ripe: and the other basket had very naughty figs, which could not be eaten, they were so bad. 3Then said the LORD unto me, What seest thou, Jeremiah? and I said, Figs; the good figs, very good; and the evil, very evil, that can not be eaten, they are so evil.

4Again the word of the LORD came unto

me, saying, 5Thus saith the LORD, the God of Israel; Like these good figs, so will I acknowledge them that are carried away captive of Judah, whom I have sent out of this place into the land of the Chaldeans for their good. 6For I will set mine eyes upon them for good, and I will bring them again to this land: and I will build them, and not pull them down; and I will plant them, and not pluck them up. 7And I will give them a heart to know me, that I am the LORD; and they shall be my people, and I will be their God: for they shall return unto me with their whole heart.

8And as the evil figs, which can not be eaten, they are so evil; surely thus saith the LORD, So will I give Zedekiah the king of Judah, and his princes, and the residue of Jerusalem, that remain in this land, and them that dwell in the land of Egypt: 9And I will deliver them to be removed into all the kingdoms of the earth for their hurt, to be a reproach and a proverb, a taunt and a curse, in all places whither I shall drive them. 10And I will send the sword, the famine, and the pestilence, among them, till they be consumed from off the land that I gave unto them and to their fathers.

Jeremiah Threatened with Death

Jer. 26 7So the priests and the prophets and all the people heard Jeremiah speaking these words in the house of the LORD.

8Now it came to pass, when Jeremiah had made an end of speaking all that the LORD had commanded him to speak unto all the people, that the priests and the prophets and all the people took him, saying, Thou shalt surely die. 9Why hast thou prophesied in the name of the LORD, saying, This house shall be like Shiloh, and this city shall be desolate without an inhabitant? And all the people were gathered against Jeremiah in the house of the LORD.

10When the princes of Judah heard these things, then they came up from the king's house unto the house of the LORD, and sat down in the entry of the new gate of the LORD's house. 11Then spake the priests and the prophets unto the princes and to all the people, saying, This man is worthy to die; for he hath prophesied against this city, as ye have heard with your ears.

12Then spake Jeremiah unto all the princes and to all the people, saying, The LORD sent me to prophesy against this house and against this city all the words that ye have heard. 13Therefore now amend your ways and your doings, and obey the voice of the LORD your God; and the LORD will repent him of the evil that he hath pronounced against you. 14As for me, behold, I am in your hand: do with me as seemeth good and meet unto you. 15But know ye for certain, that if ye put me to death, ye shall surely bring innocent blood upon yourselves, and upon this city, and upon the inhabitants thereof: for of a truth the LORD hath sent me unto you to speak all these words in your ears.

16Then said the princes and all the people unto the priests and to the prophets; This man is not worthy to die: for he hath spoken to us in the name of the LORD our God. 24Nevertheless, the hand of Ahikam the son of Shaphan was with Jeremiah, that they should not give him into the hand of the people to put him to death.

The Sign of the Yoke-Bars

Jer. 27 1In the beginning of the reign of Jehoiakim the son of Josiah king of Judah came this word unto Jeremiah from the LORD, saying, 2Thus saith the LORD to me; Make thee bonds and yokes, and put them upon thy neck, 3And send them to the

king of Edom, and to the king of Moab,
and to the king of the Ammonites, and to
the king of Tyrus, and to the king of Zidon,
by the hand of the messengers which come
to Jerusalem unto Zedekiah king of Judah;
4And command them to say unto their
masters, Thus saith the LORD of hosts, the
God of Israel; Thus shall ye say unto your
masters; 5I have made the earth, the man
and the beast that are upon the ground, by
my great power and by my outstretched
arm, and have given it unto whom it
seemed meet unto me. 6And now have I
given all these lands into the hand of Nebuchadnezzar the king of Babylon, my servant; and the beasts of the field have I given
him also to serve him. 7And all nations
shall serve him, and his son, and his son's
son, until the very time of his land come:
and then many nations and great kings
shall serve themselves of him.

Jer. 28 1And it came to pass the same
year, in the beginning of the reign of Zedekiah king of Judah, in the fourth year, and
in the fifth month, that Hananiah the son
of Azur the prophet, which was of Gibeon,
spake unto me in the house of the LORD, in
the presence of the priests and of all the
people, saying, 2Thus speaketh the LORD
of hosts, the God of Israel, saying, I have
broken the yoke of the king of Babylon.
3Within two full years will I bring again
into this place all the vessels of the LORD's
house, that Nebuchadnezzar king of Babylon took away from this place, and carried
them to Babylon: 4And I will bring again
to this place Jeconiah the son of Jehoiakim
king of Judah, with all the captives of Judah, that went into Babylon, saith the
LORD: for I will break the yoke of the king
of Babylon.

10Then Hananiah the prophet took the
yoke from off the prophet Jeremiah's neck,
and brake it. 11And Hananiah spake in the
presence of all the people, saying, Thus
saith the LORD; Even so will I break the
yoke of Nebuchadnezzar king of Babylon
from the neck of all nations within the
space of two full years. And the prophet
Jeremiah went his way.

12Then the word of the LORD came unto
Jeremiah the prophet, after that Hananiah
the prophet had broken the yoke from off
the neck of the prophet Jeremiah, saying,
13Go and tell Hananiah, saying, Thus saith
the LORD; Thou hast broken the yokes of
wood; but thou shalt make for them yokes
of iron. 14For thus saith the LORD of hosts,
the God of Israel; I have put a yoke of iron
upon the neck of all these nations, that
they may serve Nebuchadnezzar king of
Babylon; and they shall serve him: and I
have given him the beasts of the field also.

15Then said the prophet Jeremiah unto
Hananiah the prophet, Hear now, Hananiah; The LORD hath not sent thee; but
thou makest this people to trust in a lie.
16Therefore thus saith the LORD; Behold, I
will cast thee from off the face of the earth:
this year thou shalt die, because thou hast
taught rebellion against the LORD. 17So
Hananiah the prophet died the same year
in the seventh month.

Jeremiah's Letter to the Exiles

Jer. 29 4Thus saith the LORD of hosts,
the God of Israel, unto all that are carried
away captives, whom I have caused to be
carried away from Jerusalem unto Babylon; 5Build ye houses, and dwell in them;
and plant gardens, and eat the fruit of
them; 6Take ye wives, and beget sons and
daughters; and take wives for your sons,
and give your daughters to husbands, that
they may bear sons and daughters; that ye
may be increased there, and not diminished. 7And seek the peace of the city
whither I have caused you to be carried

away captives, and pray unto the LORD for it: for in the peace thereof shall ye have peace.

[8]For thus saith the LORD of hosts, the God of Israel; Let not your prophets and your diviners, that be in the midst of you, deceive you, neither hearken to your dreams which ye cause to be dreamed. [9]For they prophesy falsely unto you in my name: I have not sent them, saith the LORD.

[10]For thus saith the LORD, That after seventy years be accomplished at Babylon I will visit you, and perform my good word toward you, in causing you to return to this place. [11]For I know the thoughts that I think toward you, saith the LORD, thoughts of peace, and not of evil, to give you an expected end. [12]Then shall ye call upon me, and ye shall go and pray unto me, and I will hearken unto you. [13]And ye shall seek me, and find me, when ye shall search for me with all your heart. [14]And I will be found of you, saith the LORD: and I will turn away your captivity, and I will gather you from all the nations, and from all the places whither I have driven you, saith the LORD; and I will bring you again into the place whence I caused you to be carried away captive.

Jehoiakim Burns Jeremiah's Scroll

Jer. 36 [11]When Michaiah the son of Gemariah, the son of Shaphan, had heard out of the book all the words of the LORD, [12]Then he went down into the king's house, into the scribe's chamber: and, lo, all the princes sat there, even Elishama the scribe, and Delaiah the son of Shemaiah, and Elnathan the son of Achbor, and Gemariah the son of Shaphan, and Zedekiah the son of Hananiah, and all the princes. [13]Then Michaiah declared unto them all the words that he had heard, when Baruch read the book in the ears of the people. [14]Therefore all the princess sent Jehudi the son of Nethaniah, the son of Shelemiah, the son of Cushi, unto Baruch, saying, Take in thine hand the roll wherein thou hast read in the ears of the people, and come. So Baruch the son of Neriah took the roll in his hand, and came unto them. [15]And they said unto him, Sit down now, and read it in our ears. So Baruch read it in their ears. [16]Now it came to pass, when they had heard all the words, they were afraid both one and other, and said unto Baruch, We will surely tell the king of all these words. [17]And they asked Baruch, saying, Tell us now, How didst thou write all these words at his mouth? [18]Then Baruch answered them, He pronounced all these words unto me with his mouth, and I wrote them with ink in the book. [19]Then said the princes unto Baruch, Go, hide thee, thou and Jeremiah; and let no man know where ye be.

[20]And they went in to the king into the court, but they laid up the roll in the chamber of Elishama the scribe, and told all the words in the ears of the king. [21]So the king sent Jehudi to fetch the roll; and he took it out of Elishama the scribe's chamber. And Jehudi read it in the ears of the king, and in the ears of all the princes which stood beside the king. [22]Now the king sat in the winter house in the ninth month: and there was a fire on the hearth burning before him. [23]And it came to pass, that when Jehudi had read three or four leaves, he cut it with the penknife, and cast it into the fire that was on the hearth, until all the roll was consumed in the fire that was on the hearth. [24]Yet they were not afraid, nor rent their garments, neither the king, nor any of his servants that heard all these words. [25]Nevertheless Elnathan and Delaiah and Gemariah had made intercession to the king that he would not burn the roll;

but he would not hear them. 26But the king commanded Jerahmeel the son of Hammelech, and Seraiah the son of Azriel, and Shelemiah the son of Abdeel, to take Baruch the scribe and Jeremiah the prophet: but the LORD hid them.

27Then the word of the LORD came to Jeremiah, after that the king had burned the roll, and the words which Baruch wrote at the mouth of Jeremiah, saying, 28Take thee again another roll, and write in it all the former words that were in the first roll, which Jehoiakim the king of Judah hath burned. 29And thou shalt say to Jehoiakim king of Judah, Thus saith the LORD; Thou hast burned this roll, saying, Why hast thou written therein, saying, The king of Babylon shall certainly come and destroy this land, and shall cause to cease from thence man and beast? 30Therefore thus saith the LORD of Jehoiakim king of Judah; He shall have none to sit upon the throne of David: and his dead body shall be cast out in the day to the heat, and in the night to the frost. 31And I will punish him and his seed and his servants for their iniquity; and I will bring upon them, and upon the inhabitants of Jerusalem, and upon the men of Judah, all the evil that I have pronounced against them; but they hearkened not.

32Then took Jeremiah another roll, and gave it to Baruch the scribe, the son of Neriah; who wrote therein from the mouth of Jeremiah all the words of the book which Jehoiakim king of Judah had burned in the fire: and there were added besides unto them many like words.

Jeremiah Is Imprisoned

Jer. 37 11And it came to pass, that when the army of the Chaldeans was broken up from Jerusalem for fear of Pharaoh's army, 12Then Jeremiah went forth out of Jerusalem to go into the land of Benjamin, to separate himself thence in the midst of the people. 13And when he was in the gate of Benjamin, a captain of the ward was there, whose name was Irijah, the son of Shelemiah, the son of Hananiah; and he took Jeremiah the prophet, saying, Thou fallest away to the Chaldeans. 14Then said Jeremiah, It is false; I fall not away to the Chaldeans. But he hearkened not to him: so Irijah took Jeremiah, and brought him to the princes. 15Wherefore the princes were wroth with Jeremiah, and smote him, and put him in prison in the house of Jonathan the scribe; for they had made that the prison.

Jer. 38 4Therefore the princes said unto the king, We beseech thee, let this man be put to death: for thus he weakeneth the hands of the men of war that remain in this city, and the hands of all the people, in speaking such words unto them: for this man seeketh not the welfare of this people, but the hurt. 5Then Zedekiah the king said, Behold, he is in your hand: for the king is not he that can do any thing against you. 6Then took they Jeremiah, and cast him into the dungeon of Malchiah the son of Hammelech, that was in the court of the prison: and they let down Jeremiah with cords. And in the dungeon there was no water, but mire: so Jeremiah sunk in the mire.

Rescued by Ebed-melech

Jer. 38 7Now when Ebed-melech the Ethiopian, one of the eunuchs which was in the king's house, heard that they had put Jeremiah in the dungeon; the king then sitting in the gate of Benjamin; 8Ebed-melech went forth out of the king's house, and spake to the king, saying, 9My lord the king, these men have done evil in all that they have done to Jeremiah the prophet, whom they have cast into the dungeon; and he is like to die for hunger in the place where he is: for there is no more bread in the city. [10]Then the king commanded Ebed-melech the Ethiopian, saying, Take from hence thirty men with thee, and take up Jeremiah the prophet out of the dungeon, before he die. [11]So Ebed-melech took the men with him, and went into the house of the king under the treasury, and took thence old cast clouts and old rotten rags, and let them down by cords into the dungeon to Jeremiah. [12]And Ebed-melech the Ethiopian said unto Jeremiah, Put now these old cast clouts and rotten rags under thine armholes under the cords. And Jeremiah did so. [13]So they drew up Jeremiah with cords, and took him up out of the dungeon: and Jeremiah remained in the court of the prison.

Warns Survivors of Captivity Not to Go to Egypt

Jer. 42 [18]For thus saith the LORD of hosts, the God of Israel; As mine anger and my fury hath been poured forth upon the inhabitants of Jerusalem; so shall my fury be poured forth upon you, when ye shall enter into Egypt: and ye shall be an execration and an astonishment, and a curse, and a reproach; and ye shall see this place no more.

[19]The LORD hath said concerning you, O ye remnant of Judah; Go ye not into Egypt: know certainly that I have admonished you this day. [20]For ye dissembled in your hearts, when ye sent me unto the LORD your God, saying, Pray for us unto the LORD our God; and according unto all that the LORD our God shall say, so declare unto us, and we will do it. [21]And now I have this day declared it to you; but ye have not obeyed the voice of the LORD your God, nor any thing for the which he hath sent me unto you. [22]Now therefore know certainly that ye shall die by the sword, by the famine, and by the pestilence, in the place whither ye desire to go and to sojourn.

Forced to Go to Egypt

Jer. 43 [1]And it came to pass, that when Jeremiah had made an end of speaking unto all the people all the words of the LORD their God, for which the LORD their God had sent him to them, even all these words, [2]Then spake Azariah the son of Hoshaiah, and Johanan the son of Kareah, and all the proud men, saying unto Jeremiah, Thou speakest falsely: the LORD our God hath not sent thee to say, Go not into Egypt to sojourn there: [3]But Baruch the son of Neriah setteth thee on against us, for to deliver us into the hand of the Chaldeans, that they might put us to death, and carry us away captives into Babylon. [4]So Johanan the son of Kareah, and all the captains of the forces, and all the people, obeyed not the voice of the LORD, to dwell in the land of Judah. [5]But Johanan the son of Kareah, and all the captains of the forces, took all the remnant of Judah, that were returned from all nations, whither they had been driven, to dwell in the land of Judah; [6]Even men, and women, and children, and the king's daughters, and every person the Nebuzaradan the captain of the guard had left with Gedaliah the son of Ahikam the son of Shaphan, and Jeremiah the prophet, and Baruch the son of Neriah. [7]So they came into the land of Egypt: for they obeyed not the voice of the LORD: thus came they even to Tahpanhes.

REFERENCE: The Book of *Jeremiah* and sections in *Kings* and *Chronicles* relating to the above-mentioned kings.

JERICHO

[jer'i kō] A city on the plains just west of the river Jordan, about twenty miles northeast of Jerusalem. Jericho is first mentioned as the city to which the two spies were sent by Joshua from Shittim (*Josh. 2:1-21*). There they were shielded from the town authorities by Rahab the harlot, who was rewarded for her actions by being spared when the city was destroyed (*Josh. 2:1-21*). The story of its marvelous destruction is told in *Josh. 6*. In Elisha's time Jericho was the location of a school of prophets (*2 Kin. 2:5*). Jesus' story of the Good Samaritan is set between Jerusalem and Jericho.

SCRIPTURE

The Spies Visit Rahab in Jericho

Josh. 2 [1]And Joshua the son of Nun sent out of Shittim two men to spy secretly, saying, Go view the land, even Jericho. And they went, and came into a harlot's house, named Rahab, and lodged there. [2]And it was told the king of Jericho, saying, Behold, there came men in hither to-night of the children of Israel to search out the country. [3]And the king of Jericho sent unto Rahab, saying, Bring forth the men that are come to thee, which are entered into thine house: for they be come to search out all the country. [4]And the woman took the two men, and hid them, and said thus, There came men unto me, but I wist not whence they were: [5]And it came to pass about the time of shutting of the gate, when it was dark, that the men went out; whither the men went, I wot not: pursue after them quickly; for ye shall overtake them. [6]But she had brought them up to the roof of the house, and hid them with the stalks of flax, which she had laid in order upon the roof. [7]And the men pursued after them the way to Jordan unto the fords: and as soon as they which pursued after them were gone out, they shut the gate.

[8]And before they were laid down, she came up unto them upon the roof; [9]And she said unto the men, I know that the LORD hath given you the land, and that your terror is fallen upon us, and that all the inhabitants of the land faint because of you. [10]For we have heard how the LORD dried up the water of the Red sea for you, when ye came out of Egypt; and what ye did unto the two kings of the Amorites, that were on the other side Jordan, Sihon and Og, whom ye utterly destroyed. [11]And as soon as we had heard these things, our hearts did melt, neither did there remain any more courage in any man, because of you: for the LORD your God, he is God in heaven above, and in earth beneath. [12]Now therefore, I pray you, swear unto me by the LORD, since I have shewed you kindness, that ye will also shew kindness unto my father's house, and give me a true token: [13]And that ye will save alive my father, and my mother, and my brethren, and my sisters, and all that they have, and deliver our lives from death. [14]And the men answered her, Our life for yours, if ye utter not this our business. And it shall be, when the LORD hath given us the land, that we will deal kindly and truly with thee. [15]Then she let them down by a cord through the window: for her house was upon the town wall, and she dwelt upon the wall.

Destruction of Jericho

Josh. 6 [1]Now Jericho was straitly shut up because of the children of Israel: none went out, and none came in. [2]And the LORD said unto Joshua, See, I have given into thine hand Jericho, and the king thereof, and the mighty men of valour.

3 And ye shall compass the city, all ye men of war, and go round about the city once. Thus shalt thou do six days. 4 And seven priests shall bear before the ark seven trumpets of rams' horns: and the seventh day ye shall compass the city seven times, and the priests shall blow with the trumpets. 5 And it shall come to pass, that when they make a long blast with the ram's horn, and when ye hear the sound of the trumpet, all the people shall shout with a great shout; and the wall of the city shall fall down flat, and the people shall ascend up every man straight before him.

12 And Joshua rose early in the morning, and the priests took up the ark of the LORD. 13 And seven priests bearing seven trumpets of rams' horns before the ark of the LORD went on continually, and blew with the trumpets: and the armed men went before them; but the rearward came after the ark of the LORD, the priests going on, and blowing with the trumpets. 14 And the second day they compassed the city once, and returned into the camp. So they did six days. 15 And it came to pass on the seventh day, that they rose early about the dawning of the day, and compassed the city after the same manner seven times: only on that day they compassed the city seven times. 16 And it came to pass at the seventh time, when the priests blew with the trumpets, Joshua said unto the people, Shout; for the LORD hath given you the city.

20 So the people shouted when the priests blew with the trumpets: and it came to pass, when the people heard the sound of the trumpet, and the people shouted with a great shout, that the wall fell down flat, so that the people went up into the city, every man straight before him, and they took the city. 21 And they utterly destroyed all that was in the city, both man and woman, young and old, and ox, and sheep, and ass, with the edge of the sword.

Jesus Heals Blind Man in Jericho

Matt. 20 29 And as they departed from Jericho, a great multitude followed him. 30 And, behold, two blind men sitting by the way side, when they heard that Jesus passed by, cried out, saying, Have mercy on us, O Lord, thou Son of David. 31 And the multitude rebuked them, because they should hold their peace: but they cried the more, saying, Have mercy on us, O Lord, thou Son of David. 32 And Jesus stood still, and called them, and said, What will ye that I shall do unto you? 33 They say unto him, Lord, that our eyes may be opened. 34 So Jesus had compassion on them, and touched their eyes: and immediately their eyes received sight, and they followed him.

JEROBOAM I

[jer ô bō′am] An Ephrainite, the son of Nebat and Zeruah, and first king of Israel after the division of the kingdom in 922 BC. Under Solomon, Jeroboam served as an officer in charge of the state building programs in the land of Joseph. During this time Ahijah, the prophet of Shiloh, symbolically tore a garment into twelve pieces, giving ten of them to Jeroboam, indicating that he would become king over ten of the twelve tribes of Israel. When Solomon learned of this, he sought to kill Jeroboam; the young man fled to Egypt where he enjoyed the favor of Shishak, the Egyptian king.

At the death of Solomon, the resentment which had been stirred by oppressive taxation and forced labor came to a head. The northern tribes met at a great assembly in Shechem to accept as their king Rehoboam, who had already been proclaimed king in Jerusalem, but only on the condition that he would ease the load which had been placed upon them. In his immaturity, Rehoboam gave a harsh answer which cost him the loyalty of these tribes. His efforts to force their allegiance failed and he returned ignominiously to Jerusalem for safety. Jeroboam had returned from Egypt and was now chosen to lead the northern tribes. The rupture was complete and the great empire of David and Solomon began to decline. The first taste of enemy aggression came from Shishak, Jeroboam's old friend, who destroyed one hundred fifty towns in Palestine, including cities of the northern kingdom.

Jeroboam is perhaps best remembered for his institution of the bull cultus. Fearing that regular religious pilgrimages to Jerusalem by his subjects might lead to a reaction in favor of Rehoboam and thus cost him his kingdom, Jeroboam established a counter-cultus at two ancient sanctuaries in the northern territory, Bethel and Dan. In these sanctuaries he placed figures of bulls or calves, designed to call to mind the strength and power of God. It is probable that Jeroboam intended for the calves to serve not as an object of worship in themselves, but merely as a pedestal for the invisible God, much in the same manner as the cherubim on the ark of the covenant. (*See* CHERUBIM) When left to the unsophisticated masses, however, the cult apparently degenerated into simple idolatry. At any rate, this new institution received the constant opposition of the prophets and was responsible in a large measure for much of the upheaval which marked the history of the northern kingdom. It is characterized as "the sin of Jeroboam the son of Nebat, wherewith he made Israel to sin" (*1 Kin. 12:30; 16:26*).

Near the end of Jeroboam's reign, his son Abijah fell ill and the king sent his wife to ask assistance of Ahijah, the old prophet who had first told Jeroboam he was to be king. The prophet received her harshly, informed her that the boy would die and that, for the sin of Jeroboam, the entire family would be wiped out, a prophecy fulfilled by the usurper Baasha in 900 BC. Jeroboam died in 901 BC after a reign of twenty-two years.

See KINGS, AHIJAH

SCRIPTURE

1 Kin. 11 [26]And Jeroboam the son of Nebat, an Ephrathite of Zereda, Solomon's servant, whose mother's name was Zeruah, a widow woman, even he lifted up his hand against the king. [27]And this was the cause that he lifted up his hand against the king: Solomon built Millo, and repaired the breaches of the city of David his father. [28]And the man Jeroboam was a mighty man of valour: and Solomon seeing the young man that he was industrious, he made him ruler over all the charge of the house of Joseph. [29]And it came to pass at that time when Jeroboam went out of Jerusalem, that the prophet Ahijah the Shilonite found him in the way; and he had clad himself with a new garment; and they two were alone in the field: [30]And Ahijah caught the new garment that was on him, and rent it in twelve pieces: [31]And he said to Jeroboam, Take thee ten pieces: for thus saith the LORD, the God of Israel, Behold, I will rend the kingdom out of the hand of Solomon, and will give ten tribes to thee: [37]And I will take thee, and thou shalt reign according to all that thy soul desireth, and shalt be king over Israel. [40]Solomon sought therefore to kill Jeroboam. And Jeroboam arose, and fled into Egypt, unto Shishak king of Egypt, and was in Egypt until the death of Solomon.

1 Kin. 12 [1]And Rehoboam went to Shechem: for all Israel were come to Shechem to make him king. [2]And it came to pass, when Jeroboam the son of Nebat, who was yet in Egypt, heard of it, (for he was fled from the presence of king Solomon, and Jeroboam dwelt in Egypt;) [3]That they sent and called him. And Jeroboam and all the congregation of Israel came, and spake unto Rehoboam, saying, [4]Thy father made our yoke grievous: now therefore make thou the grievous service of thy father, and his heavy yoke which he put upon us, lighter, and we will serve thee.

5And he said unto them, Depart yet for three days, then come again to me. And the people departed.

12So Jeroboam and all the people came to Rehoboam the third day, as the king had appointed, saying, Come to me again the third day. 13And the king answered the people roughly, and forsook the old men's counsel that they gave him;

19So Israel rebelled against the house of David unto this day. 20And it came to pass when all Israel heard that Jeroboam was come again, that they sent and called him unto the congregation, and made him king over all Israel: there was none that followed the house of David, but the tribe of Judah only.

See 2 Chr. 10:1-11:4; 11:14-16; 12:15; 13:3-20

JEROBOAM II

[jer ô bō′am] The son of Jehoash (Joash) and the thirteenth king of Israel (783-748 BC). Jeroboam's father had opened the way for a prosperous reign by his recovery of the territory which had been lost to Syria under Jehoahaz. Jeroboam II resolved to carry this program even further and extended the northern frontier to Hamath, the boundary of Solomon's empire. It is also to be assumed that he subdued Moab and Ammon, reestablishing the Davidic boundaries to the East. The revenue which poured into Samaria from these tributaries brought Israel to a period of prosperity unknown since Solomon. The effects of this are graphically described in the writings of Amos, who prophesied during the reign of Jeroboam II. The rich lived in great stone houses decorated with ivory (*Amos 3:15; 5:11*); in their shadows, however, the poor were in poverty and distress. Men were sold into slavery for a pair of shoes (*Amos 2:6*; *8:6*). Vital religion was replaced by elaborate but empty ritual, performed in the grossest spirit of hypocrisy. A great part of Amos' prophecy is a severe judgment upon the social injustice which was rife in the kingdom. After the long reign of Jeroboam II, Israel never again regained her former glory, but began the downward spiral which led ultimately to Assyrian captivity.

See AMOS, JEHOASH, KINGS

SCRIPTURE

2 Kin. 14 23In the fifteenth year of Amaziah the son of Joash king of Judah, Jeroboam the son of Joash king of Israel began to reign in Samaria, and reigned forty and one years. 24And he did that which was evil in the sight of the LORD: he departed not from all the sins of Jeroboam the son of Nebat, who made Israel to sin. 25He restored the coast of Israel from the entering of Hamath unto the sea of the plain, according to the word of the LORD God of Israel, which he spake by the hand of his servant Jonah, the son of Amittai, the prophet, which was of Gathhepher. 26For the LORD saw the affliction of Israel, that it was very bitter: for there was not any shut up, nor any left, nor any helper for Israel. 27And the LORD said not that he would blot out the name of Israel from under heaven: but he saved them by the hand of Jeroboam the son of Joash.

28Now the rest of the acts of Jeroboam, and all that he did, and his might, how he warred, and how he recovered Damascus, and Hamath, which belonged to Judah, for Israel, are they not written in the book of the Chronicles of the kings of Israel? 29And Jeroboam slept with his fathers, even with the kings of Israel; and Zachariah his son reigned in his stead.

REFERENCE: The Book of *Amos*.

JERUSALEM

[je rōō′sa lem] The chief city of Palestine. Contrary to the popular notion that the name means "city of peace," its real meaning is "foundation of Shalem," indicating probably that it was an ancient center of worship of the pagan deity Shalem. Jerusalem is situated 32 miles east of the Mediterranean sea and 18 miles west of the Jordan River. It is surrounded on the west and south by the Valley of Hinnom and on the east by the Kidron Valley. A valley, unnamed in the Bible, also runs through the city from north to south. East of this central valley is a long hill; the temple stood at the north end of this hill and the ancient City of David at the south end.

In *Gen. 14*, Abraham is said to have paid a tithe to Melchizedek king of Salem. It is quite probable that this refers to Jerusalem. The first definite mention of the city in the Bible occurs in connection with the conquest of Canaan. Alarmed by the early victories of the Israelites and angered by the surrender of the Gibeonites (*see* GIBEONITES), Adonizedek king of Jerusalem and several other chieftains of the region formed a coalition to resist the onslaught. The coalition was crushed, but Jerusalem was not taken at that time, probably because it was too strong (*Josh. 10*). The city is mentioned next in *Josh. 15:7-8*, in which "the southern shoulder of the Jebusite, that is Jerusalem," is named in the description of the boundaries of Judah and Benjamin. The first siege of Jerusalem appears to have taken place after the death of Joshua. Judah and Simeon "fought against it and took it, and smote it with the edge of the sword, and set the city on fire" (*Judg. 1:8*). They were not, however, able to drive the Jebusites out of the city (*Josh. 15:63*; *Judg. 1:21*) and it is probable that they soon reoccupied all or part of it. This situation lasted until David managed to capture the city, turning it into his capital. Since the city had belonged to none of the tribes, its neutrality was useful in unifying the Israelites. By bringing the ark of the covenant to Jerusalem, David made it the religious as well as the political capital. The reign of his son and successor, Solomon, was marked by extensive construction. In addition to the temple, he built a palace for himself, the House of the Forest of Lebanon, the Hall of Pillars, the Hall of the Throne, and rebuilt the wall around the city.

After the division of the kingdom in 922 BC, the ten northern tribes made Samaria their capital, but Jerusalem remained the capital of the southern kingdom of Judah. During the reign of the various kings of Judah, Jerusalem was attacked numerous times and came under the role of various foreign powers, but she managed to weather these storms until 587 BC, at which time the Babylonian armies of Nebuchadnezzar overran Jerusalem, destroyed the temple and left the city desolate, taking many of its inhabitants captive to Babylonia. In 538 BC, one year after his conquest of the Babylonian empire, Cyrus the Persian granted permission to a group of Jews to return to Jerusalem to rebuild the temple and reestablish the Jewish faith and life. Through the efforts of Sheshbazzar, Zerubbabel, Jeshua, Haggai, and Zechariah, the work of rebuilding the temple was completed about 515 BC. About the middle of the fifth century BC, Nehemiah gained permission from Artaxerxes king of Persia to rebuild the wall of the city. The book of *Nehemiah* tells of the bravery and determination which enabled the Jews to carry out this project, despite intense opposition from neighboring rulers.

The next serious threat to Jerusalem came during the reign of the Seleucid king Antiochus Epiphanes (175-163 BC). Antiochus was determined to destroy every vestige of Jewish faith and culture and to this end he plundered the temple, converting it into a heathen temple, burned or tore down much of the city, and killed or took captive many of the inhabitants. These actions led to the Jewish revolt under the Maccabees. In the century that followed, Jerusalem was the scene of frequent battles and constant tension. The Romans gained control of the city in 63 BC. In 37 BC the Idumean ruler Herod was able, with the approval and help of the Romans, to gain control over Jerusalem. Like that of Solomon, Herod's rule was marked by an extensive program of building which included the reconstruction of the temple. The Holy City of the Jews became the Holy City of Christians by virtue of the fact it was the scene of the passion of Jesus and the institutions of the Christian church.

Jerusalem was utterly destroyed in AD 70 by the Roman armies under Titus. Since that time, its fortunes have varied, although, true to its historical character, it has seldom enjoyed peace for long at a time. It is regarded as a Holy City not only by Jews and Christians, but also by Muslims. In *Rev. 21:2* we read of a "New Jerusalem." This is not to be understood as any actual geographical spot on earth, but a heavenly city fashioned by God for his people.

SCRIPTURE

Melchizedek, King of Jerusalem

Gen. 14 [17]And the king of Sodom went out to meet him, (after his return from the slaughter of Chedorlaomer, and of the kings that were with him,) at the valley of Shaveh, which is the king's dale. [18]And Melchizedek king of Salem brought forth bread and wine: and he was the priest of the most high God. [19]And he blessed him, and said, Blessed be Abram of the most high God, possessor of heaven and earth: [20]And blessed be the most high God, which hath delivered thine enemies into thy hand. And he gave him tithes of all.

Joins Coalition against Joshua

Josh. 10 [1]Now it came to pass, when Adonizedek king of Jerusalem had heard how Joshua had taken Ai, and had utterly destroyed it; as he had done to Jericho and her king, so he had done to Ai and her king; and how the inhabitants of Gibeon had made peace with Israel, and were among them; [2]That they feared greatly, because Gibeon was a great city, as one of the royal cities, and because it was greater than Ai, and all the men thereof were mighty. [3]Wherefore Adonizedek king of Jerusalem sent unto Hoham king of Hebron, and unto Piram king of Jarmuth, and unto Japhia king of Lachish, and unto Debir king of Eglon, saying, [4]Come up unto me, and help me, that we may smite Gibeon: for it hath made peace with Joshua and with the children of Israel. [5]Therefore the five kings of the Amorites, the king of Jerusalem, the king of Hebron, the king of Jarmuth, the king of Lachish, the king of Eglon, gathered themselves together, and went up, they and all their hosts, and encamped before Gibeon, and made war against it.

Inhabitants Not Expelled by Joshua

Josh. 15 [63]As for the Jebusites the inhabitants of Jerusalem, the children of Judah could not drive them out: but the Jebusites dwell with the children of Judah at Jerusalem unto this day.

Conquered by David

2 Sam. 5 [6]And the king and his men went to Jerusalem unto the Jebusites, the inhabitants of the land: which spake unto David, saying, Except thou take away the blind and the lame, thou shalt not come in hither: thinking, David can not come in hither. [7]Nevertheless, David took the strong hold of Zion: the same is the city of David.

Plundered by Shishak

1 Kin. 14 [25]And it came to pass in the fifth year of king Rehoboam, that Shishak king of Egypt came up against Jerusalem: [26]And he took away the treasures of the house of the LORD, and the treasures of the king's house; he even took away all: and he took away all the shields of gold which Solomon had made.

Captured by Nebuchadnezzar

2 Kin. 24 [10]At that time the servants of Nebuchadnezzar king of Babylon came up against Jerusalem, and the city was besieged. [11]And Nebuchadnezzar king of Babylon came against the city, and his servants did besiege it. [12]And Jehoiachin the king of Judah went out to the king of Babylon, he, and his mother, and his servants, and his princes, and his officers: and the king of Babylon took him in the eighth year of his reign. [13]And he carried out thence all the treasures of the house of the

LORD, and the treasures of the king's house,
and cut in pieces all the vessels of gold
which Solomon king of Israel had made in
the temple of the LORD, as the LORD had
said. [14]And he carried away all Jerusalem,
and all the princes, and all the mighty men
of valour, even ten thousand captives, and
all the craftsmen and smiths: none remained, save the poorest sort of the people
of the land. [15]And he carried away Jehoiachin to Babylon, and the king's mother,
and the king's wives, and his officers, and
the mighty of the land, those carried he
into captivity from Jerusalem to Babylon.
[16]And all the men of might, even seven
thousand, and craftsmen and smiths a
thousand, all that were strong and apt for
war, even them the king of Babylon
brought captive to Babylon.

Destroyed by Nebuchadnezzar

2 Kin. 25 [1]And it came to pass in the
ninth year of his reign, in the tenth month,
in the tenth day of the month, that Nebuchadnezzar king of Babylon came, he, and
all his host, against Jerusalem, and pitched
against it; and they built forts against it
round about. [2]And the city was besieged
unto the eleventh year of king Zedekiah.
[3]And on the ninth day of the fourth month
the famine prevailed in the city, and there
was no bread for the people of the land.

[4]And the city was broken up, and all the
men of war fled by night by the way of the
gate between two walls, which is by the
king's garden: (now the Chaldees were
against the city round about:) and the
king went the way toward the plain.

[8]And in the fifth month, on the seventh
day of the month, which is the nineteenth
year of king Nebuchadnezzar king of Babylon, came Nebuzar-adan, captain of the
guard, a servant of the king of Babylon,
unto Jerusalem: [9]And he burnt the house
of the LORD, and the king's house, and all
the houses of Jerusalem, and every great
man's house burnt he with fire. [10]And all
the army of the Chaldees, that were with
the captain of the guard, brake down the
walls of Jerusalem round about. [11]Now
the rest of the people that were left in the
city, and the fugitives that fell away to the
king of Babylon, with the remnant of the
multitude, did Nebuzar-adan the captain
of the guard carry away. [12]But the captain
of the guard left of the poor of the land to
be vinedressers and husbandmen.

Rebuilding of Jerusalem

PROCLAMATION OF CYRUS

Ezra 1 [1]Now in the first year of Cyrus
king of Persia, that the word of the LORD
by the mouth of Jeremiah might be fulfilled, the LORD stirred up the spirit of Cyrus king of Persia, that he made a proclamation throughout all his kingdom, and
put it also in writing, saying, [2]Thus saith
Cyrus king of Persia, The LORD God of
heaven hath given me all the kingdoms of
the earth; and he hath charged me to build
him a house at Jerusalem, which is in Judah. [3]Who is there among you of all his
people? his God be with him, and let him
go up to Jerusalem, which is in Judah, and
build the house of the LORD God of Israel,
(he is the God,) which is in Jerusalem.
[4]And whosoever remaineth in any place
where he sojourneth, let the men of his
place help him with silver, and with gold,
and with goods, and with beasts, besides
the freewill offering for the house of God
that is in Jerusalem.

[5]Then rose up the chief of the fathers of
Judah and Benjamin, and the priests, and
the Levites, with all them whose spirit
God had raised, to go up to build the house
of the LORD which is in Jerusalem.

WORK CONTINUED BY NEHEMIAH

Neh. 2 [11]So I came to Jerusalem, and was there three days.

[12]And I arose in the night, I and some few men with me; neither told I any man what my God had put in my heart to do at Jerusalem: neither was there any beast with me, save the beast that I rode upon. [13]And I went out by night by the gate of the valley, even before the dragon well, and to the dung port, and viewed the walls of Jerusalem, which were broken down, and the gates thereof were consumed with fire. [14]Then I went on to the gate of the fountain, and to the king's pool: but there was no place for the beast that was under me to pass. [15]Then went I up in the night by the brook, and viewed the wall, and turned back, and entered by the gate of the valley, and so returned. [16]And the rulers knew not whither I went, or what I did; neither had I as yet told it to the Jews, nor to the priests, nor to the nobles, nor to the rulers, nor to the rest that did the work.

[17]Then said I unto them, Ye see the distress that we are in, how Jerusalem lieth waste, and the gates thereof are burned with fire: come, and let us build up the wall of Jerusalem, that we be no more a reproach. [18]Then I told them of the hand of my God which was good upon me; as also the king's words that he had spoken unto me. And they said, Let us rise up and build. So they strengthened their hands for this good work.

Neh. 4 [6]So built we the wall; and all the wall was joined together unto the half thereof: for the people had a mind to work.

OPPOSITION TO THE BUILDING

Neh. 4 [7]But it came to pass, that when Sanballat, and Tobiah, and the Arabians, and the Ammonites, and the Ashdodites, heard that the walls of Jerusalem were made up, and that the breaches began to be stopped, then they were very wroth, [8]And conspired all of them together to come and to fight against Jerusalem, and to hinder it. [9]Nevertheless we made our prayer unto our God, and set a watch against them day and night, because of them.

[16]And it came to pass from that time forth, that the half of my servants wrought in the work, and the other half of them held both the spears, the shields, and the bows, and the habergeons; and the rulers were behind all the house of Judah. [17]They which builded on the wall, and they that bare burdens, with those that laded, every one with one of his hands wrought in the work, and with the other hand held a weapon. [18]For the builders, every one had his sword girded by his side, and so builded. And he that sounded the trumpet was by me.

[21]So we laboured in the work: and half of them held the spears from the rising of the morning till the stars appeared. [22]Likewise at the same time said I unto the people, Let every one with his servant lodge within Jerusalem, that in the night they may be a guard to us, and labour on the day. [23]So neither I, nor my brethren, nor my servants, nor the men of the guard which followed me, none of us put off our clothes, saving that every one put them off for washing.

THE BUILDING COMPLETED

Neh. 6 [15]So the wall was finished in the twenty and fifth day of the month Elul, in fifty and two days.

REFERENCE: For personal incidents occurring in Jerusalem, *see* articles on various individuals.

JESUS

[jē'zus] The personal name of Christ. The name means "Yahweh (Jehovah) is salvation" and was a common name in New Testament times. This article is concerned mainly with the earthly life of Jesus; for a discussion of Christology (the doctrine of his person), *see* the article CHRIST. The major sources for a study of the life of Jesus are, of course, the four gospels: *Matthew, Mark, Luke,* and *John.* (*See* GOSPEL) As we study these, however, it is important to remember that their purpose is not to provide us with a biography, in our modern sense of the term. They are primarily theological writings which set forth the central features of the message of salvation—the Crucifixion, Resurrection, Glorification, and Second Coming—within a broad historical framework which includes not only the major events of his life but many examples of his religious and ethical teaching, as well as accounts of his miracles. Each gospel writer had his own method of selecting and recording available data, under the guidance of the Holy Spirit. One recorded things that another chose to omit. There was little or no attempt to make certain that their account of the sequence of events in Jesus' life coincided exactly with that of the other writers. It is therefore rather fruitless to construct intricate "harmonies" of the gospels in which all the minute details of Jesus' life are woven into one continuous strand. To do this is to miss the point of the gospels. It is possible, however, to construct a broad outline of the life of Jesus with some assurance of accuracy.

Matthew and *Luke,* the only two gospels which treat the birth of Jesus, provide us with a list of Jesus' ancestors. Matthew traces Jesus' genealogy through the royal line of David back to Abraham to show that he, like the Messiah of Jewish expectation, was truly a Jew and a "son of David" (*Matt. 1:1-17*). Luke's list (*Luke 3:23-38*) extends all the way back to Adam, indicating Jesus' kinship with all humanity. The birth narratives contained in *Matthew* and *Luke,* although somewhat difficult to fit together, tell of the announcement of the angel Gabriel to Mary, a virgin, that she would bear a child "of the Holy Spirit." The angel then appeared to Joseph, the man to whom she was betrothed (*see* MARRIAGE), to prevent him from privately divorcing Mary. We are then told of the child's birth in the stable in Bethlehem, where Joseph and Mary had gone to be enrolled for tax purposes, the proclamation of his birth to the shepherds by the angels, the visit of the wise men, the visit to the temple and the prophecies of Simeon and Anna, and the flight into Egypt, occasioned by Herod's order to slay the male infants of Bethlehem. These events took place in approximately 4 BC. While this date seems strange, it is explicable by the fact that modern scholarship has shown ancient chronological schemes to have been in error and it has been less difficult to speak of Jesus' having been born in 4 BC than to redate the rest of history.

The only event we have from Jesus' childhood is the well-known visit to the temple at the age of twelve. Apart from this we are told only that "Jesus increased in wisdom and stature, and in favour with God and man" (*Luke 2:52*). We next hear of Jesus in connection with the ministry of John the Baptist, at which time he is about thirty years old. John, a world-renouncing ascetic, proclaimed a coming day of judgment, a breaking in of the Kingdom of God, calling the people to repentance—a turning from sin unto the Lord—and baptizing them as a sign of their repentance. Jesus himself, though guilty of no sin, came to the River Jordan to be baptized of John. As he arose from the baptismal waters the heavens opened, the Holy Spirit descended on him in the form of a dove, and a voice from heaven declared "Thou art my beloved son, in whom I am well-pleased" (*Mark 1:11*). This announcement served as a formal commission and marks the beginning of Jesus' earthly ministry. A similar statement was made at his transfiguration (*Matt. 17:5*). Following the baptism of Jesus, we are told of his temptation, a concentrated attempt on the part of Satan to put Jesus' divine-human nature to the full test.

Early in his ministry, Jesus chose the twelve apostles, and other disciples to assist him in his work. Jesus' personal ministry was concentrated at first in his native Galilee. From there he went on journeys into Phoenecia and into the area west of the Jordan. Finally, he came to Judaea and Jerusalem. His message was the Kingdom of God, the open manifestation of God's rule over the universe. He spoke of this kingdom in his parables and bore witness to its presence by miracles of healing and other "signs and wonders." Jesus directed his ministry not to the self-sufficient religious or intellectual leaders but to the poor and the outcast. His parables of the lost coin, the lost sheep, and the lost boy, his attention to the blind and the odious, and his description of the feast at which beggars and other pariahs receive the blessings rejected by the higher classes all served to endear Jesus to the less-favored elements of society. He declared that the practice of true religion consisted less in scrupulous tithing and ostentatious almsgiving than in love of one's neighbor (and enemy) and humble, undivided devotion to God. His criticism of the religious teaching and practice of such groups as the scribes, Pharisees, and Sadducees, served to unite them in their opposition to him. When he went up to Jerusalem at Passover, they contrived to have him crucified. His entry into Jerusalem is worthy of note. Many of the Jews had expected a military leader who would deliver them from Roman occupation and restore to Israel the glory she enjoyed in the days of Solomon. But when Jesus came into the Holy City, he rode not in a chariot or upon a warhorse, but on an ass, the symbol of meekness and quietness. He was met not by lances held aloft, but by palm branches cast in his path. His welcome was not the shout of soldiers, but the song of children. Almost immediately, however, he showed that although he was not a military leader, neither was he a man lightly to be written off. In what must have been an amazing display of charismatic force, he entered the temple and singlehandedly cleared it of moneychangers and other tradesmen who had gathered there.

On Thursday evening of that week, Jesus met with his disciples in the Upper Room and instituted what we know as the Lord's Supper, or Holy Communion. After supper, he and several of his disciples withdrew to the Garden of Gethsemane on the slope of the Mount of Olives. There, after praying for some time, Jesus was betrayed by Judas Iscariot, one of his apostles, and arrested. He was taken first before the Sanhedrin, which had met in the house of Annas, the old high priest. After being accused and questioned in highly irregular proceedings, Jesus was taken before Pilate the governor of Judaea, on the grounds that he was an insurrectionist, claiming to be King of the Jews and plotting the overthrow of Roman rule. Pilate and Herod both examined Jesus, but found he had done nothing worthy of death. It was customary for a Jewish prisoner to be released every year at Passover. Pilate sought to extricate himself from his difficulty by offering the crowd a choice between Jesus and Barabbas, a notorious criminal. The crowd chose Barabbas. At the insistence of the Mob and its leaders, Pilate ordered Jesus scourged and crucified. With the aid of Simon of Cyrene, Jesus carried his cross to Golgotha, a hill just outside of Jerusalem. There he was nailed to his cross between two thieves. Death by crucifixion ordinarily took several days but, for some reason, Jesus died rather quickly. As the Sabbath was approaching, his body was removed and placed temporarily in a tomb belonging to Joseph of Arimathea. On the day following the Sabbath, the first day of the week, certain women who were disciples of Jesus came to prepare his body for permanent burial. When they arrived at the tomb they were told, "he is risen; he is not here; behold the place where they laid him" (*Luke 16:6*). In the next forty days, the risen Lord appeared to a number of individuals. Then, shortly before Pentecost, he went out to the Mount of Olives with a few of his disciples. He spoke to them concerning their imminent baptism with the Holy Spirit and charged them to bear witness to him. "And when he had spoken these things, while they beheld, he was taken up, and a cloud received him out of their sight" (*Acts 1:9*).

Jesus' disciples were not left alone, however. True to the promises he made before his death, the void left by his departure was filled by the coming of the Holy Spirit on Pentecost, ten days after the ascension. That same Spirit still lives in the church, the Body of Christ, enabling it to confess that "Jesus is Lord" and pointing it to that great Day when he will return to claim his beloved and to bring his Kingdom to consummation.

SCRIPTURE

Birth and Infancy

ANNUNCIATION TO MARY

Luke 1 [30]And the angel said unto her,
Fear not, Mary, for thou hast found favour with God. [31]And behold, thou shalt

conceive in thy womb, and bring forth a
son, and shalt call his name JESUS. 32He
shall be great, and shall be called the son
of the Highest, and the Lord God shall
give unto him the throne of his father
David. 33And he shall reign over the
house of Jacob for ever, and of his kingdom there shall be no end.

ANNUNCIATION TO JOSEPH

Luke 2 4And Joseph also went up from
Galilee, out of the city of Nazareth, into
Judaea, unto the city of David, which is
called Bethlehem, (because he was of the
house and lineage of David,) 5To be
taxed with Mary his espoused wife, being
great with child. 6And so it was, that
while they were there, the days were accomplished that she should be delivered.
7And she brought forth her firstborn son,
and wrapped him in swaddling clothes,
and laid him in a manger, because there
was no room for them in the Inn.

ANNUNCIATION TO THE SHEPHERDS

Luke 2 10And the angel said unto
them, Fear not: For behold, I bring you
good tidings of great joy, which shall be
to all people. 11For unto you is born this
day, in the city of David, a Saviour, which
is Christ the Lord. 12And this shall be a
sign unto you; ye shall find the babe
wrapped in swaddling clothes lying in a
manger. 13And suddenly there was with
the angel a multitude of the heavenly
host praising God, and saying, 14Glory to
God in the highest, and on earth peace,
good will toward men. 15And it came to
pass, as the angels were gone away from
them into heaven, the shepherds said one
to another, Let us now go even unto Bethlehem, and see this thing which is come
to pass, which the Lord hath made known
unto us. 16And they came with haste, and
found Mary and Joseph, and the babe
lying in a manger.

ANNUNCIATION TO THE WISE MEN

Matt. 2 1Now when Jesus was born in
Bethlehem of Judaea, in the days of
Herod the king, behold, there came wise
men from the east to Jerusalem, 2Saying,
Where is he that is born King of the Jews?
for we have seen his star in the east, and
are come to worship him.

13And when they were departed, behold, the angel of the Lord appeareth to
Joseph in a dream, saying, Arise and take
the young child, and his mother, and flee
into Egypt, and be thou there until I bring
thee word: for Herod will seek the young
child, to destroy him. 14When he arose,
he took the young child and his mother
by night, and departed into Egypt: 15And
was there until the death of Herod, that
it might be fulfilled which was spoken of
the Lord by the prophet, saying, Out of
Egypt have I called my son.

Boyhood

Luke 2 41Now his parents went to Jerusalem every year, at the feast of the Passover. 42And when he was twelve years
old, they went up to Jerusalem, after the
custom of the feast. 46And it came to pass,
that after three days they found him in
the temple, sitting in the midst of the
doctors, both hearing them, and asking
them questions. 47And all that heard him
were astonished at his understanding, and
answers. 48And when they saw him, they
were amazed: and his mother said unto
him, Son, why hast thou thus dealt with
us? Behold, thy father and I have sought
thee sorrowing. 49And he said unto them,
How is it that ye sought me? Wist ye not
that I must be about my Father's business? 50And they understood not the say-

ing which he spake unto them. 51And he went down with them, and came to Nazareth, and was subject unto them: but his mother kept all these sayings in her heart. 52And Jesus increased in wisdom and stature, and in favour with God and man.

Baptism

Matt. 3 14But John forbade him, saying, I have need to be baptized of thee, and comest thou to me? 15And Jesus answering said unto him, Suffer it to be so now: for thus it becometh us to fulfil all righteousness. Then he suffered him. 16And Jesus, when he was baptized, went up straightway out of the water: and, lo, the heavens were opened unto him, and he saw the Spirit of God descending like a dove, and lighting upon him: 17And lo a voice from heaven, saying, This is my beloved Son, in whom I am well pleased.

Temptation

Matt. 4 1Then was Jesus led up of the Spirit into the wilderness to be tempted of the devil. 2And when he had fasted forty days and forty nights, he was afterward a hungered. 3And when the tempter came to him, he said, If thou be the Son of God, command that these stones be made bread. 4But he answered and said, It is written, Man shall not live by bread alone, but by every word that proceedeth out of the mouth of God. 5Then the devil taketh him up into the holy city, and setteth him on a pinnacle of the temple, 6And saith unto him, If thou be the Son of God, cast thyself down: for it is written, He shall give his angels charge concerning thee: and in their hands they shall bear thee up, lest at any time thou dash thy foot against a stone. 7Jesus said unto him, It is written again, Thou shalt not tempt the Lord thy God. 8Again, the devil taketh him up into an exceeding high mountain, and sheweth him all the kingdoms of the world, and the glory of them; 9And saith unto him, All these things will I give thee, if thou wilt fall down and worship me. 10Then saith Jesus unto him, Get thee hence, Satan: for it is written, Thou shalt worship the Lord thy God, and him only shalt thou serve. 11Then the devil leaveth him, and, behold, angels came and ministered unto him.

First Disciples Chosen

Luke 5 10And so was also James, and John, the sons of Zebedee, which were partners with Simon. And Jesus said unto Simon, Fear not; from henceforth thou shalt catch men. 11And when they had brought their ships to land, they forsook all, and followed him.

Preaching, Teaching and Healing

Matt. 9 35And Jesus went about all the cities and villages, teaching in their synagogues, and preaching the gospel of the kingdom, and healing every sickness and every disease among the people.

36But when he saw the multitudes, he was moved with compassion on them, because they fainted, and were scattered abroad, as sheep having no shepherd. 37Then saith he unto his disciples, The harvest truly is plenteous, but the labourers are few; 38Pray ye therefore the Lord of the harvest, that he will send forth labourers into his harvest.

Luke 4 16And he came to Nazareth, where he had been brought up: and, as his custom was, he went into the synagogue on the sabbath day, and stood up for to read. 17And there was delivered unto him the book of the prophet Esaias. And when he had opened the book, he found the place where it was written, [18]The Spirit of the Lord is upon me, because he hath anointed me to preach the gospel to the poor; he hath sent me to heal the broken-hearted, to preach deliverance to the captives, and recovering of sight to the blind, to set at liberty them that are bruised, [19]To preach the acceptable year of the Lord. [20]And he closed the book, and he gave it again to the minister, and sat down. And the eyes of all them that were in the synagogue were fastened on him. [21]And he began to say unto them, This day is this scripture fulfilled in your ears.

Disciples Sent Forth

Matt. 10 [1]And when he had called unto him his twelve disciples, he gave them power against unclean spirits, to cast them out, and to heal all manner of sickness and all manner of disease.

Death and Suffering Foretold

Matt. 16 [20]Then charged he his disciples that they should tell no man that he was Jesus the Christ.

[21]From that time forth began Jesus to shew unto his disciples, how that he must go unto Jerusalem, and suffer many things of the elders and chief priests and scribes, and be killed, and be raised again the third day.

The Transfiguration

Matt. 17 [1]And after six days Jesus taketh Peter, James, and John his brother, and bringeth them up into an high mountain apart, [2]And was transfigured before them: and his face did shine as the sun, and his raiment was white as the light. [9]And as they came down from the mountain, Jesus charged them, saying, Tell the vision to no man, until the Son of man be risen again from the dead.

Last Journey to Jerusalem and Triumphal Entry

Matt. 20 [17]And Jesus going up to Jerusalem took the twelve disciples apart in the way, and said unto them, [18]Behold, we go up to Jerusalem; and the Son of man shall be betrayed unto the chief priests and unto the scribes, and they shall condemn him to death, [19]And shall deliver him to the Gentiles to mock, and to scourge, and to crucify him: and the third day he shall rise again.

John 12 [12]On the next day much people that were come to the feast, when they heard that Jesus was coming to Jerusalem, [13]Took branches of palm trees, and went forth to meet him, and cried, Hosanna: Blessed is the King of Israel that cometh in the name of the Lord.

Indicates Judas as Traitor

Matt. 26 [21]And as they did eat, he said, Verily I say unto you, that one of you shall betray me. [22]And they were exceeding sorrowful, and began every one of them to say unto him, Lord, is it I? [23]And he answered and said, He that dippeth his hand with me in the dish, the same shall betray me. [24]The Son of man goeth as it is written of him: but woe unto that man by whom the Son of man is betrayed! it had been good for that man if he had not been born. [25]Then Judas, which betrayed him, answered and said, Master, is it I? He said unto him, Thou hast said.

Institutes Lord's Supper

Matt. 26 [26]And as they were eating, Jesus took bread, and blessed it, and brake it, and gave it to the disciples, and said, Take, eat; this is my body. 27And he took the cup, and gave thanks, and gave it to them, saying, Drink ye all of it; 28For this is my blood of the new testament, which is shed for many for the remission of sins.

The Agony in the Garden

Matt. 26 36Then cometh Jesus with them unto a place called Gethsemane, and saith unto the disciples, Sit ye here, while I go and pray yonder. 37And he took with him Peter and the two sons of Zebedee, and began to be sorrowful and very heavy. 38Then saith he unto them, My soul is exceeding sorrowful, even unto death: tarry ye here, and watch with me. 39And he went a little farther, and fell on his face, and prayed, saying, O my Father, if it be possible, let this cup pass from me: nevertheless not as I will, but as thou wilt. 40And he cometh unto the disciples, and findeth them asleep, and saith unto Peter, What, could ye not watch with me one hour? 41Watch and pray, that ye enter not into temptation: the spirit indeed is willing, but the flesh is weak. 42He went away again the second time, and prayed, saying, O my Father, if this cup may not pass away from me, except I drink it, thy will be done. 43And he came and found them asleep again: for their eyes were heavy. 44And he left them, and went away again, and prayed the third time, saying the same words.

The Betrayal

Matt. 26 47And while he yet spake, lo, Judas, one of the twelve, came, and with him a great multitude with swords and staves, from the chief priests and elders of the people. 48Now he that betrayed him gave them a sign, saying, Whomsoever I shall kiss, that same is he: hold him fast. 49And forthwith he came to Jesus, and said, Hail, master; and kissed him.

Trial and Condemnation

Matt. 26 59Now the chief priests, and elders, and all the council, sought false witness against Jesus, to put him to death; 60But found none: yea, though many false witnesses came, yet found they none. At the last came two false witnesses, 61And said, This fellow said, I am able to destroy the temple of God, and to build it in three days. 62And the high priest arose, and said unto him, Answerest thou nothing? what is it which these witness against thee? 63But Jesus held his peace. And the high priest answered and said unto him, I adjure thee by the living God, that thou tell us whether thou be the Christ, the Son of God. 64Jesus saith unto him, Thou hast said: nevertheless I say unto you, Hereafter shall ye see the Son of man sitting on the right hand of power, and coming in the clouds of heaven.

Matt. 27 2And when they had bound him, they led him away, and delivered him to Pontius Pilate the governor.

22Pilate saith unto them, What shall I do then with Jesus which is called Christ? They all say unto him, Let him be crucified. 23And the governor said, Why, what evil hath he done? But they cried out the more, saying, Let him be crucified.

24When Pilate saw that he could prevail nothing, but that rather a tumult was made, he took water, and washed his hands before the multitude, saying, I am innocent of the blood of this just person: see ye to it. 25Then answered all the people, and said, His blood be on us, and on our children.

The Crucifixion

Matt. 27 35And they crucified him, and

parted his garments, casting lots: that it might be fulfilled which was spoken by the prophet, They parted my garments among them, and upon my vesture did they cast lots.

[54]Now when the centurion, and they that were with him, watching Jesus, saw the earthquake, and those things that were done, they feared greatly, saying, Truly this was the Son of God.

The Burial

Matt. 27 [57]When the even was come, there came a rich man of Arimathaea, named Joseph, who also himself was Jesus' disciple: [58]He went to Pilate, and begged the body of Jesus. Then Pilate commanded the body to be delivered. [59]And when Joseph had taken the body, he wrapped it in a clean linen cloth, [60]And laid it in his own new tomb, which he had hewn out in the rock: and he rolled a great stone to the door of the sepulchre, and departed.

The Resurrection

Mark 16 [1]And when the sabbath was past, Mary Magdalene, and Mary the mother of James, and Salome, had bought sweet spices, that they might come and anoint him. [2]And very early in the morning the first day of the week, they came unto the sepulchre at the rising of the sun. [3]And they said among themselves, Who shall roll us away the stone from the door of the sepulchre? [4]And when they looked, they saw that the stone was rolled away: for it was very great. [5]And entering into the sepulchre, they saw a young man sitting on the right side, clothed in a long white garment; and they were affrighted. [6]And he saith unto them, Be not affrighted: Ye seek Jesus of Nazareth, which was crucified: he is risen; he is not here: behold the place where they laid him.

Appearances After Resurrection

1. TO MARY MAGDALENE

Mark 16 [9]Now when Jesus was risen early the first day of the week, he appeared first to Mary Magdalene, out of whom he had cast seven devils.

See John 20:11-18

2. TO OTHER WOMEN

Matt. 28 [9]And as they went to tell his disciples, behold Jesus met them, saying, All hail. And they came and held him by the feet, and worshipped him. [10]Then said Jesus unto them, Be not afraid: go tell my brethren that they go into Galilee, and there shall they see me.

3. TO TWO DISCIPLES NEAR EMMAUS

Mark 16 [12]After that he appeared in another form unto two of them, as they walked, and went into the country.

See Luke 24:13-28

4. TO SIMON

Luke 24 [34]Saying, The Lord is risen indeed, and hath appeared to Simon.

5. TO TEN APOSTLES

Luke 24 [36]And as they thus spake, Jesus himself stood in the midst of them, and saith unto them, Peace be unto you.

See John 20:19-23

6. TO ELEVEN APOSTLES

Mark 16 [14]Afterward he appeared unto the eleven as they sat at meat, and upbraided them with their unbelief and hardness of heart, because they believed not them which had seen him after he was risen. [15]And he said unto them, Go ye into all the world, and preach the gospel to every creature. [16]He that believeth and is baptized shall be saved; but he that believeth not shall be damned. [17]And these signs shall follow them that believe; In my name shall they cast out devils; they shall speak with new tongues; [18]They shall take up serpents; and if they drink any deadly thing, it shall not hurt them; they shall lay hands on the sick, and they shall recover.

See John 20:26-29

7. TO DISCIPLES AT SEA OF TIBERIAS

John 21 [1]After these things Jesus shewed himself again to the disciples at the sea of Tiberias; and on this wise shewed he himself.

See John 21:2-25

8. TO DISCIPLES ON A MOUNT IN GALILEE

Matt. 28 [16]Then the eleven disciples went away into Galilee, into a mountain where Jesus had appointed them. [17]And when they saw him, they worshipped him: but some doubted. [18]And Jesus came and spake unto them, saying, All power is given unto me in heaven and in earth.

[19]Go ye therefore, and teach all nations, baptizing them in the name of the Father, and of the Son, and of the Holy Ghost: [20]Teaching them to observe all things whatsoever I have commanded you: and, lo, I am with you alway, even unto the end of the world.

9. TO FIVE HUNDRED AT ONCE

1 Cor. 15 [6]After that, he was seen of above five hundred brethren at once; of whom the greater part remain unto this present, but some are fallen asleep.

10. TO JAMES

1 Cor. 15 [7]After that, he was seen of James; then of all the apostles.

The Ascension

Luke 24 [50]And he led them out as far as to Bethany, and he lifted up his hands, and blessed them. [51]And it came to pass, while he blessed them, he was parted from them, and carried up into heaven.

Jesus' Teaching

Preaches repentance at Galilee, *Matt. 4:17;* at Nazareth, *Luke 4:16-19.*
Preaches about the kingdom, *Matt. 4:23; Mark 1:14.*
Testimony concerning John the Baptist, *Matt. 11:7; Luke 7:24; 20:4.*
Preaches about the Father and the Son, *John 5; 8:18, 42; 10:15; 12:23;* on the bread of life, *John 6:26;* on the seed of Abraham, *John 8:21;* on the traditions of the elders, *Matt. 15:1; Mark 7:1.*
Answers Pharisees, *Matt. 12:38; 16:1; Mark 8:11; Luke 11:16; 12:54; John 2:18.*
Lesson to disciples on humility, *John 13: 14-16.*
Teaches Scribes and Pharisees, *Matt. 23; Mark 12; Luke 11:37; 20:45.*
Destruction of Jerusalem, etc., *Matt. 24; Mark 13; Luke 13:34; 17:20; 19:41; 21.*
Invites weary to rest, *Matt. 11:23.*
Talks on suffering for the Gospel, *Matt. 10: 37; Luke 14:26.*

Talks

Marriage, *Matt. 19; Mark 10.*
Riches, *Matt. 19:16; Mark 10:17; Luke 12:13; 18:18.*
Tribute, *Matt. 22:15; Mark 12:13; Luke 20: 20.*
Resurrection, *Matt. 22:23; Mark 12:18.*
Two great commandments, *Matt. 22:35; Mark 12:28.*
Widow's mite, *Mark 12:41; Luke 21:1.*
Watchfulness, *Matt. 24:42; Mark 13:33; Luke 12:35; 21:34.*
Last judgment, *Matt. 25:31.*
Faith, *Matt. 8.*
Discipleship, *Luke 9:23-57.*
Fasting, *Matt. 9:14; Mark 2:18; Luke 5:33.*

Talks (continued)

- Blasphemy, *Matt. 12:31; Mark 3:28; Luke 11:15.*
- His brethren, *Matt. 12:46; Mark 3:31; Luke 8:19.*

Sermon on the Mount—*Matthew 5, 6, and 7*

CONTAINS

- The Beatitudes (those who are blessed), *5:5-11.*
- Salt of the earth, *5:13.*
- Light of the world, *5:14.*
- Righteousness of the Scribes and Pharisees, *5:20.*
- Anger, *5:22.*
- "thou fool," *5:22.*
- Reconciliation, *5:24.*
- Adultery, *5:27.*
- The hand and the eye, *5:29, 30.*
- Divorce, *5:32, 33.*
- Oaths, *5:33.*
- Eye for an eye, *5:38.*
- Love to neighbor and enemy, *5:43.*
- Perfection, *5:48.*
- Almsgiving, *6:1.*
- Prayer, *6:5-7.*
- Lord's Prayer, *6:9-13.*
- Fasting, *6:16.*
- Treasure on earth and in heaven, *6:19-21.*
- Evil eye, *6:23.*
- Two masters, *6:24.*
- Anxiety, *6:25-33.*
- Seeking kingdom of God, *6:33.*
- Judging not, *7:1-3.*
- Ask, seek, find, *7:7-11.*
- Straight gate, *7:13.*
- False prophets, *7:15.*
- Grapes, thorns, figs, thistles, *7:16-20.*
- Good and bad trees, *7:17.*
- Hearers and doers, *7:23, 24.*
- House on sand and house on rock, *7:24-27.*

Jesus' Parables

- Wise and foolish builders, *Matt. 7:24-27.*
- Children of the bridechamber, *Matt. 9:15; Luke 5:34, 35.*
- New cloth and old garment, *Matt. 9:13; Luke 5:36.*

Jesus' Parables (continued)

- New wine and new bottles, *Matt. 9:17.*
- Unclean spirit, *Matt. 12:43.*
- Sower, *Matt. 13:3-9, 18-23; Luke 8:5-15.*
- The tares, *Matt. 13:24-43.*
- Mustard seed, *Matt. 13:31, 32; Luke 13:19.*
- Leaven, *Matt. 13:33.*
- Hidden treasure, *Matt. 13:44.*
- Pearl of great price, *Matt. 13:45, 46.*
- Net cast into the sea, *Matt. 13:47-50.*
- Meats defiling not, *Matt. 15:10-15.*
- Unmerciful servant, *Matt. 18:23-35.*
- Hired Laborers, *Matt. 20:1-16.*
- The two sons, *Matt. 21:28-32.*
- The wicked husbandmen, *Matt. 21:33-45.*
- Marriage of the king's son, *Matt. 22:2-14.*
- The fig tree, *Matt. 24:32-34.*
- Man of the house watching, *Matt. 24:43.*
- Faithful and evil servants, *Matt. 24:45-51.*
- The ten virgins, *Matt. 25:1-13.*
- The talents, *Matt. 25:14-30.*
- Kingdom divided against itself, *Mark 3:24.*
- House divided against itself, *Mark 3:25.*
- Strong man armed, *Mark 3:27; Luke 11:21.*
- Seed growing secretly, *Mark 4:26-29.*
- The lighted candle, *Mark 4:21; Luke 11:33-36.*
- Man taking a far journey, *Mark 13:34-37.*
- Blind leading the blind, *Luke 6:39.*
- The beam and the mote, *Luke 6:41, 42.*
- The tree and its fruit, *Luke 6:43-45.*
- Creditor and debtors, *Luke 7:41-47.*
- The good Samaritan, *Luke 10:30-37.*
- The friend at midnight, *Luke 11:5-9.*
- The rich fool, *Luke 12:16-21.*
- The cloud and the wind, *Luke 12:54-57.*
- The barren fig tree, *Luke 13:6-9.*
- Chief seats at the feast, *Luke 14:7-11.*
- Builder of a tower, *Luke 14:28-30, 33.*
- The king going to war, *Luke 14:31-33.*
- The savor of salt, *Luke 14:34, 35.*
- The lost sheep, *Luke 15:3-7.*
- The lost piece of silver, *Luke 15:8-10.*
- The prodigal son, *Luke 15:11-32.*
- The unjust steward, *Luke 16:1-8.*
- The rich man and Lazarus, *Luke 16:19-31.*
- Unprofitable servant, *Luke 17:7.*
- Importunate widow, *Luke 18:1-8.*
- The Pharisee and the Publican, *Luke 18:9-14.*
- The pounds, *Luke 19:12-27.*

Jesus' Parables (continued)

The Bread of Life, *John 6:47.*
The Good Shepherd, *John 10:1-6.*
The Vine and the branches, *John 15:1-5.*

Jesus' Miracles

Water turned into wine, *John 2:6-10.*
Nobleman's son healed, *John 4:46-53.*
Centurion's servant healed, *Matt. 8:5-13.*
Draughts of fishes, *Luke 5:4-6; John 21:6.*
Devils cast out, *Matt. 8:28-32; 9:32, 33; 15:22-28; 17:14-18; Mark 1:23-27.*
Peter's mother-in-law healed, *Matt. 8:14, 15.*
Lepers cleansed, *Matt. 8:3; Luke 17:14.*
Paralytic healed, *Mark 2:3-12.*
Withered hand restored, *Matt. 12:10-13.*
Impotent man healed, *John 5:5-9.*
Dead raised to life, *Matt. 9:18, 19; 9:23-25; Luke 7:12-15; John 11:11-44.*
Issue of blood stopped, *Matt. 9:20-22.*
Blind restored to sight, *Matt. 9:27-30; Mark 8:22-25; John 9:1-7.*
The deaf and dumb cured, *Mark 7:32-35.*
The multitude fed, *Matt. 14:15-21; 15:32-38.*
Walking on the sea, *Matt. 14:25-27.*
The tribute money, *Matt. 17:27.*
The tempest stilled, *Matt. 8:23-26; Mark 4:37; Luke 8:23.*
Sudden arrival of ship, *John 6:21.*
Woman healed of infirmity, *Luke 13:11-13.*
Dropsy cured, *Luke 14:2-4.*
Fig tree blighted, *Matt. 21:19.*
Malchus healed, *Luke 22:50, 51.*
Miracles performed before the messengers of John, *John 7:21, 22.*
Different diseases healed, *Matt. 4:23, 24; 14:14; 15:30; Mark 1:34; Luke 6:17, 19.*

Character of Jesus

HOLY

Luke 1 [35]And the angel answered and said unto her, The Holy Ghost shall come upon thee, and the power of the Highest shall overshadow thee: therefore also that holy thing which shall be born of thee shall be called the Son of God.

Acts 4 [27]For of a truth against thy holy child Jesus, whom thou hast anointed, both Herod, and Pontius Pilate, with the Gentiles, and the people of Israel, were gathered together.

Rev. 3 [7]And to the angel of the church in Philadelphia write; These things saith he that is holy, he that is true, he that hath the key of David, he that openeth, and no man shutteth; and shutteth, and no man openeth.

RIGHTEOUS

Heb. 1 [9]Thou hast loved righteousness, and hated iniquity; therefore God, even thy God, hath anointed thee with the oil of gladness above thy fellows.

GOOD

Matt. 19 [16]And, behold, one came and said unto him, Good Master, what good thing shall I do, that I may have eternal life?

FAITHFUL

1 Thess. 5 [24]Faithful is he that calleth you, who also will do it.

TRUE

John 1 [14]And the Word was made flesh, and dwelt among us, (and we beheld his glory, the glory as of the only begotten of the Father,) full of grace and truth.

John 7 [18]He that speaketh of himself seeketh his own glory: but he that seeketh his glory that sent him, the same is true, and no unrighteousness is in him.

1 John 5 [20]And we know that the Son of God is come, and hath given us an understanding, that we may know him that is true, and we are in him that is true, even in his Son Jesus Christ. This is the true God, and eternal life.

JUST

John 5 [30]I can of mine own self do nothing: as I hear, I judge: and my judgment is just; because I seek not mine own will, but the will of the Father which hath sent me.

Acts 22 [14]And he said, The God of our fathers hath chosen thee, that thou shouldest know his will, and see that Just One, and shouldest hear the voice of his mouth.

GUILELESS

1 Pet. 2 [22]Who did no sin, neither was guile found in his mouth.

SINLESS

2 Cor. 5 [21]For he hath made him to be sin for us, who knew no sin; that we might be made the righteousness of God in him.

SPOTLESS

1 Pet. 1 [19]But with the precious blood of Christ, as of a lamb without blemish and without spot.

INNOCENT

Matt. 27 [4]Saying, I have sinned in that I have betrayed the innocent blood. And they said, What is that to us? see thou to that.

UNDEFILED

Heb. 7 [26]For such an high priest became us, who is holy, harmless, undefiled, separate from sinners, and made higher than the heavens.

OBEDIENT TO THE FATHER

John 14 [34]Jesus saith unto them, My meat is to do the will of him that sent me, and to finish his work.

John 15 [10]If ye keep my commandments, ye shall abide in my love; even as I have kept my Father's commandments, and abide in his love.

SUBJECT TO EARTHLY PARENTS

Luke 2 [51]And he went down with them, and came to Nazareth, and was subject unto them: but his mother kept all these sayings in her heart.

ZEALOUS

Luke 2 [49]And he said unto them, How is it that ye sought me? wist ye not that I must be about my Father's business?

MEEK AND LOWLY

Isa. 53 [7]He was oppressed, and he was afflicted, yet he opened not his mouth: he is brought as a lamb to the slaughter, and as a sheep before her shearers is dumb, so he openeth not his mouth.

Matt. 11 [29]Take my yoke upon you, and learn of me: for I am meek and lowly in heart: and ye shall find rest unto your souls.

LONGSUFFERING

1 Tim. 1 [16]Howbeit for this cause I obtained mercy, that in me first Jesus Christ might shew forth all longsuffering, for a pattern to them which should hereafter believe on him to life everlasting.

COMPASSIONATE

Isa. 40 [11]He shall feed his flock like a shepherd: he shall gather the lambs with his arm, and carry them in his bosom, and shall gently lead those that are with young.

Matt. 15 [32]Then Jesus called his disciples unto him, and said, I have compassion on the multitude, because they continue with me now three days, and have nothing to eat: and I will not send them away fasting, lest they faint in the way.

Luke 7 [13]And when the Lord saw her, he had compassion on her, and said unto her, Weep not.

Luke 19 [41]And when he was come near, he beheld the city, and wept over it.

BENEVOLENT

Matt. 4 [23]And Jesus went about all Galilee, teaching in their synagogues, and preaching the gospel of the kingdom, and healing all manner of sickness and all manner of disease among the people.

Acts 10 [38]How God anointed Jesus of Nazareth with the Holy Ghost and with power: who went about doing good, and healing all that were oppressed of the devil; for God was with them.

LOVING

John 13 [1]Now before the feast of the passover, when Jesus knew that his hour was come that he should depart out of this world unto the Father, having loved his own which were in the world, he loved them unto the end.

John 15 [13]Greater love hath no man than this, that a man lay down his life for his friends.

HUMBLE

Luke 22 [27]For whether is greater, he that sitteth at meat, or he that serveth? is not he that sitteth at meat? but I am among you as he that serveth.

Phil. 2 [8]And being found in fashion as a man, He humbled himself, and became obedient unto death, even the death of the cross.

SELF-DENYING

Matt. 8 [20]And Jesus saith unto him, The foxes have holes, and the birds of the air have nests; but the Son of man hath not where to lay his head.

2 Cor. 8 [9]For ye know the grace of our Lord Jesus Christ, that, though he was rich, yet for your sakes he became poor, that ye through his poverty might be rich.

FORGIVING

Luke 23 [34]Then said Jesus, Father, forgive them; for they know not what they do. And they parted his raiment, and cast lots.

JETHRO

[jeth'rō] Priest of Midian and father-in-law of Moses, apparently also called Reuel. (*See Ex. 2: 18; 3:1*) When Moses fled from Egypt, he went to the land of Midian. After assisting a group of sisters who were herding sheep, he was introduced to their father and eventually was given one of the sisters, Zipporah, for his wife. Moses remained with Jethro for a number of years, but after the experience with the burning bush, he left to return to Egypt to deliver the Israelites from bondage. After the exodus was accomplished, Jethro and Moses were reunited at the camp near Mount Sinai. There Jethro noted that Moses' task of judging every disputation which arose among the people was a heavy burden, both on his son-in-law and on the people. He therefore suggested a division of labor whereby appointed judges handled most of the cases, only the most important being brought before Moses. Moses accepted the suggestion and quickly put it into action. After this pleasant and fruitful visit, Jethro returned to Midian and disappears from the Biblical narrative.

See Zipporah, Moses

SCRIPTURE

Ex. 2 [15]Now when Pharaoh heard this thing, he sought to slay Moses. But Moses fled from the face of Pharaoh, and dwelt in the land of Midian: and he sat down by a well. [16]Now the priest of Midian had seven daughters: and they came and drew water, and filled the troughs to water their father's flock. [17]And the shepherds came and drove them away: but Moses stood up and helped them, and watered their flock.

[18]And when they came to Reuel their father, he said, How is it that ye are come so soon to-day? [19]And they said, An Egyptian delivered us out of the hand of the shepherds, and also drew water enough for us, and watered the flock. [20]And he said unto his daughters, And where is he? why is it that ye have left the man? call him, that he may eat bread. [21]And Moses was content to dwell with the man: and he gave Moses Zipporah his daughter.

Ex. 4 [18]And Moses went and returned to Jethro his father in law, and said unto him, Let me go, I pray thee, and return unto my brethren which are in Egypt, and see whether they be yet alive. And Jethro said to Moses, Go in peace. [19]And the LORD said unto Moses in Midian, Go, return into Egypt: for all the men are dead which sought thy life.

Ex. 18 [13]And it came to pass on the morrow, that Moses sat to judge the people: and the people stood by Moses from the morning unto the evening. [14]And when Moses' father in law saw all that he did to the people, he said, What is this thing that thou doest to the people? Why sittest thou thyself alone, and all the people stand by thee from morning unto even? [15]And Moses said unto his father in law, Because the people come unto me to inquire of God: [16]When they have a matter, they come unto me; and I judge between one and another, and I do make them know the statutes of God, and his laws. [17]And Moses' father in law said unto him, The thing that thou doest is not good. [18]Thou wilt surely wear away, both thou, and this people that is with thee: for this thing is too heavy for thee; thou art not able to perform it thyself alone. [19]Hearken now unto my voice, I will give thee counsel, and God shall be with thee: Be thou for the people to God-ward, that thou mayest bring the causes unto God: [20]And thou shalt teach them ordinances and laws, and shalt shew them the way wherein they must walk, and the work that they must do. [21]Moreover thou shalt provide out of all the people able men, such as fear God, men of truth, hating covetousness; and place such over them, to be rulers of thousands, and rulers of hundreds, rulers of fifties, and rulers of tens: [22]And let them judge the people at all seasons: and it shall be, that every great matter they shall bring unto thee, but every small matter they shall judge: so shall it be easier for thyself, and they shall bear the burden with thee. [23]If thou shalt do this thing, and God command thee so, then thou shalt be able to endure, and all this people shall also go to their place in peace. [24]So Moses hearkened to the voice of his father in law, and did all that he had said.

JEW

[jōō] A word used in the Bible to designate the Israelites, as contrasted with Gentiles. This term does not seem to have been used until the last years of the southern kingdom of Judah, and did not come into general usage until after the return from the Babylonian exile. Although certainly derived from the name of the tribe or province of Judah, it came to be used of all who were Israelites by race and religion, regardless of their national origin.

JEZEBEL

[jez′ĕ bel] The daughter of the Phoenician king Ethbaal and the wife of Ahab king of Israel (869-850 BC). Jezebel must be regarded as one of the most remarkable women in history. Her great zeal for the religion of her native land is seen in her attempts to replace the worship of the true God with that of Baal and Asherah. She is said to have fed at her table 450 prophets of Baal and 400 prophets of Asherah (*1 Kin. 18:19*). She persecuted the prophets of God and proved herself almost a match for the fiery prophet Elijah. It would be difficult to condemn Jezebel too severely solely on the basis of her actions in behalf of Baalism, for she was supporting what she believed to be best. The incident of Naboth's vineyard, however, reveals her true colors. While her husband Ahab pouted over his inability to persuade Naboth to part with a vineyard which the king desired, Jezebel ruthlessly arranged for the execution of the poor farmer and thereby gained possession of the land for her husband. Because of this act Elijah pronounced a curse on the entire house of Ahab stating that dogs would eat the flesh of Jezebel in Jezreel. Years later, when Jehu's revolution ended the synasty of the Omrides, the old queen was cast down from the palace, trampled by the horses and chariots, and her flesh eaten by dogs until there was not enough left to bury, fulfilling the words of the prophet.

See AHAB, ELIJAH, JEHU, NABOTH

SCRIPTURE

Marries Ahab

1 Kin. 16 [31]And it came to pass, as if it had been a light thing for him to walk in the sins of Jeroboam the son of Nebat, that he took to wife Jezebel the daughter of Ethbaal king of the Zidonians, and went and served Baal, and worshipped him.

Slays Prophets

1 Kin. 18 [13]Was it not told my lord what I did when Jezebel slew the prophets of the LORD, how I hid a hundred men of the LORD's prophets by fifty in a cave, and fed them with bread and water?

Supports Prophets of Baal

1 Kin. 18 [19]Now therefore send, and gather to me all Israel unto mount Carmel, and the prophets of Baal four hundred and fifty, and the prophets of the groves four hundred, which eat at Jezebel's table.

Opposes Ahab

1 Kin. 19 [1]And Ahab told Jezebel all that Elijah had done, and withal how he had slain all the prophets with the sword. [2]Then Jezebel sent a messenger unto Elijah, saying, So let the gods do to me, and more also, if I make not thy life as the life of one of them by to-morrow about this time.

Arranges Naboth's Death

1 Kin. 21 [5]But Jezebel his wife came to him, and said unto him, Why is thy spirit so sad, that thou eatest no bread? [6]And he said unto her, Because I spake unto Naboth the Jezreelite, and said unto him, Give me thy vineyard for money; or else, if it please thee, I will give thee another vineyard for it: and he answered, I will not give thee my vineyard. [7]And Jezebel his wife said unto him, Dost thou now govern the kingdom of Israel? arise, and eat bread, and let thine heart be merry: I will give thee the vineyard of Naboth the Jezreelite. [8]So she wrote letters in Ahab's name, and sealed them with his seal, and sent the letters unto the elders and to the nobles that were in his city, dwelling with Naboth. [9]And she wrote in the letters, saying, Proclaim a fast, and set Naboth on high among the people: [10]And set two men, sons of Belial, before him, to bear witness against him, saying, Thou didst blaspheme God and the king. And then carry him out, and stone him, that he may die.

[15]And it came to pass, when Jezebel heard that Naboth was stoned, and was dead, that Jezebel said to Ahab, Arise, take possession of the vineyard of Naboth the Jezreelite, which he refused to give thee for money: for Naboth is not alive, but dead.

Death of Jezebel

2 Kin. 9 [30]And when Jehu was come
to Jezreel, Jezebel heard of it; and she
painted her face, and tired her head, and
looked out at a window. [31]And as Jehu entered in at the gate, she said, Had Zimri
peace, who slew his master? [32]And he
lifted up his face to the window, and said,
Who is on my side? who? And there looked
out to him two or three eunuchs. [33]And he
said, Throw her down. So they threw her
down: and some of her blood was sprinkled
on the wall, and on the horses: and he
trode her under foot. [34]And when he was
come in, he did eat and drink, and said,
Go, see now this cursed woman, and bury
her: for she is a king's daughter. [35]And
they went to bury her; but they found no
more of her than the skull, and the feet,
and the palms of her hands.

JOAB

[jō′ab] David's nephew and the commander of his army. Joab first appears at the head of David's forces in the struggle with Ishbosheth for the throne vacated by the death of Saul. At the pool of Gibeon, the troops of the two parties met and a fierce battle ensued in which Joab's men were victorious. During the battle, Abner, the commander of Ishbosheth's forces, slew Asahel, a younger brother of Joab, and thus incurred the hate of David's general. After Abner broke with Ishbosheth and made an alliance with David, Joab lured him into a private meeting where he treacherously murdered him.

Joab was doubtless a key figure in enabling David to maintain his strong position, and figured in several major battles with neighboring nations. It was he also who arranged the death of Uriah the Hittite when David sinned with his wife, Bath-sheba. Joab played a major role in securing the return of Absalom from Geshur, to which he had gone after killing Amnon for the rape of his sister Tamar. (*See* ABSALOM) When Absalom revolted, however, Joab remained with David and, in fact, personally thrust three darts into the heart of the rebel as he hung in a tree. After the revolt had been successfully defeated, David returned from Mahanaim, to which he had been forced to flee. His first official action at his return was to appoint Amasa to be commander of the army in Joab's place. In a subsequent battle against Sheba, Joab assassinated Amasa and assumed command of the king's forces once again.

At the death of David, Joab supported Adonijah instead of Solomon and was slain by Benaiah, on Solomon's orders, while holding onto the horns of the altar.

See ABSALOM, ABNER, DAVID, ISHBOSHETH, SOLOMON

SCRIPTURE

Slays Abner

2 Sam. 3 [26]And when Joab was come out
from David, he sent messengers after Abner, which brought him again from the
well of Sirah: but David knew it not.
[27]And when Abner was returned to Hebron, Joab took him aside in the gate to
speak with him quietly, and smote him
there under the fifth rib, that he died, for
the blood of Asahel his brother.

[28]And afterward when David heard it,
he said, I and my kingdom are guiltless before the LORD for ever from the blood of
Abner the son of Ner:

See 2 Sam. 2

David's General

2 Sam. 8 [15]And David reigned over all
Israel; and David executed judgment and
justice unto all his people. [16]And Joab the
son of Zeruiah was over the host; and Jehoshaphat the son of Ahilud was recorder;

Slays Absalom

2 Sam. 18 [5]And the king commanded
Joab and Abishai and Ittai, saying, Deal
gently for my sake with the young man,
even with Absalom. And all the people
heard when the king gave all the captains
charge concerning Absalom.

9And Absalom met the servants of David. And Absalom rode upon a mule, and the mule went under the thick boughs of a great oak, and his head caught hold of the oak, and he was taken up between the heaven and the earth; and the mule that was under him went away. 10And a certain man saw it, and told Joab, and said, Behold, I saw Absalom hanged in an oak. 11And Joab said unto the man that told him, And, behold, thou sawest him, and why didst thou not smite him there to the ground? and I would have given thee ten shekels of silver, and a girdle. 12And the man said unto Joab, Though I should receive a thousand shekels of silver in mine hand, yet would I not put forth mine hand against the king's son: for in our hearing the king charged thee and Abishai and Ittai, saying, Beware that none touch the young man Absalom. 13Otherwise I should have wrought falsehood against mine own life: for there is no matter hid from the king, and thou thyself wouldest have set thyself against me. 14Then said Joab, I may not tarry thus with thee. And he took three darts in his hand, and thrust them through the heart of Absalom, while he was yet alive in the midst of the oak.

Amasa Appointed to Joab's Position

2 Sam. 19 13Say ye to Amasa, Art thou not of my bone, and of my flesh? God do so to me, and more also, if thou be not captain of the host before me continually in the room of Joab.

Joab Regains His Place

2 Sam. 20 9And Joab said to Amasa, Art thou in health, my brother? And Joab took Amasa by the beard with the right hand to kiss him. 10But Amasa took no heed to the sword that was in Joab's hand: so he smote him therewith in the fifth rib, and shed out his bowels to the ground, and struck him not again; and he died. So Joab and Abishai his brother pursued after Sheba the son of Bichri.

22Then the woman went unto all the people in her wisdom: and they cut off the head of Sheba the son of Bichri, and cast it out to Joab. And he blew a trumpet, and they retired from the city, every man to his tent. And Joab returned to Jerusalem unto the king.

23Now Joab was over all the host of Israel: and Benaiah the son of Jehoiada was over the Cherethites and over the Pelethites:

Supports Adonijah Against Solomon

1 Kin. 1 5Then Adonijah the son of Haggith exalted himself, saying, I will be king: and he prepared him chariots and horsemen, and fifty men to run before him. 7And he conferred with Joab the son of Zeruiah, and with Abiathar the priest: and they following Adonijah helped him.

Slain by Order of Solomon

1 Kin. 2 12Then sat Solomon upon the throne of David his father; and his kingdom was established greatly.

28Then tidings came to Joab: for Joab had turned after Adonijah, though he turned not after Absalom. And Joab fled unto the tabernacle of the LORD, and caught hold on the horns of the altar. 29And it was told king Solomon that Joab was fled unto the tabernacle of the LORD; and, behold, he is by the altar. Then Solomon sent Benaiah the son of Jehoiada, saying, Go, fall upon him. 30And Benaiah came to the tabernacle of the LORD, and said unto him, Thus saith the king, Come forth. And he said, Nay; but I will die here. And Benaiah brought the king word again, saying, Thus said Joab, and thus he answered me. [31]And the king said unto him, Do as he hath said, and fall upon him, and bury him; that thou mayest take away the innocent blood, which Joab shed, from me, and from the house of my father. [32]And the LORD shall return his blood upon his own head, who fell upon two men more righteous and better than he, and slew them with the sword, my father David not knowing thereof, to wit, Abner the son of Ner, captain of the host of Israel, and Amasa the son of Jether, captain of the host of Judah. [33]Their blood shall therefore return upon the head of Joab, and upon the head of his seed for ever; but upon David, and upon his seed, and upon his house, and upon his throne, shall there be peace for ever from the LORD. [34]So Benaiah the son of Jehoiada went up, and fell upon him, and slew him: and he was buried in his own house in the wilderness.

JOB

[jōb] The hero of one of the most remarkable books of the Bible. The picture which is given of Job is that of a patriarch distinguished for his integrity and piety, his wealth, and the great measure of domestic happiness these things have brought. In order to prove Job's fidelity, God allowed Satan to deprive him of all these blessings, most of which are eventually restored. The book is in the form of a historical poem; that is, a poem which purports to be based on an actual event. This event was an apparently public debate over the nature and cause of Job's afflictions, the contestants being Job and his friends, Bildad, Zophar, Eliphaz, and Elihu. It is a philosophic discussion of the problem of human suffering—a classic problem which has not as yet received a classic answer. The book is a witness to the fact that God's people in all times have frustrated in their efforts to reconcile His moral law with the prosperity of the wicked and the affliction of the righteous.

Although the book of Job does not furnish a neatly organized solution to the problem of evil, it does illustrate several common shortcomings typical of man's efforts to fathom the secrets of God. The outlook of Job's friends was limited by their conception of the direct ratio between suffering and affliction. Job, although he could give no reason for the misery which was his, denied that great personal sin was the cause. The reader, informed by the prologue, is able to see in Job's affliction an indication of God's confidence in his servant rather than his displeasure. The lesson to be gained from a study of Job's life is that man, since he does not have access to the "prologue" of his own life, can never adequately plumb the depths of God's dealings with men; nevertheless, he is encouraged to maintain fidelity in his devotion to God, assured that God's ultimate purposes are loving and merciful.

SCRIPTURE

Job's Prosperity

Job 1 [1]There was a man in the land of Uz, whose name was Job; and that man was perfect and upright, and one that feared God, and eschewed evil. [2]And there were born unto him seven sons and three daughters. [3]His substance also was seven thousand sheep, and three thousand camels, and five hundred yoke of oxen, and five hundred she-asses, and a very great household; so that this man was the greatest of all the men of the east. [4]And his sons went and feasted in their houses, every one his day; and sent and called for their three sisters to eat and to drink with them. [5]And it was so, when the days of their feasting were gone about, that Job sent and sanctified them, and rose up early in the morning, and offered burnt offerings according to the number of them all: for Job said, It may be that my sons have sinned, and cursed God in their hearts. Thus did Job continually.

Satan's Bargain with God

Job 1 [6]Now there was a day when the sons of God came to present themselves

before the LORD, and Satan came also
among them. 7And the LORD said unto Satan, Whence comest thou? Then Satan answered the LORD, and said, From going to
and fro in the earth, and from walking up
and down in it. 8And the LORD said unto
Satan, Hast thou considered my servant
Job, that there is none like him in the earth,
a perfect and an upright man, one that
feareth God, and escheweth evil? 9Then
Satan answered the LORD, and said, Doth
Job fear God for nought? 10Hast not thou
made a hedge about him, and about his
house, and about all that he hath on every
side? thou hast blessed the work of his
hands, and his substance is increased in
the land. 11But put forth thine hand now,
and touch all that he hath, and he will
curse thee to thy face. 12And the LORD said
unto Satan, Behold, all that he hath is in
thy power; only upon himself put not forth
thine hand. So Satan went forth from the
presence of the LORD.

Job's Afflictions

Job 1 13And there was a day when his
sons and his daughters were eating and
drinking wine in their eldest brother's
house: 14And there came a messenger unto
Job, and said, The oxen were ploughing,
and the asses feeding beside them: 15And
the Sabeans fell upon them, and took them
away; yea, they have slain the servants
with the edge of the sword; and I only am
escaped alone to tell thee. 16While he was
yet speaking, there came also another, and
said, The fire of God is fallen from heaven,
and hath burned up the sheep, and the
servants, and consumed them; and I only
am escaped alone to tell thee. 17While he
was yet speaking, there came also another,
and said, The Chaldeans made out three
bands, and fell upon the camels, and have
carried them away, yea, and slain the servants with the edge of the sword; and I only
am escaped alone to tell thee. 18While he
was yet speaking, there came also another,
and said, Thy sons and thy daughters were
eating and drinking wine in their eldest
brother's house: 19And, behold, there
came a great wind from the wilderness,
and smote the four corners of the house,
and it fell upon the young men, and they
are dead; and I only am escaped alone to
tell thee. 20Then Job arose, and rent his
mantle, and shaved his head, and fell down
upon the ground, and worshipped, 21And
said, Naked came I out of my mother's
womb, and naked shall I return thither:
the LORD gave, and the LORD hath taken
away; blessed be the name of the LORD.
22In all this Job sinned not, nor charged
God foolishly.

Job 2 1Again there was a day when the
sons of God came to present themselves
before the LORD, and Satan came also
among them to present himself before the
LORD. 2And the LORD said unto Satan,
From whence comest thou? And Satan answered the LORD, and said, From going to
and fro in the earth, and from walking up
and down in it. 3And the LORD said unto
Satan, Hast thou considered my servant
Job, that there is none like him in the earth,
a perfect and an upright man, one that
feareth God, and escheweth evil? and still
he holdeth fast his integrity, although thou
movedst me against him, to destroy him
without cause. 4And Satan answered the
LORD, and said, Skin for skin, yea, all that a
man hath will be give for his life. 5But put
forth thine hand now, and touch his bone
and his flesh, and he will curse thee to thy
face. 6And the LORD said unto Satan, Behold, he is in thine hand; but save his life.

7So went Satan forth from the presence
of the LORD, and smote Job with sore boils
from the sole of his foot unto his crown.

8And he took him a potsherd to scrape himself withal; and he sat down among the ashes.

9Then said his wife unto him, Dost thou still retain thine integrity? curse God, and die. 10But he said unto her, Thou speakest as one of the foolish women speaketh. What? shall we receive good at the hand of God, and shall we not receive evil? In all this did not Job sin with his lips.

Job's Friends

Job 2 11Now when Job's three friends heard of all this evil that was come upon him, they came every one from his own place; Eliphaz the Temanite, and Bildad the Shuhite, and Zophar the Naamathite: for they had made an appointment together to come to mourn with him, and to comfort him. 12And when they lifted up their eyes afar off, and knew him not, they lifted up their voice, and wept; and they rent every one his mantle, and sprinkled dust upon their heads toward heaven. 13So they sat down with him upon the ground seven days and seven nights, and none spake a word unto him: for they saw that his grief was very great.

Job's Confidence in the Lord

Job 42 1Then Job answered the LORD, and said, 2I know that thou canst do every thing, and that no thought can be withholden from thee. 3Who is he that hideth counsel without knowledge? therefore have I uttered that I understood not; things too wonderful for me, which I knew not. 4Hear, I beseech thee, and I will speak: I will demand of thee, and declare thou unto me. 5I have heard of thee by the hearing of the ear; but now mine eye seeth thee: 6Wherefore I abhor myself, and repent in dust and ashes.

God's Wrath against Job's Friends

Job 42 7And it was so, that after the LORD had spoken these words unto Job, the LORD said to Eliphaz the Temanite, My wrath is kindled against thee, and against thy two friends: for ye have not spoken of me the thing that is right, as my servant Job hath. 8Therefore take unto you now seven bullocks and seven rams, and go to my servant Job, and offer up for yourselves a burnt offering; and my servant Job shall pray for you: for him will I accept: lest I deal with you after your folly, in that ye have not spoken of me the thing which is right, like my servant Job. 9So Eliphaz the Temanite and Bildad the Shuhite and Zophar the Naamathite went, and did according as the LORD commanded them: the LORD also accepted Job.

Job's Fortunes Restored

Job 42 10And the LORD turned the captivity of Job, when he prayed for his friends: also the LORD gave Job twice as much as he had before. 11Then came there unto him all his brethren, and all his sisters, and all they that had been of his acquaintance before, and did eat bread with him in his house: and they bemoaned him, and comforted him over all the evil that the LORD had brought upon him: every man also gave him a piece of money, and every one an earring of gold. 12So the LORD blessed the latter end of Job more than his beginning: for he had fourteen thousand sheep, and six thousand camels, and a thousand yoke of oxen, and a thousand she-asses. 13He had also seven sons and three daughters. 14And he called the name of the first, Jemima; and the name of the second, Kezia; and the name of the third, Keren-happuch. 15And in all the land were no women found so fair as the daughters of Job: and their father gave them inheritance among their brethren. [16]After this lived Job a hundred and forty years, and saw his sons, and his sons' sons, even four generations. [17]So Job died, being old and full of days.

JOEL

[jō'el] One of the so-called "minor" prophets. Apart from the fact that he was the son of Pethuel, nothing can be said of Joel with any degree of certainty. His many references to Jerusalem imply that he was a native of Judah. The time of his prophetic activity was probably about 400 BC, although there is considerable dispute over this point. The occasion of Joel's prophecy was an unparalleled locust plague. This great hardship offered Joel a propitious opportunity to speak of a greater judgment which was to befall the nation and to call for a season of fasting, mourning, and repentance.

The vivid description, the intense call to action, and the careful, faultless style of Joel's prophecy have made this short work a classic of Hebrew literature.

SCRIPTURE

The Vision of the Locusts

Joel 1 [4]That which the palmerworm hath left hath the locust eaten; and that which the locust hath left hath the cankerworm eaten; and that which the cankerworm hath left hath the caterpillar eaten.

The Outpouring of the Spirit of God

Joel 2 [23]Be glad then, ye children of Zion, and rejoice in the LORD your God: for he hath given you the former rain moderately, and he will cause to come down for you the rain, the former rain, and the latter rain in the first month. [24]And the floors shall be full of wheat, and the fats shall overflow with wine and oil. [25]And I will restore to you the years that the locust hath eaten, the cankerworm, and the caterpillar, and the palmerworm, my great army which I sent among you. [26]And ye shall eat in plenty, and be satisfied, and praise the name of the LORD your God, that hath dealt wondrously with you: and my people shall never be ashamed. [27]And ye shall know that I am in the midst of Israel, and that I am the LORD your God, and none else: and my people shall never be ashamed.

[28]And it shall come to pass afterward, that I will pour out my Spirit upon all flesh; and your sons and your daughters shall prophesy, your old men shall dream dreams, your young men shall see visions: [29]And also upon the servants and upon the handmaids in those days will I pour out my Spirit. [30]And I will shew wonders in the heavens and in the earth, blood, and fire, and pillars of smoke. [31]The sun shall be turned into darkness, and the moon into blood, before the great and the terrible day of the LORD come. [32]And it shall come to pass, that whosoever shall call on the name of the LORD shall be delivered: for in mount Zion and in Jerusalem shall be deliverance, as the LORD hath said, and in the remnant whom the LORD shall call.

JOHANAN

[jō hā'nan] A loyal Jewish soldier who allied himself with Gedaliah, governor of the province of Judah after the fall of Jerusalem and subsequent deportation of Babylon. It was Johanan who sought unsuccessfully to warn Gedaliah of the plot against his life which was being hatched by Ishmael, another commander in the Jewish army. After the assassination of Gedaliah, Johanan pursued Ishmael and his band but was unable to prevent his escape to the Ammonites, who had supported him in his treachery. Fearing that the Babylonians would lay the blame for Gedaliah's death on them, Johanan and his fellow-soldiers forced the group of refugees, which had gathered around Gedaliah, to emigrate to Egypt, ignoring the fervent entreaties of the prophet Jeremiah.

See Gedaliah, Ishmael, Jeremiah

SCRIPTURE

Jer. 40 [13]Moreover Johanan the son of Kareah, and all the captains of the forces that were in the fields, came to Gedaliah to Mizpah, [14]And said unto him, Dost thou certainly know that Baalis the king of the Ammonites hath sent Ishmael the son of Nethaniah to slay thee? But Gedaliah the son of Ahikam believed them not. [15]Then Johanan the son of Kareah spake to Gedaliah in Mizpah secretly, saying, Let me go, I pray thee, and I will slay Ishmael the son of Nethaniah, and no man shall know it: wherefore should he slay thee, that all the Jews which are gathered unto thee should be scattered, and the remnant in Judah perish? [16]But Gedaliah the son of Ahikam said unto Johanan the son of Kareah, Thou shalt not do this thing: for thou speakest falsely of Ishmael.

Jer. 41 [11]But when Johanan the son of Kareah, and all the captains of the forces that were with him, heard of all the evil that Ishmael the son of Nethaniah had done, [12]Then they took all the men, and went to fight with Ishmael the son of Nethaniah, and found him by the great waters that are in Gibeon. [13]Now it came to pass, that when all the people which were with Ishmael saw Johanan the son of Kareah, and all the captains of the forces that were with him, then they were glad. [14]So all the people that Ishmael had carried away captive from Mizpah cast about and returned, and went unto Johanan the son of Kareah. [15]But Ishmael the son of Nethaniah escaped from Johanan with eight men, and went to the Ammonites.

Jer. 43 [4]So Johanan the son of Kareah, and all the captains of the forces, and all the people, obeyed not the voice of the Lord, to dwell in the land of Judah. [5]But Johanan the son of Kareah, and all the captains of the forces, took all the remnant of Judah, that were returned from all nations, whither they had been driven, to dwell in the land of Judah; [6]Even men, and women, and children, and the king's daughters, and every person that Nebuzaradan the captain of the guard had left with Gedaliah the son of Ahikam the son of Shaphan, and Jeremiah the prophet, and Baruch the son of Neriah. [7]So they came into the land of Egypt: for they obeyed not the voice of the Lord: thus came they even to Tahpanhes.

JOHN

[jon] The son of Salome and Zebedee, a fisherman on the sea of Galilee, and brother of James, also an apostle. Peter, James and John formed what has been called the "inner circle" of Jesus' disciples; of the apostles, only these three were present on such occasions as the raising of Jairus' daughter, the transfiguration, and the ordeal of the Garden of Gethsemane. Peter seems to have been the leader of this group, but John is referred to as "the disciple whom Jesus loved." That he was a man of fiery zeal is indicated by the name Boanerges which was given to James and John, meaning Son of Thunder. Despite their close association with Jesus, the two brothers were rebuked by him for their misunderstanding of the nature of his kingdom and their ambition for worldly power. At the crucifixion, Jesus entrusted the care of his mother to this disciple whom he loved. John was one of the outstanding leaders in the early church and is credited with having written the fourth gospel, three epistles, and *Revelation.* Tradition has it that the latter part of his life was spent in Ephesus, where he enjoyed a fruitful ministry.

Chosen by Jesus

Matt. 4 [21]And going on from thence, he saw other two brethren, James the son of Zebedee, and John his brother, in a ship with Zebedee their father, mending their nets; and he called them. 22And they immediately left the ship and their father, and followed him.

At the Transfiguration

Matt. 17 1And after six days Jesus taketh Peter, James, and John his brother, and bringeth them up into a high mountain apart, 2And was transfigured before them: and his face did shine as the sun, and his raiment was white as the light.

Asks for Privileged Position

Mark 10 35And James and John, the sons of Zebedee, come unto him, saying, Master, we would that thou shouldest do for us whatsoever we shall desire. 36And he said unto them, What would ye that I should do for you? 37They said unto him, Grant unto us that we may sit, one on thy right hand, and the other on thy left hand, in thy glory. 38But Jesus said unto them, Ye know not what ye ask: can ye drink of the cup that I drink of? and be baptized with the baptism that I am baptized with? 39And they said unto him, We can. And Jesus said unto them, Ye shall indeed drink of the cup that I drink of; and with the baptism that I am baptized withal shall ye be baptized: 40But to sit on my right hand and on my left hand is not mine to give; but it shall be given to them for whom it is prepared. 41And when the ten heard it, they began to be much displeased with James and John.

At Gethsemane

Mark 14 32And they came to a place which was named Gethsemane: and he saith to his disciples, Sit ye here, while I shall pray. 33And he taketh with him Peter and James and John, and began to be sore amazed, and to be very heavy;

At Jesus' Trial

John 18 15And Simon Peter followed Jesus, and so did another disciple: that disciple was known unto the high priest, and went in with Jesus into the palace of the high priest. 16But Peter stood at the door without. Then went out that other disciple, which was known unto the high priest, and spake unto her that kept the door, and brought in Peter.

At the Crucifixion

John 19 26When Jesus therefore saw his mother, and the disciple standing by, whom he loved, he saith unto his mother, Woman, behold thy son! 27Then saith he to the disciple, Behold thy mother! And from that hour that disciple took her unto his own home.

Learns of the Resurrection

John 20 2Then she runneth, and cometh to Simon Peter, and to the other disciple, whom Jesus loved, and saith unto them, They have taken away the Lord out of the sepulchre, and we know not where they have laid him.

On the Isle of Patmos

Rev. 1 9I John, who also am your brother, and companion in tribulation, and in the kingdom and patience of Jesus Christ, was in the isle that is called Patmos, for the word of God, and for the testimony of Jesus Christ.

REFERENCE: *Matt. 10:3; 17:1; 20:20-24; 26:37; Mark 5:37; 9:2; Luke 5:10; Acts 1:13; 3:1-11; 4:1-9; 8:14-17; Gal. 2:9.*

JOHN THE BAPTIST

[jon, bap'tist] The forerunner of Jesus. John was the son of Zacharias and Elisabeth, who was a cousin of Mary the mother of Jesus. He was born six months prior to Jesus, his birth having been foretold by the angel Gabriel. Nothing is known of his youth, but after a long period of seclusion he came forth from the desert to take up his ministry, garbed like the ancient prophets, in garments of camel's hair fastened to his body with a leather girdle, and eating locusts and wild honey. John's hard ascetic life, his extraordinary appearance, and the character of his messages enabled him to gather a considerable band of disciples about himself. There is no question but that John could have given Jesus much trouble in the beginning of his ministry had he chosen to assume the higher office, but he was faithful to his divine trust, and always showed in his sermons that he was but the messenger of another greater than himself; this is clearly seen in his reaction to Jesus' request for baptism at his hands. After the appearance of Jesus, John's ministry becomes somewhat obscure. It is likely, however, that he continued in his work subordinate to Jesus. The manner of his death is well known. John was arrested following his rebuke of Herod Antipas for his marriage to Herodias, whom he had seduced away from his brother Herod Philip. At Herod's birthday celebration, Herodias' daughter performed a sensual dance which so pleased the king that he offered her any gift which she might request. Herodias persuaded her daughter to ask for the head of John the Baptist in a serving tray. Herod feared the reaction of the multitude who followed John, but kept his promise and ordered his execution. John is eulogized by Jesus as "the greatest of those born of woman."

See Jesus, Herod Antipas, Herodias, Zacharias, Gabriel

SCRIPTURE

Birth and Early Years

Luke 1 57 Now Elisabeth's full time
came that she should be delivered; and
she brought forth a son. 58 And her neighbours and her cousins heard how the
Lord had shewed great mercy upon her;
and they rejoiced with her. 59 And it came
to pass, that on the eighth day they came
to circumcise the child; and they called
him Zacharias, after the name of his father. 60 And his mother answered and said,
Not so; but he shall be called John. 61 And
they said unto her, There is none of thy
kindred that is called by this name. 62 And
they made signs to his father, how he
would have him called. 63 And he asked
for a writing table, and wrote, saying, His
name is John. And they marvelled all.
80 And the child grew, and waxed strong
in spirit, and was in the deserts till the day
of his shewing unto Israel.

Ministry

Matt. 3 1 In those days came John the
Baptist, preaching in the wilderness of Judea, 2 And saying, Repent ye: for the kingdom of heaven is at hand. 3 For this is he
that was spoken of by the prophet Esaias,
saying, The voice of one crying in the wilderness, Prepare ye the way of the Lord,
make his paths straight. 4 And the same
John had his raiment of camel's hair, and
a leathern girdle about his loins; and his
meat was locusts and wild honey. 5 Then
went out to him Jerusalem, and all Judea,
and all the region round about Jordan,
6 And were baptized of him in Jordan, confessing their sins.

7 But when he saw many of the Pharisees
and Sadducees come to his baptism, he
said unto them, O generation of vipers,
who hath warned you to flee from the
wrath to come? 8 Bring forth therefore
fruits meet for repentance: 9 And think
not to say within yourselves, We have
Abraham to our father: for I say unto you,
that God is able of these stones to raise up
children unto Abraham. 10 And now also
the axe is laid unto the root of the trees:
therefore every tree which bringeth not
forth good fruit is hewn down, and cast
into the fire. 11 I indeed baptize you with
water unto repentance: but he that com-

eth after me is mightier than I, whose shoes I am not worthy to bear: he shall baptize you with the Holy Ghost, and with fire: [12]Whose fan is in his hand, and he will thoroughly purge his floor, and gather his wheat into the garner; but he will burn up the chaff with unquenchable fire.

[13]Then cometh Jesus from Galilee to Jordan unto John, to be baptized of him. [14]But John forbade him, saying, I have need to be baptized of thee, and comest thou to me? [15]And Jesus answering said unto him, Suffer it to be so now: for thus it becometh us to fulfil all righteousness. Then he suffered him.

Imprisonment

Luke 3 [18]And many other things in his exhortation preached he unto the people. [19]But Herod the tetrarch, being reproved by him for Herodias his brother Philip's wife, and for all the evils which Herod had done, [20]Added yet this above all, that he shut up John in prison.

Praised by Jesus

Luke 7 [19]And John calling unto him two of his disciples sent them to Jesus, saying, Art thou he that should come? or look we for another? [20]When the men were come unto him, they said, John Baptist hath sent us unto thee, saying, Art thou he that should come? or look we for another? [21]And in that same hour he cured many of their infirmities and plagues, and of evil spirits; and unto many that were blind he gave sight. [22]Then Jesus answering said unto them, Go your way, and tell John what things ye have seen and heard; how that the blind see, the lame walk, the lepers are cleansed, the deaf hear, the dead are raised, to the poor the gospel is preached. [23]And blessed is he, whosoever shall not be offended in me.

[24]And when the messengers of John were departed, he began to speak unto the people concerning John, What went ye out into the wilderness for to see? A reed shaken with the wind? [25]But what went ye out for to see? A man clothed in soft raiment? Behold, they which are gorgeously apparelled, and live delicately, are in kings' courts. [26]But what went ye out for to see? A prophet? Yea, I say unto you, and much more than a prophet. [27]This is he, of whom it is written, Behold, I send my messenger before thy face, which shall prepare thy way before thee. [28]For I say unto you, Among those that are born of women there is not a greater prophet than John the Baptist: but he that is least in the kingdom of God is greater than he.

Death

Matt. 14 [1]At that time Herod the tetrarch heard of the fame of Jesus, [2]And said unto his servants, This is John the Baptist; he is risen from the dead; and therefore mighty works do shew forth themselves in him.

[3]For Herod had laid hold on John, and bound him, and put him in prison for Herodias' sake, his brother Philip's wife. [4]For John said unto him, It is not lawful for thee to have her. [5]And when he would have put him to death, he feared the multitude, because they counted him as a prophet. [6]But when Herod's birthday was kept, the daughter of Herodias danced before them, and pleased Herod. [7]Whereupon he promised with an oath to give her whatsoever she would ask. [8]And she, being before instructed of her mother, said, Give me here John the Baptist's head in a

charger. [9]And the king was sorry: nevertheless for the oath's sake, and them that sat with him at meat, he commanded it to be given her. [10]And he sent, and beheaded John in the prison. [11]And his head was brought in a charger, and given to the damsel: and she brought it to her mother. [12]And his disciples came, and took up the body, and buried it, and went and told Jesus.

A Second Elijah

Matt. 17 [9]And as they came down from the mountain, Jesus charged them, saying, Tell the vision to no man, until the Son of man be risen again from the dead. [10]And the disciples asked him, saying, Why then say the scribes that Elias must first come? [11]And Jesus answered and said unto them, Elias truly shall first come, and restore all things. [12]But I say unto you, that Elias is come already, and they knew him not, but have done unto him whatsoever they listed. Likewise shall also the Son of man suffer of them. [13]Then the disciples understood that he spake unto them of John the Baptist.

JONAH

[jō′na] The chief character of the book which bears his name. The story of Jonah is one of the most familiar of the Old Testament. Jonah, a prophet of God, is called to deliver a message of repentance to Nineveh, the capital city of the Assyrians. Since Nineveh was already in the process of destroying the Jews, Jonah sought to avoid discharging his commission and boarded a ship bound for Tarshish. He was cast overboard by the sailors in the midst of a storm and swallowed by a great sea monster which the LORD had provided for this purpose.

After being released from the fish, Jonah preached his message to Nineveh and was able to bring about their repentance. Because of his hostility toward this Gentile nation, Jonah began to brood. God, by the lesson of the gourd, showed Jonah that he was concerned for other nations besides Israel.

SCRIPTURE

God's Charge to Jonah

Jonah 1 [1]Now the word of the LORD came unto Jonah the son of Amittai, saying, [2]Arise, go to Nineveh, that great city, and cry against it; for their wickedness is come up before me.

Jonah Tries to Escape

Jonah 1 [3]But Jonah rose up to flee unto Tarshish from the presence of the LORD, and went down to Joppa; and he found a ship going to Tarshish: so he paid the fare thereof, and went down into it, to go with them unto Tarshish from the presence of the LORD.

The Storm

Jonah 1 [4]But the LORD sent out a great wind into the sea, and there was a mighty tempest in the sea, so that the ship was like to be broken. [5]Then the mariners were afraid, and cried every man unto his god, and cast forth the wares that were in the ship into the sea, to lighten it of them. But Jonah was gone down into the sides of the ship; and he lay, and was fast asleep. [6]So the shipmaster came to him, and said unto him, What meanest thou, O sleeper? arise, call upon thy God, if so be that God will think upon us, that we perish not.

Jonah Cast Overboard

Jonah 1 [7]And they said every one to his fellow, Come, and let us cast lots, that we may know for whose cause this evil is upon us. So they cast lots, and the lot fell upon Jonah. [8]Then said they unto him, Tell us, we pray thee, for whose cause this evil is upon us; What is thine occupation? and whence comest thou? what is thy country? and of what people art thou? 9And he said unto them, I am a Hebrew; and I fear the LORD, the God of heaven, which hath made the sea and the dry land. 10Then were the men exceedingly afraid, and said unto him, Why hast thou done this? For the men knew that he fled from the presence of the LORD, because he had told them.

11Then said they unto him, What shall we do unto thee, that the sea may be calm unto us? for the sea wrought, and was tempestuous. 12And he said unto them, Take me up, and cast me forth into the sea; so shall the sea be calm unto you: for I know that for my sake this great tempest is upon you. 13Nevertheless the men rowed hard to bring it to the land; but they could not: for the sea wrought, and was tempestuous against them. 14Wherefore they cried unto the LORD, and said, We beseech thee, O LORD, we beseech thee, let us not perish for this man's life, and lay not upon us innocent blood: for thou, O LORD, hast done as it pleased thee. 15So they took up Jonah, and cast him forth into the sea: and the sea ceased from her raging. 16Then the men feared the LORD exceedingly, and offered a sacrifice unto the LORD, and made vows.

Swallowed by Great Fish

Jonah 1 17Now the LORD had prepared a great fish to swallow up Jonah. And Jonah was in the belly of the fish three days and three nights.

Released from the Fish

Jonah 2 10And the LORD spake unto the fish, and it vomited out Jonah upon the dry land.

Preaches in Nineveh

Jonah 3 1And the word of the LORD came unto Jonah the second time, saying, 2Arise, go unto Nineveh, that great city, and preach unto it the preaching that I bid thee. 3So Jonah arose, and went unto Nineveh, according to the word of the LORD. Now Nineveh was an exceeding great city of three days' journey. 4And Jonah began to enter into the city a day's journey, and he cried, and said, Yet forty days, and Nineveh shall be overthrown.

5So the people of Nineveh believed God, and proclaimed a fast, and put on sackcloth, from the greatest of them even to the least of them.

Jonah Sulks Over Nineveh's Repentance

Jonah 4 1But it displeased Jonah exceedingly, and he was very angry. 2And he prayed unto the LORD and said, I pray thee, O LORD, was not this my saying, when I was yet in my country? Therefore I fled before unto Tarshish: for I knew that thou art a gracious God, and merciful, slow to anger, and of great kindness, and repentest thee of the evil. 3Therefore now, O LORD, take, I beseech thee, my life from me; for it is better for me to die than to live.

4Then said the LORD, Doest thou well to be angry? 5So Jonah went out of the city, and sat on the east side of the city, and there made him a booth, and sat under it in the shadow, till he might see what would become of the city.

God's Lesson to Jonah

Jonah 4 6And the LORD God prepared a gourd, and made it to come up over Jonah, that it might be a shadow over his head, to deliver him from his grief. So Jonah was exceeding glad of the gourd.

7 But God prepared a worm when the morning rose the next day, and it smote the gourd that it withered. 8 And it came to pass, when the sun did arise, that God prepared a vehement east wind; and the sun beat upon the head of Jonah, that he fainted, and wished in himself to die, and said, It is better for me to die than to live. 9 And God said to Jonah, Doest thou well to be angry for the gourd? And he said, I do well to be angry, even unto death. *10* Then said the LORD, Thou hast had pity on the gourd, for the which thou hast not laboured, neither madest it grow; which came up in a night, and perished in a night: *11* And should not I spare Nineveh, that great city, wherein are more than sixscore thousand persons that can not discern between their right hand and their left hand; and also much cattle?

JONATHAN

[jon'a than] The eldest son of King Saul. Jonathan first appears as a daring and courageous soldier, serving in his father's army. His position seems to have been that of commander of the garrison at Gibeah, Saul's headquarters. In a campaign against the Philistines, Jonathan and his armor-bearer audaciously slaughtered an outpost of about twenty men. This bold venture threw the Philistine camp into a panic and enabled Israel to effect a complete rout. Despite his contribution to this victory, Jonathan was nearly executed because he had unwittingly broken a foolish vow of abstinence from food which Saul had made. The people, however, out of gratitude for Jonathan's bravery refused to allow Saul to put him to death.

A warm friendship of the most devoted type developed between Jonathan and David after the latter came to the court of Saul, enduring through the terrible days when Saul was seeking David's life. In fact, it was through information relayed by Jonathan that David was warned to flee for his life after Saul grew insanely jealous of him. When Jonathan was killed alongside his father in the battle with the Philistines at Giboa, his body was hung, with those of his brethren and his father, on the walls of Bethshan. They were removed under cover of darkness by the men of Jabesh-gilead, who then burned them and buried the bones. In later years, David recovered the bones and reburied them in the tomb of Kish, Saul's father. David's lament over Saul and Jonathan is a eulogy of exquisite dignity and pathos:

"Saul and Jonathan were lovely and pleasant in their lives, and in their death they were not divided: they were swifter than eagles, they were stronger than lions. Ye daughters of Israel, weep over Saul, who clothed you in scarlet, with other delights; who put on ornaments of gold upon your apparel. How are the mighty fallen in the midst of the battle! O Jonathan, thou wast slain in thine high places. I am distressed for thee, my brother Jonathan: very pleasant hast thou been unto me: thy love to me was wonderful, passing the love of women. How are the mighty fallen, and the weapons of war perished!" (*2 Sam. 1:23-27*).

See DAVID, SAUL

SCRIPTURE

Defeats the Philistines

1 Sam. 14 1 Now it came to pass upon a day, that Jonathan the son of Saul said unto the young man that bare his armour, Come, and let us go over to the Philistines' garrison, that is on the other side. But he told not his father.

13 And Jonathan climbed up upon his hands and upon his feet, and his armourbearer after him: and they fell before Jonathan; and his armourbearer slew after him. *14* And that first slaughter, which Jonathan and his armourbearer made, was about twenty men, within as it were a half acre of land, which a yoke of oxen might plough.

Breaks Saul's Foolish Vow

1 Sam. 14 27 But Jonathan heard not

when his father charged the people with the oath: wherefore he put forth the end of the rod that was in his hand, and dipped it in a honeycomb, and put his hand to his mouth; and his eyes were enlightened. [28]Then answered one of the people, and said, Thy father straitly charged the people with an oath, saying, Cursed be the man that eateth any food this day. And the people were faint. [29]Then said Jonathan, My father hath troubled the land: see, I pray you, how mine eyes have been enlightened, because I tasted a little of this honey.

[43]Then Saul said to Jonathan, Tell me what thou hast done. And Jonathan told him, and said, I did but taste a little honey with the end of the rod that was in mine hand, and, lo, I must die. [44]And Saul answered, God do so and more also: for thou shalt surely die, Jonathan. [45]And the people said unto Saul, Shall Jonathan die, who hath wrought this great salvation in Israel? God forbid: as the LORD liveth, there shall not one hair of his head fall to the ground; for he hath wrought with God this day. So the people rescued Jonathan, that he died not.

Friendship with David

1 Sam. 18 [1]And it came to pass, when he had made an end of speaking unto Saul, that the soul of Jonathan was knit with the soul of David, and Jonathan loved him as his own soul. [2]And Saul took him that day, and would let him go no more home to his father's house. [3]Then Jonathan and David made a covenant, because he loved him as his own soul. [4]And Jonathan stripped himself of the robe that was upon him, and gave it to David, and his garments, even to his sword, and to his bow, and to his girdle.

1 Sam. 19 [4]And Jonathan spake good of David unto Saul his father, and said unto him, Let not the king sin against his servant, against David; because he hath not sinned against thee, and because his works have been to thee-ward very good:

Warns David of Saul's Anger

1 Sam. 20 [13]The LORD do so much more to Jonathan: but if it please my father to do thee evil, then I will shew it thee, and send thee away, that thou mayest go in peace: and the LORD be with thee, as he hath been with my father. [20]And I will shoot three arrows on the side thereof, as though I shot at a mark. [21]And, behold, I will send a lad, saying, Go, find out the arrows. If I expressly say unto the lad, Behold, the arrows are on this side of thee, take them; then come thou: for there is peace to thee, and no hurt; as the LORD liveth. [22]But if I say thus unto the young man, Behold, the arrows are beyond thee; go thy way: for the LORD hath sent thee away.

[36]And he said unto his lad, Run, find out now the arrows which I shoot. And as the lad ran, he shot an arrow beyond him. [37]And when the lad was come to the place of the arrow which Jonathan had shot, Jonathan cried after the lad, and said, Is not the arrow beyond thee? [38]And Jonathan cried after the lad, Make speed, haste, stay not. And Jonathan's lad gathered up the arrows, and came to his master. [39]But the lad knew not any thing: only Jonathan and David knew the matter. [40]And Jonathan gave his artillery unto his lad, and said unto him, Go, carry them to the city.

[41]And as soon as the lad was gone, David arose out of a place toward the south, and fell on his face to the ground, and bowed himself three times: and they kissed one another, and wept one with

another, until David exceeded. [42]And Jonathan said to David, Go in peace, forasmuch as we have sworn both of us in the name of the LORD, saying, The LORD be between me and thee, and between my seed and thy seed for ever. And he arose and departed: and Jonathan went into the city.

Death of Jonathan

1 Sam. 31 [1]Now the Philistines fought against Israel: and the men of Israel fled from before the Philistines, and fell down slain in mount Gilboa. [2]And the Philistines followed hard upon Saul and upon his sons: and the Philistines slew Jonathan, and Abinadab, and Melchishua, Saul's sons.

JOPPA

[jop′a] A town on the southwest coast of Palestine which served as the Mediterranean harbor for Jerusalem, also referred to as Japho (*Josh. 19:46*), and now called Jaffa. We are told that it was to this harbor that Jonah came to find a ship on which he could flee from the presence of the LORD (*Jonah 1:3*). On at least two occasions the harbor is mentioned in connection with the transportation of cedars from the forest of Lebanon for use in building projects in Jerusalem (*2 Chr. 2:16; Ezra 3:7*). In the New Testament Joppa was the scene of Peter's raising Dorcas to life (*Acts 9:36-42*) and of the vision in which he learned that the gospel message was not to be withheld from the Gentiles (*Acts 9:43-10:16, 34; 11:1-10*).

See CORNELIUS, JONAH

SCRIPTURE

A Seaport

2 Chr. 2 [16]And we will cut wood out of Lebanon, as much as thou shalt need: and we will bring it to thee in floats by sea to Joppa; and thou shalt carry it up to Jerusalem.

Ezra 3 [7]They gave money also unto the masons, and to the carpenters; and meat, and drink, and oil, unto them of Zidon, and to them of Tyre, to bring cedar trees from Lebanon to the sea of Joppa, according to the grant that they had of Cyrus king of Persia.

Peter Performs Miracle at Joppa

Acts 9 [36]Now there was at Joppa a certain disciple named Tabitha, which by interpretation is called Dorcas: this woman was full of good works and almsdeeds which she did. [37]And it came to pass in those days, that she was sick, and died: whom when they had washed, they laid her in an upper chamber. [38]And forasmuch as Lydda was nigh to Joppa, and the disciples had heard that Peter was there, they sent unto him two men, desiring him that he would not delay to come to them. [39]Then Peter arose and went with them. When he was come, they brought him into the upper chamber: and all the widows stood by him weeping, and shewing the coats and garments which Dorcas made, while she was with them. [40]But Peter put them all forth, and kneeled down, and prayed; and turning him to the body said, Tabitha, arise. And she opened her eyes: and when she saw Peter, she sat up. [41]And he gave her his hand, and lifted her up; and when he had called the saints and widows, he presented her alive. [42]And it was known throughout all Joppa; and many believed in the Lord. [43]And it came to pass, that he tarried many days in Joppa with one Simon a tanner.

JORAM

[jō′ram, je hō′ram] The son of Ahab and Jezebel, brother of Ahaziah, and the ninth king of Israel (849-842 BC). He made some attempt to remove the more objectionable objects of idol-worship, but did not carry out a thorough reform. Jehoram's reign was a benevolent one. When Mesha, king of Moab, who had been a vassal of Israel since the days of Omri, rebelled against Israel, Joram enlisted the aid of Judah in recovering the territory. Although he apparently was victorious, he was never completely able to subdue the Moabite king. Difficulties with Syria also continued throughout his reign. In a battle with Hazael, king of Syria, Joram was wounded and retired to Jezreel to recover. Meanwhile, the prophet Elisha stirred up a revolt under the military leadership of Jehu whom he had anointed as king of Israel. Jehu went to Jezreel where he found Joram and his nephew, Ahaziah king of Judah. Jehu and his bowmen slew them both and the body of Jehoram was thrown onto the plot of ground which had once been the vineyard of Naboth. The death of Joram marked the end of the dynasty of Omri.

See KINGS, AHAB, ELISHA, etc.

SCRIPTURE

Makes War against Ramoth-gilead

2 Kin. 8 [28]And he went with Joram the son of Ahab to the war against Hazael king of Syria in Ramoth-gilead; and the Syrians wounded Joram. [29]And king Joram went back to be healed in Jezreel of the wounds which the Syrians had given him at Ramah, when he fought against Hazael king of Syria. And Ahaziah the son of Jehoram king of Judah went down to see Joram the son of Ahab in Jezreel, because he was sick.

Slain by the Usurper, Jehu

2 Kin. 9 [14]So Jehu the son of Jehoshaphat the son of Nimshi conspired against Joram. (Now Joram had kept Ramoth-gilead, he and all Israel, because of Hazael king of Syria. [15]But king Joram was returned to be healed in Jezreel of the wounds which the Syrians had given him, when he fought with Hazael king of Syria.) And Jehu said, If it be your minds, then let none go forth nor escape out of the city to go to tell it in Jezreel. [16]So Jehu rode in a chariot, and went to Jezreel; for Joram lay there. And Ahaziah king of Judah was come down to see Joram. [17]And there stood a watchman on the tower in Jezreel, and he spied the company of Jehu as he came, and said, I see a company. And Joram said, Take a horseman, and send to meet them, and let him say, Is it peace? [18]So there went one on horseback to meet him, and said, Thus saith the king, Is it peace? And Jehu said, What hast thou to do with peace? turn thee behind me. And the watchman told, saying, The messenger came to them, but he cometh not again. [19]Then he sent out a second on horseback, which came to them, and said, Thus saith the king, Is it peace? And Jehu answered, What hast thou to do with peace? turn thee behind me. [20]And the watchman told, saying, He came even unto them, and cometh not again: and the driving is like the driving of Jehu the son of Nimshi; for he driveth furiously. [21]And Joram said, Make ready. And his chariot was made ready. And Joram king of Israel and Ahaziah king of Judah went out, each in his chariot, and they went out against Jehu, and met him in the portion of Naboth the Jezreelite. [22]And it came to pass, when Joram saw Jehu, that he said, Is it peace, Jehu? And he answered, What peace, so long as the whoredoms of thy mother Jezebel and her witchcrafts are so many? [23]And Joram turned his hands, and fled, and said to Ahaziah, There is treachery, O Ahaziah. [24]And Jehu drew a bow with his full strength, and smote Jehoram between his arms, and the arrow went out at his heart, and he sunk down in his chariot. [25]Then said Jehu to Bidkar his captain, Take up, and cast him in the portion of

the field of Naboth the Jezreelite: for remember how that, when I and thou rode
together after Ahab his father, the LORD
laid this burden upon him; 26Surely I have
seen yesterday the blood of Naboth, and
the blood of his sons, saith the LORD; and
I will requite thee in this plat, saith the
LORD. Now therefore take and cast him
into the plat of ground, according to the
word of the LORD.

JORDAN

[jôr′dan] The river which begins in Northern Palestine at the junction of four streams and winds its way southward until it empties in the Dead Sea. After passing through the small Lake Huleh, it descends 689 feet in nine miles, running into the Sea of Galilee. (*See* SEA OF GALILEE) From this sea to the Dead Sea, the Jordan descends another 650 feet, reaching a level of 1300 feet below the Mediterranean Sea. (*See* DEAD SEA) Although it is only about seventy air miles from the Sea of Galilee to the Dead Sea, the course of the Jordan is so crooked that its actual length is approximately 200 miles. The river normally averages about 100 feet in width, but in the spring it overflows its banks and is much wider. (*See 1 Chr. 12:15*) There are many places at which it is possible to cross the river rather easily, but very few of these are close enough to any lines of travel to be of any practical use. There were fords near Jericho, to which point the men of Jericho pursued the spies (*Josh. 2:7*). Higher up at Succoth were the fords of Beth-barah, where Gideon lay in wait for the Midianites (*Judg. 7:24*), and where the men of Gilead slew the Ephraimites (*Judg. 12:6*). The Bible contains accounts of the waters having been miraculously parted in order to permit the crossing of the children of Israel (*Josh. 3:14-17*), of Elijah (*2 Kin. 2:6-8*), and of Elisha (*2 Kin. 2:14*). When Naaman the leper came to Elisha to be cleansed of his leprosy, he was instructed to dip himself in the Jordan (*2 Kin. 5:10-14*). John the Baptist did much of his baptizing in the Jordan; Jesus himself was baptized there (*Matt. 3:19*).

SCRIPTURE

Waters Separated for Israelites

Josh. 3 7And the LORD said unto Joshua,
This day will I begin to magnify thee in the
sight of all Israel, that they may know that,
as I was with Moses, so I will be with thee.
8And thou shalt command the priests that
bear the ark of the covenant, saying, When
ye are come to the brink of the water of
Jordan, ye shall stand still in Jordan.
9And Joshua said unto the children of
Israel, Come hither, and hear the words of
the LORD your God. 10And Joshua said,
Hereby ye shall know that the living God
is among you, and that he will without fail
drive out from before you the Canaanites,
and the Hittites, and the Hivites, and the
Perrizzites, and the Girgashites, and the
Amorites, and the Jebusites. 11Behold, the
ark of the covenant of the LORD of all the
earth passeth over before you into Jordan.
12Now therefore take you twelve men out
of the tribes of Israel, out of every tribe a
man. 13And it shall come to pass, as soon
as the soles of the feet of the priests that
bear the ark of the LORD, the Lord of all
the earth, shall rest in the waters of Jordan, that the waters of Jordan shall be
cut off from the waters that come down
from above; and they shall stand upon a
heap.
14And it came to pass, when the people
removed from their tents, to pass over Jordan, and the priests bearing the ark of the
covenant before the people; 15And as they
that bare the ark were come unto Jordan,
and the feet of the priests that bare the ark
were dipped in the brim of the water, (for
Jordan overfloweth all his banks all the
time of harvest,) 16That the waters which
came down from above stood and rose up
upon a heap very far from the city Adam,

that is beside Zaretan; and those that came down toward the sea of the plain, even the salt sea, failed, and were cut off: and the people passed over right against Jericho. [17]And the priests that bare the ark of the covenant of the LORD stood firm on dry ground in the midst of Jordan, and all the Israelites passed over on dry ground, until all the people were passed clean over Jordan.

Naaman Healed of Leprosy in Its Waters

2 Kin. 5 [10]And Elisha sent a messenger unto him, saying, Go and wash in Jordan seven times, and thy flesh shall come again to thee, and thou shalt be clean. [11]But Naaman was wroth, and went away, and said, Behold, I thought, He will surely come out to me, and stand, and call on the name of the LORD his God, and strike his hand over the place, and recover the leper. [12]Are not Abana and Pharpar, rivers of Damascus, better than all the waters of Israel? may I not wash in them, and be clean? So he turned and went away in a rage. [13]And his servants came near, and spake unto him, and said, My father, if the prophet had bid thee do some great thing, wouldest thou not have done it? how much rather then, when he saith to thee, Wash, and be clean? [14]Then went he down, and dipped himself seven times in Jordan, according to the saying of the man of God: and his flesh came again like unto the flesh of a little child, and he was clean.

John Baptizes in the Jordan

Matt. 3 [5]Then went out to him Jerusalem, and all Judea, and all the region round about Jordan, [6]And were baptized of him in Jordan, confessing their sins.

Jesus Baptized in the Jordan

Matt. 3 [13]Then cometh Jesus from Galilee to Jordan unto John, to be baptized of him. [14]But John forbade him, saying, I have need to be baptized of thee, and comest thou to me? [15]And Jesus answering said unto him, Suffer it to be so now: for thus it becometh us to fulfil all righteousness. Then he suffered him. [16]And Jesus, when he was baptized, went up straightway out of the water: and, lo, the heavens were opened unto him, and he saw the Spirit of God descending like a dove, and lighting upon him: [17]And lo a voice from heaven, saying, This is my beloved Son, in whom I am well pleased.

JOSEPH

[jō′sef] 1. A son of Jacob, the first by his favorite wife Rachel. Joseph incurred the envy and jealousy of his brothers by reason of his father's love and by his predictions of his own greatness, and they secretly sold him as a slave to a band of merchantmen, who took him to Egypt. The brothers deluded Jacob into believing the boy was dead. The traders, on reaching Egypt, sold Joseph to Potiphar, a high official of the government, and he rose to power and influence in Potiphar's household. Because of his refusal to commit adultery with Potiphar's wife, she had him cast into prison on false charges, but through the interpretation of dreams for the head of the prison and the pharaoh, he was released and raised to the position of second ruler of the land. Pharaoh called him by the Egyptian name Zaphenath-paneah. Not long after this Joseph's brethren came to Egypt to secure corn, as there was a great famine in the land. After several audiences, he made himself known to them. The pharaoh, through favor to Joseph, told him to invite his family to settle in the land; this was done, thus laying the foundation for the future bondage of the Israelites.

Joseph was married to Asenath, who bore him two sons, Manasseh and Ephraim. His embalmed body was carried by the Israelites through the wilderness and finally buried at Shechem. (*See* POTIPHAR)

2. Joseph, the husband of Mary, the son of Heli (or Jacob), and a descendant of David.

Tradition says that he was well advanced in years when Jesus was born, but there is no means of verifying this. After the birth of Jesus and the return from Egypt, Joseph gradually disappears, the last mention of him being with reference to the trip to Jerusalem on which Jesus was found disputing with the doctors. He is thought to have died a considerable time prior to the crucifixion. (*See* MARY, JESUS)

3. Joseph of Arimathea, a wealthy Hebrew, and a follower of Jesus. After the crucifixion he obtained permission to bury the body of Jesus in his new private tomb.

SCRIPTURE

Joseph, the Son of Jacob

BIRTH

Gen. 30 24 And she called his name Joseph; and said, The LORD shall add to me another son.

SOLD INTO EGYPT

Gen. 37 3 Now Israel loved Joseph more than all his children, because he was the son of his old age: and he made him a coat of many colours. 4 And when his brethren saw that their father loved him more than all his brethren, they hated him, and could not speak peaceably unto him.

28 Then there passed by Midianites, merchantmen; and they drew and lifted up Joseph out of the pit, and sold Joseph to the Ishmaelites for twenty pieces of silver: and they brought Joseph into Egypt.

Gen. 39 1 And Joseph was brought down to Egypt: and Potiphar, an officer of Pharaoh, captain of the guard, an Egyptian, bought him of the hands of the Ishmaelites, which had brought him down thither.

FALSELY ACCUSED AND IMPRISONED

Gen. 39 19 And it came to pass, when his master heard the words of his wife, which she spake unto him, saying, After this manner did thy servant to me; that his wrath was kindled. 20 And Joseph's master took him, and put him into the prison, a place where the king's prisoners were bound: and he was there in the prison.

21 But the LORD was with Joseph, and shewed him mercy, and gave him favour in the sight of the keeper of the prison.

RISES TO POSITION OF IMPORTANCE

Gen. 41 38 And Pharaoh said unto his servants, Can we find such a one as this is, a man in whom the spirit of God is? 39 And Pharaoh said unto Joseph, Forasmuch as God hath shewed thee all this, there is none so discreet and wise as thou art: 40 Thou shalt be over my house, and according unto thy word shall all my people be ruled: only in the throne will I be greater than thou.

RECEIVES HIS BRETHREN

Gen. 42 5 And the sons of Israel came to buy corn among those that came: for the famine was in the land of Canaan. 6 And Joseph was the governor over the land, and he it was that sold to all the people of the land: and Joseph's brethren came, and bowed down themselves before him with their faces to the earth. 7 And Joseph saw his brethren, and he knew them, but made himself strange unto them, and spake roughly unto them; and he said unto them, Whence come ye? And they said, From the land of Canaan to buy food. 8 And Joseph knew his brethren, but they knew not him.

Gen. 45 1 Then Joseph could not refrain himself before all them that stood by him; and he cried, Cause every man to go out from me. And there stood no man with him, while Joseph made himself known unto his brethren.

HIS FAMILY INVITED TO EGYPT

Gen. 45 [17]And Pharaoh said unto Joseph, Say unto thy brethren, This do ye; lade your beasts, and go, get you unto the land of Canaan; [18]And take your father and your households, and come unto me: and I will give you the good of the land of Egypt, and ye shall eat the fat of the land.

Gen. 50 [22]And Joseph dwelt in Egypt, he, and his father's house: and Joseph lived a hundred and ten years. [23]And Joseph saw Ephraim's children of the third generation: the children also of Machir the son of Manasseh were brought up upon Joseph's knees. [24]And Joseph said unto his brethren, I die; and God will surely visit you, and bring you out of this land unto the land which he sware to Abraham, to Isaac, and to Jacob.

Joseph, the Husband of Mary

Matt. 1 [16]And Jacob begat Joseph the husband of Mary, of whom was born Jesus, who is called Christ.

[19]Then Joseph, her husband, being a just man, and not willing to make her a publick example, was minded to put her away privily. [20]But while he thought on these things, behold, the angel of the Lord appeared unto him in a dream, saying, Joseph, thou son of David, fear not to take unto thee Mary thy wife: for that which is conceived in her is of the Holy Ghost. [24]Then Joseph being raised from sleep did as the angel of the Lord had bidden him, and took unto him his wife.

Matt. 2 [13]And when they were departed, behold, the angel of the Lord appeareth to Joseph in a dream, saying, Arise, and take the young child and his mother, and flee into Egypt, and be thou there until I bring thee word: for Herod will seek the young child to destroy him. [14]When he arose, he took the young child and his mother by night, and departed into Egypt.

[19]But when Herod was dead, behold, an angel of the Lord appeareth in a dream to Joseph in Egypt, [20]Saying, Arise, and take the young child and his mother, and go into the land of Israel: for they are dead which sought the young child's life. [21]And he arose, and took the young child and his mother, and came into the land of Israel.

Joseph of Arimathea

Matt. 27 [57]When the even was come, there came a rich man of Arimathaea, named Joseph, who also himself was Jesus' disciple: [58]He went to Pilate, and begged the body of Jesus. Then Pilate commanded the body to be delivered. [59]And when Joseph had taken the body, he wrapped it in a clean linen cloth, [60]And laid it in his own new tomb, which he had hewn out in the rock: and he rolled a great stone to the door of the sepulchre, and departed.

JOSHUA

[josh'ū a] The son of Nun and the successor of Moses as the leader of the Israelites. Joshua first appears in the Biblical narrative as the leader of the Israelite fighting forces in a battle with the Amalekites at Rephidim, early in the period of wilderness wanderings. The manner in which he is introduced indicates that he was already recognized as a man of considerable ability. Of the twelve spies sent from Kadesh to survey the condition of the land of Canaan and the resistance capability of its inhabitants, only Joshua and Caleb encouraged the Israelites to go up and take the land. They are said to be the only members of the host which left Egypt as adults who were permitted to enter the promised land. Apart from these two incidents, Joshua appears only as an assistant to Moses in the rest of the period of wandering. As Moses approached death, he named

Joshua as his successor and instructed him to assist Eleazar the priest in the apportionment of the land. As the new leader of Israel, Joshua led his army on a remarkable series of conquests, much of which has been confirmed by recent archaeological data. (*See* CONQUEST) At the close of his life Joshua summoned a popular assembly at Shechem; after a historical review in which he brought to their minds the mighty acts of God in Israel's behalf, he urged them to remain faithful to God, climaxing his speech with the famous challenge: "Choose you this day whom ye will serve; . . . but as for me and my house, we will serve the LORD."

SCRIPTURE

An Assistant of Moses

Ex. 24 13 And Moses rose up, and his minister Joshua; and Moses went up into the mount of God.

Ex. 32 17 And when Joshua heard the noise of the people as they shouted, he said unto Moses, There is a noise of war in the camp.

Ex. 33 11 And the LORD spake unto Moses face to face, as a man speaketh unto his friend. And he turned again into the camp; but his servant Joshua, the son of Nun, a young man, departed not out of the tabernacle.

One of Twelve Spies

Num. 14 6 And Joshua the son of Nun, and Caleb the son of Jephunneh, which were of them that searched the land, rent their clothes: 7 And they spake unto all the company of the children of Israel, saying, The land, which we passed through to search it, is an exceeding good land. 8 If the LORD delight in us, then he will bring us into this land, and give it us; a land which floweth with milk and honey. 9 Only rebel not ye against the LORD, neither fear ye the people of the land; for they are bread for us: their defence is departed from them, and the LORD is with us: fear them not. 10 But all the congregation bade stone them with stones. And the glory of the LORD appeared in the tabernacle of the congregation before all the children of Israel.

Appointed to Succeed Moses

Num. 27 18 And the LORD said unto Moses, Take thee Joshua the son of Nun, a man in whom is the spirit, and lay thine hand upon him; 19 And set him before Eleazar the priest, and before all the congregation; and give him a charge in their sight. 20 And thou shalt put some of thine honour upon him, that all the congregation of the children of Israel may be obedient. 21 And he shall stand before Eleazar the priest, who shall ask counsel for him after the judgment of Urim before the LORD: at his word shall they go out, and at his word they shall come in, both he, and all the children of Israel with him, even all the congregation. 22 And Moses did as the LORD commanded him: and he took Joshua, and set him before Eleazar the priest, and before all the congregation: 23 And he laid his hands upon him, and gave him a charge, as the LORD commanded by the hand of Moses.

God Charges Joshua

Josh. 1 5 There shall not any man be able to stand before thee all the days of thy life: as I was with Moses, so I will be with thee: I will not fail thee, nor forsake thee. 6 Be strong and of a good courage: for unto this people shalt thou divide for an inheritance the land, which I sware unto their fathers to give them. 7 Only be thou strong and very courageous, that thou mayest observe to do according to all the law, which Moses my servant commanded thee: turn not from it to the right hand or to the left, that thou mayest prosper whithersoever thou goest. [8]This book of the law shall not depart out of thy mouth; but thou shalt meditate therein day and night, that thou mayest observe to do according to all that is written therein: for then thou shalt make thy way prosperous, and then thou shalt have good success. [9]Have not I commanded thee? Be strong and of a good courage; be not afraid, neither be thou dismayed: for the LORD thy God is with thee whithersoever thou goest.

Joshua Charges the People

Josh. 24 [14]Now therefore fear the LORD, and serve him in sincerity and in truth; and put away the gods which your fathers served on the other side of the flood, and in Egypt; and serve ye the LORD. [15]And if it seem evil unto you to serve the LORD, choose you this day whom ye will serve; whether the gods which your fathers served that were on the other side of the flood, or the gods of the Amorites, in whose land ye dwell: but as for me and my house, we will serve the LORD.

JOSIAH

[jȯ sī'a] The son of Amon and king of Judah (640/39-609/8 BC). At the assassination of Amon, Josiah was set up as king by "the people of the land." At the time Josiah was only eight years old and it is assumed that the actual government of Judah was left to the young monarch's advisers. Assyria was losing control of her empire and Judah was once more virtually a free country. In the eighth year of his reign, Josiah turned to the true God; in effect, this amounted to a political declaration of independence, since a vassalage relationship ordinarily involved the worship of the gods of the conquering nation. In the twelfth year, at the death of the Assyrian ruler Asshurbanipal, Josiah made further reforms and then accomplished the bold move of capturing for Judah the Assyrian provinces of Gilead, Megiddo, and Samaria. It was at one time thought that this was incredible, but archaeological evidence has confirmed its truth. Apparently, these provinces had been abandoned by Assyria and could offer little resistance. In 622 BC, the eighteenth year of Josiah's reign, the reform reached its peak with the discovery of "the book of the Law" by the workmen who were cleaning out the temple. It is generally agreed today that this was some form of the book of *Deuteronomy*. Josiah summoned the people together, read the law to them and entered with them into a renewal of the covenant with God. What followed was apparently the most throughgoing reform in the history of Judah. The various cults were cast out of Jerusalem. The shrines of Samaria were destroyed. Josiah even succeeded where all his predecessors had failed, in tearing down the "high places" where God had been worshipped apart from the temple. Now, worship was centralized around the sanctuary in Jerusalem as in the days of David and Solomon.

In 609 BC, Pharaoh Necho II of Egypt tried to prevent the destruction of the rump nation of Assyria by Babylon. Josiah rode out to delay Necho and was killed. Among those who mourned his death was the great prophet Jeremiah, whose preaching had doubtless been influential in the remarkable reform measures of the admirable young ruler.

See JEREMIAH, KINGS

SCRIPTURE

The Young King

2 Kin. 22 [1]Josiah was eight years old when he began to reign, and he reigned thirty and one years in Jerusalem. And his mother's name was Jedidah, the daughter of Adaiah of Boscath. [2]And he did that which was right in the sight of the LORD, and walked in all the way of David his father, and turned not aside to the right hand or to the left.

Josiah's Reforms

2 Kin. 22 [8]And Hilkiah the high priest

said unto Shaphan the scribe, I have found the book of the law in the house of the LORD. And Hilkiah gave the book to Shaphan, and he read it.

2 Kin. 23 1And the king sent, and they gathered unto him all the elders of Judah and of Jerusalem. 2And the king went up into the house of the LORD, and all the men of Judah and all the inhabitants of Jerusalem with him, and the priests, and the prophets, and all the people, both small and great: and he read in their ears all the words of the book of the covenant which was found in the house of the LORD.

3And the king stood by a pillar, and made a covenant before the LORD, to walk after the LORD, and to keep his commandments and his testimonies and his statutes with all their heart and all their soul, to perform the words of this covenant that were written in this book. And all the people stood to the covenant. 4And the king commanded Hilkiah the high priest, and the priests of the second order, and the keepers of the door, to bring forth out of the temple of the LORD all the vessels that were made for Baal, and for the grove, and for all the host of heaven: and he burned them without Jerusalem in the fields of Kidron, and carried the ashes of them unto Bethel. 5And he put down the idolatrous priests, whom the kings of Judah had ordained to burn incense in the high places in the cities of Judah, and in the places round about Jerusalem; them also that burned incense unto Baal, to the sun, and to the moon, and to the planets, and to all the host of heaven. 6And he brought out the grove from the house of the LORD, without Jerusalem, unto the brook Kidron, and burned it at the brook Kidron, and stamped it small to powder, and cast the powder thereof upon the graves of the children of the people. 7And he brake down the houses of the sodomites that were by the house of the LORD, where the women wove hangings for the grove.

21And the king commanded all the people, saying, Keep the passover unto the LORD your God, as it is written in the book of this covenant. 22Surely there was not holden such a passover from the days of the judges that judged Israel, nor in all the days of the kings of Israel, nor of the kings of Judah; 23But in the eighteenth year of king Josiah, wherein this passover was holden to the LORD in Jerusalem.

25And like unto him was there no king before him, that turned to the LORD with all his heart, and with all his soul, and with all his might, according to all the law of Moses; neither after him arose there any like him.

Josiah's Death

2 Kin. 23 29In his days Pharaoh-nechoh king of Egypt went up against the king of Assyria to the river Euphrates: and king Josiah went against him; and he slew him at Megiddo, when he had seen him. 30And his servants carried him in a chariot dead from Megiddo, and brought him to Jerusalem, and buried him in his own sepulchre. And the people of the land took Jehoahaz the son of Josiah, and anointed him, and made him king in his father's stead.

JOTHAM

[jō'tham] The son of Uzziah and the twelfth king of Judah. After his father became a leper and retired from public life, the official administration of the kingdom fell to Jotham. Except for a successful campaign against the Ammonites little mention is made of military matters; it is to be assumed, therefore, that Jotham was able to maintain control of the great kingdom which Uzziah had built up. He continued the building programs which his energetic father had begun, and appears to have been reasonably faithful to the true religion. At his death he was succeeded by his son Ahaz.

See KINGS, UZZIAH

SCRIPTURE

2 Kin. 15 [32]In the second year of Pekah the son of Remaliah king of Israel began Jotham the son of Uzziah king of Judah to reign. [33]Five and twenty years old was he when he began to reign, and he reigned sixteen years in Jerusalem. And his mother's name was Jerusha, the daughter of Zadok. [34]And he did that which was right in the sight of the LORD: he did according to all that his father Uzziah had done.

[35]Howbeit the high places were not removed: the people sacrificed and burned incense still in the high places. He built the higher gate of the house of the LORD.

[36]Now the rest of the acts of Jotham, and all that he did, are they not written in the book of the Chronicles of the kings of Judah? [37]In those days the LORD began to send against Judah Rezin the king of Syria, and Pekah the son of Remaliah. [38]And Jotham slept with his fathers, and was buried with his fathers in the city of David his father: and Ahaz his son reigned in his stead.

JOTHAM

[jō'tham] The youngest son of Jerubbael (Gideon) and the only one of seventy brothers to survive the massacre by Abimelech, the son of Gideon by a concubine. After Abimelech became king of Shechem, Jotham went to the top of Mount Gerizim and proclaimed his famous parable of the bramble and the trees. The gist of the parable is this: when the trees tried to select a king, all of the trees in order refused the task until it was finally accepted by the bramble, the most lowly of those consulted; the bramble accepted and pompously offered its shade to the other trees. After speaking this fable, Jotham applied it to the situation at hand, implying that both Abimelech and his new subjects would get what they deserve. Realizing that he was powerless to do anything more, Jotham, fearing for his life, fled to Beer. Nothing more is heard of him, but the ignominious end which came to the reign of Abimelech is described as a part of "the curse of Jotham" (*Judg.* 9:57).

See ABIMELECH, GIDEON

SCRIPTURE

Judg. 9 [1]And Abimelech the son of Jerubbaal went to Shechem unto his mother's brethren, and communed with them, and with all the family of the house of his mother's father, saying, [2]Speak, I pray you, in the ears of all the men of Shechem, Whether is better for you, either that all the sons of Jerubbaal, which are threescore and ten persons, reign over you, or that one reign over you? remember also that I am your bone and your flesh. [3]And his mother's brethren spake of him in the ears of all the men of Shechem all these words: and their hearts inclined to follow Abimelech; for they said, He is our brother. [4]And they gave him threescore and ten pieces of silver out of the house of Baal-berith, wherewith Abimelech hired vain and light persons, which followed him. [5]And he went unto his father's house at Ophrah, and slew his brethren the sons of Jerubbaal, being threescore and ten persons, upon one stone: notwithstanding, yet Jotham the youngest son of Jerubbaal was left; for he hid himself. [6]And all the men of Shechem gathered together, and all the house of Millo, and went and made Abimelech king, by the plain of the pillar that was in Shechem.

[7]And when they told it to Jotham, he went and stood in the top of mount Gerizim, and lifted up his voice, and cried, and said unto them, Hearken unto me, ye men

of Shechem, that God may hearken unto you. [8]The trees went forth on a time to anoint a king over them; and they said unto the olive tree, Reign thou over us. [9]But the olive tree said unto them, Should I leave my fatness, wherewith by me they honour God and man, and go to be promoted over the trees? [10]And the trees said to the fig tree, Come thou, and reign over us. [11]But the fig tree said unto them, Should I forsake my sweetness, and my good fruit, and go to be promoted over the trees? [12]Then said the trees unto the vine, Come thou, and reign over us. [13]And the vine said unto them, Should I leave my wine, which cheereth God and man, and go to be promoted over the trees? [14]Then said all the trees unto the bramble, Come thou, and reign over us. [15]And the bramble said unto the trees, If in truth ye anoint me king over you, then come and put your trust in my shadow; and if not, let fire come out of the bramble, and devour the cedars of Lebanon. [16]Now therefore, if ye have done truly and sincerely, in that ye have made Abimelech king, and if ye have dealt well with Jerubbaal and his house, and have done unto him according to the deserving of his hands: [17](For my father fought for you, and adventured his life far, and delivered you out of the hand of Midian: [18]And ye are risen up against my father's house this day, and have slain his sons, threescore and ten persons, upon one stone, and have made Abimelech, the son of his maidservant, king over the men of Shechem, because he is your brother:) [19]If ye then have dealt truly and sincerely with Jerubbaal and with his house this day, then rejoice ye in Abimelech, and let him also rejoice in you: [20]But if not, let fire come out from Abimelech, and devour the men of Shechem, and the house of Millo; and let fire come out from the men of Shechem, and from the house of Millo, and devour Abimelech. [21]And Jotham ran away, and fled, and went to Beer, and dwelt there, for fear of Abimelech his brother.

[57]And all the evil of the men of Shechem did God render upon their heads: and upon them came the curse of Jotham the son of Jerubbaal.

JOY

[joi] The emotion excited by the acquisition or the expectation of good; pleasure caused by good fortune, or the like; gladness, delight. Throughout the Bible, joy and gladness are related to the life of Israel and the Church. This joy is not only a response to the present blessings of a covenant relationship with God but is also an anticipation of the future state, when redeemed man will be able to enjoy the fullness of the presence of God.

SCRIPTURE

General

Neh. 8 [10]Then he said unto them, Go your way, eat the fat, and drink the sweet, and send portions unto them for whom nothing is prepared: for this day is holy unto our LORD: neither be ye sorry; for the joy of the LORD is your strength.

Psa. 16 [11]Thou wilt shew me the path of life: in thy presence is fulness of joy; at thy right hand there are pleasures for evermore.

Psa. 89 [16]In thy name shall they rejoice all the day: and in thy righteousness shall they be exalted.

Psa. 149 [2]Let Israel rejoice in him that made him: let the children of Zion be joyful in their King.

Isa. 35 [2]It shall blossom abundantly, and rejoice, even with joy and singing: the glory of Lebanon shall be given unto it, the excellency of Carmel and Sharon, they shall see the glory of the LORD, and the excellency of our God.

Isa. 60 [15]Whereas thou hast been forsaken and hated, so that no man went through thee, I will make thee an eternal excellency, a joy of many generations.

Isa. 61 [10]I will greatly rejoice in the LORD, my soul shall be joyful in my God; for he hath clothed me with the garments of salvation, he hath covered me with the robe of righteousness, as a bridegroom decketh himself with ornaments, and as a bride adorneth herself with her jewels.

Luke 10 [20]Notwithstanding in this rejoice not, that the spirits are subject unto you; but rather rejoice, because your names are written in heaven.

John 15 [11]These things have I spoken unto you, that my joy might remain in you, and that your joy might be full.

Rom. 14 [17]For the kingdom of God is not meat and drink; but righteousness, and peace, and joy in the Holy Ghost.

1 Thess. 1 [6]And ye became followers of us, and of the Lord, having received the word in much affliction, with joy of the Holy Ghost.

Joy of Wicked Is Short-lived

Job 20 [5]That the triumphing of the wicked is short, and the joy of the hypocrite but for a moment.

Prov. 15 [21]Folly is joy to him that is destitute of wisdom: but a man of understanding walketh uprightly.

Eccl. 2 [10]And whatsoever mine eyes desired I kept not from them, I withheld not my heart from any joy; for my heart rejoiced in all my labour: and this was my portion of all my labour.

Isa. 16 [10]And gladness is taken away, and joy out of the plentiful field; and in the vineyards there shall be no singing, neither shall there be shouting: the treaders shall tread out no wine in their presses; I have made their vintage shouting to cease.

Jas. 4 [9]Be afflicted, and mourn, and weep: let your laughter be turned to mourning, and your joy to heaviness.

Joy Follows Grief

Psa. 30 [5]For his anger endureth but a moment; in his favour is life: weeping may endure for a night, but joy cometh in the morning.

Psa. 125 [5]They that sow in tears shall reap in joy. [6]He that goeth forth and weepeth, bearing precious seed, shall doubtless come again with rejoicing, bringing his sheaves with him.

Isa. 35 [10]And the ransomed of the LORD shall return, and come to Zion with songs and everlasting joy upon their heads: they shall obtain joy and gladness, and sorrow and sighing shall flee away.

Isa. 61 [3]To appoint unto them that mourn in Zion, to give unto them beauty for ashes, the oil of joy for mourning, the garment of praise for the spirit of heaviness; that they might be called Trees of righteousness, The planting of the LORD, that he might be glorified.

Isa. 66 [10]Rejoice ye with Jerusalem, and be glad with her, all ye that love her: rejoice for joy with her, all ye that mourn for her.

Jer. 31 [13]Then shall the virgin rejoice in the dance, both young men and old together, for I will turn their mourning into joy, and will comfort them, and make them rejoice from their sorrow.

John 16 [20]Verily, verily, I say unto you, That ye shall weep and lament, but the world shall rejoice: and ye shall be sorrowful, but your sorrow shall be turned into joy.

2 Cor. 6 [10]As sorrowful, yet alway rejoicing; as poor, yet making many rich; as having nothing, and yet possessing all things.

Jas. 1 [2]My brethren, count it all joy when ye fall into divers temptations.

Joy Over Repenting Sinner

Luke 15 [7]I say unto you, that likewise joy shall be in heaven over one sinner that repenteth, more than over ninety and nine just persons, which need no repentance.

[10]Likewise, I say unto you, there is joy in the presence of the angels of God over one sinner that repenteth.

Joy in Hymns

Eph. 5 [19]Speaking to yourselves in psalms and hymns and spiritual songs, singing and making melody in your heart to the LORD.

Col. 3 [16]Let the word of Christ dwell in you richly in all wisdom; teaching and admonishing one another in psalms and hymns and spiritual songs, singing with grace in your hearts to the Lord.

Jas. 5 [13]Is any among you afflicted? let him pray. Is any merry? let him sing psalms.

JUBAL

[jōō'bal] A son of Lamech; said to be "the father of all such as handle the harp and organ" (*Gen. 4:21*).

JUBILEE

[jōō'bi lē] The fiftieth year, falling on the year after a succession of seven Sabbatical years (49 years), in which liberty was proclaimed to all Hebrew bondmen and all property which had been sold or leased reverted to the original owner. In addition, the land was allowed to lie fallow as in a regular sabbatical year. (*See* SABBATICAL YEAR) The year was inaugurated on the Day of Atonement, the tenth day of the seventh month, by the blowing of trumpets throughout the land, and by a proclamation of universal liberty. There is some doubt as to whether the year of Jubilee was ever actually observed.

SCRIPTURE

Lev. 25 [8]And thou shalt number seven sabbaths of years unto thee, seven times seven years; and the space of the seven sabbaths of years shall be unto thee forty and nine years. [9]Then shalt thou cause the trumpet of the jubilee to sound on the tenth day of the seventh month, in the day of atonement shall ye make the trumpet sound throughout all your land. [10]And ye shall hallow the fiftieth year, and proclaim liberty throughout all the land unto all the inhabitants thereof: it shall be a jubilee unto you; and ye shall return every man unto his possession, and ye shall return every man unto his family. [11]A jubilee shall that fiftieth year be unto you: ye shall not sow, neither reap that which groweth of itself in it, nor gather the grapes in it of thy vine undressed. [12]For it is the jubilee; it shall be holy unto you: ye shall eat the increase thereof out of the field. [13]In the year of this jubilee ye shall return every man unto his possession. [14]And if thou sell aught unto thy neighbour, or buyest aught of thy neighbour's hand, ye shall not oppress one another: [15]According to the number of years after the jubilee thou shalt buy of thy neighbour, and according unto the number of years of the fruits he shall sell unto thee: [16]According to the multitude of years thou shalt increase the price thereof, and according to the fewness of years thou shalt diminish the price of it: for according to the number of the years of the fruits doth he sell unto thee. [17]Ye shall not therefore oppress one another; but thou shalt fear thy God: for I am the LORD your God.

[18]Wherefore ye shall do my statutes, and keep my judgments, and do them; and ye shall dwell in the land in safety. [19]And the land shall yield her fruit, and ye shall eat your fill, and dwell therein in safety. [20]And if ye shall say, What shall we eat the seventh year? behold, we shall not sow, nor gather in our increase: [21]Then I will command my blessing upon you in the sixth year, and it shall bring forth fruit for three years. [22]And ye shall sow the eighth year, and eat yet of old fruit until the ninth year; until her fruits come in ye shall eat of the old store.

[23]The land shall not be sold for ever: for the land is mine; for ye are strangers and sojourners with me. [24]And in all the land of your possession ye shall grant a redemption for the land.

[25]If thy brother be waxen poor, and hath sold away some of his possession, and if any of his kin come to redeem it, then shall he redeem that which his brother sold. [26]And if the man have none to redeem it, and himself be able to redeem it; [27]Then let him count the years of the sale thereof, and restore the overplus unto the man to whom he sold it; that he may return unto his possession. [28]But if he be not able to restore it to him, then that which is sold shall remain in the hand of him that hath bought it until the year of jubilee: and in the jubilee it shall go out, and he shall return unto his possession. [29]And if a man sell a dwellinghouse in a walled city, then he may redeem it within a whole year after it is sold; within a full year may he redeem it. [30]And if it be not redeemed within the space of a full year, then the house that is in the walled city shall be established for ever to him that bought it throughout his generations: it shall not go out in the jubilee. [31]But the houses of the villages which have no wall round about them shall be counted as the fields of the country: they may be redeemed, and they shall go out in the jubilee. [32]Notwithstanding the cities of the Levites, and the houses of the cities of their possession, may the Levites redeem at any time. [33]And if a man purchase of the Levites, then the house that was sold, and the city of his possession, shall go out in the year of jubilee: for the houses of the cities of the Levites are their possession among the children of Israel. [34]But the field of the suburbs of their cities may not be sold; for it is their perpetual possession.

[35]And if thy brother be waxen poor, and fallen in decay with thee; then thou shalt relieve him: yea, though he be a stranger, or a sojourner; that he may live with thee. [36]Take thou no usury of him, or increase: but fear thy God; that thy brother may live with thee. [37]Thou shalt not give him thy money upon usury, nor lend him thy victuals for increase. [38]I am the LORD your God, which brought you forth out of the land of Egypt, to give you the land of Canaan, and to be your God.

[39]And if thy brother that dwelleth by thee be waxen poor, and be sold unto thee; thou shalt not compel him to serve as a bondservant: [40]But as a hired servant, and as a sojourner, he shall be with thee, and shall serve thee unto the year of jubilee: [41]And then shall he depart from thee, both he and his children with him, and shall return unto his own family, and unto the possession of his fathers shall he return. [42]For they are my servants, which I brought forth out of the land of Egypt: they shall not be sold as bondmen. [43]Thou shalt not rule over him with rigour, but shalt fear thy God. [44]Both thy bondmen, and thy bondmaids, which thou shalt have, shall be of the heathen that are round about

you; of them shall ye buy bondmen and
bondmaids. 45Moreover, of the children
of the strangers that do sojourn among
you, of them shall ye buy, and of their families that are with you, which they begat
in your land: and they shall be your possession. 46And ye shall take them as an
inheritance for your children after you, to
inherit them for a possession; they shall be
your bondmen for ever: but over your
brethren the children of Israel, ye shall not
rule one over another with rigour.
47And if a sojourner or stranger wax rich
by thee, and thy brother that dwelleth by
him wax poor, and sell himself unto the
stranger or sojourner by thee, or to the
stock of the stranger's family: 48After that
he is sold he may be redeemed again; one
of his brethren may redeem him: 49Either
his uncle, or his uncle's son, may redeem
him, or any that is nigh of kin unto him of
his family may redeem him; or if he be
able, he may redeem himself. 50And he
shall reckon with him that bought him
from the year that he was sold to him unto
the year of jubilee: and the price of his
sale shall be according unto the number of
years, according to the time of a hired servant shall it be with him. 51If there be yet
many years behind, according unto them
he shall give again the price of his redemption out of the money that he was bought
for. 52And if there remain but few years
unto the year of jubilee, then he shall count
with him, and according unto his years
shall he give him again the price of his redemption. 53And as a yearly hired servant shall he be with him: and the other
shall not rule with rigour over him in thy
sight. 54And if he be not redeemed in these
years, then he shall go out in the year of
jubilee, both he, and his children with him.
55For unto me the children of Israel are
servants; they are my servants whom I
brought forth out of the land of Egypt: I
am the LORD your God.

JUDAEA

[jōō dē′a] This was the name given to the southernmost of the three districts of Palestine west of the Jordan, the other two being Samaria and Galilee. It extended from the Jordan and Dead Sea to the Mediterranean, and from Shiloh on the north to the wilderness on the South. It was the result of the division of the Persian empire under Darius. The first mention of the "province of Judaea" is in *Ezra 5:8*. The designation is quite common in the New Testament.

JUDAH

[jōō′da] The territory which occupied, roughly speaking, the southern one-third of Palestine west of the Jordan River and the Dead Sea. Under Saul, David, and Solomon, Judah was joined with the land occupied by the other tribes in the Kingdom which was known simply as Israel. After the split under Rehoboam, the ten northern tribes were called Israel, and the tribe of Judah, along with the tribe of Benjamin, became the kingdom of Judah. In the *Chronicles*, however, it is still referred to as Israel. For the history of Judah during the period of the divided kingdom, the reader is invited to consult the chart of kings in the appendix and the articles on the individual kings and other subjects related to this period. The kingdom of Judah lasted from 922 BC until 586 BC, at which time it fell to Nebuchadnezzar, many of its inhabitants being deported to Babylon. Although the split between Israel and Judah served to weaken both considerably, it is inconceivable that they could have withstood the assaults of Assyria and Babylon, even if they had remained united. After the Persian empire gained control of Palestine, the territory which included Judah became known as Judaea (*Ezra 5:8*), and is so designated in the New Testament.

See JUDAEA

JUDAH

[jōō′da] Son of Jacob and Leah. Judah saved the life of Joseph by persuading his brothers to sell him to the Midianite traders instead of killing him. He also assumed a role of leadership when the brothers travelled to Egypt to secure corn in time of famine. As a result of his disgraceful relationship with his daughter-in-law Tamar, Judah became the father of Perez and Zerah, the former of whom figures in the genealogy of Jesus (*Matt. 1:3*). Although he was the fourth son, Judah received the paternal blessing because of the sins of his three older brothers, Reuben, Simeon, and Levi. Judah was regarded as the ancestor of the Israelite tribe which bore his name.

SCRIPTURE

Saves Joseph's Life

Gen. 37 [26]And Judah said unto his
brethren, What profit is it if we slay our
brother, and conceal his blood? [27]Come,
and let us sell him to the Ishmaelites, and
let not our hand be upon him; for he is our
brother, and our flesh: and his brethren
were content.

Judah and Tamar

Gen. 38 [12]And in process of time the
daughter of Shuah Judah's wife died; and
Judah was comforted, and went up unto
his sheepshearers to Timnath, he and his
friend Hirah the Adullamite. [13]And it was
told Tamar, saying, Behold, thy father in
law goeth up to Timnath to shear his
sheep. [14]And she put her widow's garments off from her, and covered her with
a veil, and wrapped herself, and sat in an
open place, which is by the way to Timnath; for she saw that Shelah was grown,
and she was not given unto him to wife.
[15]When Judah saw her, he thought her to
be a harlot; because she had covered her
face. [16]And he turned unto her by the
way, and said, Go to, I pray thee, let me
come in unto thee; (for he knew not that
she was his daughter in law.) And she said,
What wilt thou give me, that thou mayest
come in unto me? [17]And he said, I will
send thee a kid from the flock. And she
said, Wilt thou give me a pledge, till thou
send it? [18]And he said, What pledge shall
I give thee? And she said, Thy signet, and
thy bracelets, and thy staff that is in thine
hand. And he gave it her, and came in unto
her, and she conceived by him. [19]And she
arose, and went away, and laid by her veil
from her, and put on the garments of her
widowhood. [20]And Judah sent the kid by
the hand of his friend the Adullamite, to
receive his pledge from the woman's hand:
but he found her not. [21]Then he asked the
men of that place, saying, Where is the
harlot, that was openly by the way side?
And they said, There was no harlot in this
place. [22]And he returned to Judah, and
said, I can not find her; and also the men of
the place said, that there was no harlot in
this place. [23]And Judah said, Let her take
it to her, lest we be shamed: behold, I sent
this kid, and thou hast not found her.

[24]And it came to pass about three
months after, that it was told Judah, saying, Tamar thy daughter in law hath
played the harlot; and also, behold, she is
with child by whoredom. And Judah said,
Bring her forth, and let her be burnt.
[25]When she was brought forth, she sent to
her father in law, saying, By the man
whose these are, am I with child: and she
said, Discern, I pray thee, whose are these,
the signet, and bracelets, and staff. [26]And
Judah acknowledged them, and said, She
hath been more righteous than I; because
that I gave her not to Shelah my son. And
he knew her again no more.

[27]And it came to pass in the time of her
travail, that, behold, twins were in her
womb. [28]And it came to pass, when she
travailed, that the one put out his hand:
and the midwife took and bound upon his
hand a scarlet thread, saying, This came
out first. [29]And it came to pass, as he drew

back his hand, that, behold, his brother came out: and she said, How hast thou broken forth? this breach be upon thee: therefore his name was called Pharez. [30]And afterward came out his brother, that had the scarlet thread upon his hand: and his name was called Zarah.

Prophecy Concerning Judah

Gen. 49 [8]Judah, thou art he whom thy brethren shall praise: thy hand shall be in the neck of thine enemies; thy father's children shall bow down before thee. [9]Judah is a lion's whelp: from the prey, my son, thou art gone up: he stooped down, he couched as a lion, and as an old lion; who shall rouse him up? [10]The sceptre shall not depart from Judah, nor a lawgiver from between his feet, until Shiloh come; and unto him shall the gathering of the people be. [11]Binding his foal unto the vine, and his ass's colt unto the choice vine; he washed his garments in wine, and his clothes in the blood of grapes: [12]His eyes shall be red with wine, and his teeth white with milk.

REFERENCE: *Gen. 35:23; 43:3, 8-10; 44:14-34; 46:28; Matt. 1:2, 3.*

JUDAISM

[jōō'da izm] The religion and life of the Jews, especially after the return from the Babylonian exile. There were several sects within Judaism (*see* PHARISEES, SADDUCEES), but all had in common belief in one God and the Law. The term appears in the Bible only in *Gal. 1:13-14.*

JUDAS ISCARIOT

[jōō'das is kar'i ot] The apostle who betrayed Jesus. The name Iscariot implies that Judas was a native of the Judaean village of Kerioth. The gospel of John contains several statements which indicate that Jesus was aware that Judas would betray him, yet he served as treasurer for the band of apostles apparently until the night of the betrayal itself. He used this position for personal gain, while pretending to be interested only in the proper use of the group funds. On the night of the Last Supper, Jesus indicated by a sign which of the disciples would betray him. Later, having conspired with the chief priests, Judas led a mob to the Garden of Gethsemane where he betrayed the Lord with a kiss. We are told that he became so remorseful and guilt-ridden that he returned the small amount of money he had received for his heinous crime, throwing it down in the temple, and then went out and hanged himself. The money was used to purchase a potter's field for the burial of strangers.

See JESUS, ACELDAMA

SCRIPTURE

An Apostle

Matt. 10 [1]And when he had called unto him his twelve disciples, he gave them power against unclean spirits, to cast them out, and to heal all manner of sickness and all manner of disease. [2]Now the names of the twelve apostles are these; . . . [4]. . . and Judas Iscariot, who also betrayed him.

His Hypocrisy

John 12 [3]Then took Mary a pound of ointment of spikenard, very costly, and anointed the feet of Jesus, and wiped his feet with her hair: and the house was filled with the odor of the ointment. [4]Then saith one of his disciples, Judas Iscariot, Simon's son, which should betray him. [5]Why was not this ointment sold for three hundred pence, and given to the poor? [6]This he said, not that he cared for the poor; but because he was a thief, and had the bag, and bare what was put therein.

Jesus Speaks of His Betrayal

John 6 [70]Jesus answered them, Have not I chosen you twelve, and one of you is a devil? [71]He spake of Judas Iscariot the

son of Simon: for he it was that should betray him, being one of the twelve.

John 13 [10]Jesus saith to him, He that is
washed needeth not save to wash his feet,
but is clean every whit: and ye are clean,
but not all. [11]For he knew who should betray him; therefore said he, Ye are not all
clean.

[18]I speak not of you all: I know whom
I have chosen: but that the scripture may
be fulfilled, He that eateth bread with me
hath lifted up his heel against me. [21]When
Jesus had thus said, he was troubled in
spirit, and testified, and said, Verily, verily, I say unto you, that one of you shall
betray me. [26]Jesus answered, He it is, to
whom I shall give a sop, when I have
dipped it. And when he had dipped the
sop, he gave it to Judas Iscariot, the son of
Simon.

Judas Betrays Jesus

Matt. 26 [14]Then one of the twelve,
called Judas Iscariot, went unto the chief
priests, [15]And said unto them, What will
ye give me, and I will deliver him unto
you? And they covenanted with him for
thirty pieces of silver. [16]And from that
time he sought opportunity to betray him.

[47]And while he yet spake, lo, Judas, one
of the twelve, came, and with him a great
multitude with swords and staves, from
the chief priests and elders of the people.
[48]Now he that betrayed him gave them a
sign, saying, Whomsoever I shall kiss, that
same is he; hold him fast. [49]And forthwith
he came to Jesus, and said, Hail, Master;
and kissed him. [50]And Jesus said unto
him, Friend, wherefore art thou come?
Then came they, and laid hands on Jesus,
and took him.

Judas' Sorrow and Death

Matt. 27 [3]Then Judas, which had betrayed him, when he saw that he was condemned, repented himself, and brought
again the thirty pieces of silver to the chief
priests and elders, [4]Saying, I have sinned
in that I have betrayed the innocent blood.
And they said, What is that to us? see thou
to that. [5]And he cast down the pieces of
silver in the temple, and departed, and
went and hanged himself. [6]And the chief
priests took the silver pieces, and said,
It is not lawful for to put them into the
treasury, because it is the price of blood.
[7]And they took counsel, and bought with
them the potter's field, to bury strangers
in.

JUDE

[jo͞od] The author of the book of Jude, "a servant of Jesus Christ and brother of James" (*Jude 1:1*). He is commonly thought to have been the brother of Jesus as well. If this is the case, he was at one time an unbeliever (*John 7:5*), yet he appeared in the upper room with his mother and the other disciples after the ascension of Jesus (*Acts 1:14*). *1 Cor. 9:5* implies that he was married.

JUDGES OF ISRAEL

When Israel was in the wilderness, Moses served as the only judge for some time. At the advice of his father-in-law, Jethro, he divided the people up into sub-groups and appointed a judge over each of these groups, handling only the most important cases himself. The classic period of the Judges of Israel came after the conquest of Canaan. Israel was settled in Palestine in a loosely-knit league of the twelve tribes, centering around the ark of the covenant, located at Shiloh. There was no organized leadership, but the people depended on spontaneous leadership to arise at the crucial times. These leaders were followed because they possessed some special gift, or "charisma," such as outstanding military prowess, wisdom, or physical strength. At least the following individuals served as judges of Israel during this period:

1. Othniel, *Judg. 3:9-11.*
2. Ehud, *Judg. 3:15-30.*

3. Shamgar, *Judg. 3:31.*
4. Deborah, *Judg. 4:5.*
5. Gideon, *Judg. 6:11-40; 7; 8.*
6. Abimelech, *Judg. 9:1-54.*
7. Tola, *Judg. 10:1, 2.*
8. Jair, *Judg. 10:3-5.*
9. Jephthah, *Judg. 11; 12:1-7.*
10. Ibzan, *Judg. 12:8-10.*
11. Elon, *Judg. 12:11-12.*
12. Abdon, *Judg. 12:13-14.*
13. Samson, *Judg. 13-16.*
14. Eli, *1 Sam. 1-4:18.*

At the end of this period, Samuel served as judge, establishing a circuit court and appointing his sons as judges. With the rise of the monarchy the classic judge disappeared, his functions being absorbed by the king.

The judges were commanded to render impartial justice, favoring neither rich nor poor, Jew nor foreigner, and refusing to be swayed by bribes or public opinion.

See articles on individual judges

SCRIPTURE

Jethro's Advice to Moses

Ex. 18 [21]Moreover thou shalt provide out of all the people able men, such as fear God, men of truth, hating covetousness; and place such over them, to be rulers of thousands, and rulers of hundreds, rulers of fifties, and rulers of tens:
[22]And let them judge the people at all seasons: and it shall be, that every great matter they shall bring unto thee, but every small matter they shall judge: so shall it be easier for thyself, and they shall bear the burden with thee.

See Deut. 1:12-17

Admonitions to Judges

Lev. 19 [15]Ye shall do no unrighteousness in judgment; thou shalt not respect the person of the poor, not honor the person of the mighty: but in righteousness shalt thou judge thy neighbor.

Deut. 1 [16]And I charged your judges at that time, saying, Hear the causes between your brethren, and judge righteously between every man and his brother, and the stranger that is with him.

2 Chr. 19 [6]And said to the judges, Take heed what ye do: for ye judge not for man, but for the LORD, who is with you in the
judgment. [7]Wherefore now let the fear of the LORD be upon you; take heed and do it: for there is no iniquity with the LORD our God, nor respect of persons, nor taking of gifts.

Isa. 10 [1]Woe unto them that decree unrighteous decrees, and that write grievousness which they have prescribed; [2]To turn aside the needy from judgment, and to take away the right from the poor of my people, that widows may be their prey, and that they may rob the fatherless!

JUDGMENT

[juj'ment] This word is used in several senses in the Bible: (1) It may refer to the statutes or commandments of God; when used in this sense, it is usually found in the plural. (2) Calamities sent by God as punishment are also viewed as judgments. (3) Finally, it may refer to God's judgment on the deeds of men, both in history and at the final Day of Judgment when history is brought to its fulfillment. This article is concerned primarily with the third of these meanings. There is frequent reference in the prophetic literature to the Day of the LORD. In the writings of Amos, it is clear the people regarded this as a day when God would visit his wrath on the enemies of Israel. Amos warns that it will be a day in which all who are disobedient to God will be judged, whether Israelites or aliens. In the later prophets, this Day of God's judgment is once more viewed as a day of rejoicing for Israel. (*See* DAY OF THE LORD) In the New Testament, the judgment on the sinfulness of the world is said to have begun with the coming of Jesus (*John 3:19; 9:39; 12:31*), but there is also unmistakable reference to a coming Day of Judgment in which the unrighteous shall be judged and punished according to their deeds and the salvation of those made righteous by the blood of Christ shall be consummated.

SCRIPTURE

God's Judgment

1 Chr. 16 [33]Then shall the trees of the wood sing out at the presence of the LORD, because he cometh to judge the earth.

Psa. 9 [7]But the LORD shall endure for ever: he hath prepared his throne for judgment. [8]And he shall judge the world in righteousness, he shall minister judgment to the people in uprightness.

Psa. 96 [13]Before the LORD; for he cometh, for he cometh to judge the earth: he shall judge the world with righteousness, and the people with his truth.

Eccl. 3 [17]I said in mine heart, God shall judge the righteous and the wicked: for there is a time there for every purpose and for every work.

Eccl. 12 [14]For God shall bring every work into judgment, with every secret thing, whether it be good, or whether it be evil.

Acts 17 [31]Because he hath appointed a day, in the which he will judge the world in righteousness by that man whom he hath ordained; whereof he hath given assurance unto all men, in that he hath raised him from the dead.

Rom. 2 [16]In the day when God shall judge the secrets of men by Jesus Christ according to my gospel.

2 Cor. 5 [10]For we must all appear before the judgment seat of Christ; that every one may receive the things done in his body, according to that he hath done, whether it be good or bad.

Heb. 9 [27]And as it is appointed unto men once to die, but after this the judgment: [28]So Christ was once offered to bear the sins of many; and unto them that look for him shall he appear the second time without sin unto salvation.

2 Pet. 3 [7]But the heavens and the earth, which are now, by the same word are kept in store, reserved unto fire against the day of judgment and perdition of ungodly men.

The Last Judgment Described

Dan. 7 [9]I beheld till the thrones were cast down, and the Ancient of days did sit, whose garment was white as snow, and the hair of his head like the pure wool: his throne was like the fiery flame, and his wheels as burning fire. [10]A fiery stream issued and came forth from before him: thousand thousands ministered unto him, and ten thousand times ten thousand stood before him: the judgment was set, and the books were opened.

Matt. 25 [31]When the Son of man shall come in his glory, and all the holy angels with him, then shall he sit upon the throne of his glory: [32]And before him shall be gathered all nations; and he shall separate them one from another, as a shepherd divideth his sheep from the goats: [33]And he shall set the sheep on his right hand, but the goats on the left.

2 Thess. 1 [8]In flaming fire taking vengeance on them that know not God, and that obey not the gospel of our Lord Jesus Christ.

Rev. 6 [12]And I beheld when he had opened the sixth seal, and, lo, there was a great earthquake; and the sun became black as sackcloth of hair, and the moon became as blood; [13]And the stars of heaven fell unto the earth, even as a fig tree casteth her untimely figs, when she is shaken of a mighty wind. [14]And the heaven departed as a scroll when it is rolled together; and every mountain and island were moved out of their places.

[15]And the kings of the earth, and the great men, and the rich men, and the chief captains, and the mighty men, and every bondman, and every free man, hid themselves in the dens and in the rocks of the mountains; [16]And said to the mountains and rocks, Fall on us, and hide us from the face of him that sitteth on the throne, and from the wrath of the Lamb: [17]For the great day of his wrath is come; and who shall be able to stand?

Rev. 20 [11]And I saw a great white throne, and him that sat on it, from whose face the earth and the heaven fled away; and there was found no place for them. [12]And I saw the dead, small and great, stand before God; and the books were opened: and another book was opened, which is the book of life: and the dead were judged out of those things which were written in the books, according to their works. [13]And the sea gave up the dead which were in it; and death and hell delivered up the dead which were in them: and they were judged every man according to their works. [14]And death and hell were cast into the lake of fire. This is the second death. [15]And whosoever was not found written in the book of life was cast into the lake of fire.

Hope of Christians in Last Judgment

1 Cor. 4 [5]Therefore judge nothing before the time, until the Lord come, who both will bring to light the hidden things of darkness, and will make manifest the counsels of the hearts: and then shall every man have praise of God.

2 Tim. 4 [6]For I am now ready to be offered, and the time of my departure is at hand. [7]I have fought a good fight, I have finished my course, I have kept the faith: [8]Henceforth there is laid up for me a crown of righteousness, which the Lord, the righteous judge, shall give me at that day: and not to me only, but unto all them also that love his appearing.

1 John 4 [17]Herein is our love made perfect, that we may have boldness in the day of judgment: because as he is, so are we in this world.

JUSTICE

[jus'tis] The rendering to every one of his due right, reward, or punishment; conformity to the principles of righteousness and rectitude; conformity to truth and reality in thoughts or opinions and conduct. In many modern speech versions of the Bible, this word is translated "righteousness." God's justice is that perfection whereby He is infinitely righteous in all His dealings with man. His justice is pictured as of two sorts: remunerative, by which He gives rewards for goodness, and punitive, by which He deals out punishment.

SCRIPTURE

God's Justice

Deut. 32 [4]He is the Rock, his work is perfect: for all his ways are judgment: a God of truth and without iniquity, just and right is he.

Job 4 [17]Shall mortal man be more just than God? shall a man be more pure than his Maker?

Job 8 [3]Doth God pervert judgment? or doth the Almighty pervert justice?

Job 34 [12]Yea, surely God will not do wickedly, neither will the Almighty pervert judgment.

Zeph. 3 [5]The just LORD is in the midst thereof; he will not do iniquity: every morning doth he bring his judgment to light, he faileth not; but the unjust knoweth no shame.

1 John 1 [9]If we confess our sins, he is faithful and just to forgive us our sins, and to cleanse us from all unrighteousness.

Rev. 15 [3]And they sing the song of Moses the servant of God, and the song of the Lamb, saying, Great and marvellous are thy works, Lord God Almighty; just and true are thy ways, thou King of saints.

Man Commanded to Do Justice

Lev. 19 [35]Ye shall do no unrighteousness in judgment, in meteyard, in weight, or in measure. [36]Just balances, just weights, a just ephah, and a just hin shall ye have: I am the LORD your God, which brought you out of the land of Egypt.

Deut. 16 [18]Judges and officers shalt thou make thee in all thy gates, which the LORD thy God giveth thee, throughout thy tribes: and they shall judge the people with just judgment.

Psa. 82 [3]Defend the poor and fatherless: do justice to the afflicted and needy.

Prov. 3 [33]The curse of the LORD is in the house of the wicked: but he blesseth the habitation of the just.

Jer. 22 [3]Thus saith the LORD; Execute ye judgment and righteousness, and deliver the spoiled out of the hand of the oppressor: and do no wrong, do no violence to the stranger, the fatherless, nor the widow, neither shed innocent blood in this place.

Mic. 6 [8]He hath shewed thee, O man, what is good; and what doth the LORD require of thee, but to do justly, and to love mercy, and to walk humbly with thy God?

Matt. 7 [12]Therefore all things whatsoever ye would that men should do to you, do ye even so to them: for this is the law and the prophets.

Phil. 4 [8]Finally, brethren, whatsoever things are true, whatsoever things are honest, whatsoever things are just, whatsoever things are pure, whatsoever things are lovely, whatsoever things are of good report; if there be any virtue, and if there be any praise, think on these things.

Rom. 13 [7]Render therefore to all their dues: tribute to whom tribute is due; custom to whom custom; fear to whom fear; honour to whom honour. [8]Owe no man anything, but to love one another: for he that loveth another hath fulfilled the law.

Col. 4 [1]Masters, give unto your servants that which is just and equal; knowing that ye also have a Master in heaven.

JUSTIFICATION

[jus ti fi kā'shun] In Christian theology this word is used primarily to indicate the establishment of a right relationship between man and God. Because of the inherent sinfulness of human nature, man is separated from God. Left to his own devices, there is no possibility of his being delivered from sin and reconciled to God. As an expression of his grace toward man, however, God, through the life and death of Jesus, has made this deliverance and salvation possible, contingent only on obedient faith. Thus, what the believer cannot earn—justification—he receives freely in return for his faith, which expresses itself in a desire to be freed from sin, in complete trust that Christ has redeemed man, and in obedience to God's commands.

See RECONCILIATION, ATONEMENT, SIN

SCRIPTURE

Hab. 2 [4]Behold, his soul which is lifted up, is not upright in him: but the just shall live by his faith.

Acts 13 [39]And by him all that believe are justified from all things, from which ye could not be justified by the law of Moses.

Rom. 1 [17]For therein is the righteousness of God revealed from faith to faith: as it is written, The just shall live by faith.

Rom. 3 [20]Therefore by the deeds of the law there shall no flesh be justified in his sight: for by the law is the knowledge of sin. [21]But now the righteousness of God

without the law is manifested, being witnessed by the law and the prophets;
[22]Even the righteousness of God which is
by faith of Jesus Christ unto all and upon
all them that believe: for there is no difference:
[23]For all have sinned, and come
short of the glory of God; [24]Being justified
freely by his grace through the redemption that is in Christ Jesus: [25]Whom God
hath set forth to be a propitiation through
faith in his blood, to declare his righteousness for the remission of sins that are past,
through the forbearance of God; [26]To declare, I say, at this time his righteousness:
that he might be just, and the justifier of
him which believeth in Jesus. [27]Where is
boasting then? It is excluded. By what
law? of works? Nay: but by the law of
faith. [28]Therefore we conclude that a man
is justified by faith without the deeds of
the law.

Rom. 5 [1]Therefore being justified by
faith, we have peace with God through
our Lord Jesus Christ: [2]By whom also we
have access by faith into this grace
wherein we stand, and rejoice in hope
of the glory of God.

Gal. 3 [11]But that no man is justified by
the law in the sight of God, it is evident:
for, The just shall live by faith. [12]And the
law is not of faith: but, The man that
doeth them shall live in them.

KADESH, KADESH-BARNEA

[kā′desh-bär′nê a] A region situated in the wilderness of Zin (*Num. 20:1*), on the western edge of the territory of the Edomites, and on the southern border of what was later to be the territory of Judah. It was from Kadesh that the spies were sent out to survey the land of Canaan; when the majority returned with a negative report and convinced the Israelites of the difficulty of taking Canaan, they were sentenced to a long period of wandering about in the wilderness south of Palestine, during which time Kadesh continued to serve as headquarters (*Num. 13*). Here Miriam died and was buried (*Num. 20:1*). Here also the people murmured over the lack of water, at which time Moses brought forth water from the rock (*Num. 20:2-13*).

SCRIPTURE

Report of the Spies

Num. 13 [25]And they returned from
searching of the land after forty days.

[26]And they went and came to Moses,
and to Aaron, and to all the congregation
of the children of Israel, unto the wilderness of Paran, to Kadesh; and brought
back word unto them, and unto all the congregation, and shewed them the fruit of
the land.

Death of Miriam

Num. 20 [1]Then came the children of
Israel, even the whole congregation, into
the desert of Zin in the first month: and the
people abode in Kadesh; and Miriam died
there, and was buried there.

Moses Brings Forth Water

Num. 20 [2]And there was no water for
the congregation: and they gathered themselves together against Moses and against
Aaron. [3]And the people chode with Moses, and spake, saying, Would God that we
had died when our brethren died before
the LORD! [4]And why have ye brought up
the congregation of the LORD into this wilderness, that we and our cattle should die
there? [5]And wherefore have ye made us
to come up out of Egypt, to bring us unto
this evil place? it is no place of seed, or of
figs, or of vines, or of pomegranates; neither is there any water to drink. [6]And Moses and Aaron went from the presence of
the assembly unto the door of the taber-

nacle of the congregation, and they fell upon their faces: and the glory of the LORD appeared unto them.

7 And the LORD spake unto Moses, saying, 8 Take the rod, and gather thou the assembly together, thou and Aaron thy brother, and speak ye unto the rock before their eyes; and it shall give forth his water, and thou shalt bring forth to them water out of the rock: so thou shalt give the congregation and their beasts drink. 9 And Moses took the rod from before the LORD, as he commanded him. 10 And Moses and Aaron gathered the congregation together before the rock, and he said unto them, Hear now, ye rebels; must we fetch you water out of this rock? 11 And Moses lifted up his hand, and with his rod he smote the rock twice: and the water came out abundantly, and the congregation drank, and their beasts also.

12 And the LORD spake unto Moses and Aaron, Because ye believed me not, to sanctify me in the eyes of the children of Israel, therefore ye shall not bring this congregation into the land which I have given them. 13 This is the water of Meribah; because the children of Israel strove with the LORD, and he was sanctified in them.

A Major Dwelling-Place in the Wilderness

Num. 33 36 And they removed from Ezion-gaber, and pitched in the wilderness of Zin, which is Kadesh. 37 And they removed from Kadesh, and pitched in mount Hor, in the edge of the land of Edom.

Canaanites Defeated by Joshua at Kadesh-barnea

Josh. 10 41 And Joshua smote them from Kadesh-barnea even unto Gaza, and all the country of Goshen, even unto Gibeon.

KINDNESS

[kīnd'nes] The state or quality of being kind; beneficence; benevolence; goodness of heart or disposition.

See GENTLENESS, BENEFICENCE

SCRIPTURE

Prov. 19 22 The desire of a man is his kindness: and a poor man is better than a liar.

Prov. 31 26 She openeth her mouth with wisdom; and in her tongue is the law of kindness.

Rom. 12 10 Be kindly affectioned one to another with brotherly love; in honour preferring one another.

1 Cor. 13 4 Charity suffereth long, and is kind; charity envieth not; charity vaunteth not itself, is not puffed up.

2 Cor. 6 6 By pureness, by knowledge, by longsuffering, by kindness, by the Holy Ghost, by love unfeigned.

Eph. 4 32 And be ye kind one to another, tender-hearted, forgiving one another, even as God for Christ's sake hath forgiven you.

Col. 3 12 Put on therefore, as the elect of God, holy and beloved, bowels of mercies, kindness, humbleness of mind, meekness, longsuffering.

2 Pet. 1 7 And to godliness brotherly kindness; and to brotherly kindness charity.

KING

[king] A title given to a male monarch who rules over an independent people, usually having the right to transmit his power to his descendants. When the Israelites first settled in Palestine, they were divided into tribes and clans, each having its local chieftain. In addition to these chieftains, there were specially gifted men known as judges who were raised up by God in times of distress.

Eventually, foreign oppression became so severe that the Israelites clamored for a king to unite them and correct their desperate situation. Samuel, the last of the judges, regarded this as a rejection of God's divine kingship and warned of the abuses which would result; nevertheless, Saul was selected and anointed to be king. At Saul's death, there was uncertainty as to whether his successor should be chosen on the basis of heredity or natural ability. Both Saul's son Ishbosheth and David claimed the throne; David, of course, was the eventual victor. At his death, Solomon became king and the hereditary principle was firmly established. For further information regarding the kings of Israel and Judah, see chart in Appendix and articles on individual kings.

See SAMUEL, SAUL, DAVID, SOLOMON, JUDGES

SCRIPTURE

Kings Chosen by God

Deut. 17 [14]When thou art come unto the land which the LORD thy God giveth thee, and shalt possess it, and shalt dwell therein, and shalt say, I will set a king over me, like as all the nations that are about me.

1 Sam. 9 [17]And when Samuel saw Saul, the LORD said unto him, Behold the man whom I spake to thee of! this same shall reign over my people.

1 Sam. 16 [1]And the LORD said unto Samuel, How long wilt thou mourn for Saul, seeing I have rejected him from reigning over Israel? fill thine horn with oil, and go, I will send thee to Jesse the Bethlehemite: for I have provided me a king among his sons.

1 Kin. 11 [35]But I will take the kingdom out of his son's hand, and will give it unto thee, even ten tribes.

1 Kin. 19 [15]And the LORD said unto him, Go, return on thy way to the wilderness of Damascus: and when thou comest, anoint Hazael to be king over Syria.

1 Chr. 28 [4]Howbeit the LORD God of Israel chose me before all the house of my father to be king over Israel for ever: for he hath chosen Judah to be the ruler; and of the house of Judah, the house of my father; and among the sons of my father he liked me to make me king over all Israel.

Dan. 2 [21]And he changeth the times and the seasons: he removeth kings, and setteth up kings; he giveth wisdom unto the wise, and knowledge to them that know understanding.

Duties and Admonitions

Psa. 2 [10]Be wise now therefore, O ye kings: be instructed, ye judges of the earth.

Prov. 25 [2]It is the glory of God to conceal a thing: but the honour of kings is to search out a matter, [3]The heaven for height, and the earth for depth, and the heart of kings is unsearchable.

Prov. 31 [4]It is not for kings, O Lemuel, it is not for kings to drink wine; nor for princes strong drink: [5]Lest they drink, and forget the law, and pervert the judgment of any of the afflicted.

Honor Due to Kings

Prov. 24 [21]My son, fear thou the LORD and the king: and meddle not with them that are given to change.

Prov. 25 [6]Put not forth thyself in the presence of the king, and stand not in the place of great men.

Eccl. 8 [2]I counsel thee to keep the king's commandment, and that in regard of the oath of God.

Eccl. 10 [20]Curse not the king, no not in thy thought; and curse not the rich in thy bedchamber: for a bird of the air shall carry the voice, and that which hath wings shall tell the matter.

KINGDOM OF GOD

The Kingdom of God, or Kingdom of Heaven, as it is also called, especially in *Matthew*, was the central theme of the preaching and teaching of Jesus. It refers to the visible manifestation of God's reign over the universe. John the Baptist and Jesus announced that this long-awaited day had finally arrived, or was so near at hand that its effect could already be felt, and summoned men to prepare for its coming by repentance, a turning from sin unto God. Jesus bore witness to this kingdom by his mighty works, primarily his miracles of healing and exorcism of demons, and by his parables, many of which have as their theme the worth of the kingdom or the manner of its operation in the world. As a tiny seed grows secretly, ultimately becoming a tree, so the kingdom, whose beginnings are almost imperceptible, moves inexorably toward its final consummation.

The imminent breaking in of this kingdom demanded that men respond to God's call while there was yet time. A decision for the Kingdom of God would prove costly—indeed, it might well mean the surrender of all a man held dear—but its blessings were of such inestimable value as to make any sacrifice worthwhile. Response to the call to the Kingdom is made in terms of response to Christ, through whom God's assault on the powers of this world was made and in whom His rule is perfectly embodied.

The Kingdom of God is both present and future. With the activity of Jesus, the task of setting the world right was begun. God began to rule in a new way. The great Church of God, animated by the Spirit of the New Age, is a real, if imperfect, participation in that rule. In this sense, the Kingdom is present. But the Kingdom still awaits its fulfillment, its being brought to the perfection for which it is intended. As disciples of Christ, we look forward to the Day of Our Lord's return and the consummation of the Messianic Kingdom which is the heavenly goal of our life here below.

SCRIPTURE

Psa. 145 [11]They shall speak of the glory of thy kingdom, and talk of thy power; [12]To make known to the sons of men his mighty acts, and the glorious majesty of his kingdom. [13]Thy kingdom is an everlasting kingdom, and thy dominion endureth throughout all generations.

Isa. 24 [23]Then the moon shall be confounded, and the sun ashamed, when the LORD of hosts shall reign in mount Zion, and in Jerusalem, and before his ancients gloriously.

Dan. 2 [44]And in the days of these kings shall the God of heaven set up a kingdom, which shall never be destroyed: and the kingdom shall not be left to other people, but it shall break in pieces and consume all these kingdoms, and it shall stand for ever.

Matt. 3 [1]In those days came John the Baptist, preaching in the wilderness of Judaea, [2]And saying, Repent ye: for the kingdom of heaven is at hand.

Matt. 5 [3]Blessed are the poor in spirit: for theirs is the kingdom of heaven.

Matt. 7 [21]Not every one that saith unto me, Lord, Lord, shall enter into the kingdom of heaven; but he that doeth the will of my Father which is in heaven.

Matt. 8 [11]And I say unto you, That many shall come from the east and west, and shall sit down with Abraham, and Isaac, and Jacob, in the kingdom of heaven.

Matt. 11 [11]Verily I say unto you, Among them that are born of women there hath not risen a greater than John the Baptist: notwithstanding he that is least in the kingdom of heaven is greater than he.

Matt. 13 [11]He answered and said unto them, Because it is given unto you to know the mysteries of the kingdom of heaven, but to them it is not given.

Matt. 16 [28]Verily I say unto you, There be some standing here, which shall not taste of death, till they see the Son of man coming in his kingdom.

Luke 9 [62]And Jesus said unto him, No man, having put his hand to the plow, and looking back, is fit for the kingdom of God.

John 3 [3]Jesus answered and said unto him, Verily, verily, I say unto thee, Except a man be born again, he cannot see the kingdom of God.

John 18 [36]Jesus answered, My kingdom is not of this world: if my kingdom were of this world, then would my servants fight, that I should not be delivered to the Jews: but now is my kingdom not from hence.

Acts 14 [22]Confirming the souls of the disciples, and exhorting them to continue in the faith, and that we must through much tribulation enter into the kingdom of God.

Rom. 14 [17]For the kingdom of God is not meat and drink; but righteousness, and peace, and joy in the Holy Ghost.

1 Cor. 15 [50]Now this I say, brethren, that flesh and blood cannot inherit the kingdom of God; neither doth corruption inherit incorruption.

2 Thess. 1 [5]Which is a manifest token of the righteous judgment of God, that ye may be counted worthy of the kingdom of God, for which ye also suffer: [6]Seeing it is a righteous thing with God to recompense tribulation to them that trouble you.

2 Pet. 1 [11]For so an entrance shall be ministered unto you abundantly into the everlasting kingdom of our Lord and Saviour Jesus Christ.

KISS

[kis] To touch or press with the lips, as in love, affection, greeting, etc. The ancients used it to symbolize various things—affection, salutation, respect, veneration, submission, homage, and even worship and the end of enmity. Many references to it and its various uses are to be found in the Bible.

SCRIPTURE

Kiss a Holy Salute

Rom. 16 [16]Salute one another with an holy kiss. The churches of Christ salute you.

1 Cor. 16 [20]All the brethren greet you. Greet ye one another with an holy kiss.

2 Cor. 13 [12]Greet one another with an holy kiss.

Kiss a Mark of Affection

Gen. 27 [27]And he came near, and kissed him: and he smelled the smell of his raiment, and blessed him, and said, See, the smell of my son is as the smell of a field which the LORD hath blessed.

Gen. 29 [11]And Jacob kissed Rachel, and lifted up his voice, and wept.

Gen. 45 [15]Moreover, he kissed all his brethren, and wept upon them: and after that his brethren talked with him.

1 Sam. 10 [1]Then Samuel took a vial of oil, and poured it upon his head, and kissed him, and said, Is it not because the LORD hath anointed thee to be captain over his inheritance?

1 Sam. 20 [41]And as soon as the lad was gone, David arose out of a place toward the south, and fell on his face to the ground, and bowed himself three times: and they kissed one another, and wept one with another, until David exceeded.

Luke 7 [38]And stood at his feet behind him weeping, and began to wash his feet with tears, and did wipe them with the hairs of her head, and kissed his feet, and anointed them with the ointment.

Luke 15 [20]And he arose, and came to his father. But when he was yet a great way off, his father saw him, and had compassion, and ran, and fell on his neck, and kissed him.

Acts 20 [37]And they all wept sore, and fell on Paul's neck, and kissed him.

Treacherous Kiss

2 Sam. 20 [9]And Joab said to Amasa, Art thou in health, my brother? And Joab took Amasa by the beard with the right hand to kiss him. [10]But Amasa took no heed to the sword that was in Joab's hand: so he smote him therewith in the fifth rib, and shed out his bowels to the ground, and struck him not again; and he died. So Joab and Abishai his brother pursued after Sheba the son of Bichri.

Matt. 26 [48]Now he that betrayed him gave them a sign, saying, Whomsoever I shall kiss, that same is he: hold him fast. [49]And forthwith he came to Jesus, and said, Hail, master; and kissed him.

KNOWLEDGE

[nol'ej] In the Bible the word "know" has a much wider range of meaning than does our English word. It includes not only the ordinary meanings of perception, sensing, and understanding, but also the deepest and most profound experiences, including sexual experience, in which one apprehends reality. To know God in this sense—to understand his will, and to live in accordance with it—is the chief duty of man.

SCRIPTURE

Knowledge Given by God

Ex. 31 [3]And I have filled him with the spirit of God, in wisdom, and in understanding, and in knowledge, and in all manner of workmanship.

2 Chr. 1 [11]And God said to Solomon, Because this was in thine heart, and thou hast not asked riches, wealth, or honour, nor the life of thine enemies, neither yet hast asked long life; but hast asked wisdom and knowledge for thyself, that thou mayest judge my people, over whom I have made thee king: [12]Wisdom and knowledge is granted unto thee; and I will give thee riches, and wealth, and honour, such as none of the kings have had that have been before thee, neither shall there any after thee have the like.

Psa. 119 [66]Teach me good judgment and knowledge: for I have believed thy commandments.

Prov. 2 [6]For the LORD giveth wisdom: out of his mouth cometh knowledge and understanding.

Eccl. 2 [26]For God giveth to a man that is good in his sight, wisdom, and knowledge, and joy: but to the sinner he giveth travail, to gather and to heap up, that he may give to him that is good before God. This also is vanity and vexation of spirit.

Isa. 28 [9]Whom shall he teach knowledge? and whom shall he make to understand doctrine? them that are weaned from the milk, and drawn from the breasts. [10]For precept must be upon precept, precept upon precept; line upon line, line upon line; here a little, and there a little.

Dan. 2 [21]And he changeth the times and the seasons: he removeth kings, and setteth up kings; he giveth wisdom unto the wise, and knowledge to them that know understanding.

Matt. 11 [25]At that time Jesus answered and said, I thank thee, O Father, Lord of heaven and earth, because thou hast hid these things from the wise and prudent, and hast revealed them unto babes.

Matt. 13 [11]He answered and said unto them, Because it is given unto you to know the mysteries of the kingdom of heaven, but to them it is not given.

1 Cor. 2 [12]Now we have received, not the spirit of the world, but the spirit which is of God; that we might know the things that are freely given to us of God. [13]Which things also we speak, not in the words which man's wisdom teacheth, but which the Holy Ghost teacheth; comparing spiritual things with spiritual.

1 Cor. 12 [8]For to one is given by the Spirit the word of wisdom; to another the word of knowledge by the same Spirit.

Benefits of Knowledge

Prov. 1 [7]The fear of the LORD is the beginning of knowledge: but fools despise wisdom and instruction.

Prov. 4 [5]Get wisdom, get understanding: forget it not; neither decline from the words of my mouth. [6]Forsake her not, and she shall preserve thee: love her, and she shall keep thee. [7]Wisdom is the principal thing; therefore get wisdom: and with all thy getting get understanding.

Prov. 9 [9]Give instruction to a wise man, and he will be yet wiser: teach a just man, and he will increase in learning. [10]The fear of the LORD is the beginning of wisdom: and the knowledge of the Holy is understanding.

Prov. 10 [14]Wise men lay up knowledge: but the mouth of the foolish is near destruction.

Prov. 12 [1]Whoso loveth instruction loveth knowledge: but he that hateth reproof is brutish.

Prov. 13 [16]Every prudent man dealeth with knowledge: but a fool layeth open his folly.

Eccl. 7 [12]For wisdom is a defence, and money is a defence: but the excellency of knowledge is, that wisdom giveth life to them that have it.

Eph. 4 [13]Till we all come in the unity of the faith, and of the knowledge of the Son of God, unto a perfect man, unto the measure of the stature of the fulness of Christ.

Jas. 3 [13]Who is a wise man and endued with knowledge among you? let him shew out of a good conversation his works with meekness of wisdom.

2 Pet. 2 [20]For if after they have escaped the pollutions of the world through the knowledge of the Lord and Saviour Jesus Christ, they are again entangled therein, and overcome, the latter end is worse with them than the beginning.

Lack of Knowledge

Prov. 1 [22]How long, ye simple ones, will ye love simplicity? and the scorners delight in their scorning, and fools hate knowledge?

Prov. 19 [2]Also, that the soul be without knowledge, it is not good; and he that hasteth with his feet sinneth.

Jer. 4 [22]For my people is foolish, they have not known me; they are sottish children, and they have none understanding; they are wise to do evil, but to do good they have no knowledge.

Hos. 4 [6]My people are destroyed for lack of knowledge: because thou hast rejected knowledge, I will also reject thee, that thou shalt be no priest to me: seeing thou hast forgotten the law of thy God, I will also forget thy children.

Rom. 1 [28]And even as they did not like to retain God in their knowledge, God gave them over to a reprobate mind, to do those things which are not convenient.

Rom. 15 [34]Awake to righteousness, and sin not; for some have not the knowledge of God: I speak this to your shame.

Knowledge Prayed for and Sought

Col. 1 [9]For this cause we also, since the day we heard it, do not cease to pray for you, and to desire that ye might be filled with the knowledge of his will in all wisdom and spiritual understanding; [10]That ye might walk worthy of the Lord unto all pleasing, being fruitful in every good work, and increasing in the knowledge of God.

2 Pet. 3 [18]But grow in grace, and in the
knowledge of our Lord and Saviour Jesus
Christ. To him be glory both now and for
ever. Amen.

Knowledge's Responsibility

Rom. 1 [22]Professing themselves to be
wise, they became fools.

Rom. 2 [17]Behold, thou art called a Jew,
and restest in the law, and makest thy
boast of God, [18]And knowest his will, and
approvest the things that are more excellent, being instructed out of the law;
[19]And art confident that thou thyself art a
guide of the blind, a light of them which
are in darkness, [20]An instructor of the
foolish, a teacher of babes, which hast the
form of knowledge and of the truth in the
law.

Jas. 4 [17]Therefore to him that knoweth
to do good, and doeth it not, to him it is sin.

Imperfection of Man's Knowledge

Eccl. 2 [21]For there is a man whose labour is in wisdom, and in knowledge, and
in equity; yet to a man that hath not laboured therein shall he leave it for his portion. This also is vanity and a great evil.

Isa. 44 [25]That frustrateth the tokens of
the liars, and maketh diviners mad; that
turneth wise men backward, and maketh
their knowledge foolish.

1 Cor. 1 [19]For it is written, I will destroy
the wisdom of the wise, and will bring to
nothing the understanding of the prudent.
[20]Where is the wise? where is the scribe?
where is the disputer of this world? hath
not God made foolish the wisdom of this
world? [21]For after that in the wisdom of
God the world by wisdom knew not God,
it pleased God by the foolishness of
preaching to save them that believe.

1 Cor. 3 [18]Let no man deceive himself.
If any man among you seemeth to be wise
in this world, let him become a fool, that
he may be wise. [19]For the wisdom of this
world is foolishness with God. For it is
written, He taketh the wise in their own
craftiness. [20]And again, The Lord knoweth the thoughts of the wise, that they are
vain.

KORAH

[kō′ra] A contemporary of Moses, best known as the main character of the story of the ill-fated rebellion in the wilderness. In company with Dathan and Abiram, Korah led 250 "princes of the assembly" in a public complaint against Moses and Aaron, asserting that they had unjustifiably usurped the authority which they held. In order to determine whom God had chosen, Moses bade the malcontents to gather the next morning at the door of the tabernacle. Korah and the 250 made their appearance on schedule, but Dathan and Abiram refused to come. Going to the tents of these men, Moses instructed all those nearby to withdraw. The narrative states that the earth then opened up, swallowing "all those that appertained unto" the leaders of the rebellion. At the same time, fire consumed those who were before the door of the tabernacle. This was then followed by a general plague which caused great destruction in the camp.

SCRIPTURE

Num. 16 [1]Now Korah, the son of Izhar,
the son of Kohath, the son of Levi, and Dathan and Abiram, the sons of Eliab, and
On, the son of Peleth, sons of Reuben, took
men: [2]And they rose up before Moses,
with certain of the children of Israel, two
hundred and fifty princes of the assembly,
famous in the congregation, men of renown: [3]And they gathered themselves together against Moses and against Aaron,
and said unto them, Ye take too much
upon you, seeing all the congregation are
holy, every one of them, and the LORD is
among them: wherefore then lift ye up
yourselves above the congregation of the

LORD? 4And when Moses heard it, he fell
upon his face: 5And he spake unto Korah
and unto all his company, saying, Even to-
morrow the LORD will shew who are his,
and who is holy; and will cause him to
come near unto him: even him whom he
hath chosen will he cause to come near
unto him. 6This do; Take you censers, Korah, and all his company; 7And put fire
therein, and put incense in them before the
LORD to-morrow: and it shall be that the
man whom the LORD doth choose, he shall
be holy: ye take too much upon you, ye
sons of Levi. 8And Moses said unto Korah, Hear, I pray you, ye sons of Levi:
9Seemeth it but a small thing unto you,
that the God of Israel hath separated you
from the congregation of Israel, to bring
you near to himself to do the service of the
tabernacle of the LORD, and to stand before the congregation to minister unto
them? 10And he hath brought thee near to
him, and all thy brethren the sons of Levi
with thee: and seek ye the priesthood also?
11For which cause both thou and all thy
company are gathered together against the
LORD: and what is Aaron, that ye murmur
against him?

12And Moses sent to call Dathan and
Abiram, the sons of Eliab; which said, We
will not come up: 13Is it a small thing that
thou hast brought us up out of a land that
floweth with milk and honey, to kill us in
the wilderness, except thou make thyself
altogether a prince over us? 14Moreover,
thou hast not brought us into a land that
floweth with milk and honey, or given us
inheritance of fields and vineyards: wilt
thou put out the eyes of these men? we
will not come up. 15And Moses was very
wroth, and said unto the LORD, Respect
not thou their offering: I have not taken
one ass from them, neither have I hurt one
of them. 16And Moses said unto Korah, Be
thou and all thy company before the LORD,
thou, and they, and Aaron, to-morrow:
17And take every man his censer, and put
incense in them, and bring ye before the
LORD every man his censer, two hundred
and fifty censers; thou also, and Aaron,
each of you his censer. 18And they took
every man his censer, and put fire in them,
and laid incense thereon, and stood in the
door of the tabernacle of the congregation
with Moses and Aaron. 19And Korah gathered all the congregation against them
unto the door of the tabernacle of the congregation: and the glory of the LORD appeared unto all the congregation. 20And
the LORD spake unto Moses and unto Aaron, saying, 21Separate yourselves from
among this congregation, that I may consume them in a moment. 22And they fell
upon their faces, and said, O God, the God
of the spirits of all flesh, shall one man sin,
and wilt thou be wroth with all the congregation?

23And the LORD spake unto Moses, saying, 24Speak unto the congregation, saying, Get you up from about the tabernacle
of Korah, Dathan, and Abiram. 25And Moses rose up and went unto Dathan and
Abiram; and the elders of Israel followed
him. 26And he spake unto the congregation, saying, Depart, I pray you, from the
tents of these wicked men, and touch nothing of theirs, lest ye be consumed in all
their sins. 27So they gat up from the tabernacle of Korah, Dathan, and Abiram,
on every side: and Dathan and Abiram
came out, and stood in the door of their
tents, and their wives, and their sons,
and their little children. 28And Moses said,
Hereby ye shall know that the LORD hath
sent me to do all these works; for I have
not done them of mine own mind. 29If
these men die the common death of all
men, or if they be visited after the visita-

tion of all men; then the LORD hath not
sent me. 30 But if the LORD make a new
thing, and the earth open her mouth, and
swallow them up, with all that appertain
unto them, and they go down quick into
the pit; then ye shall understand that these
men have provoked the LORD.
31 And it came to pass, as he had made an
end of speaking all these words, that the
ground clave asunder that was under
them: 32 And the earth opened her mouth,
and swallowed them up, and their houses,
and all the men that appertained unto Korah, and all their goods. 33 They, and all
that appertained to them, went down alive
into the pit, and the earth closed upon
them: and they perished from among the
congregation. 34 And all Israel that were
round about them fled at the cry of them:
for they said, Lest the earth swallow us up
also. 35 And there came out a fire from the
LORD, and consumed the two hundred and
fifty men that offered incense.

LABAN

[lā′ban] Son of Bethuel, brother of Rebekah, father of Leah and Rachel. Laban was a member of that segment of the family of Terah which had remained in Haran when Abraham and Lot migrated to Canaan. He first appears in the incident concerning the giving of his sister Rebekah as a wife for Isaac. He is best known, however, for his craft and deceit in dealing with Jacob. In order to win Rachel for his wife, Jacob served Laban seven years; at the end of that time, Laban gave him Leah and made him work an additional seven years for Rachel. When these fourteen years were completed, Jacob served Laban six additional years, working for a stipulated wage. In these six years, Jacob proved himself a match for Laban's shrewdness and emerged a wealthy man. Although there was considerable furor over the departure of Jacob and his company for Canaan, Laban was reconciled to his son-in-law in the famous covenant of Mizpah—"The Lord watch between me and thee, when we are absent one from another."

See JACOB, LEAH, RACHEL

SCRIPTURE

Rebekah's Brother

Gen. 28 5 And Isaac sent away Jacob:
and he went to Padanaram unto Laban,
son of Bethuel the Syrian, the brother of
Rebekah, Jacob's and Esau's mother.

Welcomes Jacob

Gen. 29 13 And it came to pass, when Laban heard the tidings of Jacob his sister's
son, that he ran to meet him, and embraced
him, and kissed him, and brought him to
his house. And he told Laban all these
things. 14 And Laban said to him, Surely
thou art my bone and my flesh. And he
abode with him the space of a month.

Deceives Jacob

Gen. 29 15 And Laban said unto Jacob,
Because thou art my brother, shouldest
thou therefore serve me for nought? tell
me, what shall thy wages be? 16 And Laban had two daughters: the name of the
elder was Leah, and the name of the
younger was Rachel. 17 Leah was tender
eyed; but Rachel was beautiful and well
favoured. 18 And Jacob loved Rachel; and
said, I will serve thee seven years for Rachel thy younger daughter. 19 And Laban
said, It is better that I give her to thee, than
that I should give her to another man:
abide with me. 20 And Jacob served seven
years for Rachel; and they seemed unto
him but a few days, for the love he had to
her.
21 And Jacob said unto Laban, Give me
my wife, for my days are fulfilled, that I
may go in unto her. 22 And Laban gathered

together all the men of the place, and made a feast. [23]And it came to pass in the evening, that he took Leah his daughter, and brought her to him; and he went in unto her. [24]And Laban gave unto his daughter Leah Zilpah his maid for a handmaid. [25]And it came to pass, that in the morning, behold, it was Leah: and he said to Laban, What is this thou hast done unto me? did not I serve with thee for Rachel? wherefore then hast thou beguiled me? [26]And Laban said, It must not be so done in our country, to give the younger before the firstborn. [27]Fulfil her week, and we will give thee this also for the service which thou shalt serve with me yet seven other years. [28]And Jacob did so, and fulfilled her week: and he gave him Rachel his daughter to wife also. [29]And Laban gave to Rachel his daughter Bilhah his handmaid to be her maid. [30]And he went in also unto Rachel, and he loved also Rachel more than Leah, and served with him yet seven other years.

Outwitted by Jacob

Gen. 30 [25]And it came to pass, when Rachel had borne Joseph, that Jacob said unto Laban, Send me away, that I may go unto mine own place, and to my country. [26]Give me my wives and my children, for whom I have served thee, and let me go: for thou knowest my service which I have done thee. [27]And Laban said unto him, I pray thee, if I have found favour in thine eyes, tarry: for I have learned by experience that the LORD hath blessed me for thy sake. [28]And he said, Appoint me thy wages, and I will give it. [29]And he said unto him, Thou knowest how I have served thee, and how thy cattle was with me. [30]For it was little which thou hadst before I came, and it is now increased unto a multitude; and the LORD hath blessed thee since my coming: and now, when shall I provide for mine own house also? [31]And he said, What shall I give thee? and Jacob said, Thou shalt not give me anything: if thou wilt do this thing for me, I will again feed and keep thy flock. [32]I will pass through all thy flock to-day, removing from thence all the speckled and spotted cattle, and all the brown cattle among the sheep, and the spotted and speckled among the goats: and of such shall be my hire. [33]So shall my righteousness answer for me in time to come, when it shall come for my hire before thy face: every one that is not speckled and spotted among the goats, and brown among the sheep, that shall be counted stolen with me. [34]And Laban said, Behold, I would it might be according to thy word. [35]And he removed that day the he-goats that were ringstreaked and spotted, and all the she-goats that were speckled and spotted, and every one that had some white in it, and all the brown among the sheep, and gave them into the hand of his sons. [36]And he set three days' journey betwixt himself and Jacob: and Jacob fed the rest of Laban's flocks.

[37]And Jacob took him rods of green poplar, and of the hazel and chestnut tree; and pilled white streaks in them, and made the white appear which was in the rods. [38]And he set the rods which he had pilled before the flocks in the gutters in the watering troughs when the flocks came to drink, that they should conceive when they came to drink. [39]And the flocks conceived before the rods, and brought forth cattle ringstreaked, speckled, and spotted. [40]And Jacob did separate the lambs, and set the faces of the flocks toward the ringstreaked, and all the brown in the flock

of Laban; and he put his own flocks by
themselves, and put them not unto Laban's cattle. 41And it came to pass, whensoever the stronger cattle did conceive,
that Jacob laid the rods before the eyes of
the cattle in the gutters, that they might
conceive among the rods. 42But when the
cattle were feeble, he put them not in: so
the feebler were Laban's, and the stronger
Jacob's. 43And the man increased exceedingly, and had much cattle, and maidservants, and menservants, and camels, and
asses.

Covenants with Jacob after the Latter Flees

Gen. 31 17Then Jacob rose up, and set
his sons and his wives upon camels; 18And
he carried away all his cattle, and all his
goods which he had gotten, the cattle of
his getting, which he had gotten in Padan-
aram, for to go to Isaac his father in the
land of Canaan. 19And Laban went to
shear his sheep: and Rachel had stolen the
images that were her father's. 20And Jacob
stole away unawares to Laban the Syrian,
in that he told him not that he fled. 21So he
fled with all that he had; and he rose up,
and passed over the river, and set his face
toward the mount Gilead. 22And it was
told Laban on the third day, that Jacob
was fled. 23And he took his brethren with
him, and pursued after him seven days'
journey; and they overtook him in the
mount Gilead. 24And God came to Laban
the Syrian in a dream by night, and said
unto him, Take heed that thou speak not to
Jacob either good or bad.

25Then Laban overtook Jacob. Now Jacob had pitched his tent in the mount: and
Laban with his brethren pitched in the
mount of Gilead.

44Now therefore come thou, let us make
a covenant, I and thou; and let it be for a
witness between me and thee. 45And Jacob took a stone, and set it up for a pillar.
46And Jacob said unto his brethren, Gather
stones; and they took stones, and made a
heap: and they did eat there upon the
heap. 47And Laban called it Jegarsaha-
dutha: but Jacob called it Galeed. 48And
Laban said, This heap is a witness between me and thee this day. Therefore
was the name of it called Galeed; 49And
Mizpah; for he said, The LORD watch between me and thee, when we are absent
one from another.

LABOR

[lā′bẽr] Physical or mental toil or exertion; effort directed toward some useful end work. The Hebrews viewed work as a divine ordinance for human life, binding on all men. It is frequently stated that labor was a curse of the Fall of man; an examination of *Gen. 1-3*, however, shows this to be an erroneous view. Adam was placed in the garden with the responsibility to care for it and to exercise his dominion over the creation. The effect of the curse was to introduce drudgery, bitterness, and suffering into what was originally designed to be man's proper function. To those who are redeemed in Christ, this curse is removed and work once again becomes joyful service given for the greater glory of God. Although work is a natural part of man's existence, it is not the only part; God has set aside one day in seven as a sabbath on which man properly ceases his work and gives himself to the worship and enjoyment of God.

SCRIPTURE

Labor Ordained for Man

Gen. 3 19In the sweat of thy face shalt thou eat bread, till thou return unto the ground; for out of it wast thou taken: for dust thou art, and unto dust shalt thou return.

Psa. 104 23Man goeth forth unto his work and to his labour until the evening.

Labor Blessed by God

Prov. 10 [16]The labour of the righteous tendeth to life: the fruit of the wicked to sin.

Prov. 13 [11]Wealth gotten by vanity shall be diminished: but he that gathereth by labour shall increase.

Eccl. 2 [24]There is nothing better for a man than that he should eat and drink, and that he should make his soul enjoy good in his labour. This also I saw, that it was from the hand of God.

Eccl. 5 [12]The sleep of a labouring man is sweet, whether he eat little or much: but the abundance of the rich will not suffer him to sleep.

[19]Every man also to whom God hath given riches and wealth, and hath given him power to eat thereof, and to take his portion, and to rejoice in his labour; this is the gift of God.

Labor Forbidden on the Sabbath

Ex. 20 [8]Remember the sabbath day, to keep it holy. [9]Six days shalt thou labour, and do all thy work: [10]But the seventh day is the sabbath of the LORD thy God: in it thou shalt not do any work, thou, nor thy son, nor thy daughter, thy manservant, nor thy maidservant, nor thy cattle, nor thy stranger that is within thy gates: [11]For in six days the LORD made heaven and earth, the sea, and all that in them is, and rested the seventh day: wherefore the LORD blessed the sabbath day, and hallowed it.

Lawful to Labor for Good on Sabbath

Luke 13 [14]And the ruler of the synagogue answered with indignation, because that Jesus had healed on the sabbath day, and said unto the people, There are six days in which men ought to work: in them therefore come and be healed, and not on the sabbath day. [15]The Lord then answered him, and said, Thou hypocrite, doth not each one of you on the sabbath loose his ox or his ass from the stall, and lead him away to watering?

Luke 14 [3]And Jesus answering spake unto the lawyers and Pharisees, saying, Is it lawful to heal on the sabbath day? [4]And they held their peace. And he took him, and healed him, and let him go; [5]And answered them, saying, Which of you shall have an ass or an ox fallen into a pit, and will not straightway pull him out on the sabbath day? [6]And they could not answer him again to these things.

The Laborer's Hire

Luke 10 [7]And in the same house remain, eating and drinking such things as they give: for the labourer is worthy of his hire. Go not from house to house.

2 Thess. 3 [10]For even when we were with you, this we commanded you, that if any would not work, neither should he eat.

1 Tim. 5 [18]For the scripture saith, Thou shalt not muzzle the ox that treadeth out the corn. And, The labourer is worthy of his reward.

LAODICEA

[lā od i sē′a] A city in the Roman province of Asia, situated in the valley of the Maeander River on a smaller river called the Lycus, near Colossae and Hierapolis. It was founded by Antiochus II of Syria, and named in honor of his wife Laodike. Under the Romans, Laodicea became a city of considerable importance and wealth. Little is known of the early history of Christianity there, although it was probably introduced by Paul or his companions. It is best remembered as the home of one of the letters to the Seven Churches in Asia, in which it is admonished for being "lukewarm" (*Rev 3:14-22*).

LASCIVIOUSNESS

[la siv′i us ness] Licentiousness; wantonness; unbridled lust; conduct and character that is indecent, unbecoming, and shameless.

See ADULTERY, LUST, SENSUALITY

SCRIPTURE

Ex. 32 6And they rose up early on the morrow, and offered burnt offerings, and brought peace offerings; and the people sat down to eat and to drink, and rose up to play.

Mark 7 21For from within, out of the heart of men, proceed evil thoughts, adulteries, fornications, murders, 22Thefts, covetousness, wickedness, deceit, lasciviousness, an evil eye, blasphemy, pride, foolishness:

Rom. 1 29Being filled with all unrighteousness, fornication, wickedness.

Rom. 13 13Let us walk honestly, as in the day: not in rioting and drunkenness, not in chambering and wantonness, not in strife and envying.

1 Cor. 6 9Know ye not that the unrighteous shall not inherit the kingdom of God? Be not deceived: neither fornicators, nor idolaters, nor adulterers, nor effeminate, nor abusers of themselves with mankind, 10Nor thieves, nor covetous, nor drunkards, nor revilers, nor extortioners, shall inherit the kingdom of God.

2 Cor. 12 21I shall bewail many which have sinned already, and have not repented of the uncleanness and fornication and lasciviousness which they have committed.

Gal. 5 19Now the works of the flesh are manifest, which are these; Adultery, fornication, uncleanness, lasciviousness, 20Idolatry, witchcraft, hatred, variance, emulations, wrath, strife, seditions, heresies. 21Envyings, murders, drunkenness, revellings, and such like: of the which I tell you before, as I have also told you in time past, that they which do such things shall not inherit the kingdom of God.

Eph. 4 17This I say therefore, and testify in the Lord, that ye henceforth walk not as other Gentiles walk, in the vanity of their mind, 18Having the understanding darened, being alienated from the life of God through the ignorance that is in them, because of the blindness of their heart. 19Who being past feeling have given themselves over unto lasciviousness, to work all uncleanness with greediness.

Eph. 5 5For this ye know, that no whoremonger, nor unclean person, nor covetous man, who is an idolater, hath any inheritance in the kingdom of Christ and of God.

Col. 3 5Mortify therefore your members which are upon the earth; fornication, uncleanness, inordinate affection, evil concupiscence, and covetousness, which is idolatry:

2 Tim. 3 6For of this sort are they which creep into houses, and lead captive silly women laden with sins, led away with divers lusts.

1 Pet. 4 2That he no longer should live the rest of his time in the flesh to the lusts of men, but to the will of God. 3For the time past of our life may suffice us to have wrought the will of the Gentiles, when ye walked in lasciviousness, lusts, excess of wine, revellings, banquetings, and abominable idolatries.

Jude 1 4For there are certain men crept in unawares, who were before of old ordained to this condemnation, ungodly men, turning the grace of our God into lasciviousness, and denying the only Lord God, and our Lord Jesus Christ. 7Even as

Sodom and Gomorrah, and the cities about them in like manner, giving themselves over to fornication, and going after strange flesh, are set forth for an example, suffering the vengeance of eternal fire.

LAVER

[lā'vĕr] A vessel for washing; a basin or bowl. Every priest who served at the altar of God was required to wash his hands and feet before entering upon his duties. (*See Ex. 30:19ff*) To facilitate this, a brazen laver was constructed and placed on a pedestal between the altar and the tabernacle itself. In the great temple of Solomon, the vessel in which the priests washed was called a "molten sea." There were also ten lavers in the court of the temple which were used to wash the sacrifices for burnt offerings. These were large tanks of water, each having a capacity of over 300 gallons, and were ornamented with lions, oxen, cherubim, and wreaths of flowers. They were mounted on wheels, which enabled them to be moved about within the court. The use of these vessels emphasizes the role of physical purity in the religion of Israel.

See TABERNACLE, TEMPLE

SCRIPTURE

In the Tabernacle

Ex. 30 [18]Thou shalt also make a laver of
brass, and his foot also of brass, to wash
withal: and thou shalt put it between the
tabernacle of the congregation and the altar, and thou shalt put water therein. [19]For
Aaron and his sons shall wash their hands
and their feet thereat: [20]When they go
into the tabernacle of the congregation,
they shall wash with water, that they die
not; or when the come near to the altar to
minister, to burn offering made by fire
unto the LORD:

Ex. 40 [7]And thou shalt set the laver between the tent of the congregation and the
altar, and shalt put water therein.
[30]And he set the laver between the tent
of the congregation and the altar, and put
water there, to wash withal. [31]And Moses
and Aaron and his sons washed their hands
and their feet thereat: [32]When they went
into the tent of the congregation, and
when they came near unto the altar, they
washed; as the LORD commanded Moses.

In the Temple

1 Kin. 7 [23]And he made a molten sea,
ten cubits from the one brim to the other:
it was round all about, and his height was
five cubits: and a line of thirty cubits did
compass it round about. [25]It stood upon
twelve oxen, three looking toward the
north, and three looking toward the west,
and three looking toward the south, and
three looking toward the east: and the sea
was set above upon them, and all their
hinder parts were inward.
[27]And he made ten bases of brass; four
cubits was the length of one base, and four
cubits the breadth thereof, and three cubits the height of it. [28]And the work of the
bases was on this manner: they had borders, and the borders were between the
ledges: [29]And on the borders that were
between the ledges were lions, oxen, and
cherubims: and upon the ledges there was
a base above: and beneath the lions and
oxen were certain additions made of thin
work. [30]And every base had four brasen
wheels, and plates of brass: and the four
corners thereof had undersetters: under
the laver were undersetters molten, at the
side of every addition.
[38]Then made he ten lavers of brass: one
laver contained forty baths: and every laver was four cubits: and upon every one of
the ten bases one laver. [39]And he put five
bases on the right side of the house, and
five on the left side of the house: and he

set the sea on the right side of the house eastward over against the south.

LAW

[lô] The Hebrew word for law is *Torah.* This term includes not only legal prescriptions, but also the wider range of instruction and guidance which is required to maintain life in a community. As used in the Bible, law refers primarily to the Law of Moses, that body of material contained in and derived from God's covenant with the children of Israel and delivered to Moses on Mt. Sinai. The Law of Moses was a covenant law, accepted by the people of Israel in gratitude for God's mighty acts of deliverance from Egyptian bondage. The basic document of the Mosaic law was the Decalogue, or Ten Commandments (*Ex. 20:1-17*). In addition to this there were the various codes, such as that contained in *Ex. 21-23,* which dealt with more specific matters and which set forth the manner in which the law was to be implemented. The Law furnished the structure of Israel's life and instructed each man in his relation to God and to his fellow-covenanter. When the stipulations of the covenant law were disregarded, God's judgment broke out on his people. The chief work of the prophets was to call attention to these breaches of the covenant and to call the nation to repentance, warning them of the consequences of continued disobedience.

During the period of the Babylonian exile, there was a notable development with respect to the attitude toward the law. The truth of the message of the prophets had finally been brought home to Israel. As a consequence there arose a great concern for rigid observance of the Law. In some respects this was a healthy attitude, but it too often degenerated into a legalistic attitude in which the spirit of thankful response to God's grace gave way to a doctrine of merit, in which one kept the law simply in view of the blessings which flow from obedience and the punishment for disobedience. In conjunction with this, there arose the feeling that all who did not observe the law in this strict, legalistic manner were to be shunned as spiritually and socially inferior.

As historical circumstances changed it became clear that the written law made no provision for a number of situations. Hence, there developed alongside the written an oral law, an unwritten tradition containing regulations and prescriptions growing out of long-established customs and interpolations on the written law. In New Testament times the Jews were divided in their attitude toward this law. The Pharisees accepted it as valid but the Sadducees refused to acknowledge its authority. Jesus was referring to this oral law when he spoke of the "tradition of the elders" or "the tradition of men." Most references to law in the New Testament refer not to the idea of law in general, but to the Law of Moses in particular. There we learn that the function of the Law in God's plan was to convict man of his sinfulness and to make him aware of his inability to attain salvation apart from God's grace. The law thus served as a schoolmaster to direct men to Christ, whose perfect obedience brought it to fulfillment and set it aside in favor of the Law of Christ, which could deal effectively with sin and guilt.

The fact that there could be no salvation under the law has led many to characterize the Old Testament as a book of law, in the legalistic sense, and the New Testament as a book of grace. In any study of law and grace in the Bible, however, one must remember that the provisions of the Law presuppose God's grace and mercy and the grace set forth in the New Covenant enjoins certain "legal" obligations.

SCRIPTURE

Law Proclaimed through Moses

Ex. 19 [3]And Moses went up unto God,
and the LORD called unto him out of the
mountain, saying, Thus shalt thou say to
the house of Jacob, and tell the children
of Israel; [4]Ye have seen what I did unto
the Egyptians, and how I bare you on
eagles' wings, and brought you unto myself. [5]Now therefore, if ye will obey my
voice indeed, and keep my covenant, then
ye shall be a peculiar treasure unto me
above all people: for all the earth is mine:
[6]And ye shall be unto me a kingdom of
priests, and a holy nation. These are the

words which thou shalt speak unto the children of Israel.

Deut. 5 [1]And Moses called all Israel, and said unto them, Hear, O Israel, the statutes and judgments which I speak in your ears this day, that ye may learn them, and keep and do them.

Entire Obedience Demanded

Deut. 27 [26]Cursed be he that confirmeth not all the words of this law to do them: and all the people shall say, Amen.

Gal. 3 [10]For as many as are of the works of the law are under the curse: for it is written, Cursed is every one that continueth not in all things which are written in the book of the law to do them.

Jas. 2 [10]For whosoever shall keep the whole law, and yet offend in one point, he is guilty of all.

The Law Good

Psa. 19 [7]The law of the LORD is perfect, converting the soul: the testimony of the LORD is sure, making wise the simple. [8]The statutes of the LORD are right, rejoicing the heart: the commandment of the LORD is pure, enlightening the eyes.

Rom. 7 [12]Wherefore the law is holy, and the commandment holy, and just, and good.

All Men Guilty under the Law

Rom. 3 [19]Now we know that what things soever the law saith, it saith to them who are under the law: that every mouth may be stopped, and all the world may become guilty before God. [20]Therefore by the deeds of the law there shall no flesh be justified in his sight: for by the law is the knowledge of sin.

Fulfilled in Christ

Matt. 5 [17]Think not that I am come to destroy the law, or the prophets: I am not come to destroy, but to fulfil. [18]For verily I say unto you, Till heaven and earth pass, one jot or one tittle shall in no wise pass from the law, till all be fulfilled. [19]Whosoever therefore shall break one of these least commandments, and shall teach men so, he shall be called the least in the kingdom of heaven: but whosoever shall do and teach them, the same shall be called great in the kingdom of heaven.

Rom. 5 [18]Therefore as by the offence of one judgment came upon all men to condemnation; even so by the righteousness of one the free gift came upon all men unto justification of life. [19]For as by one man's disobedience many were made sinners, so by the obedience of one shall many be made righteous. [20]Moreover the law entered, that the offence might abound. But where sin abounded, grace did much more abound: [21]That as sin hath reigned unto death, even so might grace reign through righteousness unto eternal life by Jesus Christ our Lord.

Abolished in Christ

Acts 15 [24]Forasmuch as we have heard, that certain which went out from us have troubled you with words, subverting your souls, saying, Ye must be circumcised, and keep the law: to whom we gave no such commandment.

Gal. 2 [16]Knowing that a man is not justified by the works of the law, but by the faith of Jesus Christ, even we have believed in Jesus Christ, that we might be justified by the faith of Christ, and not by the works of the law: for by the works of the law shall no flesh be justified.

Gal. 3 [17]And this I say, that the covenant, that was confirmed before of God in Christ, the law, which was four hundred and thirty years after, cannot disannul, that it should make the promise of none effect. [18]For if the inheritance be of the law, it is no more of promise: but God gave it to Abraham by promise. [19]Wherefore then serveth the law? It was added because of transgressions, till the seed should come to whom the promise was made; and it was ordained by angels in the hand of a mediator. [20]Now a mediator is not a mediator of one, but God is one. [21]Is the law then against the promises of God? God forbid: for if there had been a law given which could have given life, verily righteousness should have been by the law. [22]But the scripture hath concluded all under sin, that the promise by faith of Jesus Christ might be given to them that believe. [23]But before faith came, we were kept under the law, shut up unto the faith which should afterwards be revealed. [24]Wherefore the law was our schoolmaster to bring us unto Christ, that we might be justified by faith. [25]But after that faith is come, we are no longer under a schoolmaster.

Eph. 2 [13]But now in Christ Jesus ye who sometimes were far off are made nigh by the blood of Christ. [14]For he is our peace, who hath made both one, and hath broken down the middle wall of partition between us; [15]Having abolished in his flesh the enmity, even the law of commandments contained in ordinances; for to make in himself of twain one new man, so making peace; [16]And that he might reconcile both unto God in one body by the cross, having slain the enmity thereby.

Col. 2 [14]Blotting out the handwriting of ordinances that was against us, which was contrary to us, and took it out of the way, nailing it to his cross.

Heb. 7 [19]For the law made nothing perfect, but the bringing in of a better hope did; by the which we draw nigh unto God. [20]And inasmuch as not without an oath he was made priest: [21](For those priests were made without an oath; but this with an oath by him that said unto him, The Lord sware and will not repent, Thou art a priest for ever after the order of Melchisedec:) [22]By so much was Jesus made a surety of a better testament.

Christians Redeemed

John 1 [17]For the law was given by Moses, but grace and truth came by Jesus Christ.

Acts 13 [39]And by him all that believe are justified from all things, from which ye could not be justified by the law of Moses.

Rom. 10 [4]For Christ is the end of the law for righteousness to every one that believeth. [5]For Moses describeth the righteousness which is of the law, That the man which doeth those things shall live by them. [6]But the righteousness which is of faith speaketh on this wise, Say not in thine heart, Who shall ascend into heaven? (that is, to bring Christ down from above:) [7]Or, who shall descend into the deep? (that is, to bring up Christ again from the dead.) [8]But what saith it? The word is nigh thee, even in thy mouth, and in thy heart: that is, the word of faith, which we preach; [9]That if thou shalt confess with thy mouth the Lord Jesus, and shalt believe in thine heart that God hath raised him from the dead, thou shalt be saved.

Gal. 3 [1]O foolish Galatians, who hath bewitched you, that ye should not obey the truth, before whose eyes Jesus Christ hath been evidently set forth, crucified among you? [2]This only would I learn of you, Received ye the Spirit by the works of the law, or by the hearing of faith?

[3]Are ye so foolish? having begun in the Spirit, are ye now made perfect by the flesh? [4]Have ye suffered so many things in vain? if it be yet in vain. [5]He therefore that ministereth to you the Spirit, and worketh miracles among you, doeth he it by the works of the law, or by the hearing of faith? [6]Even as Abraham believed God, and it was accounted to him for righteousness. [7]Know ye therefore that they which are of faith, the same are the children of Abraham. [8]And the scripture, foreseeing that God would justify the heathen through faith, preached before the gospel unto Abraham, saying, In thee shall all nations be blessed. [9]So then they which be of faith are blessed with faithful Abraham. [10]For as many as are of the works of the law are under the curse: for it is written, Cursed is every one that continueth not in all things which are written in the book of the law to do them. [11]But that no man is justified by the law in the sight of God, it is evident: for, The just shall live by faith. [12]And the law is not of faith: but, The man that doeth them shall live in them. [13]Christ hath redeemed us from the curse of the law, being made a curse for us: for it is written, Cursed is every one that hangeth on a tree: [14]That the blessing of Abraham might come on the Gentiles through Jesus Christ; that we might receive the promise of the Spirit through faith.

LAZARUS

[laz′a rus] 1. The brother of Martha and Mary at whose home in Bethany Jesus was accustomed to visit. During a period in which Jesus was absent from the area, Lazarus fell ill and died; after lying in the tomb for four days, however, he was raised from the dead by Jesus. The spectacular character of this miracle aroused a tremendous popular following for Jesus and moved the priests of Jerusalem to plot to kill Lazarus in order to eliminate the proof of the event. Nothing further is known of Lazarus, but since no mention is made of his death, it is to be presumed that he survived the plot.

2. The name given to the chief character in one of Jesus' most noted stories, the rich man and the beggar.

SCRIPTURE

Lazarus of Bethany

John 11 [1]Now a certain man was sick, named Lazarus, of Bethany, the town of Mary and her sister Martha. [2](It was that Mary which anointed the Lord with ointment, and wiped his feet with her hair, whose brother Lazarus was sick.) [3]Therefore his sisters sent unto him, saying, Lord, behold, he whom thou lovest is sick. [4]When Jesus heard that, he said, This sickness is not unto death, but for the glory of God, that the Son of God might be glorified thereby. [5]Now Jesus loved Martha, and her sister, and Lazarus. [6]When he had heard therefore that he was sick, he abode two days still in the same place where he was. [11]These things said he: and after that he saith unto them, Our friend Lazarus sleepeth; but I go, that I may awake him out of sleep. [12]Then said his disciples, Lord, if he sleep, he shall do well. [13]Howbeit Jesus spake of his death: but they thought that he had spoken of taking of rest in sleep. [14]Then said Jesus unto them plainly, Lazarus is dead. [15]And I am glad for your sakes that I was not there, to the intent ye may believe; nevertheless let us go unto him. [17]Then when Jesus came, he found that he had lain in the grave four days already. [39]Jesus said, Take ye away the stone. Martha, the sister of him that was dead, saith unto him, Lord, by this time he stinketh: for he hath been dead four days. [40]Jesus saith unto her, Said I not unto thee, that, if thou wouldest believe, thou shouldest see the glory of God? 41 Then they took away the stone from the place where the dead was laid. And Jesus lifted up his eyes, and said, Father, I thank thee that thou hast heard me. 42 And I knew that thou hearest me always: but because of the people which stand by I said it, that they may believe that thou hast sent me. 43 And when he thus had spoken, he cried with a loud voice, Lazarus, come forth. 44 And he that was dead came forth, bound hand and foot with graveclothes: and his face was bound about with a napkin. Jesus said unto them, Loose him, and let him go.

John 12 1 Then Jesus six days before the passover came to Bethany, where Lazarus was which had been dead, whom he raised from the dead. 2 There they made him a supper; and Martha served: but Lazarus was one of them that sat at the table with him. 9 Much people of the Jews therefore knew that he was there: and they came not for Jesus' sake only, but that they might see Lazarus also, whom he had raised from the dead.

10 But the chief priests consulted that they might put Lazarus also to death; 11 Because that by reason of him many of the Jews went away, and believed on Jesus.

Lazarus the Beggar

Luke 16 19 There was a certain rich man, which was clothed in purple and fine linen, and fared sumptuously every day: 20 And there was a certain beggar named Lazarus, which was laid at his gate, full of sores, 21 And desiring to be fed with the crumbs which fell from the rich man's table: moreover the dogs came and licked his sores. 22 And it came to pass, that the beggar died, and was carried by the angels into Abraham's bosom: the rich man also died, and was buried; 23 And in hell he lift up his eyes, being in torments, and seeth Abraham afar off, and Lazarus in his bosom. 24 And he cried and said, Father Abraham, have mercy on me, and send Lazarus, that he may dip the tip of his finger in water, and cool my tongue; for I am tormented in this flame. 25 But Abraham said, Son, remember that thou in thy lifetime receivedst thy good things, and likewise Lazarus evil things: but now he is comforted, and thou art tormented.

LEAH

[lē′a] The daughter of Laban, sister of Rachel, and wife of Jacob. She is described as "tender-eyed," in contrast to Rachel, who was "beautiful and well-favoured." Jacob loved Rachel and worked seven years to gain her for his wife. On the wedding night, Laban substituted Leah in Rachel's place—an error which Jacob did not discover until the next morning. When Jacob confronted Laban with his deception, the father lamely excused himself on the grounds that "it must not so be done in our country, to give the younger before the firstborn." After a week, Jacob received Rachel also, but was compelled to work an additional seven years for her. Leah was the mother of Reuben, Simeon, Levi, Judah, Issachar, Zebulun, and Dinah. Her handmaid Zilpah also bore Jacob two sons, Gad and Asher. The Israelite tribes who later bore the names of these sons are commonly referred to as the "Leah tribes" and the "Zilpah tribes." According to *Gen. 9:31*, Leah was buried at the family burial plot at Machpelah.

See JACOB, RACHEL, LABAN

SCRIPTURE

Gen. 29 16 And Laban had two daughters: the name of the elder was Leah, and the name of the younger was Rachel. 17 Leah was tender eyed; but Rachel was beautiful and well favoured. 18 And Jacob loved Rachel; and said, I will serve thee seven years for Rachel thy younger daughter. 19 And Laban said, It is better that I give her to thee, than that I should give her to another man: abide with me. [20]And Jacob served seven years for Rachel; and they seemed unto him but a few days, for the love he had to her.

[21]And Jacob said unto Laban, Give me my wife, for my days are fulfilled, that I may go in unto her. [22]And Laban gathered together all the men of the place, and made a feast. [23]And it came to pass in the evening, that he took Leah his daughter, and brought her to him; and he went in unto her. [24]And Laban gave unto his daughter Leah Zilpah his maid for a handmaid. [25]And it came to pass, that in the morning, behold, it was Leah: and he said to Laban, What is this thou hast done unto me? did not I serve with thee for Rachel? wherefore then hast thou beguiled me? [26]And Laban said, It must not be so done in our country, to give the younger before the firstborn. [27]Fulfil her week, and we will give thee this also for the service which thou shalt serve with me yet seven other years. [28]And Jacob did so, and fulfilled her week: and he gave him Rachel his daughter to wife also.

[31]And when the LORD saw that Leah was hated, he opened her womb: but Rachel was barren. [32]And Leah conceived, and bare a son; and she called his name Reuben: for she said, Surely the LORD hath looked upon my affliction; now therefore my husband will love me. [33]And she conceived again, and bare a son; and said, Because the LORD hath heard that I was hated, he hath therefore given me this son also: and she called his name Simeon. [34]And she conceived again, and bare a son; and said, Now this time will my husband be joined unto me, because I have borne him three sons: therefore was his name called Levi. [35]And she conceived again, and bare a son; and she said, Now will I praise the LORD: therefore she called his name Judah; and left bearing.

Gen. 30 [18]And Leah said, God hath given me my hire, because I have given my maiden to my husband: and she called his name Issachar. [19]And Leah conceived again, and bare Jacob the sixth son. [20]And Leah said, God hath endued me with a good dowry; now will my husband dwell with me, because I have borne him six sons: and she called his name Zebulun. [21]And afterwards she bare a daughter, and called her name Dinah.

LEAVEN

[lev′ ′n] Any substance used to produce fermentation, as in dough or liquids. The leaven of the Bible was a piece of fermented dough reserved from a former baking; this was kneaded into the new batch of dough causing it to become fermented, or leavened. Most bread which was offered or eaten in the various rituals of the Jews was unleavened, since leaven implied a process of corruption. The power of a small portion of leaven to pervade and transform a much greater quantity of dough is referred to in a figurative sense several times in the New Testament.

SCRIPTURE

General

Ex. 12 [15]Seven days shall ye eat unleavened bread; even the first day ye shall put away leaven out of your houses: for whosoever eateth leavened bread from the first day until the seventh day, that soul shall be cut off from Israel.

[19]Seven days shall there be no leaven found in your houses: for whosoever eateth that which is leavened, even that soul shall be cut off from the congregation of Israel, whether he be a stranger, or born in the land.

Ex. 13 [7]Unleavened bread shall be eaten seven days; and there shall no leavened bread be seen with thee, neither shall there be leaven seen with thee in all thy quarters.

Lev. 2 [11]No meat offering, which ye shall bring unto the LORD, shall be made with leaven: for ye shall burn no leaven, nor any honey, in any offering of the LORD made by fire.

Deut. 16 [4]And there shall be no leavened bread seen with thee in all thy coast seven days; neither shall there any thing of the flesh, which thou sacrificedst the first day at even, remain all night until the morning.

Figurative

Matt. 13 [33]Another parable spake he unto them; The kingdom of heaven is like unto leaven, which a woman took, and hid in three measures of meal, till the whole was leavened.

Matt. 16 [5]And when his disciples were come to the other side, they had forgotten to take bread.

[6]Then Jesus said unto them, Take heed and beware of the leaven of the Pharisees and of the Sadducees. [7]And they reasoned among themselves, saying, It is because we have taken no bread. [11]How is it that ye do not understand that I spake it not to you concerning bread, that ye should beware of the leaven of the Pharisees and of the Sadducees? [12]Then understood they how that he bade them not beware of the leaven of bread, but of the doctrine of the Pharisees and of the Sadducees.

Mark 8 [15]And he charged them, saying, Take heed, beware of the leaven of the Pharisees, and of the leaven of Herod. [16]And they reasoned among themselves, saying, It is because we have no bread.

Luke 12 [1]In the mean time, when there were gathered together an innumerable multitude of people, insomuch that they trode one upon another, he began to say unto his disciples first of all, Beware ye of the leaven of the Pharisees, which is hypocrisy.

Luke 13 [21]It (the kingdom of God) is like leaven, which a woman took and hid in three measures of meal, till the whole was leavened.

1 Cor. 5 [6]Your glorying is not good. Know ye not that a little leaven leaveneth the whole lump? [7]Purge out therefore the old leaven, that ye may be a new lump, as ye are unleavened. For even Christ our passover is sacrificed for us:

Gal. 5 [9]A little leaven leaveneth the whole lump.

LEBANON

[leb′a non] A mountainous region north of Palestine, bordering on the east coast of the Mediterranean Sea for a distance of about 100 miles. In Biblical times Lebanon was subject to the Phoenicians and was famous for its forests, most of which are no longer standing. One of the great buildings which Solomon erected was the "House of the Forest of Lebanon," constructed of the legendary "cedars of Lebanon."

See 1 Kin. 7:1-5

LENDING

[lend′ing] The letting out of money or goods for temporary use on condition of return of same or an equivalent. Lending on interest (usury) to the poor is prohibited in the Old Testament codes of law. It was not the taking of interest in itself which the law sought to prohibit, but the making of a profit of a brother's distress. This is made quite clear by the fact that it was allowable to take interest of foreigners, or non-Israelites. The law also stipulated that a debtor was to obtain release from his debt in the seventh year, the so-called year of release. There is dispute among scholars as to whether this meant actual cancellation of the debt or merely the suspension of payment for that year. Not withstanding the prohibitions against the taking of interests from fellow Israelites, usury was apparently practiced both before and after the Babylonian exile, and was one of the problems with which Nehemiah had to deal. Jesus taught his disciples to be free in making loans, even to enemies, remembering the gracious gifts which they had received from God.

See BORROWING

SCRIPTURE

Ex. 22 [25]If thou lend money to any of my people that is poor by thee, thou shalt not be to him as a usurer, neither shalt thou lay upon him usury. [26]If thou at all take thy neighbour's raiment to pledge, thou shalt deliver it unto him by that the sun goeth down: [27]For that is his covering only, it is his raiment for his skin: wherein shall he sleep? and it shall come to pass, when he crieth unto me, that I will hear; for I am gracious.

Lev. 25 [35]And if thy brother be waxen poor, and fallen in decay with thee; then thou shalt relieve him: yea, though he be a stranger, or a sojourner; that he may live with thee. [36]Take thou no usury of him, or increase; but fear thy God; that thy brother may live with thee. [37]Thou shalt not give him thy money upon usury, nor lend him thy victuals for increase.

Deut. 23 [19]Thou shalt not lend upon usury to thy brother; usury of money, usury of victuals, usury of any thing that is lent upon usury: [20]Unto a stranger thou mayest lend upon usury; but unto thy brother thou shalt not lend upon usury: that the LORD thy God may bless thee in all that thou settest thine hand to in the land whither thou goest to possess it.

Psa. 37 [21]The wicked borroweth, and payeth not again: but the righteous showeth mercy, and giveth.

Isa. 24 [2]And it shall be, as with the people, so with the priest; as with the servant, so with his master; as with the maid, so with her mistress; as with the buyer, so with the seller; as with the lender, so with the borrower; as with the taker of usury, so with the giver of usury to him.

Jer. 15 [10]Woe is me, my mother, that thou hast borne me a man of strife and a man of contention to the whole earth! I have neither lent on usury, nor men have lent me on usury; yet every one of them doth curse me.

Matt. 5 [42]Give to him that asketh thee, and from him that would borrow of thee turn not thou away.

Luke 6 [34]And if ye lend to them of whom ye hope to receive, what thank have ye? for sinners also lend to sinners, to receive as much again. [35]But love ye your enemies, and do good, and lend, hoping for nothing again; and your reward shall be great, and ye shall be the children of the Highest: for he is kind unto the unthankful and to the evil.

LEPROSY

[lep'ro si] A slowly progressing and intractable disease characterized by the formation of nodules, ulcerations, scabs, and deformities of the skin, together with disturbances of sensation. The hair of the affected area turns white and the flesh sometimes appears raw. Persons afflicted with leprosy were regarded as unclean and were usually forced to separate themselves from healthy persons, since mere contact with a leper rendered one "unclean." (*See* CLEANNESS AND UNCLEANNESS) The Law contained detailed instructions treating of the recognition of the disease, the quarantine of persons suspected of having leprosy, and rules for ceremonial cleansing; it is noteworthy, however, that it is never implied leprosy can be cured by non-miraculous process. There are several types of leprosy; most authorities feel the type referred to in the Bible was a form in which the whole body becomes white and scaly, without much interference with the general health. This particular form of the disease is rare nowadays.

SCRIPTURE

Laws Concerning Leprosy

See Lev. 13; 14; 22:4; Num. 5:1-3; Deut. 24: 8; Matt. 8:4; Luke 5:14; 17:14

Leprosy Sent as a Judgment

On Miriam, *Num. 12:1-10.*
On Gehazi, *2 Kin. 5:27.*
On Uzziah, *2 Chr. 26:20, 21.*

Leprosy Healed

Miriam, *Num. 12:13, 14.*
Naaman, *2 Kin. 5:8-14.*
Unnamed persons healed by Jesus, *Luke 17: 12; Matt. 8:2; Mark 1:40, Luke 5:12.*

LEVI

[lē'vī] The son of Jacob and Leah. Levi was involved with Simeon in the treacherous slaughter of the people of Shechem after the prince of that city had assaulted their sister Dinah. For their bloody vengeance, the two brothers incurred the lasting disfavor of their father Jacob. It is often suggested that various elements of this story indicate a tribal rather than a personal involvement. Levi is regarded as the ancestor of the priestly tribe of Israel.

See PRIESTHOOD

SCRIPTURE

Son of Jacob

Gen. 29 34And she conceived again, and bare a son; and said, Now this time will my husband be joined unto me, because I have borne him three sons: therefore was his name called Levi.

Slays the Men of Shechem

Gen. 34 25And it came to pass on the third day, when they were sore, that two of the sons of Jacob, Simeon and Levi, Dinah's brethren, took each man his sword, and came upon the city boldly, and slew all the males. 26And they slew Hamor and Shechem his son with the edge of the sword, and took Dinah out of Shechem's house, and went out. 27The sons of Jacob came upon the slain, and spoiled the city, because they had defiled their sister. 28They took their sheep, and their oxen, and their asses, and that which was in the city, and that which was in the field, 29And all their wealth, and all their little ones, and their wives took they captive, and spoiled even all that was in the house. 30And Jacob said to Simeon and Levi, Ye have troubled me to make me to stink among the inhabitants of the land, among the Canaanites and the Perizzites: and I being few in number, they shall gather themselves together against me, and slay me; and I shall be destroyed, I and my house. 31And they said, Should he deal with our sister as with a harlot?

Jacob's Prophecy Concerning Levi

Gen. 49 5Simeon and Levi are brethren; instruments of cruelty are in their habitations. 6O my soul, come not thou into their secret; unto their assembly, mine honour, be not thou united: for in their anger they slew a man, and in their selfwill they digged down a wall. 7Cursed be their anger, for it was fierce; and their wrath, for it was cruel: I will divide them in Jacob, and scatter them in Israel.

LEVIATHAN

[lê vī'a than] A sea-monster in Semitic mythology, representing the forces of chaos over which God triumphed in bringing order to the creation. In several Old Testament passages, this mythological language is used as a literary device to describe the great power of God.

See RAHAB

SCRIPTURE

Job 41 1Canst thou draw out leviathan

with a hook? or his tongue with a cord which thou lettest down? [2]Canst thou put a hook into his nose? or bore his jaw through with a thorn?

LEVITES

[lē'vīts] The priestly tribe descended from Levi.

See PRIESTHOOD

Set Apart to Serve the Lord

Num. 1 [47]But the Levites, after the tribe of their fathers, were not numbered among them. [48]For the LORD had spoken unto Moses, saying, [49]Only thou shalt not number the tribe of Levi, neither take the sum of them among the children of Israel: [50]But thou shalt appoint the Levites over the tabernacle of testimony, and over all the vessels thereof, and over all things that belong to it: they shall bear the tabernacle, and all the vessels thereof; and they shall minister unto it, and shall encamp round about the tabernacle. [51]And when the tabernacle setteth forward, the Levites shall take it down; and when the tabernacle is to be pitched, the Levites shall set it up: and the stranger that cometh nigh shall be put to death. [52]And the children of Israel shall pitch their tents, every man by his own camp, and every man by his own standard, throughout their hosts. [53]But the Levites shall pitch round about the tabernacle of testimony, that there be no wrath upon the congregation of the children of Israel: and the Levites shall keep the charge of the tabernacle of testimony. [54]And the children of Israel did according to all that the LORD commanded Moses, so did they.

Num. 3 [12]And I, behold, I have taken the Levites from among the children of Israel instead of all the firstborn that openeth the matrix among the children of Israel: therefore the Levites shall be mine; [13]Because all the firstborn are mine; for on the day that I smote all the firstborn in the land of Egypt I hallowed unto me all the firstborn in Israel, both man and beast: mine they shall be: I am the LORD.

[41]And thou shalt take the Levites for me (I am the LORD) instead of all the firstborn among the children of Israel; and the cattle of the Levites instead of all the firstlings among the cattle of the children of Israel. [42]And Moses numbered, as the LORD commanded him, all the firstborn among the children of Israel. [43]And all the firstborn males by the number of names, from a month old and upward, of those that were numbered of them, were twenty and two thousand two hundred and threescore and thirteen.

[44]And the LORD spake unto Moses, saying, [45]Take the Levites instead of all the firstborn among the children of Israel, and the cattle of the Levites instead of their cattle; and the Levites shall be mine: I am the LORD. [46]And for those that are to be redeemed of the two hundred and threescore and thirteen of the firstborn of the children of Israel, which are more than the Levites; [47]Thou shalt even take five shekels apiece by the poll, after the shekel of the sanctuary shalt thou take them: (the shekel is twenty gerahs:) [48]And thou shalt give the money, wherewith the odd number of them is to be redeemed, unto Aaron and to his sons. [49]And Moses took the redemption money of them that were over and above them that were redeemed by the Levites: [50]Of the firstborn of the children of Israel took he the money; a thousand three hundred and threescore and five shekels, after the shekel of the sanctuary: [51]And Moses gave the money of them that were redeemed unto Aaron and

to his sons, according to the word of the LORD, as the LORD commanded Moses.

LIBERALITY

[lib er al′i ti] The act, quality, or state of being liberal; generosity; charity. The Bible enjoins the faithful to cultivate the grace of liberality, not only in giving to God and the poor but in our relations to our fellow-men.

See ALMS, GIVING, BENEFICENCE

SCRIPTURE

Ex. 36 [5]And they spake unto Moses, saying, The people bring much more than enough for the service of the work, which the LORD commanded to make.

Deut. 15 [7]If there be among you a poor man of one of thy brethren within any of thy gates in thy land which the LORD thy God giveth thee, thou shalt not harden thine heart, nor shut thine hand from thy poor brother: [8]But thou shalt open thine hand wide unto him, and shalt surely lend him sufficient for his need, in that which he wanteth. [9]Beware that there be not a thought in thy wicked heart, saying, The seventh year, the year of release, is at hand; and thine eye be evil against thy poor brother, and thou givest him nought; and he cry unto the LORD against thee, and it be sin unto thee. [10]Thou shalt surely give him, and thine heart shall not be grieved when thou givest unto him: because that for this thing the LORD thy God shall bless thee in all thy works, and in all that thou puttest thine hand unto. [11]For the poor shall never cease out of the land: therefore I command thee, saying, Thou shalt open thine hand wide unto thy brother, to thy poor, and to thy needy, in thy land.

[12]And if thy brother, a Hebrew man, or a Hebrew woman, be sold unto thee, and serve thee six years; then in the seventh year thou shalt let him go free from thee. [13]And when thou sendest him out free from thee, thou shalt not let him go away empty. [14]Thou shalt furnish him liberally out of thy flock, and out of thy floor, and out of thy winepress: of that wherewith the LORD thy God hath blessed thee thou shalt give unto him. [15]And thou shalt remember that thou wast a bondman in the land of Egypt, and the LORD thy God redeemed thee: therefore I command thee this thing today.

Prov. 3 [9]Honour the LORD with thy substance, and with the first-fruits of all thine increase: [10]So shall thy barns be filled with plenty, and thy presses shall burst out with new wine.

Prov. 11 [25]The liberal soul shall be made fat: and he that watereth shall be watered also himself.

Prov. 28 [27]He that giveth unto the poor shall not lack:

Eccl. 11 [1]Cast thy bread upon the waters: for thou shalt find it after many days.

Luke 6 [38]Give, and it shall be given unto you; good measure, pressed down, and shaken together, and running over, shall men give into your bosom. For with the same measure that ye mete withal it shall be measured to you again.

2 Cor. 8 [7]Therefore, as ye abound in every thing, in faith, and utterance, and knowledge, and in all diligence, and in your love to us, see that ye abound in this grace also. [9]Ye know the grace of our Lord Jesus Christ, that, though he was rich, yet for your sakes he became poor, that ye through his poverty might be rich. [11]Now therefore perform the doing of it; that as there was a readiness to will, so there may be a performance also out of that which ye have. [12]If there be first a willing mind, it is accepted according to that a man hath, and not according to that he hath not. [13]I mean not that other men be eased, and ye burdened: [14]But by an equality, that now at this time your abundance may be a supply for their want, that their abundance also may be a supply for your want: that there may be equality. [24]Shew ye to them, and before the churches, the proof of your love, and of our boasting on your behalf.

2 Cor. 9 [7]God loveth a cheerful giver.

1 John 3 [17]But whoso hath this world's good, and seeth his brother have need, and shutteth up his bowels of compassion from him, how dwelleth the love of God in him?

LIBERTY

[lib'ĕr ti] Freedom from oppression, slavery, bondage, imprisonment, etc. Jesus characterized his mission by quoting the words of the prophet Isaiah: "The Spirit of the Lord . . . hath sent me . . . to preach deliverance to the captives, . . . to set at liberty them that are bruised" (*Luke 4:18*). Paul confirmed this in the following words: "Stand fast therefore in the liberty wherewith *Christ hath made us free*, and be not entangled again with the yoke of bondage" (*Gal. 5:1*). The freedom which Christ brought to mankind is freedom from the Law, and so from Sin and Death, which are bound up with the Law. The condemnation of the Law has been removed and the regenerate Christian lives as a free son of God. Through God's grace, he possesses the will and ability to do good. The scriptures warn against abusing this liberty by using it as an excuse for licence. The freedman of God is not at liberty to sin, but to perform the will of God; he has become the bondservant of righteousness.

SCRIPTURE

Liberty Bestowed by the Gospel

Rom. 8 [21]Because the creature itself also shall be delivered from the bondage of corruption into the glorious liberty of the children of God.

2 Cor. 3 [17]Now the Lord is that Spirit: and where the Spirit of the Lord is, there is liberty.

Gal. 5 [1]Stand fast therefore in the liberty wherewith Christ hath made us free, and be not entangled again with the yoke of bondage.

Jas. 1 [25]But whoso looketh into the perfect law of liberty, and continueth therein, he being not a forgetful hearer, but a doer of the work, this man shall be blessed in his deed.

Isa. 61 [1]The Spirit of the LORD God is upon me, because the LORD hath anointed me to preach good tidings unto the meek; he hath sent me to bind up the brokenhearted, to proclaim liberty to the captives, and the opening of the prison to them that are bound.

The Nature of Christian Liberty

Rom. 6 [17]But God be thanked, that ye were the servants of sin, but ye have obeyed from the heart that form of doctrine which was delivered you. [18]Being then made free from sin, ye became the servants of righteousness. [22]But now being made free from sin, and become servants to God, ye have your fruit unto holiness, and the end everlasting life.

Rom. 7 [6]But now we are delivered from the law, that being dead wherein we were held; that we should serve in newness of spirit, and not in the oldness of the latter.

Rom. 8 [2]For the law of the Spirit of life in Christ Jesus hath made me free from the law of sin and death.

Liberty Not to be Abused

Rom. 3 [8]And not rather, (as we be slanderously reported, and as some affirm that we say,) Let us do evil, that good may come? whose damnation is just.

Rom. 6 [1]What shall we say then? Shall

we continue in sin, that grace may abound?

1 Cor. 8 [9]But take heed lest by any means this liberty of yours become a stumblingblock to them that are weak.

Gal. 5 [13]For, brethren, ye have been called unto liberty; only use not liberty for an occasion to the flesh, but by love serve one another.

1 Pet. 2 [15]For so is the will of God, that with well doing ye may put to silence the ignorance of foolish men: [16]As free, and not using your liberty for a cloke of maliciousness, but as the servants of God. [19]For this is thankworthy, if a man for conscience toward God endure grief, suffering wrongfully. [20]For what glory is it, if, when ye be buffeted for your faults, ye shall take it patiently? but if, when ye do well, and suffer for it, ye take it patiently, this is acceptable with God.

LIFE

[līf] In its simplest sense, this word refers to existence, as opposed to non-existence, or death. The Bible does not divide human life into physical, intellectual, and spiritual compartments, as we tend to do, but views it as a unity, the totality of activities and experiences of an individual or a community. To be sure, we read of soul and spirit, but these are to be understood as the principle of life and personal identity, not unlike that in animals. When the soul or spirit "leave" a man, he cannot be said to continue to exist in a disembodied form. Thus, the soul and spirit, as well as the body, are mortal and the present life is life unto death. (For a wider use of "spirit", *see* SPIRIT)

There is a life which is higher than this mere existence, a life nourished on obedience to the word of God. Jesus came that we might possess this life "which is life indeed." As a consequence of his redemptive activity, our lives are transformed by faith from lives of rebellion and pride to lives of grateful surrender to his will. In contrast to natural human life, which ends at death, this new, true life is indestructible. In fact, the blessings we now enjoy as reborn men are but an installment of the life which is to come. The continuation of this new life is set forth not in terms of the Greek concept of the immortality of the soul, but in terms of the doctrine of personal bodily resurrection, based on the resurrection of Jesus. We do not know the nature of that "spiritual body" which shall live forever in the presence of God, but we are assured that our heavenly existence will be fully personal.

The source of all life is God, whose very nature is life. To speak of him as the "living God" is to distinguish him from dumb idols which have no life of their own and to acknowledge that he not only gives life to all things but that he is providentially active in guiding and sustaining his creation.

See DEATH, SOUL, SPIRIT, RESURRECTION

SCRIPTURE

Life the Gift of God

Gen. 2 [7]And the LORD God formed man of the dust of the ground, and breathed into his nostrils the breath of life; and man became a living soul.

Job 12 [9]Who knoweth not in all these that the hand of the LORD hath wrought this? [10]In whose hand is the soul of every living thing, and the breath of all mankind.

Psa. 36 [6]Thy righteousness is like the great mountains; thy judgments are a great deep: O LORD, thou preservest man and beast.

Acts 17 [28]For in him we live, and move, and have our being; as certain also of your own poets have said, For we are also his offspring.

Long Life Promised

Ex. 20 [12]Honour thy father and thy mother: that thy days may be long upon the land which the LORD thy God giveth thee.

Deut. 5 [33]Ye shall walk in all the ways

which the LORD your God hath commanded you, that ye may live, and that it may be well with you, and that ye may prolong your days in the land which ye shall possess.

Prov. 3 [1]My son, forget not my law; but let thine heart keep my commandments: [2]For length of days, and long life, and peace shall they add to thee.

Life's Vanity, Brevity, and Uncertainty

Job 7 [1]Is there not an appointed time to man upon earth? are not his days also like the days of a hireling?

Job 9 [25]Now my days are swifter than a post: they flee away, they see no good. [26]They are passed away as the swift ships: as the eagle that hasteth to the prey.

Job 14 [1]Man that is born of a woman is of few days, and full of trouble. [2]He cometh forth like a flower, and is cut down: he fleeth also as a shadow, and continueth not.

Psa. 39 [5]Behold, thou hast made my days as a handbreadth; and mine age is as nothing before thee: verily every man at his best state is altogether vanity. Selah. [6]Surely every man walketh in a vain shew: surely they are disquieted in vain: he heapeth up riches, and knoweth not who shall gather them.

Psa. 89 [47]Remember how short my time is: wherefore hast thou made all men in vain? [48]What man is he that liveth, and shall not see death? shall he deliver his soul from the hand of the grave? Selah.

Psa. 90 [4]For a thousand years in thy sight are but as yesterday when it is past, and as a watch in the night. [5]Thou carriest them away as with a flood; they are as a sleep; in the morning they are like grass which groweth up. [6]In the morning it flourisheth, and groweth up; in the evening it is cut down, and withereth.

Eccl. 6 [12]For who knoweth what is good for man in this life, all the days of his vain life which he spendeth as a shadow? for who can tell a man what shall be after him under the sun?

Isa. 38 [12]Mine age is departed, and is removed from me as a shepherd's tent: I have cut off like a weaver my life: he will cut me off with pining sickness: from day even to night wilt thou make an end of me.

Jas. 4 [13]Go to now, ye that say, To day or to morrow we will go into such a city, and continue there a year, and buy and sell, and get gain: [14]Whereas ye know not what shall be on the morrow. For what is your life? It is even a vapour, that appeareth for a little time, and then vanisheth away. [15]For that ye ought to say, If the Lord will, we shall live, and do this, or that.

1 Pet. 1 [24]For all flesh is as grass, and all the glory of man as the flower of grass. The grass withereth, and the flower thereof falleth away.

The Right Mode of Living

Luke 1 [75]In holiness and righteousness before him, all the days of our life.

Rom. 12 [18]If it be possible, as much as lieth in you, live peaceably with all men.

Rom. 14 [7]For none of us liveth to himself, and no man dieth to himself. [8]For whether we live, we live unto the Lord; and whether we die, we die unto the Lord: whether we live therefore, or die, we are the Lord's.

Phil. 1 [21]For to me to live is Christ, and to die is gain. [22]But if I live in the flesh, this is the fruit of my labour: yet what I shall choose I wot not.

Spiritual Life

Rom. 6 [4]Therefore we are buried with him by baptism into death: that like as

Christ was raised up from the dead by the glory of the Father, even so we also should walk in newness of life.

Gal. 2 [20]I am crucified with Christ: nevertheless I live; yet not I, but Christ liveth in me: and the life which I now live in the flesh I live by the faith of the Son of God, who loved me, and gave himself for me.

Eph. 2 [1]And you hath he quickened, who were dead in trespasses and sins.

Col. 3 [3]For ye are dead, and your life is hid with Christ in God.

Eternal Life

Psa. 133 [3]As the dew of Hermon, and as the dew that descended upon the mountains of Zion: for there the LORD commanded the blessing, even life for evermore.

John 6 [27]Labour not for the meat which perisheth, but for that meat which endureth unto everlasting life, which the Son of man shall give unto you: for him hath God the Father sealed. [54]Whoso eateth my flesh, and drinketh my blood, hath eternal life; and I will raise him up at the last day.

John 10 [28]And I give unto them eternal life; and they shall never perish, neither shall any man pluck them out of my hand.

John 17 [2]As thou hast given him power over all flesh, that he should give eternal life to as many as thou hast given him. [3]And this is life eternal, that they might know thee the only true God, and Jesus Christ whom thou hast sent.

Rom. 2 [6]Who will render to every man according to his deeds: [7]To them who by patient continuance in well doing seek for glory and honour and immortality, eternal life.

Rom. 6 [23]For the wages of sin is death; but the gift of God is eternal life through Jesus Christ our Lord.

1 John 1 [2]For the life was manifested, and we have seen it, and bear witness, and shew unto you that eternal life, which was with the Father, and was manifested unto us.

1 John 2 [25]And this is the promise that he hath promised us, even eternal life.

Jude 1 [21]Keep yourselves in the love of God, looking for the mercy of our Lord Jesus Christ unto eternal life.

Rev. 2 [7]He that hath an ear, let him hear what the Spirit saith unto the churches; To him that overcometh will I give to eat of the tree of life, which is in the midst of the paradise of God.

Rev. 21 [6]And he said unto me, It is done. I am Alpha and Omega, the beginning and the end. I will give unto him that is athirst of the fountain of the water of life freely.

John 3 [14]And as Moses lifted up the serpent in the wilderness, even so must the Son of man be lifted up: [15]That whosoever believeth in him should not perish, but have eternal life.

[16]For God so loved the world, that he gave his only begotten Son, that whosoever believeth in him should not perish, but have everlasting life.

[24]Verily, verily, I say unto you, He that heareth my word, and believeth on him that sent me, hath everlasting life, and shall not come into condemnation; but is passed from death unto life.

[25]Verily, verily, I say unto you, The hour is coming, and now is, when the dead shall hear the voice of the Son of God: and they that hear shall live. [26]For as the Father hath life in himself; so hath he given to the Son to have life in himself.

LIGHT

[līt] The opposite of dark. Light is that force, agent, or action in nature which by its operation upon the organs of sight renders objects visable. The word is used in a figurative sense to denote illumination of the mind, prosperity, purity, etc. Jesus Christ is called the Light of the world because of his power of illuminating the mind of man and of acting as a guiding beacon to his followers, who serve, in turn, as lights to their fellowmen.

See DARKNESS

SCRIPTURE

Light Comes from God

Gen. 1 [3]And God said, Let there be light: and there was light. [4]And God saw the light, that it was good: and God divided the light from the darkness. [5]And God called the light Day, and the darkness he called Night. And the evening and the morning were the first day.

Jer. 31 [35]Thus saith the LORD, which giveth the sun for a light by day, and the ordinances of the moon and of the stars for a light by night, which divideth the sea when the waves thereof roar; The LORD of hosts is his name.

Rev. 21 [23]And the city had no need of the sun, neither of the moon, to shine in it: for the glory of God did lighten it, and the Lamb is the light thereof. [24]And the nations of them which saved shall walk in the light of it: and the kings of the earth do bring their glory and honor into it.

Rev. 22 [5]And there shall be no night there; and they need no candle, neither light of the sun; for the Lord God giveth them light: and they shall reign for ever and ever.

Light a Type of God's Favor

Psa. 4 [6]There be many that say, Who will shew us any good? LORD, lift thou up the light of thy countenance upon us.

Psa. 27 [1]The LORD is my light and my salvation; whom shall I fear? the LORD is the strength of my life; of whom shall I be afraid?

Psa. 97 [11]Light is sown for the righteous, and gladness for the upright in heart.

Isa. 9 [2]The people that walked in darkness have seen a great light: they that dwell in the land of the shadow of death, upon them hath the light shined.

Isa. 45 [6]That they may know from the rising of the sun, and from the west, that there is none besides me. I am the LORD, and there is none else. [7]I form the light, and create darkness; I make peace, and create evil: I the LORD do all these things.

Isa. 60 [19]The sun shall be no more thy light by day; neither for brightness shall the moon give light unto thee: but the LORD shall be unto thee an everlasting light, and thy God thy glory.

Amos 5 [20]Shall not the day of the LORD be darkness, and not light? even very dark, and no brightness in it?

God's Word Produces Light

Psa. 19 [8]The statutes of the LORD are right, rejoicing the heart: the commandment of the LORD is pure, enlightening the eyes.

Psa. 119 [105]Thy word is a lamp unto my feet, and a light unto my path. [130]The entrance of thy words giveth light; it giveth understanding unto the simple.

Prov. 6 [23]For the commandment is a lamp; and the law is light; and reproofs of instruction are the way of life.

John the Baptist was a Light

John 5 [35]He was a burning and a shining light: and ye were willing for a season to rejoice in his light.

Christ the Light of the World

Luke 2 [32]A light to lighten the Gentiles, and the glory of thy people Israel.

John 1 [4]In him was life; and the life was the light of men. [5]And the light shineth in darkness; and the darkness comprehended it not.

John 3 [19]And this is the condemnation, that light is come into the world, and men loved darkness rather than light, because their deeds were evil. [20]For every one that doeth evil hateth the light, neither cometh to the light, lest his deeds should be reproved.

John 8 [12]Then spake Jesus again unto them, saying, I am the light of the world: he that followeth me shall not walk in darkness, but shall have the light of life.

John 12 [35]Then Jesus said unto them, Yet a little while is the light with you. Walk while ye have the light, lest darkness come upon you: for he that walketh in darkness knoweth not whither he goeth. [36]While ye have light, believe in the light, that ye may be the children of light. These things spake Jesus, and departed, and did hide himself from them.

Rev. 21 [23]And the city had no need of the sun, neither of the moon, to shine in it: for the glory of God did lighten it, and the Lamb is the light thereof. [24]And the nations of them which are saved shall walk in the light of it: and the kings of the earth do bring their glory and honour into it.

Christians as Light

Matt. 5 [14]Ye are the light of the world. A city that is set on a hill cannot be hid.

Luke 16 [8]And the lord commended the unjust steward, because he had done wisely, for the children of this world are in their generation wiser than the children of light.

John 12 [36]While ye have light, believe in the light, that ye may be the children of light. These things spake Jesus, and departed, and did hide himself from them.

2 Cor. 6 [14]Be ye not unequally yoked together with unbelievers: for what fellowship hath righteousness with unrighteousness? and what communion hath light with darkness?

Eph. 5 [8]For ye were sometimes darkness but now are ye light in the Lord: walk as children of light:

Phil. 2 [15]That ye may be blameless and harmless, the sons of God, without rebuke, in the midst of a crooked and perverse nation, among whom ye shine as lights in the world.

Other Figurative Uses

Esth. 8 [16]The Jews had light, and gladness, and joy, and honor.

Job 30 [26]When I looked for good, then evil came unto me: and when I waited for light, there came darkness.

Psa. 97 [11]Light is sown for the righteous, and gladness for the upright in heart.

Prov. 16 [15]In the light of the king's countenance is life; and his favor is as a cloud of the latter rain.

Rom. 13 [12]The night is far spent, the day is at hand: let us therefore cast off the works of darkness, and let us put on the armor of light.

Col. 1 [12]Giving thanks unto the Father, which hath made us meet to be partakers of the inheritance of the saints in light:

LORD

[lord] The Hebrew and Greek words of which "Lord" is a translation in the English Bible have the general meaning of "ruler," "commander," or "one who possesses authority." It is used of temporal rulers, of masters of servants, of those to whom one wishes to show respect, as a term of courtesy much like the English "sir," and in reference to God and Christ.

The references given below illustrate the various uses of the term, as described above, and are by no means exhaustive.

Note that in *Matt. 21:30* the same Greek word translated "sir" is elsewhere rendered "Lord."

SCRIPTURE

Gen. 45 [8]So now it was not you that sent me hither, but God: and he hath made me a father to Pharaoh, and lord of all his house, and a ruler throughout all the land of Egypt.

Mark 12 [9]What shall therefore the lord of the vineyard do? he will come and destroy the husbandmen, and will give the vineyard unto others.

Matt. 9 [38]Pray ye therefore the Lord of the harvest, that he will send forth laborers into his harvest.

Matt. 21 [30]And he came to the second, and said likewise. And he answered and said, I go, sir; and went not.

Acts 25 [26]Of whom I have no certain thing to write unto my lord. Wherefore I have brought him forth before you, and specially before thee, O king Agrippa, that, after examination had, I might have somewhat to write.

Gen. 9 [26]And he said, Blessed be the LORD God of Shem; and Canaan shall be his servant.

Rom. 10 [9]That if thou shalt confess with thy mouth the Lord Jesus, and shalt believe in thine heart that God hath raised him from the dead, thou shalt be saved.

Phil. 2 [11]And that every tongue should confess that Jesus Christ is Lord, to the glory of God the Father.

LORD'S DAY

Literally, the day which belongs to the Lord. The phrase occurs only once in the New Testament, in *Rev. 1:10*, but there are several references to it in post-apostolic literature which make it clear that it was the first day of the week, or Sunday. This day was hallowed by Christians because it was the day on which Christ rose from the dead. On this day the early church met for worship. Many Jewish Christians also observed the seventh day of the week, or the Sabbath, as a day of ritual rest, but the Scriptures make it clear that this was not to be enforced as a rule binding on all Christians.

SCRIPTURE

Rev. 1 [10]I was in the Spirit on the Lord's day, and heard behind me a great voice, as of a trumpet.

Mark 16 [9]Now when Jesus was risen early the first day of the week, he appeared first to Mary Magdalene, out of whom he had cast seven devils.

John 20 [19]Then the same day at evening, being the first day of the week, when the doors were shut where the disciples were assembled for fear of the Jews, came Jesus and stood in the midst, and saith unto them, Peace be unto you.

Acts 20 [7]And upon the first day of the week, when the disciples came together to break bread, Paul preached unto them, ready to depart on the morrow; and continued his speech until midnight.

1 Cor. 16 [2]Upon the first day of the week let every one of you lay by him in store, as God hath prospered him, that there be no gatherings when I come.

See Matt. 28:1, 5, 6, 9

LORD'S PRAYER, THE

The name commonly given to the prayer of Jesus recorded in *Matt. 6:9-13* and *Luke 11:2-4*. Jesus' disciples recognized that he was supremely a man of prayer and asked him to teach them to pray. His reply was "The Lord's Prayer," a simple model of communion with God which surpasses any formal precepts about prayer.

See PRAYER

SCRIPTURE

Matt. 6 [9]After this manner therefore pray ye: Our Father which art in heaven, Hallowed be thy name. [10]Thy kingdom come. Thy will be done in earth, as it is in heaven. [11]Give us this day our daily bread. [12]And forgive us our debts, as we forgive our debtors. [13]And lead us not into temptation, but deliver us from evil: For thine is the kingdom, and the power, and the glory, for ever. Amen.

LORD'S SUPPER

The distinctive rite of Christian worship, instituted by Jesus on the night of his betrayal, consisting of a religious partaking of bread and wine, symbolizing the body and blood of Christ offered as an inexhaustible sacrifice for the sins of mankind. In the Lord's Supper, Christians discern the personal presence of Christ and look forward to the final reunion with Christ in glory; it is a pledge of their share in the new covenant. It is also an expression of fellowship between Christians, the individual members of the body of Christ. The term Eucharist, by which the Supper is sometimes called, is derived from the Greek word for thanksgiving; in remembering and celebrating the events which have made possible their redemption, Christians cannot help but partake of the Lord's Supper with thanksgiving. Inasmuch as it is a participation and sharing in the body and blood of Christ, the Supper is often referred to as Communion.

SCRIPTURE

Matt. 26 [17]Now the first day of the feast of unleavened bread the disciples came to Jesus, saying unto him, Where wilt thou that we prepare for thee to eat the passover? [18]And he said, Go into the city to such a man, and say unto him, The Master saith, My time is at hand; I will keep the passover at thy house with my disciples. [19]And the disciples did as Jesus had appointed them; and they made ready the passover. [20]Now when the even was come, he sat down with the twelve. [21]And as they did eat, he said, Verily I say unto you, that one of you shall betray me. [22]And they were exceeding sorrowful, and began every one of them to say unto him, Lord, is it I? [23]And he answered and said, He that dippeth his hand with me in the dish, the same shall betray me. [24]The Son of man goeth as it is written of him: but woe unto that man by whom the Son of man is betrayed! it had been good for that man if he had not been born. [25]Then Judas, which betrayed him, answered and said, Master, is it I? He said unto him, Thou hast said.

[26]And as they were eating, Jesus took bread, and blessed it, and brake it, and gave it to the disciples, and said, Take, eat; this is my body. [27]And he took the cup, and gave thanks, and gave it to them, saying, Drink ye all of it; [28]For this is my blood of the new testament, which is shed for many for the remission of sins. [29]But I say unto you, I will not drink henceforth of this fruit of the vine, until that day when I drink it new with you in my Father's kingdom.

1 Cor. 10 [16]The cup of blessing which we bless, is it not the communion of the blood of Christ? The bread which we break, is it not the communion of the body of Christ? [17]For we being many are one bread, and one body: for we are all partakers of that one bread. [21]Ye cannot drink the cup of the Lord, and the cup of devils: ye cannot be partakers of the Lord's table, and of the table of devils.

1 Cor. 11 [20]When ye come together therefore into one place, this is not to eat the Lord's supper. [21]For in eating every one taketh before other his own supper: and one is hungry, and another is drunken. [22]What? have ye not houses to eat and to drink in? or despise ye the church of God, and shame them that have not? What shall I say to you? shall I praise you in this? I praise you not. [23]For I have received of the Lord that which also I delivered unto you, That the Lord Jesus the same night in which he was betrayed took bread: [24]And when he had given thanks, he brake it, and said, Take, eat: this is my body, which is broken for you: this do in remembrance of me. [25]After the same manner also he took the cup, when he had supped, saying, This cup is the new testament in my blood: this do ye, as oft as ye drink it, in remembrance of me. [26]For as often as ye eat this bread, and drink this cup, ye do shew the Lord's death till he come. [27]Wherefore whosoever shall eat this bread, and drink this cup of the Lord, unworthily, shall be guilty of the body and blood of the Lord. [28]But let a man examine himself, and so let him eat of that bread, and drink of that cup. [29]For he that eateth and drinketh unworthily, eateth and drinketh damnation to himself, not discerning the Lord's body.

See John 6:48-63; Acts 2:42, 46-47; Mark 14:22-24; Luke 22:19, 20; John 1:1-4.

LOT

[lot] The son of Haran and nephew of Abraham. Lot accompanied Terah from Ur of the Chaldees to Haran; from there he migrated with Abraham to the land of Canaan. The two kinsmen journeyed together for a considerable period, but eventually Lot grew so rich in flocks, herds, and servants, that they were no longer able to swell together. When Abraham offered him the choice of the land that lay before them Lot chose the lush pasture lands toward the Jordan and "pitched his tent toward Sodom." He was to live to regret this choice. Despite his notable weaknesses, Lot had some good characteristics; we are told that God would have been willing to spare the cities of Sodom and Gomorrah from destruction had only a few more men of Lot's character lived in them. Even though the cities were destroyed, Lot and his family were given sufficient warning and were able to flee in time. The narrative tells us that his wife was turned into a pillar of salt because she looked back at the cities during their flight. In the last scene in which Lot appears, his spiral of moral deterioration has reached the bottom; in a drunken stupor, he commits incest with his two daughters and fathers Moab and Ammon, who are said to be the ancestors of the Moabites and the Ammonites, historical enemies of the Israelites nation.

See ABRAHAM, MELCHIZEDEK

SCRIPTURE

Journies with Abraham

Gen. 11 [31]And Terah took Abram his son, and Lot the son of Haran his son's son, and Sarai his daughter in law, his son Abram's wife; and they went forth with them from Ur of the Chaldees, to go into the land of Canaan; and they came unto Haran, and dwelt there.

Gen. 12 [4]So Abram departed, as the LORD had spoken unto him; and Lot went with him: and Abram was seventy and five years old when he departed out of Haran.

Abraham and Lot Part

Gen. 13 [5]And Lot also, which went with Abram, had flocks, and herds, and tents. [6]And the land was not able to bear them, that they might dwell together: for their substance was great, so that they could not dwell together. [7]And there was a strife between the herdmen of Abram's cattle and the herdmen of Lot's cattle: and the Canaanite and the Perizzite dwelt then in the land. [8]And Abram said unto Lot, Let there be no strife, I pray thee, between me and thee, and between my herdmen and thy herdmen; for we be brethren. [9]Is not the whole land before thee? Separate thyself, I pray thee, from me: if thou wilt take the left hand, then I will go to the right; or if thou depart to the right hand, then I will go to the left. [10]And Lot lifted up his eyes, and beheld all the plain of Jordan, that it was well watered every where, before the LORD destroyed Sodom and Gomorrah, even as the garden of the LORD, like the land of Egypt, as thou comest unto Zoar. [11]Then Lot chose him all the plain of Jordan; and Lot journeyed east: and they separated themselves the one from the other. [12]Abram dwelt in the land of Canaan, and Lot dwelt in the cities of the plain, and pitched his tent toward Sodom. [13]But the men of Sodom were wicked and sinners before the LORD exceedingly.

Escapes from Sodom

Gen. 19 [1]And there came two angels to Sodom at even; and Lot sat in the gate of Sodom: and Lot seeing them rose up to meet them; and he bowed himself with his face toward the ground;

[12]And the men said unto Lot, Hast thou here any besides? son in law, and thy sons, and thy daughters, and whatsoever thou hast in the city, bring them out of this place: [13]For we will destroy this place, because the cry of them is waxen great before the face of the LORD; and the LORD hath sent us to destroy it. [14]And Lot went out, and spake unto his sons in law, which married his daughters, and said, Up, get you out of this place; for the LORD will destroy this city. But he seemed as one that mocked unto his sons in law.

[15]And when the morning arose, then the angels hastened Lot, saying, Arise, take thy wife, and thy two daughters, which are here; lest thou be consumed in the iniquity of the city. [16]And while he lingered, the men laid hold upon his hand, and upon the hand of his wife, and upon the hand of his two daughters; the LORD being merciful unto him: and they brought him forth, and set him without the city.

[17]And it came to pass, when they had brought them forth abroad, that he said, Escape for thy life; look not behind thee, neither stay thou in all the plain; escape to the mountain, lest thou be consumed. [18]And Lot said unto them, Oh, not so, my Lord: [19]Behold now, thy servant hath found grace in thy sight, and thou hast magnified thy mercy, which thou hast shewed unto me in saving my life; and I can not escape to the mountain, lest some evil, take me, and I die: [20]Behold now, this city is near to flee unto, and it is a little one: Oh, let me escape thither, (is it not a little one?) and my soul shall live. [21]And he said unto him, See, I have accepted thee concerning this thing also, that I will not overthrow this city, for the which thou hast spoken. [22]Haste thee, escape thither; for I can not do any thing till thou be come thither. Therefore the name of the city was called Zoar.

[23]The sun was risen upon the earth when Lot entered into Zoar. [24]Then the LORD rained upon Sodom and upon Gomorrah brimstone and fire from the LORD out of heaven; [25]And he overthrew those cities, and all the plain, and all the inhabitants of the cities, and that which grew upon the ground.

[26]But his wife looked back from behind him, and she became a pillar of salt.

Commits Incest with His Daughters

Gen. 19 [30]And Lot went up out of Zoar, and dwelt in the mountain, and his two daughters with him; for he feared to dwell

in Zoar: and he dwelt in a cave, he and his
two daughters. 31And the firstborn said
unto the younger, Our father is old, and
there is not a man in the earth to come in
unto us after the manner of all the earth:
32Come, let us make our father drink wine,
and we will lie with him, that we may preserve seed of our father. 33And they made
their father drink wine that night: and the
firstborn went in, and lay with her father;
and he perceived not when she lay down,
nor when she arose. 34And it came to pass
on the morrow, that the firstborn said unto
the younger, Behold, I lay yesternight
with my father: let us make him drink
wine this night also; and go thou in, and lie
with him, that we may preserve seed of
our father. 35And they made their father
drink wine that night also: and the
younger arose, and lay with him; and he
perceived not when she lay down, nor
when she arose. 36Thus were both the
daughters of Lot with child by their father. 37And the firstborn bare a son, and
called his name Moab: the same is the father of the Moabites unto this day. 38And
the younger, she also bare a son, and called
his name Ben-ammi: the same is the father
of the children of Ammon unto this day.

LOVE

[luv] The Bible speaks of three types of love: the love of God for man, man's love for God, and love between men. In *1 John 4:8*, we are told that "God is Love." This means that love is rooted in the very personality of God, that no thought about God can be adequate which does not take into account his boundless love. God's love is expressed in his election of and longsuffering attitude toward Israel. Its supreme manifestation is, of course, his sending of his Son to die for our sins, that we might have life everlasting (*John 3:16; Rom. 5:8*). Man's love for God arises in response to and out of gratitude for this love which he has received through no merit of his own. This same gratitude and sense of his unworthiness of the gift of grace moves Christian man to love of other men. This love is directed not only to one's friends—for even the Pharisees love their friends—but also to those who have no worth of their own to deserve such love, even to one's enemies. It is to be specially manifested toward the fellowmembers of the Redeemed Community, for it is love which identifies them as God's children. Without love, no human community, regardless of the name it wears or the prestige it enjoys, can claim to be the church of Jesus Christ.

SCRIPTURE

God's Love

Deut. 4 37Because he loved thy fathers,
therefore he chose their seed after them,

Deut. 7 7The Lord did not set his love
upon you, nor choose you, because ye were
more in number than any people; for ye
were the fewest of all people: 8But because the Lord loved you, ...

13And he will love thee, and bless thee,
and multiply thee: . . . .

Deut. 10 15The Lord had a delight in
thy fathers to love them, and he chose
their seed after them, ... 18He doth
execute the judgment of the fatherless and
widow, and loveth the stranger, in giving
him food and raiment.

Deut. 23 5The Lord thy God turned the
curse into a blessing unto thee, because
the Lord thy God loved thee.

Deut. 33 3Yea, he loved the people; all
his saints are in thy hand: and they sat
down at thy feet; every one shall receive
of thy words.

12. . . The beloved of the Lord shall
dwell in safety by him; and the Lord shall
cover him all the day long, and he shall
dwell between his shoulders.

Jer. 31 3Yea, I have loved thee with an

everlasting love: therefore with lovingkindness have I drawn thee.

Hos. 11 1When Israel was a child, then I loved him, and called my son out of Egypt.

Mal. 1 2I have loved you, saith the LORD.

John 3 16God so loved the world, that he gave his only begotten Son, that whosoever believeth in him should not perish, but have everlasting life.

Rom. 5 8God commendeth his love toward us, in that, while we were yet sinners, Christ died for us.

Eph. 2 4God, who is rich in mercy, for his great love wherewith he loved us, 5Even when we were dead in sins, hath quickened us together with Christ, . . .

2 Thess. 2 16God, even our Father, which hath loved us, and hath given us everlasting consolation and good hope through grace,

Tit. 3 4But after that the kindness and love of God our Saviour toward man appeared,

1 John 4 8He that loveth not knoweth not God; for God is love. 9In this was manifested the love of God toward us, because that God sent his only begotten Son into the world, that we might live through him. 10Herein is love, not that we loved God, but that he loved us, and sent his Son to be the propitiation for our sins. 12God dwelleth in us, and his love is perfected in us. 13Hereby know we that we dwell in him, and he in us, because he hath given us of his Spirit. 15Whosoever shall confess that Jesus is the Son of God, God dwelleth in him, and he in God. 16And we have known and believed the love that God hath to us. God is love; and he that dwelleth in love dwelleth in God, and God in him. 19We love him, because he first loved us.

Love of Man for God

Deut. 6 5And thou shalt love the LORD thy God with all thine heart, and with all thy soul, and with all thy might.

Deut. 11 1Therefore thou shalt love the LORD thy God, and keep his charge, and his statutes, and his judgments, and his commandments, alway.

Josh. 22 5But take diligent heed to do the commandment and the law, which Moses the servant of the LORD charged you, to love the LORD your God, and to walk in all his ways, and to keep his commandments, and to cleave unto him, and to serve him with all your heart and with all your soul.

Matt. 10 37He that loveth father or mother more than me is not worthy of me: and he that loveth son or daughter more than me is not worthy of me.

Matt. 22 36Master, which is the great commandment in the law? 37Jesus said unto him, Thou shalt love the Lord thy God with all thy heart, and with all thy soul, and with all thy mind. 38This is the first and great commandment.

Mark 12 28And one of the scribes came, and having heard them reasoning together, and perceiving that he had answered them well, asked him, Which is the first commandment of all? 30And thou shalt love the Lord thy God with all thy heart, and with all thy soul, and with all thy mind, and with all thy strength: this is the first commandment. 33And to love him with all the heart, and with all the understanding, and with all the soul, and with all the strength, and to love his neighbour as himself, is more than all whole burnt offerings and sacrifices.

Deut. 30 20That thou mayest love the LORD thy God, and that thou mayest obey his voice, and that thou mayest cleave unto him: for he is thy life, and the length of thy days: that thou mayest dwell in the land which the LORD sware unto thy fathers, to Abraham, to Isaac, and to Jacob, to give them.

Psa. 91 [14]Because he hath set his love upon me, therefore will I deliver him: I will set him on high, because he hath known my name.

Psa. 145 [20]The LORD preserveth all them that love him: but all the wicked will he destroy.

Prov. 8 [17]I love them that love me; and those that seek me early shall find me.

1 Cor. 2 [9]But as it is written, Eye hath not seen, nor ear heard, neither have entered into the heart of man, the things which God hath prepared for them that love him.

1 Cor. 8 [3]But if any man love God, the same is known of him.

1 John 4 [17]Herein is our love made perfect, that we may have boldness in the day of judgment: because as he is, so are we in this world. [18]There is no fear in love; but perfect love casteth out fear: because fear hath torment. He that feareth is not made perfect in love.

Love of Man for Man

Matt. 7 [12]Therefore all things whatsoever ye would that men should do to you, do ye even so to them: for this is the law and the prophets.

Matt. 19 [19]Honour thy father and thy mother: and, Thou shalt love thy neighbour as thyself.

Matt. 22 [39]And the second is like unto it, Thou shalt love thy neighbour as thyself.

Mark 12 [31]And the second is like, namely this, Thou shalt love thy neighbour as thyself. There is none other commandment greater than these.

John 13 [34]A new commandment I give unto you, That ye love one another; as I have loved you, that ye also love one another. [35]By this shall all men know that ye are my disciples, if ye have love one to another.

John 15 [12]This is my commandment, That ye love one another, as I have loved you.

Rom. 12 [9]Let love be without dissimulation. Abhor that which is evil; cleave to that which is good. [10]Be kindly affectioned one to another with brotherly love; in honour preferring one another.

Rom. 13 [8]Owe no man anything, but to love one another: for he that loveth another hath fulfilled the law. [9]For this, Thou shalt not commit adultery, Thou shalt not kill, Thou shalt not steal, Thou shalt not bear false witness, Thou shalt not covet; and if there be any other commandment, it is briefly comprehended in this saying, namely, Thou shalt love thy neighbour as thyself. [10]Love worketh no ill to his neighbour: therefore love is the fulfilling of the law.

1 Thess. 4 [9]But as touching brotherly love ye need not that I write unto you: for ye yourselves are taught of God to love one another.

Heb. 13 [1]Let brotherly love continue.

1 Pet. 1 [22]Seeing ye have purified your souls in obeying the truth through the Spirit unto unfeigned love of the brethren, see that ye love one another with a pure heart fervently.

1 Pet. 4 [8]And above all things have fervent charity among yourselves: for charity shall cover the multitude of sins.

1 John 3 [10]In this the children of God are manifest, and the children of the devil: whosoever doeth not righteousness is not of God, neither he that loveth not his brother. [11]For this is the message that ye heard from the beginning, that we should love one another. [14]We know that we have passed from death unto life, because we love the brethren. He that loveth not his brother abideth in death.

1 John 4 [7]Beloved, let us love one another: for love is of God; and every one that loveth is born of God, and knoweth God. [11]Beloved, if God so loved us, we ought also to love one another. [20]If a man say, I love God, and hateth his brother, he is a liar: for he that loveth not his brother whom he hath seen, how can he love God whom he hath not seen? [21]And this commandment have we from him, That he who loveth God love his brother also.

1 Cor. 13 [1]Though I speak with the tongues of men and of angels, and have not charity, I am become as sounding brass, or a tinkling cymbal. [2]And though I have the gift of prophecy, and understand all mysteries, and all knowledge; and though I have all faith, so that I could remove mountains, and have not charity, I am nothing. [3]And though I bestow all my goods to feed the poor, and though I give my body to be burned, and have not charity, it profiteth me nothing. [4]Charity suffereth long, and is kind; charity envieth not; charity vaunteth not itself, is not puffed up, [5]Doth not behave itself unseemly, seeketh not her own, is not easily provoked, thinketh no evil; [6]Rejoiceth not in iniquity, but rejoiceth in the truth; [7]Beareth all things, believeth all things, hopeth all things, endureth all things. [8]Charity never faileth: but whether there be prophecies, they shall fail; whether there be tongues, they shall cease; whether there be knowledge, it shall vanish away. [13]And now abideth faith, hope, charity, these three; but the greatest of these is charity.

Gal. 5 [14]For all the law is fulfilled in one word, even in this; Thou shalt love thy neighbour as thyself.

Jas. 2 [8]If ye fulfil the royal law according to the Scripture, Thou shalt love thy neighbour as thyself, ye do well.

2 John 1 [6]And this is love, that we walk after his commandments. This is the commandment, That, as ye have heard from the beginning, ye should walk in it.

LUKE

[lo͞ok, lūk] A companion of Paul and the author of the third gospel and *Acts of Apostles*, both of which are addressed to Theophilus. Luke is described by Paul as "the beloved physician" (*Col. 4:14*). Since Paul is known to have had some sort of physical disability, it has been conjectured that Luke may have been responsible for prolonging the life of the apostle, thus enabling him to carry out his vast missionary efforts. He was a companion of Paul on many of his travels and, in the last correspondence which we have from the apostle, is mentioned as the only one who remained with him in his final trials (*2 Tim. 4:11*). That he was a Gentile is indicated in *Col. 4*, in which Epaphras, Demas, and Luke are grouped together in distinction from those "of the circumcision." At one time Luke's writings were assailed as being historically untrustworthy. As archaeological evidence from the first century has been uncovered, however, he has emerged as one of the ablest and most accurate historians of the ancient world. A noted critic of the Bible has called his version of the gospel "the most beautiful book ever written."

See THEOPHILUS, PAUL

SCRIPTURE

Col. 4 [14]Luke, the beloved physician, and Demas, greet you.

2 Tim. 4 [11]Only Luke is with me. Take Mark, and bring him with thee: for he is profitable to me for the ministry.

Philem. 1 [24]Marcus, Aristarchus, Demas, Lucas, my fellow labourers.

LUST

[lust] As used in the Bible, this term refers to any intense desire which becomes excessive or misdirected. It may be concentrated on money, personal power, or sensual pleasures such as sexual experience and drunkenness. Misdirected and excessive desires tend to throw human life into disharmony and chaos; Christians are therefore urged to control their desires in such a manner as to make their bodies instruments of righteousness rather than the prey of lusts.

See SENSUALITY

SCRIPTURE

Gen. 3 [6]And when the woman saw that the tree was good for food, and that it was pleasant to the eyes, and a tree to be desired to make one wise, she took of the fruit thereof, and did eat, and gave also unto her husband with her; and he did eat.

Matt. 5 [28]But I say unto you, That whosoever looketh on a woman to lust after her hath committed adultery with her already in his heart.

Mark 4 [19]And the cares of this world, and the deceitfulness of riches, and the lusts of other things entering in, choke the word, and it becometh unfruitful.

John 8 [44]Ye are of your father the devil, and the lusts of your father ye will do.

Rom. 13 [13]Let us walk honestly, as in the day; not in rioting and drunkenness, not in chambering and wantonness, not in strife and envying: [14]But put ye on the Lord Jesus Christ, and make not provision for the flesh, to fulfil the lusts thereof.

1 Cor. 9 [27]But I keep under my body, and bring it into subjection: lest that by any means, when I have preached to other, I myself should be a castaway.

1 Cor. 10 [6]Now these things were our examples, to the intent we should not lust after evil things, as they also lusted.

Eph. 4 [22]That ye put off concerning the former conversation the old man, which is corrupt according to the deceitful lusts;

1 Tim. 6 [9]But they that will be rich fall into temptation and a snare, and into many foolish and hurtful lusts, which drown men in destruction and perdition. [10]For the love of money is the root of all evil: which while some coveted after, they have erred from the faith, and pierced themselves through with many sorrows.

2 Tim. 2 [22]Flee also youthful lusts: but follow righteousness, faith, charity, peace, with them that call on the Lord out of a pure heart.

2 Tim. 4 [3]For the time will come when they will not endure sound doctrine; but after their own lusts shall they heap to themselves teachers, having itching ears; [4]And they shall turn away their ears from the truth, and shall be turned unto fables.

Tit. 2 [12]Teaching us that, denying ungodliness and worldly lusts, we should live soberly, righteously, and godly, in this present world;

Jas. 1 [14]But every man is tempted, when he is drawn away of his own lust, and enticed. [15]Then when lust hath conceived, it bringeth forth sin; and sin, when it is finished, bringeth forth death.

Jas. 4 [1]From whence come wars and fightings among you? come they not hence, even of your lusts that war in your members? [2]Ye lust, and have not: ye kill, and desire to have, and cannot obtain: ye fight and war, yet ye have not, because ye ask not. [3]Ye ask, and receive not, because ye ask amiss, that ye may consume it upon your lusts.

1 Pet. 2 [11]Dearly beloved, I beseech you as strangers and pilgrims, abstain from fleshly lusts, which war against the soul;

1 Pet. 4 [3]For the time past of our life may suffice us to have wrought the will of the Gentiles, when we walked in lasciviousness, lusts, excess of wine, revellings, banquetings, and abominable idolatries:

1 John 2 [16]For all that is in the world, the lust of the flesh, and the lust of the eyes, and the pride of life, is not of the Father, but is of the world. [17]And the world passeth away, and the lust thereof: but he that doeth the will of God abideth for ever.

Jude 1 [16]These are murmurers, complainers, walking after their own lusts; and their mouth speaketh great swelling words, having men's persons in admiration because of advantage. [18]How that they told you there should be mockers in the last time, who should walk after their own ungodly lusts.

LYDIA

[lid'i a] A woman of Thyatira, who was converted through the preaching of Paul. At the time of her contact with Paul, Lydia was living in Philippi, engaged in her trade of selling the purple garments produced in her home town. She was one "which worshipped God", a phrase which probably implies she was a proselyte to Judaism. Paul came in contact with her at a place by a river where Jews came to offer prayer. After being taught of Christ, Lydia and her household were baptized and she persuaded Paul and his companions to make their headquarters in her home.

See Paul

SCRIPTURE

Acts 16 [14]And a certain woman named Lydia, a seller of purple, of the city of Thyatira, which worshipped God, heard us: whose heart the Lord opened, that she attended unto the things which were spoken of Paul. [15]And when she was baptized, and her household, she besought us, saying, If ye have judged me to be faithful to the Lord, come into my house, and abide there. And she constrained us.

LYING

[lī'ing] To lie is to speak falsely, to fabricate, to make a statement with intent to deceive. The term may also be used of anything which is vain, empty, lacking stability, or which causes distrust and disharmony. Lying is one of the sins against which the Bible strongly inveighs; the punishment of liars is explicitly declared to be exclusion from heaven and banishment to the lake of fire.

SCRIPTURE

Prov. 6 [16]These six things doth the Lord hate; yea, seven are an abomination unto him: [17]A proud look, a lying tongue, and hands that shed innocent blood, [18]A heart that deviseth wicked imaginations, feet that be swift in running to mischief, [19]A false witness that speaketh lies, and he that soweth discord among brethren.

Prov. 12 [22]Lying lips are abomination to the Lord: but they that deal truly are his delight.

Lev. 19 [11]Ye shall not steal, neither deal falsely, neither lie one to another.

Col. 3 [9]Lie not one to another, seeing that ye have put off the old man with his deeds.

John 8 [44]Ye are of your father the devil, and the lusts of your father ye will do. He was a murderer from the beginning, and abode not in the truth, because there is no truth in him. When he speaketh a lie, he speaketh of his own: for he is a liar, and the father of it.

Rev. 21 [8]But the fearful, and unbelieving, and the abominable, and murderers, and whoremongers, and sorcerers, and idolaters, and all liars, shall have their part in the lake which burneth with fire and brimstone: which is the second death. [27]And there shall in no wise enter into it any thing that defileth, neither whatsoever worketh abomination, or maketh a lie: but they which are written in the Lamb's book of life.

Rev. 22 [15]For without are dogs, and sorcerers, and whoremongers, and murderers, and idolaters, and whosoever loveth and maketh a lie.

MACEDONIA

[mas ê dō′ni a] A country north of Greece. The Macedonian tribes were united into a single powerful nation by Philip of Macedon who ruled from 359 BC until 336 BC, at which time he was assassinated in a plot engineered by his wife Olympias. He was succeeded by his son, Alexander the Great, who, in a dazzling display of military genius, consolidated his power over Greece, Thrace, and Illyria, and then accomplished the overthrow of the Persian Empire. Shortly after his death in 323 BC, the Empire was divided into the kingdoms of Macedonia, Syria, and Egypt. In New Testament times, the country of Macedonia had been enlarged into a Roman province. It was the scene of some of Paul's most fruitful labors. While in Troas, he received the "Macedonian call" (*Acts 16:8-10*) and embarked for Macedonia. The churches in Philippi, Thessalonica, and Berea are ample attestation to his effectiveness in the province (see articles on these churches).

SCRIPTURE

The Macedonian Call

Acts 16 [9]And a vision appeared to Paul in the night; There stood a man of Macedonia, and prayed him, saying, Come over into Macedonia, and help us. [10]And after he had seen the vision, immediately we endeavored to go into Macedonia, assuredly gathering that the Lord had called us for to preach the gospel unto them.

Paul Preaches in Macedonia

Acts 16 [11]Therefore loosing from Troas, we came with a straight course to Samothracia, and the next day to Neapolis; [12]And from thence to Philippi, which is the chief city of that part of Macedonia, and a colony: and we were in that city abiding certain days.

Acts 20 [1]And after the uproar was ceased, Paul called unto him the disciples, and embraced them, and departed for to go into Macedonia. [2]And when he had gone over those parts, and had given them much exhortation, he came into Greece, [3]And there abode three months. And when the Jews laid wait for him, as he was about to sail into Syria, he purposed to return through Macedonia. [4]And there accompanied him into Asia Sopater of Berea; and of the Thessalonians, Aristarchus and Secundus; and Gaius of Derbe, and Timotheus; and of Asia, Tychicus and Trophimus. [5]These going before tarried for us at Troas. [6]And we sailed away from Philippi after the days of unleavened bread, and came unto them to Troas in five days; where we abode seven days.

Liberality of the Macedonians

Rom. 15 [26]For it hath pleased them of Macedonia and Achaia to make a certain contribution for the poor saints which are at Jerusalem. [27]It hath pleased them verily; and their debtors they are. For if the Gentiles have been made partakers of their spiritual things, their duty is also to minister unto them in carnal things.

2 Cor. 8 [1]Moreover, brethren, we do you to wit of the grace of God bestowed on the churches of Macedonia; [2]How that in a great trial of affliction, the abundance of their joy and their deep poverty abounded unto the riches of their liberality. [3]For to their power, I bear record, yea, and beyond their power they were willing of themselves; [4]Praying us with much en-

treaty that we would receive the gift, and
take upon us the fellowship of the ministering to the saints. [5]And this they did, not
as we hoped, but first gave their own selves
to the Lord, and unto us by the will of God.

MACHPELAH

[mak pē'la] The name of the field and cave which Abraham purchased from Ephron the Hittite as a burial plot. The bodies of Abraham and Sarah, Isaac and Rebekah, and Jacob and Leah are said to have been placed there. For hundreds of years the traditional site has been a jealously guarded Moslem sanctuary.

SCRIPTURE

Gen. 23 [8]And he communed with them,
saying, If it be your mind that I should
bury my dead out of my sight, hear me,
and entreat for me to Ephron the son of
Zohar, [9]That he may give me the cave of
Machpelah, which he hath, which is in the
end of his field; for as much money as it is
worth he shall give it me for a possession
of a buryingplace amongst you. [10]And
Ephron dwelt among the children of Heth:
and Ephron the Hittite answered Abraham in the audience of the children of
Heth, even of all that went in at the gate
of his city, saying, [11]Nay, my lord, hear
me: the field give I thee, and the cave that
is therein, I give it thee; in the presence of
the sons of my people give I it thee: bury
thy dead. [12]And Abraham bowed down
himself before the people of the land.
[13]And he spake unto Ephron in the audience of the people of the land, saying, But
if thou wilt give it, I pray thee, hear me: I
will give thee money for the field; take it of
me, and I will bury my dead there. [14]And
Ephron answered Abraham, saying unto
him, [15]My lord, hearken unto me: the land
is worth four hundred shekels of silver;
what is that betwixt me and thee?
bury therefore thy dead. [16]And Abraham hearkened unto Ephron; and Abraham weighed to Ephron the silver, which
he had named in the audience of the sons
of Heth, four hundred shekels of silver,
current money with the merchant.
[17]And the field of Ephron, which was in
Machpelah, which was before Mamre, the
field, and the cave which was therein, and
all the trees that were in the field, that
were in all the borders round about, were
made sure [18]Unto Abraham for a possession in the presence of the children of
Heth, before all that went in at the gate of
his city. [19]And after this, Abraham buried
Sarah his wife in the cave of the field of
Machpelah before Mamre: the same is Hebron in the land of Canaan. [20]And the
field, and the cave that is therein, were
made sure unto Abraham for a possession
of a buryingplace by the sons of Heth.

MAGADAN

[mag'a dan] An area to which Jesus and his disciples came after the feeding of the 4,000 (*Matt. 15:39*). In the King James Version this is translated Magdala. In the parallel passage in *Mark 8:10,* Dalmanutha is substituted for Magadan; it seems reasonable to infer from this that the regions of Magadan and Dalmanutha adjoined one another. The area is thought to be on the Western shore of the Sea of Galilee, somewhere south of the plain of Gennesaret.

MAGI

[mā'jī] A term used by Herodotus to refer to a Medean tribe which had a priestly function in the Persian Empire. In *Dan. 1:20, 2:27,* and *5:15,* the term is applied to astrologers or "wise men" who interpret dreams and divine the will of God. In New Testament usage the word usually means all who practice magical arts (*Acts 8:9; 13:6, 8*). Shortly after his birth the infant Jesus was visited by several magi (or wise men) from "the East" who had inferred from the brightness of a star which they had seen that a king had been born and who had come to honor him with gifts of gold, frankincense, and myrrh (*Matt. 2:1-12*).

SCRIPTURE

Matt. 2 [1]Now when Jesus was born in Bethlehem of Judaea in the days of Herod the king, behold, there came wise men from the east to Jerusalem, [2]Saying, Where is he that is born King of the Jews? for we have seen his star in the east, and are come to worship him. [3]When Herod the king had heard these things, he was troubled, and all Jerusalem with him. [4]And when he had gathered all the chief priests and scribes of the people together, he demanded of them where Christ should be born. [5]And they said unto him, In Bethlehem of Judaea: for thus it is written by the prophet, [6]And thou Bethlehem, in the land of Juda, art not the least among the princes of Juda: for out of thee shall come a Governor, that shall rule my people Israel. [7]Then Herod, when he had privily called the wise men, enquired of them diligently what time the star appeared. [8]And he sent them to Bethlehem, and said, Go and search diligently for the young child; and when ye have found him, bring me word again, that I may come and worship him also. [9]When they had heard the king, they departed; and, lo, the star, which they saw in the east, went before them, till it came and stood over where the young child was. [10]When they saw the star, they rejoiced with exceeding great joy.

[11]And when they were come into the house, they saw the young child with Mary his mother, and fell down, and worshipped him: and when they had opened their treasures, they presented unto him gifts; gold, and frankincense, and myrrh. [12]And being warned of God in a dream that they should not return to Herod, they departed into their own country another way.

MAJESTY

[maj'es ti] The dignity and authority of sovereign power, used in the Bible to indicate the sublimity of God and Christ.

SCRIPTURE

1 Chr. 29 [11]Thine, O LORD, is the greatness, and the power, and the glory, and the victory, and the majesty: for all that is in the heaven and in the earth is thine; thine is the kingdom, O LORD, and thou art exalted as head above all.

Job 37 [22]Fair weather cometh out of the north: with God is terrible majesty.

Psa. 93 [1]The LORD reigneth, he is clothed with majesty; the LORD is clothed with strength, wherewith he hath girded himself: the world also is stablished, that it cannot be moved.

Psa. 96 [6]Honour and majesty are before him: strength and beauty are in his sanctuary.

Isa. 24 [14]They shall lift up their voice, they shall sing for the majesty of the LORD, they shall cry aloud from the sea.

2 Pet. 1 [16]For we have not followed cunningly devised fables, when we made known unto you the power and coming of our Lord Jesus Christ, but were eyewitnesses of his majesty.

MALACHI

[mal'a kī] A prophet of the early post-exilic era. The conditions described in Malachi's prophecy are similar to those which prompted the reforms of Ezra and Nehemiah; since their work is dated about 445-400 BC, sometime around 450 is probably the correct date for Malachi. The Jews had returned from captivity a zealous and hopeful people. They had, however, become disillusioned; things simply were not as good as they had hoped. Drought and its accompanying crop failure, together with opposition from various enemies, had made life difficult. Skepticism, doubt, and general neglect of spiritual matters had crept in. They were offering imperfect sacrifices and failing to give their tithes. The priests were lax and did little to encourage them. Mixed marriages with the heathen and divorce had become common.

The heart of Malachi's message was to point out to the people that they could never expect prosperity as long as they continued in the sins described. The work of Malachi closes the period of prophetic activity. After this time, the scribes and priests came to the fore of religious leadership in the activity of expounding that which had already been written.

See EZRA, NEHEMIAH

SCRIPTURE

On Divorce

Mal. 2 [13]And this have ye done again, covering the altar of the LORD with tears, with weeping, and with crying out, insomuch that he regarded not the offering any more, or receiveth it with good will at your hand.

[14]Yet ye say, Wherefore? Because the LORD hath been witness between thee and the wife of thy youth, against whom thou hast dealt treacherously: yet is she thy companion, and the wife of thy covenant. [15]And did not he make one? Yet had he the residue of the Spirit. And wherefore one? That he might seek a godly seed. Therefore take heed to your spirit, and let none deal treacherously against the wife of his youth. [16]For the LORD, the God of Israel, saith that he hateth putting away: for one covereth violence with his garment, saith the LORD of hosts: therefore take heed to your spirit, that ye deal not treacherously.

On Robbing God

Mal. 3 [8]Will a man rob God? Yet ye have robbed me. But ye say, Wherein have we robbed thee? In tithes and offerings. [9]Ye are cursed with a curse: for ye have robbed me, even this whole nation. [10]Bring ye all the tithes into the storehouse, that there may be meat in mine house, and prove me now herewith, saith the LORD of hosts, if I will not open you the windows of heaven, and pour you out a blessing, that there shall not be room enough to receive it. [11]And I will rebuke the devourer for your sakes, and he shall not destroy the fruits of your ground; neither shall your vine cast her fruit before the time in the field, saith the LORD of hosts. [12]And all nations shall call you blessed: for ye shall be a delightsome land, saith the LORD of hosts.

On the Elijah Who Was to Come

Mal. 4 [5]Behold, I will send you Elijah the prophet before the coming of the great and dreadful day of the LORD: [6]And he shall turn the heart of the fathers to the children, and the heart of the children to their fathers, lest I come and smite the earth with a curse.

MALCHUS

[mal'kus] A servant of the high priest Caiaphas. At the arrest of Jesus in the Garden of Gethsemane, the impetuous apostle Peter, unable to stand by helplessly, took out his sword and cut off Malchus' right ear. Jesus rebuked the disciples for this show of violence and restored the severed ear. It is interesting to note that one of the men who later put a question to Peter which caused him to deny the Master is identified as a kinsman of Malchus.

See PETER

SCRIPTURE

John 18 [10]Then Simon Peter having a sword drew it, and smote the high priest's servant, and cut off his right ear. The servant's name was Malchus.

See Matt. 26:51; Mark 14:47; Luke 22:50-51; John 18:26.

MALICE

[mal'is] A deep-seated and often unreasonable dislike that takes pleasure in seeing others suffer; a disposition of the mind which leads to the performance of harmful acts against the object of one's ill will; confirmed anger. The Bible admonishes all men who would be godly to purge their hearts of malice.

SCRIPTURE

Lev. 19 [14]Thou shalt not curse the deaf, nor put a stumblingblock before the blind, but shalt fear thy God:

[17]Thou shalt not hate thy brother in thine heart:

[18]Thou shalt not avenge, nor bear any grudge against the children of thy people, but thou shalt love thy neighbour as thyself:

Deut. 32 [32]For their vine is of the vine of Sodom, and of the fields of Gomorrah: their grapes are grapes of gall, their clusters are bitter: [33]Their wine is the poison of dragons, and the cruel venom of asps.

Psa. 10 [7]His mouth is full of cursing and deceit and fraud: under his tongue is mischief and vanity. [8]He sitteth in the lurking places of the villages: in the secret places doth he murder the innocent: his eyes are privily set against the poor. [9]He lieth in wait secretly as a lion in his den: he lieth in wait to catch the poor: he doth catch the poor, when he draweth him into his net. [10]He croucheth, and humbleth himself, that the poor may fall by his strong ones.

Matt. 5 [38]Ye have heard that it hath been said, An eye for an eye, and a tooth for a tooth: [39]But I say unto you, That ye resist not evil: but whosoever shall smite thee on thy right cheek, turn to him the other also. [40]And if any man will sue thee at the law, and take away thy coat, let him have thy cloke also. [41]And whosoever shall compel thee to go a mile, go with him twain.

Mark 15 [10]For he knew that the chief priests had delivered him for envy.

Rom. 1 [29]Being filled with all unrighteousness, fornication, wickedness, covetousness, maliciousness; full of envy, murder, debate, deceit, malignity, whisperers, [30]Backbiters, haters of God, despiteful, proud, boasters, inventors of evil things, disobedient to parents, [31]Without understanding, covenant-breakers, without natural affection, implacable, unmerciful: [32]Who knowing the judgment of God, that they which commit such things are worthy of death, not only do the same, but hath pleasure in them that do them.

Eph. 4 [31]Let all bitterness, and wrath, and anger, and clamour, and evil speaking, be put away from you, with all malice:

Col. 3 [8]But now ye also put off all these: anger, wrath, malice, blasphemy, filthy communication out of your mouth.

Tit. 3 [3]We ourselves also were sometimes . . . living in malice and envy, hateful, and hating one another.

1 John 3 [15]Whosoever hateth his brother is a murderer: and ye know that no murderer hath eternal life abiding in him.

3 John 1 [10]Wherefore, if I come, I will remember his deeds which he doeth, prating against us with malicious words: and not content therewith, neither doth he himself receive the brethren, and forbiddeth them that would, and casteth them out of the church.

See Luke 6:29

MAMMON

[mam'un] The word for riches in Aramaic, the language spoken by Jesus and most of the common people of Judaea in his day. In *Luke 16:13* —"Ye cannot serve God and mammon"—there is a personification of mammon, but it cannot be proven that there was a Near Eastern deity by this name, as is sometimes claimed.

SCRIPTURE

Matt. 6 24No man can serve two masters: for either he will hate the one, and love the other; or else he will hold to the one, and despise the other. Ye cannot serve God and mammon.

Luke 16 9And I say unto you, Make to yourselves friends of the mammon of unrighteousness; that, when ye fail, they may receive you into everlasting habitations. 11If therefore ye have not been faithful in the unrighteous mammon, who will commit to your trust the true riches? 13No servant can serve two masters: for either he will hate the one, and love the other; or else he will hold to the one, and despise the other. Ye cannot serve God and mammon.

MAN

[man] The opening chapters of *Genesis* provide us with the view of man which is held consistently throughout the Bible. There man is seen to be the crown of God's creation. He is a being created in the image of God, indicating his authority over creation and his capacities for creativity and goodness. In the Fall, Man expresses his unwillingness to accept his limitations and attempts to become like God. As a consequence he thwarts God's original purpose for him and becomes a slave to sin. Thenceforth all his acts are tainted by his sinfulness. Freedom from this servitude to sin comes only through the redemption wrought through Christ. As in Adam all die, so in Christ, the True Man, all may be made alive to fulfill the purposes for which God originally created mankind. Co-laboring with God's Holy Spirit, redeemed man seeks to bring his life into conformity with God's will and word, perfectly revealed in Christ.

Contrary to the oft-expressed notion, the Bible does not view man as a soul which possesses a body. The soul does not exist independent of the body, but is regarded as the life principle of the body. When the soul "leaves" the body, it does not continue to exist in a disembodied state. Christian belief in a continuation of life after death is based not on the Greek concept of the immortal soul, but on belief in the resurrection of the body. We cannot comprehend the nature of the resurrection body, but we may infer that life after death involves the whole man in the fullness of personal existence.

See LIFE, DEATH, RESURRECTION, SOUL

SCRIPTURE

Man's Creation and Fall

Gen. 1 26And God said, Let us make man in our image, after our likeness: and let them have dominion over the fish of the sea, and over the fowl of the air, and over the cattle, and over all the earth, and over every creeping thing that creepeth upon the earth. 27So God created man in his own image, in the image of God created he him; male and female created he them.

Gen. 2 7And the LORD God formed man of the dust of the ground, and breathed into his nostrils the breath of life; and man became a living soul.

Gen. 3 9And the LORD God called unto Adam, and said unto him, Where art thou? 10And he said, I heard thy voice in the garden: and I was afraid, because I was naked; and I hid myself. 11And he said, Who told thee that thou wast naked? Hast thou eaten of the tree whereof I commanded thee, that thou shouldest not eat? 12And the man said, The woman whom thou gavest to be with me, she gave me of the tree, and I did eat.

[22]And the Lord God said, Behold, the man is become as one of us, to know good and evil: and now, lest he put forth his hand, and take also of the tree of life, and eat, and live for ever: [23]Therefore the Lord God sent him forth from the garden of Eden, to till the ground from whence he was taken. [24]So he drove out the man: and he placed at the east of the garden of Eden cherubim, and a flaming sword which turned every way, to keep the way of the tree of life.

Man's Position in Creation

Gen. 1 [28]And God blessed them, and God said unto them, Be fruitful, and multiply, and replenish the earth, and subdue it: and have dominion over the fish of the sea, and over the fowl of the air, and over every living thing that moveth upon the earth.

[29]And God said, Behold, I have given you every herb bearing seed, which is upon the face of all the earth, and every tree, in the which is the fruit of a tree yielding seed; to you it shall be for meat. [30]And to every beast of the earth, and to every fowl of the air, and to every thing that creepeth upon the earth, wherein there is life, I have given every green herb for meat: and it was so.

Man's Sinfulness

Gen. 6 [5]And God saw that the wickedness of man was great in the earth, and that every imagination of the thoughts of his heart was only evil continually. [11]The earth also was corrupt before God; and the earth was filled with violence. [12]And God looked upon the earth, and, behold, it was corrupt; for all flesh had corrupted his way upon the earth.

Deut. 32 [5]They have corrupted themselves, their spot is not the spot of his children: they are a perverse and crooked generation.

Psa. 14 [1]The fool hath said in his heart, There is no God. They are corrupt, they have done abominable works, there is none that doeth good. [2]The Lord looked down from heaven upon the children of men, to see if there were any that did understand, and seek God. [3]They are all gone aside, they are all together become filthy: there is none that doeth good, no, not one.

Psa. 53 [1]The fool hath said in his heart, There is no God. Corrupt are they, and have done abominable iniquity: there is none that doeth good. [2]God looked down from heaven upon the children of men, to see if they were any that did understand, that did seek God. [3]Every one of them is gone back: they are altogether become filthy; there is none that doeth good, no, not one.

Psa. 78 [32]For all this they sinned still, and believed not for his wondrous works.

Prov. 20 [6]Most men will proclaim every one his own goodness: but a faithful man who can find? [9]Who can say, I have made my heart clean, I am pure from my sin?

Eccl. 7 [27]Behold, this have I found, saith the Preacher, counting one by one, to find out the account; [28]Which yet my soul seeketh, but I find not: one man among a thousand have I found; but a woman among all those have I not found. [29]Lo, this only have I found, that God hath made man upright; but they have sought out many inventions.

Eccl. 8 [11]Because sentence against an evil work is not executed speedily, therefore the heart of the sons of men is fully set in them to do evil.

Jer. 2 [29]Wherefore will ye plead with me? ye all have transgressed against me, saith the Lord.

Man's Imperfection and Weakness

2 Chr. 20 [12]O our God, wilt thou not judge them? for we have no might against this great company that cometh against us; neither know we what to do: but our eyes are upon thee.

Matt. 6 [27]Which of you by taking thought can add one cubit unto his stature?

Rom. 9 [16]So then it is not of him that willeth, nor of him that runneth, but of God that sheweth mercy.

1 Cor. 3 [7]So then neither is he that planteth any thing, neither he that watereth; but God that giveth the increase.

2 Cor. 3 [5]Not that we are sufficient of ourselves to think any thing as of ourselves; but our sufficiency is of God.

Man Made to Suffer

Job 5 [6]Although affliction cometh not forth of the dust, neither doth trouble spring out of the ground: [7]Yet man is born unto trouble, as the sparks fly upward.

Job 14 [1]Man that is born of a woman is of few days, and full of trouble. [2]He cometh forth like a flower, and is cut down: he fleeth also as a shadow, and continueth not.

Psa. 39 [4]LORD, make me to know mine end, and the measure of my days, what it is; that I may know how frail I am.

Acts 14 [22]Confirming the souls of the disciples, and exhorting them to continue in the faith, and that we must through much tribulation enter into the kingdom of God.

Rom. 8 [22]For we know that the whole creation groaneth and travaileth in pain together until now. [23]And not only they, but ourselves also, which have the firstfruits of the Spirit, even we ourselves groan within ourselves, waiting for the adoption, to wit, the redemption of our body.

Ignorance of Man

Job 8 [8]For inquire, I pray thee, of the former age, and prepare thyself to the search of thy fathers: [9](For we are but of yesterday, and know nothing, because our days upon earth are a shadow:) [10]Shall not they teach thee, and tell thee, and utter words out of their heart?

Job 11 [12]For vain man would be wise, though man be born like a wild ass's colt.

Job 28 [12]But where shall wisdom be found? and where is the place of understanding? [13]Man knoweth not the price thereof; neither is it found in the land of the living.

Prov. 16 [25]There is a way that seemeth right unto a man; but the end thereof are the ways of death.

Prov. 27 [1]Boast not thyself of tomorrow; for thou knowest not what a day may bring forth.

Eccl. 8 [17]Then I beheld all the work of God, that a man cannot find out the work that is done under the sun: because though a man labour to seek it out, yet he shall not find it; yea further; though a wise man think to know it yet shall he not be able to find it.

Isa. 59 [10]We grope for the wall like the blind, and we grope as if we had no eyes: we stumble at noonday as in the night; we are in desolate places as dead men.

1 Cor. 1 [20]Where is the wise? where is the scribe? where is the disputer of this world? hath not God made foolish the wisdom of this world? [21]For after that in the wisdom of God the world by wisdom knew not God, it pleased God by the foolishness of preaching to save them that believe.

1 Cor. 8 [2]And if any man think that he knoweth any thing, he knoweth nothing yet as he ought to know.

Jas. 4 [14]Whereas ye know not what shall be on the morrow. For what is your life? It is even a vapour, that appeareth for a little time, and then vanisheth away.

Mortality of Man

Job 21 [32]Yet ye shall be brought to the grave, and shall remain in the tomb.
[33]The clods of the valley shall be sweet unto him, and every man shall draw after him, as there are innumerable before him.

Psa. 22 [29]All they that be fat upon earth shall eat and worship: all they that go down to the dust shall bow before him: and none can keep alive his own soul.

Psa. 79 [48]What man is he that liveth, and shall not see death? shall he deliver his soul from the hand of the grave? Selah.

Eccl. 1 [4]One generation passeth away, and another generation cometh: but the earth abideth for ever.

Eccl. 4 [15]I considered all the living which walk under the sun, with the second child that shall stand up in his stead.

Eccl. 6 [6]Yea, though he live a thousand years twice told, yet hath he seen no good: do not all go to one place?

Eccl. 8 [8]There is no man that hath power over the spirit to retain the spirit; neither hath he power in the day of death: and there is no discharge in that war; neither shall wickedness deliver those that are given to it.

Zech. 1 [5]Your fathers, where are they? and the prophets, do they live for ever?

Heb. 7 [23]And they truly were many priests, because they were not suffered to continue by reason of death.

Vanity of Man's Life

Psa. 49 [14]Like sheep they are laid in the grave; death shall feed on them; and the upright shall have dominion over them in the morning; and their beauty shall consume in the grave from their dwelling.

Eccl. 1 [2]Vanity of vanities, saith the Preacher, vanity of vanities; all is vanity.
[3]What profit hath a man of all his labour which he taketh under the sun? [4]One generation passeth away, and another generation cometh: but the earth abideth for ever.

Man's Duty

Eccl. 12 [13]Let us hear the conclusion of the whole matter: Fear God, and keep his commandments: for this is the whole duty of man.

Mic. 6 [8]He hath shewed thee, O man, what is good; and what doth the LORD require of thee, but to do justly, and to love mercy, and to walk humbly with thy God?

1 John 3 [23]And this is his commandment, That we should believe on the name of his Son Jesus Christ, and love one another, as he gave us commandment.

Man's Redemption

Rom. 5 [8]But God commendeth his love toward us, in that, while we were yet sinners, Christ died for us. [9]Much more then, being now justified by his blood, we shall be saved from wrath through him. [10]For if, when we were enemies, we were reconciled to God by the death of his Son, much more, being reconciled, we shall be saved by his life. [11]And not only so, but we also joy in God through our Lord Jesus Christ, by whom we have now received the atonement. [12]Wherefore, as by one man sin entered into the world, and death by sin; and so death passed upon all men, for that all have sinned: [13](For until the law sin was in the world: but sin is not imputed when there is no law.

[14]Nevertheless death reigned from Adam to Moses, even over them that had not sinned after the similitude of Adam's transgression, who is the figure of him that was to come. [15]But not as the offence, so also is the free gift. For if through the offence of one many be dead, much more the grace of God, and the gift by grace, which is by one man, Jesus Christ, hath abounded unto many. [16]And not as it was by one that sinned, so is the gift: for the judgment was by one to condemnation, but the free gift is of many offences unto justification. [17]For if by one man's offence death reigned by one; much more they which receive abundance of grace and of the gift of righteousness shall reign in life by one, Jesus Christ.) [18]Therefore as by the offence of one judgment came upon all men to condemnation; even so by the righteousness of one the free gift came upon all men unto justification of life. [19]For as by one man's disobedience many were made sinners, so by the obedience of one shall many be made righteous.

1 Cor. 15 [49]And as we have borne the image of the earthy, we shall also bear the image of the heavenly.

Phil. 3 [20]For our conversation is in heaven; from whence also we look for the Saviour, the Lord Jesus Christ: [21]Who shall change our vile body, that it may be fashioned like unto his glorious body, according to the working whereby he is able even to subdue all things unto himself.

Col. 1 [12]Giving thanks unto the Father, which hath made us meet to be partakers of the inheritance of the saints in light: [13]Who hath delivered us from the power of darkness, and hath translated us into the kingdom of his dear Son: [14]In whom we have redemption through his blood, even the forgiveness of sins.

Heb. 2 [6]But one in a certain place testified, saying, What is man, that thou art mindful of him? or the son of man, that thou visitest him? [7]Thou madest him a little lower than the angels; thou crownedst him with glory and honour, and didst set him over the works of thy hands: [8]Thou hast put all things in subjection under his feet. For in that he put all in subjection under him, he left nothing that is not put under him. But now we see not yet all things put under him. [9]But we see Jesus, who was made a little lower than the angels for the suffering of death, crowned with glory and honour; that he by the grace of God should taste death for every man. [10]For it became him, for whom are all things, and by whom are all things, in bringing many sons unto glory, to make the captain of their salvation perfect through sufferings. [11]For both he that sanctifieth and they who are sanctified are all of one: for which cause he is not ashamed to call them brethren, [12]Saying, I will declare thy name unto my brethren, in the midst of the church will I sing praise unto thee. [13]And again, I will put my trust in him. And again, Behold I and the children which God hath given me. [14]Forasmuch then as the children are partakers of flesh and blood, he also himself likewise took part of the same; that through death he might destroy him that had the power of death, that is, the devil; [15]And deliver them who through fear of death were all their lifetime subject to bondage. [16]For verily he took not on him the nature of angels; but he took on him the seed of Abraham. [17]Wherefore in all things it behoved him to be made like unto his brethren, that he might be a merciful and faithful high priest in things pertaining to God, to make reconciliation for the sins of the people.

MANASSEH, Son of Joseph

[ma nas′e] The son of Joseph and his wife Asenath, the daughter of Potiphera priest of On. Manasseh's birth brought such joy to Joseph that he was finally able to forget the wrongs which he had suffered at the hands of his brethren. Two Israelite tribes traced their lineage to Joseph, calling themselves by the names of his two sons, Manasseh and Ephraim. The relative importance of these two tribes is traced to the giving of the paternal blessing by Jacob, in which Ephraim was favored, although younger than Manasseh.

SCRIPTURE

Gen. 41 50 And unto Joseph were born two sons, before the years of famine came: which Asenath the daughter of Potipherah priest of On bare unto him. 51 And Joseph called the name of the firstborn Manasseh: For God, said he, hath made me forget all my toil, and all my father's house.

Gen. 48 1 And it came to pass after these things, that one told Joseph, Behold, thy father is sick: and he took with him his two sons, Manasseh and Ephraim.

5 And now thy two sons, Ephraim and Manasseh, which were born unto thee in the land of Egypt, before I came unto thee into Egypt, are mine; as Reuben and Simeon, they shall be mine. 6 And thy issue, which thou begettest after them, shall be thine, and shall be called after the name of their brethren in their inheritance. 7 And as for me, when I came from Padan, Rachel died by me in the land of Canaan in the way, when yet there was but a little way to come unto Ephrath: and I buried her there in the way of Ephrath; the same is Bethlehem. 8 And Israel beheld Joseph's sons, and said, Who are these? 9 And Joseph said unto his father, They are my sons, whom God hath given me in this place. And he said, Bring them, I pray thee, unto me, and I will bless them. 10 Now the eyes of Israel were dim for age, so that he could not see. And he brought them near unto him; and he kissed them, and embraced them. 11 And Israel said unto Joseph, I had not thought to see thy face: and, lo, God hath shewed me also thy seed. 12 And Joseph brought them out from between his knees, and he bowed himself with his face to the earth. 13 And Joseph took them both, Ephraim in his right hand toward Israel's left hand, and Manasseh in his left hand toward Israel's right hand, and brought them near unto him. 14 And Israel stretched out his right hand, and laid it upon Ephraim's head, who was the younger, and his left hand upon Manasseh's head, guiding his hands wittingly; for Manasseh was the firstborn.

15 And he blessed Joseph, and said, God, before whom my fathers Abraham and Isaac did walk, the God which fed me all my life long unto this day, 16 The Angel which redeemed me from all evil, bless the lads; and let my name be named on them, and the name of my fathers Abraham and Isaac; and let them grow into a multitude in the midst of the earth. 17 And when Joseph saw that his father laid his right hand upon the head of Ephraim, it displeased him: and he held up his father's hand, to remove it from Ephraim's head unto Manasseh's head. 18 And Joseph said unto his father, Not so, my father: for this is the firstborn; put thy right hand upon his head. 19 And his father refused, and said, I know it, my son, I know it: he also shall become a people, and he also shall be great: but truly his younger brother shall be greater than he, and his seed shall become a multitude of nations. 20 And he blessed them that day, saying, In thee shall Israel bless, saying, God make thee as Ephraim and as Manasseh: and he set Ephraim before Manasseh.

MANASSEH, King of Judah

[ma nas′e] The son of Hezekiah and king of Judah (687-642 BC). The Biblical record of Manasseh's reign is almost entirely a censure of the religious practices which he allowed and encouraged. Contrary to the patriotic, if fruitless, efforts of his father to assert the independence of Judah, Manasseh abandoned resistance to Assyria and was apparently a loyal vassal-king throughout his long reign. As a part of this vassalage relationship, the official Assyrian cults were set up; in addition, every sort of idolatrous practice which seemed good to Manasseh found a place in the worship of Judah. Human sacrifice became a regular practice. Those who supported a return to the true religion were persecuted severely; tradition has it that Isaiah was placed in a log and sawn asunder during this period. *2 Chr. 33:1-13* states that Manasseh was carried to Assyria in chains at some time during his reign and that while there he learned that "the Lord he was God." On his return he is said to have made some efforts at reform. Despite this late change of heart, Manasseh is usually thought of as the most wicked of Judah's kings.

See ISAIAH

SCRIPTURE

2 Kin. 21 1Manasseh was twelve years
old when he began to reign, and reigned
fifty and five years in Jerusalem. And his
mother's name was Hephzibah. 2And he
did that which was evil in the sight of the
LORD, after the abominations of the
heathen, whom the LORD cast out before
the children of Israel. 3For he built up
again the high places which Hezekiah his
father had destroyed; and he reared up
altars for Baal, and made a grove, as did
Ahab king of Israel; and worshipped all
the host of heaven, and served them. 4And
he built altars in the house of the LORD, of
which the LORD said, In Jerusalem will I
put my name. 5And he built altars for all
the host of heaven in the two courts of the
house of the LORD. 6And he made his son
pass through the fire, and observed times,
and used enchantments, and dealt with
familiar spirits and wizards: he wrought
much wickedness in the sight of the LORD,
to provoke him to anger. 7And he set a
graven image of the grove that he had
made in the house, of which the LORD said
to David, and to Solomon his son, In this
house, and in Jerusalem, which I have
chosen out of all the tribes of Israel, will I
put my name for ever: 8Neither will I
make the feet of Israel move any more out
of the land which I gave their fathers; only
if they will observe to do according to all
that I have commanded them, and according
to all the law that my servant Moses
commanded them. 9But they hearkened
not: and Manasseh seduced them to do
more evil than did the nations whom the
LORD destroyed before the children of Israel.

10And the LORD spake by his servants
the prophets, saying, 11Because Manasseh
king of Judah hath done these abominations,
and hath done wickedly above all
that the Amorites did, which were before
him, and hath made Judah also to sin with
his idols: 12Therefore thus saith the LORD
God of Israel, Behold, I am bringing such
evil upon Jerusalem and Judah, that whosoever
heareth of it, both his ears shall
tingle. 13And I will stretch over Jerusalem
the line of Samaria, and the plummet of
the house of Ahab: and I will wipe Jerusalem
as a man wipeth a dish, wiping it,
and turning it upside down. 14And I will
forsake the remnant of mine inheritance,
and deliver them into the hand of their
enemies; and they shall become a prey and
a spoil to all their enemies; 15Because they
have done that which was evil in my sight,
and have provoked me to anger, since the
day their fathers came forth out of Egypt,
even unto this day. 16Moreover Manasseh

shed innocent blood very much, till he had filled Jerusalem from one end to another; besides his sin wherewith he made Judah to sin, in doing that which was evil in the sight of the LORD.

[17]Now the rest of the acts of Manasseh, and all that he did, and his sin that he sinned, are they not written in the book of the Chronicles of the kings of Judah? [18]And Manasseh slept with his fathers, and was buried in the garden of his own house, in the garden of Uzza: and Amon his son reigned in his stead.

MANDRAKES

[man'drāks] A plant common in Palestine and used in folk medicine. In ancient times it was used as an aphrodisiac. In the Old Testament they figure in a transaction between Leah and Rachel.

SCRIPTURE

Gen. 30 [14]And Reuben went in the days of wheat harvest, and found mandrakes in the field, and brought them unto his mother Leah. Then Rachel said to Leah, Give me, I pray thee, of thy son's mandrakes. [15]And she said unto her, Is it a small matter that thou hast taken my husband? and wouldest thou take away my son's mandrakes also? And Rachel said, Therefore he shall lie with thee to-night for thy son's mandrakes. [16]And Jacob came out of the field in the evening, and Leah went out to meet him, and said, Thou must come in unto me; for surely I have hired thee with my son's mandrakes. And he lay with her that night.

MANNA

[man'a] An item in the diet of the Israelites during the period of wilderness wanderings. In *Ex. 16:15* we are told that the name is derived from the inquiry (*man hu?*, or *What is this?*) made by the Hebrews when they first saw it upon the ground.

A description of the phenomenon, together with the restrictions concerning its use, is found in the references below. Contrary to popular belief manna was not the sole article in the diet of the Israelites; numerous passages mention the presence of other articles of food. There have been various naturalistic explanations of the manna, none of which is entirely satisfactory. The substance which most nearly fits the Biblical record is the honeydew excretion produced by insects feeding on a certain species of tamarisk. It is sweet and is considered a real delicacy. As in the Biblical account, it disappears shortly after the sun rises, not because of melting, but because it is carried away by ants. The Arabs refer to this substance as *man es-simma* (the manna of heaven).

SCRIPTURE

Description of Manna

Ex. 16 [4]Then said the LORD unto Moses, Behold, I will rain bread from heaven for you; and the people shall go out and gather a certain rate every day, that I may prove them, whether they will walk in my law, or no.

[12]I have heard the murmurings of the children of Israel: speak unto them, saying, At even ye shall eat flesh, and in the morning ye shall be filled with bread; and ye shall know that I am the LORD your God. [13]And it came to pass, that at even the quails came up, and covered the camp: and in the morning the dew lay round about the host. [14]And when the dew that lay was gone up, behold, upon the face of the wilderness there lay a small round thing, as small as the hoar frost on the ground. [15]And when the children of Israel saw it, they said one to another, It is manna: for they wist not what it was. And Moses said unto them, This is the bread which the LORD hath given you to eat.

[16]This is the thing which the LORD hath commanded, Gather of it every man according to his eating, an omer for every man, according to the number of your persons; take ye every man for them which are in his tents. [17]And the children of Israel did so, and gathered, some more, some less. [18]And when they did mete it with an omer, he that gathered much had nothing over, and he that gathered little had no lack; they gathered every man according to his eating. [19]And Moses said, Let no man leave of it till the morning. [20]Notwithstanding they hearkened not unto Moses; but some of them left of it until the morning, and it bred worms, and stank: and Moses was wroth with them. [21]And they gathered it every morning, every man according to his eating: and when the sun waxed hot, it melted.

[22]And it came to pass, that on the sixth day they gathered twice as much bread, two omers for one man: and all the rulers of the congregation came and told Moses. [23]And he said unto them, This is that which the LORD hath said, To-morrow is the rest of the holy sabbath unto the LORD: bake that which ye will bake to-day, and seethe that ye will seethe; and that which remaineth over lay up for you to be kept until the morning. [24]And they laid it up till the morning, as Moses bade: and it did not stink, neither was there any worm therein. [25]And Moses said, Eat that to-day; for to-day is a sabbath unto the LORD: to-day ye shall not find it in the field. [26]Six days ye shall gather it; but on the seventh day, which is the sabbath, in it there shall be none.

[31]And the house of Israel called the name thereof Manna: and it was like coriander seed, white; and the taste of it was like wafers made with honey.

[32]And Moses said, This is the thing which the LORD commandeth, Fill an omer of it to be kept for your generations; that they may see the bread wherewith I have fed you in the wilderness, when I brought you forth from the land of Egypt. [33]And Moses said unto Aaron, Take a pot, and put an omer full of manna therein, and lay it up before the LORD, to be kept for your generations. [34]As the LORD commanded Moses, so Aaron laid it up before the Testimony, to be kept. [35]And the children of Israel did eat manna forty years, until they came to a land inhabited: they did eat manna, until they came unto the borders of the land of Canaan.

Josh. 5 [12]And the manna ceased on the morrow after they had eaten of the old corn of the land; neither had the children of Israel manna any more; but they did eat of the fruit of the land of Canaan that year.

Other Food Available

Ex. 24 [5]And he sent young men of the children of Israel, which offered burnt offerings, and sacrificed peace offerings of oxen unto the LORD.

Ex. 34 [3]Neither let the flocks nor herds feed before that mount.

Lev. 8 [2]Take Aaron and his sons with him, and the garments, and the anointing oil, and a bullock for the sin offering, and two rams, and a basket of unleavened bread;

[31]And Moses said unto Aaron and to his sons, Boil the flesh at the door of the tabernacle of the congregation; and there eat it with the bread that is in the basket of consecrations, as I commanded, saying, Aaron and his sons shall eat it.

Lev. 10 [12]Take the meat offering that remaineth of the offerings of the LORD made by fire, and eat it without leaven beside the altar: for it is most holy:

Figurative

John 6 [48]I am that bread of life. [49]Your fathers did eat manna in the wilderness, and are dead. [50]This is the bread which cometh down from heaven, that a man may eat thereof, and not die. [51]I am the living bread which came down from heaven: if any man eat of this bread, he shall live forever: and the bread that I will give is my flesh, which I will give for the life of the world.

Rev. 2 [17]He that hath an ear, let him hear what the Spirit saith unto the churches; To him that overcometh will I give to eat of the hidden manna, and will give him a white stone, and in the stone a new name written, which no man knoweth saving he that receiveth it.

MARK, JOHN

[märk, jon] Mark was the Roman name and John the Jewish name of the young man who was from time to time a companion of Paul and to whom the second gospel is almost unanimously ascribed. He is known to have been a Palestinian Jew who was closely associated with the teaching of Jesus and his apostles. His mother's home was apparently a favorite gathering place of Christians in Jerusalem. In *1 Pet. 5:13*, the great apostle speaks of him as "my son Mark," which is taken by some to mean that Mark was converted by Peter. Mark was a companion of Paul and Barnabas on the early portion of the first missionary tour, but left the party at Perga in Pamphylia, incurring the sharp disapproval of Paul. Because of Paul's refusal to take him on the second journey, Barnabas separated from Paul and set out with Mark for Cyprus. In later years, however, we learn that Mark had regained Paul's confidence and was singled out by the apostle as being particularly useful to him.

See Barnabas, Paul

SCRIPTURE

Acts 12 [12]And when he had considered the thing, he came to the house of Mary the mother of John, whose surname was Mark; where many were gathered together praying.

[25]And Barnabas and Saul returned from Jerusalem, when they had fulfilled their ministry, and took with them John, whose surname was Mark.

Acts 13 [5]And when they were at Salamis, they preached the word of God in the synagogues of the Jews: and they had also John to their minister. [13]Now when Paul and his company loosed from Paphos, they came to Perga in Pamphylia: and John departing from them returned to Jerusalem.

Acts 15 [36]And some days after, Paul said unto Barnabas, Let us go again and visit our brethren in every city where we have preached the word of the Lord, and see how they do. [37]And Barnabas determined to take with them John, whose surname was Mark. [38]But Paul thought not good to take him with them, who departed from them from Pamphylia, and went not with them to the work. [39]And the contention was so sharp between them, that they departed asunder one from the other: and so Barnabas took Mark, and sailed unto Cyprus;

II Tim. 4 [11]Only Luke is with me. Take Mark, and bring him with thee: for he is profitable to me for the ministry.

MARRIAGE

[mar′ij] The mutual relation of husband and wife; wedlock; the social institution whereby men and women are joined in a special kind of social and legal dependence for the purpose of founding and maintaining a family. The creation account indicates clearly that the family is the central unit in society and that its character and maintenance is determined by marriage. Here man is seen to be less than complete man without a helper and companion. To remedy this, he is given woman, who is created out of something taken from man and is dependent upon him.

In the Old Testament it was deemed preferable for a man to choose as his bride a woman not so far removed from his own family as to be unfamiliar or unsympathetic with the prevailing customs and religious beliefs. There were, however, certain close relatives with whom marriage was prevented. When a marriage was contracted the bridegroom paid to the bride's family a "bride price" to offset, symbolically as well as materially, the loss of the daughter. Before the actual consummation of the marriage there was a period of betrothal, during which the couple were considered to be man and wife. The marriage ceremony itself consisted mainly in the transferring of the bride from her father's house to that of the bridegroom. Accompanied by their attendants the bride and groom proceeded to the place where the wedding feast was to be held. The feast itself was often a gala affair and was climaxed by the preparation of a special tent or room which served as a bridal chamber in which the husband took physical possession of his bride.

The primary duty of the wife was to provide heirs for her husband. (*See* FAMILY) Because of the emphasis on large families, polygamy was common in early Israel. If several wives did not produce a sufficient number of children, it was not uncommon for a man to take additional concubines or handmaidens as secondary wives.

The law of Levirate marriage was designed to insure every man of male descendants to carry on his line. The term "levirate" comes from the word "levir" meaning "a husband's brother." The law stated that if a man died leaving no heirs, his nearest male kin was to take the widow as his wife, if he refused, he was subjected to the general disapproval of the community (*Deut. 25:5-10*).

In *1 Cor. 7,* Paul deals with the problems of maintaining Christian marriage in a pagan society. He averred that marriage made people anxious about the wrong things and that, in view of the expected imminent return of Christ, it was best to remain unmarried. If, however, one were married, it was best to remain so. Neither was it a sin for the unmarried to marry; in fact, it may be necessary because of the temptation to incontinence. If marriage is undertaken, both partners accept full responsibilities of the union.

The metaphor of marriage is used as descriptive of the intimate relationship between God and Israel and between Christ and the church.

See CELIBACY, DIVORCE, ADULTERY, FAMILY

SCRIPTURE

Marriage Instituted by God

Gen. 2 [18]And the LORD God said, It is not good that the man should be alone: I will make him a help meet for him. [19]And out of the ground the LORD God formed every beast of the field, and every fowl of the air; and brought them unto Adam to see what he would call them: and whatsoever Adam called every living creature, that was the name thereof: [20]And Adam gave names to all cattle, and to the fowl of the air, and to every beast of the field: but for Adam there was not found a help meet for him. [21]And the LORD God caused a deep sleep to fall upon Adam, and he slept; and he took one of his ribs, and closed up the flesh instead thereof. [22]And the rib, which the LORD God had taken from man, made he a woman, and brought her unto the man. [23]And Adam said, This is now bone of my bones, and flesh of my flesh: she shall be called Woman, because she was taken out of man. [24]Therefore shall a man leave his father and his mother, and shall cleave unto his wife: and they shall be one flesh.

Marriage under the Law

Lev. 20 [14]And if a man take a wife and her mother, it is wickedness: they shall be burnt with fire, both he and they; that there be no wickedness among you. [17]And if a man shall take his sister, his father's daughter, or his mother's daughter, and see her nakedness, and she see his nakedness; it is a wicked thing; and they shall

be cut off in the sight of their people: he
hath uncovered his sister's nakedness: he
shall bear his iniquity. [19]And thou shalt
not uncover the nakedness of thy mother's
sister, nor of thy father's sister: for he uncovereth his near kin: they shall bear their
iniquity. [20]And if a man shall lie with his
uncle's wife, he hath uncovered his uncle's
nakedness: they shall bear their sin; they
shall die childless. [21]And if a man shall
take his brother's wife, it is an unclean
thing: he hath uncovered his brother's
nakedness; they shall be childless.

Lev. 21 [1]And the LORD said unto Moses,
Speak unto the priests the sons of Aaron,
and say unto them, . . . [7]They shall not
take a wife that is a whore, or profane;
neither shall they take a woman put away
from her husband: for he is holy unto his
God.

[13]And he shall take a wife in her virginity. [14]A widow, or a divorced woman, or
profane, or an harlot, these shall he not
take: but he shall take a virgin of his own
people to wife.

Jesus' Teaching on Marriage

Matt. 19 [3]The Pharisees also came unto
him, tempting him, and saying unto him,
Is it lawful for a man to put away his wife
for every cause? [4]And he answered and
said unto them, Have ye not read that he
which made them at the beginning made
them male and female, [5]And said, For
this cause shall a man leave father and
mother, and shall cleave to his wife: and
they twain shall be one flesh? [6]Wherefore
they are no more twain, but one flesh.
What therefore God hath joined together,
let not man put asunder. [7]They say unto
him, Why did Moses then command to
give a writing of divorcement, and to put
her away? [8]He saith unto them, Moses
because of the hardness of your hearts
suffered you to put away your wives: but
from the beginning it was not so. [9]And I
say unto you, Whosoever shall put away
his wife, except it be for fornication, and
shall marry another, committeth adultery:
and whoso marrieth her which is put away
doth commit adultery.

Mark 10 [2]And the Pharisees came to
him, and asked him, Is it lawful for a man
to put away his wife? tempting him. [3]And
he answered and said unto them, What
did Moses command you? [4]And they said,
Moses suffered to write a bill of divorcement, and to put her away. [5]And Jesus
answered and said unto them, For the
hardness of your heart he wrote you this
precept. [6]But from the beginning of the
creation God made them male and female.
[7]For this cause shall a man leave his father and mother, and cleave to his wife;
[8]And they twain shall be one flesh: so then
they are no more twain, but one flesh.
[9]What therefore God hath joined together,
let not man put asunder. [10]And in the
house his disciples asked him again of the
same matter. [11]And he saith unto them,
Whosoever shall put away his wife,
and marry another, committeth adultery
against her. [12]And if a woman shall put
away her husband, and be married to another, she committeth adultery.

Matt. 22 [23]The same day came to him
the Sadducees, which say that there is no
resurrection, and asked him, [24]Saying,
Master, Moses said, If a man die, having
no children, his brother shall marry his
wife, and raise up seed unto his brother.
[25]Now there were with us seven brethren:
and the first, when he had married a wife,
deceased, and, having no issue, left his
wife unto his brother: [26]Likewise the second also, and the third, unto the seventh.
[27]And last of all the woman died also.
[28]Therefore in the resurrection whose

wife shall she be of the seven? for they all had her. [29]Jesus answered and said unto them, Ye do err, not knowing the scriptures, nor the power of God. [30]For in the resurrection they neither marry, nor are given in marriage, but are as the angels of God in heaven.

General

Rom. 7 [1]Know ye not, brethren, (for I speak to them that know the law,) how that the law hath dominion over a man as long as he liveth? [2]For the woman which hath an husband is bound by the law to her husband so long as he liveth; but if the husband be dead, she is loosed from the law of her husband. [3]So then if, while her husband liveth, she be married to another man, she shall be called an adulteress: but if her husband be dead, she is free from that law; so that she is no adulteress, though she be married to another man.

1 Cor. 7 [1]Now concerning the things whereof ye wrote unto me: It is good for a man not to touch a woman. [2]Nevertheless, to avoid fornication, let every man have his own wife, and let every woman have her own husband. [3]Let the husband render unto the wife due benevolence: and likewise also the wife unto the husband. [4]The wife hath not power of her own body, but the husband: and likewise also the husband hath not power of his own body, but the wife. [5]Defraud ye not one the other, except it be with consent for a time, that ye may give yourselves to fasting and prayer; and come together again, that Satan tempt you not for your incontinency. [6]But I speak this by permission, and not of commandment. [7]For I would that all men were even as I myself. But every man hath his proper gift of God, one after this manner, and another after that. [8]I say therefore to the unmarried and widows, It is good for them if they abide even as I. [9]But if they cannot contain, let them marry: for it is better to marry than to burn. [10]And unto the married I command, yet not I, but the Lord, Let not the wife depart from her husband: [11]But and if she depart, let her remain unmarried, or be reconciled to her husband: and let not the husband put away his wife. [12]But to the rest speak I, not the Lord: If any brother hath a wife that believeth not, and she be pleased to dwell with him, let him not put her away. [13]And the woman which hath an husband that believeth not, and if he be pleased to dwell with her, let her not leave him. [14]For the unbelieving husband is sanctified by the wife, and the unbelieving wife is sanctified by the husband: else were your children unclean; but now are they holy. [15]But if the unbelieving depart, let him depart. A brother or a sister is not under bondage in such cases: but God hath called us to peace. [16]For what knowest thou, O wife, whether thou shalt save thy husband? or how knowest thou, O man, whether thou shalt save thy wife? [25]Now concerning virgins I have no commandment of the Lord: yet I give my judgment, as one that hath obtained mercy of the Lord to be faithful. [26]I suppose therefore that this is good for the present distress, I say, that it is good for a man so to be. [27]Art thou bound unto a wife? seek not to be loosed. Art thou loosed from a wife? seek not a wife. [28]But and if thou marry, thou hast not sinned; and if a virgin marry, she hath not sinned. Nevertheless such shall have trouble in the flesh: but I spare you. [32]But I would have you without carefulness. He that is unmarried careth for the things that belong to the Lord, how he may please the Lord: [33]But he that is married careth for the things that are of the world, how he may please his wife. [34]There is difference also between a wife and a virgin. The unmarried woman careth for the things of the Lord, that she may be holy both in body and in spirit: but she that is married careth for the things of the world, how she may please her husband. [35]And this I speak for your own profit; not that I may cast a snare upon you, but for that which is comely, and that ye may attend upon the Lord without distraction. [36]But if any man think that he behaveth himself uncomely toward his virgin, if she pass the flower of her age, and need so require, let him do what he will, he sinneth not: let them marry. [37]Nevertheless he that standeth stedfast in his heart, having no necessity, but hath power over his own will, and hath so decreed in his heart that he will keep his virgin, doeth well. [38]So then he that giveth her in marriage doeth well; but he that giveth her not in marriage doeth better. [39]The wife is bound by the law as long as her husband liveth; but if her husband be dead, she is at liberty to be married to whom she will; only in the Lord. [40]But she is happier if she so abide, after my judgment: and I think also that I have the Spirit of God.

Eph. 5 [22]Wives, submit yourselves unto your own husbands, as unto the Lord. [23]For the husband is the head of the wife, even as Christ is the head of the Church: and he is the saviour of the body. [24]Therefore as the Church is subject unto Christ, so let the wives be to their own husbands in every thing. [25]Husbands, love your wives, even as Christ also loved the Church, and gave himself for it: [26]That he might sanctify and cleanse it with the washing of water, by the word, [27]That he might present it to himself a glorious Church, not having spot or wrinkle, or any such thing: but that it should be holy and without blemish. [28]So ought men to love their wives, as their own bodies: he that loveth his wife, loveth himself. [29]For no man ever yet hated his own flesh: but nourisheth and cherisheth it, even as the Lord the Church: [30]For we are members of his body, of his flesh, and of his bones. [31]For this cause shall a man leave his father and mother, and shall be joined unto his wife, and they two shall be one flesh. [32]This is a great mystery: but I speak concerning Christ and the Church. [33]Nevertheless, let every one of you in particular, so love his wife even as himself, and the wife see that she reverence her husband.

1 Tim. 4 [1]Now the Spirit speaketh expressly, that in the latter times some shall depart from the faith, giving heed to seducing spirits, and doctrines of devils; [3]Forbidding to marry, ...

1 Tim. 5 [14]I will therefore that the younger women marry, bear children, guide the house, give none occasion to the adversary to speak reproachfully.

Heb. 13 [4]Marriage is honourable in all, and the bed undefiled: but whoremongers and adulterers God will judge.

MARTHA

[mär′tha] The sister of Mary and Lazarus, and a resident of Bethany, at whose home it was Jesus' custom to visit. She appears as the bustling energetic housewife, who, when visited by the Master, gave her whole attention to his entertainment as a guest worthy of the best her house afforded. When her sister Mary failed to help her, spending her time listening to the words of Jesus instead, Martha became irritated and complained to Jesus. Jesus' gentle reproach is one which Christians in a busy world do well to remember: "Martha, Martha, thou art careful and troubled about many things: But one thing is needful; and Mary hath chosen that good part, which shall not be taken away from her."

When her brother Lazarus lay gravely ill, it was Martha who sought out Jesus to ask him to come to Bethany. In order to demonstrate his power more effectively, Jesus did not immediately go to Bethany, but waited until Lazarus had died and lain in the tomb for four days. When the Lord finally came, Martha came out to meet him; she expressed disappointment that Jesus had not come sooner and displayed some confusion at his subsequent statements to her, but her attitude throughout is one of great faith in his power. After Jesus raised Lazarus from the dead, he spent some time in a town called Ephraim. On his return to Bethany, he visited once more in the house of Lazarus and his sisters. It was on this occasion that Mary anointed Jesus' feet with expensive ointment. The only mention of Martha is that she "served," indicating probably that she had charge of the feast.

See LAZARUS, MARY

SCRIPTURE

Luke 10 38 Now it came to pass, as they
went, that he entered into a certain village: and a certain woman named Martha
received him into her house. 39 And she
had a sister called Mary, which also sat at
Jesus' feet, and heard his word. 40 But
Martha was cumbered about much serving, and came to him, and said, Lord,
dost thou not care that my sister hath left
me to serve alone? bid her therefore that
she help me. 41 And Jesus answered and
said unto her, Martha, Martha, thou art
careful and troubled about many things:
42 But one thing is needful: and Mary hath
chosen that good part, which shall not be
taken away from her.

John 11 1 Now a certain man was sick,
named Lazarus, of Bethany, the town of
Mary and her sister Martha. 2 (It was that
Mary which anointed the Lord with ointment, and wiped his feet with her hair,
whose brother Lazarus was sick.) 3 Therefore his sisters sent unto him, saying,
Lord, behold, he whom thou lovest is sick.
4 When Jesus heard that, he said, This sickness is not unto death, but for the glory of
God, that the Son of God might be glorified thereby. 5 Now Jesus loved Martha,
and her sister, and Lazarus.

MARY

[mā'ri, mâr'i] This name is applied to six different women mentioned in the New Testament:

1. Mary, the mother of Jesus. The first event of her life of which we have any knowledge is known as the Annunciation—that is, the notification to her by the angel Gabriel that she was to become the mother of the Christ or Messiah, an honor that every woman of Israel desired by reason of the favor God would thus show her. She communicated the news immediately to Elisabeth, also highly favored of God through becoming the mother of John the Baptist (*Luke 1:26-40*). Mary's song of rejoicing (*Luke 1:46-55*) has come down to us in the Scripture as one of the most beautiful hymns of adoration ever uttered. After the birth of the Lord, Mary is seen in Scripture only in glimpses. They are: the appearance of the Magi, or wise men (*Matt. 2:1-12*); making offerings in the temple in Jerusalem (*Luke 1:22ff*); the flight to Egypt and the return to Nazareth after the death of Herod (*Matt. 2:13-23*); the visit to Jerusalem during which Jesus, at the age of twelve, conversed with the doctors of the law in the temple (*Luke 2:42-52*); her appearance and conduct at the marriage feast in Cana of Galilee (*John 2:1-11*); her attempt in the synagogue at Capernaum to induce Jesus to cease his teaching (*Matt. 12:46-50*); her accompanying of her son when he went up to Jerusalem immediately before his crucifixion; her following him to Calvary; her being consigned by him while hanging on the cross to the care of his beloved apostle John, who from that time took her to reside in his house (*John 19:25-27*); and her associating with the disciples at Jerusalem after his ascension (*Acts 1:14*). We have no exact knowledge as to when and where she died. There are traditions that she lived in Ephesus in the household of John, "the beloved disciple," and that she died there about AD 63. Her character, as the Bible gives it to us, was that of the most tender, patient, faithful, devout, loving, and humble of women, immeasurably thankful for the blessedness bestowed upon her.

2. Mary Magdalene. The name Magdalene was derived from Magdala, the Galilean town from which she came. She had been possessed of "seven devils" and was cured by Jesus, after which she ministered to him. In the Master's last hours and at his Resurrection she was an important witness; it was she, in fact, to whom the risen Saviour first showed himself. Mary Magdalene's character has suffered injustice by her identification with the sinful woman of *Luke 7:36-50* and the consequent use of the word "Magdalene" to refer to fallen womanhood; there is, however, nothing in scripture to support this identification.

3. Mary, the sister of Lazarus and Martha. She was a woman of deep spiritual interests, a fact which is seen in a study of her actions in the presence of the Lord and a comparison of them with those of her sister Martha. (*See* MARTHA) She showed her love and veneration of Jesus by anointing his feet with costly ointment.

4. Mary, the mother of James and Joses. This Mary was one of the women who supported Jesus in his ministry and who were witnesses of his death and resurrection (*Mark 15:40; 16:1; Luke 24:10*).

5. Mary, the mother of John, surnamed Mark. Little is known of her save that the apostles were accustomed to assemble at her home (*Acts 12:12*).

6. Mary, a Christian woman in Rome, mentioned by Paul in *Rom. 16:6*. Nothing is known of her except that she was a hard worker for the Lord.

SCRIPTURE

Mary, the Mother of Jesus

GABRIEL APPEARS TO MARY

Luke 1 [26]And in the sixth month the angel Gabriel was sent from God unto a city of Galilee, named Nazareth, [27]To a virgin espoused to a man whose name was Joseph, of the house of David; and the virgin's name was Mary. [28]And the angel came in unto her, and said, Hail, thou that art highly favoured, the Lord is with thee: blessed art thou among women. [29]And when she saw him, she was troubled at his saying, and cast in her mind what manner of salutation this should be. [30]And the angel said unto her, Fear not, Mary: for thou hast found favour with God. [31]And, behold, thou shalt conceive in thy womb, and bring forth a son, and shalt call his name JESUS. [32]He shall be great, and shall be called the Son of the Highest; and the Lord God shall give unto him the throne of his father David: [33]And he shall reign over the house of Jacob for ever; and of his kingdom there shall be no end. [34]Then said Mary unto the angel, How shall this be, seeing I know not a man? [35]And the angel answered and said unto her, The Holy Ghost shall come upon thee, and the power of the Highest shall overshadow thee: therefore also that holy thing which shall be born of thee shall be called the Son of God. [36]And, behold, thy cousin Elisabeth, she hath also conceived a son in her old age; and this is the sixth month with her, who was called barren. [37]For with God nothing shall be impossible. [38]And Mary said, Behold the handmaid of the Lord; be it unto me according to thy word. And the angel departed from her. [39]And Mary arose in those days, and went into the hill country with haste, into a city of Juda; [40]And entered into the house of Zacharias, and saluted Elisabeth.

GIVES BIRTH TO JESUS

Luke 2 [4]And Joseph also went up from Galilee, out of the city of Nazareth, into Judea, unto the city of David, which is called Bethlehem, (because he was of the house and lineage of David,) [5]To be taxed with Mary his espoused wife, being great with child. [6]And so it was, that, while they were there, the days were accomplished that she should be delivered. [7]And she brought forth her firstborn son, and wrapped him in swaddling clothes, and laid him in a manger; because there was no room for them in the inn.

AT THE CROSS OF JESUS

John 19 [25]Now there stood by the cross of Jesus his mother, and his mother's sister, Mary the wife of Cleophas, and Mary Magdalene. [26]When Jesus therefore saw his mother, and the disciple standing by, whom he loved, he saith unto his mother, Woman, behold thy son! [27]Then saith he to the disciple, Behold thy mother! And from that hour that disciple took her unto his own home.

Mary Magdalene

SUPPORTS JESUS' MINISTRY

Luke 8 [1]And it came to pass afterward, that he went throughout every city and village, preaching and shewing the glad tidings of the kingdom of God: and the twelve were with him, [2]And certain women, which had been healed of evil spirits and infirmities, Mary called Magdalene, out of whom went seven devils, [3]And Joanna the wife of Chuza Herod's steward, and Susanna, and many others, which ministered unto him of their substance.

AT THE CRUCIFIXION

Mark 15 [40]There were also women looking on afar off: among whom was Mary Magdalene, and Mary the mother of James the less and of Joses, and Salome;

JESUS APPEARS TO HER AFTER RESURRECTION

Mark 16 [1]And when the sabbath was past, Mary Magdalene, and Mary the mother of James, and Salome, had bought sweet spices, that they might come and anoint him.

[9]Now when Jesus was risen early the first day of the week, he appeared first to Mary Magdalene, out of whom he had cast seven devils.

See Matt. 27:56, 61; Mark 15:40, 47

Mary, the Sister of Martha and Lazarus

Luke 10 [38]Now it came to pass, as they went, that he entered into a certain village: and a certain woman named Martha received him into her house. [39]And she had a sister called Mary, which also sat at Jesus' feet, and heard his word. [40]But Martha was cumbered about much serving, and came to him, and said, Lord, dost thou not care that my sister hath left me to serve alone? bid her therefore that she help me. [41]And Jesus answered and said unto her, Martha, Martha, thou art careful and troubled about many things: [42]But one thing is needful; and Mary hath chosen that good part, which shall not be taken away from her.

John 11 [1]Now a certain man was sick, named Lazarus, of Bethany, the town of Mary and her sister Martha. [2](It was that Mary which anointed the Lord with ointment, and wiped his feet with her hair, whose brother Lazarus was sick.) [3]Therefore his sisters sent unto him, saying, Lord, behold, he whom thou lovest is sick. [4]When Jesus heard that, he said, This sickness is not unto death, but for the glory of God, that the Son of God might be glorified thereby. [5]Now Jesus loved Martha, and her sister, and Lazarus.

John 12 [1]Then Jesus six days before the passover came to Bethany, where Lazarus was which had been dead, whom he raised from the dead. [2]There they made him a supper; and Martha served: but

Lazarus was one of them that sat at the table with him. [3]Then took Mary a pound of ointment of spikenard, very costly, and anointed the feet of Jesus, and wiped his feet with her hair: and the house was filled with the odour of the ointment.

MASTER

[mas′ter] This word is used in a number of different senses in the Bible, including owner, lord, chief, instructor, and head of a household. In the New Testament it is frequently used of Jesus.

See JESUS

SCRIPTURE

Ex. 21 [20]And if a man smite his servant, or his maid, with a rod, and he die under his hand; he shall be surely punished. [21]Notwithstanding, if he continue a day or two, he shall not be punished: for he is his money.

[26]And if a man smite the eye of his servant, or the eye of his maid, that it perish; he shall let him go free for his eye's sake. [27]And if he smite out his manservant's tooth, or his maidservant's tooth; he shall let him go free for his tooth's sake.

Lev. 25 [43]Thou shalt not rule over him with rigour; but shalt fear thy God.

Deut. 24 [14]Thou shalt not oppress an hired servant that is poor and needy, whether he be of thy brethren, or of thy strangers that are in thy land within thy gates: [15]At his day thou shalt give him his hire, neither shall the sun go down upon it; for he is poor, and setteth his heart upon it: lest he cry against thee unto the LORD, and it be sin unto thee.

Eph. 6 [9]Ye masters, do the same things unto them, forbearing threatening: knowing that your Master also in his heaven; neither is there respect of persons with him.

Col. 4 [1]Masters, give unto your servants that which is just and equal; knowing that ye also have a Master in heaven.

See Lev. 19:13

Title Applied to Jesus

Matt. 10 [25]It is enough for the disciple that he be as his master, and the servant as his lord. If they have called the master of the house Beelzebub, how much more shall they call them of his household?

Matt. 26 [49]And forthwith he came to Jesus, and said, Hail, Master; and kissed him.

Mark 14 [45]And as soon as he was come, he goeth straightway to him, and saith, Master, Master; and kissed him.

Luke 8 [24]And they came to him, and awoke him, saying, Master, Master, we perish. Then he arose, and rebuked the wind and the raging of the water: and they ceased and there was a calm.

John 13 [13]Ye call me Master and Lord: and ye say well; for so I am. [14]If I then, your Lord and Master, have washed your feet; ye also ought to wash one another's feet.

MATTHEW

[math′ū] An apostle of Christ and the individual to whom tradition has ascribed the first gospel. The sum of the information which the Bible provides on Matthew, or Levi, as he was sometimes called, is that he was a tax collector whom Jesus summoned to be an apostle and that he entertained several of his friends at a banquet at which Jesus was the guest of honor.

SCRIPTURE

Matt. 9 [9]And as Jesus passed forth from thence, he saw a man, named Matthew, sitting at the receipt of custom: and he saith unto him, Follow me. And he arose, and followed him.

Mark 2 14 And as he passed by, he saw
Levi the son of Alphaeus sitting at the receipt of custom, and said unto him, Follow me. And he arose and followed him.
15 And it came to pass, that, as Jesus sat at
meat in his house, many publicans and
sinners sat also together with Jesus and his
disciples: for there were many, and they
followed him.

See Matt. 10:3; Mark 3:18; Luke 5:27; 6:15; Acts 1:13

MATTHIAS

[ma thī′as] The individual chosen to take Judas Iscariot's place as one of the twelve apostles. When the apostles sought a replacement for Judas, they chose two "of the men which have companied with us all the time that the Lord Jesus went in and out among us"—Joseph called Barsabas and Matthias. After praying for the Lord's guidance in their decision, they drew lots and "the lot fell upon Matthias; and he was numbered with the eleven apostles."

SCRIPTURE

Acts 1 21 Wherefore of these men which
have companied with us all the time that
the Lord Jesus went in and out among us,
22 Beginning from the baptism of John,
unto that same day that he was taken up
from us, must one be ordained to be a witness with us of his resurrection. 23 And
they appointed two, Joseph called Barsabas, who was surnamed Justus, and
Matthias. 24 And they prayed, and said,
Thou, Lord, which knowest the hearts of
all men, shew whether of these two thou
hast chosen, 25 That he may take part of
this ministry and apostleship, from which
Judas by transgression fell, that he might
go to his own place. 26 And they gave forth
their lots; and the lot fell upon Matthias;
and he was numbered with the eleven
apostles.

MEDES

[mēdz] An Indo-Aryan people who settled in what is now northern Iran, in the ninth century BC. By the end of the seventh century BC, they had developed into a nation strong enough to pose a threat to Assyria. In 614 BC, the Median ruler Cyarxes took Asshur, the ancient Assyrian capital and made a treaty with Nabopolassar king of Babylon. In 612 BC, his armies marched on and took the chief Assyrian city of Nineveh. Subsequently, while Nebuchadnezzar was absorbing Mesopotamia, Syria, and Palestine into the Babylonian empire, Cyarxes consolidated his power and built a massive state with its capital at Ecbatana. In 585 BC, Cyarxes was succeeded by his son Astyages. The latter's reign—and the Median Empire—ended in the revolt led by Cyrus the Persian. Nabonidus, who succeeded Nebuchadnezzar to the Babylonian throne, saw the possibility of ridding himself of Babylon's chief rival and threw his support behind Cyrus. In 550 BC, Cyrus dethroned Astyages and took Ecbatana as the first major victory in the campaign which, with the conquest of Babylon in 539 BC, was to make him master of the world, as the first ruler of the vast Persian Empire.

See CYRUS

MEDIATOR

[mē′di ā tẽr] Usually, one who intervenes between two parties at variance with one another, for the purpose of effecting a reconciliation. In the Bible, it has the additional meaning of drawing together two parties into a covenant or agreement, without the necessary implication of previous enmity. The role of mediator has always been vital in the relationship between God and man. Moses and the prophets served to convey to Israel the will of God which they had received directly. In turn, they also made intercession before God on behalf of the community, although this function eventually came to be concentrated in the priesthood. The doctrine of mediation reaches its pinnacle in Christ, who served both as God's representative to man and man's representative to God. The theme of the mediatorial work of Christ is expounded fully in the book of *Hebrews*, where its perfection is shown by comparison with the similiar functions performed by the Jewish priesthood.

See INTERCESSION, CHRIST, JESUS, ADVOCATE

SCRIPTURE

Mediation of Moses

Ex. 32 [11]And Moses besought the LORD his God, and said, LORD, why doth thy wrath wax hot against thy people, which thou hast brought forth out of the land of Egypt with great power, and with a mighty hand? [12]Wherefore should the Egyptians speak, and say, For mischief did he bring them out, to slay them in the mountains, and to consume them from the face of the earth? Turn from thy fierce wrath, and repent of this evil against thy people. [13]Remember Abraham, Isaac, and Israel, thy servants, to whom thou swarest by thine own self, and saidst unto them, I will multiply your seed as the stars of heaven, and all this land that I have spoken of will I give unto your seed, and they shall inherit it for ever. [14]And the LORD repented of the evil which he thought to do unto his people.

[30]And it came to pass on the morrow, that Moses said unto the people, Ye have sinned a great sin: and now I will go up unto the LORD; peradventure I shall make an atonement for your sin. [31]And Moses returned unto the LORD, and said, Oh, this people have sinned a great sin, and have made them gods of gold. [32]Yet now, if thou wilt forgive their sin—; and if not, blot me, I pray thee, out of thy book which thou hast written.

Ex. 33 [11]And the LORD spake unto Moses face to face, as a man speaketh unto his friend. . . .

Num. 12 [6]And he said, Hear now my words: If there be a prophet among you, I the LORD will make myself known unto him in a vision, and will speak unto him in a dream. [7]My servant Moses is not so, who is faithful in all mine house. [8]With him will I speak mouth to mouth, even apparently, and not in dark speeches; and the similitude of the LORD shall he behold: wherefore then were ye not afraid to speak against my servant Moses?

Deut. 5 [5](I stood between the LORD and you at that time, to show you the word of the LORD: for ye were afraid by reason of the fire, and went not up into the mouth,)

Mediation of Christ

Rom. 5 [10]For if, when we were enemies, we were reconciled to God by the death of his Son; much more, being reconciled, we shall be saved by his life.

Gal. 3 [19]Wherefore then serveth the law? It was added because of transgressions, till the seed should come to whom the promise was made; and it was ordained by angels in the hand of a mediator. [20]Now a mediator is not a mediator of one, but God is one.

1 Tim. 2 [5]For there is one God, and one mediator between God and men, the man Christ Jesus;

Heb. 1 [1]God, who at sundry times and in divers manners spake in time past unto the fathers by the prophets, [2]Hath in these last days spoken unto us by his Son, whom he hath appointed heir of all things, by whom also he made the worlds; [3]Who being the brightness of his glory, and the express image of his person, and upholding all things by the word of his power, when he had himself purged our sins, sat down on the right hand of the Majesty on high;

Heb. 4 [15]For we have not a high priest which cannot be touched with the feeling of our infirmities; but was in all points tempted like as we are, yet without sin.

Heb. 8 [6]But now hath he obtained a more excellent ministry, by how much also he is the mediator of a better covenant, which was established upon better promises.

Heb. 9 [15]And for this cause he is the mediator of the new testament, that by means of death, for the redemption of the transgressions that were under the first testament, they which are called might receive the promise of eternal inheritance.

Heb. 12 [24]And to Jesus the mediator of the new covenant, and to the blood of sprinkling, that speaketh better things than that of Abel.

MEDITATION

[med i tā'shun] A form of private devotion consisting of deep, continued reflection on some religious theme. The word seldom occurs outside of *Psalms*, but the practice of meditation is clearly regarded as beneficial for Christians. The objects of meditation mentioned in the *Psalms* are God, his law, and his works. It appears that meditation means active contemplation of its object, a deliberate effort being made to put all distractions out of one's mind. In the Bible it does not have reference to the contemplative mysticism common to Oriental religions and which has had its devotees in Christianity.

SCRIPTURE

Deut. 6 [6]And these words which I command thee this day, shall be in thine heart.

Deut. 11 [18]Therefore shall ye lay up these my words in your heart and in your soul, and bind them for a sign upon your hand, that they may be as frontlets between your eyes.

Deut. 32 [46]And he said unto them, Set your hearts unto all the words which I testify among you this day, which ye shall command your children to observe to do, all the words of this law.

Josh. 1 [8]This book of the law shall not depart out of thy mouth; but thou shalt meditate therein day and night, that thou mayest observe to do according to all that is written therein: for then thou shalt make thy way prosperous, and then thou shalt have good success.

Psa. 1 [2]But his delight is in the law of the LORD: and in his law doth he meditate day and night. [3]And he shall be like a tree planted by the rivers of water, that bringeth forth his fruit in his season; his leaf also shall not wither; and whatsoever he doeth shall prosper.

Psa. 119 [15]I will meditate in thy precepts, and have respect unto thy ways. [23]Princes also did sit and speak against me: but thy servant did meditate in thy statutes. [97]O how love I thy law! it is my meditation all the day. [148]Mine eyes prevent the night watches, that I might meditate in thy word.

1 Tim. 4 [15]Meditate upon these things; give thyself wholly to them; that thy profiting may appear to all. [16]Take heed unto thyself, and unto the doctrine; continue in them: for in doing this thou shalt both save thyself, and them that hear thee.

MEEKNESS

[mēk'nes] Mildness of temper, patience under injuries; long-suffering; submissiveness. It is commonly associated with humility, the quality of which Jesus himself was the essence. Christians are exhorted to cultivate meekness and to demonstrate it in their relations with the world and with one another.

See HUMILITY, PRIDE, PEACE,
JESUS (MEEKNESS OF)

SCRIPTURE

Psa. 22 [26]The meek shall eat and be

satisfied: they shall praise the LORD that seek him: your heart shall live for ever.

Psa. 25 [9]The meek will he guide in judgment: and the meek will he teach his way.

Psa. 37 [11]But the meek shall inherit the earth; and shall delight themselves in the abundance of peace.

Psa. 147 [6]The LORD lifteth up the meek: he casteth the wicked down to the ground.

Psa. 149 [4]For the LORD taketh pleasure in his people: he will beautify the meek with salvation.

Prov. 17 [1]Better is a dry morsel, and quietness therewith, than an house full of sacrifices with strife.

Isa. 29 [19]The meek also shall increase their joy in the LORD, and the poor among men shall rejoice in the Holy One of Israel.

Zeph. 2 [3]Seek ye the LORD, all ye meek of the earth, which have wrought his judgment: seek righteousness, seek meekness:

Matt. 5 [5]Blessed are the meek: for they shall inherit the earth.

[38]Ye have heard that it hath been said, An eye for an eye, and a tooth for a tooth: [39]But I say unto you, That ye resist not evil: but whosoever shall smite thee on thy right cheek, turn to him the other also. [40]And if any man will sue thee at the law, and take away thy coat, let him have thy cloke also. [41]And whosoever shall compel thee to go a mile, go with him twain. [42]Give to him that asketh thee, and from him that would borrow of thee turn not thou away.

Matt. 11 [29]Take my yoke upon you, and learn of me; for I am meek and lowly in heart: and ye shall find rest unto your souls.

Gal. 5 [22]The fruit of the Spirit is love, joy, peace, longsuffering, gentleness, goodness, faith, [23]Meekness, temperance: against such there is no law.

Gal. 6 [1]Brethren, if a man be overtaken in a fault, ye which are spiritual, restore such an one in the spirit of meekness; considering thyself, lest thou also be tempted.

2 Tim. 2 [24]The servant of the Lord must not strive; but be gentle unto all men, apt to teach, patient, [25]In meekness instructing those that oppose themselves; . . .

Tit. 3 [2]To speak evil of no man, to be no brawlers, but gentle, shewing all meekness unto all men.

1 Pet. 3 [4]But let it be the hidden man of the heart, in that which is not corruptible, even the ornament of a meek and quiet spirit, which is in the sight of God of great price. [11]Let him eschew evil, and do good; let him seek peace, and ensue it. [15]. . . Be ready always to give an answer to every man that asketh you a reason of the hope that is in you with meekness and fear:

MELCHIZEDEK

[mel kiz′ê dek] "King of Salem" (*see* SALEM) and "the priest of the most high God" in the time of Abraham. On his return from the defeat of the coalition of kings who had raided Sodom and had taken his nephew Lot captive, Abraham was met by Melchizedek who brought him bread and wine and bestowed on him the blessing of "the most high God." Abraham in turn recognized Melchizedek's kingly and priestly dignity by paying tithes to him. In *Hebrews*, Christ is called a priest "after the order of Melchizedek." Their respective priesthoods are alike in that (1) neither was of the Levitical tribe; (2) both were superior to Abraham; (3) the beginning and end of both is unknown; and (4) each is not only a priest, but a king as well.

See PRIESTHOOD

SCRIPTURE

Melchizedek Blesses Abraham

Gen. 14 [18]And Melchizedek king of Salem brought forth bread and wine: and he was the priest of the most high God.

19And he blessed him, and said, Blessed
be Abram of the most high God, possessor of heaven and earth: 20And blessed
be the most high God, which hath delivered thine enemies into thy hand. And
he gave him tithes of all.

Psa. 110 4The LORD hath sworn, and
will not repent, Thou art a priest for ever
after the order of Melchizedek.

Melchizedek and Christ

Heb. 5 4And no man taketh this honour unto himself, but he that is called of
God, as was Aaron. 5So also, Christ glorified not himself, to be made an high
priest: but he that said unto him, Thou
art my Son, to day have I begotten thee.
6As he saith also in another place, Thou
art a priest for ever after the order of Melchisedec. 7Who in the days of his flesh,
when he had offered up prayers and supplications, with strong crying and tears,
unto him that was able to save him from
death, and was heard, in that he feared.
8Though he were a Son, yet learned he
obedience by the things which he suffered:
9And being made perfect, he became the
author of eternal salvation unto all them
that obey him, 10Called of God an high
priest after the order of Melchisedec:
11Of whom we have many things to say,
and hard to be uttered, seeing ye are dull
of hearing.

Heb. 6 13For when God made promise
to Abraham, because he could swear by
no greater, he sware by himself, 14Saying,
Surely, blessing I will bless thee, and multiplying I will multiply thee. 15And so
after he had patiently endured, he obtained the promise. 16For men verily
swear by the greater, and an oath for confirmation is to them an end of all strife.
17Wherein God willing more abundantly
to shew unto the heirs of promise the immutability of his counsel, confirmed it by
an oath: 18That by two immutable things,
in which it was impossible for God to lie,
we might have a strong consolation, who
have fled for refuge to lay hold upon the
hope set before us. 19Which hope we have
as an anchor of the soul both sure and stedfast, and which entereth into that within
the veil, 20Whither the forerunner is for us
entered; even Jesus, made an high priest
for ever after the order of Melchisedec.

Heb. 7 1For this Melchisedec, king of
Salem, priest of the most high God, who
met Abraham returning from the slaughter of the kings, and blessed him; 2To
whom also Abraham gave a tenth part of
all; first being by interpretation King of
righteousness, and after that also King of
Salem, which is, King of peace; 3Without
father, without mother, without descent,
having neither beginning of days, nor end
of life; but made like unto the Son of God;
abideth a priest continually.

MELITA

[mel'i ta] An island, now generally identified with Malta (and so translated in the Revised Standard Version), on which Paul and his companions took refuge when the ship bearing him to Rome ran aground and was broken up by the surf. While on the island, Paul was bitten by a viper, which he shook off without suffering harm. The inhabitants of the island were naturally quite impressed and many of them, including the chief man of the island, Publius, came to be healed of various diseases and infirmities.

SCRIPTURE

Acts 28 1And when they were escaped,
then they knew that the island was
called Melita. 2And the barbarous people shewed us no little kindness: for they
kindled a fire, and received us every one,
because of the present rain, and because

of the cold. 3And when Paul had gathered a bundle of sticks, and laid them on the fire, there came a viper out of the heat, and fastened on his hand. 4And when the barbarians saw the venomous beast hang on his hand, they said among themselves, No doubt this man is a murderer, whom, though he hath escaped the sea, yet vengeance suffereth not to live. 5And he shook off the beast into the fire, and felt no harm. 6Howbeit they looked when he should have swollen, or fallen down dead suddenly: but after they had looked a great while, and saw no harm come to him, they changed their minds, and said that he was a god. 7In the same quarters were possessions of the chief man of the island, whose name was Publius; who received us, and lodged us three days courteously. 8And it came to pass, that the father of Publius lay sick of a fever and of a bloody flux: to whom Paul entered in, and prayed, and laid his hands on him, and healed him. 9So when this was done, others also, which had diseases in the island, came, and were healed: 10Who also honoured us with many honours; and when we departed, they laded us with such things as were necessary.

MENAHEM

[men'a hem] The son of Gadi and the sixteenth king of Israel (748-738 BC). On learning of the assassination of Zechariah by the usurper Shallum, Manahem marched from Tirzah, a minor capital of the northern kingdom, and slew Shallum, taking the throne for himself. His savage reprisal at the refusal of the town of Tipsah to accept his rule (*2 Kin. 15:16*) apparently served as a warning to any other area which might be tempted to withhold its allegiance, as no other revolts within the kingdom are mentioned. The greatest threat to Israel during Menahem's reign came from Assyria. To avoid being overrun and to confirm his hold of the royal power, Menahem chose to pay a heavy tribute rather than to resist the forces of Pul (Tiglath-Pileser). This tribute was exacted from the citizens and was a heavy burden on the land. Menahem was succeeded by his son Pekahiah.

See PEKAHIAH, PUL, SHALLUM

SCRIPTURE

2 Kin. 15 13Shallum the son of Jabesh began to reign in the nine and thirtieth year of Uzziah king of Judah; and he reigned a full month in Samaria. 14For Menahem the son of Gadi went up from Tirzah, and came to Samaria, and smote Shallum the son of Jabesh in Samaria, and slew him, and reigned in his stead. 15And the rest of the acts of Shallum, and his conspiracy which he made, behold, they are written in the book of the Chronicles of the kings of Israel.

16Then Menahem smote Tiphsah, and all that were therein, and the coasts thereof from Tirzah: because they opened not to him, therefore he smote it; and all the women therein that were with child he ripped up. 17In the nine and thirtieth year of Azariah king of Judah began Menahem the son of Gadi to reign over Israel, and reigned ten years in Samaria. 18And he did that which was evil in the sight of the LORD: he departed not all his days from the sins of Jeroboam the son of Nebat, who made Israel to sin. 19And Pul the king of Assyria came against the land: and Menahem gave Pul a thousand talents of silver, that his hand might be with him to confirm the kingdom in his hand. 20And Menahem exacted the money of Israel, even of all the mighty men of wealth, of each man fifty shekels of silver, to give to the king of Assyria. So the king of Assyria turned back, and stayed not there in the land.

21And the rest of the acts of Menahem, and all that he did, are they not written in the book of the Chronicles of the kings of

Israel? [22]And Menahem slept with his fathers; and Pekahiah his son reigned in his stead.

MEPHIBOSHETH

[mē fib′ô sheth] Son of Jonathan and grandson of Saul. Mephibosheth was five years old when Saul and Jonathan were killed at the hands of the Philistines in the disaster of Mount Gilboa. When his nurse heard of the defeat of the Israelite forces, she fled with Mephibosheth in her arms; in her haste, the child was apparently dropped and became crippled in both feet. In later years, when David sought to show his love for Jonathan by bestowing favor on some survivor of the house of Saul, he was put in contact with a man named Ziba who told him of Mephibosheth. David summoned Mephibosheth to the court and presented him with land and possessions which had belonged to Saul, appointing Ziba to act as overseer of the land. In addition, Mephibosheth was invited to be a daily guest at the king's table.

Nothing further is heard of Mephibosheth until the rebellion of Absalom. At that time, Ziba met the fleeing David and deceived him concerning his master, asserting that Mephibosheth had remained in Jerusalem, hoping to take advantage of the confusion to seize the throne for himself. David believed him and gave to Ziba the property which had been Mephibosheth's. When the rebellion had been crushed, David returned to Jerusalem and was met by Mephibosheth, whom he questioned with regard to his remaining in Jerusalem. Then Mephibosheth revealed that he had instructed Ziba to saddle an ass for him, but the crafty servant had disobeyed and had slandered him to David. Perhaps unsure as to the truth in the matter, and too weary to pursue it further, David resolved to divide the land between Ziba and Mephibosheth. Mephibosheth protested that he would be willing for Ziba to have everything, as long as the king remained friendly to him; the narrative does not tell us of the final outcome of the matter. Sometime thereafter, the Gibeonites demanded blood revenge on the house of Saul for his slaughter of some of their number. David sought to dissuade them, but finally complied by surrendering seven of Saul's descendants. Mephibosheth, however, was spared, indicating that he and David had been fully reconciled.

See ZIBA

SCRIPTURE

Jonathan's Son

2 Sam. 4 [4]And Jonathan, Saul's son, had a son that was lame of his feet. He was five years old when the tidings came of Saul and Jonathan out of Jezreel, and his nurse took him up, and fled: and it came to pass, as she made haste to flee, that he fell, and became lame. And his name was Mephibosheth.

Shown Kindness by David

2 Sam. 9 [6]Now when Mephibosheth, the son of Jonathan, the son of Saul, was come unto David, he fell on his face, and did reverence. And David said, Mephibosheth. And he answered, Behold thy servant!

[7]And David said unto him, Fear not: for I will surely shew thee kindness for Jonathan thy father's sake, and will restore thee all the land of Saul thy father; and thou shalt eat bread at my table continually. [8]And he bowed himself, and said, What is thy servant, that thou shouldest look upon such a dead dog as I am?

[9]Then the king called to Ziba, Saul's servant, and said unto him, I have given unto thy master's son all that pertained to Saul and to all his house. [10]Thou therefore, and thy sons, and thy servants, shall till the land for him, and thou shalt bring in the fruits that thy master's son may have food to eat: but Mephibosheth thy master's son shall eat bread alway at my table. . . .

Defrauded by Ziba

2 Sam. 16 1And when David was a little
past the top of the hill, behold, Ziba the
servant of Mephibosheth met him, with
a couple of asses saddled, and upon them
two hundred loaves of bread, and a hundred bunches of raisins, and a hundred
of summer fruits, and a bottle of wine.
2And the king said unto Ziba, What meanest thou by these? And Ziba said, The
asses be for the king's household to ride
on; and the bread and summer fruit for
the young men to eat; and the wine, that
such as be faint in the wilderness may
drink. 3And the king said, And where is
thy master's son? And Ziba said unto the
king, Behold, he abideth at Jerusalem: for
he said, To-day shall the house of Israel
restore me the kingdom of my father.
4Then said the king to Ziba, Behold, thine
are all that pertained unto Mephibosheth.
And Ziba said, I humbly beseech thee that
I may find grace in thy sight, my lord, O
king.

His Defense before David

2 Sam. 19 24And Mephibosheth the son
of Saul came down to meet the king, and
had neither dressed his feet, nor trimmed
his beard, nor washed his clothes, from
the day the king departed until the day he
came again in peace. 25And it came to
pass, when he was come to Jerusalem to
meet the king, that the king said unto him,
Wherefore wentest not thou with me, Mephibosheth? 26And he answered, My lord,
O king, my servant deceived me: for thy
servant said, I will saddle me an ass, that
I may ride thereon, and go to the king; because thy servant is lame. 27And he hath
slandered thy servant unto my lord the
king; but my lord the king is as an angel
of God: do therefore what is good in thine
eyes. 28For all of my father's house were
but dead men before my lord the king: yet
didst thou set thy servant among them
that did eat at thine own table. What right
therefore have I yet to cry any more unto
the king? 29And the king said unto him,
Why speakest thou any more of thy matters? I have said, Thou and Ziba divide the
land. 30And Mephibosheth said unto the
king, Yea, let him take all, forasmuch as
my lord the king is come again in peace
unto his own house.

Spared by David

2 Sam. 21 1Then there was a famine in
the days of David three years, year after
year; and David inquired of the Lord.
And the Lord answered, It is for Saul, and
for his bloody house, because he slew the
Gibeonites. 2And the king called the Gibeonites, and said unto them; (now the
Gibeonites were not of the children of
Israel, but of the remnant of the Amorites;
and the children of Israel had sworn unto
them: and Saul sought to slay them in his
zeal to the children of Israel and Judah:)
3Wherefore David said unto the Gibeonites, What shall I do for you? and wherewith shall I make the atonement, that ye
may bless the inheritance of the Lord?
4And the Gibeonites said unto him, We
will have no silver nor gold of Saul, nor
of his house; neither for us shalt thou kill
any man in Israel. And he said, What ye
shall say, that will I do for you. 5And they
answered the king, The man that consumed us, and that devised against us that
we should be destroyed from remaining
in any of the coasts of Israel, 6Let seven
men of his sons be delivered unto us, and
we will hang them up unto the Lord in
Gibeah of Saul, whom the Lord did

choose. And the king said, I will give them. [7]But the king spared Mephibosheth, the son of Jonathan the son of Saul, because of the LORD's oath that was between them, between David and Jonathan the son of Saul.

MERCY

[mûr'si] Affectionate pity to those who are needy, distressed, or suffering in mind, body, or estate; kindness or compassion to those who are in need of them. As used in the Bible, mercy generally refers either to God's willingness to remain in covenant with disobedient and rebellious Israel or to his compassion for man in his weakness and misery. Only occasionally is the word actually used in connection with forgiveness of sins; nevertheless, our current definition of the word demands that we consider this to be a cardinal manifestation of God's mercy. Numerous biblical passages make it clear that man is required to show mercy, on pain of exclusion from the kingdom.

SCRIPTURE

2 Sam. 22 [26]With the merciful thou wilt shew thyself merciful, and with the upright man thou wilt shew thyself upright.

Prov. 3 [3]Let not mercy and truth forsake thee: bind them about thy neck; write them upon the table of thine heart: [4]So shalt thou find favour and good understanding in the sight of God and man.

Prov. 11 [17]The merciful man doeth good to his own soul: but he that is cruel troubleth his own flesh.

Prov. 14 [21]He that despiseth his neighbor sinneth: but he that hath mercy on the poor, happy is he. [22]Do they not err that devise evil? but mercy and truth shall be to them that devise good. [31]He that oppresseth the poor reproacheth his Maker: but he that honoureth him hath mercy on the poor.

Prov. 20 [28]Mercy and truth preserve the king: and his throne is upholden by mercy.

Hos. 12 [6]Therefore turn thou to thy God: keep mercy and judgment, and wait on thy God continually.

Mic. 6 [8]He hath shewed thee, O man, what is good; and what doth the LORD require of thee, but to do justly, and to love mercy, and to walk humbly with thy God?

Matt. 5 [7]Blessed are the merciful: for they shall obtain mercy.

Matt. 23 [23]Woe unto you, scribes and Pharisees, hypocrites! for ye pay tithe of mint and anise and cummin, and have omitted the weightier matters of the law, judgment, mercy, and faith: these ought ye to have done, and not to leave the other undone.

Luke 6 [36]Be ye therefore merciful, as your Father also is merciful.

Col. 3 [12]Put on therefore, as the elect of God, holy and beloved, bowels of mercies, kindness, humbleness of mind, meekness, longsuffering; [13]Forbearing one another, and forgiving one another, if any man have a quarrel against any: even as Christ forgave you, so also do ye.

Jas. 2 [13]For he shall have judgment without mercy, that hath shewed no mercy; and mercy rejoiceth against judgment.

See Psa. 18:25

MESOPOTAMIA

[me sô pô tā'mi a] Literally, "between the two rivers." Mesopotamia is the land which corresponds to modern Eastern Syria and Northern Iraq. It includes the area of Haran, to which Abraham journied after leaving Ur of the Chaldees (*Gen. 11:31*) and from which Eliezer, Abraham's servant, brought Rebekah to be Isaac's wife (*Gen. 24:10*). The diviner Balaam was also a resident of Mesopotamia (*Deut. 23: 4*). In the New Testament, Mesopotamia refers to the entire valley of the Tigris and Euphrates rivers, corresponding to modern Iraq. For further history of this region, see articles on ASSYRIA and BABYLONIA.

METHUSELAH

[mê thū'ze la] In *Gen. 5:21, 27*, Methuselah is said to have been the son of Enoch and to have lived 969 years, the greatest age attributed to any person in the Bible.

SCRIPTURE

Gen. 5 [25]And Methuselah lived a hundred eighty and seven years, and begat Lamech: [26]And Methuselah lived after he begat Lamech seven hundred eighty and two years, and begat sons and daughters: [27]And all the days of Methuselah were nine hundred sixty and nine years: and he died.

MICAH

[mī'ka] A prophet of Judah "in the days of Jotham, Ahaz, and Hezekiah," and thus a contemporary of Isaiah. Micah was called the "Morasthite" because he was a native of Moresheth, sometimes called Moresheth-gath due to its location in the southwestern part of Judah near the Philistine city of Gath. Little is known of Micah apart from his prophecy. Micah's oracles are directed to Samaria and Jerusalem, the respective capitals of Israel and Judah and therefore responsible to some degree for the corruption which had overtaken these two kingdoms. Micah is credited by Jeremiah as having influenced Hezekiah.

SCRIPTURE

The Peace of the Last Days

Mic. 4 [1]But in the last days it shall come to pass, that the mountain of the house of the LORD shall be established in the top of the mountains, and it shall be exalted above the hills; and people shall flow unto it. [2]And many nations shall come, and say, Come, and let us go up to the mountain of the LORD, and to the house of the God of Jacob; and he will teach us of his ways, and we will walk in his paths: for the law shall go forth of Zion, and the word of the LORD from Jerusalem.

[3]And he shall judge among many people, and rebuke strong nations afar off; and they shall beat their swords into ploughshares, and their spears into pruninghooks: nation shall not lift up a sword against nation, neither shall they learn war any more. [4]But they shall sit every man under his vine and under his fig tree; and none shall make them afraid: for the mouth of the LORD of hosts hath spoken it.

The Deliverer to Come from Bethlehem

Mic. 5 [2]But thou, Beth-lehem Ephratah, though thou be little among the thousands of Judah, yet out of thee shall he come forth unto me that is to be ruler in Israel; whose goings forth have been from of old, from everlasting.

What the Lord Requires

Mic. 6 [8]He hath shewed thee, O man, what is good; and what doth the LORD require of thee, but to do justly, and to love mercy, and to walk humbly with thy God?

The Moral Corruption of Israel

Mic. 7 [1]Woe is me! for I am as when they have gathered the summer fruits, as the grape gleanings of the vintage: there is no cluster to eat: my soul desired the first ripe fruit. [2]The good man is perished out of the earth; and there is none upright among men: they all lie in wait for blood; they hunt every man his brother with a net.

[3]That they may do evil with both hands earnestly, the prince asketh, and the judge asketh for a reward; and the great man, he uttereth his mischievous desire: so they

wrap it up. [4]The best of them is as a brier: the most upright is sharper than a thorn hedge: the day of thy watchmen and thy visitation cometh; now shall be their perplexity.

[5]Trust ye not in a friend, put ye not confidence in a guide: keep the doors of thy mouth from her that lieth in thy bosom. [6]For the son dishonoureth the father, the daughter riseth up against her mother, the daughter in law against her mother in law; a man's enemies are the men of his own house. [7]Therefore I will look unto the LORD; I will wait for the God of my salvation: my God will hear me.

MICAIAH

[mī kī′a] The son of Imlah and a prophet of God. In about 850 BC, Ahab king of Israel enlisted the aid of Jehoshaphat king of Judah to resist the pressure of the Syrian king, Ben-hadad. Seeking to learn the will of God concerning this venture, Ahab summoned a band of 400 prophets, all of whom presented a picture of easy victory. Jehoshaphat, uneasy at such a unanimous report, asked if there were not other prophets who might be consulted. Ahab reluctantly summoned Micaiah, whom he referred to as a prophet of doom, and the prophet reluctantly came to the court. At first Micaiah simply repeated the favorable report of the 400, but admitted under pressure that the venture would end in disaster. When challenged on the accuracy of his prophecy, Micaiah described a council of the LORD from which a lying spirit was dispatched to enter the mouths of the prophets and deceive the king. At this Zedekiah, the most outspoken of the group of prophets, struck Micaiah, implying that it was Micaiah and not the 400 in whom the lying spirit dwelt. Ahab, angered by this prophecy, had Micaiah put in prison. Undaunted, the prophet declared that he was willing to let the outcome of the events serve as his vindication or condemnation. Although nothing further is heard of Micaiah, the campaign cost the life of Ahab and ended in defeat for the Israelite coalition.

SCRIPTURE

1 Kin. 22 [5]And Jehoshaphat said unto the king of Israel, Inquire, I pray thee, at the word of the LORD to-day. [6]Then the king of Israel gathered the prophets together, about four hundred men, and said unto them, Shall I go against Ramoth-gilead to battle, or shall I forbear? And they said, Go up; for the Lord shall deliver it into the hand of the king. [7]And Jehoshaphat said, Is there not here a prophet of the LORD besides, that we might inquire of him? [8]And the king of Israel said unto Jehoshaphat, There is yet one man, Micaiah the son of Imlah, by whom we may inquire of the LORD: but I hate him; for he doth not prophesy good concerning me, but evil. And Jehoshaphat said, Let not the king say so. [9]Then the king of Israel called an officer, and said, Hasten hither Micaiah the son of Imlah. [10]And the king of Israel and Jehoshaphat the king of Judah sat each on his throne, having put on their robes, in a void place in the entrance of the gate of Samaria; and all the prophets prophesied before them. [11]And Zedekiah the son of Chenaanah made him horns of iron: and he said, Thus saith the LORD, With these shalt thou push the Syrians, until thou have consumed them. [12]And all the prophets prophesied so, saying, Go up to Ramoth-gilead, and prosper: for the LORD shall deliver it into the king's hand. [13]And the messenger that was gone to call Micaiah spake unto him, saying, Behold now, the words of the prophets declare good unto the king with one mouth: let thy word, I pray thee, be like the word of one of them, and speak that which is good. [14]And Micaiah said, As the LORD liveth, what the LORD saith unto me, that will I speak.

15 So he came to the king. And the king said unto him, Micaiah, shall we go against Ramoth-gilead to battle, or shall we forbear? And he answered him, Go, and prosper: for the LORD shall deliver it into the hand of the king. 16 And the king said unto him, How many times shall I adjure thee that thou tell me nothing but that which is true in the name of the LORD? 17 And he said, I saw all Israel scattered upon the hills, as sheep that have not a shepherd: and the LORD said, These have no master: let them return every man to his house in peace. 18 And the king of Israel said unto Jehoshaphat, Did I not tell thee that he would prophesy no good concerning me, but evil? 19 And he said, Hear thou therefore the word of the LORD: I saw the LORD sitting on his throne, and all the host of heaven standing by him on his right hand and on his left. 20 And the LORD said, Who shall persuade Ahab, that he may go up and fall at Ramoth-gilead? And one said on this manner, and another said on that manner. 21 And there came forth a spirit, and stood before the LORD, and said, I will persuade him. 22 And the LORD said unto him, Wherewith? And he said, I will go forth, and I will be a lying spirit in the mouth of all his prophets. And he said, Thou shalt persuade him, and prevail also: go forth, and do so. 23 Now therefore, behold, the LORD hath put a lying spirit in the mouth of all these thy prophets, and the LORD hath spoken evil concerning thee. 24 But Zedekiah the son of Chenaanah went near, and smote Micaiah on the cheek, and said, Which way went the Spirit of the LORD from me to speak unto thee? 25 And Micaiah said, Behold, thou shalt see in that day, when thou shalt go into an inner chamber to hide thyself. 26 And the king of Israel said, Take Micaiah, and carry him back unto Amon the governor of the city, and to Joash the king's son; 27 And say, Thus saith the king, Put this fellow in the prison, and feed him with bread of affliction and with water of affliction, until I come in peace. 28 And Micaiah said, If thou return at all in peace, the LORD hath not spoken by me. And he said, Hearken, O people, every one of you.

MICHAEL

[mī′kȧ el, mī′kel] One of the two named angels in Scripture, the other being Gabriel. Michael is consistently pictured as possessing a warlike character. In the book of *Daniel,* he appears as a heavenly champion of the people of Israel. Jude refers to him as having opposed the devil in a contest over the body of Moses. In *Rev. 12: 7-12,* it is Michael who leads the angelic host against the dragon Satan and his forces, casting them out of heaven.

SCRIPTURE

Dan. 10 13 But the prince of the kingdom of Persia withstood me one and twenty days: but, lo, Michael, one of the chief princes, came to help me; and I remained there with the kings of Persia. 21 But I will shew thee that which is noted in the scripture of truth: and there is none that holdeth with me in these things, but Michael your prince.

Dan. 12 1 And at that time shall Michael stand up, the great prince which standeth for the children of thy people: and there shall be a time of trouble, such as never was since there was a nation even to that same time: and at that time thy people shall be delivered, every one that shall be found written in the book.

Jude 1 9 Yet Michael the archangel, when contending with the devil he disputed about the body of Moses, durst not

bring against him a railing accusation, but
said, The Lord rebuke thee.

Rev. 12 [7]And there was war in heaven:
Michael and his angels fought against the
dragon; and the dragon fought and his
angels, [8]And prevailed not; neither was
their place found any more in heaven.
[9]And the great dragon was cast out, that
old serpent, called the Devil, and Satan,
which deceiveth the whole world: he was
cast out into the earth, and his angels were
cast out with him. [10]And I heard a loud
voice saying in heaven, Now is come salvation, and strength, and the kingdom of
our God, and the power of his Christ: for
the accuser of our brethren is cast down,
which accused them before our God day
and night. [11]And they overcame him by
the blood of the Lamb, and by the word of
their testimony; and they loved not their
lives unto the death. [12]Therefore rejoice,
ye heavens, and ye that dwell in them.
Woe to the inhabiters of the earth and of
the sea! for the devil is come down unto
you, having great wrath, because he knoweth that he hath but a short time.

MICHAL

[mī'kal] Saul's younger daughter, and a wife of David. After his fabled defeat of the giant Goliah, David became a court hero. Michal fell in love with David and let it be known to her father. Arrangements were made and she became David's wife after he had presented Saul with the fantastic marriage present of a basket of foreskins taken from two hundred slain Philistines. Michal showed herself to be a woman of cleverness and loyalty to her husband when she aided David in his escape from the jealous Saul. During the period when David was treated as an enemy of the state, Michal was given in marriage to a man named Phalti. When David gained undisputed control of the kingdom after the death of Saul, the one thing he demanded of his defeated rival Ishbosheth was the return of his wife Michal, which thing was done despite the weeping protests of her husband. Michal's last appearance is as a disenchanted wife, critical and contemptuous of David's ecstatic exhibition at the arrival of the Ark of the Covenant in Jerusalem. David's reaction to her criticism indicates that love's flame was burning less brightly for both than it once had. The Biblical record informs us that "Michal the daughter of Saul had no child unto the day of her death."

SCRIPTURE

Given to David by Saul

1 Sam. 18 [20]And Michal Saul's daughter loved David: and they told Saul, and
the thing pleased him. [21]And Saul said, I
will give him her, that she may be a snare
to him, and that the hand of the Philistines may be against him. Wherefore Saul
said to David, Thou shalt this day be my
son in law in the one of the twain.

[22]And Saul commanded his servants,
saying, Commune with David secretly,
and say, Behold, the king hath delight in
thee, and all his servants love thee: now
therefore be the king's son in law. [23]And
Saul's servants spake those words in the
ears of David. And David said, Seemeth it
to you a light thing to be a king's son in
law, seeing that I am a poor man, and
lightly esteemed? [24]And the servants of
Saul told him, saying, On this manner
spake David. [25]And Saul said, Thus shall
ye say to David, The king desireth not any
dowry, but a hundred foreskins of the Philistines, to be avenged of the king's enemies. But Saul thought to make David fall
by the hand of the Philistines. [26]And when
his servants told David these words, it
pleased David well to be the king's son
in law: and the days were not expired.
[27]Wherefore David arose and went, he and
his men, and slew of the Philistines two
hundred men; and David brought their
foreskins, and they gave them in full tale

to the king, that he might be the king's son in law. And Saul gave him Michal his daughter to wife.

Rescues David from Death

1 Sam. 19 [11]Saul also sent messengers unto David's house, to watch him, and to slay him in the morning: and Michal David's wife told him, saying, If thou save not thy life to-night, to-morrow thou shalt be slain.

[12]So Michal let David down through a window: and he went, and fled, and escaped. [13]And Michal took an image, and laid it in the bed, and put a pillow of goats' hair for his bolster, and covered it with a cloth. [14]And when Saul sent messengers to take David, she said, He is sick. [15]And Saul sent the messengers again to see David, saying, Bring him up to me in the bed, that I may slay him. [16]And when the messengers were come in, behold, there was an image in the bed, with a pillow of goats' hair for his bolster. [17]And Saul said unto Michal, Why hast thou deceived me so, and sent away mine enemy, that he is escaped? And Michal answered Saul, He said unto me, Let me go; why should I kill thee?

Taken from David by Saul

1 Sam. 25 [44]But Saul had given Michal his daughter, David's wife, to Phalti the son of Laish, which was of Gallim.

Recovered by David

2 Sam. 3 [12]And Abner sent messengers to David on his behalf, saying, Whose is the land? saying also, Make thy league with me, and, behold, my hand shall be with thee, to bring about all Israel unto thee.

[13]And he said, Well; I will make a league with thee: but one thing I require of thee, that is, Thou shalt not see my face, except thou first bring Michal Saul's daughter, when thou comest to see my face. [14]And David sent messengers to Ish-bosheth Saul's son, saying, Deliver me my wife Michal, which I espoused to me for a hundred foreskins of the Philistines. [15]And Ish-bosheth sent, and took her from her husband, even from Phaltiel the son of Laish. [16]And her husband went with her along weeping behind her to Bahurim. Then said Abner unto him, Go, return. And he returned.

Despises David for His Religious Ecstasy

2 Sam. 6 [16]And as the ark of the LORD came into the city of David, Michal Saul's daughter looked through a window, and saw king David leaping and dancing before the LORD; and she despised him in her heart.

[20]Then David returned to bless his household. And Michal the daughter of Saul came out to meet David, and said, How glorious was the king of Israel to-day, who uncovered himself to-day in the eyes of the handmaids of his servants, as one of the vain fellows shamelessly uncovereth himself! [21]And David said unto Michal, It was before the LORD, which chose me before thy father, and before all his house, to appoint me ruler over the people of the LORD, over Israel: therefore will I play before the LORD. [22]And I will yet be more vile than thus, and will be base in mine own sight: and of the maidservants which thou hast spoken of, of them shall I be had in honour. [23]Therefore Michal the daughter of Saul had no child unto the day of her death.

MIDIAN, MIDIANITES

[mid'i an, mid'i an its] An Arabian tribe living in "the east country" (*Gen. 25:6*). It was a caravan of Midianites to whom Joseph was sold by his brothers and by whom he was transported to Egypt (*Gen. 37:25*). In later years, when Moses fled from Egypt, he found refuge with Jethro, priest of Midian, whose daughter he married (*Ex. 2:15-31*); while there he received his commission from God to deliver his people from Egypt (*Ex. 4:19*). Midianites are said to have been in league with Balak king of Moab when he hired Balaam to curse the Israelites (*Num. 22:4-7*). As a result of Balaam's efforts to thwart Israel, a great number of the Midianites were ruthlessly slain (*Num. 25:15, 17; 31:2ff*). During the period of the judges, we hear of the Midianites swarming across the desert on camels to make raids on Israel and to subject them to a seven-year period of oppression; this, incidentally, is the first historical mention of the domestication of camels. Israel was delivered from this oppression through the efforts of Gideon (*Judg. 6-8*).

See GIDEON, BALAAM, JETHROL, etc.

SCRIPTURE

Joseph Sold to Midianites

Gen. 37 [28]Then there passed by Midianites, merchantmen; and they drew and lifted up Joseph out of the pit, and sold Joseph to the Ishmaelites for twenty pieces of silver: and they brought Joseph into Egypt.

Moses Dwells in Midian

Ex. 2 [15]... But Moses fled from the face of Pharaoh, and dwelt in the land of Midian: and he sat down by a well. [16]Now the priest of Midian had seven daughters: and they came and drew water, and filled the troughs to water their father's flock. [17]And the shepherds came and drove them away: but Moses stood up and helped them, and watered their flock. [18]And when they came to Reuel their father, he said, How is it that ye are come so soon to-day? [19]And they said, An Egyptian delivered us out of the hand of the shepherds, and also drew water enough for us, and watered the flock. [20]And he said unto his daughters, And where is he? why is it that ye have left the man? call him, that he may eat bread. [21]And Moses was content to dwell with the man: and he gave Moses Zipporah his daughter. [22]And she bare him a son, and he called his name Gershom: for he said, I have been a stranger in a strange land.

Ex. 4 [19]And the LORD said unto Moses in Midian, Go, return into Egypt: for all the men are dead which sought thy life. [20]And Moses took his wife and his sons, and set them upon an ass, and he returned to the land of Egypt: and Moses took the rod of God in his hand.

Midianites Slain for Their Part in Hiring Balaam

Num. 25 [16]And the LORD spake unto Moses, saying, [17]Vex the Midianites, and smite them: [18]For they vex you with their wiles, wherewith they have beguiled you in the matter of Peor, and in the matter of Cozbi, the daughter of a prince of Midian, their sister, which was slain in the day of the plague for Peor's sake.

Num. 31 [1]And the LORD spake unto Moses, saying, [2]Avenge the children of Israel of the Midianites: afterward shalt thou be gathered unto thy people. [3]And Moses spake unto the people, saying, Arm some of yourselves unto the war, and let them go against the Midianites, and avenge the LORD of Midian. [4]Of every tribe a thousand, throughout all the tribes of Israel, shall ye send to the war. [5]So there were delivered out of the thousands of Israel, a thousand of every tribe, twelve thousand armed for war. [6]And Moses sent them to the war, a thousand of every tribe, them and Phinehas the son of Eleazar the priest, to the war, with the holy instruments, and the trumpets to blow in his hand. [7]And they warred against the Midianites, as the LORD commanded Moses; and they slew all the males. [8]And they slew the kings of Midian, beside the rest of them that were slain; namely, Evi, and Rekem, and Zur, and Hur, and Reba, five kings of Midian: Balaam also the son of Beor they slew with the sword. [9]And the children of Israel took all the women of Midian captives, and their little ones, and took the spoil of all their cattle, and all their flocks, and all their goods. [10]And they burnt all their cities wherein they dwelt, and all their goodly castles, with fire. [11]And they took all the spoil, and all the prey, both of men and of beasts.

Midian Oppresses Israel

Judg. 6 [1]And the children of Israel did evil in the sight of the LORD: and the LORD delivered them into the hand of Midian seven years. [2]And the hand of Midian prevailed against Israel: and because of the Midianites the children of Israel made them the dens which are in the mountains, and caves, and strong holds. [3]And so it was, when Israel had sown, that the Midianites came up, and the Amalekites, and the children of the east, even they came up against them; [4]And they encamped against them, and destroyed the increase of the earth, till thou come unto Gaza, and left no sustenance for Israel, neither sheep, nor ox, nor ass. [5]For they came up with their cattle and their tents, and they came as grasshoppers for multitude; for both they and their camels were without number: and they entered into the land to destroy it. [6]And Israel was greatly impoverished because of the Midianites; and the children of Israel cried unto the LORD.

Gideon Delivers Israel

Judg. 6 [11]And there came an angel of the LORD, and sat under an oak which was in Ophrah, that pertained unto Joash the Abi-ezrite: and his son Gideon threshed wheat by the winepress, to hide it from the Midianites. [12]And the angel of the LORD appeared unto him, and said unto him, The LORD is with thee, thou mighty man of valour. [13]And Gideon said unto him, O my Lord, if the LORD be with us, why then is all this befallen us? and where be all his miracles which our fathers told us of, saying, Did not the LORD bring us up from Egypt? but now the LORD hath forsaken us, and delivered us into the hands of the Midianites. [14]And the LORD looked upon him, and said, Go in this thy might, and thou shalt save Israel from the hand of the Midianites: have not I sent thee? [15]And he said unto him, O my Lord, wherewith shall I save Israel? behold, my family is poor in Manasseh, and I am the least in my father's house. [16]And the LORD said unto him, Surely I will be with thee, and thou shalt smite the Midianites as one man.

Judg. 7 [19]So Gideon, and the hundred men that were with him came unto the outside of the camp in the beginning of the middle watch; and they had but newly set the watch: and they blew the trumpets, and brake the pitchers that were in their hands. [20]And the three companies blew the trumpets, and brake the pitchers, and held the lamps in their left hands, and the trumpets in their right hands to blow withal: and they cried, The sword of the LORD, and of Gideon. [21]And they stood every man in his place round about the camp: and all the host ran, and cried, and fled. [22]And the three hundred blew the trumpets, and the LORD set every man's sword against his fellow, even throughout all the host: and the host fled to Beth-shittah in Zererath, and to the border of Abel-meholah, unto Tabbath. [23]And the men of Israel gathered themselves together out of Naphtali, and out of Asher, and out of all Manasseh, and pursued after the Midianites.

[24]And Gideon sent messengers throughout all mount Ephraim, saying, Come down against the Midianites, and take before them the waters unto Beth-barah and Jordan. Then all the men of Ephraim gathered themselves together, and took the waters unto Beth-barah and Jordan. [25]And they took two princes of the Midianites, Oreb and Zeeb; and they slew Oreb upon the rock Oreb, and Zeeb they slew at the winepress of Zeeb, and pursued Midian, and brought the heads of Oreb and Zeeb to Gideon on the other side Jordan.

MILLENNIUM

[mil len′ni um] As used by Bible students this word refers to the thousand-year reign of Christ which many believe will occur between this present age in which Satan rules and the future age in which God shall reign eternally. Belief in the millennium is based on *Rev. 20.* In this passage, the Devil is bound and cast into a bottomless pit for a thousand years, during which time those who have been martyrs for Christ shall reign with him (*Rev. 20:4*). At the end of the thousand-year reign, Satan is to be loosed for a final assault on the nation, to be followed by the general resurrection of the dead, the final judgment, and the casting into hell of all those whose names are "not found written in the book of life."

In the early years of the church, the millenial hope, often referred to as "chiliasm," was a popular theme of Christian writers. It is still a widely held article of faith in the Christian church. Beliefs with respect to the millennium may be arranged for convenience in three groups: Premillennialism, Postmillennialism, and Amillennialism. In the first of these the second coming of Christ is placed before the millennium; in the second, it is placed afterward. Amillennialists—those who do not believe in a literal millennium—content either that the writer was mistaken in his expectations or that the language is figurative. Those who interpret the millennium figuratively may feel, for instance, that it is to be equated with the present reign of Christ in the church, or they may simply hold that *Rev. 20* is a symbolic picture of the final triumph of God's truth and righteousness over Satan and the forces of evil.

SCRIPTURE

Rev. 20 [1]And I saw an angel come down from heaven, having the key of the bottomless pit and a great chain in his hand. [2]And he laid hold on the dragon, that old serpent, which is the Devil, and Satan, and bound him a thousand years, [3]And cast him into the bottomless pit, and shut him up, and set a seal upon him, that he should deceive the nations no more, till the thousand years should be fulfilled: and after that he must be loosed a little season. [4]And I saw thrones, and they sat upon them, and judgment was given unto them: and I saw the souls of them that were beheaded for the witness of Jesus, and for the word of God, and which had not worshipped the beast, neither his image, neither had received his mark upon their foreheads, or in their hands; and they lived and reigned with Christ a thousand years. [5]But the rest of the dead lived not again until the thousand years were finished. This is the first resurrection. [6]Blessed and holy is he that hath part in the first resurrection: on such the second death hath no power, but they shall be priests of God and of Christ, and shall reign with him a thousand years. [7]And when the thousand years are expired, Satan shall be loosed out of his prison, [8]And shall go out to deceive the nations which are in the four quarters of the earth, Gog and Magog, to gather them together to battle: the number of whom is as the sand of the sea. [9]And they went up on the breadth of the earth, and compassed the camp of the saints about, and the beloved city: and fire came down from God out of heaven, and devoured them. [10]And the devil that deceived them was cast into the lake of fire and brimstone, where the beast and the false prophet are, and shall be tormented day and night for ever and ever.

MINISTER

[min′is tẽr] The essence of the Christian ministry is personal service. In *Luke 22:25-27*, Jesus sets forth the principle that one's readiness to serve is the standard by which his greatness as a minister is to be assessed. Those who hold a special position within the church are thus to regard it not as an opportunity to wield authority, but as a commission to perform the service corresponding to the office.

The earliest ministry of the church was that of the *Apostles*. As the meaning of the word "apostle" indicates, they were men "sent out on a mission" to continue the work of Christ. The number of the apostles is usually restricted to the Twelve and to Paul. These men were empowered by the Spirit of God to bear witness to Christ, to impart information pertinent to salvation, and to make decisions with regard to church order and discipline. A second group of inspired ministers were called *Prophets*. In *1 Cor. 14:3*, we are told that "he that prophesieth speaketh unto men to edification, and exhortation, and comfort." The book of *Acts* mentions several individuals who were said to prophesy (*Acts 11:28; 21:20; 15:32; 21:29*). The gift of prophecy sometimes followed the imparting of the Spirit by the laying on of hands by the apostles (*Acts 19:6*).

Those designated as *Evangelists* probably travelled from place to place proclaiming the good news of salvation (the "evangel"), refuting false doctrine, strengthening the faith of believers, and organizing churches. Following up the work of the evangelist was the Teacher, whose duty it was to build up the life of the church by offering instruction in the Old Testament scriptures and the teachings of Christ and the apostles, and by applying these teachings to the ethical and moral life. A teacher might be a man or a woman, but women were not permitted to teach in a public assembly (*1 Cor. 14:34-35*).

As the church grew, the apostles appointed men in each congregation to oversee the work in that place. In *Acts 20:28*, Paul charges the overseers of the church in Ephesus to "take heed therefore unto yourselves, and to all the flock, over the which the Holy Ghost hath made you overseers, to feed the church of God, which he hath purchased with his own blood." In the New Testament, the terms *Bishop, Presbyter, Pastor,* and *Elder* seem to be used interchangeably for this office of spiritual shepherd. By the second century, however, each city or region usually had but a single Bishop and the college of presbyters, or elders, worked under his authority.

The last order of ministers to be considered here is that of the *Deacon*. The function of the deacon appears to have been to perform various services, at the direction of the elders, such as the administration of charitable goods. In *Rom. 16:1*, Phoebe is referred to as a "deaconess," and in *1 Tim. 3:11* instructions are given for "the women." We cannot be certain whether the women referred to here are a special order of women called deaconesses or whether they are simply the wives of the deacons. Apart from *Rom. 16:1*, we have no other clear reference to deaconesses until the third century, indicating perhaps that Phoebe was simply a woman engaged in various forms of personal service.

The New Testament portrays the church as the Spirit-filled body of Christ, whose life is sustained and enriched by each member's exercise of his particular gift. In this sense every member of the church may be considered a true minister of Christ.

See DEACON, ELDER, PROPHET

SCRIPTURE

General

Acts 6 [4]But we will give ourselves continually to prayer, and to the ministry of the word.

Acts 20 24But none of these things move me, neither count I my life dear unto myself, so that I might finish my course with joy, and the ministry which I have received of the Lord Jesus, to testify the Gospel of the grace of God.

Rom. 12 6Having then gifts, differing according to the grace that is given to us, whether prophecy, let us prophesy according to the proportion of faith. 7Or ministry, let us wait on our ministering: or he that teacheth, on teaching: 8Or he that exhorteth, on exhortation: he that giveth, let him do it with simplicity: he that ruleth, with diligence: he that sheweth mercy, with cheerfulness.

1 Cor. 16 15I beseech you, brethren, (ye know the house of Stephanas, that it is the firstfruits of Achaia, and that they have addicted themselves to the ministry of the Saints,) 16That ye submit yourselves unto such, and to every one that helpeth with us and laboureth.

Heb. 3 1Wherefore holy brethren, partakers of the heavenly calling, consider the Apostle and high Priest of our profession Christ Jesus, 2Who was faithful to him that appointed him, as also Moses was faithful in all his house. 3For this man was counted worthy of more glory than Moses, inasmuch as he who hath builded the house hath more honour than the house. 4For every house is builded by some man, but he that built all things is God. 5And Moses verily was faithful in all his house as a servant, for a testimony of those things which were to be spoken after.

2 Tim. 1 8Be not thou therefore ashamed of the testimony of our Lord, nor of me his prisoner, but be thou partaker of the afflictions of the Gospel according to the power of God, 9Who hath saved us, and called us with an holy calling, not according to our works, but according to his own purpose and grace, which was given us in Christ Jesus, before the world began, 10But is now made manifest by the appearing of our Saviour Jesus Christ, who hath abolished death, and hath brought life and immortality to light, through the Gospel: 11Whereunto I am appointed a preacher, and an apostle, and a teacher of the Gentiles.

1 Pet. 2 9But ye are a chosen generation, a royal Priesthood, an holy nation, a peculiar people, that ye should shew forth the praises of him who hath called you out of darkness into his marvellous light.

Divine Appointment

Ex. 4 12Now therefore go, and I will be with thy mouth, and teach thee what thou shalt say. 13And he said, O my LORD, send, I pray thee, by the hand of him whom thou wilt send.

Rom. 1 1Paul, a servant of Jesus Christ, called to be an apostle, separated unto the gospel of God.

2 Cor. 1 21Now he which stablisheth us with you in Christ, and hath anointed us, is God.

2 Cor. 2 15For we are unto God a sweet savour of Christ, in them that are saved, and in them that perish: 16To the one we are the savour of death unto death; and to the other the savour of life unto life. And who is sufficient for these things? 17For we are not as many, which corrupt the word of God: but as of sincerity, but as of God, in the sight of God speak we in Christ.

2 Cor. 5 20Now then we are ambassadors for Christ, as though God did beseech you by us: we pray you in Christ's stead, be ye reconciled to God.

Gal. 1 1Paul, an apostle, (not of men, neither by man, but by Jesus Christ, and

God the Father, who raised him from the dead.)

1 Tim. 4 [14]Neglect not the gift that is in thee, which was given thee by prophecy, with the laying on of the hands of the presbytery.

Christ's Commission to Ministers

Matt. 28 [19]Go ye therefore, and teach all nations, baptizing them in the name of the Father, and of the Son, and of the Holy Ghost: [20]Teaching them to observe all things whatsoever I have commanded you: and, lo, I am with you alway, even unto the end of the world. Amen.

John 4 [35]Say not ye, There are yet four months, and then cometh harvest? behold, I say unto you, Lift up your eyes, and look on the fields; for they are white already to harvest.

Duties of Ministers

TO PREACH TRUE DOCTRINE

1 Cor. 1 [23]But we preach Christ crucified, unto the Jews a stumblingblock, and unto the Greeks foolishness: [24]But unto them which are called, both Jews and Greeks, Christ, the power of God, and the wisdom of God.

1 Cor. 2 [1]And I, brethren, when I came to you, came not with excellency of speech, or of wisdom, declaring unto you the testimony of God. [2]For I determined not to know any thing among you, save Jesus Christ, and him crucified. [3]And I was with you in weakness, and in fear, and in much trembling. [4]And my speech and my preaching was not with enticing words of man's wisdom, but in demonstration of the Spirit and of power: [5]That your faith should not stand in the wisdom of men, but in the power of God.

1 Cor. 3 [9]For we are labourers together with God, ye are God's husbandry, ye are God's building. [10]According to the grace of God which is given unto me, as a wise master-builder I have laid the foundation, and another buildeth thereon. But let every man take heed how he buildeth thereupon. [11]For other foundation can no man lay, than that is laid, which is Jesus Christ. [12]Now if any man build upon this foundation, gold, silver, precious stones, wood, hay, stubble: [13]Every man's work shall be made manifest. For the day shall declare it, because it shall be revealed by fire, and the fire shall try every man's work of what sort it is.

2 Cor. 4 [5]For we preach not ourselves, but Christ Jesus the Lord, and ourselves your servants for Jesus' sake. [6]For God who commanded the light to shine out of darkness, hath shined in our hearts, to give the light of the knowledge of the glory of God in the face of Jesus Christ. [7]But we have this treasure in earthen vessels, that the excellency of the power may be of God, and not of us.

2 Cor. 5 [11]Knowing therefore the terror of the Lord, we persuade men; but we are made manifest unto God, and I trust also, are made manifest in your consciences. [12]For we commend not ourselves again unto you, but give you occasion to glory on our behalf, that you may have somewhat to answer them which glory in appearance, and not in heart. [13]For whether we be beside ourselves, it is to God: or whether we be sober, it is for your cause.

TO SHUN ERROR

Acts 20 [29]For I know this, that after my departing shall grievous wolves enter in among you, not sparing the flock. [30]Also of your own selves shall men arise, speaking perverse things, to draw away disciples after them. [31]Therefore watch, and remember, that by the space of three years I ceased not to warn every one night and day with tears.

1 Tim. 1 [6]From which some having swerved have turned aside into vain jangling; [7]Desiring to be teachers of the law; understanding neither what they say, nor whereof they affirm.

1 Tim. 6 [3]If any man teach otherwise, and consent not to wholesome words, even the words of our Lord Jesus Christ, and to the doctrine which is according to godliness; [4]He is proud, knowing nothing, but doting about questions and strifes of words, whereof cometh envy, strife, railings, evil surmisings, [5]Perverse disputings of men of corrupt minds, and destitute of the truth, supposing that gain is godliness: from such withdraw thyself.

2 Tim. 2 [16]But shun profane and vain babblings: for they will increase unto more ungodliness. [17]And their word will eat as doth a canker: of whom is Hymeneus and Philetus; [18]Who concerning the truth have erred, saying that the resurrection is past already; and overthrow the faith of some.

TO AVOID USELESS OR HARMFUL DISCUSSIONS

1 Tim. 1 [4]Neither give heed to fables and endless genealogies, which minister questions, rather than godly edifying which is in faith: so do.

1 Tim. 4 [6]If thou put the brethren in remembrance of these things, thou shalt be a good minister of Jesus Christ, nourished up in the words of faith and of good doctrine, whereunto thou hast attained. [7]But refuse profane and old wives' fables, and exercise thyself rather unto godliness.

1 Tim. 6 [20]O Timothy, keep that which is committed to thy trust, avoiding profane and vain babblings, and oppositions of science falsely so called.

2 Tim. 2 [14]Of these things put them in remembrance, charging them before the Lord, that they strive not about words to no profit, but to the subverting of the hearers. [15]Study to shew thyself approved unto God, a workman that needeth not to be ashamed, rightly dividing the word of truth. [23]But foolish and unlearned questions avoid, knowing that they do gender strifes.

Tit. 3 [9]But avoid foolish questions, and genealogies, and contentions, and strivings about the law; for they are unprofitable and vain.

TO REPROVE, KINDLY YET WITH FORCE

Gal. 4 [12]Brethren, I beseech you, be as I am; for I am as ye are: ye have not injured me at all. [13]Ye know how through infirmity of the flesh I preached the gospel unto you at the first. [14]And my temptation which was in my flesh ye despised not, nor rejected; but received me as an angel of God, even as Christ Jesus. [15]Where is then the blessedness ye spake of? for I bear you record, that, if it had been possible, ye would have plucked out your own eyes, and have given them to me. [16]Am I therefore become your enemy, because I tell you the truth?

1 Cor. 4 [18]Now some are puffed up, as though I would not come to you. [19]But I will come to you shortly, if the Lord will, and will know, not the speech of them which are puffed up, but the power. [21]What will ye? shall I come unto you with a rod, or in love, and in the spirit of meekness?

1 Cor. 11 [17]Now in this that I declare unto you I praise you not, that ye come together not for the better, but for the worse. [18]For first of all, when ye come together in the church, I hear that there be divisions among you; and I partly believe it.

2 Cor. 13 [1]This is the third time I am coming to you. In the mouth of two or three witnesses shall every word be established. [2]I told you before, and foretell you, as if I were present, the second time; and being absent now I write to them which heretofore have sinned, and to all other, that, if I come again, I will not spare. [10]Therefore I write these things being absent, lest being present I should use sharpness, according to the power which the Lord hath given me to edification, and not to destruction.

Gal. 1 [10]For do I now persuade men, or God? or do I seek to please men? for if I yet pleased men, I should not be the servant of Christ.

TO SET A GOOD EXAMPLE

Tit. 2 [7]In all things shewing thyself a pattern of good works: in doctrine shewing uncorruptness, gravity, sincerity, [8]Sound speech, that cannot be condemned; that he that is of the contrary part may be ashamed, having no evil thing to say of you.

TO MAINTAIN DECENCY AND ORDER

1 Cor. 14 [26]How is it then, brethren? when ye come together, every one of you hath a psalm, hath a doctrine, hath a tongue, hath a revelation, hath an interpretation. Let all things be done unto edifying. [27]If any man speak in an unknown tongue, let it be by two, or at the most by three, and that by course; and let one interpret. [28]But if there be no interpreter, let him keep silence in the church; and let him speak to himself, and to God. [34]Let your women keep silence in the churches: for it is not permitted unto them to speak; but they are commanded to be under obedience, as also saith the law. [35]And if they will learn any thing, let them ask their husbands at home: for it is a shame for women to speak in the church. [40]Let all things be done decently and in order.

Character and Qualifications of a Minister

KNOWLEDGE AND DISCRETION

Luke 6 [39]And he spake a parable unto them; Can the blind lead the blind? shall they not both fall into the ditch?

2 Cor. 11 [12]But what I do, that I will do, that I may cut off occasion from them which desire occasion; that wherein they glory, they may be found even as we. [13]For such are false apostles, deceitful workers, transforming themselves into the apostles of Christ.

Gal. 2 [2]And I went up by revelation, and communicated unto them that gospel which I preach among the Gentiles, but privately to them which were of reputation, lest by any means I should run, or had run, in vain.

TRUTHFULNESS

2 Cor. 1 [18]But as God is true, our word toward you was not yea and nay.

2 Cor. 4 [1]Therefore, seeing we have this ministry, as we have received mercy, we faint not; [2]But have renounced the hidden things of dishonesty, not walking in craftiness, nor handling the word of God deceitfully; but, by manifestation of the truth, commending ourselves to every man's conscience in the sight of God.

2 Cor. 13 [8]For we can do nothing against the truth, but for the truth.

1 Thess. 2 [1]For yourselves, brethren,

know our entrance in unto you, that it was
not in vain: 2But even after that we had
suffered before, and were shamefully entreated, as ye know, at Philippi, we were
bold in our God to speak unto you the
gospel of God with much contention.
5For neither at any time used we flattering
words, as ye know, nor a cloak of covetousness; God is witness.

GENTLENESS

1 Cor. 4 14I write not these things to
shame you, but as my beloved sons I warn
you. 15For though ye have ten thousand
instructors in Christ, yet have ye not many
fathers: for in Christ Jesus I have forgotten you through the gospel. 16Wherefore
I beseech you, be ye followers of me.

2 Cor. 2 4For out of much affliction and
anguish of heart I wrote unto you with
many tears; not that ye should be grieved,
but that ye might know the love which I
have more abundantly unto you. 5But if
any have caused grief, he hath not grieved
me, but in part: that I may not overcharge
you all. 6Sufficient to such a man is this
punishment, which was inflicted of many.
7So that contrariwise ye ought rather to
forgive him, and comfort him, lest perhaps
such a one should be swallowed up with
overmuch sorrow. 8Wherefore I beseech
you that ye would confirm your love toward him. 9For to this end also did I
write, that I might know the proof of you,
whether ye be obedient in all things. 10To
whom ye forgive any thing, I forgive also:
for if I forgave any thing, to whom I forgave it, for your sakes forgave I it in the
person of Christ.

1 Thess. 2 7But we were gentle among
you, even as a nurse cherisheth her children: 8So being affectionately desirous of
you, we were willing to have imparted
unto you, not the gospel of God only, but
also our own souls, because ye were dear
unto us.

FORBEARANCE

Phil. 1 15Some indeed preach Christ
even of envy and strife; and some also of
good will: 16The one preach Christ of
contention, not sincerely, supposing to
add affliction to my bonds: 17But the
other of love, knowing that I am set for the
defence of the gospel. 18What then? notwithstanding, every way, whether in pretence, or in truth, Christ is preached;
and I therein do rejoice, yea, and will
rejoice.

MEEKNESS AND HUMILITY

Luke 22 27For whether is greater, he
that sitteth at meat, or he that serveth? is
not he that sitteth at meat? but I am
among you as he that serveth.

John 13 14If I then, your Lord and Master, have washed your feet; ye also ought
to wash one another's feet.

1 Cor. 3 6I have planted, Apollos watered; but God gave the increase. 7So
then neither is he that planteth any thing,
neither he that watereth; but God that
giveth the increase.

1 Cor. 4 10We are fools for Christ's sake,
but ye are wise in Christ; we are weak,
but ye are strong; ye are honourable, but
we are despised.

2 Cor. 4 7But we have this treasure in
earthen vessels, that the excellency of the
power may be of God, and not of us.

2 Cor. 10 1Now I Paul myself beseech
you by the meekness and gentleness of
Christ, who in presence am base among
you, but being absent am bold toward
you: 2But I beseech you, that I may not
be bold when I am present with that con-

fidence, wherewith I think to be bold against some, which think of us as if we walked according to the flesh.

2 Tim. 2 [24]And the servant of the Lord must not strive; but be gentle unto all men, apt to teach, patient; [25]In meekness instructing those that oppose themselves; if God peradventure will give them repentance to the acknowledging of the truth.

Tit. 3 [2]To speak evil of no man, to be no brawlers, but gentle, shewing all meekness unto all men.

FIRMNESS

Gal. 2 [3]But neither Titus, who was with me, being a Greek, was compelled to be circumcised: [4]And that because of false brethren unawares brought in, who came in privily to spy out our liberty which we have in Christ Jesus, that they might bring us into bondage: [5]To whom we gave place by subjection, no, not for an hour; that the truth of the gospel might continue with you.

BLAMELESSNESS

2 Cor. 6 [3]Giving no offence in any thing, that the ministry be not blamed. [6]By pureness, by knowledge, by longsuffering, by kindness, by the Holy Ghost, by love unfeigned, [7]By the word of truth, by the power of God, by the armour of righteousness on the right hand and on the left.

1 Thess. 2 [10]Ye are witnesses, and God also, how holily and justly and unblameably we behaved ourselves among you that believe.

1 Tim. 6 [11]But thou, O man of God, flee these things; and follow after righteousness, godliness, faith, love, patience, meekness.

2 Tim. 2 [22]Flee also youthful lusts: but follow righteousness, faith, charity, peace, with them that call on the Lord out of a pure heart.

ZEAL AND DEVOTION

Rom. 1 [9]For God is my witness, whom I serve with my spirit in the gospel of his Son, that without ceasing I make mention of you always in my prayers; [10]Making request, if by any means now at length I might have a prosperous journey by the will of God to come unto you. [11]For I long to see you, that I may impart unto you some spiritual gift, to the end ye may be established; [12]That is, that I may be comforted together with you by the mutual faith both of you and me.

Rom. 14 [7]For none of us liveth to himself, and no man dieth to himself.

2 Cor. 5 [12]For we commend not ourselves again unto you, but give you occasion to glory on our behalf, that ye may have somewhat to answer them which glory in appearance, and not in heart. [13]For whether we be beside ourselves, it is to God: or whether we be sober, it is for your cause.

The Reward of Christian Ministry

John 4 [35]Say not ye, There are yet four months, and then cometh harvest? behold, I say unto you, Lift up your eyes, and look on the fields; for they are white already to harvest. [36]And he that reapeth receiveth wages, and gathereth fruit unto life eternal: that both he that soweth and he that reapeth may rejoice together. [37]And herein is that saying true, One soweth, and another reapeth. [38]I sent you to reap that whereon ye bestowed no labour: other men laboured, and ye are entered into their labours.

Phil. 1 [19]For I know that this shall turn to my salvation through your prayer, and

the supply of the spirit of Jesus Christ,
[20]According to my earnest expectation, and my hope, that in nothing I shall be ashamed, but that with all boldness, as always, so now also Christ shall be magnified in my body, whether it be by life or by death. [21]For to me to live is Christ, and to die is gain.

2 Tim. 4 [6]For I am now ready to be offered, and the time of my departure is at hand. [7]I have fought a good fight, I have finished my course, I have kept the faith. [8]Henceforth there is laid up for me a crown of righteousness, which the Lord the righteous judge shall give me at that day: and not to me only, but unto them also that love his appearing.

Types of Ministry

1 Cor. 12 [28]And God hath set some in the church, first apostles, secondarily prophets, thirdly teachers, after that miracles, then gifts of healings, helps, governments, diversities of tongues.

Acts 14 [23]And when they had ordained them elders in every church, and had prayed with fasting, they commended them to the Lord, on whom they believed.

1 Tim. 3 [1]This is a true saying, If a man desire the office of a bishop, he desireth a good work. [8]Likewise must the deacons be grave, not double-tongued, not given to much wine, not greedy of filthy lucre.

Rom. 16 [1]I commend unto you Phebe our sister, which is a servant of the church which is at Cenchrea.

Acts 21 [8]We entered into the house of Philip the evangelist, which was one of the seven, and abode with him.

MIRACLES

[mir'a k'l] In the Biblical sense, a miracle is an extraordinary event which takes place in a manner contrary to the regularly observed processes of nature. Regardless of who the direct agent of the miraculous occurrence happens to be, the Bible always recognizes the power of God as the ultimate source of such events. The principle groups of miraculous events in the Old Testament are those connected with the Exodus and wilderness wanderings, and the groups of miracles attributed to Elijah and Elisha. The supreme miracle recorded in the Bible is, of course, the resurrection of Jesus Christ, turning what appeared to be a supreme tragedy into a supreme triumph over the forces of evil and the power of death. During Jesus' life, he performed many miracles, a fact which even his enemies admitted (*Mark 3:22*). These were not done merely to dazzle his audience or to gain a reputation as a wonder-worker; this is made clear by his refusal to comply with requests for a "sign" (*Matt. 12:38-40; 16:4;* etc.). They served rather as heralds of the messianic age (*Matt. 11:4-5; Luke 7:22*) and were designed to stir the people to belief and repentance (*Matt. 11:20-21; Luke 10:13*).

Jesus' apostles were also endowed with the power to perform miracles. (*See Matt. 10:1, 8; 6:7; Luke 8:1; 10:19; John 14:12; Acts 1:8; 2:43; 3:6-7; 9:36-42; 16:16-18*) These miracles confirmed the Christian gospel and assisted in the establishment of a firm foundation for the church. After this was achieved, the need for miracles disappeared and they ceased to be performed.

See List of Miracles in Appendix

MIRIAM

[mir'i am] Daughter of Amram and Jochebed, and sister of Aaron and Moses. She is probably the sister who watched the basket of bulrushes as it drifted to the place where Pharaoh's daughter was bathing. She joined with Aaron in criticizing Moses for the wife he had chosen and was struck with leprosy. At Aaron's intercession, however, she was healed. She was buried at Kadesh, during the wilderness wanderings.

SCRIPTURE

Watches over Moses

Ex. 2 [1]And there went a man of the

house of Levi, and took to wife a daughter of Levi. 2And the woman conceived and bare a son: and when she saw him that he was a goodly child, she hid him three months. 3And when she could not longer hide him, she took for him an ark of bulrushes, and daubed it with slime and with pitch, and put the child therein; and she laid it in the flags by the river's brink. 4And his sister stood afar off, to wit what would be done to him.

5And the daughter of Pharaoh came down to wash herself at the river; and her maidens walked along by the river's side: and when she saw the ark among the flags, she sent her maid to fetch it. 6And when she had opened it, she saw the child and, behold, the babe wept. And she had compassion on him, and said, This is one of the Hebrews' children. 7Then said his sister to Pharaoh's daughter, Shall I go and call to thee a nurse of the Hebrew women, that she may nurse the child for thee? 8And Pharaoh's daughter said to her, Go. And the maid went and called the child's mother.

Murmurs against Moses

Num. 12 1And Miriam and Aaron spake against Moses because of the Ethiopian woman whom he had married: for he had married an Ethiopian woman. 2And they said, Hath the LORD indeed spoken only by Moses? hath he not spoken also by us? And the LORD heard it. 3(Now the man Moses was very meek, above all the men which were upon the face of the earth.) 4And the LORD spake suddenly unto Moses, and unto Aaron, and unto Miriam, Come out ye three unto the tabernacle of the congregation. And they three came out. 5And the LORD came down in the pillar of the cloud, and stood in the door of the tabernacle, and called Aaron and Miriam: and they both came forth. 6And he said, Hear now my words: If there be a prophet among you, I the LORD will make myself known unto him in a vision, and will speak unto him in a dream. 7My servant Moses is not so, who is faithful in all mine house. 8With him will I speak mouth to mouth, even apparently, and not in dark speeches; and the similitude of the LORD shall he behold: wherefore then were ye not afraid to speak against my servant Moses? 9And the anger of the LORD was kindled against them; and he departed. 10And the cloud departed from off the tabernacle; and, behold, Miriam became leprous, white as snow: and Aaron looked upon Miriam, and, behold, she was leprous. 11And Aaron said unto Moses, Alas, my lord, I beseech thee, lay not the sin upon us, wherein we have done foolishly, and wherein we have sinned. 12Let her not be as one dead, of whom the flesh is half consumed when he cometh out of his mother's womb. 13And Moses cried unto the LORD, saying, Heal her now, O God, I beseech thee.

14And the LORD said unto Moses, If her father had but spit in her face, should she not be ashamed seven days? let her be shut out from the camp seven days, and after that let her be received in again. 15And Miriam was shut out from the camp seven days: and the people journeyed not till Miriam was brought in again.

Miriam's Death

Num. 20 1Then came the children of Israel, even the whole congregation, into the desert of Zin in the first month: and the people abode in Kadesh; and Miriam died there, and was buried there.

MISCHIEF

[mis′chif] Harm or damage befalling, plotted

against, or done to anyone; disarrangement of order caused by some human agency.

SCRIPTURE

Psa. 7 [14]Behold, he travaileth with iniquity, and hath conceived mischief, and brought forth falsehood. [15]He made a pit, and digged it, and is fallen into the ditch which he made. [16]His mischief shall return upon his own head, and his violent dealing shall come down upon his own pate.

Psa. 140 [1]Deliver me, O LORD, from the evil man: preserve me from the violent man; [2]Which imagine mischiefs in their heart; continually are they gathered together for war.

Prov. 26 [27]Whoso diggeth a pit shall fall therein: and he that rolleth a stone, it will return upon him.

Isa. 33 [1]Woe to thee that spoilest, and thou wast not spoiled; and dealest treacherously, and they dealt not treacherously with thee! when thou shalt cease to spoil, thou shalt be spoiled; and when thou shalt make an end to deal treacherously, they shall deal treacherously with thee.

Acts 13 [10]And said, O full of all subtilty and all mischief, thou child of the devil, thou enemy of all righteousness, wilt thou not cease to pervert the right ways of the Lord?

MISSIONARY

[mish'un ẽr i] One who goes forth as a representative of God, propagating a message with a view to making converts. After the return from Babylonian exile, the Jews apparently engaged in extensive and successful mission work; Jesus refers to the zeal of the Pharisees in this matter (*Matt. 23:15*) and the book of *Acts* refers to proselytes—Gentiles who had been converted to Judaism (*Acts 2:11; 6:5; 13:43*).

John the Baptist and Jesus himself may properly be spoken of as missionaries, for they had truly been "sent" to proclaim the will of God to men. From the beginning of the Christian era, proclamation of the gospel has been regarded as a central task of the Christian community. Jesus' most intimate associates were called "apostles"; the meaning of this word is "one who is sent forth." Both these and the Seventy were sent out by the Lord to spread the tidings of the coming kingdom. The book of *Acts* is, to a great extent, a chronicle of the missionary activities of the early church. Here we read of the spread of the gospel which arose as a result of the persecution which followed the martyrdom of Stephen. Especially prominent in this period is the work of Philip the Evangelist (*Acts 8*). The last half of *Acts* is devoted to the labor of that greatest of all missionaries, the Apostle Paul. (*See* PAUL) It is clear from the commands of Christ and the examples of these early Christians that everyone who would be a child of God must also be, in some sense of the word, a missionary.

SCRIPTURE

Matt. 24 [14]And this gospel of the kingdom shall be preached in all the world for a witness unto all nations; and then shall the end come.

Matt. 28 [19]Go ye therefore, and teach all nations, baptizing them in the name of the Father, and of the Son, and of the Holy Ghost:

Mark 13 [10]And the gospel must first be published among all nations.

Luke 24 [47]And that repentance and remission of sins should be preached in his name among all nations, beginning at Jerusalem.

Acts 13 [2]As they ministered to the Lord, and fasted, the Holy Ghost said, Separate me Barnabas and Saul for the work whereunto I have called them. [3]And when they had fasted and prayed, and laid their hands on them they sent them away.

[4]So they, being sent forth by the Holy Ghost, departed unto Seleucia; and from thence they sailed to Cyprus.

[47]For so hath the Lord commanded us,

saying, I have set thee to be a light of the Gentiles, that thou shouldest be for salvation unto the ends of the earth.

MITE

[mīt] The smallest copper or bronze coin known to the Hebrews at the time of Christ. Its value seems to have been less than a quarter of a cent. Bible students remember it in connection with the words of Christ in reference to the poor widow who donated her last two mites into the treasury of the temple.

SCRIPTURE

Mark 12 [42]And there came a certain poor widow, and she threw in two mites, which make a farthing. [43]And he called unto him his disciples, and saith unto them, Verily I say unto you, That this poor widow hath cast more in, than all they which have cast into the treasury: [44]For all they did cast in of their abundance; but she of her want did cast in all that she had, even all her living.

MOAB, MOABITES

[mō′ab, mō′ab īts] Moab was the district east of the Dead Sea, extending northward about fifty miles from its southern tip, with an average breadth of about thirty miles. From the scriptures and from the famous Moabite Stone, a monument of King Mesha, erected about 850 BC and discovered in 1868, we learn that there were numerous towns in the area, including Dibon, Nebo, Beth-diblaim, Kerioth, and Zoar. In *Gen. 19:30-37*, the Moabites are said to have descended from Moab, the son of the incestuous union of Lot and his daughter. The relationship between Moab and Israel is marked by almost constant enmity, beginning with the effort of Balak king of Moab to thwart the Israelites' march to Canaan by hiring the Mesopotamian diviner, Balaam (*Num. 22, 24*). During the period of the judges, the Moabites oppressed the Hebrew tribes for eighteen years, until their king, Eglon, was assassinated by Ehud (*Judg. 3:12-30*). Moab became a vassal of Israel under the military leadership of David (*2 Sam. 8:2*) and remained such until after the schism between Israel and Judah, at which time it revolted, but was reconquered by Omri king of Israel. The remaining years of the kingdom of Israel saw frequent clashes with Moab, with first one and then the other gaining the upper hand. It appears that, at the fall of Judah to Nebuchadnezzar, Moab was able to escape total destructions, but in succeeding centuries it almost completely lost its identity.

SCRIPTURE

Descended from Lot

Gen. 19 [36]Thus were both the daughters of Lot with child by their father. [37]And the firstborn bare a son, and called his name Moab: the same is the father of the Moabites unto this day.

Hire Balaam to Curse Israel

Num. 22 [1]And the children of Israel set forward, and pitched in the plains of Moab on this side Jordan by Jericho.

[2]And Balak the son of Zippor saw all that Israel had done to the Amorites. [3]And Moab was sore afraid of the people, because they were many: and Moab was distressed because of the children of Israel. [4]And Moab said unto the elders of Midian, Now shall this company lick up all that are round about us, as the ox licketh up the grass of the field. And Balak the son of Zippor was king of the Moabites at that time. [5]He sent messengers therefore unto Balaam the son of Beor to Pethor, which is by the river of the land of the children of his people, to call him, saying, Behold, there is a people come out from Egypt: behold, they cover the face of the earth, and they abide over against me: [6]Come now therefore, I pray thee, curse me this people; for they are too mighty for me: peradventure I shall prevail, that we may smite them, and that I may drive them out

of the land: for I wot that he whom thou blessest is blessed, and he whom thou cursest is cursed. 7And the elders of Moab and the elders of Midian departed with the rewards of divination in their hand; and they came unto Balaam, and spake unto him the words of Balak. 8And he said unto them, Lodge here this night, and I will bring you word again, as the LORD shall speak unto me: and the princes of Moab abode with Balaam. 9And God came unto Balaam, and said, What men are these with thee? 10And Balaam said unto God, Balak the son of Zippor, king of Moab, hath sent unto me, saying, 11Behold, there is a people come out of Egypt, which covereth the face of the earth: come now, curse me them; peradventure I shall be able to overcome them, and drive them out. 12And God said unto Balaam, Thou shalt not go with them; thou shalt not curse the people: for they are blessed. 13And Balaam rose up in the morning, and said unto the princes of Balak, Get you into your land: for the LORD refuseth to give me leave to go with you. 14And the princes of Moab rose up, and they went unto Balak, and said, Balaam refuseth to come with us.

15And Balak sent yet again princes, more, and more honourable than they. 16And they came to Balaam, and said to him, Thus saith Balak the son of Zippor, Let nothing, I pray thee, hinder thee from coming unto me: 17For I will promote thee unto very great honour, and I will do whatsoever thou sayest unto me: come therefore, I pray thee, curse me this people. 18And Balaam answered and said unto the servants of Balak, If Balak would give me his house full of silver and gold, I can not go beyond the word of the LORD my God, to do less or more. 19Now therefore, I pray you, tarry ye also here this night, that I may know what the LORD will say unto me more. 20And God came unto Balaam at night, and said unto him, If the men come to call thee, rise up, and go with them; but yet the word which I shall say unto thee, that shalt thou do. 21And Balaam rose up in the morning, and saddled his ass, and went with the princes of Moab.

Are a Snare to Israel

Num. 25 1And Israel abode in Shittim, and the people began to commit whoredom with the daughters of Moab. 2And they called the people unto the sacrifices of their gods: and the people did eat, and bowed down to their gods. 3And Israel joined himself unto Baal-peor: and the anger of the LORD was kindled against Israel.

Israel Oppressed by Moab, Delivered by Ehud

Judg. 3 12And all the children of Israel did evil again in the sight of the LORD: and the LORD strengthened Eglon the king of Moab against Israel, because they had done evil in the sight of the LORD. 13And he gathered unto him the children of Ammon and Amalek, and went and smote Israel, and possessed the city of palm trees. 14So the children of Israel served Eglon the king of Moab eighteen years. 15But when the children of Israel cried unto the LORD, the LORD raised them up a deliverer, Ehud the son of Gera, a Benjamite, a man lefthanded: and by him the children of Israel sent a present unto Eglon the king of Moab. 16But Ehud made him a dagger which had two edges, of a cubit length; and he did gird it under his raiment upon his right thigh. 17And he brought the present unto Eglon king of Moab: and Eglon was a very fat man. 18And when he had made an end to offer the present, he sent away the people that bare the present. [19]But he himself turned again from the quarries that were by Gilgal, and said, I have a secret errand unto thee, O king: who said, Keep silence. And all that stood by him went out from him. [20]And Ehud came unto him; and he was sitting in a summer parlour, which he had for himself alone: and Ehud said, I have a message from God unto thee. And he arose out of his seat. [21]And Ehud put forth his left hand, and took the dagger from his right thigh, and thrust it into his belly: [22]And the haft also went in after the blade; and the fat closed upon the blade, so that he could not draw the dagger out of his belly; and the dirt came out. [23]Then Ehud went forth through the porch, and shut the doors of the parlour upon him, and locked them. [24]When he was gone out, his servants came; and when they saw that, behold, the doors of the parlour were locked, they said, Surely he covereth his feet in his summer chamber. [25]And they tarried till they were ashamed: and, behold, he opened not the doors of the parlour; therefore they took a key, and opened them: and, behold, their lord was fallen down dead on the earth. [26]And Ehud escaped while they tarried, and passed beyond the quarries, and escaped unto Seirath. [27]And it came to pass, when he was come, that he blew a trumpet in the mountain of Ephraim, and the children of Israel went down with him from the mount, and he before them. [28]And he said unto them, Follow after me: for the LORD hath delivered your enemies the Moabites into your hand. And they went down after him, and took the fords of Jordan toward Moab, and suffered not a man to pass over. [29]And they slew of Moab at that time about ten thousand men, all lusty, and all men of valour; and there escaped not a man. [30]So Moab was subdued that day under the hand of Israel. And the land had rest fourscore years.

Israelites at War with Moab

UNDER KING JEHORAM

2 Kin. 3 [4]And Mesha king of Moab was a sheepmaster, and rendered unto the king of Israel a hundred thousand lambs, and a hundred thousand rams, with the wool. [5]But it came to pass, when Ahab was dead, that the king of Moab rebelled against the king of Israel.

[6]And king Jehoram went out of Samaria the same time, and numbered all Israel.

[21]And when all the Moabites heard that the kings were come up to fight against them, they gathered all that were able to put on armour, and upward, and stood in the border. [22]And they rose up early in the morning, and the sun shone upon the water, and the Moabites saw the water on the other side as red as blood: [23]And they said, This is blood: the kings are surely slain, and they have smitten one another: now therefore, Moab, to the spoil. [24]And when they came to the camp of Israel, the Israelites rose up and smote the Moabites, so that they fled before them: but they went forward smiting the Moabites, even in their country. [25]And they beat down the cities, and on every good piece of land cast every man his stone, and filled it; and they stopped all the wells of water, and felled all the good trees: only in Kirharaseth left they the stones thereof; howbeit the slingers went about it, and smote it.

[26]And when the king of Moab saw that the battle was too sore for him, he took with him seven hundred men that drew swords, to break through even unto the king of Edom: but they could not. [27]Then

he took his eldest son that should have reigned in his stead, and offered him for a burnt offering upon the wall. And there was great indignation against Israel: and they departed from him, and returned to their own land.

UNDER JEHOIAKIM

2 Kin. 24 2And the LORD sent against him bands of the Chaldees, and bands of the Syrians, and bands of the Moabites, and bands of the children of Ammon, and sent them against Judah to destroy it, according to the word of the LORD, which he spake by his servants the prophets.

Judgment against Moab

Jer. 48 1Against Moab thus saith the LORD of hosts, the God of Israel; Woe unto Nebo! for it is spoiled: Kiriathaim is confounded and taken: Misgab is confounded and dismayed. 2There shall be no more praise of Moab: in Heshbon they have devised evil against it; come, and let us cut it off from being a nation. Also thou shalt be cut down, O Madmen; the sword shall pursue thee.

8And the spoiler shall come upon every city, and no city shall escape: the valley also shall perish, and the plain shall be destroyed, as the LORD hath spoken. 9Give wings unto Moab, that it may flee and get away: for the cities thereof shall be desolate, without any to dwell therein.

11Moab hath been at ease from his youth, and he hath settled on his lees, and hath not been emptied from vessel to vessel, neither hath he gone into captivity: therefore his taste remained in him, and his scent is not changed.

20Moab is confounded; for it is broken down: howl and cry; tell ye it in Arnon, that Moab is spoiled, 25The horn of Moab is cut off, and his arm is broken, saith the LORD.

26Make ye him drunken; for he magnified himself against the LORD: Moab also shall wallow in his vomit, and he also shall be in derision. 28O ye that dwell in Moab, leave the cities, and dwell in the rock, and be like the dove that maketh her nest in the sides of the hole's mouth. 29We have heard the pride of Moab, (he is exceeding proud,) his loftiness, and his arrogancy, and his pride, and the haughtiness of his heart. 30I know his wrath, saith the LORD; but it shall not be so; his lies shall not so effect it. 31Therefore will I howl for Moab, and I will cry out for all Moab; mine heart shall mourn for the men of Kir-heres. 35Moreover I will cause to cease in Moab, saith the LORD, him that offereth in the high places, and him that burneth incense to his gods. 36Therefore mine heart shall sound for Moab like pipes, and mine heart shall sound like pipes for the men of Kir-heres: because the riches that he hath gotten are perished. 40For thus saith the LORD; Behold, he shall fly as an eagle, and shall spread his wings over Moab. 41Kerioth is taken, and the strong holds are surprised, and the mighty men's hearts in Moab at that day shall be as the heart of a woman in her pangs. 42And Moab shall be destroyed from being a people, because he hath magnified himself against the LORD. 43Fear, and the pit, and the snare, shall be upon thee, O inhabitant of Moab, saith the LORD. 44He that fleeth from the fear shall fall into the pit; and he that getteth up out of the pit shall be taken in the snare: for I will bring upon it, even upon Moab, the year of their visitation, saith the LORD.

47Yet will I bring again the captivity of Moab in the latter days, saith the LORD. Thus far is the judgment of Moab.

MOLECH, MOLOCH

[mō′lek, mō′lok] A deity of the Ammonites, also called Milcom or Malcam. The worship of Molech involved the sacrifice of children as burnt offerings. We are told that Solomon, under the influence of his idolatrous wives, built an altar to this "abomination of the children of Ammon." Molech-worship figured rather prominently in the history of the kingdom of Judah, especially during the reigns of Ahaz and Manasseh, both of whom are said to have made their own children "pass through the fire." Josiah's reform brought a temporary halt to these practices, but the writings of the later prophets indicate that they were revived. The chief site of this worship was Topheth in the Valley of Hinnom, near Jerusalem.

The word Gehenna, used in reference to the place of torment of the wicked, derives its name from this infamous valley.

See AHAZ, MANASSEH, GEHENNA

SCRIPTURE

Lev. 18 [21]And thou shalt not let any of thy seed pass through the fire to Molech, neither shalt thou profane the name of thy God: I am the LORD.

Lev. 20 [2]Again, thou shalt say to the children of Israel, Whosoever he be of the children of Israel, or of the strangers that sojourn in Israel, that giveth any of his seed unto Molech; he shall surely be put to death: the people of the land shall stone him with stones. [3]And I will set my face against that man, and will cut him off from among his people; because he hath given of his seed unto Molech, to defile my sanctuary, and to profane my holy name. [4]And if the people of the land do any ways hide their eyes from the man, when he giveth of his seed unto Molech, and kill him not; [5]Then I will set my face against that man, and against his family, and will cut him off, and all that go a whoring after him, to commit whoredom with Molech, from among their people.

1 Kin. 11 [7]Then did Solomon build a high place for Chemosh, the abomination of Moab, in the hill that is before Jerusalem, and for Molech, the abomination of the children of Ammon.

2 Kin. 16 [3]But he walked in the way of the kings of Israel, yea, and made his son to pass through the fire, according to the abominations of the heathen, whom the LORD cast out from before the children of Israel.

2 Kin. 21 [6]And he made his son pass through the fire, and observed times, and used enchantments, and dealt with familiar spirits and wizards: he wrought much wickedness in the sight of the LORD, to provoke him to anger.

2 Kin. 23 [10]And he defiled Topheth, which is in the valley of the children of Hinnom, that no man might make his son or his daughter to pass through the fire to Molech.

2 Chr. 28 [3]Moreover he burnt incense in the valley of the son of Hinnom, and burnt his children in the fire, after the abominations of the heathen whom the LORD had cast out before the children of Israel.

Jer. 7 [31]And they have built the high places of Tophet, which is in the valley of the son of Hinnom, to burn their sons and their daughters in the fire; which I commanded them not, neither came it into my heart.

See Isa. 47:5; Ezek. 16:20, 21; 20:26, 31; 23:37, 39

MONEY

[mun′i] Anything customarily used as a medium of exchange and measure of value. The barter system was the first phase in the development of our modern conception of money. Bartering consisted in offering various commodities in return for desired commodities of similar value or in payment of obligations such as taxes or tribute. Cattle and produce were common items of barter. Because of inconvenience and difficulty in fixing the value on such items, this gave way to the use of metals such as gold, silver, copper, and iron, which could be used to make various objects or retained for reuse in future transactions. The purchasing power of these pieces of metal was usually determined by weight. From the use of scaled pieces of metal it was but a step to minted coins. The first coins of which we have any knowledge, like our present coins, were small pieces of metal stamped with an indication of value. The first mention of coins in the Bible is in *Ezra 2:69*, in which it is stated that the Jews in Babylonian exile contributed "threescore and one thousand crowns of gold" to be used in the reconstruction of the temple. It is fairly certain that the coin named here is the Persian daric.

Due to the vast difference in purchasing power between Biblical times and the present, it is quite difficult to convey an accurate idea of the value of the various monetary units mentioned in the Bible, but the following table will give some idea as to the relative value of these units.

Monetary Unit	*Modern Equivalent*	*Reference*
farthing	1 1/5 cts.	*Matt. 10:29*
gold shekel	$4.85 or $9.69	*1 Chr. 21:25*
mina or maneh		*Ezek. 45:12*
Gold	$242 or $484	
Silver	$16 or $32	
mite	3/20 ct.	*Luke 12:59*
penny	19 cts.	*Matt. 20:2*
pound	$20	*Luke 19:16*
talent	$970 or $1940	*Ex. 38:25*
talent of Gold	$14, 542 or $29,085	*1 Kin. 9:14*

MORDECAI

[môr′dē kī] A Jew in the period of exile who served in the Persian government of Ahasuerus (485-465 BC). When his young cousin Esther's parents died, Mordecai adopted her as his daughter and reared her. After Esther became Ahasuerus' queen (*see* ESTHER), Mordecai discovered a plot against the life of the king, but somehow failed to be rewarded for his service. Later, because of the refusal of Mordecai to pay homage to Haman, a chief minister in the Persian empire, the latter influenced the king to issue a decree calling for the extermination of the Jews. Mordecai persuaded Esther to intervene, at the risk of her life, on the Jews' behalf. Esther's efforts were successful; the plot was counteracted, Haman was hanged, and Mordecai received his long-deserved honor for having saved the king's life. Archaeology has found ancient texts which contain references to Mordecai, a high official at court during the reign of Xerxes I, who is almost certainly to be identified with Ahasuerus.

See HAMAN, PURIM, AHASUERUS

REFERENCE: The entire Book of *Esther*.

SCRIPTURE

Adopts and Rears Esther

Esth. 2 [5]Now in Shushan the palace there was a certain Jew, whose name was Mordecai, the son of Jair, the son of Shimei, the son of Kish, a Benjamite; [6]Who had been carried away from Jerusalem with the captivity which had been carried away with Jeconiah king of Judah, whom Nebuchadnezzar the king of Babylon had carried away. [7]And he brought up Hadassah, that is Esther, his uncle's daughter; for she had neither father nor mother, and the maid was fair and beautiful; whom Mordecai, when her father and mother were dead, took for his own daughter.

[11]And Mordecai walked every day before the court of the women's house, to know how Esther did, and what should become of her.

Saves the King's Life

Esth. 2 [21]In those days, while Mordecai sat in the king's gate, two of the king's chamberlains, Bigthan and Teresh, of those which kept the door, were wroth, and sought to lay hand on the king Ahasuerus. [22]And the thing was known to Mordecai, who told it unto Esther the queen:

and Esther certified the king thereof in Mordecai's name. [23]And when inquisition was made of the matter, it was found out; therefore they were both hanged on a tree: and it was written in the book of the Chronicles before the king.

Refuses to Pay Homage to Haman

Esth. 3 [1]After these things did king Ahasuerus promote Haman the son of Hammedatha the Agagite, and advanced him, and set his seat above all the princes that were with him. [2]And all the king's servants, that were in the king's gate, bowed, and reverenced Haman: for the king had so commanded concerning him. But Mordecai bowed not, nor did him reverence. [5]And when Haman saw that Mordecai bowed not, nor did him reverence, then was Haman full of wrath. [6]And he thought scorn to lay hands on Mordecai alone; for they had shewed him the people of Mordecai: wherefore Haman sought to destroy all the Jews that were throughout the whole kingdom of Ahasuerus, even the people of Mordecai.

Urges Esther to Intervene

Esth. 4 [13]Then Mordecai commanded to answer Esther, Think not with thyself that thou shalt escape in the king's house, more than all the Jews. [14]For if thou altogether holdest thy peace at this time, then shall there enlargement and deliverance arise to the Jews from another place; but thou and thy father's house shall be destroyed: and who knoweth, whether thou art come to the kingdom for such a time as this?

The King Rewards Mordecai

Esth. 6 [1]On that night could not the king sleep, and he commanded to bring the book of records of the chronicles; and they were read before the king. [2]And it was found written, that Mordecai had told of Bigthana and Teresh, two of the king's chamberlains, the keepers of the door, who sought to lay hand on the king Ahasuerus. [3]And the king said, What honour and dignity hath been done to Mordecai for this? Then said the king's servants that ministered unto him, There is nothing done for him.

[11]Then took Haman the apparel and the horse, and arrayed Mordecai, and brought him on horseback through the street of the city, and proclaimed before him, Thus shall it be done unto the man whom the king delighteth to honour.

Mordecai Succeeds Haman

Esth. 8 [1]On that day did the king Ahasuerus give the house of Haman the Jews' enemy unto Esther the queen. And Mordecai came before the king; for Esther had told what he was unto her. [2]And the king took off his ring, which he had taken from Haman, and gave it unto Mordecai. And Esther set Mordecai over the house of Haman.

Esth. 10 [3]For Mordecai the Jew was next unto king Ahasuerus, and great among the Jews, and accepted of the multitude of his brethren, seeking the wealth of his people, and speaking peace to all his seed.

MOSES

[mō′ziz] The leader of the Israelites in the exodus from Egypt and in the period of wanderings in the wilderness, during which time the covenant with God was made at Mt. Sinai. Moses was the son of Amram and Jochebed, and the brother of Aaron and Miriam. His dates were probably about 1355-1235 BC. Amram and Jochebed were descendants of Levi, one of the children of Jacob, or Israel, who had entered Egypt about 1700 BC (*see* EXODUS) at the request of the Pharaoh whom Joseph served. Centuries passed and "there arose a Pharaoh who knew not Joseph." This ruler, fearing that the now numerous Hebrews might start an uprising, issued an order to slay all infant males born to the Hebrews. To save the life of her infant son, Jochebed placed him in a little basket made of bulrushes, slime, and pitch, and left the basket among the reeds at the spot where Pharaoh's daughter was accustomed to bathe. When this princess found the child, she had compassion on him and, after the child was weaned, she adopted him and named him Moses. We know nothing of Moses' life in the Egyptian court. At the age of forty he fled from Egypt after having slain an Egyptian who was taskmaster over the Israelites. He came to the land of Midian where he met his wife Zipporah and became a shepherd under her father, Jethro. While tending his sheep one day in the region of Mt. Sinai, the LORD spoke to him from the midst of a burning bush, commissioning him to deliver his people from Egyptian bondage. Although skeptical of his ability to fulfil this task, he returned to Egypt and, with the aid of his brother Aaron and the ten plagues, led the children of Israel out of captivity. (*See* EXODUS) It was through Moses that God made the covenant with the Israelites. Thus, the law which grew out of the central document of that covenant, the Ten Commandments came to be called "the law of Moses." Despite Moses' central role in the making of the covenant, he was not indispensable to the continuance of Israel's religion. In fact, due to his failure to show proper honor to God at the waters of Meribah, he was not allowed to enter into the promised land to which he led his people. We are told that he died at the age of 120 in the land of Moab after having viewed the land of Canaan from atop Mt. Pisgah and that he was buried by the Lord in an unknown place. Moses is the chief figure of the religion of Israel. He is mentioned in the New Testament more than any other Old Testament character, and appeared with Elijah on the mountain of Jesus' transfiguration.

SCRIPTURE

Birth and Early History

Ex. 2 2 And the woman conceived and
bare a son: and when she saw him that he
was a goodly child, she hid him three
months. 3 And when she could not longer
hide him, she took for him an ark of bulrushes, and daubed it with slime and with
pitch, and put the child therein; and she
laid it in the flags by the river's brink.
4 And his sister stood afar off, to wit what
would be done to him.

5 And the daughter of Pharaoh came
down to wash herself at the river; and her
maidens walked along by the river's side:
and when she saw the ark among the flags,
she sent her maid to fetch it. 6 And when
she had opened it, she saw the child: and,
behold, the babe wept. And she had compassion on him, and said, This is one of the
Hebrews' children. 7 Then said his sister to
Pharaoh's daughter, Shall I go and call to
thee a nurse of the Hebrew women, that
she may nurse the child for thee? 8 And
Pharaoh's daughter said to her, Go. And
the maid went and called the child's
mother. 9 And Pharaoh's daughter said
unto her, Take this child away, and nurse
it for me, and I will give thee thy wages.
And the woman took the child, and nursed
it. 10 And the child grew, and she brought
him unto Pharaoh's daughter, and he became her son. And she called his name
Moses: and she said, Because I drew him
out of the water.

His Call to Leadership

Ex. 2 23 And it came to pass, in process
of time, that the king of Egypt died: and
the children of Israel sighed by reason of
the bondage, and they cried, and their cry
came up unto God by reason of the bondage.

Ex. 3 1 Now Moses kept the flock of
Jethro his father in law, the priest of
Midian: and he led the flock to the back
side of the desert, and came to the moun-

tain of God, even to Horeb. [2]And the angel of the LORD appeared unto him in a flame of fire out of the midst of a bush: and he looked, and, behold, the bush burned with fire, and the bush was not consumed. [3]And Moses said, I will now turn aside, and see this great sight, why the bush is not burnt. [4]And when the LORD saw that he turned aside to see, God called unto him out of the midst of the bush, and said, Moses, Moses. And he said, Here am I.

[10]Come now therefore, and I will send thee unto Pharaoh, that thou mayest bring forth my people the children of Israel out of Egypt.

[11]And Moses said unto God, Who am I, that I should go unto Pharaoh, and that I should bring forth the children of Israel out of Egypt? [12]And he said, Certainly I will be with thee; and this shall be a token unto thee, that I have sent thee: When thou hast brought forth the people out of Egypt, ye shall serve God upon this mountain.

The Exodus

Ex. 12 [40]Now the sojourning of the children of Israel who dwelt in Egypt was four hundred and thirty years. [41]And it came to pass at the end of the four hundred and thirty years, even the selfsame day it came to pass, that all the hosts of the LORD went out from the land of Egypt.

Ex. 14 [23]And the Egyptians pursued, and went in after them to the midst of the sea, even all Pharaoh's horses, his chariots, and his horsemen. [24]And it came to pass, that in the morning watch the LORD looked unto the host of the Egyptians through the pillar of fire and of the cloud, and troubled the host of the Egyptians. [25]And took off their chariot wheels, that they drave them heavily: so that the Egyptians said, Let us flee from the face of Israel; for the LORD fighteth for them against the Egyptians.

[26]And the LORD said unto Moses, Stretch out thine hand over the sea, that the waters may come again upon the Egyptians, upon their chariots, and upon their horsemen. [27]And Moses stretched forth his hand over the sea, and the sea returned to his strength when the morning appeared; and the Egyptians fled against it; and the LORD overthrew the Egyptians in the midst of the sea. [28]And the waters returned, and covered the chariots, and the horsemen, and all the host of Pharaoh that came into the sea after them; there remained not so much as one of them. [29]But the children of Israel walked upon dry land in the midst of the sea; and the waters were a wall unto them on their right hand, and on their left. [30]Thus the LORD saved Israel that day out of the hand of the Egyptians; and Israel saw the Egyptians dead upon the sea shore. [31]And Israel saw that great work which the LORD did upon the Egyptians: and the people feared the LORD, and believed the LORD, and his servant Moses.

Receives the Law

Ex. 24 [12]And the LORD said unto Moses, Come up to me into the mount, and be there: and I will give thee tables of stone, and a law, and commandments which I have written; that thou mayest teach them. [13]And Moses rose up, and his minister Joshua; and Moses went up into the mount of God. [14]And he said unto the elders, Tarry ye here for us, until we come again unto you: and, behold, Aaron and Hur are with you: if any man have any matters to do, let him come unto them. [15]And Moses went up into the mount, and a cloud covered the mount. [16]And the glory of the LORD abode upon mount Sinai, and the cloud covered it six days;

and the seventh day he called unto Moses out of the midst of the cloud. 17And the sight of the glory of the LORD was like devouring fire on the top of the mount in the eyes of the children of Israel. 18And Moses went into the midst of the cloud, and gat him up into the mount: and Moses was in the mount forty days and forty nights.

Ex. 32 15And Moses turned, and went down from the mount, and the two tables of the testimony were in his hand: the tables were written on both their sides; on the one side and on the other were they written. 16And the tables were the work of God, and the writing was the writing of God, graven upon the tables.

19And it came to pass, as soon as he came nigh unto the camp, that he saw the calf, and the dancing: and Moses' anger waxed hot, and he cast the tables out of his hands, and brake them beneath the mount.

Ex. 34 1And the LORD said unto Moses, Hew thee two tables of stone like unto the first: and I will write upon these tables the words that were in the first tables, which thou brakest.

28And he was there with the LORD forty days and forty nights; he did neither eat bread, nor drink water. And he wrote upon the tables the words of the covenant, the ten commandments.

29And it came to pass, when Moses came down from mount Sinai with the two tables of testimony in Moses' hand, when he came down from the mount, that Moses wist not that the skin of his face shone while he talked with him.

Moses' Sin

Num. 20 7And the LORD spake unto Moses, saying, 8Take the rod, and gather thou the assembly together, thou and Aaron thy brother, and speak ye unto the rock before their eyes; and it shall give forth his water, and thou shalt bring forth to them water out of the rock: so thou shalt give the congregation and their beasts drink. 9And Moses took the rod from before the LORD, as he commanded him. 10And Moses and Aaron gathered the congregation together before the rock, and he said unto them, Hear now, ye rebels; must we fetch you water out of this rock? 11And Moses lifted up his hand, and with his rod he smote the rock twice: and the water came out abundantly, and the congregation drank, and their beasts also.

12And the LORD spake unto Moses and Aaron, Because ye believed me not, to sanctify me in the eyes of the children of Israel, therefore ye shall not bring this congregation into the land which I have given them.

Told of His Coming Death

Num. 27 12And the LORD said unto Moses, Get thee up into this mount Abarim, and see the land which I have given unto the children of Israel. 13And when thou hast seen it, thou also shalt be gathered unto thy people, as Aaron thy brother was gathered. 14For ye rebelled against my commandment in the desert of Zin, in the strife of the congregation, to sanctify me at the water before their eyes: that is the water of Meribah in Kadesh in the wilderness of Zin.

15And Moses spake unto the LORD, saying, 16Let the LORD, the God of the spirits of all flesh, set a man over the congregation, 17Which may go out before them, and which may go in before them, and which may lead them out, and which may bring them in; that the congregation of the LORD be not as sheep which have no shepherd.

18And the LORD said unto Moses, Take

thee Joshua the son of Nun, a man in
whom is the spirit, and lay thine hand
upon him.

Moses' Death

Deut. 34 [1]And Moses went up from
the plains of Moab unto the mountain of
Nebo, to the top of Pisgah, that is over
against Jericho: and the LORD shewed him
all the land of Gilead, unto Dan, [2]And all
Naphtali, and the land of Ephraim, and
Manasseh, and all the land of Judah, unto
the utmost sea, [3]And the south, and the
plain of the valley of Jericho, the city of
palm trees, unto Zoar. [4]And the LORD said
unto him, This is the land which I sware
unto Abraham, unto Isaac, and unto Jacob, saying, I will give it unto thy seed: I
have caused thee to see it with thine eyes,
but thou shalt not go over thither.
[5]So Moses the servant of the LORD died
there in the land of Moab, according to
the word of the LORD. [6]And he buried him
in a valley in the land of Moab, over
against Bethpeor: but no man knoweth
of his sepulchre unto this day.

Seen at the Transfiguration

Mark 9 [4]And there appeared unto them
Elias with Moses: and they were talking
with Jesus.

MOTHER

[muth'ẽr] A female parent. The Bible enjoins upon us the obligation to show respect and veneration for motherhood.

See CHILDREN, FAMILY, MARRIAGE, HUSBAND, FATHER

SCRIPTURE

Ex. 20 [12]Honour thy father and thy
mother: that thy days may be long upon
the land which the LORD thy God giveth
thee.

Prov. 1 [8]My son, hear the instruction of
thy father, and forsake not the law of thy
mother.

Prov. 19 [26]He that wasteth his father,
and chaseth away his mother, is a son that
causeth shame, and bringeth reproach.

Prov. 23 [22]Hearken unto thy father that
begat thee, and despise not thy mother
when she is old.

MOUTH

[mowth] The opening in the head of all types of the animal kingdom through which food is taken and from which the sounds of the voice issue. There are numerous passages in the Bible which refer to the mouth, both in a figurative and a literal sense.

SCRIPTURE

Mouth of God

Deut. 8 [3]And he humbled thee, and
suffered thee to hunger, and fed thee with
manna, which thou knewest not, neither
did thy fathers know; that he might make
thee know that man doth not live by bread
only, but by every word that proceedeth
out of the mouth of the LORD, doth man
live.

Matt. 4 [4]But he answered and said, It
is written, Man shall not live by bread
alone, but by every word that proceedeth
out of the mouth of God.

Mouth of Babes

Psa. 8 [2]Out of the mouth of babes and
sucklings hast thou ordained strength because of thine enemies, that thou mightest still the enemy and the avenger.

Matt. 21 [16]And said unto him, Hearest
thou what these say? And Jesus saith unto
them, Yea; have ye never read, Out of the
mouth of babes and sucklings thou hast
perfected praise?

Mouth of the Wicked

Psa. 63 [11]But the king shall rejoice in God; every one that sweareth by him shall glory: but the mouth of them that speak lies shall be stopped.

Psa. 107 [42]The righteous shall see it, and rejoice: and all iniquity shall stop her mouth.

Psa. 109 [2]For the mouth of the wicked and the mouth of the deceitful are opened against me; they have spoken against me with a lying tongue.

Prov. 4 [24]Put away from thee a froward mouth, and perverse lips put far from thee.

Prov. 6 [12]A naughty person, a wicked man, walketh with a froward mouth.

Prov. 19 [28]An ungodly witness scorneth judgment: and the mouth of the wicked devoureth iniquity.

Rom. 3 [19]Now we know that what things soever the law saith, it saith to them who are under the law: that every mouth may be stopped, and all the world may become guilty before God.

Mouth of the Righteous

Psa. 37 [30]The mouth of the righteous speaketh wisdom, and his tongue talketh of judgment.

Prov. 10 [31]The mouth of the just bringeth forth wisdom: but the froward tongue shall be cut out.

Eccl. 10 [12]The words of a wise man's mouth are gracious; but the lips of a fool will swallow up himself.

Mouth of the Fool

Prov. 14 [3]In the mouth of the foolish is a rod of pride: but the lips of the wise shall preserve them.

Prov. 15 [2]The tongue of the wise useth knowledge aright: but the mouth of fools poureth out foolishness.

Prov. 18 [7]A fool's mouth is his destruction, and his lips are the snare of his soul.

Prov. 26 [7]The legs of the lame are not equal: so is a parable in the mouth of fools.

MURDER

[mûr′dẽr] The malicious killing of a human being. In virtually all times and civilizations, murder has been recognized as a cardinal offence against society. Killings done in accident or in the defense of life are not to be regarded as murders, although many of the ancient races did not so distinguish, and permitted blood-revenge for them the same as for actual murders. Israelite law recognized this distinction and made provision for the man who had taken life accidentally. (*See* REFUGE, CITIES OF) In the sixth commandment of the Decalogue, the verb translated "kill" is best translated "murder", and does not refer to killing to avenge a murder, to capital punishment, or to killing in war. The concern here is with the protection of human life within the community of Israel and the prevention of the weakening of society brought about by murder. Jesus struck at the very heart of murders when he condemned even the attitudes which, when fully developed, lead to murders.

SCRIPTURE

Gen. 4 [9]And the LORD said . . .
[10]What hast thou done? the voice of thy brother's blood crieth unto me from the ground. [11]And now art thou cursed from the earth, which hath opened her mouth to receive thy brother's blood from thy hand;

Gen. 9 [5]Surely your blood of your lives will I require; at the hand of every beast will I require it, and at the hand of man; at the hand of every man's brother will I require the life of man. [6]Whoso sheddeth man's blood, by man shall his blood be shed: for in the image of God made he man.

Ex. 20 [13]Thou shalt not kill.

Num. 35 [16]And if he smite him with an

instrument of iron, so that he die, he is a murderer: the murderer shall surely be put to death. [17]And if he smite him with throwing a stone, wherewith he may die, and he die, he is a murderer: the murderer shall surely be put to death. [18]Or if he smite him with an hand weapon of wood, wherewith he may die, and he die, he is a murderer: the murderer shall surely be put to death. [19]The revenger of blood himself shall slay the murderer: when he meeteth him, he shall slay him. [20]But if he thrust him of hatred, or hurl at him by laying of wait, that he die; [21]Or in enmity smite him with his hand, that he die: he that smote him shall surely be put to death; for he is a murderer: the revenger of blood shall slay the murderer, when he meeteth him. [22]But if he thrust him suddenly without enmity, or have cast upon him any thing without laying of wait, [30]Whoso killeth any person, the murderer shall be put to death by the mouth of witnesses: but one witness shall not testify against any person to cause him to die. [31]Moreover ye shall take no satisfaction for the life of a murderer, which is guilty of death: but he shall be surely put to death.

Matt. 5 [21]Ye have heard that it was said by them of old time, Thou shalt not kill; and whosoever shall kill shall be in danger of the judgment: [22]But I say unto you, That whosoever is angry with his brother without a cause shall be in danger of the judgment: and whosoever shall say to his brother, Raca, shall be in danger of the council: but whosoever shall say, Thou fool, shall be in danger of hell fire.

Matt. 15 [19]Out of the heart proceed evil thoughts, murders, ...

Matt. 19 [18]He saith unto him, Which? Jesus said, Thou shalt do no murder, ...

Gal. 5 [19]Now the works of the flesh are manifest, which are these; Adultery, fornication, uncleanness, lasciviousness, [20]Idolatry, witchcraft, hatred, variance, emulations, wrath, strife, seditions, heresies, [21]Envyings, murders, drunkenness, revellings, and such like: of the which I tell you before, as I have also told you in time past, that they which do such things shall not inherit the kingdom of God.

1 Tim. 1 [9]Knowing this, that the law is not made for a righteous man, but for the lawless and disobedient, for the ungodly and for sinners, for unholy and profane, for murderers of fathers and murderers of mothers, for manslayers,

Jas. 2 [11]For he that said, Do not commit adultery, said also, Do not kill. Now if thou commit no adultery, yet if thou kill, thou art become a transgressor of the law.

1 Pet. 4 [15]Let none of you suffer as a murderer,

1 John 3 [15]Whosoever hateth his brother is a murderer: and ye know that no murderer hath eternal life abiding in him.

Rev. 9 [21]Neither repented they of their murders,

Rev. 21 [8]Murderers . . . shall have their part in the lake which burneth with fire and brimstone: which is the second death.

See Mark 7:21

MUSIC

[myōō′zik] Music was an integral part of the lives of ancient people. It was used in war, in magic incanation, in worship, in work, and in various sorts of social activities such as parties, banquets, and parades. It was a regular part of court and harem life. In *Gen. 4:21* Jubal is credited with being "the father of all those who handle the harp and organ." The most famous musician in the Old Testament is, of course, King David, a talented composer, singer, and player.

A number of musical instruments are mentioned in the Old Testament. Among these were instruments whose purpose was primarily noise-making. The timbrel, or tabret, was probably a portable drum, perhaps having some kind of jingling contrivance like a modern tambourine. It is usually associated with merrymaking. The sistrum, erroneously translated "cornet" in the King James Version, was really little more than a rattle. The frame of a sistrum was a metal loop fastened to a handle. Wires were strung across the loops and rings of metal hung on the wires so as to produce a jingling sound when shaken. Cymbals were also widely used. We know of two types of ancient cymbals. Vertical cymbals, so called because they were struck together vertically, were harsh in tone. The lighter, clear-toned cymbals were horizontally struck.

The word translated "harp" in the King James Version is more properly translated "lyre." The ancient lyre was probably constructed by stretching string made from the intestines of sheep across a sounding board, over a bland space, and attaching them to a cross bar. That the lyre was also an instrument of joy may be seen from the references which tell us it was hung on the willows in Babylonia, for the exiles had not the heart to play. The terms trigon, sackbut, lute, viol, and psaltery all refer to stringed instruments ranging in construction from the lyre just described to a crude form of the modern Irish harp.

Among the woodwinds we read of the flute, or pipe, which was simply a hollow reed with finger holes drilled near one end. A rudimentary form of the oboe and clarinet were also known to ancient musicians. The instrument most often named in the Bible is the *shophar* ("ram's horn") or trumpet, also translated "cornet." This was made by heating a ram's horn with steam until it became soft and shaping it into the desired form. The *shophar* was primarily a signalling instrument, used to alert the people in time of danger, to summon them to worship and war, to announce the beginning of the sabbath or other religious holidays, or to signal the death of a well-known individual. The blast of the *shophar* was loud and demanding. It was this kind of horn which was used at the defeat of Jericho. A second type of trumpet was constructed of metal and was also used to sound war alarms and in the temple worship.

There is much less talk of music and musical instruments in the New Testament than in the Old Testament. This is probably explained by the fact that most of the early Jewish Christians came from the Synagogues. Although instrumental music was still used in the temple, unaccompanied vocal music was the rule in the synagogues. Opposition to instrumental music in early Christian worship was based mainly on its use in the pagan theatre and circus. Nevertheless, there is frequent reference to instrumental music in the book of *Revelation* and in other early apocalypic writing.

SCRIPTURE

Gen. 4 21And his brother's name was Jubal: he was the father of all such as handle the harp and organ.

Psa. 33 2Praise the LORD with harp: sing unto him with the psaltery and an instrument of ten strings. 3Sing unto him a new song; play skilfully with a loud noise.

Psa. 81 1Sing aloud unto God our strength: make a joyful noise unto the God of Jacob. 2Take a psalm, and bring hither the timbrel, the pleasant harp with the psaltery. 3Blow up the trumpet in the new moon, in the time appointed, on our solemn feast day.

Psa. 98 4Make a joyful noise unto the LORD, all the earth: make a loud noise, and rejoice, and sing praise. 5Sing unto the LORD with the harp; with the harp, and the voice of a psalm. 6With trumpets and sound of cornet make a joyful noise before the LORD, the King.

Psa. 105 2Sing unto him, sing psalms unto him; talk ye of all his wondrous works.

Eph. 5 19Speaking to yourselves in psalms and hymns and spiritual songs, singing and making melody in your heart to the Lord.

Col. 3 16Let the word of Christ dwell in you richly in all wisdom; teaching and admonishing one another in psalms and hymns and spiritual songs, singing with grace in your hearts to the Lord.

MYRRH

[mûr] An aromatic gum resin with a bitter, slightly pungent taste. It is mentioned in the Bible as valuable for its perfume (*Esth. 2:12, Psa. 45:8*) and was used in the preparation of the holy anointing oil (*Ex. 30:23*). Myrrh is mentioned three times in connection with Jesus: it was one of the gifts brought to him by the Magi, or "wise men" (*Matt. 2:11*); it was offered to him on the cross, perhaps as an anasthetic (*Matt. 15:23*); and it was used in preparation of his body for burial (*John 19:39*).

SCRIPTURE

Ex. 30 23Take thou also unto thee principal spices, of pure myrrh five hundred shekels, and of sweet cinnamon half so much, even two hundred and fifty shekels, and of sweet calamus two hundred and fifty shekels,

Esth. 2 12Now when every maid's turn was come to go in to king Ahasuerus, after that she had been twelve months, according to the manner of the women, (for so were the days of their purifications accomplished, to wit, six months with oil of myrrh, and six months with sweet odours, and with other things for the purifying of the women;)

Psa. 45 8All thy garments smell of myrrh, and aloes, and cassia, out of the ivory palaces, whereby they have made thee glad.

Matt. 2 11And when they were come into the house, they saw the young child with Mary his mother, and fell down, and worshipped him: and when they had opened their treasures, they presented unto him gifts; gold, and frankincense, and myrrh.

Matt. 15 23But he answered her not a word. And his disciples came and besought him, saying, Send her away; for she crieth after us.

John 19 39And there came also Nicodemus, (which at the first came to Jesus by night,) and brought a mixture of myrrh and aloes, about a hundred pound weight.

MYSTERY

[mis′tẽr i] In our times, the word mystery signifies a secret or puzzle to which the answer has not yet been discovered. As used in the Bible, it refers to a divine secret which has been, or is being, disclosed; since it is divine, however, it is not completely transparent to man and remains something of a mystery. The term is used of the plan of redemption, of the kingdom of God, and, in a derivative sense, of the "man of sin," the "mother of harlots," and the institution of marriage.

SCRIPTURE

Mystery of the Plan of Redemption

Deut. 29 29The secret things belong unto the LORD our God: but those things which are revealed belong unto us and to our children for ever, that we may do all the words of this law.

Psa. 25 14The secret of the LORD is with them that fear him; and he will shew them his covenant.

Prov. 3 32His secret is with the righteous.

Amos 3 7Surely the Lord GOD will do nothing, but he revealeth his secret unto his servants the prophets.

Matt. 11 25At that time Jesus answered and said, I thank thee, O Father, Lord of heaven and earth, because thou hast hid these things from the wise and prudent, and hast revealed them unto babes.

John 3 8The wind bloweth where it listeth, and thou hearest the sound thereof, but canst not tell whence it cometh, and whither it goeth: so is every one that is born of the Spirit. [9]Nicodemus answered and said unto him, How can these things be? [10]Jesus answered and said unto him, Art thou a master of Israel, and knowest not these things? [11]Verily, verily, I say unto thee, We speak that we do know, and testify that we have seen; and ye receive not our witness. [12]If I have told you earthly things, and ye believe not, how shall ye believe, if I tell you of heavenly things?

Rom. 16 [25]Now to him that is of power to stablish you according to my gospel, and the preaching of Jesus Christ, according to the revelation of the mystery, which was kept secret since the world began, [26]But now is made manifest, and by the scriptures of the prophets, according to the commandment of the everlasting God, made known to all nations for the obedience of faith:

Eph. 3 [3]How that by revelation he made known unto me the mystery; (as I wrote afore in few words, [4]Whereby, when ye read, ye may understand my knowledge in the mystery of Christ) [5]Which in other ages was not made known unto the sons of men, as it is now revealed unto his holy apostles and prophets by the Spirit; [9]And to make all men see what is the fellowship of the mystery, which from the beginning of the world hath been hid in God, who created all things by Jesus Christ: [18]May be able to comprehend with all saints what is the breadth, and length, and depth, and height; [19]And to know the love of Christ, which passeth knowledge, that ye might be filled with all the fulness of God.

Eph. 6 [19]And for me, that utterance may be given unto me, that I may open my mouth boldly, to make known the mystery of the gospel,

Col. 1 [25]Whereof I am made a minister, according to the dispensation of God which is given to me for you, to fulfil the word of God; [26]Even the mystery which hath been hid from ages and from generations, but now is made manifest to his saints: [27]To whom God would make known what is the riches of the glory of this mystery among the Gentiles; which is Christ in you, the hope of glory:

Col. 4 [3]Withal praying also for us, that God would open unto us a door of utterance, to speak the mystery of Christ, for which I am also in bonds:

1 Tim. 3 [9]Holding the mystery of the faith in a pure conscience. [16]And without controversy great is the mystery of godliness: God was manifest in the flesh, justified in the Spirit, seen of angels, preached unto the Gentiles, believed on in the world, received up into glory.

Rev. 10 [7]But in the days of the voice of the seventh angel, when he shall begin to sound, the mystery of God should be finished, as he hath declared to his servants the prophets.

NAAMAN

[nā'a man] A leprous commander of the army of Damascus. Through the efforts of a young servant girl, Naaman learned of the marvelous deeds of the prophet Elisha and sought him out in order to have his leprosy cleansed. Elisha declined to see him, but sent word for him to bathe seven times in the Jordan River. Naaman was angered at this apparently trivial command, but was finally persuaded by his companions to obey. He was cured and became a worshipper of the God of Israel.

SCRIPTURE

2 Kin. 5 [1]Now Naaman, captain of the host of the king of Syria, was a great man with his master, and honourable, because by him the LORD had given deliverance unto Syria: he was also a mighty man in valour, but he was a leper. 2And the Syrians had gone out by companies, and had brought away captive out of the land of Israel a little maid; and she waited on Naaman's wife. 3And she said unto her mistress, Would God my lord were with the prophet that is in Samaria! for he would recover him of his leprosy. 4And one went in, and told his lord, saying, Thus and thus said the maid that is of the land of Israel. 5And the king of Syria said, Go to, go, and I will send a letter unto the king of Israel. And he departed, and took with him ten talents of silver, and six thousand pieces of gold, and ten changes of raiment.

9So Naaman came with his horses and with his chariot, and stood at the door of the house of Elisha. 10And Elisha sent a messenger unto him, saying, Go and wash in Jordan seven times, and thy flesh shall come again to thee, and thou shalt be clean. 11But Naaman was wroth, and went away, and said, Behold, I thought he will surely come out to me, and stand, and call on the name of the LORD his God, and strike his hand over the place, and recover the leper. 12Are not Abana and Pharpar, rivers of Damascus, better than all the waters of Israel? may I not wash in them, and be clean? So he turned and went away in a rage. 13And his servants came near, and spake unto him, and said, My father, if the prophet had bid thee do some great thing, wouldest thou not have done it? how much rather then, when he saith to thee, Wash, and be clean? 14Then went he down, and dipped himself seven times in Jordan, according to the saying of the man of God: and his flesh came again like unto the flesh of a little child, and he was clean.

15And he returned to the man of God, he and all his company, and came, and stood before him: and he said, Behold, now I know that there is no God in all the earth, but in Israel: now therefore, I pray thee, take a blessing of thy servant. 16But he said, As the LORD liveth, before whom I stand, I will receive none. And he urged him to take it; but he refused. 17And Naaman said, Shall there not then, I pray thee, be given to thy servant two mules' burden of earth? for thy servant will henceforth offer neither burnt offering nor sacrifice unto other gods, but unto the LORD.

NABAL

[nā'bal] A wealthy farmer and stock-raiser in the region of Maon, in southern Judea. When David was a fugitive from Saul, he and his men encamped near the flocks of Nabal and protected them from harm. In return for this favor, David sent men to Nabal to ask for food and other provisions. Nabal was a man of a terrible disposition and insolently refused any aid to David. This so enraged the young warrior that he determined to punish Nabal and set out for his home with an army of four hundred men. He was dissuaded from his purpose by Nabal's beautiful and tactful wife, Abigail, who met with him with a present and apologized for the churlish actions of her husband. When Abigail returned home, her husband was engaged in a drunken feast; the next morning, however, she related to him the calamity which had been so narrowly averted. Nabal's "heart died within him, and he became as a stone", within ten days he was dead. Shortly afterward, David chose Abigail to be one of his wives.

See ABIGAIL

SCRIPTURE

1 Sam. 25 2And there was a man in Maon, whose possessions were in Carmel; and the man was very great, and he had three thousand sheep, and a thousand goats: and he was shearing his sheep in Carmel. 3Now the name of the man was Nabal, and the name of his wife Abigail;

and she was a woman of good understanding, and of a beautiful countenance: but
the man was churlish and evil in his doings; and he was of the house of Caleb.
4And David heard in the wilderness that
Nabal did shear his sheep. 5And David
sent out ten young men, and David said
unto the young men, Get you up to Carmel, and go to Nabal, and greet him in my
name:
10And Nabal answered David's servants,
and said, Who is David? and who is the
son of Jesse? there be many servants nowadays that break away every man from his
master. 11Shall I then take my bread, and
my water, and my flesh that I have killed
for my shearers, and give it unto men,
whom I know not whence they be? 12So
David's young men turned their way, and
went again, and came and told him all
those sayings. 13And David said unto his
men, Gird ye on every man his sword. And
they girded on every man his sword; and
David also girded on his sword: and there
went up after David about four hundred
men; and two hundred abode by the stuff.
14But one of the young men told Abigail, Nabal's wife, saying, Behold, David
sent messengers out of the wilderness to
salute our master; and he railed on them.
18Then Abigail made haste, and took
two hundred loaves, and two bottles of
wine, and five sheep ready dressed, and
five measures of parched corn, and a hundred clusters of raisins, and two hundred
cakes of figs, and laid them on asses.
19And she said unto her servants, Go on
before me; behold, I come after you. But
she told not her husband Nabal. 23And
when Abigail saw David, she hasted, and
lighted off the ass, and fell before David
on her face, and bowed herself to the
ground. 24And fell at his feet, and said,
Upon me, my lord, upon me let this iniquity be: and let thine handmaid, I pray
thee, speak in thine audience, and hear
the words of thine handmaid. 25Let not
my lord, I pray thee, regard this man of
Belial, even Nabal: for as his name is, so
is he; Nabal is his name, and folly is with
him: but I thine handmaid saw not the
young men of my lord, whom thou didst
send. 26Now therefore, my lord, as the
LORD liveth, and as thy soul liveth, seeing
the LORD hath withholden thee from coming to shed blood, and from avenging thyself with thine own hand, now let thine
enemies, and they that seek evil to my
lord, be as Nabal.
36And Abigail came to Nabal; and, behold, he held a feast in his house, like the
feast of a king; and Nabal's heart was
merry within him, for he was very
drunken: wherefore she told him nothing,
less or more, until the morning light.
37But it came to pass in the morning, when
the wine was gone out of Nabal, and his
wife had told him these things, that his
heart died within him, and he became as
a stone. 38And it came to pass about ten
days after, that the LORD smote Nabal,
that he died.

NABOTH

[nā'both] The owner of a vineyard adjoining the palace of Ahab, king of Israel. Ahab desired the plot of land for his own, but Naboth refused to part with it, in accordance with the custom concerning paternal inheritances. Ahab's ruthless wife, Jezebel, noticed her husband's sullen attitude about the refusal of Naboth and promised to secure the vineyard for him. She arranged to have Naboth tried and executed on a trumped-up charge of blasphemy and announced to Ahab that the vineyard was his. While Ahab was inspecting his new possession, the prophet Elijah confronted him and pronounced a curse on him and his descendants for this egregious injustice. Ahab made a show of repentance and gained a temporary postponement of the wrath of God, but when it eventually fell upon him, both at his own death and at the extermination of his house by Jehu, the incident of Naboth's vineyard was recalled.

See Ahab, Elijah, Jehu, Jezebel

SCRIPTURE

1 Kin. 21 [1]And it came to pass after these things, that Naboth the Jezreelite had a vineyard, which was in Jezreel, hard by the palace of Ahab king of Samaria. [2]And Ahab spake unto Naboth, saying, Give me thy vineyard, that I may have it for a garden of herbs, because it is near unto my house: and I will give thee for it a better vineyard than it; or if it seem good to thee, I will give thee the worth of it in money. [3]And Naboth said to Ahab, The Lord forbid it me, that I should give the inheritance of my fathers unto thee. [4]And Ahab came into his house heavy and displeased because of the word which Naboth the Jezreelite had spoken to him: for he had said, I will not give thee the inheritance of my fathers. And he laid him down upon his bed, and turned away his face, and would eat no bread.

[5]But Jezebel his wife came to him, and said unto him, Why is thy spirit so sad, that thou eatest no bread? [6]And he said unto her, Because I spake unto Naboth the Jezreelite, and said unto him, Give me thy vineyard for money; or else, if it please thee, I will give thee another vineyard for it: and he answered, I will not give thee my vineyard. [7]And Jezebel his wife said unto him, Dost thou now govern the kingdom of Israel? arise, and eat bread, and let thine heart be merry: I will give thee the vineyard of Naboth the Jezreelite. [8]So she wrote letters in Ahab's name, and sealed them with his seal, and sent the letters unto the elders and to the nobles that were in his city, dwelling with Naboth. [9]And she wrote in the letters, saying, Proclaim a fast, and set Naboth on high among the people: [10]And set two men, sons of Belial, before him, to bear witness against him, saying, Thou didst blaspheme God and the king. And then carry him out and stone him, that he may die. [11]And the men of his city, even the elders and the nobles who were the inhabitants in his city, did as Jezebel had sent unto them, and as it was written in the letters which she had sent unto them. [12]They proclaimed a fast, and set Naboth on high among the people. [13]And there came in two men, children of Belial, and sat before him: and the men of Belial witnessed against him, even against Naboth, in the presence of the people, saying, Naboth did blaspheme God and the king. Then they carried him forth out of the city, and stoned him with stones, that he died. [14]Then they sent to Jezebel, saying, Naboth is stoned, and is dead.

[15]And it came to pass, when Jezebel heard that Naboth was stoned, and was dead, that Jezebel said to Ahab, Arise, take possession of the vineyard of Naboth the Jezreelite, which he refused to give thee for money: for Naboth is not alive, but dead. [16]And it came to pass, when Ahab heard that Naboth was dead, that Ahab rose up to go down to the vineyard of Naboth the Jezreelite, to take possession of it.

2 Kin. 9 [25]Then said Jehu to Bidkar his captain, Take up, and cast him in the portion of the field of Naboth the Jezreelite: for remember how that, when I and thou rode together after Ahab his father, the Lord laid this burden upon him; [26]Surely I have seen yesterday the blood of Naboth, and the blood of his sons, saith the Lord; and I will requite thee in this plat, saith the Lord. Now therefore take and cast him into the plat of ground, according to the word of the LORD.

NADAB

[nā'dab] Two rather prominent Biblical characters bear this name.

1. Nadab, the son of Aaron and Elisheba. This man was among the select leaders of Israel who accompanied Moses when he ascended Mount Sinai to receive the covenant from God. He was later chosen for the priesthood and was struck dead along with his brother Abihu, when they used "strange fire" in offering incense.

See ABIHU

2. Nadab, the son of Jeroboam I and ruler of the Northern Kingdom for two years (901-900 BC). While Nadab and his army were laying siege to Gibbethon, a stronghold of the Philistines, he was slain by Baasha, who then became king of Israel. Baasha's first recorded act as king was to kill the rest of the house of Jeroboam, thus fulfilling the prophecy which Ahijah had made to Jeroboam.

See AHIJAH, KINGS

SCRIPTURE

Nadab, the Son of Aaron

WITH MOSES AT MT. SINAI

Ex. 24 [1]And he said unto Moses, Come up unto the LORD, thou, and Aaron, Nadab, and Abihu, and seventy of the elders of Israel; and worship ye afar off.

[9]Then went up Moses, and Aaron, Nadab, and Abihu, and seventy of the elders of Israel; [10]And they saw the God of Israel: and there was under his feet as it were a paved work of a sapphire stone, and as it were the body of heaven in his clearness. [11]And upon the nobles of the children of Israel he laid not his hand: also they saw God, and did eat and drink.

APPOINTED AS PRIEST

Ex. 28 [1]And take thou unto thee Aaron thy brother, and his sons with him, from among the children of Israel, that he may minister unto me in the priest's office, even Aaron, Nadab and Abihu, Eleazar and Ithamar, Aaron's sons.

OFFERS STRANGE FIRE

Lev. 10 [1]And Nadab and Abihu, the sons of Aaron, took either of them his censer, and put fire therein, and put incense thereon, and offered strange fire before the LORD, which he commanded them not. [2]And there went out fire from the LORD, and devoured them, and they died before the LORD.

Nadab, King of Israel

1 Kin. 14 [20]And the days which Jeroboam reigned were two and twenty years: and he slept with his fathers, and Nadab his son reigned in his stead.

1 Kin. 15 [25]And Nadab the son of Jeroboam began to reign over Israel in the second year of Asa king of Judah, and reigned over Israel two years. [26]And he did evil in the sight of the LORD, and walked in the way of his father, and in his sin wherewith he made Israel to sin.

[27]And Baasha the son of Ahijah, of the house of Issachar, conspired against him; and Baasha smote him at Gibbethon, which belonged to the Philistines; for Nadab and all Israel laid siege to Gibbethon. [28]Even in the third year of Asa king of Judah did Baasha slay him, and reigned in his stead. [29]And it came to pass, when he reigned, that he smote all the house of Jeroboam; he left not to Jeroboam any that breathed, until he had destroyed him, according unto the saying of the LORD, which he spake by his servant Ahijah the Shilonite: [30]Because of the sins of Jeroboam which he sinned, and which he made Israel sin, by his provocation wherewith he

provoked the LORD GOD of Israel to anger.
31 Now the rest of the acts of Nadab, and
all that he did, are they not written in the
book of the Chronicles of the kings of
Israel?

NAHUM

[nā'hum] A prophet of Judah. Little is known of the personal life of Nahum. He is called the "Elkoshite" in *Nah. 1:1*, which would suggest that he was from a locality known as Elkosh. The date of Nahum's prophecy may be fixed somewhere shortly before 612 BC, the date of the fall of the Assyrian capital Nineveh. The prophecy centers on the impending destruction of this city and is of a nationalistic, chauvinistic type, marked by a feeling of satisfaction which almost approaches glee in anticipation of Nineveh's receiving the punishment which is her just due.

SCRIPTURE

Oracle against Nineveh

Nah. 3 1 Woe to the bloody city! it is all
full of lies and robbery; the prey departeth
not; 2 The noise of a whip, and the noise of
the rattling of the wheels, and of the
prancing horses, and of the jumping chariots. 3 The horseman lifteth up both the
bright sword and the glittering spear: and
there is a multitude of slain, and a great
number of carcasses; and there is none end
of their corpses; they stumble upon their
corpses: 4 Because of the multitude of the
whoredoms of the well favoured harlot,
the mistress of witchcrafts, that selleth nations through her whoredoms, and families
through her witchcrafts. 5 Behold, I am
against thee, saith the LORD of hosts; and
I will discover thy skirts upon thy face, and
I will shew the nations thy nakedness, and
the kingdoms thy shame. 6 And I will cast
abominable filth upon thee, and make thee
vile, and will set thee as a gazingstock.
7 And it shall come to pass, that all they
that look upon thee shall flee from thee,
and say, Nineveh is laid waste: who will
bemoan her? whence shall I seek comforters for thee? 11 Thou also shalt be
drunken: thou shalt be hid, thou also shalt
seek strength because of the enemy. 12 All
thy strong holds shall be like fig trees with
the first ripe figs: if they be shaken, they
shall even fall into the mouth of the eater.
13 Behold, thy people in the midst of thee
are women: the gates of thy land shall be
set wide open unto thine enemies: the fire
shall devour thy bars. 18 Thy shepherds
slumber, O king of Assyria: thy nobles
shall dwell in the dust: thy people is scattered upon the mountains, and no man
gathereth them. 19 There is no healing of
thy bruise; thy wound is grievous: all that
hear the bruit of thee shall clap the hands
over thee: for upon whom hath not thy
wickedness passed continually?

NAME

[nām] The word or title by which a person, place, or thing is known. In Biblical times, much more so than in our times, names were regarded as closely related to the nature of the bearer. This was especially true in the case of deity. The Hebrew sanctuary was spoken of as the place where God had recorded his name, or caused his name to be remembered, or the place where he had caused his name to dwell. To refer to God's name is often nothing more than another way of referring to God himself; that is, the name of God signifies the presence of God. This idea is carried over into the New Testament in such phrases as "hallowed be thy name" (*Matt. 6:9*), "blaspheme his name" (*Rev. 13:6*), and "call on the name" (*Acts 2:21;* cf. *Rom. 15:9*). The name of God may also denote the nature, will, or purpose of God (cf. *John 17:6; Acts 9:15*). Most Christian prayers are uttered "in the name of Jesus"; to many, this has come to be nothing more than a phrase little different from a complimentary close of a letter. To pray in the name of Jesus, however, is to pray in the character, spirit, and attitude of Jesus; it implies that we are his representatives on earth and, as such, are united with him and his purposes.

SCRIPTURE

General

Prov. 22 [1]A good name is rather to be chosen than great riches, and loving favor rather than silver and gold.

Eccl. 7 [1]A good name is better than precious ointment; and the day of death than the day of one's birth.

The Name of God

Ex. 6 [3]And I appeared unto Abraham, unto Isaac, and unto Jacob, by the name of God Almighty; but by my name Jehovah was I not known to them.

Psa. 20 [7]Some trust in chariots, and some in horses: but we will remember the name of the LORD our God.

Psa. 83 [18]That men may know that thou, whose name alone is Jehovah, art the Most High over all the earth.

John 17 [6]I have manifested thy name unto the men which thou gavest me out of the world: thine they were, and thou gavest them me; and they have kept thy word.

Acts 9 [15]But the Lord said unto him, Go thy way: for he is a chosen vessel unto me, to bear my name before the Gentiles, and kings, and the children of Israel:

Heb. 13 [15]By him therefore let us offer the sacrifice of praise to God continually, that is, the fruit of our lips, giving thanks to his name.

The Name of Christ

Matt. 18 [20]For where two or three are gathered together in my name, there am I in the midst of them.

1 Cor. 1 [13]Is Christ divided? was Paul crucified for you? or were ye baptized in the name of Paul? [14]I thank God that I baptized none of you, but Crispus and Gaius; [15]Lest any should say that I had baptized in mine own name.

Prayer in Name of Christ

John 14 [13]And whatsoever ye shall ask in my name, that will I do, that the Father may be glorified in the Son. [14]If ye shall ask any thing in my name, I will do it.

John 16 [23]And in that day ye shall ask me nothing. Verily, verily, I say unto you, Whatsoever ye shall ask the Father in my name, he will give it you. [24]Hitherto have ye asked nothing in my name: ask, and ye shall receive, that your joy may be full.

Eph. 5 [20]Giving thanks always for all things unto God, and the Father, in the Name of our Lord Jesus Christ.

Col. 3 [17]And whatsoever ye do in word or deed, do all in the Name of the Lord Jesus, giving thanks to God and the Father, by him.

Miracles in Christ's Name

Acts 3 [6]Then Peter said, Silver and gold have I none, but such as I have, give I thee: In the Name of Jesus Christ of Nazareth, rise up and walk.

Acts 4 [10]Be it known unto you all, and to all the people of Israel, that by the Name of Jesus Christ of Nazareth, whom ye crucified, whom God raised from the dead, even by him, doth this man stand here before you, whole.

Acts 19 [13]Then certain of the vagabond Jews, exorcists, took upon them to call over them which had evil spirits the Name of the Lord Jesus, saying, We adjure you by Jesus whom Paul preacheth. [14]And there were seven sons of one Sceva, a Jew, and chief of the Priests, which did so.

15 And the evil spirit answered, and said,
Jesus I know, and Paul I know, but who
are ye? 16 And the man in whom the evil
spirit was, leapt on them, and overcame
them, and prevailed against them, so that
they fled out of that house naked and
wounded.

NATHAN

[nā'than] A prophet in the time of David and Solomon. Nathan first came to prominence in connection with David's desire to build a temple for the LORD. At first he encouraged the king but later reported a vision in which he had been told that instead, the LORD would establish a house for David in his descendants and that his son and successor would build a house for the LORD.

His next appearance came after David's sin with Bath-sheba, the wife of Uriah the Hittite. Nathan told a parable of a rich man who stole a poor man's only ewe lamb, which he dearly loved. David was incensed at the injustice and demanded that the man be duly punished. Nathan's answer has become classic: "Thou art the man." He then upbraided the king severely and prophesied the death of the child born of the adulterous union.

In *1 Kin. 1*, Nathan appears in a different role —that of a court politician. David was old and feeble and there was a struggle developing between Adonijah and Solomon as to who would succeed to the throne. Adonijah made a great feast and invited a great number of royal officials, conspicuously overlooking Solomon and his supporters, Nathan, Benaiah, Zadok, and the "mighty men." Nathan instructed Bath-sheba to remind the aged king of his promise that Solomon should succeed him; as she spoke to David, Nathan dramatically burst in and announced that Adonijah had been proclaimed king. This stirred David to action and he quickly had Solomon anointed king. For his support in Solomon's campaign for the throne, Nathan escaped the bloodbath which brought an end to Adonijah and his more prominent supporters.

See ADONIJAH, BATH-SHEBA, DAVID, URIAH, etc.

SCRIPTURE

Speaks to David Concerning a Temple

2 Sam. 7 1 And it came to pass, when the
king sat in his house, and the LORD had
given him rest round about from all his enemies; 2 That the king said unto Nathan
the prophet, See now, I dwell in a house
of cedar, but the ark of God dwelleth
within curtains. 3 And Nathan said to the
king, Go, do all that is in thine heart; for
the LORD is with thee.

4 And it came to pass that night, that the
word of the LORD came unto Nathan, saying, 5 Go and tell my servant David, Thus
saith the LORD, Shalt thou build me a
house for me to dwell in?

12 And when thy days be fulfilled, and
thou shalt sleep with thy fathers, I will set
up thy seed after thee, which shall proceed
out of thy bowels, and I will establish his
kingdom. 13 He shall build a house for my
name, and I will stablish the throne of his
kingdom for ever. 17 According to all these
words, and according to all this vision, so
did Nathan speak unto David.

Rebukes David for His Sin

2 Sam. 12 1 And the LORD sent Nathan
unto David. And he came unto him, and
said unto him, There were two men in one
city; the one rich, and the other poor. 2 The
rich man had exceeding many flocks and
herds: 3 But the poor man had nothing,
save one little ewe lamb, which he had
bought and nourished up: and it grew up
together with him, and with his children;
it did eat of his own meat, and drank of his
own cup, and lay in his bosom, and was
unto him as a daughter. 4 And there came
a traveller unto the rich man, and he
spared to take of his own flock and of his

own herd, to dress for the wayfaring man that was come unto him; but took the poor man's lamb, and dressed it for the man that was come to him. 5And David's anger was greatly kindled against the man; and he said to Nathan, As the LORD liveth, the man that hath done this thing shall surely die. 6And he shall restore the lamb fourfold, because he did this thing, and because he had no pity.

7And Nathan said to David, Thou art the man. Thus saith the LORD God of Israel, I anointed thee king over Israel, and I delivered thee out of the hand of Saul: 8And I gave thee thy master's house, and thy master's wives into thy bosom, and gave thee the house of Israel and of Judah; and if that had been too little, I would moreover have given unto thee such and such things. 9Wherefore hast thou despised the commandment of the LORD, to do evil in his sight? thou hast killed Uriah the Hittite with the sword, and hast taken his wife to be thy wife, and hast slain him with the sword of the children of Ammon. 10Now therefore the sword shall never depart from thine house; because thou hast despised me, and hast taken the wife of Uriah the Hittite to be thy wife. 11Thus saith the LORD, Behold, I will raise up evil against thee out of thine own house, and I will take thy wives before thine eyes, and give them unto thy neighbour, and he shall lie with thy wives in the sight of this sun. 12For thou didst it secretly: but I will do this thing before all Israel, and before the sun. 13And David said unto Nathan, I have sinned against the LORD. And Nathan said unto David, The LORD also hath put away thy sin; thou shalt not die. 14Howbeit, because by this deed thou hast given great occasion to the enemies of the LORD to blaspheme, the child also that is born unto thee shall surely die.

15And Nathan departed unto his house. And the LORD struck the child that Uriah's wife bare unto David, and it was very sick.

Supports Solomon against Adonijah

1 Kin. 1 11Wherefore Nathan spake unto Bath-sheba the mother of Solomon, saying, Hast thou not heard that Adonijah the son of Haggith doth reign, and David our lord knoweth it not? 12Now therefore come, let me, I pray thee, give thee counsel, that thou mayest save thine own life, and the life of thy son Solomon. 13Go and get thee in unto king David, and say unto him, Didst not thou, my lord, O king, swear unto thine handmaid, saying, Assuredly Solomon thy son shall reign after me, and he shall sit upon my throne? why then doth Adonijah reign? 14Behold, while thou yet talkest there with the king, I also will come in after thee, and confirm thy words.

22And, lo, while she yet talked with the king, Nathan the prophet also came in. 23And they told the king, saying, Behold Nathan the prophet. And when he was come in before the king, he bowed himself before the king with his face to the ground.

32And king David said, Call me Zadok the priest, and Nathan the prophet, and Benaiah the son of Jehoiada. And they came before the king. 33The king also said unto them, Take with you the servants of your lord, and cause Solomon my son to ride upon mine own mule, and bring him down to Gihon: 34And let Zadok the priest and Nathan the prophet anoint him there king over Israel: and blow ye with the trumpet, and say, God save king Solomon.

NATHANAEL

[na than'â el] A disciple of Jesus, seemingly regarded in the fourth gospel as one of the Twelve.

Nathanael is often identified with Bartholomew, on the following grounds: Nathanael is never mentioned by Matthew, Mark, or Luke, while Bartholomew is never mentioned by John. In the first three gospels, Philip is closely associated with Bartholomew, but in the gospel of John, he is associated with Nathanael. This hypothesis is entirely possible, since most of the apostles had two names. Nathanael was from Cana of Galilee and was brought to the Lord by Philip. When he was first told of Jesus, he expressed his surprise in the famous statement, "Can any good thing come out of Nazareth?" He was paid a remarkable compliment by Jesus who, on first seeing him said, "Behold an Israelites indeed, in whom is no guile!" After a brief conversation Nathanael confessed, "Rabbi, thou art the Son of God; thou art the King of Israel." He appears to have been faithful to his confessed Lord for the remainder of his life.

SCRIPTURE

Chosen to Be Disciple of Jesus

John 1 [45]Philip findeth Nathanael, and saith unto him, We have found him, of whom Moses in the law, and the prophets, did write, Jesus of Nazareth, the son of Joseph. [46]And Nathanael said unto him, Can there any good thing come out of Nazareth? Philip saith unto him, Come and see. [47]Jesus saw Nathanael coming to him, and saith of him, Behold an Israelite indeed, in whom is no guile! [48]Nathanael saith unto him, Whence knowest thou me? Jesus answered and said unto him, Before that Philip called thee, when thou wast under the fig tree, I saw thee. [49]Nathanael answered and saith unto him, Rabbi, thou art the Son of God; thou art the King of Israel.

Witness of the Resurrection

John 21 [2]There were together Simon Peter, and Thomas called Didymus, and Nathanael of Cana in Galilee, and the sons of Zebedee, and two other of his disciples.

NAZARETH

[naz'a reth] A town of Galilee, situated among the southern ridges of Lebanon, just before they sink down into the Plain of Esdraelon. It was the home of Joseph, Mary, and Jesus. Although his birthplace was actually Bethlehem, Jesus was referred to as Jesus of Nazareth, and his followers were for a long time called Nazarenes.

SCRIPTURE

Matt. 2 [23]And he came and dwelt in a city called Nazareth: that it might be fulfilled which was spoken by the prophets, He shall be called a Nazarene.

Matt. 21 [11]And the multitude said, This is Jesus the prophet of Nazareth of Galilee.

John 1 [46]And Nathanael said unto him, Can there any good thing come out of Nazareth? Philip saith unto him, Come and see.

Acts 24 [5]For we have found this man a pestilent fellow, and a mover of sedition among all the Jews throughout the world, and ringleader of the sect of the Nazarenes.

See Mark 1:9, 24; 10:47; Luke 2:39, 41, etc.

NAZIRITE

[naz'i rīt] An individual who consecrated himself to the LORD and took a special vow of separation. During the period of his vow, the Nazirite was forbidden to eat or drink of any product of the vine, to cut his hair or beard, to touch a dead body, and to eat unclean food. At the close of the period of consecration, he made various offerings, shaved his head and burnt the hair, after which he returned to normal life. If the vow was accidentally violated at any time before its completion, the entire process had to be repeated from the beginning.

SCRIPTURE

Num. 6 [1]And the LORD spake unto Moses, saying, [2]Speak unto the children of Israel, and say unto them, When either man or woman shall separate themselves to vow a vow of a Nazarite, to separate themselves unto the LORD; [3]He shall separate himself from wine and strong drink, and shall drink no vinegar of wine, or vinegar of strong drink, neither shall he drink any liquor of grapes, nor eat moist grapes, or dried. [4]All the days of his separation shall he eat nothing that is made of the vine tree, from the kernals even to the husk. [5]All the days of the vow of his separation there shall no razor come upon his head: until the days be fulfilled, in the which he separateth himself unto the LORD, he shall be holy, and shall let the locks of the hair of his head grow. [6]All the days that he separateth himself unto the LORD he shall come at no dead body. [7]He shall not make himself unclean for his father, or for his mother, for his brother, or for his sister, when they die: because the consecration of his God is upon his head. [8]All the days of his separation he is holy unto the LORD.

Judg. 13 [5]For, lo, thou shalt conceive, and bear a son; and no razor shall come on his head: for the child shall be a Nazarite unto God from the womb: and he shall begin to deliver Israel out of the hand of the Philistines.

[6]Then the woman came and told her husband, saying, A man of God came unto me, and his countenance was like the countenance of an angel of God, very terrible: but I asked him not whence he was, neither told he me his name: [7]But he said unto me, Behold, thou shalt conceive, and bear a son; and now drink no wine nor strong drink, neither eat any unclean thing: for the child shall be a Nazarite to God from the womb to the day of his death.

Judg. 16 [17]That he told her all his heart, and said unto her, There hath not come a razor upon mine head; for I have been a Nazarite unto God from my mother's womb: if I be shaven, then my strength will go from me, and I shall become weak, and be like any other man.

Amos 2 [11]And I raised up of your sons for prophets, and of your young men for Nazarites. Is it not even thus, O ye children of Israel? saith the LORD. [12]But ye gave the Nazarites wine to drink; and commanded the prophets, saying, Prophesy not.

See Num. 6:9-21

NEBO

[nē'bō] The mountain from which Moses took his first and last view of the Promised Land. It is described as in the land of Moab, facing Jericho, and is apparently identical with the "top of Pisgah." It has not been possible to settle on its exact location.

SCRIPTURE

Deut. 32 [49]Get thee up into this mountain Abarim, unto mount Nebo, which is in the land of Moab, that is over against Jericho; and behold the land of Canaan, which I give unto the children of Israel for a possession:

Deut. 34 [1]And Moses went up from the plains of Moab unto the mountain of Nebo, to the top of Pisgah, that is over against Jericho. And the LORD shewed him all the land of Gilead, unto Dan,

NEBUCHADNEZZAR

[neb'yo͞o k'd nez'ẽr] (Also called Nebuchadrezzar) King of Babylonia (605-562 BC), son of Nabopolassar and father of Evil-Merodach. In 605 BC, Nebuchadnezzar defeated Pharaoh Necho II at Carchemish, thus gaining control over Syria and Palestine. Jehoiakim king of Judah, who had been placed on the throne by Pharaoh Necho, quickly submitted to Nebuchadnezzar. Whatever plans Nebuchadnezzar might have had for further activity in the West was thwarted by the death of his father, which necessitated his return to Babylon. Shortly afterward, he returned to Jerusalem and received tribute from Jehoiakim. In 597 BC, Jehoiakim was succeeded by his son Jehoiachin. Within a few weeks after Jehoiachin's accession, Nebuchadnezzar again marched on Jerusalem, stripping it of many of its treasures and carrying a number of its inhabitants, including Jehoiachin, into captivity. In 586 BC, Nebuchadnezzar laid siege to Jerusalem for the second time, destroying it completely and taking thousands of its citizens to Babylonia.

The history of the remainder of Nebuchadnezzar's long reign is less well-known than that of the early years. Doubtless his rule was strengthened by his marriage to the daughter of the king of the powerful kingdom of the Medes. Nebuchadnezzar is also remembered for his having built the famous hanging gardens, one of the seven wonders of the ancient world.

SCRIPTURE

2 Kin. 24 [1]In his days Nebuchadnezzar
king of Babylon came up, and Jehoiakim
became his servant three years: then he
turned and rebelled against him.
[11]And Nebuchadnezzar king of Babylon
came against the city, and his servants did
besiege it. [12]And Jehoiachin the king of
Judah went out to the king of Babylon, he,
and his mother, and his servants, and his
princes, and his officers: and the king of
Babylon took him in the eighth year of his
reign. [13]And he carried out thence all the
treasures of the house of the LORD, and the
treasures of the king's house, and cut in
pieces all the vessels of gold which Solomon king of Israel had made in the temple
of the LORD, as the LORD had said. [14]And
he carried away all Jerusalem, and all the
princes, and all the mighty men of valour,
even ten thousand captives, and all the
craftsmen and smiths: none remained,
save the poorest sort of the people of the
land. [15]And he carried away Jehoiachin to
Babylon, and the king's mother, and the
king's wives, and his officers, and the
mighty of the land, those carried he into
captivity from Jerusalem to Babylon.
[16]And all the men of might, even seven
thousand, and craftsmen and smiths a
thousand, all that were strong and apt for
war, even them the king of Babylon
brought captive to Babylon.

2 Kin. 25 [1]And it came to pass in the
ninth year of his reign, in the tenth month,
in the tenth day of the month, that Nebuchadnezzar king of Babylon came, he, and
all his host, against Jerusalem, and pitched
against it; and they built forts against it
round about. [2]And the city was besieged
unto the eleventh year of king Zedekiah.
[3]And on the ninth day of the fourth month
the famine prevailed in the city, and there
was no bread for the people of the land.
[4]And the city was broken up, and all the
men of war fled by night by the way of the
gate between two walls, which is by the
king's garden: (now the Chaldees were
against the city round about:) and the
king went the way toward the plain. [5]And
the army of the Chaldees pursued after
the king, and overtook him in the plains of
Jericho: and all his army were scattered
from him. [6]So they took the king, and
brought him up to the king of Babylon to
Riblah; and they gave judgment upon him.
[7]And they slew the sons of Zedekiah before his eyes, and put out the eyes of Zedekiah, and bound him with fetters of brass,
and carried him to Babylon.

NEHEMIAH

[nē hē mī'a] The reorganization of the Jewish community after the return from Babylonian exile was largely the work of two men: Nehemiah and Ezra. Ezra's task was to reconstitute the Jewish community on the basis of the law of God. Nehemiah's was to provide political and administrative stability. Nehemiah's career as a leader of Israel began in the twentieth year of

Artaxerxes I, or 445 BC. Disturbed at a report of the deplorable conditions in Judah, he petitioned the king, whom he served as cupbearer, to allow him to go to Jerusalem and take such steps as might be necessary to put the city on a sound footing. The stability of Judah was of considerable advantage to the Persian king and he quickly acceded to Nehemiah's request, making him governor of the province and granting him supplies to carry out the task of rebuilding the wall of Jerusalem. By 440 BC, Nehemiah had arrived in Jerusalem and, after an inspection of the wall, had set about to rebuild it. In spite of harassment of the most persistant and troublesome sort led by Sanballat, Tobiah, and Geshem, the work was finally brought to completion. In his two terms as governor of the province, Nehemiah brought about a number of desperately needed reforms; political, social and religious. His advocacy of strict Jewish purity doubtlessly proved helpful in enforcing the reforms which took place under Ezra.

See EZRA, GESHEM, SANBALLAT, TOBIAH

SCRIPTURE

Obtains Permission to Return to Jerusalem

Neh. 2 1And it came to pass in the month Nisan, in the twentieth year of Artaxerxes the king, that wine was before him: and I took up the wine, and gave it unto the king. Now I had not been beforetime sad in his presence. 2Wherefore the king said unto me, Why is thy countenance sad, seeing thou art not sick? this is nothing else but sorrow of heart. Then I was very sore afraid, 3And said unto the king, Let the king live for ever: why should not my countenance be sad, when the city, the place of my fathers' sepulchres, lieth waste, and the gates thereof are consumed with fire? 4Then the king said unto me, For what dost thou make request? So I prayed to the God of heaven. 5And I said unto the king, If it please the king, and if thy servant have found favour in thy sight, that thou wouldest send me unto Judah, unto the city of my fathers' sepulchres, that I may build it. 6And the king said unto me, (the queen also sitting by him,) For how long shall thy journey be? and when wilt thou return? So it pleased the king to send me; and I set him a time. 7Moreover I said unto the king, If it please the king, let letters be given me to the governors beyond the river, that they may convey me over till I come into Judah; 8And a letter unto Asaph the keeper of the king's forest, that he may give me timber to make beams for the gates of the palace which appertained to the house, and for the wall of the city, and for the house that I shall enter into. And the king granted me, according to the good hand of my God upon me.

11So I came to Jerusalem, and was there three days.

Rebuilds the Wall of Jerusalem

Neh. 4 6So built we the wall; and all the wall was joined together unto the half thereof: for the people had a mind to work.

7But it came to pass, that when Sanballat, and Tobiah, and the Arabians, and the Ammonites, and the Ashdodites, heard that the walls of Jerusalem were made up, and that the breaches began to be stopped, then they were very wroth. 8And conspired all of them together to come and to fight against Jerusalem, and to hinder it.

13Therefore set I in the lower places behind the wall, and on the higher places, I even set the people after their families with their swords, their spears, and their bows. 16And it came to pass from that time forth, that the half of my servants wrought in the work, and the other half of them held both the spears, the shields, and the bows, and the habergeons; and the rulers were behind all the house of Judah. 17 They which builded on the wall, and they that bare burdens, with those that laded, every one with one of his hands wrought in the work, and with the other hand held a weapon. 18 For the builders, every one had his sword girded by his side, and so builded. And he that sounded the trumpet was by me.

23 So neither I, nor my brethren, nor my servants, nor the men of the guard which followed me, none of us put off our clothes, saving that every one put them off for washing.

Neh. 6 15 So the wall was finished in the twenty and fifth day of the month Elul, in fifty and two days. 16 And it came to pass, that when all our enemies heard thereof, and all the heathen that were about us saw these things, they were much cast down in their own eyes: for they perceived that this work was wrought of our God.

Reforms Effected by Nehemiah

Neh. 13 6 But in all this time was not I at Jerusalem: for in the two and thirtieth year of Artaxerxes king of Babylon came I unto the king, and after certain days obtained I leave of the king: 7 And I came to Jerusalem, and understood of the evil that Eliashib did for Tobiah, in preparing him a chamber in the courts of the house of God. 8 And it grieved me sore: therefore I cast forth all the household stuff of Tobiah out of the chamber. 9 Then I commanded, and they cleansed the chambers: and thither brought I again the vessels of the house of God, with the meat offering and the frankincense.

10 And I perceived that the portions of the Levites had not been given them: for the Levites and the singers, that did the work, were fled every one to his field. 11 Then contended I with the rulers and said, Why is the house of God forsaken? And I gathered them together, and set them in their place. 12 Then brought all Judah the tithe of the corn and the new wine and the oil unto the treasuries. 13 And I made treasurers over the treasuries, Shelemiah the priest, and Zadok the scribe, and of the Levites, Pedaiah: and next to them was Hanan the son of Zaccur, the son of Mattaniah: for they were counted faithful, and their office was to distribute unto their brethren. 14 Remember me, O my God, concerning this, and wipe not out my good deeds that I have done for the house of my God, and for the officers thereof.

15 In those days saw I in Judah some treading winepresses on the sabbath, and bringing in sheaves, and lading asses; as also wine, grapes, and figs, and all manner of burdens, which they brought into Jerusalem on the sabbath day: and I testified against them in the day wherein they sold victuals. 16 There dwelt men of Tyre also therein, which brought fish, and all manner of ware, and sold on the sabbath unto the children of Judah, and in Jerusalem. 17 Then I contended with the nobles of Judah, and said unto them, What evil thing is this that ye do, and profane the sabbath day? 18 Did not your fathers thus, and did not our God bring all this evil upon us, and upon this city? yet ye bring more wrath upon Israel by profaning the sabbath. 19 And it came to pass, that when the gates of Jerusalem began to be dark before the sabbath, I commanded that the gates should be shut, and charged that they should not be opened till after the sabbath: and some of my servants set I at the gates, that there should no burden be brought in on the sabbath day. 20 So the merchants and sellers of all kind of ware

lodged without Jerusalem once or twice. [21]Then I testified against them, and said unto them, Why lodge ye about the wall? if ye do so again, I will lay hands on you. From that time forth came they no more on the sabbath. [22]And I commanded the Levites, that they should cleanse themselves, and that they should come and keep the gates, to sanctify the sabbath day. Remember me, O my God, concerning this also, and spare me according to the greatness of thy mercy.

[23]In those days also saw I Jews that had married wives of Ashdod, of Ammon, and of Moab: [24]And their children spake half in the speech of Ashdod, and could not speak in the Jews' language, but according to the language of each people. [25]And I contended with them, and cursed them, and smote certain of them, and plucked off their hair, and made them swear by God, saying, Ye shall not give your daughters unto their sons, nor take their daughters unto your sons, or for yourselves. [30]Thus cleansed I them from all strangers, and appointed the wards of the priests and the Levites, every one in his business;

NEIGHBOR

[nā'bẽr] In the Old Testament, this word signified one related by the bond of nationality or religion; specifically, another Israelite. This near equation of the neighbor with the brother, or fellow-covenanter, is essentially retained in the New Testament despite popular belief to the contrary. Virtually all New Testament statements which treat of one's duty to his neighbor are in reference to relations between Christians and not between Christians and non-Christians.

The parable of the Good Samaritan has often been cited as evidence that the neighbor is anyone who is in need; the main point of the parable, however, is not that the wounded man was a neighbor, but that the Samaritan proved himself a neighbor, or brother, through his charitable action. This is not to be taken to mean that the Christian bears no responsibility to the non-Christian. To be sure, the New Testament clearly implies that we are to show due regard for the rights and needs of our fellowmen, as expressed by Paul in *Gal. 6:10*—"Do good to all men." But even this statement has the corollary "especially unto them that are of the household of faith."

SCRIPTURE

Ex. 20 [16]Thou shalt not bear false witness against thy neighbour. [17]Thou shalt not covet thy neighbour's house, thou shalt not covet thy neighbour's wife, nor his manservant, nor his maidservant, nor his ox, nor his ass, nor any thing that is thy neighbour's.

Lev. 19 [18]Thou shalt not avenge, nor bear any grudge against the children of thy people, but thou shalt love thy neighbour as thyself: I am the LORD.

Deut. 27 [17]Cursed be he that removeth his neighbour's landmark: and all the people shall say, Amen.

Prov. 3 [28]Say not unto thy neighbour, Go, and come again, and to-morrow I will give; when thou hast it by thee.

Prov. 24 [28]Be not a witness against thy neighbour without cause; and deceive not with thy lips. [29]Say not, I will do so to him as he hath done to me: I will render to the man according to his work.

Prov. 25 [8]Go not forth hastily to strive, lest thou know not what to do in the end thereof, when thy neighbour hath put thee to shame. [17]Withdraw thy foot from thy neighbour's house; lest he be weary of thee, and so hate thee. [18]A man that beareth false witness against his neighbour is a maul, and a sword, and a sharp arrow.

Mark 12 [31]And the second is like, namely this, Thou shalt love thy neighbour as thyself. There is none other commandment greater than these. [32]And the scribe said unto him, Well, Master, thou

hast said the truth: for there is one God;
and there is none other but he: 33 And to
love him with all the heart, and with all
the understanding, and with all the soul,
and with all the strength, and to love his
neighbour as himself, is more than all
whole burnt offerings and sacrifices.
34 And when Jesus saw that he answered
discreetly, he said unto him, Thou art not
far from the kingdom of God. And no man
after that durst ask him any question.

Rom. 13 9 For this, Thou shalt not commit adultery, Thou shalt not kill, Thou
shalt not steal, Thou shalt not bear false
witness, Thou shalt not covet; and if there
be any other commandment, it is briefly
comprehended in this saying, namely,
Thou shalt love thy neighbour as thyself.
10 Love worketh no ill to his neighbour:
therefore love is the fulfilling of the law.

Gal. 5 14 For all the law is fulfilled in one
word, even in this; Thou shalt love thy
neighbour as thyself. 15 But if ye bite and
devour one another, take heed that ye be
not consumed one of another.

Jas. 2 8 If ye fulfil the royal law, according to the Scripture, Thou shalt love thy
neighbour as thyself, ye do well.

NERO

[nē′rō] Emperor of Rome (AD 54-68). His mother, Agrippina, was married to the Emperor Claudius I. (*See* CLAUDIUS) Through her machinations, Nero became the adopted son and son-in-law of Claudius and gained the throne when she poisoned Claudius in AD 54. Nero was a vain and cowardly ruler who fancied himself a musician and poet. The early years of his reign were successful, due to the efforts of his able advisers. After about five years, however these had passed from the scene and Nero's true colors began to appear. In AD 64, a nine-day fire destroyed a great portion of Rome. Persistent tradition has it that Nero himself was responsible for starting the fire. Whether this is true or not, he shifted the blame to the suspicious group of people known as Christians and instigated a rather severe persecution of this new religion. Some were covered with the skins of animals and torn by dogs, while others were covered with pitch and burned as torches in Nero's garden. The historian Tacitus makes it clear that the Christians were generally regarded as innocent victims of the excessive cruelty of a warped monster in need of a scapegoat.

In AD 68, the governors of Africa, Gaul, and Spain revolted; when Nero learned of this, he fled from the city and committed suicide. Nero was the Caesar to whom Paul appealed (*Acts 25: 11*) and by whom he was probably executed. There is a strong tradition that the apostle Peter also met his death at the hands of this ruler.

NICODEMUS

[nik ô dē′mus] A Pharisee and a "ruler of the Jews." He was impressed by Jesus' teachings, but being afraid to seek Him openly, paid a visit by night to receive further instruction from the Master and was taught the doctrine of the New Birth. There is no record of his having openly declared himself a follower of Jesus, but that he remained in sympathy with his work is evident in his defence of the Lord before the Sanhedrin and in his assisting Joseph of Arimathea in Jesus' burial.

SCRIPTURE

Comes to Jesus by Night

John 3 1 There was a man of the Pharisees, named Nicodemus, a ruler of the
Jews: 2 The same came to Jesus by night,
and said unto him, Rabbi, we know that
thou art a teacher come from God: for no
man can do these miracles that thou doest,
except God be with him. 3 Jesus answered
and said unto him, Verily, verily, I say
unto thee, Except a man be born again,
he cannot see the kingdom of God. 4 Nicodemus saith unto him, How can a man be
born when he is old? can he enter the second time into his mother's womb, and be
born? 5 Jesus answered, Verily, verily, I
say unto thee, Except a man be born of

water and of the Spirit, he cannot enter into the kingdom of God. [9]Nicodemus answered and said unto him, How can these things be? [10]Jesus answered and said unto him, Art thou a master of Israel, and knowest not these things? [11]Verily, verily, I say unto thee, We speak that we do know, and testify that we have seen; and ye receive not our witness. [12]If I have told you earthly things, and ye believe not, how shall ye believe, if I tell you of heavenly things? [13]And no man hath ascended up to heaven, but he that came down from heaven, even the Son of man which is in heaven.

Defends Jesus

John 7 [45]Then came the officers to the chief priests and Pharisees; and they said unto them, Why have ye not brought him? [46]The officers answered, Never man spake like this man. [47]Then answered them the Pharisees, Are ye also deceived? [48]Have any of the rulers or of the Pharisees believed on him? [49]But this people who knoweth not the law are cursed. [50]Nicodemus saith unto them, (he that came to Jesus by night, being one of them,) [51]Doth our law judge any man, before it hear him, and know what he doeth? [52]They answered and said unto him, Art thou also of Galilee? Search, and look: for out of Galilee ariseth no prophet. [53]And every man went unto his own house.

Assists in Jesus' Burial

John 19 [39]And there came also Nicodemus, which at the first came to Jesus by night, and brought a mixture of myrrh and aloes, about an hundred pound weight. [40]Then took they the body of Jesus, and wound it in linen clothes with the spices, as the manner of the Jews is to bury. [41]Now in the place where he was crucified there was a garden; and in the garden a new sepulchre, wherein was never man yet laid. [42]There laid they Jesus therefore because of the Jews' preparation day; for the sepulchre was nigh at hand.

NICOLAITANS

[nik ô lā'i tanz] A sect or party of evil influence in early Christianity, mentioned in *Rev. 2:6, 15.* Although we cannot be certain, it appears that the Nicolaitans held that it was lawful "to eat things sacrificed to idols and to commit fornication." The church in Ephesus is praised for "hating their works", while the church at Pergamum is censured for having in its number those who accepted the teaching and practice of the Nicolaitans.

SCRIPTURE

Rev. 2 [6]But this thou hast, that thou hatest the deeds of the Nicolaitans, which I also hate. [15]So hast thou also them that hold the doctrine of the Nicolaitans, which thing I hate.

NIGHT

[nīt] Literally, the time from dusk to dawn, when no light of the sun is visable; used often in Scripture in a figurative sense, either to express intellectual, moral, or spiritual darkness or the time of the end of one's activity.

SCRIPTURE

General

Gen. 1 [5]And God called the light Day, and the darkness he called Night: and the evening and the morning were the first day.

Psa. 19 [2]Day unto day uttereth speech, and night unto night sheweth knowledge.

Rev. 21 [25]And the gates of it shall not be shut at all by day: for there shall be no night there.

Isa. 60 [20]Thy sun shall no more go

down; neither shall thy moon withdraw itself: for the LORD shall be thine everlasting light, and the days of thy mourning shall be ended.

Spiritual Night

Rom. 13 [12]The night is far spent, the day is at hand: let us therefore cast off the works of darkness, and let us put on the armour of light.

1 Thess. 5 [5]Ye are all the children of light, and the children of the day: we are not of the night nor of darkness. [6]Therefore let us not sleep, as do others; but let us watch and be sober. [7]For they that sleep, sleep in the night; and they that be drunken are drunken in the night.

The End of Labor

John 9 [4]I must work the works of him that sent me, while it is day: the night cometh, when no man can work.

NIMROD

[nim'rod] An Old Testament character described as "a mighty hunter before the LORD" and a builder of cities.

SCRIPTURE

Gen. 10 [8]And Cush begat Nimrod: he began to be a mighty one in the earth. [9]He was a mighty hunter before the LORD: wherefore it is said, Even as Nimrod the mighty hunter before the LORD.

1 Chr. 1 [10]And Cush begat Nimrod: he began to be mighty upon the earth.

NINEVEH

[nin'ĕ ve] The capital city of the Assyrian empire. Nineveh was located on the eastern bank of the Tigris River, at the point where it is joined by the Khost. It was destroyed in 612 BC by the Medo-Babylonian forces led by Cyarxes and Nabopolassar. Nineveh figures prominently in the prophetic books of *Jonah* and *Nahum*; the former contains an account of the city's reception of Jonah's message of repentance and the latter is a song of jubilation over its destruction.

See JONAH, NAHUM, ASSYRIA and related articles

NOAH

[nō'ah] One of the best-known characters in the Bible, Noah is pictured as a righteous man in the midst of a wicked generation. For his righteousness, Noah and his family were chosen by God to be spared from the destruction of civilization in the Flood. According to the divine commands, Noah built an ark and gathered specimens of the various kinds of animal life. After the deluge God made a covenant with Noah in which He pledged never again to destroy civilization by water. The narrative states that the rainbow was given as a sign of this covenant.

The last recorded episode of Noah's life pictures him in a less favorable light. He is seen to have become drunk on the wine from his vineyard. His youngest son, Ham, irreverently exposed the nakedness of his father; as a result, Noah placed a curse on the descendants of Ham to the effect that they would be the slaves and servants of the descendants of Noah's other two sons, Shem and Japheth.

See ARK, FLOOD, HAM, JAPHETH, RAINBOW, SHEM

SCRIPTURE

Gen. 5 [28]And Lamech lived a hundred eighty and two years, and begat a son: [29]And he called his name Noah, saying, This same shall comfort us concerning our work and toil of our hands, because of the ground which the LORD hath cursed.

Gen. 6 [7]And the LORD said, I will destroy man whom I have created from the face of the earth; both man and beast, and the creeping thing, and the fowls of the air; for it repenteth me that I have made them. [8]But Noah found grace in the eyes of the LORD.

[9]These are the generations of Noah:

Noah was a just man and perfect in his generations, and Noah walked with God. [10]And Noah begat three sons, Shem, Ham, and Japheth. [11]The earth also was corrupt before God; and the earth was filled with violence. [12]And God looked upon the earth, and behold, it was corrupt; for all flesh had corrupted his way upon the earth. [13]And God said unto Noah, The end of all flesh is come before me; for the earth is filled with violence through them; and behold, I will destroy them with the earth.

[14]Make thee an ark of gopher wood; rooms shalt thou make in the ark, and shalt pitch it within and without with pitch.

Gen. 7 [1]And the LORD said unto Noah, Come thou and all thy house into the ark; for thee have I seen righteous before me in this generation. [2]Of every clean beast thou shalt take to thee by sevens, the male and his female: and of beasts that are not clean by two, the male and his female. [3]Of fowls also of the air by sevens, the male and the female; to keep seed alive upon the face of all the earth. [6]And Noah was six hundred years old when the flood of waters was upon the earth.

[7]And Noah went in, and his sons, and his wife, and his sons' wives with him, into the ark, because of the waters of the flood.

Gen. 8 [14]And in the second month, on the seven and twentieth day of the month, was the earth dried.

[15]And God spake unto Noah, saying, [16]Go forth of the ark, thou, and thy wife, and thy sons, and thy sons' wives with thee. [17]Bring forth with thee every living thing that is with thee, of all flesh, both of fowl, and of cattle, and of every creeping thing that creepeth upon the earth; that they may breed abundantly in the earth, and be fruitful, and multiply upon the earth. [18]And Noah went forth, and his sons, and his wife, and his sons' wives with him: [19]Every beast, every creeping thing, and every fowl, and whatsoever creepeth upon the earth, after their kinds, went forth out of the ark.

[20]And Noah builded an altar unto the LORD; and took of every clean beast, and of every clean fowl, and offered burnt offerings on the altar.

Gen. 9 [20]And Noah began to be a husbandman, and he planted a vineyard: [21]And he drank of the wine, and was drunken; and he was uncovered within his tent. [22]And Ham, the father of Canaan, saw the nakedness of his father, and told his two brethren without. [23]And Shem and Japheth took a garment, and laid it upon both their shoulders, and went backward, and covered the nakedness of their father; and their faces were backward, and they saw not their father's nakedness. [24]And Noah awoke from his wine, and knew what his younger son had done unto him. [25]And he said, Cursed be Canaan; a servant of servants shall he be unto his brethren. [26]And he said, Blessed be the LORD God of Shem; and Canaan shall be his servant. [27]God shall enlarge Japheth, and he shall dwell in the tents of Shem; and Canaan shall be his servant.

[28]And Noah lived after the flood three hundred and fifty years. [29]And all the days of Noah were nine hundred and fifty years: and he died.

NOB

[nob] An ancient priestly town in the territory of Benjamin. When David was a fugitive from the jealous king Saul, he fled to Nob and found refuge with Ahimelech the high priest, who fed him with the shewbread from the tabernacle and gave him the sword which had belonged to Goliath (*1 Sam. 21:1-9*). Doeg the Edomite witnessed this and, on reporting it to Saul, was com-

missioned to take vengeance on the city of Nob. We are told that Doeg "fell upon the priests, and slew on that day fourscore and five persons that did wear a linen ephod. (*See* EPHOD) And Nob, the city of the priests, smote he with the edge of the sword, both men and women, children and sucklings, and oxen, and asses, and sheep, with the edge of the sword" (*1 Sam. 22:18-19*).

See ABIATHAR

SCRIPTURE

David Flees to Nob

1 Sam. 21 [1]Then came David to Nob to Ahimelech the priest: and Ahimelech was afraid at the meeting of David, and said unto him, Why art thou alone, and no man with thee? [2]And David said unto Ahimelech the priest, The king hath commanded me a business, and hath said unto me, Let no man know any thing of the business whereabout I send thee, and what I have commanded thee: and I have appointed my servants to such and such a place. [3]Now therefore what is under thine hand? give me five loaves of bread in mine hand, or what there is present. [4]And the priest answered David, and said, There is no common bread under mine hand, but there is hallowed bread; if the young men have kept themselves at least from women. [5]And David answered the priest, and said unto him, Of a truth women have been kept from us about these three days, since I came out, and the vessels of the young men are holy, and the bread is in a manner common, yea, though it were sanctified this day in the vessel. [6]So the priest gave him hallowed bread: for there was no bread there but the shewbread, that was taken from before the LORD, to put hot bread in the day when it was taken away. [7]Now a certain man of the servants of Saul was there that day, detained before the LORD; and his name was Doeg, an Edomite, the chiefest of the herdmen that belonged to Saul.

[8]And David said unto Ahimelech, And is there not here under thine hand spear or sword? for I have neither brought my sword nor my weapons with me, because the king's business required haste. [9]And the priest said, The sword of Goliath the Philistine, whom thou slewest in the valley of Elah, behold, it is here wrapped in a cloth behind the ephod: if thou wilt take that, take it: for there is no other save that here. And David said, There is none like that; give it me.

Destroyed by Order of Saul

1 Sam. 22 [18]And the king said to Doeg, Turn thou, and fall upon the priests. And Doeg the Edomite turned, and he fell upon the priests, and slew on that day fourscore and five persons that did wear a linen ephod. [19]And Nob, the city of the priests, smote he with the edge of the sword, both men and women, children and sucklings, and oxen, and asses, and sheep, with the edge of the sword.

OATH

[ōth] A solemn appeal to God or other revered person or object as a means of attesting the truth of one's word; the invoking of a curse on oneself if one has not spoken the truth or fails to keep a promise. Israelite Law sought to impress upon the people the sacredness of an oath, forbidding the swearing of a false oath and swearing by a false god. Since there is no evidence the profanity was a serious evil in this period, it is quite likely that the third commandment of the Decalogue (*see* DECALOGUE) is a prohibition against speaking the name of the LORD without result—without doing what is vowed. The fundamental idea of this commandment was probably an injunction against breaking an oath. Oaths were sworn in the name of the LORD, by the life of the king (*1 Sam. 17:55; 25:26; 2 Sam. 11:11*), by heaven (*Matt. 5:34; 23:22*), by the earth (*Matt. 5:35*), by one's own head or life (*Matt. 5:36*), by the temple, and by articles in it (*Matt. 23:16*). Jesus' command in *Matt 5:34* to "swear not at all" was probably not intended to imply that oaths in themselves are sinful (*see*, for example *Matt. 26:63-64; 2 Cor. 1:23; Gal. 1:20; Heb. 6:13-18*), but to assert that the Christian has no double standard of truth, that is, his simple affirmative or negative is just as binding as any oath he might make.

SCRIPTURE

General

Ex. 20 [7]Thou shalt not take the name of
the LORD thy God in vain: for the LORD
will not hold him guiltless that taketh his
name in vain.

Ex. 22 [11]Then shall an oath of the LORD
be between them both, that he hath not
put his hand unto his neighbor's goods;
and the owner of it shall accept thereof,
and he shall not make it good.

Lev. 5 [1]And if a soul sin, and hear the
voice of swearing, and is a witness,
whether he hath seen or known of it; if
he do not utter it, then he shall bear his iniquity.

Lev. 6 [2]If a soul sin, and commit a trespass against the LORD, and lie unto his
neighbor in that which was delivered him
to keep, or in fellowship, or in a thing taken
away by violence, or hath deceived his
neighbor; [3]Or have found that which was
lost, and lieth concerning it, and sweareth
falsely; in any of all these that a man doeth, sinning therein: [5]Or all that about
which he hath sworn falsely; he shall even
restore it in the principal, and shall add
the fifth part more thereto, and give it unto
him to whom it appertaineth, in the day of
his trespass offering.

Lev. 19 [12]And ye shall not swear by my
name falsely, neither shalt thou profane
the name of thy God: I am the LORD.

Jer. 12 [16]And it shall come to pass, if
they will diligently learn the ways of my
people, to swear by my name, The LORD
liveth; as they taught my people to swear
by Baal; then shall they be built in the
midst of my people.

Amos 8 [14]They that swear by the sin of
Samaria, and say, Thy god, O Dan, liveth;
and, The manner of Beer-sheba liveth;
even they shall fall, and never rise up
again.

Matt. 5 [33]Again, ye have heard that it
hath been said by them of old time, Thou
shalt not forswear thyself, but shalt perform unto the Lord thine oaths: [34]But I
say unto you, Swear not at all; neither by
heaven; for it is God's throne: [35]Nor by the
earth; for it is his footstool: neither by Jerusalem; for it is the city of the great King.
[36]Neither shalt thou swear by thy head, because thou canst not make one hair white
or black. [37]But let your communication
be, Yea, yea; Nay, nay: for whatsoever is
more than these cometh of evil.

Matt. 23 [18]And, Whosoever shall swear
by the altar, it is nothing; but whosoever
sweareth by the gift that is upon it, he is
guilty. [19]Ye fools and blind: for whether is
greater, the gold, or the temple that sanctifieth the gold? [20]Whoso therefore shall
swear by the altar, sweareth by it, and by
all things thereon. [21]And whoso shall
swear by the temple, sweareth by it, and
by him that dwelleth therein. [22]And he
that shall swear by heaven, sweareth by
the throne of God, and by him that sitteth
thereon.

Jas. 5 [12]But above all things, my brethren, swear not, neither by heaven, neither
by the earth, neither by any other oath:
but let your yea by yea; and your nay, nay;
lest ye fall into condemnation.

Examples of Oaths

Gen. 14 [22]And Abram said to the king of

Sodom, I have lifted up mine hand unto the LORD, the most high God, the possessor of heaven and earth, [23]That I will not take from a thread even to a shoe-latchet, and that I will not take any thing that is thine, lest thou shouldest say, I have made Abram rich:

Gen. 25 [33]And Jacob said, Swear to me this day; and he sware unto him: and he sold his birthright unto Jacob.

Judg. 11 [10]And the elders of Gilead said unto Jephthah, The LORD be witness between us, if we do not so according to thy words.

1 Kin. 1 [28]Then king David answered and said, Call me Bath-sheba. And she came into the king's presence, and stood before the king. [29]And the king sware, and said, As the LORD liveth, that hath redeemed my soul out of all distress,

Matt. 26 [71]And when he was gone out into the porch, another maid saw him, and said unto them that were there, This fellow was also with Jesus of Nazareth. [72]And again he denied with an oath, I do not know the man. [73]And after a while came unto him they that stood by, and said to Peter, Surely thou also art one of them; for thy speech bewrayeth thee. [74]Then began he to curse and to swear, saying, I know not the man.

2 Cor. 1 [23]Moreover I call God for a record upon my soul, that to spare you I came not as yet unto Corinth.

Gal. 1 [20]Now the things which I write unto you, behold, before God, I lie not.

Heb. 6 [13]For when God made promise to Abraham, because he could swear by no greater, he sware by himself, [14]Saying, Surely blessing I will bless thee, and multiplying I will multiply thee. [15]And so, after he had patiently endured, he obtained the promise. [16]For men verily swear by the greater: and an oath for confirmation is to them an end of all strife. [17]Wherein God, willing more abundantly to show unto the heirs of promise the immutability of his counsel, confirmed it by an oath: [18]That by two immutable things, in which it was impossible for God to lie, we might have a strong consolation, who have fled for refuge to lay hold upon the hope set before us:

OBADIAH

[ō ba dī'a] The name of several characters in the Bible, the most important of whom is the prophet Obadiah, whose book has as its theme the destruction of Edom.

See EDOM, EDOMITES

SCRIPTURE

Oracle Concerning Edom

Obad. 1 [1]The vision of Obadiah. Thus saith the Lord GOD concerning Edom; We have heard a rumour from the LORD, and an ambassador is sent among the heathen, Arise ye, and let us rise up against her in battle. [2]Behold, I have made thee small among the heathen: thou art greatly despised.

[3]The pride of thine heart hath deceived thee, thou that dwellest in the clefts of the rock, whose habitation is high; that saith in his heart, Who shall bring me down to the ground? [4]Though thou exalt thyself as the eagle, and though thou set thy nest among the stars, thence will I bring thee down, saith the LORD.

[15]For the day of the LORD is near upon all the heathen: as thou hast done, it shall be done unto thee: thy reward shall return upon thine own head. [16]For as ye have drunk upon my holy mountain, so shall all the heathen drink continually; yea, they shall drink, and they shall swallow down, and they shall be as though they had not been.

[17]But upon mount Zion shall be deliverance, and there shall be holiness; and the house of Jacob shall possess their possessions. [18]And the house of Jacob shall be a fire, and the house of Joseph a flame, and the house of Esau for stubble, and they shall kindle in them, and devour them; and there shall not be any remaining of the house of Esau; for the LORD hath spoken it.

OBEDIENCE

[ō bē′di ens] The act of conforming to the command of a superior out of due regard for his authority. As used in the Bible, it indicates the proper response to God's acts, promises, and commands. This response is conformity with what God prescribes, not purely mechanical, but arising out of love and gratitude. The supreme illustration of a spirit of obedience to God is found in Jesus' prayer in the garden of Gethsemane that the cup of sorrow and death might pass from him, if it were God's will. Yet, despite this obvious desire to avoid the awful agonies he knew he was to undergo on the cross, Jesus went out from the garden with a faith in God and a loyalty to His will that neither nails, nor spear, nor jibes could shake. Through his obedience, expiation for sin was effected and those who are joined with him in faithful obedience have the promise of eternal salvation. As a part of their obedience to the LORD, Christians are admonished to be subject in domestic and civil matters as well as in those which are specifically religious.

See DISOBEDIENCE

SCRIPTURE

Obedience to God Enjoined

Ex. 19 [5]Now therefore, if ye will obey my voice indeed, and keep my covenant, then ye shall be a peculiar treasure unto me above all people: for all the earth is mine.

Ex. 23 [21]Beware of him, and obey his voice, provoke him not; for he will not pardon your transgressions: for my name is in him. [22]But if thou shalt indeed obey his voice, and do all that I speak; then I will be an enemy unto thine enemies, and an adversary unto thine adversaries.

Deut. 11 [1]Therefore thou shalt love the LORD thy God, and keep his charge, and his statutes, and his judgments, and his commandments, always.

[26]Behold, I set before you this day a blessing and a curse: [27]A blessing, if ye obey the commandments of the LORD your God which I command you this day; [28]And a curse, if ye will not obey the commandments of the LORD your God, but turn aside out of the way which I command you this day, to go after other gods which ye have not known.

Isa. 1 [19]If ye be willing and obedient, ye shall eat the good of the land: [20]But if ye refuse and rebel, ye shall be devoured with the sword: for the mouth of the LORD hath spoken it.

Jer. 7 [23]But this thing commanded I them, saying, Obey my voice, and I will be your God, and ye shall be my people: and walk ye in all the ways that I have commanded you, that it may be well unto you.

Jer. 26 [13]Therefore now amend your ways and your doings, and obey the voice of the LORD your God; and the LORD will repent him of the evil that he hath pronounced against you.

Acts 5 [29]Then Peter and the other apostles answered, and said, We ought to obey God rather than men.

Jas. 1 [25]But whoso looketh into the perfect law of liberty, and continueth therein, he being not a forgetful hearer, but a doer of the work, this man shall be blessed in his deed.

Obedience Preferred Before Sacrifice

1 Sam. 15 22And Samuel said, Hath the LORD as great delight in burnt-offerings and sacrifices, as in obeying the voice of the LORD? Behold, to obey is better than sacrifice, and to hearken than the fat of rams.

Obedience of Christ

Mark 14 33And he taketh with him Peter and James and John, and began to be sore amazed, and to be very heavy; 34And saith unto them, My soul is exceeding sorrowful unto death: tarry ye here, and watch. 35And he went forward a little, and fell on the ground, and prayed that, if it were possible, the hour might pass from him. 36And he said, Abba, Father, all things are possible unto thee; take away this cup from me: nevertheless not what I will, but what thou wilt. 37And he cometh, and findeth them sleeping, and saith unto Peter, Simon, sleepest thou? couldest not thou watch one hour? 38Watch ye and pray, lest ye enter into temptation. The spirit truly is ready, but the flesh is weak. 39And again he went away, and prayed, and spake the same words. 40And when he returned, he found them asleep again, (for their eyes were heavy,) neither wist they what to answer him. 41And he cometh the third time, and saith unto them, Sleep on now, and take your rest: it is enough, the hour is come; behold, the Son of man is betrayed into the hands of sinners. 42Rise up, let us go; lo, he that betrayeth me is at hand.

Rom. 5 19For as by one man's disobedience many were made sinners: so by the obedience of one shall many be made righteous.

Phil. 2 8And being found in fashion as a man, he humbled himself, and became obedient unto death, even the death of the Cross.

Heb. 5 7Who in the days of his flesh, when he had offered up prayers and supplications with strong crying and tears unto him that was able to save him from death, and was heard in that he feared; 8Though he were a Son, yet learned he obedience by the things which he suffered.

Blessings of Obedience

Deut. 28 1And it shall come to pass, if thou shalt hearken diligently unto the voice of the LORD thy God, to observe and to do all his commandments which I command thee this day: that the LORD thy God will set thee on high above all nations of the earth: 2And all these blessings shall come on thee, and overtake thee, if thou shalt hearken unto the voice of the LORD thy God. 3Blessed shalt thou be in the city, and blessed shalt thou be in the field. 4Blessed shall be the fruit of thy body, and the fruit of thy ground, and the fruit of thy cattle, the increase of thy kine, and the flocks of thy sheep. 5Blessed shall be thy basket and thy store. 6Blessed shalt thou be when thou comest in, and blessed shalt thou be when thou goest out.

Matt. 7 21Not every one that saith unto me, Lord, Lord, shall enter into the kingdom of heaven; but he that doeth the will of my Father which is in heaven. 22Many will say to me in that day, Lord, Lord, have we not prophesied in thy name? and in thy name have cast out devils? and in thy name done many wonderful works? 23And then will I profess unto them, I never knew you: depart from me, ye that work iniquity.

24Therefore whosoever heareth these sayings of mine, and doeth them, I will liken him unto a wise man, which built his house upon a rock: [25]And the rain descended, and the floods came, and the winds blew, and beat upon that house; and it fell not: for it was founded upon a rock. [26]And every one that heareth these sayings of mine, and doeth them not, shall be likened unto a foolish man, which built his house upon the sand: [27]And the rain descended, and the floods came, and the winds blew, and beat upon that house, and it fell: and great was the fall of it.

Heb. 11 [8]By faith Abraham, when he was called to go out into a place which he should after receive for an inheritance, obeyed; and he went out, not knowing whither he went.

1 Pet. 1 [22]Seeing ye have purified your souls in obeying the truth to the Spirit, unto unfeigned love of the brethren: see that ye love one another with a pure heart fervently.

Rev. 22 [14]Blessed are they that do his commandments, that they may have right to the tree of life, and may enter in through the gates into the city.

Obedience in the Home

Eph. 6 [1]Children, obey your parents in the Lord: for this is right.

Col. 3 [20]Children, obey your parents in all things, for this is well pleasing unto the Lord.

Tit. 2 [5]To be discreet, chaste, keepers at home, good, obedient to their own husbands, that the word of God be not blasphemed.

Eph. 6 [5]Servants, be obedient to them that are your masters according to the flesh, with fear and trembling, in singleness of your heart, as unto Christ: [6]Not with eyeservice as menpleasers, but as the servants of Christ, doing the will of God from the heart.

Civil Obedience

Rom. 13 [1]Let every soul be subject unto the higher powers. For there is no power but of God: the powers that be are ordained of God. [2]Whosoever therefore resisteth the power, resisteth the ordinance of God: and they that resist shall receive to themselves damnation.

Heb. 13 [17]Obey them that have the rule over you, and submit yourselves: for they watch for your souls, as they that must give account, that they may do it with joy, and not with grief: for that is unprofitable for you.

OFFENCE, OFFEND

[o fens′, o fend′] To offend is to do harm to, to affront; in Scripture it has the meaning of "to cause to sin" or, in its intransitive form, "to be caused to sin." An offence is either the cause of anger, displeasure, etc., and therefore a "stumbling-block," or it is a sin.

See Temptation

SCRIPTURE

Warnings against Giving Offence

Matt. 5 [19]Whosoever therefore shall break one of these least commandments, and shall teach men so, he shall be called the least in the kingdom of heaven: but whosoever shall do and teach them, the same shall be called great in the kingdom of heaven.

Mark 9 [42]And whosoever shall offend one of these little ones that believe in me, it is better for him that a millstone were hanged about his neck, and he were cast into the sea.

1 Cor. 8 [9]But take heed lest by any means this liberty of yours become a stumblingblock to them that are weak.

[10]For if any man see thee which hast knowledge sit at meat in the idol's temple, shall not the conscience of him which is weak be emboldened to eat those things which are offered to idols; [11]And through thy knowledge shall the weak brother perish, for whom Christ died? [12]But when ye sin so against the brethren, and wound their weak conscience, ye sin against Christ. [13]Wherefore, if meat make my brother to offend, I will eat no flesh while the world standeth, lest I make my brother to offend.

1 Cor. 10 [32]Give none offense, neither to the Jews, nor to the Gentiles, nor to the church of God.

Remedies for Offenses

Matt. 5 [29]And if thy right eye offend thee, pluck it out, and cast it from thee: for it is profitable for thee that one of thy members should perish, and not that thy whole body should be cast into hell. [30]And if thy right hand offend thee, cut it off, and cast it from thee: for it is profitable for thee that one of thy members should perish, and not that thy whole body should be cast into hell.

Matt. 18 [8]Wherefore if thy hand or thy foot offend thee, cut them off, and cast them from thee: it is better for thee to enter into life halt or maimed, rather than having two hands or two feet to be cast into everlasting fire. [9]And if thine eye offend thee, pluck it out, and cast it from thee: it is better for thee to enter into life with one eye, rather than having two eyes to be cast into hell fire.

Christ Delivered for Our Offenses

Rom. 4 [24]But for us also, to whom it shall be imputed, if we believe on him that raised up Jesus our Lord from the dead; [25]Who was delivered for our offences, and was raised again for our justification.

Christ an Offence

Gal. 5 [11]And I, brethren, if I yet preach circumcision, why do I yet suffer persecution? then is the offense of the cross ceased.

1 Pet. 2 [8]And a stone of stumbling, and a rock of offense, even to them which stumble at the word, being disobedient.

OG

[og] The king of Bashan mentioned in the conquest of that territory by Moses and the wandering tribes. Og and his people are said to have been "utterly destroyed." He was especially remembered by the Israelites for his great size; his iron bedstead measured nine by four cubits, or about thirteen by six feet. The account of the conquest in *Deuteronomy* speaks of him as the last of the Rephaim, a giant-race of that region.

SCRIPTURE

Num. 21 [33]And they turned and went up by the way of Bashan: and Og the king of Bashan went out against them, he, and all his people, to the battle at Edrei. [34]And the LORD said unto Moses, Fear him not: for I have delivered him into thy hand, and all his people, and his land; and thou shalt do to him as thou didst unto Sihon king of the Amorites, which dwelt at Heshbon. [35]So they smote him, and his sons, and all his people, until there was none left him alive: and they possessed his land.

Deut. 3 [1]Then we turned, and went up the way to Bashan: and Og the king of Bashan came out against us, he and all his people, to battle at Edrei. [2]And the LORD said unto me, Fear him not: for I will deliver him, and all his people, and his land, into thy hand; and thou shalt do unto him as thou didst unto Sihon king of the Amo-

rites, which dwelt at Heshbon. 3So the
LORD our God delivered into our hands Og
also, the king of Bashan, and all his people: and we smote him until none was left
to him remaining. 4And we took all his
cities at that time, there was not a city
which we took not from them threescore
cities, all the region of Argob, the kingdom
of Og in Bashan. 5All these cities were
fenced with high walls, gates, and bars;
besides unwalled towns a great many.
6And we utterly destroyed them, as we did
unto Sihon king of Heshbon, utterly destroying the men, women, and children, of
every city. 7But all the cattle, and the spoil
of the cities, we took for a prey to ourselves. 8And we took at that time out of
the hand of the two kings of the Amorites
the land that was on this side Jordan, from
the river of Arnon unto mount Hermon;
9(Which Hermon the Sidonians call Sir-
ion; and the Amorites call it Shenir;) 10All
the cities of the plain, and all Gilead, and
all Bashan, unto Salchah and Edrei, cities
of the kingdom of Og in Bashan. 11For
only Og king of Bashan remained of the
remnant of giants; behold, his bedstead
was a bedstead of iron; is it not in Rabbath
of the children of Ammon? nine cubits was
the length thereof, and four cubits the
breadth of it, after the cubit of a man.
12And this land, which we possessed at
that time, from Aroer, which is by the river
Arnon, and half mount Gilead, and the
cities thereof, gave I unto the Reubenites
and to the Gadites.

OLIVES, MOUNT OF

[ol'ivz] A mountain ridge east of Jerusalem, also called Olivet. We first hear of the Mount of Olives when David, fleeing from Absalom, "went up by the ascent of mount Olivet" (*2 Sam. 15:30*). In connection with this event, it is mentioned that David worshipped God on this mountain (*2 Sam. 15:32*), from which we can infer that there was some type of sanctuary there. Zechariah prophesied that in the Day of the LORD, God would stand upon the Mount of Olives "and the mount of Olives shall cleave in the midst thereof toward the east and toward the west, and there shall be a very great valley; and half of the mountain shall remove toward the north, and half of it toward the south" (*Zech. 14:4, Ezek. 11:23*). The Mount of Olives is, of course, better known for its association with the last days in the life of Jesus. The village of Bethany, in which Jesus seems to have made his home while in Judaea, was situated "at the mount of Olives" (*Mark 11:1; Matt. 21:1; Luke 19:29*). The triumphal entry into Jerusalem was made over a portion of this mountain (*Luke 19:29, 37*), and his sermon on the coming of the Son of man was delivered "as he sat upon the Mount of Olives" (*Matt. 24:3*). The Garden of Gethsemane, in which Jesus prayed in agony, and in which he was betrayed by Judas and arrested, was situated on the lower slopes of Olivet. (*See* GETHSEMANE) The Mount of Olives is best known, perhaps, as the scene of Jesus' last appearance to his disciples and his ascension to the right hand of God (*Luke 24:50-52; Acts 1:1-12*).

SCRIPTURE

Scene of David's Worship

2 Sam. 15 30And David went up by the ascent of mount Olivet, and wept as he went up, and had his head covered, and he went barefoot: and all the people that was with him covered every man his head, and they went up, weeping as they went up.

32And it came to pass, that when David was come to the top of the mount, where he worshipped God, behold, Hushai the Archite came to meet him with his coat rent, and earth upon his head:

Scene of Jesus' Preaching

Matt. 24 3And as he sat upon the mount of Olives, the disciples came unto him privately, saying, Tell us, when shall these

things be? and what shall be the sign of
thy coming, and of the end of the world?

Scene of Ascension

Acts 1 [1]The former treatise have I
made, O Theophilus, of all that Jesus began both to do and to teach, [2]Until the
day in which he was taken up, after that
he through the Holy Ghost had given commandments unto the apostles whom he
had chosen: [3]To whom also he shewed himself alive after his passion by many infal-
lible proofs, being seen of them forty days,
and speaking of the things pertaining to
the kingdom of God: [4]And, being assembled together with them, commanded
them that they should not depart from
Jerusalem, but wait for the promise of the
Father, which, saith he, ye have heard of
me. [5]For John truly baptized with water;
but ye shall be baptized with the Holy
Ghost not many days hence. [6]When they
therefore were come together, they asked
of him, saying, Lord, wilt thou at this time
restore again the kingdom to Israel? [7]And
he said unto them, It is not for you to know
the times or the seasons, which the Father
hath put in his own power. [8]But ye shall
receive power, after that the Holy Ghost
is come upon you: and ye shall be witnesses unto me both in Jerusalem, and in
all Judea, and in Samaria, and unto the uttermost part of the earth. [9]And when he
had spoken these things, while they beheld, he was taken up; and a cloud received him out of their sight. [10]And while
they looked steadfastly toward heaven as
he went up, behold, two men stood by
them in white apparel; [11]Which also said,
Ye men of Galilee, why stand ye gazing
up into heaven? this same Jesus, which is
taken up from you into heaven, shall so
come in like manner as ye have seen him
go into heaven. [12]Then returned they
unto Jerusalem from the mount called
Olivet, which is from Jerusalem a sabbath day's journey.

OMRI

[om'rī] The sixth king of Northern Israel, reigning about 876-869 BC. Omri was commander of the army of King Elah and was away on a mission against the Philistine city of Gibbethon when that king was slain by Zimri, another commander in the army. When the army repudiated the claims of Zimri and named Omri as king, he quickly returned to the capital city of Tirzah to claim his throne. Zimri committed suicide (*see* ZIMRI), but Omri still had to contend with Tibni, who had considerable popular support. After about four years Omri gained undisputed control of the northern kingdom and set about to establish what was to become one of the strongest reigns of all the northern kings. One of his first moves was to transfer the capital from Tirzah to the hill of Samaria. This was an impressive site from a strategic point of view, being surrounded on all sides by a valley, thus making it a strong natural fortification. (*See* SAMARIA) Foreign sources from this period speak of Samaria as "Beth-Omri," the house of Omri. He further solidified his position by reestablishing the treaty with Tyre which had been so beneficial to King Solomon. (*See* SOLOMON) Although the Bible is silent on this point, the Moabite stone, discovered in 1868, informs us that Omri also defeated Moab, reestablishing large areas of the Solomonic empire. Omri was a king of enormous vigor and ability, but is characterized as a man who "wrought evil in the eyes of the LORD, and did worse than all that were before him, for he walked in all the way of Jeroboam the son of Nebat, and in his sin wherewith he made Israel to sin, to provoke the LORD God of Israel to anger with their vanities" (*1 Kin. 16:25-26*).

See KINGS

SCRIPTURE

1 Kin. 16 [15]In the twenty and seventh
year of Asa king of Judah did Zimri reign
seven days in Tirzah. And the people were
encamped against Gibbethon, which be-

longed to the Philistines. [16]And the people that were encamped heard say, Zimri hath conspired, and hath also slain the king: wherefore all Israel made Omri, the captain of the host, king over Israel that day in the camp. [17]And Omri went up from Gibbethon, and all Israel with him, and they besieged Tirzah. [18]And it came to pass, when Zimri saw that the city was taken, that he went into the palace of the king's house, and burnt the king's house over him with fire, and died, [19]For his sins which he sinned in doing evil in the sight of the LORD, in walking in the way of Jeroboam, and in his sin which he did, to make Israel to sin. [20]Now the rest of the acts of Zimri, and his treason that he wrought, are they not written in the book of the Chronicles of the kings of Israel?

[21]Then were the people of Israel divided into two parts: half of the people followed Tibni the son of Ginath, to make him king; and half followed Omri. [22]But the people that followed Omri prevailed against the people that followed Tibni the son of Ginath: so Tibni died, and Omri reigned. [23]In the thirty and first year of Asa king of Judah began Omri to reign over Israel, twelve years: six years reigned he in Tirzah. [24]And he bought the hill Samaria of Shemer for two talents of silver, and built on the hill, and called the name of the city which he built, after the name of Shemer, owner of the hill, Samaria.

[25]But Omri wrought evil in the eyes of the LORD, and did worse than all that were before him. [26]For he walked in all the way of Jeroboam the son of Nebat, and in his sin wherewith he made Israel to sin, to provoke the LORD God of Israel to anger with their vanities. [27]Now the rest of the acts of Omri which he did, and his might that he shewed, are they not written in the book of the Chronicles of the kings of Israel? [28]So Omri slept with his fathers, and was buried in Samaria: and Ahab his son reigned in his stead.

ONESIMUS

[ō nes′i mus] A fugitive slave of Philemon who absconded, possibly with some money, seeking refuge in Rome. While in Rome, he came in contact with Paul in some way, was brought to faith and repentance, and became a source of great comfort to the apostle. Although Paul appreciated the aid which Onesimus had given him, he felt that the slave should be restored to his master and persuaded him to return to the household of his rightful owner. Philemon had the legal right to take the life of the slave, as Onesimus had committed one of the gravest offences in ancient law; therefore, the Letter to Philemon was written for the purpose of assuring a merciful reception for Onesimus. The slave returned to Colossae in company with Tychicus, carrying both the letter to Philemon and the epistle to the Colossian church.

See PHILEMON

SCRIPTURE

Philem. 1 [10]I beseech thee for my son Onesimus, whom I have begotten in my bonds: [11]Which in time past was to thee unprofitable, but now profitable to thee and to me: [12]Whom I have sent again: thou therefore receive him, that is, mine own bowels: [13]Whom I would have retained with me, that in thy stead he might have ministered unto me in the bonds of the gospel: [14]But without thy mind would I do nothing; that thy benefit should not be as it were of necessity, but willingly. [15]For perhaps he therefore departed for a season, that thou shouldest receive him for ever; [16]Not now as a servant, but above a servant, a brother beloved, specially to me, but how much more unto thee, both in the flesh, and in the Lord? [17]If thou count me therefore a partner, receive him as myself.

[18]If he hath wronged thee, or oweth thee ought, put that on mine account;

ONESIPHORUS

[ō nê sif′ô rus] A Christian of Ephesus. In writing to Timothy from prison, Paul noted that the Christians of Asia had deserted him. One exception was Onesiphorus, who had come to Rome at some risk, sought Paul out, and ministered to him. The apostle also mentions that Onesiphorus had already established a well-known record of selfless service in Ephesus and expresses a fervant desire that he might "find mercy of the Lord in that day."

SCRIPTURE

2 Tim. 1 [16]The Lord give mercy unto the house of Onesiphorus; for he oft refreshed me, and was not ashamed of my chain: [17]But, when he was in Rome, he sought me out very diligently, and found me. [18]The Lord grant unto him that he may find mercy of the Lord in that day: and in how many things he ministered unto me at Ephesus, thou knowest very well.

See 2 Tim. 4:19

OPPRESSION

[ô presh′un] Unjust or cruel exercise of authority or power, especially by the imposition of burdens; tyranny; unnecessary severity or cruelty. Man seems inclined to oppression in that he often seeks to demonstrate his power over such persons as are weaker than he. The Bible warns us against oppression, contrasting it with the merciful treatment of mankind by God.

SCRIPTURE

Ex. 22 [21]Thou shalt neither vex a stranger, nor oppress him: for ye were strangers in the land of Egypt.

[22]Ye shall not afflict any widow, or fatherless child. [23]If thou afflict them in any wise, and they cry at all unto me, I will surely hear their cry; [24]And my wrath shall wax hot, and I will kill you with the sword; and your wives shall be widows, and your children fatherless.

Lev. 25 [14]And if thou sell aught unto thy neighbour, or buyest aught of thy neighbour's hand, ye shall not oppress one another.

Deut. 23 [16]He shall dwell with thee, even among you in that place which he shall choose in one of thy gates where it liketh him best: thou shalt not oppress him.

Deut. 24 [14]Thou shalt not oppress an hired servant that is poor and needy, whether he be of thy brethren, or of thy strangers that are in thy land within thy gates.

Psa. 12 [5]For the oppression of the poor, for the sighing of the needy, now will I arise, saith the LORD; I will set him in safety from him that puffeth at him.

Psa. 62 [10]Trust not in oppression, and become not vain in robbery: if riches increase, set not your heart upon them.

Eccl. 4 [1]So I returned, and considered all the oppressions that are done under the sun: and behold the tears of such as were oppressed, and they had no comforter; and on the side of their oppressors there was power; but they had no comforter.

Eccl. 5 [8]If thou seest the oppression of the poor, and violent perverting of judgment and justice in a province, marvel not at the matter: for he that is higher than the highest regardeth; and there be higher than they.

Isa. 1 [17]Learn to do well; seek judgment, relieve the oppressed, judge the fatherless, plead for the widow.

Isa. 10 [1]Woe unto them that decree unrighteous decrees, and that write grievousness which they have prescribed; [2]To turn aside the needy from judgment, and to take away the right from the poor of my people, that widows may be their prey, and that they may rob the fatherless! 3And what will ye do in the day of visitation, and in the desolation which shall come from far? to whom will ye flee for help? and where will ye leave your glory? 4Without me they shall bow down under the prisoners, and they shall fall under the slain. For all this his anger is not turned away, but his hand is stretched out still.

Isa. 58 6Is not this the fast that I have chosen? to loose the bands of wickedness, to undo the heavy burdens, and to let the oppressed go free, and that ye break every yoke?

Ezek. 22 7In thee have they set light by father and mother: in the midst of thee have they dealt by oppression with the stranger: in thee have they vexed the fatherless and the widow.

Mic. 2 1Woe to them that devise iniquity, and work evil upon their beds! when the morning is light, they practise it, because it is in the power of their hand. 2And they covet fields, and take them by violence; and houses, and take them away: so they oppress a man and his house, even a man and his heritage. 3Therefore thus saith the LORD; Behold, against this family do I devise an evil, from which ye shall not remove your necks; neither shall ye go haughtily: for this time is evil.

Mal. 3 5And I will come near to you to judgment: and I will be a swift witness against the sorcerers, and against the adulterers, and against false swearers, and against those that oppress the hireling in his wages, the widow, and the fatherless, and that turn aside the stranger from his right, and fear not me, saith the LORD of hosts.

Jas. 5 4Behold, the hire of the labourers which have reaped down your fields, which is of you kept back by fraud, crieth: and the cries of them which have reaped are entered into the ears of the Lord of Sabaoth.

ORACLE

[or'a k'l] A divine utterance delivered to man, either directly or through some medium, such as a prophet or written scriptures.

SCRIPTURE

The Scriptures as Oracles

Acts 7 38This is he that was in the Church in the wilderness with the angel which spake to him in the mount Sina, and with our fathers: who received the lively oracles, to give unto us.

Rom. 3 1What advantage then hath the Jew? or what profit is there of circumcision? 2Much every way: chiefly, because that unto them were committed the Oracles of God.

Heb. 5 12For when for the time ye ought to be teachers, ye have need that one teach you again which be the first principles of the oracles of God; and are become such as have need of milk, and not of strong meat.

1 Pet. 4 11If any man speak, let him speak as the oracles of God: if any man minister, let him do it as of the ability which God giveth, that God in all things may be glorified through Jesus Christ, to whom be praise and dominion for ever and ever. Amen.

ORDINATION

[ôr di nā'shun] As currently used, this word refers to the investing of individuals with ministerial or other ecclesiastical rank. The New Testament contains several references to ordination, but is neither explicit nor detailed in its statements. We can only infer that it was thought desirable for people who were to hold church office to be publicly recognized in some way.

SCRIPTURE

Acts 13 [3]And when they had fasted and prayed, and laid their hands on them, they sent them away.

Acts 14 [23]And when they had ordained them elders in every church, and had prayed with fasting, they commended them to the Lord, on whom they believed.

1 Tim. 4 [14]Neglect not the gift that is in thee, which was given thee by prophecy, with the laying on of the hands of the presbytery.

2 Tim. 1 [6]Wherefore I put thee in remembrance, that thou stir up the gift of God, which is in thee by the putting on of my hands.

Tit. 1 [5]For this cause left I thee in Crete, that thou shouldest set in order the things that are wanting, and ordain elders in every city, as I had appointed thee:

Heb. 6 [2]Of the doctrine of baptisms, and of laying on of hands, and of resurrection of the dead, and of eternal judgment.

ORPHAN

[or'fan] As used in the Bible, this word refers to the fatherless and does not necessarily imply that a child has been deprived of both parents. The Scriptures are solicitous of orphans and contain provisions for their welfare.

SCRIPTURE

Ex. 22 [22]Ye shall not afflict any widow, or fatherless child. [23]If thou afflict them in any wise, and they cry at all unto me, I will surely hear their cry; [24]And my wrath shall wax hot, and I will kill you with the sword; and your wives shall be widows, and your children fatherless.

Deut. 14 [28]At the end of three years thou shalt bring forth all the tithe of thine increase the same year, and shalt lay it up within thy gates: [29]And the Levite, (because he hath no part nor inheritance with thee,) and the stranger, and the fatherless, and the widow, which are within thy gates, shall come, and shall eat and be satisfied; that the LORD thy God may bless thee in all the work of thine hand which thou doest.

Deut. 24 [19]When thou cuttest down thine harvest in thy field, and hast forgot a sheaf in the field, thou shalt not go again to fetch it: it shall be for the stranger, for the fatherless, and for the widow: that the LORD thy God may bless thee in all the work of thine hands. [20]When thou beatest thine olive tree, thou shalt not go over the boughs again: it shall be for the stranger, for the fatherless, and for the widow. [21]When thou gatherest the grapes of thy vineyard, thou shalt not glean it afterward: it shall be for the stranger, for the fatherless, and for the widow.

Deut. 26 [12]When thou hast made an end of tithing all the tithes of thine increase the third year, which is the year of tithing, and hast given it unto the Levite, the stranger, the fatherless, and the widow, that they may eat within thy gates, and be filled;

Deut. 27 [19]Cursed be he that perverteth the judgment of the stranger, fatherless, and widow.

Psa. 68 [5]A father of the fatherless, and a judge of the widows, is God in his holy habitation.

Psa. 82 [3]Defend the poor and fatherless: do justice to the afflicted and needy.

Psa. 146 [9]The LORD preserveth the strangers; he relieveth the fatherless and widow:

Jas. 1 [27]Pure religion and undefiled before God and the Father is this, To visit the fatherless and widows in their affliction, and to keep himself unspotted from the world.

OSTENTATION

[os′ten tā′shun] Ambitious, proud, and unnecessary display, pretentious parade of one's wealth or accomplishments in dress, manner, speech, or mode of living. In addition to being a useless and foolish vanity, ostentation runs counter to the very principle and theory of Christianity.

See VANITY

SCRIPTURE

Prov. 25 [14]Whoso boasteth himself of a false gift is like clouds and wind without rain.

Prov. 27 [1]Boast not thyself of tomorrow; for thou knowest not what a day may bring forth. [2]Let another man praise thee, and not thine own mouth; a stranger, and not thine own lips.

Matt. 6 [1]Take heed that ye do not your alms before men, to be seen of them; otherwise ye have no reward of your Father which is in heaven. [2]Therefore when thou doest thine alms, do not sound a trumpet before thee, as the hypocrites do in the synagogues and in the streets, that they may have glory of men. Verily I say unto you, They have their reward. [3]But when thou doest alms, let not thy left hand know what thy right hand doeth: [4]That thine alms may be in secret: and thy Father which seeth in secret himself shall reward thee openly.

OTHNIEL

[oth′ni el] The son of Kenaz and brother of Caleb. Othniel led an army to victory over Kiriath-sepher, later called Debir. As a reward he received Achsah, the daughter of Caleb, to be his wife. After Israel settled in Canaan, she was oppressed by Cushan-rishathaim, king of Mesopotamia; Othniel delivered Israel from this ruler's hand and is regarded as the first of the Israelite heroes known as "judges."

See JUDGES

SCRIPTURE

Conquers Kirjath-sepher

Josh. 15 [16]And Caleb said, He that smiteth Kirjath-sepher, and taketh it, to him will I give Achsah my daughter to wife. [17]And Othniel the son of Kenaz, the brother of Caleb, took it: and he gave him Achsah his daughter to wife. [18]And it came to pass, as she came unto him, that she moved him to ask of her father a field: and she lighted off her ass; and Caleb said unto her, What wouldest thou? [19]Who answered, Give me a blessing; for thou hast given me a south land; give me also springs of water. And he gave her the upper springs, and the nether springs. [20]This is the inheritance of the tribe of the children of Judah according to their families.

Judge of Israel

Judg. 3 [8]Therefore the anger of the LORD was hot against Israel, and he sold them into the hand of Chushan-rishathaim king of Mesopotamia: and the children of Israel served Chushan-rishathaim eight years. [9]And when the children of Israel cried unto the LORD, the LORD raised up a deliverer to the children of Israel, who delivered them, even Othniel the son of Kenaz, Caleb's younger brother. [10]And the Spirit of the LORD came upon him, and he judged Israel, and went out to war: and the LORD delivered Chushan-rishathaim king of Mesopotamia into his hand; and his hand prevailed against Chushan-rishathaim. [11]And the land had rest forty years: and Othniel the son of Kenaz died.

PALESTINE

[pal′es tīn] The designation of the land in which most of Biblical history takes place. It extends northward to the Amanus-Taurus mountains and southward to the Indian Ocean. Its eastern boundary is formed by the Zagros mountains and the Persian Gulf. On the west it is bounded by the Red Sea and the Mediterranean.

The name "Palestine" was derived from the tribe of invaders who settled in the area in the twelfth century BC; they are well-known to Bible students as the Philistines. For the history of this area, see ISRAEL, JUDAH, PHILISTINES, SYRIA, etc. For geography, see DEAD SEA, GALILEE, JORDAN, etc.

PAMPHYLIA

[pam fil'i a] A country on the southern coast of Asia Minor, lying just south of Pisidia. Paul, Barnabas, and John Mark introduced Christianity into Pamphylia while on their first missionary journey, preaching especially in the cities of Perga and Attalia. It was in Perga that John Mark left the party and returned to Jerusalem.

See PAUL, BARNABAS, MARK

SCRIPTURE

Visited by Paul

Acts 13 13Now when Paul and his company loosed from Paphos, they came to Perga in Pamphylia: and John departing from them returned to Jerusalem.
14But when they departed from Perga, they came to Antioch in Pisidia, and went into the synagogue on the sabbath day, and sat down.
24When John had first preached before his coming the baptism of repentance to all the people of Israel.

PARABLES

[par'a b'l] A short, fictitious, and comparative narrative of something which might occur in real life, from which a moral is pointed or a lesson taught. The parable as a means of teaching was used by the Hebrew teachers from the earliest times, and arrived at its highest development in the parables of Jesus. The most ignorant people could absorb and digest a parable where direct language might prove to be beyond their comprehension.

Jesus made His parables things of actual life, and they form the most characteristic and beautiful passages of his teachings. The gospels contain over fifty parabolic utterances of Jesus, though he doubtless spoke many more in the course of his ministry.

Old Testament Parables

- The Trees Choosing a King—Jotham to the Shechemites, *Judg. 9:7-15.*
- The Ewe Lamb—Nathan to David, *2 Sam. 12:1-4.*
- The Two Brethren—by the widow of Tekoah, *2 Sam. 14:1-11.*
- The Escaped Captive—by one of the sons of the prophets to Ahab, *1 Kin. 20:35-40.*
- The Thistle and the Cedar—Jehoash to Amaziah, *2 Kin. 14:9.*
- The Vineyard and the Grapes—Isaiah to Judah and Jerusalem, *Isa. 5:1-7.*
- The Eagle and the Vine—Ezekiel to Israel, *Ezek. 17:3-10.*
- The Lion's Whelps—Ezekiel to Israel, *Ezek. 19:2-9.*
- The Boiling Pot—Ezekiel to Israel, *Ezek. 24:3-5.*

Parables of Jesus

See JESUS

PARACLETE

[par'a klēt] A transliteration of the Greek word *parakletos*, translated in the various English versions as Comforter, Counselor, Advocate, Intercessor, or Helper. The literature of the ancient world has been ransacked in an effort to discover why the author of the Fourth Gospel used this word of the Holy Spirit. Its literal meaning is "one called to the side of", but this is not sufficiently illuminating. In *1 John 2:1*, the term is used of Christ, in the legal sense of Advocate or Intercessor. This meaning, however, does not sufficiently sound the depths of the term as used in the "paraclete passages" in *John 14-16.* From these passages the Paraclete, or Holy Spirit, may be seen as a vindicating and punishing witness, as a counselor and tutor, and as one who assists and supports. This makes it clear that no one English word is broad enough to include all these meanings. To avoid confusion, the Bible student will do well simply to read "Paraclete" in these passages and to fill in its meaning from the functions attributed to him therein.

See SPIRIT

SCRIPTURE

Christ as the Paraclete

1 John 2 [1]My little children, these things write I unto you, that ye sin not. And if any man sin, we have an advocate (paraclete) with the Father, Jesus Christ the righteous.

Holy Spirit as the Paraclete

See SPIRIT

PARADISE

[par′a dīs] Originally a Persian word for a royal park or garden, this term has been used to refer to several different places or states. The Garden of Eden is often referred to as Paradise. It is also used to refer to the pleasant abode of the righteous dead, in opposition to Gehenna. In post-Biblical Christian theology, the term used interchangeably with "heaven." Jewish and later Christian speculations about Paradise as a place where souls are purged and fitted for heaven find no support in the New Testament. It is difficult to determine precisely what Jesus was referring to when he assured the thief on the cross that "today thou shalt be with me in Paradise." The primary implication of the statement is that the thief was justified from his sins through his faith; it cannot be cited as a positive support for any theory about the condition of the departed.

See GEHENNA, SHEOL, HELL, HEAVEN

SCRIPTURE

Luke 23 [43]And Jesus said unto him, Verily I say unto thee, To-day shalt thou be with me in paradise.

2 Cor. 12 [4]How that he was caught up into paradise, and heard unspeakable words, which it is not lawful for a man to utter.

Rev. 2 [7]He that hath an ear, let him hear what the Spirit saith unto the churches; To him that overcometh will I give to eat of the tree of life, which is in the midst of the paradise of God.

PARDON

[par′d′n] Forgiveness; remission of punishment for an act of sin or injury. Pardon is a prerequisite to full fellowship between God and man.

See FORGIVENESS

SCRIPTURE

Job 7 [21]And why dost thou not pardon my transgression, and take away mine iniquity? for now shall I sleep in the dust; and thou shalt seek me in the morning, but I shall not be.

Psa. 25 [7]Remember not the sins of my youth, nor my transgressions: according to thy mercy remember thou me for thy goodness' sake, O LORD. [11]For thy name's sake, O LORD, pardon mine iniquity; for it is great. [18]Look upon mine affliction and my pain; and forgive all my sins.

Psa. 39 [8]Deliver me from all my transgressions: make me not the reproach of the foolish.

Psa. 51 [1]Have mercy upon me, O God, according to thy lovingkindness: according unto the multitude of thy tender mercies blot out my transgressions. [8]Make me to hear joy and gladness; that the bones which thou hast broken may rejoice. [9]Hide thy face from my sins, and blot out all mine iniquities. [14]Deliver me from bloodguiltiness, O God, thou God of my salvation: and my tongue shall sing aloud of thy righteousness.

PARENT

[pâr′ent] One who begets or brings forth offspring; a father or a mother. The fifth commandment of the Decalogue enjoins upon children of

God the responsibility of showing due honor and respect to one's parents. This commandment provides for the preservation of the basic unit of society, the family. Parents likewise receive a number of admonitions concerning their responsibilities toward their children.

See CHILDREN, RESPECT, FATHER, MOTHER

SCRIPTURE

Duty to Parents

Ex. 20 [12]Honour thy father and thy mother: that thy days may be long upon the land which the LORD thy God giveth thee.

Lev. 19 [3]Ye shall fear every man his mother and his father, and keep my sabbaths: I am the LORD your God.

Matt. 15 [4]For God commanded, saying, Honour thy father and mother: and, He that curseth father or mother, let him die the death. [5]But ye say, Whosoever shall say to his father or his mother, It is a gift, by whatsoever thou mightest be profited by me; [6]And honour not his father or his mother, he shall be free. Thus have ye made the commandment of God of none effect by your tradition.

Matt. 19 [19]Honour thy father and thy mother: and, Thou shalt love thy neighbour as thyself.

Eph. 6 [2]Honour thy father and mother; which is the first commandment with promise; [3]That it may be well with thee, and thou mayest live long on the earth.

Duty of Parents

Prov. 13 [24]He that spareth his rod hateth his son: but he that loveth him chasteneth him betimes.

Prov. 19 [18]Chasten thy son while there is hope, and let not thy soul spare for his crying.

Prov. 22 [6]Train up a child in the way he should go: and when he is old, he will not depart from it. [15]Foolishness is bound in the heart of a child; but the rod of correction shall drive it far from him.

Prov. 23 [13]Withhold not correction from the child: for if thou beatest him with the rod, he shall not die. [14]Thou shalt beat him with the rod, and shalt deliver his soul from hell.

Luke 11 [11]If a son shall ask bread of any of you that is a father, will ye give him a stone? or if he ask a fish, will he for a fish give him a serpent? [12]Or if he shall ask an egg, will he offer him a scorpion? [13]If ye then, being evil, know how to give good gifts unto your children: how much more shall your heavenly Father give the Holy Spirit to them that ask him?

Eph. 6 [4]And, ye fathers, provoke not your children to wrath: but bring them up in the nurture and admonition of the Lord.

Col. 3 [21]Fathers, provoke not your children to anger, lest they be discouraged.

1 Tim. 5 [8]But if any provide not for his own, and specially for those of his own house, he hath denied the faith, and is worse than an infidel.

PARTIALITY

[pär shē al'i tē] The showing of undue favor to one person or thing over another person or thing; unjust bias of mind.

See RESPECT

SCRIPTURE

Lev. 19 [15]Ye shall do no unrighteousness in judgment; thou shalt not respect the person of the poor, nor honour the person of the mighty: but in righteousness shalt thou judge thy neighbour.

Deut. 1 [17]Ye shall not respect persons in judgment; but ye shall hear the small as well as the great; ye shall not be afraid of the face of man; for the judgment is God's:

and the cause that is too hard for you, bring it unto me, and I will hear it.

Mal. 2 [9]Therefore have I also made you contemptible and base before all the people, according as ye have not kept my ways, but have been partial in the law.

Acts 10 [34]Then Peter opened his mouth, and said, Of a truth I perceive that God is no respecter of persons.

Rom. 2 [11]For there is no respect of persons with God.

1 Tim. 5 [21]I charge thee before God, and the Lord Jesus Christ, and the elect angels, that thou observe these things without preferring one before another, doing nothing by partiality.

Jas. 2 [4]Are ye not then partial in yourselves, and are become judges of evil thoughts?

Jas. 3 [17]But the wisdom that is from above, is first pure, then peaceable, gentle, and easy to be intreated, full of mercy, and good fruits, without partiality, and without hypocrisy.

1 Pet. 1 [17]And if ye call on the Father, who without respect of persons judgeth according to every man's work, pass the time of your sojourning here in fear.

PATIENCE

[pā′shens] The state or quality of being patient; bearing suffering, trouble, disappointment, waiting, or trials with fortitude; uncomplaining endurance of evils or wrongs. This is to be distinguished from resignation. Patience implies self-possession and indicates a certain quietness and repose; resignation is submission. The cultivation of a patient spirit aids one in avoiding a sinful reaction to the many petty annoyances and harassments which face each of us.

SCRIPTURE

Patience under Affliction

Job 34 [31]Surely it is meet to be said unto God, I have borne chastisement, I will not offend any more: [32]That which I see not teach thou me: If I have done iniquity, I will do no more.

Prov. 3 [11]My son, despise not the chastening of the LORD; neither be weary of his correction.

Lam. 3 [27]It is good for a man that he bear the yoke in his youth. [28]He sitteth alone and keepeth silence, because he hath borne it upon him. [29]He putteth his mouth in the dust; if so be there may be hope.

Heb. 12 [5]And ye have forgotten the exhortation which speaketh unto you as unto children, My son, despise not thou the chastening of the Lord, nor faint when thou art rebuked of him.

Exhortations to Patience

Eccl. 7 [8]Better is the end of a thing than the beginning thereof: and the patient in spirit is better than the proud in spirit.

Luke 21 [19]In your patience possess ye your souls.

Col. 1 [11]Strengthened with all might, according to his glorious power, unto all patience and longsuffering with joyfulness.

1 Thess. 5 [14]Now we exhort you, brethren, warn them that are unruly, comfort the feebleminded, support the weak, be patient toward all men.

Heb. 6 [15]And so, after he had patiently endured, he obtained the promise.

Heb. 10 [36]For ye have need of patience, that, after ye have done the will of God, ye might receive the promise.

Jas. 1 [3]Knowing this, that the trying of your faith worketh patience. [4]But let patience have her perfect work, that ye may be perfect and entire, wanting nothing.

Jas. 5 [7]Be patient therefore, brethren, unto the coming of the Lord. Behold, the husbandman waiteth for the precious

fruit of the earth, and hath long patience
for it, until he receive the early and latter
rain. [8]Be ye also patient; stablish your
hearts: for the coming of the Lord draweth
nigh. [11]Behold, we count them happy
which endure. Ye have heard of the patience of Job, and have seen the end of the Lord; that the Lord is very pitiful, and of tender mercy.

PATMOS

[pat′mos] An island of the Southern Sporades group, situated off the southwest coast of Turkey. It is a rocky treeless island, about ten miles long and six miles wide at the widest point. Patmos is mentioned once in the Bible, in *Rev. 1:9*, as the scene of John's revelation.

PATRIARCH

[pā′tri ark] The term commonly used to refer to the forefathers of the Israelites nation, especially Abraham, Isaac, Jacob, and the twelve sons of Jacob.

SCRIPTURE

Acts 7 [8]And he gave him the covenant
of circumcision: and so Abraham begat Isaac, and circumcised him the eighth day; and Isaac begat Jacob; and Jacob begat
the twelve patriarchs. [9]And the patri-
archs, moved with envy, sold Joseph into Egypt: but God was with him.

Heb. 7 [4]Now consider how great this man was, unto whom even the patriarch Abraham gave the tenth of the spoils.

PAUL

[pôl] The Greek form of the name of the great "apostle of the Gentiles" (*Rom. 11:13*), the Hebrew form of which is Saul, who changed from a persecutor of Christians to a missionary and writer whose influence on Christianity is second only to Jesus himself. Our information on the life of Paul is taken from the *Acts of Apostles* and from his own letters. Paul was born in the city of Tarsus, in Cilicia, early in the first century AD. His father, a Jew, probably rendered some service to the Roman government for which he was given the right of free Roman citizenship which, under Roman law, descended to his son. Tarsus was a leading educational center in those days and it is probable that part of the knowledge of Greek and Roman thought which Paul manifests in his speeches and letters may be traced to his early training there. Although his family was probably well-to-do, Paul learned a trade. This was standard procedure for any young man who was a student of the Law. After he became an apostle, he used his trade, that of making tentcloth and tents, as a means of self-support in his mission work. When he reached the proper age, he was sent to Jerusalem to study under the well-known scholar and teacher, Gamaliel, a strict Pharisee. We can imagine him as a young man about the time of Jesus' death, full of zeal for the Jewish faith, with nothing but contempt for the religious movement which had sprung up around Jesus and his teachings. Perhaps Jesus' denunciations of the Pharisees particularly irked him. At any rate, he was a leader in the early persecution of Christians by the Jews, having a part in the stoning of Stephen.

But God had a use for this persecutor. He was to be a "chosen vessel" in which the gospel would be carried to the Gentiles. While on his way to Damascus to carry out plans for further persecution of Christians, Paul was overwhelmed by a blinding light from heaven and voice which inquired, "Saul, Saul, why persecutest thou me?" When he asked of the voice, "Who art thou?" he was told it was the risen Jesus who spoke to him. He was bidden to go to Damascus and after three days, during which time he neither ate nor drank, he was confronted by a disciple named Ananias who instructed him as to what was expected of him and baptized him. After a brief period of preaching and debating with the Jews, he seems to have gone to Arabia, perhaps to prepare his mind for the great task which lay before him. He returned to Damascus from whence he made his first visit to Jerusalem since his conversion. He was received with suspicion until Barnabas took him to the apostles and explained to them about his conversion, after which he was constantly seen in their company. He then began a ministry in Syria and Cilicia which probably lasted ten or eleven years. Toward the end of this period he labored alongside Barnabas in Antioch of Syria. Then, in AD 46, Barnabas and Saul journeyed to Jerusalem to carry famine relief money to the brethren in Judaea. On returning to Antioch, Paul and Barnabas were charged to go on an evangelistic tour which is commonly referred to as the First Missionary Journey. This tour took them to the island of Cyprus and to Southern Galatia and other cities in that area of Asia Minor. (*See Acts 13-14*) Following this trip, he traveled to Jerusalem for a conference dealing with the various problems which had arisen over the admittance of Gentiles to a community of faith which had originally been wholly Jewish (*Acts 15*). The second missionary journey, which took about three years, carried the new faith across the continental boundary into Europe, to such cities as Philippi, Athens, and Corinth (*Acts 16-18*). On the third journey many of the areas previously evangelized were revisited. A great portion of this tour—about two and a half years—was spent in the work at Ephesus (*Acts 19-21*). Paul completed this journey by returning to Jerusalem, at which time he was thrown into prison on the false charge of having brought a Gentile into the inner court of the temple. Because of plots of the Jews to kill him, he was soon transferred to Caesarea. There he appeared before the governors, Felix and Festus, and King Agrippa. By virtue of his Roman citizenship and the right of appeal to Caesar it carried with it, Paul was sent to Rome. After an exciting and dangerous voyage, which included a shipwreck, Paul came to Rome, where he was imprisoned. In the last definite statement we have concerning Paul's life, we are told that he "dwelt two years in his own hired house, and received all that came in unto him, preaching the kingdom of God, and teaching those things which concern the Lord Jesus Christ, with all confidence, no man forbidding him" (*Acts 28: 30-31*). After this, we can be certain of nothing. That he felt he was going to be released is made clear by his letters to the Philippians and to Philemon, informing them that he intended to visit them soon. The favorable treatment he had received while in prison would certainly seem to support his optimism. In addition, there are references in early Christian literature to Paul's having been released, after which he continued his missionary efforts, preaching in places as far away as Spain. If this tradition is true, it is probable he was imprisoned a second time. At any rate, it seems unquestionable he was beheaded outside Rome in about AD 67, during the persecutions under Nero.

An early extra-Biblical description of Paul pictures him as small in stature, bald-headed, bowlegged, of rugged physique, with meeting eyebrows and a slightly hooked nose. We know he possessed a "thorn in the flesh" which he regarded as a serious disability, although we cannot be sure as to its nature. All in all, there seems to have been little in personal appearance to command admiration. Yet his spirit and courage, his indomitable energy and tireless devotion to the cause of Christ set him apart as one of the most remarkable religious leaders in the history of the world.

SCRIPTURE

Paul as a Persecutor

Acts 7 [58]And cast him out of the city, and stoned him: and the witnesses laid down their clothes at a young man's feet, whose name was Saul.

Acts 8 [1]And Saul was consenting unto his death. And at that time there was a great persecution against the Church which was at Jerusalem, and they were all scattered abroad throughout the regions of Judaea, and Samaria, except the apostles. [2]And devout men carried Stephen to his burial, and made great lamentation over him. [3]As for Saul, he made havoc of the Church, entering into every house, and haling men and women committed them to prison.

Acts 9 [1]And Saul, yet breathing out threatenings and slaughter against the disciples of the Lord, went unto the high Priest, [2]And desired of him letters to Damascus, to the Synagogues, that if he found any of this way, whether they were men or women, he might bring them bound unto Jerusalem.

Acts 22 [4]And I persecuted this way unto the death, binding and delivering into prisons both men and women. [5]As also the high Priest doth bear me witness, and all the estate of the elders: from whom also I received letters unto the brethren, and went to Damascus, to bring them which were there, bound unto Jerusalem, for to be punished.

Acts 26 [9]I verily thought with myself, that I ought to do many things contrary to the name of Jesus of Nazareth: [10]Which thing I also did in Jerusalem, and many of the Saints did I shut up in prison, having received authority from the chief Priests, and when they were put to death, I gave my voice against them. [11]And I punished them oft in every Synagogue, and compelled them to blaspheme, and being exceedingly mad against them, I persecuted them even unto strange cities.

1 Cor. 15 [9]For I am the least of the apostles, that am not meet to be called an apostle, because I persecuted the Church of God.

Gal. 1 [13]For ye have heard of my conversation in time past in the Jews' religion, how that beyond measure I persecuted the Church of God, and wasted it: [14]And profited in the Jews' religion above many my equals in mine own nation, being more exceedingly zealous of the traditions of my fathers.

Phil. 3 [6]Concerning zeal, persecuting the Church; touching the righteousness which is in the law, blameless.

1 Tim. 1 [13]Who was before a blasphemer, and a persecutor, and injurious. But I obtained mercy, because I did it ignorantly, in unbelief.

Paul's Conversion

Acts 9 [3]And as he journeyed, he came near Damascus: and suddenly there shined round about him a light from heaven: [4]And he fell to the earth, and heard a voice saying unto him, Saul, Saul, why persecutest thou me? [5]And he said, Who art thou, Lord? And the Lord said, I am Jesus whom thou persecutest: it is hard for thee to kick against the pricks. [6]And he trembling and astonished said, Lord, what wilt thou have me to do? And the Lord said unto him, Arise, and go into the city, and it shall be told thee what thou must do. [7]And the men which journeyed with him stood speechless, hearing a voice, but seeing no man. [8]And Saul arose from the earth; and when his eyes were opened, he saw no man: but they led him by the hand, and brought him into Damascus. [9]And he was three days without sight, and neither did eat nor drink.

[10]And there was a certain disciple at Damascus, named Ananias; and to him said the Lord in a vision, Ananias. And he said, Behold, I am here, Lord. [11]And the Lord said unto him, Arise, and go into the street which is called Straight, and enquire in the house of Judas for one called Saul, of Tarsus: for, behold, he prayeth, [12]And hath seen in a vision a man named Ananias coming in, and putting his hand on him, that he might receive his sight. [13]Then Ananias answered, Lord, I have heard by many of this man, how much evil he hath done to thy saints at Jerusalem: [14]And here he hath authority from the chief priests to bind all that call on thy name. [15]But the Lord said unto him, Go thy way: for he is a chosen vessel unto me, to bear my name before the Gentiles, and kings, and the children of Israel: [16]For I will shew him how great things he must suffer for my name's sake. [17]And Ananias went his way, and entered into the house; and putting his hands on him said, Brother Saul, the Lord, even Jesus, that appeared

unto thee in the way as thou camest, hath sent me, that thou mightest receive thy sight, and be filled with the Holy Ghost. 18And immediately there fell from his eyes as it had been scales: and he received sight forthwith, and arose, and was baptized. 19And when he had received meat, he was strengthened. Then was Saul certain days with the disciples which were at Damascus. 20And straightway he preached Christ in the synagogues, that he is the Son of God.

The First Missionary Journey

Acts 13 1Now there were in the church that was at Antioch certain prophets and teachers; as Barnabas, and Simeon that was called Niger, and Lucius of Cyrene, and Manaen, which had been brought up with Herod the tetrarch, and Saul. 2As they ministered to the Lord, and fasted, the Holy Ghost said, Separate me Barnabas and Saul for the work whereunto I have called them. 3And when they had fasted and prayed, and laid their hands on them, they sent them away.

14But when they departed from Perga, they came to Antioch in Pisidia, and went into the synagogue on the sabbath day, and sat down.

Acts 14 1And it came to pass in Iconium, that they went both together into the synagogue of the Jews, and so spake, that a great multitude both of the Jews and also of the Greeks believed.

21And when they had preached the gospel to that city, and had taught many, they returned again to Lystra, and to Iconium, and Antioch, 22Confirming the souls of the disciples, and exhorting them to continue in the faith, and that we must through much tribulation enter into the kingdom of God. 23And when they had ordained them elders in every church, and had prayed with fasting, they commended them to the Lord, on whom they believed. 24And after they had passed throughout Pisidia, they came to Pamphylia. 25And when they had preached the word in Perga, they went down into Attalia: 26And thence sailed to Antioch, from whence they had been recommended to the grace of God for the work which they fulfilled.

The Second Missionary Journey

Acts 15 35Paul also and Barnabas continued in Antioch, teaching and preaching the word of the Lord, with many others also.

36And some days after Paul said unto Barnabas, Let us go again and visit our brethren in every city where we have preached the word of the Lord, and see how they do. 37And Barnabas determined to take with them John, whose surname was Mark. 38But Paul thought not good to take him with them, who departed from them from Pamphylia, and went not with them to the work. 39And the contention was so sharp between them, that they departed asunder one from the other: and so Barnabas took Mark, and sailed unto Cyprus; 40And Paul chose Silas, and departed, being recommended by the brethren unto the grace of God. 41And he went through Syria and Cilicia, confirming the churches.

Acts 16 7After they were come to Mysia, they assayed to go into Bithynia: but the Spirit suffered them not.

THE MACEDONIAN CALL

Acts 16 8And they passing by Mysia came down to Troas. 9And a vision appeared to Paul in the night; There stood a man of Macedonia, and prayed him, saying, Come over into Macedonia, and help us. 10And after he had seen the vision,

immediately we endeavoured to go into
Macedonia, assuredly gathering that the
Lord had called us for to preach the gos-
pel unto them. [11]Therefore loosing from
Troas, we came with a straight course to
Samothracia, and the next day to Neapolis;

IN PHILIPPI

Acts 16 [12]And from thence to Philippi,
which is the chief city of that part of Macedonia, and a colony: and we were in that
city abiding certain days. [13]And on the
sabbath we went out of the city by a river
side, where prayer was wont to be made;
and we sat down, and spake unto the
women which resorted thither.

[14]And a certain woman named Lydia,
a seller of purple, of the city of Thyatira,
which worshipped God, heard us: whose
heart the Lord opened, that she attended
unto the things which were spoken of Paul.
[15]And when she was baptized, and her
household, she besought us, saying, If ye
have judged me to be faithful to the Lord,
come into my house, and abide there. And
she constrained us.

[16]And it came to pass, as we went to
prayer, a certain damsel possessed with a
spirit of divination met us, which brought
her masters much gain by soothsaying:
[17]The same followed Paul and us, and
cried, saying, These men are the servants
of the most high God, which shew unto us
the way of salvation. [18]And this did she
many days. But Paul, being grieved,
turned and said to the spirit, I command
thee in the name of Jesus Christ to come
out of her. And he came out the same hour.

[19]And when her masters saw that the
hope of their gains was gone, they caught
Paul and Silas, and drew them into the
marketplace unto the rulers, [20]And
brought them to the magistrates, saying,
These men, being Jews, do exceedingly
trouble our city, [21]And teach customs,
which are not lawful for us to receive, neither to observe, being Romans. [22]And the
multitude rose up together against them;
and the magistrates rent off their clothes,
and commanded to beat them. [23]And
when they had laid many stripes upon
them, they cast them into prison, charging
the jailer to keep them safely: [24]Who,
having received such a charge, thrust them
into the inner prison, and made their feet
fast in the stocks.

[25]And at midnight Paul and Silas
prayed, and sang praises unto God: and
the prisoners heard them. [26]And suddenly
there was a great earthquake, so that the
foundations of the prison were shaken: and
immediately all the doors were opened,
and every one's bands were loosed. [27]And
the keeper of the prison awaking out of
his sleep, and seeing the prison doors open,
he drew out his sword, and would have
killed himself, supposing that the prisoners had been fled. [28]But Paul cried with
a loud voice, saying, Do thyself no harm:
for we are all here. [29]Then he called for a
light, and sprang in, and came trembling,
and fell down before Paul and Silas,
[30]And brought them out, and said, Sirs,
what must I do to be saved? [31]And they
said, Believe on the Lord Jesus Christ, and
thou shalt be saved, and thy house. [32]And
they spake unto him the word of the Lord,
and to all that were in his house. [33]And he
took them the same hour of the night, and
washed their stripes; and was baptized, he
and all his, straightway.

IN ATHENS

Acts 17 [14]And then immediately the
brethren sent away Paul to go as it were to
the sea: but Silas and Timotheus abode
there still. [15]And they that conducted Paul
brought him unto Athens: and receiving

a commandment unto Silas and Timotheus for to come to him with all speed, they departed.

[16]Now while Paul waited for them at Athens, his spirit was stirred in him, when he saw the city wholly given to idolatry. [17]Therefore disputed he in the synagogue with the Jews, and with the devout persons, and in the market daily with them that met with him.

[32]And when they heard of the resurrection of the dead, some mocked: and others said, We will hear thee again of this matter. [33]So Paul departed from among them. [34]Howbeit certain men clave unto him, and believed: among the which was Dionysius the Areopagite, and a woman named Damaris, and others with them.

IN CORINTH

Acts 18 [1]After these things Paul departed from Athens, and came to Corinth; [2]And found a certain Jew named Aquila, born in Pontus, lately come from Italy, with his wife Priscilla, (because that Claudius had commanded all Jews to depart from Rome,) and came unto them. [3]And because he was of the same craft, he abode with them, and wrought: (for by their occupation they were tentmakers.) [4]And he reasoned in the synagogue every sabbath, and persuaded the Jews and the Greeks.

[9]Then spake the Lord to Paul in the night by a vision, Be not afraid, but speak, and hold not thy peace: [10]For I am with thee, and no man shall set on thee to hurt thee: for I have much people in this city. [11]And he continued there a year and six months, teaching the word of God among them.

The Third Missionary Journey

Acts 18 [22]And when he had landed at Cesarea, and gone up, and saluted the church, he went down to Antioch. [23]And after he had spent some time there, he departed, and went over all the country of Galatia and Phrygia in order, strengthening all the disciples.

IN EPHESUS

Acts 19 [1]And it came to pass, that, while Apollos was at Corinth, Paul having passed through the upper coasts came to Ephesus: and finding certain disciples, [2]He said unto them, Have ye received the Holy Ghost since ye believed? And they said unto him, We have not so much as heard whether there be any Holy Ghost. [3]And he said unto them, Unto what then were ye baptized? And they said, Unto John's baptism. [4]Then said Paul, John verily baptized with the baptism of repentance, saying unto the people, that they should believe on him which should come after him, that is, on Christ Jesus. [5]When they heard this, they were baptized in the name of the Lord Jesus. [6]And when Paul had laid his hands upon them, the Holy Ghost came on them; and they spake with tongues, and prophesied. [7]And all the men were about twelve. [8]And he went into the synagogue, and spake boldly for the space of three months, disputing and persuading the things concerning the kingdom of God. [9]But when divers were hardened, and believed not, but spake evil of that way before the multitude, he departed from them, and separated the disciples, disputing daily in the school of one Tyrannus. [10]And this continued by the space of two years; so that all they which dwelt in Asia heard the word of the Lord Jesus, both Jews and Greeks. [11]And God wrought special miracles by the hands of Paul: [12]So that from his body were brought unto the sick handkerchiefs or aprons, and the diseases de-

parted from them, and the evil spirits went
out of them.

IN TROAS

Acts 20 7And upon the first day of the
week, when the disciples came together to
break bread, Paul preached unto them,
ready to depart on the morrow; and continued his speech until midnight. 8And
there were many lights in the upper chamber, where they were gathered together.
9And there sat in a window a certain
young man named Eutychus, being fallen
into a deep sleep: and as Paul was long
preaching, he sunk down with sleep, and
fell down from the third loft, and was
taken up dead. 10And Paul went down,
and fell on him, and embracing him said,
Trouble not yourselves; for his life is in
him. 11When he therefore was come up
again, and had broken bread, and eaten,
and talked a long while, even till break of
day, so he departed. 12And they brought
the young man alive, and were not a little
comforted.

IN MILETUS

Acts 20 17And from Miletus he sent to
Ephesus, and called the elders of the
church.

36And when he had thus spoken, he
kneeled down, and prayed with them all.
37And they all wept sore, and fell on Paul's
neck, and kissed him, 38Sorrowing most
of all for the words which he spake, that
they should see his face no more. And
they accompanied him unto the ship.

Imprisonment Prophesied

Acts 21 8And the next day we that were
of Paul's company departed, and came
unto Caesarea: and we entered into the
house of Philip the evangelist, which was
one of the seven; and abode with him.
9And the same man had four daughters,
virgins, which did prophesy. 10And as we
tarried there many days, there came down
from Judaea a certain prophet, named
Agabus. 11And when he was come unto
us, he took Paul's girdle, and bound his
own hands and feet, and said, Thus saith
the Holy Ghost, So shall the Jews at Jerusalem bind the man that owneth this girdle, and shall deliver him into the hands
of the Gentiles. 12And when we heard
these things, both we, and they of that
place, besought him not to go up to Jerusalem. 13Then Paul answered, What
mean ye to weep and to break mine heart?
for I am ready not to be bound only, but
also to die at Jerusalem for the name of
the Lord Jesus. 14And when he would not
be persuaded, we ceased, saying, The will
of the Lord be done. 27And when the
seven days were almost ended, the Jews
which were of Asia, when they saw him
in the temple, stirred up all the people,
and laid hands on him, 28Crying out,
Men of Israel, help: This is the man, that
teacheth all men every where against the
people, and the law, and this place: and
further brought Greeks also into the temple, and hath polluted this holy place.

Acts 22 25And as they bound him with
thongs, Paul said unto the centurion that
stood by, Is it lawful for you to scourge
a man that is a Roman, and uncondemned? 26When the centurion heard that,
he went and told the chief captain, saying, Take heed what thou doest: for this
man is a Roman. 27Then the chief captain came, and said unto him, Tell me, art
thou a Roman? He said, Yea. 28And the
chief captain answered, With a great sum
obtained I this freedom. And Paul said,
But I was free born. 29Then straightway
they departed from him which should
have examined him: and the chief captain

also was afraid, after he knew that he was a Roman, and because he had bound him.

Acts 23 [11]And the night following the Lord stood by him, and said, Be of good cheer, Paul: for as thou hast testified of me in Jerusalem, so must thou bear witness also at Rome. [31]Then the soldiers, as it was commanded them, took Paul, and brought him by night to Antipatris. [32]On the morrow they left the horsemen to go with him, and returned to the castle: [33]Who, when they came to Caesarea, and delivered the epistle to the governor, presented Paul also before him.

Appeals to Caesar

Acts 24 [23]And he commanded a centurion to keep Paul, and to let him have liberty, and that he should forbid none of his acquaintance to minister or come unto him. [24]And after certain days, when Felix came with his wife Drusilla, which was a Jewess, he sent for Paul, and heard him concerning the faith in Christ. [25]And as he reasoned of righteousness, temperance, and judgment to come, Felix trembled, and answered, Go thy way for this time; when I have a convenient season, I will call for thee. [26]He hoped also that money should have been given him of Paul, that he might loose him: wherefore he sent for him the oftener, and communed with him. [27]But after two years Porcius Festus came into Felix' room: and Felix, willing to shew the Jews a pleasure, left Paul bound.

Acts 25 [12]Then Festus, when he had conferred with the council, answered, Hast thou appealed unto Caesar? unto Caesar shalt thou go.

Before Agrippa

Acts 26 [1]Then Agrippa said unto Paul, Thou art permitted to speak for thyself. Then Paul stretched forth the hand, and answered for himself. [24]And as he thus spake for himself, Festus said with a loud voice, Paul, thou art beside thyself; much learning doth make thee mad. [25]But he said, I am not mad, most noble Festus; but speak forth the words of truth and soberness. [26]For the king knoweth of these things, before whom also I speak freely: for I am persuaded that none of these things are hidden from him; for this thing was not done in a corner. [27]King Agrippa, believest thou the prophets? I know that thou believest. [28]Then Agrippa said unto Paul, Almost thou persuadest me to be a Christian. [29]And Paul said, I would to God, that not only thou, but also all that hear me this day, were both almost, and altogether such as I am, except these bonds.

Sets Out for Rome

Acts 27 [1]And when it was determined that we should sail into Italy, they delivered Paul and certain other prisoners unto one named Julius, a centurion of Augustus' band. [20]And when neither sun nor stars in many days appeared, and no small tempest lay on us, all hope that we should be saved was then taken away.

Storm and Shipwreck

Acts 27 [22]And now I exhort you to be of good cheer: for there shall be no loss of any man's life among you, but of the ship. [23]For there stood by me this night the angel of God, whose I am, and whom I serve, [24]Saying, Fear not, Paul; thou must be brought before Caesar: and, lo, God hath given thee all them that sail with thee. [25]Wherefore, sirs, be of good cheer: for I believe God, that it shall be even as it was told me. [41]And falling into a place where two seas met, they ran the ship aground;

and the forepart stuck fast, and remained
unmoveable, but the hinder part was
broken with the violence of the waves.

Acts 28 [1]And when they were escaped,
then they knew that the island was called
Melita. [2]And the barbarous people
shewed us no little kindness: for they kindled a fire, and received us every one, because of the present rain, and because of
the cold. [3]And when Paul had gathered
a bundle of sticks, and laid them on the
fire, there came a viper out of the heat,
and fastened on his hand. [4]And when the
barbarians saw the venomous beast hang
on his hand, they said among themselves,
No doubt this man is a murderer, whom,
though he hath escaped the sea, yet vengeance suffereth not to live. [5]And he shook
off the beast into the fire, and felt no harm.
[6]Howbeit they looked when he should
have swollen, or fallen down dead suddenly: but after they had looked a great
while, and saw no harm come to him, they
changed their minds, and said that he was
a god.

Dwells in Rome

Acts 28 [16]And when we came to Rome,
the Centurion delivered the prisoners to
the Captain of the guard: but Paul was
suffered to dwell by himself, with a soldier that kept him. [30]And Paul dwelt two
whole years in his own hired house, and
received all that came in unto him,
[31]Preaching the kingdom of God, and
teaching those things which concern the
Lord Jesus Christ, with all confidence, no
man forbidding him.

Foretells His Death

2 Tim. 4 [5]But watch thou in all things,
endure afflictions, do the work of an evangelist, make full proof of thy ministry.
[6]For I am now ready to be offered, and the
time of my departure is at hand. [7]I have
fought a good fight, I have finished my
course, I have kept the faith: [8]Henceforth
there is laid up for me a crown of righteousness, which the Lord, the righteous
judge, shall give me at that day: and not
to me only, but unto all them also that
love his appearing.

Paul's Writings

CHRONOLOGICALLY

(The dates suggested here are uncertain and subject to considerable debate.)

Galatians, written AD 49, probably from Syrian Antioch.
1 and 2 Thessalonians, AD 51-52, from Corinth.
1 and 2 Corinthians, AD 53-56, from Ephesus.
Romans, AD 55-56, from Corinth.
Colossians, AD 61, from Rome.
Philemon, AD 61, from Rome.
Ephesians, AD 61, from Rome.
Philippians, AD 62-64, from Rome.
Titus, AD 65-66, from Rome.
1 Timothy, AD 65-66, from Rome.
2 Timothy, AD 67, from Rome.

TOPICALLY

Galatians—Law and gospel, sin and grace.
1 and 2 Thessalonians—The Second Coming.
1 Corinthians—Moral and practical problems, unity, spiritual gifts, the resurrection.
2 Corinthians—Defense of Paul's ministry in Corinth.
Romans—Justification by faith, Law and gospel, sin and grace, destiny of the Jews.
Colossians—The person and work of Christ.
Philemon—Concerning the slave, Onesimus.
Ephesians—The church.
Philippians—The person of Christ; expressions of thanksgiving and joy.
Titus—Church government, pastoral care.
1 Timothy—Church government, pastoral care, false teachers.
2 Timothy—False teachers, personal matters.

PEACE

[pēs] Freedom from disturbance or agitation;

calm; repose; a state of quiet or tranquillity. The ideal of peace plays a prominent role in both Judaism and Christianity. The common Hebrew greeting, *Shalom*, means "peace" and is used in such phrases as "Is there peace to you" (How are you?) and "Peace be with you." One of the great desires of the Israelites, expressed in the priestly benediction—"The LORD lift up his countenance upon thee and give thee peace" (*Num. 6:26*)—was peace from enemies and the attendant material prosperity. Those who trusted in God were promised inward, or spiritual peace. Christians, as children of the God of Peace, are exhorted to be at peace with one another. The gospel of Christ may aptly be described as a message of spiritual peace from God to man.

SCRIPTURE

Peace to Be Sought of God

Jer. 29 [7]And seek the peace of the city whither I have caused you to be carried away captives, and pray unto the LORD for it: for in the peace thereof shall ye have peace.

1 Tim. 2 [1]I exhort therefore, that, first of all, supplications, prayers, intercessions, and giving of thanks, be made for all men; [2]For kings, and for all that are in authority; that we may lead a quiet and peaceable life in all godliness and honesty.

Bestowed by God

Lev. 26 [6]And I will give peace in the land, and ye shall lie down, and none shall make you afraid: and I will rid evil beasts out of the land, neither shall the sword go through your land.

1 Kin. 2 [33]Their blood shall therefore return upon the head of Joab, and upon the head of his seed for ever: but upon David, and upon his seed, and upon his house, and upon his throne, shall there be peace for ever from the LORD.

Prov. 16 [7]When a man's ways please the LORD, he maketh even his enemies to be at peace with him.

Isa. 45 [7]I form the light, and create darkness: I make peace, and create evil: I the LORD do all these things.

Jer. 14 [13]Then said I, Ah Lord GOD! behold, the prophets say unto them, Ye shall not see the sword, neither shall ye have famine; but I will give you assured peace in this place.

Peace Should Be Maintained

Psa. 34 [14]Depart from evil, and do good; seek peace, and pursue it.

Matt. 5 [9]Blessed are the peacemakers: for they shall be called the children of God.

Rom. 12 [18]If it be possible, as much as lieth in you, live peaceably with all men.

Rom. 14 [19]Let us therefore follow after the things which make for peace, and things wherewith one may edify another.

1 Cor. 7 [15]But if the unbelieving depart, let him depart. A brother or a sister is not under bondage in such cases: but God hath called us to peace.

Eph. 4 [3]Endeavouring to keep the unity of the Spirit in the bond of peace.

1 Thess. 5 [13]And to esteem them very highly in love for their work's sake. And be at peace among yourselves.

2 Tim. 2 [22]Flee also youthful lusts: but follow righteousness, faith, charity, peace, with them that call on the Lord out of a pure heart.

Jas. 3 [18]And the fruit of righteousness is sown in peace of them that make peace.

1 Pet. 3 [11]Let him eschew evil, and do good; let him seek peace, and ensue it.

Spiritual Peace God's Gift

John 14 [27]Peace I leave with you, my peace I give unto you: not as the world giveth, give I unto you. Let not your heart be troubled, neither let it be afraid.

Acts 10 [36]The word which God sent unto the children of Israel, preaching peace by Jesus Christ: (he is Lord of all).

Rom. 1 [7]To all that be in Rome, beloved of God, called to be saints: Grace to you and peace from God our Father, and the Lord Jesus Christ.

Rom. 5 [1]Therefore being justified by faith, we have peace with God through our Lord Jesus Christ.

Rom. 8 [6]For to be carnally minded is death; but to be spiritually minded is life and peace.

Rom. 14 [17]For the kingdom of God is not meat and drink; but righteousness, and peace, and joy in the Holy Ghost.

Phil. 4 [7]And the peace of God, which passeth all understanding, shall keep your hearts and minds through Christ Jesus.

Col. 3 [15]And let the peace of God rule in your hearts, to the which also ye are called in one body; and be ye thankful.

1 Thess. 5 [23]And the very God of peace sanctify you wholly; and I pray God your whole spirit and soul and body be preserved blameless unto the coming of our Lord Jesus Christ.

2 Thess. 3 [16]Now the Lord of peace himself give you peace always by all means. The Lord be with you all.

Rev. 1 [4]John to the seven churches which are in Asia: Grace be unto you, and peace, from him which is, and which was, and which is to come; and from the seven Spirits which are before his throne.

Peace Denied to the Wicked

2 Kin. 9 [31]And as Jehu entered in at the gate, she said, Had Zimri peace, who slew his master?

Isa. 48 [22]There is no peace, saith the LORD, unto the wicked.

Isa. 59 [8]The way of peace they know not: and there is no judgment in their goings: they have made them crooked paths; whosoever goeth therein shall not know peace.

Jer. 12 [12]The spoilers are come upon all high places through the wilderness: for the sword of the LORD shall devour from the one end of the land even to the other end of the land: no flesh shall have peace.

Ezek. 7 [25]Destruction cometh; and they shall seek peace, and there shall be none.

Peace Promised

Psa. 29 [11]The LORD will give strength unto his people; the LORD will bless his people with peace.

Psa. 85 [8]I will hear what God the LORD will speak: for he will speak peace unto his people, and to his saints: but let them not turn again to folly.

John 14 [27]Peace I leave with you, my peace I give unto you: not as the world giveth, give I unto you. Let not your heart be troubled, neither let it be afraid.

Gal. 6 [16]And as many as walk according to this rule, peace be on them, and mercy, and upon the Israel of God.

Eph. 6 [23]Peace be to the brethren, and love with faith, from God the Father and the Lord Jesus Christ.

Peace in Earth and Heaven

Luke 2 [13]And suddenly there was with the angel a multitude of the heavenly host praising God, and saying, [14]Glory to God in the highest, and on earth peace, good will toward men.

Luke 19 [37]And when he was come nigh, even now at the descent of the mount of Olives, the whole multitude of the disciples began to rejoice and praise God with a loud voice for all the mighty works that they had seen; [38]Saying, Blessed be the King that cometh in the name of the Lord: peace in heaven, and glory in the highest.

PEKAH

[pē'ka] The son of Remaliah and eighteenth king of Israel (736-732/1 BC). Pekah gained the throne through a conspiracy which resulted in the assassination of his predecessor, Pekahiah. It is probable that this plot was a reflection of resentment toward the national policy which had been established by Pekahiah's father, Menahem. At any rate, Pekah quickly joined with Rezin of Syria to form a coalition to withstand the relentless advance of Tiglath-Pileser III of Assyria. At Ahaz' refusal to join this confederacy, troops were sent against Judah; the Southern Kingdom held, but with great loss of life and at the price of many captives, some of whom were later returned. (*See 2 Chr. 28:5-15*) By this time, Tiglath-Pileser had begun the march which was to put the world at his feet. Syria was leveled and Pekah was left with but a remnant of his kingdom, consisting of Ephraim and Western Manasseh. In an attempt to break down nationalistic patterns, Tiglath-Pileser deported thousands of Israelites and other vanquished peoples and organized the conquered lands into Assyrian provinces. Pekah was shortly thereafter assassinated and succeeded by the last of the monarchs of Israel, Hoshea.

See AHAZ, TIGLATH-PILESER, HOSHEA

SCRIPTURE

2 Kin. 15 [23]In the fiftieth year of Azariah king of Judah, Pekahiah the son of Menahem began to reign over Israel in Samaria, and reigned two years. [24]And he did that which was evil in the sight of the LORD: he departed not from the sins of Jeroboam the son of Nebat, who made Israel to sin. [25]But Pekah the son of Remaliah, a captain of his, conspired against him, and smote him in Samaria, in the palace of the king's house, with Argob and Arieh, and with him fifty men of the Gileadites: and he killed him, and reigned in his room. [26]And the rest of the acts of Pekahiah, and all that he did, behold, they are written in the book of the Chronicles of the kings of Israel.

[27]In the two and fiftieth year of Azariah king of Judah, Pekah the son of Remaliah began to reign over Israel in Samaria, and reigned twenty years. [28]And he did that which was evil in the sight of the LORD: he departed not from the sins of Jeroboam the son of Nebat, who made Israel to sin. [29]In the days of Pekah king of Israel came Tiglath-pileser king of Assyria, and took Ijon and Abel-beth-maachah, and Janoah, and Kedesh, and Hazor, and Gilead, and Galilee, all the land of Naphtali, and carried them captive to Assyria. [30]And Hoshea the son of Elah made a conspiracy against Pekah the son of Remaliah, and smote him, and slew him, and reigned in his stead, in the twentieth year of Jotham the son of Uzziah. [31]And the rest of the acts of Pekah, and all that he did, behold, they are written in the book of the Chronicles of the kings of Israel.

PEKAHIAH

[pek a hī'a] The son of Menahem and the seventeenth king of Israel (738-736 BC). After a reign of two years, Pekahiah was slain by conspiracy led by Pekah, one of his own captains. It may be assumed that at least part of the resentment against Pekahiah stemmed from the submission of his father the Assyrian rule and the consequent tribute which drained Israel of its financial resources.

See MENAHEM, PEKAH

SCRIPTURE

2 Kin. 15 [23]In the fiftieth year of Azariah king of Judah, Pekahiah the son of Menahem began to reign over Israel in

Samaria, and reigned two years. 24 And he
did that which was evil in the sight of the
LORD: he departed not from the sins of
Jeroboam the son of Nebat, who made
Israel to sin. 25 But Pekah the son of Remaliah, a captain of his, conspired against
him, and smote him in Samaria, in the palace of the king's house, with Argob and
Arieh, and with him fifty men of the Gileadites: and he killed him, and reigned in
his room. 26 And the rest of the acts of
Pekahiah, and all that he did, behold, they
are written in the book of the Chronicles
of the kings of Israel.

PENTATEUCH

[pen′ta tūk] Literally, a "five-fold book." This is the Greek term used to refer to the first five books of the Bible. These five books form a unit which contain an account of creation, the early history of the ancestors of Israel, and the Mosaic Law. The Jews referred to the Pentateuch as the *Torah*, or the Law. For some time most Biblical critics have rejected the traditional view that Moses was the author of these five books, asserting that the Pentateuch is comprised of different documents or strata of material which originated at various stages in Israel's history. As one might expect, a tremendous amount of literature on this subject has been produced; conclusions vary widely. Some claim that Moses had very little, if anything, to do with the composition of the Pentateuch; others, that it was compiled or edited at a later date, but largely from genuine Mosaic material; still others hold to the traditional theory of Mosaic authorship. Since the limits of this article do not permit an adequate discussion of this problem, the reader is referred to a standard introductory works on the Old Testament. In an effort to solve the problem of the authorship of the Pentateuch, scholars have sometimes separated *Deuteronomy* from the first four books and these became known as the Tetrateuch or "four-fold book." Similarly, the book of *Joshua* has been added to the Pentateuch to form what is known as the Hexateuch, or "six-fold book."

PERAEA

[pė rē′a] The province designated in the Bible as "the land beyond the Jordan." It appears that Jesus was baptized in Peraea and that he spent a considerable portion of his ministry in that region.

REFERENCE: *Matt. 19; Mark 10:1-31; Luke 18:15-30; John 10:40.*

PERFECTION

[pẽr fek′shun] The quality or state of being perfect or complete, so that nothing is wanting; the highest attainable state of excellence. Absolute perfection—the perfection of God—is set before man as an ideal and aim, but cannot be attained in this life. Through God's grace, however, the Christian may achieve a state of relative excellence which is termed perfection.

SCRIPTURE

Perfection Not in Man

Job 9 20 If I justify myself, mine own
mouth shall condemn me: if I say, I am
perfect, it shall also prove me perverse.
21 Though I were perfect, yet would I not
know my soul: I would despise my life.

Psa. 143 2 And enter not into judgment
with thy servant: for in thy sight shall no
man living be justified.

Eccl. 7 20 For there is not a just man
upon earth, that doeth good, and sinneth
not.

Phil. 3 12 Not as though I had already
attained, either were already perfect: but
I follow after, if that I may apprehend
that for which also I am apprehended of
Christ Jesus. 13 Brethren, I count not myself to have apprehended: but this one
thing I do, forgetting those things which
are behind, and reaching forth unto those
things which are before, 14 I press toward
the mark for the prize of the high calling
of God in Christ Jesus.

1 John 1 [8]If we say that we have no sin, we deceive ourselves, and the truth is not in us. [10]If we say that we have not sinned, we make him a liar, and his word is not in us.

Perfection to Be Striven For

Deut. 5 [32]Ye shall observe to do therefore as the LORD your God hath commanded you: ye shall not turn aside to the right hand or to the left.

Deut. 18 [13]Thou shalt be perfect with the LORD thy God.

Josh. 23 [6]Be ye therefore very courageous to keep and to do all that is written in the book of the law of Moses, that ye turn not aside therefrom to the right hand or to the left.

1 Kin. 8 [61]Let your heart therefore be perfect with the LORD our God, to walk in his statutes, and to keep his commandments, as at this day.

Psa. 101 [2]I will behave myself wisely in a perfect way. O when wilt thou come unto me? I will walk within my house with a perfect heart.

Matt. 5 [48]Be ye therefore perfect, even as your Father which is in heaven is perfect.

Rom. 13 [14]But put ye on the Lord Jesus Christ, and make not provision for the flesh, to fulfil the lusts thereof,

2 Cor. 7 [1]Having therefore these promises, dearly beloved, let us cleanse ourselves from all filthiness of the flesh and spirit, perfecting holiness in the fear of God.

2 Cor. 13 [9]For we are glad, when we are weak, and ye are strong: and this also we wish, even your perfection. [11]Finally, brethren, farewell. Be perfect, be of good comfort, be of one mind, live in peace; and the God of love and peace shall be with you.

Eph. 4 [13]Till we all come in the unity of the faith, and of the knowledge of the Son of God, unto a perfect man, unto the measure of the stature of the fulness of Christ: [14]That we henceforth be no more children, tossed to and fro, and carried about with every wind of doctrine, by the sleight of men, and cunning craftiness, whereby they lie in wait to deceive.

Phil. 1 [10]That ye may approve things that are excellent; that ye may be sincere and without offence till the day of Christ.

Phil. 2 [15]That ye may be blameless and harmless, the sons of God, without rebuke, in the midst of a crooked and perverse nation, among whom ye shine as lights in the world.

Col. 1 [21]And you, that were sometime alienated and enemies in your mind by wicked works, yet now hath he reconciled [22]In the body of his flesh through death, to present you holy and unblameable and unreproveable in his sight.

PERIZZITES

[per'i zīts] One of the seven nations of the land of Canaan who were to be driven out by the conquering Israelites. Israel failed to expel these peoples completely "and they took their daughters to be their wives, and gave their daughters to their sons, and served their gods." The same problems of toleration and intermarriage with these groups were an object of the reforming efforts of Ezra and Nehemiah after the return of Israel from Babylonian exile.

SCRIPTURE

Land Given to Israel

Deut. 20 [16]But of the cities of these people, which the LORD thy God doth give thee for an inheritance, thou shalt save alive nothing that breatheth: [17]But thou shalt utterly destroy them; namely, the Hittites, and the Amorites, the Canaanites, and the Perizzites, the Hivites, and the Jebusites; as the LORD thy God hath commanded thee: [18]That they teach you not to do after all their abominations, which they have done unto their gods; so should ye sin against the LORD your God.

Intermarry with Israel

Judg. 3 [5]And the children of Israel dwelt among the Canaanites, Hittites, and Amorites, and Perizzites, and Hivites and Jebusites: [6]And they took their daughters to be their wives, and gave their daughters to their sons, and served their gods.

Israel Urged to Separate From

Ezra 9 [1]Now when these things were done, the princes came to me, saying, The people of Israel, and the priests, and the Levites, have not separated themselves from the people of the lands, doing according to their abominations, even of the Canaanites, the Hittites, the Perizzites, the Jebusites, the Ammonites, the Moabites, the Egyptians, and the Amorites. [2]For they have taken of their daughters for themselves, and for their sons: so that the holy seed have mingled themselves with the people of those lands: yea, the hand of the princes and rulers hath been chief in this trespass.

PERJURY

[pẽr′jŏŏ ri] The act of swearing falsely or breaking an oath, particularly in court. No legal system can be maintained without safeguards against perjury. The ninth commandment of the Decalogue prohibits such false swearing.

SCRIPTURE

Ex. 20 [16]Thou shalt not bear false witness against thy neighbour.

Lev. 19 [12]And ye shall not swear by my name falsely, neither shalt thou profane the name of thy God: I am the LORD.

Zech. 5 [3]Then said he unto me, This is the curse that goeth forth over the face of the whole earth: for every one that stealeth shall be cut off as on this side, according to it; and every one that sweareth shall be cut off as on that side, according to it. [4]I will bring it forth, saith the LORD of hosts, and it shall enter into the house of the thief, and into the house of him that sweareth falsely by my name: and it shall remain in the midst of his house, and shall consume it with the timber thereof and the stones thereof.

Zech. 8 [17]And let none of you imagine evil in your hearts against his neighbour; and love no false oath.

PERSECUTION

[pûr sė kū′shun] The act of pursuing with hostile intentions; specifically, to cause to suffer because of belief, especially religious belief. Persecution is usually associated only with the Christian era, but the worshippers of the true God underwent severe trials in the Old Testament period also. This is summed up by the writer of *Hebrews* in the following words: "others were tortured, not accepting deliverance; that they might obtain a better resurrection: And others had trial of cruel mockings and scourgings, yea, moreover of bonds and imprisonment: They were stoned, they were sawn asunder, were tempted, were slain with the sword: they wandered about in sheepskins and goatskins; being destitute, afflicted, tormented; Of whom the world was not worthy: they wandered in deserts, and in mountains, and in dens and caves of the earth" (*Heb. 11:35-38*).

Beginning with the persecution which scattered the church in Jerusalem and resulted in the death of Stephen, there have been few periods in the history of the Church in which Christians were not persecuted for their loyalty to Christ. Jesus promised his disciples that they could and should expect severe treatment at the hands of those who were opposed to the gospel message and its implications. If men had persecuted him, they would surely persecute his disciples; faithfulness unto death, however, carried with it the assurance of eternal life.

See MARTYR

SCRIPTURE

Persecution Foretold and Expected

Matt. 23 [34]Wherefore, behold, I send unto you prophets, and wise men, and scribes: and some of them ye shall kill and crucify; and some of them shall ye scourge in your synagogues, and persecute them from city to city.

Mark 13 [12]Now the brother shall betray the brother to death, and the father the son; and children shall rise up against their parents, and shall cause them to be put to death.

Luke 10 [3]Go your ways: behold, I send you forth as lambs among wolves.

Luke 11 [49]Therefore also said the wisdom of God, I will send them prophets and apostles, and some of them they shall slay and persecute.

Luke 12 [49]I am come to send fire on the earth; and what will I, if it be already kindled? [50]But I have a baptism to be baptized with; and how am I straitened till it be accomplished! [51]Suppose ye that I am come to give peace on earth? I tell you, Nay; but rather division: [52]For from henceforth there shall be five in one house divided, three against two, and two against three. [53]The father shall be divided against the son, and the son against the father; the mother against the daughter, and the daughter against the mother; the mother in law against her daughter in law, and the daughter in law against her mother in law.

Luke 21 [12]But before all these, they shall lay their hands on you, and persecute you, delivering you up to the synagogues, and into prisons, being brought before kings and rulers for my name's sake. [13]And it shall turn to you for a testimony. [16]And ye shall be betrayed both by parents, and brethren, and kinsfolk, and friends; and some of you shall they cause to be put to death.

John 15 [20]Remember the word that I said unto you, The servant is not greater than his lord. If they have persecuted me, they will also persecute you; if they have kept my saying, they will keep yours also. [21]But all these things will they do unto you for my name's sake, because they know not him that sent me.

John 16 [2]They shall put you out of the synagogues: yea, the time cometh, that whosoever killeth you will think that he doeth God service. [3]And these things will they do unto you, because they have not known the Father, nor me.

Acts 9 [16]For I will shew him how great things he must suffer for my name's sake.

Acts 14 [22]Confirming the souls of the disciples, and exhorting them to continue in the faith, and that we must through much tribulation enter into the kingdom of God.

Acts 20 [22]And now, behold, I go bound in the spirit unto Jerusalem, not knowing the things that shall befall me there: [23]Save that the Holy Ghost witnesseth in every city, saying that bonds and afflictions abide me.

1 Cor. 4 [9]For I think that God hath set forth us the apostles last, as it were appointed to death: for we are made a spectacle unto the world, and to angels, and to men.

1 Thess. 3 [3]That no man should be moved by these afflictions: for yourselves know that we are appointed thereunto. [4]For verily, when we were with you, we told you before that we should suffer tribulation; even as it came to pass, and ye know.

2 Tim. 3 [12]Yea, and all that will live godly in Christ Jesus shall suffer persecution.

Heb. 12 [4]Ye have not yet resisted unto blood, striving against sin.

Endurance of Persecution

2 Cor. 4 [8]We are troubled on every side, yet not distressed; we are perplexed, but not in despair; [9]Persecuted, but not forsaken; cast down, but not destroyed.

Phil. 1 [28]And in nothing terrified by your adversaries: which is to them an evident token of perdition, but to you of salvation, and that of God.

2 Tim. 1 [12]For the which cause I also suffer these things: nevertheless I am not ashamed; for I know whom I have believed, and am persuaded that he is able to keep that which I have committed unto him against that day.

1 Pet. 4 [12]Beloved, think it not strange concerning the fiery trial which is to try you, as though some strange thing happened unto you: [13]But rejoice, inasmuch as ye are partakers of Christ's sufferings; that, when his glory shall be revealed, ye may be glad also with exceeding joy. [16]Yet if any man suffer as a Christian, let him not be ashamed; but let him glorify God on this behalf.

Persecution Blessed

Matt. 5 [10]Blessed are they which are persecuted for righteousness' sake: for theirs is the kingdom of heaven. [11]Blessed are ye, when men shall revile you, and persecute you, and shall say all manner of evil against you falsely, for my sake. [12]Rejoice, and be exceeding glad: for great is your reward in heaven: for so persecuted they the prophets which were before you.

Matt. 10 [32]Whosoever therefore shall confess me before men, him will I confess also before my Father which is in heaven. [33]But whosoever shall deny me before men, him will I also deny before my Father which is in heaven.

Mark 8 [35]For whosoever will save his life shall lose it: but whosoever shall lose his life for my sake and the gospel's, the same shall save it.

Mark 10 [29]And Jesus answered and said, Verily I say unto you, There is no man that hath left house, or brethren, or sisters, or father, or mother, or wife, or children, or lands, for my sake, and the gospel's, [30]But he shall receive a hundredfold now in this time, houses, and brethren, and sisters, and mothers, and children, and lands, with persecutions; and in the world to come eternal life.

Mark 13 [13]And ye shall be hated of all men for my name's sake: but he that shall endure unto the end, the same shall be saved.

PERSEVERANCE

[pûr sḗ vẽr′ans] The act or state of persisting in anything undertaken; continued pursuit or prosecution of any business, plan, or effort. The term is used in a technical sense to denote the continuance of Christians in the life appropriate to the regenerate child of God. There has been considerable debate within the Christian religion as to whether or not it is possible for a man, once having begun the New Life, to fail to persevere. Although it is impossible in an article of this scope to treat this complex subject, the scriptures which are usually referred to in such discussions are assembled below.

See STEADFASTNESS

SCRIPTURE

Matt. 24 [13]But he that shall endure unto the end, the same shall be saved.

Luke 9 [62]And Jesus said unto him, No man, having put his hand to the plow, and looking back, is fit for the kingdom of God.

John 10 [28]I give unto them eternal life; and they shall never perish, neither shall any man pluck them out of my hand. [29]My Father, which gave them me, is greater than all; and no man is able to pluck them out of my Father's hand.

Acts 14 [21]And when they had preached the gospel to that city, and had taught many, they returned again to Lystra, and to Iconium, and Antioch, [22]Confirming the souls of the disciples, and exhorting them to continue in the faith, and that we must through much tribulation enter into the kingdom of God.

Rom. 8 [38]For I am persuaded, that neither death, nor life, nor angels, nor principalities, nor powers, nor things present, nor things to come, [39]Nor height, nor depth, nor any other creature, shall be able to separate us from the love of God, which is in Jesus Christ our Lord.

1 Cor. 15 [58]Therefore my beloved brethren, be ye stedfast, unmoveable, always abounding in the work of the Lord, forasmuch as you know that your labour is not in vain in the Lord.

1 Cor. 16 [13]Watch ye, stand fast in the faith, quit you like men: be strong.

Gal. 6 [9]And let us not be weary in well doing: for in due season we shall reap, if we faint not.

Eph. 6 [18]Praying always with all prayer and supplication in the Spirit, and watching thereunto with all perseverance and supplication for all saints.

Phil. 1 [27]Let your conversation be as it becometh the gospel of Christ: that whether I come and see you, or else be absent, I may hear of your affairs, that ye stand fast in one spirit, with one mind striving together for the faith of the gospel:

Col. 1 [23]If ye continue in the faith grounded and settled, and be not moved away from the hope of the gospel, which ye have heard, and which was preached to every creature which is under heaven; whereof I Paul am made a minister.

1 Thess. 5 [21]Prove all things; hold fast that which is good.

2 Thess. 3 [13]But ye, brethren, be not weary in well doing.

1 Tim. 6 [14]That thou keep this commandment without spot, unrebukeable, until the appearing of our Lord Jesus Christ.

Heb. 2 [1]Therefore we ought to give the more earnest heed to the things which we have heard, lest at any time we should let them slip.

Heb. 3 [6]But Christ as a son over his own house; whose house are we, if we hold fast the confidence and the rejoicing of the hope firm unto the end. [13]But exhort one another daily, while it is called To day; lest any of you be hardened through the deceitfulness of sin. [14]For we are made partakers of Christ, if we hold the beginning of our confidence stedfast unto the end.

Heb. 10 [23]Let us hold fast the profession of our faith without wavering (for he is faithful that promised). [38]Now the just shall live by faith: but if any man draw back, my soul shall have no pleasure in him. [39]But we are not of them who draw back unto perdition: but of them that believe, to the saving of the soul.

Jas. 1 [12]Blessed is the man that endureth temptation: for when he is tried, he shall receive the crown of life, which the Lord hath promised to them that love him.

Jas. 5 [11]Behold we count them happy which endure. Ye have heard of the patience of Job, and have seen the end of the Lord; that the Lord is very pitiful, and of tender mercy.

1 Pet. 1 [4]To an inheritance incorruptible, and undefiled, and that fadeth not away, reserved in heaven for you, [5]Who are kept by the power of God through faith unto salvation ready to be revealed in the last time.

1 Pet. 5 [8]Be sober, be vigilant; because your adversary the devil, as a roaring lion, walketh about, seeking whom he may devour:

2 Pet. 1 [10]Wherefore the rather, brethren, give diligence to make your calling and election sure: for if ye do these things, ye shall never fall: [11]For so an entrance shall be ministered unto you abundantly into the everlasting kingdom of our Lord and Saviour Jesus Christ.

2 Pet. 3 [17]Ye therefore, beloved, seeing ye know these things before, beware lest ye also being led away with the error of the wicked, fall from your own stedfastness.

Rev. 2 [10]Fear none of those things which thou shalt suffer: behold, the devil shall cast some of you into prison, that ye may be tried, and ye shall have tribulation ten days: be thou faithful unto death, and I will give thee a crown of life. [25]But that which ye have already, hold fast till I come. [26]And he that overcometh, and keepeth my works unto the end, to him will I give power over the nations.

PERSIA

[pûr′sha] Persia, located in what is now Iran, first comes into prominence in Biblical history with the rise of Cyrus. It was this magnificent ruler who conquered Babylon in 539 BC, thus completing a campaign which had made him master of the world. In 538 BC, Cyrus issued the decree which enabled the first group of exiles to return to Jerusalem to reestablish the Jewish faith and life under the governorship of Sheshbazzar. Moreover, he returned the sacred vessels which Nebuchadnezzar had removed from Solomon's Temple. In 520 BC, the governor of the land west of the Euphrates, ordered the work at Jerusalem halted. Cyrus' original decree was recovered, however, and the reigning king Darius I (522-486 BC) confirmed it and offered the Jews any assistance which might be required to complete the job. Darius is remembered as one of the greatest of ancient rulers. He instituted systems of coinage, postage, and justice which lasted for centuries. In addition he organized the empire into administrative units called satrapies, each of which was semi-autonomous. These factors gave considerable stability to the small states within the empire and made it possible for a dependent people such as the Jews to survive.

Under Artaxerxes I (465-424 BC), Ezra was designated to return to Jerusalem to reorganize the temple worship, and the royal cupbearer Nehemiah was appointed governor of the province with authority to rebuild the walls of the city. After this period, we have no further record of the relation between Persian and Jewish rulers. Although there are difficulties in dating the events with which the book of *Esther* deals, these are also to be placed within the period of the Persian Empire.

See ESTHER, EZRA, NEHEMIAH

SCRIPTURE

Extent of the Persian Empire

Esth. 1 [1]Now it came to pass in the days of Ahasuerus, (this is Ahasuerus which reigned from India even unto Ethiopia, over a hundred and seven and twenty provinces:)

Administration

Dan. 6 [1]It pleased Darius to set over the kingdom a hundred and twenty princes, which should be over the whole kingdom; [2]And over these three presidents; of whom Daniel was first: that the princes might give accounts unto them, and the king should have no damage.

Israel Captive in Persia

2 Chr. 36 [20]And them that had escaped from the sword carried he away to Babylon; where they were servants to him and his sons until the reign of the kingdom of Persia:

Rulers of Persia

AHASUERUS

Esth. 1 [3]In the third year of his reign, he made a feast unto all his princes and his servants; the power of Persia and Media, the nobles and princes of the provinces, being before him:

DARIUS

Dan. 5 [31]And Darius the Median took the kingdom, being about threescore and two years old.

ARTAXERXES I

Ezra 4 [7]And in the days of Artaxerxes wrote Bishlam, Mithredath, Tabeel, and the rest of their companions, unto Artaxerxes king of Persia; and the writing of the letter was written in the Syrian tongue, and interpreted in the Syrian tongue.

CYRUS

2 Chr. 36 [22]Now in the first year of Cyrus king of Persia, that the word of the Lord spoken by the mouth of Jeremiah might be accomplished, the Lord stirred up the spirit of Cyrus king of Persia, that he made a proclamation throughout all his kingdom, and put it also in writing, saying, [23]Thus saith Cyrus king of Persia, All the kingdoms of the earth hath the Lord God of heaven given me; and he hath charged me to build him a house in Jerusalem, which is in Judah. Who is there among you of all his people? The Lord his God be with him, and let him go up.

PETER, SIMON

[pē′tẽr, sī′mon] One of the best-known of the twelve apostles, also called Simon Bar-jona and Cephas. Peter was a native of Bethsaida, a town of Galilee, and, with his brother Andrew, operated a fishing business. He was probably a disciple of John the Baptist before the ministry of Jesus began. His first contact with Jesus came when Andrew, having talked with Jesus, "first findeth his own brother Simon and saith unto him, We have found the Messiah." Eventually, Peter was selected as an apostle and from the first assumed a sort of leadership, acting as spokesman for the apostles in their conversations with Jesus, and generally showing those qualities of ardent attachment and zeal which were so strong a part of his nature. He, along with James and John, was a member of the "inner circle" of Jesus' companions who were found with him on the mount of transfiguration and in the Garden of Gethsemane. The incidents of the gospels throw much light upon Peter's character—the attempt to walk upon the sea to meet Jesus, his unhesitating confession of faith in Jesus as the son of God, his rash but affectionate rebuke of the Lord for speaking of suffering and death as a part of His divine mission, his horror at the thought that his Master desired to wash his feet, his severing the ear of Malchus at the arrest of Jesus, his denial of the Lord following so closely on his boast of unwavering loyalty, and his bitter sorrow at his failure in this regard.

After figuring as a prominent witness of the resurrection and ascension of Christ, Peter is seen once more as the leader of the apostles in the early days of the Christian church. It was he who delivered the sermon on Pentecost which resulted in three thousand baptisms. The early chapters of the book of *Acts* are largely an account of Peter's activities in the days which followed. In the company of John, he healed the lame man at the Beautiful gate of the temple, was arrested for a sermon which he gave on that occasion, defended himself before the Sanhedren, and obtained his release. Subsequently he was arrested again and beaten, with the rest of the apostles, but did not cease preaching the gospel at every opportunity. He then apparently embarked on a series of journeys throughout Palestine, during which he raised Dorcas from the dead and took the gospel to the Gentile centurion, Cornelius. After this latter event, Peter returned to Jerusalem to defend his action concerning Cornelius to "the circumcision party." While there, he was arrested by Herod Agrippa I, who had already put the apostle James to death; however, the church prayed on his behalf and he was miraculously delivered from prison. Nothing more is heard of Peter until the synod at which Paul and Barnabas discussed with the brethren in Jerusalem the problems connected with taking the gospel to Gentiles. Paul informs us that Peter subsequently went to Antioch and displayed some duplicity concerning the Gentile question, drawing a sharp rebuke from Paul. Little more is known of Peter. Two New Testament epistles are ascribed to him. There is a persistent tradition that he was crucified head downward during the persecution under Nero, fulfilling Christ's prophecy of a violent death.

See PAUL, JESUS, etc.

REFERENCE: *Matt. 1-28; Mark 1-16; Luke 1-24; John 1-21; Acts 1-5; 10-12; 15.*

SCRIPTURE

Called by Jesus

Matt. 4 18And Jesus, walking by the sea
of Galilee, saw two brethren, Simon called
Peter, and Andrew his brother, casting a
net into the sea: for they were fishers.
19And he saith unto them, Follow me, and
I will make you fishers of men.

Tries to Walk on Water

Matt. 14 28And Peter answered him and
said, Lord, if it be thou, bid me come unto
thee on the water. 29And he said, Come.
And when Peter was come down out of the
ship, he walked on the water, to go to Jesus. 30But when he saw the wind boister-
ous, he was afraid; and beginning to sink,
he cried, saying, Lord, save me. 31And immediately Jesus stretched forth his hand,
and caught him, and said unto him, O thou
of little faith, wherefore didst thou doubt?

Confesses Jesus' Messiahship

Matt. 16 16And Simon Peter answered
and said, Thou art the Christ, the Son of
the living God. 17And Jesus answered and
said unto him, Blessed art thou, Simon
Bar-jona: for flesh and blood hath not revealed it unto thee, but my Father which
is in heaven. 18And I say also unto thee,
That thou art Peter, and upon this rock I
will build my church; and the gates of hell
shall not prevail against it. 19And I will
give unto thee the keys of the kingdom of
heaven: and whatsoever thou shalt bind
on earth shall be bound in heaven: and
whatsoever thou shalt loose on earth shall
be loosed in heaven.

Witnesses the Transfiguration

Matt. 17 1And after six days Jesus taketh Peter, James, and John his brother,
and bringeth them up into an high mountain apart, 2And was transfigured before
them: and his face did shine as the sun,
and his raiment was white as the light.
3And, behold, there appeared unto them
Moses and Elias talking with him. 4Then
answered Peter, and said unto Jesus, Lord,
it is good for us to be here: if thou wilt, let
us make here three tabernacles; one for
thee, and one for Moses, and one for Elias.

Boasts of His Loyalty

Matt. 26 33Peter answered and said
unto him, Though all men shall be offended because of thee, yet will I never
be offended. 34Jesus said unto him, Verily
I say unto thee, That this night, before the
cock crow, thou shalt deny me thrice.
35Peter said unto him, Though I should die
with thee, yet will I not deny thee. Likewise also said all the disciples.

Denies Christ

Luke 22 31And the Lord said, Simon,
Simon, behold, Satan hath desired to have
you, that he may sift you as wheat: 32But
I have prayed for thee, that thy faith fail
not: and when thou art converted,
strengthen thy brethren. 33And he said
unto him, Lord, I am ready to go with thee,

both into prison, and to death. 34And he said, I tell thee, Peter, the cock shall not crow this day, before that thou shalt thrice deny that thou knowest me.

54Then took they him, and led him, and brought him into the high priest's house. And Peter followed afar off. 55And when they had kindled a fire in the midst of the hall, and were set down together, Peter sat down among them. 56But a certain maid beheld him as he sat by the fire, and earnestly looked upon him, and said, This man was also with him. 57And he denied him, saying, Woman, I know him not. 58And after a little while another saw him, and said, Thou art also of them. And Peter said, Man, I am not. 59And about the space of one hour after another confidently affirmed, saying, Of a truth this fellow also was with him: for he is a Galilaean. 60And Peter said, Man, I know not what thou sayest. And immediately, while he yet spake, the cock crew. 61And the Lord turned, and looked upon Peter. And Peter remembered the word of the Lord, how he had said unto him, Before the cock crow, thou shalt deny me thrice. 62And Peter went out, and wept bitterly.

His Martyrdom Foretold

John 21 17He saith unto him the third time, Simon, son of Jonas, lovest thou me? Peter was grieved because he said unto him the third time, Lovest thou me? And he said unto him, Lord, thou knowest all things; thou knowest that I love thee. Jesus saith unto him, Feed my sheep. 18Verily, verily, I say unto thee, When thou wast young, thou girdedst thyself, and walkedst whither thou wouldest: but when thou shalt be old, thou shalt stretch forth thy hands, and another shall gird thee, and carry thee whither thou wouldest not. 19This spake he, signifying by what death he should glorify God. And when he had spoken this, he saith unto him, Follow me.

Teaches Boldly

Acts 4 18And they called them, and commanded them not to speak at all nor teach in the name of Jesus. 19But Peter and John answered and said unto them, Whether it be right in the sight of God to hearken unto you more than unto God, judge ye. 20For we cannot but speak the things which we have seen and heard. 21So when they had further threatened them, they let them go, finding nothing how they might punish them, because of the people: for all men glorified God for that which was done.

Rebuked by Paul

Gal. 2 11But when Peter was come to Antioch, I withstood him to the face, because he was to be blamed. 12For before that certain came from James, he did eat with the Gentiles: but when they were come, he withdrew and separated himself, fearing them which were of the circumcision. 13And the other Jews dissembled likewise with him; insomuch that Barnabas also was carried away with their dissimulation. 14But when I saw that they walked not uprightly according to the truth of the gospel, I said unto Peter before them all, If thou, being a Jew, livest after the manner of Gentiles, and not as do the Jews, why compellest thou the Gentiles to live as do the Jews?

PHARAOH

[fā′ rō] A title used as a name, or part of a name, of the kings of ancient Egypt. Among the most important Pharaoh mentioned in the Bible are:

1. The Pharaoh whose dream was interpreted by Joseph and who promoted him to a position in the kingdom second only to the Pharaoh himself.

This ruler cannot be satisfactorily identified. (*See Gen. 40-50*)

2. The Pharaoh under whom the Israelites were forced to work, under oppressive conditions, on the store cities of Pithom and Rameses. It is quite possible that this work was carried on during the reigns of several Pharaohs, namely Ramses I, Sethos, and Ramses II, the latter of whom was probably ruling at the time of the Exodus. (*See* EXODUS and *Ex. 1-15*)

3. Pharaoh Necho II (609-594 BC). Shortly after his accession to the throne, Necho set about to enlarge Egyptian holdings. He met resistance from Josiah king of Judah and slew that great reformer. (*See* JOSIAH) Josiah was succeeded by Jehoahaz, but because of the latter's anti-Egyptian sentiments, Necho deposed him and replaced him with Eliakim, whose name was subsequently changed to Jehoiakim.

After a few years of success in Asian campaigns, Necho suffered severe defeat at Carchemish in 605 BC, at the hands of Nebuchadnezzar. After another battle in 601-600 BC, in which both the Babylonians and Egyptians sustained heavy losses, Necho gave up his plans of expansion and led no further campaigns during his reign. (*See 2 Kin. 23:39-35; 24:7; 2 Chr. 35: 20-34; 36:3, 4; Jer. 46:2; 47:1*)

4. Pharaoh Hophra (588-569 BC). It was this ruler who invited Zedekiah to revolt against Babylon, thus precipitating the final downfall of Judah in 586 BC. Jeremiah prophesied that Hophra would suffer a fate similar to that of Zedekiah (*Jer. 44:30*). In 569 BC, Hophra was dethroned and replaced by Amasis. In 566, he lost his life in an attempt to regain the throne. (*See Jer. 46:25, 26*)

SCRIPTURE

Ruler in Time of Joseph

APPOINTS JOSEPH TO HIGH POSITION

Gen. 41 [41]And Pharaoh said unto Joseph, See I have set thee over all the land of Egypt. [42]And Pharaoh took off his ring from his hand, and put it upon Joseph's hand, and arrayed him in vestures of fine linen, and put a gold chain about his neck; [43]And he made him to ride in the second chariot which he had; and they cried before him, Bow the knee: and he made him ruler over all the land of Egypt. [44]And Pharaoh said unto Joseph, I am Pharaoh, and without thee shall no man lift up his hand or foot in all the land of Egypt. [45]And Pharaoh called Joseph's name Zaphnath-paaneah; and he gave him to wife Asenath the daughter of Potipherah priest of On. And Joseph went out over all the land of Egypt.

SENDS FOR JOSEPH'S FAMILY

Gen. 45 [16]And the fame thereof was heard in Pharaoh's house, saying, Joseph's brethren are come: and it pleased Pharaoh well, and his servants. [17]And Pharaoh said unto Joseph, Say unto thy brethren, This do ye; lade your beasts, and go, get you unto the land of Canaan; [18]And take your father and your households, and come unto me: and I will give you the good of the land of Egypt, and ye shall eat the fat of the land. [19]Now thou art commanded, this do ye; take you wagons out of the land of Egypt for your little ones, and for your wives, and bring your father, and come. [20]Also regard not your stuff; for the good of all the land of Egypt is yours. [21]And the children of Israel did so: and Joseph gave them wagons, according to the commandment of Pharaoh, and gave them provision for the way.

Ruler at the Time of the Exodus

A PHARAOH WHO "KNEW NOT JOSEPH"

Ex. 1 [8]Now there arose up a new king over Egypt, which knew not Joseph. [9]And he said unto his people, Behold, the people of the children of Israel are more and mightier than we: [10]Come on, let us deal wisely with them; lest they multiply, and it come to pass, that, when there falleth out any war, they join also unto our enemies, and fight against us, and so get them up out of the land. 11Therefore they did set over them taskmasters to afflict them with their burdens. And they built for Pharaoh treasure cities, Pithom and Raamses.

MOSES' FOSTER GRANDFATHER

Ex. 2 1And there went a man of the house of Levi, and took to wife a daughter of Levi. 2And the woman conceived, and bare a son: and when she saw him that he was a goodly child, she hid him three months. 3And when she could not longer hide him, she took for him an ark of bulrushes, and daubed it with slime and with pitch, and put the child therein; and she laid it in the flags by the river's brink. 4And his sister stood afar off, to wit what would be done to him.

5And the daughter of Pharaoh came down to wash herself at the river; and her maidens walked along by the river's side: and when she saw the ark among the flags, she sent her maid to fetch it. 6And when she had opened it, she saw the child: and, behold, the babe wept. And she had compassion on him, and said, This is one of the Hebrews' children. 7Then said his sister to Pharaoh's daughter, Shall I go and call to thee a nurse of the Hebrew women, that she may nurse the child for thee? 8And Pharaoh's daughter said to her, Go. And the maid went and called the child's mother. 9And Pharaoh's daughter said unto her, Take this child away, and nurse it for me, and I will give thee thy wages. And the woman took the child, and nursed it. 10And the child grew, and she brought him unto Pharaoh's daughter, and he became her son. And she called his name Moses: and she said, Because I drew him out of the water.

REFUSES TO LET ISRAELITES GO

Ex. 5 1And afterward Moses and Aaron went in, and told Pharaoh, Thus saith the LORD God of Israel, Let my people go, that they may hold a feast unto me in the wilderness. 2And Pharaoh said, Who is the LORD, that I should obey his voice to let Israel go? I know not the LORD, neither will I let Israel go. 3And they said, The God of the Hebrews hath met with us: let us go, we pray thee, three days' journey into the desert, and sacrifice unto the LORD our God; lest he fall upon us with pestilence, or with the sword. 4And the king of Egypt said unto them, Wherefore do ye, Moses and Aaron, let the people from their works? get you unto your burdens. 5And Pharaoh said, Behold, the people of the land now are many, and ye make them rest from their burdens. 6And Pharaoh commanded the same day the taskmasters of the people, and their officers, saying, 7Ye shall no more give the people straw to make brick, as heretofore: let them go and gather straw for themselves. 8And the tale of the bricks, which they did make heretofore, ye shall lay upon them; ye shall not diminish aught thereof: for they be idle; therefore they cry, saying, Let us go and sacrifice to our God. 9Let there more work be laid upon the men, that they may labour therein; and let them not regard vain words.

Ex. 7 10And Moses and Aaron went in unto Pharaoh, and they did so as the LORD had commanded: and Aaron cast down his rod before Pharaoh, and before his servants, and it became a serpent. 11Then Pharaoh also called the wise men and the sorcerers: now the magicians of Egypt, they also did in like manner with their enchantments. 12For they cast down every man his rod, and they became serpents:

but Aaron's rod swallowed up their rods. [13]And he hardened Pharaoh's heart that he hearkened not unto them; as the LORD had said.

PHARAOH HARDENS HIS HEART

Ex. 8 [8]Then Pharaoh called for Moses and Aaron, and said, Entreat the LORD, that he may take away the frogs from me, and from my people; and I will let the people go, that they may do sacrifice unto the LORD. [13]And the LORD did according to the word of Moses; and the frogs died out of the houses, out of the villages, and out of the fields. [14]And they gathered them together upon heaps; and the land stank. [15]But when Pharaoh saw that there was respite, he hardened his heart, and hearkened not unto them; as the LORD had said.

HIS ARMY SWALLOWED IN THE SEA

Ex. 14 [26]And the LORD said unto Moses, Stretch out thine hand over the sea, that the waters may come again upon the Egyptians, upon their chariots, and upon their horsemen. [27]And Moses stretched forth his hand over the sea, and the sea returned to his strength when the morning appeared; and the Egyptians fled against it; and the LORD overthrew the Egyptians in the midst of the sea. [28]And the waters returned, and covered the chariots, and the horsemen, and all the host of Pharaoh that came into the sea after them; there remained not so much as one of them. [29]But the children of Israel walked upon dry land in the midst of the sea; and the waters were a wall unto them on their right hand, and on their left.

Pharaoh Necho (Necoh)

SLAYS JOSIAH

2 Kin. 23 [29]In his days Pharaoh-nechoh king of Egypt went up against the king of Assyria to the river Euphrates: and king Josiah went against him; and he slew him at Megiddo, when he had seen him.

APPOINTS A KING FOR JUDAH

2 Kin. 23 [31]Jehoahaz was twenty and three years old when he began to reign; and he reigned three months in Jerusalem. And his mother's name was Hamutal, the daughter of Jeremiah of Libnah. [32]And he did that which was evil in the sight of the LORD, according to all that his fathers had done. [33]And Pharaoh-nechoh put him in bands at Riblah in the land of Hamath, that he might not reign in Jerusalem; and put the land to a tribute of a hundred talents of silver, and a talent of gold. [34]And Pharaoh-nechoh made Eliakim the son of Josiah king in the room of Josiah his father, and turned his name to Jehoiakim, and took Jehoahaz away: and he came to Egypt, and died there. [35]And Jehoiakim gave the silver and the gold to Pharaoh; but he taxed the land to give the money according to the commandment of Pharaoh: he exacted the silver and the gold of the people of the land, of every one according to his taxation, to give it unto Pharaoh-nechoh.

CONTAINED BY BABYLON

2 Kin. 24 [7]And the king of Egypt came not again any more out of his land: for the king of Babylon had taken from the river of Egypt unto the river Euphrates all that pertained to the king of Egypt.

Pharaoh Hophra

Jer. 37 [4]Now Jeremiah came in and went out among the people: for they had not put him into prison. [5]Then Pharaoh's army was come forth out of Egypt: and when the Chaldeans that besieged Jerusalem heard tidings of them, they departed from Jerusalem.

[6]Then came the word of the LORD unto the prophet Jeremiah, saying, [7]Thus saith the LORD, the God of Israel; Thus shall ye say to the king of Judah, that sent you unto me to inquire of me; Behold, Pharaoh's army, which is come forth to help you, shall return to Egypt into their own land.

Jer. 44 [30]Thus saith the LORD; Behold, I will give Pharaoh-hophra king of Egypt into the hand of his enemies, and into the hand of them that seek his life; as I gave Zedekiah king of Judah into the hand of Nebuchadrezzar king of Babylon, his enemy, and that sought his life.

PHARISEES

[far′i sēz] A religious party of the Jews, mentioned prominently in the New Testament. The Pharisees emerged from the period of the Maccabean conflict, during the time of John Hyrcanus (135-105 BC), and survived until the annihilation of Jewish national life in 135 AD, in the reign of Hadrian. The origin of the name "Pharisee" is an unsolved problem. It is generally agreed that the name means "the separated ones"; this, however, is still somewhat indefinite, since the Pharisees could properly be spoken of as separating themselves from the king, the Sadducees, various sorts of impurity, and the *'Am ha-aretz*, the "people of the land" who made little attempt at strict observance of the Law.

Prior to the development of Pharisaism, a group of religious leaders known as *Soferim* had made some attempt to apply the Law to the practical matters of life. For the most part these were very simple, and it was felt by some that a more elaborate method should be devised for adapting the Law to new customs and developments. From this desire came the *Midrash,* a body of material consisting of deductions from the Law in justification of current rules and customs. In addition, there was developed the concept of "Oral Law," that is, the position that not all of the Law had been written, but that some had been handed down orally from the Fathers and was to be considered as authoritative as the written law. This was later embodied in the *Mishnah* to provide authority for customs which had developed but could find no support in the written law. The Sadducees, who had control of the priesthood, strongly opposed the Pharisees on this question, maintaining that only those things found in the written law could be considered as permanently authoritative. Behind this stand, at least to some extent, was the desire of the Sadducees to regulate custom and practice by priestly decrees which could be issued and revoked at will. (*See* SADDUCEES)

The Pharisees were drawn largely from among the people, in contrast to the aristocratic Sadducees, and therefore commanded wide influence with the common people. Consequently, they were able to force the Sadducees to follow their bidding on many matters, on pain of losing the support of the people. The Pharisees used their influence in an attempt to bring religion into the common life of the people. As a result of their efforts, the Sabbath and other holy days were endowed with great sanctity, daily prayers were encouraged and practiced widely, divorces were made more difficult to obtain and the general status of women was greatly improved, the synagogue service was fully developed, and the canon of Scripture was fixed. They also furthered belief in the resurrection of the body and in angels and spirits.

The Pharisees eventually came to stress religious observance for its educational worth, believing that it had great benefit in impressing upon the mind the truth behind the observance. Doubtless, this often resulted in genuine and profound piety; on the other hand, it also produced a legalistic spirit which could justifiably be charged with formalism and hypocrisy. It is against this narrow and exclusive element in Pharisaism that Jesus spoke so strongly in the gospels. It should not be forgotten that, despite the unfavorable picture presented in the New Testament, the Pharisees performed a valuable service in protecting the worship of the one true God against idolatrous innovations.

SCRIPTURE

Characteristics of Pharisees

Matt. 9 [14]Then came to him the disciples of John, saying, Why do we and the

Pharisees fast oft, but thy disciples fast not?

Matt. 12 2 But when the Pharisees saw it, they said unto him, Behold, thy disciples do that which is not lawful to do upon the sabbath day.

Matt. 15 1 Then came to Jesus scribes and Pharisees, which were of Jerusalem, saying, 2 Why do thy disciples transgress the tradition of the elders? for they wash not their hands when they eat bread.

Acts 23 8 For the Sadducees say that there is no resurrection, neither angel, nor spirit: but the Pharisees confess both.

Rebuked by Jesus

Matt. 23 1 Then spake Jesus to the multitude, and to his disciples, 2 Saying, The scribes and the Pharisees sit in Moses' seat: 3 All therefore whatsoever they bid you observe, that observe and do; but do not ye after their works: for they say, and do not. 4 For they bind heavy burdens and grievous to be borne, and lay them on men's shoulders; but they themselves will not move them with one of their fingers. 5 But all their works they do for to be seen of men: they make broad their phylacteries, and enlarge the borders of their garments, 6 And love the uppermost rooms at feasts, and the chief seats in the synagogues, 7 And greetings in the markets, and to be called of men, Rabbi, Rabbi. 8 But be not ye called Rabbi: for one is your Master, even Christ; and all ye are brethren. 9 And call no man your father upon the earth: for one is your Father, which is in heaven. 10 Neither be ye called masters: for one is your Master, even Christ. 11 But he that is greatest among you shall be your servant. 12 And whosoever shall exalt himself shall be abased; and he that shall humble himself shall be exalted.

13 But woe unto you, scribes and Pharisees, hypocrites! for ye shut up the kingdom of heaven against men: for ye neither go in yourselves, neither suffer ye them that are entering to go in. 14 Woe unto you, scribes and Pharisees, hypocrites! for ye devour widows' houses, and for a pretence make long prayer: therefore ye shall receive the greater damnation. 15 Woe unto you, scribes and Pharisees, hypocrites! for ye compass sea and land to make one proselyte; and when he is made, ye make him twofold more the child of hell than yourselves. 16 Woe unto you, ye blind guides, which say, Whosoever shall swear by the temple, it is nothing; but whosoever shall swear by the gold of the temple, he is a debtor! 17 Ye fools and blind: for whether is greater, the gold, or the temple that sanctifieth the gold? 18 And, Whosoever shall swear by the altar, it is nothing; but whosoever sweareth by the gift that is upon it, he is guilty. 19 Ye fools and blind: for whether is greater, the gift, or the altar that sanctifieth the gift? 20 Whoso therefore shall swear by the altar, sweareth by it, and by all things thereon. 21 And whoso shall swear by the temple, sweareth by it, and by him that dwelleth therein. 22 And he that shall swear by heaven, sweareth by the throne of God, and by him that sitteth thereon. 23 Woe unto you, scribes and Pharisees, hypocrites! for ye pay tithe of mint and anise and cummin, and have omitted the weightier matters of the law, judgment, mercy, and faith: these ought ye to have done, and not to leave the other undone. 24 Ye blind guides, which strain at a gnat, and swallow a camel. 25 Woe unto you, scribes and Pharisees, hypocrites! for ye make clean the outside of the cup and of the platter, but within they are full of extortion and excess. 26 Thou blind Pharisee, cleanse first that which is within the cup and platter, that the outside of them may

be clean also. [27]Woe unto you, scribes and Pharisees, hypocrites! for ye are like unto whited sepulchres, which indeed appear beautiful outward, but are within full of dead men's bones, and of all uncleanness. [28]Even so ye also outwardly appear righteous unto men, but within ye are full of hypocrisy and iniquity. [29]Woe unto you, scribes and Pharisees, hypocrites! because ye build the tombs of the prophets, and garnish the sepulchres of the righteous, [30]And say, If we had been in the days of our fathers, we would not have been partakers with them in the blood of the prophets. [31]Wherefore ye be witnesses unto yourselves, that ye are the children of them which killed the prophets. [32]Fill ye up then the measure of your fathers. [33]Ye serpents, ye generation of vipers, how can ye escape the damnation of hell?

Mark 7 [5]Then the Pharisees and the scribes asked him, Why walk not thy disciples according to the tradition of the elders, but eat bread with unwashen hands? [6]He answered and said unto them, Well hath Esaias prophesied of you hypocrites, as it is written, This people honoureth me with their lips, but their heart is far from me. [7]Howbeit in vain do they worship me, teaching for doctrines the commandments of men. [8]For laying aside the commandment of God, ye hold the tradition of men, as the washing of pots and cups: and many other such like things ye do. [9]And he said unto them, Full well ye reject the commandment of God, that ye may keep your own tradition. [10]For Moses said, Honour thy father and thy mother; and, Whoso curseth father or mother, let him die the death: [11]But ye say, If a man shall say to his father or mother, It is Corban, that is to say, a gift, by whatsoever thou mightest be profited by me; he shall be free. [12]And ye suffer him no more to do aught for his father or his mother; [13]Making the word of God of none effect through your tradition, which ye have delivered: and many such like things do ye.

Luke 18 [10]Two men went up into the temple to pray; the one a Pharisee, and the other a publican. [11]The Pharisee stood and prayed thus with himself, God, I thank thee, that I am not as other men are, extortioners, unjust, adulterers, or even as this publican. [12]I fast twice in the week, I give tithes of all that I possess. [13]And the publican, standing afar off, would not lift up so much as his eyes unto heaven, but smote upon his breast, saying, God be merciful to me a sinner. [14]I tell you, this man went down to his house justified rather than the other: for every one that exalteth himself shall be abased; and he that humbleth himself shall be exalted.

PHILEMON

[fi lē′mon] A leader in the Colossian church to whom Paul addressed an epistle. Philemon was probably a man of some means, known to be warmhearted and hospitable. He appears to have been a good friend of Paul, having been with him in some former work, and having carried on a good work in the apostle's absence. Paul was acquainted not only with Philemon but with what appears to be his family (Apphi and Archippus), and sent his greeting to them. The purpose of Paul's letter was to encourage Philemon to receive as a Christian brother the runaway slave Onesimus, who had been of assistance to Paul in his Roman imprisonment.

See ONESIMUS

SCRIPTURE

Philem. 1 [1]Paul, a prisoner of Jesus Christ, and Timothy our brother, unto Philemon our dearly beloved, and fellowlabourer, [2]And to our beloved Apphia, and Archippus our fellowsoldier, and to the church in thy house: [3]Grace to you, and peace, from God our Father and the Lord Jesus Christ. [4]I thank my God, making mention of thee always in my prayers, [5]Hearing of thy love and faith, which thou hast toward the Lord Jesus, and toward all saints; [6]That the communication of thy faith may become effectual by the acknowledging of every good thing which is in you in Christ Jesus. [7]For we have great joy and consolation in thy love, because the bowels of the saints are refreshed by thee, brother. [8]Wherefore, though I might be much bold in Christ to enjoin thee that which is convenient, [9]Yet for love's sake I rather beseech thee, being such an one as Paul the aged, and now also a prisoner of Jesus Christ. [10]I beseech thee for my son Onesimus, whom I have begotten in my bonds: [11]Which in time past was to thee unprofitable, but now profitable to thee and to me: [12]Whom I have sent again: thou therefore receive him, that is, mine own bowels: [13]Whom I would have retained with me, that in thy stead he might have ministered unto me in the bonds of the gospel: [14]But without thy mind would I do nothing; that thy benefit should not be as it were of necessity, but willingly. [15]For perhaps he therefore departed for a season, that thou shouldest receive him for ever; [16]Not now as a servant, but above a servant, a brother beloved, specially to me, but how much more unto thee, both in the flesh, and in the Lord? [17]If thou count me therefore a partner, receive him as myself. [18]If he hath wronged thee, or oweth thee ought, put that on mine account; [19]I Paul have written it with mine own hand, I will repay it: albeit I do not say to thee how thou owest unto me even thine own self besides. [20]Yea, brother, let me have joy of thee in the Lord: refresh my bowels in the Lord. [21]Having confidence in thy obedience I wrote unto thee, knowing that thou wilt also do more than I say. [22]But withal prepare me also a lodging: for I trust that through your prayers I shall be given unto you. [23]There salute thee Epaphras, my fellow-prisoner in Christ Jesus; [24]Marcus, Aristarchus, Demas, Lucas, my fellowlabourers. [25]The grace of our Lord Jesus Christ be with your spirit. Amen.

PHILIP

[fil′ip] One of the twelve apostles, a resident of Bethsaida of Galilee. Philip first came in contact with Jesus in Bethany, where he and Andrew had gone to hear John the Baptist. His first reaction on learning that Jesus was the Messiah and accepting the call which Jesus had extended to him was to tell the grand news to Nathanael, who was also won to the Lord. Philip is mentioned briefly in several incidents during the Lord's ministry, each illustrating his close relationship to the Master.

SCRIPTURE

John 1 [43]The day following Jesus would go forth into Galilee, and findeth Philip, and saith unto him, Follow me. [44]Now Philip was of Bethsaida, the city of Andrew and Peter. [45]Philip findeth Nathanael, and saith unto him, We have found him, of whom Moses in the law, and the prophets, did write, Jesus of Nazareth, the son of Joseph. [46]And Nathanael said unto him, Can there any good thing come out of Nazareth? Philip saith unto him, Come and see.

John 6 [5]When Jesus then lifted up his eyes, and saw a great company come unto him, he saith unto Philip, Whence shall we buy bread, that these may eat? [6]And this he said to prove him: for he himself knew what he would do. [7]Philip answered him, Two hundred pennyworth of bread is not sufficient for them, that every one of them may take a little.

John 12 [20]And there were certain

Greeks among them, that came up to worship at the feast: 21The same came therefore to Philip, which was of Bethsaida of
Galilee, and desired him, saying, Sir, we
would see Jesus. 22Philip cometh and telleth Andrew: and again Andrew and Philip
tell Jesus.

REFERENCE: *Matt. 10:3; Mark 3:18; Luke 6:14; Acts 1:13; John 14:8-13.*

PHILIP THE EVANGELIST

[fil'ip, ē van'gel ist] One of the seven chosen to serve in the daily distribution of food and supplies to the Christian community in Jerusalem. (*Acts 6:1ff*) During the persecution which brought the death of Stephen and scattered the Jerusalem Christians over Judaea and Samaria, Philip carried on an effective evangelistic work in a city of Samaria. Among those who were baptized was a magician named Simon who had a great following of his own and who later sought to buy the power of the Holy Spirit from the apostles. (*See* SIMON MAGUS) From Samaria, Philip was instructed to "go toward the south, unto the way that goeth down from Jerusalem unto Gaza," there he came across an official of the government of Candace queen of the Ethiopians. Beginning with a passage in *Isa. 53* which the man happened to be reading, Philip "preached unto him Jesus", and soon baptized him into Christ. Philip then preached in a number of towns, finally settling in Caesarea, where he made his home. A number of years later, Paul and his companions on returning from the third missionary journey, stayed for a few days in Philip's home in Caesarea.

SCRIPTURE

Acts 8 4Therefore they that were scattered abroad went every where preaching
the word. 5Then Philip went down to the
city of Samaria, and preached Christ unto
them. 6And the people with one accord
gave heed unto those things which Philip
spake, hearing and seeing the miracles
which he did. 7For unclean spirits, crying
with loud voice, came out of many that
were possessed with them: and many
taken with palsies, and that were lame,
were healed. 8And there was great joy in
that city. 12But when they believed Philip
preaching the things concerning the kingdom of God, and the name of Jesus Christ,
they were baptized, both men and women.
13Then Simon himself believed also: and
when he was baptized, he continued with
Philip, and wondered, beholding the miracles and signs which were done. 26And
the angel of the Lord spake unto Philip,
saying, Arise, and go toward the south
unto the way that goeth down from Jerusalem unto Gaza, which is desert. 27And
he arose and went: and, behold, a man of
Ethiopia, an eunuch of great authority
under Candace, queen of the Ethiopians,
who had the charge of all her treasure, and
had come to Jerusalem for to worship,
28Was returning, and sitting in his chariot
read Esaias the prophet. 29Then the Spirit
said unto Philip, Go near, and join thyself
to this chariot. 30And Philip ran thither
to him, and heard him read the prophet
Esaias, and said, Understandest thou what
thou readest? 31And he said, How can I,
except some man should guide me? And he
desired Philip that he would come up and
sit with him. 32The place of the scripture
which he read was this, He was led as a
sheep to the slaughter; and like a lamb
dumb before his shearer, so opened he not
his mouth: 33In his humiliation his judgment was taken away: and who shall declare his generation? for his life is taken
from the earth. 34And the eunuch answered Philip, and said, I pray thee, of
whom speaketh the prophet this? of himself, or of some other man? 35Then Philip
opened his mouth, and began at the same
scripture, and preached unto him Jesus.
36And as they went on their way, they
came unto a certain water; and the eunuch

said, See, here is water; what doth hinder
me to be baptized? 37And Philip said, If
thou believest with all thine heart, thou
mayest. And he answered and said, I believe that Jesus Christ is the Son of God.
38And he commanded the chariot to stand
still: and they went down both into the
water, both Philip and the eunuch; and he
baptized him. 39And when they were
come up out of the water, the Spirit of the
Lord caught away Philip, that the eunuch
saw him no more: and he went on his way
rejoicing. 40But Philip was found at Azotus: and passing through he preached in
all the cities, till he came to Caesarea.

Acts 21 8And the next day we that were
of Paul's company departed, and came
unto Caesarea: and we entered into the
house of Philip the evangelist, which was
one of the seven; and abode with him.
9And the same man had four daughters,
virgins, which did prophesy. 10And as we
tarried there many days, there came down
from Judaea a certain prophet, named
Agabus.

PHILIPPI

[fi lip'ī] The leading city of Macedonia, situated on the famous Egnatian road, about nine miles from the sea, and named for Philip of Macedon. Its inhabitants were Roman citizens and enjoyed all the attendant privileges. There were few Jews in the city; there was, in fact, not even a synagogue. The only place of worship was a "place for prayer" by the river Angites which flowed by the city (*Acts 16:12*).

Paul and Silas visited Philippi on the second missionary journey, having received the "Macedonian call" while in Troas (*Acts 16:9*). It was at the "place for prayer" mentioned above that Paul met and converted Lydia, a seller of purple from Thyatira. Shortly after this he cured a girl who was "possessed with a spirit of divination . . . which brought her masters much gain by soothsaying." Enraged at having lost the profit which she had brought them, her owners dragged Paul and Silas before the magistrates of the city and accused them of having created a disturbance. As a result, Paul and Silas were beaten and cast into prison. The story of their marvelous release and subsequent conversion of the jailer is one of the most familiar to students of the New Testament (*Acts 16:16-34*). After his release from prison, Paul went to Thessalonica and did not return to Philippi until the third missionary tour (*Acts 19:22; 20:3-6*). Apart from this we have no record of the apostle's ever having visited the city again; he was, however, in close contact with the church in Philippi, as they sent gifts of money to him on several occasions, (*see Phil. 4:15-16; 2 Cor. 11:9*) and comforted him while he was imprisoned at Rome by sending Epaphroditus to bear a gift and to minister to the apostle (*Phil. 2:25*). It was the return of Epaphroditus to Philippi that occasioned Paul's heartwarming epistle to the wonderful Christians who must have comprised the church in that city. Despite its apparent strength little is known of the Philippian church outside the New Testament.

SCRIPTURE

Paul Preaches in Philippi

Acts 16 11Therefore loosing from Troas,
we came with a straight course to Samothracia, and the next day to Neapolis;
12And from thence to Philippi, which is the
chief city of that part of Macedonia, and a
colony: and we were in that city abiding
certain days.

Paul Cast into Prison

Acts 16 22And the multitude rose up together against them: and the magistrates
rent off their clothes, and commanded to
beat them. 23And when they had laid
many stripes upon them, they cast them
into prison, charging the jailor to keep
them safely: 24Who, having received such
a charge, thrust them into the inner prison,
and made their feet fast in the stocks.

Paul Before the Magistrates

Acts 16 34And when he had brought

them into his house, he set meat before them, and rejoiced, believing in God with all his house. [35]And when it was day, the magistrates sent the serjeants, saying, Let those men go. [36]And the keeper of the prison told this saying to Paul, The magistrates have sent to let you go: now therefore depart, and go in peace. [37]But Paul said unto them, They have beaten us openly uncondemned, being Romans, and have cast us into prison; and now do they thrust us out privily? nay verily; but let them come themselves and fetch us out. [38]And the serjeants told these words unto the magistrates: and they feared, when they heard that they were Romans. [39]And they came and besought them, and brought them out, and desired them to depart out of the city. [40]And they went out of the prison, and entered into the house of Lydia: and when they had seen the brethren, they comforted them, and departed.

Paul Shamefully Treated

1 Thess. 2 [1]For yourselves, brethren, know our entrance in unto you, that it was not in vain: [2]But even after that we had suffered before, and were shamefully entreated, as ye know, at Philippi, we were bold in our God to speak unto you the gospel of God with much contention.

Church in Philippi Aids Paul

Phil. 4 [10]But I rejoiced in the Lord greatly, that now at the last your care of me hath flourished again; wherein ye were also careful, but ye lacked opportunity. [11]Not that I speak in respect of want: for I have learned, in whatsoever state I am, therewith to be content. [12]I know both how to be abased, and I know how to abound: every where and in all things I am instructed both to be full and to be hungry, both to abound and to suffer need. [13]I can do all things through Christ which strengtheneth me. [14]Notwithstanding, ye have well done, that ye did communicate with my affliction. [15]Now ye Philippians know also, that in the beginning of the gospel, when I departed from Macedonia, no church communicated with me as concerning giving and receiving, but ye only. [16]For even in Thessalonica ye sent once and again unto my necessity. [17]Not because I desire a gift: but I desire fruit that may abound to your account. [18]But I have all, and abound: I am full, having received of Epaphroditus the things which were sent from you, an odour of a sweet smell, a sacrifice acceptable, well pleasing to God. [19]But my God shall supply all your need according to his riches in glory by Christ Jesus.

Paul Writes to Philippian Church

Phil. 1 [1]Paul and Timotheus, the servants of Jesus Christ, to all the saints in Christ Jesus which are at Philippi, with the bishops and deacons:

PHILISTINES

[fil is'tēnz] A people who held the coastal area of southern Palestine and were frequently at war with the Israelites in the period of the judges and the early years of the monarchy. The land which they inhabited was called Philistia and contained five major cities: Gaza, Ashkelon, Ashdod, Ekron, and Gath. Each of these cities was governed by a tyrant.

Although of Aegean origin, the Philistines assimilated much of the religion and culture common to most of the inhabitants of Canaan. (*See* CANAAN) They held a local monopoly on the smelting of iron, a fact which gave them no little military advantage over their enemies. Although not especially numerous, the Philistines were well-disciplined, skillful warriors whose superior weapons and chariots enabled them to pose a serious threat to the nation of Israel. In about 1050 BC, near Aphek, at the edge of the coastal plain, the Philistines cut the Israelite army to pieces, captured the ark of the covenant, and destroyed the central shrine at Shiloh. King Saul was able to recoup some of Israel's losses; it was David, however, who finally broke the power of Philistia and reduced it to a vassal state.

See SAUL, DAVID

SCRIPTURE

Defeated by Various Judges

SHAMGAR

Judg. 3 [31]And after him was Shamgar the son of Anath, which slew of the Philistines six hundred men with an oxgoad; and he also delivered Israel.

SAMSON

Judg. 14 [19]And the Spirit of the LORD came upon him, and he went down to Ashkelon, and slew thirty men of them, and took their spoil, and gave change of garments unto them which expounded the riddle. And his anger was kindled, and he went up to his father's house.

Judg. 15 [3]And Samson said concerning them, Now shall I be more blameless than the Philistines, though I do them a displeasure. [4]And Samson went and caught three hundred foxes, and took firebrands, and turned tail to tail, and put a firebrand in the midst between two tails. [5]And when he had set the brands on fire, he let them go into the standing corn of the Philistines, and burnt up both the shocks, and also the standing corn, with the vineyards and olives.

[6]Then the Philistines said, Who hath done this? And they answered, Samson, the son in law of the Timnite, because he had taken his wife, and given her to his companion. And the Philistines came up, and burnt her and her father with fire. [7]And Samson said unto them, Though ye have done this, yet will I be avenged of you, and after that I will cease. [8]And he smote them hip and thigh with a great slaughter: and he went down and dwelt in the top of the rock Etam.

[14]And when he came unto Lehi, the Philistines shouted against him: and the Spirit of the LORD came mightily upon him, and the cords that were upon his arms became as flax that was burnt with fire, and his bands loosed from off his hands. [15]And he found a new jawbone of an ass, and put forth his hand, and took it, and slew a thousand men therewith. [16]And Samson said, With the jawbone of an ass, heaps upon heaps, with the jaw of an ass have I slain a thousand men.

Judg. 16 [29]And Samson took hold of the two middle pillars upon which the house stood, and on which it was borne up, of the one with his right hand, and of the other with his left. [30]And Samson said, Let me die with the Philistines. And he bowed himself with all his might; and the house fell upon the lords, and upon all the people that were therein. So the dead which he slew at his death were more than they which he slew in his life.

Defeat the Israelites and Take the Ark

1 Sam. 4 [1]And the word of Samuel came to all Israel. Now Israel went out against the Philistines to battle, and pitched beside Ebenezer: and the Philistines pitched in Aphek. [2]And the Philistines put themselves in array against Israel: and when they joined battle, Israel was smitten before the Philistines: and they slew of the army in the field about four thousand men.

[3]And when the people were come into the camp, the elders of Israel said, Wherefore hath the LORD smitten us to-day before the Philistines? Let us fetch the ark of the covenant of the LORD out of Shiloh

unto us, that, when it cometh among us, it may save us out of the hand of our enemies. 4 So the people sent to Shiloh, that they might bring from thence the ark of the covenant of the LORD of hosts, which dwelleth between the cherubim: and the two sons of Eli, Hophni and Phinehas, were there with the ark of the covenant of God. 5 And when the ark of the covenant of the LORD came into the camp, all Israel shouted with a great shout, so that the earth rang again. 6 And when the Philistines heard the noise of the shout, they said, What meaneth the noise of this great shout in the camp of the Hebrews? And they understood that the ark of the LORD was come into the camp. 7 And the Philistines were afraid; for they said, God is come into the camp. And they said, Woe unto us! for there hath not been such a thing heretofore. 8 Woe unto us! who shall deliver us out of the hand of these mighty Gods? these are the Gods that smote the Egyptians with all the plagues in the wilderness. 9 Be strong, and quit yourselves like men, O ye Philistines, that ye be not servants unto the Hebrews, as they have been to you: quit yourselves like men, and fight.

10 And the Philistines fought, and Israel was smitten, and they fled every man into his tent: and there was a very great slaughter; for there fell of Israel thirty thousand footmen. 11 And the ark of God was taken; and the two sons of Eli, Hophni and Phinehas, were slain.

Suffer Plagues and Return the Ark

1 Sam. 5 8 They sent therefore and gathered all the lords of the Philistines unto them, and said, What shall we do with the ark of the God of Israel? And they answered, Let the ark of the God of Israel be carried about unto Gath. And they carried the ark of the God of Israel about thither. 9 And it was so, that, after they had carried it about, the hand of the LORD was against the city with a very great destruction: and he smote the men of the city, both small and great, and they had emerods in their secret parts.

10 Therefore they sent the ark of God to Ekron. And it came to pass, as the ark of God came to Ekron, that the Ekronites cried out, saying, They have brought about the ark of the God of Israel to us, to slay us and our people. 11 So they sent and gathered together all the lords of the Philistines, and said, Send away the ark of the God of Israel, and let it go again to his own place, that it slay us not, and our people: for there was a deadly destruction throughout all the city; the hand of God was very heavy there. 12 And the men that died not were smitten with the emerods: and the cry of the city went up to heaven.

1 Sam. 6 1 And the ark of the LORD was in the country of the Philistines seven months. 2 And the Philistines called for the priests and the diviners, saying, What shall we do to the ark of the LORD? tell us wherewith we shall send it to his place. 3 And they said, If ye send away the ark of the God of Israel, send it not empty; but in any wise return him a trespass offering: then ye shall be healed, and it shall be known to you why his hand is not removed from you.

10 And the men did so; and took two milch kine, and tied them to the cart, and shut up their calves at home: 11 And they laid the ark of the LORD upon the cart, and the coffer with the mice of gold and the images of their emerods. 12 And the kine took the straight way to the way of Bethshemesh, and went along the highway, lowing as they went, and turned not aside to the right hand or to the left; and the

lords of the Philistines went after them unto the border of Beth-shemesh.

Defeated by Samuel

1 Sam. 7 [3]And Samuel spake unto all the house of Israel, saying, If ye do return unto the LORD with all your hearts, then put away the strange gods and Ashtaroth from among you, and prepare your hearts unto the LORD, and serve him only: and he will deliver you out of the hand of the Philistines. [4]Then the children of Israel did put away Baalim and Ashtaroth, and served the LORD only. [5]And Samuel said, Gather all Israel to Mizpeh, and I will pray for you unto the LORD. [6]And they gathered together to Mizpeh, and drew water, and poured it out before the LORD, and fasted on that day, and said there, We have sinned against the LORD. And Samuel judged the children of Israel in Mizpeh. [7]And when the Philistines heard that the children of Israel were gathered together to Mizpeh, the lords of the Philistines went up against Israel. And when the children of Israel heard it, they were afraid of the Philistines. [8]And the children of Israel said to Samuel, Cease not to cry unto the LORD our God for us, that he will save us out of the hand of the Philistines.

[9]And Samuel took a sucking lamb, and offered it for a burnt offering wholly unto the LORD: and Samuel cried unto the LORD for Israel; and the LORD heard him. [10]And as Samuel was offering up the burnt offering, the Philistines drew near to battle against Israel: but the LORD thundered with a great thunder on that day upon the Philistines, and discomfited them; and they were smitten before Israel. [11]And the men of Israel went out of Mizpeh, and pursued the Philistines, and smote them, until they came under Beth-car. [12]Then Samuel took a stone, and set it between Mizpeh and Shen, and called the name of it Ebenezer, saying, Hitherto hath the LORD helped us.

[13]So the Philistines were subdued, and they came no more into the coast of Israel: and the hand of the LORD was against the Philistines all the days of Samuel.

Defeated by Saul and Jonathan

1 Sam. 13 [3]And Jonathan smote the garrison of the Philistines that was in Geba; and the Philistines heard of it. And Saul blew the trumpet throughout all the land, saying, Let the Hebrews hear. [4]And all Israel heard say that Saul had smitten a garrison of the Philistines, and that Israel also was had in abomination with the Philistines. And the people were called together after Saul to Gilgal.

The Philistines' Advantage in War

1 Sam. 13 [19]Now there was no smith found throughout all the land of Israel: for the Philistines said, Lest the Hebrews make them swords or spears: [20]But all the Israelites went down to the Philistines, to sharpen every man his share, and his coulter, and his axe, and his mattock. [21]Yet they had a file for the mattocks, and for the coulters, and for the forks, and for the axes, and to sharpen the goads. [22]So it came to pass in the day of battle, that there was neither sword nor spear found in the hand of any of the people that were with Saul and Jonathan: but with Saul and with Jonathan his son was there found. [23]And the garrison of the Philistines went out to the passage of Michmash.

David Slays Their Champion, Goliath

1 Sam. 17 [1]Now the Philistines gathered together their armies to battle, and were gathered together at Shochoh, which belongeth to Judah, and pitched between

Shochoh and Azekah, in Ephes-dammim. 2And Saul and the men of Israel were gathered together, and pitched by the valley of Elah, and set the battle in array against the Philistines. 3And the Philistines stood on a mountain on the one side, and Israel stood on a mountain on the other side: and there was a valley between them.

4And there went out a champion out of the camp of the Philistines, named Goliath, of Gath, whose height was six cubits and a span. 5And he had a helmet of brass upon his head, and he was armed with a coat of mail; and the weight of the coat was five thousand shekels of brass. 6And he had greaves of brass upon his legs, and a target of brass between his shoulders. 7And the staff of his spear was like a weaver's beam; and his spear's head weighed six hundred shekels of iron: and one bearing a shield went before him. 8And he stood and cried unto the armies of Israel, and said unto them, Why are ye come out to set your battle in array? am not I a Philistine, and ye servants to Saul? choose you a man for you, and let him come down to me. 9If he be able to fight with me, and to kill me, then will we be your servants: but if I prevail against him, and kill him, then shall ye be our servants, and serve us. 10And the Philistine said, I defy the armies of Israel this day; give me a man, that we may fight together. 11When Saul and all Israel heard those words of the Philistine, they were dismayed, and greatly afraid.

37David said moreover, The LORD that delivered me out of the paw of the lion, and out of the paw of the bear, he will deliver me out of the hand of this Philistine. And Saul said unto David, Go, and the LORD be with thee.

38And Saul armed David with his armour, and he put a helmet of brass upon his head; also he armed him with a coat of mail. 39And David girded his sword upon his armour, and he assayed to go; for he had not proved it. And David said unto Saul, I can not go with these, for I have not proved them. And David put them off him. 40And he took his staff in his hand, and chose him five smooth stones out of the brook, and put them in a shepherd's bag which he had, even in a scrip; and his sling was in his hand: and he drew near to the Philistine. 48And it came to pass, when the Philistine arose, and came and drew nigh to meet David, that David hasted, and ran toward the army to meet the Philistine. 49And David put his hand in his bag, and took thence a stone, and slang it, and smote the Philistine in his forehead, that the stone sunk into his forehead; and he fell upon his face to the earth. 50So David prevailed over the Philistine with a sling and with a stone, and smote the Philistine, and slew him; but there was no sword in the hand of David. 51Therefore David ran, and stood upon the Philistine, and took his sword, and drew it out of the sheath thereof, and slew him, and cut off his head therewith. And when the Philistines saw their champion was dead, they fled. 52And the men of Israel and of Judah arose, and shouted, and pursued the Philistines, until thou come to the valley, and to the gates of Ekron. And the wounded of the Philistines fell down by the way to Shaaraim, even unto Gath, and unto Ekron. 53And the children of Israel returned from chasing after the Philistines, and they spoiled their tents. 54And David took the head of the Philistine, and brought it to Jerusalem; but he put his armour in his tent.

Saul and His Sons Slain by Philistines

1 Sam. 31 1Now the Philistines fought against Israel: and the men of Israel fled from before the Philistines, and fell down slain in mount Gilboa. 2And the Philistines followed hard upon Saul and upon his sons: and the Philistines slew Jonathan, and Abinadab, and Melchi-shua, Saul's sons. 3And the battle went sore against Saul, and the archers hit him; and he was sore wounded of the archers. 4Then said Saul unto his armourbearer, Draw thy sword, and thrust me through therewith: lest these uncircumcised come and thrust me through, and abuse me. But his armourbearer would not; for he was sore afraid. Therefore Saul took a sword, and fell upon it. 5And when his armourbearer saw that Saul was dead, he fell likewise upon his sword, and died with him. 6So Saul died, and his three sons, and his armourbearer, and all his men, that same day together.

7And when the men of Israel that were on the other side of the valley, and they that were on the other side Jordan, saw that the men of Israel fled, and that Saul and his sons were dead, they forsook the cities, and fled; and the Philistines came and dwelt in them.

Defeated by David

2 Sam. 5 17But when the Philistines heard that they had anointed David king over Israel, all the Philistines came up to seek David; and David heard of it, and went down to the hold. 18The Philistines also came and spread themselves in the valley of Rephaim. 19And David inquired of the LORD, saying, Shall I go up to the Philistines? wilt thou deliver them into mine hand? And the LORD said unto David, Go up: for I will doubtless deliver the Philistines into thine hand. 20And David came to Baal-perazim, and David smote them there, and said, The LORD hath broken forth upon mine enemies before me, as the breach of waters. Therefore he called the name of that place Baal-perazim. 21And there they left their images, and David and his men burned them.

22And the Philistines came up yet again, and spread themselves in the valley of Rephaim. 23And when David inquired of the LORD, he said, Thou shalt not go up; but fetch a compass behind them, and come upon them over against the mulberry trees. 24And let it be, when thou hearest the sound of a going in the tops of the mulberry trees, that then thou shalt bestir thyself: for then shall the LORD go out before thee, to smite the host of the Philistines. 25And David did so, as the LORD had commanded him, and smote the Philistines from Geba until thou come to Gazer.

Defeated by David's Mighty Men

2 Sam. 23 9And after him was Eleazar the son of Dodo the Ahohite, one of the three mighty men with David, when they defied the Philistines that were there gathered together to battle, and the men of Israel were gone away: 10He arose, and smote the Philistines until his hand was weary, and his hand clave unto the sword: and the LORD wrought a great victory that day; and the people returned after him only to spoil. 11And after him was Shammah the son of Agee the Hararite. And the Philistines were gathered together into a troop, where was a piece of ground full of lentiles: and the people fled from the Philistines. 12But he stood in the midst of the ground, and defended it, and slew the Philistines: and the LORD wrought a great victory. 13And three of the thirty chief went down, and came to David in the harvest time unto the cave of Adullam: and the troop of the Philistines pitched in the valley of Rephaim. 14And David was then in a hold, and the garrison of the Philistines was then in Beth-lehem. [15]And David longed, and said, Oh that one would give me drink of the water of the well of Beth-lehem, which is by the gate! [16]And the three mighty men brake through the host of the Philistines, and drew water out of the well of Beth-lehem, that was by the gate, and took it, and brought it to David: nevertheless he would not drink thereof, but poured it out unto the LORD.

Pay Tribute to Jehoshaphat

2 Chr. 17 [11]Also some of the Philistines brought Jehoshaphat presents, and tribute silver; and the Arabians brought him flocks, seven thousand and seven hundred rams, and seven thousand and seven hundred he-goats.

Defeated by Hezekiah

2 Kin. 18 [1]Now it came to pass in the third year of Hoshea son of Elah king of Israel, that Hezekiah the son of Ahaz king of Judah began to reign.

[8]He smote the Philistines, even unto Gaza, and the borders thereof, from the tower of the watchmen to the fenced city.

PHINEHAS

[fin′ê as] 1. Son of Eleazar and grandson of Aaron. Phinehas is best known as a leader in helping to clean out the widespread adultery at Shittim by slaying an Israelite named Zimri and his Midianite consort. As a reward, he received for himself and his descendants the promise of succession to the priesthood.

2. The younger son of Eli.

See HOPHNI AND PHINEHAS

SCRIPTURE

Phinehas, the Son of Eleazar

Ex. 6 [25]And Eleazar Aaron's son took him one of the daughters of Putiel to wife; and she bare him Phinehas: these are the heads of the fathers of the Levites according to their families.

Num. 25 [6]And, behold, one of the children of Israel came and brought unto his brethren a Midianitish woman in the sight of Moses, and in the sight of all the congregation of the children of Israel, who were weeping before the door of the tabernacle of the congregation. [7]And when Phinehas, the son of Eleazar, the son of Aaron the priest, saw it, he rose up from among the congregation, and took a javelin in his hand; [8]And he went after the man of Israel into the tent, and thrust both of them through, the man of Israel, and the woman through her belly. So the plague was stayed from the children of Israel. [9]And those that died in the plague were twenty and four thousand.

[10]And the LORD spake unto Moses, saying, [11]Phinehas, the son of Eleazar, the son of Aaron the priest, hath turned my wrath away from the children of Israel, while he was zealous for my sake among them, that I consumed not the children of Israel in my jealousy. [12]Wherefore say, Behold, I give unto him my covenant of peace: [13]And he shall have it, and his seed after him, even the covenant of an everlasting priesthood; because he was zealous for his God, and made an atonement for the children of Israel.

Phinehas, the Son of Eli

WICKEDNESS OF

1 Sam. 2 [12]Now the sons of Eli were sons of Belial; they knew not the LORD. [13]And the priest's custom with the people was, that, when any man offered sacrifice, the priest's servant came, while the flesh was in seething, with a fleshhook of three teeth in his hand; [14]And he struck it into the

pan, or kettle, or caldron, or pot; all that
the fleshhook brought up the priest took
for himself. So they did in Shiloh unto all
the Israelites that came thither. [15]Also before they burnt the fat, the priest's servant
came, and said to the man that sacrificed,
Give flesh to roast for the priest; for he will
not have sodden flesh of thee, but raw.
[16]And if any man said unto him, Let them
not fail to burn the fat presently, and then
take as much as thy soul desireth; then he
would answer him, Nay; but thou shalt
give it me now: and if not, I will take it by
force. [17]Wherefore the sin of the young
men was very great before the LORD: for
men abhorred the offering of the LORD.

[22]Now Eli was very old, and heard all
that his sons did unto all Israel; and how
they lay with the women that assembled at
the door of the tabernacle of the congregation. [23]And he said unto them, Why do
ye such things? for I hear of your evil
dealings by all this people. [24]Nay, my
sons; for it is no good report that I hear: ye
make the LORD's people to transgress. [25]If
one man sin against another, the judge
shall judge him: but if a man sin against
the LORD, who shall entreat for him? Notwithstanding, they hearkened not unto the
voice of their father, because the LORD
would slay them.

GOD'S JUDGMENT ON PHINEHAS

1 Sam. 2 [34]And this shall be a sign unto
thee, that shall come upon thy two sons, on
Hophni and Phinehas; in one day they
shall die both of them.

SLAIN BY PHILISTINES

1 Sam. 4 [10]And the Philistines fought,
and Israel was smitten, and they fled every
man into his tent: and there was a very
great slaughter; for there fell of Israel
thirty thousand foot men. [11]And the ark of
God was taken; and the two sons of Eli,
Hophni and Phinehas, were slain.

PHOEBE

[fē′bê] Described in *Rom. 16:1-2* as a "sister, which is a servant of the church which is at Cenchrea." Paul urges the Roman church to receive her "in the Lord, as becometh saints", and to "assist her in whatsoever business she hath need of you: for she hath been a succourer of many, and of myself also." It is usually assumed that Phoebe was the bearer of the Roman letter and that these words served as introduction for her.

See DEACON

PHOENICIA

[fê nish′i a] The territory on the east coast of the Mediterranean Sea, covering about 150 miles between the rivers Litani and Arvad, corresponding to modern Lebanon and Southern Latakia. For historical information directly related to the Bible, see TYRE, SIDON, LEBANON.

PHRYGIA

[frij′i a] An extensive district in central Asia Minor. Paul preached in this region while on the first and second missionary journies.

SCRIPTURE

Acts 16 [6]Now when they had gone
throughout Phrygia and the region of Galatia, and were forbidden of the Holy
Ghost to preach the word in Asia,

Acts 18 [22]And when he had landed at
Caesarea, and gone up, and saluted the
church, he went down to Antioch. [23]And
after he had spent some time there, he departed, and went over all the country of
Galatia and Phrygia in order, strengthening all the disciples.

PHYLACTERY (Frontlet)

[fi lak′tēr i] A cube-shaped leather box, containing lips on which are written certain passages of scripture. There were bound to the forehead and left arm by means of leather thongs. Every Jewish male over thirteen years of age wore phylacteries at the time of morning prayer, except on Sabbaths and other special days of observance. Theoretically, they served as a reminder of the Law, but it is quite probable that they were also regarded as an amulet to ward off evil. Jesus condemned the practice, current in his day, of enlarging the phylactery and making it an occasion of religious ostentation.

SCRIPTURE

Deut. 6 [6]And these words which I command thee this day, shall be in thine heart: [7]And thou shalt teach them diligently unto thy children, and shalt talk of them when thou sittest in thine house, and when thou walkest by the way, and when thou liest down, and when thou risest up. [8]And thou shalt bind them for a sign upon thine hand, and they shall be as frontlets between thine eyes.

Deut. 11 [18]Therefore shall ye lay up these my words in your heart and in your soul, and bind them for a sign upon your hand, that they may be as frontlets between your eyes.

Matt. 23 [5]But all their works they do for to be seen of men: they make broad their phylacteries, and enlarge the borders of their garments,

PILATE, PONTIUS

[pī'lǎt, pon'shi us] Procurator of Judaea at the time of the trial and crucifixion of Jesus. According to Roman law in Judaea, the Jewish Sanhedrin had the right to try cases, but could hand down a death sentence only on the approval of the procurator; it was for this reason that Jesus was brought before Pontius Pilate. Although surprised by Jesus' refusal to answer the accusations which were brought against him, Pilate recognized his innocence and favored his release. Warned by his wife not to harm Jesus, he sought to extricate himself from a difficult situation by means of the annual custom of releasing one prisoner of the people's choice. He offered them the choice between the innocent Jesus and a notorious criminal, Barabbas, feeling sure that they would choose Jesus, but the crowd chose Barabbas. Pilate then washed his hands in front of the mob, indicating that the guilt in the matter lay with them and not himself. He made several more attempts to spare Jesus from the crucifixion which they demanded but eventually acceded to their will and gave him up to be executed. That he was irritated at the perverseness of the Jews is reflected in his refusal to altar the title which he had affixed to the cross of Jesus—"JESUS OF NAZARETH, THE KING OF THE JEWS." Shortly after the crucifixion, Pilate got into political trouble and was summoned back to Rome to appear before the emperor. In the meantime, however, the emperor died and Pilate escaped punishment. Tradition has it that he eventually committed suicide while in exile.

SCRIPTURE

Matt. 27 [1]When the morning was come, all the chief priests and elders of the people took counsel against Jesus to put him to death: [2]And when they had bound him, they led him away, and delivered him to Pontius Pilate the governor.

John 18 [29]Pilate then went out unto them, and said, What accusation bring ye against this man? [30]They answered and said unto him, If he were not a malefactor, we would not have delivered him up unto thee. [31]Then said Pilate unto them, Take ye him, and judge him according to your law. The Jews therefore said unto him, It is not lawful for us to put any man to death: [32]That the saying of Jesus might be fulfilled, which he spake, signifying what death he should die.

Matt. 27 [19]When he was set down on the judgment seat, his wife sent unto him, saying, Have thou nothing to do with that just man: for I have suffered many things this day in a dream because of him.

John 18 [33]Then Pilate entered into the judgment hall again, and called Jesus, and said unto him, Art thou the King of the Jews? [34]Jesus answered him, Sayest thou this thing of thyself, or did others tell it thee of me? [35]Pilate answered, Am I a Jew? Thine own nation and the chief priests have delivered thee unto me: what hast thou done? [36]Jesus answered, My kingdom is not of this world: if my kingdom were of this world, then would my servants fight, that I should not be delivered to the Jews: but now is my kingdom not from hence. [37]Pilate therefore said unto him, Art thou a king then? Jesus answered, Thou sayest that I am a king. To this end was I born, and for this cause came I into the world, that I should bear witness unto the truth. Every one that is of the truth heareth my voice. [38]Pilate saith unto him, What is truth? And when he had said this, he went out again unto the Jews, and saith unto them, I find in him no fault at all. [39]But ye have a custom, that I should release unto you one at the passover: will ye therefore that I release unto you the King of the Jews? [40]Then cried they all again, saying, Not this man, but Barabbas. Now Barabbas was a robber.

John 19 [1]Then Pilate therefore took Jesus, and scourged him. [2]And the soldiers platted a crown of thorns, and put it on his head, and they put on him a purple robe, [3]And said, Hail, King of the Jews! and they smote him with their hands. [4]Pilate therefore went forth again, and saith unto them, Behold, I bring him forth to you, that ye may know that I find no fault in him. [5]Then came Jesus forth, wearing the crown of thorns, and the purple robe. And Pilate saith unto them, Behold the man! [6]When the chief priests therefore and officers saw him, they cried out, saying, Crucify him, crucify him. Pilate saith unto them, Take ye him, and crucify him: for I find no fault in him. [7]The Jews answered him, We have a law, and by our law he ought to die, because he made himself the Son of God.

[8]When Pilate therefore heard that saying, he was the more afraid; [9]And went again into the judgment hall, and saith unto Jesus, Whence art thou? But Jesus gave him no answer. [10]Then saith Pilate unto him, Speakest thou not unto me? knowest thou not that I have power to crucify thee, and have power to release thee? [11]Jesus answered, Thou couldest have no power at all against me, except it were given thee from above: therefore he that delivered me unto thee hath the greater sin. [12]And from thenceforth Pilate sought to release him: but the Jews cried out, saying, If thou let this man go, thou art not Caesar's friend: whosoever maketh himself a king speaketh against Caesar.

[13]When Pilate therefore heard that saying, he brought Jesus forth, and sat down in the judgment seat in a place that is called the Pavement, but in the Hebrew, Gabbatha. [14]And it was the preparation of the passover, and about the sixth hour: and he saith unto the Jews, Behold your King! [15]But they cried out, Away with him, away with him, crucify him. Pilate saith unto them, Shall I crucify your King? The chief priests answered, We have no king but Caesar. [16]Then delivered he him therefore unto them to be crucified. And they took Jesus, and led him away. [17]And he bearing his cross went forth into a place called the place of a skull, which is called in the Hebrew Golgotha: [18]Where they crucified him, and two other with him, on either side one, and Jesus in the midst.

[19]And Pilate wrote a title, and put it on the cross. And the writing was, JESUS OF NAZARETH THE KING OF THE JEWS. [20]This title then read many of the Jews: for the place where Jesus was crucified was nigh

to the city: and it was written in Hebrew, and Greek, and Latin. [21]Then said the chief priests of the Jews to Pilate, Write not, The King of the Jews; but that he said, I am King of the Jews. [22]Pilate answered, What I have written I have written.

PISGAH

[piz'ga] Pisgah is identified with Nebo in *Deut. 34:1.* Although it is impossible to be certain, many scholars have set forth the opinion that the name Pisgah applies to the mountain range at the western end of the Moab plateau. Here, a summit which may possibly be the "top" of "head" of Pisgah commands a wide view of the desert below answering to the description in *Num. 21:20.*

See NEBO

SCRIPTURE

Balaam Prophesies on Pisgah

Num. 23 [13]And Balak said unto him, Come, I pray thee, with me unto another place, from whence thou mayest see them: thou shalt see but the utmost part of them, and shalt not see them all: and curse me them from thence.

[14]And he brought him into the field of Zophim, to the top of Pisgah, and built seven altars, and offered a bullock and a ram on every altar.

Moses Views Canaan from Pisgah

Deut. 34 [1]And Moses went up from the plains of Moab unto the mountain of Nebo, to the top of Pisgah, that is over against Jericho: and the LORD shewed him all the land of Gilead, unto Dan, [2]And all Naphtali, and the land of Ephraim, and Manasseh, and all the land of Judah, unto the utmost sea, [3]And the south, and the plain of the valley of Jericho, the city of palm trees, unto Zoar.

PITY

[pit'i] Compassion or mercy for the suffering or distress of others.

SCRIPTURE

The Pity of God

Isa. 63 [9]In all their affliction he was afflicted, and the angel of his presence saved them: in his love and in his pity he redeemed them; and he bare them, and carried them all the days of old.

Jas. 5 [11]Behold, we count them happy which endure. Ye have heard of the patience of Job, and have seen the end of the Lord; that the Lord is very pitiful, and of tender mercy.

The Pity of Jesus

Matt. 18 [33]Shouldest not thou also have had compassion on thy fellowservant, even as I had pity on thee?

Mark 6 [34]And Jesus, when he came out, saw much people, and was moved with compassion toward them, because they were as sheep not having a shepherd: and he began to teach them many things.

The Pity of Men

Job 19 [21]Have pity upon me, have pity upon me, O ye my friends; for the hand of God hath touched me.

Prov. 69 [20]Reproach hath broken my heart; and I am full of heaviness: and I looked for some to take pity, but there was none; and for comforters, but I found none.

Prov. 19 [17]He that hath pity upon the poor, lendeth unto the LORD; and that which he hath given will he pay him again.

Pity Not to Be Shown Offenders against the Law

Deut. 7 [16]And thou shalt consume all

the people which the LORD thy God shall deliver thee; thine eye shall have no pity upon them: neither shalt thou serve their gods; for that will be a snare unto thee.

See Deut. 13:8; 19:13, 21; 25:11, 12

PLAGUE

[plāg] Any afflictive evil; scourge; infestation. As used in the Bible it usually refers to sudden outbursts of pestilence which are regarded as coming from God as a punishment for evil. The term is used of several epidemics which attacked Israel as a result of their sinfulness, but it is applied in a special sense to the ten afflictions which were visited upon the Egyptians because of the Pharaoh's refusal to allow the Israelites to leave Egypt. These Ten Plagues included the turning of water into blood, the plagues of frogs, lice, flies, murrain on the cattle of the land, boils, hail, locusts, darkness, and the death of the first-born of Egypt.

SCRIPTURE

Water Turned to Blood

Ex. 7 [20]And Moses and Aaron did so, as the LORD commanded; and he lifted up the rod, and smote the waters that were in the river, in the sight of Pharaoh, and in the sight of his servants; and all the waters that were in the river were turned to blood. [21]And the fish that was in the river died; and the river stank, and the Egyptians could not drink of the water of the river; and there was blood throughout all the land of Egypt.

Frogs

Ex. 8 [5]And the LORD spake unto Moses, Say unto Aaron, Stretch forth thine hand with thy rod over the streams, over the rivers, and over the ponds, and cause frogs to come up upon the land of Egypt. [6]And Aaron stretched out his hand over the waters of Egypt; and the frogs came up, and covered the land of Egypt.

Lice

Ex. 8 [16]And the LORD said unto Moses, Say unto Aaron, Stretch out thy rod, and smite the dust of the land, that it may become lice throughout all the land of Egypt. [17]And they did so; for Aaron stretched out his hand with his rod, and smote the dust of the earth, and it became lice in man, and in beast; all the dust of the land became lice throughout all the land of Egypt.

Flies

Ex. 8 [20]And the LORD said unto Moses, Rise up early in the morning, and stand before Pharaoh; lo, he cometh forth to the water; and say unto him, Thus saith the LORD, Let my people go, that they may serve me. [21]Else, if thou wilt not let my people go, behold, I will send swarms of flies upon thee, and upon thy servants, and upon thy people, and into thy houses: and the houses of the Egyptians shall be full of swarms of flies, and also the ground whereon they are. [22]And I will sever in that day the land of Goshen, in which my people dwell, that no swarms of flies shall be there; to the end thou mayest know that I am the LORD in the midst of the earth. [23]And I will put a division between my people and thy people: to-morrow shall this sign be. [24]And the LORD did so; and there came a grievous swarm of flies into the house of Pharaoh, and into his servants' houses, and into all the land of Egypt: the land was corrupted by reason of the swarm of flies.

Murrain

Ex. 9 [6]And the LORD did that thing on the morrow, and all the cattle of Egypt died: but of the cattle of the children of Israel died not one. [7]And Pharaoh sent, and, behold, there was not one of the cattle of the Israelites dead. And the heart of Pharaoh was hardened, and he did not let the people go.

Boils

Ex. 9 [8]And the LORD said unto Moses and unto Aaron, Take to you handfuls of ashes of the furnace, and let Moses sprinkle it toward the heaven in the sight of Pharaoh. [9]And it shall become small dust in all the land of Egypt, and shall be a boil breaking forth with blains upon man, and upon beast, throughout all the land of Egypt. [10]And they took ashes of the furnace, and stood before Pharaoh; and Moses sprinkled it up toward heaven; and it became a boil breaking forth with blains upon man, and upon beast. [11]And the magicians could not stand before Moses because of the boils; for the boil was upon the magicians, and upon all the Egyptians. [12]And the LORD hardened the heart of Pharaoh, and he hearkened not unto them; as the LORD had spoken unto Moses.

Hail

Ex. 9 [22]And the LORD said unto Moses, Stretch forth thine hand toward heaven, that there may be hail in all the land of Egypt, upon man, and upon beast, and upon every herb of the field, throughout the land of Egypt. [23]And Moses stretched forth his rod toward heaven: and the LORD sent thunder and hail, and the fire ran along upon the ground; and the LORD rained hail upon the land of Egypt. [24]So there was hail, and fire mingled with the hail, very grievous, such as there was none like it in all the land of Egypt since it became a nation. [25]And the hail smote throughout all the land of Egypt all that was in the field, both man and beast; and the hail smote every herb of the field, and brake every tree of the field. [26]Only in the land of Goshen, where the children of Israel were, was there no hail.

Locusts

Ex. 10 [12]And the LORD said unto Moses, Stretch out thine hand over the land of Egypt for the locusts, that they may come up upon the land of Egypt, and eat every herb of the land, even all that the hail hath left. [13]And Moses stretched forth his rod over the land of Egypt, and the LORD brought an east wind upon the land all that day, and all that night; and when it was morning, the east wind brought the locusts. [14]And the locusts went up over all the land of Egypt, and rested in all the coasts of Egypt: very grievous were they; before them there were no such locusts as they, neither after them shall be such. [15]For they covered the face of the whole earth, so that the land was darkened; and they did eat every herb of the land, and all the fruit of the trees which the hail had left: and there remained not any green thing in the trees, or in the herbs of the field, through all the land of Egypt.

[16]Then Pharaoh called for Moses and Aaron in haste; and he said, I have sinned against the LORD your God, and against you. [17]Now therefore forgive, I pray thee, my sin only this once, and entreat the LORD your God, that he may take away from me this death only. [18]And he went out from Pharaoh, and entreated the LORD. [19]And the LORD turned a mighty strong west wind, which took away the locusts, and cast them into the Red sea; there remained not one locust in all the coasts of Egypt.

Darkness

Ex. 10 [21]And the LORD said unto Moses, Stretch out thine hand toward heaven, that there may be darkness over the land of

Egypt, even darkness which may be felt.
[22]And Moses stretched forth his hand toward heaven; and there was a thick darkness in all the land of Egypt three days:
[23]They saw not one another, neither rose
any from his place for three days: but all
the children of Israel had light in their
dwellings.

Death of the Firstborn

Ex. 12 [29]And it came to pass, that at
midnight the LORD smote all the firstborn
in the land of Egypt, from the firstborn of
Pharaoh that sat on his throne unto the
firstborn of the captive that was in the
dungeon; and all the firstborn of cattle.
[30]And Pharaoh rose up in the night, he,
and all his servants, and all the Egyptians;
and there was a great cry in Egypt: for
there was not a house where there was not
one dead.

[31]And he called for Moses and Aaron by
night, and said, Rise up, and get you forth
from among my people, both ye and the
children of Israel; and go, serve the LORD,
as ye have said. [32]Also take your flocks and
your herds, as ye have said, and be gone;
and bless me also. [33]And the Egyptians
were urgent upon the people, that they
might send them out of the land in haste;
for they said, We be all dead men. [34]And
the people took their dough before it was
leavened, their kneadingtroughs being
bound up in their clothes upon their
shoulders. [35]And the children of Israel did
according to the word of Moses; and they
borrowed of the Egyptians jewels of silver,
and jewels of gold, and raiment: [36]And
the LORD gave the people favour in the
sight of the Egyptians, so that they lent
unto them such things as they required:
and they spoiled the Egyptians.

REFERENCE: Plagues on Israel: Because of Idolatry, *Ex. 32:35;* After Eating Quail, *Num. 11:33;* On Refusing to Enter the Promised Land, *Num. 14:37;* After Korah's Rebellion, *Num. 16:41-50;* Of Serpents, *Num. 21:6;* For the Sin of Peor, *Josh. 22:17;* KORAH.

PLEASURE

[plezh'ûr] The gratification of the senses or the mind; agreeable sensations or emotions; amusement. Pleasures are of two sorts—those that make us enjoy this life better by making us realize the extent of God's plans for us by giving us good things, and "worldly pleasures"—those that are harmful to body and mind and thereby to the Christian and religious life in general. The Bible contains numerous statements concerning the necessity for avoiding worldly pleasures.

See HAPPINESS, JOY, AMUSEMENTS

SCRIPTURE

Vanity of Worldly Pleasures

Eccl. 2 [1]I said in mine heart, Go to now,
I will prove thee with mirth; therefore enjoy pleasure: and behold, this also is vanity. [2]I said of laughter, It is mad: and of
mirth, What doeth it? [3]I sought in mine
heart to give myself unto wine, yet ac-
quainting mine heart with wisdom; and to
lay hold on folly, till I might see what was
that good for the sons of men, which they
should do under the heaven all the days of
their life. [4]I made me great works; I
builded me houses; I planted me vineyards; [5]I made me gardens and orchards,
and I planted trees in them of all kind of
fruits: [6]I made me pools of water, to water
therewith the wood that bringeth forth
trees: [7]I got me servants and maidens,
and had servants born in my house; also I
had great possessions of great and small
cattle above all that were in Jerusalem before me; [8]I gathered me also silver and
gold, and the peculiar treasure of kings,
and of the provinces; I gat me men-singers
and women-singers, and the delights of

the sons of men, as musical instruments,
and that of all sorts. 9So I was great, and
increased more than all that were before
me in Jerusalem: also my wisdom remained with me. 10And whatsoever mine
eyes desired I kept not from them, I withheld not my heart from any joy; for my
heart rejoiced in all my labour: and this
was my portion of all my labour. 11Then I
looked on all the works that my hands had
wrought, and on the labour that I had laboured to do: and behold, all was vanity
and vexation of spirit, and there was no
profit under the sun.

Effects of Worldly Pleasure

Luke 8 14And that which fell among
thorns are they, which, when they have
heard, go forth, and are choked with cares
and riches and pleasures of this life, and
bring no fruit to perfection.

Jas. 5 1Go to now, ye rich men, weep
and howl for your miseries that shall come
upon you. 2Your riches are corrupted, and
your garments are motheaten. 3Your gold
and silver is cankered; and the rust of them
shall be a witness against you, and shall eat
your flesh as it were fire. Ye have heaped
treasure together for the last days. 4Be-
hold, the hire of the labourers who have
reaped down your fields, which is of you
kept back by fraud, crieth: and the cries of
them which have reaped are entered into
the ears of the Lord of sabaoth. 5Ye have
lived in pleasure on the earth, and been
wanton; ye have nourished your hearts, as
in a day of slaughter.

2 Pet. 2 12But these, as natural brute
beasts made to be taken and destroyed,
speak evil of the things that they understand not, and shall utterly perish in their
own corruption, 13And shall receive the
reward of unrighteousness, as they that
count it pleasure to riot in the day time:
Spots they are and blemishes, sporting
themselves with their own deceivings,
while they feast with you: 14Having eyes
full of adultery and that cannot cease from
sin, beguiling unstable souls: an heart they
have exercised with covetous practices:
cursed children.

Commands and Warnings against Worldly Pleasure

2 Tim. 3 4Traitors, heady, highminded,
lovers of pleasures more than lovers of
God, 5Having a form of godliness, but
denying the power thereof: from such turn
away. 6For of this sort are they which
creep into houses, and lead captive silly
women laden with sins, led away with divers lusts, 7Ever learning, and never able
to come to the knowledge of the truth.

Tit. 3 3For we ourselves also were sometimes foolish, disobedient, deceived, serving divers lusts and pleasures, living in
malice and envy, hateful, and hating one
another.

1 Pet. 4 1Forasmuch then as Christ hath
suffered for us in the flesh, arm yourselves
likewise with the same mind: for he that
hath suffered in the flesh hath ceased from
sin; 2That he no longer should live the rest
of his time in the flesh to the lusts of men,
but to the will of God. 3For the time past
of our life may suffice us to have wrought
the will of the Gentiles, when we walked
in lasciviousness, lusts, excess of wine, rev-
elings, banquetings, and abominable idolatries: 4Wherein they think it strange that
ye run not with them to the same excess of
riot, speaking evil of you: 5Who shall give
account to him that is ready to judge the
quick and the dead. 6For, for this cause
was the gospel preached also to them that
are dead, that they might be judged according to men in the flesh, but live according to God in the spirit.

POETRY

[pō′et ri] Speech or writing that formulates an imaginative awareness of experience in language chosen and arranged to create a specific emotional response through its meaning, sound, and rhythm. A good portion of the Hebrew Old Testament is poetry; in addition to *Job*, *Psalms*, *Proverbs*, *Song of Solomon*, and most of the utterances of the prophets, the Pentateuch and other historical books contain examples of early poetry. (*See*, for example, *Ex. 15* and *Judg. 5*) Hebrew poetry has few, if any, deliberate rhymes; rather, it depends on rhythm and parallelism for poetic effect. The rhythm of Hebrew poetry depends on stressed syllables within a line or a section of a line. Each section usually contains two or three stressed syllables. The "three-three" pattern (three stressed syllables in each section) is perhaps the most common pattern in Hebrew poetry. The "three-two" pattern (three stresses in the first section, two in the second) is also common, being found most often in laments. These patterns are, of course, based on the Hebrew text and are not discernible in English.

Unlike rhythm, the curious aspect of Hebrew poetry known as parallelism can easily be detected in translation. There are three main types of parallelism. The first of these is synonomous parallelism, in which a second line repeats the meaning of the first line, but in different words, as in *Psa. 2:9*:

> "Thou shalt break them with a rod of iron;
> Thou shalt dash them in pieces like a potter's vessel."

The second type is a parallelism in which opposite thoughts are expressed, as in *Psa. 30:5*:

> "Weeping may endure for a night,
> But joy cometh in the morning."

Finally, there is a "climbing" parallelism in which part of the first line is repeated with an additional phrase or thought, as in *Psa. 93:3*:

> "The floods have lifted up, O Lord,
> The floods have lifted up their voice;
> The floods lift up their waves."

A recent development in the analysis of Hebrew poetry is the method of counting the syllables in the lines of a poem to discover if any discernible pattern of arrangement appears. This method has produced some striking results; numerous poems have been found in which it appears quite likely that the author consciously controlled the length of his lines and the number of syllables within them to form a symmetrical pattern. As in the case of rhythm, these patterns can be seen only in the original Hebrew text.

POOR

[po͞or] The word "poor" is used in the Bible to indicate a number of different conditions, namely: (1) destitute of property or the good things of life; needy or indigent; (2) destitute of such qualities as are desirable or might be expected; (3) worthy of pity or sympathy; (4) free from self-assertion or not proud or arrogant, as the meek.

The Bible instructs us to be good to the poor in that it advises almsgiving and kindness to those who have less of material goods than we. It also counsels us to be generous, kind, and considerate toward those things or persons that are poor in the sense of qualities, giving from our own store of qualities to help them. To the "poor in spirit" or the meek are promised great rewards.

SCRIPTURE

The Poor Always to Be Found

Deut. 15 11For the poor shall never cease out of the land: therefore I command thee, saying, Thou shalt open thine hand wide unto thy brother, to thy poor, and to thy needy, in thy land.

Matt. 26 11For ye have the poor always with you; but me ye have not always.

Mark 14 7For ye have the poor with you always, and whensoever ye will ye may do them good: but me ye have not always.

The Condition of the Poor

Job 24 4They turn the needy out of the way: the poor of the earth hide themselves together.

Prov. 13 7There is that maketh himself rich, yet hath nothing: there is that maketh himself poor, yet hath great riches. 8The ransom of a man's life are his riches: but the poor heareth not rebuke.

Prov. 18 [23]The poor useth entreaties; but the rich answereth roughly.

Prov. 19 [4]Wealth maketh many friends; but the poor is separated from his neighbour.

Eccl. 9 [15]Now there was found in it a poor wise man, and he by his wisdom delivered the city; yet no man remembered that same poor man. [16]Then said I, Wisdom is better than strength: nevertheless the poor man's wisdom is despised, and his words are not heard.

Jas. 2 [5]Hearken, my beloved brethren, Hath not God chosen the poor of this world rich in faith, and heirs of the kingdom which he hath promised to them that love him?

Causes for Poverty

Prov. 6 [9]How long wilt thou sleep, O sluggard? when wilt thou arise out of thy sleep? [10]Yet a little sleep, a little slumber, a little folding of the hands to sleep: [11]So shall thy poverty come as one that travelleth, and thy want as an armed man.

Prov. 10 [4]He becometh poor that dealeth with a slack hand; but the hand of the diligent maketh rich.

Prov. 23 [21]For the drunkard and the glutton shall come to poverty: and drowsiness shall clothe a man with rags.

Prov. 28 [19]He that tilleth his land shall have plenty of bread: but he that followeth after vain persons shall have poverty enough. [22]He that hasteth to be rich hath an evil eye, and considereth not that poverty shall come upon him.

Oppression of Poor Condemned

Ex. 22 [25]If thou lend money to any of my people that is poor by thee, thou shalt not be to him as an usurer, neither shalt thou lay upon him usury.

Deut. 15 [7]If there be among you a poor man of one of thy brethren within any of thy gates in thy land which the LORD thy God giveth thee, thou shalt not harden thy heart, nor shut thine hand from thy poor brother.

Psa. 82 [3]Defend the poor and fatherless: do justice to the afflicted and needy. [4]Deliver the poor and needy: rid them out of the hand of the wicked.

Prov. 14 [31]He that oppresseth the poor reproacheth his Maker: but he that honoureth him hath mercy on the poor.

Prov. 17 [5]Whoso mocketh the poor reproacheth his Maker: and he that is glad at calamities shall not be unpunished.

Prov. 22 [16]He that oppresseth the poor to increase his riches, and he that giveth to the rich, shall surely come to want. [22]Rob not the poor, because he is poor; neither oppress the afflicted in the gate: [23]For the LORD will plead their cause, and spoil the soul of those that spoiled them.

Isa. 3 [14]The LORD will enter into judgment with the ancients of his people, and the princes thereof; for ye have eaten up the vineyard; the spoil of the poor is in your houses. [15]What mean ye that ye beat my people to pieces, and grind the faces of the poor? saith the Lord GOD of hosts.

Amos 2 [6]Thus saith the LORD; For three transgressions of Israel, and for four, I will not turn away the punishment thereof: because they sold the righteous for silver, and the poor for a pair of shoes; [7]That pant after the dust of the earth on the head of the poor, and turn aside the way of the meek.

Amos 5 [11]Forasmuch, therefore, as your treading is upon the poor, and ye take from him burdens of wheat: ye have built houses of hewn stone, but ye shall not dwell in them; ye have planted pleasant vineyards, but ye shall not drink wine of them.

Zech. 7 [10]And oppress not the widow, nor the fatherless, the stranger, nor the poor; and let none of you imagine evil against his brother in your heart.

Jas. 2 [2]For if there come unto your assembly a man with a gold ring, in goodly apparel, and there come in also a poor man in vile raiment; [3]And ye have respect to him that weareth the gay clothing, and say unto him, Sit thou here in a good place; and say to the poor, Stand thou there, or sit here under my footstool: [4]Are ye not then partial in yourselves, and are become judges of evil thoughts?

Poor to Be Kindly Treated

Ex. 23 [10]And six years thou shalt sow thy land, and shalt gather in the fruits thereof: [11]But the seventh year thou shalt let it rest and lie still; that the poor of thy people may eat: and what they leave the beasts of the field shall eat. In like manner thou shalt deal with thy vineyard, and with thy oliveyard.

Lev. 19 [10]And thou shalt not glean thy vineyard, neither shalt thou gather every grape of thy vineyard; thou shalt leave them for the poor and stranger: I am the LORD your God.

Lev. 25 [25]If thy brother be waxen poor, and hath sold away some of his possession, and if any of his kin come to redeem it, then shall he redeem that which his brother sold.

Deut. 15 [7]If there be among you a poor man of one of thy brethren within any of thy gates in thy land which the LORD thy God giveth thee, thou shalt not harden thine heart, nor shut thine hand from thy poor brother: [8]But thou shalt open thine hand wide unto him, and shalt surely lend him sufficient for his need, in that which he wanteth.

Psa. 41 [1]Blessed is he that considereth the poor: the LORD will deliver him in time of trouble. [2]The LORD will preserve him, and keep him alive; and he shall be blessed upon the earth: and thou wilt not deliver him unto the will of his enemies. [3]The LORD will strengthen him upon the bed of languishing: thou wilt make all his bed in his sickness.

Prov. 14 [21]He that despiseth his neighbour sinneth: but he that hath mercy on the poor, happy is he.

Gal. 2 [10]Only they would that we should remember the poor, the same which I also was forward to do.

God Considers the Poor

Job 5 [15]But he saveth the poor from the sword, from their mouth, and from the hand of the mighty. [16]So the poor hath hope, and iniquity stoppeth her mouth.

Psa. 9 [18]For the needy shall not always be forgotten: the expectation of the poor shall not perish for ever.

Psa. 68 [10]Thy congregation hath dwelt therein: thou, O God, hast prepared of thy goodness for the poor.

Psa. 69 [33]For the LORD heareth the poor, and despiseth not his prisoners.

Psa. 72 [2]He shall judge thy people with righteousness, and thy poor with judgment.

Psa. 102 [17]He will regard the prayer of the destitute, and not despise their prayer.

Psa. 113 [7]He raiseth up the poor out of the dust, and lifteth the needy out of the dunghill; [8]That he may set him with princes, even with the princes of his people.

Psa. 132 [15]I will abundantly bless her provision: I will satisfy her poor with bread.

Luke 12 [22]And he said unto his disciples, Therefore I say unto you, Take no thought for your life, what ye shall eat;

neither for the body, what ye shall put on. 23The life is more than meat, and the body is more than raiment. 24Consider the ravens: for they neither sow nor reap; which neither have storehouse nor barn; and God feedeth them: how much more are ye better than the fowls? 25And which of you with taking thought can add to his stature one cubit? 26If ye then be not able to do that thing which is least, why take ye thought for the rest? 27Consider the lilies how they grow: they toil not, they spin not; and yet I say unto you, that Solomon in all his glory was not arrayed like one of these. 28If then God so clothe the grass, which is to day in the field, and to morrow is cast into the oven; how much more will he clothe you, O ye of little faith? 29And seek not ye what ye shall eat, or what ye shall drink, neither be ye of doubtful mind. 30For all these things do the nations of the world seek after: and your Father knoweth that ye have need of these things.

31But rather seek ye the kingdom of God; and all these things shall be added unto you. 32Fear not, little flock; for it is your Father's good pleasure to give you the kingdom.

The Church's Care for the Poor

Acts 6 1And in those days when the number of the disciples was multiplied, there arose a murmuring of the Grecians against the Hebrews, because their widows were neglected in the daily ministration. 2Then the twelve called the multitude of the disciples unto them, and said, It is not reason that we should leave the word of God, and serve tables. 3Wherefore, brethren, look ye out among you seven men of honest report, full of the Holy Ghost, and wisdom, whom we may appoint over this business.

2 Cor. 9 5Therefore I thought it necessary to exhort the brethren, that they would go before unto you, and make up beforehand your bounty, whereof ye had notice before, that the same might be ready, as a matter of bounty, and not as of covetousness. 6But this I say, He which soweth sparingly shall reap also sparingly; and he which soweth bountifully shall reap also bountifully. 7Every man according as he purposeth in his heart, so let him give; not grudgingly, or of necessity: for God loveth a cheerful giver. 8And God is able to make all grace abound toward you; that ye, always having all sufficiency in all things, may abound to every good work: 9(As it is written, He hath dispersed abroad; he hath given to the poor: his righteousness remaineth for ever. 10Now he that ministereth seed to the sower both minister bread for your food, and multiply your seed sown, and increase the fruits of your righteousness;) 11Being enriched in every thing to all bountifulness, which causeth through us thanksgiving to God.

Gal. 2 10Only they would that we should remember the poor; the same which I also was forward to do.

Christ Blesses the Poor in Spirit

Isa. 66 2For all those things hath mine hand made, and all those things have been, saith the LORD: but to this man will I look, even to him that is poor and of a contrite spirit, and trembleth at my word.

Matt. 5 3Blessed are the poor in spirit: for theirs is the kingdom of heaven.

Luke 6 20And he lifted up his eyes on his disciples, and said, Blessed be ye poor: for yours is the kingdom of God.

POTIPHAR

[pot'i far] An officer of Pharaoh to whom Joseph was sold by the Midianite traders. It was Potiphar's wife who was responsible for Joseph's being imprisoned after he refused to betray his master's trust by committing adultery with her.

See JOSEPH

SCRIPTURE

Gen. 39 [1]And Joseph was brought down to Egypt; and Potiphar, an officer of Pharaoh, captain of the guard, an Egyptian, bought him of the hands of the Ishmaelites, which had brought him down thither.

See Gen. 37:36; 39:1-20

POTTAGE

[pot′ȧj] A dish made by boiling lentils, rice, parsley, or flour with bits of meat, forming a thick, meaty soup. This has long been a favorite article of diet in the Near East. In the Bible, pottage figures in the story of Esau's sale of his birthright to Jacob for a mess of pottage (*Gen. 25:19-28*).

SCRIPTURE

Gen. 25 [29]And Jacob sod pottage: and Esau came from the field, and he was faint:
[30]And Esau said to Jacob, Feed me, I pray thee, with that same red pottage; for I am faint: therefore was his name called Edom.
[31]And Jacob said, Sell me this day thy birthright. [32]And Esau said, Behold, I am at the point to die: and what profit shall this birthright do to me? [33]And Jacob said, Swear to me this day; and he sware unto him: and he sold his birthright unto Jacob.
[34]Then Jacob gave Esau bread and pottage of lentils; and he did eat and drink, and rose up, and went his way: thus Esau despised his birthright.

POWER

[pou′ẽr] Strength, might, force; the possession of sway or controlling influence over others; also, a person, government, etc., invested with authority or influence or exercising control. In the King James Version of the Bible, there is often little distinction made between "power" and "authority", that they are quite closely related is seen in the fact that authority is valueless without the power to enforce it. Power is attributed primarily to God, but may be applied to any holder of power, whether human or superhuman. The "Powers", mentioned several times in the New Testament, often refer to an order of angelic beings believed to exercise power both on earth and in "the heavenly places"; according to the scriptures, these have been overcome by Christ.

SCRIPTURE

The Power of God

Ex. 15 [11]Who is like unto thee, O LORD, among the gods? who is like thee, glorious in holiness, fearful in praises, doing wonders? [12]Thou stretchedst out thy right hand, the earth swallowed them.

1 Chr. 29 [12]Both riches and honor come of thee, and thou reignest over all; and in thine hand is power and might; and in thine hand it is to make great, and to give strength unto all.

Psa. 62 [11]God had spoken once; twice have I heard this; that power belongeth unto God.

Matt. 19 [26]But Jesus beheld them, and said unto them, With men this is impossible; but with God all things are possible.

Eph. 1 [19]And what is the exceeding greatness of his power to us-ward who believe, according to the working of his mighty power, [20]Which he wrought in Christ, when he raised him from the dead, and set him at his own right hand in the heavenly places.

See GOD, OMNIPOTENCE OF

The Power of Christ

Matt. 9 [6]But that ye may know that the Son of man hath power on earth to forgive sins, (then saith he to the sick of the palsy), Arise, take up thy bed, and go unto thine house.

Luke 4 [32]And they were astonished at his doctrine: for his word was with power.

2 Cor. 12 [9]And he said unto me, My grace is sufficient for thee: for my strength is made perfect in weakness. Most gladly therefore will I rather glory in my infirmities, that the power of Christ may rest upon me.

Spiritual Power

Gen. 32 [28]And he said, Thy name shall be called no more Jacob, but Israel: for as a prince hast thou power with God and with men, and hast prevailed.

Isa. 40 [29]He giveth power to the faint; and to them that have no might he increaseth strength. [30]Even the youths shall faint and be weary, and the young men shall utterly fall: [31]But they that wait upon the LORD shall renew their strength; they shall mount up with wings as eagles; they shall run, and not be weary; and they shall walk, and not faint.

Luke 24 [49]And, behold, I send the promise of my Father upon you: but tarry ye in the city of Jerusalem, until ye be endued with power from on high.

Acts 1 [8]But ye shall receive power, after that the Holy Ghost is come upon you: and ye shall be witnesses unto me both in Jerusalem, and in all Judaea, and in Samaria, and unto the uttermost part of the earth.

Acts 6 [8]And Stephen, full of faith and power, did great wonders and miracles among the people.

2 Tim. 1 [7]For God hath not given us the spirit of fear; but of power, and of love, and of a sound mind.

The "Powers"

Matt. 24 [49]Immediately after the tribulation of those days shall the sun be darkened, and the moon shall not give her light, and the stars shall fall from heaven, and the powers of the heavens shall be shaken.

Luke 12 [11]And when they bring you unto the synagogues, and unto magistrates, and powers, take ye no thought how or what thing ye shall answer, or what ye shall say:

Rom. 8 [38]For I am persuaded, that neither death, nor life, nor angels, nor principalities, nor powers, nor things present, nor things to come.

Rom. 13 [1]Let every soul be subject unto the higher powers. For there is no power but of God: the powers that be are ordained of God.

Eph. 3 [10]To the intent that now unto the principalities and powers in heavenly places might be known by the church the manifold wisdom of God.

Eph. 6 [12]For we wrestle not against flesh and blood, but against principalities, against powers, against the rulers of the darkness of this world, against spiritual wickedness in high places.

Col. 1 [16]For by him were all things created, that are in heaven, and that are in earth, visible and invisible, whether they be thrones, or dominions, or principalities, or powers; all things were created by him, and for him:

Col. 2 [15]And having spoiled principalities and powers, he made a show of them openly, triumphing over them in it.

Tit. 3 [1]Put them in mind to be subject to principalities and powers, to obey magistrates, to be ready to every good work.

1 Pet. 3 [22]Who is gone into heaven, and is on the right hand of God; angels and authorities and powers being made subject unto him.

See Mark 13:25; Luke 21:26

PRAISE

[prāz] Honor rendered for worth; approval;

laudation; joyful tribute or homage rendered to God. The Bible makes it clear that Christians are to render to God proper praise and honor, with gladness and thanksgiving for His manifold mercies and goodness to mankind.

SCRIPTURE

Praise to God

Ex. 15 [2]The LORD is my strength and song, and he is become my salvation: he is my God, and I will prepare him a habitation; my father's God, and I will exalt him.

Judg. 5 [3]Hear, O ye kings; give ear, O ye princes; I, even I, will sing unto the LORD; I will sing praise to the LORD God of Israel.

2 Sam. 22 [50]Therefore I will give thanks unto thee, O LORD, among the heathen, and I will sing praises unto thy name.

1 Chr. 16 [9]Sing unto him, sing psalms unto him, talk ye of all his wondrous works. [24]Declare his glory among the heathen; his marvelous works among all nations. [36]Blessed be the LORD God of Israel for ever and ever. And all the people said, Amen, and praised the LORD.

1 Chr. 29 [13]Now, therefore, our God, we thank thee, and praise thy glorious name.

Psa. 5 [17]I will praise the LORD according to his righteousness: and will sing praise to the name of the LORD most high.

Psa. 9 [1]I will praise thee, O LORD, with my whole heart; I will shew forth all thy marvellous works. [11]Sing praises to the LORD, which dwelleth in Zion: declare among the people his doings.

Psa. 21 [13]Be thou exalted, LORD, in thine own strength: so will we sing and praise thy power.

Psa. 22 [23]Ye that fear the LORD, praise him; all ye the seed of Jacob, glorify him; and fear him, all ye the seed of Israel.

Psa. 34 [3]O magnify the LORD with me, and let us exalt his name together.

Isa. 12 [4]And in that day shall ye say, Praise the LORD, call upon his name, declare his doings among the people, make mention that his name is exalted.

Jer. 51 [10]The LORD hath brought forth our righteousness: come, and let us declare in Zion the work of the LORD our God.

Dan. 4 [37]Now I Nebuchadnezzar praise and extol and honour the King of heaven, all whose works are truth, and his ways judgment: and those that walk in pride he is able to abase.

Joel 2 [26]And ye shall eat in plenty, and be satisfied, and praise the name of the LORD your God, that hath dealt wondrously with you: and my people shall never be ashamed.

Luke 1 [46]And Mary said, My soul doth magnify the Lord, [47]And my spirit hath rejoiced in God my Saviour.

Luke 2 [20]And the shepherds returned, glorifying and praising God for all the things that they had heard and seen, as it was told unto them.

Luke 19 [37]And when he was come nigh, even now at the descent of the mount of Olives, the whole multitude of the disciples began to rejoice and praise God with a loud voice for all the mighty works that they had seen; [38]Saying, Blessed be the King that cometh in the name of the Lord: peace in heaven, and glory in the highest.

1 Pet. 2 [9]But ye are a chosen generation, a royal priesthood, a holy nation, a peculiar people; that ye should show forth the praises of him who hath called you out of darkness into his marvelous light.

Praise in Worship

Psa. 26 [12]My foot standeth in an even place; in the congregations will I bless the LORD.

Psa. 35 [18]I will give thee thanks in the great congregation: I will praise thee among much people.

Psa. 68 [26]Bless ye God in the congregations, even the LORD, from the fountain of Israel.

Psa. 89 [5]And the heavens shall praise thy wonders, O LORD: thy faithfulness also in the congregation of the saints.

Psa. 100 [4]Enter into his gates with thanksgiving, and into his courts with praise: be thankful unto him, and bless his name.

Psa. 107 [32]Let them exalt him also in the congregation of the people, and praise him in the assembly of the elders.

Acts 2 [46]And they, continuing daily with one accord in the temple, and breaking bread from house to house, did eat their meat with gladness and singleness of heart, [47]Praising God, and having favor with all the people. And the Lord added to the church daily such as should be saved.

Acts 16 [25]And at midnight Paul and Silas prayed, and sang praises unto God: and the prisoners heard them.

Eph. 5 [19]Speaking to yourselves in psalms and hymns and spiritual songs, singing and making melody in your heart to the Lord;

Heb. 2 [12]Saying, I will declare thy name unto my brethren, in the midst of the church will I sing praise unto thee.

Heb. 13 [15]By him therefore let us offer the sacrifice of praise to God continually, that is, the fruit of our lips, giving thanks to his name.

PRAYER

[prar] Prayer is the characteristic activity of the Christian life. It is impossible to contain the magnitude of this experience in a single definition. It is a communication between man and God. It is the opening of the skylight of the soul to the life that is above. When Paul summarizes God's work of salvation in *Gal. 4:4-7*, he places the right of calling on God as Father at the pinnacle. It is truly a profound expression of God's grace toward us; as one writer has put it, "In prayer God invites us to live with him." In allowing us to approach him in prayer, God shows his great love for us, and in praying we formulate and manifest our devotion to him. Prayer offered in faith in man's most powerful resource, for by it we may induce almighty God to grant that which we desire; but prayer offered in faith is at the same time a request that he induce us to desire that which he wills to grant, that we may earnestly say, "Thy will be done" (*Matt. 6:10*).

Jesus' disciples recognized the need for meaningful communication with the Father and asked the Master to "teach us to pray." In reply, Jesus gave them the model prayer we know as "The Lord's Prayer" (*Luke 11:24; Matt. 6:9-13*). From this example, we learn that the criterion of acceptable prayer is not length or poetic grandeur, but the expression of submission to his will, desire for the advance and consummation of his work among men, and praise to his holy name. This model prayer, and other instruction as to the mode and content of prayer are not the only assistance we receive. Paul tells us the Holy Spirit, who perfectly knows both our mind and the mind of God, prays alongside us and intercedes for us "with sighs too deep for words" (*Rom.8:26*,RSV). In addition, the Risen Christ serves as mediator between man and God, always making intercession for the saints (*Heb. 4:14; 7:25; 1 Tim. 2:5*).

The Bible presents us with a wide spectrum of men and women at prayer. Some stand with hands lifted up to God, others kneel, and still others prostrate themselves before the majesty of their LORD. Some mumble inaudibly, while others cry aloud as if to bridge the gap between heaven and earth by sheer vocal power. Some pray in temples and synagogues, while others withdraw to hills or gardens to be alone with God. Some prayers are completely spontaneous, others are liturgical and oft-repeated. Prayer is often accompanied by sacrifice, sometimes by fasting or humiliation in sackcloth and ashes. It may be an expression of thanksgiving, a confession of sin and guilt and a request for forgiveness, intercession on behalf of others—rulers, the sick, the church, the brother, the enemy, etc.—or petition for the granting of one's own plea. Man may approach God in prayer in any or all or none of these ways, for these are to some extent incidental. Those things which are vital to meaningful prayer are the absence of hypocrisy, perseverance in pursuing the object of prayer until one is satisfied as to the will of God, unquestioning faith in God's ability to perform that which he wills, and utterance in the name and spirit of Christ, the spirit of submission to the divine purpose.

SCRIPTURE

Objects and Occasions of Prayer

1 Chr. 16 35 And say ye, Save us, O God of our salvation, and gather us together, and deliver us from the heathen, that we may give thanks to thy holy name, and glory in thy praise.

Job 33 26 He shall pray unto God, and he will be favourable unto him: and he shall see his face with joy: for he will render unto man his righteousness.

Psa. 132 6 Pray for the peace of Jerusalem: they shall prosper that love thee.

Matt. 5 44 But I say unto you, Love your enemies, bless them that curse you, do good to them that hate you, and pray for them which despitefully use you, and persecute you.

Matt. 9 38 Pray ye therefore the Lord of the harvest, that he will send forth labourers into his harvest.

Matt. 26 41 Watch and pray, that ye enter not into temptation: the spirit indeed is willing, but the flesh is weak.

Luke 18 13 And the publican, standing afar off, would not lift up so much as his eyes unto heaven, but smote upon his breast, saying, God be merciful to me a sinner.

38 And he cried, saying, Jesus, thou son of David, have mercy on me.

Rom. 15 30 Now I beseech you, brethren, for the Lord Jesus Christ's sake, and for the love of the Spirit, that ye strive together with me in your prayers to God for me.

Jas. 5 13 Is any among you afflicted? let him pray. Is any merry? let him sing Psalms.

1 Pet. 4 7 But the end of all things is at hand: be ye therefore sober and watch unto prayer.

Prayer Commanded

Isa. 55 6 Seek ye the LORD while he may be found, call ye upon him while he is near.

Matt. 7 7 Ask, and it shall be given you; seek, and ye shall find; knock, and it shall be opened unto you: 8 For every one that asketh receiveth; and he that seeketh findeth; and to him that knocketh it shall be opened.

Matt. 26 41 Watch and pray, that ye enter not into temptation: the spirit indeed is willing, but the flesh is weak.

Luke 18 1 And he spake a parable unto them to this end, that men ought always to pray, and not to faint.

Luke 21 36 Watch ye therefore, and pray always, that ye may be accounted worthy to escape all these things that shall come to pass, and to stand before the Son of man.

Eph. 6 18 Praying always with all prayer and supplication in the Spirit, and watching thereunto with all perseverance and supplication for all saints.

Phil. 4 6 Be careful for nothing: but in every thing by prayer and supplication with thanksgiving let your request be made known unto God.

Col. 4 2 Continue in prayer, and watch in the same with thanksgiving.

1 Thess. 5 17 Pray without ceasing. 25 Brethren, pray for us.

1 Tim. 2 1 I exhort therefore, that, first of all, supplications, prayers, intercessions, and giving of thanks, be made for all men;

[2]For kings, and for all that are in authority;
that we may lead a quiet and peaceable
life in all godliness and honesty. [3]For this
is good and acceptable in the sight of God
our Saviour; [4]Who will have all men to be
saved, and to come unto the knowledge of
the truth. [8]I will therefore that men pray
every where, lifting up holy hands, without wrath and doubting.

Encouragement to Prayer

Job 33 [26]He shall pray unto God, and he will be favourable unto him: and he shall see his face with joy: for he will render unto man his righteousness.

Psa. 6 [9]The LORD hath heard my supplication; the LORD will receive my prayer.

Psa. 32 [6]For this shall every one that is godly pray unto thee in a time when thou mayest be found: surely in the floods of great waters they shall not come nigh unto him.

Psa. 66 [19]But verily God hath heard me;
he hath attended to the voice of my prayer.
[20]Blessed be God, which hath not turned
away my prayer, nor his mercy from me.

Isa. 65 [24]And it shall come to pass, that before they call, I will answer; and while they are yet speaking, I will hear.

Zech. 13 [9]And I will bring the third part through the fire, and will refine them as silver is refined, and will try them as gold is tried: they shall call on my name, and I will hear them; I will say, It is my people; and they shall say, The LORD is my God.

Matt. 18 [19]Again I say unto you, That if two of you shall agree on earth as touching any thing that they shall ask, it shall be done for them of my Father which is in heaven.

Matt. 21 [22]And all things, whatsoever ye shall ask in prayer, believing, ye shall receive.

Mark 11 [24]Therefore I say unto you, What things soever ye desire, when ye pray, believe that ye receive them, and ye shall have them.

Luke 11 [9]And I say unto you, Ask, and it shall be given you; seek, and ye shall find; knock, and it shall be opened unto you.

Rom. 8 [26]Likewise the Spirit also helpeth our infirmities: for we know not what we should pray for as we ought: but the Spirit itself maketh intercession for us with groanings which cannot be uttered.

Rom. 10 [13]For whosoever shall call upon the Name of the Lord, shall be saved.

Jas. 1 [5]If any of you lack wisdom, let him
ask of God, that giveth to all men liberally,
and upbraideth not: and it shall be given
him. [6]But let him ask in faith, nothing wavering: for he that wavereth is like a wave of the sea, driven with the wind, and tossed.

Prayers Heard and Answered

Psa. 10 [17]LORD, thou hast heard the desire of the humble: thou wilt prepare their heart, thou wilt cause thine ear to hear.

Psa. 65 [2]O thou that hearest prayer, unto thee shall all flesh come.

Psa. 99 [6]Moses and Aaron among his priests, and Samuel among them that call upon his name; they called upon the LORD, and he answered them.

Isa. 58 [9]Then shalt thou call, and the LORD shall answer; thou shalt cry, and he shall say, Here I am. If thou take away from the midst of thee the yoke, the putting forth of the finger, and speaking vanity.

Proper Offering of Prayer

Psa. 145 [18]The LORD is nigh unto all them that call upon him, to all that call upon him in truth.

Eccl. 5 [2]Be not rash with thy mouth, and let not thine heart be hasty to utter any thing before God: for God is in heaven, and thou upon earth: therefore let thy words be few.

Matt. 6 [5]And when thou prayest, thou shalt not be as the hypocrites are: for they love to pray standing in the synagogues and in the corners of the streets, that they may be seen of men. Verily I say unto you, They have their reward. [6]But thou, when thou prayest, enter into thy closet, and when thou hast shut thy door, pray to thy Father which is in secret; and thy Father which seeth in secret shall reward thee openly. [7]But when ye pray, use not vain repetitions, as the heathen do: for they think that they shall be heard for their much speaking. [8]Be not ye therefore like unto them: for your Father knoweth what things ye have need of, before ye ask him.

Matt. 26 [39]And he went a little farther, and fell on his face, and prayed, saying, O my Father, if it be possible, let this cup pass from me: nevertheless not as I will, but as thou wilt.

Mark 11 [25]And when ye stand praying, forgive, if ye have ought against any: that your Father also which is in heaven may forgive you your trespasses. [26]But if ye do not forgive, neither will your Father which is in heaven forgive your trespasses.

John 9 [31]Now we know that God heareth not sinners: but if any man be a worshipper of God, and doeth his will, him he heareth.

John 15 [7]If ye abide in me, and my words abide in you, ye shall ask what ye will, and it shall be done unto you.

Rom. 12 [12]Rejoicing in hope; patient in tribulation; continuing instant in prayer.

Col. 4 [2]Continue in prayer, and watch in the same with thanksgiving.

1 Tim. 5 [5]Now she that is a widow indeed, and desolate, trusteth in God, and continueth in supplications and prayers night and day.

Heb. 11 [6]But without faith it is impossible to please him: for he that cometh to God, must believe that he is, and that he is a rewarder of them that diligently seek him.

Jas. 4 [8]Draw nigh to God, and he will draw nigh to you: cleanse your hands ye sinners, and purify your hearts ye double minded.

Pray through and in the Name of Christ

John 16 [26]At that day ye shall ask in my name: and I say not unto you, that I will pray the Father for you.

Eph. 2 [18]For through him we both have an access by one Spirit unto the Father.

Heb. 10 [19]Having therefore, brethren, boldness to enter into the Holiest by the blood of Jesus.

Posture for Prayer

Num. 16 [22]And they fell upon their faces, and said, O God, the God of the spirits of all flesh, shall one man sin, and wilt thou be wroth with all the congregation?

1 Kin. 8 [22]And Solomon stood before the altar of the LORD in the presence of all the congregation of Israel, and spread forth his hands toward heaven: [23]And he said, LORD God of Israel, there is no God like thee, in heaven above, or on earth beneath, who keepest covenant and mercy with thy servants that walk before thee with all their heart.

1 Chr. 21 [16]And David lifted up his eyes, and saw the angel of the LORD stand between the earth and the heaven, having a drawn sword in his hand, stretched out over Jerusalem. Then David and the elders of Israel, who were clothed in sackcloth, fell upon their faces.

Psa. 28 [2]Hear the voice of my supplications, when I cry unto thee, when I lift up my hands toward thy holy oracle.

Psa. 95 [6]O come, let us worship and bow down: let us kneel before the LORD our maker.

Lam. 2 [19]Arise, cry out in the night: in the beginning of the watches pour out thy heart like water before the face of the LORD: lift up thine hands toward him for the life of thy young children, that faint for hunger in the top of every street.

Luke 22 [41]And he was withdrawn from them about a stone's cast, and kneeled down, and prayed.

Wicked and Hypocritical Prayer Condemned

Psa. 109 [6]Set thou a wicked man over him: and let Satan stand at his right hand. [7]When he shall be judged, let him be condemned: and let his prayer become sin.

Prov. 28 [9]He that turneth away his ear from hearing the law, even his prayer shall be abomination.

Matt. 6 [5]And when thou prayest, thou shalt not be as the hypocrites are: for they love to pray standing in the synagogues and in the corners of the streets, that they may be seen of men. Verily I say unto you, They have their reward.

The Lord's Prayer

MATTHEW'S FORM

Matt. 6 [9]After this manner therefore pray ye: Our Father which art in heaven, Hallowed be thy name. [10]Thy kingdom come. Thy will be done in earth, as it is in heaven. [11]Give us this day our daily bread. [12]And forgive us our debts, as we forgive our debtors. [13]And lead us not into temptation, but deliver us from evil: For thine is the kingdom, and the power, and the glory, for ever. Amen.

LUKE'S FORM

Luke 11 [1]And it came to pass, that, as he was praying in a certain place, when he ceased, one of his disciples said unto him, Lord, teach us to pray, as John also taught his disciples. [2]And he said unto them, When ye pray, say, Our Father which art in heaven, Hallowed be thy name. Thy kingdom come. Thy will be done, as in heaven, so in earth. [3]Give us day by day our daily bread. [4]And forgive us our sins; for we also forgive every one that is indebted to us. And lead us not into temptation; but deliver us from evil.

PREACHING

[prēch'ing] In the New Testament "preaching" refers to proclamation of the gospel to non-Christians, as distinguished from "teaching," which refers to moral, ethical, and doctrinal instruction to those who are already Christians. The Greek word for proclamation is *kerygma*; this word is frequently used by Biblical scholars to describe the characteristic message of early Christian evangelists. It is generally believed this kerygma contained the following items: (1) a brief outline of Jesus' ministry, (2) an account of his death, resurrection, and exaltation, (3) a proclamation of his Second Coming, and (4) a call to repentance and an offer of forgiveness of sins and the gift of the Holy Spirit. The preaching of the apostles and early evangelists was thus the proclamation of the salvation wrought by God in Christ, together with a summons to believe it and be saved.

SCRIPTURE

General

Matt. 4 [17]From that time Jesus began to preach, and to say, Repent: for the kingdom of heaven is at hand.

Matt. 28 [19]Go ye therefore, and teach all nations, baptizing them in the name of the Father, and of the Son, and of the Holy Ghost.

Mark 1 [14]Now after that John was put in prison, Jesus came into Galilee, preaching the gospel of the kingdom of God.

Mark 16 [15]And he said unto them, Go ye into all the world, and preach the gospel to every creature.

Luke 4 [17]And there was delivered unto him the book of the prophet Esaias. And when he had opened the book, he found the place where it was written, [18]The Spirit of the Lord is upon me, because he hath anointed me to preach the gospel to the poor; he hath sent me to heal the brokenhearted, to preach deliverance to the captives, and recovering of sight to the blind, to set at liberty them that are bruised, [19]To preach the acceptable year of the Lord.

Luke 9 [60]Jesus said unto him, Let the dead bury their dead: but go thou and preach the kingdom of God.

Luke 24 [47]And that repentance and remission of sins should be preached in his name among all nations, beginning at Jerusalem.

Acts 10 [40]But Philip was found at Azotus: and passing through he preached in all the cities, till he came to Caesarea.

Rom. 10 [13]For whosoever shall call upon the name of the Lord shall be saved. [14]How then shall they call on him in whom they have not believed? and how shall they believe in him of whom they have not heard? and how shall they hear without a preacher? [15]And how shall they preach, except they be sent? as it is written, How beautiful are the feet of them that preach the gospel of peace, and bring glad tidings of good things!

1 Cor. 1 [17]For Christ sent me not to baptize, but to preach the gospel: not with wisdom of words, lest the cross of Christ should be made of none effect. [18]For the preaching of the cross is to them that perish foolishness; but unto us which are saved it is the power of God. [21]For after that in the wisdom of God the world by wisdom knew not God, it pleased God by the foolishness of preaching to save them that believe. [23]We preach Christ crucified, unto the Jews a stumblingblock, and unto the Greeks foolishness; [27]God hath chosen the foolish things of the world to confound the wise; and God hath chosen the weak things of the world to confound the things which are mighty; [28]And base things of the world, and things which are despised, hath God chosen, yea, and things which are not, to bring to nought things that are: [29]That no flesh should glory in his presence.

1 Cor. 2 [1]And I, brethren, when I came to you, came not with excellency of speech or of wisdom, declaring unto you the testimony of God. [2]For I determined not to know any thing among you, save Jesus Christ, and him crucified. [3]And I was with you in weakness, and in fear, and in much trembling. [4]And my speech and my preaching was not with enticing words of man's wisdom, but in demonstration of the Spirit and of power:

Content of Early Christian Preaching

Acts 13 [17]The God of this people of Israel chose our fathers, and exalted the people when they dwelt as strangers in the land of Egypt, and with a high arm brought he them out of it.

Acts 3 [18]But those things, which God before had showed by the mouth of all his prophets, that Christ should suffer, he hath so fulfilled.

[24]Yea, and all the prophets from Samuel

and those that follow after, as many as have spoken, have likewise foretold of these days.

Rom. 1 [3]Concerning his Son Jesus Christ our Lord, which was made of the seed of David according to the flesh;

Acts 10 [37]And began from Galilee, after the baptism which John preached; [38]How God anointed Jesus of Nazareth with the Holy Ghost and with power: who went about doing good, and healing all that were oppressed of the devil; for God was with him. [39]And we are witnesses of all things which he did both in the land of the Jews, and in Jerusalem;

Acts 13 [27]For they that dwell at Jerusalem, and their rulers, because they knew him not, nor yet the voices of the prophets which are read every sabbath day, they have fulfilled them in condemning him. [28]And though they found no cause of death in him, yet desired they Pilate that he should be slain. [29]And when they had fulfilled all that was written of him, they took him down from the tree, and laid him in a sepulchre.

Rom. 1 [4]And declared to be the Son of God with power, according to the Spirit of holiness, by the resurrection from the dead:

Acts 5 [31]Him hath God exalted with his right hand to be a Prince and a Saviour, for to give repentance to Israel, and forgiveness of sins. [32]And we are his witnesses of these things; and so is also the Holy Ghost, whom God hath given to them that obey him.

Acts 10 [42]And he commanded us to preach unto the people, and to testify that it is he which was ordained of God to be the Judge of quick and dead.

Acts 2 [38]Then Peter said unto them, Repent, and be baptized every one of you in the name of Jesus Christ for the remission of sins, and ye shall receive the gift of the Holy Ghost.

Rom. 10 [8]But what saith it? The word is nigh thee, even in thy mouth, and in thy heart: that is, the word of faith, which we preach; [9]That if thou shalt confess with thy mouth the Lord Jesus, and shalt believe in thine heart that God hath raised him from the dead, thou shalt be saved.

PREDESTINATION

[prē des ti nā′shun] To settle beforehand; to foreordain to an earthly or eternal lot or destiny. The doctrine of predestination is based upon belief in a living, acting God who orders events, things, and men. As a part of this activity he has set aside certain groups and individuals to sustain a definite relationship to him. The nation of Israel, the house of David, and the prophet Jeremiah (*see Jer. 1:5*) were all chosen by God "beforehand" to serve a special end. God's determination to reconcile the world to himself through the agency of Jesus Christ is perhaps the clearest instance of the divine predestination.

The New Testament speaks of the members of the church as the elect, the called, the chosen, and the predestined. There is great joy in believing some have been predestined to a special relationship with the God of the Universe, but there is also a dark side to this belief, for if some have been predestined to eternal life by divine decree, then it follows logically that others have not. This doctrine of "double predestination" has been one of the thorniest with which Christian theologians have had to deal. The apostle Paul treats this problem in *Rom. 8-11* and in *Eph. 1.* In *Rom. 8:28,* he encourages his readers by assuring them that, despite whatever tribulations might befall them, their salvation is secure, since they have been predestined to be "conformed to the image of his Son." In the remaining portion of these chapters, he makes it clear that this election rests not upon race or merit, but upon God's sovereign will and grace. In *Eph. 1:3-14,* we see clearly that this grace is made known in Jesus Christ and that however we are to understand predestination it is not to be separated from the work of Christ, who takes part in the determinations that are made with regard to mankind.

Paul does not deny that God has predestined some to life and others to death. He is unwilling, however, to draw the lines with any certainty, or to declare unequivocally that God has predestined some to eternal damnation. In *Rom. 11:7-16,* he contrasts Israel with "the elect" but speaks of the possibility of their eventual salvation. In *Tit. 1:1,* he speaks of furthering the faith of the elect "in hope of eternal life" indicating that the final salvation even of the elect is not entirely certain. It would appear, therefore, that we can never plumb the depths of the divine mind deeply enough to arrive at an answer that will be satisfactory to all. It is doubtful the tension between predestination and free will can ever be completely resolved. We must content ourselves with the knowledge that our final destiny will be determined by our relation to Christ and that God is "not willing that any should perish, but that all should come to repentance" (*2 Pet. 3:9*).

See ELECTION

SCRIPTURE

Rom. 8 29 For whom he did foreknow, he also did predestinate to be conformed to the image of his Son, that he might be the firstborn among many brethren. 30 Moreover whom he did predestinate, them he also called: and whom he called, them he also justified: and whom he justified, them he also glorified.

Rom. 9 18 Therefore hath he mercy on whom he will have mercy, and whom he will he hardeneth. 19 Thou wilt say then unto me, Why doth he yet find fault? For who hath resisted his will? 20 Nay but, O man, who art thou that repliest against God? Shall the thing formed say to him that formed it, Why hast thou made me thus? 21 Hath not the potter power over the clay, of the same lump to make one vessel unto honour, and another unto dishonour? 22 What if God, willing to shew his wrath, and to make his power known, endured with much longsuffering the vessels of wrath fitted to destruction: 23 And that he might make known the riches of his glory on the vessels of mercy, which he had afore prepared unto glory, 24 Even us, whom he hath called, not of the Jews only, but also of the Gentiles? 25 As he saith also in Osee, I will call them my people, which were not my people; and her beloved, which was not beloved. 26 And it shall come to pass, that in the place where it was said unto them, Ye are not my people; there shall they be called the children of the living God.

Rom. 10 8 But what saith it? The word is nigh thee, even in thy mouth, and in thy heart: that is, the word of faith, which we preach; 9 That if thou shalt confess with thy mouth the Lord Jesus, and shalt believe in thine heart that God hath raised him from the dead, thou shalt be saved. 10 For with the heart man believeth unto righteousness; and with the mouth confession is made unto salvation. 11 For the scripture saith, Whosoever believeth on him shall not be ashamed. 12 For there is no difference between the Jew and the Greek: for the same Lord over all is rich unto all that call upon him. 13 For whosoever shall call upon the name of the Lord shall be saved. 14 How then shall they call on him in whom they have not believed? and how shall they believe in him of whom they have not heard? and how shall they hear without a preacher? 15 And how shall they preach, except they be sent? as it is written, How beautiful are the feet of them that preach the gospel of peace, and bring glad tidings of good things! 16 But they have not all obeyed the gospel. For Esaias saith, Lord, who hath believed our report?

Eph. 1 1 Paul, an apostle of Jesus Christ by the will of God, to the saints which are at Ephesus, and to the faithful in Christ Jesus: 2 Grace be to you, and peace, from God our Father, and from the Lord Jesus

Christ. [3]Blessed be the God and Father of our Lord Jesus Christ, who hath blessed us with all spiritual blessings in heavenly places in Christ: [4]According as he hath chosen us in him before the foundation of the world, that we should be holy and without blame before him in love: [5]Having predestinated us unto the adoption of children by Jesus Christ to himself, according to the good pleasure of his will, [6]To the praise of the glory of his grace, wherein he hath made us accepted in the beloved. [7]In whom we have redemption through his blood, the forgiveness of sins, according to the riches of his grace; [8]Wherein he hath abounded toward us in all wisdom and prudence; [9]Having made known unto us the mystery of his will, according to his good pleasure which he hath purposed in himself: [10]That in the dispensation of the fulness of times he might gather together in one all things in Christ, both which are in heaven, and which are on earth; even in him: [11]In whom also we have obtained an inheritance, being predestinated according to the purpose of him who worketh all things after the counsel of his own will: [12]That we should be to the praise of his glory, who first trusted in Christ. [13]In whom ye also trusted, after that ye heard the word of truth, the gospel of your salvation: in whom also after that ye believed, ye were sealed with that Holy Spirit of promise, [14]Which is the earnest of our inheritance until the redemption of the purchased possession, unto the praise of his glory.

PRIDE

[prīd] The state or quality of being proud or having inordinate self-esteem; conceit concerning one's talents, ability, wealth, station, etc.; disdainful behavior. The abundant teaching on pride and humility is a distinctive feature of biblical religion. Beginning with the story of the Fall in *Gen. 3* (*see* FALL), pride is viewed as the root and essence of sin; it is seeking for oneself the honor and glory that properly belong to God. The most profound teaching on pride comes from the life and words of the Master himself. He condemned racial pride, the spiritual pride of the Pharisees which manifested itself in ostentatious religious practices, and other forms of social pride, while urging his disciples to assume an attitude of childlike humility. He was, of course, the finest example of his teaching, as seen in his washing the feet of the disciples and in his submission to death on the cross. Paul instructs us that the cross is the proper ground for Christian humility, for apart from it neither Jew nor Gentile has any grounds for boasting concerning his salvation.

See VANITY, OSTENTATION, CONCEIT, HUMILITY

SCRIPTURE

General

1 Sam. 2 [3]Talk no more so exceeding proudly; let not arrogancy come out of your mouth: for the LORD is a God of knowledge, and by him actions are weighed.

Prov. 6 [16]These six things doth the LORD hate; yea, seven are an abomination unto him: [17]A proud look, a lying tongue, and hands that shed innocent blood.

Prov. 8 [13]The fear of the LORD is to hate evil: pride, and arrogancy, and the evil way, and the froward mouth, do I hate.

Prov. 16 [5]Every one that is proud in heart is an abomination to the LORD: though hand join in hand, he shall not be unpunished.

Prov. 21 [4]A high look and a proud heart, and the ploughing of the wicked, is sin.

Dan. 5 [20]But when his heart was lifted up, and his mind hardened in pride, he was deposed from his kingly throne, and they took his glory from him.

Rom. 12 [3]For I say, through the grace given unto me, to every man that is among you, not to think of himself more highly than he ought to think; but to think soberly, according as God hath dealt to every man the measure of faith. [16]Be of the same mind one toward another. Mind not high things, but condescend to men of low estate. Be not wise in your own conceits.

Luke 18 [11]The Pharisee stood and prayed thus with himself, God, I thank thee, that I am not as other men are, extortioners, unjust, adulterers, or even as this publican. [12]I fast twice in the week, I give tithes of all that I possess.

1 Cor. 8 [1]Now as touching things offered unto idols, we know that we all have knowledge. Knowledge puffeth up: but Charity edifieth. [2]And if any man think that he knoweth any thing, he knoweth nothing yet as he ought to know.

1 Tim. 3 [6]Not a novice, lest being lifted up with pride, he fall into the condemnation of the devil.

Evil Results of Pride

Psa. 10 [2]The wicked in his pride doth persecute the poor: let them be taken in the devices that they have imagined.

Prov. 13 [10]Only by pride cometh contention: but with the well-advised is wisdom.

Prov. 21 [24]Proud and haughty scorner is his name, who dealeth in proud wrath.

Prov. 28 [25]He that is of a proud heart stirreth up strife: but he that putteth his trust in the LORD shall be made fat.

Jer. 49 [16]Thy terribleness hath deceived thee, and the pride of thine heart, O thou that dwellest in the clefts of the rock, that holdest the height of the hill: though thou shouldest make thy nest as high as the eagle, I will bring thee down from thence, saith the LORD.

Shame and Destruction Follows Pride

Prov. 11 [2]When pride cometh, then cometh shame: but with the lowly is wisdom.

Prov. 16 [18]Pride goeth before destruction, and an haughty spirit before a fall. [19]Better it is to be of an humble spirit with the lowly, than to divide the spoil with the proud.

Prov. 18 [12]Before destruction the heart of man is haughty, and before honour is humility.

Isa. 28 [3]The crown of pride, the drunkards of Ephraim, shall be trodden under feet.

PRIEST, PRIESTHOOD

[prēst, prēst′ho͝od] One authorized or ordained to perform special sacerdotal functions; office of a priest. The priests of the religion of Israel were set aside as men "holy unto the Lord". (*See* HOLINESS) They were to be free from physical defect or infirmity and were subject to numerous restrictions and ceremonial obligations designed to protect this holiness. The priesthood of Israel consisted of three levels arranged in hierarchical fashion. At the top of the structure was the high priest, whose duty it was to represent the whole people before the mercy seat of God and to make atonement for their sins. His mediatorship was symbolized by his breastplate, on which were inscribed the names of the twelve tribes of Israel. At the second level were the priests. The primary tasks of the priests were officiating at religious feasts and festivals (*see* FEASTS), regulating and offering the sacrifices in the elaborate sacrificial system (*see* SACRIFICES), providing answers to various problems of the people, and, in general, serving as intermediaries between man and God. After the exile, the priesthood attained enormous prestige and power and largely comprised the educated class which guarded the traditions of the fathers, developed Jewish theology, and was instrumental in compiling and editing of the writings which form our Old Testament. During David's reign the priesthood was divided into twenty-four "courses", each course consisting of descendants of one of the twenty-four grandsons of Aaron. (*See 1 Chr. 24:1-19*) These officiated in the temple service in rotation, each division serving for one week, beginning with the Sabbath, except at the major religious festivals, when the entire priesthood was on duty at once. All members of the priesthood were Levites in that they were of the tribe of Levi, which was consecrated to the service of the LORD as a substitute for the first-born sons of all Israel. (*See Num. 3:12-13*) The term "Levite," however, is used in a technical sense to refer to the third and lowest level of the priestly class, which consisted of members of the tribe of Levi not descended from Aaron. They were charged with the subordinate functions of the temple service, such as caring for the building and grounds, gatekeeping, preparation of offerings, and assisting the priests in whatever way was necessary. In the division of the land at Shiloh, the Levites received no major land area of their own, but were assigned forty-eight cities scattered throughout the territory of the other tribes. They were maintained by the tithe of the congregation and in turn gave a tithe of this to support the regular priests.

By the time of Jesus' ministry the priesthood had developed into an aristocratic ruling class, with the high priest a virtual sovereign. Jesus did not question the legitimacy of the priesthood for its time, but in his ministry the necessity for such an earthly priesthood was abolished. The temporal priesthood of the sons of Aaron was superseded by the Great High Priest after the order of Melchizedek who, having offered himself as an all-sufficient sacrifice, has entered into the Most Holy Place of the heavenly sanctuary and exercises his mediatorship not within the framework of an earthly institution, but eternally, at the right hand of God.

There is a sense in which every Christian may properly be called a priest (*1 Pet. 2:5; Rev. 1:6; 5:10; 20:6*). He is made "holy unto the Lord," is sanctified by his baptism and anointing with the Holy Spirit. He is clothed with the vestments of Jesus' righteousness. He offers praise to God that is sweeter far than any incense burned in the temple. He proclaims the Lordship of Christ and prays on behalf of his fellowman. In offering himself as a "living sacrifice" (*Rom. 12:1*), he shares in the sufferings of the Lamb of God and demonstrates his fitness for the "holy priesthood, to offer up spiritual sacrifices, acceptable to God by Jesus Christ" (*1 Pet. 2:5*).

SCRIPTURE

The Priesthood of Jesus

Heb. 2 17Wherefore in all things it behooved him to be made like unto his brethren, that he might be a merciful and faithful high priest in things pertaining to God, to make reconciliation for the sins of the people.

Heb. 4 14Seeing then that we have a great high priest, that is passed into the heavens, Jesus the Son of God, let us hold fast our profession.
15For we have not a high priest which cannot be touched with the feeling of our infirmities; but was in all points tempted like as we are, yet without sin.

Heb. 5 5So also Christ glorified not himself to be made a high priest; but he that said unto him, Thou art my Son, today have I begotten thee.
6As he saith also in another place, Thou art a priest for ever after the order of Melchisedec.
7Who in the days of his flesh, when he had offered up prayers and supplications with strong crying and tears unto him that was able to save him from death, and was heard in that he feared;
8Though he were a Son, yet learned he obedience by the things which he suffered;
9And being made perfect, he became the author of eternal salvation unto all them that obey him;
10Called of God a high priest after the order of Melchisedec.

Heb. 6 20Whither the forerunner is for us entered, even Jesus, made a high priest for ever after the order of Melchisedec.

Heb. 7 26For such a high priest became us, who is holy, harmless, undefiled, separate from sinners, and made higher than the heavens;

Heb. 8 1Now of the things which we

have spoken this is the sum: We have such a high priest, who is set on the right hand of the throne of the Majesty in the heavens;

Heb. 9 [11]But Christ being come a high priest of good things to come, by a greater and more perfect tabernacle, not made with hands, that is to say, not of this building; [12]Neither by the blood of goats and calves, but by his own blood he entered in once into the holy place, having obtained eternal redemption for us. [13]For if the blood of bulls and of goats, and the ashes of a heifer sprinkling the unclean, sanctifieth to the purifying of the flesh; [14]How much more shall the blood of Christ, who through the eternal Spirit offered himself without spot to God, purge your conscience from dead works to serve the living God?

REFERENCE: High Priest, *Ex. 28:2-43; 39:1-31; Lev. 16; 21:10-15; Num. 5:15; 18:2-7; Deut. 17:8-13;* Priests, *Ex. 28-29; Lev. 2:3; 10:8-20; 21:1, 5, 6; 1 Chr. 24;* Levites, *Num. 1:47-54; 3:14-19; 4:1-17; 8:5-23; Deut. 18:1-2;* Levitical cities, *Lev. 25:32-4; Num. 35:2-8; Josh. 21: 1-4, 13-19, 41, 42;* Support of Priests, *Ex. 29: 27-34; Lev. 2, 5-7; 23:20; Num. 18:8-18, 26-32.*

PRINCE

[prins] The son of a king or ruler; a person high in authority as a noble; also used as a generic term for a ruler or sovereign. Christ is referred to as the Prince of Life and Peace and the evil one is called a prince to indicate his sovereignty over evil things.

SCRIPTURE

The Prince of Peace and Life

Isa. 9 [6]For unto us a child is born, unto us a son is given: and the government shall be upon his shoulder: and his name shall be called Wonderful, Counsellor, The mighty God, The everlasting Father, The Prince of Peace.

Acts 3 [15]And killed the Prince of life, whom God hath raised from the dead, whereof we are witnesses.

The Prince of This World and Power of the Air

John 12 [31]Now is the judgment of this world: now shall the prince of this world be cast out.

John 14 [30]Hereafter I will not talk much with you: for the prince of this world cometh, and hath nothing in me.

Eph. 2 [2]Wherein in time past ye walked according to the course of this world, according to the prince of the power of the air, the spirit that now worketh in the children of disobedience.

Christ's Miracles Ascribed to Prince of Devils

Matt. 9 [34]But the Pharisees said, He casteth out devils through the prince of the devils.

Matt. 12 [24]But when the Pharisees heard it, they said, This fellow doth not cast out devils, but by Beelzebub the prince of the devils.

Mark 3 [22]And the scribes which came down from Jerusalem said, He hath Beelzebub, and by the prince of the devils casteth he out devils. [23]And he called them unto him, and said unto them in parables, How can Satan cast out Satan?

PROFESSION

[prō fesh'un] Public avowal or declaration; open acknowledgment; also a solemn vow or promise. Profession of faith, or open acknowledgment of belief in Christ, is a fundamental requirement of Christianity. This is a declaration of allegiance and definite act of enlistment under the banner of Christ, who died for our salvation. To this profession we are told to hold fast, since through it we and our principles are known to the world.

See CONFESSION

SCRIPTURE

1 Tim. 6 [12]Fight the good fight of faith, lay hold on eternal life, whereunto thou art also called, and hast professed a good profession before many witnesses.

Heb. 4 [14]Seeing then that we have a great high Priest, that is passed into the heavens, Jesus the Son of God, let us hold fast our profession.

Heb. 10 [23]Let us hold fast the profession of our faith without wavering; (for he is faithful that promised;) [24]And let us consider one another to provoke unto love and to good works.

PROMISE

[prom'is] A declaration made by one person to another to do, or to refrain from doing, a thing; a declaration which gives the person receiving it the right to expect the performance of the thing or its non-performance, according to the nature of the declaration.

The Bible is replete with the promises of God to man, the greatest of which is the promise of salvation through faith.

SCRIPTURE

Promises of God

TO MANKIND FROM THE FALL

Gen. 3 [15]And I will put enmity between thee and the woman, and between thy seed and her seed; it shall bruise thy head, and thou shalt bruise his heel.

TO NOAH

Gen. 8 [21]And the Lord smelled a sweet savour; and the Lord said in his heart, I will not again curse the ground any more for man's sake; for the imagination of man's heart is evil from his youth: neither will I again smite any more every thing living, as I have done. [22]While the earth remaineth, seedtime and harvest, and cold and heat, and summer and winter, and day and night, shall not cease.

Gen. 9 [9]And I, behold, I establish my covenant with you, and with your seed after you; [10]And with every living creature that is with you, of the fowl, of the cattle, and of every beast of the earth with you, from all that go out of the ark, to every beast of the earth. [11]And I will establish my covenant with you; neither shall all flesh be cut off any more by the waters of a flood; neither shall there any more be a flood to destroy the earth.

TO ABRAHAM

Gen. 13 [15]For all the land which thou seest, to thee will I give it, and to thy seed for ever. [16]And I will make thy seed as the dust of the earth: so that if a man can number the dust of the earth, then shall thy seed also be numbered.

Gen. 17 [6]And I will make thee exceedingly fruitful, and I will make nations of thee; and kings shall come out of thee. [7]And I will establish my covenant between me and thee, and thy seed after thee, in their generations, for an everlasting covenant; to be a God unto thee, and to thy seed after thee.

Gen. 22 [16]And said, By myself have I sworn, saith the Lord, for because thou hast done this thing, and hast not withheld thy son, thine only son: [17]That in blessing I will bless thee, and in multiplying I will multiply thy seed as the stars of the heaven, and as the sand which is upon the seashore; and thy seed shall possess the gate of his enemies; [18]And in thy seed shall all the nations of the earth be blessed; because thou hast obeyed my voice.

TO DAVID

2 Sam. 7 [11]And as since the time that I

commanded judges to be over my people Israel, and have caused thee to rest from all thine enemies. Also the LORD telleth thee that he will make thee an house.

[12]And when thy days be fulfilled, and thou shalt sleep with thy fathers, I will set up thy seed after thee, which shall proceed out of thy bowels, and I will establish his kingdom. [13]He shall build an house for my name, and I will stablish the throne of his kingdom for ever. [14]I will be his father, and he shall be my son. If he commit iniquity, I will chasten him with the rod of men, and with the stripes of the children of men.

Promises of Christ

Matt. 6 [33]But seek ye first the kingdom of God, and his righteousness; and all these things shall be added unto you.

Matt. 7 [7]Ask, and it shall be given you; seek, and ye shall find; knock, and it shall be opened unto you.

Matt. 10 [40]He that receiveth you receiveth me, and he that receiveth me receiveth him that sent me. [41]He that receiveth a prophet in the name of a prophet shall receive a prophet's reward; and he that receiveth a righteous man in the name of a righteous man shall receive a righteous man's reward. [42]And whosoever shall give to drink unto one of these little ones a cup of cold water only in the name of a disciple, verily I say unto you, he shall in no wise lose his reward.

Matt. 11 [28]Come unto me, all ye that labour and are heavy laden, and I will give you rest.

Matt. 12 [50]For whosoever shall do the will of my Father which is in heaven, the same is my brother, and sister, and mother.

Matt. 16 [18]And I say also unto thee, That thou art Peter, and upon this rock I will build my church; and the gates of hell shall not prevail against it. [19]And I will give unto thee the keys of the kingdom of heaven: and whatsoever thou shalt bind on earth shall be bound in heaven: and whatsoever thou shalt loose on earth shall be loosed in heaven.

[24]Then said Jesus unto his disciples, If any man will come after me, let him deny himself, and take up his cross, and follow me. [25]For whosoever will save his life shall lose it: and whosoever will lose his life for my sake shall find it.

Matt. 17 [20]And Jesus said unto them, Because of your unbelief: for verily I say unto you, If ye have faith as a grain of mustard seed, ye shall say unto this mountain, Remove hence to yonder place; and it shall remove; and nothing shall be impossible unto you.

Matt. 19 [28]And Jesus said unto them, Verily I say unto you, That ye which have followed me, in the regeneration when the Son of man shall sit in the throne of his glory, ye also shall sit upon twelve thrones, judging the twelve tribes of Israel. [29]And every one that hath forsaken houses, or brethren, or sisters, or father, or mother, or wife, or children, or lands, for my name's sake, shall receive an hundredfold, and shall inherit everlasting life. [30]But many that are first shall be last; and the last shall be first.

Matt. 28 [20]Teaching them to observe all things whatsoever I have commanded you: and, lo, I am with you alway, even unto the end of the world. Amen.

Luke 12 [32]Fear not, little flock; for it is your Father's good pleasure to give you the kingdom.

John 14 [12]Verily, verily, I say unto you, He that believeth on me, the works that I do shall he do also; and greater works than these shall he do; because I go unto my Father. [13]And whatsoever ye shall ask in my name, that will I do, that the Father may be glorified in the Son. [14]If ye shall ask any thing in my name, I will do it.

Promise of the Gospel

Psa. 89 [3]I have made a covenant with my chosen, I have sworn unto David my servant, [4]Thy seed will I establish for ever, and build up thy throne to all generations. Selah.

Rom. 1 [1]Paul, a servant of Jesus Christ, called to be an apostle, separated unto the gospel of God, [2](Which he had promised afore by his prophets in the holy Scriptures,) [3]Concerning his Son Jesus Christ our Lord, which was made of the seed of David according to the flesh, [4]And declared to be the Son of God, with power, according to the Spirit of holiness, by the resurrection from the dead.

Eph. 3 [6]That the Gentiles should be fellowheirs, and of the same body, and partakers of his promise in Christ, by the gospel.

2 Tim. 1 [1]Paul an apostle of Jesus Christ by the will of God, according to the promise of life, which is in Christ Jesus.

Heb. 6 [13]For when God made promise to Abraham, because he could swear by no greater, he sware by himself, [14]Saying, Surely blessing I will bless thee, and multiplying I will multiply thee. [15]And so, after he had patiently endured, he obtained the promise. [16]For men verily swear by the greater: and an oath for confirmation is to them an end of all strife. [17]Wherein God, willing more abundantly to shew unto the heirs of promise the immutability of his counsel, confirmed it by an oath: [18]That by two immutable things, in which it was impossible for God to lie, we might have a strong consolation, who have fled for refuge to lay hold upon the hope set before us: [19]Which hope we have as an anchor of the soul, both sure and stedfast, and which entereth into that within the veil; [20]Whither the forerunner is for us entered, even Jesus, made an high priest for ever after the order of Melchisedec.

God's Promises Unbreakable and Precious

Num. 23 [19]God is not a man, that he should lie; neither the son of man, that he should repent: hath he said, and shall he not do it? or hath he spoken, and shall he not make it good?

Deut. 7 [9]Know therefore that the LORD thy God, he is God, the faithful God, which keepeth covenant and mercy with them that love him and keep his commandments to a thousand generations.

Josh. 23 [14]And behold, this day I am going the way of all the earth; and ye know in all your hearts and in all your souls, that not one thing hath failed of all the good things which the LORD your God spake concerning you; all are come to pass unto you, and not one thing hath failed thereof. [15]Therefore it shall come to pass, that as all good things are come upon you, which the LORD your God promised you; so shall the LORD bring upon you all evil things, until he have destroyed you from off this good land which the LORD your God hath given you.

1 Kin. 8 [56]Blessed be the LORD, that hath given rest unto his people Israel, according to all that he promised: there hath not failed one word of all his good promise, which he promised by the hand of Moses his servant.

2 Cor. 1 [20]For all the promises of God in him are Yea, and in him Amen, unto the glory of God by us.

Gal. 3 [21]Is the law then against the promises of God? God forbid: for if there had been a law given which could have given life, verily righteousness should have been by the law. [22]But the Scripture hath concluded all under sin, that the promise by faith of Jesus Christ might be given to them that believe.

2 Pet. 1 [4]Whereby are given unto us exceeding great and precious promises, that by these you might be partakers of the divine nature, having escaped the corruption that is in the world through lust.

God Remembers His Promises

Psa. 105 [42]For he remembered his holy promise, and Abraham his servant.

Luke 1 [54]He hath holpen his servant Israel, in remembrance of his mercy, [55]As he spake to our fathers, to Abraham, and to his seed for ever.

Isa. 1 [18]Come now, and let us reason together, saith the LORD: though your sins be as scarlet, they shall be as white as snow; though they be red like crimson, they shall be as wool. [19]If ye be willing and obedient, ye shall eat the good of the land: [20]But if ye refuse and rebel, ye shall be devoured with the sword: for the mouth of the LORD hath spoken it.

Isa. 27 [5]Or let him take hold of my strength, that he may make peace with me, and he shall make peace with me.

Isa. 43 [25]I, even I, am he that blotteth out thy transgressions for mine own sake, and will not remember thy sins.

Isa. 44 [22]I have blotted out, as a thick cloud, thy transgressions, and as a cloud, thy sins: return unto me; for I have redeemed thee.

Promises to the Repentant and Returning

Isa. 55 [1]Ho, every one that thirsteth, come ye to the waters, and he that hath no money; come ye, buy, and eat; yea, come, buy wine and milk without money and without price. [2]Wherefore do ye spend money for that which is not bread? and your labour for that which satisfieth not? hearken diligently unto me, and eat ye that which is good, and let your soul delight itself in fatness. [3]Incline your ear, and come unto me: hear, and your soul shall live; and I will make an everlasting covenant with you, even the sure mercies of David. [4]Behold, I have given him for a witness to the people, a leader and commander to the people.

Jer. 31 [34]And they shall teach no more every man his neighbour, and every man his brother, saying, Know the LORD: for they shall all know me, from the least of them unto the greatest of them, saith the LORD: for I will forgive their iniquity, and I will remember their sin no more.

Jer. 33 [8]And I will cleanse them from all their iniquity, whereby they have sinned against me; and I will pardon all their iniquities, whereby they have sinned, and whereby they have transgressed against me.

Ezek. 33 [16]None of his sins that he hath committed shall be mentioned unto him: he hath done that which is lawful and right; he shall surely live.

2 Cor. 6 [18]And will be a Father unto you, and ye shall be my sons and daughters, saith the Lord Almighty.

2 Cor. 7 [1]Having therefore these promises, dearly beloved, let us cleanse ourselves from all filthiness of the flesh and spirit, perfecting holiness in the fear of God.

God Promises to Uphold and Perfect

Psa. 37 [17]For the arms of the wicked shall be broken: but the LORD upholdeth the righteous.

Psa. 73 [26]My flesh and my heart faileth: but God is the strength of my heart, and my portion for ever.

Psa. 84 [11]For the LORD God is a sun and shield: the LORD will give grace and glory; no good thing will he withhold from them that walk uprightly.

Isa. 40 [29]He giveth power to the faint; and to them that have no might he increaseth strength.

Isa. 41 [10]Fear thou not; for I am with thee: be not dismayed; for I am thy God: I will strengthen thee; yea, I will help thee; yea, I will uphold thee with the right hand of my righteousness.

Isa. 46 [4]And even to your old age I am he: and even to hoar hairs will I carry you: I have made, and I will bear; even I will carry, and will deliver you.

Zech. 2 [8]For thus saith the LORD of hosts: After the glory hath he sent me unto the nations which spoiled you: for he that toucheth you, toucheth the apple of his eye. [9]For behold, I will shake my hand upon them, and they shall be a spoil to their servants: and ye shall know that the LORD of hosts hath sent me.

Zech. 10 [12]And I will strengthen them in the Lord; and they shall walk up and down in his name, saith the Lord.

John 14 [26]But the Comforter, which is the Holy Ghost, whom the Father will send in my name, he shall teach you all things, and bring all things to your remembrance, whatsoever I have said unto you.

Rom. 16 [20]And the God of peace shall bruise Satan under your feet shortly. The grace of our Lord Jesus Christ be with you. Amen.

1 Cor. 10 [13]There hath no temptation taken you, but such as is common to man: but God is faithful, who will not suffer you to be tempted above that you are able: but will with the temptation also make a way to escape, that ye may be able to bear it.

1 Cor. 15 [57]But thanks be to God, which giveth us the victory, through our Lord Jesus Christ.

1 Cor. 12 [9]And he said unto me, My grace is sufficient for thee: for my strength is made perfect in weakness. Most gladly therefore will I rather glory in my infirmities, that the power of Christ may rest upon me.

Eph. 1 [3]Blessed be the God and Father of our Lord Jesus Christ, who hath blessed us with all spiritual blessings in heavenly places in Christ.

Promises to the Poor and Fatherless

Deut. 10 [18]He doth execute the judgment of the fatherless and widow, and loveth the stranger, in giving him food and raiment.

Psa. 9 [8]And he shall judge the world in righteousness, he shall minister judgment to the people in uprightness. [9]The LORD also will be a refuge for the oppressed, a refuge in times of trouble.

Psa. 10 [14]Thou hast seen it; for thou beholdest mischief and spite, to requite it with thy hand: the poor committeth himself unto thee; thou art the helper of the fatherless.

Psa. 68 [5]A father of the fatherless, and a judge of the widows, is God in his holy habitation. [6]God setteth the solitary in families: he bringeth out those which are bound with chains: but the rebellious dwell in a dry land.

Psa. 69 [33]For the LORD heareth the poor, and despiseth not his prisoners.

Psa. 72 [12]For he shall deliver the needy when he crieth; the poor also, and him that hath no helper. [13]He shall spare the poor and needy, and shall save the souls of the needy. [14]He shall redeem their soul from deceit and violence. and precious shall their blood be in his sight.

Psa. 102 [17]He will regard the prayer of the destitute, and not despise their prayer.

Psa. 109 [31]For he shall stand at the right hand of the poor, to save him from those that condemn his soul.

Psa. 113 [7]He raiseth up the poor out of the dust, and lifteth the needy out of the dunghill; [8]That he may set him with princes, even with the princes of his people. [9]He maketh the barren woman to keep house, and to be a joyful mother of children. Praise ye the LORD.

Jer. 49 [11]Leave thy fatherless children, I will preserve them alive; and let thy widows trust in me.

Promises of Temporal Blessings

Ex. 23 [25]And ye shall serve the LORD your God, and he shall bless thy bread, and thy water; and I will take sickness away from the midst of thee.

Lev. 26 [60]And I will give peace in the land, and ye shall lie down, and none shall make you afraid: and I will rid evil beasts out of the land, neither shall the sword go through your land.

Psa. 34 [9]O fear the LORD, ye his saints; for there is no want to them that fear him. [10]The young lions do lack, and suffer hunger: but they that seek the LORD shall not want any good thing.

Psa. 37 [3]Trust in the LORD, and do good; so shalt thou dwell in the land, and verily thou shalt be fed.

Prov. 3 [9]Honour the LORD with thy substance, and with the firstfruits of all thine increase: [10]So shall thy barns be filled with plenty, and thy presses shall burst out with new wine.

Matt. 6 [25]Therefore I say unto you, Take no thought for your life, what ye shall eat, or what ye shall drink; nor yet for your body, what ye shall put on. Is not the life more than meat, and the body than raiment? [26]Behold the fowls of the air: for they sow not, neither do they reap, nor gather into barns; yet your heavenly Father feedeth them. Are ye not much better than they?

Phil. 4 [19]But my God shall supply all your need according to his riches in glory by Christ Jesus.

1 Tim. 4 [8]For bodily exercise profiteth little: but godliness is profitable unto all things, having promise of the life that now is, and of that which is to come.

PROPHETS, PROPHECY

[prof'ets, prof'ĕ si] The prophets were human beings to whom God made revelations regarding His will for communication to mankind. There are apparently two general types of prophets in the Old Testament. The first class are diviners, seers, and cultic preachers and priests. These disappear largely after the rise of the Israelite monarchy and are replaced by a new type of prophet. This latter type has been described variously as literary, reactionary, and revolutionary. It is to this type of prophecy that the sixteen prophetic books in the Old Testament belong. These prophets often formed themselves into guilds, referred to in the Bible as "the sons of the prophets." Elijah was apparently the chief prophet of such a guild. Although the prophets deliver a wide variety of messages, their major functions can be conveniently narrowed to three. (1) They were "king-makers and king-breakers." They are often seen repudiating the kings of Israel, usually resulting in the fall of the dynasty of that king. Ordinarily, the reason for this repudiation was flagrant violation of the true worship of God. (2) The prophets are also seen as declarers of Holy War. (*See* WAR) (3) Finally, the prophets were guardians of the tradition of the central sanctuary. Throughout the prophetic literature the people are summoned back to the true worship at the temple in Jerusalem.

These prophets were messengers of the Great God. The oracles which they delivered may also be grouped into three categories. (1) Oracles of

God, the Divine Warrior. These messages speak of future, imminent, or eschatological war. They contain descriptions of the destruction which is to come and recall the previous mighty acts of God in support of their statements. This class also includes oracles summoning Israel to Holy War, oracles promising destruction on Israel for covenant-breaking, oracles against the nations around Israel, and oracles speaking of the future and ultimate triumphs of God over the forces of evil. (2) Oracles of God, the Divine Judge. In these oracles, God presents his case against the people. His faithfulness is contrasted with their unfaithfulness and a verdict is announced by the prophet. *Mic. 6:1-8* is a good example of this type of oracle. (3) Oracles of the Divine Kingship. In these much use is made of the language of royalty. A striking example of this is *Isa. 6:1-8.* This class also includes the whole sequence of oracles in which the prophets deal with a king who shall arise to redeem Israel from her current troubles.

The prophets were the attackers of idolatry in Judah and Israel and constantly fought a heartbreaking battle against this recurring evil. They also possessed a keen sense of social responsibility and display a passion for equality and justice, emphasizing the point that man does not stand alone before God but is always viewed in his relation to his fellowman as well. The language of the prophets characteristically fluctuates between weal and woe; judgment of the present is offset by expressions of hope for the future. Western man is greatly indebted to the Old Testament prophets for an historical interpretation of man. In their work is found the basis for the view that God is sovereign over history and is working out his purposes in accord with an overall plan, sometimes indiscernible, but always in the hands of the LORD.

For further information, see articles on the individual prophets and the chronological chart of the era of the prophets in the appendix.

SCRIPTURE

God the Author of Prophecy

Luke 1 [70]As he spake by the mouth of his holy prophets, which have been since the world began.

2 Pet. 1 [19]We have also a more sure word of prophecy; whereunto ye do well that ye take heed, as unto a light that shineth in a dark place, until the day dawn, and the day star arise in your hearts: [20]Knowing this first, that no prophecy of the scripture is of any private interpretation. [21]For the prophecy came not in old time by the will of man: but holy men of God spake as they were moved by the Holy Ghost.

Rev. 1 [1]The Revelation of Jesus Christ, which God gave unto him, to shew unto his servants things which must shortly come to pass; and he sent and signified it by his angel unto his servant John: [2]Who bare record of the word of God, and of the testimony of Jesus Christ, and of all things that he saw. [3]Blessed is he that readeth, and they that hear the words of this prophecy, and keep those things which are written therein: for the time is at hand.

Prophecy the Gift of Christ and the Holy Ghost

1 Cor. 12 [8]For to one is given by the Spirit the word of wisdom; to another the word of knowledge by the same Spirit; [9]To another faith by the same Spirit; to another the gifts of healing by the same Spirit; [10]To another the working of miracles; to another prophecy; to another discerning of spirits; to another divers kinds of tongues; to another the interpretation of tongues: [11]But all these worketh that one and the self-same Spirit, dividing to every man severally as he will. [12]For as the body is one, and hath many members, and all the members of that one body, being many, are one body: so also is Christ.

Eph. 4 [11]And he gave some, apostles; and some, prophets; and some, evangelists; and some, pastors and teachers.

Rev. 11 [3]And I will give power unto my two witnesses, and they shall prophesy a thousand two hundred and threescore days, clothed in sackcloth.

Prophecy to Be Received with Faith

2 Chr. 20 [20]And they rose early in the morning, and went forth into the wilderness of Tekoa: and as they went forth, Jehoshaphat stood and said, Hear me, O Judah, and ye inhabitants of Jerusalem; Believe in the LORD your God, so shall ye be established; believe his prophets, so shall ye prosper.

Luke 24 [25]Then he said unto them, O fools, and slow of heart to believe all that the prophets have spoken.

1 Thess. 5 [20]Despise not prophesyings.

PROSPERITY

[pros per'i ti] The quality or state of being prosperous, or having plenty of anything or things good or desirable; successful progress in any business or enterprise.

SCRIPTURE

Prosperity of the Righteous

Psa. 36 [8]They shall be abundantly satisfied with the fatness of thy house; and thou shalt make them drink of the river of thy pleasures.

Psa. 37 [11]But the meek shall inherit the earth; and shall delight themselves in the abundance of peace. [18]The LORD knoweth the days of the upright: and their inheritance shall be for ever. [19]They shall not be ashamed in the evil time: and in the days of famine they shall be satisfied.

Psa. 75 [10]All the horns of the wicked also will I cut off; but the horns of the righteous shall be exalted.

Psa. 84 [11]For the LORD God is a sun and shield: the LORD will give grace and glory; no good thing will he withhold from them that walk uprightly.

Psa. 92 [12]The righteous shall flourish like the palm tree; he shall grow like a cedar in Lebanon.

Prosperity of the Wicked

Job 5 [3]I have seen the foolish taking root: but suddenly I cursed his habitation.

Job 9 [24]The earth is given into the hand of the wicked: he covereth the faces of the judges thereof; if not, where, and who is he?

Job 12 [6]The tabernacles of robbers prosper, and they that provoke God are secure; into whose hand God bringeth abundantly.

Job 21 [13]They spend their days in wealth, and in a moment go down to the grave.

Job 22 [18]Yet he filled their houses with good things: but the counsel of the wicked is far from me.

Job 24 [22]He draweth also the mighty with his power: he riseth up, and no man is sure of life. [23]Though it be given him to be in safety, whereon he resteth; yet his eyes are upon their ways. [24]They are exalted for a little while, but are gone and brought low: they are taken out of the way as all other, and cut off as the tops of the ears of corn.

Psa. 73 [5]They are not in trouble as other men; neither are they plagued like other men. [6]Therefore pride compasseth them about as a chain; violence covereth them as a garment. [7]Their eyes stand out with fatness: they have more than heart could wish. [12]Behold, these are the ungodly, who prosper in the world; they increase in riches.

Eccl. 8 [12]Though a sinner do evil a hundred times, and his days be prolonged, yet surely I know that it shall be well with them that fear God, which fear before him: [13]But it shall not be well with the wicked, neither shall he prolong his days, which are as a shadow; because he feareth not before God.

Jer. 5 [27]As a cage is full of birds, so are their houses full of deceit: therefore they are become great and waxen rich.

Dangers of Prosperity

Deut. 6 [10]And it shall be, when the LORD thy God shall have brought thee into the land which he sware unto thy fathers, to Abraham, to Isaac, and to Jacob, to give thee great and goodly cities, which thou buildedst not, [11]And houses full of all good things, which thou filledst not, and wells digged, which thou diggedst not, vineyards and olive trees, which thou plantedst not; when thou shalt have eaten and be full; [12]Then beware lest thou forget the LORD, which brought thee forth out of the land of Egypt, from the house of bondage.

Prov. 1 [32]For the turning away of the simple shall slay them, and the prosperity of fools shall destroy them.

Prov. 30 [8]Remove far from me vanity and lies; give me neither poverty nor riches; feed me with food convenient for me: [9]Lest I be full, and deny thee, and say, Who is the LORD? or lest I be poor, and steal, and take the name of my God in vain.

Luke 6 [24]But woe unto you that are rich! for ye have received your consolation. [25]Woe unto you that are full! for ye shall hunger. Woe unto you that laugh now! for ye shall mourn and weep.

Luke 12 [16]And he spake a parable unto them, saying, The ground of a certain rich man brought forth plentifully: [17]And he thought within himself, saying, What shall I do, because I have no room where to bestow my fruits? [18]And he said, This will I do: I will pull down my barns, and build greater; and there will I bestow all my fruits and my goods. [19]And I will say to my soul, Soul, thou hast much goods laid up for many years; take thine ease, eat, drink, and be merry. [20]But God said unto him, Thou fool, this night thy soul shall be required of thee: then whose shall those things be, which thou hast provided? [21]So is he that layeth up treasure for himself, and is not rich toward God.

Luke 16 [19]There was a certain rich man, which was clothed in purple and fine linen, and fared sumptuously every day: [20]And there was a certain beggar named Lazarus, which was laid at his gate, full of sores, [21]And desiring to be fed with the crumbs which fell from the rich man's table: moreover the dogs came and licked his sores. [22]And it came to pass, that the beggar died, and was carried by the angels into Abraham's bosom: the rich man also died, and was buried; [23]And in hell he lift up his eyes, being in torments, and seeth Abraham afar off, and Lazarus in his bosom. [24]And he cried and said, Father Abraham, have mercy on me, and send Lazarus, that he may dip the tip of his finger in water, and cool my tongue; for I am tormented in this flame. [25]But Abraham said, Son, remember that thou in thy lifetime receivedst thy good things, and likewise Lazarus evil things: but now he is comforted, and thou art tormented.

Jas. 5 [1]Go to now, ye rich men, weep and howl for your miseries that shall come upon you. [2]Your riches are corrupted, and your garments are motheaten. [3]Your gold and silver is cankered; and the rust of them shall be a witness against you, and shall eat your flesh as it were fire. Ye have heaped treasure together for the last days.

PROVIDENCE

[prov'i dens] Although it is never used in the sense in the Bible, this word has come to signify the fatherly love and care with which God controls all that happens.

SCRIPTURE

Gen. 8 [22]While the earth remaineth,
seedtime and harvest, and cold and heat,
and summer and winter, and day and night
shall not cease.

Psa. 36 [6]Thy righteousness is like the
great mountains; thy judgments are a
great deep: O LORD, thou preservest man
and beast. [7]How excellent is thy lovingkindness, O God! therefore the children of
men put their trust under the shadow of
thy wings.

Psa. 104 [28]That thou givest them they
gather: thou openest thine hand, they are
filled with good. [29]Thou hidest thy face,
they are troubled: thou takest away their
breath, they die, and return to their dust.
[30]Thou sendest forth thy spirit, they are
created: and thou renewest the face of the
earth.

Psa. 136 [23]Who remembered us in our
low estate: for his mercy endureth for
ever: [24]And hath redeemed us from our
enemies: for his mercy endureth for ever.
[25]Who giveth food to all flesh: for his
mercy endureth for ever. [26]O give thanks
unto the God of heaven: for his mercy endureth for ever.

Psa. 145 [14]The LORD upholdeth all that
fall, and raiseth up all those that be bowed
down. [15]The eyes of all wait upon thee;
and thou givest them their meat in due
season. [16]Thou openest thine hand, and
satisfiest the desire of every living thing.
[17]The LORD is righteous in all his ways, and
holy in all his works. [18]The LORD is nigh
unto all them that call upon him, to all that
call upon him in truth.

Matt. 6 [26]Behold the fowls of the air:
for they sow not, neither do they reap, nor
gather into barns; yet your heavenly Father feedeth them. Are ye not much better
than they? [27]Which of you by taking
thought can add one cubit unto his stature? [28]And why take ye thought for raiment? Consider the lilies of the field, how
they grow; they toil not, neither do they
spin: [29]And yet I say unto you, That even
Solomon in all his glory was not arrayed
like one of these.

Matt. 10 [29]Are not two sparrows sold
for a farthing? and one of them shall not
fall on the ground without your Father.
[30]But the very hairs of your head are all
numbered. [31]Fear ye not therefore, ye are
of more value than many sparrows.

Acts 17 [26]And hath made of one blood
all nations of men for to dwell on all the
face of the earth, and hath determined the
times before appointed, and the bounds
of their habitation; [27]That they should
seek the Lord, if haply they might feel
after him, and find him, though he be not
far from every one of us.

PSALM

[säm] A sacred song or poem. See article on the Book of *Psalms* in the appendix.

PUBLICAN

[pub'li kan] A collector of customs or tolls on imports, exports, and goods in the hands of merchants passing through the province. Publicans obtained their posts by paying a stipulated sum; they then kept for themselves whatever they could collect in excess of this amount. Because of this policy, the publicans were charged with being extortioners, which, in most cases, was probably true. This, combined with the fact that the customs tax itself was looked upon as an unjust imposition by Rome, made the publicans the object of insult, opprobrium, and hatred. The manner in which Jesus referred to them reflects the popular attitude toward the publican. Despite his apparent recognition of their faults, however, Jesus did not accept the dictum that they were unfit for companionship; this is clearly indicated by his choice of Levi (Matthew) as an apostle, by his visiting in the home of Zacchaeus, and by the parable of the Pharisee and the publican, in which the humble outcast was seen to be more acceptable to God than the self-righteous religious leader.

See TAXES

SCRIPTURE

Matt. 5 [46]For if ye love them which love you, what reward have ye? do not even the publicans the same? [47]And if ye salute your brethren only, what do ye more than others? do not even the publicans so?

Matt. 21 [32]For John came unto you in the way of righteousness, and ye believed him not: but the publicans and the harlots believed him: and ye, when ye had seen it, repented not afterward, that he might believe him.

Luke 3 [12]Then came also publicans to be baptized, and said unto him, Master, what shall we do? [13]And he said unto them, Exact no more than that which is appointed you.

Luke 18 [10]Two men went up into the temple to pray; the one a Pharisee, and the other a publican. [11]The Pharisee stood and prayed thus with himself, God, I thank thee, that I am not as other men are, extortioners, unjust, adulterers, or even as this publican. [12]I fast twice in the week, I give tithes of all that I possess. [13]And the publican, standing afar off, would not lift up so much as his eyes unto heaven, but smote upon his breast, saying, God be merciful to me a sinner. [14]I tell you, this man went down to his house justified rather than the other: for every one that exalteth himself shall be abased; and he that humbleth himself shall be exalted.

See Matt. 9:9, 11; 10:3; 11:19; 18:17; Luke 19:2-10

PUNISHMENT

[pun'ish ment] A penalty inflicted on an offender as a retribution, and incidentally for reformation and prevention. In the Bible, punishment may refer to the retribution for wrongs committed against another man as provided for in the Law—"And if any mischief follow, then thou shalt give life for life, Eye for eye, tooth for tooth, hand for hand, foot for foot, Burning for burning, wound for wound, stripe for stripe" (*Ex. 21:23-25*). Jesus sought to replace this policy of "an eye for an eye" by insistence on forgiveness up to "seventy times seven" (*Matt. 18:22*); nevertheless, he was even stricter than the law in some respects, as seen in his extension of the condemnation of murder to include anger and abuse and of adultery to include lust (*Matt. 5:21-32*).

In both the Old and New Testaments, punishment is seen to be God's reaction to sin. His wrath is constantly leveled at sin; therefore, unrepentant, persistent sinfulness on the part of man can result in nothing less than condemnation and punishment. Punishment is also used of the consequences for sin, since sin has as an inevitable sequel pain, suffering, and death.

Types of Punishment: Under the Law, capital punishment was prescribed for a number of offenses, including murder (*Num. 35:16-21, 30-33*); adultery (*Lev. 20:10*); incest (*Lev. 20:11, 12, 14*); bestiality (*Lev. 20:15-16*); sodomy (*Lev. 18:22; 20:13*); rape of a betrothed virgin (*Deut. 22:25*); kidnapping (*Ex. 21:16*); witchcraft (*Ex. 22:18*); offering human sacrifice (*Lev. 20:2-5*); striking, cursing, or disobeying parents (*Ex. 21:15, 17; Lev. 20:9; Deut. 21:18-21*); blasphemy (*Lev. 24:11-14, 16, 23*); breaking the Sabbath (*Ex. 35:2*). The death penalty was executed in biblical times by burning (*Lev. 20:14; 21:9*); stoning (*Lev. 20:2, 27*); hanging (*Deut. 21:22, 23*); beheading (*Matt. 14:10*); crucifixion (*Matt. 27:35, 38*); and the sword (*Ex. 32:27, 28; Acts 12:2*). The death penalty could not be inflicted on testimony of less than two witnesses (*Num. 35:30; Deut. 17:6; 19:15*).

SCRIPTURE

Punishment According to Deeds

Jer. 17 [10]I the LORD search the heart, I try the reins, even to give every man according to his ways, and according to the fruit of his doings.

Ezek. 7 [3]Now is the end come upon thee, and I will send mine anger upon thee, and will judge thee according to thy ways, and will recompense upon thee all thine abominations. [27]. . . I will do unto them after their way, and according to their deserts will I judge them; and they shall know that I am the LORD.

Ezek. 16 [59]For thus saith the Lord GOD; I will even deal with thee as thou hast done, which hast despised the oath in breaking the covenant.

Zech. 1 [6]Like as the LORD of hosts thought to do unto us, according to our ways, and according to our doings, so hath he dealt with us.

Matt. 5 [22]But I say unto you, that whosoever is angry with his brother without a cause shall be in danger of the judgment; and whosoever shall say to his brother, Raca, shall be in danger of the council: but whosoever shall say, Thou fool, shall be in danger of hell fire.

Matt. 23 [14]Woe unto you, scribes and Pharisees, hypocrites! for ye devour widows' houses, and for a pretence make long prayer: Therefore ye shall receive the greater damnation.

See Luke 20:47

Given to Secure Repentance and Obedience

Lev. 26 [14]But if ye will not hearken unto me, and will not do all these commandments; [15]And if ye shall despise my statutes, or if your soul abhor my judgments, so that ye will not do all my commandments, but that ye break my covenant: [16]I also will do this unto you; I will even appoint over you terror, consumption, and the burning ague, that shall consume the eyes, and cause sorrow of heart: and ye shall sow your seed in vain, for your enemies shall eat it. [17]And I will set my face against you, and ye shall be slain before your enemies: they that hate you shall reign over you; and ye shall flee when none pursueth you. [18]And if ye will not yet for all this hearken unto me, then I will punish you seven times more for your sins.

Deut. 13 [10]And thou shalt stone him with stones, that he die; because he hath sought to thrust thee away from the LORD thy God, which brought thee out of the land of Egypt, from the house of bondage. [11]And all Israel shall hear, and fear, and shall do no more any such wickedness as this is among you.

Deut. 21 [21]And all the men of his city shall stone him with stones, that he die: so shalt thou put evil away from among you: and all Israel shall hear, and fear.

Prov. 19 [25]Smite a scorner, and the simple will beware: and reprove one that hath understanding, and he will understand knowledge.

Prov. 21 [11]When the scorner is punished, the simple is made wise:

Prov. 26 [3]A whip for the horse, a bridle for the ass, and a rod for the fool's back.

See Lev. 26:25-28

Punishment of the Wicked Is Sure

Prov. 11 [21]Though hand join in hand, the wicked shall not be unpunished:

Prov. 16 [5]Every one that is proud in heart is an abomination to the LORD: though hand join in hand, he shall not be unpunished.

Jer. 11 [11]Therefore thus saith the LORD, Behold, I will bring evil upon them, which they shall not be able to escape; and though they shall cry unto me, I will not hearken unto them.

Jer. 25 [29]For, lo, I begin to bring evil on the city which is called by my name, and should ye be utterly unpunished? Ye shall not be unpunished: for I will call for a sword upon all the inhabitants of the earth, saith the LORD of hosts.

Matt. 23 [33]Ye serpents, ye generation of vipers, how can ye escape the damnation of hell?

Rom. 2 [3]Thinkest thou this, O man, that judgest them which do such things, and doest the same, that thou shalt escape the judgment of God?

Col. 3 [25]He that doeth wrong shall receive for the wrong which he hath done: and there is no respect of persons.

Heb. 2 [3]How shall we escape, if we neglect so great salvation;

Heb. 12 [25]If they escaped not who refused him that spake on earth, much more shall not we escape, if we turn away from him that speaketh from heaven:

Eternal Punishment

Dan. 12 [2]And many of them that sleep in the dust of the earth shall awake, some to everlasting life, and some to shame and everlasting contempt.

Matt. 3 [12]He will burn up the chaff with unquenchable fire.

Matt. 10 [28]And fear not them which kill the body, but are not able to kill the soul: but rather fear him which is able to destroy both soul and body in hell.

Matt. 18 [8]Wherefore if thy hand or thy foot offend thee, cut them off, and cast them from thee: it is better for thee to enter into life halt or maimed, rather than having two hands or two feet to be cast into everlasting fire.

Matt. 25 [41]Then shall he say also unto them on the left hand, Depart from me, ye cursed, into everlasting fire, prepared for the devil and his angels: [46]And these shall go away into everlasting punishment: but the righteous into life eternal.

Mark 3 [29]But he that shall blaspheme against the Holy Ghost hath never forgiveness, but is in danger of eternal damnation:

Luke 3 [17]Whose fan is in his hand, and he will throughly purge his floor, and will gather the wheat into his garner; but the chaff he will burn with fire unquenchable.

Rev. 14 [10]The same shall drink of the wine of the wrath of God, which is poured out without mixture into the cup of his indignation; and he shall be tormented with fire and brimstone in the presence of the holy angels, and in the presence of the Lamb: [11]And the smoke of their torment ascendeth up for ever and ever: and they have no rest day nor night, who worship the beast and his image, and whosoever receiveth the mark of his name.

PURIFY, PURIFICATION

[pū'ri fī, pū ri fi kā'shun] To free from impurities or noxious matter; to clear from material or spiritual defilement. Ritual purity was a vital part of the life and worship of the Hebrews. In order to take part in the worship of the tabernacle or temple, it was necessary to be free from every sort of "uncleanness". (*See* CLEANNESS AND UNCLEANNESS) Uncleanness was generally removed by washings, coupled with sacrifices of various sorts, depending on the nature of the uncleanness. For example, contact with a dead body rendered one unclean for a period of seven days; purification was secured by sprinkling the ashes of a red heifer mixed with water upon the unclean person on the third and seventh day.

In the New Testament, Jesus makes it clear that inward purity is superior to ritual purity. (*See Matt. 15:3-20*) Christians may enter into the holy place of God's spiritual temple having their hearts cleansed of evil and their bodies washed with the pure water of baptism. The "washing of regeneration and renewing of the Holy Spirit" is part of God's purpose to "purify unto himself a people for his own possession" (*Tit. 2:14; 3:5; Eph. 5:26-27*).

SCRIPTURE

Ritual Purification

Lev. 14 8And he that is to be cleansed shall wash his clothes, and shave off all his hair, and wash himself in water, that he may be clean: and after that he shall come into the camp, and shall tarry abroad out of his tent seven days. 9But it shall be on the seventh day, that he shall shave all his hair off his head and his beard and his eyebrows, even all his hair he shall shave off: and he shall wash his clothes, also he shall wash his flesh in water, and he shall be clean.

Num. 8 6Take the Levites from among the children of Israel, and cleanse them. 7And thus shalt thou do unto them, to cleanse them: Sprinkle water of purifying upon them, and let them shave all their flesh, and let them wash their clothes, and so make themselves clean. 21And the Levites were purified, and they washed their clothes; and Aaron offered them as an offering before the LORD; and Aaron made an atonement for them to cleanse them.

Num. 19 1And the LORD spake unto Moses and unto Aaron, saying, 2This is the ordinance of the law which the LORD hath commanded, saying, Speak unto the children of Israel, that they bring thee a red heifer without spot, wherein is no blemish, and upon which never came yoke. 3And ye shall give her unto Eleazar the priest, that he may bring her forth without the camp, and one shall slay her before his face: 4And Eleazar the priest shall take of her blood with his finger, and sprinkle of her blood directly before the tabernacle of the congregation seven times. 5And one shall burn the heifer in his sight; her skin, and her flesh, and her blood, with her dung, shall he burn: 6And the priest shall take cedar wood, and hyssop, and scarlet, and cast it into the midst of the burning of the heifer. 9And a man that is clean shall gather up the ashes of the heifer, and lay them up without the camp in a clean place, and it shall be kept for the congregation of the children of Israel for a water of separation: it is a purification for sin.

17And for an unclean person they shall take of the ashes of the burnt heifer of purification for sin, and running water shall be put thereto in a vessel: 18And a clean person shall take hyssop, and dip it in the water, and sprinkle it upon the tent, and upon all the vessels, and upon the persons that were there, and upon him that touched a bone, or one slain, or one dead, or a grave: 19And the clean person shall sprinkle upon the unclean on the third day, and on the seventh day: and on the seventh day he shall purify himself, and wash his clothes, and bathe himself in water, and shall be clean at even.

Jesus' Teaching on Purification

Mark 7 2And when they saw some of his disciples eat bread with defiled, that is to say, with unwashen hands, they found fault. 3For the Pharisees, and all the Jews, except they wash their hands oft, eat not, holding the tradition of the elders. 4And when they come from the market, except they wash, they eat not. And many other things there be, which they have received to hold, as the washing of cups, and pots, brazen vessels, and of tables. 5Then the Pharisees and scribes asked him, Why walk not thy disciples according to the tradition of the elders, but eat bread with unwashen hands?

Matt. 15 10And he called the multitude, and said unto them, Hear, and understand:

[11]Not that which goeth into the mouth defileth a man; but that which cometh out of
the mouth, this defileth a man.

PURIM

[pū'rim] The plural form of *Pur*, meaning "lots." It is the name of a feast which, according to the book of *Esther*, was first celebrated in commemoration of the deliverance of the Jews from the fate intended for them by Haman, a vain noble in the court of Ahasuerus, king of Persia during a part (485-465 BC) of the Babylonian exile. The feast derives its name from the circumstance that Haman cast lots to ascertain the best day for destroying the Jews (*Esth. 3:7; 9:26*). The date of the proposed extermination was to be the 13th day of the month of Adar, the twelfth month of the Hebrew calendar. (*See* FEASTS) The feast was a two-day celebration and was held on the 14th and 15th days of Adar. There is still some observance of Purim.

See ESTHER, HAMAN, MORDECAI

SCRIPTURE

Esth. 3 [7]In the first month, that is, the
month Nisan, in the twelfth year of king
Ahasuerus, they cast Pur, that is, the lot,
before Haman from day to day, and from
month to month, to the twelfth month,
that is, the month Adar.

Esth. 9 [16]But the other Jews that were
in the king's province gathered themselves
together, and stood for their lives, and had
rest from their enemies, and slew of their
foes seventy and five thousand, but they
laid not their hands on the prey, [17]On the
thirteenth day of the month Adar; and on
the fourteenth day of the same rested they,
and made it a day of feasting and gladness.
[18]But the Jews that were at Shushan assembled together on the thirteenth day
thereof, and on the fourteenth thereof;
and on the fifteenth day of the same they
rested, and made it a day of feasting and
gladness. [19]Therefore the Jews of the villages, that dwelt in the unwalled towns,
made the fourteenth day of the month
Adar a day of gladness and feasting, and
a good day, and of sending portions one to
another.
[20]And Mordecai wrote these things, and
sent letters unto all the Jews that were in
all the provinces of the king Ahasuerus,
both nigh and far, [21]To establish this
among them, that they should keep the
fourteenth day of the month Adar, and the
fifteenth day of the same, yearly, [22]As the
days wherein the Jews rested from their
enemies, and the month which was turned
unto them from sorrow to joy, and from
mourning into a good day: that they
should make them days of feasting and
joy, and of sending portions one to another, and gifts to the poor. [23]And the
Jews undertook to do as they had begun,
and as Mordecai had written unto them;
[24]Because Haman the son of Hammedatha, the Agagite, the enemy of all the Jews,
had devised against the Jews to destroy
them, and had cast Pur, that is, the lot, to
consume them, and to destroy them;
[26]Wherefore they called these days Purim
after the name of Pur. Therefore, for all
the words of this letter, and of that which
they had seen concerning this matter, and
which had come unto them, [32]And the decree of Esther confirmed these matters of
Purim; and it was written in the book.

PURITY

[pū'ri ti] Quality or state of being pure; cleanness; freedom from foulness; freedom from guilt; innocence; chastity; freedom from sinister or improper motive. Ceremonial or ritual purity was an integral part of life and worship under the Law of Moses. (*See* CLEANNESS AND UNCLEANNESS, PURIFY) Jesus placed the emphasis on inward or ethical purity, impressing upon his disciples that "not that which goeth into the mouth defileth a man; but that which cometh out of the mouth, this defileth a man" (*Matt. 15:11*).

SCRIPTURE

Psa. 24 [3]Who shall ascend into the hill of the LORD? or who shall stand in his holy place? [4]He that hath clean hands, and a pure heart; who hath not lifted up his soul unto vanity, nor sworn deceitfully. [5]He shall receive the blessing from the LORD, and righteousness from the God of his salvation.

Psa. 51 [7]Purge me with hyssop, and I shall be clean: wash me, and I shall be whiter than snow.

Prov. 15 [26]The words of the pure are pleasant words.

Prov. 20 [9]Who can say, I have made my heart clean, I am pure from my sin?

Prov. 21 [8]The way of man is froward and strange: but as for the pure, his work is right.

Prov. 30 [12]There is a generation that are pure in their own eyes, and yet is not washed from their filthiness.

Isa. 6 [7]And he laid it upon my mouth, and said, Lo, this hath touched thy lips; and thine iniquity is taken away, and thy sin purged.

Matt. 5 [8]Blessed are the pure in heart: for they shall see God.

Phil. 4 [8]Finally, brethren, whatsoever things are true, whatsoever things are honest, whatsoever things are just, whatsoever things are pure, whatsoever things are lovely, whatsoever things are of good report; if there be any virtue, and if there be any praise, think on these things.

1 Tim. 1 [5]Now the end of the commandment is charity out of a pure heart, and of a good conscience, and of faith unfeigned:

1 Tim. 5 [22]Keep thyself pure.

Tit. 1 [15]Unto the pure all things are pure.

1 John 3 [3]And every man that hath this hope in him purifieth himself, even as he is pure.

QUICK, QUICKEN

[kwik, kwik'n] As used in the King James Version of the Bible, the word "quick" ordinarily refers to something that has life. To quicken is to give life; in a religious sense, it refers to the giving of spiritual life to men dead in sin, removing their guilt, and reconciling them to God.

SCRIPTURE

General

Psa. 71 [20]Thou, which hast shewed me great and sore troubles, shalt quicken me again, and shalt bring me up again from the depths of the earth.

Psa. 80 [18]So will not we go back from thee: quicken us, and we will call upon thy name.

John 5 [21]For as the Father raiseth up the dead, and quickeneth them; even so the Son quickeneth whom he will.

John 6 [63]It is the spirit that quickeneth; the flesh profiteth nothing: the words that I speak unto you, they are spirit, and they are life.

Rom. 4 [17](As it is written, I have made thee a father of many nations,) before him whom he believed, even God, who quickeneth the dead, and calleth those things which be not as though they were.

Rom. 8 [11]But if the Spirit of him that raised up Jesus from the dead dwell in you, he that raised up Christ from the dead shall also quicken your mortal bodies by his Spirit that dwelleth in you.

1 Cor. 15 [45]And so it is written, The first man Adam was made a living soul; the last Adam was made a quickening spirit.

2 Cor. 3 [6]Who also hath made us able ministers of the new testament; not of the letter, but of the spirit: for the letter killeth, but the spirit giveth life.

Eph. 2 [1]And you hath he quickened, who were dead in trespasses and sins.

1 Pet. 3 [18]For Christ also hath once suffered for sins, the just for the unjust, that he might bring us to God, being put to death in the flesh, but quickened by the Spirit.

"The Quick and the Dead"

Acts 10 [42]And he commanded us to preach unto the people, and to testify that it is he which was ordained of God to be the Judge of quick and dead.

2 Tim. 4 [1]I charge thee therefore before God, and the Lord Jesus Christ, who shall judge the quick and the dead at his appearing and his kingdom.

1 Pet. 4 [5]Who shall give account to him that is ready to judge the quick and the dead.

QUIET

[kwī'et] Rest, peace, absence of noise or turmoil, an undisturbed state.

See Peace

SCRIPTURE

Quiet for the Faithful

Prov. 1 [33]But whoso hearkeneth unto me shall dwell safely, and shall be quiet from fear of evil.

Isa. 30 [15]For thus saith the Lord God, the Holy One of Israel; In returning and rest shall ye be saved; in quietness and in confidence shall be your strength: and ye would not.

Isa. 32 [17]And the work of righteousness shall be peace; and the effect of righteousness, quietness and assurance for ever.
[18]And my people shall dwell in a peaceable habitation, and in sure dwellings, and in quiet resting places.

Quietness Enjoined

1 Thess. 4 [11]And that ye study to be quiet, and to do your own business, and to work with your own hands, as we commanded you.

2 Thess. 3 [12]Now them that are such we command and exhort by our Lord Jesus Christ, that with quietness they work, and eat their own bread.

1 Tim. 2 [1]I exhort therefore, that, first of all, supplications, prayers, intercessions, and giving of thanks, be made for all men;
[2]For kings, and for all that are in authority; that we may lead a quiet and peaceable life in all godliness and honesty. [3]For this is good and acceptable in the sight of God our Saviour.

RABBI

[rab'ī] Literally, "my great one," a term used by the Jews of religious leaders. Jesus was often referred to as Rabbi, frequently translated in the King James Version as "Master." Another term of respect derived from Rabbi is Rabboni, meaning "my great master."

SCRIPTURE

Matt. 23 [7]And greetings in the markets, and to be called of men, Rabbi, Rabbi.
[8]But be not ye called Rabbi: for one is your Master, even Christ; and all ye are brethren.

John 1 [49]Nathanael answered and saith unto him, Rabbi, thou art the Son of God: thou art the King of Israel.

John 3 [26]And they came unto John, and said unto him, Rabbi, he that was with thee beyond Jordan, to whom thou barest witness, behold, the same baptizeth, and all men come to him.

John 6 [25]And when they had found him on the other side of the sea, they said unto him, Rabbi, when camest thou hither?

RABSHAKEH

[rab'sha ke, rab shā'ke] An officer of Sennacherib king of Assyria during the reign of Hezekiah king of Judah. The Rabshakeh appeared at Jerusalem with two other Assyrian officers called the Tartan and the Rabsaris. Standing "by the conduit of the upper pool", the Rabshakeh loudly addressed several representatives of King Hezekiah. He ridiculed the king for his dependence on Egypt and the LORD, asserting that God would aid the Assyrians. The king's representatives asked him to speak in Aramaic, that the people on the wall might not hear, but the Rabshakeh refused, speaking more loudly than before and offering various enticements in order to induce the citizens of Jerusalem to revolt against their king. The people displayed their loyalty to Hezekiah by refusing to answer a word, in keeping with a command which had been given. The Assyrian might with which the Rabshakeh was threatening Jerusalem was hurled back by a devastating plague which is said to have slain 185,000 of Sennacharib's soldiers.

SCRIPTURE

2 Kin. 18 [17]And the king of Assyria sent
Tartan and Rabsaris and Rabshakeh from
Lachish to king Hezekiah with a great host
against Jerusalem: and they went up, and
came to Jerusalem. And when they were
come up, they came and stood by the conduit of the upper pool, which is in the
highway of the fuller's field. [18]And when
they had called to the king, there came out
to them Eliakim the son of Hilkiah, which
was over the household, and Shebna the
scribe, and Joah the son of Asaph the recorder. [19]And Rabshakeh said unto them,
Speak ye now to Hezekiah, Thus saith the
great king, the king of Assyria, What confidence is this wherein thou trustest?
[20]Thou sayest, (but they are but vain
words,) I have counsel and strength for
the war. Now on whom dost thou trust,
that thou rebellest against me? [21]Now, behold, thou trustest upon the staff of this
bruised reed, even upon Egypt, on which
if a man lean, it will go into his hand, and
pierce it: so is Pharaoh king of Egypt unto
all that trust on him. [22]But if ye say unto
me, We trust in the LORD our God: is not
that he whose high places and whose altars
Hezekiah hath taken away, and hath said
to Judah and Jerusalem, Ye shall worship
before this altar in Jerusalem? [23]Now
therefore, I pray thee, give pledges to my
lord the king of Assyria, and I will deliver
thee two thousand horses, if thou be
able on thy part to set riders upon them.
[24]How then wilt thou turn away the face of
one captain of the least of my master's
servants, and put thy trust on Egypt for
chariots and for horsemen? [25]Am I now
come up without the LORD against this
place to destroy it? The LORD said to me,
Go up against this land, and destroy it.
[26]Then said Eliakim the son of Hilkiah,
and Shebna, and Joah, unto Rabshakeh,
Speak, I pray thee, to thy servants in the
Syrian language; for we understand it; and
talk not with us in the Jews' language in
the ears of the people that are on the wall.
[27]But Rabshakeh said unto them, Hath my
master sent me to thy master, and to thee,
to speak these words? hath he not sent me
to the men which sit on the wall, that they
may eat their own dung, and drink their
own piss with you? [28]Then Rabshakeh
stood and cried with a loud voice in the
Jews' language, and spake, saying, Hear
the word of the great king, the king of Assyria: [29]Thus saith the king, Let not Hezekiah deceive you: for he shall not be able to
deliver you out of his hand: [30]Neither let
Hezekiah make you trust in the LORD, saying, The LORD will surely deliver us, and
this city shall not be delivered into the
hand of the king of Assyria. [31]Hearken not
to Hezekiah: for thus saith the king of Assyria, Make an agreement with me by a
present, and come out to me, and then eat
ye every man of his own vine, and every
one of his fig tree, and drink ye every one
the waters of his cistern: [32]Until I come

and take you away to a land like your own
land, a land of corn and wine, a land of
bread and vineyards, a land of oil olive and
of honey, that ye may live, and not die:
and hearken not unto Hezekiah, when he
persuadeth you, saying, The LORD will deliver us. 33Hath any of the gods of the nations delivered at all his land out of the
hand of the king of Assyria? 34Where are
the gods of Hamath, and of Arpad? where
are the gods of Sepharvaim, Hena, and
Ivah? have they delivered Samaria out of
mine hand? 35Who are they among all the
gods of the countries that have delivered
their country out of mine hand, that the
LORD should deliver Jerusalem out of mine
hand? 36But the people held their peace,
and answered him not a word: for the
king's commandment was, saying, Answer
him not. 37Then came Eliakim the son of
Hilkiah, which was over the household,
and Shebna the scribe, and Joah the son of
Asaph the recorder, to Hezekiah with their
clothes rent, and told him the words of
Rabshakeh.

2 Kin. 19 8So Rabshakeh returned, and
found the king of Assyria warring against
Libnah: for he had heard that he was departed from Lachish.

RACA

[rā'ka] A word of contempt or scorn, used by Jews in the time of Jesus, meaning "empty" or "worthless." Jesus condemned the use of this term in *Matt. 5:22.* Since it was not the word itself, but the attitude of the speaker which Jesus was condemning, any modern expression which expresses contempt for one's fellowman is likewise prohibited.

SCRIPTURE

Matt. 5 22But I say unto you, That whosoever is angry with his brother without a
cause shall be in danger of the judgment:
and whosoever shall say to his brother,
Raca, shall be in danger of the council: but
whosoever shall say, Thou fool, shall be in
danger of hell fire.

RACHEL

[rā'chel] The daughter of Laban, sister of Rachel, and wife of Jacob. Jacob was sent by his parents to Haran to find a wife among the daughters of Laban. He seems to have been immediately attracted to Rachel, whom he found tending sheep. After contracting with Laban to receive her after seven years of service, Jacob received Leah instead, by a deception. After a week, he also received Rachel, but was compelled to work an additional seven years. Although Jacob favored Rachel, it was not she, but the "tender-eyed" Leah who bore him children. (*See* LEAH) Dismayed, Rachel gave him her handmaid Bilhah, the arrangement being that all children born to Bilhah would be reckoned as Rachel's; the handmaid bore him two sons, Dan and Naphtali. Finally, Rachel conceived and gave birth to Joseph. After Jacob and his family returned to Canaan, Rachel died in giving birth to a second son, Benjamin. The tribes which later bore the names of these two women are commonly referred to as the "Bilhah tribes" and the "Rachel tribes." Rachel seems to have inherited something of the duplicity and cunning of her father, as seen in the episode of her theft and concealment of Laban's household gods when Jacob's party departed from Haran.

See LEAH, JACOB, LABAN

SCRIPTURE

Becomes Jacob's Wife

Gen. 29 10And it came to pass, when Jacob saw Rachel the daughter of Laban his
mother's brother, and the sheep of Laban
his mother's brother, that Jacob went near,
and rolled the stone from the well's mouth,
and watered the flock of Laban his mother's brother. 11And Jacob kissed Rachel,
and lifted up his voice, and wept. 12And
Jacob told Rachel that he was her father's

brother, and that he was Rebekah's son: and she ran and told her father. 13And it came to pass, when Laban heard the tidings of Jacob his sister's son, that he ran to meet him, and embraced him, and kissed him, and brought him to his house. And he told Laban all these things. 14And Laban said to him, Surely thou art my bone and my flesh. And he abode with him the space of a month.

15And Laban said unto Jacob, Because thou art my brother, shouldest thou therefore serve me for nought? tell me, what shall thy wages be? 16And Laban had two daughters: the name of the elder was Leah, and the name of the younger was Rachel. 17Leah was tender eyed; but Rachel was beautiful and well favoured. 18And Jacob loved Rachel; and said, I will serve thee seven years for Rachel thy younger daughter. 19And Laban said, It is better that I give her to thee, than that I should give her to another man: abide with me. 20And Jacob served seven years for Rachel; and they seemed unto him but a few days, for the love he had to her.

21And Jacob said unto Laban, Give me my wife, for my days are fulfilled, that I may go in unto her. 22And Laban gathered together all the men of the place, and made a feast. 23And it came to pass in the evening, that he took Leah his daughter, and brought her to him; and he went in unto her. 24And Laban gave unto his daughter Leah Zilpah his maid for a handmaid. 25And it came to pass, that in the morning, behold, it was Leah: and he said to Laban, What is this thou hast done unto me? did not I serve with thee for Rachel? wherefore then hast thou beguiled me? 26And Laban said, It must not be so done in our country, to give the younger before the firstborn. 27Fulfil her week, and we will give thee this also for the service which thou shalt serve with me yet seven other years. 28And Jacob did so, and fulfilled her week: and he gave him Rachel his daughter to wife also.

Steals Laban's Idols

Gen. 31 19And Laban went to shear his sheep: and Rachel had stolen the images that were her father's. 20And Jacob stole away unawares to Laban the Syrian, in that he told him not that he fled.

25Then Laban overtook Jacob. Now Jacob had pitched his tent in the mount: and Laban with his brethren pitched in the mount of Gilead. 26And Laban said to Jacob, What hast thou done, that thou hast stolen away unawares to me, and carried away my daughters, as captives taken with the sword? 30And now, though thou wouldest needs be gone, because thou sore longedst after thy father's house, yet wherefore hast thou stolen my gods? 31And Jacob answered and said to Laban, Because I was afraid: for I said, Peradventure thou wouldest take by force thy daughters from me. 32With whomsoever thou findest thy gods, let him not live: before our brethren discern thou what is thine with me, and take it to thee. For Jacob knew not that Rachel had stolen them. 33And Laban went into Jacob's tent, and into Leah's tent, and into the two maidservants' tents; but he found them not. Then went he out of Leah's tent, and entered into Rachel's tent. 34Now Rachel had taken the images, and put them in the camel's furniture, and sat upon them. And Laban searched all the tent, but found them not. 35And she said to her father, Let it not displease my lord that I can not rise up before thee; for the custom of women is upon me. And he searched, but found not the images.

See Gen. 29-35; 48:7

RAHAB

[rā'hab] 1. A harlot of Jericho who protected two spies sent from Joshua. When they were pursued by the king of Jericho, Rahab hid them on her rooftop, later letting them down over the wall with a scarlet cord. For this act of kindness, she and her family were spared when Israel overran Jericho. The scarlet cord was hung in a window as a sign that her house was not to be destroyed. Rachab is listed in the genealogy of Jesus (*Matt. 1:5*).

REFERENCE: *Josh. 2; 6:17-25.*

2. A sea-monster in Semitic mythology, representing the forces of chaos over which God triumphed in bringing order to the creation. In several Old Testament passages, this mythological language is used as a literary device to describe the great power of God.

See LEVIATHAN

SCRIPTURE

Psa. 89 [10]Thou hast broken Rahab in pieces, as one that is slain; thou hast scattered thine enemies with thy strong arm.

Isa. 51 [9]Awake, awake, put on strength, O arm of the LORD; awake, as in the ancient days, in the generations of old. Art thou not it that hath cut Rahab, and wounded the dragon? [10]Art thou not it which hath dried the sea, the waters of the great deep; that hath made the depths of the sea a way for the ransomed to pass over?

RAIN

[rān] Water falling in drops condensed from vapor in the atmosphere; also, the descent of such drops. In Scripture, rain is viewed as being within the providential control of God. Rain is referred to in several passages as a figure of speech.

SCRIPTURE

Rain the Gift of God

Gen. 2 [5]And every plant of the field before it was in the earth, and every herb of the field before it grew: for the LORD God had not caused it to rain upon the earth, and there was not a man to till the ground.

1 Sam. 12 [17]Is it not wheat harvest today? I will call unto the LORD, and he shall send thunder and rain; that ye may perceive that your wickedness is great, which ye have done in the sight of the LORD, in asking you a king.

Job 36 [27]For he maketh small the drops of water: they pour down rain according to the vapor thereof:

Job 37 [6]For he saith to the snow, Be thou on the earth; likewise to the small rain, and to the great rain of his strength.

Matt. 5 [45]That ye may be the children of your Father which is in heaven: for he maketh his sun to rise on the evil and on the good, and sendeth rain on the just and on the unjust.

Acts 14 [17]Nevertheless he left not himself without witness, in that he did good, and gave us rain from heaven, and fruitful seasons, filling our hearts with food and gladness.

Rain Withheld

1 Kin. 17 [1]And Elijah the Tishbite, who was of the inhabitants of Gilead, said unto Ahab, As the LORD God of Israel liveth, before whom I stand, there shall not be dew nor rain these years, but according to my word.

Zech. 14 [17]And it shall be, that whoso will not come up of all the families of the earth unto Jerusalem to worship the King, the LORD of hosts, even upon them shall be no rain.

Jas. 5 [17]Elias was a man subject to like passions as we are, and he prayed earnestly that it might not rain: and it rained not on the earth by the space of three years and six months.

Rain as an Emblem

Deut. 32 [2]My doctrine shall drop as the rain, my speech shall distil as the dew, as the small rain upon the tender herb, and as the showers upon the grass.

2 Sam. 23 [4]And he shall be as the light of the morning, when the sun riseth, even a morning without clouds; as the tender grass springing out of the earth by clear shining after rain.

Psa. 68 [9]Thou, O God, didst send a plentiful rain, whereby thou didst confirm thine inheritance, when it was weary.

Hos. 10 [12]Sow to yourselves in righteousness, reap in mercy; break up your fallow ground: for it is time to seek the LORD, till he come and rain righteousness upon you.

RAINBOW

[rān′bo] A bow or arch showing the seven basic colors and seen in the heavens. It is formed by the reflection and refraction of the sun's rays in drops of falling rain or moisture. It is seen at its greatest brilliancy when the spectator is between the sun and the raincloud. It is also to be seen in spraying fountains and waterfalls. The Bible alludes to it as a symbol of God's mercy (*Gen. 9: 13*).

SCRIPTURE

Gen. 9 [13]I do set my bow in the cloud, and it shall be for a token of a covenant between me and the earth.

RAMOTH-GILEAD

[rā′moth gil′ē ad] A city of the territory assigned to Gad, east of the Jordan River, and one of the cities of refuge. (*See* REFUGE, CITIES OF) During the period of conflict between Israel and Syria, Ramoth-Gilead changed hands several times. Ahab king of Israel received fatal wounds in an attempt to regain control of the city (*1 Kin. 22:1-40*). His son Joram attempted to succeed where his father had failed, but he too was wounded and had to withdraw from the battle. While Joram was recuperating, the army at Ramoth-Gilead rallied behind Jehu and enabled him to carry out his bloody purge of the house of Ahab. *See* JEHU

SCRIPTURE

A City of Refuge

Deut. 4 [41]Then Moses severed three cities on this side Jordan toward the sunrising; [42]That the slayer might flee thither, which should kill his neighbor unawares, and hated him not in times past; and that fleeing unto one of these cities he might live. [43]Namely, Bezer in the wilderness, in the plain country, of the Reubenites; and Ramoth in Gilead, of the Gadites; and Golan in Bashan, of the Manassites.

Ahab Slain There

1 Kin. 22 [29]So the king of Israel and Jehoshaphat the king of Judah went up to Ramoth-gilead. [30]And the king of Israel said unto Jehoshaphat, I will disguise myself, and enter into the battle; but put thou on thy robes. And the king of Israel disguised himself, and went into the battle. [31]But the king of Syria commanded his thirty and two captains that had rule over his chariots, saying, Fight neither with small nor great, save only with the king of Israel. [32]And it came to pass, when the captains of the chariots saw Jehoshaphat, that they said, Surely it is the king of Israel. And they turned aside to fight against him: and Jehoshaphat cried out. [33]And it came to pass, when the captains of the chariots perceived that it was not the king of Israel, that they turned back from pursuing him. [34]And a certain man drew a bow at a venture, and smote the king of Israel between the joints of the harness: wherefore he said unto the driver of his chariot, Turn thine hand, and carry me out of the host; for I am wounded. [35]And the battle increased that day: and the king was stayed up in his chariot against the Syrians, and died at even: and the blood ran out of the wound into the midst of the chariot. [36]And there went a proclamation throughout the host about the going down of the sun, saying, Every man to his city, and every man to his own country.

Recovered by Joram

2 Kin. 8 [28]And he went with Joram the son of Ahab to the war against Hazael king of Syria in Ramoth-gilead; and the Syrians wounded Joram. [29]And king Joram went back to be healed in Jezreel of the wounds which the Syrians had given him at Ramah, when he fought against Hazael king of Syria. And Ahaziah the son of Jehoram king of Judah went down to see Joram the son of Ahab in Jezreel, because he was sick.

2 Kin. 9 [14]So Jehu the son of Jehoshaphat the son of Nimshi conspired against Joram. (Now Joram had kept Ramoth-gilead, he and all Israel, because of Hazael king of Syria. [15]But king Joram was returned to be healed in Jezreel of the wounds which the Syrians had given him, when he fought with Hazael king of Syria.) And Jehu said, If it be your minds, then let none go forth nor escape out of the city to go to tell it in Jezreel.

REAPING

[rēp'ing] The cutting down or harvesting a crop of anything, especially grains. Reaping is often used in the Bible as a figure of speech.

See AGRICULTURE

SCRIPTURE

Job 4 [8]Even as I have seen, they that plough iniquity, and sow wickedness, reap the same.

Psa. 126 [5]They that sow in tears shall reap in joy.

Prov. 22 [8]He that soweth iniquity shall reap vanity: and the rod of his anger shall fail.

Matt. 13 [30]Let both grow together until the harvest: and in the time of harvest I will say to the reapers, Gather ye together first the tares, and bind them in bundles to burn them: but gather the wheat into my barn.

John 4 [36]And he that reapeth receiveth wages, and gathereth fruit unto life eternal: that both he that soweth and he that reapeth may rejoice together. [37]And herein is that saying true, One soweth, and another reapeth. [38]I sent you to reap that whereon ye bestowed no labour: other men laboured, and ye are entered into their labours.

1 Cor. 9 [11]If we have sown unto you spiritual things, is it a great thing if we shall reap your carnal things?

2 Cor. 9 [6]But this I say, He which soweth sparingly shall reap also sparingly; and he which soweth bountifully shall reap also bountifully.

Gal. 6 [7]Be not deceived; God is not mocked: for whatsoever a man soweth, that shall he also reap.

Rev. 14 [15]And another angel came out of the temple, crying with a loud voice to him that sat on the cloud, Thrust in thy sickle, and reap: for the time is come for thee to reap; for the harvest of the earth is ripe. [16]And he that sat on the cloud thrust in his sickle on the earth; and the earth was reaped.

REBEKAH

[rê bek'a] Daughter of Bethuel, sister of Laban, wife of Isaac, mother of Esau and Jacob. When Abraham desired to find a wife for his Isaac, he sent a servant to "the city of Nahor", in Mesopotamia, to choose a woman from among Abraham's kinsmen who had remained in the region when Abraham and Lot moved to Canaan. In that city the servant met Rebekah and persuaded her to return with him. After twenty years of marriage to Isaac, she finally became the mother of Esau and Jacob. Although Esau was the elder, Rebekah favored Jacob and helped him in the deception to gain the blessing which properly belonged to Esau. She protected Jacob from Esau's subsequent wrath by sending him to stay with her brother Laban in Haran. Apparently, the mother and her beloved son were never reunited. Rebekah was buried in the family burial ground at Macpelsh.

See ISAAC, ESAU, JACOB, LABAN

SCRIPTURE

Chosen to Become Isaac's Wife

Gen. 24 1 And Abraham was old, and well stricken in age: and the LORD had blessed Abraham in all things. 2 And Abraham said unto his eldest servant of his house, that ruled over all that he had, Put, I pray thee, thy hand under my thigh: 3 And I will make thee swear by the LORD, the God of heaven, and the God of the earth, that thou shalt not take a wife unto my son of the daughters of the Canaanites, among whom I dwell: 4 But thou shalt go unto my country, and to my kindred, and take a wife unto my son Isaac.

15 And it came to pass, before he had done speaking, that, behold, Rebekah came out, who was born to Bethuel, son of Milcah, the wife of Nahor, Abraham's brother, with her pitcher upon her shoulder. 16 And the damsel was very fair to look upon, a virgin, neither had any man known her: and she went down to the well, and filled her pitcher, and came up. 17 And the servant ran to meet her, and said, Let me, I pray thee, drink a little water of thy pitcher. 18 And she said, Drink, my lord: and she hasted, and let down her pitcher upon her hand, and gave him drink. 19 And when she had done giving him drink, she said, I will draw water for thy camels also, unitl they have done drinking. 20 And she hasted, and emptied her pitcher into the trough, and ran again unto the well to draw water, and drew for all his camels. 21 And the man wondering at her held his peace, to wit whether the LORD had made his journey prosperous or not. 22 And it came to pass, as the camels had done drinking, that the man took a golden earring of half a shekel weight, and two bracelets for her hands of ten shekels weight of gold; 23 And said, Whose daughter art thou? tell me, I pray thee: is there room in thy father's house for us to lodge in? 24 And she said unto him, I am the daughter of Bethuel the son of Milcah, which she bare unto Nahor.

32 And the man came into the house: and he ungirded his camels, and gave straw and provender for the camels, and water to wash his feet, and the men's feet that were with him. 33 And there was set meat before him to eat: but he said, I will not eat, until I have told mine errand. And he said, Speak on. 34 And he said, I am Abraham's servant. 48 And I bowed down my head, and worshipped the LORD, and blessed the LORD God of my master Abraham, which had led me in the right way to take my master's brother's daughter unto his son. 49 And now, if ye will deal kindly and truly with my master, tell me: and if not, tell me; that I may turn to the right hand, or to the left. 50 Then Laban and Bethuel answered and said, The thing proceedeth from the LORD: we can not speak unto thee bad or good. 51 Behold, Rebekah is before thee; take her, and go, and let her be thy master's son's wife, as the LORD hath spoken. 58 And they called Rebekah, and said unto her, Wilt thou go with this man?

And she said, I will go. 59And they sent away Rebekah their sister, and her nurse, and Abraham's servant, and his men. 60And they blessed Rebekah, and said unto her, Thou art our sister; be thou the mother of thousands of millions, and let thy seed possess the gate of those which hate them.

61And Rebekah arose, and her damsels, and they rode upon the camels, and followed the man: and the servant took Rebekah, and went his way. 62And Isaac came from the way of the well Lahai-roi; for he dwelt in the south country. 63And Isaac went out to meditate in the field at the eventide: and he lifted up his eyes, and saw, and, behold, the camels were coming. 64And Rebekah lifted up her eyes, and when she saw Isaac, she lighted off the camel. 65For she had said unto the servant, What man is this that walketh in the field to meet us? And the servant had said, It is my master: therefore she took a veil, and covered herself. 66And the servant told Isaac all things that he had done. 67And Isaac brought her into his mother Sarah's tent, and took Rebekah, and she became his wife; and he loved her: and Isaac was comforted after his mother's death.

Bears Esau and Jacob

Gen. 25 21And Isaac entreated the LORD for his wife, because she was barren: and the LORD was entreated of him, and Rebekah his wife conceived. 22And the children struggled together within her; and she said, If it be so, why am I thus? And she went to inquire of the LORD. 23And the LORD said unto her, Two nations are in thy womb, and two manner of people shall be separated from thy bowels; and the one people shall be stronger than the other people; and the elder shall serve the younger.

24And when her days to be delivered were fulfilled, behold, there were twins in her womb. 25And the first came out red, all over like a hairy garment; and they called his name Esau. 26And after that came his brother out, and his hand took hold on Esau's heel; and his name was called Jacob: . . . .

Isaac Deceives Abimelech concerning Rebekah

Gen. 26 6And Isaac dwelt in Gerar. 7And the men of the place asked him of his wife; and he said, She is my sister: for he feared to say, She is my wife; lest, said he, the men of the place should kill me for Rebekah; because she was fair to look upon. 8And it came to pass, when he had been there a long time, that Abimelech king of the Philistines looked out at a window, and saw, and, behold, Isaac was sporting with Rebekah his wife. 9And Abimelech called Isaac, and said, Behold, of a surety she is thy wife: and how saidst thou, She is my sister? And Isaac said unto him, Because I said, Lest I die for her. 10And Abimelech said, What is this thou hast done unto us? one of the people might lightly have lain with thy wife, and thou shouldest have brought guiltiness upon us. 11And Abimelech charged all his people, saying, He that toucheth this man or his wife shall surely be put to death.

Rebekah Helps Jacob Deceive Isaac

Gen. 27 6And Rebekah spake unto Jacob her son, saying, Behold, I heard thy father speak unto Esau thy brother, saying, 7Bring me venison, and make me savoury meat, that I may eat, and bless thee before the LORD before my death. 8Now therefore, my son, obey my voice according to that which I command thee. 9Go now to the flock, and fetch me from thence

two good kids of the goats; and I will make
them savoury meat for thy father, such as
he loveth: 10 And thou shalt bring it to thy
father, that he may eat, and that he may
bless thee before his death.

See Gen. 22-27; 49:31

RECHABITES

[rek′a bīts] A primitivist order in Palestine which had its origin in the period of the kings. In the midst of the cosmopolitan world which had existed in Palestine since the reigns of David and Solomon, the Rechabites clung to the simple nomadic life. Each took a vow that he would neither live in houses nor have anything to do with vineyards or wine; it was felt that these marks of civilization were detrimental to strict obedience to God. They traced this vow to Jehonadab, or Jonadab, the son of Rechab who took part in the extirpation of the worshippers of Baal during the revolution of Jehu (*2 Kin. 10*). In one of the illustrated parables for which he is noted, Jeremiah contrasted the fidelity of the Rechabites to their covenant with the refusal of Judah to heed the covenant which it had made with God (*Jer. 35*).

SCRIPTURE

Jonadab the Rechabites

2 Kin. 10 15 And when he was departed
thence, he lighted on Jehonadab the son
of Rechab coming to meet him: and he
saluted him, and said to him, Is thine heart
right, as my heart is with thy heart? And
Jehonadab answered, It is. If it be, give me
thine hand. And he gave him his hand; and
he took him up to him into the chariot.
16 And he said, Come with me, and see my
zeal for the LORD. So they made him ride
in his chariot. 17 And when he came to Samaria,
he slew all that remained unto Ahab
in Samaria, till he had destroyed him, according
to the saying of the LORD, which
he spake to Elijah.

Jeremiah Lauds the Rechabites

Jer. 35 1 The word which came unto Jeremiah
from the LORD, in the days of Jehoiakim
the son of Josiah king of Judah, saying,
2 Go unto the house of the Rechabites,
and speak unto them, and bring them into
the house of the LORD, into one of the
chambers, and give them wine to drink.
3 Then I took Jaazaniah the son of Jeremiah,
the son of Habaziniah, and his
brethren, and all his sons, and the whole
house of the Rechabites; 4 And I brought
them into the house of the LORD, into the
chamber of the sons of Hanan, the son of
Igdaliah, a man of God, which was by the
chamber of the princes, which was above
the chamber of Maaseiah the son of Shallum,
the keeper of the door: 5 And I set before
the sons of the house of the Rechabites
pots full of wine, and cups; and I said
unto them, Drink ye wine. 6 But they said,
We will drink no wine: for Jonadab the
son of Rechab our father commanded us,
saying, Ye shall drink no wine, neither ye,
nor your sons for ever: 7 Neither shall ye
build house, nor sow seed, nor plant vineyard,
nor have any: but all your days ye
shall dwell in tents; that ye may live many
days in the land where ye be strangers.
8 Thus have we obeyed the voice of Jonadab
the son of Rechab our father in all that
he hath charged us, to drink no wine all
our days, we, our wives, our sons, nor our
daughters; 9 Nor to build houses for us to
dwell in; neither have we vineyard, nor
field, nor seed: 10 But we have dwelt in
tents, and have obeyed, and done according
to all that Jonadab our father commanded
us. 11 But it came to pass, when
Nebuchadrezzar king of Babylon came up
into the land, that we said, Come, and let
us go to Jerusalem for fear of the army of
the Chaldeans, and for fear of the army of
the Syrians: so we dwell at Jerusalem.

12 Then came the word of the LORD unto
Jeremiah, saying, 13 Thus saith the LORD

of hosts, the God of Israel; Go and tell the
men of Judah and the inhabitants of Jerusalem, Will ye not receive instruction to
hearken to my words? saith the LORD.
14The words of Jonadab the son of Rechab,
that he commanded his sons not to drink
wine, are performed; for unto this day
they drink none, but obey their father's
commandment: notwithstanding I have
spoken unto you, rising early and speaking; but ye hearkened not unto me. 15I
have sent also unto you all my servants the
prophets, rising up early and sending
them, saying, Return ye now every man
from his evil way, and amend your doings,
and go not after other gods to serve them,
and ye shall dwell in the land which I
have given to you and to your fathers: but
ye have not inclined your ear, nor hearkened unto me. 16Because the sons of Jonadab the son of Rechab have performed the
commandment of their father, which he
commanded them; but this people hath
not hearkened unto me: 17Therefore thus
saith the LORD God of hosts, the God of
Israel; Behold, I will bring upon Judah
and upon all the inhabitants of Jerusalem
all the evil that I have pronounced against
them: because I have spoken unto them,
but they have not heard; and I have called
unto them, but they have not answered.

18And Jeremiah said unto the house of
the Rechabites, Thus saith the LORD of
hosts, the God of Israel; Because ye have
obeyed the commandment of Jonadab
your father, and kept all his precepts, and
done according unto all that he hath commanded you: 19Therefore thus saith the
LORD of hosts, the God of Israel; Jonadab
the son of Rechab shall not want a man to
stand before me for ever.

RECONCILIATION

[rek on sil i ā'shun] The act of reconciling or bringing harmony into personal relationships in which hostility has previously existed. Reconciliation is used in the Testament to refer to the changed relationship between God and man which is the result of the death and resurrection of Christ. Through the death of Christ and the consequent exercise of the power of divine forgiveness, the barriers between God and man have been removed and both are able to enjoy full fellowship with the other.

See REDEMPTION, ATONEMENT, SALVATION, etc.

SCRIPTURE

Rom. 5 10For if, when we were enemies,
we were reconciled to God by the death of
his Son; much more, being reconciled, we
shall be saved by his life. 11And not only
so, but we also joy in God through our
Lord Jesus Christ, by whom we have now
received the atonement.

Rom. 11 15For if the casting away of
them be the reconciling of the world, what
shall the receiving of them be, but life
from the dead?

2 Cor. 5 18And all things are of God,
who hath reconciled us to himself by Jesus
Christ, and hath given to us the ministry
of reconciliation; 19To wit, that God was
in Christ, reconciling the world unto himself, not imputing their trespasses unto
them; and hath committed unto us the
word of reconciliation. 20Now then we are
ambassadors for Christ, as though God did
beseech you by us: we pray you in Christ's
stead, be ye reconciled to God.

Eph. 2 16And that he might reconcile
both unto God in one body by the cross,
having slain the enmity thereby:

Col. 1 19For it pleased the Father that
in him should all fulness dwell; 20And,
having made peace through the blood of
his cross, by him to reconcile all things
unto himself; by him, I say, whether they
be things in earth, or things in heaven.
21And you, that were sometime alienated

and enemies in your mind by wicked works, yet now hath he reconciled [22]In the body of his flesh through death, to present you holy and unblamable and unreprovable in his sight:

RED SEA

[red sē] The sea between Egypt and Arabia. The upper part of this sea has two arms; the western arm is called the Gulf of Suez and is 190 miles long; the eastern arm is called the Gulf of Akaba and is about 112 miles in length. The children of Israel are said to have passed over the Red Sea on their flight from Egypt; there is, however, considerable difficulty concerning this traditional view. In the first place, the tip of the Gulf of Suez is so far to the south that it is unlikely they would have chosen such a route, in view of the pursuing Egyptian cavalry. It has been contended that this gulf once extended about fifty miles farther northward than it now does, but there is insufficient evidence to support such a claim. Moreover, the Hebrew text of the Old Testament does not state that the Israelites crossed the Red Sea. The words which are so translated in the English Bible (*Yam Suf*) do not mean *Red* Sea, but *Reed* Sea, or Sea of Reeds. It is quite possible, therefore, that the Israelites actually crossed some body of water much nearer their point of departure.

See Exodus

SCRIPTURE

Ex. 10 [19]And the Lord turned a mighty strong west wind, which took away the locusts, and cast them into the Red Sea; there remained not one locust in all the coasts of Egypt.

Ex. 13 [18]But God led the people about, through the way of the wilderness of the Red Sea: and the children of Israel went up harnessed out of the land of Egypt.

Ex. 14 [21]And Moses stretched out his hand over the sea; and the Lord caused the sea to go back by a strong east wind all that night, and made the sea dry land, and the waters were divided. [22]And the children of Israel went into the midst of the sea upon the dry ground: and the waters were a wall unto them on their right hand, and on their left.

[23]And the Egyptians pursued, and went in after them to the midst of the sea, even all Pharaoh's horses, his chariots, and his horsemen. [24]And it came to pass, that in the morning watch the Lord looked unto the host of the Egyptians through the pillar of fire and of the cloud, and troubled the host of the Egyptians, [25]And took off their chariot wheels, that they drave them heavily: so that the Egyptians said, Let us flee from the face of Israel; for the Lord fighteth for them against the Egyptians.

Ex. 15 [4]Pharaoh's chariots and his host hath he cast into the sea: his chosen captains also are drowned in the Red Sea.

Josh. 2 [10]For we have heard how the Lord dried up the water of the Red Sea for you, when ye came out of Egypt; and what ye did unto the two kings of the Amorites, that were on the other side Jordan, Sihon and Og, whom ye utterly destroyed.

Neh. 9 [9]And didst see the affliction of our fathers in Egypt, and heardest their cry by the Red Sea;

Heb. 11 [29]By faith they passed through the Red Sea as by dry land: which the Egyptians assaying to do were drowned.

REDEMPTION (Redeem, Redeemer)

[rē demp′shun, rē dēm′, rē dēm′er] The biblical concept of redemption is based upon the Hebrew practice of buying back something, such as land or a slave, which formerly belonged to the purchaser, but for one reason or another has passed from his possession. The term was also used of a man's paying the price of release for a kinsman who had sold himself into slavery. In present religious usage it refers primarily to God's saving activity, especially as manifested in the work of Christ. In the Old Testament redemption is primarily from physical bondage or peril, but this is far from being divorced from an element of spiritual well-being. The theme of the divine initiative in the redemption of Israel informs the whole of Old Testament literature. Jesus may properly be spoken of as the Redeemer inasmuch as he has done for man what man could not do for himself by giving his life as a ransom for many, he has released those who obey him from the guilt and power of sin. Those who were formerly slaves have been purchased by the blood of Christ and are now sons of God in the divine household and await that final consummation of redemption whose scope will embrace all history and nature.

See Atonement, Jesus, Salvation

SCRIPTURE

God as Redeemer

Job 19 [25]For I know that my Redeemer liveth, and that he shall stand at the latter day upon the earth.

Psa. 19 [14]Let the words of my mouth, and the meditation of my heart, be acceptable in thy sight, O Lord, my strength, and my redeemer.

Psa. 78 [35]And they remembered that God was their rock, and the high God their redeemer.

Prov. 23 [11]For their Redeemer is mighty; he shall plead their cause with thee.

Isa. 41 [14]Fear not, thou worm Jacob, and ye men of Israel; I will help thee, saith the Lord, and thy Redeemer, the Holy One of Israel.

Isa. 47 [4]As for our Redeemer, the Lord of hosts is his name, the Holy One of Israel.

Isa. 59 [20]And the Redeemer shall come to Zion, and unto them that turn from transgression in Jacob, saith the Lord.

Isa. 63 [16]Doubtless thou art our Father, though Abraham be ignorant of us, and Israel acknowledge us not: thou, O Lord, art our Father, our Redeemer; thy name is from everlasting.

Jer. 50 [34]Their Redeemer is strong; The Lord of hosts is his name: he shall thoroughly plead their cause, that he may give rest to the land, and disquiet the inhabitants of Babylon.

Hos. 13 [14]I will ransom them from the power of the grave; I will redeem them from death: O death, I will be thy plagues, O grave, I will be thy destruction: repentance shall be hid from mine eyes.

Christ as Redeemer

Matt. 20 [28]Even as the Son of man came not to be ministered unto, but to minister, and to give his life a ransom for many.

Rom. 3 [24]Being justified freely by his grace through the redemption that is in Christ Jesus: [25]Whom God hath set forth to be a propitiation through faith in his blood, to declare his righteousness for the remission of sins that are past, through the forbearance of God.

1 Cor. 1 [30]But of him are ye in Christ Jesus, who of God is made unto us wisdom, and righteousness, and sanctification, and redemption:

1 Cor. 6 [20]For ye are bought with a price: therefore glorify God in your body, and in your spirit, which are God's.

1 Cor. 7 [23]Ye are bought with a price; be not ye the servants of men.

Gal. 1 [3]Grace be to you and peace from God the Father, and from our Lord Jesus Christ, [4]Who gave himself for our sins, that he might deliver us from this present evil world, according to the will of God and our Father.

Gal. 3 [13]Christ hath redeemed us from the curse of the law, being made a curse for us: for it is written, Cursed is every one that hangeth on a tree.

Gal. 4 [4]But when the fulness of the time was come, God sent forth his Son, made of a woman, made under the law, [5]To redeem them that were under the law, that we might receive the adoption of sons.

Eph. 1 [5]Having predestinated us unto the adoption of children by Jesus Christ to himself, according to the good pleasure of his will, [6]To the praise of the glory of his grace, wherein he hath made us accepted in the beloved. [7]In whom we have redemption through his blood, the forgiveness of sins, according to the riches of his grace.

Col. 1 [14]In whom we have redemption through his blood, even the forgiveness of sins:

1 Tim. 2 [6]Who gave himself a ransom for all, to be testified in due time.

Tit. 2 [14]Who gave himself for us, that he might redeem us from all iniquity, and purify unto himself a peculiar people, zealous of good works.

Heb. 9 [12]Neither by the blood of goats and calves, but by his own blood he entered in once into the holy place, having obtained eternal redemption for us. [15]And for this cause he is the mediator of the new testament, that by means of death, for the redemption of the transgressions that were under the first testament, they which are called might receive the promise of eternal inheritance.

1 Pet. 1 [18]Forasmuch as ye know that ye were not redeemed with corruptible things, as silver and gold, from your vain conversation received by tradition from your fathers.

Rev. 5 [9]And they sung a new song, saying, Thou art worthy to take the book, and to open the seals thereof: for thou wast slain, and hast redeemed us to God by thy blood out of every kindred, and tongue, and people, and nation.

See Mark 10:45

REFUGE

[ref'ūj] A hiding-place, place of safety, or sanctuary from foes or danger. The word is used of God as the One to whom sinners may flee for safety and salvation through belief, repentance, and obedience.

SCRIPTURE

God as a Refuge

Deut. 33 [27]The eternal God is thy refuge, and underneath are the everlasting arms: and he shall thrust out the enemy from before thee; and shall say, Destroy them.

2 Sam. 22 [3]The God of my rock; in him will I trust: he is my shield, and the horn of my salvation, my high tower, and my refuge, my saviour; thou savest me from violence.

Psa. 9 [9]The Lord also will be a refuge for the oppressed, a refuge in times of trouble.

Psa. 46 [1]God is our refuge and strength, a very present help in trouble.

Heb. 6 [17]Wherein God, willing more abundantly to shew unto the heirs of promise the immutability of his counsel, confirmed it by an oath: [18]That by two immutable things, in which it was impossible for God to lie, we might have a strong consolation, who have fled for refuge to lay hold upon the hope set before us: [19]Which hope we have as an anchor of the soul, both sure and stedfast, and which entereth into that within the vail.

Cities of Refuge

Num. 35 [9]And the Lord spake unto Moses, saying, [10]Speak unto the children of Israel, and say unto them, When ye be come over Jordan into the land of Canaan, [11]Then ye shall appoint you cities to be cities of refuge for you; that the slayer may

flee thither, which killeth any person at
unawares. [12]And they shall be unto you
cities for refuge from the avenger; that the
manslayer die not, until he stand before
the congregation in judgment. [13]And of
these cities which ye shall give, six cities
shall ye have for refuge. [14]Ye shall give
three cities on this side Jordan, and three
cities shall ye give in the land of Canaan,
which shall be cities of refuge. [15]These six
cities shall be a refuge, both for the children of Israel, and for the stranger, and for
the sojourner among them; that every one
that killeth any person unawares may flee
thither. [22]But if he thrust him suddenly
without enmity, or have cast upon him any
thing without laying of wait, [23]Or with
any stone, wherewith a man may die, seeing him not, and cast it upon him, that he
die, and was not his enemy, neither sought
his harm: [24]Then the congregation shall
judge between the slayer and the revenger
of blood according to these judgments:
[25]And the congregation shall deliver the
slayer out of the hand of the revenger of
blood, and the congregation shall restore
him to the city of his refuge, whither he
was fled: and he shall abide in it unto
the death of the high priest, which was
anointed with the holy oil. [26]But if the
slayer shall at any time come without the
border of the city of his refuge, whither he
was fled; [27]And the revenger of blood find
him without the borders of the city of his
refuge, and the revenger of blood kill the
slayer; he shall not be guilty of blood:
[28]Because he should have remained in the
city of his refuge until the death of the
high priest: but after the death of the high
priest the slayer shall return into the land
of his possession.

REFUGE, CITIES OF

[ref'ūj] A term used to designate six cities, three on each side of the Jordan, which were designed to act as places of asylum for people who had accidentally taken a human life. Among most peoples of the Ancient Near East, it was customary for the nearest relative of a slain man to take vengeance on the slayer, whether the death was the result of premeditated homicide or came about by pure accident. According to the Law, if the slayer could reach one of the cities of refuge before he was overtaken by the pursuing relative of the slain man, called the avenger of blood, he was received into the city and his case heard by the elders of the city. If this preliminary hearing proved favorable, he was allowed to remain in the city until a formal trial could be held. If he was found guilty, he was turned over to the avenger of blood and slain. If, however, he was declared innocent of willful murder, he was allowed to remain in the city until the death of the high priest, at which time he was free to return home. If at any time before the death of the high priest, he chose to leave the city, the avenger of blood was free to take his life without guilt.

The six cities appointed for this purpose were Bezer, Ramoth-gilead, and Golan on the east of the Jordan, and Hebron, Shechem, and Kedesh west of the Jordan.

REFERENCE: *Ex. 21:13, 14; Num. 35:11-32; Deut. 4:41-43; 19:2-13; Josh. 20:1-9.*

REGENERATION

[rē jen ẽr ā'shun] Act or condition of rebirth; spiritual revival, rebirth, renewal, or recreation. The difference between natural life and life "in Christ" is so striking that Jesus described the transition as a radical renewal, a new creation, a being "born again," a regeneration. This regeneration is not a second natural birth, but a being "begotten from above" by God's Holy Spirit. It is associated with baptism, in which one puts off the old man of sin and is clothed with Christ. The new life thus bestowed on the reborn individual is a real foretaste of that which will be brought to completion at the end of this age.

SCRIPTURE

Matt. 19 [28]And Jesus said unto them,
Verily I say unto you, That ye which have
followed me, in the regeneration when the

Son of man shall sit in the throne of his glory, ye also shall sit upon twelve thrones, judging the twelve tribes of Israel.

John 1 [12]But as many as received him, to them gave he power to become the sons of God, even to them that believe on his name: [13]Which were born, not of blood, nor of the will of the flesh, nor of the will of man, but of God.

John 3 [3]Jesus answered and said unto him, Verily, verily, I say unto thee, Except a man be born again, he cannot see the kingdom of God. [4]Nicodemus saith unto him, How can a man be born when he is old? can he enter the second time into his mother's womb, and be born? [5]Jesus answered, Verily, verily, I say unto thee, Except a man be born of water and of the Spirit, he cannot enter into the kingdom of God. [6]That which is born of the flesh is flesh; and that which is born of the Spirit is spirit. [7]Marvel not that I said unto thee, Ye must be born again. [8]The wind bloweth where it listeth, and thou hearest the sound thereof, but canst not tell whence it cometh, and whither it goeth: so is every one that is born of the Spirit.

2 Cor. 5 [5]Now he that hath wrought us for the selfsame thing is God, who also hath given unto us the earnest of the Spirit. [17]If any man be in Christ, he is a new creature: old things are passed away; behold, all things are become new.

Gal. 4 [29]As then he that was born after the flesh persecuted him that was born after the Spirit, even so it is now.

Gal. 6 [15]In Christ Jesus neither circumcision availeth any thing, nor uncircumcision, but a new creature.

Eph. 2 [1]You hath he quickened, who were dead in trespasses and sins; [5]Even when we were dead in sins, hath quickened us together with Christ, (by grace ye are saved;) [6]And hath raised us up together, and made us sit together in heavenly places in Christ Jesus: [8]For by grace are ye saved through faith; and that not of yourselves: it is the gift of God: [10]We are his workmanship, created in Christ Jesus unto good works, which God hath before ordained that we should walk in them.

Col. 2 [11]In whom also ye are circumcised with the circumcision made without hands, in putting off the body of the sins of the flesh by the circumcision of Christ: [12]Buried with him in baptism, wherein also ye are risen with him through the faith of the operation of God, who hath raised him from the dead. [13]And you, being dead in your sins and the uncircumcision of your flesh, hath he quickened together with him, having forgiven you all trespasses;

Tit. 3 [4]But after that the kindness and love of God our Saviour toward man appeared, [5]Not by works of righteousness which we have done, but according to his mercy he saved us, by the washing of regeneration, and renewing of the Holy Ghost; [6]Which he shed on us abundantly through Jesus Christ our Saviour.

REHOBOAM

[rē hô bō′am] Son of Solomon and first king of Judah after the division of the kingdom (922-915 BC). Immediately after Solomon's death, Rehoboam ascended to the throne in Jerusalem with little opposition. The people of Northern Israel, however, insisted that he appear before them in an assembly at Shechem. There they stipulated as condition of their allegiance the lightening of the oppressive tax load which Solomon had levied. On the advice of immature counsellors, Rehoboam harshly replied that his rule would be even more severe than his father's. At this the people turned away from Rehoboam and sent for Jeroboam to be their king. In an effort to salvage his kingdom, Rehoboam sent Adoram, his taskmaster, to force the people into line, but this man was stoned and Rehoboam was forced to flee back to Jerusalem and to be content with his greatly reduced territory.

Rehoboam immediately collected a large army to take vengeance on Israel, but was dissuaded by the prophet Shemaiah from making a concerted attack. Nevertheless, we are told that "there was war between Rehoboam and Jeroboam continually" (*1 Kin. 14:30; 2 Chr. 12:15*).

In the year 918 BC Shishak king of Egypt attacked Palestine, destroying 150 towns. It was during this invasion that the magnificent temple of Solomon was plundered of its treasures. It is plausible that, had Rehoboam displayed more wisdom at Shechem and thus averted the schism, this invasion of Shishak might have been resisted more successfully.

Rehoboam followed in the steps of his father by allowing idolatrous worship and in keeping a sizable harem. He was succeeded by his son Abijah.

See JEROBOAM, KINGS

SCRIPTURE

Division of Kingdom under Rehoboam

1 Kin. 12 [1]And Rehoboam went to Shechem: for all Israel were come to Shechem to make him king. [2]And it came to pass, when Jeroboam the son of Nebat, who was yet in Egypt, heard of it, (for he was fled from the presence of king Solomon, and Jeroboam dwelt in Egypt,) [3]That they sent and called him. And Jeroboam and all the congregation of Israel came, and spake unto Rehoboam, saying, [4]Thy father made our yoke grievous: now therefore make thou the grievous service of thy father, and his heavy yoke which he put upon us, lighter, and we will serve thee. [5]And he said unto them, Depart yet for three days, then come again to me. And the people departed.

[12]So Jeroboam and all the people came to Rehoboam the third day, as the king had appointed, saying, Come to me again the third day. [13]And the king answered the people roughly, and forsook the old men's counsel that they gave him; [14]And spake to them after the counsel of the young men, saying, My father made your yoke heavy, and I will add to your yoke: my father also chastised you with whips, but I will chastise you with scorpions. [15]Wherefore the king hearkened not unto the people; for the cause was from the LORD, that he might perform his saying, which the LORD spake by Ahijah the Shilonite unto Jeroboam the son of Nebat.

[16]So when all Israel saw that the king hearkened not unto them, the people answered the king, saying, What portion have we in David? neither have we inheritance in the son of Jesse: to your tents, O Israel: now see to thine own house, David. So Israel departed unto their tents. [17]But as for the children of Israel which dwelt in the cities of Judah, Rehoboam reigned over them.

Summary of Rehoboam's Reign

1 Kin. 14 [21]And Rehoboam the son of Solomon reigned in Judah. Rehoboam was forty and one years old when he began to reign, and he reigned seventeen years in Jerusalem, the city which the LORD did choose out of all the tribes of Israel, to put his name there. And his mother's name was Naamah an Ammonitess. [22]And Judah did evil in the sight of the LORD, and they provoked him to jealousy with their sins which they had committed, above all that their fathers had done. [23]For they also built them high places, and images, and groves, on every high hill, and under every green tree. [24]And there were also sodomites in the land: and they did according to all the abominations of the nations which the LORD cast out before the children of Israel.

[25]And it came to pass in the fifth year of king Rehoboam, that Shishak king of

Egypt came up against Jerusalem: [26]And he took away the treasures of the house of the LORD, and the treasures of the king's house; he even took away all: and he took away all the shields of gold which Solomon had made. [27]And king Rehoboam made in their stead brazen shields, and committed them unto the hands of the chief of the guard, which kept the door of the king's house. [28]And it was so, when the king went into the house of the LORD, that the guard bare them, and brought them back into the guardchamber.

[29]Now the rest of the acts of Rehoboam, and all that he did, are they not written in the book of the Chronicles of the kings of Judah? [30]And there was war between Rehoboam and Jeroboam all their days. [31]And Rehoboam slept with his fathers, and was buried with his fathers in the city of David. And his mother's name was Naamah an Ammonitess. And Abijam his son reigned in his stead.

REJOICING

[rē jois′ing] Joy, gladness, delight; an occasion or expression of joy. The child of God is exhorted to rejoice over the mercies and goodness of his heavenly Father.

SCRIPTURE

Deut. 12 [12]And ye shall rejoice before the LORD your God, ye, and your sons, and your daughters, and your menservants, and your maidservants, and the Levite that is within your gates; forasmuch as he hath no part nor inheritance with you.

1 Chr. 16 [10]Glory ye in his holy name: let the heart of them rejoice that seek the LORD.

2 Chr. 6 [41]Now therefore arise, O LORD God, into thy resting place, thou, and the ark of thy strength: let thy priests, O LORD God, be clothed with salvation, and let thy saints rejoice in goodness.

Psa. 5 [11]But let all those that put their trust in thee rejoice: let them ever shout for joy, because thou defendest them: let them also that love thy name be joyful in thee.

Psa. 33 [1]Rejoice in the LORD, O ye righteous: for praise is comely for the upright.

Psa. 68 [4]Sing unto God, sing praises to his name: extol him that rideth upon the heavens by his name JAH, and rejoice before him.

Psa. 89 [16]In thy name shall they rejoice all the day: and in thy righteousness shall they be exalted.

Psa. 97 [12]Rejoice in the LORD, ye righteous; and give thanks at the remembrance of his holiness.

Rom. 12 [15]Rejoice with them that do rejoice, and weep with them that weep.

Phil. 3 [1]Finally, my brethren, rejoice in the Lord. To write the same things to you, to me indeed is not grievous, but for you it is safe.

Phil. 4 [4]Rejoice in the Lord alway: and again I say, Rejoice.

1 Thess. 5 [16]Rejoice evermore.

Rev. 12 [12]Therefore rejoice, ye heavens, and ye that dwell in them. Woe to the inhabiters of the earth and of the sea! for the devil is come down unto you, having great wrath, because he knoweth that he hath but a short time.

Rev. 18 [20]Rejoice over her, thou heaven, and ye holy apostles and prophets; for God hath avenged you on her.

REMISSION

[rē mish′un] Forgiveness; exemption from the consequences of an offense; relinquishment of a claim or obligation; pardon for transgression. The scriptures teach us that Christ's blood was shed for the remission of the sins of mankind.

SCRIPTURE

Matt. 26 [28]For this is my blood of the

new testament, which is shed for many for the remission of sins.

Mark 1 [4]John did baptize in the wilderness, and preach the baptism of repentance for the remission of sins.

Luke 24 [46]And said unto them, Thus it is written, and thus it behoved Christ to suffer, and to rise from the dead the third day: [47]And that repentance and remission of sins should be preached in his name among all nations, beginning at Jerusalem.

Acts 2 [38]Then Peter said unto them, Repent, and be baptized every one of you in the name of Jesus Christ for the remission of sins, and ye shall receive the gift of the Holy Ghost.

Acts 10 [42]And he commanded us to preach unto the people, and to testify that it is he which was ordained of God to be the Judge of quick and dead. [43]To him give all the prophets witness, that through his name whosoever believeth in him shall receive remission of sins.

Heb. 9 [22]And almost all things are by the law purged with blood; and without shedding of blood is no remission.

Heb. 10 [18]Now where remission of these is, there is no more offering for sin.

REMORSE

[rê môrs'] Distress, like gnawing pain, excited by a sense of guilt; repentant regret. The Scriptures contain several references to and examples of remorse over sinfulness.

See PENITENCE, REPENTANCE

SCRIPTURE

Psa. 31 [10]My life is spent with grief, and my years with sighing: my strength faileth because of mine iniquity, and my bones are consumed.

Psa. 38 [2]Thine arrows stick fast in me, and thy hand presseth me sore. [3]There is no soundness in my flesh because of thine anger; neither is there any rest in my bones because of my sin. [4]For mine iniquities are gone over mine head: as an heavy burden they are too heavy for me. [5]My wounds stink and are corrupt because of my foolishness. [6]I am troubled; I am bowed down greatly; I go mourning all the day long.

Psa. 51 [1]Have mercy upon me, O God, according to thy lovingkindness: according unto the multitude of thy tender mercies blot out my transgressions. [2]Wash me throughly from mine iniquity, and cleanse me from my sin. [3]For I acknowledge my transgressions: and my sin is ever before me. [4]Against thee, thee only, have I sinned, and done this evil in thy sight: [7]Purge me with hyssop, and I shall be clean: wash me, and I shall be whiter than snow.

Prov. 5 [7]Hear me now therefore, O ye children, and depart not from the words of my mouth. [8]Remove thy way far from her, and come not nigh the door of her house: [9]Lest thou give thine honour unto others, and thy years unto the cruel: [10]Lest strangers be filled with thy wealth; and thy labours be in the house of a stranger; [11]And thou mourn at the last, when thy flesh and thy body are consumed, [12]And say, How have I hated instruction, and my heart despised reproof; [13]And have not obeyed the voice of my teachers, nor inclined mine ear to them that instructed me!

Lam. 1 [20]Behold, O LORD; for I am in distress; my bowels are troubled: mine heart is turned within me; for I have grievously rebelled:

Ezek. 33 [10]Thus ye speak, saying, If our transgressions and our sins be upon us, and we pine away in them, how should we then live?

Luke 13 [28]There shall be weeping and

gnashing of teeth, when ye shall see Abraham, and Isaac, and Jacob, and all the prophets, in the kingdom of God, and you yourselves thrust out.

Acts 2 [37]Now when they heard this, they were pricked in their heart, and said unto Peter and to the rest of the apostles, Men and brethren, what shall we do?

REPENTANCE

[rē pen'tans] In *Gen. 6:6* we read that "it repented the LORD that he had made man on the earth, and it grieved him at his heart," and in *1 Sam. 15:35* that "the LORD repented that he had made Saul king over Israel." When applied to God "repent" signifies that, due to human failure, he has deemed it best to achieve his purposes by a course of action different from that he had originally willed. When used of human beings, it ordinarily indicates a complete change of mind, a forsaking of one's past existence and an acceptance of a whole new approach to life.

The fundamental message of the Hebrew prophets was repentance, a call to forsake the worship of Baal or other sins which characterized the lives of their hearers and to return to the faithful practice of the worship of the God of Israel. When John the Baptist came with the spirit of Elijah he proclaimed repentance as the necessary condition for escape from the imminent judgment entrance into the kingdom of God. In Jesus' preaching, repentance was closely connected with belief in the gospel (*Mark 1:15*). Repentance affects the whole man. It is not merely a substitution of one set of external actions and observances for another set, but an inward turning, a recognition and disavowal of one's sin coupled with the embracing of a new way of life, a life in conformity with the teachings of Christ, a life characterized by "fruits meet for repentance."

SCRIPTURE

Nature of Repentance

SENSE OF GUILT

Psa. 51 [1]Have mercy upon me, O God, according to thy lovingkindness: according unto the multitude of thy tender mercies blot out my transgressions. [2]Wash me throughly from mine iniquity, and cleanse me from my sin. [3]For I acknowledge my transgressions: and my sin is ever before me. [4]Against thee, thee only, have I sinned, and done this evil in thy sight: that thou mightest be justified when thou speakest, and be clear when thou judgest. [5]Behold, I was shapen in iniquity; and in sin did my mother conceive me. [6]Behold, thou desirest truth in the inward parts: and in the hidden part thou shalt make me to know wisdom. [7]Purge me with hyssop, and I shall be clean: wash me, and I shall be whiter than snow.

Isa. 64 [6]But we are all as an unclean thing, and all our righteousnesses are as filthy rags; and we all do fade as a leaf; and our iniquities, like the wind, have taken us away.

Acts 2 [37]Now when they heard this, they were pricked in their heart, and said unto Peter and to the rest of the apostles, Men and brethren, what shall we do?

Acts 16 [30]And brought them out, and said, Sirs, what must I do to be saved?

2 Cor. 7 [9]Now I rejoice, not that ye were made sorry, but that ye sorrowed to repentance: for ye were made sorry after a godly manner, that ye might receive damage by us in nothing. [10]For godly sorrow worketh repentance to salvation not to be repented of: but the sorrow of the world worketh death.

The Command to Repent

Job 11 [14]If iniquity be in thine hand, put it far away, and let not wickedness dwell in thy tabernacles. [15]For then shalt thou lift up thy face without spot; yea, thou shalt be steadfast, and shalt not fear.

Jer. 7 [3]Thus saith the LORD of hosts,

the God of Israel, Amend your ways and your doings, and I will cause you to dwell in this place.

Jer. 18 [11]Now therefore go to, speak to the men of Judah, and to the inhabitants of Jerusalem, saying, Thus saith the LORD; Behold, I frame evil against you, and devise a device against you: return ye now every one from his evil way, and make your ways and your doings good.

Jer. 26 [13]Therefore now amend your ways and your doings, and obey the voice of the LORD your God; and the LORD will repent him of the evil that he hath pronounced against you.

Ezek. 18 [30]Therefore I will judge you, O house of Israel, every one according to his ways, saith the LORD God. Repent, and turn yourselves from all your transgressions; so iniquity shall not be your ruin.

Dan. 4 [27]Wherefore, O king, let my counsel be acceptable unto thee, and break off thy sins by righteousness, and thine iniquities by shewing mercy to the poor; if it may be a lengthening of thy tranquillity.

Zech. 1 [2]The LORD hath been sore displeased with your fathers. [3]Therefore say thou unto them, Thus saith the LORD of hosts; Turn ye unto me, saith the LORD of hosts, and I will turn unto you, saith the LORD of hosts.

Matt. 3 [7]But when he saw many of the Pharisees and Sadducees come to his baptism, he said unto them, O generation of vipers, who hath warned you to flee from the wrath to come? [8]Bring forth therefore fruits meet for repentance.

Repentance a Divine Call

Matt. 4 [17]From that time Jesus began to preach, and to say, Repent: for the kingdom of heaven is at hand.

Matt. 9 [13]But go ye and learn what that meaneth, I will have mercy, and not sacrifice: for I am not come to call the righteous, but sinners to repentance.

Mark 1 [15]And saying, The time is fulfilled, and the kingdom of God is at hand: repent ye, and believe the gospel.

Mark 6 [12]And they went out, and preached that men should repent.

Acts 8 [21]Thou hast neither part nor lot in this matter: for thy heart is not right in the sight of God. [22]Repent therefore of this thy wickedness, and pray God, if perhaps the thought of thine heart may be forgiven thee.

Promises to the Penitent

Deut. 30 [1]And it shall come to pass, when all these things are come upon thee, the blessing and the curse, which I have set before thee, and thou shalt call them to mind among all the nations, whither the LORD thy God hath driven thee, [2]And shalt return unto the LORD thy God, and shalt obey his voice according to all that I command thee this day, thou and thy children, with all thine heart, and with all thy soul; [3]That then the LORD thy God will turn thy captivity, and have compassion upon thee, and will return and gather thee from all the nations, whither the LORD thy God hath scattered thee.

Psa. 34 [18]The LORD is nigh unto them that are of a broken heart; and saveth such as be of a contrite spirit.

Psa. 147 [3]He healeth the broken in heart, and bindeth up their wounds.

Jer. 4 [1]If thou wilt return, O Israel, saith the LORD, return unto me: and if thou wilt put away thine abominations out of my sight, then shalt thou not remove.

Ezek. 18 [21]But if the wicked will turn from all his sins that he hath committed, and keep all my statutes, and do that which is lawful and right, he shall surely live, he shall not die. [22]All his transgressions that he hath committed, they shall not be mentioned unto him: in his righteousness that he hath done he shall live.

27 Again, when the wicked man turneth away from his wickedness that he hath committed, and doeth that which is lawful and right, he shall save his soul alive. 28 Because he considereth, and turneth away from all his transgressions that he hath committed, he shall surely live, he shall not die.

Ezek. 33 10 Therefore, O thou son of man, speak unto the house of Israel; Thus ye speak, saying, If our transgressions and our sins be upon us, and we pine away in them, how should we then live? 11 Say unto them, As I live, saith the Lord GOD, I have no pleasure in the death of the wicked; but that the wicked turn from his way and live: turn ye, turn ye from your evil ways; for why will ye die, O house of Israel? 12 Therefore, thou son of man, say unto the children of thy people, The righteousness of the righteous shall not deliver him in the day of his transgression: as for the wickedness of the wicked, he shall not fall thereby in the day that he turneth from his wickedness; neither shall the righteous be able to live for his righteousness in the day that he sinneth. 14 Again, when I say unto the wicked, Thou shalt surely die; if he turn from his sin, and do that which is lawful and right; 15 If the wicked restore the pledge, give again that he had robbed, walk in the statutes of life, without committing iniquity; he shall surely live, he shall not die. 16 None of his sins that he hath committed shall be mentioned unto him: he hath done that which is lawful and right; he shall surely live.

17 Yet the children of thy people say, The way of the LORD is not equal: but as for them, their way is not equal. 18 When the righteous turneth from his righteousness, and committeth iniquity, he shall even die thereby. 19 But if the wicked turn from his wickedness, and do that which is lawful and right, he shall live thereby.

20 Yet ye say, The way of the LORD is not equal, O ye house of Israel, I will judge you every one after his ways.

The Impenitent

Prov. 21 29 A wicked man hardeneth his face: but as for the upright, he directeth his way.

Matt. 11 20 Then began he to upbraid the cities wherein most of his mighty works were done, because they repented not: 21 Woe unto thee, Chorazin! woe unto thee, Bethsaida! for if the mighty works, which were done in you, had been done in Tyre and Sidon, they would have repented long ago in sackcloth and ashes. 22 But I say unto you, It shall be more tolerable for Tyre and Sidon at the day of judgment, than for you.

Luke 13 1 There were present at that season some that told him of the Galileans, whose blood Pilate had mingled with their sacrifices. 2 And Jesus answering said unto them, Suppose ye that these Galileans were sinners above all the Galileans, because they suffered such things? 3 I tell you, Nay: but, except ye repent, ye shall all likewise perish. 4 Or those eighteen, upon whom the tower in Siloam fell, and slew them, think ye that they were sinners above all men that dwelt in Jerusalem? 5 I tell you, Nay: but, except ye repent, ye shall all likewise perish.

Rom. 2 5 But, after thy hardness and impenitent heart, treasurest up unto thyself wrath against the day of wrath and revelation of the righteous judgment of God.

2 Cor. 12 21 And lest, when I come again, my God will humble me among you, and that I shall bewail many which have sinned already, and have not repented of the uncleanness and fornication and lasciviousness which they have committed.

Heb. 12 [17]For ye know how that afterward, when he would have inherited the blessing, he was rejected: for he found no place of repentance, though he sought it carefully with tears.

Rev. 2 [21]And I gave her space to repent of her fornication; and she repented not.

Rev. 9 [21]Neither repented they of their murders, nor of their sorceries, nor of their fornication, nor of their thefts.

REPROOF

[rē prūf′] Generally speaking, rebuke or reprehension spoken to one's face; reprimand. The Bible teaches us that the young should take reproof from elders and should not be forward in reproving elders. Reproof spoken in the proper spirit to one in error is entirely proper, but care should be taken that such reproof remain within reasonable bounds.

SCRIPTURE

Psa. 141 [5]Let the righteous smite me; it shall be a kindness: and let him reprove me; it shall be an excellent oil, which shall not break my head: for yet my prayer also shall be in their calamities. [6]When their judges are overthrown in stony places, they shall hear my words; for they are sweet.

Prov. 9 [7]He that reproveth a scorner getteth to himself shame: and he that rebuketh a wicked man getteth himself a blot. [8]Reprove not a scorner, lest he hate thee: rebuke a wise man, and he will love thee. [9]Give instruction to a wise man, and he will be yet wiser: teach a just man, and he will increase in learning.

Prov. 10 [17]He is in the way of life that keepeth instruction: but he that refuseth reproof erreth.

Prov. 13 [18]Poverty and shame shall be to him that refuseth instruction: but he that regardeth reproof shall be honoured.

Prov. 15 [10]Correction is grievous unto him that forsaketh the way: and he that hateth reproof shall die. [12]A scorner loveth not one that reproveth him: neither will he go unto the wise. [32]He that refuseth instruction despiseth his own soul: but he that heareth reproof getteth understanding.

Prov. 17 [10]A reproof entereth more into a wise man than a hundred stripes into a fool.

Prov. 24 [25]But to them that rebuke him shall be delight, and a good blessing shall come upon them.

Prov. 25 [12]As an earring of gold, and an ornament of fine gold, so is a wise reprover upon an obedient ear.

2 Thess. 3 [14]And if any man obey not our word by this epistle, note that man, and have no company with him, that he may be ashamed. [15]Yet count him not as an enemy, but admonish him as a brother.

1 Tim. 5 [1]Rebuke not an elder, but entreat him as a father; and the younger men as brethren; [20]Them that sin rebuke before all, that others also may fear.

2 Tim. 4 [2]Preach the word; be instant in season, out of season; reprove, rebuke, exhort with all long-suffering and doctrine.

Tit. 1 [13]This witness is true. Wherefore rebuke them sharply, that they may be sound in the faith;

RESPECT

[rê spekt′] To consider worthy of esteem or honor; to receive with favor; to show partiality.

SCRIPTURE

Respect for Aged

Lev. 19 [32]Thou shalt rise up before the hoary head, and honor the face of the old man, and fear thy God: I am the LORD.

Respect for Rulers

Prov. 25 [6]Put not forth thyself in the presence of the king, and stand not in the place of great men:

Rom. 13 [1]Let every soul be subject unto the higher powers. For there is no power but of God: the powers that be are ordained of God. [7]Render therefore to all their dues: tribute to whom tribute is due; custom to whom custom; fear to whom fear; honor to whom honor.

1 Pet. 2 [17]Honor the king.

Respect for Fellow Christians

Rom. 12 [10]Be kindly affectioned one to another with brotherly love; in honor preferring one another;

Phil. 2 [3]Let nothing be done through strife or vainglory; but in lowliness of mind let each esteem other better than themselves.

1 Pet. 2 [17]Honor all men. Love the brotherhood.

Respect of Persons

Prov. 24 [23]These things also belong to the wise. It is not good to have respect of persons in judgment.

Prov. 28 [21]To have respect of persons is not good: for, for a piece of bread that man will transgress.

Jas. 2 [1]My brethren, have not the faith of our Lord Jesus Christ, the Lord of glory, with respect of persons. [2]For if there come unto your assembly a man with a gold ring, in goodly apparel, and there come in also a poor man in vile raiment; [3]And ye have respect to him that weareth the gay clothing, and say unto him, Sit thou here in a good place; and say to the poor, Stand thou there, or sit here under my footstool: [4]Are ye not then partial in yourselves, and are become judges of evil thoughts? [5]Hearken, my beloved brethren, Hath not God chosen the poor of this world rich in faith, and heirs of the kingdom which he hath promised to them that love him? [6]But ye have despised the poor. Do not rich men oppress you, and draw you before the judgment seats? [7]Do not they blaspheme that worthy name by the which ye are called? [8]If ye fulfil the royal law according to the Scripture, Thou shalt love thy neighbor as thyself, ye do well: [9]But if ye have respect to persons, ye commit sin, and are convinced of the law as transgressors.

God Not a Respecter of Persons

Deut. 10 [17]For the LORD your God is God of gods, and LORD of lords, a great God, a mighty, and a terrible, which regardeth not persons, nor taketh reward:

Job 34 [19]How much less to him that accepteth not the persons of princes, nor regardeth the rich more than the poor? for they all are the work of his hands.

Acts 10 [34]Then Peter opened his mouth, and said, Of a truth I perceive that God is no respecter of persons:

Rom. 2 [11]For there is no respect of persons with God.

Rom. 10 [12]For there is no difference between the Jew and the Greek: for the same Lord over all is rich unto all that call upon him.

1 Pet. 1 [17]And if ye call on the Father, who without respect of persons judgeth according to every man's work, pass the time of your sojourning here in fear:

See 2 Chr. 19:7; Eph. 6:8-9; Col. 3:25

RESPONSIBILITY

[re spon si bil'i ti] Accountability; moral accountability, as responsibility of parents or responsibility for sin; reliability. The Bible contains a number of passages which indicate that men are held responsible to God in proportion to their abilities and the privileges which have been accorded them.

SCRIPTURE

Ezek. 18 [1]The word of the LORD came unto me again, saying, [2]What mean ye, that ye use this proverb concerning the land of Israel, saying, The fathers have eaten sour grapes, and the children's teeth are set on edge? [3]As I live, saith the Lord GOD, ye shall not have occasion any more to use this proverb in Israel. [4]Behold, all souls are mine; as the soul of the father, so also the soul of the son is mine: the soul that sinneth, it shall die.

[18]As for his father, because he cruelly oppressed, spoiled his brother by violence, and did that which is not good among his people, lo, even he shall die in his iniquity.

[19]Yet say ye, Why? doth not the son bear the iniquity of the father? When the son hath done that which is lawful and right, and hath kept all my statutes, and hath done them, he shall surely live. [20]The soul that sinneth, it shall die. The son shall not bear the iniquity of the father, neither shall the father bear the iniquity of the son: The righteousness of the righteous shall be upon him, and the wickedness of the wicked shall be upon him.

[30]Therefore I will judge you, O house of Israel, every one according to his ways, saith the Lord GOD. Repent, and turn yourselves from all your transgressions; so iniquity shall not be your ruin.

Ezek. 33 [4]Then whosoever heareth the sound of the trumpet, and taketh not warning; if the sword come, and take him away, his blood shall be upon his own head.

Matt. 10 [11]And into whatsoever city or town ye shall enter, enquire who in it is worthy; and there abide till ye go thence. [12]And when ye come into an house, salute it. [13]And if the house be worthy, let your peace come upon it: but if it be not worthy, let your peace return to you. [14]And whosoever shall not receive you, nor hear your words, when ye depart out of that house or city, shake off the dust of your feet. [15]Verily I say unto you, It shall be more tolerable for the land of Sodom and Gomorrah in the day of judgment, than for that city.

Matt. 11 [20]Then began he to upbraid the cities wherein most of his mighty works were done, because they repented not: [21]Woe unto thee, Chorazin! woe unto thee, Bethsaida! for if the mighty works, which were done in you, had been done in Tyre and Sidon, they would have repented long ago in sackcloth and ashes. [22]But I say unto you, It shall be more tolerable for Tyre and Sidon at the day of judgment, than for you. [23]And thou, Capernaum, which art exalted unto heaven, shalt be brought down to hell: for if the mighty works, which have been done in thee, had been done in Sodom, it would have remained until this day. [24]But I say unto you, That it shall be more tolerable for the land of Sodom in the day of judgment, than for thee.

Matt. 12 [41]The men of Nineveh shall rise in judgment with this generation, and shall condemn it: because they repented at the preaching of Jonas; and, behold, a greater than Jonas is here. [42]The queen of the south shall rise up in the judgment with this generation, and shall condemn it: for she came from the uttermost parts of the earth to hear the wisdom of Solomon; and, behold, a greater than Solomon is here.

Matt. 23 [31]Wherefore ye be witnesses unto yourselves, that ye are the children of them which killed the prophets. [32]Fill ye up then the measure of your fathers. 33Ye serpents, ye generation of vipers, how can ye escape the damnation of hell?

34Wherefore, behold, I send unto you prophets and wise men, and scribes: and some of them ye shall kill and crucify, and some of them shall ye scourge in your synagogues, and persecute them from city to city: 35That upon you may come all the righteous blood shed upon the earth, from the blood of righteous Abel unto the blood of Zacharias son of Barachias, whom ye slew between the temple and the altar.

Luke 21 1And he looked up, and saw the rich men casting their gifts into the treasury. 2And he saw also a certain poor widow casting in thither two mites. 3And he said, Of a truth I say unto you, that this poor widow hath cast in more than they all: 4For all these have of their abundance cast in unto the offerings of God: but she of her penury hath cast in all the living that she had.

John 15 22If I had not come and spoken unto them, they had not had sin: but now they have no cloke for their sin. 24If I had not done among them the works which none other man did, they had not had sin: but now have they both seen and hated both me and my Father.

Acts 17 30And the times of this ignorance God winked at; but now commandeth all men everywhere to repent: 31Because he hath appointed a day, in the which he will judge the world in righteousness by that man whom he hath ordained; whereof he hath given assurance unto all men, in that he hath raised him from the dead.

Rom. 12 3For I say, through the grace given unto me, to every man that is among you, not to think of himself more highly than he ought to think; but to think soberly, according as God hath dealt to every man the measure of faith. 6Having then gifts differing according to the grace that is given to us, whether prophecy, let us prophesy according to the proportion of faith; 7Or ministry, let us wait on our ministering: or he that teacheth, on teaching; 8Or he that exhorteth, on exhortation: he that giveth, let him do it with simplicity; he that ruleth, with diligence; he that sheweth mercy, with cheerfulness.

Eph. 4 7But unto every one of us is given grace according to the measure of the gift of Christ.

1 Tim. 6 20O Timothy, keep that which is committed to thy trust.

REFERENCE: *Matt. 25:14-30; Luke 9:5; 10:10-15; 11:31, 32, 49-51.*

REST

[rest] Repose; freedom from anything that disturbs; peace or security; sleep or slumber, and thence, figuratively, death. God promises rest for the weary who come to Him as well as rest to the faithful in the afterlife.

See PEACE, QUIET, etc.

SCRIPTURE

Isa. 11 10And in that day there shall be a root of Jesse, which shall stand for an ensign of the people; to it shall the Gentiles seek: and his rest shall be glorious.

Isa. 14 3And it shall come to pass in the day that the LORD shall give thee rest from thy sorrow, and from thy fear, and from the hard bondage wherein thou wast made to serve.

Isa. 30 15For thus saith the Lord GOD, the Holy One of Israel; In returning and rest shall ye be saved; in quietness and in confidence shall be your strength: and ye would not.

Jer. 6 16Thus saith the LORD, Stand ye in the ways, and see, and ask for the old paths, where is the good way, and walk therein, and ye shall find rest for your souls. But they said, We will not walk therein.

Matt. 11 [28]Come unto me, all ye that labour and are heavy laden, and I will give you rest.

Heb. 3 [11]So I sware in my wrath, They shall not enter into my rest.

Heb. 4 [1]Let us therefore fear, lest, a
promise being left us of entering into his
rest, any of you should seem to come
short of it. [2]For unto us was the gospel
preached, as well as unto them: but the
word preached did not profit them, not
being mixed with faith in them that heard
it. [3]For we which have believed do enter
into rest, as he said, As I have sworn in my
wrath, if they shall enter into my rest: although the works were finished from the
foundation of the world. [4]For he spake in
a certain place of the seventh day on this
wise, And God did rest the seventh day
from all his works. [5]And in this place
again, If they shall enter into my rest.
[6]Seeing therefore it remaineth that some
must enter therein, and they to whom it
was first preached entered not in because
of unbelief: [7]Again, he limiteth a certain
day, saying in David, To day, after so long
a time; as it is said, To day if ye will hear
his voice, harden not your hearts. [8]For if
Jesus had given them rest, then would he
not afterward have spoken of another day.
[9]There remaineth therefore a rest to the
people of God. [10]For he that is entered
into his rest, he also hath ceased from his
own works, as God did from his. [11]Let us
labour therefore to enter into that rest, lest
any man fall after the same example of
unbelief.

RESURRECTION

[rez u rek'shun] A restoration to life; revivification of a dead body. Although there are some earlier references to the idea of a resurrection, the doctrine receives its first real development in the period of the Babylonian exile, in the sixth century BC. It was applied to David (*Ezek. 34:23-31; 37:24-8*) and to Israel as a whole (*Ezek. 37:1-14*). In both these cases resurrection was to lead to glory and exaltation, but in *Dan. 12:1-2* resurrection is associated with a Day of Judgment in which some shall awake "some to everlasting life, and some to shame and everlasting contempt." Jewish thought was divided on the matter of the resurrection. In Jesus' time the Pharisees were the chief representatives of those who believed in a resurrection, while the Sadducees denied any meaningful life after death.

The doctrine of the resurrection is of central importance in the New Testament. At the heart of early Christian preaching lay the proclamation of Jesus' bodily resurrection from the dead on the third day after his crucifixion. This was viewed not as an afterthought which God had used to rescue a plan that had gone awry, but as an integral part of his program for the redemption of mankind. How such an event could take place is beyond our comprehension, for it flied in the face of all we regard as "natural." It is only by faith we can accept the resurrection as historical fact and understand it to be the sign of God's ultimate victory over Satan's power, as manifested in sin and death.

The Christian hope for life after death rests not upon any speculative theory of the intrinsic immortality of the soul, for the Bible does not teach the soul is immortal (*see* ETERNAL LIFE, SOUL), but squarely upon the basis of Jesus' resurrection. Jesus, as representative man, has triumphed over death on behalf of the whole human race. For those who are united with him, the old man of sin is crucified and eternal life is begun. This does not mean, of course, that Christians are exempted from physical death, but death is no longer viewed as the end of existence, that one already shares in Christ's victory over sin and the grave and may look forward with confidence to the final resurrection when the salvation now enjoyed in part bursts forth in glorious fullness. The form we shall have in the resurrection is described by Paul as a "spiritual body" (*1 Cor. 15:50-57*). It is impossible to comprehend fully what is meant by this apparently self-contradictory term, but it would seem to indicate the form we shall have in the resurrection will be neither "pure spirit" nor the corporeal flesh of our present bodies, but a "body" fashioned by God for eternal citizenship in the city of heaven.

SCRIPTURE

General

Psa. 17 15As for me, I will behold thy face in righteousness: I shall be satisfied, when I awake, with thy likeness.

Isa. 26 19Thy dead men shall live, together with my dead body shall they arise. Awake and sing, ye that dwell in dust: for thy dew is as the dew of herbs, and the earth shall cast out the dead.

Ezek. 37 1The hand of the LORD was upon me, and carried me out in the Spirit of the LORD, and set me down in the midst of the valley which was full of bones, 2And caused me to pass by them round about: and, behold, there were very many in the open valley; and, lo, they were very dry. 3And he said unto me, Son of man, can these bones live? And I answered, O Lord GOD, thou knowest. 4Again he said unto me, Prophesy upon these bones, and say unto them, O ye dry bones, hear the word of the LORD. 5Thus saith the Lord GOD unto these bones: Behold, I will cause breath to enter into you, and ye shall live: 6And I will lay sinews upon you, and will bring up flesh upon you, and cover you with skin, and put breath in you, and ye shall live; and ye shall know that I am the LORD. 7So I prophesied as I was commanded: and as I prophesied, there was a noise, and behold a shaking, and the bones came together, bone to his bone. 8And when I beheld, lo, the sinews and the flesh came up upon them, and the skin covered them above: but there was no breath in them. 9Then said he unto me, Prophesy unto the wind, prophesy, son of man, and say to the wind, Thus saith the Lord GOD; Come from the four winds, O breath, and breathe upon these slain, that they may live. 10So I prophesied as he commanded me, and the breath came into them, and they lived, and stood up upon their feet, an exceeding great army.

11Then he said unto me, Son of man, these bones are the whole house of Israel: behold, they say, Our bones are dried, and our hope is lost: we are cut off for our parts. 12Therefore prophesy and say unto them, Thus saith the Lord GOD; Behold, O my people, I will open your graves, and cause you to come up out of your graves, and bring you into the land of Israel. 13And ye shall know that I am the LORD, when I have opened your graves, O my people, and brought you up out of your graves, 14And shall put my Spirit in you, and ye shall live, and I shall place you in your own land: then shall ye know that I the LORD have spoken it, and performed it, saith the LORD.

Dan. 12 1And at that time shall Michael stand up, the great prince which standeth for the children of thy people: and there shall be a time of trouble, such as never was since there was a nation even to that same time: and at that time thy people shall be delivered, every one that shall be found written in the book. 2And many of them that sleep in the dust of the earth shall awake, some to everlasting life, and some to shame and everlasting contempt. 3And they that be wise, shall shine as the brightness of the firmament; and they that turn many to righteousness, as the stars for ever and ever.

Matt. 22 23The same day came to him the Sadducees, which say that there is no resurrection, and asked him, 24Saying, Master, Moses said, If a man die, having no children, his brother shall marry his wife, and raise up seed unto his brother. 25Now there were with us seven brethren:

and the first, when he had married a wife,
deceased, and, having no issue, left his
wife unto his brother: [26]Likewise the second also, and the third, unto the seventh.
[27]And last of all the woman died also.
[28]Therefore in the resurrection whose wife
shall she be of the seven? for they all had
her. [29]Jesus answered and said unto them,
Ye do err, not knowing the scriptures, nor
the power of God. [30]For in the resurrection they neither marry, nor are given in
marriage, but are as the angels of God in
heaven. [31]But as touching the resurrection
of the dead, have ye not read that which
was spoken unto you by God, saying, [32]I
am the God of Abraham, and the God of
Isaac, and the God of Jacob? God is not the
God of the dead, but of the living.

John 5 [28]Marvel not at this: for the hour
is coming, in the which all that are in the
graves shall hear his voice, [29]And shall
come forth; they that have done good, unto
the resurrection of life; and they that have
done evil, unto the resurrection of damnation.

John 11 [21]Then said Martha unto Jesus,
Lord, if thou hadst been here, my brother
had not died. [22]But I know, that even now,
whatsoever thou wilt ask of God, God will
give it thee. [23]Jesus saith unto her, Thy
brother shall rise again. [24]Martha saith
unto him, I know that he shall rise again
in the resurrection at the last day. [25]Jesus
said unto her, I am the resurrection, and
the life: he that believeth in me, though he
were dead, yet shall he live: [26]And whosoever liveth and believeth in me shall never
die. Believest thou this?

Acts 4 [1]And as they spake unto the people, the priests, and the captain of the temple, and the Sadducees, came upon them,
[2]Being grieved that they taught the people, and preached through Jesus the resurrection from the dead.

Acts 17 [18]Then certain philosophers of
the Epicureans, and of the Stoicks, encountered him. And some said, What will
this babbler say? other some, He seemeth
to be a setter forth of strange gods: because he preached unto them Jesus, and
the resurrection.

Acts 24 [15]And have hope toward God,
which they themselves also allow, that
there shall be a resurrection of the dead,
both of the just and unjust.

Acts 26 [8]Why should it be thought a
thing incredible with you, that God should
raise the dead?

Rom. 6 [5]For if we have been planted together in the likeness of his death, we shall
be also in the likeness of his resurrection:
[6]Knowing this, that our old man is crucified with him, that the body of sin might be
destroyed, that henceforth we should not
serve sin. [7]For he that is dead is freed from
sin. [8]Now if we be dead with Christ, we
believe that we shall also live with him:
[9]Knowing that Christ being raised from
the dead dieth no more; death hath no
more dominion over him. [10]For in that he
died, he died unto sin once: but in that he
liveth, he liveth unto God. [11]Likewise
reckon ye also yourselves to be dead indeed unto sin, but alive unto God through
Jesus Christ our Lord.

1 Cor. 15 [12]Now if Christ be preached
that he rose from the dead, how say some
among you that there is no resurrection of
the dead? [13]But if there be no resurrection
of the dead, then is Christ not risen: [14]And
if Christ be not risen, then is our preaching
vain, and your faith is also vain. [15]Yea,
and we are found false witnesses of God;
because we have testified of God that he
raised up Christ: whom he raised not up,
if so be that the dead rise not. [16]For if the
dead rise not, then is not Christ raised.
[17]And if Christ be not raised, your faith is

vain; ye are yet in your sins. [18]Then they also which are fallen asleep in Christ are perished. [29]Else what shall they do which are baptized for the dead, if the dead rise not at all? why are they then baptized for the dead? [30]And why stand we in jeopardy every hour? [31]I protest by your rejoicing which I have in Christ Jesus our Lord, I die daily. [32]If after the manner of men I have fought with beasts at Ephesus, what advantageth it me, if the dead rise not? let us eat and drink; for to morrow we die.

1 Thess. 4 [13]But I would not have you to be ignorant, brethren, concerning them which are asleep, that ye sorrow not, even as others, which have no hope. [14]For if we believe that Jesus died and rose again, even so them also which sleep in Jesus will God bring with him. [15]For this we say unto you by the word of the Lord, that we which are alive and remain unto the coming of the Lord shall not prevent them which are asleep. [16]For the Lord himself shall descend from heaven with a shout, with the voice of the archangel, and with the trump of God: and the dead in Christ shall rise first. [17]Then we which are alive and remain shall be caught up together with them in the clouds, to meet the Lord in the air: and so shall we ever be with the Lord. [18]Wherefore comfort one another with these words.

Nature of the Resurrected

John 11 [23]Jesus saith unto her, Thy brother shall rise again. [24]Martha saith unto him, I know that he shall rise again in the resurrection at the last day.

1 Cor. 15 [35]But some man will say, How are the dead raised up? and with what body do they come? [36]Thou fool, that which thou sowest is not quickened, except it die: [37]And that which thou sowest, thou sowest not that body which shall be, but bare grain, it may chance of wheat, or of some other grain: [38]But God giveth it a body as it hath pleased him, and to every seed his own body. [42]So also is the resurrection of the dead. It is sown in corruption, it is raised in incorruption: [43] It is sown in dishonour, it is raised in glory: it is sown in weakness, it is raised in power: [44]It is sown a natural body, it is raised a spiritual body. There is a natural body, and there is a spiritual body. [45]And so it is written, The first man Adam was made a living soul; the last Adam was made a quickening spirit. [46]Howbeit that was not first which is spiritual, but that which is natural; and afterward that which is spiritual. [50]Now this I say, brethren, that flesh and blood cannot inherit the kingdom of God; neither doth corruption inherit incorruption.

2 Cor. 5 [1]For we know that, if our earthly house of this tabernacle were dissolved, we have a building of God, a house not made with hands, eternal in the heavens. [2]For in this we groan, earnestly desiring to be clothed upon with our house which is from heaven: [3]If so be that being clothed we shall not be found naked. [4]For we that are in this tabernacle do groan, being burdened: not for that we would be unclothed, but clothed upon, that mortality might be swallowed up of life.

1 Cor. 15 [51]Behold, I shew you a mystery; We shall not all sleep, but we shall all be changed, [52]In a moment, in the twinkling of an eye, at the last trump: for the trumpet shall sound, and the dead shall be raised incorruptible, and we shall be changed. [53]For this corruptible must put on incorruption, and this mortal must put on immortality. [54]So when this corruptible shall have put on incorruption, and this mortal shall have put on immortality, then shall be brought to pass the saying that is written, Death is swallowed up in victory.

55O death, where is thy sting? O grave, where is thy victory? 56The sting of death is sin; and the strength of sin is the law.

The Believers' Hope

Rom. 8 23And not only they, but ourselves also, which have the firstfruits of the Spirit, even we ourselves groan within ourselves, waiting for the adoption, to wit, the redemption of our body.

Phil. 3 10That I may know him, and the power of his resurrection, and the fellowship of his sufferings, being made conformable unto his death; 11If by any means I might attain unto the resurrection of the dead.

REUBEN

[rōō'ben] The eldest son of Jacob, by his wife Leah. Reuben's rights as eldest son were forfeited by his relations with Bilhah, Jacob's concubine. He was responsible for saving the life of Joseph by persuading his brethren to put the young man in a pit instead of slaying him as they had intended. He later displays considerable guilt-feeling at the wrong which was committed against Joseph. Reuben was regarded as the ancestor of the Israelite tribe which bore his name.

See JOSEPH

SCRIPTURE

Son of Leah

Gen. 29 32And Leah conceived, and bare a son; and she called his name Reuben; for she said, Surely the LORD hath looked upon my affliction; now therefore my husband will love me.

Sins against His Father

Gen. 35 22And it came to pass, when Israel dwelt in that land, that Reuben went and lay with Bilhah his father's concubine: and Israel heard it.

Saves Joseph's Life

Gen. 37 19And they said one to another, Behold, this dreamer cometh. 20Come now therefore, and let us slay him, and cast him into some pit, and we will say, Some evil beast hath devoured him; and we shall see what will become of his dreams. 21And Reuben heard it, and he delivered him out of their hands; and said, Let us not kill him. 22And Reuben said unto them, Shed no blood, but cast him into this pit that is in the wilderness, and lay no hand upon him; that he might rid him out of their hands, to deliver him to his father again.

29And Reuben returned unto the pit; and, behold, Joseph was not in the pit; and he rent his clothes. 30And he returned unto his brethren, and said, The child is not; and I, whither shall I go?

Feels Guilt about Joseph

Gen. 42 22And Reuben answered them, saying, Spake I not unto you, saying, Do not sin against the child; and ye would not hear? therefore, behold, also his blood is required.

37And Reuben spake unto his father, saying, Slay my two sons, if I bring him not to thee: deliver him into my hand, and I will bring him to thee again.

REVELATION

[rev e lā'shun] The act or process of revealing that which has previously been unknown; specifically, God's disclosure of himself or his will to man. God is both the subject and object of divine revelation. Man can know nothing of God save that which he chooses to communicate to us. Happily, God has revealed himself in a number of ways in the course of history and has enabled man to apprehend that revelation. In the period of biblical history he made "personal appearances" to men, taking the form of a human being or an angel or appearing in a cloud, in fire, or as a bright light. On occasion, he appeared to men in direct visions, while at other times he made himself known in a dream. He revealed himself in various phenomena of nature such as wind, thunder, storm, and earthquake, and in a less direct way in the splendor and intricacy of the universe. But God's primary mode of revelation is through his word. This word is communicated to men in direct commandments such as those contained in the Decalogue or Ten Commandments (*see* DECALOGUE), in the oracles of his spokesmen the prophets, and through the writers of such material as the *Psalms* and the "wisdom literature" (*Proverbs, Ecclesiastes,* etc.). God's self-revelation to man reaches its climax in the Incarnate Word, Jesus Christ. In Christ, God makes himself known as one who loves men so much that he is willing to suffer and die for them that they might be freed from sin and death and be reconciled to him. The New Testament writings are our most valuable witnesses to this revelation and serve as an authoritative standard—a canon—which guides the church in its proclamation of the revelation and in its communal life.

A distinctive feature of the religion of Israel and the Christian religion is that the revelation of God is bound up within a concrete historical framework. The formative event in the religion of Israel was the exodus from Egypt, an event which may be charted and dated with some accuracy. (*See* EXODUS) But God did not stop there. The Old Testament is a record of his continuous intervention in history, of his execution of his plan for the redemption of mankind, which culminates in the sending of his son to usher in the Kingdom of God. We look forward to that day when his purposes will be fully accomplished, when history will be brought to fulfillment, when the Kingdom of God is consummated, when that which we have known in part will be made known in full and we shall see God as he is in himself.

SCRIPTURE

Deut. 29 [29]The secret things belong unto the LORD our God: but those things which are revealed belong unto us, and to our children for ever, that we may do all the words of this law.

Job 33 [16]Then he openeth the ears of men, and sealeth their instruction.

Isa. 40 [5]And the glory of the LORD shall be revealed, and all flesh shall see it together: for the mouth of the LORD hath spoken it.

Jer. 33 [6]Behold, I will bring it health and cure, and I will cure them, and will reveal unto them the abundance of peace and truth.

Dan. 2 [22]He revealeth the deep and secret things: he knoweth what is in the darkness, and the light dwelleth with him.

Amos 3 [7]Surely the Lord GOD will do nothing, but he revealeth his secret unto his servants the prophets.

Matt. 10 [26]Fear them not therefore: for there is nothing covered, that shall not be revealed; and hid, that shall not be known.

Matt. 11 [25]At that time Jesus answered and said, I thank thee, O Father, Lord of heaven and earth, because thou hast hid these things from the wise and prudent, and hast revealed them unto babes. [26]Even so, Father: for so it seemed good in thy sight. [27]All things are delivered unto me of my Father: and no man knoweth the Son, but the Father; neither knoweth any man the Father, save the Son, and he to whomsoever the Son will reveal him.

Matt. 16 [17]And Jesus answered and said unto him, Blessed art thou, Simon Barjona: for flesh and blood hath not revealed it unto thee, but my Father which is in heaven.

1 Cor. 2 [9]But as it is written, Eye hath not seen, nor ear heard, neither have entered into the heart of man, the things which God hath prepared for them that love him. [10]But God hath revealed them unto us by his Spirit: for the Spirit searcheth all things, yea, the deep things of God.

Gal. 1 [12]For I neither received it of man, neither was I taught it, but by the revelation of Jesus Christ.

Phil. 3 [15]Let us therefore, as many as be

perfect, be thus minded: and if in any thing ye be otherwise minded, God shall reveal even this unto you.

1 Pet. 1 5Who are kept by the power of God through faith unto salvation ready to be revealed in the last time.

1 Pet. 4 13But rejoice, inasmuch as ye are partakers of Christ's sufferings; that, when his glory shall be revealed, ye may be glad also with exceeding joy.

Rev. 1 1The Revelation of Jesus Christ, which God gave unto him, to shew unto his servants things which must shortly come to pass; and he sent and signified it by his angel unto his servant John: 2Who bare record of the word of God, and of the testimony of Jesus Christ, and of all things that he saw.

REVENGE

[rē venj′] The returning of evil for evil - retaliation. Although the Law of Moses sanctioned the principle of "an eye for an eye and a tooth for a tooth", as a deterrent to aggressive action, the general tenor of scripture is against retaliation, instructing us that vengeance for wrongs committed against us should be left in the hands of the LORD.

SCRIPTURE

Retaliation

Ex. 21 23And if any mischief follow, then thou shalt give life for life, 24Eye for eye, tooth for tooth, hand for hand, foot for foot, 25Burning for burning, wound for wound, stripe for stripe.

Lev. 19 18Thou shalt not avenge, nor bear any grudge against the children of thy people, but thou shalt love thy neighbour as thyself: I am the LORD.

Prov. 20 22Say not thou, I will recompense evil; but wait on the LORD, and he shall save thee.

Prov. 24 29Say not, I will do so to him as he hath done to me: I will render to the man according to his work.

Matt. 5 38Ye have heard that it hath been said, An eye for an eye, and a tooth for a tooth: 39But I say unto you, That ye resist not evil: but whosoever shall smite thee on thy right cheek, turn to him the other also. 40And if any man will sue thee at the law, and take away thy coat, let him have thy cloke also. 41And whosoever shall compel thee to go a mile, go with him twain. 42Give to him that asketh thee, and from him that would borrow of thee turn not thou away.

43Ye have heard that it hath been said, Thou shalt love thy neighbour, and hate thine enemy. 44But I say unto you, Love your enemies, bless them that curse you, do good to them that hate you, and pray for them which despitefully use you, and persecute you;

Luke 9 52They went, and entered into a village of the Samaritans, to make ready for him. 53And they did not receive him, because his face was as though he would go to Jerusalem. 54And when his disciples James and John saw this, they said, Lord, wilt thou that we command fire to come down from heaven, and consume them, even as Elias did? 55But he turned, and rebuked them, and said, Ye know not what manner of spirit ye are of. 56For the Son of man is not come to destroy men's lives, but to save them.

Rom. 12 17Recompense to no man evil for evil. 19Dearly beloved, avenge not yourselves, but rather give place unto wrath: for it is written, Vengeance is mine; I will repay, saith the Lord.

1 Cor. 6 7Now therefore there is utterly a fault among you, because ye go to law one with another. Why do ye not rather take wrong? why do ye not rather suffer yourselves to be defrauded? 8Nay, ye do

wrong, and defraud, and that your brethren.
1 Thess. 5 [15]See that none render evil
for evil unto any man; but ever follow that
which is good, both among yourselves, and
to all men.
1 Pet. 3 [9]Not rendering evil for evil, or
railing for railing: but contrariwise blessing; knowing that ye are thereunto called,
that ye should inherit a blessing.

REVERENCE

[rev′ẽr ens] A respectful and submissive disposition of mind, arising from affection, esteem, fear, awe, and a sense of the superiority of the person reverenced. Worshippers of God are commanded to show reverence toward God and the things that are his.

See RESPECT

SCRIPTURE

Ex. 3 [5]And he said, Draw not nigh
hither: put off thy shoes from off thy feet;
for the place whereon thou standest is holy
ground. [6]Moreover he said, I am the God
of thy father, the God of Abraham, the
God of Isaac, and the God of Jacob. And
Moses hid his face; for he was afraid to look
upon God.
Lev. 19 [30]Ye shall keep my sabbaths,
and reverence my sanctuary: I am the
LORD.
Psa. 89 [7]God is greatly to be feared in
the assembly of the saints, and to be had in
reverence of all them that are about him.
Psa. 111 [9]He sent redemption unto his
people: he hath commanded his covenant
for ever: holy and reverend is his name.
[10]The fear of the LORD is the beginning of
wisdom: a good understanding have all
they that do his commandments: his praise
endureth for ever.
Heb. 12 [28]Wherefore we receiving a
kingdom which cannot be moved, let us
have grace, whereby we may serve God
acceptably with reverence and godly fear:
[29]For our God is a consuming fire.

REWARD

[rê wôrd′] To requite; to recompense; to repay; to compensate; also, that which is given in recognition of an act. The scriptures teach us that God rewards those who obey him with the blessings of salvation from sin and eternal life. The evil also receive a reward appropriate to their wickedness.

SCRIPTURE

Rewards for the Righteous

Deut. 5 [33]Ye shall walk in all the ways
which the LORD your God hath commanded you, that ye may live, and that it
may be well with you, and that ye may
prolong your days in the land which ye
shall possess.
Deut. 6 [17]Ye shall diligently keep the
commandments of the LORD your God,
and his testimonies, and his statutes,
which he hath commanded thee. [18]And
thou shalt do that which is right and good
in the sight of the LORD; that it may be well
with thee, and that thou mayest go in and
possess the good land which the LORD
sware unto thy fathers, [19]To cast out all
thine enemies from before thee, as the
LORD hath spoken.
Deut. 8 [1]All the commandments which
I command thee this day shall ye observe
to do, that ye may live, and multiply, and
go in and possess the land which the LORD
sware unto your fathers.
2 Sam. 22 [20]He brought me forth also
into a large place: he delivered me, because he delighted in me. [21]The LORD rewarded me according to my righteousness;
according to the cleanness of my hands
hath he recompensed me. [25]Therefore the

LORD hath recompensed me according to my righteousness; according to my cleanness in his eyesight.

Psa. 18 [19]He brought me forth also into a large place; he delivereth me, because he delighted in me. [20]The Lord rewarded me according to my righteousness; according to the cleanness of my hands hath he recompensed me.

Prov. 2 [1]My son, if thou wilt receive my words, and hide my commandments with thee; [2]So that thou incline thine ear unto wisdom, and apply thine heart to understanding; [3]Yea, if thou criest after knowledge, and liftest up thy voice for understanding; [4]If thou seekest her as silver, and searchest for her as for hid treasures; [5]Then shalt thou understand the fear of the Lord, and find the knowledge of God.

Prov. 3 [21]My son, let not them depart from thine eyes: keep sound wisdom and discretion: [22]So shall they be life unto thy soul, and grace to thy neck.

Ezek. 11 [20]That they may walk in my statutes, and keep mine ordinances, and do them: and they shall be my people, and I will be their God.

Matt. 7 [21]Not every one that saith unto me, Lord, Lord, shall enter into the kingdom of heaven; but he that doeth the will of my Father which is in heaven.

Matt. 24 [13]But he that shall endure unto the end, the same shall be saved.

Luke 12 [31]But rather seek ye the kingdom of God; and all these things shall be added unto you.

Luke 22 [28]Ye are they which have continued with me in my temptations. [29]And I appoint unto you a kingdom, as my Father hath appointed unto me.

Rom. 8 [32]He that spared not his own Son, but delivered him up for us all, how shall he not with him also freely give us all things?

Gal. 6 [9]And let us not be weary in well doing: for in due season we shall reap, if we faint not.

1 Tim. 4 [8]For bodily exercise profiteth little: but godliness is profitable unto all things, having promise of the life that now is, and of that which is to come.

2 Tim. 4 [7]I have fought a good fight, I have finished my course, I have kept the faith: [8]Henceforth there is laid up for me a crown of righteousness, which the Lord, the righteous judge, shall give me at that day: and not to me only, but unto all them also that love his appearing.

Heb. 3 [14]For we are made partakers of Christ, if we hold the beginning of our confidence steadfast unto the end.

Heb. 10 [39]But we are not of them who draw back unto perdition; but of them that believe to the saving of the soul.

Jas. 1 [2]My brethren, count it all joy when ye fall into divers temptations. [12]Blessed is the man that endureth temptation: for when he is tried, he shall receive the crown of life, which the Lord hath promised to them that love him.

Reward of Faithful Ministry

Prov. 11 [30]The fruit of the righteous is a tree of life; and he that winneth souls is wise.

John 4 [36]And he that reapeth receiveth wages, and gathereth fruit unto life eternal: that both he that soweth and he that reapeth may rejoice together. [37]And herein is that saying true, One soweth, and another reapeth. [38]I sent you to reap that whereon ye bestowed no labour: other men laboured, and ye are entered into their labours.

Phil. 1 [19]For I know that this shall turn to my salvation through your prayer, and the supply of the Spirit of Jesus Christ, [20]According to my earnest expectation and my hope, that in nothing I shall be ashamed, but that with all boldness, as always, so now also Christ shall be magnified in my body, whether it be by life, or by death. [21]For to me to live is Christ, and to die is gain.

1 Pet. 5 [4]And when the chief Shepherd shall appear, ye shall receive a crown of glory that fadeth not away.

Reward of the Wicked

Deut. 32 [41]If I whet my glittering sword, and mine hand take hold on judgment; I will render vengeance to mine enemies, and will reward them that hate me.

2 Sam. 3 [39]And I am this day weak, though anointed king; and these men the sons of Zeruiah be too hard for me: the LORD shall reward the doer of evil according to his wickedness.

Psa. 54 [5]He shall reward evil unto mine enemies; cut them off in thy truth.

2 Pet. 2 [13]And shall receive the reward of unrighteousness, as they that count it pleasure to riot in the day time. Spots they are and blemishes, sporting themselves with their own deceivings while they feast with you.

Rev. 20 [15]And whosoever was not found written in the book of life was cast into the lake of fire.

RHODA

[rō'da] A maid in the house of Mary, mother of John Mark. It was Rhoda who answered the door when Peter knocked at Mary's house after having been miraculously released from prison. She was so excited that she did not open the door, but ran to tell those assembled in the house. She had considerable difficulty in convincing them of the truth of her story.

SCRIPTURE

Acts 12 [13]And as Peter knocked at the door of the gate, a damsel came to hearken, named Rhoda.

RICHES (Rich, Wealth)

[rich'ez] That which makes one rich; wealth; an abundant supply of money, land, or goods; also, wealth of a mental or spiritual order, such as righteousness, godliness, love, wisdom, knowledge, etc. The Bible does not teach that the possessions of an abundance of material goods is evil in itself, but that the greed and desire which frequently accompany the accumulation of riches are sources of social misery and spiritual danger. Riches may quite easily lead to pride, self-esteem, and contempt for those who are less successful or less endowed materially. Jesus recognized this and urged indifference to possessions, reminding his disciples that "a man's life consisteth not in the abundance of his possessions" (*Luke 12:15*). To place one's trust in riches rather than in God is practical atheism.

See PROSPERITY, POOR

SCRIPTURE

Worldly Riches

THEIR VANITY

Job 31 [24]If I have made gold my hope, or have said to the fine gold, Thou art my confidence; [25]If I rejoiced because my wealth was great, and because mine hand had gotten much.

Prov. 13 [7]There is that maketh himself rich, yet hath nothing: there is that maketh himself poor, yet hath great riches. [8]The ransom of a man's life are his riches: but the poor heareth not rebuke.

Prov. 23 [4]Labour not to be rich: cease from thine own wisdom. [5]Wilt thou set thine eyes upon that which is not? for riches certainly make themselves wings; they fly away as an eagle toward heaven.

Eccl. 4 [8]There is one alone, and there is not a second; yea, he hath neither child nor brother: yet is there no end of all his labour; neither is his eye satisfied with riches; neither saith he, For whom do I labour, and bereave my soul of good? This is also vanity, yea, it is a sore travail.

Eccl. 5 [10]He that loveth silver shall not be satisfied with silver; nor he that loveth abundance with increase: this is also vanity. [11]When goods increase, they are increased that eat them: and what good is there to the owners thereof, saving the beholding of them with their eyes?

Eccl. 6 [1]There is an evil which I have seen under the sun, and it is common among men: [2]A man to whom God hath given riches, wealth, and honour, so that he wanteth nothing for his soul of all that he desireth, yet God giveth him not power to eat thereof, but a stranger eateth it: this is vanity, and it is an evil disease.

1 Tim. 6 [17]Charge them that are rich in this world, that they be not highminded, nor trust in uncertain riches, but in the living God, who giveth us richly all things to enjoy.

THEIR TEMPTATION AND USELESSNESS

Deut. 8 [11]Beware that thou forget not the LORD thy God, in not keeping his commandments, and his judgments, and his statutes, which I command thee this day: [12]Lest when thou hast eaten and art full, and hast built goodly houses, and dwelt therein; [13]And when thy herds and thy flocks multiply, and thy silver and thy gold is multiplied, and all that thou hast is multiplied; [14]Then thine heart be lifted up, and thou forget the LORD thy God, which brought thee forth out of the land of Egypt, from the house of bondage. [17]And thou say in thine heart, My power and the might of mine hand hath gotten me this wealth. [18]But thou shalt remember the LORD thy God: for it is he that giveth thee power to get wealth, that he may establish his covenant which he sware unto thy fathers, as it is this day.

Prov. 28 [20]A faithful man shall abound with blessings: but he that maketh haste to be rich shall not be innocent. [22]He that hasteth to be rich hath an evil eye, and considereth not that poverty shall come upon him.

Luke 12 [15]And he said unto them, Take heed, and beware of covetousness: for a man's life consisteth not in the abundance of the things which he possesseth. [16]And he spake a parable unto them, saying, The ground of a certain rich man brought forth plentifully: [17]And he thought within himself, saying, What shall I do, because I have no room where to bestow my fruits? [18]And he said, This will I do: I will pull down my barns, and build greater; and there will I bestow all my fruits and my goods. [19]And I will say to my soul, Soul, thou hast much goods laid up for many years; take thine ease, eat, drink, and be merry. [20]But God said unto him, Thou fool, this night thy soul shall be required of thee: then whose shall those things be, which thou hast provided? [21]So is he that layeth up treasure for himself, and is not rich toward God.

[34]For where your treasure is, there will your heart be also.

Luke 18 [18]And a certain ruler asked him, saying, Good Master, what shall I do to inherit eternal life? [19]And Jesus said unto him, Why callest thou me good? none is good, save one, that is, God. [20]Thou knowest the commandments, Do not commit adultery, Do not kill, Do not steal, Do not bear false witness, Honour thy father and thy mother. [21]And he said, All these have I kept from my youth up. [22]Now when Jesus heard these things, he said unto him, Yet lackest thou one thing: sell all that thou hast, and distribute unto the poor, and thou shalt have treasure in heaven: and come, follow me. [23]And when he heard this, he was very sorrowful: for he was very rich. [24]And when Jesus saw that he was very sorrowful, he said, How hardly shall they that have riches enter into the kingdom of God! [25]For it is easier for a camel to go through a needle's eye, than for a rich man to enter into the kingdom of God. [26]And they that heard it said, Who then can be saved? [27]And he said, The things which are impossible with men are possible with God.

1 Tim. 6 [10]For the love of money is the root of all evil: which while some coveted after, they have erred from the faith, and pierced themselves through with many sorrows.

See Mark 10:17-27

RICHES PROFITLESS TO THE WICKED

Job 20 [15]He hath swallowed down riches, and he shall vomit them up again: God shall cast them out of his belly.

Psa. 37 [16]A little that a righteous man hath is better than the riches of many wicked.

Prov. 10 [2]Treasures of wickedness profit nothing: but righteousness delivereth from death. [3]The LORD will not suffer the soul of the righteous to famish: but he casteth away the substance of the wicked.

Prov. 11 [4]Riches profit not in the day of wrath: but righteousness delivereth from death. [28]He that trusteth in his riches shall fall: but the righteous shall flourish as a branch.

Prov. 15 [6]In the house of the righteous is much treasure: but in the revenues of the wicked is trouble.

Prov. 20 [21]An inheritance may be gotten hastily at the beginning; but the end thereof shall not be blessed.

Prov. 21 [6]The getting of treasures by a lying tongue is a vanity tossed to and fro of them that seek death.

Eccl. 5 [13]There is a sore evil which I have seen under the sun, namely, riches kept for the owners thereof to their hurt. [14]But those riches perish by evil travail: and he begetteth a son, and there is nothing in his hand.

Ezek. 7 [19]They shall cast their silver in the streets, and their gold shall be removed: their silver and their gold shall not be able to deliver them in the day of the wrath of the LORD: they shall not satisfy their souls, neither fill their bowels: because it is the stumblingblock of their iniquity.

True Riches

Matt. 13 [44]Again, the kingdom of heaven is like unto treasure hid in a field; the which when a man hath found, he hideth, and for joy thereof goeth and selleth all that he hath, and buyeth that field. [45]Again, the kingdom of heaven is like unto a merchant man, seeking goodly pearls: [46]Who, when he had found one pearl of great price, went and sold all that he had, and bought it.

Luke 16 [11]If therefore ye have not been faithful in the unrighteous mammon, who will commit to your trust the true riches?

Eph. 3 [8]Unto me, who am less than the least of all saints, is this grace given, that I should preach among the Gentiles the unsearchable riches of Christ.

Col. 2 [2]That their hearts might be comforted, being knit together in love, and unto all riches of the full assurance of understanding, to the acknowledgment of the mystery of God, and of the Father, and of Christ; [3]In whom are hid all the treasures of wisdom and knowledge.

RIGHTEOUSNESS

[rī′chus nes] The state or quality of being righteous, of being free from wrong or sin, of being just. The Hebrew words which are translated "righteousness" in the Old Testament originally signified that which conforms to a norm; this norm was God himself. The prophets emphasized what God must do if he was to be consistent with himself as a righteous being. This included not only ethical righteousness, or the establishment of equal justice and rights for all, but came to include benevolence and salvation for those who were faithful to him. In the New Testament, Paul uses the word righteousness much more frequently than other writers. In his epistles, the word has three different meanings: first, it is used of the ethical conduct demanded by the Law of Moses; second, of the even higher standard of holiness, purity, and uprightness expected of the Christian; and third, of the righteousness of God, which, to Paul, was represented by the gift of salvation through Jesus Christ.

See PURITY, WICKED, etc.

SCRIPTURE

Righteousness of God

Ezra 9 [15]O LORD God of Israel, thou art righteous:

Job 36 [3]I will fetch my knowledge from afar, and will ascribe righteousness to my Maker.

Psa. 5 [8]Lead me, O LORD, in thy righteousness because of mine enemies;

Psa. 50 [6]And the heavens shall declare his righteousness: for God is judge himself.

Psa. 88 [12]Shall thy wonders be known in the dark? and thy righteousness in the land of forgetfulness?

Psa. 89 [16]In thy name shall they rejoice all the day: and in thy righteousness shall they be exalted.

Psa. 112 [4]He is gracious, and full of compassion, and righteous.

Psa. 116 [5]Gracious is the LORD, and righteous; yea, our God is merciful.

Psa. 119 [40]Behold, I have longed after thy precepts: quicken me in thy righteousness. [137]Righteous art thou, O LORD, and upright are thy judgments. [142]Thy righteousness is an everlasting righteousness, and thy law is the truth.

Isa. 51 [8]My righteousness shall be for ever, and my salvation from generation to generation.

Isa. 56 [1]Thus saith the LORD, Keep ye judgment, and do justice: for my salvation is near to come, and my righteousness to be revealed.

Hos. 14 [9]The ways of the LORD are right, and the just shall walk in them:

Mic. 7 [9]He will bring me forth to the light, and I shall behold his righteousness.

Matt. 6 [33]But seek ye first the kingdom of God, and his righteousness; and all these things shall be added unto you.

Rom. 3 [5]But if our unrighteousness commend the righteousness of God, what shall we say? Is God unrighteous who taketh vengeance? (I speak as a man) [6]God forbid: for then how shall God judge the world? [21]But now the righteousness of God without the law is manifested, being witnessed by the law and the prophets; [22]Even the righteousness of God which is by faith of Jesus Christ unto all and upon all them that believe: for there is no difference:

Rom. 9 [14]What shall we say then? Is there unrighteousness with God? God forbid.

Rom. 10 [3]For they being ignorant of God's righteousness, and going about to establish their own righteousness, have not submitted themselves unto the righteousness of God. [4]For Christ is the end of the law for righteousness to every one that believeth.

2 Tim. 4 8 Henceforth there is laid up for me a crown of righteousness, which the Lord, the righteous judge, shall give me at that day: and not to me only, but unto all them also that love his appearing.

Righteousness of Men Described

Psa. 1 1 Blessed is the man that walketh not in the counsel of the ungodly, nor standeth in the way of sinners, nor sitteth in the seat of the scornful. 2 But his delight is in the law of the LORD; and in his law doth he meditate day and night. 3 And he shall be like a tree planted by the rivers of water, that bringeth forth his fruit in his season; his leaf also shall not wither; and whatsoever he doeth shall prosper.

Psa. 4 3 But know that the LORD hath set apart him that is godly for himself:

Psa. 15 1 LORD, who shall abide in thy tabernacle? who shall dwell in thy holy hill? 2 He that walketh uprightly, and worketh righteousness, and speaketh the truth in his heart. 3 He that backbiteth not with his tongue, nor doeth evil to his neighbour, nor taketh up a reproach against his neighbour. 4 In whose eyes a vile person is contemned; but he honoureth them that fear the LORD. He that sweareth to his own hurt, and changeth not. 5 He that putteth not out his money to usury, nor taketh reward against the innocent.

Isa. 33 15 He that walketh righteously, and speaketh uprightly; he that despiseth the gain of oppressions, that shaketh his hands from holding of bribes, that stoppeth his ears from hearing of blood, and shutteth his eyes from seeing evil; 16 He shall dwell on high; his place of defence shall be the munitions of rocks: bread shall be given him; his waters shall be sure.

Luke 6 45 A good man out of the good treasure of his heart bringeth forth that which is good; . . . for of the abundance of the heart his mouth speaketh.

John 13 35 By this shall all men know that ye are my disciples, if ye have love one to another.

John 15 14 Ye are my friends, if ye do whatsoever I command you.

Rom. 4 3 For what saith the Scripture? Abraham believed God, and it was counted unto him for righteousness. 4 Now to him that worketh is the reward not reckoned of grace, but of debt. 5 But to him that worketh not, but believeth on him that justifieth the ungodly, his faith is counted for righteousness. 9 Cometh this blessedness then upon the circumcision only, or upon the uncircumcision also? for we say that faith was reckoned to Abraham for righteousness. 10 How was it then reckoned? when he was in circumcision, or in uncircumcision? Not in circumcision, but in uncircumcision. 11 And he received the sign of circumcision, a seal of the righteousness of the faith which he had yet being uncircumcised: that he might be the father of all them that believe, though they be not circumcised; that righteousness might be imputed unto them also:

Rom. 6 13 Neither yield ye your members as instruments of unrighteousness unto sin: but yield yourselves unto God, as those that are alive from the dead, and your members as instruments of righteousness unto God. 14 For sin shall not have dominion over you: for ye are not under the law, but under grace. 15 What then? shall we sin, because we are not under the law, but under grace? God forbid. 16 Know ye not, that to whom ye yield yourselves servants to obey, his servants ye are to whom ye obey; whether of sin unto death, or of obedience unto righteousness? 17 But God be thanked, that ye were the servants of sin, but ye have obeyed from the heart that form of doctrine which was delivered you. [18]Being then made free from sin, ye became the servants of righteousness.

Eph. 4 [13]Till we all come in the unity of the faith, and of the knowledge of the Son of God, unto a perfect man, unto the measure of the stature of the fulness of Christ: [14]That we henceforth be no more children, tossed to and fro, and carried about with every wind of doctrine, by the sleight of men, and cunning craftiness, whereby they lie in wait to deceive; [15]But speaking the truth in love, may grow up into him in all things, which is the head, even Christ: [16]From whom the whole body fitly joined together and compacted by that which every joint supplieth, according to the effectual working in the measure of every part, maketh increase of the body unto the edifying of itself in love. [23]And be renewed in the spirit of your mind; [24]And that ye put on the new man, which after God is created in righteousness and true holiness. [25]Wherefore putting away lying, speak every man truth with his neighbour: for we are members one of another. [26]Be ye angry, and sin not: let not the sun go down upon your wrath: [27]Neither give place to the devil. [28]Let him that stole steal no more: but rather let him labour, working with his hands the thing which is good, that he may have to give to him that needeth. [29]Let no corrupt communication proceed out of your mouth, but that which is good to the use of edifying, that it may minister grace unto the hearers. [30]And grieve not the holy Spirit of God, whereby ye are sealed unto the day of redemption. [31]Let all bitterness, and wrath, and anger, and clamour, and evil speaking, be put away from you, with all malice: [32]And be ye kind one to another, tenderhearted, forgiving one another, even as God for Christ's sake hath forgiven you.

1 John 3 [7]Little children, let no man deceive you: he that doeth righteousness is righteous, even as he is righteous. [9]Whosoever is born of God doth not commit sin; for his seed remaineth in him: and he cannot sin, because he is born of God. [14]We know that we have passed from death unto life, because we love the brethren. He that loveth not his brother abideth in death. [18]My little children, let us not love in word, neither in tongue; but in deed and in truth. [19]And hereby we know that we are of the truth, and shall assure our hearts before him.

Promises to the Righteous

Job 36 [7]He withdraweth not his eyes from the righteous: but with kings are they on the throne; yea, he doth establish them for ever, and they are exalted.

Psa. 15 [1]LORD, who shall abide in thy tabernacle? who shall dwell in thy holy hill? [2]He that walketh uprightly, and worketh righteousness, and speaketh the truth in his heart.

Psa. 37 [16]A little that a righteous man hath is better than the riches of many wicked.

Psa. 55 [22]Cast thy burden upon the LORD, and he shall sustain thee: he shall never suffer the righteous to be moved.

Psa. 64 [10]The righteous shall be glad in the LORD, and shall trust in him; and all the upright in heart shall glory.

Prov. 2 [7]He layeth up sound wisdom for the righteous: he is a buckler to them that walk uprightly.

Prov. 10 [30]The righteous shall never be removed: but the wicked shall not inhabit the earth.

Prov. 11 [4]Riches profit not in the day of

wrath: but righteousness delivereth from
death. [5]The righteousness of the perfect
shall direct his way: but the wicked shall
fall by his own wickedness. [6]The righteousness of the upright shall deliver them:
but transgressors shall be taken in their
own naughtiness. [10]When it goeth well
with the righteous, the city rejoiceth: and
when the wicked perish, there is shouting.
[11]By the blessing of the upright the city
is exalted: but it is overthrown by the
mouth of the wicked.

Isa. 3 [10]Say ye to the righteous, that it shall be well with him: for they shall eat the fruit of their doings.

Isa. 26 [2]Open ye the gates, that the righteous nation which keepeth the truth may enter in.

Matt. 13 [43]Then shall the righteous shine forth as the sun in the kingdom of their Father. Who hath ears to hear, let him hear.

Acts 10 [35]But in every nation he that feareth him, and worketh righteousness, is accepted with him.

Rom. 2 [10]But glory, honour, and peace, to every man that worketh good, to the Jew first, and also to the Gentile.

1 Pet. 3 [12]For the eyes of the Lord are over the righteous, and his ears are open unto their prayers: but the face of the Lord is against them that do evil.

ROME

[rōm] The most powerful city in the ancient world and capital of the vast empire which bears its name. Traditionally founded in 753 BC and located on the Tiber River in Central Italy, Rome was a truly cosmopolitan city, attracting people from all over the Mediterranean world.

In the first century AD, Rome was in a high period of her development. The influence of the Roman Empire is writ large on the pages of the New Testament. (*See*, for example, articles on CAESAR or HEROD) *Acts of Apostles* may be viewed as the story of the spread of the gospel from Jerusalem to Rome. We cannot be certain as to how Christianity was planted in Rome. Paul's epistle to the Romans, written about 55 AD, makes it clear that the church had already been established before the apostle visited Rome. The personal references in the epistle, however, indicate that a number of the Christians in Rome were people whom Paul had known elsewhere, so it is not impossible that he was indirectly responsible for the work there. The book of *Acts* ends with Paul's commitment to a Roman prison. Strong tradition has it that he was later beheaded there, although many scholars feel that he was released, that he engaged in further mission efforts, and that his death came during a second Roman imprisonment.

Most scholars feel that many of the references in the *Revelation* refer to Rome and the Roman Empire. (*See*, for example, *Rev. 17:6, 9, 15, 18, 22; 18:3, 9, 12, 13, 22*) For a fuller treatment of this enormous subject, the reader should consult standard religions and secular encyclopedias.

SCRIPTURE

Paul Desires to Preach in Rome

Rom. 1 [15]So, as much as in me is, I am ready to preach the gospel to you that are at Rome also.

Paul in Rome

Acts 28 [14]. . . and so we went toward
Rome. [15]And from thence, when the
brethren heard of us, they came to meet
us as far as Appii Forum, and the Three
Taverns: whom when Paul saw, he
thanked God, and took courage. [16]And
when we came to Rome, the centurion
delivered the prisoners to the captain of
the guard: but Paul was suffered to dwell
by himself with a soldier that kept him.
[17]And it came to pass, that after three days
Paul called the chief of the Jews together:
and when they were come together, he

said unto them, Men and brethren, though I have committed nothing against the people, or customs of our fathers, yet was I delivered prisoner from Jerusalem into the hands of the Romans. [18]Who, when they had examined me, would have let me go, because there was no cause of death in me. [19]But when the Jews spake against it, I was constrained to appeal unto Caesar; not that I had ought to accuse my nation of. [20]For this cause therefore have I called for you, to see you, and to speak with you: because that for the hope of Israel I am bound with this chain. [21]And they said unto him, We neither received letters out of Judaea concerning thee, neither any of the brethren that came shewed or spake any harm of thee. [22]But we desire to hear of thee what thou thinkest: for as concerning this sect, we know that every where it is spoken against. [23]And when they had appointed him a day, there came many to him into his lodging; to whom he expounded and testified the kingdom of God, persuading them concerning Jesus, both out of the law of Moses, and out of the prophets, from morning till evening. [24]And some believed the things which were spoken, and some believed not. [30]And Paul dwelt two whole years in his own hired house, and received all that came in unto him, [31]Preaching the kingdom of God, and teaching those things which concern the Lord Jesus Christ, with all confidence, no man forbidding him.

RULER

[rōōl′ĕr] One who has dominion over someone else. In the Bible, this term is used in a wide variety of ways, referring to princes, magistrates, nobles, commanders, judges, members of the Jewish Sanhedrin, leaders in the synagogues, and virtually any other sort of person in authority. The Scriptures contain numerous passages setting forth the qualifications of a just ruler and exhort the righteous to be subject to those who have the rule over them.

SCRIPTURE

Character and Qualifications of a Ruler

Ex. 18 [21]Moreover thou shalt provide out of all the people able men, such as fear God, men of truth, hating covetousness; and place such over them, to be rulers of thousands, and rulers of hundreds, rulers of fifties, and rulers of tens: [22]And let them judge the people at all seasons: and it shall be, that every great matter they shall bring unto thee, but every small matter they shall judge: so shall it be easier for thyself, and they shall bear the burden with thee.

Ex. 23 [8]And thou shalt take no gift: for the gift blindeth the wise, and perverteth the words of the righteous.

Deut. 16 [18]Judges and officers shalt thou make thee in all thy gates, which the LORD thy God giveth thee, throughout thy tribes: and they shall judge the people with just judgment. [19]Thou shalt not wrest judgment; thou shalt not respect persons, neither take a gift: for a gift doth blind the eyes of the wise, and pervert the words of the righteous. [20]That which is altogether just shalt thou follow, that thou mayest live, and inherit the land which the LORD thy God giveth thee.

2 Sam. 23 [3]The God of Israel said, The Rock of Israel spake to me, He that ruleth over men must be just, ruling in the fear of God.

Prov. 16 [12]It is an abomination to kings to commit wickedness: for the throne is established by righteousness.

Prov. 20 [8]A king that sitteth in the throne of judgment scattereth away all evil with his eyes. [26]A wise king scattereth the wicked, and bringeth the wheel over them. [28]Mercy and truth preserve the king: and his throne is upholden by mercy.

Duties of Rulers

Ex. 18 [16]When they have a matter, they come unto me; and I judge between one and another, and I do make them know the statutes of God, and his laws. [20]And thou shalt teach them ordinances and laws, and shalt shew them the way wherein they must walk, and the work that they must do.

Ex. 23 [3]Neither shalt thou countenance a poor man in his cause.

[6]Thou shall not wrest the judgment of thy poor in his cause. [7]Keep thee far from a false matter; and the innocent and righteous slay thou not: for I will not justify the wicked.

[9]Also thou shalt not oppress a stranger: for ye know the heart of a stranger, seeing ye were strangers in the land of Egypt.

Lev. 19 [15]Ye shall do no unrighteousness in judgment: thou shalt not respect the person of the poor, nor honour the person of the mighty: but in righteousness shalt thou judge thy neighbour.

Lev. 24 [22]Ye shall have one manner of law, as well for the stranger, as for one of your own country: for I am the LORD your God.

Deut. 1 [16]And I charged your judges at that time, saying, Hear the causes between your brethren, and judge righteously between every man and his brother, and the stranger that is with him. [17]Ye shall not respect persons in judgment; but ye shall hear the small as well as the great; ye shall not be afraid of the face of man; for the judgment is God's.

Deut. 17 [18]And it shall be, when he sitteth upon the throne of his kingdom, that he shall write him a copy of this law in a book out of that which is before the priests the Levites. [19]And it shall be with him, and he shall read therein all the days of his life; that he may learn to fear the LORD his God, to keep all the words of this law and these statutes, to do them: [20]That his heart be not lifted up above his brethren, and that he turn not aside from the commandment, to the right hand, or to the left: to the end that he may prolong his days in his kingdom, he, and his children, in the midst of Israel.

Josh. 1 [8]This book of the law shall not depart out of thy mouth; but thou shalt meditate therein day and night, that thou mayest observe to do according to all that is written therein: for then thou shalt make thy way prosperous, and then thou shalt have good success.

2 Chr. 9 [8]God loved Israel, to establish them for ever, therefore made he thee king over them, to do judgment and justice.

Responsibility of the Righteous Toward Their Rulers

Matt. 22 [17]Tell us therefore, What thinkest thou? Is it lawful to give tribute unto Caesar, or not? [18]But Jesus perceived their wickedness, and said, Why tempt ye me, ye hypocrites? [19]Shew me the tribute money. And they brought unto him a penny. [20]And he saith unto them, Whose is this image and superscription? [21]They say unto him, Caesar's. Then saith he unto them, Render therefore unto Caesar the things which are Caesar's; and unto God the things that are God's.

Rom. 13 [1]Let every soul be subject unto the higher powers. For there is no power but of God: the powers that be are ordained of God. [2]Whosoever therefore resisteth the power, resisteth the ordinance of God: and they that resist shall receive to themselves damnation. [3]For rulers are not a terror to good works, but to the evil.

Wilt thou then not be afraid of the power? do that which is good, and thou shalt have praise of the same: [4]For he is the minister of God to thee for good. But if thou do that which is evil, be afraid; for he beareth not the sword in vain: for he is the minister of God, a revenger to execute wrath upon him that doeth evil. [5]Wherefore ye must needs be subject, not only for wrath, but also for conscience' sake. [6]For for this cause pay ye tribute also: for they are God's ministers, attending continually upon this very thing. [7]Render therefore to all their dues: tribute to whom tribute is due; custom to whom custom; fear to whom fear; honour to whom honour.

1 Tim. 2 [1]I exhort therefore, that, first of all, supplications, prayers, intercessions, and giving of thanks, be made for all men; [2]For kings, and for all that are in authority; that we may lead a quiet and peaceable life in all godliness and honesty.

Tit. 3 [1]Put them in mind to be subject to principalities and powers, to obey magistrates, to be ready to every good work.

1 Pet. 2 [13]Submit yourselves to every ordinance of man for the Lord's sake: whether it be to the king, as supreme; [14]Or unto governors, as unto them that are sent by him for the punishment of evildoers, and for the praise of them that do well. [15]For so is the will of God, that with well doing ye may put to silence the ignorance of foolish men: [16]As free, and not using your liberty for a cloke of maliciousness, but as the servants of God. [17]Honour all men. Love the brotherhood. Fear God. Honour the king.

RUTH

[rōōth] Daughter-in-law of Naomi, wife of Boaz, and great-grandmother of David. Due to a severe famine in the land of Judah, Elimelech, a native of Bethlehem, emigrated to Moab with his wife and two sons, who married two Moabite women, Ruth and Orpah. At the end of ten years, all three of the women were left widows and Naomi decided to return to Bethlehem. Despite Naomi's protests, Ruth determined to return to Bethlehem with her. Ruth's dedication to Naomi and to the religion of the God of Israel is stated in *Ruth 1:16-17*: "Intreat me not to leave thee, or to return from following after thee: for whither thou goest, I will go; and where thou lodgest, I will lodge: thy people shall be my people, and thy God my God; where thou diest, will I die, and there will I be buried: the Lord do so to me and more also, if ought but death part thee and me."

They arrived in Bethlehem at the time of the barley harvest. Ruth went out to glean in the fields of Boaz, a wealthy man whose relationship with his servants eloquently attests to his character (*Ruth 2:4*). According to Hebrew law, Ruth had a right to demand that a near kinsman of her late husband take her for his wife. Boaz had been related to Ruth's husband and was willing to marry her, but since there was another man of closer kinship, it was necessary to go through certain customary and legal measures before he could rightfully claim her. This being done, the two were married with the blessings of their neighbors and eventually became the parents of Obed, the grandfather of David.

SCRIPTURE

Refuses to Leave Naomi

Ruth 1 [16]And Ruth said, Entreat me not to leave thee, or to return from following after thee: for whither thou goest, I will go; and where thou lodgest, I will lodge: thy people shall be my people, and thy God my God: [17]Where thou diest, will I die, and there will I be buried: the Lord do so to me, and more also, if aught but death part thee and me. [18]When she saw that she was steadfastly minded to go with her, then she left speaking unto her.

[22]So Naomi returned, and Ruth the Moabitess, her daughter in law, with her, which returned out of the country of

Moab: and they came to Bethlehem in the beginning of barley harvest.

Gleans in the Field of Boaz

Ruth 2 1And Naomi had a kinsman of her husband's, a mighty man of wealth, of the family of Elimelech; and his name was Boaz. 2And Ruth the Moabitess said unto Naomi, Let me now go to the field, and glean ears of corn after him in whose sight I shall find grace. And she said unto her, Go, my daughter. 3And she went, and came, and gleaned in the field after the reapers; and her hap was to light on a part of the field belonging unto Boaz, who was of the kindred of Elimelech.

4And, behold, Boaz came from Bethlehem, and said unto the reapers, The LORD be with you. And they answered him, The LORD bless thee. 5Then said Boaz unto his servant that was set over the reapers, Whose damsel is this? 6And the servant that was set over the reapers answered and said, It is the Moabitish damsel that came back with Naomi out of the country of Moab: 7And she said, I pray you, let me glean and gather after the reapers among the sheaves: so she came, and hath continued even from the morning until now, that she tarried a little in the house.

Boaz' Kindness Toward Her

Ruth 2 8Then said Boaz unto Ruth, Hearest thou not, my daughter? Go not to glean in another field, neither go from hence, but abide here fast by my maidens: 9Let thine eyes be on the field that they do reap, and go thou after them: have I not charged the young men that they shall not touch thee? and when thou art athirst, go unto the vessels, and drink of that which the young men have drawn. 10Then she fell on her face, and bowed herself to the ground, and said unto him, Why have I found grace in thine eyes, that thou shouldest take knowledge of me, seeing I am a stranger? 11And Boaz answered and said unto her, It hath fully been shewed me, all that thou hast done unto thy mother in law since the death of thine husband; and how thou hast left thy father and thy mother, and the land of thy nativity, and art come unto a people which thou knewest not heretofore. 12The LORD recompense thy work, and a full reward be given thee of the LORD God of Israel, under whose wings thou art come to trust. 13Then she said, Let me find favour in thy sight, my lord; for that thou hast comforted me, and for that thou hast spoken friendly unto thine handmaid, though I be not like unto one of thine handmaidens. 14And Boaz said unto her, At mealtime come thou hither, and eat of the bread, and dip thy morsel in the vinegar. And she sat beside the reapers: and he reached her parched corn, and she did eat, and was sufficed, and left. 15And when she was risen up to glean, Boaz commanded his young men, saying, Let her glean even among the sheaves, and reproach her not: 16And let fall also some of the handfuls of purpose for her, and leave them, that she may glean them, and rebuke her not. 17So she gleaned in the field until even, and beat out that she had gleaned: and it was about an ephah of barley.

18And she took it up, and went into the city; and her mother in law saw what she had gleaned: and she brought forth, and gave to her that she had reserved after she was sufficed. 19And her mother in law said unto her, Where hast thou gleaned to-day? and where wroughtest thou? blessed be he that did take knowledge of thee. And she shewed her mother in law with whom she had wrought, and said, The man's name with whom I wrought to-day is Boaz.

Sleeps at Boaz' Feet

Ruth 3 [7]And when Boaz had eaten and drunk, and his heart was merry, he went to lie down at the end of the heap of corn: and she came softly, and uncovered his feet, and laid her down.

Becomes Boaz' Wife

Ruth 4 [13]So Boaz took Ruth, and she was his wife: and when he went in unto her, the LORD gave her conception, and she bare a son. [14]And the women said unto Naomi, Blessed be the LORD, which hath not left thee this day without a kinsman, that his name may be famous in Israel. [15]And he shall be unto thee a restorer of thy life, and a nourisher of thine old age: for thy daughter in law, which loveth thee, which is better to thee than seven sons, hath borne him. [16]And Naomi took the child, and laid it in her bosom, and became nurse unto it. [17]And the women her neighbours gave it a name, saying, There is a son born to Naomi; and they called his name Obed: he is the father of Jesse, the father of David.

SABAOTH

[sab'ȧ oth] The Greek transliteration of the Hebrew word for "hosts." In the Old Testament God is often spoken of as the LORD of Hosts. When the equivalent phrase was found in the New Testament in *Rom. 9:29* and *Jas. 5:4*, the translators of the King James Version simply transliterated it into the form "Lord of Sabaoth." In more recent versions, this is rendered "Lord of Hosts." Although the word bears a similarity to "Sabbath", there is no connection between the two and they should not be confused.

SABBATH

[sab'ath] "Sabbath" is derived from a Hebrew word meaning "to cease, abstain, or desist." It refers to the last day of a seven-day week which, in the Jewish religion, is a day on which one rests from his normal activity, devoting himself to the service of God. The observance of the Sabbath was one of the Ten Commandments (*see* DECALOGUE) and is traced back to God's resting on the seventh day of his creative activity. Breaking of the Sabbath by performance of proscribed labor was punishable by death (*Ex. 31:14; Num. 15:32-6*).

By the time of Jesus' ministry, Sabbath-keeping was regarded as one of the distinctive features of Jewish religion, and proper observance had developed into a highly technical affair, with ingenious methods of avoiding certain regulations. The true spirit and purpose of the Sabbath, however, had been obscured. When Jesus plucked grain for food or healed on the Sabbath, the Jews reacted violently. His answers showed them the Sabbath had not been given to test their obedience or ingenuity, but to assist them in maintaining their physical and spiritual strength. His actions were in fact a fulfillment of God's original purpose in giving the Sabbath and demonstrated the superficiality of the legalistic restrictions the Rabbis had placed upon Sabbath-keeping.

The "Sabbath day's journey" mentioned in the New Testament (*see Acts 1:12*) was about 2,000 cubits, or from 3,000 to 3,600 feet, depending on the length of the cubit. The calculation of this distance was based upon the approximate distance from the tabernacle to the outer edge of the camp during the period of wandering in the wilderness. According to rabbinic law, all activity on the Sabbath had to be confined to an area within this distance of one's home, although there was some latitude in establishing the location of "home."

In the beginning of the church, Christians observed the Sabbath, but gradually shifted their worship to the Lord's Day, the first day of the week, in commemoration of Jesus' resurrection on that day.

See LORD'S DAY

SCRIPTURE

General

Gen. 2 [2]On the seventh day God ended

his work which he had made; and he rested on the seventh day from all his work which he had made. [3]And God blessed the seventh day, and sanctified it; because that in it he had rested from all his work which God created and made.

Ex. 20 [8]Remember the sabbath day, to keep it holy. [9]Six days shalt thou labour, and do all thy work: [10]But the seventh day is the sabbath of the LORD thy God: in it thou shalt not do any work, thou, nor thy son, nor thy daughter, thy manservant, nor thy maidservant, nor thy cattle, nor thy stranger that is within thy gates: [11]For in six days the LORD made heaven and earth, the sea, and all that in them is, and rested the seventh day: wherefore the LORD blessed the sabbath day, and hallowed it.

Ex. 31 [13]Speak thou also unto the children of Israel, saying, Verily my sabbaths ye shall keep: for it is a sign between me and you throughout your generations; that ye may know that I am the LORD that doth sanctify you. [14]Ye shall keep the sabbath therefore; for it is holy unto you: every one that defileth it shall surely be put to death: for whosoever doeth any work therein, that soul shall be cut off from among his people. [15]Six days may work be done; but in the seventh is the sabbath of rest, holy to the LORD: whosoever doeth any work in the sabbath day, he shall surely be put to death. [16]Wherefore the children of Israel shall keep the sabbath, to observe the sabbath throughout their generations, for a perpetual covenant. [17]It is a sign between me and the children of Israel for ever: for in six days the LORD made heaven and earth, and on the seventh day he rested, and was refreshed.

Neh. 10 [31]And if the people of the land bring ware or any victuals on the sabbath day to sell, that we would not buy it of them on the sabbath, or on the holy day:

Psa. 118 [24]This is the day which the LORD hath made; we will rejoice and be glad in it.

Jer. 17 [21]Thus saith the LORD; Take heed to yourselves, and bear no burden on the sabbath day, nor bring it in by the gates of Jerusalem; [22]Neither carry forth a burden out of your houses on the sabbath day, neither do ye any work, but hallow ye the sabbath day, as I commanded your fathers.

Jesus' Attitude Toward the Sabbath

Matt. 12 [1]At that time Jesus went on the sabbath day through the corn; and his disciples were an hungred, and began to pluck the ears of corn, and to eat. [2]But when the Pharisees saw it, they said unto him, Behold, thy disciples do that which is not lawful to do upon the sabbath day. [3]But he said unto them, Have ye not read what David did, when he was an hungred, and they that were with him; [4]How he entered into the house of God, and did eat the shewbread, which was not lawful for him to eat, neither for them which were with him, but only for the priests? [5]Or have ye not read in the law, how that on the sabbath days the priests in the temple profane the sabbath, and are blameless? [6]But I say unto you, That in this place is one greater than the temple. [7]But if ye had known what this meaneth, I will have mercy, and not sacrifice, ye would not have condemned the guiltless. [8]For the Son of man is Lord even of the sabbath day.

[10]And, behold, there was a man which had his hand withered. And they asked him, saying, Is it lawful to heal on the sabbath days? that they might accuse him. [11]And he said unto them, What man shall there be among you, that shall have one sheep, and if it fall into a pit on the sabbath day, will he not lay hold on it, and lift it

out? [12]How much then is a man better
than a sheep? Wherefore it is lawful to do
well on the sabbath days. [13]Then saith he
to the man, Stretch forth thine hand. And
he stretched it forth; and it was restored
whole, like as the other.

Mark 16 [1]And when the sabbath was
past, Mary Magdalene, and Mary the
mother of James, and Salome, had bought
sweet spices, that they might come and
anoint him.

Luke 13 [10]He was teaching in one of the
synagogues on the sabbath.

[11]And, behold, there was a woman
which had a spirit of infirmity eighteen
years, and was bowed together, and could
in no wise lift up herself. [12]And when Jesus saw her, he called her to him, and said
unto her, Woman, thou art loosed from
thine infirmity. [13]And he laid his hands on
her: and immediately she was made
straight, and glorified God. [14]And the
ruler of the synagogue answered with indignation, because that Jesus had healed
on the sabbath day, and said unto the people, There are six days in which men ought
to work: in them therefore come and be
healed, and not on the sabbath day. [15]The
Lord then answered him, and said, Thou
hypocrite, doth not each one of you on the
sabbath loose his ox or his ass from the
stall, and lead him away to watering?
[16]And ought not this woman, being a
daughter of Abraham, whom Satan hath
bound, lo, these eighteen years, be loosed
from this bond on the sabbath day? [17]And
when he had said these things, all his adversaries were ashamed:

Luke 14 [1]And it came to pass, as he
went into the house of one of the chief
Pharisees to eat bread on the sabbath day,
that they watched him. [2]And, behold,
there was a certain man before him which
had the dropsy. [3]And Jesus answering
spake unto the lawyers and Pharisees, saying, Is it lawful to heal on the sabbath day?
[4]And they held their peace. And he took
him, and healed him, and let him go; [5]And
answered them, saying, Which of you shall
have an ass or an ox fallen into a pit, and
will not straightway pull him out on the
sabbath day? [6]And they could not answer
him again to these things.

John 5 [5]And a certain man was there,
which had an infirmity thirty and eight
years. [6]When Jesus saw him lie, and knew
that he had been now a long time in that
case, he saith unto him, Wilt thou be made
whole? [7]The impotent man answered
him, Sir, I have no man, when the water is
troubled, to put me into the pool: but
while I am coming, another steppeth down
before me. [8]Jesus saith unto him, Rise,
take up thy bed, and walk. [9]And immediately the man was made whole, and took
up his bed, and walked: and on the same
day was the sabbath.

[10]The Jews therefore said unto him that
was cured, It is the sabbath day: it is not
lawful for thee to carry thy bed. [11]He answered them, He that made me whole, the
same said unto me, Take up thy bed, and
walk. [12]Then asked they him, What man
is that which said unto thee, Take up thy
bed, and walk? [13]And he that was healed
wist not who it was: for Jesus had conveyed himself away, a multitude being in
that place. [14]Afterward Jesus findeth him
in the temple, and said unto him, Behold,
thou art made whole: sin no more, lest a
worse thing come unto thee.

John 7 [21]Jesus answered and said unto
them, I have done one work, and ye all
marvel. [22]Moses therefore gave unto you
circumcision; (not because it is of Moses,
but of the fathers;) and ye on the sabbath
day circumcise a man. [23]If a man on the
sabbath day receive circumcision, that the

law of Moses should not be broken; are ye angry at me, because I have made a man every whit whole on the sabbath day? [24]Judge not according to the appearance, but judge righteous judgment.

John 19 [31]The Jews therefore, because it was the preparation, that the bodies should not remain upon the cross on the sabbath day, (for that sabbath day was an high day,) besought Pilate that their legs might be broken, and that they might be taken away.

See Mark 2:28; Luke 6:1-10; John 9:1-34

SABBATICAL YEAR

[sa bat′ik al] The seventh year, in which all field-work was to cease; this brought relief to the poor by allowing them to harvest whatever the unfilled fields produced and it also enabled the land to lie fallow for a period, that it might be more productive. The sabbatical year served to remind Israel of the authority and goodness of God to inculcate humanity, and to give time for devotion and deeds of mercy. It is often mistakenly supposed that all Hebrew slaves were released in the Sabbatical year. It should be noted, however, that although Hebrew slaves were released in the seventh year of their bondage (*Ex. 21:2-6*), there is no reason to connect this with any particular year.

See JUBILEE

SCRIPTURE

Ex. 23 [10]And six years thou shalt sow thy land, and shalt gather in the fruits thereof: [11]But the seventh year thou shalt let it rest and lie still; that the poor of thy people may eat: and what they leave the beasts of the field shall eat. In like manner thou shalt deal with thy vineyard, and with thy oliveyard.

Deut. 15 [1]At the end of every seven years thou shalt make a release. [2]And this is the manner of the release: Every creditor that lendeth aught unto his neighbour shall release it; he shall not exact it of his neighbour, or of his brother; because it is called the LORD's release. [3]Of a foreigner thou mayest exact it again: but that which is thine with thy brother thine hand shall release;

SACKCLOTH

[sak′kloth] Cloth of a coarse texture, of a dark color, made of goat's hair and worn as an indication of mourning or utter humility.

SCRIPTURE

Gen. 37 [34]And Jacob rent his clothes, and put sackcloth upon his loins, and mourned for his son many days.

1 Kin. 20 [31]And his servants said unto him, Behold now, we have heard that the kings of the house of Israel are merciful kings: let us, I pray thee, put sackcloth on our loins, and ropes upon our heads, and go out to the king of Israel: peradventure he will save thy life. [32]So they girded sackcloth on their loins, and put ropes on their heads, and came to the king of Israel, and said, Thy servant Benhadad saith, I pray thee, let me live. And he said, Is he yet alive? he is my brother.

Job 16 [15]I have sewed sackcloth upon my skin, and defiled my horn in the dust. [16]My face is foul with weeping, and on my eyelids is the shadow of death;

Isa. 15 [3]In their streets they shall gird themselves with sackcloth: on the tops of their houses, and in their streets, every one shall howl, weeping abundantly.

Jonah 3 [8]But let man and beast be covered with sackcloth, and cry mightily unto God: yea, let them turn every one from his evil way, and from the violence that is in their hands.

Rev. 6 [12]And I beheld when he had opened the sixth seal, and, lo, there was a great earthquake; and the sun became black as sackcloth of hair, and the moon became as blood;

SACRIFICE

[sak'ri fīs] An offering to a deity of animal or vegetable life or of food, drink, incense, etc. The offering of one's possessions in sacrifice to a deity or deities was common to virtually all ancient societies. Although the formal sacrificial system was not instituted in Israel until the time of Moses, there is frequent reference to sacrifices in the previous periods of biblical history; the story of Cain and Abel indicates that offering sacrifice had been a part of life as long as anyone could remember. Sacrifices were offered as a sign of calling God to witness alliances or covenants made between men (*Gen. 31:44-54*) or between men and God (*Ex. 24:3-8*). They were offered simply as a gift of gratitude and thanksgiving for blessings received, as an accompaniment of a request for some favor or blessing from the deity, and in atonement for certain sins.

The Israelite sacrificial system contained five main sacrifices. The burnt-offering was a public ceremony, performed each morning and evening, with special offerings on the Sabbath and various other religious holidays. In this ceremony, the offered animal, always an unblemished male, was completely burned, nothing being left for the priests or the worshipper who provided the sacrifice. A second class of offerings was the meal-offering, or cereal-offering, which consisted of fine flour, or unleavened cakes or wafers. A portion of this was mixed with oil and frankincense and offered in the fire, the rest going to the priests for their own consumption. It was frequently the accompaniment of meat and drink-offerings. The peace-offering, so called because it promoted a peaceful relationship with God, was ordinarily a private affair, except at the feast of Pentecost (*Lev. 23:19* and *Lev. 9:4*). In this sacrifice, only the fat of the entrails, the kidneys, and a portion of the liver were burnt on the altar; the remainder was divided between the priests and the family of the offerer. The sin-offering was not, as its name might imply, an expiation for every sort of sin, but only for those sins which were committed unwittingly. In this ceremony, the fat of the entrails, the kidneys, and the appendage of the liver were burnt, as in the peace-offering, but the remainder, instead of being eaten, was taken outside the camp and burnt on a wood fire near the place where the ashes from the altar were poured out. The guilt-offering was made in atonement for sins which, though not always unwitting, seem to be restricted to a certain class of sins, such as failure to testify on some matter before the courts, accidentally touching some unclean thing, neglecting to pay the required religious taxes, or failure to return borrowed property. The mode of offering seems to be the same as in the sin-offering. In all of the flesh offerings, the sacrifice might range in value from a bull to a pair of turtledoves, depending on the economic status of the worshipper. The terms "heave-offering" and "wave-offering" refer to the priests' portion of the offering which was waved in the air, perhaps as a sign that it was being offered to God but that God "waves it back" to those who minister to him. There are numerous variations on these main sacrifices. The reader who wishes to delve further into this subject should read carefully *Lev. 1-9*.

When Jesus offered himself in sacrifice for the sins of mankind, there was no further need for the sacrificial system of Judaism. The daily sacrifices were supplanted by the one sacrifice which was all sufficient and eternally valid. To be sure, the old system had been instituted by God, but in Christ that toward which it had pointed was realized. The blood of bulls and goats has been superseded by the blood of the Lamb of God, and the mortal priests who annually entered into the Holy of Holies by the Great High Priest who has penetrated the veil of death and intercedes for us eternally before God's mercy-seat in the sanctuary of heaven.

SCRIPTURE

Before the Law of Moses

Gen. 4 [3]And in process of time it came
to pass, that Cain brought of the fruit of the
ground an offering unto the LORD. [4]And
Abel, he also brought of the firstlings of his
flock and of the fat thereof. And the LORD
had respect unto Abel and to his offering:
[5]But unto Cain and to his offering he had

not respect. And Cain was very wroth, and his countenance fell.

Gen. 22 [1]And it came to pass after these things, that God did tempt Abraham, and said unto him, Abraham: and he said, Behold, here I am. [2]And he said, Take now thy son, thine only son Isaac, whom thou lovest, and get thee into the land of Moriah; and offer him there for a burnt offering upon one of the mountains which I will tell thee of. [3]And Abraham rose up early in the morning, and saddled his ass, and took two of his young men with him, and Isaac his son, and clave the wood for the burnt offering, and rose up, and went unto the place of which God had told him.

Gen. 31 [54]Then Jacob offered sacrifice upon the mouth, and called his brethren to eat bread: and they did eat bread, and tarried all night in the mount.

Under the Law

THE SACRIFICIAL SYSTEM

See Lev. 1-9

HUMAN SACRIFICE FORBIDDEN

Deut. 12 [31]Thou shalt not do so unto the LORD thy God: for every abomination to the LORD which he hateth have they done unto their gods; for even their sons and their daughters they have burnt in the fire to their gods.

OBEDIENCE BETTER THAN SACRIFICE

1 Sam. 15 [22]And Samuel said, Hath the LORD as great delight in burnt offerings and sacrifices, as in obeying the voice of the LORD? Behold, to obey is better than sacrifice, and to hearken than the fat of rams.

Christian Sacrifice

Luke 5 [27]And after these things he went forth, and saw a publican, named Levi, sitting at the receipt of custom: and he said unto him, Follow me. [28]And he left all, rose up, and followed him.

Luke 18 [18]And a certain ruler asked him, saying, Good Master, what shall I do to inherit eternal life? [19]And Jesus said unto him, Why callest thou me good? none is good, save one, that is, God. [20]Thou knowest the commandments, Do not commit adultery, Do not kill, Do not steal, Do not bear false witness, Honor thy father and thy mother. [21]And he said, All these have I kept from my youth up. [22]Now when Jesus heard these things, he said unto him, Yet lackest thou one thing: sell all that thou hast, and distribute unto the poor, and thou shalt have treasure in heaven: and come, follow me. [23]And when he heard this, he was very sorrowful: for he was very rich.

Rom. 12 [1]I beseech you therefore, brethren, by the mercies of God, that ye present your bodies a living sacrifice, holy, acceptable unto God, which is your reasonable service.

Heb. 9 [24]For Christ is not entered into the holy places made with hands, which are the figures of the true; but into heaven itself, now to appear in the presence of God for us: [25]Now yet that he should offer himself often, as the high priest entereth into the holy place every year with blood of others; [26]For then must he often have suffered since the foundation of the world: but now once in the end of the world hath he appeared to put away sin by the sacrifice of himself.

SADDUCEES

[sad'ū sēz] A religious party of the Jews, mentioned prominently in the New Testament. There is some difficulty in ascertaining the true character of the Sadducees since virtually all the information we have of them comes from their opponents. Nevertheless, it seems certain that they were the old priestly party, intent on protecting their conservative interests against the innovations of the Pharisees. (*See* PHARISEES) The name is probably derived from the word Zadokite. The "Sons of Zadok" were members of a priestly party who traced themselves back to Zadok, the head of the priesthood under David and Solomon (*1 Kin. 1:34; 2:35*). In contrast to the desire of the Pharisees to accept a body of oral tradition as equal in authority to the written law, the Sadducees insisted that all doctrine receive its support directly from the written law. Consequently they rejected the Pharisaic ideas of a Messiah, the belief in the resurrection of the body, and, according to *Acts 23:8,* belief in angels and spirits. This last matter is somewhat confusing, as the Pentateuch contains several references to these beings; it is possible that the writer of *Acts* had reference to the absence of any developed system of belief in angels and demons. As noted in the article on the PHARISEES, the Sadducees were often forced to do the bidding of the Pharisees, due to the wide popular support which the latter enjoyed. As a result, the power of the Sadducees was seriously impaired and, after the destruction of Jerusalem in AD 70, the Pharisees gained the undisputed ascendancy.

SCRIPTURE

Rebuked by John

Matt. 3 [7]But when he saw many of the
Pharisees and Sadducees come to his baptism, he said unto them, O generation of
vipers, who hath warned you to flee from
the wrath to come? [8]Bring forth therefore
fruits meet for repentance: [9]And think not
to say within yourselves, We have Abraham to our father: for I say unto you, that
God is able of these stones to raise up children unto Abraham.

Disbelieve Doctrine of Resurrection

Matt. 22 [23]The same day came to him
the Sadducees, which say that there is no
resurrection, and asked him, [24]Saying,
Master, Moses said, If a man die, having no
children, his brother shall marry his wife,
and raise up seed unto his brother. [25]Now
there were with us seven brethren: and the
first, when he had married a wife, deceased, and, having no issue, left his wife
unto his brother: [26]Likewise the second
also, and the third, unto the seventh.
[27]And last of all the woman died also.
[28]Therefore in the resurrection whose wife
shall she be of the seven? for they all had
her. [29]Jesus answered and said unto them,
Ye do err, not knowing the scriptures, nor
the power of God. [30]For in the resurrection they neither marry, nor are given in
marriage, but are as the angels of God in
heaven. [31]But as touching the resurrection
of the dead, have ye not read that which
was spoken unto you by God, saying, [32]I
am the God of Abraham, and the God of
Isaac, and the God of Jacob? God is not
the God of the dead, but of the living.
[33]And when the multitude heard this, they
were astonished at his doctrine.

Persecute the Apostles

Acts 4 [1]And as they spake unto the people, the priests, and the captain of the temple, and the Sadducees, came upon them,
[2]Being grieved that they taught the people, and preached through Jesus the resurrection from the dead. [3]And they laid
hands on them, and put them in hold unto
the next day: for it was now eventide.

Acts 5 [17]Then the high priest rose up,
and all they that were with him, (which is
the sect of the Sadducees,) and were filled
with indignation, [18]And laid their hands
on the apostles, and put them in the common prison.

SAINT

[sānt] In the Bible, this term is usually applied to the whole company of God's people rather than to any single individual. In modern times we are prone to think of a "saint" as a person of almost superhuman purity and goodness; the Hebrew and Greek terms which are translated "saint" in the Bible, however, generally refer to one set apart by God for his own. The primary aspect of sainthood is, therefore, the fact that one has been consecrated by God for his service; although moral purity and a godly character ought always to follow immediately, they are a secondary consideration.

See HOLINESS, SANCTIFICATION

SCRIPTURE

The Saints of God

Deut. 33 [2]And he said, The LORD came from Sinai, and rose up from Seir unto them; he shined forth from mount Paran, and he came with ten thousands of saints: from his right hand went a fiery law for them.

1 Sam. 2 [9]He will keep the feet of his saints, and the wicked shall be silent in darkness; for by strength shall no man prevail.

Psa. 145 [10]All thy works shall praise thee, O LORD; and thy saints shall bless thee.

Psa. 149 [1]Praise ye the LORD. Sing unto the LORD a new song, and his praise in the congregation of saints.

Prov. 2 [8]He keepeth the paths of judgment, and preserveth the way of his saints.

Dan. 7 [18]But the saints of the Most High shall take the kingdom, and possess the kingdom for ever, even for ever and ever.

Believers as Saints

Rom. 8 [27]And he that searcheth the hearts knoweth what is the mind of the Spirit, because he maketh intercession for the saints according to the will of God.

Eph. 2 [19]Now therefore ye are no more strangers and foreigners, but fellow-citizens with the saints, and of the household of God.

Col. 1 [12]Giving thanks unto the Father, which hath made us meet to be partakers of the inheritance of the saints in light.

Jude 1 [3]Beloved, when I gave all diligence to write unto you of the common salvation, it was needful for me to write unto you, and exhort you that ye should earnestly contend for the faith which was once delivered unto the saints.

Rev. 5 [8]And when he had taken the book, the four beasts and four and twenty elders fell down before the Lamb, having every one of them harps, and golden vials full of odours, which are the prayers of saints.

Obligations and Blessings of the Saints

2 Chr. 6 [41]Now therefore arise, O LORD God, into thy resting place, thou, and the ark of thy strength: let thy priests, O LORD God, be clothed with salvation, and let thy saints rejoice in goodness.

Psa. 30 [4]Sing unto the LORD, O ye saints of his, and give thanks at the remembrance of his holiness.

Psa. 31 [23]O love the LORD, all ye his saints: for the LORD preserveth the faithful, and plentifully rewardeth the proud doer.

Psa. 132 [9]Let thy priests be clothed with righteousness; and let thy saints shout for joy.

Rom. 16 [2]That ye receive her in the Lord, as becometh saints, and that ye assist her in whatsoever business she hath need of you: for she hath been a succourer of
many, and of myself also. [15]Salute Philo-
logus, and Julia, Nereus, and his sister, and Olympas, and all the saints which are with them.

1 Cor. 6 [1]Dare any of you, having a matter against another, go to law before
the unjust, and not before the saints? [2]Do
ye not know that the saints shall judge the world? and if the world shall be judged by

you, are ye unworthy to judge the smallest matters?

2 Cor. 8 [4]Praying us with much intreaty that we would receive the gift, and take upon us the fellowship of the ministering to the saints.

Eph. 4 [11]And he gave some, apostles; and some, prophets; and some, evangelists; and some, pastors and teachers; [12]For the perfecting of the saints, for the work of the ministry, for the edifying of the body of Christ.

Eph. 6 [18]Praying always with all prayer and supplication in the Spirit, and watching thereunto with all perseverance and supplication for all saints.

Philem. 1 [4]I thank my God, making mention of thee always in my prayers, [5]Hearing of thy love and faith, which thou hast toward the Lord Jesus, and toward all saints.

Heb. 6 [10]For God is not unrighteous to forget your work and labour of love, which ye have shewed toward his name, in that ye have ministered to the saints, and do minister.

Heb. 13 [24]Salute all them, that have the rule over you, and all the saints. They of Italy salute you.

SALEM

[sā'lem] A locality of which Melchizedek was king. It is often assumed that Salem is simply an abbreviated form of Jerusalem, but this is an erroneous view. There is, in fact, no way in which we can decide with certainty as to the identification of this ancient city or region.

SCRIPTURE

Gen. 14 [18]And Melchizedek king of Salem brought forth bread and wine: and he was the priest of the most high God.

SALVATION

[sal vā'shun] The act, process, or result of deliverance or preservation from danger, bondage, disease, or sin. In the Bible salvation usually refers to deliverance from some physical danger or distress. Anyone able to effect this deliverance, whether judge, prophet, priest, or king, might be referred to as a "saviour." In the later writings of the Old Testament and in the New Testament, however, there is greater emphasis on moral and spiritual deliverance and on physical deliverance which transcends the realm of ordinary human experience. Man is seen as universally in need of a salvation which he is unable of himself to bring about. His lost condition may be variously described as corruption, disease, death, falling short of the glory of God, a feeling of being trapped—"alone and afraid in a world I never made," bondage to sin and its consequences, alienation from one's fellowmen and from God, rebellion against God, guilt, anxiety, etc. His own unaided efforts to solve his problems through intellectual, economic, political, social, or psychological skills and techniques are doomed to futility. The Law of Moses, though incapable of procuring complete salvation, served its purpose well in convicting men of their sinfulness and demonstrating the impossibility of salvation apart from the grace of God.

The supreme manifestation of God's grace, the focal point in the history of salvation, is the cross of Jesus Christ. The significance of this act is viewed under several figures of speech in the New Testament (*see* ATONEMENT); whether it is spoken of as a ransom paid to redeem enslaved man, an acquittal before the divine bar of justice, or a victory over sin and death, it is clear throughout that the effective power in salvation belongs to God and not to man. Salvation is a free gift of God granted to lost and undeserving men who trust in the righteousness of Christ and humble themselves in submission to his will.

We may distinguish three aspects of salvation: past, present, and future. The salvation of regenerate man has already been accomplished in that his former sins have been forgiven and forgotten. He has passed from death to life and stands justified before God as one of his children. His heart has been sealed with the first fruits of the Spirit as a guarantee of his salvation, and eternal life is a present possession, freeing him from the fear of death. (*See* ETERNAL LIFE) In addition to this, however, there is a need for the "working out" of his salvation (*Phil. 2:12*), for the continual effort to make his "calling and election sure" (*2 Pet. 1:10*), for the denial of "ungodliness and worldly lusts" (*Tit. 2:12*) and the performance of "works of righteousness" as an external manifestation of a genuine inward transformation (*Jas. 2:14-26*). Finally, salvation is regarded as future in that the full measure of that for which we hope and now enjoy in part—the complete destruction of evil by the forces of good, the regeneration of heaven and earth, and eternal life in the presence of Father, Son, and Holy Spirit—will be made actual at the end of the age, when Christ comes again to reclaim his own.

See ATONEMENT, ELECTION, JUSTIFICATION, SANCTIFICATION, etc.

SCRIPTURE

Prayer for Salvation

Psa. 20 [9]Save, LORD: let the king hear us
when we call.

Psa. 54 [1]Save me, O God, by thy name,
and judge me by thy strength.

Psa. 71 [3]Be thou my strong habitation,
whereunto I may continually resort: thou
hast given commandment to save me; for
thou art my rock and my fortress.

Psa. 85 [7]Shew us thy mercy, O LORD,
and grant us thy salvation.

Psa. 86 [16]O turn unto me, and have
mercy upon me; give thy strength unto thy
servant, and save the son of thine handmaid.

Salvation by Grace

Acts 20 [24]But none of these things move
me, neither count I my life dear unto myself, so that I might finish my course with
joy, and the ministry, which I have received of the Lord Jesus, to testify the gospel of the grace of God.

Rom. 3 [24]Being justified freely by his
grace through the redemption that is in
Christ Jesus.

Rom. 5 [15]But not as the offence, so also
is the free gift. For if through the offence
of one many be dead, much more the grace
of God, and the gift by grace, which is by
one man, Jesus Christ, hath abounded unto
many. [16]And not as it was by one that
sinned, so is the gift: for the judgment was
by one to condemnation, but the free gift
is of many offences unto justification.
[17]For if by one man's offence death reigned
by one; much more they which receive
abundance of grace and of the gift of
righteousness shall reign in life by one,
Jesus Christ.

Rom. 11 [5]Even so then at this present
time also there is a remnant according to
the election of grace. [6]And if by grace,
then is it no more of works: otherwise
grace is no more grace. But if it be of
works, then is it no more grace: otherwise
work is no more work.

Eph. 1 [5]Having predestinated us unto
the adoption of children by Jesus Christ to
himself, according to the good pleasure of
his will, [6]To the praise of the glory of his
grace, wherein he hath made us accepted
in the beloved. [7]In whom we have redemption through his blood, the forgiveness of sins, according to the riches of his
grace.

Eph. 2 [4]But God who is rich in mercy,
for his great love wherewith he loved us,
[5]Even when we were dead in sins, hath
quickened us together with Christ, (by
grace ye are saved) [6]And hath raised us
up together, and made us sit together in
heavenly places in Christ Jesus: [7]That in
the ages to come he might shew the exceeding riches of his grace, in his kindness
towards us, through Christ Jesus. [8]For by
grace are ye saved, through faith, and that
not of yourselves: it is the gift of God:
[9]Not of works, lest any man should boast.
[10]For we are his workmanship, created in
Christ Jesus unto good works, which God

hath before ordained, that we should walk in them.

2 Tim. 1 [9]Who hath saved us, and called us with an holy calling, not according to our works, but according to his own purpose and grace, which was given us in Christ Jesus before the world began, [10]But is now made manifest by the appearing of our Saviour Jesus Christ, who hath abolished death, and hath brought life and immortality to light through the gospel.

Tit. 3 [5]Not by works of righteousness which we have done, but according to his mercy he saved us, by the washing of regeneration, and renewing of the Holy Ghost.

1 Pet. 1 [9]Receiving the end of your faith, even the salvation of your souls. [10]Of which salvation the prophets have enquired and searched diligently, who prophesied of the grace that should come unto you.

Salvation by Christ

Matt. 18 [14]For the Son of man is come to save that which was lost.

Luke 2 [10]And the angel said unto them, Fear not: for, behold, I bring you good tidings of great joy, which shall be to all people. [11]For unto you is born this day in the city of David a Saviour, which is Christ the Lord.

Luke 9 [56]For the Son of man is not come to destroy men's lives, but to save them. And they went to another village.

Luke 19 [10]For the Son of man is come to seek and to save that which was lost.

John 3 [17]For God sent not his Son into the world to condemn the world; but that the world through him might be saved.

Acts 4 [12]Neither is there salvation in any other: for there is none other name under heaven given among men, whereby we must be saved.

1 Thess. 5 [9]For God hath not appointed us to wrath, but to obtain salvation by our Lord Jesus Christ.

1 Tim. 1 [15]This is a faithful saying, and worthy of all acceptation, that Christ Jesus came into the world to save sinners; of whom I am chief.

1 John 2 [22]Who is a liar but he that denieth that Jesus is the Christ? He is antichrist, that denieth the Father and the Son.

1 John 4 [14]And we have seen and do testify that the Father sent the Son to be the Saviour of the world.

Conditions of Salvation

Matt. 3 [2]Repent ye: for the kingdom of heaven is at hand.

Matt. 18 [3]And said, Verily I say unto you, Except ye be converted, and become as little children, ye shall not enter into the kingdom of heaven.

Matt. 19 [16]And, behold, one came and said unto him, Good Master, what good thing shall I do, that I may have eternal life? [17]And he said unto him, Why callest thou me good? there is none good but one, that is, God: but if thou wilt enter into life, keep the commandments. [18]He saith unto him, Which? Jesus said, Thou shalt do no murder, Thou shalt not commit adultery, Thou shalt not steal, Thou shalt not bear false witness, [19]Honour thy father and thy mother: and, Thou shalt love thy neighbour as thyself. [20]The young man saith unto him, All these things have I kept from my youth up: what lack I yet? [21]Jesus said unto him, If thou wilt be perfect, go and sell that thou hast, and give to the poor, and thou shalt have treasure in heaven: and come and follow me.

Matt. 24 [13]But he that shall endure unto the end, the same shall be saved.

John 3 [3]Jesus answered and said unto him, Verily, verily, I say unto thee, Except

a man be born again, he cannot see the
kingdom of God. [4]Nicodemus saith unto
him, How can a man be born when he is
old? can he enter the second time into
his mother's womb, and be born? [5]Jesus
answered, Verily, verily I say unto thee,
Except a man be born of water and of the
Spirit, he cannot enter into the kingdom
of God.

[14]And as Moses lifted up the serpent in
the wilderness, even so must the Son of
man be lifted up: [15]That whosoever believeth in him should not perish, but have
eternal life.

[16]For God so loved the world, that he
gave his only begotten Son, that whosoever believeth in him should not perish,
but have everlasting life. [17]For God sent
not his Son into the world to condemn the
world; but that the world through him
might be saved.

[18]He that believeth on him is not condemned: but he that believeth not is condemned already, because he hath not believed in the name of the only begotten
Son of God.

John 5 [24]Verily, verily, I say unto you,
He that heareth my word, and believeth on
him that sent me, hath everlasting life, and
shall not come into condemnation; but is
passed from death unto life.

John 6 [28]Then said they unto him, What
shall we do, that we might work the works
of God? [29]Jesus answered and said unto
them, This is the work of God, that ye believe on him whom he hath sent.

Acts 2 [38]Then Peter said unto them, Repent, and be baptized every one of you in
the name of Jesus Christ for the remission
of sins, and ye shall receive the gift of the
Holy Ghost.

All Men May Accept Salvation

John 6 [37]All that the Father giveth me
shall come to me; and him that cometh to
me I will in no wise cast out.

Acts 2 [21]And it shall come to pass, that
whosoever shall call on the name of the
Lord shall be saved.

Rom. 5 [15]But not as the offence, so also
is the free gift: for if through the offence
of one many be dead, much more the grace
of God, and the gift by grace, which is by
one man, Jesus Christ, hath abounded unto
many. [16]And not as it was by one that
sinned, so is the gift: for the judgment was
by one to condemnation, but the free gift
is of many offences unto justification.
[17]For if by one man's offence death reigned
by one; much more they which receive
abundance of grace and of the gift of
righteousness shall reign in life by one,
Jesus Christ. [18]Therefore, as by the offence of one judgment came upon all men
to condemnation; even so by the righteousness of one the free gift came upon all
men unto justification of life. [19]For as by
one man's disobedience many were made
sinners, so by the obedience of one shall
many be made righteous. [20]Moreover the
law entered, that the offence might
abound. But where sin abounded, grace
did much more abound.

Rom. 10 [11]For the Scripture saith,
Whosoever believeth on him shall not be
ashamed. [13]For whosoever shall call upon
the name of the Lord shall be saved.

2 Cor. 5 [14]For the love of Christ con-
straineth us; because we thus judge, that
if one died for all, then were all dead:
[15]And that he died for all, that they which
live should not henceforth live unto themselves, but unto him which died for them,
and rose again.

1 Tim. 2 [3]For this is good and acceptable in the sight of God our Saviour;
[4]Who will have all men to be saved, and to
come unto the knowledge of the truth.

1 Tim. 4 9 This is a faithful saying, and
worthy of all acceptation. 10 For therefore
we both labour and suffer reproach, because we trust in the living God, who is
the Saviour of all men, specially of those
that believe.

2 Tim. 2 21 If a man therefore purge
himself from these, he shall be a vessel
unto honour, sanctified, and meet for the
master's use, and prepared unto every
good work.

Tit. 2 11 For the grace of God that bringeth salvation hath appeared to all men.

1 John 2 2 And he is the propitiation for
our sins: and not for ours only, but also for
the sins of the whole world.

Rev. 22 17 And the Spirit and the bride
say, Come. And let him that heareth say,
Come. And let him that is athirst come.
And whosoever will, let him take the water
of life freely.

But Few Are Saved

Matt. 7 13 Enter ye in at the strait gate:
for wide is the gate, and broad is the way,
that leadeth to destruction, and many
there be which go in thereat: 14 Because
strait is the gate, and narrow is the way,
which leadeth unto life, and few there be
that find it.

Luke 13 23 Then said one unto him,
Lord, are there few that be saved? And he
said unto them, 24 Strive to enter in at the
strait gate: for many, I say unto you, will
seek to enter in, and shall not be able.

Thanksgiving for Salvation

Luke 1 68 Blessed be the Lord God of
Israel; for he hath visited and redeemed
his people, 69 And hath raised up a horn
of salvation for us in the house of his servant David; 70 As he spake by the mouth of
his holy prophets, which have been since
the world began.

1 Cor. 15 57 But thanks be to God, which
giveth us the victory through our Lord
Jesus Christ.

2 Cor. 2 14 Now thanks be unto God,
which always causeth us to triumph in
Christ, and maketh manifest the savour of
his knowledge by us in every place.

2 Cor. 9 15 Thanks be unto God for his
unspeakable gift.

Eph. 1 3 Blessed be the God and Father
of our Lord Jesus Christ, who hath blessed
us with all spiritual blessings in heavenly
places in Christ.

Col. 1 12 Giving thanks unto the Father,
which hath made us meet to be partakers
of the inheritance of the saints in light:
13 Who hath delivered us from the power of
darkness, and hath translated us into the
kingdom of his dear Son.

1 Pet. 1 3 Blessed be the God and Father
of our Lord Jesus Christ, which according
to his abundant mercy hath begotten us
again unto a lively hope by the resurrection of Jesus Christ from the dead.

Salvation Past, Present, and Future

ALREADY ACCOMPLISHED

Rom. 8 16 The Spirit itself beareth witness with our spirit, that we are the children of God.

1 Cor. 1 18 For the preaching of the cross
is to them that perish, foolishness; but unto
us which are saved, it is the power of God.

Eph. 2 8 For by grace are ye saved
through faith; and that not of yourselves:
it is the gift of God:

IN PROCESS

Phil. 2 12 Wherefore, my beloved, as ye
have always obeyed, not as in my presence
only, but now much more in my absence,
work out your own salvation with fear and
trembling.

2 Pet. 1 10 Wherefore the rather, brethren, give diligence to make your calling and election sure: for if ye do these things, ye shall never fall: [11]For so an entrance shall be ministered unto you abundantly into the everlasting kingdom of our Lord and Saviour Jesus Christ.

YET TO BE COMPLETED

Matt. 10 [22]He that endureth to the end shall be saved.

Rom. 5 [9]Much more then, being now justified by his blood, we shall be saved from wrath through him. [10]For if, when we were enemies, we were reconciled to God by the death of his Son; much more, being reconciled, we shall be saved by his life.

Rom. 13 [11]For now is our salvation nearer than when we believed.

Phil. 3 [21]Who shall change our vile body, that it may be fashioned like unto his glorious body, according to the working whereby he is able even to subdue all things unto himself.

1 Thess. 5 [9]For God hath not appointed us to wrath, but to obtain salvation by our Lord Jesus Christ.

2 Tim. 2 [10]Therefore I endure all things for the elect's sake, that they may also obtain the salvation which is in Christ Jesus with eternal glory.

Heb. 1 [14]Are they not all ministering spirits, sent forth to minister for them who shall be heirs of salvation?

Heb. 9 [28]So Christ was once offered to bear the sins of many; and unto them that look for him shall he appear the second time without sin unto salvation.

1 Pet. 1 [5]Who are kept by the power of God through faith unto salvation ready to be revealed in the last time.

SAMARIA, SAMARITANS

[sa mā'ri a, sa mār'i tanz] Under Omri king of Israel (876-869 BC), the hill of Samaria in central Palestine became the site of the capital city of the northern kingdom. The hill was a natural fortress of great strength; it is a tribute to Omri's judgment that he chose it for his capital. The history of Samaria through the fall of the northern kingdom may be learned by consulting the articles in this book on the kings of Israel. (*See* KINGS OF JUDAH AND ISRAEL) When Sargon II took Samaria in 722 BC, a large number of its inhabitants were deported and replaced by elements from other parts of the empire. The Samaritans of which we read in post-exilic literature were the products of this mixed population. We know little of the history of Samaria under Assyrian and Babylonian rulers; however, when the exiles returned from Babylon under the edict of the Persian ruler, a group of Samaritans sought to aid in the rebuilding of the temple and wall of Jerusalem, but were refused any part in the proceedings. Angered by this rebuff they sought to thwart the building programs and were for a time successful. This enmity apparently continued to develop, for in the New Testament times we find Jews journeying from Galilee to Jerusalem by way of Perea instead of going through Samaria, simply in order to avoid any contact with the hated Samaritans. When this is understood, Jesus' story of the Good Samaritan becomes even more meaningful. In New Testament times, Samaria referred to the middle of the three provinces West of the Jordan, the others being Galilee to the North and Judaea to the South. There is to this day a religious division between Jews and Samaritans. The Samaritans carry on their worship in the ancient sanctuary on Mount Gerizim and stedfastly maintain that their copy of the Law of Moses was the only authentic one.

See OMRI, AMOS, HOSEA, NEHEMIAH, SANBALLAT, etc.

SCRIPTURE

Built by Omri

1 Kin. 16 [23]In the thirty and first year of Asa king of Judah began Omri to reign over Israel, twelve years: six years reigned he in Tirzah. [24]And he bought the hill Samaria of Shemer for two talents of silver, and built on the hill, and called the name of the city which he built, after the name of Shemer, owner of the hill, Samaria.

Defeated by Assyrians

2 Kin. 17 [5]Then the king of Assyria came up throughout all the land, and went up to Samaria, and besieged it three years.

[6]In the ninth year of Hoshea the king of Assyria took Samaria, and carried Israel away into Assyria, and placed them in Halah and in Habor by the river of Gozan, and in the cities of the Medes.

Hinder Rebuilding of Jerusalem

Neh. 4 [1]But it came to pass, that when Sanballat heard that we builded the wall, he was wroth, and took great indignation, and mocked the Jews. [2]And he spake before his brethren and the army of Samaria, and said, What do these feeble Jews? will they fortify themselves? will they sacrifice? will they make an end in a day? will they revive the stones out of the heaps of the rubbish which are burned?

[7]But it came to pass, that when Sanballat, and Tobiah, and the Arabians, and the Ammonites, and the Ashdodites, heard that the walls of Jerusalem were made up, and that the breaches began to be stopped, then they were very wroth.

Animosity Between Jews and Samaritans

John 4 [9]Then saith the woman of Samaria unto him, How is it that thou, being a Jew, askest drink of me, which am a woman of Samaria? for the Jews have no dealings with the Samaritans.

Jesus Speaks to Woman at the Well in Samaria

John 4 [1]When therefore the Lord knew how the Pharisees had heard that Jesus made and baptized more disciples than John, [2](Though Jesus himself baptized not, but his disciples,) [3]He left Judaea, and departed again into Galilee. [4]And he must needs go through Samaria. [5]Then cometh he to a city of Samaria, which is called Sychar, near to the parcel of ground that Jacob gave to his son Joseph. [6]Now Jacob's well was there. Jesus therefore, being wearied with his journey, sat thus on the well: and it was about the sixth hour. [7]There cometh a woman of Samaria to draw water: Jesus saith unto her, Give me to drink. [8](For his disciples were gone away unto the city to buy meat.) [9]Then saith the woman of Samaria unto him, How is it that thou, being a Jew, askest drink of me, which am a woman of Samaria? for the Jews have no dealings with the Samaritans. [10]Jesus answered and said unto her, If thou knewest the gift of God, and who it is that saith to thee, Give me to drink; thou wouldest have asked of him, and he would have given thee living water.

Samaritans Become Disciples

John 4 [39]And many of the Samaritans of that city believed on him for the saying of the woman, which testified, He told me all that ever I did. [40]So when the Samaritans were come unto him, they besought him that he would tarry with them: and he abode there two days. [41]And many more believed because of his own word; [42]And said unto the woman, Now we believe, not because of thy saying: for we have heard him ourselves, and know that this is indeed the Christ, the Saviour of the world.

Philip, Peter, and John Preach in Samaria

Acts 8 [4]Therefore they that were scattered abroad went everywhere preaching the word. [5]Then Philip went down to the city of Samaria, and preached Christ unto them. [14]Now when the apostles which were at Jerusalem heard that Samaria had received the word of God, they sent unto them Peter and John: [25]And they, when they had testified and preached the word of the Lord, returned to Jerusalem, and preached the gospel in many villages of the Samaritans.

SAMSON

[sam′sun] Samson is one of the most remarkable characters in the biblical narratives. He was the son of Manoah, a Danite, to whom his birth was announced by an angel. He served as a judge for twenty years and was a great champion of Israel in her conflicts with the Philistines. He was noted for his superhuman strength and his moral weakness. He married a Philistine woman against the wishes of his parents but later left her because she had revealed the secret of a riddle which he had put to the guests at the wedding feast. Among the great acts of strength with which Samson is credited are the burning of the crops of the Philistines by tying torches between the tails of 150 pairs of foxes, the slaying of 3,000 Philistines with the jawbone of an ass, and the uprooting of the city gates of Gaza. The secret of his phenomenal strength—which lay in his great mass of hair—was discovered by Delilah, a woman with whom he was in love, and he was betrayed by her after he had been shorn of his hair. His eyes were put out and he was taken to Gaza to work in the grinding house at the prison mill. At a great festival celebrating his capture, Samson pulled down the temple of Dagon. It is said of this last feat that "the dead that he slew at his death were more than they that he slew in his life" (*Judg. 16:29-30*).

See Judges, Delilah

SCRIPTURE

Birth Announced by Angel

Judg. 13 [2]And there was a certain man of Zorah, of the family of the Danites, whose name was Manoah; and his wife was barren, and bare not. [3]And the angel of the Lord appeared unto the woman, and said unto her, Behold, now, thou art barren, and bearest not: but thou shalt conceive, and bear a son. [4]Now therefore, beware I pray thee, and drink not wine, nor strong drink, and eat not any unclean thing: [5]For, lo, thou shalt conceive, and bear a son; and no razor shall come on his head: for the child shall be a Nazarite unto God from the womb: and he shall begin to deliver Israel out of the hand of the Philistines.

[24]And the woman bare a son, and called his name Samson. And the child grew, and the Lord blessed him.

Seeks a Wife Among the Philistines

Judg. 14 [1]And Samson went down to Timnath, and saw a woman in Timnath of the daughters of the Philistines. [2]And he came up, and told his father and his mother, and said, I have seen a woman in Timnath of the daughters of the Philistines: now therefore get her for me to wife. [3]Then his father and his mother said unto him, Is there never a woman among the daughters of thy brethren, or among all my people, that thou goest to take a wife of the uncircumcised Philistines? And Samson said unto his father, Get her for me; for she pleaseth me well. [4]But his father and his mother knew not that it was of the Lord, that he sought an occasion against the Philistines: for at that time the Philistines had dominion over Israel.

[5]Then went Samson down, and his father and his mother, to Timnath, and came to the vineyards of Timnath: and, behold, a young lion roared against him. [6]And the Spirit of the Lord came mightily upon him, and he rent him as he would have rent a kid, and he had nothing in his hand: but he told not his father or his mother what he

had done. [7]And he went down, and talked with the woman; and she pleased Samson well.

Defrauded by the Philistines

Judg. 14 [8]And after a time he returned to take her, and he turned aside to see the carcass of the lion: and, behold, there was a swarm of bees and honey in the carcass of the lion. [9]And he took thereof in his hands, and went on eating, and came to his father and mother, and he gave them, and they did eat: but he told not them that he had taken the honey out of the carcass of the lion.

[10]So his father went down unto the woman: and Samson made there a feast; for so used the young men to do. [11]And it came to pass, when they saw him, that they brought thirty companions to be with him.

[12]And Samson said unto them, I will now put forth a riddle unto you: if ye can certainly declare it me within the seven days of the feast, and find it out, then I will give you thirty sheets and thirty change of garments: [13]But if ye cannot declare it me, then shall ye give me thirty sheets and thirty change of garments. And they said unto him, Put forth thy riddle, that we may hear it. [14]And he said unto them, Out of the eater came forth meat, and out of the strong came forth sweetness. And they could not in three days expound the riddle. [15]And it came to pass on the seventh day, that they said unto Samson's wife, Entice thy husband, that he may declare unto us the riddle, lest we burn thee and thy father's house with fire: have ye called us to take that we have? is it not so? [16]And Samson's wife wept before him, and said, Thou dost but hate me, and lovest me not: thou hast put forth a riddle unto the children of my people, and hast not told it me. And he said unto her, Behold, I have not told it my father nor my mother, and shall I tell it thee? [17]And she wept before him the seven days, while their feast lasted: and it came to pass on the seventh day, that he told her, because she lay sore upon him: and she told the riddle to the children of her people. [18]And the men of the city said unto him on the seventh day before the sun went down, What is sweeter than honey? and what is stronger than a lion? And he said unto them, If ye had not ploughed with my heifer, ye had not found out my riddle.

His Revenge

Judg. 14 [19]And the Spirit of the LORD came upon him, and he went down to Ashkelon, and slew thirty men of them, and took their spoil, and gave change of garments unto them which expounded the riddle. And his anger was kindled, and he went up to his father's house. [20]But Samson's wife was given to his companion, whom he had used as his friend.

Judg. 15 [1]But it came to pass within a while after, in the time of wheat harvest, that Samson visited his wife with a kid; and he said, I will go in to my wife into the chamber. But her father would not suffer him to go in. [2]And her father said, I verily thought that thou hadst utterly hated her; therefore I gave her to thy companion: is not her younger sister fairer than she? take her, I pray thee, instead of her.

[3]And Samson said concerning them, Now shall I be more blameless than the Philistines, though I do them a displeasure. [4]And Samson went and caught three hundred foxes, and took firebrands, and turned tail to tail, and put a firebrand in the midst between two tails. [5]And when he had set the brands on fire, he let them go into the standing corn of the Philistines,

and burnt up both the shocks, and also the standing corn, with the vineyards and olives.

6Then the Philistines said, Who hath done this? And they answered, Samson, the son in law of the Timnite, because he had taken his wife, and given her to his companion. And the Philistines came up, and burnt her and her father with fire.

7And Samson said unto them, Though ye have done this, yet will I be avenged of you, and after that I will cease. 8And he smote them hip and thigh with a great slaughter: and he went down and dwelt in the top of the rock Etam.

Slays a Thousand with the Jawbone of an Ass

Judg. 15 9Then the Philistines went up, and pitched in Judah, and spread themselves in Lehi. 10And the men of Judah said, Why are ye come up against us? And they answered, To bind Samson are we come up, to do to him as he hath done to us. 11Then three thousand men of Judah went to the top of the rock Etam, and said to Samson, Knowest thou not that the Philistines are rulers over us? what is this that thou hast done unto us? And he said unto them, As they did unto me, so have I done unto them. 12And they said unto him, We are come down to bind thee, that we may deliver thee into the hand of the Philistines. And Samson said unto them, Swear unto me, that ye will not fall upon me yourselves. 13And they spake unto him, saying, No; but we will bind thee fast, and deliver thee into their hand: but surely we will not kill thee. And they bound him with two new cords, and brought him up from the rock.

14And when he came unto Lehi, the Philistines shouted against him: and the Spirit of the LORD came mightily upon him, and the cords that were upon his arms became as flax that was burnt with fire, and his bands loosed from off his hands. 15And he found a new jawbone of an ass, and put forth his hand, and took it, and slew a thousand men therewith. 16And Samson said, With the jawbone of an ass, heaps upon heaps, with the jaw of an ass have I slain a thousand men. 17And it came to pass, when he had made an end of speaking, that he cast away the jawbone out of his hand, and called that place Ramath-lehi.

Samson in Gaza

Judg. 16 1Then went Samson to Gaza, and saw there a harlot, and went in unto her. 2And it was told the Gazites, saying, Samson is come hither. And they compassed him in, and laid wait for him all night in the gate of the city, and were quiet all the night, saying, In the morning when it is day we shall kill him. 3And Samson lay till midnight, and arose at midnight, and took the doors of the gate of the city, and the two posts, and went away with them, bar and all, and put them upon his shoulders, and carried them up to the top of a hill that is before Hebron.

Samson and Delilah

Judg. 16 4And it came to pass afterward, that he loved a woman in the valley of Sorek, whose name was Delilah. 5And the lords of the Philistines came up unto her, and said unto her, Entice him, and see wherein his great strength lieth, and by what means we may prevail against him, that we may bind him to afflict him: and we will give thee every one of us eleven hundred pieces of silver.

6And Delilah said to Samson, Tell me, I pray thee, wherein thy great strength lieth, and wherewith thou mightest be bound to afflict thee. 7And Samson said unto her, If they bind me with seven green withs that were never dried, then shall I be weak, and be as another man. 8Then the lords of the Philistines brought up to her seven green withs which had not been dried, and she bound him with them. 9Now there were men lying in wait, abiding with her in the chamber. And she said unto him, The Philistines be upon thee, Samson. And he brake the withs, as a thread of tow is broken when it toucheth the fire. So his strength was not known. 10And Delilah said unto Samson, Behold, thou hast mocked me, and told me lies: now tell me, I pray thee, wherewith thou mightest be bound. 11And he said unto her, If they bind me fast with new ropes that never were occupied, then shall I be weak, and be as another man. 12Delilah therefore took new ropes, and bound him therewith, and said unto him, The Philistines be upon thee, Samson. And there were liers in wait abiding in the chamber. And he brake them from off his arms like a thread. 13And Delilah said unto Samson, Hitherto thou hast mocked me, and told me lies: tell me wherewith thou mightest be bound. And he said unto her, If thou weavest the seven locks of my head with the web. 14And she fastened it with the pin, and said unto him, The Philistines be upon thee, Samson. And he awaked out of his sleep, and went away with the pin of the beam, and with the web.

15And she said unto him, How canst thou say, I love thee, when thine heart is not with me? Thou hast mocked me these three times, and hast not told me wherein thy great strength lieth. 16And it came to pass, when she pressed him daily with her words, and urged him, so that his soul was vexed unto death; 17That he told her all his heart, and said unto her, There hath not come a razor upon mine head; for I have been a Nazarite unto God from my mother's womb: if I be shaven, then my strength will go from me, and I shall become weak, and be like any other man. 18And when Delilah saw that he had told her all his heart, she sent and called for the lords of the Philistines, saying, Come up this once, for he hath shewed me all his heart. Then the lords of the Philistines came up unto her, and brought money in their hand. 19And she made him sleep upon her knees; and she called for a man, and she caused him to shave off the seven locks of his head; and she began to afflict him, and his strength went from him. 20And she said, The Philistines be upon thee, Samson. And he awoke out of his sleep, and said, I will go out as at other times before, and shake myself. And he wist not that the LORD was departed from him.

21But the Philistines took him, and put out his eyes, and brought him down to Gaza, and bound him with fetters of brass; and he did grind in the prison house. 22Howbeit the hair of his head began to grow again after he was shaven.

The Death of Samson

Judg. 16 23Then the lords of the Philistines gathered them together for to offer a great sacrifice unto Dagon their god, and to rejoice: for they said, Our god hath delivered Samson our enemy into our hand. 24And when the people saw him, they praised their god: for they said, Our god hath delivered into our hands our enemy, and the destroyer of our country, which slew many of us. 25And it came to pass, when their hearts were merry, that they said, Call for Samson, that he may make us sport. And they called for Samson out of the prison house; and he made them sport:

and they set him between the pillars.
26And Samson said unto the lad that held
him by the hand, Suffer me that I may feel
the pillars whereupon the house standeth,
that I may lean upon them. 27Now the
house was full of men and women; and all
the lords of the Philistines were there; and
there were upon the roof about three thousand men and women, that beheld while
Samson made sport. 28And Samson called
unto the LORD, and said, O Lord GOD, remember me, I pray thee, and strengthen
me, I pray thee, only this once, O God, that
I may be at once avenged of the Philistines
for my two eyes. 29And Samson took hold
of the two middle pillars upon which the
house stood, and on which it was borne
up, of the one with his right hand, and of
the other with his left. 30And Samson said,
Let me die with the Philistines. And he
bowed himself with all his might; and the
house fell upon the lords, and upon all the
people that were therein. So the dead
which he slew at his death were more than
they which he slew in his life.

SAMUEL

[sam'û el] A judge and prophet of Israel, the son of Elkanah and Hannah. Hannah, who had been childless many years, prayed to God to give her a son, vowing to consecrate him to the LORD's service. Her prayer was answered and the child, Samuel, was put under the care of Eli, priest of the central sanctuary at Shiloh. While there, Samuel was used by God to inform Eli that his house would be punished for the abuses to which his sons had subjected the priesthood. (*See* HOPHNI AND PHINEHAS) Samuel next appears as the head of an assembly called at Mizpah. Here he offered sacrifice and assured the Israelites of victory over the Philistines. This is followed by the narrative of the defeat of the Philistines and the erection of the memorial stone, Ebenezer, the "stone of help." (*See* EBENEZER) From that time forward he served in the capacity of prophet and judge, traveling a yearly circuit which included Bethel, Gilgal, Mizpah, and his home, Ramah. When Israel insisted upon a king to rule over it, Samuel anointed Saul privately in Ramah and then presided over the formal election at Mizpah. Samuel's attitude toward the new monarchy is a bit ambiguous, but he displayed an awareness of the abuses which could arise in such an arrangement. Samuel's relationship to Saul is an interesting one in that he seems to have possessed more authority than did the king; in fact, the function of the prophet as a king-maker and king-breaker (*see* PROPHETS AND PROPHECY) is especially clear in Samuel, not only in the incidents noted above but in his denunciation of Saul for his usurpation of the priestly functions at Gilgal (*1 Sam. 13*) and his disobedience concerning Agag (*1 Sam. 15*) and in his anointing of David to succeed Saul while the latter was still flourishing. At Samuel's death he was widely lamented and buried at his home in Ramah.

See HANNAH, ELI, SAUL, AGAG, etc.

SCRIPTURE

Birth and Dedication to God

1 Sam. 1 20Wherefore it came to pass,
when the time was come about after Hannah had conceived, that she bare a son, and
called his name Samuel, saying, Because
I have asked him of the LORD.
26And she said, O my lord, as thy soul
liveth, my lord, I am the woman that stood
by thee here, praying unto the LORD. 27For
this child I prayed; and the LORD hath
given me my petition which I asked of him:
28Therefore also I have lent him to the
LORD; as long as he liveth he shall be lent
to the LORD. And he worshipped the LORD
there.

Samuel's Call

1 Sam. 3 8And the LORD called Samuel
again the third time. And he arose and
went to Eli, and said, Here am I; for thou
didst call me. And Eli perceived that the
LORD had called the child. 10And the
LORD came, and stood, and called as at

other times, Samuel, Samuel. Then Samuel answered, Speak; for thy servant heareth.

[19]And Samuel grew, and the LORD was with him, and did let none of his words fall to the ground. [20]And all Israel, from Dan even to Beersheba, knew that Samuel was established to be a prophet of the LORD.

Samuel Judges Israel

1 Sam. 7 [15]And Samuel judged Israel all the days of his life. [16]And he went from year to year in circuit to Bethel, and Gilgal, and Mizpeh, and judged Israel in all those places. [17]And his return was to Ramah; for there was his house; and there he judged Israel; and there he built an altar unto the LORD.

Samuel Asked to Make a King

1 Sam. 8 [5]And said unto him, Behold, thou art old, and thy sons walk not in thy ways: now make us a king to judge us like all the nations.

[6]But the thing displeased Samuel, when they said, Give us a king to judge us. And Samuel prayed unto the LORD. [7]And the LORD said unto Samuel, Hearken unto the voice of the people in all that they say unto thee: for they have not rejected thee, but they have rejected me, that I should not reign over them. [8]According to all the works which they have done since the day that I brought them up out of Egypt even unto this day, wherewith they have forsaken me, and served other gods, so do they also unto thee. [9]Now therefore hearken unto their voice: howbeit yet protest solemnly unto them, and shew them the manner of the king that shall reign over them.

[10]And Samuel told all the words of the LORD unto the people that asked of him a king.

Samuel Makes Saul King

1 Sam. 9 [15]Now the LORD had told Samuel in his ear a day before Saul came, saying, [16]Tomorrow about this time, I will send thee a man out of the land of Benjamin, and thou shalt anoint him to be captain over my people Israel, that he may save my people out of the hand of the Philistines: for I have looked upon my people, because their cry is come unto me. [17]And when Samuel saw Saul, the LORD said unto him, Behold the man whom I spake to thee of! this same shall reign over my people.

1 Sam. 10 [1]Then Samuel took a vial of oil, and poured it upon his head, and kissed him, and said, Is it not because the LORD hath anointed thee to be captain over his inheritance?

David Anointed by Samuel

1 Sam. 16 [1]And the Lord said unto Samuel, How long wilt thou mourn for Saul, seeing I have rejected him from reigning over Israel? fill thine horn with oil, and go, I will send thee to Jesse the Bethlehemite: for I have provided me a king among his sons.

[13]Then Samuel took the horn of oil, and anointed him in the midst of his brethren: and the Spirit of the Lord came upon David from that day forward. So Samuel rose up, and went to Ramah.

Samuel's Death

1 Sam. 25 [1]And Samuel died: and all the Israelites were gathered together, and lamented him, and buried him in his house at Ramah. And David arose, and went down to the wilderness of Paran.

SANBALLAT, TOBIAH, AND GESHEM

[san bal′at, tō̂ bī′a, gē̆′shem] The individuals

who offered continual harassment to Nehemiah during the period in which he was rebuilding the wall of Jerusalem after the return from Babylonian captivity (c. 440 BC). Sanballat was governor of the province of Samaria, Tobiah was governor of the province of Ammon in Transjordan, and Geshem was a chieftain who governed the province of Arabia. The tactics which they used to discourage Nehemiah's project included ridicule, threats of attack, and a plot to murder Nehemiah. Nehemiah proved to be more than a match for them. He refused to be intimidated by any of their ruses and counteracted threats of attack by dividing his men into two forces, one to work and the other to stand ready to fight. After the walls were finally brought to completion, no further harassment is mentioned. Tobiah appears once more during Nehemiah's second term in office. He had taken advantage of Nehemiah's temporary return to Babylon, and, with the approval of Eliashib the priest, had moved into one of the rooms in the temple normally used to store offerings. When Nehemiah returned from Babylon and learned of this, he reported that "it grieved me sore: therefore I cast forth all the household stuff of Tobiah out of the chamber."

See EZRA, NEHEMIAH

SCRIPTURE

Oppose Nehemiah

Neh. 4 1 But it came to pass, that when
Sanballat heard that we builded the wall,
he was wroth, and took great indignation,
and mocked the Jews. 2 And he spake before his brethren and the army of Samaria,
and said, What do these feeble Jews? will
they fortify themselves? will they sacrifice? will they make an end in a day? will
they revive the stones out of the heaps of
the rubbish which are burned? 3 Now Tobiah the Ammonite was by him, and he
said, Even that which they build, if a fox
go up, he shall even break down their stone
wall. 4 Hear, O our God; for we are despised: and turn their reproach upon their
own head, and give them for a prey in the
land of captivity: 5 And cover not their iniquity, and let not their sin be blotted out
from before thee: for they have provoked
thee to anger before the builders. 6 So
built we the wall; and all the wall was
joined together unto the half thereof: for
the people had a mind to work.

7 But it came to pass, that when Sanballat, and Tobiah, and the Arabians, and
the Ammonites, and the Ashdodites, heard
that the walls of Jerusalem were made up,
and that the breaches began to be stopped,
then they were very wroth, 8 And conspired all of them together to come and to
fight against Jerusalem, and to hinder it.

Foiled by Nehemiah

Neh. 6 1 Now it came to pass, when Sanballat, and Tobiah, and Geshem the Arabian, and the rest of our enemies, heard
that I had builded the wall, and that there
was no breach left therein; (though at that
time I had not set up the doors upon the
gates;) 2 That Sanballat and Geshem sent
unto me, saying, Come, let us meet together in some one of the villages in the
plain of Ono. But they thought to do me
mischief. 3 And I sent messengers unto
them, saying, I am doing a great work, so
that I can not come down: why should the
work cease, whilst I leave it, and come
down to you? 4 Yet they sent unto me four
times after this sort; and I answered them
after the same manner.

15 So the wall was finished in the twenty
and fifth day of the month Elul, in fifty and
two days.

SANCTIFY, SANCTIFICATION

[sank'ti fī, sank ti fi kā'shun] To make holy; the process of being made or becoming holy. Holiness belongs properly to God and it is he alone who can impart holiness, who can effect sanctification in our lives. The long history of his efforts to redeem humanity, culminating in Jesus Christ, is an expression of his desire to sanctify men, to set them apart for his purposes. The teaching of the New Testament compels us to view sanctification in a double aspect: it is accomplished not through achievement of moral perfection but in the reception of the gift of the Holy Spirit; yet, the saint—one who has been sanctified—must constantly seek to bring his sanctification to completion through consecration to Christ which manifests itself in turning from worldliness to the service of righteousness and perfect holiness.

SCRIPTURE

Sanctification by Christ

John 17 19And for their sakes I sanctify myself, that they also might be sanctified through the truth.

1 Cor. 1 2Unto the church of God which is at Corinth, to them that are sanctified in Christ Jesus, called to be saints, with all that in every place call upon the name of Jesus Christ our Lord, both theirs and ours.
30But of him are ye in Christ Jesus, who of God is made unto us wisdom, and righteousness, and sanctification, and redemption.

1 Cor. 6 11And such were some of you: but ye are washed, but ye are sanctified, but ye are justified in the name of the Lord Jesus, and by the Spirit of our God.

Eph. 5 26That he might sanctify and cleanse it with the washing of water by the word.

Heb. 2 11For both he that sanctifieth and they who are sanctified are all of one: for which cause he is not ashamed to call them brethren.

Heb. 10 10By the which will we are sanctified through the offering of the body of Jesus Christ once for all.

Jude 1 1Jude, the servant of Jesus Christ, and brother of James, to them that are sanctified by God the Father, and preserved in Jesus Christ, and called.

Sanctification by the Holy Ghost

Rom. 15 16That I should be the minister of Jesus Christ to the Gentiles, ministering the gospel of God, that the offering up of the Gentiles might be acceptable, being sanctified by the Holy Ghost.

2 Thess. 2 13But we are bound to give thanks alway to God for you, brethren beloved of the Lord, because God hath from the beginning chosen you to salvation through sanctification of the Spirit and belief of the truth.

1 Pet. 1 2Elect according to the foreknowledge of God the Father, through sanctification of the Spirit, unto obedience and sprinkling of the blood of Jesus Christ: Grace unto you, and peace, be multiplied.

SANCTUARY

[sank′tů å ri] A sacred spot; a consecrated place; the most sacred part of any religious edifice; a building consecrated to the worship of God; also, a sacred asylum or place of refuge.

See TABERNACLE; TEMPLE; REFUGE, CITIES OF

SCRIPTURE

Ex. 25 8And let them make me a sanctuary; that I may dwell among them.

Lev. 19 30Ye shall keep my sabbaths, and reverence my sanctuary: I am the LORD.

Num. 18 5And ye shall keep the charge of the sanctuary, and the charge of the altar: that there be no wrath any more upon the children of Israel.

Lam. 2 7The LORD hath cast off his altar, he hath abhorred his sanctuary, he hath given up into the hand of the enemy the walls of her palaces; they have made a noise in the house of the LORD, as in the day of a solemn feast.

[20]Behold, O LORD, and consider to whom thou hast done this. Shall the women eat their fruit, and children of a span long? shall the priest and the prophet be slain in the sanctuary of the LORD?

Ezek. 11 [16]Therefore say, Thus saith the Lord GOD; Although I have cast them far off among the heathen, and although I have scattered them among the countries, yet will I be to them as a little sanctuary in the countries where they shall come.

Ezek. 42 [20]He measured it by the four sides: it had a wall round about, five hundred reeds long, and five hundred broad, to make a separation between the sanctuary and the profane place.

Heb. 8 [2]A minister of the sanctuary, and of the true tabernacle, which the Lord pitched, and not man.

Heb. 9 [2]For there was a tabernacle made; the first, wherein was the candlestick, and the table, and the shewbread, which is called the sanctuary.

SANHEDRIN

[san'hê drin] The supreme council of the Jews in the time of Christ and earlier, before which Jesus, Stephen, Peter, John, Paul, and others of the apostles appeared. In the New Testament it is usually referred to simply as "the council." It consisted of seventy-one members and sat at Jerusalem. Although its origins are somewhat uncertain, it is generally thought to have begun during the era of Alexander the Great. The power and influence of the Sanhedrin were greatest during the period of Roman rule in Palestine. It served as a major instrument of justice among the Jews, handling all matters pertaining to the Jewish Law and many criminal matters. It was not empowered to administer capital punishment, but, in most cases, it seems that the Roman official handed down judgments in line with the recommendations of the Sanhedrin. Less important tribunals, consisting of twenty-three members each, were also designated by this term.

SCRIPTURE

Matt. 26 [59]Now the chief priests, and elders, and all the council, sought false witness against Jesus, to put him to death.

Acts 4 [15]But when they had commanded them to go aside out of the council, they conferred among themselves.

Acts 5 [21]And when they heard that, they entered into the temple early in the morning, and taught. But the high priest came, and they that were with him, and called the council together, and all the senate of the children of Israel, and sent to the prison to have them brought.

Acts 6 [12]And they stirred up the people, and the elders, and the scribes, and came upon him, and caught him, and brought him to the council,

Acts 22 [30]On the morrow, because he would have known the certainty wherefore he was accused of the Jews, he loosed him from his bands, and commanded the chief priests and all their council to appear, and brought Paul down, and set him before them.

Acts 24 [20]Or else let these same here say, if they have found any evil doing in me, while I stood before the council,

SARAH, SARAI

[sā'ra, sā'rī] The wife of Abraham and mother of Isaac, called Sarai before her name was changed. Sarah became Abraham's wife while he was still a resident in Ur of the Chaldees. She was also a half-sister to Abraham; the brief story of Abraham's life contains two accounts of his having made use of this fact to save his life. To both the Egyptian Pharaoh and Abimelech king of Gerar, Abraham presented Sarah as his sister and allowed her to be taken into the royal harem, fearing that he would be killed if the rulers desired her, but knew she was his wife. In both cases she was returned untouched but the kings involved were understandably vexed at Abraham.

In the first passage which mentions Sarah, she

is described as follows: "But Sarai was barren; she had no child." Apart from the two narratives noted above, the bulk of the material concerning Sarai centers around her barrenness and eventually childbearing. Despairing of bearing a child for Abraham, she gave him her handmaid Hagar, the arrangement being that all children born of this union would be reckoned as Sarah's. When the slave-woman became contemptuous of her mistress, Sarah sent her away; Hagar returned, however, and gave birth to Ishmael. Finally, after mocking the word of the LORD that she should bear a child, Sarah became the mother of the promised son Isaac. Despite the blessing of the LORD which she had received, Sarah marred the feast celebrating the weaning of this child by insisting that Hagar and Ishmael be expelled from the camp. At Sarah's death, Abraham purchased from Ephron the Hittite the cave in the field of Machpelah which was to become the burial ground of the classic ancestors of Israel.

See HAGAR, ISHMAEL

SCRIPTURE

Abraham's Wife

Gen. 11 [29]And Abram and Nahor took them wives: the name of Abram's wife was Sarai; and the name of Nahor's wife, Milcah, the daughter of Haran, the father of Milcah, and the father of Iscah. [30]But Sarai was barren; she had no child.

Abraham Deceives Pharaoh Concerning Sarah

Gen. 12 [10]And there was a famine in the land: and Abram went down into Egypt to sojourn there; for the famine was grievous in the land.

[14]And it came to pass, that, when Abram was come into Egypt, the Egyptians beheld the woman that she was very fair. [15]The princes also of Pharaoh saw her, and commended her before Pharaoh: and the woman was taken into Pharaoh's house. [16]And he entreated Abram well for her sake: and he had sheep, and oxen, and he-asses, and menservants, and maidservants, and she-asses, and camels. [17]And the LORD plagued Pharaoh and his house with great plagues, because of Sarai, Abram's wife. [18]And Pharaoh called Abram, and said, What is this that thou hast done unto me? why didst thou not tell me that she was thy wife? [19]Why saidst thou, She is my sister? so I might have taken her to me to wife: now therefore behold thy wife, take her, and go thy way. [20]And Pharaoh commanded his men concerning him: and they sent him away, and his wife, and all that he had.

Gives Hagar to Abraham

Gen. 16 [1]Now Sarai, Abram's wife, bare him no children: and she had a handmaid, an Egyptian, whose name was Hagar. [2]And Sarai said unto Abram, Behold now, the LORD hath restrained me from bearing: I pray thee, go in unto my maid; it may be that I may obtain children by her. And Abram hearkened to the voice of Sarai. [3]And Sarai, Abram's wife, took Hagar her maid the Egyptian, after Abram had dwelt ten years in the land of Canaan, and gave her to her husband Abram to be his wife.

Sends Hagar Away

Gen. 16 [4]And he went in unto Hagar, and she conceived: and when she saw that she had conceived, her mistress was despised in her eyes. [5]And Sarai said unto Abram, My wrong be upon thee: I have given my maid into thy bosom; and when she saw that she had conceived, I was despised in her eyes: the LORD judge between me and thee. [6]But Abram said unto Sarai, Behold, thy maid is in thy hand; do to her as it pleaseth thee. And when Sarai dealt hardly with her, she fled from her face.

Sarah Bears a Son

Gen. 21 [1]And the LORD visited Sarah as

he had said, and the LORD did unto Sarah
as he had spoken. [2]For Sarah conceived,
and bare Abraham a son in his old age, at
the set time of which God had spoken to
him. [3]And Abraham called the name of
his son that was born unto him, whom
Sarah bare to him, Isaac.

Death and Burial

Gen. 23 [1]And Sarah was a hundred and
seven and twenty years old: these were the
years of the life of Sarah. [2]And Sarah died
in Kirjath-arba; the same is Hebron in the
land of Canaan: and Abraham came to
mourn for Sarah, and to weep for her.
[19]And after this, Abraham buried Sarah
his wife in the cave of the field of Machpelah before Mamre: the same is Hebron
in the land of Canaan.

SARGON

[sär'gon] King of Assyria (722-705 BC). Although Shalmaneser V began the campaign which resulted in the final overthrow of the northern kingdom of Israel, archaeological findings indicate that he died before bringing it to completion and that the city actually fell to his successor, Sargon II. It was apparently during Sargon's reign that various tribes of people were brought into Israel to replace those who had been taken captive to Assyria. The people designated in the Bible as Samaritans are descendent of this stock.

During the reign of Hezekiah a coalition was formed to rebel against Sargon. There was pressure upon Judah to join, but the sentiment represented by Isaiah (*see Isa. 20*) was apparently stronger and Hezekiah seems to have refused to take part in the rebellion. This proved to be a prudent policy, as the allies suffered a thoroughly crushing defeat. Hezekiah remained a tributary of Assyria throughout the rest of Sargon's reign, although he did attempt revolt under Sennacherib, Sargon's successor.

See SENNACHERIB, HEZEKIAH

REFERENCE: *Isa. 20.*

SATAN

[sā'tan] Literally, an adversary or accuser; one who distresses or strives against another. This word is used in portions of the Old Testament and throughout the New Testament as the proper name of the supreme supernatural adversary, also called the Devil. The opposition between Satan and God is made clear in the New Testament, in which Satan is seen as a leader of the forces of evil (*Matt. 12:26*) and the agent in the temptations of Jesus (*Matt. 4:10*), Peter (*Matt. 16:23*), Judas (*Luke 22:3*), and Ananias (*Acts 5:3*). Through the life and atoning acts of Jesus, Satan has been overcome, but he still seeks to gain the advantage over us (*2 Cor. 2:11*).

See BEELZEBUB, DEMONS

SCRIPTURE

Matt. 4 [10]Then saith Jesus unto him,
Get thee hence, Satan: for it is written,
Thou shalt worship the Lord thy God, and
him only shalt thou serve.
Matt. 12 [26]And if Satan cast out Satan,
he is divided against himself; how shall
then his kingdom stand?
Matt. 16 [23]But he turned, and said unto
Peter, Get thee behind me, Satan: thou art
an offense unto me: for thou savorest not
the things that be of God, but those that be
of men.
Luke 22 [3]Then entered Satan into Judas
surnamed Iscariot, being of the number of
the twelve.
Acts 4 [3]But Peter said, Ananias, why
hath Satan filled thine heart to lie to the
Holy Ghost, and to keep back part of the
price of the land?
2 Cor. 2 [11]Lest Satan should get an advantage of us: for we are not ignorant of
his devices.

SAUL

[sôl] A Benjaminite, the son of Kish, and the first king of Israel. When Israel clamored for a king, Saul was privately anointed by Samuel in

Ramah and later elected by a popular assembly at Mizpah. Saul's strength as a king was derived mainly from his success as a warrior and commander. The official acceptance of his leadership seems to have come at Gilagal after he had delivered Jabesh-gilead from the Ammonites. With the aid of his son Jonathan at Michmash he climaxed a series of encounters which resulted in the successful overthrow of the Philistines, Israel's constant foe. It is said of Saul that "he fought against all his enemies on every side . . . wherever he turned he put them to the worse" (*1 Sam. 14:47*). A number of the judges had also been outstanding military leaders, but Saul was distinguished from them by a leadership which was national in scope and a permanence of office which the judges did not possess. (*See* JUDGES) In most other respects, however, his rule was not greatly unlike theirs. He possessed no harem or staff of attendants. His royal dwelling place at Gibeah, which has been excavated by archaeologists, more closely resembled a large fortress than the palaces of later kings.

Despite an auspicious beginning, the greater part of Saul's reign was a disappointing and tragic affair. Toward the end of his life, he seems to have been quite close to insanity. The deterioration began with his break with Samuel, arising over his assumption of the priestly privileges at Gilgal, before the battle with the Philistines (*see 1 Sam. 13*), and becoming complete with his sparing of Agag king of the Amalekites in opposition to the laws of Holy Warfare. (*See* WAR) The latter phase of Saul's reign is best remembered for his unbalanced behavior toward David. After his introduction at the court of Saul, David had become an extremely popular figure with the people of Israel. Filled with insane jealousy, Saul spent his last years in repeated efforts to track down and kill him, despite David's repeated expression of loyalty. One particularly shocking episode in connection with this mad pursuit was Saul's slaughter of the priests at Nob after they had given aid to the fleeing David. Saul's obsession with David caused him to neglect other matters of the new kingdom; foremost among these was the Philistine problem. In the interim since Michmash, the Philitines had strengthened their forces and were awaiting the opportunity to strike back at Israel. Despite the prediction of tragedy received through the medium at Endor, Saul encamped against the Philistines at the foot of Mount Gilboa. The Philistines scored a complete victory; Saul's three sons were slain and the king took his own life after being wounded. The Philistines cut off Saul's head and hung his body, along with those of his sons, on the wall of Beth-shan. The men of Jabesh-gilead, still loyal to Saul, removed the bodies, burned them and buried the bones in Jabesh.

See DAVID, SAMUEL

SCRIPTURE

Parentage and Choice as King

1 Sam. 9 [1]Now there was a man of Benjamin, whose name was Kish, the son of Abiel, the son of Zeror, the son of Bechorath, the son of Aphiah, a Benjamite, a mighty man of power. [2]And he had a son, whose name was Saul, a choice young man, and a goodly: and there was not among the children of Israel a goodlier person than he: from his shoulders and upward he was higher than any of the people.

[17]And when Samuel saw Saul, the LORD said unto him, Behold the man whom I spake to thee of! this same shall reign over my people.

1 Sam. 10 [1]Then Samuel took a vial of oil, and poured it upon his head, and kissed him, and said, Is it not because the LORD hath anointed thee to be captain over his inheritance?

1 Sam. 11 [15]And all the people went to Gilgal; and there they made Saul king before the LORD in Gilgal; there they sacrificed sacrifices of peace offerings before the LORD, and there Saul and all the men of Israel rejoiced greatly.

1 Sam. 15 [7]And Saul smote the Amalekites from Havilah until thou comest to Shur, that is over against Egypt. [8]And he took Agag the king of the Amalekites alive, and utterly destroyed all the people with the edge of the sword. [9]But Saul and the people spared Agag, and the best of the sheep, and of the oxen, and of the fatlings, and the lambs, and all that was good, and would not utterly destroy them: but every thing that was vile and refuse, that they destroyed utterly.

[10]Then came the word of the LORD unto Samuel, saying, [11]It repenteth me that I have set up Saul to be king: for he is turned back from following me, and hath not performed my commandments. And it grieved Samuel; and he cried unto the LORD all night.

See 1 Sam. 15:22-23

Jealousy and Fear of David

1 Sam. 18 [7]And the women answered one another as they played, and said, Saul hath slain his thousands, and David his ten thousands. [8]And Saul was very wroth, and the saying displeased him; and he said, They have ascribed unto David ten thousands, and to me they have ascribed but thousands: and what can he have more but the kingdom? [9]And Saul eyed David from that day and forward.

[10]And it came to pass on the morrow, that the evil spirit from God came upon Saul, and he prophesied in the midst of the house: and David played with his hand, as at other times: and there was a javelin in Saul's hand. [11]And Saul cast the javelin; for he said, I will smite David even to the wall with it. And David avoided out of his presence twice.

[12]And Saul was afraid of David, because the LORD was with him, and was departed from Saul.

Tries to Kill David

1 Sam. 23 [8]And Saul called all the people together to war, to go down to Keilah, to besiege David and his men.

[14]And David abode in the wilderness in strong holds, and remained in a mountain in the wilderness of Ziph. And Saul sought him every day, but God delivered him not into his hand.

Life Spared by David

1 Sam. 24 [1]And it came to pass, when Saul was returned from following the Philistines, that it was told him, saying, Behold, David is in the wilderness of Engedi. [2]Then Saul took three thousand chosen men out of all Israel, and went to seek David and his men upon the rocks of the wild goats. [3]And he came to the sheepcotes by the way, where was a cave; and Saul went in to cover his feet: and David and his men remained in the sides of the cave. [4]And the men of David said unto him, Behold the day of which the LORD said unto thee, Behold, I will deliver thine enemy into thine hand, that thou mayest do to him as it shall seem good unto thee. Then David arose, and cut off the skirt of Saul's robe privily.

1 Sam. 26 [7]So David and Abishai came to the people by night: and, behold, Saul lay sleeping within the trench, and his spear stuck in the ground at his bolster: but Abner and the people lay round about him. [8]Then said Abishai to David, God hath delivered thine enemy into thine hand this day: now therefore let me smite him, I pray thee, with the spear even to the earth at once, and I will not smite him the second time. [9]And David said to Abishai, Destroy him not: for who can stretch forth his hand against the LORD's anointed, and be guiltless? [10]David said furthermore, As the LORD liveth, the LORD shall smite him; or his day shall come to die; or he shall descend into battle, and perish. [11]The LORD forbid that I should stretch forth mine hand against the LORD's anointed: but, I pray thee, take thou now the spear that is at his bolster, and the cruse of water, and let us go. [12]So David took the spear and the cruse of water from Saul's bolster; and they gat them away, and no man saw it, nor knew it, neither awaked: for they were all asleep; because a deep sleep from the LORD was fallen upon them.

Consults Medium and Hears His Doom

1 Sam. 28 [7]Then said Saul unto his servants, Seek me a woman that hath a familiar spirit, that I may go to her, and inquire of her. And his servants said to him, Behold, there is a woman that hath a familiar spirit at Endor. [8]And Saul disguised himself, and put on other raiment, and he went, and two men with him, and they came to the woman by night: and he said, I pray thee, divine unto me by the familiar spirit, and bring me him up, whom I shall name unto thee. [9]And the woman said unto him, Behold, thou knowest what Saul hath done, how he hath cut off those that have familiar spirits, and the wizards, out of the land: wherefore then layest thou a snare for my life, to cause me to die? [10]And Saul sware to her by the LORD, saying, As the LORD liveth, there shall no punishment happen to thee for this thing. [11]Then said the woman, Whom shall I bring up unto thee? And he said, Bring me up Samuel.

[16]Then said Samuel, Wherefore then dost thou ask of me, seeing the LORD is departed from thee, and is become thine enemy? [17]And the LORD hath done to him, as he spake by me: for the LORD hath rent the kingdom out of thine hand, and given it to thy neighbour, even to David: [18]Because thou obeyedst not the voice of the LORD, nor executedst his fierce wrath upon Amalek, therefore hath the LORD done this thing unto thee this day. [19]Moreover the LORD will also deliver Israel with thee into the hand of the Philistines: and to-morrow shalt thou and thy sons be with me: the LORD also shall deliver the host of Israel into the hand of the Philistines. [20]Then Saul fell straightway all along on the earth, and was sore afraid, because of the words of Samuel: and there was no strength in him; for he had eaten no bread all the day, nor all the night.

Saul's Defeat and Suicide

1 Sam. 31 [1]Now the Philistines fought against Israel: and the men of Israel fled from before the Philistines, and fell down slain in mount Gilboa. [2]And the Philistines followed hard upon Saul and upon his sons: and the Philistines slew Jonathan, and Abinadab, and Melchishua, Saul's sons. [3]And the battle went sore against Saul, and the archers hit him; and he was sore wounded of the archers. [4]Then said Saul unto his armourbearer, Draw thy sword, and thrust me through therewith; lest these uncircumcised come and thrust me through, and abuse me. But his armourbearer would not: for he was sore afraid. Therefore Saul took a sword, and fell upon it. [5]And when his armourbearer saw that Saul was dead, he fell likewise upon his sword, and died with him. [6]So Saul died, and his three sons, and his armourbearer, and all his men, that same day together.

See 1 Sam. 9-31

SAVIOUR

[sāv′yẽr] The Bible sometimes describes outstanding rulers and military leaders who deliver their people from oppression or danger as "saviours," but the term is used primarily as a title of God or Jesus Christ, in whom God's saving activity reaches its climax. For discussion concerning Jesus' work.

See ATONEMENT, CHRIST, JESUS

SCRIPTURE

2 Sam. 22 [3]The God of my rock; in him will I trust: he is my shield, and the horn of my salvation, my high tower, and my refuge, my saviour; thou savest me from violence.

2 Kin. 13 [5]And the LORD gave Israel a saviour, so that they went out from under the hands of the Syrians: and the children of Israel dwelt in their tents, as beforetime.

Matt. 1 [21]Thou shalt call his name JESUS: for he shall save his people from their sins.

Luke 1 [68]Blessed be the Lord God of Israel; for he hath visited and redeemed his people, [69]And hath raised up an horn of salvation for us in the house of his servant David; [70]As he spake by the mouth of his holy prophets, which have been since the world began:

Luke 2 [11]Unto you is born this day in the city of David a Saviour, which is Christ the Lord. [30]Mine eyes have seen thy salvation,

Luke 19 [10]The Son of man is come to seek and to save that which was lost.

John 3 [16]God so loved the world, that he gave his only begotten Son, that whosoever believeth in him should not perish, but have everlasting life. [17]God sent not his Son into the world to condemn the world; but that the world through him might be saved.

John 10 [7]I am the door of the sheep. [9]I am the door: by me if any man enter in, he shall be saved, and shall go in and out, and find pasture. [10]I am come that they might have life, and that they might have it more abundantly.

Acts 4 [12]Neither is there salvation in any other: for there is none other name under heaven given among men, whereby we must be saved.

Acts 5 [31]Him hath God exalted with his right hand to be a Prince and a Saviour, for to give repentance to Israel, and forgiveness of sins.

Acts 15 [11]We believe that through the grace of the Lord Jesus Christ we shall be saved,

Acts 16 [31]Believe on the Lord Jesus Christ, and thou shalt be saved, and thy house.

2 Tim. 1 [1]According to the promise of life which is in Christ Jesus, [9]Who hath saved us, and called us with an holy calling, not according to our works, but according to his own purpose and grace, which was given us in Christ Jesus before the world began, [10]But is now made manifest by the appearing of our Saviour Jesus Christ, who hath abolished death, and hath brought life and immortality to light through the gospel: [12]I know whom I have believed, and am persuaded that he is able to keep that which I have committed unto him against that day.

See Luke 15:4-10

SCAPEGOAT

[skāp′gōt] The term used to designate one of the animals in the ritual of the Day of Atonement. Two goats were taken before the high priests, one of which was killed for a sin offering. The priest then laid his hands on the head of the remaining goat, the scapegoat; he confessed the sins of the people, symbolically transferring them to the goat, who was then led away into the wilderness, where he was let go. In most modern translations of the Bible, the scapegoat is called Azazel.

See FEASTS AND FESTIVALS

SCRIPTURE

Lev. 16 [7]And he shall take the two goats, and present them before the LORD at the door of the tabernacle of the congregation. [8]And Aaron shall cast lots upon the two goats; one lot for the LORD, and the other lot for the scapegoat. 9And Aaron shall bring the goat upon which the LORD's lot fell, and offer him for a sin offering. 10But the goat, on which the lot fell to be the scapegoat, shall be presented alive before the LORD, to make an atonement with him, and to let him go for a scapegoat into the wilderness.

21And Aaron shall lay both his hands upon the head of the live goat, and confess over him all the iniquities of the children of Israel, and all their transgressions in all their sins, putting them upon the head of the goat, and shall send him away by the hand of a fit man into the wilderness: 22And the goat shall bear upon him all their iniquities unto a land not inhabited: and he shall let go the goat in the wilderness.

SCOFF, SCOFFER

[skof, skof′ĕr] To scoff is to manifest scorn or contempt by a derisive or mocking expression or action.

SCRIPTURE

2 Chr. 36 16But they mocked the messengers of God, and despised his words, and misused his prophets, until the wrath of the LORD arose against his people, till there was no remedy.

Psa. 1 1Blessed is the man that walketh not in the counsel of the ungodly, nor standeth in the way of sinners, nor sitteth in the seat of the scornful.

Prov. 1 22How long, ye simple ones, will ye love simplicity? and the scorners delight in their scorning, and fools hate knowledge? 25But ye have set at nought all my counsel, and would none of my reproof:

Prov. 3 34Surely he scorneth the scorners: but he giveth grace unto the lowly.

Prov. 9 12If thou be wise, thou shalt be wise for thyself: but if thou scornest, thou alone shalt bear it.

Prov. 13 1A wise son heareth his father's instruction: but a scorner heareth not rebuke.

Prov. 14 6A scorner seeketh wisdom, and findeth it not: 9Fools make a mock at sin:

Prov. 19 29Judgments are prepared for scorners, and stripes for the back of fools.

Prov. 21 11When the scorner is punished, the simple is made wise:

Prov. 22 10Cast out the scorner, and contention shall go out; yea, strife and reproach shall cease.

Matt. 12 24When the Pharisees heard it, they said, This fellow doth not cast out devils, but by Beelzebub the prince of the devils.

Luke 4 23And he said unto them, Ye will surely say unto me this proverb, Physician, heal thyself: whatsoever we have heard done in Capernaum, do also here in thy country.

Luke 16 14And the Pharisees also, who were covetous, heard all these things: and they derided him.

Acts 2 13Others mocking said, These men are full of new wine.

Acts 17 18Then certain philosophers of the Epicureans, and of the Stoicks, encountered him. And some said, What will this babbler say? other some, He seemeth to be a setter forth of strange gods: because he preached unto them Jesus, and the resurrection.

32And when they heard of the resurrection of the dead, some mocked: and others said, We will hear thee again of this matter.

2 Pet. 3 3Knowing this first, that there shall come in the last days scoffers, walking after their own lusts, 4And saying, Where is the promise of his coming? for since the fathers fell asleep, all things continue as they were from the beginning of the creation.

See Mark 3:22; Luke 11:15

SCOURGE, SCOURGING

[skurj', skur'jing] A whip designed for severe beatings. It consisted of a handle to which several cords or leather thongs were fastened; these were often knotted or weighted with pieces of bone or metal, which served to make the blow more painful. The victim of scourging was tied to a post and beaten across the back and loins; in some cases, the front of the body and the face were also struck. Scourging was often administered preceding capital punishment, doubtless to weaken the victim and hasten his death. Jesus himself was scourged before his crucifixion (*Matt. 27:26, Mark 15:15*). It was also used to obtain confession from accused persons (*Acts 22:24*). Paul claims to have received on five occasions "forty stripes save one" (*2 Cor. 11:23-25*). This odd figure is explained by the fact that the Law prohibited the giving of any more than forty stripes (*Deut. 25:3*); it is quite likely that thirty-nine stripes were given to allow for an error in counting. It was against Roman law to scourge a Roman citizen, as noted by Paul in *Acts 22:25*, but this seems not to have been rigidly observed in outlying districts.

SCRIPTURE

Deut. 25 [3]Forty stripes he may give him, and not exceed: lest, if he should exceed, and beat him above these with many stripes, then thy brother should seem vile unto thee.

Matt. 27 [26]Then released he Barabbas unto them: and when he had scourged Jesus, he delivered him to be crucified.

Acts 22 [24]The chief captain commanded him to be brought into the castle, and bade that he should be examined by scourging; that he might know wherefore they cried so against him. [25]And as they bound him with thongs, Paul said unto the centurion that stood by, Is it lawful for you to scourge a man that is a Roman, and uncondemned?

SCRIBES

[scrībz] The importance of the Law in Judaism cannot be exaggerated. After the return from Babylonian exile, there arose a class of professional scholars, called scribes, whose duty it was to interpret the Law and apply it to every aspect of life. The origin of this class is obscure, but at the time of Jesus they formed a solid profession with wide influence over the people. It is probable that most of the scribes belonged to the party of the Pharisees, since this group recognized as binding the traditions which had grown up alongside the Law as a result of the type of interpretation in which the scribes were engaged (*see* PHARISEES); doubtless, however, some scribes also adhered to the sect of the Sadducees. (*See* SADDUCEES)

The scribes were held in high honor among the Jews and were commonly addressed by the title "Rabbi", meaning "my Lord" or "my Master." In addition to their scholarly duties, they also sat in the judgment on cases which were brought before them; they received no remuneration for this activity but derived their living from the pursuit of some trade which they practiced on the side.

The work of the scribes had many good results. It made the Jews truly a people of the Law, bringing some familiarity with the Law to the commonest peasant. On the other hand, the endless interpretations and applications which were placed on various laws often obscured the motive behind them, resulting in a superficial legalism.

See Matt. 23

SCRIPTURE

An Interpreter of the Law

Ezra 7 [6]This Ezra went up from Babylon; and he was a ready scribe in the law of Moses, which the LORD God of Israel had given: and the king granted him all his request, according to the hand of the LORD his God upon him.

Falsely Accuse Jesus

Matt. 9 [3]And, behold, certain of the scribes said within themselves, This man blasphemeth.

Censured by Jesus

Matt. 15 [1]Then came to Jesus scribes and Pharisees, which were of Jerusalem, saying, [2]Why do thy disciples transgress the tradition of the elders? for they wash not their hands when they eat bread. [3]But he answered and said unto them, Why do ye also transgress the commandment of God by your tradition?

Matt. 23 [1]Then spake Jesus to the multitude, and to his disciples, [2]Saying, The scribes and the Pharisees sit in Moses' seat: [3]All therefore whatsoever they bid you observe, that observe and do; but do not ye after their works: for they say, and do not. [4]For they bind heavy burdens and grievous to be borne, and lay them on men's shoulders; but they themselves will not move them with one of their fingers. [5]But all their works they do for to be seen of men: they make broad their phylacteries, and enlarge the borders of their garments, [6]And love the uppermost rooms at feasts, and the chief seats in the synagogues, [7]And greetings in the markets, and to be called of men, Rabbi, Rabbi. [8]But be not ye called Rabbi: for one is your Master, even Christ; and all ye are brethren. [9]And call no man your father upon the earth: for one is your Father, which is in heaven. [10]Neither be ye called masters: for one is your Master, even Christ. [11]But he that is greatest among you shall be your servant. [12]And whosoever shall exalt himself shall be abased; and he that shall humble himself shall be exalted.

[13]But woe unto you, scribes and Pharisees, hypocrites! for ye shut up the kingdom of heaven against men: for ye neither go in yourselves, neither suffer ye them that are entering to go in. [14]Woe unto you, scribes and Pharisees, hypocrites! for ye devour widows' houses, and for a pretence make long prayer: therefore ye shall receive the greater damnation. [15]Woe unto you, scribes and Pharisees, hypocrites! for ye compass sea and land to make one proselyte; and when he is made, ye make him twofold more the child of hell than yourselves. [16]Woe unto you, ye blind guides, which say, Whosoever shall swear by the temple, it is nothing; but whosoever shall swear by the gold of the temple, he is a debtor! [17]Ye fools and blind: for whether is greater, the gold, or the temple that sanctifieth the gold? [18]And, Whosoever shall swear by the altar, it is nothing; but whosoever sweareth by the gift that is upon it, he is guilty. [19]Ye fools and blind: for whether is greater, the gift, or the altar that sanctifieth the gift? [20]Whoso therefore shall swear by the altar, sweareth by it, and by all things thereon. [21]And whoso shall swear by the temple, sweareth by it, and by him that dwelleth therein. [22]And he that shall swear by heaven, sweareth by the throne of God, and by him that sitteth thereon. [23]Woe unto you, scribes and Pharisees, hypocrites! for ye pay tithe of mint and anise and cummin, and have omitted the weightier matters of the law, judgment, mercy, and faith: these ought ye to have done, and not to leave the other undone. [24]Ye blind guides, which strain at a gnat, and swallow a camel. [25]Woe unto you, scribes and Pharisees, hypocrites! for ye make clean the outside of the cup and of the platter, but within they are full of extortion and excess. [26]Thou blind Pharisee, cleanse first that which is within the cup and platter, that the outside of them may be clean also. [27]Woe unto you, scribes and

Pharisees, hypocrites! for ye are like unto
whited sepulchres, which indeed appear
beautiful outward, but are within full of
dead men's bones, and of all uncleanness.
28 Even so ye also outwardly appear righteous unto men, but within ye are full of
hypocrisy and iniquity. 29 Woe unto you,
scribes and Pharisees, hypocrites! because
ye build the tombs of the prophets, and
garnish the sepulchres of the righteous,
30 And say, If we had been in the days of
our fathers, we would not have been partakers with them in the blood of the prophets. 31 Wherefore ye be witnesses unto
yourselves, that ye are the children of them
which killed the prophets. 32 Fill ye up
then the measure of your fathers. 33 Ye serpents, ye generation of vipers, how can ye
escape the damnation of hell?

34 Wherefore, behold, I send unto you
prophets, and wise men, and scribes: and
some of them ye shall kill and crucify; and
some of them shall ye scourge in your synagogues, and persecute them from city to
city: 35 That upon you may come all the
righteous blood shed upon the earth, from
the blood of righteous Abel unto the blood
of Zacharias son of Barachias, whom ye
slew between the temple and the altar.
36 Verily I say unto you, All these things
shall come upon this generation.

SCRIPTURE

[scrip'tûr] Literally, anything written; a document or inscription. As used by Christians this term usually refers to the books of the Bible. The Holy Scriptures, inspired of God, contain various revelations of Himself, culminating in the record of his supreme revelation in Jesus Christ. They also reveal his plans for man, together with various rules, precepts, and examples designed to guide man in his efforts to order his life in accordance with the will of God. As used in the New Testament, scripture refers to the Old Testament writings. Several of the passages cited below have a wilder meaning than the written word, but would certainly contain reference to Scripture.

SCRIPTURE

Characteristics of Scripture

INSPIRED OF GOD

2 Sam. 23 1 Now these be the last words
of David. David the son of Jesse said, and
the man who was raised up on high, the
anointed of the God of Jacob, and the
sweet psalmist of Israel, said, 2 The Spirit
of the LORD spake by me and his word was
in my tongue.

2 Kin. 21 10 And the LORD spake by his
servants the prophets,

Neh. 9 13 Thou camest down also upon
mount Sinai, and spakest with them from
heaven, and gavest them right judgments,
and true laws, good statutes and commandments: 14 And madest known to
them thy holy sabbath, and command-
edst them precepts, statutes, and laws, by
the hand of Moses thy servant.

Rom. 1 2 (Which he had promised afore
by his prophets in the holy Scriptures.)

1 Cor. 2 13 Which things also we speak,
not in the words which man's wisdom
teacheth, but which the Holy Ghost teacheth; comparing spiritual things with spiritual.

1 Cor. 7 40 But she is happier if she so
abide, after my judgment: and I think also
that I have the Spirit of God.

1 Cor. 14 36 What! came the word of
God out from you? or came it unto you
only? 37 If any man think himself to be a
prophet, or spiritual, let him acknowledge
that the things that I write unto you are
the commandments of the Lord.

Gal. 1 11 But I certify you, brethren, that
the gospel which was preached of me is
not after man. 12 For I neither received it

of man, neither was I taught it, but by the revelation of Jesus Christ.

Eph. 3 [3]How that by revelation he made known unto me the mystery; (as I wrote afore in few words.)

1 Thess. 2 [13]For this cause also thank we God without ceasing, because, when ye received the word of God which ye heard of us, ye received it not as the word of men, but, as it is in truth, the word of God, which effectually worketh also in you that believe.

2 Tim. 3 [16]All Scripture is given by inspiration of God, and is profitable for doctrine, for reproof, for correction, for instruction in righteousness.

1 Pet. 1 [10]Of which salvation the prophets have inquired and searched diligently, who prophesied of the grace that should come unto you. [11]Searching what, or what manner of time the Spirit of Christ which was in them did signify, when it testified beforehand the sufferings of Christ, and the glory that should follow. [12]Unto whom it was revealed, that not unto themselves, but unto us they did minister the things, which are now reported unto you by them that have preached the gospel unto you with the Holy Ghost sent down from heaven; which things the angels desire to look into.

2 Pet. 1 [20]Knowing this first, that no prophecy of the Scripture is of any private interpretation. [21]For the prophecy came not in old time by the will of man: but holy men of God spake as they were moved by the Holy Ghost.

1 John 5 [9]If we receive the witness of men, the witness of God is greater: for this is the witness of God which he has testified of his Son.

EFFICACIOUS

Isa. 55 [10]For as the rain cometh down and the snow from heaven, and returneth not thither, but watereth the earth, and maketh it bring forth and bud, that it may give seed to the sower, and bread to the eater: [11]So shall my word be that goeth forth out of my mouth; it shall not return unto me void, but it shall accomplish that which I please, and it shall prosper in the thing whereto I sent it.

Eph. 6 [17]And take the helmet of salvation, and the sword of the Spirit, which is the word of God.

Heb. 4 [12]For the word of God is quick, and powerful, and sharper than any two-edged sword, piercing even to the dividing asunder of soul and spirit, and of the joints and marrow, and is a discerner of the thoughts and intents of the heart.

CONTAIN EVERLASTING TRUTHS; MUST BE FULFILLED

Psa. 119 [144]The righteousness of thy testimonies is everlasting: give me understanding, and I shall live. [152]Concerning thy testimonies, I have known of old that thou hast founded them for ever.

Isa. 40 [8]The grass withereth, the flower fadeth: but the word of our God shall stand for ever.

Matt. 5 [17]Think not that I am come to destroy the law, or the prophets: I am not come to destroy, but to fulfil. [18]For verily I say unto you, Till heaven and earth pass, one jot or one tittle shall in no wise pass from the law, till all be fulfilled.

Luke 16 [16]The law and the prophets were until John: since that time the kingdom of God is preached, and every man presseth into it. [17]And it is easier for heaven and earth to pass, than one tittle of the law to fall.

Luke 21 [33]Heaven and earth shall pass away, but my words shall not pass away.

Luke 24 [44]And he said unto them, These are the words which I spake unto you, while I was yet with you, that all things must be fulfilled, which were written in the law of Moses, and in the prophets, and in the psalms, concerning me.

John 10 [35]If he called them gods, unto whom the word of God came, and the Scripture cannot be broken.

1 Pet. 1 [25]But the word of the Lord endureth for ever. And this is the word which by the gospel is preached unto you.

THE STANDARD OF TRUTH

Isa. 8 [20]To the law and to the testimony: if they speak not according to this word, it is because there is no light in them.

Matt. 15 [1]Then came to Jesus scribes and Pharisees, which were of Jerusalem, saying, [2]Why do thy disciples transgress the tradition of the elders? for they wash not their hands when they eat bread. [3]But he answered and said unto them, Why do ye also transgress the commandment of God by your tradition?

Mark 7 [7]Howbeit in vain do they worship me, teaching for doctrines the commandments of men. [8]For laying aside the commandment of God, ye hold the tradition of men, as the washing of pots and cups: and many other such like things ye do. [9]And he said unto them, Full well ye reject the commandment of God, that ye may keep your own tradition. [13]Making the word of God of none effect through your tradition, which ye have delivered: and many such like things do ye.

John 5 [46]For had ye believed Moses, ye would have believed me: for he wrote of me. [47]But if ye believe not his writings, how shall ye believe my words?

Acts 18 [28]For he mightily convinced the Jews, and that publicly, shewing by the Scriptures that Jesus was Christ.

Col. 2 [8]Beware lest any man spoil you through philosophy and vain deceit, after the tradition of men, after the rudiments of the world, and not after Christ.

PURE

Psa. 12 [6]The words of the LORD are pure words: as silver tried in a furnace of earth, purified seven times.

Psa. 119 [140]Thy word is very pure: therefore thy servant loveth it.

Prov. 30 [5]Every word of God is pure: he is a shield unto them that put their trust in him.

Rom. 7 [12]Wherefore the law is holy, and the commandment holy, and just, and good.

ILLUMINATING

Psa. 119 [105]Thy word is a lamp unto my feet, and a light unto my path.

Prov. 6 [23]For the commandment is a lamp; and the law is light; and reproofs of instruction are the way of life.

2 Pet. 1 [19]We have also a more sure word of prophecy; whereunto ye do well that ye take heed, as unto a light that shineth in a dark place, until the day dawn, and the daystar arise in your hearts.

1 John 2 [8]Again, a new commandment I write unto you, which thing is true in him and in you: because the darkness is past, and the true light now shineth.

FULL OF WISDOM

Psa. 119 [98]Thou through thy commandments hast made me wiser than mine enemies; for they are ever with me. [99]I have more understanding than all my teachers: for thy testimonies are my meditation. [100]I understand more than the ancients, because I keep thy precepts. [104]Through thy precepts I get understanding: therefore I hate every false way. [130]The entrance of thy words giveth light; it giveth understanding unto the simple.

Prov. 1 [2]To know wisdom and instruction; to perceive the words of understanding; [3]To receive the instruction of wisdom, justice, and judgment, and equity; [4]To give subtilty to the simple, to the young man knowledge and discretion.

Matt. 13 [51]Jesus saith unto them, Have ye understood all these things? They say unto him, Yea, Lord. [52]Then said he unto them, Therefore every scribe which is instructed unto the kingdom of heaven, is like unto a man that is a householder, which bringeth forth out of his treasure things new and old.

Mark 12 [24]And Jesus answering said unto them, Do ye not therefore err, because ye know not the Scriptures, neither the power of God?

1 Cor. 10 [11]Now all these things happened unto them for ensamples: and they are written for our admonition upon whom the ends of the world are come.

Eph. 3 [4]Whereby, when ye read, ye may understand my knowledge in the mystery of Christ.

SATISFYING

Job 23 [12]Neither have I gone back from the commandment of his lips; I have esteemed the words of his mouth more than my necessary food.

Psa. 19 [10]More to be desired are they than gold, yea, than much fine gold: sweeter also than honey and the honeycomb.

Psa. 119 [20]My soul breaketh for the longing that it hath unto thy judgments at all times. [47]And I will delight myself in thy commandments, which I have loved. [48]My hands also will I lift up unto thy commandments, which I have loved; and I will meditate in thy statutes. [72]The law of thy mouth is better unto me than thousands of gold and silver. [103]How sweet are thy words unto my taste! yea, sweeter than honey to my mouth.

1 Pet. 2 [2]As newborn babes, desire the sincere milk of the word, that ye may grow thereby.

INSPIRE HOPE

Psa. 119 [81]My soul fainteth for thy salvation: but I hope in thy word. [147]I prevented the dawning of the morning, and cried: I hoped in thy word.

Rom. 15 [4]For whatsoever things were written aforetime were written for our learning, that we through patience and comfort of the Scriptures might have hope.

INSPIRE JOY

Psa. 19 [8]The statutes of the LORD are right, rejoicing the heart: the commandment of the LORD is pure, enlightening the eyes.

Psa. 119 [14]I have rejoiced in the way of thy testimonies, as much as in all riches. [16]I will delight myself in thy statutes; I will not forget thy word. [162]I rejoice at thy word, as one that findeth great spoil.

1 John 1 [4]And these things write we unto you, that your joy may be full.

COMFORTING AND CONSOLING

Psa. 119 [50]This is my comfort in my affliction: for thy word hath quickened me. [92]Unless thy law had been my delights, I should then have perished in mine affliction. [93]I will never forget thy precepts: for with them thou hast quickened me.

Acts 15 [30]So when they were dismissed, they came to Antioch: and when they had gathered the multitude together, they delivered the epistle: [31]Which when they had read, they rejoiced for the consolation.

SANCTIFYING AND SAVING

Psa. 17 [4]Concerning the works of men, by the word of thy lips I have kept me from the paths of the destroyer.

Psa. 119 [9]Wherewithal shall a young man cleanse his way? by taking heed thereto according to thy word.

John 20 [31]But these are written, that ye might believe that Jesus is the Christ, the Son of God; and that believing ye might have life through his name.

Rom. 1 [16]For I am not ashamed of the gospel of Christ: for it is the power of God unto salvation to every one that believeth; to the Jew first, and also to the Greek.

Rom. 10 [17]So then faith cometh by hearing, and hearing by the word of God.

2 Tim. 3 [15]And that from a child thou hast known the holy Scriptures, which are able to make thee wise unto salvation through faith which is in Christ Jesus.

Jas. 1 [21]Wherefore lay apart all filthiness and superfluity of naughtiness, and receive with meekness the engrafted word, which is able to save your souls.

FULL OF INSTRUCTION

Deut. 6 [7]And thou shalt teach them diligently unto thy children, and shall talk of them when thou sittest in thine house, and when thou walkest by the way, and when thou liest down, and when thou risest up. [8]And thou shalt bind them for a sign upon thine hand, and they shall be as frontlets between thine eyes.

2 Chr. 12 [9]And they taught in Judah, and had the book of the law of the LORD with them, and went about throughout all the cities of Judah, and taught the people.

Ezra 7 [10]For Ezra had prepared his heart to seek the law of the LORD, and to do it, and to teach in Israel statutes and judgments.

Neh. 8 [7]Also Jeshua, and Bani, and Sherebiah, Jamin, Akkub, Shabbethai, Hodijah, Maaseiah, Kelita, Azariah, Jozabad, Hanan, Pelaiah, and the Levites, caused the people to understand the law: and the people stood in their place. [8]So they read in the book in the law of God distinctly, and gave the sense, and caused them to understand the reading.

Isa. 28 [10]For precept must be upon precept, precept upon precept; line upon line, line upon line; here a little, and there a little.

Dan. 7 [16]I came near unto one of them that stood by, and asked him the truth of all this. So he told me, and made me know the interpretation of the things.

Luke 24 [27]And beginning at Moses and all the prophets, he expounded unto them in all the scriptures the things concerning himself.

[45]Then opened he their understanding, that they might understand the Scriptures.

Acts 8 [31]And he said, How can I, except some man should guide me? And he desired Philip that he would come up and sit with him.

Acts 18 [26]And he began to speak boldly in the synagogue: whom when Aquila and Priscilla had heard, they took him unto them, and expounded unto him the way of God more perfectly.

SEA OF GALILEE

[sē, gal′i lē] The name given in the New Testament to the lake in the northern province of Galilee. Most of the public life of Jesus was spent in the neighborhood of the sea of Galilee. This region was then the most densely populated in all Palestine. No less than nine cities stood on its shores. The lake is of an oval shape, about thirteen miles long, and six broad. The river Jordan enters it at its northern end, and passes out at its southern end. The scenery is bleak and monotonous, but the water of the lake is sweet, cool, and transparent and abounds in fish. Several of the apostles were engaged in the fishing industry on this lake. Other names by which this body of water is known in the Bible include "the sea of Chinnereth (sometimes Chinneroth)" (*Num. 34:11; Josh. 12:3; 13:27*), from a town near its shore (*Josh. 19:35*); "the sea of Tiberias" (*John 21:1*) from another nearby city (*John 6:1*); "the lake of Gennesaret" (*Luke 5:1*), from the fertile plain to the northwest; and simply "the Sea" (*John 6:16*).

See GALILEE

SCRIPTURE

Jesus Calls Disciples

Matt. 4 [18]And Jesus, walking by the sea of Galilee, saw two brethren, Simon called Peter, and Andrew his brother, casting a net into the sea: for they were fishers. [19]And he saith unto them, Follow me, and I will make you fishers of men. [20]And they straightway left their nets, and followed him. [21]And going on from thence, he saw other two brethren, James the son of Zebedee, and John his brother, in a ship with Zebedee their father, mending their nets; and he called them. [22]And they immediately left the ship and their father, and followed him.

Jesus Teaches from Boat on Its Waters

Matt. 13 [1]The same day went Jesus out of the house, and sat by the sea side. [2]And great multitudes were gathered together unto him, so that he went into a ship, and sat; and the whole multitude stood on the shore.

Jesus Performs Miracles

Matt. 8 [24]And, behold, there arose a great tempest in the sea, insomuch that the ship was covered with the waves: but he was asleep. [25]And his disciples came to him, and awoke him, saying, Lord, save us: we perish. [26]And he saith unto them, Why are ye fearful, O ye of little faith? Then he arose, and rebuked the winds and the sea; and there was a great calm. [27]But the men marvelled, saying, What manner of man is this, that even the winds and the sea obey him!

[28]And when he was come to the other side into the country of the Gergesenes, there met him two possessed with devils, coming out of the tombs, exceeding fierce, so that no man might pass by that way. [29]And, behold, they cried out, saying, What have we to do with thee, Jesus, thou Son of God? art thou come hither to torment us before the time? [30]And there was a good way off from them an herd of many swine feeding. [31]So the devils besought him, saying, If thou cast us out, suffer us to go away into the herd of swine. [32]And he said unto them, Go. And when they were come out, they went into the herd of swine: and, behold, the whole herd of swine ran violently down a steep place into the sea, and perished in the waters.

Luke 5 [1]And it came to pass, that, as the people pressed upon him to hear the word of God, he stood by the lake of Gennesaret, [2]And saw two ships standing by the lake: but the fishermen were gone out of them, and were washing their nets. [3]And he entered into one of the ships, which was Simon's, and prayed him that he would thrust out a little from the land. And he sat down, and taught the people out of the ship. [4]Now when he had left speaking, he said unto Simon, Launch out into the deep, and let down your nets for a draught. [5]And Simon answering said unto him, Master, we have toiled all the night, and have taken nothing: nevertheless at thy word I will let down the net. [6]And when they had this done, they inclosed a great multitude of fishes: and their net brake. 7And they beckoned unto their partners, which were in the other ship, that they should come and help them. And they came, and filled both the ships, so that they began to sink. 8When Simon Peter saw it, he fell down at Jesus' knees, saying, Depart from me; for I am a sinful man, O Lord. 9For he was astonished, and all that were with him, at the draught of the fishes which they had taken:

John 21 4But when the morning was now come, Jesus stood on the shore: but the disciples knew not that it was Jesus. 5Then Jesus saith unto them, Children, have ye any meat? They answered him, No. 6And he said unto them, Cast the net on the right side of the ship, and ye shall find. They cast therefore, and now they were not able to draw it for the multitude of fishes. 7Therefore that disciple whom Jesus loved saith unto Peter, It is the Lord. Now when Simon Peter heard that it was the Lord, he girt his fisher's coat unto him, (for he was naked,) and did cast himself into the sea. 8And the other disciples came in a little ship; (for they were not far from land, but as it were two hundred cubits,) dragging the net with fishes.

SEAL

[sēl] Literally, an instrument of stone, metal, wood, etc., on which is engraved a figure, often of intricate design; a signet. In ancient times, seals were pressed into wax or clay and affixed to royal commands, deeds, letters, and other objects as a mark of authenticity or ownership. These seals were often affixed to rings, known as signet rings. A large number of ancient seals have been discovered and can be seen in many museums. When a man presented his seal to another it was a sign that he had invested him with the power to act in his stead as an official deputy. The word "seal" is often used figuratively in the Bible (see scripture below).

SCRIPTURE

General

Gen. 41 41And Pharaoh said unto Joseph, See, I have set thee over all the land of Egypt. 42And Pharaoh took off his ring from his hand, and put it upon Joseph's hand, and arrayed him in vestures of fine linen, and put a gold chain about his neck;

1 Kin. 21 8So she wrote letters in Ahab's name, and sealed them with his seal, and sent the letters unto the elders and to the nobles that were in his city, dwelling with Naboth.

Esth. 3 12In the name of king Ahasuerus was it written, and sealed with the king's ring.

Esth. 8 8Write ye also for the Jews, as it liketh you, in the king's name, and seal it with the king's ring: for the writing which is written in the king's name, and sealed with the king's ring, may no man reverse.

Dan. 6 17And a stone was brought, and laid upon the mouth of the den; and the king sealed it with his own signet, and with the signet of his lords; that the purpose might not be changed concerning Daniel.

Rev. 5 1And I saw in the right hand of him that sat on the throne a book written within and on the backside, sealed with seven seals.

Figurative

Deut. 32 34Is not this laid up in store with me, and sealed up among my treasures?

Song 8 6Set me as a seal upon thine heart, as a seal upon thine arm: for love is strong as death; jealousy is cruel as the grave: the coals thereof are coals of fire, which hath a most vehement flame.

Isa. 29 [11]And the vision of all is become unto you as the words of a book that is sealed, which men deliver to one that is learned, saying, Read this, I pray thee: and he saith, I cannot; for it is sealed. [12]And the book is delivered to him that is not learned, saying, Read this, I pray thee: and he saith, I am not learned.

John 3 [33]He that hath received his testimony hath set to his seal that God is true.

John 6 [27]Labour not for the meat which perisheth, but for that meat which endureth unto everlasting life, which the Son of man shall give unto you: for him hath God the Father sealed.

Rom. 4 [11]And he received the sign of circumcision, a seal of the righteousness of the faith which he had yet being uncircumcised: that he might be the father of all them that believe, though they be not circumcised; that righteousness might be imputed unto them also:

1 Cor. 9 [2]If I be not an apostle unto others, yet doubtless I am to you: for the seal of mine apostleship are ye in the Lord.

Eph. 1 [13]In whom ye also trusted, after that ye heard the word of truth, the gospel of your salvation: in whom also after that ye believed, ye were sealed with that holy Spirit of promise,

Eph. 4 [30]And grieve not the holy Spirit of God, whereby ye are sealed unto the day of redemption.

2 Tim. 2 [19]Nevertheless the foundation of God standeth sure, having this seal, The Lord knoweth them that are his. And, Let every one that nameth the name of Christ depart from iniquity.

Rev. 7 [2]And I saw another angel ascending from the east, having the seal of the living God: and he cried with a loud voice to the four angels, to whom it was given to hurt the earth and the sea, [3]Saying, Hurt not the earth, neither the sea, nor the trees, till we have sealed the servants of our God in their foreheads. [4]And I heard the number of them which were sealed: and there were sealed an hundred and forty and four thousand of all the tribes of the children of Israel.

SECOND COMING

[sek'und kum'ing] The return of Christ at the end of this age to bring to triumphant completion the work begun in his ministry, death, and resurrection. The Greek word for the Second Coming is *parousia* and is often found in discussions of the subject. Belief in the Second Coming was a vital part of early Christian faith and the New Testament contains frequent references to it. For further discussion see MILLENIUM, SON OF MAN.

SCRIPTURE

Matt. 24 [42]Watch therefore; for ye know not what hour your Lord doth come. [43]But know this, that if the goodman of the house had known in what watch the thief would come, he would have watched, and would not have suffered his house to be broken up. [44]Therefore be ye also ready: for in such an hour as ye think not the Son of man cometh.

Matt. 26 [64]Hereafter shall ye see the Son of man sitting on the right hand of power, and coming in the clouds of heaven.

Mark 13 [27]Then shall he send his angels, and shall gather together his elect from the four winds, from the uttermost part of the earth to the uttermost part of heaven.

[32]But of that day and that hour knoweth no man, no, not the angels which are in heaven, neither the Son, but the Father. [35]Watch ye therefore: for ye know not when the master of the house cometh, at even, or at midnight, or at the cockcrow-

ing, or in the morning: 36 Lest coming suddenly he find you sleeping.

Mark 14 62 Ye shall see the Son of man sitting on the right hand of power, and coming in the clouds of heaven.

John 14 3 If I go and prepare a place for you, I will come again, and receive you unto myself; that where I am, there ye may be also.

18 I will not leave you comfortless: I will come to you. 28 Ye have heard how I said unto you, I go away, and come again unto you. If ye loved me, ye would rejoice, because I said, I go unto the Father: for my Father is greater than I. 29 And now I have told you before it come to pass, that, when it is come to pass, ye might believe.

Acts 1 11 This same Jesus, which is taken up from you into heaven, shall so come in like manner as ye have seen him go into heaven.

1 Cor. 1 7 So that ye come behind in no gift; waiting for the coming of our Lord Jesus Christ: 8 Who shall also confirm you unto the end, that ye may be blameless in the day of our Lord Jesus Christ.

1 Cor. 11 26 As often as ye eat this bread, and drink this cup, ye do shew the Lord's death till he come.

1 Cor. 15 23 Christ the firstfruits; afterward they that are Christ's at his coming.

1 Thess. 3 13 To the end he may stablish your hearts unblameable in holiness before God, even our Father, at the coming of our Lord Jesus Christ with all his saints.

1 Thess. 4 15 For this we say unto you by the word of the Lord, that we which are alive and remain unto the coming of the Lord shall not prevent them which are asleep. 16 For the Lord himself shall descend from heaven with a shout, with the voice of the archangel, and with the trump of God: and the dead in Christ shall rise first: 17 Then we which are alive and remain shall be caught up together with them in the clouds, to meet the Lord in the air: and so shall we ever be with the Lord.

1 Thess. 5 2 Yourselves know perfectly that the day of the Lord so cometh as a thief in the night. 3 For when they shall say, Peace and safety; then sudden destruction cometh upon them, as travail upon a woman with child; and they shall not escape. 23 . . . I pray God your whole spirit and soul and body be preserved blameless unto the coming of our Lord Jesus Christ.

2 Thess. 1 7 To you who are troubled rest with us, when the Lord Jesus shall be revealed from heaven with his mighty angels, 8 In flaming fire taking vengeance on them that know not God, and that obey not the gospel of our Lord Jesus Christ: 9 Who shall be punished with everlasting destruction from the presence of the Lord, and from the glory of his power; 10 When he shall come to be glorified in his saints, and to be admired in all them that believe (because our testimony among you was believed) in that day.

2 Thess. 2 1 We beseech you, brethren, by the coming of our Lord Jesus Christ, and by our gathering together unto him, 2 That ye be not soon shaken in mind, or be troubled, neither by spirit, nor by word, nor by letter as from us, as that the day of Christ is at hand. 3 Let no man deceive you by any means: for that day shall not come, except there come a falling away first, and that man of sin be revealed, the son of perdition; 5 Remember ye not, that, when I was yet with you, I told you these things? 8 Then shall that Wicked be revealed, whom the Lord shall consume with the spirit of his mouth, and shall destroy with the brightness of his coming:

Heb. 9 [28]So Christ was once offered to bear the sins of many; and unto them that look for him shall he appear the second time without sin unto salvation.

2 Pet. 1 [16]We have not followed cunningly devised fables, when we made known unto you the power and coming of our Lord Jesus Christ,

2 Pet. 3 [3]Knowing this first, that there shall come in the last days scoffers, walking after their own lusts, [4]And saying, Where is the promise of his coming? for since the fathers fell asleep, all things continue as they were from the beginning of the creation. [10]But the day of the Lord will come as a thief in the night; in the which the heavens shall pass away with a great noise, and the elements shall melt with fervent heat, the earth also and the works that are therein shall be burned up. [11]Seeing then that all these things shall be dissolved, what manner of persons ought ye to be in all holy conversation and godliness. [12]Looking for and hasting unto the coming of the day of God, wherein the heavens being on fire shall be dissolved, and the elements shall melt with fervent heat?

1 John 2 [28]Little children, abide in him; that, when he shall appear, we may have confidence, and not be ashamed before him at his coming.

1 John 3 [2]But we know that, when he shall appear, we shall be like him; for we shall see him as he is.

Jude 1 [14]Enoch also, the seventh from Adam, prophesied of these, saying, Behold, the Lord cometh with ten thousands of his saints, [15]To execute judgment upon all,

Rev. 1 [7]Behold, he cometh with clouds; and every eye shall see him, and they also which pierced him: and all kindreds of the earth shall wail because of him.

Rev. 22 [12]Behold, I come quickly; and my reward is with me, to give every man according as his work shall be. [20]He which testifieth these things saith, Surely I come quickly. Amen. Even so, come, Lord Jesus.

See Matt. 24:36; 2 Pet. 3:8, 9, 13, 14

SECOND DEATH

[sek′und deth] An expression found only in the book of *Revelation*, referring to the final penalty of the wicked.

SCRIPTURE

Rev. 2 [11]He that hath an ear, let him hear what the Spirit saith unto the churches; He that overcometh shall not be hurt of the second death.

Rev. 20 [6]Blessed and holy is he that hath part in the first resurrection: on such the second death hath no power, but they shall be priests of God and of Christ, and shall reign with him a thousand years. [14]And death and hell were cast into the lake of fire. This is the second death.

Rev. 21 [8]But the fearful, and unbelieving, and the abominable, and murderers, and whoremongers, and sorcerers, and idolaters, and all liars, shall have their part in the lake which burneth with fire and brimstone: which is the second death.

SECRET

[sē′kret] Something undisclosed or unrevealed; something confided in a man which he ought not to disclose; anything concealed from public conversation. The Bible speaks of the secrets of wisdom and the secrets of God—those mysteries of the past, present, and future which God either keeps from man entirely or makes known in his divine revelation. We are told that nothing can be kept secret from God.

See God, Omniscience of; Mystery

SCRIPTURE

Secret Things Belong to God

Deut. 15 [8]The secret things belong unto

the LORD our God: but those things which are revealed belong unto us and to our children for ever, that we may do all the words of this law.

Job 15 [8]Hast thou heard the secret of God? and dost thou restrain wisdom to thyself?

Secrets Revealed by God

Psa. 25 [14]The secret of the LORD is with them that fear him; and he will shew them his covenant.

Prov. 3 [32]For the froward is abomination to the LORD: but his secret is with the righteous.

Amos 3 [7]Surely the Lord GOD will do nothing, but he revealeth his secret unto his servants the prophets.

Matt. 11 [25]At that time Jesus answered and said, I thank thee, O Father, Lord of heaven and earth, because thou hast hid these things from the wise and prudent, and hast revealed them unto babes.

Matt. 13 [35]That it might be fulfilled which was spoken by the prophet, saying, I will open my mouth in parables; I will utter things which have been kept secret from the foundation of the world.

Rom. 16 [25]Now to him that is of power to stablish you according to my gospel, and the preaching of Jesus Christ, according to the revelation of the mystery, which was kept secret since the world began, [26]But now is made manifest, and by the scriptures of the prophets, according to the commandment of the everlasting God, made known to all nations for the obedience of faith.

All Secrets Known to God

Psa. 44 [21]Shall not God search this out? for he knoweth the secrets of the heart.

Psa. 90 [8]Thou hast set our iniquities before thee, our secret sins in the light of thy countenance.

Eccl. 12 [14]For God shall bring every work into judgment, with every secret thing, whether it be good, or whether it be evil.

Matt. 6 [4]That thine alms may be in secret: and thy Father which seeth in secret himself shall reward thee openly.

Mark 4 [22]For there is nothing hid, which shall not be manifested; neither was any thing kept secret, but that it should come abroad.

Rom. 2 [16]In the day when God shall judge the secrets of men by Jesus Christ according to my gospel.

Some Secrets Not to Be Revealed

Prov. 25 [9]Debate thy cause with thy neighbour himself; and discover not a secret to another: [10]Lest he that heareth it put thee to shame, and thine infamy turn not away.

Matt. 18 [15]Moreover if thy brother shall trespass against thee, go and tell him his fault between thee and him alone: if he shall hear thee, thou hast gained thy brother.

SELAH

[sē′la] A Hebrew word, occurring frequently at the end of a verse in the *Psalms* and other poetic literature. It is thought that this is a musical or liturgical symbol, perhaps indicating pause or rest.

SELF-DENIAL

[self-dē nī′l] The act of denying oneself; forbearance from gratification of one's desires. Self-denial is one of the foremost attributes which the Christian is urged to cultivate, taking as the perfect model the Master himself. Men ordinarily finds self-denial one of the most difficult of the Christian graces to attain, since it conflicts with his inclination to seek his own pleasure and comfort before giving thought to that of his neighbor. Christians may sometimes be called upon to deny themselves of things which are basically harmless, but which might be misunderstood and cause a weaker individual to stumble.

See OFFENSE

SCRIPTURE

General

Prov. 23 [1]When thou sittest to eat with
a ruler, consider diligently what is before
thee: [2]And put a knife to thy throat, if thou
be a man given to appetite. [3]Be not desirous of his dainties: for they are deceitful
meat. [4]Labour not to be rich: cease from
thine own wisdom. [5]Wilt thou set thine
eyes upon that which is not? for riches certainly make themselves wings; they fly away as an eagle toward heaven.

Jer. 35 [6]But they said, We will drink no
wine: for Jonadab the son of Rechab our father commanded us, saying, Ye shall drink no wine, neither ye, nor your sons for
ever: [7]Neither shall ye build house, nor sow seed, nor plant vineyard, nor have any: but all your days ye shall dwell in tents; that ye may live many days in the
land where ye be strangers. [8]Thus have we obeyed the voice of Jonadab the son of Rechab our father in all that he hath charged us, to drink no wine all our days, we, our wives, our sons, nor our daughters;
[9]Nor to build houses for us to dwell in; neither have we vineyard, nor field, nor seed:
[10]But we have dwelt in tents, and have obeyed, and done according to all that Jonadab our father commanded us.

Christ's Example of Self-Denial

Rom. 15 [3]For even Christ pleased not himself; but, as it is written, The reproaches of them that reproached thee fell on me.

Phil. 2 [7]But made himself of no reputation, and took upon him the form of a servant, and was made in the likeness of men:
[8]And being found in fashion as a man, he humbled himself, and became obedient unto death, even the death of the cross.

Self-Denial Expected of Christians

Matt. 10 [38]And he that taketh not his cross, and followeth after me, is not worthy of me.

Matt. 16 [24]Then said Jesus unto his disciples, If any man will come after me, let him deny himself, and take up his cross, and follow me.

Luke 3 [11]He answereth and saith unto them, He that hath two coats, let him impart to him that hath none; and he that hath meat, let him do likewise.

Luke 14 [33]So likewise, whosoever he be of you that forsaketh not all that he hath, he cannot be my disciple.

Acts 2 [45]And sold their possessions and goods, and parted them to all men, as every man had need.

Rom. 6 [12]Let not sin therefore reign in
your mortal body, that ye should obey it in
the lusts thereof. [13]Neither yield ye your members as instruments of unrighteousness unto sin: but yield yourselves unto God, as those that are alive from the dead, and your members as instruments of righteousness unto God.

Rom. 8 [13]For if ye live after the flesh, ye shall die: but if ye through the Spirit do mortify the deeds of the body, ye shall live.

Rom. 14 [20]For meat destroy not the
work of God. All things indeed are pure; but it is evil for that man who eateth with
offence. [21]It is good neither to eat flesh, nor to drink wine, nor any thing whereby thy brother stumbleth, or is offended, or is made weak.

Rom. 15 [1]We then that are strong ought to bear the infirmities of the weak, and not to please ourselves. [2]Let every one of us please his neighbour for his good to edification. [3]For even Christ pleased not himself; but, as it is written, The reproaches of them that reproached thee fell on me.

1 Cor. 10 [23]All things are lawful for me, but all things are not expedient: all things are lawful for me, but all things edify not.

Tit. 2 [12]Teaching us that, denying ungodliness and worldly lusts, we should live soberly, righteously, and godly, in this present world.

SELF-EXAMINATION

[self-ex am i nā′shun] An inspection or analysis of one's own conduct, motive and state. The Bible urges constant self-examination as a means of maintaining a covenant relation with God.

SCRIPTURE

Job 13 [23]How many are mine iniquities and sins? make me to know my transgression and my sin.

Psa. 4 [4]Stand in awe, and sin not: commune with your own heart upon your bed, and be still.

Psa. 77 [6]I call to remembrance my song in the night: I commune with mine own heart: and my spirit made diligent search.

Psa. 119 [59]I thought on my ways, and turned my feet unto thy testimonies.

Lam. 3 [40]Let us search and try our ways, and turn again to the LORD.

Hag. 1 [7]Thus saith the LORD of hosts; Consider your ways.

1 Cor. 11 [27]Wherefore whosoever shall eat this bread, and drink this cup of the Lord, unworthily, shall be guilty of the body and blood of the Lord. [28]But let a man examine himself, and so let him eat of that bread, and drink of that cup. [31]For if we would judge ourselves, we should not be judged.

2 Cor. 13 [5]Examine yourselves, whether ye be in the faith; prove your own selves. Know ye not your own selves, how that Jesus Christ is in you, except ye be reprobates?

Gal. 6 [3]For if a man think himself to be something, when he is nothing, he deceiveth himself. [4]But let every man prove his own work, and then shall he have rejoicing in himself alone, and not in another.

SELFISHNESS

[self′ish nes] Exclusive regard for one's own interest or happiness; a sort of self-love or self-interest which leads its possessor purposely to ignore the interest and happiness, rights and privileges of others. The Bible contains numerous warnings against the sin of selfishness.

SCRIPTURE

Isa. 56 [11]Yea, they are greedy dogs which can never have enough, and they are shepherds that cannot understand: they all look to their own way, every one for his gain, from his quarter.

Rom. 15 [1]We then that are strong ought to bear the infirmities of the weak, and not to please ourselves.

1 Cor. 10 [24]Let no man seek his own, but every man another's wealth.

2 Cor. 5 [15]And that he died for all, that they which live should not henceforth live unto themselves, but unto him which died for them, and rose again.

Phil. 2 [4]Look not every man on his own things, but every man also on the things of others.

Jas. 2 [8]If ye fulfil the royal law according to the scripture, Thou shalt love thy neighbour as thyself, ye do well.

SELF-RIGHTEOUSNESS

[self-rī′chus nes] Righteous in one's own esteem; it is used in a perjorative sense of men who take great pride in the high outward moral quality of their lives and feel that they can attain salvation by their own efforts, not recognizing their miserable spiritual condition and their need for the grace of God.

SCRIPTURE

Deut. 9 [4]Speak not thou in thine heart, after that the LORD thy God hath cast them out from before thee, saying, For my righteousness the LORD hath brought me in to possess this land: but for the wickedness of these nations the LORD doth drive them out
from before thee. [5]Not for thy righteousness, or for the uprightness of thine heart, dost thou go to possess their land: but for the wickedness of these nations the LORD thy God doth drive them out from before thee, and that he may perform the word which the LORD sware unto thy fathers,
Abraham, Isaac, and Jacob. [6]Understand therefore, that the LORD thy God giveth thee not this good land to possess it for thy righteousness; for thou art a stiffnecked people.

Prov. 16 [2]All the ways of a man are clean in his own eyes; but the LORD weigheth the spirits.

Prov. 20 [6]Most men will proclaim every one his own goodness: but a faithful man who can find?

Prov. 21 [2]Every way of a man is right in his own eyes: but the LORD pondereth the hearts.

Luke 16 [14]And the Pharisees also, who were covetous, heard all these things: and
they derided him. [15]And he said unto them, Ye are they which justify yourselves before men; but God knoweth your hearts: for that which is highly esteemed among men is abomination in the sight of God.

Luke 18 [9]And he spake this parable unto certain which trusted in themselves that they were righteous, and despised
others: [10]Two men went up into the temple to pray; the one a Pharisee, and the
other a publican. [11]The Pharisee stood and prayed thus with himself, God, I thank thee, that I am not as other men are, extortioners, unjust, adulterers, or even as this
publican. [12]I fast twice in the week, I give
tithes of all that I possess. [13]And the publican, standing afar off, would not lift up so much as his eyes unto heaven, but smote upon his breast, saying, God be merciful to
me a sinner. [14]I tell you, this man went down to his house justified rather than the other: for every one that exalteth himself shall be abased; and he that humbleth himself shall be exalted.

John 9 [41]Jesus said unto them, If ye were blind, ye should have no sin: but now ye say, We see; therefore your sin remaineth.

Rom. 3 [27]Where is boasting then? It is excluded. By what law? of works? Nay: but by the law of faith.

Rom. 10 [3]For they being ignorant of God's righteousness, and going about to establish their own righteousness, have not submitted themselves unto the righteousness of God.

2 Cor. 1 [9]But we had the sentence of death in ourselves, that we should not trust in ourselves, but in God which raiseth the dead.

2 Cor. 10 [17]But he that glorieth, let him
glory in the Lord. [18]For not he that commendeth himself is approved, but whom the Lord commendeth.

Gal. 6 [3]For if a man think himself to be something, when he is nothing, he deceiveth himself.

SENNACHERIB

[se nak′ẽr ib] King of Assyria (704-682 BC). Upon his accession to the throne of Assyria after the death of Sargon, Sennacherib found himself faced with revolt at both ends of his empire. In the East he was threatened by Marduk-apaliddina

(The Merodach-baladan of the Bible); the western rebellion consisted of a coalition in which Hezekiah king of Judah played a leading role. By 701, Sennacherib regained control, forcing Hezekiah to give up a considerable portion of his territory as well as greatly increasing the annual tribute. It is difficult to harmonize the biblical account with the Assyrian archives of this period, but it appears that Sennacherib then returned to Assyria, according to the agreement made at Lachish. After about a decade, revolt flared in the West once again. Eastern troubles prevented immediate action, but by 688 Sennacherib was free to move westward to crush the opposition. It was apparently in this campaign that the army of Sennacherib was decimated by a terrible plague, forcing him to return home without destroying Jerusalem. Although Assyrian records break off after about 689 BC, *2 Kin. 19:37* informs us that Sennacherib met his death at the hands of two of his sons and was replaced by a third son, Esarhaddon.

See HEZEKIAH, RABSHAKEH

SCRIPTURE

2 Kin. 19 32 Therefore thus saith the LORD concerning the king of Assyria, He shall not come into this city, nor shoot an arrow there, nor come before it with shield, nor cast a bank against it. 33 By the way that he came, by the same shall he return, and shall not come into this city, saith the LORD. 34 For I will defend this city, to save it, for mine own sake, and for my servant David's sake.

35 And it came to pass that night, that the angel of the LORD went out, and smote in the camp of the Assyrians a hundred fourscore and five thousand: and when they arose early in the morning, behold, they were all dead corpses. 36 So Sennacherib king of Assyria departed, and went and returned, and dwelt at Nineveh. 37 And it came to pass, as he was worshipping in the house of Nisroch his god, that Adrammelech and Sharezer his sons smote him with the sword: and they escaped into the land of Armenia. And Esarhaddon his son reigned in his stead.

SENSUAL

[sen'shōō al] Pertaining to the gratification of the senses, or the indulgence of appetites; voluptuous; sometimes, lewd.

SCRIPTURE

Eccl. 2 24 There is nothing better for a man, than that he should eat and drink, and that he should make his soul enjoy good in his labour. This also I saw, that it was from the hand of God.

Eccl. 8 15 Then I commended mirth, because a man hath no better thing under the sun, than to eat, and to drink, and to be merry: for that shall abide with him of his labour the days of his life, which God giveth him under the sun.

Eccl. 11 9 Rejoice, O young man, in thy youth; and let thy heart cheer thee in the days of thy youth, and walk in the ways of thine heart, and in the sight of thine eyes: but know thou, that for all these things God will bring thee into judgment.

Isa. 22 13 And behold joy and gladness, slaying oxen, and killing sheep, eating flesh, and drinking wine: let us eat and drink; for to morrow we shall die.

Isa. 56 12 Come ye, say they, I will fetch wine, and we will fill ourselves with strong drink; and to morrow shall be as this day, and much more abundant.

Luke 12 19 And I will say to my soul, Soul, thou hast much goods laid up for many years; take thine ease, eat, drink, and be merry. 20 But God said unto him, Thou fool, this night thy soul shall be required of thee: then whose shall those things be, which thou hast provided?

Jas. 5 5 Ye have lived in pleasure on the earth, and been wanton; ye have nourished your hearts, as in a day of slaughter.

Jude 1 [18]They told you there should be mockers in the last time, who should walk after their own ungodly lusts. [19]These be they who separate themselves, sensual, having not the Spirit.

SERAPHIM

[ser′a fim] Mythological creature mentioned in Isaiah's inaugural vision (*Isa. 6*). These creatures are not fully described, but from the mention of faces, hands, feet, and wings, it is probable that they correspond to the eagle-headed, lion-bodied, winged "griffins" which have been found on many Hebrew seals.

See CHERUBIM

SCRIPTURE

Isa. 6 [1]In the year that king Uzziah died I saw also the LORD sitting upon a throne, high and lifted up, and his train filled the temple. [2]Above it stood the seraphim: each one had six wings: with twain he covered his face, and with twain he covered his feet, and with twain he did fly.

[6]Then flew one of the seraphim unto me, having a live coal in his hand, which he had taken with the tongs from off the altar:

SEVEN CHURCHES OF ASIA

This phrase commonly denotes the seven churches in Asia Minor to whom the short "letters" in the first three chapters of *Revelation* are addressed. The cities in which these churches were located are Ephesus, Smyrna, Pergamum, Thyatira, Sardis, Philadelphia, and Laodicea. These three chapters give a thumbnail sketch of these churches as they appeared near the end of the first century AD.

See EPHESUS, LAODICEA

SCRIPTURE

The Church in Ephesus

Rev. 2 [1]Unto the angel of the church of Ephesus write; These things saith he that holdeth the seven stars in his right hand, who walketh in the midst of the seven golden candlesticks; [2]I know thy works, and thy labour, and thy patience, and how thou canst not bear them which are evil: and thou hast tried them which say they are apostles, and are not, and hast found them liars: [3]And hast borne, and hast patience, and for my name's sake hast laboured, and hast not fainted. [4]Nevertheless I have somewhat against thee, because thou hast left thy first love. [5]Remember therefore from whence thou art fallen, and repent, and do the first works; or else I will come unto thee quickly, and will remove thy candlestick out of his place, except thou repent. [6]But this thou hast, that thou hatest the deeds of the Nicolaitans, which I also hate. [7]He that hath an ear, let him hear what the Spirit saith unto the churches; To him that overcometh will I give to eat of the tree of life, which is in the midst of the paradise of God.

The Church in Smyrna

Rev. 2 [8]And unto the angel of the church in Smyrna write; These things saith the first and the last, which was dead, and is alive; [9]I know thy works, and tribulation, and poverty, (but thou art rich) and I know the blasphemy of them which say they are Jews, and are not, but are the synagogue of Satan. [10]Fear none of those things which thou shalt suffer: behold, the devil shall cast some of you into prison, that ye may be tried; and ye shall have tribulation ten days: be thou faithful unto death, and I will give thee a crown of life. [11]He that hath an ear, let him hear what the Spirit saith unto the churches; He that overcometh shall not be hurt of the second death.

The Church in Pergamos

Rev. 2 [12]And to the angel of the church in Pergamos write; These things saith he which hath the sharp sword with two edges; [13]I know thy works, and where thou dwellest, even where Satan's seat is: and thou holdest fast my name, and hast not denied my faith, even in those days wherein Antipas was my faithful martyr, who was slain among you, where Satan dwelleth. [14]But I have a few things against thee, because thou hast there them that hold the doctrine of Balaam, who taught Balak to cast a stumblingblock before the children of Israel, to eat things sacrificed unto idols, and to commit fornication. [15]So hast thou also them that hold the doctrine of the Nicolaitans, which thing I hate. [16]Repent; or else I will come unto thee quickly, and will fight against them with the sword of my mouth. [17]He that hath an ear, let him hear what the Spirit saith unto the churches; To him that overcometh will I give to eat of the hidden manna, and will give him a white stone, and in the stone a new name written, which no man knoweth saving he that receiveth it.

The Church in Thyatira

Rev. 2 [18]And unto the angel of the church in Thyatira write; These things saith the Son of God, who hath his eyes like unto a flame of fire, and his feet are like fine brass; [19]I know thy works, and charity, and service, and faith, and thy patience, and thy works; and the last to be more than the first. [20]Notwithstanding I have a few things against thee, because thou sufferest that woman Jezebel, which calleth herself a prophetess, to teach and to seduce my servants to commit fornication, and to eat things sacrificed unto idols. [21]And I gave her space to repent of her fornication; and she repented not. [22]Behold, I will cast her into a bed, and them that commit adultery with her into great tribulation, except they repent of their deeds. [23]And I will kill her children with death; and all the churches shall know that I am he which searcheth the reins and hearts: and I will give unto every one of you according to your works. [24]But unto you I say, and unto the rest in Thyatira, as many as have not this doctrine, and which have not known the depths of Satan, as they speak; I will put upon you none other burden. [25]But that which ye have already hold fast till I come. [26]And he that overcometh, and keepeth my works unto the end, to him will I give power over the nations: [27]And he shall rule them with a rod of iron; as the vessels of a potter shall they be broken to shivers: even as I received of my Father. [28]And I will give him the morning star. [29]He that hath an ear, let him hear what the Spirit saith unto the churches.

The Church in Sardis

Rev. 3 [1]And unto the angel of the church in Sardis write; These things saith he that hath the seven Spirits of God, and the seven stars; I know thy works, that thou hast a name that thou livest, and art dead. [2]Be watchful, and strengthen the things which remain, that are ready to die: for I have not found thy works perfect before God. [3]Remember therefore how thou hast received and heard, and hold fast, and repent. If therefore thou shalt not watch, I will come on thee as a thief, and thou shalt not know what hour I will come upon thee. [4]Thou hast a few names even in Sardis which have not defiled their garments; and they shall walk with me in white: for they are worthy. 5 He that overcometh, the same shall be clothed in white raiment; and I will not blot out his name out of the book of life, but I will confess his name before my Father, and before his angels. 6 He that hath an ear, let him hear what the Spirit saith unto the churches.

The Church in Philadelphia

Rev. 3 7 And to the angel of the church in Philadelphia write; These things saith he that is holy, he that is true, he that hath the key of David, he that openeth, and no man shutteth; and shutteth, and no man openeth; 8 I know thy works: behold, I have set before thee an open door, and no man can shut it: for thou hast a little strength, and hast kept my word, and hast not denied my name. 9 Behold, I will make them of the synagogue of Satan, which say they are Jews, and are not, but do lie; behold, I will make them to come and worship before thy feet, and to know that I have loved thee. 10 Because thou hast kept the word of my patience, I also will keep thee from the hour of temptation, which shall come upon all the world, to try them that dwell upon the earth. 11 Behold, I come quickly: hold that fast which thou hast, that no man take thy crown. 12 Him that overcometh will I make a pillar in the temple of my God, and he shall go no more out: and I will write upon him the name of my God, and the name of the city of my God, which is new Jerusalem, which cometh down out of heaven from my God: and I will write upon him my new name. 13 He that hath an ear, let him hear what the Spirit saith unto the churches.

The Church in Laodicea

Rev. 3 14 And unto the angel of the church of the Laodiceans write; These things saith the Amen, the faithful and true witness, the beginning of the creation of God; 15 I know thy works, that thou art neither cold nor hot: I would thou wert cold or hot. 16 So then because thou art lukewarm, and neither cold nor hot, I will spue thee out of my mouth. 17 Because thou sayest, I am rich, and increased with goods, and have need of nothing; and knowest not that thou art wretched, and miserable, and poor, and blind, and naked: 18 I counsel thee to buy of me gold tried in the fire, that thou mayest be rich; and white raiment, that thou mayest be clothed, and that the shame of thy nakedness do not appear; and anoint thine eyes with eyesalve, that thou mayest see. 19 As many as I love, I rebuke and chasten: be zealous therefore, and repent. 20 Behold, I stand at the door, and knock: if any man hear my voice, and open the door, I will come in to him, and will sup with him, and he with me. 21 To him that overcometh will I grant to sit with me in my throne, even as I also overcame, and am set down with my Father in his throne. 22 He that hath an ear, let him hear what the Spirit saith unto the churches.

SHADRACH, MESHACH, AND ABEDNEGO

[shad′rak, mē′shak, å bed′ne gō] The Chaldean names given to Hananiah, Mishael, and Azariah, who, with Daniel, came to Babylon in the first deportation of Hebrews from Jerusalem by Nebuchadnezzar in 597 BC. Because of their ability and integrity, these men gained positions of importance in the Babylonian government. For their refusal to worship a great image of Nebuchadnezzar, Shadrach, Meshach, and Abednego were cast into a fiery furnace from which they were miraculously delivered. After this incident, they were restored to their former positions.

See Captivity, Babylon

SCRIPTURE

Dan. 1 1 In the third year of the reign of

Jehoiakim king of Judah came Nebuchadnezzar king of Babylon unto Jerusalem, and besieged it. 2 And the LORD gave Jehoiakim king of Judah into his hand, with part of the vessels of the house of God: which he carried into the land of Shinar to the house of his god; and he brought the vessels into the treasure house of his god.

3 And the king spake unto Ashpenaz the master of his eunuchs, that he should bring certain of the children of Israel, and of the king's seed, and of the princes; 4 Children in whom was no blemish, but well favoured, and skilful in all wisdom, and cunning in knowledge, and understanding science, and such as had ability in them to stand in the king's palace, and whom they might teach the learning and the tongue of the Chaldeans. 5 And the king appointed them a daily provision of the king's meat, and of the wine which he drank: so nourishing them three years, that at the end thereof they might stand before the king. 6 Now among these were of the children of Judah, Daniel, Hananiah, Mishael, and Azariah: 7 Unto whom the prince of the eunuchs gave names: for he gave unto Daniel the name of Belteshazzar; and to Hananiah, of Shadrach; and to Mishael, of Meshach; and to Azariah, of Abednego.

11 Then said Daniel to Melzar, whom the prince of the eunuchs had set over Daniel, Hananiah, Mishael, and Azariah, 12 Prove thy servants, I beseech thee, ten days; and let them give us pulse to eat, and water to drink. 13 Then let our countenances be looked upon before thee, and the countenance of the children that eat of the portion of the king's meat: and as thou seest, deal with thy servants. 14 So he consented to them in this matter, and proved them ten days. 15 And at the end of ten days their countenances appeared fairer and fatter in flesh than all the children which did eat the portion of the king's meat. 16 Thus Melzar took away the portion of their meat, and the wine that they should drink; and gave them pulse.

17 As for these four children, God gave them knowledge and skill in all learning and wisdom: and Daniel had understanding in all visions and dreams. 18 Now at the end of the days that the king had said he should bring them in, then the prince of the eunuchs brought them in before Nebuchadnezzar. 19 And the king communed with them; and among them all was found none like Daniel, Hananiah, Mishael, and Azariah: therefore stood they before the king. 20 And in all matters of wisdom and understanding, that the king inquired of them, he found them ten times better than all the magicians and astrologers that were in all his realm.

Dan. 3 1 Nebuchadnezzar the king made an image of gold, whose height was threescore cubits, and the breadth thereof six cubits: he set it up in the plain of Dura, in the province of Babylon.

13 Then Nebuchadnezzar in his rage and fury commanded to bring Shadrach, Meshach, and Abednego. Then they brought these men before the king. 14 Nebuchadnezzar spake and said unto them, Is it true, O Shadrach, Meshach, and Abednego? do not ye serve my gods, nor worship the golden image which I have set up? 16 Shadrach, Meshach, and Abednego, answered and said to the king, O Nebuchadnezzar, we are not careful to answer thee in this matter. 17 If it be so, our God whom we serve is able to deliver us from the burning fiery furnace, and he will deliver us out of thine hand, O king. 18 But if not, be it known unto thee, O king, that we will not serve thy gods, nor worship the golden image which thou hast set up.

19 Then was Nebuchadnezzar full of
fury, and the form of his visage was
changed against Shadrach, Meshach, and
Abednego: therefore he spake, and commanded that they should heat the furnace
one seven times more than it was wont
to be heated. 20 And he commanded the
most mighty men that were in his army to
bind Shadrach, Meshach, and Abednego,
and to cast them into the burning fiery
furnace. 21 Then these men were bound
in their coats, their hosen, and their hats,
and their other garments, and were cast
into the midst of the burning fiery furnace. 22 Therefore because the king's commandment was urgent, and the furnace exceeding hot, the flame of the fire slew those
men that took up Shadrach, Meshach, and
Abednego. 23 And these three men, Shadrach, Meshach, and Abednego, fell down
bound into the midst of the burning fiery
furnace. 24 Then Nebuchadnezzar the
king was astonied, and rose up in haste,
and spake, and said unto his counsellors,
Did not we cast three men bound into the
midst of the fire? They answered and said
unto the king, True, O king. 25 He answered and said, Lo, I see four men loose,
walking in the midst of the fire, and they
have no hurt; and the form of the fourth is
like the Son of God.

26 Then Nebuchadnezzar came near to
the mouth of the burning fiery furnace,
and spake, and said, Shadrach, Meshach,
and Abednego, ye servants of the most
high God, come forth, and come hither.
Then Shadrach, Meshach, and Abednego,
came forth of the midst of the fire. 27 And
the princes, governors, and captains, and
the king's counsellors, being gathered together, saw these men, upon whose bodies
the fire had no power, nor was a hair of
their head singed, neither were their coats
changed, nor the smell of fire had passed
on them. 28 Then Nebuchadnezzar spake,
and said, Blessed be the God of Shadrach,
Meshach, and Abednego, who hath sent
his angel, and delivered his servants that
trusted in him, and have changed the
king's word, and yielded their bodies, that
they might not serve nor worship any god,
except their own God. 29 Therefore I make
a decree, That every people, nation, and
language, which speak any thing amiss
against the God of Shadrach, Meshach,
and Abednego, shall be cut in pieces, and
their houses shall be made a dunghill; because there is no other God that can
deliver after this sort. 30 Then the king
promoted Shadrach, Meshach, and Abednego, in the province of Babylon.

SHALLUM

[shal'um] The fifteenth king of Israel who reigned only one month (c. 748 BC) after publicly assassinating his predecessor, Zachariah, in the seventh month of his reign. Shallum's reign is distinguished only by the fact that it was the shortest in the history of the northern kingdom. He was slain by Menahem after one month on the throne.

See KINGS, ZECHARIAH, MENAHEM

SCRIPTURE

2 Kin. 15 8 In the thirty and eighth year
of Azariah king of Judah did Zachariah the
son of Jeroboam reign over Israel in Samaria six months. 9 And he did that which
was evil in the sight of the LORD, as his fathers had done: he departed not from the
sins of Jeroboam the son of Nebat, who
made Israel to sin. 10 And Shallum the son
of Jabesh conspired against him, and
smote him before the people, and slew
him, and reigned in his stead. 11 And the
rest of the acts of Zachariah, behold, they
are written in the book of the Chronicles
of the kings of Israel. 12 This was the word

of the Lord which he spake unto Jehu, saying, Thy sons shall sit on the throne of Israel unto the fourth generation. And so it
came to pass.
[13]Shallum the son of Jabesh began to
reign in the nine and thirtieth year of Uzziah king of Judah; and he reigned a full
month in Samaria. [14]For Menahem the
son of Gadi went up from Tirzah, and
came to Samaria, and smote Shallum the
son of Jabesh in Samaria, and slew him,
and reigned in his stead. [15]And the rest
of the acts of Shallum, and his conspiracy
which he made, behold, they are written in
the book of the Chronicles of the kings of
Israel.

SHALMANESER

[shal ma nē′zẽr] The name of several Assyrian kings. It is Shalmaneser V who is mentioned in the Bible. He succeeded Tiglath-Pileser to the throne in 727 BC and reigned until 722 BC. At his accession, Hoshea was serving as a vassal king of Israel. Shortly afterward, relying on expected help from So king of Egypt—which never materialized—Hoshea made the suicidal mistake of refusing to pay the annual tribute. In 724, Shalmaneser took Hoshea captive and laid siege to Samaria. After a long struggle the great city fell and Israel was no more. Archaeological records indicate that Shalmaneser died during the course of the campaign and that it was Sargon II (722-795 BC) to whom the city actually fell in 721 BC.

See Sargon, Hoshea

SCRIPTURE

2 Kin. 17 [1]In the twelfth year of Ahaz
king of Judah began Hoshea the son of
Elah to reign in Samaria over Israel nine
years. [2]And he did that which was evil
in the sight of the Lord, but not as the
kings of Israel that were before him.
[3]Against him came up Shalmaneser king
of Assyria; and Hoshea became his servant, and gave him presents. [4]And the king
of Assyria found conspiracy in Hoshea: for
he had sent messengers to So king of
Egypt, and brought no present to the king
of Assyria, as he had done year by year:
therefore the king of Assyria shut him up,
and bound him in prison.
[5]Then the king of Assyria came up
throughout all the land, and went up to
Samaria, and besieged it three years.
[6]In the ninth year of Hoshea, the king of
Assyria took Samaria, and carried Israel
away into Assyria, and placed them in Halah and in Habor by the river of Gozan,
and in the cities of the Medes.
2 Kin. 18 [9]And it came to pass in the
fourth year of king Hezekiah, which was
the seventh year of Hoshea son of Elah
king of Israel, that Shalmaneser king of
Assyria came up against Samaria, and besieged it. [10]And at the end of three years
they took it: even in the sixth year of Hezekiah, that is, the ninth year of Hoshea
king of Israel, Samaria was taken. [11]And
the king of Assyria did carry away Israel
unto Assyria, and put them in Halah and
in Habor by the river of Gozan, and in
the cities of the Medes: [12]Because they
obeyed not the voice of the Lord their
God, but transgressed his covenant, and
all that Moses the servant of the Lord
commanded, and would not hear them,
nor do them.

SHAMGAR

[sham′gar] The son of Anath and a judge of Israel who delivered his people from oppression under the Philistines. He is best noted for the feat of killing six hundred Philistines with an ox goad.

See Judges of Israel

SCRIPTURE

Judg. 3 [31]And after him was Shamgar
the son of Anath, which slew of the Philistines six hundred men with an ox goad:
and he also delivered Israel.

Judg. 5 [6]In the days of Shamgar the son of Anath, in the days of Jael, the highways were unoccupied, and the travelers walked through byways.

SHEBA, QUEEN OF

[shē'ba] The Queen of Sheba is said to have visited Solomon "to prove him with hard questions." After she tested his fabled wisdom to her satisfaction and surveyed the vast riches of his empire, "there was no more spirit in her", and she uttered the famous phrase, "the half was not told me." The biblical record notes that after a lavish exchange of gifts she returned to her native land. It is quite probable, however, that this visit was promoted by more than a simple interest in riddles. The land over which this queen ruled was in control of the spice and incense trade for which southwestern Arabia was famous. It is likely that the queen's visit had as a major purpose the establishment of a suitable trade agreement with the Israelite king.

See Solomon

SCRIPTURE

1 Kin. 10 [1]And when the queen of Sheba heard of the fame of Solomon concerning the name of the Lord, she came to prove him with hard questions. [2]And she came to Jerusalem with a very great train, with camels that bare spices, and very much gold and precious stones: and when she was come to Solomon, she communed with him of all that was in her heart. [3]And Solomon told her all her questions: there was not any thing hid from the king, which he told her not. [4]And when the queen of Sheba had seen all Solomon's wisdom, and the house that he had built, [5]And the meat of his table, and the sitting of his servants, and the attendance of his ministers, and their apparel, and his cupbearers, and his ascent by which he went up unto the house of the Lord; there was no more spirit in her. [6]And she said to the king, It was a true report that I heard in mine own land of thy acts and of thy wisdom. [7]Howbeit I believed not the words, until I came, and mine eyes had seen it; and, behold, the half was not told me: thy wisdom and prosperity exceedeth the fame which I heard. [8]Happy are thy men, happy are these thy servants, which stand continually before thee, and that hear thy wisdom. [9]Blessed be the Lord thy God, which delighted in thee, to set thee on the throne of Israel: because the Lord loved Israel for ever, therefore made he thee king, to do judgment and justice. [10]And she gave the king a hundred and twenty talents of gold, and of spices very great store, and precious stones: there came no more such abundance of spices as these which the queen of Sheba gave to king Solomon. [11]And the navy also of Hiram, that brought gold from Ophir, brought in from Ophir great plenty of almug trees, and precious stones. [12]And the king made of the almug trees pillars for the house of the Lord, and for the king's house, harps also and psalteries for singers: there came no such almug trees, nor were seen unto this day. [13]And king Solomon gave unto the queen of Sheba all her desire, whatsoever she asked, besides that which Solomon gave her of his royal bounty. So she turned and went to her own country, she and her servants.

See 2 Chr. 9:1-12

SHECHEM

[shē'kem] An ancient city situated in the pass between Mount Ebal and Mount Gerizim, about five miles southeast of Samaria, also referred to as Sichem (*Gen. 12:6*) and Sychem (*Acts 7:16*). The first mention of Shechem is in connection with Abram's journey from Haran, during which he stopped in Shechem, at the oak of Moreh and erected an altar to the Lord (*Gen. 12:4-7*). The city figures more prominently in the account of Dinah's defilement by Shechem prince of the city and the subsequent vengeance on the men of the city by her brother's Simeon and Levi (*Gen. 34*). It was here that Joshua summoned the tribes together for his last meeting with them (*Josh. 24*). Shechem next figures in the narrative concerning Jotham and Abimelech (*Judg. 9*). The latter became king over Shechem but was later rejected, at which time he captured and burned the city. By the time of the schism of the kingdom of Israel, Shechem was once more an important center, for it was there that Rehoboam met with the representatives of the northern tribes, in an effort to confirm his rule over them, and it was there that he was rejected in favor of Jeroboam, who made Shechem his capital for a time. After the capital was transferred to Samaria, Shechem declined and was apparently of little significance until it became the central city of the Samaritan party (*see* SAMARITANS), whose sanctuary was erected on Mount Gerizim. Some scholars identify Shechem with the Sychar of *John 4:5*, but this cannot be definitely established. Archaeologists have recently discovered the ancient site of Shechem.

SCRIPTURE

Abraham Builds an Altar

Gen. 12 6And Abram passed through
the land unto the place of Sichem, unto
the plain of Moreh. And the Canaanite was
then in the land. 7And the LORD appeared
unto Abram, and said, Unto thy seed will I
give this land: and there builded he an altar unto the LORD, who appeared unto him.

Simeon and Levi Slay Inhabitants to Avenge Dinah's Defilement

Gen. 34 1And Dinah the daughter of
Leah, which she bare unto Jacob, went out
to see the daughters of the land. 2And
when Shechem the son of Hamor the Hivite, prince of the country, saw her, he took
her, and lay with her, and defiled her.
3And his soul clave unto Dinah the daughter of Jacob, and he loved the damsel, and
spake kindly unto the damsel. 4And Shechem spake unto his father Hamor, saying,
Get me this damsel to wife. 5And Jacob
heard that he had defiled Dinah his daughter: (now his sons were with his cattle in
the field: and Jacob held his peace until
they were come.)

6And Hamor the father of Shechem
went out unto Jacob to commune with
him. 7And the sons of Jacob came out of
the field when they heard it: and the men
were grieved, and they were very wroth,
because he had wrought folly in Israel in
lying with Jacob's daughter, which thing
ought not to be done. 8And Hamor communed with them, saying, The soul of my
son Shechem longeth for your daughter: I
pray you give her him to wife. 9And make
ye marriages with us, and give your daughters unto us, and take our daughters unto
you. 10And ye shall dwell with us: and the
land shall be before you; dwell and trade
ye therein, and get you possessions therein.
11And Shechem said unto her father and
unto her brethren, Let me find grace in your
eyes, and what ye shall say unto me I will
give. 12Ask me never so much dowry and
gift, and I will give according as ye shall
say unto me: but give me the damsel to
wife. 13And the sons of Jacob answered
Shechem and Hamor his father deceitfully,
and said, because he had defiled Dinah
their sister: 14And they said unto them,
We cannot do this thing, to give our sister
to one that is uncircumcised; for that were
a reproach unto us: 15But in this will we
consent unto you: If ye will be as we be,
that every male of you be circumcised:
16Then will we give our daughters unto
you, and we will take your daughters to us,
and we will dwell with you, and we will
become one people. 17But if ye will not
hearken unto us, to be circumcised; then
will we take our daughter, and we will be
gone. 18And their words pleased Hamor

and Shechem Hamor's son. [19]And the young man deferred not to do the thing, because he had delight in Jacob's daughter: and he was more honourable than all the house of his father.

[20]And Hamor and Shechem his son came unto the gate of their city, and communed with the men of their city, saying [21]These men are peaceable with us; therefore let them dwell in the land, and trade therein: for the land, behold, it is large enough for them; let us take their daughters to us for wives, and let us give them our daughters. [22]Only herein will the men consent unto us for to dwell with us, to be one people, if every male among us be circumcised, as they are circumcised. [23]Shall not their cattle and their substance and every beast of theirs be ours? only let us consent unto them, and they will dwell with us. [24]And unto Hamor and unto Shechem his son hearkened all that went out of the gate of his city; and every male was circumcised, all that went out of the gate of his city.

[25]And it came to pass on the third day, when they were sore, that two of the sons of Jacob, Simeon and Levi, Dinah's brethren, took each man his sword, and came upon the city boldly, and slew all the males. [26]And they slew Hamor and Shechem his son with the edge of the sword, and took Dinah out of Shechem's house, and went out. [27]The sons of Jacob came upon the slain, and spoiled the city, because they had defiled their sister. [28]They took their sheep, and their oxen, and their asses, and that which was in the city, and that which was in the field, [29]And all their wealth, and all their little ones, and their wives took they captive, and spoiled even all that was in the house. [30]And Jacob said to Simeon and Levi, Ye have troubled me to make me to stink among the inhabitants of the land, among the Canaanites and the Perizzites: and I being few in number, they shall gather themselves together against me, and slay me; and I shall be destroyed, I and my house. [31]And they said, Should he deal with our sister as with a harlot?

Joshua Summons the Tribes to Shechem

Josh. 24 [1]And Joshua gathered all the tribes of Israel to Shechem, and called for the elders of Israel, and for their heads, and for their judges, and for their officers; and they presented themselves before God.

Abimelech Becomes King of Shechem

Judg. 9 [1]And Abimelech the son of Jerubbaal went to Shechem unto his mother's brethren, and communed with them, and with all the family of the house of his mother's father, saying, [2]Speak, I pray you, in the ears of all the men of Shechem, Whether is better for you, either that all the sons of Jerubbaal, which are threescore and ten persons, reign over you, or that one reign over you? remember also that I am your bone and your flesh. [3]And his mother's brethren spake of him in the ears of all the men of Shechem all these words: and their hearts inclined to follow Abimelech; for they said, He is our brother. [4]And they gave him threescore and ten pieces of silver out of the house of Baalberith, wherewith Abimelech hired vain and light persons, which followed him. [5]And he went unto his father's house at Ophrah, and slew his brethren the sons of Jerubbaal, being threescore and ten persons, upon one stone: notwithstanding, yet Jotham the youngest son of Jerubbaal was left; for he hid himself. [6]And all the men of Shechem gathered together, and all the house of Millo, and went and made Abimelech king, by the plain of the pillar that was in Shechem.

Shechem Revolts against Abimelech

Judg. 9 [22]When Abimelech had reigned three years over Israel, [23]Then God sent an evil spirit between Abimelech and the men of Shechem; and the men of Shechem dealt treacherously with Abimelech: [24]That the cruelty done to the threescore and ten sons of Jerubbaal might come, and their blood be laid upon Abimelech their brother, which slew them, and upon the men of Shechem, which aided him in the killing of his brethren. [25]And the men of Shechem set liers in wait for him in the top of the mountains, and they robbed all that came along that way by them: and it was told Abimelech. [26]And Gaal the son of Ebed came with his brethren, and went over to Shechem: and the men of Shechem put their confidence in him. [27]And they went out into the fields, and gathered their vineyards, and trode the grapes, and made merry, and went into the house of their god, and did eat and drink, and cursed Abimelech. [28]And Gaal the son of Ebed said, Who is Abimelech, and who is Shechem, that we should serve him? is not he the son of Jerubbaal? and Zebul his officer? serve the men of Hamor the father of Shechem: for why should we serve him? [29]And would to God this people were under my hand! then would I remove Abimelech. And he said to Abimelech, Increase thine army, and come out.

Abimelech Quells Revolt

Judg. 9 [34]And Abimelech rose up, and all the people that were with him, by night, and they laid wait against Shechem in four companies. [35]And Gaal the son of Ebed went out, and stood in the entering of the gate of the city: and Abimelech rose up, and the people that were with him, from lying in wait. [36]And when Gaal saw the people, he said to Zebul, Behold, there come people down from the top of the mountains. And Zebul said unto him, Thou seest the shadow of the mountains as if they were men. [37]And Gaal spake again, and said, See, there come people down by the middle of the land, and another company come along by the plain of Meonenim. [38]Then said Zebul unto him, Where is now thy mouth, wherewith thou saidst, Who is Abimelech, that we should serve him? is not this the people that thou hast despised? go out, I pray now, and fight with them. [39]And Gaal went out before the men of Shechem, and fought with Abimelech. [40]And Abimelech chased him, and he fled before him, and many were overthrown and wounded, even unto the entering of the gate. [41]And Abimelech dwelt at Arumah: and Zebul thrust out Gaal and his brethren, that they should not dwell in Shechem. [42]And it came to pass on the morrow, that the people went out into the field; and they told Abimelech. [43]And he took the people, and divided them into three companies, and laid wait in the field, and looked, and, behold, the people were come forth out of the city; and he rose up against them, and smote them. [44]And Abimelech, and the company that was with him, rushed forward, and stood in the entering of the gate of the city: and the two other companies ran upon all the people that were in the fields, and slew them. [45]And Abimelech fought against the city all that day; and he took the city, and slew the people that was therein, and beat down the city, and sowed it with salt.

[46]And when all the men of the tower of Shechem heard that, they entered into a hold of the house of the god Berith. [47]And it was told Abimelech, that all the men of the tower of Shechem were gathered together. [48]And Abimelech gat him up to

mount Zalmon, he and all the people that were with him; and Abimelech took an axe in his hand, and cut down a bough from the trees, and took it, and laid it on his shoulder, and said unto the people that were with him, What ye have seen me do, make haste, and do as I have done. [49]And all the people likewise cut down every man his bough, and followed Abimelech, and put them to the hold, and set the hold on fire upon them; so that all the men of the tower of Shechem died also, about a thousand men and women.

Rehoboam Crowned at Shechem

1 Kin. 12 [1]And Rehoboam went to Shechem: for all Israel were come to Shechem to make him king.

Rebuilt by Jeroboam

1 Kin. 12 [25]Then Jeroboam built Shechem in mount Ephraim, and dwelt therein; and went out from thence, and built Penuel.

SHEM

[shem] A son of Noah, regarded as the progenitor of tribes in Syria, Canaan, Chaldaea, Assyria, Persia, and Arabia.

See HAM, NOAH, JAPHETH

SCRIPTURE

Gen. 9 [18]And the sons of Noah, that went forth of the ark, were Shem, and Ham, and Japheth: and Ham is the father of Canaan. [19]These are the three sons of Noah: and of them was the whole earth overspread. [20]And Noah began to be a husbandman, and he planted a vineyard: [21]And he drank of the wine, and was drunken; and he was uncovered within his tent. [22]And Ham, the father of Canaan, saw the nakedness of his father, and told his two brethren without. [23]And Shem and Japheth took a garment, and laid it upon both their shoulders, and went backward, and covered the nakedness of their father; and their faces were backward, and they saw not their father's nakedness.

SHEOL

[shē′ōl] The underworld; the unseen state of the dead; the region of shadows, silence, and forgetting in which the dead reside. The Hebrews did not view death as total extinction; rather, they felt that when a man was "gathered to his fathers", he entered the gloomy nether world known as Sheol. There virtually all contact with God and the living was severed; therefore, Sheol was viewed by the Hebrew with horror and dismay. In the King James Version of the Bible, Sheol is translated by "grave" (*Gen. 37:35; 1 Sam. 2:6; Job 7:9; Psa. 6:5; 49:14; Isa. 14:11;* etc.), "hell" (*Deut. 32:22; Psa. 9:17; 18:5; Isa. 14:9; Amos 9:2;* etc.), or "pit" (*Num. 16:30, 33; Job 17:16*). It is the equivalent of the Greek word "Hades" and is so rendered in the Septuagint, the Greek translation of the Hebrew Old Testament.

See HELL, HADES, PARADISE, GEHENNA

SHEPHERD

[shep′ẽrd] One who cares for flocks. The keeping of sheep was and is a principle means of livelihood in Palestine. (*See* AGRICULTURE) The shepherd's primary duties are to see that his flocks find plenty to eat and drink, to care for any that are injured or ill, and to find any that may become lost. The Bible contains numerous references to the pastoral life in a figurative sense. The term "pastor" is still in use in the Christian church and signifies those who have the spiritual oversight over "flocks", or congregations (*1 Pet. 5:1-4*). "Sheep which have no shepherd" is a phrase used to refer to people without a leader or a sense of direction and, therefore, lost (*Num. 27:17; 1 Kin. 22:17; Ezek. 35:5, 8; Matt. 9:36*). As the supreme spiritual overseer, Jesus is spoken of as "The Good Shepherd" (*John 10:14*), Chief Shepherd (*1 Pet. 5:4*), Great Shepherd (*Heb. 13:20*), and the One Shepherd (*John 10:16*).

SCRIPTURE

God's People Compared to Sheep

Psa. 74 [1]O God, why hast thou cast us off for ever? why doth thine anger smoke against the sheep of thy pasture?

Psa. 79 [13]So we thy people and sheep of thy pasture will give thee thanks for ever: we will shew forth thy praise to all generations.

Psa. 95 [7]For he is our God; and we are the people of his pasture, and the sheep of his hand. To day if ye will hear his voice.

Psa. 100 [3]Know ye that the LORD he is God: it is he that hath made us, and not we ourselves; we are his people, and the sheep of his pasture.

Ezek. 34 [2]Son of man, prophesy against the shepherds of Israel, prophesy, and say unto them, Thus saith the Lord GOD unto the shepherds; Woe be to the shepherds of Israel that do feed themselves! should not the shepherds feed the flocks?

[11]For thus saith the Lord GOD; Behold, I, even I, will both search my sheep, and seek them out. [12]As a shepherd seeketh out his flock in the day that he is among his sheep that are scattered; so will I seek out my sheep, and will deliver them out of all places where they have been scattered in the cloudy and dark day. [13]And I will bring them out from the people, and gather them from the countries, and will bring them to their own land, and feed them upon the mountains of Israel by the rivers, and in all the inhabited places of the country. [14]I will feed them in a good pasture, and upon the high mountains of Israel shall their fold be: there shall they lie in a good fold, and in a fat pasture shall they feed upon the mountains of Israel. [15]I will feed my flock, and I will cause them to lie down, saith the Lord GOD. [16]I will seek that which was lost, and bring again that which was driven away, and will bind up that which was broken, and will strengthen that which was sick: but I will destroy the fat and the strong; I will feed them with judgment.

Matt. 15 [24]But he answered and said, I am not sent but unto the lost sheep of the house of Israel.

Matt. 25 [32]And before him shall be gathered all nations: and he shall separate them one from another, as a shepherd divideth his sheep from the goats.

John 10 [2]But he that entereth in by the door is the shepherd of the sheep. [3]To him the porter openeth; and the sheep hear his voice: and he calleth his own sheep by name, and leadeth them out. [4]And when he putteth forth his own sheep, he goeth before them, and the sheep follow him: for they know his voice.

1 Pet. 2 [25]For ye were as sheep going astray; but are now returned unto the Shepherd and Bishop of your souls.

Lamb as Emblem of Christ

John 1 [29]The next day John seeth Jesus coming unto him, and saith, Behold the Lamb of God, which taketh away the sin of the world.

The Good Shepherd

Isa. 40 [11]He shall feed his flock like a shepherd: he shall gather the lambs with his arm, and carry them in his bosom, and shall gently lead those that are with young.

Zech. 11 [16]For, lo, I will raise up a shepherd in the land, which shall not visit those that be cut off, neither shall seek the young one, nor heal that that is broken, nor feed that that standeth still: but he shall eat the flesh of the fat, and tear their claws in pieces.

John 10 [14]I am the good shepherd, and

know my sheep, and am known of mine.

Heb. 13 20 Now the God of peace, that brought again from the dead our Lord Jesus, that great shepherd of the sheep, through the blood of the everlasting covenant.

1 Pet. 2 25 For ye were as sheep going astray; but are now returned unto the Shepherd and Bishop of your souls.

1 Pet. 5 4 And when the chief Shepherd shall appear, ye shall receive a crown of glory that fadeth not away.

SHEWBREAD (Showbread)

[shō′bred] The bread which was arranged in two piles of six loaves each on a table situated in the Holy Place of both the Tabernacle and the Temple. (*See* TABERNACLE and TEMPLE) The table of shewbread also held a number of vessels which probably contained grain, wine, and oil, offered to God as representative of the chief products of the land. The loaves of shewbread were changed every Sabbath, at which time the old loaves were eaten by the priests. The shewbread is sometimes referred to in the Bible as the "bread of the presence" (*Ex. 25:30; Heb. 9:2*), and the "continual showbread" (*Num. 4:7; 2 Chr. 2:4*). Detailed instructions for preparation of the shewbread may be found in *Lev. 24:5-9.*

SCRIPTURE

Instructions for Preparation

Lev. 24 5 And thou shalt take fine flour, and bake twelve cakes thereof: two tenth deals shall be in one cake. 6 And thou shalt set them in two rows, six on a row, upon the pure table before the LORD. 7 And thou shalt put pure frankincense upon each row, that it may be on the bread for a memorial, even an offering made by fire unto the LORD. 8 Every sabbath he shall set it in order before the LORD continually, being taken from the children of Israel by an everlasting covenant. 9 And it shall be Aaron's and his sons'; and they shall eat it in the holy place: for it is most holy unto him of the offerings of the LORD made by fire by a perpetual statute.

To Be Kept Before the Lord Continually

Ex. 25 30 And thou shalt set upon the table showbread before me always.

Num. 4 7 And upon the table of showbread they shall spread a cloth of blue, and put thereon the dishes, and the spoons, and the bowls, and covers to cover withal: and the continual bread shall be thereon.

David Eats Shewbread

1 Sam. 21 1 Then came David to Nob to Ahimelech the priest: and Ahimelech was afraid at the meeting of David, and said unto him, Why art thou alone, and no man with thee? 2 And David said unto Ahimelech the priest, The king hath commanded me a business, and hath said unto me, Let no man know any thing of the business whereabout I send thee, and what I have commanded thee: and I have appointed my servants to such and such a place. 3 Now therefore what is under thine hand? give me five loaves of bread in mine hand, or what there is present. 4 And the priest answered David, and said, There is no common bread under mine hand, but there is hallowed bread; if the young men have kept themselves at least from women. 5 And David answered the priest and said unto him, Of a truth women have been kept from us about these three days, since I came out, and the vessels of the young men are holy, and the bread is in a manner common, yea, though it were sanctified this day in the vessel. 6 So the priest gave him hallowed bread: for there was no bread there but the shewbread, that was taken from before the LORD, to put hot bread in the day when it was taken away.

SHIBBOLETH

[shib'ô leth] A test word which the men of Gilead applied to the Ephraimites who tried to escape across the Jordan after having been defeated by the Gileadites. When asked to pronounce this word, the Ephraimites were betrayed by their dialect and the Gileadites were able to identify and slay them.

SCRIPTURE

Judg. 12 [1]And the men of Ephraim
gathered themselves together, and went
northward, and said unto Jephthath,
Wherefore passedst thou over to fight
against the children of Ammon, and didst
not call us to go with thee? we will burn
thine house upon thee with fire. [2]And
Jephthah said unto them, I and my people
were at great strife with the children of
Ammon; and when I called you, ye delivered me not out of their hands. [3]And
when I saw that ye delivered me not, I put
my life in my hands, and passed over
against the children of Ammon, and the
LORD delivered them into my hand:
wherefore then are ye come up unto me
this day, to fight against me? [4]Then Jephthah gathered together all the men of Gilead, and fought with Ephraim: and the
men of Gilead smote Ephraim, because
they said, Ye Gileadites are fugitives of
Ephraim among the Ephraimites, and
among the Manassites. [5]And the Gileadites took the passages of Jordan before the
Ephraimites: and it was so, that when those
Ephraimites which were escaped said, Let
me go over, that the men of Gilead said
unto him, Art thou an Ephraimite? If he
said, Nay; [6]Then said they unto him, Say
now Shibboleth: and he said Sibboleth: for
he could not frame to pronounce it right.
Then they took him and slew him at the
passages of Jordan. And there fell at that
time of the Ephraimites forty and two
thousand.

SHILOH

[shi'lō] A town in the land assigned to Ephraim, situated "on the north of Beth-el, on the east side of the highway that goeth up from Beth-el to Shechem, and on the south of Lebonah" (*Judg. 21:19*). From the time of the assembly after the wars of conquest (*Josh. 18-21*), until its capture by the Philistines, the ark of the covenant rested at Shiloh, making that place the central sanctuary of Israel (*Judg. 18:31; 1 Sam. 1:3; 3, 4*). The Bible contains no direct account of the destruction of Shiloh, but the event is referred to in *Psa. 78:60* and in *Jer. 7:12, 14; 26:6.*

SCRIPTURE

Site of the Ark of the Covenant

Josh. 18 [1]And the whole congregation
of the children of Israel assembled together at Shiloh, and set up the tabernacle
of the congregation there: and the land
was subdued before them.

The Promised Land Apportioned at Shiloh

Josh. 18 [9]And the men went and passed
through the land, and described it by cities
into seven parts in a book, and came again
to Joshua to the host at Shiloh.
[10]And Joshua cast lots for them in Shiloh
before the LORD: and there Joshua divided
the land unto the children of Israel according to their divisions.

The Early Center of Israelite Government

Josh. 21 [1]Then came near the heads of
the fathers of the Levites unto Eleazar the
priest, and unto Joshua the son of Nun,
and unto the heads of the fathers of the
tribes of the children of Israel; [2]And they
spake unto them at Shiloh in the land of
Canaan, saying, The LORD commanded by
the hand of Moses to give us cities to dwell
in, with the suburbs thereof for our cattle.
[12]But the fields of the city, and the villages thereof, gave they to Caleb the son
of Jephunneh for his possession.

Josh. 22 [9]And the children of Reuben and the children of Gad and the half tribe of Manasseh returned, and departed from the children of Israel out of Shiloh, which is in the land of Canaan, to go unto the country of Gilead, to the land of their possession, whereof they were possessed, according to the word of the LORD by the hand of Moses.

[12]And when the children of Israel heard of it, the whole congregation of the children of Israel gathered themselves together at Shiloh, to go up to war against them.

Judg. 21 [12]And they found among the inhabitants of Jabesh-gilead four hundred young virgins that had known no man by lying with any male: and they brought them unto the camp to Shiloh, which is in the land of Canaan.

1 Sam. 1 [9]So Hannah rose up after they had eaten in Shiloh, and after they had drunk. Now Eli the priest sat upon a seat by a post of the temple of the LORD.

SHIPHRAH AND PUAH

[shif'ra, pū'a] The two Hebrew midwives whom the king of Egypt commanded to kill all male children born to Hebrew women. They avoided carrying out this command, excusing themselves on the grounds that the vigorous Hebrew women delivered their own children before the midwives could arrive.

SCRIPTURE

Ex. 1 [15]And the king of Egypt spake to the Hebrew midwives, of which the name of the one was Shiphrah, and the name of the other Puah; [16]And he said, When ye do the office of a midwife to the Hebrew women, and see them upon the stools, if it be a son, then ye shall kill him; but if it be a daughter, then she shall live. [17]But the midwives feared God, and did not as the king of Egypt commanded them, but saved the men children alive. [18]And the king of Egypt called for the midwives, and said unto them, Why have ye done this thing, and have saved the men children alive? [19]And the midwives said unto Pharaoh, Because the Hebrew women are not as the Egyptian women; for they are lively, and are delivered ere the midwives come in unto them. [20]Therefore God dealt well with the midwives: and the people multiplied, and waxed very mighty. [21]And it came to pass, because the midwives feared God, that he made them houses. [22]And Pharaoh charged all his people, saying, Every son that is born ye shall cast into the river, and every daughter ye shall save alive.

SHISHAK

[shī'shak] King of Egypt (c. 935-914 BC) and founder of the Twenty-second (Bubastite) dynasty. It was this king who gave asylum to Jeroboam when he fled to Egypt to escape possible death at the hands of Solomon. His friendship seems to have been motivated merely by a desire to foster any weakness in Israel, for when Jeroboam became king over northern Israel after the schism under Rehoboam, Shishak showed him no favoritism in a campaign of pillage and destruction which resulted in the conquest of 150 towns of Palestine, according to an inscription found at Karnack. Jerusalem itself escaped destruction, but the fabled treasures of the temple and the royal palace were plundered and Rehoboam was placed under a heavy tribute. Although the internal weakness of the Egyptian state made it impossible for Shishak to re-establish the Egyptian empire, he had so weakened Israel and Judah as to make it impossible for either to force the other into a union with itself, thus assuring the permanency of the division between the two kingdoms.

See JEROBOAM, REHOBOAM

SCRIPTURE

Gives Asylum to Jeroboam

1 Kin. 11 40Solomon sought therefore to kill Jeroboam. And Jeroboam arose, and fled into Egypt, unto Shishak king of Egypt, and was in Egypt until the death of Solomon.

Spoils Jerusalem

2 Chr. 12 2And it came to pass, that in
the fifth year of king Rehoboam, Shishak
king of Egypt came up against Jerusalem,
because they had transgressed against the
LORD, 3With twelve hundred chariots, and
threescore thousand horsemen: and the
people were without number that came
with him out of Egypt; the Lubim, the Sukkiim, and the Ethiopians. 4And he took the
fenced cities which pertained to Judah,
and came to Jerusalem.
5Then came Shemaiah the prophet to
Rehoboam, and to the princes of Judah,
that were gathered together to Jerusalem
because of Shishak, and said unto them,
Thus saith the LORD, Ye have forsaken me,
and therefore have I also left you in the
hand of Shishak. 6Whereupon the prin-
ces of Israel and the king humbled themselves; and they said, The LORD is righteous. 7And when the LORD saw that they
humbled themselves, the word of the LORD
came to Shemaiah, saying, They have
humbled themselves; therefore I will not
destroy them, but I will grant them some
deliverance; and my wrath shall not be
poured out upon Jerusalem by the hand of
Shishak. 8Nevertheless they shall be his
servants; that they may know my service,
and the service of the kingdoms of the
countries. 9So Shishak king of Egypt came
up against Jerusalem, and took away the
treasures of the house of the LORD, and the
treasures of the king's house; he took all:
he carried away also the shields of gold
which Solomon had made.

SHITTIM

[shit′im] The last place at which Israel camped before crossing the Jordan to begin the conquest of Palestine. It was here that the evil counsel of Balaam brought disaster to the Israelites and, ultimately, to the Midianites and Balaam himself (*Num. 25:1ff; 31:16*). In *Num. 33:49*, it is called Abel-Shittim.

REFERENCE: *Num. 33:49; Josh. 2:1; 3:1.*

SHITTIM WOOD

[shit′im] A species of Acacia, the Shittah tree is a gnarled, thorny tree found in the Sinaitic peninsula and in Egypt. It produces a hard, close-grained wood, from which the ark of the covenant and several other articles of the tabernacle were made. It yields gum arabic, which is obtained by incisions in the bark. In most revised versions of the Bible, the wood of this tree is called Acacia wood.

REFERENCE: *Ex. 25:5, 10, 13; 26:15, 26; 27:1, 2; Deut. 10:3.*

SIDON

[sī′don] Also written Zidon, this is the name of one of the oldest Phoenician cities, located about twenty miles north of Tyre. Sidon was an early leader in maritime commerce, as its sailors were the first to sail out of sight of land and by night, guiding themselves by the position of the stars. The citizens of Sidon are characterized in *Judg. 18:7* as "quiet and unsuspecting, lacking nothing that is in the earth, and possessing wealth." They are mentioned as aiding in the shipping of timber from Lebanon for Solomon's building projects in Jerusalem (*1 Kin. 5:6*). During the prosperous period of Omri's reign over Israel (*see* OMRI), an alliance with Sidon was cemented by the marriage of Omri's son Ahab to Jezebel, the daughter of Ethbaal king of Sidon.

Sidon is mentioned in the New Testament in

connection with Jesus' healing of the Syro-phoenician woman's daughter (*Matt. 15:21-28*), and with Paul's visit with some friends while on his way to Rome (*Acts 27:3; Matt. 11:21-22; Mark 3:8*).

SIHON

[sī′hon] King of the Amorites at the time of the Exodus. Operating out of Heshbon, Sihon had apparently built up a formidable nation. He resisted the Israelites on their journey from Egypt to Palestine and, consequently, "Israel smote him with the edge of the sword, and possessed his land from Arnon unto Jabbok, even unto the children of Ammon." In the historical books, there is occasional reference to the victory over Sihon as a warning to any other nation which might threaten or oppose Israel.

SCRIPTURE

Num. 21 [21]And Israel sent messengers unto Sihon king of the Amorites, saying, [22]Let me pass through thy land: we will not turn into the fields, or into the vineyards; we will not drink of the waters of the well: but we will go along by the king's high way until we be past thy borders. [23]And Sihon would not suffer Israel to pass through his border: but Sihon gathered all his people together, and went out against Israel into the wilderness: and he came to Jahaz, and fought against Israel. [24]And Israel smote him with the edge of the sword, and possessed his land from Arnon unto Jabbok, even unto the children of Ammon: for the border of the children of Ammon was strong. [25]And Israel took all these cities: and Israel dwelt in all the cities of the Amorites, Heshbon, and in all the villages thereof. [26]For Heshbon was the city of Sihon the king of the Amorites, who had fought against the former king of Moab, and taken all his land out of his hand, even unto Arnon. [27]Wherefore they that speak in proverbs say, Come into Heshbon, let the city of Sihon be built and prepared: [28]For there is a fire gone out of Heshbon, a flame from the city of Sihon: it hath consumed Ar of Moab, and the lords of the high places of Arnon. [29]Woe to thee, Moab! thou art undone, O people of Chemosh: he hath given his sons that escaped, and his daughters, into captivity unto Sihon king of the Amorites. [30]We have shot at them; Heshbon is perished even unto Dibon, and we have laid them waste even unto Nophah, which reacheth unto Medeba.

SILAS

[sī′las] A Christian of Jerusalem, probably identical with the Silvanus of the epistles. Silas first appears as one of those appointed by the synod in Jerusalem to convey to the churches in Antioch, Syria, and Cilicia the letter containing the decisions reached by that synod with regard to the obligation of Gentile Christians toward the Law of Moses. Shortly afterward, Paul and Barnabas prepared to embark on their second missionary journey; when they disagreed over whether or not John Mark should be allowed to accompany them, Barnabas departed with Mark for Cyprus and Silas was chosen to be Paul's co-worker. Silas is best remembered, perhaps, as Paul's companion in the prison in Philippi; while there, an earthquake made possible their escape, but they remained within the prison and siezed the opportunity to teach the jailer of Christ, converting him to the Way; "and he took them the same hour of the night, and washed their stripes; and was baptized, he and all his, straightway."

See PAUL

SCRIPTURE

Acts 15 [22]Then pleased it the apostles and elders, with the whole church, to send chosen men of their own company to Antioch with Paul and Barnabas; namely, Judas surnamed Barsabas, and Silas, chief men among the brethren: [32]And Judas and Silas, being prophets also themselves, exhorted the brethren with many words, and confirmed them. [33]And after they had tarried there a space, they were let go in peace from the brethren unto the apostles. [34]Notwithstanding it pleased Silas to abide there still. [35]Paul also and Barnabas continued in Antioch, teaching and preaching the word of the Lord, with many others also.

[36]And some days after Paul said unto Barnabas, Let us go again and visit our brethren in every city where we have preached the word of the Lord, and see how they do. [37]And Barnabas determined to take with them John, whose surname was Mark. [38]But Paul thought not good to take him with them, who departed from them from Pamphylia, and went not with them to the work. [39]And the contention was so sharp between them, that they departed asunder one from the other: and so Barnabas took Mark, and sailed unto Cyprus; [40]And Paul chose Silas, and departed, being recommended by the brethren unto the grace of God. [41]And he went through Syria and Cilicia, confirming the churches.

Acts 16 [25]And at midnight Paul and Silas prayed, and sang praises unto God: and the prisoners heard them. [26]And suddenly there was a great earthquake, so that the foundations of the prison were shaken: and immediately all the doors were opened, and every one's bands were loosed.

Acts 17 [10]And the brethren immediately sent away Paul and Silas by night unto Berea: who coming thither went into the synagogue of the Jews. [13]But when the Jews of Thessalonica had knowledge that the word of God was preached of Paul at Berea, they came thither also, and stirred up the people. [14]And then immediately the brethren sent away Paul to go as it were to the sea: but Silas and Timotheus abode there still. [15]And they that conducted Paul brought him unto Athens: and receiving a commandment unto Silas and Timotheus for to come to him with all speed, they departed.

REFERENCE: *Acts 15:22-18:23; 2 Cor. 1:19; 1 Thess. 1:1; 2 Thess. 1:1; 1 Pet. 5:12.*

SILOAM

[si lō′am] Also spelled Siloah, Shelah, and Shiloah, this is the name of the pool in which Jesus directed the blind man to wash, after which he was cured of his blindness. Jews also made reference to a tower in Siloam.

SCRIPTURE

Isa. 8 [6]Forasmuch as this people refuseth the waters of Shiloah that go softly, and rejoice in Rezin and Remaliah's son;

John 9 [7]And said unto him, Go, wash in the pool of Siloam, (which is by interpretation, Sent.) He went his way therefore, and washed, and came seeing.

Luke 13 [4]Or those eighteen, upon whom the tower in Siloam fell, and slew them, think ye that they were sinners above all men that dwelt in Jerusalem?

SIMEON

[sim′ē on] 1. The son of Jacob and Leah. Because of the terrible vengeance which Simeon and Levi took upon the city of Shechem after the prince of that city assaulted their sister Dinah, they were looked upon with disfavor in the eyes of their father. It is often suggested that various elements of this story indicate a tribal rather than a personal involvement. When the brethren of Joseph journeyed to Egypt to secure corn, it was Simeon who was retained by Joseph as a hostage. Simeon was regarded as the ancestor of the Israelite tribe which bore his name.

See DINAH

2. The aged man in Jerusalem who took Jesus in his arms and blessed him when the child was brought into the temple.

SCRIPTURE

Simeon, the Son of Jacob

BIRTH

Gen. 29 [33]And she conceived again, and bare a son; and said, Because the LORD hath heard that I was hated, he hath therefore given me this son also: and she called his name Simeon.

SLAYS THE INHABITANTS OF SHECHEM

Gen. 34 [25]And it came to pass on the third day, when they were sore, that two of the sons of Jacob, Simeon and Levi, Dinah's brethren, took each man his sword, and came upon the city boldly, and slew all the males. [26]And they slew Hamor and Shechem his son with the edge of the sword, and took Dinah out of Shechem's house, and went out. [27]The sons of Jacob came upon the slain, and spoiled the city, because they had defiled their sister. [28]They took their sheep, and their oxen, and their asses, and that which was in the city, and that which was in the field, [29]And all their wealth, and all their little ones, and their wives took they captive, and spoiled even all that was in the house. [30]And Jacob said to Simeon and Levi, Ye have troubled me to make me to stink among the inhabitants of the land, among the Canaanites and the Perizzites: and I being few in number, they shall gather themselves together against me, and slay me; and I shall be destroyed, I and my house. [31]And they said, Should he deal with our sister as with a harlot?

RETAINED BY JOSEPH AS A HOSTAGE

Gen. 42 [24]And he turned himself about from them, and wept; and returned to them again, and communed with them, and took from them Simeon, and bound him before their eyes.

RELEASED BY JOSEPH

Gen. 43 [23]And he said, Peace be to you, fear not: your God, and the God of your father, hath given you treasure in your sacks: I had your money. And he brought Simeon out unto them.

JACOB'S PROPHECY CONCERNING SIMEON

Gen. 49 [5]Simeon and Levi are brethren; instruments of cruelty are in their habitations. [6]O my soul, come not thou into their secret; unto their assembly, mine honour, be not thou united: for in their anger they slew a man, and in their self-will they digged down a wall. [7]Cursed be their anger, for it was fierce; and their wrath for it was cruel: I will divide them in Jacob and scatter them in Israel.

Simeon of Jerusalem

Luke 2 [22]And when the days of her purification according to the law of Moses were accomplished, they brought him to Jerusalem, to present him to the Lord; [23](As it is written in the law of the Lord, Every male that openeth the womb shall be called holy to the Lord;) [24]And to offer a sacrifice according to that which is said in the law of the Lord, A pair of turtledoves, or two young pigeons. [25]And, behold, there was a man in Jerusalem, whose name was Simeon; and the same man was just and devout, waiting for the consolation of Israel: and the Holy Ghost was upon him. [26]And it was revealed unto him by the Holy Ghost, that he should not see death, before he had seen the Lord's Christ. [27]And he came by the Spirit into the temple: and when the parents brought in the child Jesus, to do for him after the

custom of the law, [28]Then took he him up
in his arms, and blessed God, and said,
[29]Lord, now lettest thou thy servant depart in peace, according to thy word:
[30]For mine eyes have seen thy salvation,
[31]Which thou hast prepared before the
face of all people; [32]A light to lighten the
Gentiles, and the glory of thy people
Israel. [33]And Joseph and his mother marvelled at those things which were spoken
of him. [34]And Simeon blessed them, and
said unto Mary his mother, Behold, this
child is set for the fall and rising again of
many in Israel; and for a sign which shall
be spoken against; [35](Yea, a sword shall
pierce through thy own soul also,) that
the thoughts of many hearts may be revealed.

SIMON

[sī′mon] The Bible mentions a number of persons bearing this name, the more important of whom are:

1. Simon Peter. (*See* PETER)
2. Simon the Canaanite, also called Simon Zelotes. He was one of the apostles (*Matt. 10:4; Mark 3:18; Luke 6:15; Acts 1:13*).
3. Simon the leper, a man of Bethany with whom Jesus dined (*Matt. 26:6; Mark 14:3*).
4. Simon the Pharisee, with whom Jesus dined; possibly identical with 3 above (*Luke 7:36-44*).
5. Simon of Cyrene, who helped carry Jesus' cross to the site of his crucifixion. He was the father of Alexander and Rufus (*Matt. 27:32; Mark 15:21; Luke 23:26*).
6. Simon the tanner, a resident of Joppa with whom the apostle Peter lodged (*Acts 9:43; 10:6, 17, 32*).
7. Simon Magus, a sorceror of Samaria. The term "Magus" is not used of him in the New Testament but has been applied to him because of his practice of sorcery, or magic. We are told that, through his sorcery, he had "bewitched the people of Samaria, giving out that himself was some great one: To whom they all gave heed, from the least to the greatest, saying, This man is the great power of God" (*Acts 8:13*). When Philip the evangelist came to Samaria preaching of Jesus and performing miracles, Simon was attracted to him, was baptized, and "continued with Philip, and wondered, beholding the miracles and signs which were done" (*Acts 8:13*). Later, when Peter and John came down from Jerusalem and imparted the Holy Spirit to the believers, Simon tried to buy this miraculous gift and was severely rebuked by Peter (*Acts 8:14-24*). He and his sin have been immortalized in the word "simony", a term used to indicate the buying of an office in the church for money.

SCRIPTURE

Simon the Canaanite

Matt. 10 [2]Now the names of the twelve
apostles are these . . . [4]Simon the Canaanite . . . .

Simon the Leper

Mark 14 [3]And being in Bethany, in the house of Simon the leper, as he sat at meat, there came a woman having an alabaster box of ointment of spikenard very precious; and she brake the box, and poured it on his head.

Simon the Pharisee

Luke 7 [36]And one of the Pharisees desired him that he would eat with him.
And he went into the Pharisee's house,
and sat down to meat. [40]And Jesus . . .
said unto him, Simon, I have somewhat to
say unto thee. And he saith, Master, say
on.

Simon of Cyrene

Mark 15 [21]And they compel one Simon a Cyrenian, who passed by, coming out of the country, the father of Alexander and Rufus, to bear his cross.

Simon the Tanner

Acts 10 [5]And now send men to Joppa,

and call for one Simon, whose surname is Peter: 6He lodgeth with one Simon a tanner whose house is by the sea side: he shall tell thee what thou oughtest to do.

Simon Magus

Acts 8 5Then Philip went down to the city of Samaria, and preached Christ unto them. 6And the people with one accord gave heed unto those things which Philip spake, hearing and seeing the miracles which he did. 7For unclean spirits, crying with loud voice, came out of many that were possessed with them: and many taken with palsies, and that were lame, were healed. 8And there was great joy in that city. 9But there was a certain man, called Simon, which beforetime in the same city used sorcery, and bewitched the people of Samaria, giving out that himself was some great one: 10To whom they all gave heed, from the least to the greatest, saying, This man is the great power of God. 11And to him they had regard, because that of long time he had bewitched them with sorceries. 12And when they believed Philip preaching the things concerning the kingdom of God, and the name of Jesus Christ, they were baptized, both men and women. 13Then Simon himself believed also: and when he was baptized, he continued with Philip, and wondered, beholding the miracles and signs which were done. 18And when Simon saw that through laying on of the apostles' hands the Holy Ghost was given, he offered them money, 19Saying, Give me also this power, that on whomsoever I lay hands, he may receive the Holy Ghost. 20But Peter said unto him, Thy money perish with thee, because thou hast thought that the gift of God may be purchased with money. 21Thou hast neither part nor lot in this matter: for thy heart is not right in the sight of God. 22Repent therefore of this thy wickedness, and pray God, if perhaps the thought of thine heart may be forgiven thee. 23For I perceive that thou art in the gall of bitterness, and in the bond of iniquity. 24Then answered Simon, and said, Pray ye to the Lord for me, that none of these things which ye have spoken come upon me.

SIN

[sin] The word "sin" has various shades of meaning in the Bible. If we are to assign a primary meaning to the word, it should probably be "missing the mark," having reference to any thought or action which fails to achieve a positive result. In the Old Testament sin is not viewed in isolation, but with respect to one's relationship to God and his fellowman. The formal expression of this relationship was the covenant. Any violation of the precepts of the covenant, whether unwitting or intentional, was a threat to the covenant community. Alongside this view that every sin has its effect upon other men and upon one's relationship to God stood the view that every misfortune suffered was a direct consequence of one's sins. The difficulty of squaring this view with observable fact is reflected in the book of *Job*. Here we see that the problem of individual suffering is often impossible to explain. (*See* JOB) Nevertheless, the consistent teaching of the Bible from the story of the Fall onward is that the suffering and sorrow characteristic of human existence is a consequence of man's sinfulness.

The doctrine of sin reaches its full development in the New Testament. In reducing the many specific commandments of the Law to the two commands to love God and the neighbor, Jesus made it clear that every thought or action not motivated by love was sinful. This underlay his condemnations of the legalism and hypocrisy of the Scribes and Pharisees who gave scrupulous attention to the most minute points of the Law, but whose lack of love for God and men betrayed a complete failure to understand the nature of true piety.

The story of the Fall in *Gen. 3* and Paul's references to it in the New Testament tell us something of the origin and consequences of sin. Paul associates the sinfulness of humanity and the corruption of nature with the sin of Adam. Adam's experience is that of everyman. Unable to accept the limitations placed upon him by God and tempted to believe he can overcome these limitations by his own power, he reaches for forbidden fruits, in disobedience to the divine command. As a consequence he is cut off from God, the source of meaningful life. The relation of Adam to the race has been the subject of intense theological dispute in the history of the church. Some have contended that a sinful nature, together with the guilt for sin, was transmitted to all men through sexual intercourse. Others have argued that man is born free of sin, but sins by imitation, as all have done since the time of Adam. Paul teaches not that every man is held guilty before God because of the sin of Adam, but that all humanity possesses a corrupted nature which is incapable of perfect obedience to the divine will. Paul frequently speaks of a "law in our members" (*Rom. 6:13-14; 7:21-23*) and "flesh" (*Rom. 7:5-8:13; 13:14; Gal. 5:16-21*) as that which induces man to sin, even though his "spirit" may desire to be righteous. He does not mean by this that the physical matter of our bodies is intrinsically evil, for the "works of the flesh" include sins of the mind as well as the body (*Gal. 5:19-21*); rather, he is using the term to refer to the life of the creature apart from the guiding power of the Spirit of God. The nature of this "flesh" is so perverse that the law itself becomes an occasion of sin, arousing men to commit the very sins it prohibits (*Rom. 7:7-8*).

An integral part of the preaching of the prophets of God and of the early Christian evangelists was repentance, turning from sin to a life of positive good. God became man to save us from our sin (*Matt. 1:21; 9:13; Luke 19:10; John 1:29*) and the Christian gospel promised that by faith one could avail himself of the atoning blood of Christ and receive forgiveness of sin. Men are forgiven not because of their merit, but because of the grace of God. We are not to abuse this gift by "sinning more, that grace may abound" (*Rom. 6:1*) but are to lead lives of love far removed from those things which lead to sin. In order to help us put the law of love into practice, Paul gives specific moral instructions, not unlike the "vice lists" of Stoic moralists of the first century (*1 Cor. 5:9-11; 6:9-10; Gal. 5:16-21; 1 Tim. 6:4-5; 2 Tim. 3:1-7*). (*See* Stoics) In addition to this specific instruction we must be careful that we do nothing which, although harmless in itself, but which might be misunderstood by a weaker brother and "cause him to stumble" (*1 Cor. 8:7-13; Rom. 14*).

The question of whether or not it is possible to live a sinless life is one to which the Bible seems to say both yes and no. Paul clearly indicates that we can never completely conquer the "flesh" in this life. (*See Rom. 7:24-25*) In *1 John*, however, the implication seems to be that true Christians not only can but do lead sinless lives (*1 John 3:5-8; 5:18-19*). But *1 John 1:8-10* asserts that any man who says he has no sin is a liar. It appears to this writer that the passages in *1 John 1:3* and *5* refer to the "ideal", the goal for which Christians should strive, but that the statement in *1 John 1:1* and those of Paul describe the actual situation.

reference: For Sin against the Holy Spirit, *see* Spirit, Atonement, Fall, Flesh

SCRIPTURE

Origin of Sin

Gen. 3 1Now the serpent was more subtile than any beast of the field which the
Lord God had made. And he said unto the
woman, Yea, hath God said, Ye shall not
eat of every tree of the garden? 2And the
woman said unto the serpent, We may eat
of the fruit of the trees of the garden: 3But
of the fruit of the tree which is in the midst
of the garden, God hath said, Ye shall not
eat of it, neither shall ye touch it, lest ye
die. 4And the serpent said unto the
woman, Ye shall not surely die: 5For God
doth know that in the day ye eat thereof,
then your eyes shall be opened, and ye shall
be as gods, knowing good and evil. 6And
when the woman saw that the tree was
good for food, and that it was pleasant to
the eyes, and a tree to be desired to make
one wise, she took of the fruit thereof, and

did eat, and gave also unto her husband
with her; and he did eat. [7]And the eyes of
them both were opened, and they knew
that they were naked; and they sewed fig
leaves together, and made themselves
aprons. [8]And they heard the voice of the
LORD God walking in the garden in the
cool of the day: and Adam and his wife hid
themselves from the presence of the LORD
God amongst the trees of the garden.

Matt. 15 [18]But those things which proceed out of the mouth come forth from the
heart; and they defile the man. [19]For out
of the heart proceed evil thoughts, murders, adulteries, fornications, thefts, false witness, blasphemies.

John 8 [44]Ye are of your father the devil, and the lusts of your father ye will do. He was a murderer from the beginning, and abode not in the truth, because there is no truth in him. When he speaketh a lie, he speaketh of his own: for he is a liar, and the father of it.

Rom. 5 [12]Wherefore, as by one man sin
entered into the world, and death by sin;
and so death passed upon all men, for that
all have sinned: [13]For until the law sin was
in the world: but sin is not imputed when
there is no law. [14]Nevertheless death
reigned from Adam to Moses, even over them that had not sinned after the similitude of Adam's transgression, who is the figure of him that was to come.

1 John 3 [8]He that committeth sin is of the devil; for the devil sinneth from the beginning. For this purpose the Son of God was manifested, that he might destroy the works of the devil.

Nature and Characteristics of Sin

Deut. 9 [7]Remember, and forget not, how thou provokedst the LORD thy God to wrath in the wilderness: from the day that thou didst depart out of the land of Egypt, until ye came unto this place, ye have been rebellious against the LORD.

Josh. 1 [18]Whosoever he be that doth rebel against thy commandment, and will not hearken unto thy words in all that thou commandest him, he shall be put to death: only be strong and of a good courage.

Sin's Characteristics

Prov. 14 [34]Righteousness exalteth a nation: but sin is a reproach to any people.

Prov. 15 [9]The way of the wicked is an abomination unto the LORD: but he loveth him that followeth after righteousness.

Prov. 24 [9]The thought of foolishness is sin: and the scorner is an abomination to men.

Isa. 1 [18]Come now, and let us reason together, saith the LORD: though your sins be as scarlet, they shall be as white as snow; though they be red like crimson, they shall be as wool.

Isa. 59 [2]But your iniquities have separated between you and your God, and your
sins have hid his face from you, that he will
not hear. [3]For your hands are defiled with
blood, and your fingers with iniquity; your lips have spoken lies, your tongue hath muttered perverseness.

Jer. 44 [4]Howbeit, I sent unto you all
my servants the prophets, rising early and
sending them, saying, Oh, do not this
abominable thing that I hate. [5]But they
hearkened not, nor inclined their ear to turn from their wickedness, to burn no incense unto other gods.

Rom. 14 [23]And he that doubteth is damned if he eat, because he eateth not of faith: for whatsoever is not of faith is sin.

Eph. 5 [11]And have no fellowship with the unfruitful works of darkness, but rather reprove them.

Heb. 3 [13]But exhort one another daily, while it is called To day; lest any of you be hardened through the deceitfulness of sin. [15]While it is said, To day if ye will hear his voice, harden not your hearts, as in the provocation.

Heb. 9 [14]How much more shall the blood of Christ, who through the eternal Spirit offered himself without spot to God, purge your conscience from dead works to serve the living God?

Jas. 4 [17]Therefore to him that knoweth to do good, and doeth it not, to him it is sin.

1 John 3 [4]Whosoever committeth sin transgresseth also the law: for sin is the transgression of the law.

1 John 5 [17]All unrighteousness is sin: and there is a sin not unto death.

Universality of Sin

Job 15 [14]What is man, that he should be clean? and he which is born of a woman, that he should be righteous?

Job 25 [4]How then can man be justified with God? or how can he be clean that is born of a woman?

Psa. 51 [5]Behold, I was shapen in iniquity; and in sin did my mother conceive me.

Rom. 3 [9]What then? are we better than they? No, in no wise: for we have before proved both Jews and Gentiles, that they are all under sin; [10]As it is written, There is none righteous, no, not one: [23]For all have sinned and come short of the glory of God.

1 John 1 [8]If we say that we have no sin, we deceive ourselves, and the truth is not in us. [10]If we say that we have not sinned, we make him a liar, and his word is not in us.

Gal. 3 [22]But the scripture hath concluded all under sin, that the promise by faith of Jesus Christ might be given to them that believe.

Christ Alone Sinless

2 Cor. 5 [21]For he hath made him to be sin for us, who knew no sin; that we might be made the righteousness of God in him.

Heb. 4 [15]For we have not an high priest which cannot be touched with the feeling of our infirmities; but was in all points tempted like as we are, yet without sin.

Heb. 7 [26]For such an high priest became us, who is holy, harmless, undefiled, separate from sinners, and made higher than the heavens; [27]Who needeth not daily, as those high priests, to offer up sacrifice, first for his own sins, and then for the people's: for this he did once, when he offered up himself.

1 John 3 [5]And ye know that he was manifested to take away our sins; and in him is no sin.

Christ's Blood Redeems from Sin

John 1 [29]The next day John seeth Jesus coming unto him, and saith, Behold the Lamb of God, which taketh away the sin of the world.

Eph. 1 [7]In whom we have redemption through his blood, the forgiveness of sins, according to the riches of his grace.

1 John 1 [7]But if we walk in the light, as he is in the light, we have fellowship one with another, and the blood of Jesus Christ his Son cleanseth us from all sin.

1 John 3 [5]And ye know that he was manifested to take away our sins; and in him is no sin.

Repentance and Confession of Sin

Psa. 38 [18]For I will declare mine iniquity; I will be sorry for my sin.

Prov. 28 [13]He that covereth his sins shall

not prosper: but whoso confesseth and forsaketh them shall have mercy.

Jer. 3 [21]A voice was heard upon the high places, weeping and supplications of the children of Israel: for they have perverted their way, and they have forgotten the LORD their God. [22]Return, ye backsliding children, and I will heal your backslidings. Behold, we come unto thee, for thou art the LORD our God.

1 John 1 [9]If we confess our sins, he is faithful and just to forgive us our sins, and to cleanse us from all unrighteousness.

The Fight Against Sin

WITH PRAYER

Psa. 19 [13]Keep back thy servant also from presumptuous sins; let them not have dominion over me: then shall I be upright, and I shall be innocent from the great transgression.

Psa. 39 [1]I said, I will take heed to my ways, that I sin not with my tongue: I will keep my mouth with a bridle, while the wicked is before me.

Psa. 51 [2]Wash me thoroughly from mine iniquity, and cleanse me from my sin. [3]For I acknowledge my transgressions: and my sin is ever before me. [4]Against thee, thee only, have I sinned, and done this evil in thy sight: that thou mightest be justified when thou speakest, and be clear when thou judgest.

Psa. 139 [23]Search me, O God, and know my heart: try me, and know my thoughts: [24]And see if there be any wicked way in me, and lead me in the way everlasting.

Matt. 6 [12]And forgive us our debts, as we forgive our debtors. [13]And lead us not into temptation, but deliver us from evil: For thine is the kingdom, and the power, and the glory, for ever. Amen.

WITH MORTIFYING THE FLESH

Rom. 8 [13]For if ye live after the flesh, ye shall die: but if ye through the Spirit do mortify the deeds of the body, ye shall live.

Col. 3 [5]Mortify therefore your members which are upon the earth; fornication, uncleanness, inordinate affection, evil concupiscence, and covetousness, which is idolatry.

WITH STRIVING

Heb. 12 [4]Ye have not yet resisted unto blood, striving against sin.

Punishment of Sin

Gen. 2 [17]But of the tree of the knowledge of good and evil, thou shalt not eat of it: for in the day that thou eatest thereof thou shalt surely die.

Ezek. 18 [4]Behold, all souls are mine; as the soul of the father, so also the soul of the son is mine: the soul that sinneth, it shall die.

Rom. 6 [23]For the wages of sin is death; but the gift of God is eternal life through Jesus Christ our Lord.

Gal. 5 [19]Now the works of the flesh are manifest, which are these; Adultery, fornication, uncleanness, lasciviousness, [20]Idolatry, witchcraft, hatred, variance, emulations, wrath, strife, seditions, heresies, [21]Envyings, murders, drunkenness, revellings, and such like: of the which I tell you before, as I have also told you in time past, that they which do such things shall not inherit the kingdom of God.

Eph. 5 [5]For this ye know, that no whoremonger, nor unclean person, nor covetous man, who is an idolater, hath an inheritance in the kingdom of Christ and of God.

Jas. 1 [15]Then when lust hath conceived, it bringeth forth sin: and sin, when it is finished, bringeth forth death.

Rev. 21 27 And there shall in no wise enter into it any thing that defileth, neither
whatsoever worketh abomination, or maketh a lie: but they which are written in the
Lamb's book of life.

The Ideal of a Sinless Life

1 John 3 5 And ye know that he was manifested to take away our sins; and in him is
no sin. 6 Whosoever abideth in him sinneth
not: whosoever sinneth hath not seen him,
neither known him. 7 Little children, let no
man deceive you: he that doeth righteousness is righteous, even as he is righteous.
8 He that committeth sin is of the devil; for
the devil sinneth from the beginning. For
this purpose the Son of God was manifested, that he might destroy the works of
the devil.

1 John 5 18 We know that whosoever is
born of God, sinneth not; but he that is begotten of God, keepeth himself, and that
wicked one toucheth him not. 19 And we
know that we are of God, and the whole
world lieth in wickedness.

SINAI

[sī′nī, sī′nȧ ī] The mountain on which the Lord appeared to Moses and gave the Law. The name is also applied to the desert around the mountain. In a number of passages this same mountain and desert are called Horeb. The mountain which is traditionally identified with Sinai stands in Arabia Petraea, and is called by the Arabs *Jebel Mousa*, or the Mountain of Moses.

See MOSES, COVENANT

SCRIPTURE

Ex. 19 1 In the third month, when the
children of Israel were gone forth out of
the land of Egypt, the same day came they
into the wilderness of Sinai. 2 For they
were departed from Rephidim, and were
come to the desert of Sinai, and had
pitched in the wilderness; and there Israel
camped before the mount.

10 And the LORD said unto Moses, Go
unto the people, and sanctify them to-day
and to-morrow, and let them wash their
clothes, 11 And be ready against the third
day: for the third day the LORD will come
down in the sight of all the people upon
mount Sinai. 12 And thou shalt set bounds
unto the people round about, saying, Take
heed to yourselves, that ye go not up into
the mount, or touch the border of it: whosoever toucheth the mount shall be surely
put to death: 13 There shall not a hand
touch it, but he shall surely be stoned, or
shot through; whether it be beast or man,
it shall not live: when the trumpet sound-
eth long, they shall come up to the mount.

16 And it came to pass on the third day,
in the morning, that there were thunders
and lightnings, and a thick cloud upon the
mount, and the voice of the trumpet exceeding loud; so that all the people that
was in the camp trembled. 17 And Moses
brought forth the people out of the camp
to meet with God; and they stood at the
nether part of the mount. 18 And mount
Sinai was altogether on a smoke, because
the LORD descended upon it in fire: and the
smoke thereof ascended as the smoke of a
furnace, and the whole mount quaked
greatly. 19 And when the voice of the trumpet sounded long, and waxed louder and
louder, Moses spake, and God answered
him by a voice. 20 And the LORD came
down upon mount Sinai, on the top of the
mount: and the LORD called Moses up to
the top of the mount; and Moses went up.
21 And the LORD said unto Moses, Go down,
charge the people, lest they break through
unto the LORD, to gaze, and many of them
perish. 22 And let the priests also, which
come near to the LORD, sanctify themselves, lest the LORD break forth upon

them. 23 And Moses said unto the LORD, The people can not come up to mount Sinai: for thou chargedst us, saying, Set bounds about the mount, and sanctify it.

SISERA

[sis′ẽr a] The general of the armies of Jabin, a Canaanite king who ruled in Hazor. Sisera's army was decimated by the forces led by Deborah and Barak, but Sisera himself escaped. He found refuge in the tent of Jael, the wife of Heber the Kenite. After putting him to sleep with a glass of milk, however, this woman slew Sisera by driving a tent peg into his temple.

See BARAK, DEBORAH

SCRIPTURE

Judg. 4 13 And Sisera gathered together all his chariots, even nine hundred chariots of iron, and all the people that were with him, from Harosheth of the Gentiles unto the river of Kishon. 14 And Deborah said unto Barak, Up; for this is the day in which the LORD hath delivered Sisera into thine hand: is not the LORD gone out before thee? So Barak went down from mount Tabor, and ten thousand men after him. 15 And the LORD discomfited Sisera, and all his chariots, and all his host, with the edge of the sword before Barak; so that Sisera lighted down off his chariot, and fled away on his feet. 16 But Barak pursued after the chariots, and after the host, unto Harosheth of the Gentiles: and all the host of Sisera fell upon the edge of the sword; and there was not a man left. 17 Howbeit Sisera fled away on his feet to the tent of Jael the wife of Heber the Kenite: for there was peace between Jabin the king of Hazor and the house of Heber the Kenite.

18 And Jael went out to meet Sisera, and said unto him, Turn in, my lord, turn in to me; fear not. And when he had turned in unto her into the tent, she covered him with a mantle. 19 And he said unto her, Give me, I pray thee, a little water to drink; for I am thirsty. And she opened a bottle of milk, and gave him drink, and covered him. 20 Again he said unto her, Stand in the door of the tent, and it shall be, when any man doth come and inquire of thee, and say, Is there any man here? thou shalt say, No. 21 Then Jael Heber's wife took a nail of the tent, and took a hammer in her hand, and went softly unto him, and smote the nail into his temples, and fastened it into the ground: for he was fast asleep, and weary. So he died. 22 And, behold, as Barak pursued Sisera, Jael came out to meet him, and said unto him, Come, and I will shew thee the man whom thou seekest. And when he came into her tent, behold, Sisera lay dead, and the nail was in his temples.

SLANDER

[slan′dẽr] A false or untruthful report or charge; also a truth circulated with a hostile purpose. The Bible contains numerous warnings against tale-bearing, gossip, and other forms of evil-speaking. Paul especially condemns slander, perhaps as a result of his experience with those who slandered him and his work.

SCRIPTURE

General

Rom. 1 29 Being filled with all unrighteousness, fornication, wickedness, covetousness, maliciousness; full of envy, murder, debate, deceit, malignity; whisperers, 30 Backbiters, haters of God, despiteful, proud, boasters, inventors of evil things, disobedient to parents.

Rom. 3 8 And not rather, (as we be slanderously reported, and as some affirm that we say,) Let us do evil, that good may come? whose damnation is just.

2 Cor. 12 [20]For I fear, lest, when I come, I shall not find you such as I would, and that I shall be found unto you such as ye would not: lest there be debates, envyings, wraths, strifes, backbitings, whisperings, swellings, tumults:

1 Tim. 3 [11]Even so must their wives be grave, not slanderers, sober, faithful in all things.

2 Tim. 3 [3]Without natural affection, truce-breakers, false accusers, incontinent, fierce, despisers of those that are good,

Tit. 2 [3]The aged women likewise, that they be in behaviour as becometh holiness, not false accusers, not given to much wine, teachers of good things;

Warnings against Slander

Ex. 20 [16]Thou shalt not bear false witness against thy neighbour.

Ex. 23 [1]Thou shalt not raise a false report: put not thine hand with the wicked to be an unrighteous witness.

Psa. 34 [13]Keep thy tongue from evil, and thy lips from speaking guile.

Psa. 50 [20]Thou sittest and speakest against thy brother; thou slanderest thine own mother's son. [21]These things hast thou done, and I kept silence; thou thoughtest that I was altogether such a one as thyself: but I will reprove thee, and set them in order before thine eyes.

Psa. 101 [5]Whoso privily slandereth his neighbour, him will I cut off: him that hath a high look and a proud heart will I not suffer.

Prov. 10 [18]He that hideth hatred with lying lips, and he that uttereth a slander, is a fool.

Jer. 9 [4]Take ye heed every one of his neighbour, and trust ye not in any brother: for every brother will utterly supplant, and every neighbour will walk with slanders.

Eph. 4 [31]Let all bitterness, and wrath, and anger, and clamour, and evil speaking, be put away from you, with all malice.

1 Tim. 3 [11]Even so must their wives be grave, not slanderers, sober, faithful in all things.

Effects of and Conduct Under Slander

Prov. 17 [9]He that covereth a transgression seeketh love; but he that repeateth a matter separateth very friends.

Prov. 26 [20]Where no wood is, there the fire goeth out: so where there is no talebearer, the strife ceaseth. [21]As coals are to burning coals, and wood to fire; so is a contentious man to kindle strife. [22]The words of a talebearer are as wounds, and they go down into the innermost parts of the belly.

Matt. 5 [11]Blessed are ye, when men shall revile you, and persecute you, and shall say all manner of evil against you falsely, for my sake. [12]Rejoice, and be exceeding glad: for great is your reward in heaven: for so persecuted they the prophets which were before you.

1 Cor. 4 [12]And labour, working with our own hands: being reviled, we bless; being persecuted, we suffer it: [13]Being defamed, we intreat: we are made as the filth of the world, and are the offscouring of all things unto this day.

SLAVERY

[slāv′ẽr i] The condition of bondage; the institution of slaveholding. Slavery was a commonplace throughout virtually all of the biblical period. A man might become a slave as a result of his being taken captive in a war or being captured and sold by slave-traders. In times of famine or other distress, parents might sell their children into slavery or, especially if in debt, voluntarily become slaves themselves. In addition, any child born of slave parents automatically became the property of the master.

In most ancient societies, the slave was treated as a piece of property with few rights of his own. In general, the Old Testament follows this pattern, but there is some attempt at humanization of regulations regarding slaves. If a slave were injured or killed, not he but his master was considered the injured party and all reparation was made to the latter. A master was free to treat his slaves any way he chose; if, however, he injured a slave permanently, he was obligated to free him as compensation for this injury. Israelite law contained further provision for the release of slaves. After a six year period of service, a slave was given the opportunity to go free, together with his wife and children. If he chose to remain in his master's house, his ear was pierced with an awl and be became a permanent slave. If a girl had been sold by her father with the understanding that she would become the wife of one of the men in the household and the agreement was subsequently not fulfilled, she was entitled to her release. Also, in the year of Jubilee there was to be a general release of all bondservants. (*See* JUBILEE)

Somewhat surprising to our modern sense of the dignity of humanity is the fact that Jesus nor the New Testament writers came out strongly in opposition to the institution of slavery. Instead, by showing that all men are in need of deliverance and that none is able to provide it of himself, Jesus bestowed a dignity on the slave that he had not hitherto enjoyed. He raised his status even further in his own assumption of the role of one who came not to be served but to serve, to be a slave in the household of the Father, to devote his whole earthly existence to ministering to the needs of humanity.

When Paul writes of slavery, he does not recommend revolt, but recognition of the fact that in Christ there is neither master nor slave. There are only men who have been saved by God's grace and who are therefore brethren. This does not mean Paul was blind to the evils of slavery; he urged slaves to accept freedom if given an opportunity. It means he viewed slavery as part of an order which would pass away and that physical emancipation was entirely secondary to liberation from the bonds of sin and death.

SCRIPTURE

Gen. 17 27And all the men of his house,
born in the house, and bought with money
of the stranger, were circumcised with
him.

Ex. 21 2If thou buy a Hebrew servant,
six years he shall serve: and in the seventh
he shall go out free for nothing. 3If he
came in by himself, he shall go out by himself: if he were married, then his wife shall
go out with him. 4If his master have given
him a wife, and she have borne him sons or
daughters; the wife and her children shall
be her master's, and he shall go out by himself. 5And if the servant shall plainly say,
I love my master, my wife, and my children; I will not go out free: 6Then his master shall bring him unto the judges; he shall
also bring him to the door, or unto the door
post; and his master shall bore his ear
through with an awl; and he shall serve
him for ever.

7And if a man sell his daughter to be a
maidservant, she shall not go out as the
menservants do.

32If the ox shall push a manservant or a
maidservant; he shall give unto their master thirty shekels of silver, and the ox shall
be stoned.

Ex. 22 2If a thief be found breaking up,
and be smitten that he die, there shall no
blood be shed for him. 3If the sun be risen
upon him, there shall be blood shed for
him; for he should make full restitution: if
he have nothing, then he shall be sold for
his theft.

Num. 31 9And the children of Israel
took all the women of Midian captives, and
their little ones, and took the spoil of all
their cattle, and all their flocks, and all
their goods.

1 Kin. 9 21Their children that were left
after them in the land, whom the children
of Israel also were not able utterly to destroy, upon those did Solomon levy a tribute of bondservice unto this day.

Ezek. 27 [13]Javan, Tubal, and Meshech, they were thy merchants: they traded the persons of men and vessels of brass in thy market.

SLING

[sling] An ancient weapon for hurling stones or pebbles. A sling consists of two strips of leather or heavy cord, joined in the middle by a flat, broader piece of leather, in which the stone was placed. One of the two loose ends was tied to the hand or wrist and the other held in the hand. The stone usually about two or three inches in diameter, was then swung around with great force and sent toward its mark by releasing the end held in the hand. The sling is still used by many Palestinian shepherds and can be a fearful weapon in the hands of an expert. The tribe of Benjamin is said to have had a force of 700 left-handed slingers; "everyone could sling stones at an hair breadth, and not miss" (*Judg. 20:16*). It was this type of weapon which was used by the shepherd-boy David to fell the giant Goliath (*1 Sam. 17:49*). That the sling served as a major weapon in times of war is attested to by the fact that archaeologists have found great numbers of these slingstones in many of the ancient cities which have been excavated.

SLOTHFULNESS

[slōth'ful nes] The state or quality of being indolent, inactive, lazy, without diligence; disinclination to action or labor.

See DILIGENCE

SCRIPTURE

Prov. 6 [6]Go to the ant, thou sluggard; consider her ways, and be wise: [7]Which having no guide, overseer, or ruler, [8]Provideth her meat in the summer, and gathereth her food in the harvest. [9]How long wilt thou sleep, O sluggard? when wilt thou arise out of thy sleep? [10]Yet a little sleep, a little slumber, a little folding of the hands to sleep: [11]So shall thy poverty come as one that travelleth, and thy want as an armed man.

Prov. 10 [4]He becometh poor that dealeth with a slack hand: but the hand of the diligent maketh rich.

Prov. 12 [24]The hand of the diligent shall bear rule: but the slothful shall be under tribute.

Prov. 13 [4]The soul of the sluggard desireth, and hath nothing: but the soul of the diligent shall be made fat.

Prov. 18 [9]He also that is slothful in his work is brother to him that is a great waster.

Prov. 19 [15]Slothfulness casteth into a deep sleep; and an idle soul shall suffer hunger.

Prov. 20 [4]The sluggard will not plough by reason of the cold; therefore shall he beg in harvest, and have nothing.

Prov. 21 [25]The desire of the slothful killeth him; for his hands refuse to labour.

Prov. 24 [30]I went by the field of the slothful, and by the vineyard of the man void of understanding; [31]And, lo, it was all grown over with thorns, and nettles had covered the face thereof, and the stone wall thereof was broken down. [32]Then I saw, and considered it well: I looked upon it, and received instruction.

Matt. 25 [26]His lord answered and said unto him, Thou wicked and slothful servant, thou knewest that I reap where I sowed not, and gather where I have not strawed: [27]Thou oughtest therefore to have put my money to the exchangers, and then at my coming I should have received mine own with usury.

Rom. 12 [11]Not slothful in business; fervent in spirit; serving the Lord;

2 Thess. 3 [10]For even when we were with you, this we commanded you, that if any would not work, neither should he eat.

[11]For we hear that there are some which walk among you disorderly, working not at all, but are busybodies. [12]Now them that are such we command and exhort by our Lord Jesus Christ, that with quietness they work, and eat their own bread.

Heb. 6 [12]That ye be not slothful, but followers of them who through faith and patience inherit the promises.

SOBER

[sō'ber] In addition to habitual temperance in the use of liquor, sobriety has reference to temperance of thought and action, calmness, seriousness, gravity, etc.

SCRIPTURE

Rom. 12 [3]For I say, through the grace given unto me, to every man that is among you, not to think of himself more highly than he ought to think; but to think soberly, according as God hath dealt to every man the measure of faith.

1 Thess. 5 [6]Therefore let us not sleep, as do others; but let us watch and be sober.

1 Tim. 2 [9]In like manner also, that women adorn themselves in modest apparel, with shamefacedness and sobriety; not with broided hair, or gold, or pearls, or costly array.

Tit. 1 [8]But a lover of hospitality, a lover of good men, sober, just, holy, temperate.

Tit. 2 [4]That they may teach the young women to be sober, to love their husbands, to love their children, [5]To be discreet, chaste, keepers at home, good, obedient to their own husbands, that the word of God be not blasphemed. [6]Young men likewise exhort to be sober-minded. [12]Teaching us that, denying ungodliness and worldly lusts, we should live soberly, righteously, and godly, in this present world.

1 Pet. 1 [13]Wherefore gird up the loins of your mind, be sober, and hope to the end for the grace that is to be brought unto you at the revelation of Jesus Christ.

1 Pet. 4 [7]But the end of all things is at hand: be ye therefore sober, and watch unto prayer.

1 Pet. 5 [8]Be sober, be vigilant; because your adversary the devil, as a roaring lion, walketh about, seeking whom he may devour.

SODOM

[sod'um] One of the cities destroyed by fire in the time of Abraham and Lot (*Gen. 19:24*). This city, which Lot chose as his residence after separating from Abraham, was proverbial for its wickedness; homosexuality seems to have been a special mark of its evil—hence, the term sodomy. Sodom is thought by many to have been located in the plain south of the Dead Sea, now covered with water.

See LOT, GOMORRAH

SCRIPTURE

Lot Moves to Sodom

Gen. 13 [10]And Lot lifted up his eyes, and beheld all the plain of Jordan, that it was well watered every where, before the Lord destroyed Sodom and Gomorrah, even as the garden of the LORD, like the land of Egypt, as thou comest unto Zoar. [11]Then Lot chose him all the plain of Jordan; and Lot journeyed east: and they separated themselves the one from the other. [12]Abram dwelt in the land of Canaan, and Lot dwelt in the cities of the plain, and pitched his tent toward Sodom.

Character of the Sodomites

Gen. 13 [13]But the men of Sodom were wicked and sinners before the LORD exceedingly.

Gen. 19 [1]And there came two angels to Sodom at even; and Lot sat in the gate of Sodom: and Lot seeing them rose up to meet them; and he bowed himself with his face toward the ground; [2]And he said, Behold now, my lords, turn in, I pray you, into your servant's house, and tarry all night, and wash your feet, and ye shall rise up early, and go on your ways.

[4]But before they lay down, the men of the city, even the men of Sodom, compassed the house round, both old and young, all the people from every quarter:
[5]And they called unto Lot, and said unto him, Where are the men which came in to thee this night? bring them out unto us, that we may know them.

The Destruction of Sodom

Gen. 18 [20]And the LORD said, Because the cry of Sodom and Gomorrah is great, and because their sin is very grievous, [21]I will go down now, and see whether they have done altogether according to the cry of it, which is come unto me; and if not, I will know.

Gen. 19 [14]And Lot went out, and spake unto his sons-in-law, which married his daughters, and said, Up, get you out of this place; for the LORD will destroy this city. But he seemed as one that mocked unto his sons-in-law.

[24]Then the LORD rained upon Sodom and upon Gomorrah brimstone and fire from the Lord out of heaven; [25]And he overthrew those cities, and all the plain, and all the inhabitants of the cities, and that which grew upon the ground.

New Testament References

Matt. 10 [15]Verily I say unto you, It shall be more tolerable for the land of Sodom and Gomorrah in the day of judgment, than for that city.

2 Pet. 2 [6]And turning the cities of Sodom and Gomorrah into ashes condemned them with an overthrow, making them an ensample unto those that after should live ungodly;

See Matt. 10:15; Jude 1:7

SOLOMON

[sol'ô mun] The son of David and Bath-sheba, and the third of the three great kings of the united kingdom of Israel, reigning from about 961-922 BC. After the death of David, Solomon consolidated his empire in a bloodbath which saw the murder of his brother Adonijah and Joab, the strong figure of David's regime, and the banishment of Abiathar the priest to Anathoth. Benaiah, Zadok, and Nathan backed Solomon and thus escaped death.

Solomon then set about to establish himself as an Oriental emperor. He possessed great wisdom and was probably responsible for the collection of proverbs and other types of wisdom literature, much of which he himself is said to be the author. Through strategic treaties and diplomacy-by-marriage, Solomon was able to increase his power and property even beyond the level which David had achieved. He was clearly an economic genius, bringing the nation to its greatest heights. By means of an alliance with the Queen of Sheba, he gained control of the myrrh and frankincense of South Arabia. He built control points along the great trade routes of that part of the world. He was a supplier of horses and chariots to Near Eastern rulers. Stables which he built have been found at Hazor and Megiddo. With the Phoenecians, he established a shipping cartel and operated a fleet of refinery ships. He established a system of royal provinces, appointing a governor over each territory and making him responsible for a month's provisions for the royal court. Solomon is perhaps best remembered for his great building program in Jerusalem. The most famous of the great buildings which he erected was the Temple of the LORD. (*See* TEMPLE)

Solomon is said to have had at least 700 wives and 300 concubines. They were gathered from all nations and represented all shades of religious faith. Many of them were utterly pagan, and to please them Solomon permitted the erection of shrines and temples of their gods in which they could worship. Thus there crept into Israel the worst phases of idolatry and part of the cause for the future break-up of the nation.

Toward the end of his life troubles began to appear through powerful factions, and enemies raised up both within and without the nation. After his death, which occurred about 922 BC, the kingdom split into the dual monarchies of Israel and Judah. (*See* REHOBOAM, JEROBOAM)

Solomon's character is difficult to estimate properly, for the reason that it is so complex as it is given in the Bible that there is no means of arriving at the true nature of the man. He was a wise administrator of his own affairs; but he seems to have lacked the wisdom to leave a compact and united kingdom behind him. He was a great builder, but a vast amount of it was built for his own glory or pleasure. He built up a huge magnificence to God in the Temple, and yet worshipped heathen gods of all sorts for the pleasure of his wives and concubines. He glorified the throne at the cost of his nation and left to his heir only an empty shell of richness and splendor that collapsed when the pressure of trouble came. He is credited with words of deepest wisdom, yet he seemed unable to abide by them.

See BATH-SHEBA, DAVID, JUDAH, TEMPLE, etc.

SCRIPTURE

Birth of Solomon

2 Sam. 12 24And David comforted Bath-sheba his wife, and went in unto her, and lay with her: and she bare a son, and he called his name Solomon: and the LORD loved him.

Choice of Solomon as King

1 Kin. 1 11Wherefore Nathan spake unto Bath-sheba the mother of Solomon, saying, Hast thou not heard that Adonijah the son of Haggith doth reign, and David our lord knoweth it not? 12Now therefore come, let me, I pray thee, give thee counsel, that thou mayest save thine own life, and the life of thy son Solomon. 13Go and get thee in unto king David, and say unto him, Didst not thou, my lord, O king, swear unto thine handmaid, saying, Assuredly Solomon thy son shall reign after me, and he shall sit upon my throne? why then doth Adonijah reign? 14Behold, while thou yet talkest there with the king, I also will come in after thee, and confirm thy words.

29And the king sware, and said, As the LORD liveth, that hath redeemed my soul out of all distress, 30Even as I sware unto thee by the LORD God of Israel, saying, Assuredly Solomon thy son shall reign after me, and he shall sit upon my throne in my stead; even so will I certainly do this day. 31Then Bath-sheba bowed with her face to the earth, and did reverence to the king, and said, Let my lord king David live for ever.

32And king David said, Call me Zadok the priest, and Nathan the prophet, and Benaiah the son of Jehoiada. And they came before the king. 33The king also said unto them, Take with you the servants of your lord, and cause Solomon my son to ride upon mine own mule, and bring him down to Gihon: 34And let Zadok the priest and Nathan the prophet anoint him there king over Israel: and blow ye with the trumpet, and say, God save king Solomon.

Solomon Asks God for Wisdom

1 Kin. 3 5In Gibeon the LORD appeared to Solomon in a dream by night: and God said, Ask what I shall give thee. 6And Solomon said, Thou hast shewed unto thy servant David my father great mercy, according as he walked before thee in truth, and in righteousness, and in uprightness of heart with thee; and thou hast kept for him this great kindness, that thou hast given him a son to sit on his throne, as it is this day. 7And now, O LORD my God, thou hast made thy servant king instead of Da-

vid my father: and I am but a little child:
I know now how to go out or come in.
[8]And thy servant is in the midst of thy
people which thou hast chosen, a great
people, that cannot be numbered nor
counted for multitude. [9]Give therefore
thy servant an understanding heart to
judge thy people, that I may discern between good and bad: for who is able to
judge this thy so great a people? [10]And
the speech pleased the LORD, that Solomon
had asked this thing. [11]And God said unto
him, Because thou hast asked this thing,
and hast not asked for thyself long life;
neither hast asked riches for thyself, nor
hast asked the life of thine enemies; but
hast asked for thyself understanding to
discern judgment; [12]Behold, I have done
according to thy word: lo, I have given
thee a wise and an understanding heart;
so that there was none like thee before
thee, neither after thee shall any arise like
unto thee. [13]And I have also given thee
that which thou hast not asked, both
riches, and honour: so that there shall not
be any among the kings like unto thee all
thy days.

Builds the Temple

1 Kin. 6 [1]And it came to pass in the four
hundred and eightieth year after the children of Israel were come out of the land
of Egypt, in the fourth year of Solomon's
reign over Israel, in the month Zif, which
is the second month, that he began to build
the house of the LORD.

[37]In the fourth year was the foundation
of the house of the LORD laid, in the month
Zif: [38]And in the eleventh year, in the
month Bul, which is the eighth month,
was the house finished throughout all the
parts thereof, and according to all the fashion of it. So was he seven years in building
it.

God Warns Solomon

1 Kin. 9 [1]And it came to pass, when
Solomon had finished the building of the
house of the LORD, and the king's house,
and all Solomon's desire which he was
pleased to do, [2]That the LORD appeared to
Solomon the second time, as he had appeared unto him at Gibeon. [3]And the
LORD said unto him, I have heard thy
prayer and thy supplication, that thou hast
made before me: I have hallowed this
house, which thou hast built, to put my
name there for ever; and mine eyes and
mine heart shall be there perpetually.
[4]And if thou wilt walk before me, as David
thy father walked, in integrity of heart,
and in uprightness, to do according to all
that I have commanded thee, and wilt
keep my statutes and my judgments:
[5]Then I will establish the throne of thy
kingdom upon Israel for ever, as I promised to David thy father, saying, There
shall not fail thee a man upon the throne
of Israel. [6]But if ye shall at all turn from
following me, ye or your children, and
will not keep my commandments and
my statutes which I have set before you,
but go and serve other gods, and worship
them: [7]Then will I cut off Israel out of
the land which I have given them; and
this house, which I have hallowed for my
name, will I cast out of my sight; and Israel shall be a proverb and a byword
among all people: [8]And at this house,
which is high, every one that passeth by
it shall be astonished, and shall hiss; and
they shall say, Why hath the LORD done
thus unto this land, and to this house?
[9]And they shall answer, Because they forsook the LORD their God, who brought
forth their fathers out of the land of Egypt,
and have taken hold upon other gods, and
have worshipped them, and served them:

therefore hath the LORD brought upon
them all this evil.

Solomon's Sins and Death

1 Kin. 11 1But king Solomon loved
many strange women, together with the
daughter of Pharaoh, women of the Moabites, Ammonites, Edomites, Zidonians, and
Hittites; 2Of the nations concerning
which the LORD said unto the children of
Israel, Ye shall not go in to them, neither
shall they come in unto you: for surely
they will turn away your heart after their
gods: Solomon clave unto these in love.
3And he had seven hundred wives, princesses, and three hundred concubines: and
his wives turned away his heart. 4For it
came to pass, when Solomon was old, that
his wives turned away his heart after other
gods: and his heart was not perfect with
the LORD his God, as was the heart of David his father. 5For Solomon went after
Ashtoreth the goddess of the Zidonians,
and after Milcom the abomination of the
Ammonites. 6And Solomon did evil in the
sight of the LORD, and went not fully after
the LORD, as did David his father. 7Then
did Solomon build a high place for Chemosh, the abomination of Moab, in the hill
that is before Jerusalem, and for Molech,
the abomination of the children of Ammon. 8And likewise did he for all his
strange wives, which burnt incense and
sacrificed unto their gods.

9And the LORD was angry with Solomon,
because his heart was turned from the
LORD God of Israel, which had appeared
unto him twice, 10And had commanded
him concerning this thing, that he should
not go after other gods: but he kept
not that which the LORD commanded.
11Wherefore the LORD said unto Solomon,
Forasmuch as this is done of thee, and
thou hast not kept my covenant and my
statutes, which I have commanded thee,
I will surely rend the kingdom from thee,
and will give it to thy servant. 12Notwith-
standing, in thy days I will not do it for
David thy father's sake: but I will rend it
out of the hand of thy son. 13Howbeit I
will not rend away all the kingdom; but
will give one tribe to thy son for David
my servant's sake, and for Jerusalem's
sake which I have chosen.

41And the rest of the acts of Solomon,
and all that he did, and his wisdom, are
they not written in the book of the acts of
Solomon? 42And the time that Solomon
reigned in Jerusalem over all Israel was
forty years. 43And Solomon slept with his
fathers, and was buried in the city of David his father: and Rehoboam his son
reigned in his stead.

SON OF MAN

This term is used in three ways in the Bible. Frequently it means simply "human being" or "man." In *Dan. 7:13* a figure "like unto a son of man" symbolizes the Kingdom of God which is to be established in future ages. In the New Testament Jesus often speaks of himself as the Son of Man. It is difficult to know precisely what Jesus meant by this self-designation, since neither he nor the gospel writers ever explain its significance. For many years scholars understood it as an affirmation of his humanity, his solidarity with the human race. The trend in recent biblical scholarship has been to see this phrase as a messianic title. The study of ancient Jewish texts such as the newly discovered Dead Sea Scrolls has shown that in the first century there was widespread expectation of a Messiah who would come to deliver his people from oppression. In one Jewish book, the *Book of Enoch*, such a messianic figure is called "Son of Man." Although Jesus may well have used this title to express his humanity, it seems highly probable that he intended it in a messianic sense also. There is as yet, however, no way of achieving absolute certainty with regard to his use of his puzzling term.

SCRIPTURE

"Human Being"

Num. 23 [19]God is not a man, that he should lie; neither the son of man, that he should repent: hath he said, and shall he not do it? or hath he spoken, and shall he not make it good?

Job 35 [8]Thy wickedness may hurt a man as thou art; and thy righteousness may profit the son of man.

Jer. 49 [18]As in the overthrow of Sodom and Gomorrah and the neighbor cities thereof, saith the LORD, no man shall abide there, neither shall a son of man dwell in it.

Ezek. 2 [1]And he said unto me, Son of man, stand upon thy feet, and I will speak unto thee.

A Figure of the Kingdom

Dan. 7 [13]I saw in the night visions, and, behold, one like the Son of man came with the clouds of heaven, and came to the Ancient of days, and they brought him near before him.

Jesus as the Son of Man

See Scripture under CHRIST

SORROW

[sor′ō] Grief; sadness; pain of mind at the loss or absence or failure of something or someone; unhappiness; mourning.

See REMORSE, AFFLICTION

SCRIPTURE

Gen. 42 [38]And he said, My son shall not go down with you; for his brother is dead, and he is left alone: if mischief befall him by the way in the which ye go, then shall ye bring down my gray hairs with sorrow to the grave.

Job 17 [7]Mine eye also is dim by reason of sorrow, and all my members are as a shadow.

Psa. 90 [10]The days of our years are threescore years and ten; and if by reason of strength they be fourscore years, yet is their strength labour and sorrow; for it is soon cut off, and we fly away.

Isa. 35 [10]And the ransomed of the LORD shall return, and come to Zion with songs and everlasting joy upon their heads: they shall obtain joy and gladness, and sorrow and sighing shall flee away.

Matt. 8 [12]But the children of the kingdom shall be cast out into outer darkness: there shall be weeping and gnashing of teeth.

Luke 22 [45]And when he rose up from prayer, and was come to his disciples, he found them sleeping for sorrow.

Rom. 9 [2]That I have great heaviness and continual sorrow in my heart.

2 Cor. 7 [10]For godly sorrow worketh repentance to salvation not to be repented of: but the sorrow of the world worketh death.

Rev. 21 [4]And God shall wipe away all tears from their eyes; and there shall be no more death, neither sorrow, nor crying, neither shall there be any more pain: for the former things are passed away.

See Matt. 13:42, 50

SOSTHENES

[sos′the nēz] 1. The ruler of the synagogue at Corinth who was beaten by a frustrated and angry mob when Gallio, proconsul of Achaia, refused to pay attention to their complaints against Paul (*Acts 18:12-17*).

2. A companion of Paul at the time of the writing of *1 Corinthians* (*1 Cor. 1:1*).

SCRIPTURE

Ruler of the Synagogue

Acts 18 [12]And when Gallio was the

deputy of Achaia, the Jews made insurrection with one accord against Paul, and brought him to the judgment seat, [13]Saying, This fellow persuadeth men to worship God contrary to the law. [14]And when Paul was now about to open his mouth, Gallio said unto the Jews, If it were a matter of wrong or wicked lewdness, O ye Jews, reason would that I should bear with you: [15]But if it be a question of words and names, and of your law, look ye to it; for I will be no judge of such matters. [16]And he drave them from the judgment seat. [17]Then all the Greeks took Sosthenes, the chief ruler of the synagogue, and beat him before the judgment seat. And Gallio cared for none of those things.

A Companion of Paul

1 Cor. 1 [1]Paul, called to be an apostle of Jesus Christ through the will of God, and Sosthenes our brother,

SOUL

[sōl] As used in the Old Testament soul (Hebrew *nephesh*) designates men or animals in their total being (*Gen. 1:30; Ex. 46:26, 27*). When God breathed the breath of life into man, he became a living *nephesh* (*Gen. 2:7; 1 Cor. 15:45*). Soul is the life principle. Man is "body-soul", for the Hebrews did not think in terms of disembodied souls. Men after death go to Sheol where they exist in utter weakness with the life principle departed (*Isa. 14:9, 10*).

In the New Testament the idea of "soul" (Greek *psyche*) as life principle continues (*Acts 20:10*), but the term may mean "person" (*Acts 2:43*). At death the believer enters the presence of Christ (*2 Cor. 5:8; Phil. 1:23*). It continues after death (*Matt. 10:28; Rev. 6:9, 20:4*). The intermediate state will be completed in the resurrection (*1 Cor. 15:22, 23; 1 Thess. 4:14*).

See LIFE, MAN, SPIRIT

SCRIPTURE

Gen. 1 [30]And to every beast of the earth, and to every fowl of the air, and to everything that creepeth upon the earth, wherein there is life (a living soul), I have given every green herb for meat: and it was so.

Gen. 2 [7]And the LORD God formed man of the dust of the ground, and breathed into his nostrils the breath of life; and man became a living soul.

Gen. 46 [26]All the souls that came with Jacob into Egypt, which came out of his loins, besides Jacob's sons' wives, all the souls were threescore and six; [27]And the sons of Joseph, which were borne him in Egypt, were two souls: all the souls of the house of Jacob, which came into Egypt, were threescore and ten.

Isa. 14 [9]Hell (Sheol) from beneath is moved for thee to meet thee at thy coming: it stirreth up the dead for thee, even all the chief ones of the earth; it hath raised up from their thrones all the kings of the nations. [10]All they shall speak and say unto thee, Art thou also become weak as we? Art thou become like unto us?

Matt. 28 [10]And fear not them which kill the body, but are not able to kill the soul: but rather fear him which is able to destroy both soul and body in hell.

Acts 2 [43]And fear came upon every soul: and many wonders and signs were done by the apostles.

Acts 20 [10]And Paul went down, and fell on him, and embracing him said, Trouble not yourselves; for his life is in him.

1 Cor. 15 [22]For as in Adam all die, even so in Christ shall all be made alive. [23]But every man in his own order: Christ the firstfruits; afterward they that are Christ's at his coming. [45]And so it is written, The first man Adam was made a living soul; the last Adam was made a quickening (life-giving) spirit.

2 Cor. 5 [8]We are confident (of good

courage), I say, and willing rather to be absent from the body, and to be present (at home) with the Lord.

Phil. 1 [23]For I am in a strait betwixt two, having a desire to depart, and to be with Christ; which is far better:

1 Thess. 4 [14]For if we believe that Jesus died and rose again, even so them also which sleep in Jesus will God bring with him.

Rev. 6 [9]And when he had opened the fifth seal, I saw under the altar the souls of them that were slain for the word of God, and for the testimony which they held:

Rev. 20 [6]And I saw thrones, and they sat upon them, and judgment was given unto them: and I saw the souls of them that were beheaded for the witness of Jesus, and for the word of God, and which had not worshipped the beast, neither his image, neither had received his mark upon their foreheads, or in their hands; and they lived and reigned with Christ a thousand years.

SPEECH

[spēch] The faculty of uttering articulate sounds or words to express thought; the power of speaking; that which is spoken; talk; conversation. The Bible contains references to three kinds of speech: (1) wise speech, whose ends are good; (2) evil speech, whose ends are malicious; and (3) vain speech, whose ends are empty or foolish.

SCRIPTURE

Wise Speech

Psa. 37 [30]The mouth of the righteous speaketh wisdom, and his tongue talketh of judgment.

Psa. 77 [12]I will meditate also of all thy work, and talk of thy doings.

Psa. 119 [13]With my lips have I declared all the judgments of thy mouth. [27]Make me to understand the way of thy precepts: so shall I talk of thy wondrous works. [46]I will speak of thy testimonies also before kings, and will not be ashamed. [54]Thy statutes have been my songs in the house of my pilgrimage. [172]My tongue shall speak of thy word: for all thy commandments are righteousness.

Psa. 141 [3]Set a watch, O LORD, before my mouth; keep the door of my lips.

Prov. 10 [13]In the lips of him that hath understanding wisdom is found: but a rod if for the back of him that is void of understanding. [21]The lips of the righteous feed many: . . . .

Prov. 15 [1]A soft answer turneth away wrath: . . . .

Prov. 20 [15]There is gold, and a multitude of rubies: but the lips of knowledge are a precious jewel.

Prov. 25 [11]A word fitly spoken is like apples of gold in pictures of silver.

Matt. 12 [37]For by thy words thou shalt be justified, and by thy words thou shalt be condemned.

Luke 6 [45]A good man out of the good treasure of his heart bringeth forth that which is good; and an evil man out of the evil treasure of his heart bringeth forth that which is evil: for of the abundance of the heart his mouth speaketh.

Eph. 4 [29]Let no corrupt communication proceed out of your mouth, but that which is good to the use of edifying, that it may minister grace unto the hearers.

Col. 4 [6]Let your speech be alway with grace, seasoned with salt, that ye may know how ye ought to answer every man.

Evil Speech

Psa. 12 [3]The LORD shall cut off all flattering lips, and the tongue that speaketh proud things: [4]Who have said, With our tongue will we prevail; our lips are our own: who is lord over us?

Psa. 34 [13]Keep thy tongue from evil, and thy lips from speaking guile.

Prov. 4 [24]Put away from thee a froward mouth, and perverse lips put far from thee.

Prov. 15 [1]A soft answer turneth away wrath: but grievous words stir up anger. [4]A wholesome tongue is a tree of life: but perverseness therein is a breach in the spirit. [28]The heart of the righteous studieth to answer: but the mouth of the wicked poureth out evil things.

Prov. 16 [27]An ungodly man diggeth up evil: and in his lips there is as a burning fire. [28]A froward man soweth strife: and a whisperer separateth chief friends.

Prov. 17 [4]A wicked doer giveth heed to false lips; and a liar giveth ear to a naughty tongue. [9]He that covereth a transgression seeketh love; but he that repeateth a matter separateth very friends. [20]He that hath a froward heart findeth no good: and he that hath a perverse tongue falleth into mischief.

Matt. 5 [37]But let your communication be, Yea, yea; Nay, nay: for whatsoever is more than these cometh of evil.

Rom. 3 [13]Their throat is an open sepulchre; with their tongues they have used deceit; the poison of asps is under their lips: [14]Whose mouth is full of cursing and bitterness:

Eph. 4 [31]Let all bitterness, and wrath, and anger, and clamour, and evil speaking, be put away from you, with all malice:

Col. 3 [8]But now ye also put off all these; anger, wrath, malice, blasphemy, filthy communication out of your mouth.

Jas. 1 [26]If any man among you seem to be religious, and bridleth not his tongue, but deceiveth his own heart, this man's religion is vain.

Jas. 3 [5]Even so the tongue is a little member, and boasteth great things. Behold, how great a matter a little fire kindleth! [6]And the tongue is a fire, a world of iniquity: so is the tongue among our members, that it defileth the whole body, and setteth on fire the course of nature; and it is set on fire of hell. [8]But the tongue can no man tame; it is an unruly evil, full of deadly poison.

Jas. 4 [11]Speak not evil one of another, brethren. He that speaketh evil of his brother, and judgeth his brother, speaketh evil of the law, and judgeth the law: but if thou judge the law, thou art not a doer of the law, but a judge.

Vain Speech

Prov. 10 [14]Wise men lay up knowledge: but the mouth of the foolish is near destruction.

Prov. 12 [23]A prudent man concealeth knowledge: but the heart of fools proclaimeth foolishness.

Prov. 26 [4]Answer not a fool according to his folly, lest thou also be like unto him. [7]The legs of the lame are not equal: so is a parable in the mouth of fools. [13]The slothful man saith, There is a lion in the way; a lion is in the streets.

Prov. 29 [20]Seest thou a man that is hasty in his words? there is more hope of a fool than of him.

Matt. 12 [36]But I say unto you, That every idle word that men shall speak, they shall give account thereof in the day of judgment.

Eph. 5 [4]Neither filthiness, nor foolish talking, nor jesting, which are not convenient: but rather giving of thanks.

SPIKENARD

[spīk'nard] An aromatic plant from which was taken nard, the expensive perfume used for anointing and in ancient baths.

See NARD

SCRIPTURE

Mark 14 [3]And being in Bethany in the house of Simon the leper, as he sat at meat, there came a woman having an alabaster box of ointment of spikenard very precious; and she brake the box, and poured it on his head.

John 12 [3]Then took Mary a pound of ointment of spikenard, very costly, and anointed the feet of Jesus, and wiped his feet with her hair: and the house was filled with the odour of the ointment.

SPIRIT

[spir'it] The Hebrew word for spirit is *ruach.* In the Old Testament it frequently means "wind." The Greek equivalent *pneuma* is used in this sense only twice in the New Testament. These terms are also used to denote "breath," the vital stuff of life in default of which man ceases to live. In neither of these usages is it difficult to make an association with God. The wind was thought to be the unseen instrument of an unseen God, and, as God was viewed as the source of life, it was natural to associate spirit with the life created by God. "Spirit" is also found with the meaning "soul" or "heart," the seat of the intelligence and emotions, the principle of life which God imparts to man at his beginning and recalls from him at his death. In the Old Testament the Spirit of God is viewed as having been sent forth for the creation and sustenance of human life and as endowing men with special abilities and gifts such as leadership, craftsmanship, and wisdom. The gift of prophecy, however, was considered the characteristic mark of the presence of the Spirit. In short, the Spirit of God was viewed as the divine power immanent in Israel's history.

It is not until the New Testament that the doctrine of the Spirit reaches full development. The events connected with the nativity of Jesus and John heralded the dawn of a new age of the Spirit. The child which Mary bore was to be a "child of the Holy Spirit" (*Matt. 1:20; Luke 1: 35*). Elisabeth and Zecharias, the parents of John the Baptist, were both "filled with the Holy Spirit" and prophesied (*Luke 1:41-45, 67-79*). Likewise, when Jesus was presented in the temple as an infant, the aged Simeon was inspired to proclaim the role of the Christ in bringing the knowledge of God to the Gentiles (*Luke 2: 27-35*). When John the Baptist began his ministry, he informed his hearers that the one to whom he bore witness would effect an outpouring of the Holy Spirit. Jesus himself was anointed with the Holy Spirit at the time of his baptism at the hands of John in the river Jordan. We are told the Spirit descended "in a bodily shape like a dove upon him" (*Luke 3:22*), symbolic of the fullness of the divine power with which he was endowed. There are occasional references to the Spirit in the ministry of Jesus and blasphemy against the Spirit—the ascription of the miraculous signs of the presence of the Kingdom of God to the power of the devil—is regarded as the ultimate, unforgivable sin. (*See Mark 3:22-30*) The activity of the Spirit was, however, not fully manifested until Jesus' earthly ministry was completed (*John 7:39*).

The Holy Spirit first came "with power" on the day of Pentecost (*Acts 2*). With the sound of "a rushing mighty wind" and the appearance of "cloven tongues like as of fire," the Spirit "sat upon" each of the apostles, enabling them to preach to the multi-lingual assembly concerning Christ and verifying the truth of their proclamation. A similar manifestation at the household of Cornelius made it plain that the Kingdom of God was inclusive of Gentiles as well as Jews (*Acts 10:44-47*). Many of the early leaders of the church, such as Peter, Stephen, Paul, and Barnabas, were recipients of a special measure of the power of the Spirit. In addition, numerous other members of the church were endowed by the Spirit with gifts of healing, prophecy, speaking in and interpretation of tongues, etc., designed to strengthen the church inwardly and to aid in evangelism. (*See* SPIRITUAL GIFTS)

The Spirit may properly be thought of as the link between Christ and his church, the agency by which he dwells within it and guides its life. One becomes a Christian through a new birth, a birth of water and of spirit which is contrasted with fleshly birth. This new birth, often associated with baptism (*John 3:3-5; Tit. 3:5; Rom. 6: 3, 4*), is birth into a new life "in the Spirit" (*Rom. 8:9*). The effects of this new life are seen not simply in moments of ecstatic frenzy, but in every aspect of the Christian's life. It is the Spirit of God active in believers which makes Christ present to them, which unites them in personal fellowship, which enables them to confess Jesus as Lord (*1 Cor. 12:3*) and to call upon God as their Father (*Gal. 4:6*). The Spirit is the principle of the new age, the principle of the Law of Christ which replaces the Law of Moses, the principle of life which replaces the principle of death. As the common experience of regenerate men, he produces Christian community, the "fellowship of the Holy Spirit" and is the ground of church unity (*1 Cor. 12:4-13*). Life in the Spirit is marked by joy and gladness, even in times of trial, by the fruits of the Spirit (*Gal. 5: 22-26*), and, supremely, by unself-seeking love (*1 Cor. 13*). His present indwelling is the down payment and guarantee of the fullness of salvation which will be ours in the life to come (*2 Cor. 1:22*).

The high water mark of New Testament teaching on the Holy Spirit is reached in *John 14-16.* These chapters contain the five "paraclete sayings" (*John 14:15-17; 14:26; 15:26, 27; 16:5-11, 12-15; see* PARACLETE) which constitute the classical statement of the person and work of the Holy Spirit. There is a marked tendency toward personalization in these passages. The use of masculine pronouns and adjectives indicate we are to think of the Holy Spirit as a fully personal being. In these five passages, considered here as a group instead of individually, the Spirit of Truth is seen preeminently as the revealer of Christ. As Jesus is the truth, the Spirit of Truth (*John 14:17; 15:26; 16:13*) leads the disciples to a full appreciation of his life and teachings. The functions attributed to him in this capacity are teaching (*John 14:26*), guiding into truth (*John 16:13*), bringing to remembrance (*John 14:26*), bearing witness (*John 15: 26*), "declaring the things to come" (*John 16: 13*), and glorifying Christ, taking the things that are his and declaring them to the disciples (*John 16:14*). In these various facets of his activity, the Spirit recalls the teachings of Jesus which have not yet been fully grasped, confirms and expands them, and brings home their meaning in new ways and under fresh conditions until the revelation of God's grace and truth are complete. In addition, he instructs the disciples in those things which pertain to the new dispensation—the dispensation of the Spirit—and to final judgment. It is not difficult to see in this an affinity with the Old Testament conception of the Spirit as inspirer of prophecy.

As a part of his revealing and witnessing ministry, the Spirit acts as a Convincer or Convicter, putting into full operation the work which Christ had effected. Through the Christian ministry, the Spirit convicts the world of sin, exposing all claims of righteousness outside Christ; he bears witness to and glorifies Christ by proclaiming that the truly Righteous One has returned to his Father in heaven; and through proclamation of the resurrection, he announces the judgment which has been passed on Satan (*John 16:8-11*).

In these passages the mission of the Spirit is attributed now to the Father and then to the Son (*John 14:16, 26; 15:26; 16:7*). We are probably to understand by this that the Spirit is sent from the Father, as is the Son, but in this particular mission, the immediate sender is the Son, in whose name the Paraclete is sent as a fruit of and sequel to the mission or the Incarnate Word.

It is not improper to think of the Spirit as the *alter ego* ("other self") of Christ, continuing, developing, and complementing the earthly ministry of Jesus. The similarities between their ministries are considerable: both are sent by the Father (*John 14:24-26*), proceed from him (*John 16:27; 15:26*), and derive their authority from him (*John 14:10; 16:13*); both teach (*John 7:14; 14:26*), bear witness (*John 8:14; 15:26*), and convict the world of sin (*John 3:18-20; 16: 8-11*). Further, *John 14:7* implies that the one who is to come is already present—"he *dwells with* you, and *will be in* you." In *1 John 2:1*, Jesus is described as the Paraclete. In *John 14:1-14*, he describes himself as performing the same functions implied in *1 John 2:1*. Then, in *John 14:16*, he says, "I will pray the Father, and he will give you *another* paraclete." It is clear then, that, at least in John's writings, the Spirit is in some sense Christ's *alter ego*, the form of his manifestation to the church in the period between his glorification and the Second Coming.

The role of the Spirit as *alter ego*, whose primary function is to expound the significance of the life and death of Jesus, ruled out the possibility of his full manifestation while Jesus was still on earth (*John 16:7; 7:39*). In preparing his disciples for the reception of the Holy Spirit, Jesus assured them it was to their advantage that he leave them (*John 16:7*). It has been suggested that perhaps Jesus was thinking of the possibility that his continued presence would impede their development into full Christian manhood because of the overpowering force of his personality. Another, and perhaps more probable, suggestion is that spatial and temporal limitations would be overcome in the ministry of the Spirit, allowing him to be present in the universal church until the end of the dispensation.

The gospel of John contains no sharply delineated doctrine of the Trinity, but in the picture of three divine persons, distinct yet at times scarcely indistinguishable, there is a more highly developed idea of the godhead than is found elsewhere in the New Testament. As viewed by John the Spirit is in intimate relation with ultimate reality and is its primary vehicle in the new age. Through him men experience spiritual rebirth, participate in eternal truth and life, and bear witness to Christ, reversing the judgment which the world has placed upon him.

SCRIPTURE

Holy Spirit

Gen. 1 [2]And the Spirit of God moved upon the face of the waters.

Ex. 31 [3]And I have filled him with the spirit of God, in wisdom, and in understanding, and in knowledge, and in all manner of workmanship,

Isa. 11 [2]And the spirit of the LORD shall rest upon him, the spirit of wisdom and understanding, the spirit of counsel and might, the spirit of knowledge and of the fear of the LORD;

Isa. 61 [1]The Spirit of the LORD God is upon me; because the LORD hath anointed me to preach good tidings unto the meek; he hath sent me to bind up the brokenhearted, to proclaim liberty to the captives, and the opening of the prison to
them that are bound; [2]To proclaim the acceptable year of the LORD, and the day of vengeance of our God; to comfort all that mourn.

Mic. 3 [8]But truly I am full of power by the spirit of the LORD, and of judgment, and of might,

Hag. 2 [5]According to the word that I covenanted with you when ye came out of Egypt, so my spirit remaineth among you:

Matt. 1 [18]Now the birth of Jesus Christ was on this wise: When as his mother Mary was espoused to Joseph, before they came together, she was found with child of the Holy Ghost.

Matt. 3 [11]I indeed baptize you with water unto repentance: but . . . he shall baptize you with the Holy Ghost, and with fire:
[16]And Jesus, when he was baptized, went up straightway out of the water: and lo, the heavens were opened unto him, and he saw the Spirit of God descending like a dove, and lighting upon him: [17]And lo a
voice from heaven, saying, This is my beloved Son, in whom I am well pleased.

Matt. 4 [1]Then was Jesus led up of the spirit into the wilderness to be tempted of the devil.

Matt. 10 [20]For it is not ye that speak, but the Spirit of your Father which speaketh in you.

Matt. 12 [28]But if I cast out devils by the Spirit of God, then the kingdom of God is come unto you.

Luke 2 [25]And, behold, there was a man in Jerusalem, whose name was Simeon; and the same man was just and devout, waiting for the consolation of Israel: and the Holy Ghost was upon him. [26]And it was revealed unto him by the Holy Ghost, that he should not see death, before he had seen the Lord's Christ. [27]And he came by the Spirit into the temple: and when the parents brought in the child Jesus, to do for him after the custom of the law,

Luke 11 [13]If ye then, being evil, know how to give good gifts unto your children; how much more shall your heavenly Father give the Holy Spirit to them that ask him?

Luke 12 [12]For the Holy Ghost shall teach you in the same hour what ye ought to say.

John 3 [3]Jesus answered and said unto him, Verily, verily, I say unto thee, Except a man be born again, he can not see the kingdom of God. [4]Nicodemus saith unto him, How can a man be born when he is old? can he enter the second time into his mother's womb, and be born? [5]Jesus answered, Verily, verily, I say unto thee, Except a man be born of water and of the Spirit, he can not enter into the kingdom of God. [6]That which is born of the flesh is flesh; and that which is born of the Spirit is spirit. [7]Marvel not that I said unto thee, Ye must be born again. [8]The wind bloweth where it listeth, and thou hearest the sound thereof, but canst not tell whence it cometh, and whither it goeth: so is every one that is born of the Spirit.

[34]For he whom God hath sent speaketh the words of God: for God giveth not the Spirit by measure unto him.

John 14 [16]I will pray the Father, and he shall give you another Comforter, that he may abide with you for ever; [17]Even the Spirit of truth; whom the world cannot receive, because it seeth him not, neither knoweth him: but ye know him; for he dwelleth with you, and shall be in you. [26]But the Comforter, which is the Holy Ghost, whom the Father will send in my name, he shall teach you all things, and bring all things to your remembrance, whatsoever I have said unto you.

John 15 [26]When the Comforter is come, whom I will send unto you from the Father, even the Spirit of truth, which proceedeth from the Father, he shall testify of me:

John 16 [7]Nevertheless I tell you the truth; It is expedient for you that I go away: for if I go not away, the Comforter will not come unto you; but if I depart, I will send him unto you. [8]And when he is come, he will reprove the world of sin, and of righteousness, and of judgment: [9]Of sin, because they believe not on me; [10]Of righteousness, because I go to my Father, and ye see me no more; [11]Of judgment, because the prince of this world is judged. [12]I have yet many things to say unto you, but ye cannot bear them now. [13]Howbeit when he, the Spirit of truth, is come, he will guide you into all truth: for he shall not speak of himself; but whatsoever he shall hear, that shall he speak: and he will shew you things to come. [14]He shall glorify me: for he shall receive of mine, and shall shew it unto you.

John 20 [22]He breathed on them, and saith unto them, Receive ye the Holy Ghost:

Acts 1 [2]Until the day in which he was taken up, after that he through the Holy Ghost had given commandments unto the apostles whom he had chosen: [5]For John truly baptized with water; but ye shall be baptized with the Holy Ghost not many days hence. [8]But ye shall receive power, after that the Holy Ghost is come upon you:

[16]Men and brethren, this scripture must needs have been fulfilled, which the Holy Ghost by the mouth of David spake before

concerning Judas, which was guide to them that took Jesus.

Acts 2 [2]And suddenly there came a sound from heaven as of a rushing mighty wind, and it filled all the house where they were sitting. [3]And there appeared unto them cloven tongues like as of fire, and it sat upon each of them. [4]And they were all filled with the Holy Ghost, and began to speak with other tongues, as the Spirit gave them utterance.

[33]Therefore being by the right hand of God exalted, and having received of the Father the promise of the Holy Ghost, he hath shed forth this, which ye now see and hear.

[38]Then Peter said unto them, Repent, and be baptized . . . in the name of Jesus Christ for the remission of sins, and ye shall receive the gift of the Holy Ghost.

Acts 4 [8]Then Peter, filled with the Holy Ghost, said unto them, Ye rulers of the people, and elders of Israel,

[31]And when they had prayed, the place was shaken where they were assembled together; and they were all filled with the Holy Ghost, and they spake the word of God with boldness.

Acts 5 [32]We are his witnesses . . . and so is also the Holy Ghost, whom God hath given to them that obey him.

Acts 6 [5]They chose Stephen, a man full of faith and of the Holy Ghost,

Acts 7 [51]Ye stiffnecked and uncircumcised in heart and ears, ye do always resist the Holy Ghost: as your fathers did, so do ye.

Acts 8 [15]Who, when they were come down, prayed for them, that they might receive the Holy Ghost: [16](For as yet he was fallen upon none of them: only they were baptized in the name of the Lord Jesus.) [17]Then laid they their hands on them, and they received the Holy Ghost.

Acts 10 [44]While Peter yet spake these words, the Holy Ghost fell on all them which heard the word. [45]And they of the circumcision which believed were astonished, as many as came with Peter, because that on the Gentiles also was poured out the gift of the Holy Ghost. [46]For they heard them speak with tongues, and magnify God. Then answered Peter, [47]Can any man forbid water, that these should not be baptized, which have received the Holy Ghost as well as we?

Rom. 8 [1]There is therefore now no condemnation to them which are in Christ Jesus, who walk not after the flesh, but after the Spirit. [2]For the law of the Spirit of life in Christ Jesus hath made me free from the law of sin and death. [3]For what the law could not do, in that it was weak through the flesh, God sending his own Son in the likeness of sinful flesh, and for sin, condemned sin in the flesh: [4]That the righteousness of the law might be fulfilled in us, who walk not after the flesh, but after the Spirit. [9]But ye are not in the flesh, but in the Spirit, if so be that the Spirit of God dwell in you. Now if any man have not the Spirit of Christ, he is none of his. [10]And if Christ be in you, the body is dead because of sin; but the Spirit is life because of righteousness. [11]But if the Spirit of him that raised up Jesus from the dead dwell in you, he that raised up Christ from the dead shall also quicken your mortal bodies by his Spirit that dwelleth in you. [12]Therefore, brethren, we are debtors, not to the flesh, to live after the flesh. [13]For if ye live after the flesh, ye shall die: but if ye through the Spirit do mortify the deeds of the body, ye shall live. [14]For as many as are led by the Spirit of God, they are the sons of God. [15]For ye have not received the spirit of bondage again to fear; but ye have received the Spirit of adoption, whereby we cry, Abba, Father. [16]The Spirit itself beareth witness with our spirit, that we are the children of God: [23]And not only they, but ourselves also, which have the firstfruits of the Spirit, even we ourselves groan within ourselves, waiting for the adoption, to wit, the redemption of our body. [24]For we are saved by hope: but hope that is seen is not hope: for what a man seeth, why doth he yet hope for? [25]But if we hope for that we see not, then do we with patience wait for it. [26]Likewise the Spirit also helpeth our infirmities: for we know not what we should pray for as we ought: but the Spirit itself maketh intercession for us with groanings which can not be uttered. [27]And he that searcheth the hearts knoweth what is the mind of the Spirit, because he maketh intercession for the saints according to the will of God.

Rom. 15 [30]Now I beseech you, brethren, for the Lord Jesus Christ's sake, and for the love of the Spirit, that ye strive together with me in your prayers to God for me;

1 Cor. 2 [4]And my speech and my preaching was not with enticing words of man's wisdom, but in demonstration of the Spirit and of power: [11]For what man knoweth the things of a man, save the spirit of man which is in him? even so the things of God knoweth no man, but the Spirit of God. [12]Now we have received, not the spirit of the world, but the Spirit which is of God; that we might know the things that are freely given to us of God. [13]Which things also we speak, not in the words which man's wisdom teacheth, but which the Holy Ghost teacheth; comparing spiritual things with spiritual. [14]But the natural man receiveth not the things of the Spirit of God: for they are foolishness unto him: neither can he know them, because they are spiritually discerned. [15]But he that is spiritual judgeth all things, yet he himself is judged of no man.

1 Cor. 3 [16]Know ye not that ye are the temple of God, and that the Spirit of God dwelleth in you?

1 Cor. 6 [11]And such were some of you: but ye are washed, but ye are sanctified, but ye are justified in the name of the Lord Jesus, and by the Spirit of our God. [19]What? know ye not that your body is the temple of the Holy Ghost which is in you, which ye have of God, and ye are not your own?

1 Cor. 12 [3]Wherefore I give you to understand, that no man speaking by the Spirit of God calleth Jesus accursed: and that no man can say that Jesus is the Lord, but by the Holy Ghost. [4]Now there are diversities of gifts, but the same Spirit. [5]And there are differences of administrations, but the same Lord. [6]And there are diversities of operations, but it is the same God which worketh all in all. [7]But the manifestation of the Spirit is given to every man to profit withal. [8]For to one is given by the Spirit the word of wisdom; to another the word of knowledge by the same Spirit; [9]To another faith by the same Spirit; to another the gifts of healing by the same Spirit; [10]To another the working of miracles; to another prophecy; to another discerning of spirits; to another divers kinds of tongues; to another the interpretation of tongues: [11]But all these worketh that one and the selfsame Spirit, dividing to every man severally as he will.

2 Cor. 1 [22]Who hath also sealed us, and given the earnest of the Spirit in our hearts.

2 Cor. 3 [3]Forasmuch as ye are manifestly declared to be the epistle of Christ ministered by us, written not with ink, but with the Spirit of the living God; not in tables of stone, but in fleshly tables of the heart. [6]Ministers of the new testament;

not of the letter, but of the spirit: for the letter killeth, but the spirit giveth life. [8]How shall not the ministration of the spirit be rather glorious? [17]Now the Lord is that Spirit: and where the Spirit of the Lord is, there is liberty. [18]But we all, with open face beholding as in a glass the glory of the Lord, are changed into the same image from glory to glory, even as by the Spirit of the Lord.

2 Cor. 5 [5]Now he that hath wrought us for the selfsame thing is God, who also hath given unto us the earnest of the Spirit.

2 Cor. 13 [14]The grace of the Lord Jesus Christ, and the love of God, and the communion of the Holy Ghost, be with you all.

Gal. 4 [6]Because ye are sons, God hath sent forth the Spirit of his Son into your hearts, crying, Abba, Father.

Gal. 5 [5]We through the Spirit wait for the hope of righteousness by faith. [16]Walk in the Spirit, and ye shall not fulfil the lust of the flesh. [17]For the flesh lusteth against the Spirit, and the Spirit against the flesh: and these are contrary the one to the other: so that ye cannot do the things that ye would. [18]But if ye be led of the Spirit, ye are not under the law. [22]But the fruit of the Spirit is love, joy, peace, longsuffering, gentleness, goodness, faith, [23]Meekness, temperance: against such there is no law. [25]If we live in the Spirit, let us also walk in the Spirit.

Gal. 6 [8]He that soweth to the Spirit shall of the Spirit reap life everlasting.

Eph. 1 [12]That we should be to the praise of his glory, who first trusted in Christ. [13]In whom also after that ye believed, ye were sealed with that holy Spirit of promise, [14]Which is the earnest of our inheritance until the redemption of the purchased possession, unto the praise of his glory.

Eph. 2 [18]Through him (Jesus Christ) we both have access by one Spirit unto the Father. [22]In whom ye also are builded together for an habitation of God through the Spirit.

Eph. 3 [5]Which in other ages was not made known unto the sons of men, as it is now revealed unto his holy apostles and prophets by the Spirit; [16]Strengthened with might by his Spirit in the inner man;

Eph. 4 [3]Endeavouring to keep the unity of the Spirit in the bond of peace. [4]There is one body, and one Spirit, even as ye are called in one hope of your calling; [30]Grieve not the holy Spirit of God, whereby ye are sealed unto the day of redemption.

Eph. 5 [9](The fruit of the Spirit is in all goodness and righteousness and truth;)

Eph. 6 [17]And take the . . . sword of the Spirit, which is the word of God; [18]Praying always with all prayer and supplication in the Spirit,

Phil. 2 [1]If there be . . . any fellowship of the Spirit,

1 Thess. 5 [19]Quench not the Spirit.

2 Thess. 2 [13]But we are bound to give thanks alway to God for you, brethren beloved of the Lord, because God hath from the beginning chosen you to salvation through sanctification of the Spirit and belief of the truth:

1 Tim. 4 [1]Now the Spirit speaketh expressly, that in the latter times some shall depart from the faith, giving heed to seducing spirits, and doctrines of devils;

Tit. 3 [5]Not by works of righteousness which we have done, but according to his mercy he saved us, by the washing of regeneration, and renewing of the Holy Ghost: [6]Which he shed on us abundantly through Jesus Christ our Saviour;

1 Pet. 1 [2]Elect according to the foreknowledge of God the Father, through sanctification of the Spirit, unto obedience

and sprinkling of the blood of Jesus Christ:
[11]Searching what, or what manner of time the Spirit of Christ which was in them did signify, when it testified beforehand the sufferings of Christ, and the glory that should follow.
[12]Unto whom it was revealed, that not unto themselves, but unto us they did minister the things, which are now reported unto you by them that have preached the gospel unto you with the Holy Ghost sent down from heaven; which things the angels desire to look into.
[22]Seeing ye have purified your souls in obeying the truth through the Spirit unto unfeigned love of the brethren, see that ye love one another with a pure heart fervently:

1 John 4 [2]Hereby know ye the Spirit of God: Every spirit that confesseth that Jesus Christ is come in the flesh is of God:
[13]Hereby know we that we dwell in him, and he in us, because he hath given us of his Spirit.

1 John 5 [6]. . . It is the Spirit that beareth witness, because the Spirit is truth.
[7]For there are three that bear record in heaven, the Father, the Word, and the Holy Ghost: and these three are one.
[8]And there are three that bear witness in earth, the spirit, and the water, and the blood: and these three agree in one.

Rev. 22 [17]The Spirit and the bride say, Come . . . .

See Ex. 35:31; Matt. 1:20; John 1:33; Acts 11:16; Mark 1:10; 13:11; Luke 3:22; John 1:32; 1 Cor. 6:19; 2 Cor. 5:5

SPIRITUAL GIFTS

A term used in the New Testament to designate special abilities of Christians, bestowed by the Spirit of God for use in the service of the church. According to *Heb. 2:4*, they are used to confirm the gospel of salvation. The list of spiritual gifts in *1 Cor. 12:8-10* includes wisdom, knowledge, faith, healing, miracles, prophecy, discerning of spirits, speaking in tongues, and interpretation of tongues. Paul indicates that these gifts are equally valid, but not equally valuable. Their relative value is determined by their worth to the church. In dealing with this matter he uses the analogy of the human body, in which all members have their due function, but some are less important than others (*1 Cor. 12:12-26*). The service of each Christian is to be in proportion to the gift which he possesses. As these gifts are gifts of loving grace, so their use must be controlled by the principle of love, the greatest of all spiritual gifts.

See SPIRIT

SCRIPTURE

General Gifts

Rom. 1 [11]For I long to see you, that I may impart unto you some spiritual gift, to the end ye may be established;

1 Cor. 1 [7]So that ye come behind in no gift; waiting for the coming of our Lord Jesus Christ:

1 Cor. 7 [7]For I would that all men were even as I myself. But every man hath his proper gift of God, one after this manner, and another after that.

2 Cor. 1 [11]Ye also helping together by prayer for us, that for the gift bestowed upon us by the means of many persons thanks may be given by many on our behalf.

Particular Gifts

Rom. 12 [6]Having then gifts differing according to the grace that is given to us, whether prophecy, let us prophesy according to the proportion of faith;
[7]Or ministry, let us wait on our ministering: or he that teacheth, on teaching;
[8]Or he that exhorteth, on exhortation: he that giveth, let him do it with simplicity; he that ruleth, with diligence; he that sheweth mercy, with cheerfulness.

1 Cor. 12 [8]For to one is given by the Spirit the word of wisdom; to another the word of knowledge by the same Spirit; [9]To another faith by the same Spirit; to another the gifts of healing by the same Spirit; [10]To another the working of miracles; to another prophecy; to another discerning of spirits; to another divers kinds of tongues; to another the interpretation of tongues: [28]And God hath set some in the church, first apostles, secondarily prophets, thirdly teachers, after that miracles, then gifts of healings, helps, governments, diversities of tongues. [29]Are all apostles? are all prophets? are all teachers? are all workers of miracles? [30]Have all the gifts of healing? do all speak with tongues? do all interpret?

Instruction Concerning Use of Spiritual Gifts

Rom. 12 [3]For I say, through the grace given unto me, to every man that is among you, not to think of himself more highly than he ought to think; but to think soberly, according as God hath dealt to every man the measure of faith. [4]For as we have many members in one body, and all members have not the same office: [5]So we, being many, are one body in Christ, and every one members one of another. [6]Having then gifts differing according to the grace that is given to us, whether prophecy, let us prophesy according to the proportion of faith; [7]Or ministry, let us wait on our ministering; or he that teacheth, on teaching; [8]Or he that exhorteth, on exhortation: he that giveth, let him do it with simplicity; he that ruleth, with diligence; he that sheweth mercy, with cheerfulness.

1 Cor. 12 [1]Now concerning spiritual gifts, brethren, I would not have you ignorant. [6]And there are diversities of operations, but it is the same God which worketh all in all. [7]But the manifestation of the Spirit is given to every man to profit withal. [11]But all these worketh that one and the selfsame Spirit, dividing to every man severally as he will. [12]For as the body is one, and hath many members, and all the members of that one body, being many, are one body: so also is Christ.

1 Cor. 14 [1]Follow after charity, and desire spiritual gifts, but rather that ye may prophesy. [2]For he that speaketh in an unknown tongue speaketh not unto men, but unto God: for no man understandeth him; howbeit in the spirit he speaketh mysteries. [3]But he that prophesieth speaketh unto men to edification, and exhortation, and comfort. [4]He that speaketh in an unknown tongue edifieth himself; but he that prophesieth edifieth the church. [5]I would that ye all spake with tongues, but rather that ye prophesied: for greater is he that prophesieth than he that speaketh with tongues, except he interpret, that the church may receive edifying. [6]Now, brethren, if I come unto you speaking with tongues, what shall I profit you, except I shall speak to you either by revelation, or by knowledge, or by prophesying, or by doctrine? [7]And even things without life giving sound, whether pipe or harp, except they give a distinction in the sounds, how shall it be known what is piped or harped? [8]For if the trumpet give an uncertain sound, who shall prepare himself to the battle? [9]So likewise ye, except ye utter by the tongue words easy to be understood, how shall it be known what is spoken? for ye shall speak into the air. [10]There are, it may be, so many kinds of voices in the world, and none of them is without signification. [11]Therefore if I know not the meaning of the voice, I shall be unto him that speaketh a barbarian, and he that speaketh shall be a barbarian unto me. 12 Even so ye, forasmuch as ye are zealous of spiritual gifts, seek that ye may excel to the edifying of the church. 13 Wherefore let him that speaketh in an unknown tongue pray that he may interpret. 14 For if I pray in an unknown tongue, my spirit prayeth, but my understanding is unfruitful. 15 What is it then? I will pray with the spirit, and I will pray with the understanding also: I will sing with the spirit, and I will sing with the understanding also. 16 Else, when thou shalt bless with the spirit, how shall he that occupieth the room of the unlearned say Amen at thy giving of thanks, seeing he understandeth not what thou sayest? 17 For thou verily givest thanks well, but the other is not edified. 18 I thank my God, I speak with tongues more than ye all: 19 Yet in the church I had rather speak five words with my understanding, that by my voice I might teach others also, than ten thousand words in an unknown tongue. 22 Wherefore tongues are for a sign, not to them that believe, but to them that believe not: but prophesying serveth not for them that believe not, but for them which believe. 23 If therefore the whole church be come together into one place, and all speak with tongues, and there come in those that are unlearned, or unbelievers, will they not say that ye are mad? 24 But if all prophesy, and there come in one that believeth not, or one unlearned, he is convinced of all, he is judged of all: 25 And thus are the secrets of his heart made manifest; and so falling down on his face he will worship God, and report that God is in you of a truth. 26 How is it then, brethren? when ye come together, every one of you hath a psalm, hath a doctrine, hath a tongue, hath a revelation, hath an interpretation. Let all things be done unto edifying. 27 If any man speak in an unknown tongue, let it be by two, or at the most by three, and that by course; and let one interpret. 28 But if there be no interpreter, let him keep silence in the church; and let him speak to himself, and to God. 29 Let the prophets speak two or three, and let the other judge. 30 If any thing be revealed to another that sitteth by, let the first hold his peace. 39 Wherefore, brethren, covet to prophesy, and forbid not to speak with tongues. 40 Let all things be done decently and in order.

Eph. 4 7 But unto every one of us is given grace according to the measure of the gift of Christ. 8 Wherefore he saith, When he ascended upon high, he led captivity captive, and gave gifts unto men. 9 (Now that he ascended, what is it but that he also descended first into the lower parts of the earth? 10 He that descended is the same also that ascended up far above all heavens, that he might fill all things.) 11 And he gave some, apostles; and some, prophets; and some, evangelists; and some, pastors and teachers; 12 For the perfecting of the saints, for the work of the ministry, for the edifying of the body of Christ: 13 Till we all come in the unity of the faith, and of the knowledge of the Son of God, unto a perfect man, unto the measure of the stature of the fulness of Christ:

1 Tim. 4 13 Till I come, give attendance to reading, to exhortation, to doctrine. 14 Neglect not the gift that is in thee, which was given thee by prophecy, with the laying on of the hands of the presbytery.

Heb. 2 4 God also bearing them witness, both with signs and wonders, and with divers miracles, and gifts of the Holy Ghost, according to his own will?

1 Pet. 4 10 As every man hath received the gift, even so minister the same one to another, as good stewards of the manifold grace of God. [11]If any man speak, let him speak as the oracles of God; if any man minister, let him do it as of the ability which God giveth; that God in all things may be glorified through Jesus Christ: to whom be praise and dominion for ever and ever. Amen.

STEADFASTNESS (Stedfastness)

[sted'fast nes] The quality or state of being steadfast; firmness; constancy; resolution in a good cause; fixedness of purpose.

SCRIPTURE

Deut. 10 [20]Thou shalt fear the LORD thy God; him shalt thou serve, and to him shalt thou cleave, and swear by his name.

Job 11 [15]For then shalt thou lift up thy face without spot; yea, thou shalt be steadfast, and shalt not fear.

1 Cor. 15 [58]Therefore, my beloved brethren, be ye stedfast, unmoveable always abounding in the work of the Lord, forasmuch as ye know that your labour is not in vain in the Lord.

Col. 2 [5]For though I be absent in the flesh, yet am I with you in the spirit, joying and beholding your order, and the steadfastness of your faith in Christ.

1 Thess. 5 [21]Prove all things; hold fast that which is good.

Heb. 3 [14]For we are made partakers of Christ, if we hold the beginning of our confidence stedfast unto the end.

Heb. 4 [14]Seeing then that we have a great high priest, that is passed into the heavens, Jesus the Son of God, let us hold fast our profession.

Heb. 10 [23]Let us hold fast the profession of our faith without wavering; (for he is faithful that promised;) [24]And let us consider one another to provoke unto love and to good works.

1 Pet. 5 [9]Whom resist stedfast in the faith, knowing that the same afflictions are accomplished in your brethren that are in the world.

2 Pet. 3 [17]Ye therefore, beloved, seeing ye know these things before, beware lest ye also, being led away with the error of the wicked, fall from your own stedfastness.

STEPHEN

[stē'v'n] A Christian martyr. Stephen was among the seven chosen to serve in the daily distribution of food and supplies to the Christian community in Jerusalem. He is the first named and is designated as "a man full of faith and of the Holy Ghost" who "did great wonders and miracles among the people." In order to counteract the effect which his work was having, several Jews engaged him in controversy; "and they were not able to resist the wisdom and the spirit by which he spake." Consequently, they stirred up the people and had him arraigned before the council and charged with a number of false accusations, among which were blasphemy against the law and the temple. In his defence, Stephen recalled the long history of the people of Israel, reminding his accusers of the consistent refusal of the Hebrews to remain faithful to the covenant which they had made. At the climax of his speech, he indicted his hearers with these words: "Ye stiffnecked and uncircumcised in heart and ears, ye do always resist the Holy Ghost: as your fathers did, so do ye. Which of the prophets have not your fathers persecuted? and they have slain them which showed before of the coming of the Just One; of whom ye have been now the betrayers and murderers:" (*Acts 7:51, 52*). At this, they could no longer control their rage, but leaped upon him and "gnashed on him with their teeth." Then, in violation of Roman law, they took him outside the city and stoned him to death, apparently under the supervision of a young man named Saul, later to become the apostle Paul. In his dying moments, Stephen displayed the spirit which had made him so admirable in life. The account of his last words cannot but provoke an image of the Lord whom he served; as they stoned him he prayed, "calling upon God, and saying, Lord Jesus, receive my spirit. And he kneeled down, and cried with a loud voice, Lord, lay not this sin to their charge. And when he had said this, he fell asleep" (*Acts 7:59, 60*).

SCRIPTURE

Acts 6 [2]Then the twelve called the multitude of the disciples unto them, and said,
It is not reason that we should leave the
word of God, and serve tables. [3]Where-
fore, brethren, look ye out among you
seven men of honest report, full of the
Holy Ghost and wisdom, whom we may
appoint over this business. [4]But we will
give ourselves continually to prayer, and
to the ministry of the word.
[5]And the saying pleased the whole multitude: and they chose Stephen, a man full
of faith and of the Holy Ghost, and Philip,
and Prochorus, and Nicanor, and Timon,
and Parmenas, and Nicolas a proselyte of
Antioch: [6]Whom they set before the apostles: and when they had prayed, they laid their hands on them.
[8]And Stephen, full of faith and
power, did great wonders and miracles
among the people.
[9]Then there arose certain of the synagogue, which is called the synagogue of
the Libertines, and Cyrenians, and Alexandrians, and of them of Cilicia and of
Asia, disputing with Stephen. [10]And they
were not able to resist the wisdom and the
spirit by which he spake. [11]Then they suborned men, which said, We have heard
him speak blasphemous words against Moses, and against God. [12]And they stirred
up the people, and the elders, and the
scribes, and came upon him, and caught
him, and brought him to the council,
[13]And set up false witnesses, which said,
This man ceaseth not to speak blasphemous words against this holy place, and
the law: [14]For we have heard him say, that
this Jesus of Nazareth shall destroy this
place, and shall change the customs which
Moses delivered us. [15]And all that sat in
the council, looking stedfastly on him, saw
his face as it had been the face of an angel.
Acts 7 [54]When they heard these things,
they were cut to the heart, and they
gnashed on him with their teeth. [55]But he,
being full of the Holy Ghost, looked up
stedfastly into heaven, and saw the glory
of God, and Jesus standing on the right
hand of God, [56]And said, Behold, I see the
heavens opened, and the Son of man
standing on the right hand of God. [57]Then
they cried out with a loud voice, and
stopped their ears, and ran upon him with
one accord, [58]And cast him out of the city,
and stoned him: and the witnesses laid
down their clothes at a young man's feet,
whose name was Saul. [59]And they stoned
Stephen, calling upon God, and saying,
Lord Jesus, receive my spirit. [60]And he
kneeled down, and cried with a loud voice,
Lord, lay not this sin to their charge. And
when he had said this, he fell asleep.

STEWARD

[stū'ẽrd] An officer or employee in a family or on an estate; his task was to manage the domestic concerns, supervise the servants and possibly the children, collect income, keep accounts, etc. Stewards seem to have been commonplace throughout almost all of the period of biblical history. Elizer of Damascus is named as the steward of Abraham (*Gen. 15:2*). The role filled by Jacob in the household of Laban was that of a steward (*Gen. 29:15-30:43*). Joseph is said to have had a steward after he was raised to a position of importance in Egypt (*Gen. 44:1-4*). Several of Jesus' parables, including the Laborers in the Vineyard (*Matt. 20:1-16*) and the Unjust Steward (*Luke 16:1-8*), indicate that most households of any substance probably had stewards. In the epistles, the term is used of ministers of the gospel and overseers of the church, with reference to their obligation to care for that which had been entrusted to them by the master of the household, Jesus Christ.

SCRIPTURE

Luke 12 [35]Let your loins be girded about, and your lights burning; [36]And ye yourselves like unto men that wait for their lord, when he will return from the wedding; that, when he cometh and knocketh, they may open unto him immediately. [37]Blessed are those servants, whom the lord when he cometh shall find watching: verily I say unto you, that he shall gird himself, and make them to sit down to meat, and will come forth and serve them. [38]And if he shall come in the second watch, or come in the third watch, and find them so, blessed are those servants. [39]And this know, that if the goodman of the house had known what hour the thief would come, he would have watched, and not have suffered his house to be broken through. [40]Be ye therefore ready also: for the Son of man cometh at an hour when ye think not.

[41]Then Peter said unto him, Lord, speakest thou this parable unto us, or even to all? [42]And the Lord said, Who then is that faithful and wise steward, whom his lord shall make ruler over his household, to give them their portion of meat in due season? [43]Blessed is that servant, whom his lord when he cometh shall find so doing.

Luke 16 [1]And he said also unto his disciples, There was a certain rich man, which had a steward; and the same was accused unto him that he had wasted his goods. [2]And he called him, and said unto him, How is it that I hear this of thee? give an account of thy stewardship; for thou mayest be no longer steward. [3]Then the steward said within himself, What shall I do? for my lord taketh away from me the stewardship: I can not dig; to beg I am ashamed. [4]I am resolved what to do, that, when I am put out of the stewardship, they may receive me into their houses. [5]So he called every one of his lord's debtors unto him, and said unto the first, How much owest thou unto my lord? [6]And he said, A hundred measures of oil. And he said unto him, Take thy bill, and sit down quickly, and write fifty. [7]Then said he to another, And how much owest thou? And he said, A hundred measures of wheat. And he said unto him, Take thy bill, and write fourscore. [8]And the lord commended the unjust steward, because he had done wisely: for the children of this world are in their generation wiser than the children of light.

1 Cor. 4 [1]Let a man so account of us, as of the ministers of Christ, and stewards of the mysteries of God. [2]Moreover it is required in stewards, that a man be found faithful.

1 Pet. 4 [10]As every man hath received the gift, even so minister the same one to another, as good stewards of the manifold grace of God.

STOICS (Stoa, Stoicism)

[stō′iks, stō′a, stō′i cism] A Greek philosophical school or sect, founded by Zeno of Citium about 300 BC and continuing until at least 260 AD. Its name is derived from the Stoa Poikile, a public hall in Athens in which Zeno and his successors taught. The history of this school is usually divided into three periods: (1) The Early Stoa (from Zeno until the first half of the second century BC); (2) The Middle Stoa, (the second and first centuries BC); and (3) The Late Stoa (the period of the Roman Empire). The most important leaders of the Stoa in these periods were Zeno in the Early Stoa, Panaetius in the Middle Stoa, and Seneca, Epictetus, and Marcus Aurelius in the Late Stoa.

Zeno taught that virtue was based on knowledge; only the wise man, or sage, could be truly virtuous. The aim of the true philosopher is to live in harmony with nature. The guiding principle in nature is the Logos, or reason, which is identified with God and manifested in fate, providence, and human reason. Zeno maintained that among the elements fire was the most closely related to the Logos and that the universe was periodically consumed by fire, after which a new cycle of existence and events begins. This doctrine of a universal conflagration was rejected by Panaetius, in the period of the Middle Stoa. Zeno felt that to live in harmony with reason is the only good and that not to do so is the only evil. Everything else is of no consequence. From this stems the well-known Stoic attitude toward pain, pleasure, and death. The Stoic did not fear pain, nor death, because he did not view them as evil; he avoided pleasure, because he felt that pleasure was not a good to be sought.

In the Middle and Late Stoa, there was a great emphasis on participation in public life as the duty of the wise man; as a result, Stoic thought had great influence on the soldiers and statesmen of the Roman empire. Stoics are mentioned in *Acts 17:18* as having been among those Athenians who invited Paul to speak on the Areopagus, or Mar's Hill.

See EPICUREANS, AREOPAGUS

SCRIPTURE

Acts 17 [18]Then certain philosophers of the Epicureans, and of the Stoics, encountered him. And some said, What will this babbler say? other some, He seemeth to be a setter forth of strange gods: because he preached unto them Jesus, and the resurrection.

STONING

[stōn′ing] The most common form of execution among the Israelites. The witnesses, of whom two were required, were commanded to cast the first stone. (*See John 8:7*) If these failed to bring death, the bystanders joined the stoning until the victim was dead.

SCRIPTURE

Ex. 19 [12]And thou shalt set bounds unto the people round about, saying, take heed to yourselves, that ye go not up into the mount, or touch the border of it: whosoever toucheth the mount shall be surely put to death: [13]There shall not a hand touch it, but he shall surely be stoned, or shot through.

Lev. 20 [27]A man also or woman that hath a familiar spirit, or that is a wizard, shall surely be put to death: they shall stone them with stones; their blood shall be upon them.

Josh. 7 [25]And Joshua said, Why hast thou troubled us? the LORD shall trouble thee this day. And all Israel stoned him with stones, and burned them with fire, after they had stoned them with stones.

Luke 20 [6]But and if we say, Of men; all the people will stone us: for they be persuaded that John was a prophet.

Acts 7 [58]And cast him out of the city, and stoned him: and the witnesses laid down their clothes at a young man's feet, whose name was Saul.

Acts 14 [5]And when there was an assault made both of the Gentiles, and also of the Jews with their rulers, to use them despitefully, and to stone them.

STRANGER

[strānj′ẽr] Anyone residing or visiting in a country or town of which he is not a full citizen; a sojourner or foreigner. The Law of Moses protected the stranger against judicial inequality and contained provisions to assist him in obtaining his basic physical needs. The stranger was subject to legislation concerning most of the holy days, but he could not observe Passover until he had entered into the covenant through the rite of circumcision. Intermarriage with strangers or foreigners, although common in Israel's history, seems to have been generally disliked (*see Gen. 24:3; 27:46ff; Num. 12:1; Deut. 25:5; Judg. 14:3*) and was vigorously opposed by Ezra and Nehemiah in the post-exilic period (*Ezra 10; Neh. 13:23-31*).

See GENTILES, USURY, HOSPITALITY

SCRIPTURE

Ex. 12 [43]And the LORD said unto Moses
and Aaron, This is the ordinance of the
passover; There shall no stranger eat
thereof: [48]And when a stranger shall sojourn with thee, and will keep the passover
to the LORD, let all his males be circumcised, and then let him come near and keep
it; and he shall be as one that is born in the
land; for no uncircumcised person shall
eat thereof. [49]One law shall be to him that
is homeborn, and unto the stranger that sojourneth among you.

Ex. 20 [10]But the seventh day is the sabbath of the LORD thy God: in it thou shalt
not do any work, thou, nor thy son, nor thy
daughter, thy manservant, nor thy maidservant, nor thy cattle, nor thy stranger
that is within thy gates:

Lev. 19 [10]And thou shalt not glean thy
vineyard, neither shalt thou gather every
grape of thy vineyard; thou shalt leave
them for the poor and the stranger; I am
the LORD your God.

[33]And if a stranger sojourn with thee in
your land, ye shall not vex him. [34]But the
stranger that swelleth with you shall be
unto you as one born among you, and thou
shalt love him as thyself; for ye were
strangers in the land of Egypt: I am the
LORD your God.

Lev. 23 [22]And when ye reap the harvest
of your land, thou shalt not make clean riddance of the corners of thy field when thou
reapest, neither shalt thou gather any
gleaning of thy harvest: thou shalt leave
them unto the poor, and to the stranger: I
am the LORD your God.

Lev. 24 [22]Ye shall have one manner of
law, as well for the stranger, as for one of
your own country: for I am the LORD your
God.

Deut. 1 [16]And I charged your judges at
that time, saying, Hear the causes between
your brethren, and judge righteously between every man and his brother, and the
stranger that is with him.

Deut. 10 [18]He doth execute the judgment of the fatherless and widow, and loveth the stranger, in giving him food and
raiment. [19]Love ye therefore the stranger:
for ye were strangers in the land of Egypt.

Deut. 14 [29]And the Levite (because he
hath no part nor inheritance with thee,)
and the stranger, and the fatherless, and
the widow, which are within thy gates,
shall come, and shall eat and be satisfied;
that the LORD thy God may bless thee in all
the work of thine hand which thou doest.

Deut. 15 [3]Of a foreigner thou mayest
exact it again: but that which is thine with
thy brother thine hand shall release.

Deut. 17 [15]Thou shalt in any wise set
him king over thee, whom the LORD thy
God shall choose: one from among thy
brethren shalt thou set king over thee, thou
mayest not set a stranger over thee, which
is not thy brother.

Deut. 24 [19]When thou cuttest down
thine harvest in thy field, and hast forgot
a sheaf in the field, thou shalt not go again
to fetch it: it shall be for the stranger, for
the fatherless, and for the widow: that the
LORD thy God may bless thee in all the
work of thine hands. [20]When thou beatest
thine olive tree, thou shalt not go over the
boughs again: it shall be for the stranger,
for the fatherless, and for the widow.
[21]When thou gatherest the grapes of thy
vineyard, thou shalt not glean it afterward:
it shall be for the stranger, for the fatherless, and for the widow.

Deut. 25 [5]If brethren dwell together,
and one of them die, and have no child, the
wife of the dead shall not marry without
unto a stranger: her husband's brother
shall go in unto her, and take her to him to

wife, and perform the duty of an husband's brother unto her.

Deut. 26 [12]When thou hast made an end of tithing all the tithes of thine increase the third year, which is the year of tithing, and hast given it unto the Levite, the stranger, the fatherless, and the widow, that they may eat within your gates, and be filled;

See Deut. 23:20

STRIFE

[strif] Exertion or contention for superiority; altercation; contentiousness; quarreling; fighting. The Bible contains numerous references to strife and its effects.

SCRIPTURE

Exhortations Against Strife

Prov. 3 [30]Strive not with a man without cause, if he have done thee no harm.

Prov. 17 [14]The beginning of strife is as when one letteth out water: therefore leave off contention, before it be meddled with.

Prov. 25 [8]Go not forth hastily to strive, lest thou know not what to do in the end thereof, when thy neighbour hath put thee to shame.

Prov. 26 [17]He that passeth by, and meddleth with strife belonging not to him, is like one that taketh a dog by the ears.

Rom. 13 [13]Let us walk honestly, as in the day; not in rioting and drunkenness, not in chambering and wantonness, not in strife and envying.

1 Cor. 3 [3]For ye are yet carnal: for whereas there is among you envying, and strife, and divisions, are ye not carnal, and walk as men?

Gal. 5 [19]Now the works of the flesh are manifest, which are these; Adultery, fornication, uncleanness, lasciviousness, [20]Idolatry, witchcraft, hatred, variance, emulations, wrath, strife, seditions, heresies, [21]Envyings, murders, drunkenness, revellings, and such like: of the which I tell you before, as I have also told you in time past, that they which do such things shall not inherit the kingdom of God.

Phil. 2 [3]Let nothing be done through strife or vainglory; but in lowliness of mind let each esteem other better than themselves. [14]Do all things without murmurings and disputings.

2 Tim. 2 [23]But foolish and unlearned questions avoid, knowing that they do gender strifes.

Tit. 3 [9]But avoid foolish questions, and genealogies, and contentions, and strivings about the law; for they are unprofitable and vain.

Jas. 3 [14]But if ye have bitter envying and strife in your hearts, glory not, and lie not against the truth.

The Origin of Strife

Prov. 10 [12]Hatred stirreth up strifes: but love covereth all sins.

Prov. 13 [10]Only by pride cometh contention: but with the well advised is wisdom.

Prov. 15 [18]A wrathful man stirreth up strife: but he that is slow to anger appeaseth strife.

Prov. 16 [28]A froward man soweth strife: and a whisperer separateth chief friends.

Prov. 22 [10]Cast out the scorner, and contention shall go out; yea, strife and reproach shall cease.

Prov. 26 [20]Where no wood is, there the fire goeth out: so where there is no talebearer, the strife ceaseth.

Prov. 28 [25]He that is of a proud heart stirreth up strife: but he that putteth his trust in the LORD shall be made fat.

Prov. 30 [33]Surely the churning of milk

bringeth forth butter, and the wringing of the nose bringeth forth blood: so the forcing of wrath bringeth forth strife.

1 Tim. 6 [4]He is proud, knowing nothing, but doting about questions and strifes of words, whereof cometh envy, strife, railings, evil surmisings, [5]Perverse disputings of men of corrupt minds, and destitute of the truth, supposing that gain is godliness: from such withdraw thyself.

Results of Strife

Gal. 5 [15]But if ye bite and devour one another, take heed that ye be not consumed one of another.

Jas. 3 [16]For where envying and strife is, there is confusion and every evil work.

Strife Condemned

1 Cor. 1 [11]For it hath been declared unto me of you, my brethren, by them which are of the house of Chloe, that there are contentions among you. [12]Now this I say, that every one of you saith, I am of Paul; and I of Apollos; and I of Cephas; and I of Christ. [13]Is Christ divided? was Paul crucified for you? or were ye baptized in the name of Paul?

1 Cor. 3 [3]For ye are yet carnal: for whereas there is among you envying, and strife, and divisions, are ye not carnal, and walk as men?

1 Cor. 6 [1]Dare any of you, having a matter against another, go to law before the unjust, and not before the saints? [2]Do ye not know that the saints shall judge the world? and if the world shall be judged by you, are ye unworthy to judge the smallest matters?

STUBBORNNESS

[stub'born nes] The state or quality of being unreasonably obstinate in will or opinion; obdurate; headstrong; self-willed.

SCRIPTURE

Stubbornness Forbidden

2 Chr. 30 [8]Now be ye not stiffnecked, as your fathers were, but yield yourselves unto the LORD, and enter into his sanctuary, which he hath sanctified for ever: and serve the LORD your God, that the fierceness of his wrath may turn away from you.

Psa. 32 [9]Be ye not as the horse, or as the mule, which have no understanding: whose mouth must be held in with bit and bridle, lest they come near unto thee.

Punishment for Stubbornness

Prov. 1 [24]Because I have called, and ye refused; I have stretched out my hand, and no man regarded; [25]But ye have set at nought all my counsel, and would none of my reproof: [26]I also will laugh at your calamity; I will mock when your fear cometh.

Prov. 29 [1]He, that being often reproved hardeneth his neck, shall suddenly be destroyed, and that without remedy.

SUCCOTH

[suk'oth] 1. An ancient town, in the account of the homeward journey of Jacob from Padanaram. Jacob there put up "booths" (succoth) for his cattle, as well as a house for himself (*Gen. 33:17*).

2. The first station of the Israelites on an exodus from Egypt (*Ex. 12:37; 13:20; Num. 33:5*).

SWINE

[swīn] A stout-bodied, short-legged omnivorous mammal with a thick skin usually covered with coarse bristles, a rather long snout, small tail, and cloven feet; a pig or hog. Jews were forbidden by the law to eat the flesh of swine. The exact reason for this prohibition is unknown. It has been suggested that it may be due to the fact that pigs were considered sacred in some of the pagan religions known to the Israelites.

SCRIPTURE

Lev. 11 [4]Nevertheless, these shall ye not eat of them that chew the cud, or of them that divide the hoof: [7]And the swine, though he divide the hoof, and be cloven-footed, yet he cheweth not the cud; he is unclean to you. [8]Of their flesh shall ye not eat, and their carcass shall ye not touch; they are unclean to you.

SWORD OF THE SPIRIT

[sōrd, spir′it] One of the titles given to the word of God, the Scriptures.

SCRIPTURE

Eph. 6 [17]And take the helmet of salvation, and the sword of the Spirit, which is the word of God:

Heb. 4 [12]For the word of God is quick, and powerful, and sharper than any two-edged sword, piercing even to the dividing asunder of soul and spirit, and of the joints and marrow, and is a discerner of the thoughts and intents of the heart.

SYNAGOGUE

[sin′a gog] Literally, a "gathering-place." This is the name applied to the houses of worship in later Judaism which were found throughout Palestine and in the lands of the Dispersion. (*See* DISPERSION) It is usually thought that this institution originated during the period of Babylonian exile, as a result of the desire of devout Jews to gather together to hear an exposition of the Law. Prayers and preaching were eventually added and the synagogue became the regular place of worship. A standard synagogue service consisted of a recitation of specified verses, reading of portions from the Law and the Prophets, prayers, a sermon, and the benediction. The synagogue had a regular hierarchy of officials. The Elders had jurisdiction not only over the affairs directly connected with the synagogue, but acted as a local tribunal with judicial authority over members of the congregation. The Ruler of the synagogue was probably chosen from the elders; his duty was to appoint those who were to participate in the service and to act as a general overseer. The Ruler and the Learned men of the synagogue sat in the "chief seats", facing the congregation. In addition to these were the "delegate of the congregation", who was chosen at each meeting to conduct the prayers; the interpreter, who translated the Hebrew scriptures into the vernacular tongue; and the almoners, whose duty it was to collect and distribute alms for the poor.

TABERNACLE

[tab′ẽr nak′l] A sacred tent or portable sanctuary, fashioned and erected under the leadership of Moses. It housed the Ark of the Covenant and was the center of Israelite religion from its construction in the wilderness of Sinai until the division of the land at Shiloh, and perhaps until the time of Solomon's temple.

After the giving of the Law, God instructed Moses to construct the tabernacle out of gifts from the people (*Ex. 35:4*). We are told that the people brought "more than enough for doing the work which the LORD commanded" (*Ex. 36:5*). Moses appointed two specially gifted artisans, Bezaleel and Aholiab, to fashion the materials, and work on the tabernacle was begun. The tabernacle was placed in the western half of a courtyard of one hundred by fifty cubits, or, figuring the cubit at approximately eighteen inches, one-hundred-fifty by seventy-five feet. This courtyard consisted of a fence on which were hung fine linens. Within the courtyard, in front of the tabernacle, were the altar of burnt offerings and the laver. The altar was constructed of boards and overlaid with brass. It was here that the sacrifices were offered to God. The laver was a great brass bowl in which the priests washed their hands and feet before officiating at the altar or in the tabernacle itself. The tabernacle was a structure measuring thirty by ten cubits. Its long sides faced north and south, with the entrance facing west. It consisted of a framework ten cubits high, upon which were placed coverings of linen, goats' hair, and animal skins. The frame was constructed of acacia wood overlaid with gold and was set in silver sockets. There were two rooms within the tabernacle, separated by a veil. The larger of these rooms measured twenty cubits in length and was called the Holy Place. Immediately in front of the veil stood the altar of incense, a cube of two cubits constructed of acacia wood overlaid with gold. Along the north side of the tent was the table of shewbread, on which were placed twelve loaves, representing the twelve tribes, and various accessories such as dishes, flagons, and spoons. On the north side stood a golden lampstand and its accessories. The smaller room in the tabernacle, a ten cubit cube, was called the Most Holy Place or the Holy of Holies. Apart from preparation for moving the tabernacle, only the high priest was allowed within the Holy of Holies and he only once a year, on the Day of Atonement. (*See* FEASTS, FESTIVALS) Within this room was the Ark of the Covenant. (*See* ARK) The "mercy seat," a slab of pure gold which rested on top of the Ark, was adorned by two cherubim, or winged sphinxes; for the probable significance of these figures, *see* CHERUBIM.

The tabernacle was completed and erected on the first day of the first month after the second year of the exodus, nine months after the arrival of the Israelites at Sinai. After its completion, the glory of the LORD covered the tabernacle, taking the form of a cloud by day and a pillar of fire by night. It stood in the center of the camp of Israel. Immediately surrounding it were the tents of the Levites. The tents of the remaining tribes formed an outer circle. The tabernacle accompanied Israel into the land of Canaan and was set up in Shiloh at the time of the division of the land among the tribes (*Josh. 18:1*). After that, it is the ark and not the tabernacle, as such, which is the center of religious devotion; we cannot be sure what became of the original tabernacle.

In the New Testament the tabernacle is viewed as a copy of heavenly things and a foreshadow of things to come. The veil, the mercy seat, and the Holy of Holies are all mentioned in connection with the work of Christ and their archetypal significance is revealed.

SCRIPTURE

Instructions for Building

See Ex. 35-40

Traveled Before the Israelites

Num. 10 33And they departed from the
mount of the LORD three days' journey:
and the ark of the covenant of the LORD
went before them in the three days' journey, to search out a resting place for them.
34And the cloud of the LORD was upon
them by day, when they went out of the
camp. 35And it came to pass, when the
ark set forward, that Moses said, Rise up,
LORD, and let thine enemies be scattered;
and let them that hate thee flee before
thee. 36And when it rested, he said, Return, O LORD, unto the many thousands of
Israel.

The Lord Appears at the Tabernacle

Num. 12 4And the LORD spake suddenly
unto Moses, and unto Aaron, and unto
Miriam, Come out ye three unto the tabernacle of the congregation. And they three
came out. 5And the LORD came down in
the pillar of the cloud, and stood in the
door of the tabernacle, and called Aaron
and Miriam: and they both came forth.
6And he said, Hear now my words: If
there be a prophet among you, I the LORD
will make myself known unto him in a
vision, and will speak unto him in a dream.
7My servant Moses is not so, who is faithful in all mine house. 8With him will I
speak mouth to mouth, even apparently,
and not in dark speeches; and the similitude of the LORD shall he behold: wherefore then were ye not afraid to speak
against my servant Moses? 9And the anger of the LORD was kindled against them;

and he departed. [10]And the cloud departed from off the tabernacle; and, behold, Miriam became leprous, white as snow: and Aaron looked upon Miriam, and, behold, she was leprous.

Symbolic of Spiritual Things

Heb. 8 [1]Now of the things which we have spoken this is the sum: We have such a high priest, who is set on the right hand of the throne of the Majesty in the heavens; [2]A minister of the sanctuary, and of the true tabernacle, which the Lord pitched, and not man. [5]Who serve unto the example and shadow of heavenly things, as Moses was admonished of God when he was about to make the tabernacle: for, See, saith he, that thou make all things according to the pattern shewed to thee in the mount.

Heb. 9 [1]Then verily the first covenant had also ordinances of divine service, and a worldly sanctuary. [2]For there was a tabernacle made; the first, wherein was the candlestick, and the table, and the shewbread; which is called the sanctuary. [3]And after the second veil, the tabernacle which is called the holiest of all; [4]Which had the golden censer, and the ark of the covenant overlaid round about with gold, wherein was the golden pot that had manna, and Aaron's rod that budded, and the tables of the covenant; [5]And over it the cherubim of glory shadowing the mercy seat; of which we can not now speak particularly. [6]Now when these things were thus ordained, the priests went always into the first tabernacle, accomplishing the service of God. [7]But into the second went the high priest alone once every year, not without blood, which he offered for himself, and for the errors of the people: [8]The Holy Ghost this signifying, that the way into the holiest of all was not yet made manifest, while as the first tabernacle was yet standing: [9]Which was a figure for the time then present, in which were offered both gifts and sacrifices, that could not make him that did the service perfect, as pertaining to the conscience; [10]Which stood only in meats and drinks, and divers washings, and carnal ordinances, imposed on them until the time of reformation. [11]But Christ being come an high priest of good things to come, by a greater and more perfect tabernacle, not made with hands, that is to say, not of this building; [12]Neither by the blood of goats and calves, but by his own blood he entered in once into the holy place, having obtained eternal redemption for us. [23]It was therefore necessary that the patterns of things in the heavens should be purified with these; but the heavenly things themselves with better sacrifices than these. [24]For Christ is not entered into the holy places made with hands, which are the figures of the true; but into heaven itself, now to appear in the presence of God for us: [25]Nor yet that he should offer himself often, as the high priest entereth into the holy place every year with blood of others; [26]For then must he often have suffered since the foundation of the world: but now once in the end of the world hath he appeared to put away sin by the sacrifice of himself.

TAMMUZ

[tam'ōōz] A Sumerian deity of vegetation. In Babylonian mythology, Tammuz is pictured as having been betrayed by Ishtar, the goddess of love. The annual dying of vegetation was held to be connected with this betrayal and was celebrated with weeping and wailing. In *Ezek. 8:14*, the women of Jerusalem are said to have engaged in a form of this wailing ceremony.

SCRIPTURE

Ezek. 8 [14]Then he brought me to the door of the gate of the LORD's house which was toward the north; and, behold, there sat women weeping for Tammuz.

TARSUS

[tär′sus] The capital city of Cilicia, situated in southeastern Asia Minor on the banks of the river Cydnus, about ten miles inland from the Mediterranean. Tarsus was the site of a great university and its inhabitants are said to have had a remarkable enthusiasm for learning. It is known to Bible students as the home of the apostle Paul, although he left it at an early age to be educated in Jerusalem. Paul's Roman citizenship, which he claims to have held from birth, was probably bestowed on one of his ancestors as a reward for some outstanding service.

REFERENCE: *Acts 9:11, 30; 21:39; 22:3.*

TAX

[taks] A pecuniary burden imposed by authority; a forced contribution of wealth to meet the public needs of a government; impost, tribute, levy, duty, toll, assessment. The only fixed tax in Israel before the rise of the monarchy was the half-shekel which each male member of the community above twenty years of age was required to pay. (*See Ex. 30:11-16*) This revenue was used to defray the expenses of the tabernacle; in later years it was devoted to the service of the temple.

When the Israelites demanded that their system of judges be replaced by a monarchy, Samuel warned them of the burden of taxation which would be placed upon them by a king (*1 Sam. 8:10-18*). Under Saul and David, the spoil from their victories and tribute from conquered states kept the treasury at such a level that excessive taxation was unnecessary. In the peaceful reign of Solomon, however, it became necessary to place a greater portion of the burden on the Israelites themselves. In order to maintain the luxurious standard of living at court and to finance his ambitious building projects, Solomon found it necessary to divide the empire into twelve fiscal districts. Over each of these was placed a governor whose duty it was to provide provisions for the court for one month of the year. This burden was so excessive that the assembly which met to confirm Rehoboam's succession to the throne after the death of Solomon demanded of him that he reduce the assessment. Rehoboam's foolish decision in the matter resulted in the unfortunate seccession of the ten northern tribes, leaving the once great nation sadly weakened. In the remaining years of Israel and Judah, there was added to the burden of domestic taxation the payment of tribute money to the conquering rulers of Egypt, Assyria, Babylon, and, after the return from exile, Persia.

In the Roman period, the direct taxes upon the people were collected by imperial officials as a part of their regular duties. The customs or tolls on imports, exports, and goods in the hands of merchants passing through the province, were collected by individuals called "Publicans" who purchased their position for a fixed sum and kept for themselves anything they could collect above that amount. (*See* PUBLICAN)

During the time of Christ the taxes collected in Judaea were quite heavy and went directly into the imperial treasury. These two factors help to explain why the matter of paying taxes to Caesar was such a burning issue among the Jews. (*See Matt. 22:17; Mark 12:13-17; Luke 20:22*) Despite the fact that man seems to possess a natural disinclination for paying taxes, both Jesus and Paul recognize this to be an inevitable concomitant of organized society and instruct us to "render unto Caesar that which is Caesar's" as a part of our Christian duty.

SCRIPTURE

The "Atonement Money"

Ex. 30 [11]And the LORD spake unto Moses, saying, [12]When thou takest the sum of the children of Israel after their number, then shall they give every man a ransom for his soul unto the LORD, when thou numberest them; that there be no plague among them, when thou numberest them.

13 This they shall give, every one that passeth among them that are numbered, half a shekel after the shekel of the sanctuary: (a shekel is twenty gerahs:) a half shekel shall be the offering of the LORD. 14 Every one that passeth among them that are numbered, from twenty years old and above, shall give an offering unto the LORD. 15 The rich shall not give more, and the poor shall not give less, than half a shekel, when they give an offering unto the LORD, to make an atonement for your souls. 16 And thou shalt take the atonement money of the children of Israel, and shalt appoint it for the service of the tabernacle of the congregation; that it may be a memorial unto the children of Israel before the LORD, to make an atonement for your souls.

Samuel's Warning against the Monarch

1 Sam. 8 10 And Samuel told all the words of the LORD unto the people that asked of him a king. 11 And he said, This will be the manner of the king that shall reign over you: He will take your sons, and appoint them for himself, for his chariots, and to be his horsemen; and some shall run before his chariots. 15 And he will take the tenth of your seed, and of your vineyards, and give to his officers, and to his servants. 17 He will take the tenth of your sheep: and ye shall be his servants.

Solomon's Tax Program

1 Kin. 4 7 And Solomon had twelve officers over all Israel, which provided victuals for the king and his household: each man his month in a year made provision.

Under the Kings

Amos 5 11 Forasmuch therefore as your treading is upon the poor, and ye take from him burdens of wheat.

Isa. 3 14 The LORD will enter into judgment with the ancients of his people, and the princes thereof; for ye have eaten up the vineyard; the spoil of the poor is in your houses.

Under Conquerors

2 Kin. 17 4 And the king of Assyria found conspiracy in Hoshea: for he had sent messengers to So king of Egypt, and brought no present to the king of Assyria, as he had done year by year; therefore the king of Assyria shut him up, and bound him in prison.

2 Kin. 23 31 Jehoahaz was twenty and three years old when he began to reign; and he reigned three months in Jerusalem. And his mother's name was Hamutal, the daughter of Jeremiah of Libnah. 32 And he did that which was evil in the sight of the LORD, according to all that his fathers had done. 33 And Pharaoh-nechoh put him in bands at Riblah in the hand of Hamath, that he might not reign in Jerusalem; and put the land to a tribute of a hundred talents of silver, and a talent of gold. 34 And Pharaoh-nechoh made Eliakim the son of Josiah king in the room of Josiah his father, and turned his name to Jehoiakim, and took Jehoahaz away: and he came to Egypt, and died there. 35 And Jehoiakim gave the silver and the gold to Pharaoh; but he taxed the land to give the money according to the commandment of Pharaoh: he exacted the silver and the gold of the people of the land, of every one according to his taxation, to give it unto Pharaoh-nechoh.

Ezra 4 13 Be it known now unto the king, that, if this city be builded, and the walls set up again, then will they not pay toll, tribute, and custom, and so thou shalt endamage the revenue of the kings.

Ezra 7 24 Also we certify you, that,

touching any of the priests and Levites, singers, porters, Nethinim, or ministers of this house of God, it shall not be lawful to impose toll, tribute, or custom, upon them.

New Testament Teaching on Taxes

Matt. 17 [24]And when they were come to Capernaum, they that received tribute money came to Peter, and said, Doth not your master pay tribute? [25]He saith, Yes. And when he was come into the house, Jesus prevented him, saying, What thinkest thou, Simon? of whom do the kings of the earth take custom or tribute? of their own children, or of strangers? [26]Peter saith unto him, Of strangers. Jesus saith unto him, Then are the children free. [27]Notwithstanding, lest we should offend them, go thou to the sea, and cast a hook, and take up the fish that first cometh up; and when thou hast opened his mouth, thou shall find a piece of money: that take, and give unto them for me and thee.

Matt. 22 [17]Tell us therefore, What thinkest thou? Is it lawful to give tribute unto Caesar, or not? [18]But Jesus perceived their wickedness, and said, Why tempt ye me, ye hypocrites? [19]Shew me the tribute money. And they brought unto him a penny. [20]And he saith unto them, Whose is this image and superscription? [21]They say unto him, Caesar's. Then saith he unto them, Render therefore unto Caesar the things which are Caesar's; and unto God the things that are God's. [22]When they had heard these words, they marvelled, and left him, and went their way.

Rom. 13 [1]Let every soul be subject unto the higher powers. For there is no power but of God: the powers that be are ordained of God. [5]Wherefore ye must needs be subject, not only for wrath, but also for conscience' sake. [6]For, for this cause pay ye tribute also: for they are God's ministers, attending continually upon this very thing. [7]Render therefore to all their dues: tribute to whom tribute is due; custom to whom custom; fear to whom fear; honour to whom honour.

TEACH, TEACHER, TEACHING

[tēch] To cause to learn; to instruct; to guide the studies of; to impart the knowledge of; to make aware by information, etc.
[tēch'ẽr] One who teaches.
[tēch'ing] The act of instructing.

As used in the New Testament, teaching usually means instruction in the faith, and is to be distinguished from preaching, or the proclamation of the gospel message to the non-Christians world. (*See* PREACHING) This distinction is seen in descriptions of the work of the Great Preacher and Teacher, Jesus Christ. (*See Matt. 4:23; 9:35*) Since sound instruction in the faith is essential to the spiritual growth of Christians and the development of the Church, the scriptures contain numerous passages which deal with the duties and qualifications of those who teach. Special emphasis is laid on the danger of false teaching; Christians are warned to test those who pervert the true gospel and to refrain from listening to them.

See MINISTER, DOCTRINE, HERESY

SCRIPTURE

Jesus the Model Teacher

Matt. 4 [23]And Jesus went about all Galilee, teaching in their synagogues, and preaching the gospel of the kingdom, and healing all manner of sickness and all manner of disease among the people.

Matt. 5 [2]And he opened his mouth, and taught them . . . .

Matt. 7 [29]For he taught them as one having authority, and not as the scribes.

Luke 4 [14]And Jesus returned in the power of the Spirit into Galilee: and there went out a fame of him through all the region round about. [15]And he taught in their synagogues, being glorified of all.

Luke 24 [27]And beginning at Moses and all the prophets, he expounded unto them in all the Scriptures the things concerning himself.

John 7 [14]Now about the midst of the feast Jesus went up into the temple, and taught.

See Matt. 9:35

True Teaching from God

Psa. 7 [17]O God, thou hast taught me from my youth: and hitherto have I declared thy wondrous works. [18]Now also when I am old and greyheaded, O God, forsake me not; until I have shewed thy strength unto this generation, and thy power to every one that is to come.

Isa. 54 [13]And all thy children shall be taught of the LORD; and great shall be the peace of thy children.

John 6 [45]It is written in the prophets, And they shall be all taught of God. Every man therefore that hath heard, and hath learned of the Father, cometh unto me.

Gal. 1 [12]For I neither received it of man, neither was I taught it, but by the revelation of Jesus Christ.

God's Appointed Human Teachers

Acts 13 [1]Now there were in the church that was at Antioch certain prophets and teachers; as Barnabas, and Simeon that was called Niger, and Lucius of Cyrene, and Manaen, which had been brought up with Herod the tetrarch, and Saul. [2]As they ministered to the Lord, and fasted, the Holy Ghost said, Separate me Barnabas and Saul for the work whereunto I have called them. [3]And when they had fasted and prayed, and laid their hands on them, they sent them away.

Rom. 2 [19]And art confident that thou thyself art a guide of the blind, a light of them which are in darkness, [20]An instructor of the foolish, a teacher of babes, which hast the form of knowledge and of the truth in the law.

Rom. 12 [6]Having then gifts differing according to the grace that is given to us, whether prophecy, let us prophesy according to the proportion of faith; [7]Or ministry, let us wait on our ministering: or he that teacheth, on teaching; [8]Or he that exhorteth, on exhortation: he that giveth, let him do it with simplicity; he that ruleth, with diligence; he that sheweth mercy, with cheerfulness.

1 Cor. 12 [28]And God hath set some in the church, first apostles, secondarily prophets, thirdly teachers, after that miracles, then gifts of healings, helps, governments, diversities of tongues. [29]Are all apostles? are all prophets? are all teachers? are all workers of miracles?

Gal. 6 [6]Let him that is taught in the word communicate unto him that teacheth in all good things.

Eph. 4 [11]And he gave some, apostles; and some, prophets; and some, evangelists; and some, pastors and teachers; [12]For the perfecting of the saints, for the work of the ministry, for the edifying of the body of Christ: [13]Till we all come in the unity of the faith, and of the knowledge of the Son of God, unto a perfect man, unto the measure of the stature of the fulness of Christ.

Col. 1 [28]Whom we preach, warning every man, and teaching every man in all wisdom; that we may present every man perfect in Christ Jesus:

Col. 3 [16]Let the word of Christ dwell in you richly in all wisdom; teaching and admonishing one another in psalms and hymns and spiritual songs, singing with grace in your hearts to the Lord.

False Teachers

FORETOLD AND DESCRIBED

Ezek. 22 25There is a conspiracy of her prophets in the midst thereof, like a roaring lion ravening the prey; they have devoured souls; they have taken the treasure and precious things; they have made her many widows in the midst thereof. 26Her priests have violated my law, and have profaned mine holy things: they have put no difference between the holy and profane, neither have they shewed difference between the unclean and the clean, and have hid their eyes from my sabbaths, and I am profaned among them.

Matt. 24 4And Jesus answered and said unto them, Take heed that no man deceive you. 5For many shall come in my name, saying, I am Christ; and shall deceive many. 6And ye shall hear of wars and rumours of wars: see that ye be not troubled: for all these things must come to pass, but the end is not yet. 7For nation shall rise against nation, and kingdom against kingdom: and there shall be famines, and pestilences, and earthquakes, in divers places. 8All these are the beginning of sorrows. 9Then shall they deliver you up to be afflicted, and shall kill you: and ye shall be hated of all nations for my name's sake. 10And then shall many be offended, and shall betray one another, and shall hate one another. 11And many false prophets shall rise, and shall deceive many. 12And because iniquity shall abound, the love of many shall wax cold. 13But he that shall endure unto the end, the same shall be saved.

Acts 20 29For I know this, that after my departing shall grievous wolves enter in among you, not sparing the flock. 30Also of your own selves shall men arise, speaking perverse things, to draw away disciples after them.

2 Cor. 11 13For such are false apostles, deceitful workers, transforming themselves into the apostles of Christ. 14And no marvel; for Satan himself is transformed into an angel of light. 15Therefore it is no great thing if his ministers also be transformed as the ministers of righteousness; whose end shall be according to their works.

1 Tim. 1 6From which some having swerved have turned aside unto vain jangling; 7Desiring to be teachers of the law; understanding neither what they say, nor whereof they affirm.

1 Tim. 4 1Now the Spirit speaketh expressly, that in the latter times some shall depart from the faith, giving heed to seducing spirits, and doctrines of devils; 2Speaking lies in hypocrisy; having their conscience seared with a hot iron; 3Forbidding to marry, and commanding to abstain from meats, which God hath created to be received with thanksgiving of them which believe and know the truth. 4For every creature of God is good, and nothing to be refused, if it be received with thanksgiving.

2 Tim. 3 1This know also, that in the last days perilous times shall come. 2For men shall be lovers of their own selves, covetous, boasters, proud, blasphemers, disobedient to parents, unthankful, unholy, 3Without natural affection, trucebreakers, false accusers, incontinent, fierce, despisers of those that are good, 4Traitors, heady, highminded, lovers of pleasures more than lovers of God; 5Having a form of godliness, but denying the power thereof: from such turn away. 6For of this sort are they which creep into houses, and lead captive silly women laden with sins, led away with divers lusts, [7]Ever learning, and never able to come to the knowledge of the truth.

2 Pet. 2 [1]But there were false prophets also among the people, even as there shall be false teachers among you, who privily shall bring in damnable heresies, even denying the Lord that brought them, and bring upon themselves swift destruction. [2]And many shall follow their pernicious ways; be reason of whom the way of truth shall be evil spoken of. [3]And through covetousness shall they with feigned words make merchandise of you: whose judgment now of a long time lingereth not, and their damnation slumbereth not.

NOT TO BE LISTENED TO

Deut. 13 [1]If there arise among you a prophet, or a dreamer of dreams, and giveth thee a sign or a wonder, [2]And the sign or the wonder come to pass, whereof he spake unto thee, saying, Let us go after other gods, which thou hast not known, and let us serve them; [3]Thou shalt not hearken unto the words of that prophet, or that dreamer of dreams: for the LORD your God proveth you, to know whether ye love the LORD your God with all your heart and with all your soul.

Col. 2 [8]Beware lest any man spoil you through philosophy and vain deceit, after the tradition of men, after the rudiments of the world, and not after Christ.

HOW TO BE TESTED

Isa. 8 [19]And when they shall say unto you, Seek unto them that have familiar spirits, and unto wizards that peep and that mutter: should not a people seek unto their God? for the living to the dead? [20]To the law and to the testimony: if they speak not according to this word, it is because there is no light in them.

Rom. 16 [17]Now I beseech you, brethren, mark them which cause divisions and offences contrary to the doctrine which ye have learned; and avoid them. [18]For they that are such serve not our Lord Jesus Christ, but their own belly; and by good words and fair speeches deceive the hearts of the simple.

Tit. 3 [9]But avoid foolish questions, and genealogies, and contentions, and strivings about the law; for they are unprofitable and vain. [10]A man that is an heretick after the first and second admonition reject; [11]Knowing that he that is such is subverted, and sinneth, being condemned of himself.

1 John 4 [1]Beloved, believe not every spirit, but try the spirits whether they are of God: because many false prophets are gone out into the world. [2]Hereby know ye the Spirit of God: Every spirit that confesseth that Jesus Christ is come in the flesh is of God: [3]And every spirit that confesseth not that Jesus Christ is come in the flesh is not of God: and this is that spirit of antichrist, whereof ye have heard that it should come; and even now already is it in the world.

TEMPERANCE

[tem′pẽr ans] Habitual moderation in the indulgence of the appetites and passions; moderation. As used in the Bible, temperance involves mastery of oneself to such a degree that one is able to abstain from anything which might hinder his effective service to God and to subject all his physical impulses to the will of Christ. Properly understood, this is an inner virtue, a condition of the heart, which cannot be replaced simply by external abstinence.

See ABSTINENCE, DRINK

SCRIPTURE

Intemperance Condemned

Prov. 20 [1]Wine is a mocker, strong drink
is raging: and whosoever is deceived
thereby is not wise.

Prov. 23 [31]Look not thou upon the wine
when it is red, when it giveth his colour in
the cup, when it moveth itself aright.

Eph. 5 [18]And be not drunk with wine,
wherein is excess; but be filled with the
Spirit.

Tit. 2 [3]The aged women likewise, that
they be in behaviour as becometh holiness,
not false accusers, not given to much wine,
teachers of good things.

Punishments of Intemperance

Deut. 29 [19]And it come to pass, when he
heareth the words of this curse, that he
bless himself in his heart, saying, I shall
have peace, though I walk in the imagination of mine heart, to add drunkenness to
thirst: [20]The LORD will not spare him, but
then the anger of the LORD and his jealousy
shall smoke against that man, and all the
curses that are written in this book shall lie
upon him, and the LORD shall blot out his
name from under heaven. [21]And the LORD
shall separate him unto evil out of all the
tribes of Israel, according to all the curses
of the covenant that are written in this
book of the law.

Prov. 23 [29]Who hath woe? who hath
sorrow? who hath contentions? who hath
babbling? who hath wounds without
cause? who hath redness of eyes? [30]They
that tarry long at the wine; they that go to
seek mixed wine.

Isa. 5 [11]Woe unto them that rise up
early in the morning, that they may follow
strong drink; that continue until night, till
wine inflame them!

[22]Woe unto them that are mighty to
drink wine, and men of strength to mingle
strong drink: [23]Which justify the wicked
for reward, and take away the righteousness of the righteous from him!

Isa. 24 [9]They shall not drink wine with
a song; strong drink shall be bitter to them
that drink it. [11]There is a crying for wine
in the streets; all joy is darkened, the mirth
of the land is gone.

Isa. 28 [1]Woe to the crown of pride, to
the drunkards of Ephraim, whose glorious
beauty is a fading flower, which are on the
head of the fat valleys of them that are
overcome with wine! [3]The crown of pride
the drunkards of Ephraim, shall be trodden under feet.

[7]But they also have erred through wine,
and through strong drink are out of the
way; the priest and the prophet have erred
through strong drink, they are swallowed
up of wine, they are out of the way through
strong drink; they err in vision, they stumble in judgment.

Joel 1 [5]Awake, ye drunkards, and weep;
and howl, all ye drinkers of wine, because
of the new wine; for it is cut off from your
mouth.

Nah. 1 [10]For while they be folden together as thorns, and while they are
drunken as drunkards, they shall be devoured as stubble fully dry.

Temperance in All Things Commended

Prov. 23 [1]When thou sittest to eat with
a ruler, consider diligently what is before
thee: [2]And put a knife to thy throat, if
thou be a man given to appetite.

1 Cor. 9 [25]And every man that striveth
for the mastery is temperate in all things.
Now they do it to obtain a corruptible
crown; but we an incorruptible. [26]I therefore so run, not as uncertainly; so fight I,

not as one that beateth the air: [27]But I keep under my body, and bring it into subjection: lest that by any means, when I have preached to others, I myself should be a castaway.

Gal. 5 [22]But the fruit of the Spirit is love, joy, peace, longsuffering, gentleness, goodness, faith, [23]Meekness, temperance: against such there is no law.

Eph. 5 [18]And be not drunk with wine, wherein is excess; but be filled with the Spirit.

Tit. 1 [8]But a lover of hospitality, a lover of good men, sober, just, holy, temperate.

TEMPLE

[tem'p'l] An edifice dedicated to the worship of a deity. There were three temples in Israel's history: Solomon's, Zerubbabel's, and Herod's.

1. The Temple of Solomon

King David desired to build a temple to the LORD, but was prevented because of his excessive occupation in war (*1 Chr. 22:5-16*). Shortly after his son Solomon acceeded to the throne of Israel, he began to bring his father's dream to reality. He raised a labor force of 30,000 men from his own nation and enlisted Hiram king of Tyre to assist him in the provision of materials and skilled workmen. Work on the temple was begun probably in 957 BC, the fourth year of Solomon's reign, and was completed about seven years later. The interior dimensions of the temple were sixty cubits in length, thirty cubits in height, and twenty cubits in width. Outside the temple proper, in the inner court, stood a large bronze altar, twenty cubits square and ten cubits high, which was the altar of burnt-offerings. Other items in this inner court before the temple were the "Molten Sea" and ten ornate wagons carrying lavers. The Molten Sea was a huge basin or tank twenty cubits in diameter and five cubits deep, with a capacity of about 10,000 gallons of water. It was situated atop twelve bronze bulls arranged in groups of three. The smaller lavers had a capacity of about 200 gallons each and were arranged in rows of five on either side of the inner court.

On the porch at the entrance of the temple stood two large bronze pillars called Jachin and Boaz. The first room in the temple proper was a vestibule or entrance hall twenty cubits wide. There were other rooms and chambers surrounding the main rooms. Passing through two large double doors which were themselves divided into folding leaves, one entered the largest room, the Holy Place, which was about forty cubits long. The walls of this room, like those of the Holy of Holies, were covered with cedar wainscoting and overlaid with gold. They were decorated with carved figures of cherubim, palm trees, gourds, and flowers. The floors were covered with cypress boards. Inside this larger room were the table of shewbread and ten lampstands, five on each side of the entrance to the Holy of Holies, plus various accessories such as incense dishes, snuffers, tongs, etc.

The Holy of Holies was a cube of twenty cubits which was separated from the Holy Place by a double door of olivewood. Inside this room were two gigantic cherubim (*see* CHERUBIM) ten cubits in height with a wingspread of ten cubits. These faced the doorway, their wing touching the walls on each side and meeting in the center. Beneath the outstretched wings stood the ark of the covenant. (*See* ARK)

This temple was the center of true worship for almost four hundred years. During the stormy history of the divided kingdom it was plundered and restored several times. It was finally destroyed in 587/586 BC by the armies of Nebuchadnezzar of Babylon.

2. The Temple of Zerubbabel

One of the first official acts of Cyrus the Persian after his conquest of the Babylonian empire in 539 BC was to allow deported peoples to return to their homeland to reestablish their culture and religious observances. Shortly thereafter, a small band of Jews set out for Jerusalem under the leadership of Shesh-bazzar and Zerubbabel. Construction was begun at the site of the first temple and; at the urging of the prophets Haggai and Zechariah, the high priest Joshua, and Zerubbabel, the second temple, often called the temple of Zerubbabel, was brought to completion in "the sixth year of the reign of Darius the king," or 516/515 BC. It is impossible to ascertain the dimensions of the second temple, except to state it was a building of rather large size. It stood until the latter part of the first century BC, nearly a century longer than Solomon's temple.

3. The Temple of Herod

Herod the Great, king of Jewish Palestine, wished to restore the temple to its former glory. The foundations of the old temple were removed and, in about 20 BC, work was begun on the third temple. Herod's temple utilized the basic floor plan of the first temple, but its architecture was Hellenistic-Roman. A remarkable feature of this temple was the use of huge white stones twenty-five by eight by twelve cubits in size. The temple proper was situated in a large paved court at least 200 yards long on all sides. A large portion of the outer court was open to Gentiles and was called the Court of the Gentiles. This was separated from a smaller court by a low stone fence which bore a warning to all non-Jews to keep out, on pain of death. Inside this smaller court was the Women's Court, where Jews could enter with their wives. This led to the Court of Israel, open only to Jewish males. Immediately surrounding the temple proper was the Priests' Court, which, as its name implies, was restricted to the priests engaged in the divine service. The basic construction of the temple was completed in a year and a half but "finishing" work was continued until at least AD 63 and perhaps was not complete at the destruction of the temple in AD 70 by the Roman army.

SCRIPTURE

The Temple of Solomon

DAVID FORBIDDEN TO BUILD

2 Sam. 7 [4]And it came to pass that night,
that the word of the LORD came unto Nathan, saying, [5]Go and tell my servant David, Thus saith the LORD, Shalt thou build
me a house for me to dwell in? [6]Whereas I
have not dwelt in any house since the time
that I brought up the children of Israel out
of Egypt, even to this day, but have walked
in a tent and in a tabernacle. [7]In all the
places wherein I have walked with all the
children of Israel spake I a word with any
of the tribes of Israel, whom I commanded
to feed my people Israel, saying, Why
build ye not me a house of cedar? [8]Now
therefore so shalt thou say unto my servant
David, Thus saith the LORD of hosts, I took
thee from the sheepcote, from following
the sheep, to be ruler over my people, over
Israel: [9]And I was with thee whithersoever thou wentest, and have cut off all
thine enemies out of thy sight, and have
made thee a great name, like unto the
name of the great men that are in the earth.
[10]Moreover I will appoint a place for my
people Israel, and will plant them, that
they may dwell in a place of their own, and
move no more; neither shall the children
of wickedness afflict them any more, as beforetime, [11]And as since the time that I
commanded judges to be over my people
Israel, and have caused thee to rest from
all thine enemies. Also the LORD telleth
thee that he will make thee a house.

[12]And when thy days be fulfilled, and
thou shalt sleep with thy fathers, I will set
up thy seed after thee, which shall proceed
out of thy bowels, and I will establish his
kingdom.

SOLOMON CONSCRIPTS WORKERS

1 Kin. 5 [13]And king Solomon raised a
levy out of all Israel; and the levy was
thirty thousand men. [14]And he sent them
to Lebanon, ten thousand a month by
courses: a month they were in Lebanon,
and two months at home: and Adoniram
was over the levy. [15]And Solomon had
threescore and ten thousand that bare burdens, and fourscore thousand hewers in
the mountains; [16]Besides the chief of Solomon's officers which were over the work,
three thousand and three hundred, which
ruled over the people that wrought in the
work.

MATERIALS FURNISHED BY HIRAM OF TYRE

1 Kin. 5 [8]And Hiram sent to Solomon, saying, I have considered the things which thou sentest to me for: and I will do all thy desire concerning timber of cedar, and concerning timber of fir. [9]My servants shall bring them down from Lebanon unto the sea; and I will convey them by sea in floats unto the place that thou shalt appoint me, and will cause them to be discharged there, and thou shalt receive them: and thou shalt accomplish my desire, in giving food for my household. [10]So Hiram gave Solomon cedar trees and fir trees according to all his desire. [11]And Solomon gave Hiram twenty thousand measures of wheat for food to his household, and twenty measures of pure oil: thus gave Solomon to Hiram year by year. [12]And the LORD gave Solomon wisdom, as he promised him: and there was peace between Hiram and Solomon; and they two made a league together.

DESCRIPTION OF THE TEMPLE

2 Chr. 3 [1]Then Solomon began to build the house of the LORD at Jerusalem in mount Moriah, where the LORD appeared unto David his father, in the place that David had prepared in the threshingfloor of Ornan the Jebusite. [2]And he began to build in the second day of the second month, in the fourth year of his reign.

[3]Now these are the things wherein Solomon was instructed for the building of the house of God. The length by cubits after the first measure was threescore cubits, and the breadth twenty cubits. [4]And the porch that was in the front of the house, the length of it was according to the breadth of the house, twenty cubits, and the height was a hundred and twenty: and he overlaid it within with pure gold. [5]And the greater house he ceiled with fir tree, which he overlaid with fine gold, and set thereon palm trees and chains. [6]And he garnished the house with precious stones for beauty: and the gold was gold of Parvaim. [7]He overlaid also the house, the beams, the posts, and the walls thereof, and the doors thereof, with gold; and graved cherubim on the walls. [8]And he made the most holy house, the length whereof was according to the breadth of the house, twenty cubits, and the breadth thereof twenty cubits; and he overlaid it with fine gold amounting to six hundred talents. [9]And the weight of the nails was fifty shekels of gold. And he overlaid the upper chambers with gold. [10]And in the most holy house he made two cherubim of image work, and overlaid them with gold.

[11]And the wings of the cherubim were twenty cubits long: one wing of the one cherub was five cubits, reaching to the wall of the house: and the other wing was likewise five cubits, reaching to the wing of the other cherub. [12]And one wing of the other cherub was five cubits, reaching to the wall of the house: and the other wing was five cubits also, joining to the wing of the other cherub. [13]The wings of these cherubim spread themselves forth twenty cubits: and they stood on their feet, and their faces were inward.

[14]And he made the veil of blue, and purple, and crimson, and fine linen, and wrought cherubim thereon. [15]Also he made before the house two pillars of thirty and five cubits high, and the chapiter that was on the top of each of them was five cubits. [16]And he made chains, as in the oracle, and put them on the heads of the pillars; and made a hundred pomegranates, and put them on the chains. [17]And he reared up the pillars before the

temple, one on the right hand, and the other on the left; and called the name of that on the right hand Jachin, and the name of that on the left Boaz.

2 Chr. 4 [1]Moreover he made an altar of brass, twenty cubits the length thereof, and twenty cubits the breadth thereof, and ten cubits the height thereof.

[2]Also he made a molten sea of ten cubits from brim to brim, round in compass, and five cubits the height thereof; and a line of thirty cubits did compass it round about. [3]And under it was the similitude of oxen, which did compass it round about: ten in a cubit, compassing the sea round about. Two rows of oxen were cast, when it was cast. [4]It stood upon twelve oxen, three looking toward the north, and three looking toward the west, and three looking toward the south, and three looking toward the east: and the sea was set above upon them, and all their hinder parts were inward. [5]And the thickness of it was a handbreadth, and the brim of it like the work of the brim of a cup, with flowers of lilies; and it received and held three thousand baths.

[6]He made also ten lavers, and put five on the right hand, and five on the left, to wash in them: such things as they offered for the burnt offering they washed in them; but the sea was for the priests to wash in. [7]And he made ten candlesticks of gold according to their form, and set them in the temple, five on the right hand, and five on the left. [8]He made also ten tables, and placed them in the temple, five on the right side, and five on the left. And he made a hundred basins of gold.

[9]Furthermore he made the court of the priests, and the great court, and doors for the court, and overlaid the doors of them with brass. [10]And he set the sea on the right side of the east end, over against the south. [11]And Huram made the pots, and the shovels, and the basins. And Huram finished the work that he was to make for king Solomon for the house of God; [12]To wit, the two pillars, and the pommels, and the chapiters which were on the top of the two pillars, and the two wreaths to cover the two pommels of the chapiters which were on the top of the pillars; [13]And four hundred pomegranates on the two wreaths, two rows of pomegranates on each wreath, to cover the two pommels of the chapiters which were upon the pillars. [14]He made also bases, and lavers made he upon the bases; [15]One sea, and twelve oxen under it. [16]The pots also, and the shovels, and the fleshhooks, and all their instruments, did Huram his father make to king Solomon for the house of the LORD, of bright brass. [17]In the plain of Jordan did the king cast them, in the clay ground between Succoth and Zeredathah. [18]Thus Solomon made all these vessels in great abundance: for the weight of the brass could not be found out.

[19]And Solomon made all the vessels that were for the house of God, the golden altar also, and the tables whereon the shewbread was set; [20]Moreover the candlesticks with their lamps, that they should burn after the manner before the oracle, of pure gold; [21]And the flowers, and the lamps, and the tongs, made he of gold, and that perfect gold; [22]And the snuffers, and the basins, and the spoons, and the censers, of pure gold: and the entry of the house, the inner doors thereof for the most holy place, and the doors of the house of the temple, were of gold.

EXCERPTS FROM SOLOMON'S DEDICATION SPEECH

1 Kin. 8 [12]Then spake Solomon, The LORD said that he would dwell in the thick darkness. [13]I have surely built thee a house to dwell in, a settled place for thee to abide in for ever.

27 But will God indeed dwell on the earth? behold, the heaven and heaven of heavens can not contain thee; how much less this house that I have builded? 28 Yet have thou respect unto the prayer of thy servant, and to his supplication, O LORD my God, to hearken unto the cry and to the prayer, which thy servant prayeth before thee to-day: 29 That thine eyes may be open toward this house night and day, even toward the place of which thou hast said, My name shall be there: that thou mayest hearken unto the prayer which thy servant shall make toward this place.

38 What prayer and supplication soever be made by any man, or by all thy people Israel, which shall know every man the plague of his own heart, and spread forth his hands toward this house: 39 Then hear thou in heaven thy dwellingplace, and forgive, and do, and give to every man according to his ways, whose heart thou knowest; (for thou, even thou only, knowest the hearts of all the children of men;) 40 That they may fear thee all the days that they live in the land which thou gavest unto our fathers.

59 And let these my words, wherewith I have made supplication before the LORD, be nigh unto the LORD our God day and night, that he maintain the cause of his servant, and the cause of his people Israel at all times, as the matter shall require: 60 That all the people of the earth may know that the LORD is God, and that there is none else. 61 Let your heart therefore be perfect with the LORD our God, to walk in his statutes, and to keep his commandments, as at this day.

PLUNDERED BY SHISHAK

1 Kin. 14 25 And it came to pass in the fifth year of king Rehoboam, that Shishak king of Egypt came up against Jerusalem: 26 And he took away the treasures of the house of the LORD, and the treasures of the king's house; he even took away all: and he took away all the shields of gold which Solomon had made.

REPAIRED BY JEHOASH, KING OF JUDAH

2 Kin. 12 4 And Jehoash said to the priests, All the money of the dedicated things that is brought into the house of the LORD, even the money of every one that passeth the account, the money that every man is set at, and all the money that cometh into any man's heart to bring into the house of the LORD, 5 Let the priests take it to them, every man of his acquaintance: and let them repair the breaches of the house, wheresoever any breach shall be found. 6 But it was so, that in the three and twentieth year of king Jehoash the priests had not repaired the breaches of the house. 7 Then king Jehoash called for Jehoiada the priest, and the other priests, and said unto them, Why repair ye not the breaches of the house? now therefore receive no more money of your acquaintance, but deliver it for the breaches of the house. 8 And the priests consented to receive no more money of the people, neither to repair the breaches of the house. 9 But Jehoiada the priest took a chest, and bored a hole in the lid of it, and set it beside the altar, on the right side as one cometh into the house of the LORD: and the priests that kept the door put therein all the money that was brought into the house of the LORD. 10 And it was so, when they saw that there was much money in the chest, that the king's scribe and the high priest came up, and they put up in bags, and told the money that was found in the house of the LORD. 11 And they gave

the money, being told, into the hands of
them that did the work, that had the oversight of the house of the LORD: and they
laid it out to the carpenters and builders,
that wrought upon the house of the LORD,
[12]And to masons, and hewers of stone, and
to buy timber and hewed stone to repair
the breaches of the house of the LORD, and
for all that was laid out for the house to
repair it. [13]Howbeit there were not made
for the house of the LORD bowls of silver,
snuffers, basins, trumpets, any vessels of
gold, or vessels of silver, of the money that
was brought into the house of the LORD:
[14]But they gave that to the workmen, and
repaired therewith the house of the LORD.

DESTROYED BY NEBUCHADNEZZAR

2 Kin. 24 [12]. . . and the king of Babylon
took him in the eighth year of his reign.
[13]And he carried out thence all the treasures of the house of the LORD, and the
treasures of the king's house, and cut in
pieces all the vessels of gold which Solomon king of Israel had made in the temple of the LORD, as the LORD had said.

2 Kin. 25 [8]And in the fifth month, on the
seventh day of the month, which is the
nineteenth year of king Nebuchadnezzar
king of Babylon, came Nebuzaradan, captain of the guard, a servant of the king of
Babylon, unto Jerusalem: [9]And he burnt
the house of the LORD, and the king's
house, and all the houses of Jerusalem, and
every great man's house burnt he with fire.
[10]And all the army of the Chaldees, that
were with the captain of the guard, brake
down the walls of Jerusalem round about.
[11]Now the rest of the people that were left
in the city, and the fugitives that fell away
to the king of Babylon, with the remnant
of the multitude, did Nebuzaradan the
captain of the guard carry away. [12]But the
captain of the guard left of the poor of the
land to be vinedressers and husbandmen.
[13]And the pillars of brass that were in the
house of the LORD, and the bases, and the
brazen sea that was in the house of the
LORD, did the Chaldees break in pieces,
and carried the brass of them to Babylon.
[14]And the pots, and the shovels, and the
snuffers, and the spoons, and all the vessels
of brass wherewith they ministered, took
they away. [15]And the firepans, and the
bowls, and such things as were of gold, in
gold, and of silver, in silver, the captain of
the guard took away. [16]The two pillars,
one sea, and the bases which Solomon had
made for the house of the LORD; the brass
of all these vessels was without weight.
[17]The height of the one pillar was eighteen
cubits, and the chapiter upon it was brass:
and the height of the chapiter three cubits;
and the wreathen work, and pomegranates
upon the chapiter round about, all of brass:
and like unto these had the second pillar
with wreathen work.

The Temple of Zerubbabel

REBUILDING ALLOWED BY CYRUS

Ezra 1 [2]Thus saith Cyrus king of Persia,
The LORD God of heaven hath given me
all the kingdoms of the earth; and he hath
charged me to build him a house at Jerusalem, which is in Judah. [3]Who is there
among you of all his people? his God be
with him, and let him go up to Jerusalem,
which is in Judah, and build the house of
the LORD God of Israel, (he is the God,)
which is in Jerusalem. [4]And whosoever
remaineth in any place where he sojourneth, let the men of his place help him with
silver, and with gold, and with goods, and
with beasts, besides the freewill offering
for the house of God that is in Jerusalem.

THE BUILDING BEGUN

Ezra 3 [10]And when the builders laid the

foundation of the temple of the LORD, they set the priests in their apparel with trumpets, and the Levites the sons of Asaph with cymbals, to praise the LORD, after the ordinance of David king of Israel.
[11]And they sang together by course in praising and giving thanks unto the LORD; because he is good, for his mercy endureth for ever toward Israel. And all the people shouted with a great shout, when they praised the LORD, because the foundation of the house of the LORD was laid.

THE BUILDING STOPPED

Ezra 4 [23]Now when the copy of king Artaxerxes' letter was read before Rehum, and Shimshai the scribe, and their companions, they went up in haste to Jerusalem unto the Jews, and made them to
cease by force and power. [24]Then ceased the work of the house of God which is at Jerusalem. So it ceased unto the second year of the reign of Darius king of Persia.

THE BUILDING COMPLETED

Ezra 6 [13]Then Tatnai, governor on this side the river, Shethar-boznai, and their companions, according to that which Darius the king had sent, so they did speedily.
[14]And the elders of the Jews builded, and they prospered through the prophesying of Haggai the prophet and Zechariah the son of Iddo. And they builded, and finished it, according to the commandment of the God of Israel, and according to the commandment of Cyrus, and Darius, and Artaxerxes king of Persia.
[15]And this house was finished on the third day of the month Adar, which was in the sixth year of the reign of Darius the king.
[16]And the children of Israel, the priests, and the Levites, and the rest of the children of the captivity, kept the dedication of this house of God with joy,

The Temple of Herod

MANY YEARS IN BUILDING

John 2 [20]Then said the Jews, Forty and six years was this temple in building, and wilt thou rear it up in three days?

MAGNIFICENCE OF THE TEMPLE

Mark 13 [1]And as he went out of the temple, one of his disciples saith unto him, Master, see what manner of stones and what buildings are here!

Matt. 24 [1]And Jesus went out, and departed from the temple: and his disciples came to him for to shew him the buildings of the temple.

JESUS CLEANSES THE TEMPLE

Mark 11 [15]And they come to Jerusalem: and Jesus went into the temple, and began to cast out them that sold and bought in the temple, and overthrew the tables of the moneychangers, and the seats of them that
sold doves; [16]And would not suffer that any man should carry any vessel through
the temple. [17]And he taught, saying unto them, Is it not written, My house shall be called of all nations the house of prayer? but ye have made it a den of thieves.

TEMPT, TEMPTATION

[tempt, temp tā'shun] In modern times, the word tempt means simply "to entice"; as used in the King James Version of the Bible, however, its primary meaning is to "prove" or "test." It is in this latter sense that God may be spoken of as tempting men. He does not entice them to sin, but he does test their faithfulness. Only Jesus was able to withstand all temptation. Throughout his life he was "tempted in all points like as we are" (*Heb. 4:15*), but the supreme trials which he faced are recorded in the classic accounts of his temptation, in *Matt. 4* and *Luke 4.* Here we are told that Jesus refused to use his supernatural powers to provide for his own physical comfort by turning the stones into bread, to draw attention to himself by casting himself from the pinnacle of the temple, or to achieve political power by submitting himself to the will of Satan. It is because of his victory over sin that he has become our high priest.

SCRIPTURE

God Tests His People

Gen. 22 1And it came to pass after these things, that God did tempt Abraham, and said unto him, Abraham: and he said, Behold, here I am.

Ex. 20 20And Moses said unto the people, Fear not: for God is come to prove you, and that his fear may be before your faces, that ye sin not.

Deut. 8 2And thou shalt remember all the way which the LORD thy God led thee these forty years in the wilderness, to humble thee, and to prove thee, to know what was in thine heart, whether thou wouldest keep his commandments, or no.

God Does Not Entice to Sin

Jas. 1 13Let no man say when he is tempted, I am tempted of God: for God cannot be tempted with evil, neither tempteth he any man:

Men Forbidden to Tempt God

Deut. 6 16Ye shall not tempt the LORD your God, as ye tempted him in Massah.

Matt. 4 7Jesus said unto him, It is written again, Thou shalt not tempt the Lord thy God.

See Luke 4:12

Temptation of Jesus

Matt. 4 1Then was Jesus led up of the Spirit into the wilderness to be tempted of the devil. 2And when he had fasted forty days and forty nights, he was afterward a hungered. 3And when the tempter came to him, he said, If thou be the Son of God, command that these stones be made bread. 4But he answered and said, It is written, Man shall not live by bread alone, but by every word that proceedeth out of the mouth of God. 5Then the devil taketh him up into the holy city, and setteth him on a pinnacle of the temple, 6And saith unto him, If thou be the Son of God, cast thyself down: for it is written, He shall give his angels charge concerning thee: and in their hands they shall bear thee up, lest at any time thou dash thy foot against a stone. 7Jesus said unto him, It is written again, Thou shalt not tempt the Lord thy God. 8Again, the devil taketh him up into an exceeding high mountain, and sheweth him all the kingdoms of the world, and the glory of them; 9And saith unto him, All these things will I give thee, if thou wilt fall down and worship me. 10Then saith Jesus unto him, Get thee hence, Satan: for it is written, Thou shalt worship the Lord thy God, and him only shalt thou serve. 11Then the devil leaveth him, and, behold, angels came and ministered unto him.

Heb. 2 17Wherefore in all things it behoved him to be made like unto his brethren, that he might be a merciful and faithful high priest in things pertaining to God, to make reconciliation for the sins of the people. 18For in that he himself hath suffered being tempted, he is able to succour them that are tempted.

Heb. 41 15For we have not an high priest which cannot be touched with the feeling of our infirmities; but was in all points tempted like as we are, yet without sin.

See Luke 4:1-13

TERAPHIM

[ter'a fim] An image of some type; probably a

household god. Such household images are never directly referred to as objects of worship, but they are mentioned in connection with certain types of divination and magical practice (*Ezek. 21:21; Zech. 10:2*). They apparently varied widely in size, some being small enough to conceal easily (*Gen. 31:30, 34*) and others being large enough to pass for a human being (*2 Sam. 19:13, 16*). A number of images which are thought to be teraphim have been discovered by archaeologists.

SCRIPTURE

Gen. 31 [30]And now, though thou wouldest needs be gone, because thou sore longedst after thy father's house, yet wherefore has thou stolen my gods? [34]Now Rachel had taken the images, and put them in the camel's furniture, and sat upon them. And Laban searched all the tent, but found them not.

Judg. 17 [5]And the man Micah had a house of gods, and made an ephod, and teraphim, and consecrated one of his sons, who became his priest.

Judg. 18 [14]Do ye know that there is in these houses an ephod, and teraphim, and a graven image, and a molten image?

1 Sam. 19 [13]And Michal took an image, and laid it in the bed, and put a pillow of goats' hair for his bolster, and covered it with a cloth.

Ezek. 21 [21]For the king of Babylon stood at the parting of the way, at the head of the two ways, to use divination: he made his arrows bright, he consulted with images, he looked in the liver.

THANK, THANKFULNESS, THANKSGIVING

[thanks, thank'ful nes, thanks'giv ing] Grateful acknowledgment of favors or gifts; the act of giving thanks, especially to God, for blessings spiritual, temporal, and eternal. The greatest of the gifts which God has given is, of course, the gift of His Son, Jesus Christ. Thankfulness for this unspeakable gift is the mainspring, the one true motive, of Christian living. The giving of thanks to God for His manifold mercies and blessings should be one of man's daily acts of devotion to his creator.

SCRIPTURE

Exhortations to Give Thanks

Psa. 50 [14]Offer unto God thanksgiving; and pay thy vows unto the most High.

Psa. 92 [1]It is a good thing to give thanks unto the LORD, and to sing praises unto thy name, O Most High:

Psa. 100 [4]Enter into his gates with thanksgiving, and into his courts with praise; be thankful unto him, and bless his name.

Psa. 107 [1]O give thanks unto the LORD, for he is good: for his mercy endureth for ever.

2 Cor. 9 [12]For the administration of this service not only supplieth the want of the saints, but is abundant also by many thanksgivings unto God.

Eph. 5 [20]Giving thanks always for all things unto God and the Father in the name of our Lord Jesus Christ;

Phil. 4 [6]Be careful for nothing; but in every thing by prayer and supplication with thanksgiving let your requests be made known unto God.

Col. 2 [7]Rooted and built up in him, and stablished in the faith, as ye have been taught, abounding therein with thanksgiving.

Col. 4 [2]Continue in prayer, and watch in the same with thanksgiving.

Rev. 7 [12]Saying, Amen: Blessing, and glory, and wisdom, and thanksgiving, and honour, and power, and might, be unto our God for ever and ever. Amen.

Giving of Thanks by Jesus

Matt. 26 [26]And as they were eating, Jesus took bread, and blessed it, and brake it, and gave it to the disciples, and said, Take, eat; this is my body. [27]And he took the cup, and gave thanks, and gave it to them, saying, Drink ye all of it.

See Mark 8:6

Giving Thanks at Meals

Mark 8 [6]And he commanded the people to sit down on the ground: and he took the seven loaves, and gave thanks, and brake, and gave to his disciples to set before them; and they did set them before the people.

Acts 27 [35]And when he had thus spoken, he took bread, and gave thanks to God in presence of them all: and when he had broken it, he began to eat.

Rom. 14 [6]He that regardeth the day, regardeth it unto the Lord; and he that regardeth not the day, to the Lord he doth not regard it. He that eateth, eateth to the Lord, for he giveth God thanks; and he that eateth not, to the Lord he eateth not, and giveth God thanks.

THEFT AND THIEVES

[theft, thēvz] Theft is the act of stealing, or taking the property of another person without his consent or knowledge; a thief is one who steals. Stealing is forbidden in the Ten Commandments and elsewhere in Scripture as destructive of social order.

SCRIPTURE

Ex. 20 [15]Thou shalt not steal.

Ex. 22 [1]If a man shall steal an ox, or a sheep, and kill it, or sell it; he shall restore five oxen for an ox, and four sheep for a sheep. [2]If a thief be found breaking up, and be smitten that he die, there shall no blood be shed for him. [3]If the sun be risen upon him, there shall be blood shed for him; for he should make full restitution; if he have nothing, then he shall be sold for his theft. [4]If the theft be certainly found in his hand alive, whether it be ox, or ass, or sheep; he shall restore double.

Lev. 19 [11]Ye shall not steal, neither deal falsely.

[13]Thou shalt not defraud thy neighbour, neither rob him:

Prov. 6 [30]Men do not despise a thief, if he steal to satisfy his soul when he is hungry; [31]But if he be found, he shall restore sevenfold; he shall give all the substance of his house.

Matt. 6 [19]Lay not up for yourselves treasures upon earth, where moth and rust doth corrupt, and where thieves break through and steal: [20]But lay up for yourselves treasures in heaven, where neither moth nor rust doth corrupt, and where thieves do not break through nor steal:

Mark 11 [17]Is it not written, My house shall be called of all nations the house of prayer? but ye have made it a den of thieves.

Mark 15 [27]And with they crucify two thieves; the one on his right hand, and the other on his left.

John 10 [1]Verily, verily, I say unto you, He that entereth not by the door into the sheepfold, but climbeth up some otherway, the same is a thief and a robber.

Rom. 2 [21]Thou therefore which teachest another, teachest thou not thyself? thou that preachest a man should not steal, dost thou steal?

1 Cor. 6 [8]Nay, ye do wrong, and defraud, and that your brethren. [10]Nor thieves, nor covetous . . . nor extortioners, shall inherit the kingdom of God.

Eph. 4 [28]Let him that stole steal no more: but rather let him labour, working with his hands the thing which is good, that he may have to give to him that needeth.

1 Pet. 4 [15]But let none of you suffer as a murderer, or as a thief, or as an evildoer, or as a busybody in other men's matters.

See Deut. 5:19; Matt. 19:18; Rom. 13:19; Matt. 27:28, 44

THEOPHILUS

[thē of'i lus] The name of, or epithet applied to, the recipient of Luke's gospel *Acts of Apostles*. It means "loved of God." Theophilus was apparently a Gentile, perhaps a new convert, who wanted to learn more of the life and teachings of Jesus. It is quite possible that he was a wealthy individual who was to serve as a patron for the book, introducing into a larger circle of readers.

See LUKE

SCRIPTURE

Luke 1 [1]Forasmuch as many have taken in hand to set forth in order a declaration of those things which are most surely believed among us, [2]Even as they delivered them unto us, which from the beginning were eyewitnesses, and ministers of the word; [3]It seemed good to me also, having had perfect understanding of all things from the very first, to write unto thee in order, most excellent Theophilus, [4]That thou mightest know the certainty of those things, wherein thou hast been instructed.

Acts 1 [1]The former treatise have I made, O Theophilus, of all that Jesus began both to do and teach, [2]Until the day in which he was taken up, after that he through the Holy Ghost had given commandments unto the apostles whom he had chosen:

THESSALONICA, THESSALONIANS

[thes a lō nī'ka, thes a lō'ni anz] The city of Thessalonica, named for the step-sister of Alexander the Great, was the leading harbor of Macedonia. It was built on a hill overlooking the Thermaic Gulf and a beautiful fertile plain. In both Macedonian and Roman times it was an important city, due to its harbor and to the great Egnatian highway which ran through it. The church was established in that city by the apostle Paul, together with Silvanus (Silas) and Timothy, on the second missionary journey, probably in AD 50 (*Acts 17:1-9*). It was composed largely of Gentile believers who "turned from idols to serve the living and true God" (*1 Thess. 1:9*). After the missionaries left Thessalonica to continue their journey on into Achaia, Paul often sought to return and visit the Christians there but was unable to fulfill this desire (*1 Thess. 2:18*). In his place he sent Timothy to encourage and further establish them in sound doctrine and to bring a report of their current spiritual condition (*1 Thess. 3:1-2, 5*). Timothy's report was generally good, but it was not without its disturbing elements, especially with regard to misconceptions concerning the second coming of Christ. For a discussion of this and other problems, the reader is urged to study the two epistles to the *Thessalonians*.

SCRIPTURE

Paul Visits

Acts 17 [1]Now when they had passed through Amphipolis and Apollonia, they came to Thessalonica, where was a synagogue of the Jews: [2]And Paul, as his manner was, went in unto them, and three sabbath days reasoned with them out of the Scriptures, [3]Opening and alleging, that Christ must needs have suffered, and risen again from the dead; and that this Jesus, whom I preach unto you, is Christ. [4]And some of them believed, and consorted with Paul and Silas; and of the devout Greeks a great multitude, and of the chief women not a few.

[5]But the Jews which believed not, moved with envy, took unto them certain lewd fellows of the baser sort, and gathered a company, and set all the city on an uproar, and assaulted the house of Jason, and sought to bring them out to the people. [6]And when they found them not, they

drew Jason and certain brethren unto the rulers of the city, crying, These that have turned the world upside down are come hither also; [7]Whom Jason hath received: and these all do contrary to the decrees of Cesar, saying that there is another king, one Jesus. [8]And they troubled the people and the rulers of the city, when they heard these things. [9]And when they had taken security of Jason, and of the others, they let them go.

[10]And the brethren immediately sent away Paul and Silas by night unto Berea: who coming thither went into the synagogue of the Jews. [11]These were more noble than those in Thessalonica, in that they received the word with all readiness of mind, and searched the Scriptures daily, whether those things were so.

Paul Writes to the Church There

1 Thess. 1 [1]Paul, and Silvanus, and Timotheus, unto the church of the Thessalonians which is in God the Father, and in the Lord Jesus Christ: Grace be unto you, and peace, from God our Father, and the Lord Jesus Christ.

2 Thess. 1 [1]Paul, and Silvanus, and Timotheus, unto the church of the Thessalonians in God our Father and the Lord Jesus Christ:

THOMAS

[tom′as] One of the twelve apostles, also called "Didymus" or "the Twin." Thomas was a courageous disciple of Christ, willing to follow him even when death seemed a likely prospect. (*See John 11:16*) He is best remembered, of course, as "the doubter." He was not present at the first appearance of the risen Christ to his disciples and expressed skepticism at their report—"Except I shall see in his hands the print of the nails, and put my finger into the print of the nails, and thrust my hand into his side, I will not believe." Despite this show of disbelief, Thomas when Jesus' appearance fulfilled the conditions which he had set, Thomas humbly acknowledged him as "my Lord and my God."

SCRIPTURE

John 11 [16]Then said Thomas, which is called Didymus, unto his fellow-disciples, Let us also go, that we may die with him.

John 14 [5]Thomas saith unto him, Lord, we know not whither thou goest; and how can we know the way?

John 20 [24]But Thomas, one of the twelve, called Didymus, was not with them when Jesus came. [25]The other disciples therefore said unto him, We have seen the Lord. But he said unto them, Except I shall see in his hands the print of the nails, and put my finger into the print of the nails, and thrust my hand into his side, I will not believe.

[26]And after eight days again his disciples were within, and Thomas with them: then came Jesus, the doors being shut, and stood in the midst, and said, Peace be unto you. [27]Then saith he to Thomas, Reach hither thy finger, and behold my hands; and reach hither thy hand, and thrust it into my side: and be not faithless, but believing. [28]And Thomas answered and said unto him, My Lord and my God. [29]Jesus saith unto him, Thomas, because thou hast seen me, thou hast believed: blessed are they that have not seen, and yet have believed.

TIBERIUS CAESAR

[tī bē′ri as cē′zēr] The second Roman Emperor, successor of Augustus. Tiberius began to reign as co-regent in AD 13, became sole Emperor in AD 14, and reigned until AD 37. He was a wise and efficient administrator, although his policies sometimes bordered on tyranny. It was he who was Caesar during the ministry of Christ.

See CAESARS

SCRIPTURE

Luke 3 [1]Now in the fifteenth year of the reign of Tiberius Caesar, Pontius Pilate being governor of Judea, and Herod being tetrarch of Galilee, and his brother Philip tetrarch of Iturea and of the region of Trachonitis, and Lysanias the tetrarch of Abilene,

TIGLATH-PILESER III

[tig'lath-pi lē'zẽr] King of Assyria during the reigns of Menahem, Pekahiah, Pekah, and Hoshea, kings of Israel, and Uzziah, Jotham, and Ahaz, kings of Judah, ruling from 745-727 BC. He is probably identical with the Pul of *2 Kin. 15:19* and *1 Chr. 5:26.* In 743 BC Tiglath-pileser set about to make a permanent conquest of the West. In order to break down nationalistic lines, he followed a policy of deporting conquered peoples, sometimes replacing them with groups of whose loyalty he could be sure. As a result of his western campaigns, Menahem king of Israel became a willing vassal of Tiglath-pileser and paid a heavy tribute. When Menahem's successor, Pekahiah, was assassinated by Pekah after a very short reign, Israel sought to break the vassalage alliance and joined with Rezin of Syria in an effort to achieve this end. When Ahaz king of Judah refused to join, Pekah and Rezin marched on the southern kingdom. Ahaz put himself in the power of Tiglath-pileser and implored him to relieve the pressure by attacking Israel and Syria. In all probability, Tiglath-pileser would have done this anyway and must have been delighted to have received a huge tribute and the allegiance of Judah in the bargain. Archaeological evidence abundantly confirms the biblical account of the overwhelming blow which Tiglath-pileser administered to the coalition forces. It seems probable that Israel would have been completely destroyed had not Hoshea, Pekah's successor, surrendered and offered tribute to Tiglath-pileser. This action, however, only postponed the final blow; the kingdom of Israel had been thoroughly crushed. The reigns of Tiglath-pileser's successors, Shalmaneser V and Sargon, were to see its disappearance from history.

See articles on the various kings noted above.

SCRIPTURE

2 Kin. 15 [29]In the days of Pekah king of Israel came Tiglath-pileser king of Assyria, and took Ijon, and Abelbethmaachah, and Janoah, and Kedesh, and Hazor, and Gilead, and Galilee, all the land of Naphtali, and carried them captive to Assyria.

2 Kin. 16 [7]So Ahaz sent messengers to Tiglath-pileser king of Assyria, saying, I am thy servant and thy son: come up, and save me out of the hand of the king of Syria, and out of the hand of the king of
Israel, which rise up against me. [8]And
Ahaz took the silver and gold that was found in the house of the LORD, and in the treasures of the king's house, and sent it for
a present to the king of Assyria. [9]And the
king of Assyria hearkened unto him: for the king of Assyria went up against Damascus, and took it, and carried the people of it captive to Kir, and slew Rezin.
[10]And king Ahaz went to Damascus to meet Tiglath-pileser king of Assyria, and saw an altar that was at Damascus: and king Ahaz sent to Urijah the priest the fashion of the altar, and the pattern of it, according to all the workmanship thereof.

TIMOTHY

[tim'ô thi] A companion and fellow-worker of Paul, also called Timotheus. Timothy was a resident of Lystra whom Paul seems to have converted on his first missionary journey. His father was a non-Christian Greek, but his mother Eunice, a Jewess, and his grandmother Lois were believers. Paul was so impressed with the young man that he chose him to accompany him on the remainder of the journey, having him circumcised to avoid any offense to the Jews with whom they would be in contact. On this and subsequent travels of Paul, Timothy served him well not only as a companion, but as a special emissary to various churches to carry out the duties which the apostle assigned him. He was found with him in Rome during the first imprisonment, after which he went to Philippi and then to Ephesus. It was during Timothy's period of service to the church in Ephesus that Paul wrote *1 Timothy*, giving instructions as to how he should conduct the affairs of Ephesian church until Paul rejoined him there. Paul's last epistle, *2 Timothy*, was written to his beloved "child in the faith" from the second imprisonment in Rome. The old apostle could see the end approaching and he desired the comfort which his younger associate could give him. It is unknown whether Timothy was able to reach Rome before Paul was executed.

See PAUL

REFERENCE: *Acts 16-20; 1* and *2 Tim.; Rom. 16:21; 1 Cor. 4:17; 2 Cor. 1:19; Col. 1:1, 2; 1 Thess. 1:1; 3:2, 6; 2 Thess. 1:1; Philem. 1:1.*

SCRIPTURE

Acts 16 [1]Then came he to Derbe and
Lystra: and, behold, a certain disciple was
there, named Timotheus, the son of a certain woman, which was a Jewess, and believed; but his father was a Greek: [2]Which
was well reported of by the brethren that
were at Lystra and Iconium. [3]Him would
Paul have to go forth with him; and took and circumcised him because of the Jews which were in those quarters: for they knew all that his father was a Greek.

1 Cor. 16 [10]Now if Timotheus come, see that he may be with you without fear: for he worketh the work of the Lord, as I also do.

Phil. 2 [19]But I trust in the Lord Jesus to send Timotheus shortly unto you, that I also may be of good comfort, when I know
your state. [20]For I have no man like-
minded, who will naturally care for your
state. [21]For all seek their own, not the
things which are Jesus Christ's. [22]But ye
know the proof of him, that, as a son with the father, he hath served with me in the
gospel. [23]Him therefore I hope to send
presently, so soon as I shall see how it will go with me.

Acts 18 [5]And when Silas and Timotheus were come from Macedonia, Paul was pressed in the spirit, and testified to the Jews that Jesus was Christ.

Acts 20 [4]And there accompanied him into Asia Sopater of Berea; and of the Thessalonians, Aristarchus and Secundus; and Gaius of Derbe, and Timotheus; and of Asia, Tychicus and Trophimus.

TITHE

[tīth] The custom of giving one-tenth of one's income and produce for religious purposes. Abram gave to Melchizedek, the Priest of God Most High, a tenth of the spoils taken in battle (*Gen. 14:20*). Jacob dedicated to God the tenth of his gain (*Gen. 28:22*). The Law enjoined upon the Israelites the duty of paying a tithe of all they had. The Levites paid to the priests the tithe of what they received from the people (*Num. 18:26*). In New Testament times, the motivation behind tithing had been perverted and we read of the Pharisees' tithing the plants of their gardens, but neglecting the more important matters of mercy, justice, and faith (*Matt. 23:23*).

SCRIPTURE

Gen. 14 [20]And blessed be the most high God, which hath delivered thine enemies into thy hand. And he gave him tithes of all.

Gen. 28 [22]And this stone, which I have set for a pillar, shall be God's house: and of all that thou shalt give me I will surely give the tenth unto thee.

Lev. 27 [30]And all the tithe of the land, whether of the seed of the land, or of the fruit of the tree, is the LORD's: it is holy
unto the LORD. [31]And if a man will at all
redeem aught of his tithes, he shall add
thereto the fifth part thereof. [32]And concerning the tithe of the herd, or of the flock, even of whatsoever passeth under the rod, the tenth shall be holy unto the LORD.

Num. 18 [26]Thus speak unto the Levites, and say unto them, When ye take of the children of Israel the tithes which I have given you from them for your inheritance, then ye shall offer up a heave offering of it for the LORD, even a tenth part of the tithe.

Deut. 14 [28]At the end of three years thou shalt bring forth all the tithe of thine increase the same year, and shalt lay it up within thy gates:

Matt. 23 [23]Woe unto you, scribes and Pharisees, hypocrites! for ye pay tithe of mint and anise and cummin, and have omitted the weightier matters of the law, judgment, mercy, and faith: these ought ye to have done, and not to leave the other undone.

TITUS

[tī'tus] A Gentile Christian and co-worker of the apostle Paul. Paul resisted the demands of the Jews at Jerusalem that Titus be circumcised on the grounds that he was to be an example of the freedom from the Law which Christianity had made possible. Titus made two trips to Corinth to deal with the various problems there and to assist in gathering the collection for the poor saints in Jerusalem. After Paul's release from his first Roman imprisonment, Titus probably accompanied him on his preaching trips and was left in Crete to assist in the work of the church there. It was to instruct him in his dealings with the Cretan church that Paul wrote the epistle to Titus. In this letter, Paul asks Titus to meet him at Nicopolis. We can infer from *2 Tim. 4:10* that Titus rejoined Paul, was with him during the second Roman imprisonment, and was then sent on some type of evangelistic mission to Dalmatia.

SCRIPTURE

A Gentile

Gal. 2 [3]But neither Titus, who was with me, being a Greek, was compelled to be circumcised:

At the Jerusalem Council

Acts 15 [2]When therefore Paul and Barnabas had no small dissension and disputation with them, they determined that Paul and Barnabas, and certain other of them, should go up to Jerusalem unto the apostles and elders about this question.

Gal. 2 [1]Then fourteen years after I went up again to Jerusalem with Barnabas, and took Titus with me also.

Paul's Associate in Corinth Ministry

2 Cor. 2 [13]I had no rest in my spirit, because I found not Titus my brother; but taking my leave of them, I went from thence into Macedonia.

2 Cor. 7 [6]Nevertheless God, that comforteth those that are cast down, comforted us by the coming of Titus; [13]Therefore we were comforted in your comfort: yea, and exceedingly the more joyed we for the joy of Titus, because his spirit was refreshed by you all.

2 Cor. 8 [6]Insomuch that we desired Titus, that as he had begun, so he would also finish in you the same grace also. [16]But thanks be to God, which put the same earnest care into the heart of Titus for you.

2 Cor. 12 [18]I desired Titus, and with him I sent a brother. Did Titus make a gain of you? walked we not in the same spirit? walked we not in the same steps?

Left in Crete

Tit. 1 [5]For this cause left I thee in Crete, that thou shouldest set in order the things that are wanting, and ordain elders in every city, as I had appointed thee:

Sent to Dalmatia

2 Tim. 4 [10]For Demas hath forsaken me, having loved this present world, and is departed unto Thessalonica; Crescens to Galatia, Titus unto Dalmatia.

TONGUES, GIFT OF

[tungz] Technically called "glossalalia," the gift of tongues was a peculiar phenomenon apparently rather common in early Christianity, especially in the churches with which the apostle Paul was associated. It seems to have consisted in ecstatic, unintelligible speech and issued from Christians who believed themselves to be specially possessed by the Holy Spirit. In writing to the church at Corinth, Paul acknowledges the gift of tongues to be one of the "gifts" of the Holy Spirit (*1 Cor. 14:5, 39*), but emphasizes the point that it is by no means the greatest of these gifts (*1 Cor. 12:10; 14:19*). On the contrary, its undisciplined use can have a detrimental effect on public worship and the unity of Christian fellowship (*1 Cor. 14:23, 26, 27*). It is especially to be refrained from where there is no one present to interpret the "words" which are being spoken (*1 Cor. 12:10, 30; 14:28*).

SCRIPTURE

1 Cor. 12 1Now concerning spiritual
gifts, brethren, I would not have you ignorant. 4Now there are diversities of gifts,
but the same Spirit. 8For to one is given
by the Spirit the word of wisdom; to another the word of knowledge by the same
Spirit; 10To another the working of miracles; to another prophecy; to another discerning of spirits; to another divers kinds
of tongues; to another the interpretation
of tongues:

1 Cor. 14 1Follow after charity, and desire spiritual gifts, but rather that ye may
prophesy. 2For he that speaketh in an unknown tongue speaketh not unto men, but
unto God: for no man understandeth him;
howbeit in the spirit he speaketh mysteries. 3But he that prophesieth speaketh
unto men to edification, and exhortation,
and comfort. 4He that speaketh in an unknown tongue edifieth himself; but he that
prophesieth edifieth the church. 5I would
that ye all spake with tongues, but rather
that ye prophesied: for greater is he that
prophesieth than he that speaketh with
tongues, except he interpret, that the
church may receive edifying. 6Now,
brethren, if I come unto you speaking with
tongues, what shall I profit you, except I
shall speak to you either by revelation, or
by knowledge, or by prophesying, or by
doctrine? 7And even things without life
giving sound, whether pipe or harp, except
they give a distinction in the sounds, how
shall it be known what is piped or harped?
8For if the trumpet give an uncertain
sound, who shall prepare himself to the
battle? 9So likewise ye, except ye utter by
the tongue words easy to be understood,
how shall it be known what is spoken? for
ye shall speak into the air. 10There are, it
may be, so many kinds of voices in the
world, and none of them is without signification. 11Therefore if I know not the
meaning of the voice, I shall be unto him
that speaketh a barbarian, and he that
speaketh shall be a barbarian unto me.
12Even so ye, forasmuch as ye are zealous
of spiritual gifts, seek that ye may excel to
the edifying of the church. 13Wherefore
let him that speaketh in an unknown
tongue pray that he may interpret. 14For
if I pray in an unknown tongue, my spirit
prayeth, but my understanding is unfruitful. 15What is it then? I will pray with the
spirit, and I will pray with the understanding also: I will sing with the spirit, and I
will sing with the understanding also.
16Else when thou shalt bless with the spirit,
how shall he that occupieth the room of
the unlearned say Amen at thy giving of
thanks, seeing he understandeth not what
thou sayest? 17For thou verily givest
thanks well, but the other is not edified.
18I thank my God, I speak with tongues
more than ye all: 19Yet in the church I had

rather speak five words with my understanding, that by my voice I might teach
others also, than ten thousand words in an
unknown tongue. 28But if there be no interpreter, let him keep silence in the
church; and let him speak to himself, and
to God. 39Wherefore, brethren, covet to
prophesy, and forbid not to speak with
tongues. 40Let all things be done decently
and in order.

TRANSFIGURATION

[trans fig û rā'shun] The changing of the form or appearance of something. The word ordinarily refers to the supernatural change in the appearance of Jesus as recorded in the Gospels. Shortly after Peter's confession of faith at Caesarea Philippi (*see Matt. 16:13-20*), Jesus, accompanied by Peter, James, and John, ascended a high mountain nearby—probably Mount Hermon—for prayer. While praying, Jesus was "transfigured"; "his face did shine as the sun", and "his raiment became shining, exceeding white as snow; so as no fuller on earth can white them." The disciples then heard Jesus talking with Elijah and Moses, who had appeared alongside him. Peter was so thrilled by the experience that he requested that booths be built that they might dwell there and preserve the marvelous moment. Suddenly, a voice from a cloud spoke, saying, "This is my beloved Son, in whom I am well pleased; hear ye him." Stricken with awe, the disciples prostrated themselves on the ground. When they arose, Moses and Elijah had disappeared, and the disciples saw Jesus only. From this incident forward, Jesus seems to have had a keener sense of the necessity of his death on the cross and a new fervor and confidence in the mission which he was to perform.

The Christian may properly be spoken of as transfigured when, through spiritual rebirth, he abandons his own will and displays the mind of Christ, being "changed into the same image from glory to glory, even as by the Spirit of the Lord" (*2 Cor. 3:18*).

SCRIPTURE

Matt. 17 1And after six days Jesus taketh Peter, James, and John his brother,
and bringeth them up into an high mountain apart, 2And was transfigured before
them: and his face did shine as the sun,
and his raiment was white as the light.
3And, behold, there appeared unto them
Moses and Elias talking with him. 4Then
answered Peter, and said unto Jesus, Lord,
it is good for us to be here: if thou wilt, let
us make here three tabernacles; one for
thee, and one for Moses, and one for Elias.
5While he yet spake, behold, a bright cloud
overshadowed them: and behold a voice
out of the cloud, which said, This is my beloved Son, in whom I am well pleased;
hear ye him. 6And when the disciples
heard it, they fell on their face, and were
sore afraid. 7And Jesus came and touched
them, and said, Arise, and be not afraid.
8And when they had lifted up their eyes,
they saw no man, save Jesus only.

See Mark 9:2-8; Luke 9:28-36

TRANSLATION

[trans lā'shun] As used in the Bible, this term refers to the passing of Enoch from the earthly state to the heavenly state, without the intervention of death. The Bible simply contains the narrative of this event and gives little hint as to its nature.

SCRIPTURE

Gen. 5 24And Enoch walked with God:
and he was not; for God took him.

Heb. 11 5By faith Enoch was translated
that he should not see death; and was not
found, because God had translated him:
for before his translation he had this testimony, that he pleased God.

TRESPASS

[tres'pas] To exceed the bounds of what is lawful, right, or just; to sin; to offend; to encroach, as on another's privileges, rights, privacy, etc.; any violations of law, civil or moral. A trespass may be against a person, a community, the state, or God. Under the Law of Moses, a special sacrifice called the trespass offering was made before reconciliation was effected when a trespass had been committed. (*See* SACRIFICES) The New Testament teaches us that reconciliation must be made between the trespasser and the offended before one's worship is acceptable to God; in all cases, the offended is bound to forgive if the offender shows true repentance. (*See Matt. 5:23, 24; 6:14, 15; 18:21, 22*)

See FORGIVENESS

TRIBULATION

[trib ū lā'shun] Distress, trouble, severe affliction.

See AFFLICTION

SCRIPTURE

Matt. 13 21Yet hath he not root in himself, but dureth for a while: for when tribulation or persecution ariseth because of the word, by and by he is offended.

Matt. 24 21For then shall be great tribulation, such as was not since the beginning of the world to this time, no, nor ever shall be.

John 16 33These things I have spoken unto you, that in me ye might have peace. In the world ye shall have tribulation: but be of good cheer; I have overcome the world.

Acts 14 22Confirming the souls of the disciples, and exhorting them to continue in the faith, and that we must through much tribulation enter into the kingdom of God.

1 Thess. 3 4For verily, when we were with you, we told you before that we should suffer tribulation; even as it came to pass, and ye know.

Rev. 7 14And I said unto him, Sir, thou knowest. And he said to me, These are they which came out of great tribulation, and have washed their robes, and made them white in the blood of the Lamb.

TROAS

[trō'as] The chief city in northwest Asia Minor, on the coast of Mysia. It was here that Paul received the "Macedonian call" while on his second missionary journey (*Acts 16:9*), after which he left for Philippi. On the third journey, he visited in Troas, at which time he raised Eytychus from the dead after he had fallen out of a window while Paul was preaching (*Acts 20:5-12*).

SCRIPTURE

Visited by Paul

Acts 16 8And they passing by Mysia came down to Troas. 11Therefore loosing from Troas, we came with a straight course to Samothracia, and the next day to Neapolis;

Acts 20 5These going before tarried for us at Troas. 6And we sailed away from Philippi after the days of unleavened bread, and came unto them to Troas in five days; where we abode seven days.
7And upon the first day of the week, when the disciples came together to break bread, Paul preached unto them, ready to depart on the morrow; and continued his speech until midnight.

TROPHIMUS

[trof'i mus] A native of Ephesus and a companion of the apostle Paul. Trophimus joined Paul on the third missionary journey and accompanied him all the way back to Jerusalem, at which time he became the occasion of a considerable disturbance when the Jews mistakenly supposed that Paul had taken him, a Gentile, into the inner court of the Temple, an offence punishable by death. We last hear of Trophimus in the second epistle to *Timothy*, in which Paul states that "Trophimus I left at Miletus sick."

SCRIPTURE

Companion of Paul

Acts 20 4And there accompanied him into Asia Sopater of Berea; and of the Thessalonians, Aristarchus and Secundus; and Gaius of Derbe, and Timotheus; and of Asia, Tychicus and Trophimus.

Cause of Disturbance in Jerusalem

Acts 21 27And when the seven days were almost ended, the Jews which were of Asia, when they saw him in the temple, stirred up all the people, and laid hands on him, 28Crying out, Men of Israel, help: This is the man, that teacheth all men every where against the people, and the law, and this place: and further brought Greeks also into the temple, and hath polluted this holy place. 29(For they had seen before with him in the city Trophimus an Ephesian, whom they supposed that Paul had brought into the temple.) 30And all the city was moved, and the people ran together: and they took Paul, and drew him out of the temple: and forthwith the doors were shut.

Left Ill at Miletus (Miletum)

2 Tim. 4 20Erastus abode at Corinth: but Trophimus have I left at Miletum sick.

TRUST

[trust] The assured resting of the mind of one person on the integrity, honor, justice, love, truth, or any other sound principle in another. The trust which the Christian has in God is an exemplification of his faith; the greater the trust the greater the degree of faith. The Bible urges complete trust in God and shows us the blessings of it.

See Faith

SCRIPTURE

Trust in God

1 Sam. 17 37David said moreover, The LORD that delivered me out of the paw of the lion, and out of the paw of the bear, he will deliver me out of the hand of this Philistine. And Saul said unto David, Go, and the LORD be with thee.

2 Kin. 18 5He trusted in the LORD God of Israel; so that after him was none like him among all the kings of Judah, nor any that were before him. 6For he clave to the LORD, and departed not from following him, but kept his commandments, which the LORD commanded Moses. 7And the LORD was with him; and he prospered whithersoever he went forth: and he rebelled against the king of Assyria, and served him not.

Psa. 4 5Offer the sacrifices of righteousness, and put your trust in the LORD.

Psa. 10 14Thou hast seen it; for thou beholdest mischief and spite, to requite it with thy hand: the poor committeth himself unto thee; thou art the helper of the fatherless.

Psa. 31 5Into thine hand I commit my spirit; thou hast redeemed me, O LORD God of truth.

Psa. 41 11By this I know that thou favourest me, because mine enemy doth not triumph over me.

Psa. 71 7I am as a wonder unto many; but thou art my strong refuge.

Psa. 112 7He shall not be afraid of evil tidings: his heart is fixed, trusting in the LORD. 8His heart is established, he shall not be afraid, until he see his desire upon his enemies.

Psa. 118 8It is better to trust in the LORD than to put confidence in man. 9It is better to trust in the LORD than to put confidence in princes.

Prov. 28 25He that is of a proud heart stirreth up strife: but he that putteth his trust in the LORD shall be made fat.

Isa. 50 10Who is among you that feareth

the LORD, that obeyeth the voice of his servant, that walketh in darkness, and hath no light? let him trust in the name of the LORD, and stay upon his God.

Matt. 6 25Therefore I say unto you, Take no thought for your life, what ye shall eat, or what ye shall drink; nor yet for your body, what ye shall put on. Is not the life more than meat, and the body than raiment? 31Therefore take no thought, saying, What shall we eat? or, What shall we drink? or, Wherewithal shall we be clothed? 32(For after all these things do the Gentiles seek:) for your heavenly Father knoweth that ye have need of all these things. 33But seek ye first the kingdom of God, and his righteousness; and all these things shall be added unto you. 34Take therefore no thought for the morrow: for the morrow shall take thought for the things of itself. Sufficient unto the day is the evil thereof.

Heb. 12 12Wherefore lift up the hands which hang down, and the feeble knees; 13And make straight paths for your feet, lest that which is lame be turned out of the way; but let it rather be healed.

1 Pet. 5 7Casting all your care upon him; for he careth for you.

Distrust Shamed

Matt. 6 30Wherefore, if God so clothe the grass of the field, which to day is, and to morrow is cast into the oven, shall he not much more clothe you, O ye of little faith?

Matt. 10 31Fear ye not therefore, ye are of more value than many sparrows.

Luke 12 23The life is more than meat, and the body is more than raiment. 24Consider the ravens: for they neither sow nor reap; which neither have storehouse nor barn; and God feedeth them: how much more are ye better than the fowls? 25And which of you with taking thought can add to his stature one cubit? 26If ye then be not able to do that thing which is least, why take ye thought for the rest? 27Consider the lilies how they grow: they toil not, they spin not; and yet I say unto you, that Solomon in all his glory was not arrayed like one of these. 28If then God so clothe the grass, which is to day in the field, and to morrow is cast into the oven; how much more will he clothe you, O ye of little faith? 30For all these things do the nations of the world seek after: and your Father knoweth that ye have need of these things.

TRUTH

[trōōth] The Old Testament views truth as an essential quality of God, signifying his reliability, dependability, and faithfulness. Derived from this is the concept of truth as a fact or state which has unalterable validity or stability and therefore has to be accepted. As applied to man, truth meant that the individual was consistent in his actions and that he conformed to God's will, as revealed in the Law. Although the New Testament concept of truth is closer to our modern view, truth is still more than something merely to be thought or believed; it is something to be done. The word is often used as an equivalent to Christianity, or the revelation of God in Christ. Acceptance of and dedication to this truth equips men for fellowship with one another and acceptance by God.

SCRIPTURE

God Is Truth

Deut. 32 4He is the Rock, his work is perfect: for all his ways are judgment: a God of truth and without iniquity, just and right is he.

1 Kin. 8 24Who has kept with thy servant David my father that thou promisedst him: thou spakest also with thy mouth, and hast fulfilled it with thine hand, as it is this day.

1 Kin. 17 [24]And the woman said to Elijah, Now by this I know that thou art a man of God, and that the word of the LORD in thy mouth is truth.

Psa. 25 [10]All the paths of the LORD are mercy and truth unto such as keep his covenant and his testimonies.

Psa. 31 [5]Into thine hand I commit my spirit: thou hast redeemed me, O LORD God of truth.

Psa. 33 [4]For the word of the LORD is right; and all his works are done in truth.

Psa. 57 [10]For thy mercy is great unto the heavens, and thy truth unto the clouds.

Psa. 96 [13]Before the LORD: for he cometh, for he cometh to judge the earth: he shall judge the world with righteousness, and the people with his truth.

Psa. 100 [5]For the LORD is good; his mercy is everlasting; and his truth endureth to all generations.

Psa. 108 [4]For thy mercy is great above the heavens: and thy truth reacheth unto the clouds.

Psa. 117 [2]For his merciful kindness is great toward us: and the truth of the LORD endureth for ever. Praise ye the LORD.

Psa. 146 [6]Which made heaven, and earth, the sea, and all that therein is: which keepeth truth for ever.

Jer. 10 [10]But the LORD is the true God.

Mic. 7 [20]Thou wilt perform the truth to Jacob, and the mercy to Abraham, which thou hast sworn unto our fathers from the days of old.

Rom. 3 [3]For what if some did not believe? shall their unbelief make the faith of God without effect? [4]God forbid: yea, let God be true, but every man a liar; as it is written, That thou mightest be justified in thy sayings, and mightest overcome when thou art judged. [5]But if our righteousness commend the righteousness of God, what shall we say? Is God unrighteous who taketh vengeance? (I speak as a man) [6]God forbid: for then how shall God judge the world? [7]For if the truth of God hath more abounded through my lie unto his glory; why yet am I also judged as a sinner?

Tit. 1 [2]In hope of eternal life, which God, that cannot lie, promised before the world began.

God's Word Is Truth

2 Sam. 22 [31]As for God, his way is perfect; the word of the LORD is tried: he is a buckler to all them that trust in him.

Psa. 119 [160]Thy word is true from the beginning: and every one of thy righteous judgments endureth for ever.

Prov. 22 [20]Have not I written to thee excellent things in counsels and knowledge, [21]That I might make thee know the certainty of the words of truth; that thou mightest answer the words of truth to them that send unto thee?

John 17 [17]Sanctify them through thy truth: thy word is truth.

John 21 [24]This is the disciple which testifieth of these things, and wrote these things: and we know that his testimony is true.

Rev. 19 [9]And he saith unto me, Write, Blessed are they which are called unto the marriage supper of the Lamb. And he saith unto me, These are the true sayings of God.

The Christian Revelation Is Truth

John 14 [6]Jesus saith unto him, I am the way, the truth, and the life: no man cometh unto the Father, but by me.

John 17 [17]Sanctify them through thy truth: thy word is truth. [19]And for their sakes I sanctify myself, that they also might be sanctified through the truth.

2 Cor. 4 [2]But have renounced the hidden things of dishonesty, not walking in craftiness, nor handling the word of God deceitfully; but, by manifestation of the truth, commending ourselves to every man's conscience in the sight of God.

Gal. 5 [7]Ye did run well; who did hinder you that ye should not obey the truth?

Eph. 1 [13]In whom ye also trusted, after that ye heard the word of truth, the gospel of your salvation:

Eph. 4 [21]If so be that ye have heard him, and have been taught by him, as the truth is in Jesus.

2 Thess. 2 [10]And with all deceivableness of unrighteousness in them that perish; because they received not the love of the truth, that they might be saved. [11]And for this cause God shall send them strong delusion, that they should believe a lie: [12]That they all might be damned who believed not the truth, but had pleasure in unrighteousness.

1 Tim. 3 [15]But if I tarry long, that thou mayest know how thou oughtest to behave thyself in the house of God, which is the church of the living God, the pillar and ground of the truth.

1 Tim. 4 [3]Forbidding to marry, and commanding to abstain from meats, which God hath created to be received with thanksgiving of them which believe and know the truth.

Heb. 10 [26] For if we sin wilfully after that we have received the knowledge of the truth, there remaineth no more sacrifice for sins.

Jas. 1 [18]Of his own will begat he us with the word of truth, that we should be a kind of firstfruits of his creatures.

Jas. 5 [19]Brethren, if any of you do err from the truth, and one convert him.

Truth Required of Men

Psa. 51 [6]Behold, thou desirest truth in the inward parts: and in the hidden part thou shalt make me to know wisdom.

John 3 [21]But he that doeth truth cometh to the light, that his deeds may be made manifest, that they are wrought in God.

1 Pet. 1 [22]Seeing ye have purified your souls in obeying the truth through the Spirit unto unfeigned love of the brethren, see that ye love one another with a pure heart fervently.

Miscellaneous

John 4 [24]God is a Spirit: and they that worship him must worship him in spirit and in truth.

2 Cor. 12 [6]For though I would desire to glory, I shall not be a fool; for I will say the truth: but now I forbear, lest any man should think of me above that which he seeth me to be, or that he heareth of me.

Gal. 4 [16]Am I therefore become your enemy, because I tell you the truth?

1 Tim. 2 [7]Whereunto I am ordained a preacher, and an apostle (I speak the truth in Christ, and lie not,) a teacher of the Gentiles in faith and verity.

2 Tim. 2 [15]Study to show thyself approved unto God, a workman that needeth not to be ashamed, rightly dividing the word of truth.

2 Tim. 4 [4]And they shall turn away their ears from the truth, and shall be turned unto fables.

TUBAL-CAIN

[tū′bal kān] A son of Lamech and brother of Jubal and Jabal. He is spoken of in *Gen. 4:22* as "an instructor of every artificer in brass and iron."

TYCHICUS

[tik′i kus] An Asian companion of Paul. Tychicus first appears as one of the friends of Paul engaged in delivering the money which had been collected among the Gentile churches for the benefit of the poor saints in Jerusalem. He was with Paul during his first Roman imprisonment and carried word of his condition to the churches of Asia-Minor, at the same time delivering the letters to the churches at Ephesus and Colossae and accompanying the runaway slave Onesimus on his return to his master, Philemon, to whom Paul had also addressed a short letter. After Paul's release, he wrote to Titus to ask him to meet him in Nicopolis, informing him that either Artemas or Tychicus would replace him in the work in Crete (*Tit. 3:12*). In the last passage in which Tychicus is mentioned (*2 Tim. 4:12*), he is once again busy with the work assigned to him by the aged apostle, who is now back in Rome awaiting death. Here Paul tells Timothy that he has already sent Tychicus to relieve him at Ephesus, that he might join the apostle in Rome. From these brief notices concerning Tychicus, we learn that he was a willing and tireless servant of Christ, a faithful companion to Paul, and a man capable of adapting to any task to which he was assigned.

SCRIPTURE

A Companion of Paul

Acts 20 [4]And there accompanied him into Asia Sopater of Berea; and of the Thessalonians, Aristarchus and Secundus; and Gaius of Derbe, and Timotheus; and of Asia, Tychicus and Trophimus.

Tit. 3 [12]When I shall send Artemas unto thee, or Tychicus, be diligent to come unto me to Nicopolis: for I have determined there to winter.

Eph. 6 [21]But that ye also may know my affairs, and how I do, Tychicus, a beloved brother and faithful minister in the Lord, shall make known to you all things:

2 Tim. 4 [12]And Tychicus have I sent to Ephesus.

TYRANNUS

[tī ran′us] An Ephesian in whose "school" Paul taught for a period of two years, about whom no further information is given. The school probably amounted to nothing more than a hall or area which Paul was allowed to use.

SCRIPTURE

Acts 19 [9]But when divers were hardened, and believed not, but spake evil of that way before the multitude, he departed from them, and separated the disciples, disputing daily in the school of one Tyrannus. [10]And this continued by the space of two years; so that all they which dwelt in Asia heard the word of the Lord Jesus, both Jews and Greeks.

TYRE

[tīr] The most famous of Phoenician cities, situated about twenty miles south of Sidon. By the 10th century BC, Tyre was the most important city of Phoenicia. It appears that Hiram king of Tyre was in control of the forests of Lebanon as he arranged to ship lumber from those forests to assist David and Solomon in their building projects in Jerusalem. This alliance with Israel was but one of the outstanding achievements in the brilliant reign of Hiram. In the first half of the ninth century Tyre became subject to Assyria, but about a century later Isaiah refers to her in such a way as to imply that her prosperity had not been seriously affected (*Isa. 23:8*). Tyre is mentioned in the New Testament in connection with Jesus' visit to Phoenicia, at which time he healed the Syrophoenician woman's daughter (*Matt. 15:21; Mark 7:24*). Paul also visited in Tyre near the end of his third missionary journey (*Acts 21:3-7*).

SCRIPTURE

Visited by Jesus

Matt. 15 [21]Then Jesus went thence, and departed into the coasts of Tyre and Sidon.

Visited by Paul

Acts 21 [3]Now when we had discovered Cyprus, we left it on the left hand, and sailed into Syria, and landed at Tyre: for there the ship was to unlade her burden. [4]And finding disciples, we tarried there seven days: who said to Paul through the Spirit, that he should not go up to Jerusalem. [5]And when we had accomplished those days, we departed and went our way; and they all brought us on our way, with wives and children, till we were out of the city: and we kneeled down on the shore, and prayed. [6]And when we had taken our leave one of another, we took ship; and they returned home again. [7]And when we had finished our course from Tyre, we came to Ptolemais, and saluted the brethren, and abode with them one day.

UNBELIEF

[un bē lēf′] The state or act of not believing; especially, the rejection of divine revelation; disobedience; the antithesis of faith. As used in the Bible, unbelief involves self-will and is not identical with lack of belief through ignorance.

SCRIPTURE

General

Mark 16 [14]Afterward he appeared unto the eleven as they sat at meat, and upbraided them with their unbelief and hardness of heart, because they believed not them which had seen him after he was risen.

Luke 8 [12]Those by the way side are they that hear; then cometh the devil, and taketh away the word out of their hearts, lest they should believe and be saved.

Luke 24 [25]Then he said unto them, O fools, and slow of heart to believe all that the prophets have spoken.

John 5 [38]And ye have not his word abiding in you: for whom he hath sent, him ye believe not.

John 8 [45]And because I tell you the truth, ye believe me not.

John 10 [26]But ye believe not, because ye are not of my sheep, as I said unto you. [27]My sheep hear my voice, and I know them, and they follow me.

Acts 19 [9]But when divers were hardened, and believed not, but spake evil of that way before the multitude, he departed from them, and separated the disciples, disputing daily in the school of one Tyrannus.

2 Cor. 4 [3]But if our gospel be hid, it is hid to them that are lost: [4]In whom the god of this world hath blinded the minds of them which believe not, lest the light of the glorious gospel of Christ, who is the image of God, should shine unto them.

Eph. 2 [2]Wherein in time past ye walked according to the course of this world, according to the prince of the power of the air, the spirit that now worketh in the children of disobedience.

2 Thess. 2 [12]That they all might be damned who believed not the truth, but had pleasure in unrighteousness.

Heb. 3 [12]Take heed, brethren, lest there be in any of you an evil heart of unbelief, in departing from the living God.

Unbelief Contrasted with Belief

John 3 [18]He that believeth on him is not condemned: but he that believeth not is condemned already, because he hath not believed in the name of the only begotten Son of God.

[36]He that believeth on the Son hath everlasting life: and he that believeth not the Son shall not see life; but the wrath of God abideth on him.

1 John 5 [10]He that believeth on the Son of God hath the witness in himself: he that believeth not God hath made him a liar; because he believeth not the record that God gave of his Son.

Mercy for Repentance After Unbelief

1 Tim. 1 [13]Who was before a blasphemer, and a persecutor, and injurious:
but I obtained mercy, because I did it
ignorantly in unbelief.

Punishment of Unbelievers

Num. 20 [12]And the LORD spake unto
Moses and Aaron, Because ye believed me
not, to sanctify me in the eyes of the children of Israel, therefore ye shall not bring
this congregation into the land which I
have given them.

Psa. 78 [21]Therefore the LORD heard this,
and was wroth: so a fire was kindled
against Jacob, and anger also came up
against Israel; [22]Because they believed
not in God, and trusted not in his salvation.

John 8 [24]I said therefore unto you, that
ye shall die in your sins: for if ye believe
not that I am he, ye shall die in your sins.

Heb. 3 [18]And to whom sware he that
they should not enter into his rest, but to
them that believed not? [19]So we see that
they could not enter in because of unbelief.

Heb. 4 [6]Seeing therefore it remaineth
that some must enter therein, and they to
whom it was first preached entered not
in because of unbelief.

Heb. 12 [25]See that ye refuse not him
that speaketh: for if they escaped not who
refused him that spake on earth, much
more shall not we escape, if we turn away
from him that speaketh from heaven.

UNFAITHFULNESS

[un fāth′ful nes] Failure or refusal to be observant of vows, allegiance, or duty; lacking in good faith; dishonest.

See BACKSLIDING, UNBELIEF, etc.

SCRIPTURE

Matt. 3 [10]Now also the ax is laid unto
the root of the trees: therefore every tree
which bringeth not forth good fruit is
hewn down, and cast into the fire.

Matt. 13 [12]Whosoever hath, to him shall
be given, and he shall have more abundance: but whosoever hath not, from him
shall be taken away even that he hath.

Luke 13 [6]He spake also this parable; A
certain man had a fig tree planted in his
vineyard; and he came and sought fruit
thereon, and found none. [7]Then said he
unto the dresser of his vineyard, Behold,
these three years I come seeking fruit on
this fig tree, and find none: cut it down;
why cumbereth it the ground? [8]And he
answering said unto him, Lord, let it alone
this year also, till I shall dig about it, and
dung it: [9]And if it bear fruit, well: and if
not, then after that thou shalt cut it down.

John 15 [2]Every branch in me that beareth not fruit he taketh away: and every
branch that beareth fruit, he purgeth it,
that it may bring forth more fruit.

2 Pet. 1 [8]For if these things be in you,
and abound, they make you that ye shall
neither be barren nor unfruitful in the
knowledge of our Lord Jesus Christ. [9]But
he that lacketh these things is blind, and
cannot see afar off, and hath forgotten that
he was purged from his old sins.

UNITY

[ū′ni ti] The state of being one; singleness; absence of diversity; concord; harmony; accord; uniformity; as a unity of sentiment. The Scriptures exhort children of God to live together in unity.

SCRIPTURE

Psa. 133 [1]Behold, how good and how
pleasant it is for brethren to dwell together
in unity!

Isa. 52 [8]Thy watchmen shall lift up the
voice; with the voice together shall they

sing: for they shall see eye to eye, when the LORD shall bring again Zion.

John 10 [16]And other sheep I have, which are not of this fold: them also I must bring, and they shall hear my voice; and there shall be one fold, and one shepherd.

Acts 4 [32]The multitude of them that believed were of one heart and of one soul: neither said any of them that ought of the things which he possessed was his own; but they had all things common.

Rom. 12 [5]So we, being many, are one body in Christ, and every one members one of another. [16]Be of the same mind one toward another. Mind not high things, but condescend to men of low estate. Be not wise in your own conceits.

Rom. 14 [19]Let us therefore follow after the things which make for peace, and things wherewith one may edify another.

Rom. 15 [5]Now the God of patience and consolation grant you to be likeminded one toward another according to Christ Jesus: [6]That ye may with one mind and one mouth glorify God, even the Father of our Lord Jesus Christ.

1 Cor. 10 [17]For we being many are one bread, and one body: for we are all partakers of that one bread.

1 Cor. 12 [13]For by one Spirit are we all baptized into one body, whether we be Jews or Gentiles, whether we be bond or free; and have been all made to drink into one Spirit. [14]For the body is not one member, but many.

2 Cor. 13 [11]Finally, brethren, farewell. Be perfect, be of good comfort, be of one mind, live in peace; and the God of love and peace shall be with you.

Gal. 3 [28]There is neither Jew nor Greek, there is neither bond nor free, there is neither male nor female: for ye are all one in Christ Jesus.

Eph. 1 [10]That in the dispensation of the fulness of times he might gather together in one all things in Christ, both which are in heaven, and which are on earth; even in him.

Eph. 2 [19]Now therefore ye are no more strangers and foreigners, but fellowcitizens with the saints, and of the household of God.

Eph. 4 [3]Endeavouring to keep the unity of the Spirit in the bond of peace. [4]There is one body, and one Spirit, even as ye are called in one hope of your calling; [5]One Lord, one faith, one baptism, [6]One God and Father of all, who is above all, and through all, and in you all.

Phil. 1 [27]Only let your conversation be as it becometh the gospel of Christ: that whether I come and see you, or else be absent, I may hear of your affairs, that ye stand fast in one spirit, with one mind striving together for the faith of the gospel.

Phil. 2 [2]Fulfil ye my joy, that ye be likeminded, having the same love, being of one accord, of one mind.

Phil. 3 [16]Let us walk by the same rule, let us mind the same thing.

1 Pet. 3 [8]Finally, be ye all of one mind, having compassion one of another, love as brethren, be pitiful, be courteous.

UNSELFISHNESS

[un self'ish nes] The quality of ordering one's conduct and actions in such a way that the needs and desires of others are considered before one's own.

SCRIPTURE

Isa. 56 [11]Yea, they are greedy dogs which can never have enough, and they are shepherds that cannot understand: they all look to their own way, every one for his gain, from his quarter.

Rom. 15 [1]We then that are strong ought to bear the infirmities of the weak, and not to please ourselves.

1 Cor. 10 [24]Let no man seek his own, but every man another's wealth.

2 Cor. 5 [15]And that he died for all, that they which live should not henceforth live unto themselves, but unto him which died for them, and rose again.

Phil. 2 [4]Look not every man on his own things, but every man also on the things of others.

Jas. 2 [8]If ye fulfil the royal law according to the scripture, Thou shalt love thy neighbour as thyself, ye do well.

UR OF THE CHALDEES

[ur, kal′dēz] The home city of the patriarch Abraham (*Gen. 11:31*). The ruins of this ancient city were discovered and extensively excavated in the third decade of this century. They are located in Southern Mesopotamia about eleven miles west of the Euphrates.

SCRIPTURE

Gen. 11 [27]Now these are the generations of Terah: Terah begat Abram, Nahor, and Haran; and Haran begat Lot. [28]And Haran died before his father Terah in the land of his nativity, in Ur of the Chaldees. [31]And Terah took Abram his son, and Lot the son of Haran his son's son, and Sarai his daughter in law.

URIAH

[ů rī′a] A Hittite soldier, numbered among David's "mighty men." He was married to a beautiful Hebrew woman, Bath-sheba, with whom David committed adultery while Uriah was away with the army in battle. In order to cover his sin, David summoned Uriah back to Jerusalem, but failed to induce him to visit his wife, apparently in keeping with a soldier's vow. In desperation, David ordered Joab, the commander of the army, to assign Uriah to the most dangerous spot in the battle. When his death was reported, David summoned Bath-sheba to his house and made her his wife. In the scathing rebuke of David by the prophet Nathan, Uriah is compared to a man who has his only lamb stolen by a man with great flocks.

See BATH-SHEBA, JOAB, DAVID, NATHAN

SCRIPTURE

One of David's Mighty Men

2 Sam. 23 [8]These be the names of the mighty men whom David had: . . . . [39]Uriah the Hittite: thirty and seven in all.

David's Adultery with His Wife

2 Sam. 11 [2]And it came to pass in an evening tide, that David arose from off his bed, and walked upon the roof of the king's house: and from the roof he saw a woman washing herself; and the woman was very beautiful to look upon. [3]And David sent and inquired after the woman. And one said, Is not this Bath-sheba, the daughter of Eliam, the wife of Uriah the Hittite? [4]And David sent messengers, and took her; and she came in unto him, and he lay with her; for she was purified from her uncleanness: and she returned unto her house. [5]And the woman conceived, and sent and told David, and said, I am with child.

Summoned Home from War

2 Sam. 11 [6]And David sent to Joab, saying, Send me Uriah the Hittite. And Joab sent Uriah to David. [7]And when Uriah was come unto him, David demanded of him how Joab did, and how the people did, and how the war prospered. [8]And David said to Uriah, Go down to thy house, and wash thy feet. And Uriah departed out of the king's house, and there followed him a mess of meat from the king. [9]But Uriah slept at the door of the king's house with all the servants of his lord, and went not down to his house. [10]And when they had told David, saying, Uriah went not down unto his house, David said unto Uriah, Camest thou not from thy journey? why then didst thou not go down unto thine house? [11]And Uriah said unto David, The ark, and Israel, and Judah, abide in tents; and my lord Joab, and the servants of my lord, are encamped in the open fields; shall I then go into mine house, to eat and to drink, and to lie with my wife? As thou livest, and as thy soul liveth, I will not do this thing. [12]And David said to Uriah, Tarry here to-day also, and to-morrow I will let thee depart. So Uriah abode in Jerusalem that day, and the morrow. [13]And when David had called him, he did eat and drink before him; and he made him drunk: and at even he went out to lie on his bed with the servants of his lord, but went not down to his house.

David Arranges His Death

2 Sam. 11 [14]And it came to pass in the morning, that David wrote a letter to Joab, and sent it by the hand of Uriah. [15]And he wrote in the letter, saying, Set ye Uriah in the forefront of the hottest battle, and retire ye from him, that he may be smitten, and die. [16]And it came to pass, when Joab observed the city, that he assigned Uriah unto a place where he knew that valiant men were. [17]And the men of the city went out, and fought with Joab: and there fell some of the people of the servants of David; and Uriah the Hittite died also.

[18]Then Joab sent and told David all the things concerning the war; [19]And charged the messenger, saying, When thou hast made an end of telling the matters of the war unto the king, [20]And if so be that the king's wrath arise, and he say unto thee, Wherefore approached ye so nigh unto the city when ye did fight? knew ye not that they would shoot from the wall? [21]Who smote Abimelech the son of Jerubbesheth? did not a woman cast a piece of a millstone upon him from the wall, that he died in Thebez? why went ye nigh the wall? Then say thou, Thy servant Uriah the Hittite is dead also.

[22]So the messenger went, and came and shewed David all that Joab had sent him for. [23]And the messenger said unto David, Surely the men prevailed against us, and came out unto us into the field, and we were upon them even unto the entering of the gate. [24]And the shooters shot from off the wall upon thy servants; and some of the king's servants be dead, and thy servant Uriah the Hittite is dead also. [25]Then David said unto the messenger, Thus shalt thou say unto Joab, Let not this thing displease thee, for the sword devoureth one as well as another: make thy battle more strong against the city, and overthrow it: and encourage thou him.

David Marries His Widow

2 Sam. 11 [26]And when the wife of Uriah heard that Uriah her husband was dead, she mourned for her husband. [27]And when the mourning was past, David sent and fetched her to his house, and she became his wife, and bare him a son. But the thing that David had done displeased the LORD.

URIM AND THUMMIM

[ū′rim, thum′im] Articles which were apparently placed in the breastplate of the high priest and used to ascertain God's will in various matters. These articles are never specifically described. Since the Scriptures are unclear in their references to Urim and Thummim, it remains a matter of conjecture both as to what they were and how they were used.

SCRIPTURE

Ex. 28 [30]And thou shalt put in the breastplate of judgment the Urim and the

Thummim; and they shall be upon Aaron's heart, when he goeth in before the LORD: and Aaron shall bear the judgment of the children of Israel upon his heart before the LORD continually.

Lev. 8 [8]And he put the breastplate upon him: also he put in the breastplate the Urim and the Thummim.

Num. 27 [21]And he shall stand before Eleazar the priest, who shall ask counsel for him after the judgment of Urim before the LORD: at his word shall they go out, and at his word they shall come in, both he, and all the children of Israel with him, even all the congregation.

1 Sam. 28 [6]And when Saul inquired of the LORD, the LORD answered him not, neither by dreams, nor by Urim, nor by prophets.

Ezra 2 [63]And the Tirshatha said unto them, that they should not eat of the most holy things, till there stood up a priest with Urim and with Thummim.

Neh. 7 [65]And the Tirshatha said unto them, that they should not eat of the most holy things, till there stood up a priest with Urim and Thummim.

UZZAH

[uz′a] One of the drivers of the cart which bore the ark of the covenant from Kiriath-jearim on its journey toward the city of David. Uzzah is remembered as the man who fell dead after having touched the ark when he apparently felt it needed steadying. His death was regarded by David as an omen and the journey was discontinued, the ark being kept in the house of Obed-Edom the Gittite for a period of three months before it was finally taken to Jerusalem.

SCRIPTURE

2 Sam. 6 [1]Again David gathered together all the chosen men of Israel, thirty thousand. [2]And David arose and went with all the people that were with him from Baale of Judah, to bring up from thence the ark of God, whose name is called by the name of the LORD of hosts that dwelleth between the cherubim. [3]And they set the ark of God upon a new cart, and brought it out of the house of Abinadab that was in Gibeah: and Uzzah and Ahio, the sons of Abinadab, drave the new cart. [4]And they brought it out of the house of Abinadab, which was at Gibeah, accompanying the ark of God: and Ahio went before the ark. [5]And David and all the house of Israel played before the LORD on all manner of instruments made of fir wood, even on harps, and on psalteries, and on timbrels, and on cornets, and on cymbals.

[6]And when they came to Nachon's threshingfloor, Uzzah put forth his hand to the ark of God, and took hold of it; for the oxen shook it. [7]And the anger of the LORD was kindled against Uzzah, and God smote him there for his error; and there he died by the ark of God.

UZZIAH

[u zī′a] The son of Amaziah and eleventh king of Judah, also called Azariah. In a period of Assyrian and Egyptian weakness, Uzziah was able to recover much of the lost glory of Judah (under Jeroboam II, Israel experienced a similar revival). Uzziah reopened the port and industries of Ezion-geber (Elath) at the head of the Red Sea; he restored and maintained control of major trade lines; he subdued the old enemies of Edom, Philistia and Arabia; and carried out an extensive program of fortification and building. Foreign sources indicate that Uzziah may have been the leader of a coalition which encountered Tiglath-Pileser in central Syria. The Bible tells us that Uzziah's pride in his successes led him to usurp the role of the priests in burning incense in the temple and that he was struck with leprosy as punishment for this sin. He then retired from public life, leaving official control of the kingdom in the hands of his son Jotham.

See JOTHAM, EZION-GEBER, TIGLATH-PILESER, KINGS

SCRIPTURE

2 Chr. 26 [1]Then all the people of Judah took Uzziah, who was sixteen years old, and made him king in the room of his father Amaziah. [2]He built Eloth, and restored it to Judah, after that the king slept with his fathers. [3]Sixteen years old was Uzziah when he began to reign, and he reigned fifty and two years in Jerusalem. His mother's name also was Jecoliah of Jerusalem. [4]And he did that which was right in the sight of the LORD, according to all that his father Amaziah did. [5]And he sought God in the days of Zechariah, who had understanding in the visions of God: and, as long as he sought the LORD, God made him to prosper. [6]And he went forth and warred against the Philistines, and brake down the wall of Gath, and the wall of Jabneh, and the wall of Ashdod and built cities about Ashdod, and among the Philistines. [7]And God helped him against the Philistines, and against the Arabians that dwelt in Gurbaal, and the Mehunim. [8]And the Ammonites gave gifts to Uzziah: and his name spread abroad even to the entering in of Egypt; for he strengthened himself exceedingly. [9]Moreover Uzziah built towers in Jerusalem at the corner gate, and at the valley gate, and at the turning of the wall, and fortified them. [10]Also he built towers in the desert, and digged many wells: for he had much cattle, both in the low country, and in the plains; husbandmen also, and vinedressers in the mountains, and in Carmel: for he loved husbandry. [11]Moreover Uzziah had a host of fighting men, that went out to war by bands, according to the number of their account by the hand of Jeiel the scribe and Maaseiah the ruler, under the hand of Hananiah, one of the king's captains. [12]The whole number of the chief of the fathers of the mighty men of valour were two thousand and six hundred. [13]And under their hand was an army, three hundred thousand and seven thousand and five hundred, that made war with mighty power, to help the king against the enemy. [14]And Uzziah prepared for them throughout all the host, shields, and spears, and helmets, and habergeons, and bows, and slings to cast stones. [15]And he made in Jerusalem engines, invented by cunning men, to be on the towers and upon the bulwarks, to shoot arrows and great stones withal. And his name spread far abroad; for he was marvellously helped, till he was strong.

[16]But when he was strong, his heart was lifted up to his destruction: for he transgressed against the LORD his God, and went into the temple of the LORD to burn incense upon the altar of incense. [17]And Azariah the priest went in after him, and with him fourscore priests of the LORD, that were valiant men. [18]And they withstood Uzziah the king, and said unto him, It appertaineth not unto thee, Uzziah, to burn incense unto the LORD, but to the priests the sons of Aaron, that are consecrated to burn incense: go out of the sanctuary; for thou hast trespassed; neither shall it be for thine honour from the LORD God. [19]Then Uzziah was wroth, and had a censer in his hand to burn incense: and while he was wroth with the priests, the leprosy even rose up in his forehead before the priests in the house of the LORD, from beside the incense altar. [20]And Azariah the chief priest, and all the priests, looked upon him, and, behold, he was leprous in his forehead, and they thrust him out from thence; yea, himself hasted also to go out, because the LORD had smitten him. [21]And Uzziah the king was a leper unto the day of his death, and dwelt in a several house,

being a leper: for he was cut off from the
house of the LORD: and Jotham his son was
over the king's house, judging the people
of the land.
22Now the rest of the acts of Uzziah, first
and last, did Isaiah the prophet, the son of
Amoz, write. 23So Uzziah slept with his fathers, and they buried him with his fathers
in the field of the burial which belonged to
the kings; for they said, He is a leper: and
Jotham his son reigned in his stead.

See 2 Kin. 14:21; 15:1-7

VANITY

[van'i ti] The quality or state of being vain; unreal; profitless; empty; unsubstantial; also inordinate pride or conceit. The Bible contains warnings against various types of vanity—of the mind, of riches, of position or social standing.

SCRIPTURE

Psa. 94 11The Lord knoweth the
thoughts of man, that they are vanity.

Eccl. 1 2Vanity of vanities, saith the
Preacher, vanity of vanities; all is vanity.
12I the Preacher was king over Israel in
Jerusalem. 13And I gave my heart to seek
and search out by wisdom concerning all
things that are done under heaven: this
sore travail hath God given to the sons of
man to be excercised therewith. 14I have
seen all the works that are done under the
sun; and, behold, all is vanity and vexation
of spirit.

Eccl. 2 1I said in mine heart, Go to now,
I will prove thee with mirth; therefore enjoy pleasure: and, behold, this also is vanity. 4I made me great works; I builded me
houses; I planted me vineyards: 5I made
me gardens and orchards, and I planted
trees in them of all kind of fruits: 6I made
me pools of water, to water therewith the
wood that bringeth forth trees: 7I got me
servants and maidens, and had servants
born in my house; also I had great possessions of great and small cattle above all
that were in Jerusalem before me: 8I gathered me also silver and gold, and the peculiar treasure of kings and of the provinces; I gat me men singers and women
singers, and the delights of the sons of
men, as musical instruments, and that of
all sorts. 9So I was great, and increased
more than all that were before me in Jerusalem: also my wisdom remained with me.
10And whatsoever mine eyes desired I kept
not from them, I withheld not my heart
from any joy; for my heart rejoiced in all
my labour: and this was my portion of all
my labour. 11Then I looked on all the
works that my hands had wrought, and on
the labour that I had laboured to do: and,
behold, all was vanity and vexation of
spirit, and there was no profit under the
sun.
15Then said I in my heart, As it happeneth to the fool, so it happeneth even to me;
and why was I then more wise? Then I
said in my heart, that this also is vanity.
18Yea, I hated all my labour which I
had taken under the sun: because I should
leave it unto the man that shall be after
me. 19And who knoweth whether he shall
be a wise man or a fool? yet shall he have
rule over all my labour wherein I have laboured, and wherein I have shewed myself wise under the sun. This is also vanity.
20Therefore I went about to cause my heart
to despair of all the labour which I took
under the sun. 21For there is a man whose
labour is in wisdom, and in knowledge,
and in equity; yet to a man that hath not
laboured therein shall he leave it for his
portion. This also is vanity and a great evil.

Eccl. 12 8Vanity of vanities, saith the
Preacher; all is vanity.

VASHTI

[vash'tī] The queen of Ahasuerus who, for her

refusal to appear before the king's guests at a royal banquet, was repudiated and deposed, to be replaced by Esther. Apart from the Bible, history gives no mention of Vashti.

See ESTHER, AHASUERUS

SCRIPTURE

Esth. 1 1 Now it came to pass in the days
of Ahasuerus, (this is Ahasuerus which
reigned from India even unto Ethiopia,
over a hundred and seven and twenty
provinces,) 2 That in those days, when the
king Ahasuerus sat on the throne of his
kingdom, which was in Shushan the palace, 3 In the third year of his reign, he
made a feast unto all his princes and his
servants; the power of Persia and Media,
the nobles and princes of the provinces,
being before him: 9 Also Vashti the queen
made a feast for the women in the royal
house which belonged to king Ahasuerus.
10 On the seventh day, when the heart of
the king was merry with wine, he commanded Mehuman, Biztha, Harbona, Big-
tha, and Abagtha, Zethar, and Carcas, the
seven chamberlains that served in the
presence of Ahasuerus the king, 11 To
bring Vashti the queen before the king
with the crown royal, to shew the people
and the princes her beauty: for she was
fair to look on. 12 But the queen Vashti refused to come at the king's commandment
by his chamberlains: therefore was the
king very wroth, and his anger burned in
him.

13 Then the king said to the wise men,
which knew the times, (for so was the
king's manner toward all that knew law
and judgment: 14 And the next unto him
was Carshena, Shethar, Admatha, Tarshish, Meres, Marsena, and Memucan, the
seven princes of Persia and Media, which
saw the king's face, and which sat the first
in the kingdom,) 15 What shall we do unto
the queen Vashti according to law, because she hath not performed the commandment of the king Ahasuerus by the
chamberlains? 16 And Memucan answered
before the king and the princes, Vashti the
queen hath not done wrong to the king
only, but also to all the princes, and to all
the people that are in all the provinces of
the king Ahasuerus. 17 For this deed of the
queen shall come abroad unto all women,
so that they shall despise their husbands
in their eyes, when it shall be reported,
The king Ahasuerus commanded Vashti
the queen to be brought in before him, but
she came not. 19 If it please the king, let
there go a royal commandment from him,
and let it be written among the laws of the
Persians and the Medes, that it be not altered, That Vashti come no more before
king Ahasuerus: and let the king give her
royal estate unto another that is better
than she. 20 And when the king's decree,
which he shall make, shall be published
throughout all his empire, (for it is great,)
all the wives shall give to their husbands
honour, both to great and small. 21 And
the saying pleased the king and the
princes; and the king did according to the
word of Memucan:

VEIL

[vāl] 1. As an article of dress in biblical times, the veil might be a light or heavy wrap which could be used to cover the face. Among Greeks and Romans, polite women seldom appeared in public with unveiled faces, but this custom was not widely followed by Hebrew women. Rebekah's example, as recorded in *Gen. 24:65* indicates that it was customary for brides to wear a veil. It also seems that a mark of a harlot was the wearing of a veil. (*See Gen. 38*)

2. The veil which hung between the two holy chambers of the tabernacle is described as having been made of blue, purple, and scarlet linen, and embroidered with cherubim (*Ex. 26:31*). When the tabernacle was moved from place to place during the wanderings in the wilderness,

the veil was used as a wrap for the ark of the covenant (*Num. 4:5*). Solomon's temple apparently contained a similar veil, protected by olivewood doors (*2 Chr. 3:14; 1 Kin. 6:31*). The veil in the temple of Herod is said to have been rent from top to bottom at the time of Jesus' death (*Matt. 27:51; Mark 15:38; Luke 23:45; Heb. 10:20*).

See TABERNACLE, TEMPLE

VINE, VINEYARD

[vīn, vin′yard] From the earliest known times, Palestine was a vine-growing region, as indicated by numerous wine-presses found in and around early centers of civilization. In addition to wine, the vine supplied the ancients with sugar and honey, which they obtained by boiling the juice of the grape to a thick "grape-honey."

To prepare a vineyard, stones were cleared from an area and used to construct a wall or terrace around the plot. The vine-stocks were usually allowed to grow along the ground, although they were sometimes elevated several inches off the ground by sticks. Care of a vineyard included plowing or harrowing the ground and clearing it of weeds, pruning dead and fruitless branches, and guarding against wild animals such as jackals and foxes. For this latter purpose a watchman was stationed in a tower or high summer house which afforded him a view of a large area of the vineyard. This structure also provided shelter for the workmen at their meals and a suitable place to keep the tools. Adjacent to the vineyard was a winepress; for a description of this and a discussion of its use, see WINE. The vine is referred to figuratively in a number of passages; in most of these, the meaning is fairly obvious.

SCRIPTURE

Lev. 25 [3]Six years thou shalt sow thy field, and six years thou shalt prune thy vineyard, and gather in the fruit thereof; [4]But in the seventh year shall be a sabbath of rest unto the land, a sabbath for the LORD: thou shalt neither sow thy field, nor prune thy vineyard.

Neh. 9 [25]And they took strong cities, and a fat land, and possessed houses full of all goods, wells digged, vineyards, and oliveyards, and fruit trees in abundance.

Prov. 24 [30]I went by the field of the slothful, and by the vineyard of the man void of understanding; [31]And lo, it was all grown over with thorns, and nettles had covered the face thereof, and the stone wall thereof was broken down.

Song 2 [15]Take us the foxes, the little foxes, that spoil the vines: for our vines have tender grapes.

Isa. 5 [1]Now will I sing to my well beloved a song of my beloved touching his vineyard. My well beloved hath a vineyard in a very fruitful hill: [2]And he fenced it, and gathered out the stones thereof, and planted it with the choicest vine, and built a tower in the midst of it, and also made a winepress therein: and he looked that it should bring forth grapes, and it brought forth wild grapes. [3]And now, O inhabitants of Jerusalem, and men of Judah, judge, I pray you, betwixt me and my vineyard. [4]What could have been done more to my vineyard, that I have not done in it? wherefore, when I looked that it should bring forth grapes, brought it forth wild grapes? [5]And now go to; I will tell you what I will do to my vineyard: I will take away the hedge thereof, and it shall be eaten up; and break down the wall thereof, and it shall be trodden down: [6]And I will lay it waste: it shall not be pruned, nor digged; but there shall come up briers and thorns: I will also command the clouds that they rain no rain upon it. [7]For the vineyard of the LORD of hosts is the house of Israel, and the men of Judah his pleasant plant: and he looked for judgment, but behold oppression; for righteousness, but behold a cry.

Matt. 21 [33]Hear another parable: There was a certain householder, which planted a vineyard, and hedged it round about,

and digged a winepress in it, and built a
tower, and let it out to husbandmen, and
went into a far country.

VIRGIN

[vûr′jin] One who has not had sexual intercourse. The word usually refers to a woman. The Old Testament offers abundant attestation to the high value which the Israelites placed on virginity. The New Testament teaches that Jesus was miraculously conceived of the Holy Spirit and born of a virgin mother, Mary. Matthew cites this as a fulfillment of the prophecy recorded in *Isa. 7:14*. "Behold, a virgin shall conceive, and bear a son, and shall call his name Immanuel." In the Revised Standard Version of the Bible, translated in 1952, this word "virgin" is replaced by "young woman." This translation has been the occasion of much confusion and misunderstanding of the aims of the translators of the Revised Standard Version. The Hebrew word in this verse simply indicates that the woman is sexually mature, without reference to whether or not she is a virgin. The immediate event of which Isaiah spoke was a natural birth which was to serve as a sign to King Ahaz (*Isa. 7:10-16*). Therefore, the young woman to whom Isaiah referred would not have been a virgin. In the application of this prophecy to the birth of Jesus, however, Matthew uses the Greek term *parthenos*, which has the specific meaning of "virgin" and is so translated in both the King James and Revised Standard Versions. Thus, despite the criticism to which the Revised Standard Version has been subjected, it has not been unfaithful in its rendering of these texts.

See JESUS, MARY

REFERENCE: *Ex. 22:17; Deut. 22:13-24; Matt. 25: 1-13.*

SCRIPTURE

The Virgin Mary

Matt. 1 [23]Behold, a virgin shall be with
child, and shall bring forth a son, and they
shall call his name Emmanuel, which being interpreted is, God with us.

Paul's Teaching concerning Virgins

1 Cor. 7 [25]Now concerning virgins I
have no commandment of the Lord: yet
I give my judgment, as one that hath obtained mercy of the Lord to be faithful.
[26]I suppose therefore that this is good for
the present distress, I say, that it is good
for a man so to be. [27]Art thou bound unto
a wife? seek not to be loosed. Art thou
loosed from a wife? seek not a wife. [28]But
and if thou marry, thou hast not sinned;
and if a virgin marry, she hath not sinned.
Nevertheless such shall have trouble in
the flesh: but I spare you. [29]But this I say,
brethren, the time is short: it remaineth,
that both they that have wives be as
though they had none; [30]And they that
weep, as though they wept not; and they
that rejoice, as though they rejoiced not;
and they that buy, as though they possessed not; [31]And they that use this world,
as not abusing it: for the fashion of this
world passeth away. [32]But I would have
you without carefulness. He that is unmarried careth for the things that belong to the
Lord, how he may please the Lord: [33]But
he that is married careth for the things that
are of the world, how he may please his
wife. [34]There is difference also between a
wife and a virgin. The unmarried woman
careth for the things of the Lord, that she
may be holy both in body and in spirit:
but she that is married careth for the things
of the world, how she may please her husband. [35]And this I speak for your own
profit; not that I may cast a snare upon you,
but for that which is comely, and that ye
may attend upon the Lord without distraction. [36]But if any man think that he
behaveth himself uncomely toward his
virgin, if she pass the flower of her age, and
need so require, let him do what he will,
he sinneth not: let them marry. [37]Never-

theless he that standeth steadfast in his heart, having no necessity, but hath power over his own will, and hath so decreed in his heart that he will keep his virgin, doeth well. [38]So then he that giveth her in marriage doeth well; but he that giveth her not in marriage doeth better.

VISION

[vizh'un] Something seen otherwise than by ordinary sight, as in a dream or ecstatic experience. The Bible indicates that visionary experiences were a rather common means of communication between God and man, especially in the case of the prophets. As used in such verses as *1 Sam. 3:1* ("And the word of the LORD was precious in those days; there was no open vision.") and *Prov. 29:18* ("Where there is no vision the people perish."), vision means the declaration of God's will vital to the continuing life of the community.

See DREAMS

VOW

[vou] A sacred promise made to God to abstain from certain things or practices or to perform certain things, such as offerings. Ordinarily these were made in return for certain benefits which it was hoped God would grant. Vows were not commanded to be made as a religious duty, but once made, the law contained detailed provisions for their execution. The vows of children were not valid except when ratified by parents, nor those of wives except when known and unforbidden by the husband. Items which were vowed, such as land, animals, or persons, could be redeemed by the paying of a sum equivalent to the worth of the vowed object plus an extra sum as a "ransom."

See OATH

REFERENCE: Vows of Jacob, *Gen. 28:20-22;* Jephthah, *Judg. 11:29-40;* Hannah, *1 Sam. 1:11, 27, 28;* Absalom, *2 Sam. 15:7, 8.*

SCRIPTURE

General

Lev. 5 [4]Or if a soul swear, pronouncing with his lips to do evil, or to do good, whatsoever it be that a man shall pronounce with an oath, and it be hid from him; when he knoweth of it, then he shall be guilty in one of these.

Num. 30 [2]If a man vow a vow unto the LORD, or swear an oath to bind his soul with a bond; he shall not break his word, he shall do according to all that proceedeth out of his mouth. [3]If a woman also vow a vow unto the LORD, and bind herself by a bond, being in her father's house in her youth; [4]And her father hear her vow, and her bond wherewith she hath bound her soul, and her father shall hold his peace at her; then all her vows shall stand, and every bond wherewith she hath bound her soul shall stand. [5]But if her father disallow her in the day that he heareth; not any of her vows, or of her bonds wherewith she hath bound her soul, shall stand; and the LORD shall forgive her, because her father disallowed her. [6]And if she had at all a husband, when she vowed, or uttered aught out of her lips, wherewith she bound her soul; [7]And her husband heard it, and held his peace at her in the day that he heard it: then her vows shall stand, and her bonds wherewith she bound her soul shall stand. [8]But if her husband disallowed her on the day that he heard it, then he shall make her vow which she vowed, and that which she uttered with her lips, wherewith she bound her soul, of none effect; and the LORD shall forgive her. [13]Every vow, and every binding oath to afflict the soul, her husband may establish it, or her husband may make it void. [14]But if her husband altogether hold his peace at her from day to day; then he establisheth all her vows, or all her bonds, which are upon her: he confirmeth them, because he held his peace at her in the day that he heard them. [15]But if he shall any ways make them void after that he hath heard them; then he shall bear her iniquity.

Psa. 22 [25]My praise shall be of thee in the great congregation: I will pay my vows before them that fear him.

Psa. 66 [13]I will go into thy house with burnt offerings: I will pay thee my vows.

Eccl. 5 [4]When thou vowest a vow unto God, defer not to pay it; for he hath no pleasure in fools: pay that which thou hast vowed. [5]Better is it that thou shouldest not vow, than that thou shouldest vow and not pay. [6]Suffer not thy mouth to cause thy flesh to sin; neither say thou before the angel, that it was an error: wherefore should God be angry at thy voice, and destroy the work of thine hands?

See Lev. 22:18-25; 23:37, 38; 27:1-25; Num. 29: 39.

WAR

[war] From the earliest days of Israel's history, war had a religious significance. It is quite proper to speak of the battles of Israel, especially in the period of the conquest of Canaan, as Holy War. A definite pattern for Holy Warfare can be discerned in the Old Testament. Regular consultation of God was made in order to insure his support of the campaign. When the time for attack came, the trumpets were blown and a cry went up. God went forth with the armies, dwelling in the midst of the camp. Since they were in the sphere of God's direct activity, the soldiers put away from themselves anything which might offend the LORD. Numbers were not a decisive factor in Holy War, since God was leading the army; this is clearly seen in the story of Gideon's defeat of the Midianites (*Judg.* 7). Ordinarily, a numinous panic siezed the enemy at the moment of attack making possible their swift and complete destruction by the Israelites. Although there was some variation as to what fell under the ban, it may be stated generally that the spoil belonged to God. Attempts to secure booty for private use could bring disaster to the entire nation, as in the case of Achan (*Josh.* 7).

In the New Testament, Jesus speaks of "wars and rumors of wars" (*Matt. 24:6; Mark 13:7; Luke 21:9*) indicating that these were to be a part of the normal world-order. In the epistles and in *Revelation,* the language of war is used to refer to the struggles and ultimate victory of Christians and the Church, under the leadership of Christ himself.

SCRIPTURE

Holy Warfare

See Deuteronomy, Joshua, and *Judges*

The Christian's Spiritual Warfare

Rom. 7 [23]But I see another law in my members, warring against the law of my mind, and bringing me into captivity to the law of sin which is in my members.

2 Cor. 10 [3]For though we walk in the flesh, we do not war after the flesh. [5]Casting down imaginations, and every high thing that exalteth itself against the knowledge of God, and bringing into captivity every thought to the obedience of Christ.

Eph. 6 [10]Finally, my brethren, be strong in the Lord, and in the power of his might. [11]Put on the whole armour of God, that ye may be able to stand against the wiles of the devil. [12]For we wrestle not against flesh and blood, but against principalities, against powers, against the rulers of the darkness of this world, against spiritual wickedness in high places. [13]Wherefore take unto you the whole armour of God, that ye may be able to withstand in the evil day, and having done all, to stand. [14]Stand therefore, having your loins girt about with truth, and having on the breastplate of righteousness; [15]And your feet shod with the preparation of the gospel of peace; [16]Above all, taking the shield of faith, wherewith ye shall be able to quench all the fiery darts of the wicked. [17]And take the helmet of salvation, and the sword of the Spirit, which is the word of God:

Rom. 8 [37]Nay, in all these things we are more than conquerors through him that loved us.

The Triumph of Christ

Col. 2 [15]And having spoiled principalities and powers, he made a show of them openly, triumphing over them in it.

Eph. 2 [16]And that he might reconcile both unto God in one body by the cross, having slain the enmity thereby: [17]And came and preached peace to you which were afar off, and to them that were nigh.

Rev. 17 [14]These shall make war with the Lamb, and the Lamb shall overcome them; for he is Lord of lords, and King of kings: and they that are with him are called, and chosen, and faithful.

Rev. 19 [14]And the armies which were in heaven followed him upon white horses, clothed in fine linen, white and clean. [15]And out of his mouth goeth a sharp sword, that with it he should smite the nations; and he shall rule them with a rod of iron: and he treadeth the winepress of the fierceness and wrath of Almighty God.

WATCHFULNESS

[woch′ful nes] The state or quality of being watchful; alertness. The Scriptures exhort us to watchfulness for a number of different reasons—that we do not fall into temptation and sin, that we walk in the ways of God, that we maintain the proper relations between ourselves and our fellow-men, and that we be ready for the second coming of Christ.

SCRIPTURE

Watchfulness against Sin, Temptation, etc.

Deut. 11 [16]Take heed to yourselves, that your heart be not deceived, and ye turn aside, and serve other gods, and worship them;

Josh. 23 [11]Take good heed therefore unto yourselves, that ye love the LORD your God.

Matt. 24 [4]And Jesus answered and said unto them, Take heed that no man deceive you.

Matt. 26 [38]Then saith he unto them, My soul is exceeding sorrowful, even unto death: tarry ye here, and watch with me. [39]And he went a little farther, and fell on his face, and prayed, saying, O my Father, if it be possible, let this cup pass from me: nevertheless not as I will, but as thou wilt. [40]And he cometh unto the disciples, and findeth them asleep, and saith unto Peter, What, could ye not watch with me one hour? [41]Watch and pray, that ye enter not into temptation: the spirit indeed is willing, but the flesh is weak.

Luke 11 [35]Take heed therefore, that the light which is in thee be not darkness.

Luke 12 [15]Take heed, and beware of covetousness; for a man's life consisteth not in the abundance of the things which he possesseth.

[35]Let your loins be girded about, and your lights burning; [36]And ye yourselves like unto men that wait for their lord, when he will return from the wedding; that when he cometh and knocketh, they may open unto him immediately. [37]Blessed are those servants, whom the lord when he cometh shall find watching: verily I say unto you, that he shall gird himself, and make them to sit down to meat, and will come forth and serve them. [38]And if he shall come in the second watch, or come in the third watch, and find them so, blessed are those servants. [39]And this know, that if the goodman of the house had known what hour the thief would come, he would have watched, and not have suffered his house to be broken through. [40]Be ye therefore ready also: for

the Son of man cometh at an hour when ye think not.

1 Cor. 10 [12]Wherefore let him that thinketh he standeth take heed lest he fall.

Eph. 6 [18]Praying always with all prayer and supplication in the Spirit, and watching thereunto with all perseverance and supplication for all saints.

Col. 4 [2]Continue in prayer, and watch in the same with thanksgiving.

2 Tim. 4 [5]But watch thou in all things, endure afflictions, do the work of an evangelist, make full proof of thy ministry.

1 Pet. 4 [7]But the end of all things is at hand: be ye therefore sober, and watch unto prayer.

1 Pet. 5 [8]Be sober, be vigilant; because your adversary the devil, as a roaring lion, walketh about, seeking whom he may devour.

Watching for Christ's Second Coming

Matt. 24 [42]Watch therefore; for ye know not what hour your Lord doth come.

Mark 13 [34]For the Son of man is as a man taking a far journey, who left his house, and gave authority to his servants, and to every man his work, and commanded the porter to watch. [35]Watch ye therefore: for ye know not when the master of the house cometh, at even, or at midnight, or at the cock-crowing, or in the morning: [36]Lest coming suddenly he find you sleeping. [37]And what I say unto you I say unto all, Watch.

Luke 21 [34]And take heed to yourselves, lest at any time your hearts be overcharged with surfeiting, and drunkenness, and cares of this life, and so that day come upon you unawares. [35]For as a snare shall it come on all of them that dwell on the face of the whole earth.

Rom. 13 [11]And that, knowing the time, that now it is high time to awake out of sleep: for now is our salvation nearer than when we believed.

1 Thess. 5 [4]But ye, brethren, are not in darkness, that that day should overtake you as a thief. [5]Ye are all the children of light, and the children of the day: we are not of the night nor of darkness. [6]Therefore let us not sleep, as do others; but let us watch and be sober.

WATER

[wô′tẽr] Water is everywhere a vital aspect of life, but it is even more highly regarded in areas in which it is in short supply. Therefore, it is not at all surprising that water is frequently used as symbolic of God's blessings. As indicated in the scripture passages given below, it is spoken of in the sense of spiritual refreshment, and as a symbol of eternal life. Another prominent use of water in the Bible is in connection with cleansing. Washings figured prominently in the consecration of priests and in other aspects of the worship of Ancient Israel. Use of water in this way led to the practice of baptism, which was widely practiced among the Essenese and other Jewish sects, thus providing a background for John's baptizing activity and for Christian baptism.

See BAPTISM

SCRIPTURE

Symbolic of Spiritual Refreshment

Psa. 23 [2]He leadeth me beside the still waters.

Isa. 35 [6]Then shall the lame man leap as a hart, and the tongue of the dumb sing: for in the wilderness shall waters break out, and streams in the desert. [7]And the parched ground shall become a pool, and the thirsty land springs of water: in the habitation of dragons, where each lay, shall be grass with reeds and rushes.

Isa. 41 [18]I will open rivers in high places, and fountains in the midst of the valleys: I will make the wilderness a pool of water, and the dry land springs of water.

Jer. 2 [13]For my people have committed two evils; they have forsaken me the fountain of living waters, and hewed them out cisterns, broken cisterns, that can hold no water.

John 7 [38]He that believeth on me, as the Scripture hath said, out of his belly shall flow rivers of living water.

Symbolic of Eternal Life

John 4 [14]But whosoever drinketh of the water that I shall give him shall never thirst; but the water that I shall give him shall be in him a well of water springing up into everlasting life.

Rev. 7 [17]For the Lamb which is in the midst of the throne shall feed them, and shall lead them unto living fountains of waters.

Rev. 21 [6]I will give unto him that is athirst of the fountain of the water of life freely.

Rev. 22 [1]And he showed me a pure river of water of life, clear as crystal, proceeding out of the throne of God and of the Lamb.

Used in Israel's Worship

Ex. 29 [4]And Aaron and his sons thou shalt bring unto the door of the tabernacle of the congregation, and shalt wash them with water.

Num. 8 [7]And thus shalt thou do unto them, to cleanse them: Sprinkle water of purifying upon them, and let them shave all their flesh, and let them wash their clothes, and so make themselves clean.

Lev. 16 [24]And he shall wash his flesh with water in the holy place, and put on his garments, and come forth, and offer his burnt offering, and the burnt offering of the people, and make an atonement for himself, and for the people.

WAY, The

[wā] Literally, a highway, path, or any customary course of travel; also, a course of human conduct. The phrase "the Way" was one of the earliest designations of the Christian religion (*Acts 9:2; 18:25, 26; 19:9, 23; 22:4; 24:22*). That the followers of Jesus should be identified by this term is entirely fitting, since the Master referred to himself as "the Way, the Truth, and the Life" (*John 14:6*).

SCRIPTURE

Jesus the Way

John 14 [6]Jesus saith unto him, I am the way, the truth, and the life: no man cometh unto the Father, but by me.

The Christian Religion

Acts 9 [2]And desired of him letters to Damascus to the synagogues, that if he found any of this way, whether they were men or women, he might bring them bound unto Jerusalem.

Acts 18 [25]This man was instructed in the way of the Lord; and being fervent in the spirit, he spake and taught diligently the things of the Lord, knowing only the baptism of John. [26]And he began to speak boldly in the synagogue: whom when Aquila and Priscilla had heard, they took him unto them, and expounded unto him the way of God more perfectly.

Acts 19 [9]But when divers were hardened, and believed not, but spake evil of that way before the multitude, he departed from them, and separated the disciples, disputing daily in the school of one Tyrannus.

[23]And the same time there arose no small stir about that way.

Acts 22 [4]And I persecuted this way unto the death, binding and delivering into prisons both men and women.

Acts 24 [22]And when Felix heard these things, having more perfect knowledge of that way, he deferred them, and said, When Lysias the chief captain shall come down, I will know the uttermost of your matter.

WEEPING

[wēp′ing] The shedding of tears; an expression of sorrow, grief, or anguish. The Scriptures offer much comfort for those who weep.

SCRIPTURE

Psa. 6 8Depart from me, all ye workers of iniquity; for the LORD hath heard the voice of my weeping.

Psa. 30 5For his anger endureth but a moment; in his favour is life: weeping may endure for a night, but joy cometh in the morning.

Lam. 1 2She weepeth sore in the night, and her tears are on her cheeks: among all her lovers she hath none to comfort her: all her friends have dealt treacherously with her, they are become her enemies.

Joel 2 12Therefore also now, saith the LORD, turn ye even to me with all your heart, and with fasting, and with weeping, and with mourning.

Matt. 8 12But the children of the kingdom shall be cast out into outer darkness: there shall be weeping and gnashing of teeth.

Matt. 22 13Then said the king to his servants, Bind him hand and foot, and take him away, and cast him into outer darkness; there shall be weeping and gnashing of teeth.

Luke 6 21Blessed are ye that hunger now: for ye shall be filled. Blessed are ye that weep now: for ye shall laugh.

Luke 7 38And stood at his feet behind him weeping, and began to wash his feet with tears, and did wipe them with the hairs of her head, and kissed his feet, and anointed them with the ointment.

John 11 32Then when Mary was come where Jesus was, and saw him, she fell down at his feet, saying unto him, Lord, if thou hadst been here, my brother had not died. 33When Jesus therefore saw her weeping, and the Jews also weeping which came with her, he groaned in the spirit, and was troubled, 34And said, Where have ye laid him? They said unto him, Lord, come and see. 35Jesus wept.

Rom. 12 15Rejoice with them that do rejoice, and weep with them that weep.

1 Cor. 7 30And they that weep, as though they wept not; and they that rejoice, as though they rejoiced not; and they that buy, as though they possessed not.

Rev. 21 4And God shall wipe away all tears from their eyes; and there shall be no more death, neither sorrow, nor crying, neither shall there be any more pain: for the former things are passed away.

WEIGHTS AND MEASURES

[wāts, mezh′ẽrs] Instruments for determining the extent, dimensions, quantity, degree, capacity, or the like, of a thing. For most forms of trading and commerce, common standards of measure are required. In earliest times, familiar items were used as points of reference, such as the weight of an egg, the capacity of a handful, the distance of a day's journey, the length of the span of a hand, or the distance between the elbow and the finger tip. Gradually, more definite standards came into use. There is still some uncertainty involved in the study of ancient metrology, but the following modern equivalents of weights and measures mentioned in the Bible are as accurate as can be provided by modern scholarship.

Measure	*Modern Equivalent*	*Reference*
MEASURES OF WEIGHT		
shekel	1/3 or 3/4 oz.	*Gen. 24:22*
bekah	1 1/2 shekel	*Ex. 38:26*
gerah	1/20 shekel	*Ex. 30:13*
mina or maneh	1 or 2 lbs.	*Ezek. 45:12*
talent	45 or 90 lbs.	*Zech. 5:7*

Measure	*Modern Equivalent*	*Reference*
	MEASURES OF LENGTH	
cubit	18 inches	*Jer. 52:21*
(Roman period)	21.6 inches	*Matt. 6:27*
fathom	6 feet	*Acts 27:28*
finger	3/4 inch	*Jer. 52:21*
furlong	606 feet	*Luke 24:13*
mile	5,000 feet	*Matt. 5:41*
palm	3 inches	*1 Kin. 7:26*
reed	8 3/4 feet	*Ezek. 40:5*
sabbath day's journey	2/3 mile	*Acts 1:12*
span	9 inches	*Ex. 28:16*
	DRY MEASURES	
cab	2 pts.	*2 Kin. 6:25*
ephah	4 gals., 7 pts.	*Lev. 19:36*
kor, or homer	48 gals., 3 pts.	*Ezek. 45:14*
letech (half-homer)	24 gals., 1 1/2 pts.	*Hos. 3:2*
omer	2 pts.	*Ex. 16:36*
seah	1 gal., 5 pts.	*Gen. 18:6*
	LIQUID MEASURES	
bath or ephah	4 gals., 7 pts.	*Isa. 5:10*
firkin	8 1/2 gals.	*John 2:6*
cab	2 pts.	*2 Kin. 6:25*
hin	6 1/2 pts.	*Ex. 29:40*
kor, or homer	48 gals., 3 pts.	*Ezek. 45:14*
log	1 pt.	*Lev. 14:10*

WICKED, WICKEDNESS

[wik′ed, wik′ed nes] To be wicked is to be morally bad, evil in thought and purpose; iniquitous; to disregard justice, righteousness, truth, honor, virtue; to be sinful, depraved, etc.

See SIN, EVIL, etc.

SCRIPTURE

Wicked and Righteous Contrasted

Job 8 [20]Behold, God will not cast away a perfect man, neither will he help the evil doers: [21]Till he fill thy mouth with laughing, and thy lips with rejoicing.

Psa. 1 [6]For the LORD knoweth the way of the righteous: but the way of the ungodly shall perish.

2 Sam. 22 [26]With the merciful thou wilt shew thyself merciful, and with the upright man thou wilt shew thyself upright. [27]With the pure thou wilt show thyself pure; and with the froward thou wilt shew thyself unsavoury. [28]And the afflicted people thou wilt save: but thine eyes are upon the haughty, that thou mayest bring them down.

2 Chr. 15 [1]And the Spirit of God came upon Azariah the son of Oded: [2]And he went out to meet Asa, and said unto him, Hear ye me, Asa, and all Judah and Benjamin; The LORD is with you, while ye be with him; and if ye seek him, he will be found of you; but if ye forsake him, he will forsake you.

Psa. 32 [10]Many sorrows shall be to the wicked: but he that trusteth in the LORD, mercy shall compass him about.

Psa. 37 [17]For the arms of the wicked shall be broken: but the LORD upholdeth the righteous. [18]The LORD knoweth the days of the upright: and their inheritance shall be for ever. [19]They shall not be ashamed in the evil time: and in the days of famine they shall be satisfied. [20]But the wicked shall perish, and the enemies of the LORD shall be as the fat of lambs: they shall consume; into smoke shall they consume away.

Prov. 10 [9]He that walketh uprightly walketh surely: but he that perverteth his ways shall be known. [24]The fear of the wicked, it shall come upon him: but the desire of the righteous shall be granted. [25]As the whirlwind passeth, so is the wicked no more: but the righteous is an everlasting foundation. [28]The hope of the righteous shall be gladness: but the expectation of the wicked shall perish. [29]The way of the LORD is strength to the upright: but destruction shall be to the workers of iniquity. [30]The righteous shall never be removed: but the wicked shall not inhabit the earth.

Prov. 21 [18]The wicked shall be a ransom for the righteous, and the transgressor for the upright.

Prov. 22 [5]Thorns and snares are in the way of the froward: he that doth keep his soul shall be far from them.

Prov. 28 [18]Whoso walketh uprightly shall be saved: but he that is perverse in his ways shall fall at once.

Isa. 65 [13]Therefore thus saith the Lord GOD, Behold, my servants shall eat, but ye shall be hungry: behold, my servants shall drink, but ye shall be thirsty: behold, my servants shall rejoice, but ye shall be ashamed: [14]Behold, my servants shall sing for joy of heart, but ye shall cry for sorrow of heart, and shall howl for vexation of spirit.

Mal. 3 [18]Then shall ye return, and discern between the righteous and the wicked, between him that serveth God and him that serveth him not.

Prosperity of the Wicked Complained About

Job 9 [24]The earth is given into the hand of the wicked: he covereth the faces of the judges thereof; if not, where, and who is he?

Job 12 [6]The tabernacles of robbers prosper, and they that provoke God are secure; into whose hand God bringeth abundantly.

Job 21 [6]Even when I remember I am afraid, and trembling taketh hold on my flesh. [7]Wherefore do the wicked live, become old, yea, are mighty in power? [8]Their seed is established in their sight with them, and their offspring before their eyes. [9]Their houses are safe from fear, neither is the rod of God upon them. [13]They spend their days in wealth, and in a moment go down to the grave.

Job 22 [18]Yet he filled their houses with good things: but the counsel of the wicked is far from me.

Jer. 12 [1]Righteous art thou, O LORD, when I plead with thee: yet let me talk with thee of thy judgments: Wherefore doth the way of the wicked prosper? wherefore are all they happy that deal very treacherously? [2]Thou hast planted them, yea, they have taken root: they grow, yea, they bring forth fruit: thou art near in their mouth, and far from their reins.

Mal. 2 [17]Ye have wearied the LORD with your words. Yet ye say, Wherein have we wearied him? When ye say, Every one that doeth evil is good in the sight of the LORD, and he delighteth in them; or, Where is the God of judgment?

Mal. 3 [15]And now we call the proud happy; yea, they that work wickedness are set up; yea, they that tempt God are even delivered.

Doom of the Wicked

PASS AWAY

Psa. 36 [12]There are the workers of iniquity fallen: they are cast down, and shall not be able to rise.

Psa. 37 [34]Wait on the LORD, and keep his way, and he shall exalt thee to inherit the land: when the wicked are cut off, thou shalt see it. [35]I have seen the wicked in great power, and spreading himself like a green bay tree. [36]Yet he passed away, and, lo, he was not: yea, I sought him, but he could not be found.

THEIR TERROR

Heb. 10 [31]It is a fearful thing to fall into the hands of the living God.

Rev. 6 [15]And the kings of the earth, and the great men, and the rich men, and the chief captains, and the mighty men, and every bond man, and every free man, hid themselves in the dens and in the rocks of the mountains; [16]And said to the mountains and rocks, Fall on us, and hide us from the face of him that sitteth on the throne, and from the wrath of the Lamb: [17]For the great day of his wrath is come; and who shall be able to stand?

THEIR SEPARATION FROM THE RIGHTEOUS

Matt. 13 [47]Again, the kingdom of heaven is like unto a net, that was cast into the sea, and gathered of every kind: [48]Which, when it was full, they drew to shore, and sat down, and gathered the good into vessels, but cast the bad away. [49]So shall it be at the end of the world: the angels shall come forth, and sever the wicked from among the just.

Matt. 25 [32]And before him shall be gathered all nations: and he shall separate them one from another, as a shepherd divideth his sheep from the goats: [33]And he shall set the sheep on his right hand, but the goats on the left.

Rev. 22 [11]He that is unjust, let him be unjust still: and he which is filthy, let him be filthy still: and he that is righteous, let him be righteous still: and he that is holy, let him be holy still.

GIVEN OVER TO SATAN

Psa. 109 [6]Set thou a wicked man over him: and let Satan stand at his right hand.

1 Cor. 5 [2]And ye are puffed up, and have not rather mourned, that he that hath done this deed might be taken away from among you. [3]For I verily, as absent in body, but present in spirit, have judged already, as though I were present, concerning him that hath so done this deed, [4]In the name of our Lord Jesus Christ, when ye are gathered together, and my spirit, with the power of our Lord Jesus Christ, [5]To deliver such a one unto Satan for the destruction of the flesh, that the spirit may be saved in the day of the Lord Jesus.

1 Tim. 1 [20]Of whom is Hymeneus and Alexander; whom I have delivered unto Satan, that they may learn not to blaspheme.

DAMNATION OF THE WICKED

Prov. 16 [25]There is a way that seemeth right unto a man; but the end thereof are the ways of death.

Matt. 13 [24]Another parable put he forth unto them, saying, The kingdom of heaven is likened unto a man which sowed good seed in his field: [25]But while men slept, his enemy came and sowed tares among the wheat, and went his way. [26]But when the blade was sprung up, and brought forth fruit, then appeared the tares also. [27]So the servants of the householder came and said unto him, Sir, didst not thou sow good seed in thy field? from whence then hath it tares? [28]He said unto them, An enemy hath done this. The servants said unto him, Wilt thou then that we go and gather them up? [29]But he said, Nay; lest while ye gather up the tares, ye root up also the wheat with them. [30]Let both grow together until the harvest: and in the time of harvest I will say to the reapers, Gather ye together first the tares, and bind them in bundles to burn them: but gather the wheat into my barn.

[40]As therefore the tares are gathered and burned in the fire; so shall it be in the end of this world. [41]The son of man shall send forth his angels, and they shall gather out of his kingdom all things that offend, and them which do iniquity; [42]And shall cast them into a furnace of fire: there shall be wailing and gnashing of teeth.

Matt. 25 [46]And these shall go away into everlasting punishment: but the righteous into life eternal.

Jas. 5 [1]Go to now, ye rich men, weep and howl for your miseries that shall come upon you. [2]Your riches are corrupted, and your garments are motheaten. [3]Your gold and silver is cankered; and the rust of them shall be a witness against you, and shall eat your flesh as it were fire. Ye have heaped treasure together for the last days.

2 Pet. 2 [2]And many shall follow their pernicious ways; by reason of whom the way of truth shall be evil spoken of. [3]And through covetousness shall they with feigned words make merchandise of you; whose judgment now for a long time lingereth not, and their damnation slumbereth not.

WIDOW

[wid'ō] A woman who has lost her husband by death. Both Old and New Testaments view the plight of the widow sympathetically and contain provisions for her welfare. Paul speaks of "widows indeed," referring, it seems, to those who are old and in need of support.

SCRIPTURE

Deut. 24 [17]Thou shalt not pervert the judgment of the stranger, nor of the fatherless; nor take a widow's raiment to pledge:

Job 31 [16]If I have withheld the poor from their desire, or have caused the eyes of the widow to fail;

Psa. 68 [5]A father of the fatherless, and a judge of the widows, is God in his holy habitation.

Psa. 146 [9]The LORD preserveth the strangers; he relieveth the fatherless and widow: but the way of the wicked he turneth upside down.

Prov. 15 [25]The LORD will destroy the house of the proud: but he will establish the border of the widow.

1 Tim. 5 [2]The elder women as mothers; the younger as sisters, with all purity. [3]Honour widows that are widows indeed. [4]But if any widow have children or nephews, let them learn first to show piety at home, and to requite their parents: for that is good and acceptable before God. [5]Now she that is a widow indeed, and desolate, trusteth in God, and continueth in supplications and prayers night and day. [6]But she that liveth in pleasure is dead while she liveth. [7]And these things give in charge, that they may be blameless. [8]But if any provide not for his own, and specially for those of his own house, he hath denied the faith, and is worse than an infidel. [9]Let not a widow be taken into the number under threescore years old, having been the wife of one man, [10]Well reported of for good works; if she have brought up children, if she have lodged strangers, if she have washed the saints' feet, if she have relieved the afflicted, if she have diligently followed every good work. [11]But the younger widows refuse: for when they have begun to wax wanton against Christ, they will marry; [12]Having damnation, because they have cast off their first faith. [13]And withal they learn to be idle, wandering about from house to house; and not only idle, but tattlers also and busybodies, speaking things which they ought not. [14]I will therefore that the younger women marry, bear children, guide the house, give none occasion to the adversary to speak reproachfully. [15]For some are already turned aside after Satan. [16]If any man or woman that believeth have widows, let them relieve them, and let not the church be charged; that it may relieve them that are widows indeed.

Jas. 1 [27]Pure religion and undefiled before God and the Father is this, To visit the fatherless and widows in their affliction, and to keep himself unspotted from the world.

WILDERNESS

[wil'dẽr nes] A term used in the Bible to translate a number of Hebrew and Greek words. A precise definition is impossible, as it may indicate pasture land, arid desert, or rocky, mountainous terrain.

WINE

[wīn] As used in the Bible this term almost always refers to fermented grape juice. Most ancient wine presses, many of which are still in existence, consisted simply of two hollowed-out areas in rocks, one on a higher elevation than the other and connected with it by a pipe or channel. The grapes were placed in the larger upper vat where they were crushed by the feet of the treaders, the juice running into the smaller, but deeper, lower vat. It was then removed in jars or allowed to remain in the lower vat for fermentation. Fermentation began almost immediately, becoming so active at its highest point that it was necessary to keep the wine in vats or jars, since it would burst even the strongest of wineskins. The fermentation process usually lasted forty days, after which the juice was considered to be real wine. Certain types of wine were allowed to remain in the vats on their lees, or the heavier matter which collected at the bottom of the vats, but usually it was strained and drawn off after the forty day period.

Wine was considered a vital aspect of normal life in Palestine, as is clearly seen in numerous Biblical references. (*See Gen. 14:18; 27:28; Deut. 28:30, 39; Lam. 2:12*) Drink offerings were a regular part of the worship and a store of wine was kept in the temple (*Lev. 23:13; 1 Chr. 9:29*). The Bible contains numerous references to wine in a figurative sense, the meaning of most of which is fairly obvious.

See WINESKINS, VINE, DRINK, ABSTINENCE

SCRIPTURE

Made from Grapes

Gen. 40 [11]And Pharaoh's cup was in my hand: and I took the grapes, and pressed them into Pharaoh's cup, and I gave the cup into Pharaoh's hand.

Kept in Jars (bottles)

Jer. 13 [12]Therefore thou shalt speak unto them this word; Thus saith the LORD God of Israel, Every bottle shall be filled with wine: and they shall say unto thee, Do we not certainly know that every bottle shall be filled with wine?

Kept in Skins (bottles)

Matt. 9 [17]Neither do men put new wine into old bottles: else the bottles break, and the wine runneth out, and the bottles perish: but they put new wine into new bottles, and both are preserved.

Stored in Cellars

1 Chr. 27 [27]And over the vineyards was Shimei the Ramathite: over the increase of the vineyards for the wine cellars was Zabdi the Shiphmite:

Medicinal Use of Wine

Prov. 31 [6]Give strong drink unto him that is ready to perish, and wine unto those that be of heavy hearts.

1 Tim. 5 [23]Drink no longer water, but use a little wine for thy stomach's sake and thine often infirmities.

Forbidden to Nazarites

Num. 6 [2]Speak unto the children of Israel, and say unto them, When either man or woman shall separate themselves to vow a vow of a Nazarite, to separate themselves unto the LORD: [3]He shall separate himself from wine and strong drink, and shall drink no vinegar of wine, or vinegar of strong drink, neither shall he drink any liquor of grapes, nor eat moist grapes, or dried.

where is the place of understanding? [21]Seeing it is hid from the eyes of all living, and kept close from the fowls of the air. [22]Destruction and death say, We have heard the fame thereof with our ears.

Eccl. 1 [16]I communed with mine own heart, saying, Lo, I am come to great estate, and have gotten more wisdom than all they that have been before me in Jerusalem: yea, my heart had great experience of wisdom and knowledge. [17]And I gave my heart to know wisdom, and to know madness and folly: I perceived that this also is vexation of spirit.

Eccl. 7 [23]All this have I proved by wisdom: I said, I will be wise; but it was far from me. [24]That which is far off, and exceeding deep, who can find it out? [25]I applied mine heart to know, and to search, and to seek out wisdom, and the reason of things, and to know the wickedness of folly, even of foolishness and madness.

Eccl. 8 [16]When I applied mine heart to know wisdom, and to see the business that is done upon the earth: (for also there is that neither day nor night seeth sleep with his eyes:) [17]Then I beheld all the work of God, that a man cannot find out the work that is done under the sun: because though a man labour to seek it out, yet he shall not find it; yea further; though a wise man think to know it, yet shall he not be able to find it.

General Remarks and Exhortations on Wisdom

Job 15 [17]I will shew thee, hear me; and that which I have seen I will declare; [18]Which wise men have told from their fathers, and have not hid it: [19]Unto whom alone the earth was given, and no stranger passed among them.

Job 22 [28]Thou shalt also decree a thing, and it shall be established unto thee: and the light shall shine upon thy ways.

Job 28 [15]It cannot be gotten for gold, neither shall silver be weighed for the price thereof.

Psa. 37 [30]The mouth of the righteous speaketh wisdom, and his tongue talketh of judgment.

Psa. 107 [43]Whoso is wise, and will observe these things, even they shall understand the loving-kindness of the LORD.

Prov. 2 [9]Then shalt thou understand righteousness, and judgment, and equity; yea, every good path.

[10]When wisdom entereth into thine heart, and knowledge is pleasant unto thy soul; [11]Discretion shall preserve thee, understanding shall keep thee.

Prov. 3 [13]Happy is the man that findeth wisdom, and the man that getteth understanding: [14]For the merchandise of it is better than the merchandise of silver, and the gain thereof than fine gold. [15]She is more precious than rubies: and all the things thou canst desire are not to be compared unto her. [16]Length of days is in her right hand; and in her left hand riches and honour. [17]Her ways are ways of pleasantness, and all her paths are peace. [18]She is a tree of life to them that lay hold upon her: and happy is every one that retaineth her.

Eccl. 7 [11]Wisdom is good with an inheritance: and by it there is profit to them that see the sun. [12]For wisdom is a defence, and money is a defence: but the excellency of knowledge is, that wisdom giveth life to them that have it.

Eccl. 10 [2]A wise man's heart is at his right hand; but a fool's heart at his left.

Matt. 6 [22]The light of the body is the eye; if therefore thine eye be single, thy whole body shall be full of light. [23]But if thine eye be evil, thy whole body shall be full of darkness. If therefore the light that is in thee be darkness, how great is that darkness!

1 Cor. 12 [1]Now concerning spiritual gifts, brethren, I would not have you ignorant.

Eph. 1 [18]The eyes of your understanding being enlightened; that ye may know what is the hope of his calling, and what the riches of the glory of his inheritance in the saints.

Jas. 3 [17]But the wisdom that is from above is first pure, then peaceable, gentle, and easy to be entreated, full of mercy and good fruits, without partiality and without hypocrisy.

Wisdom to Be Found in Scripture

Psa. 19 [11]Moreover by them is thy servant warned; and in keeping of them there is great reward.

Psa. 119 [98]Thou through thy commandments hast made me wiser than mine enemies; for they are ever with me. [99]I have more understanding than all my teachers: for thy testimonies are my meditation. [100]I understand more than the ancients, because I keep thy precepts.

Prov. 1 [2]To know wisdom and instruction; to perceive the words of understanding; [3]To receive the instruction of wisdom, justice, and judgment, and equity; [4]To give subtilty to the simple, to the young man knowledge and discretion.

Matt. 13 [51]Jesus saith unto them, Have ye understood all these things? They say unto him, Yea, Lord. [52]Then said he unto them, Therefore every scribe which is instructed unto the kingdom of heaven, is like unto a man that is a householder, which bringeth forth out of his treasure things new and old.

Mark 12 [24]And Jesus answering said unto them, Do ye not therefore err, because ye know not the Scriptures, neither the power of God?

1 Cor. 10 [11]Now all these things happened unto them for ensamples: and they are written for our admonition upon whom the ends of the world are come.

Eph. 3 [4]Whereby, when ye read, ye may understand my knowledge in the mystery of Christ.

Worldly Wisdom Foolishness with God

1 Cor. 1 [19]For it is written, I will destroy the wisdom of the wise, and will bring to nothing the understanding of the prudent. [20]Where is the wise? where is the scribe? where is the disputer of this world? hath not God made foolish the wisdom of this world? [21]For after that in the wisdom of God the world by wisdom knew not God, it pleased God by the foolishness of preaching to save them that believe. [22]For the Jews require a sign, and the Greeks seek after wisdom.

1 Cor. 2 [6]Howbeit we speak wisdom among them that are perfect: yet not the wisdom of this world, nor of the princes of this world, that come to nought.

1 Cor. 3 [18]Let no man deceive himself. If any man among you seemeth to be wise in this world, let him become a fool, that he may be wise. [19]For the wisdom of this world is foolishness with God: for it is written, He taketh the wise in their own craftiness. [20]And again, The Lord knoweth the thoughts of the wise, that they are vain.

Wisdom as Ability

Ex. 31 [3]And I have filled him with the spirit of God, in wisdom, and in understanding, and in knowledge, and in all manner of workmanship, [4]To devise cunning works, to work in gold, and in silver, and in brass, [5]And in cutting of stones, to set them, and in carving of timber, to work in all manner of workmanship. [6]And I, behold, I have given with him Aholiab the son of Ahisamach, of the tribe of Dan: and in the hearts of all that are wise hearted I have put wisdom, that they may make all that I have commanded thee;

1 Kin. 7 [14]He was a widow's son of the tribe of Naphtali, and his father was a man of Tyre, a worker in brass: and he was filled with wisdom, and understanding, and cunning to work all works in brass.

See Ex. 35:31-35; 36:1, 2; 2 Chr. 2:14

Wise Men

Gen. 41 [8]And it came to pass in the morning that his spirit was troubled; and he sent and called for all the magicians of Egypt, and all the wise men thereof: and Pharaoh told them his dream; but there was none that could interpret them unto Pharaoh.

Ex. 7 [11]Then Pharaoh also called the wise men and the sorcerers: now the magicians of Egypt, they also did in like manner with their enchantments.

1 Kin. 3 [12]Behold, I have done according to thy word: lo, I have given thee a wise and an understanding heart; so that there was none like thee before thee, neither after thee shall any arise like unto thee.

Esth. 1 [13]Then the king said to the wise men, which knew the times, (for so was the king's manner toward all that knew law and judgment:

Eccl. 12 [9]And moreover, because the Preacher was wise, he still taught the people knowledge; yea, he gave good heed, and sought out, and set in order many proverbs.

Matt. 2 [1]Now when Jesus was born in Bethlehem of Judea in the days of Herod the king, behold, there came wise men from the east to Jerusalem, [2]Saying, Where is he that is born King of the Jews? for we have seen his star in the east, and are come to worship him.

Matt. 23 [34]Wherefore, behold, I send unto you prophets, and wise men, and scribes: and some of them ye shall kill and crucify; and some of them shall ye scourge in your synagogues, and persecute them from city to city.

1 Cor. 1 [19]For it is written, I will destroy the wisdom of the wise, and will bring to nothing the understanding of the prudent.

WITCH, WITCHCRAFT

[wich, wich'kraft] In modern times, a witch is usually thought of as a woman who has made a compact with the devil or other evil spirits which enables her to work injury and misfortune on people through the use of magic spells and incantations. In Biblical times, however, a "witch" was a person who practiced the art of divination, that is, one who was regarded as being able to summon spirits from the dead in order to ask questions of them.

"Witchcraft" may refer either to divination or to sorcery, the practice of the magician's art. Individuals who practiced sorcery were believed to possess superhuman power over living creatures, including men, and over nature and natural objects as well.

SCRIPTURE

Witches

Ex. 22 [18]Thou shalt not suffer a witch to live.

Deut. 18 [10]There shall not be found among you any one that maketh his son or his daughter to pass through the fire, or that useth divination, or an observer of times, or an enchanter, or a witch.

1 Sam. 28 [7]Then said Saul unto his servants, Seek me a woman that hath a familiar spirit, that I may go to her, and inquire of her. And his servants said to him, Behold, there is a woman that hath a familiar spirit at Endor. [8]And Saul disguised himself, and put on other raiment, and he went, and two men with him, and they came to the woman by night: and he said, I pray thee, divine unto me by the familiar spirit, and bring me him up, whom I shall name unto thee. [9]And the woman said unto him, Behold, thou knowest what Saul hath done, how he hath cut off those that have familiar spirits, and the wizards, out of the land: wherefore then layest thou a snare for my life, to cause me to die? [10]And Saul sware to her by the LORD, saying, As the LORD liveth, there shall no punishment happen to thee for this thing. [11]Then said the woman, Whom shall I bring up unto thee? And he said, Bring me up Samuel. [12]And when the woman saw Samuel, she cried with a loud voice: and the woman spake to Saul, saying, Why hast thou deceived me? for thou art Saul. [13]And the king said unto her, Be not afraid: for what sawest thou? And the woman said unto Saul, I saw gods ascending out of the earth. [14]And he said unto her, What form is he of? And she said, An old man cometh up; and he is covered with a mantle. And Saul perceived that it was Samuel, and he stooped with his face to the ground, and bowed himself.

Witchcraft

1 Sam. 15 [23]For rebellion is as the sin of witchcraft, and stubbornness is as iniquity and idolatry.

2 Kin. 9 [22]And it came to pass, when Joram saw Jehu, that he said, Is it peace, Jehu? And he answered, What peace, so long as the whoredoms of thy mother Jezebel and her witchcrafts are so many?

2 Chr. 33 [6]And he caused his children to pass through the fire in the valley of the son of Hinnom: also he observed times, and used enchantments, and used witchcraft, and dealt with a familiar spirit, and with wizards: he wrought much evil in the sight of the LORD, to provoke him to anger.

Isa. 47 [9]But these two things shall come to thee in a moment in one day, the loss of children, and widowhood: they shall come upon thee in their perfection for the multitude of thy sorceries, and for the great abundance of thine enchantments.

Mic. 5 [12]And I will cut off witchcrafts out of thine hand; and thou shalt have no more soothsayers:

Acts 8 [9]But there was a certain man, called Simon, which beforetime in the same city used sorcery, and bewitched the people of Samaria, giving out that himself was some great one: [10]To whom they all gave heed, from the least to the greatest, saying, This man is the great power of God. [11]And to him they had regard because that of long time he had bewitched them with sorceries.

Gal. 5 [19]Now the works of the flesh are manifest, which are these, Adultery, fornication, uncleanness, lasciviousness, [20]Idolatry, witchcraft, hatred, variance, emulations, wrath, strife, seditions, heresies,

WITNESS

[wit′nes] This word is used in the Bible of inanimate objects, such as a heap of stones or a pillar erected as a formal attestation to a covenant or other transaction between individuals. The word is used more frequently in our modern sense of one who testifies regarding a matter before a court of law. According to Israelite law, it was necessary to have at least two witnesses to substantiate an accusation against a person (*Deut. 17:6; 19:15*). Each witness was heard separately and if their testimony was contradictory, their witness was not considered valid. If an individual was sentenced to death by stoning, the witnesses were required to lay their hands on the head of the condemned, signifying the gravity of their responsibility in presenting testimony resulting in the death penalty. The giving of false testimony in court was prohibited in the ninth commandment of the Decalogue (*see* DECALOGUE); the person guilty of such an offence was liable to the punishment intended for the individual falsely accused. Despite these prohibitions, false witnessing was apparently a common sin of the Israelites. In the New Testament, the word sometimes has the sense of martyr.

SCRIPTURE

General

Gen. 31 44 Now therefore come thou, let us make a covenant, I and thou; and let it be for a witness between me and thee. 45 And Jacob took a stone, and set it up for a pillar. 46 And Jacob said unto his brethren, Gather stones; and they took stones, and made a heap: and they did eat there upon the heap. 48 And Laban said, This heap is a witness between me and thee this day. Therefore was the name of it called Galeed, 49 And Mizpah; for he said, The LORD watch between me and thee, when we are absent one from another. 50 If thou shalt afflict my daughters, or if thou shalt take other wives besides my daughters, no man is with us; see, God is witness betwixt me and thee. 51 And Laban said to Jacob, Behold this heap, and behold this pillar, which I have cast betwixt me and thee; 52 This heap be witness, and this pillar be witness, that I will not pass over this heap to thee, and that thou shalt not pass over this heap and this pillar unto me, for harm.

Deut. 17 6 At the mouth of two witnesses, or three witnesses, shall he that is worthy of death be put to death; but at the mouth of one witness he shall not be put to death.

Deut. 19 15 One witness shall not rise up against a man for any iniquity, or for any sin, in any sin that he sinneth: at the mouth of two witnesses, or at the mouth of three witnesses, shall the matter be established.

False Witnessing Prohibited

Ex. 20 16 Thou shalt not bear false witness against thy neighbour.

Deut. 19 16 If a false witness rise up against any man to testify against him that which is wrong; 17 Then both the men, between whom the controversy is, shall stand before the LORD, before the priests and the judges, which shall be in those days; 18 And the judges shall make diligent inquisition: and, behold, if the witness be a false witness, and hath testified falsely against his brother; 19 Then shall ye do unto him, as he had thought to have done unto his brother: so shalt thou put the evil away from among you. 20 And those which remain shall hear, and fear, and shall henceforth commit no more any such evil among you. 21 And thine eye shall not pity; but life shall go for life, eye for eye, tooth for tooth, hand for hand, foot for foot.

False Witnessing Common

See above

Martyrs Called Witnesses

Acts 22 20 And when the blood of thy martyr Stephen was shed, I also was standing by, and consenting unto his death, and kept the raiment of them that slew him.

Rev. 2 13 I know thy works, and where thou dwellest, even where Satan's seat is: and thou holdest fast my name, and hast not denied my faith, even in those days wherein Antipas was my faithful martyr, who was slain among you, where Satan dwelleth.

Rev. 17 6 And I saw the woman drunken with the blood of the saints, and with the blood of the martyrs of Jesus: and when I saw her, I wondered with great admiration.

WOMAN

[wŏŏm′an] An adult female person. The social structure of ancient Israel was patriarchal; that is, the authority rested primarily in the husband and father. The principle role of the woman in this society was to bear and care for children and to perform the ordinary tasks of maintaining a household such as cooking, sewing, carrying water, etc. Her position was one of subordination and subjection to the men in her lives, her father and her husband. She married at the instruction and arrangement of her father and could be divorced by her husband if she failed to please him. (*See* DIVORCE) She was not, however, simply a piece of property, as was the case in some ancient societies. The relationship was such as to allow her to retain her individuality, to enjoy a real personal relationship with him, and to experience the kind of love we commonly associate with marriage. Her children were expected to accord her the same respect as that given to their father. On occasion, women engaged in various facets of commercial and political activity such as purchasing real estate (*Prov. 31:16*), making and selling cloth and garments (*Prov. 31:24*), and even serving as a political, spiritual, and military leader for the nation. (*See* DEBORAH)

Women figure prominently in the ministry of Jesus. He healed them, he spoke of them in his sermons and parables, and he in turn was the recipient of their ministrations and financial support. From the New Testament writings, we know they had a plane of considerable, though subordinate, importance in the early church. Women are among those who were cast into prison because of their faith (*Acts 8:3; 9:2*). Numerous women are named in the various epistles of Paul, indicating their rather extensive role in the work of the church. They were allowed to teach other women and, in a discreet manner, give instruction and counsel to men. They were not, however, to preach or teach in the public worship or to engage in other activities which would result in a man's being relegated to a subordinate position (*1 Tim. 2:12; 1 Cor. 14:34-36*). They were to be treated with respect, the older women being thought of as mothers and the younger as sisters, and through their piety and consecration, to exert the nurturing and healing influence of which women alone are capable.

SCRIPTURE

Gen. 2 18 And the LORD God said, It is not good that the man should be alone; I will make him an help meet for him. 21 And the LORD God caused a deep sleep to fall upon Adam, and he slept: and he took one of his ribs, and closed up the flesh instead thereof; 22 And the rib, which the LORD God had taken from man, made he a woman, and brought her unto the man. 23 And Adam said, This is now bone of my bones, and flesh of my flesh: she shall be called Woman, because she was taken out of Man. 24 Therefore shall a man leave his father and his mother, and shall cleave unto his wife: and they shall be one flesh.

Gen. 3 16 Unto the woman he said, I will greatly multiply thy sorrow and thy conception; in sorrow thou shalt bring forth children; and thy desire shall be to thy husband, and he shall rule over thee.

Prov. 11 16 A gracious woman retaineth honour: 22 As a jewel of gold in a swine's snout, so is a fair woman which is without discretion.

Prov. 12 4 A virtuous woman is a crown to her husband: but she that maketh ashamed is as rottenness in his bones.

Prov. 14 1 Every wise woman buildeth her house: but the foolish plucketh it down with her hands.

Prov. 31 10 Who can find a virtuous woman? for her price is far above rubies. 11 The heart of her husband doth safely trust in her, so that he shall have no need of spoil. 12 She will do him good and not evil all the days of her life. 13 She seeketh wool, and flax, and worketh willingly with her hands. 14 She is like the merchants' ships; she bringeth her food from afar. 15 She riseth also while it is yet night, and giveth meat to her household, and a portion to her maidens. 16She considereth a field, and buyeth it: with the fruit of her hands she planteth a vineyard. 17She girdeth her loins with strength, and strengtheneth her arms. 18She perceiveth that her merchandise is good: her candle goeth not out by night. 19She layeth her hands to the spindle, and her hands hold the distaff. 20She stretcheth out her hand to the poor; yea, she reacheth forth her hands to the needy. 21She is not afraid of the snow for her household: for all her household are clothed with scarlet. 22She maketh herself coverings of tapestry; her clothing is silk and purple. 23Her husband is known in the gates, when he sitteth among the elders of the land. 24She maketh fine linen, and selleth it; and delivereth girdles unto the merchant. 25Strength and honour are her clothing; and she shall rejoice in time to come. 26She openeth her mouth with wisdom; and in her tongue is the law of kindness. 27She looketh well to the ways of her household, and eateth not the bread of idleness. 28Her children arise up, and call her blessed; her husband also, and he praiseth her. 29Many daughters have done virtuously, but thou excellest them all. 30Favour is deceitful, and beauty is vain: but a woman that feareth the LORD, she shall be praised. 31Give her of the fruit of her hands; and let her own works praise her in the gates.

1 Cor. 11 3But I would have you know, that the head of every man is Christ; and the head of the woman is the man; and the head of Christ is God. 4Every man praying or prophesying, having his head covered, dishonoureth his head. 5But every woman that prayeth or prophesieth with her head uncovered dishonoureth her head: for that is even all one as if she were shaven. 6For if the woman be not covered, let her also be shorn: but if it be a shame for a woman to be shorn or shaven, let her be covered. 7For a man indeed ought not to cover his head, forasmuch as he is the image and glory of God: but the woman is the glory of the man. 8For the man is not of the woman; but the woman of the man. 9Neither was the man created for the woman; but the woman for the man. 10For this cause ought the woman to have power on her head because of the angels. 11Nevertheless neither is the man without the woman, neither the woman without the man, in the Lord. 12For as the woman is of the man, even so is the man also by the woman; but all things of God. 13Judge in yourselves: is it comely that a woman pray unto God uncovered? 14Doth not even nature itself teach you, that, if a man have long hair, it is a shame unto him? 15But if a woman have long hair, it is a glory to her: for her hair is given her for a covering.

1 Cor. 14 34Let your women keep silence in the churches: for it is not permitted unto them to speak; but they are commanded to be under obedience, as also saith the law. 35And if they will learn any thing, let them ask their husbands at home: for it is a shame for women to speak in the church.

1 Tim. 2 9In like manner also, that women adorn themselves in modest apparel, with shamefacedness and sobriety; not with broided hair, or gold, or pearls, or costly array; 10But (which becometh women professing godliness) with good works. 11Let the woman learn in silence with all subjection. 12But I suffer not a woman to teach, nor to usurp authority over the man, but to be in silence. 13For Adam was first formed, then Eve. 14And Adam was not deceived, but the woman

being deceived was in the transgression.
[15]Notwithstanding she shall be saved in
childbearing, if they continue in faith and
charity and holiness with sobriety.

See Psa. 68:11

WORKS

[wûrks] In the gospel according to John, "works" usually refers to the miracles of Jesus. Paul and James use the word in a special sense to denote the performance of certain outward acts by which men seek to be accepted of God. Paul contrasts these works with the faith in Christ through which the believer is justified apart from all works of merit. James makes it clear, however, that vital faith will always manifest itself in "works" and that without such a manifestation, faith is dead. Other passages make it clear that the performance of good "works" are an evidence of the new life in Christ.

See LABOR

SCRIPTURE

The Works of Jesus

John 5 [36]But I have greater witness
than that of John: for the works which the
Father hath given me to finish, the same
works that I do, bear witness of me, that
the Father hath sent me.
John 10 [38]But if I do, though ye believe
not me, believe the works: that ye may
know, and believe, that the Father is in
me, and I in him.

Salvation Not by Works

Rom. 3 [27]Where is boasting then? It is
excluded. By what law? of works? Nay:
but by the law of faith.
Rom. 4 [2]For if Abraham were justified
by works, he hath whereof to glory; but
not before God. [6]Even as David also describeth the blessedness of the man, unto
whom God imputeth righteousness without works,
Gal. 2 [16]Knowing that a man is not justified by the works of the law, but by the
faith of Jesus Christ, even we have believed in Jesus Christ, that we might be
justified by the faith of Christ, and not by
the works of the law: for by the works of
the law shall no flesh be justified.
Gal. 3 [2]This only would I learn of you,
Received ye the Spirit by the works of the
law, or by the hearing of faith? [5]He therefore that ministereth to you the Spirit, and
worketh miracles among you, doeth he it
by the works of the law, or by the hearing
of faith? [10]For as many as are of the works
of the law are under the curse: for it is
written, Cursed is every one that continueth not in all things which are written in
the book of the law to do them.
Heb. 9 [14]How much more shall the
blood of Christ, who through the eternal
Spirit offered himself without spot to God,
purge your conscience from dead works
to serve the living God?

True Faith Accompanied by Works

Matt. 16 [27]For the Son of man shall
come in the glory of his Father with his
angels; and then he shall reward every
man according to his works.
Rom. 2 [6]Who will render to every man
according to his deeds:
2 Cor. 9 [8]And God is able to make all
grace abound toward you; that ye, always
having all sufficiency in all things, may
abound to every good work:
Gal. 5 [6]For in Jesus Christ neither circumcision availeth any thing, nor uncircumcision; but faith which worketh by
love.
Eph. 2 [10]For we are his workmanship,
created in Christ Jesus unto good works,
which God hath before ordained that we
should walk in them.
Col. 1 [10]That ye might walk worthy of

the Lord unto all pleasing, being fruitful in every good work, and increasing in the knowledge of God;

1 Thess. 1 [3]Remembering without ceasing your work of faith, and labour of love, and patience of hope in our Lord Jesus Christ, in the sight of God and our Father;

2 Thess. 2 [17]Comfort your hearts, and stablish you in every good word and work.

Jas. 2 [14]What doth it profit, my brethren, though a man say he hath faith, and have not works? can faith save him? [15]If a brother or sister be naked, and destitute of daily food, [16]And one of you say unto them, Depart in peace, be ye warmed and filled; notwithstanding ye give them not those things which are needful to the body; what doth it profit?

1 Pet. 1 [17]And if ye call on the Father, who without respect of persons judgeth according to every man's work, pass the time of your sojourning here in fear:

WORSHIP

[wûr'ship] Act of paying honors to a deity; religious reverence and homage. In primitive times men conceived of their gods as in some respects like themselves, with similar needs and appetites. Worship of these deities was designed to meet the needs they were believed to have. The effects of this primitive conception is seen in the worship of ancient Israel, with its elaborate sacrificial system. (*See* SACRIFICE) Gradually there developed the awareness of the importance of the inward spiritual attitude of the worshipper, and worship came to be conceived of as a spiritual service to God. In ancient times, worship was offered wherever God was known to have appeared, resulting in numerous sacrifices throughout the land, many of which became corrupted through contact with local idolatry. With the building of the Temple, Jerusalem came to be regarded as the only legitimate place of worship. There is good reason to believe that the opposition of the prophets to the worship of Northern Israel after the division in 922 BC (*see* ISRAEL) was directed as much against worship in a place other than the central sanctuary as against the idolatrous practices of these northern sanctuaries. (*See* JEROBOAM) During and after the Babylonian exile the synagogues gained in importance as centers of Jewish religion, but as long as the temple stood, they remained primarily places of instruction rather than worship. For further discussion of the worship of Israel, see FEASTS AND FESTIVALS, MUSIC, PRIESTHOOD, SABBATH, and SACRIFICE.

Early Christian worship consisted mainly in preaching and teaching, prayers, and the Eucharist, or Lord's Supper (*Acts 2:42, 46*). The preaching and teaching consisted of instruction concerning the life of Jesus, exposition of scripture, and instruction in ethical matters; it is doubtful the missionary sermons of the early evangelists were delivered in the context of the worship of the Christian community. (*See* PREACHING) The prayers were frequently spontaneous, but the use of the Lord's Prayer and other short liturgical prayers such as "Maranatha" (Come, Lord!—*1 Cor. 16:22; Rev. 22:20*) are well attested to in the Bible and other early Christian literature. In addition, we know that the entire congregation spoke the Amen at the end of prayers (*1 Cor. 14:16; 2 Cor. 1:20*). The primary event of meetings for Christian worship seems to have been the celebration of the Lord's Supper, which sometimes took place in the setting of an actual meal. (*See* LORD'S SUPPER) Other elements of early Christian worship were singing (*Eph. 5:19; Col. 3:16; see* MUSIC), giving (*1 Cor. 16:2*), prophecy (*1 Cor. 14:26, 29, 32*), and speaking in and interpretation of tongues (*1 Cor. 14, see* TONGUES). The aim of this worship was to praise God and to strengthen and develop the body of Christ in the community.

See LORD'S DAY

SCRIPTURE

Worship in the Old Testament

2 Kin. 17 [36]But the LORD, who brought you up out of the land of Egypt with great power and a stretched out arm, him shall ye fear, and him shall ye worship, and to him shall ye do sacrifice.

1 Chr. 16 [29]Give unto the LORD the

glory due unto his name: bring an offering, and come before him: worship the LORD in the beauty of holiness.

2 Chr. 5 [13]It came even to pass, as the trumpeters and singers were as one, to make one sound to be heard in praising and thanking the LORD; and when they lifted up their voice with the trumpets and cymbals and instruments of musick, and praised the LORD, saying, For he is good; for his mercy endureth for ever: that then the house was filled with a cloud, even the house of the LORD; [14]So that the priests could not stand to minister by reason of the cloud: for the glory of the LORD had filled the house of God.

2 Chr. 7 [1]Now when Solomon had made an end of praying, the fire came down from heaven, and consumed the burnt offering and the sacrifices; and the glory of the LORD filled the house.

2 Chr. 30 [27]Then the priests the Levites arose and blessed the people: and their voice was heard, and their prayer came up to his holy dwelling place, even unto heaven.

Psa. 22 [22]I will declare thy name unto my brethren: in the midst of the congregation will I praise thee.

Psa. 24 [3]Who shall ascend into the hill of the LORD? or who shall stand in his holy place? [4]He that hath clean hands, and a pure heart; who hath not lifted up his soul unto vanity, nor sworn deceitfully.

Psa. 29 [2]Give unto the LORD the glory due unto his name; worship the LORD in the beauty of holiness.

Psa. 35 [18]I will give thee thanks in the great congregation: I will praise thee among much people.

Psa. 66 [4]All the earth shall worship thee, and shall sing unto thee; they shall sing to thy name. [13]I will go into thy house with burnt offerings: I will pay thee my vows, [14]Which my lips have uttered, and my mouth hath spoken, when I was in trouble.

Psa. 100 [1]Make a joyful noise unto the LORD, all ye lands. [2]Serve the LORD with gladness: come before his presence with singing. [3]Know ye that the LORD he is God: it is he that hath made us, and not we ourselves; we are his people, and the sheep of his pasture. [4]Enter into his gates with thanksgiving, and into his courts with praise: be thankful unto him, and bless his name. [5]For the LORD is good; his mercy is everlasting; and his truth endureth to all generations.

Psa. 122 [1]I was glad when they said unto me, Let us go into the house of the LORD.

Psa. 138 [2]I will worship toward thy holy temple, and praise thy name for thy lovingkindness and for thy truth: for thou hast magnified thy word above all thy name.

Psa. 149 [1]Sing unto the LORD a new song, and his praise in the congregation of saints.

Isa. 1 [11]To what purpose is the multitude of your sacrifices unto me? saith the LORD: I am full of the burnt offerings of rams, and the fat of fed beasts; and I delight not in the blood of bullocks, or of lambs, or of he goats. [12]When ye come to appear before me, who hath required this at your hand, to tread my courts? [13]Bring no more vain oblations; incense is an abomination unto me; the new moons and sabbaths, the calling of assemblies, I cannot away with; it is iniquity, even the solemn meeting. [14]Your new moons and your appointed feasts my soul hateth: they are a trouble unto me; I am weary to bear them. [15]And when ye spread forth your hands, I will hide mine eyes from you: yea, when ye make many prayers, I will not hear: your hands are full of blood.

Amos 5 [21]I hate, I despise your feast days, and I will not smell in your solemn assemblies. [22]Though ye offer me burnt offerings and your meat offerings, I will not accept them; neither will I regard the peace offerings of your fat beasts. [23]Take thou away from me the noise of thy songs; for I will not hear the melody of thy viols. [24]But let judgment run down as waters, and righteousness as a mighty stream.

Hab. 2 [20]The LORD is in his holy temple: let all the earth keep silence before him.

See Psa. 29:2; 1 Kin. 8:3-11

Christian Worship

Luke 4 [8]Thou shalt worship the Lord thy God, and him only shalt thou serve.

John 4 [23]The hour cometh, and now is, when the true worshippers shall worship the Father in spirit and in truth: for the Father seeketh such to worship him. [24]God is a Spirit: and they that worship him must worship him in spirit and in truth.

Acts 2 [42]And they continued steadfastly in the apostles' doctrine and fellowship, and in breaking of bread, and in prayers. [46]And they, continuing daily with one accord in the temple, and breaking bread from house to house, did eat their meat with gladness and singleness of heart.

Acts 20 [7]And upon the first day of the week, when the disciples came together to break bread, Paul preached unto them, ready to depart on the morrow; and continued his speech until midnight.

1 Cor. 14 [13]Wherefore let him that speaketh in an unknown tongue pray that he may interpret. [14]For if I pray in an unknown tongue, my spirit prayeth, but my understanding is unfruitful. [15]What is it then? I will pray with the spirit, and I will pray with the understanding also: I will sing with the spirit, and I will sing with the understanding also. [16]Else, when thou shalt bless with the spirit, how shall he that occupieth the room of the unlearned say Amen at thy giving of thanks, seeing he understandeth not what thou sayest? [17]For thou verily givest thanks well, but the other is not edified. [23]If therefore the whole church be come together into one place, and all speak with tongues, and there come in those that are unlearned, or unbelievers, will they not say that ye are mad? [24]But if all prophesy, and there come in one that believeth not, or one unlearned, he is convinced of all, he is judged of all: [25]And thus are the secrets of his heart made manifest; and so falling down on his face he will worship God, and report that God is in you of a truth. [26]How is it then, brethren? when ye come together, every one of you hath a psalm, hath a doctrine, hath a tongue, hath a revelation, hath an interpretation. Let all things be done unto edifying [27]If any man speak in an unknown tongue, let it be by two, or at the most by three, and that by course; and let one interpret. [28]But if there be no interpreter, let him keep silence in the church; and let him speak to himself, and to God. [29]Let the prophets speak two or three, and let the other judge. [30]If any thing be revealed to another that sitteth by, let the first hold his peace. [31]For ye may all prophesy one by one, that all may learn, and all may be comforted. [32]And the spirits of the prophets are subject to the prophets. [33]For God is not the author of confusion, but of peace, as in all churches of the saints. [34]Let your women keep silence in the churches: for it is not permitted unto them to speak; but they are commanded to be under obedience, as also saith the law. [35]And if they will learn anything, let them ask their husbands at home: for it is a shame for women to speak in the church. [40]Let all things be done decently and in order.

1 Cor. 11 [20]When ye come together therefore into one place, this is not to eat the Lord's supper. [21]For in eating every one taketh before other his own supper: and one is hungry, and another is drunken. [22]What? have ye not houses to eat and to drink in? or despise ye the church of God, and shame them that have not? What shall I say to you? shall I praise you in this? I praise you not. [23]For I have received of the Lord that which also I delivered unto you, That the Lord Jesus the same night in which he was betrayed took bread: [24]And when he had given thanks, he brake it, and said, Take, eat: this is my body, which is broken for you: this do in remembrance of me. [25]After the same manner also he took the cup, when he had supped, saying, This cup is the new testament in my blood: this do ye, as oft as ye drink it, in remembrance of me. [26]For as often as ye eat this bread, and drink this cup, ye do shew the Lord's death till he come. [27]Wherefore whosoever shall eat this bread, and drink this cup of the Lord, unworthily, shall be guilty of the body and blood of the Lord. [28]But let a man examine himself, and so let him eat of that bread, and drink of that cup. [29]For he that eateth and drinketh unworthily, eateth and drinketh damnation to himself, not discerning the Lord's body. [30]For this cause many are weak and sickly among you, and many sleep. [31]For if we would judge ourselves, we should not be judged. [32]But when we are judged, we are chastened of the Lord, that we should not be condemned with the world. [33]Wherefore, my brethren, when ye come together to eat, tarry one for another. [34]And if any man hunger, let him eat at home; that ye come not together unto condemnation. And the rest will I set in order when I come.

1 Cor. 16 [2]Upon the first day of the week let every one of you lay by him in store, as God hath prospered him, that there be no gatherings when I come. [22]. . . Maranatha.

Eph. 5 [19]Speaking to yourselves in psalms and hymns and spiritual songs, singing and making melody in your heart to the Lord.

Col. 3 [16]Let the word of Christ dwell in you richly in all wisdom; teaching and admonishing one another in psalms and hymns and spiritual songs, singing with grace in your hearts to the Lord.

WRATH

[rath] This word is used in the Bible to denote several emotions, including anger, grief, bitterness, indignation, and fury. When used of God, wrath refers to his absolute opposition to sin and evil. It is thus not a capricious anger like that of mythological deities, but a constant aspect of his holy and righteous nature. When used of man, however, wrath indicates an unholy emotion to which man should not give vent.

See ANGER

SCRIPTURE

Wrath of God

Num. 11 [1]And when the people complained, it displeased the LORD: and the LORD heard it; and his anger was kindled; and the fire of the LORD burnt among them, and consumed them that were in the uttermost parts of the camp.

Deut. 29 [27]And the anger of the LORD was kindled against this land, to bring upon it all the curses that are written in this book:

2 Sam. 6 [7]And the anger of the LORD

was kindled against Uzzah, and God smote him there for his error; and there he died by the ark of God.

Psa. 79 [6]Pour out thy wrath upon the heathen that have not known thee, and upon the kingdoms that have not called upon thy name.

Isa. 5 [25]Therefore is the anger of the LORD kindled against his people, and he hath stretched forth his hand against them, and hath smitten them: and the hills did tremble, and their carcasses were torn in the midst of the streets. For all this his anger is not turned away, but his hand is stretched out still.

Isa. 42 [25]Therefore he hath poured upon him the fury of his anger, and the strength of battle: and it hath set him on fire round about, yet he knew not; and it burned him, yet he laid it not to heart.

Jer. 44 [6]Wherefore my fury and mine anger was poured forth, and was kindled in the cities of Judah and in the streets of Jerusalem; and they are wasted and desolate, as at this day.

Human Wrath

Gen. 4 [6]And the LORD said unto Cain, Why art thou wroth? and why is thy countenance fallen?

Gen. 49 [7]Cursed be their anger, for it was fierce; and their wrath, for it was cruel:

Prov. 19 [19]A man of great wrath shall suffer punishment: for if thou deliver him, yet thou must do it again.

Matt. 5 [22]But I say unto you, That whosoever is angry with his brother without a cause shall be in danger of the judgment: and whosoever shall say to his brother, Raca, shall be in danger of the council: but whosoever shall say, Thou fool, shall be in danger of hell fire.

Luke 4 [28]And all they in the synagogue, when they heard these things, were filled with wrath,

Rom. 12 [19]Dearly beloved, avenge not yourselves, but rather give place unto wrath: for it is written, Vengeance is mine; I will repay, saith the Lord.

Eph. 4 [26]Be ye angry, and sin not: let not the sun go down upon your wrath: [31]Let all bitterness, and wrath, and anger, and clamour, and evil speaking, be put away from you, with all malice:

Eph. 6 [4]And, ye fathers, provoke not your children to wrath: but bring them up in the nurture and admonition of the Lord.

Col. 3 [8]But now ye also put off all these; anger, wrath, malice, blasphemy, filthy communication out of your mouth. [19]Husbands, love your wives, and be not bitter against them.

ZACCHAEUS

[zak kē′us] A collector of taxes, Zacchaeus was short in stature and climbed a sycamore tree in order to see Jesus as he passed. To reward him for his determination, Jesus visited in his home.

SCRIPTURE

Luke 19 [1]And Jesus entered and passed through Jericho. [2]And, behold, there was a man named Zacchaeus, which was the chief among the publicans, and he was rich. [3]And he sought to see Jesus who he was; and could not for the press, because he was little of stature. [4]And he ran before, and climbed up into a sycamore tree to see him: for he was to pass that way. [5]And when Jesus came to the place, he looked up, and saw him, and said unto him, Zacchaeus, make haste, and come down; for to day I must abide at thy house. [6]And he made haste, and came down, and received him joyfully. [7]And when they saw it, they all murmured, saying, That he was gone to be guest with a man that is a sinner. [8]And Zacchaeus stood, and said unto the Lord; Behold, Lord, the half of my goods I give to the poor; and if I have taken any thing from any man by false accusation, I restore him fourfold. [9]And Jesus said unto him, This day is salvation come to this house, forsomuch as he also is a son of Abraham. [10]For the Son of man is come to seek and to save that which was lost.

ZACHARIAS

[zak a rī′as] The father of John the Baptist and a priest of the "course of Abijah," one of the groups into which the priests were divided for purposes of arranging their service in the temple. Zacharias, with his wife Elisabeth, is described as "righteous before God, walking in all the commandments and ordinances of the Lord blameless" (*Luke 1:6*). On one occasion when it was the turn of the division of Abijah to serve in the temple, Zacharias was burning incense and was confronted by the angel Gabriel, who announced to him that Elisabeth would bear a son. Since Elisabeth was barren and well past the normal age of child-bearing, Zacharias could hardly believe the words of the angel and for his skepticism was struck dumb. At the birth of the child, Zacharias complied with the instructions of the angel and insisted that the child be named John, although no one else in the family bore this name. When this was agreed upon, Zacharias recovered his speech and uttered the hymn usually referred to as *Benedictus*.

See John the Baptist, Gabriel

SCRIPTURE

Luke 1 [5]There was in the days of Herod, the king of Judaea, a certain priest named Zacharias, of the course of Abia: and his wife was of the daughters of Aaron, and her name was Elisabeth. [6]And they were both righteous before God, walking in all the commandments and ordinances of the Lord blameless. [7]And they had no child, because that Elisabeth was barren, and they both were now well stricken in years. [8]And it came to pass, that while he executed the priest's office before God in the order of his course, [9]According to the custom of the priest's office, his lot was to burn incense when he went into the temple of the Lord. [10]And the whole multitude of the people were praying without at the time of incense. [11]And there appeared unto him an angel of the Lord standing on the right side of the altar of incense. [12]And when Zacharias saw him, he was troubled, and fear fell upon him. [13]But the angel said unto him, Fear not, Zacharias: for thy prayer is heard; and thy wife Elisabeth shall bear thee a son, and thou shalt call his name John. [18]And Zacharias said unto the angel, Whereby shall I know this? for I am an old man, and my wife well stricken in years. [19]And the angel answering said unto him, I am Gabriel, that stand in the presence of God; and am sent to speak unto thee, and to shew thee these glad tidings. [20]And, behold, thou shalt be dumb, and not able to speak, until the day that these things shall be performed, because thou believest not my words, which shall be fulfilled in their season. [21]And the people waited for Zacharias, and marvelled that he tarried so long in the temple. [22]And when he came out, he could not speak unto them: and they perceived that he had seen a vision in the temple: for he beckoned unto them, and remained speechless. [23]And it came to pass, that, as soon as the days of his ministration were accomplished, he departed to his own house. [24]And after those days his wife Elisabeth conceived, [57]Now Elisabeth's full time came that she should be delivered; and she brought forth a son. [58]And her neighbours and her cousins heard how the Lord had shewed great mercy upon her; and they rejoiced with her. [59]And it

came to pass, that on the eighth day they came to circumcise the child; and they called him Zacharias, after the name of his father.
60And his mother answered and said, Not so; but he shall be called John.
61And they said unto her, There is none of thy kindred that is called by this name.
62And they made signs to his father, how he would have him called.
63And he asked for a writing table, and wrote, saying, His name is John. And they marvelled all.
64And his mouth was opened immediately, and his tongue loosed, and he spake, and praised God.

ZADOK, ZADOKITES

[zā′dok, zā′do kīts] Several individuals in the Bible bear this name. The most important of these was the direct descendant of Aaron who, with Abiathar, served as co-high priest at the court of David (*2 Sam. 8:17*). During the rebellion of Absalom, Zadok had charge of the Ark of the Covenant (*2 Sam. 15:24-25*). In the power struggle which arose over the succession to David's throne, Zadok supported Solomon over against the claims of Adonijah, who was supported by Abiathar. By virtue of having chosen correctly in this matter, Zadok and his descendants held the high-priestly duties in Solomon's temple until its destruction in 587 BC. Ezekiel claims that the Zadokites were the only priestly family which did not commit apostasy during the period of the monarchy (*Ezek. 44:15-31*). In the second temple (*see* TEMPLE), the Zadokites retained their position until 171 BC. The Qumran community, made famous by the Dead Sea Scrolls, remained loyal to the Zadokite priesthood and looked forward to its restoration.

SCRIPTURE

High Priest in David's Time

2 Sam. 19
11And king David sent to Zadok and to Abiathar the priests, saying, speak unto the elders of Judah, saying, Why are ye the last to bring the king back to his house? seeing the speech of all Israel is come to the king, even to his house.

Has Charge of the Ark

2 Sam. 15
24And lo Zadok also, and all the Levites were with him, bearing the ark of the covenant of God: and they set down the ark of God; and Abiathar went up, until all the people had done passing out of the city.
25And the king said unto Zadok, Carry back the ark of God into the city: if I shall find favour in the eyes of the LORD, he will bring me again, and shew me both it, and his habitation:
26But if he thus say, I have no delight in thee; behold, here am I, let him do to me as seemeth good unto him.
27The king said also unto Zadok the priest, Art not thou a seer? return into the city in peace, and your two sons with you, Ahimaaz thy son, and Jonathan the son of Abiathar.
28See, I will tarry in the plain of the wilderness, until there come word from you to certify me.
29Zadok therefore and Abiathar carried the ark of God again to Jerusalem: and they tarried there.

Stands with Solomon in Struggle for David's Throne

1 Kin. 1
8But Zadok the priest, and Benaiah the son of Jehoiada, and Nathan the prophet, and Shimei, and Rei, and the mighty men which belonged to David, were not with Adonijah.

26But me, even me thy servant, and Zadok the priest, and Benaiah the son of Jehoiada, and thy servant Solomon, hath he not called.

32And king David said, Call me Zadok the priest, and Nathan the prophet, and Benaiah the son of Jehoiada. And they came before the king.
33The king also said unto them, Take with you the servants of your lord, and cause Solomon my son to ride upon mine own mule, and bring him

down to Gihon: [34]And let Zadok the priest and Nathan the prophet anoint him there king over Israel: and blow ye with the trumpet, and say, God save king Solomon. [35]Then ye shall come up after him, that he may come and sit upon my throne; for he shall be king in my stead: and I have appointed him to be ruler over Israel and over Judah. [36]And Benaiah the son of Jehoiada answered the king, and said, Amen: the LORD God of my lord the king say so too. [37]As the LORD hath been with my lord the king, even so be he with Solomon, and make his throne greater than the throne of my lord king David. [38]So Zadok the priest, and Nathan the prophet, and Benaiah the son of Jehoiada, and the Cherethites, and the Pelethites, went down, and caused Solomon to ride upon king David's mule, and brought him to Gihon. [39]And Zadok the priest took a horn of oil out of the tabernacle, and anointed Solomon. And they blew the trumpet; and all the people said, God save king Solomon. [40]And all the people came up after him, and the people piped with pipes, and rejoiced with great joy, so that the earth rent with the sound of them.

[44]And the king hath sent with him Zadok the priest, and Nathan the prophet, and Benaiah the son of Jehoiada, and the Cherethites, and the Pelethites, and they have caused him to ride upon the king's mule: [45]And Zadok the priest and Nathan the prophet have anointed him king in Gihon: and they are come up from thence rejoicing, so that the city rang again. This is the noise that ye have heard.

The Sole High Priest under Solomon

1 Kin. 2 [35]And the king put Benaiah the son of Jehoiada in his room over the host: and Zadok the priest did the king put in the room of Abiathar.

ZEAL

[zēl] Ardor in the pursuit of anything; ardent and active interest; enthusiasm; fervor. The Bible contains numerous examples of religious zeal.

SCRIPTURE

1 Chr. 29 [17]In the uprightness of mine heart I have willingly offered all these things: and now have I seen with joy thy people, which are present here, to offer willingly unto thee.

Psa. 42 [1]As the hart panteth after the water brooks, so panteth my soul after thee, O God. [2]My soul thirsteth for God, for the living God: when shall I come and appear before God?

Psa. 119 [139]My zeal hath consumed me, because mine enemies have forgotten thy words.

Matt. 5 [16]Let your light so shine before men, that they may see your good works, and glorify your Father which is in heaven.

Luke 22 [33]And he said unto him, Lord, I am ready to go with thee, both into prison, and to death.

John 9 [4]I must work the works of him that sent me, while it is day: the night cometh, when no man can work.

Acts 26 [19]I was not disobedient unto the heavenly vision. [20]But shewed first unto them of Damascus, and at Jerusalem, and throughout all the coasts of Judaea, and then to the Gentiles, that they should repent and turn to God, and do works meet for repentance. [22]Having therefore obtained help of God, I continue unto this day, witnessing both to small and great, saying none other things than those which the prophets and Moses did say should come. [23]That Christ should suffer, and that he should be the first that should rise from the dead, and should shew light unto the people, and to the Gentiles. [29]And

Paul said, I would to God, that not only thou, but also all that hear me this day, were both almost, and altogether such as I am, except these bonds.

Rom. 1 [15]So, as much as in me is, I am ready to preach the gospel to you that are at Rome also.

Rom. 15 [20]Yea, so have I strived to preach the gospel, not where Christ was named, lest I should build upon another man's foundation.

1 Cor. 14 [12]Even so ye, forasmuch as ye are zealous of spiritual gifts, seek that ye may excel to the edifying of the church.

1 Cor. 15 [58]Therefore, my beloved brethren, be ye stedfast, unmovable, always abounding in the work of the Lord, forasmuch as ye know that your labour is not in vain in the Lord.

2 Cor. 7 [11]For behold this selfsame thing, that ye sorrowed after a godly sort, what carefulness it wrought in you, yea, what clearing of yourselves, yea, what indignation, yea, what fear, yea, what vehement desire, yea, what zeal, yea, what revenge! In all things ye have approved yourselves to be clear in this matter.

Gal. 4 [18]But it is good to be zealously affected always in a good thing.

Gal. 6 [9]Let us not be weary in well doing: for in due season we shall reap, if we faint not.

Tit. 2 [14]Who gave himself for us, that he might redeem us from all iniquity, and purify unto himself a peculiar people, zealous of good works.

Rev. 3 [19]As many as I love, I rebuke and chasten: be zealous therefore and repent.

Zeal Without Knowledge

Rom. 10 [2]For I bear them record that they have a zeal of God, but not according to knowledge. [3]For they being ignorant of God's righteousness, and going about to establish their own righteousness, have not submitted themselves unto the righteousness of God.

Gal. 1 [13]For ye have heard of my conversation in time past in the Jews' religion, how that beyond measure I persecuted the church of God, and wasted it: [14]And profited in the Jews' religion above many my equals in mine own nation, being more exceedingly zealous of the traditions of my fathers.

Gal. 4 [17]They zealously affect you, but not well; yea, they would exclude you, that ye might affect them.

Phil. 1 [15]Some indeed preach Christ even of envy and strife; and some also of good will: [16]The one preach Christ of contention, not sincerely, supposing to add affliction to my bonds: [17]But the other of love, knowing that I am set for the defence of the gospel.

ZECHARIAH (The King)

[zek a rī'a] The son of Jeroboam II and fourteenth king of Israel. Jeroboam II had raised the kingdom to a height unmatched since the time of Solomon, the new sovereign was, however, given little opportunity to demonstrate his worth as a successor to his illustrious father, as he was publicly assassinated by the usurper Shallum after ruling only six months (c. 748 BC).

See KINGS, JEROBOAM II, SHALLUM

SCRIPTURE

2 Kin. 15 [8]In the thirty and eighth year of Azariah king of Judah did Zachariah the son of Jeroboam reign over Israel in Samaria six months. [9]And he did that which was evil in the sight of the LORD, as his fathers had done: he departed not from the sins of Jeroboam the son of Nebat, who made Israel to sin. [10]And Shallum the son of Jabesh conspired against him, and smote him before the people, and slew him, and reigned in his stead. [11]And the rest of the acts of Zachariah, behold, they are written in the book of the Chronicles of the kings of Israel. [12]This was the word of the LORD which he spake unto Jehu, saying, Thy sons shall sit on the throne of Israel unto the fourth generation. And so it came to pass.

ZECHARIAH (The Prophet)

[zek a rī'a] A prophet of the early post-exilic period, the son of Berechiah and the grandson of Iddo. Zechariah apparently was born in Babylon and returned to Jerusalem sixteen years previous to the time of his ministry in the group led by Zerubbabel. He was a contemporary of Haggai and began his ministry two months after that prophet had begun his, in 520 BC. The work of rebuilding the temple was already in progress. The purpose of Zechariah's preaching was to join Haggai in the task of encouraging the construction of the temple and to see it through to its completion. He and Haggai deserve much credit for the rebuilt edifice. Zechariah met his task with reproof for shortcomings, encouragement and exhortations, promises of God's blessing and statements looking forward to the Messianic era.

See HAGGAI, TEMPLE

SCRIPTURE

Supports Rebuilding of the Temple

Ezra 5 [1]Then the prophets, Haggai the prophet, and Zechariah the son of Iddo, prophesied unto the Jews that were in Judah and Jerusalem in the name of the God of Israel, even unto them. [2]Then rose up Zerubbabel the son of Shealtiel, and Jeshua the son of Jozadak, and began to build the house of God which is at Jerusalem: and with them were the prophets of God helping them.

Ezra 6 [14]And the elders of the Jews builded, and they prospered through the prophesying of Haggai the prophet and Zechariah the son of Iddo. And they builded, and finished it, according to the commandment of the God of Israel, and according to the commandment of Cyrus, and Darius, and Artaxerxes king of Persia.

Prophecies of the Messianic Era

Zech. 9 [9]Rejoice greatly, O daughter of Zion; shout, O daughter of Jerusalem: behold, thy King cometh unto thee: he is just, and having salvation; lowly, and riding upon an ass, and upon a colt the foal of an ass. [10]And I will cut off the chariot from Ephraim, and the horse from Jerusalem, and the battle bow shall be cut off: and he shall speak peace unto the heathen: and his dominion shall be from sea even to sea, and from the river even to the ends of the earth.

[16]And the LORD their God shall save them in that day as the flock of his people: for they shall be as the stones of a crown, lifted up as an ensign upon his land. [17]For how great is his goodness, and how great is his beauty! corn shall make the young men cheerful, and new wine the maids.

ZEDEKIAH (The King)

[zed ê kī'a] The uncle of Jehoiachin and the last king of Judah (597-587 BC), also called Mattaniah. Zedekiah came to the throne after the first great deportation of captives to Babylon in 597 BC had depleted the population of its better elements. He seems to have been a well-meaning but vascillating king who was swayed by the advice of his nobles. Against the constant warnings of the prophet Jeremiah, Zedekiah joined with his neighbors in a plan for rebellion against Babylon. In 588, Nebuchadnezzar set out to deal the final, crushing blow to Judah. Systematically destroying the outlying fortresses, he finally laid siege to Jerusalem. This was lifted temporarily in order to throw back an advance from Egyptian forces. The siege was then resumed and continued until the summer of 587; with the city near starvation, Nebuchadnezzar's forces managed to break through the walls and poured into the city. Zedekiah and a group of his soldiers fled but were overtaken near Jericho and brought back before Nebuchadnezzar. After witnessing the execution of his own sons, Zedekiah was blinded and carried to Babylon where he died. A short time later Nebuzaradan, an officer of Nebuchadnezzar's army, razed Jerusalem completely. At this time, further deportation of the population was made and the nation of Judah ceased to exist.

See JEREMIAH

SCRIPTURE

2 Kin. 24 [17]And the king of Babylon made Mattaniah his father's brother king in his stead, and changed his name to Zedekiah. [18]Zedekiah was twenty and one years old when he began to reign, and he reigned eleven years in Jerusalem. And his mother's name was Hamutal, the daughter of Jeremiah of Libnah. [19]And he did that which was evil in the sight of the LORD, according to all that Jehoiakim had done. [20]For through the anger of the LORD it came to pass in Jerusalem and Judah, until he had cast them out from his presence, that Zedekiah rebelled against the king of Babylon.

2 Kin. 25 [1]And it came to pass in the ninth year of his reign, in the tenth month, in the tenth day of the month, that Nebuchadnezzar king of Babylon came, he, and all his host, against Jerusalem, and pitched against it; and they built forts against it round about. [2]And the city was besieged unto the eleventh year of king Zedekiah. [3]And on the ninth day of the fourth month the famine prevailed in the city, and there was no bread for the people of the land.

[4]And the city was broken up, and all the men of war fled by night by the way of the gate between two walls, which is by the king's garden: (now the Chaldees were against the city round about:) and the king went the way toward the plain. [5]And the army of the Chaldees pursued after the king, and overtook him in the plains of Jericho: and all his army were scattered from him. [6]So they took the king, and brought him up to the king of Babylon to Riblah; and they gave judgment upon him. [7]And they slew the sons of Zedekiah before his eyes, and put out the eyes of Zedekiah, and bound him with fetters of brass, and carried him to Babylon.

ZEDEKIAH (The Prophet)

[zed ē kī'a] A court prophet in the time of King Ahab of Israel, and the leader of a band of 400 prophets summoned by Ahab when he wished to learn the future of the campaign which he and Jehoshaphat king of Judah were planning against Ramoth-gilead. Zedekiah embellished the uniformly favorable reply of the prophets by making a pair of iron horns and using them to demonstrate how the Israelites would push the Syrians around. When Micaiah was summoned and prophesied disaster for the venture, implying that Zedekiah possessed "a lying spirit", Zedekiah struck him and sarcastically questioned his prophetic authority. Micaiah was cast into prison, but the defeat of the kings vindicated his prophecy.

SCRIPTURE

1 Kin. 22 [10]And the king of Israel and Jehoshaphat the king of Judah sat each on his throne, having put on their robes, in a void place in the entrance of the gate of Samaria; and all the prophets prophesied before them. [11]And Zedekiah the son of Chenaanah made him horns of iron: and he said, Thus saith the LORD, With these shalt thou push the Syrians, until thou have consumed them. [12]And all the prophets prophesied so, saying, Go up to Ramoth-gilead, and prosper: for the LORD shall deliver it into the king's hand. [13]And the messenger that was gone to call Micaiah spake unto him, saying, Behold now, the words of the prophets declare good unto

the king with one mouth: let thy word, I
pray thee, be like the word of one of them,
and speak that which is good. [14]And Micaiah said, As the LORD liveth, what the
LORD saith unto me, that will I speak.
[15]So he came to the king. And the king
said unto him, Micaiah, shall we go against
Ramoth-gilead to battle, or shall we forbear? And he answered him, Go, and prosper: for the LORD shall deliver it into the
hand of the king. [16]And the king said unto
him, How many times shall I adjure thee
that thou tell me nothing but that which is
true in the name of the LORD? [17]And he
said, I saw all Israel scattered upon the
hills, as sheep that have not a shepherd:
and the LORD said, These have no master:
let them return every man to his house in
peace. [18]And the king of Israel said unto
Jehoshaphat, Did I not tell thee that he
would prophesy no good concerning me,
but evil? [19]And he said, Hear thou therefore the word of the LORD: I saw the LORD
sitting on his throne, and all the host of
heaven standing by him on his right hand
and on his left. [20]And the LORD said, Who
shall persuade Ahab, that he may go up
and fall at Ramoth-gilead? And one said
on this manner, and another said on that
manner. [21]And there came forth a spirit,
and stood before the LORD, and said, I will
persuade him. [22]And the LORD said unto
him, Wherewith? And he said, I will go
forth, and I will be a lying spirit in the
mouth of all his prophets. And he said,
Thou shalt persuade him, and prevail also:
go forth, and do so. [23]Now therefore, behold, the LORD hath put a lying spirit in the
mouth of all these thy prophets, and the
LORD hath spoken evil concerning thee.
[24]But Zedekiah the son of Chenaanah went
near, and smote Micaiah on the cheek, and
said, Which way went the Spirit of the
LORD from me to speak unto thee? [25]And
Micaiah said, Behold, thou shalt see in that
day, when thou shalt go into an inner
chamber to hide thyself.

ZELOPHEHAD, DAUGHTERS OF

[zê lō′fê had] Zelophehad was a member of the tribe of Manasseh who had five daughters, but no sons. Normally, the family inheritance went to the oldest male child. At the death of Zelophehad, his five daughters came to Moses and Eleazar and persuaded them to allot them a portion of land in Canaan. This story was included in the narrative to explain the origin of the law dealing with such cases.

SCRIPTURE

Num. 27 [1]Then came the daughters of
Zelophehad, the son of Hepher, the son of
Gilead, the son of Machir, the son of Manasseh, of the families of Manasseh the son
of Joseph: and these are the names of his
daughters; Mahlah, Noah, and Hoglah,
and Milcah, and Tirzah. [2]And they stood
before Moses, and before Eleazar the
priest, and before the princes and all the
congregation, by the door of the tabernacle of the congregation, saying, [3]Our father died in the wilderness, and he was not
in the company of them that gathered
themselves together against the LORD in
the company of Korah; but died in his
own sin, and had no sons. [4]Why should
the name of our father be done away from
among his family, because he hath no son?
Give unto us therefore a possession among
the brethren of our father. [5]And Moses
brought their cause before the LORD.
[6]And the LORD spake unto Moses, saying, [7]The daughters of Zelophehad speak
right: thou shalt surely give them a possession of an inheritance among their father's
brethren; and thou shalt cause the inheritance of their father to pass unto them.
[8]And thou shalt speak unto the children of
Israel, saying, If a man die, and have no

son, then ye shall cause his inheritance to pass unto his daughter. 9And if he have no daughter, then ye shall give his inheritance unto his brethren. 10And if he have no brethren, then ye shall give his inheritance unto his father's brethren. 11And if his father have no brethren, then ye shall give his inheritance unto his kinsman that is next to him of his family, and he shall possess it: and it shall be unto the children of Israel a statute of judgment, as the Lord commanded Moses.

ZEPHANIAH

[zef a nī′ a] A prophet of Judah. The first verse of Zephaniah's prophecy places his work in the reign of Josiah (c. 640-609 BC). Since the condition described is worse than might be expected after the reforms of Josiah had been carried out, the prophecy was probably uttered in the early part of that king's reign. Zephaniah traces his lineage through four generations back to Hezekiah. If this individual is to be identified with King Hezekiah, it is likely that Zephaniah sought to gain authority for his word by showing himself to be of royal blood. If this is the case, his criticism of the ruling classes becomes even more notable. Zephaniah probably lived in Judah and quite possibly in Jerusalem. In *Zeph. 1:4* he speaks of Jerusalem as "this place", and in *Zeph. 1:10-11,* he exhibits considerable knowledge of the topography of the city.

SCRIPTURE

The Day of the Lord

Zeph. 1 14The great day of the Lord is near, it is near, and hasteth greatly, even the voice of the day of the Lord: the mighty man shall cry there bitterly. 15That day is a day of wrath, a day of trouble and distress, a day of wasteness and desolation, a day of darkness and gloominess, a day of clouds and thick darkness, 16A day of the trumpet and alarm against the fenced cities, and against the high towers. 17And I will bring distress upon men, that they shall walk like blind men, because they have sinned against the Lord: and their blood shall be poured out as dust, and their flesh as the dung. 18Neither their silver nor their gold shall be able to deliver them in the day of the Lord's wrath; but the whole land shall be devoured by the fire of his jealousy: for he shall make even a speedy riddance of all them that dwell in the land.

The Restoration of Israel

Zeph. 3 14Sing, O daughter of Zion; shout, O Israel; be glad and rejoice with all the heart, O daughter of Jerusalem. 15The Lord hath taken away thy judgments, he hath cast out thine enemy: the King of Israel, even the Lord, is in the midst of thee: thou shalt not see evil any more. 16In that day it shall be said to Jerusalem, Fear thou not: and to Zion, Let not thine hands be slack. 17The Lord thy God in the midst of thee is mighty; he will save, he will rejoice over thee with joy; he will rest in his love, he will joy over thee with singing. 18I will gather them that are sorrowful for the solemn assembly, who are of thee, to whom the reproach of it was a burden. 19Behold, at that time I will undo all that afflict thee: and I will save her that halteth, and gather her that was driven out; and I will get them praise and fame in every land where they have been put to shame. 20At that time will I bring you again, even in the time that I gather you: for I will make you a name and a praise among all people of the earth, when I turn back your captivity before your eyes, saith the Lord.

ZERUBBABEL

[ze rub′a bel] A leader in the building of the second temple, after the return from Babylonian exile. Some scholars identify Zerubbabel with Sheshbazzar, since both are mentioned as leaders on the project, but it seems more probable that Sheshbazzar was perhaps the titular head, while Zerubbabel and Joshua the priest were the actual active leaders. In *Hag. 1:1* and *2:2*, Zerubbabel is referred to as the "governor" under whom the work was carried out.

SCRIPTURE

Hag. 1 12Then Zerubbabel the son of
Shealtiel, and Joshua the son of Josedech,
the high priest, with all the remnant of the
people, obeyed the voice of the LORD their
God, and the words of Haggai the prophet,
as the LORD their God had sent him, and
the people did fear before the LORD.
13Then spake Haggai the LORD's messenger in the LORD's message unto the people,
saying, I am with you, saith the LORD.
14And the LORD stirred up the spirit of Zerubbabel the son of Shealtiel, governor of
Judah, and the spirit of Joshua the son of
Josedech, the high priest, and the spirit of
all the remnant of the people; and they
came and did work in the house of the
LORD of hosts, their God,

Ezra 1 8Even those did Cyrus king of
Persia bring forth by the hand of Mithredath the treasurer, and numbered them
unto Sheshbazzar, the prince of Judah.
9And this is the number of them: thirty
chargers of gold, a thousand charges of silver, nine and twenty knives. 10Thirty basins of gold, silver basins of a second sort
four hundred and ten, and other vessels a
thousand. 11All the vessels of gold and of
silver were five thousand and four hundred. All these did Sheshbazzar bring up
with them of the captivity that were
brought up from Babylon unto Jerusalem.

Ezra 3 2Then stood up Jeshua the son of
Jozadak, and his brethren the priests, and
Zerubbabel the son of Shealtiel, and his
brethren, and builded the altar of the God
of Israel, to offer burnt offerings thereon,
as it is written in the law of Moses the man
of God.

Ezra 4 1Now when the adversaries of
Judah and Benjamin heard that the children of the captivity builded the temple
unto the LORD God of Israel; 2Then they
came to Zerubbabel, and to the chief of the
fathers, and said unto them, Let us build
with you: for we seek your God, as ye do;
and we do sacrifice unto him since the days
of Esarhaddon king of Assur, which
brought us up hither. 3But Zerubbabel,
and Jeshua, and the rest of the chief of the
fathers of Israel, said unto them, Ye have
nothing to do with us to build a house unto
our God; but we ourselves together will
build unto the LORD God of Israel, as king
Cyrus the king of Persia hath commanded
us.

Ezra 5 2Then rose up Zerubbabel the
son of Shealtiel, and Jeshua the son of Jozadak, and began to build the house of God
which is at Jerusalem: and with them were
the prophets of God helping them. 14And
the vessels also of gold and silver of the
house of God, which Nebuchadnezzar
took out of the temple that was in Jerusalem, and brought them into the temple of
Babylon, those did Cyrus the king take out
of the temple of Babylon, and they were
delivered unto one, whose name was
Sheshbazzar, whom he had made governor; 15And said unto him, Take these vessels, go, carry them into the temple that is
in Jerusalem, and let the house of God be
builded in his place. 16Then came the
same Sheshbazzar, and laid the foundation of the house of God which is in Jerusalem: and since that time even until now
hath it been in building, and yet it is not
finished.

ZIBA

[zī'ba] A servant of the house of Saul. When

David sought to show his love for Jonathan by bestowing favor on some member of Saul's house who had survived the disaster at Mount Gilboa (*see* SAUL), he was put in contact with Ziba, who told him of Mephibosheth, Jonathan's crippled son. David summoned Mephibosheth and presented him with the land which had belonged to Saul. Ziba was appointed to oversee the tilling of the land and to attend to the needs of Mephibosheth. When David was forced to flee Jerusalem during the rebellion of Absalom, Ziba met him with a considerable supply of provisions for his journey. David inquired concerning Mephibosheth and Ziba replied that his master had remained in Jerusalem, hoping to take advantage of the confusion to sieze the throne for himself. This apparent treachery moved David to bestow on Ziba all the property and goods which had belonged to Mephibosheth. After the rebellion had been crushed, David returned to his capital and was assisted in crossing the Jordan by Ziba and his sons and servants. As he approached Jerusalem, Mephibosheth came out to meet him and revealed that Ziba had hindered him from accompanying the king and had slandered him in order to receive his property. Perhaps unsure as to the truth in the matter, and too weary to pursue it further, David resolved to divide the land equally between Ziba and Mephibosheth, although Mephibosheth seemed willing for Ziba to have everything.

See MEPHIBOSHETH

SCRIPTURE

A Servant of Mephibosheth

2 Sam. 9 [1]And David said, Is there yet
any that is left of the house of Saul, that I
may shew him kindness for Jonathan's
sake? [2]And there was of the house of Saul
a servant whose name was Ziba. And
when they had called him unto David, the
king said unto him, Art thou Ziba? And
he said, Thy servant is he. [3]And the king
said, Is there not yet any of the house of
Saul, that I may shew the kindness of God
unto him? And Ziba said unto the king,
Jonathan hath yet a son, which is lame on
his feet. [4]And the king said unto him,
Where is he? And Ziba said unto the king,
Behold, he is in the house of Machir, the
son of Ammiel, in Lodebar.
[5]Then king David sent, and fetched him
out of the house of Machir, the son of Ammiel,
from Lodebar. [6]Now when Mephibosheth,
the son of Jonathan, the son of
Saul, was come unto David, he fell on his
face, and did reverence. And David said,
Mephibosheth. And he answered, Behold
thy servant!
[7]And David said unto him, Fear not:
for I will surely shew thee kindness for
Jonathan thy father's sake, and will restore
thee all the land of Saul thy father;
and thou shalt eat bread at my table
continually. [8]And he bowed himself, and
said, What is thy servant, that thou shouldest
look upon such a dead dog as I am?
[9]Then the king called to Ziba, Saul's
servant, and said unto him, I have given
unto thy master's son all that pertained to
Saul and to all his house. [10]Thou therefore,
and thy sons, and thy servants, shall till
the land for him, and thou shalt bring in
the fruits that thy master's son may have
food to eat: but Mephibosheth thy master's
son shall eat bread alway at my table.
Now Ziba had fifteen sons and twenty
servants. [11]Then said Ziba unto the king,
According to all that my lord the king hath
commanded his servant, so shall thy servant
do. As for Mephibosheth, said the king,
he shall eat at my table, as one of the king's
sons. [12]And Mephibosheth had a young
son, whose name was Micha. And all that
dwelt in the house of Ziba were servants
unto Mephibosheth. [13]So Mephibosheth
dwelt in Jerusalem: for he did eat continually
at the king's table; and was lame on
both his feet.

His Treachery

2 Sam. 16 [1]And when David was a little

past the top of the hill, behold, Ziba the
servant of Mephibosheth met him, with a
couple of asses saddled, and upon them
two hundred loaves of bread, and a hundred bunches of raisins, and a hundred of
summer fruits, and a bottle of wine. [2]And
the king said unto Ziba, What meanest
thou by these? And Ziba said, The asses be
for the king's household to ride on; and the
bread and summer fruit for the young men
to eat; and the wine, that such as be faint
in the wilderness may drink. [3]And the
king said, And where is thy master's son?
And Ziba said unto the king, Behold, he
abideth at Jerusalem: for he said, To-day
shall the house of Israel restore me the
kingdom of my father. [4]Then said the king
to Ziba, Behold, thine are all that pertained
unto Mephibosheth. And Ziba said, I humbly beseech thee that I may find grace in
thy sight, my lord, O king.

2 Sam. 19 [24]And Mephibosheth the son
of Saul came down to meet the king, and
had neither dressed his feet, nor trimmed
his beard, nor washed his clothes, from the
day the king departed until the day he
came again in peace. [25]And it came to
pass, when he was come to Jerusalem to
meet the king, that the king said unto him,
Wherefore wentest not thou with me, Mephibosheth? [26]And he answered, My lord,
O king, my servant deceived me: for thy
servant said, I will saddle me an ass, that I
may ride thereon, and go to the king; because thy servant is lame. [27]And he hath
slandered thy servant unto my lord the
king; but my lord the king is as an angel of
God: do therefore what is good in thine
eyes. [28]For all of my father's house were
but dead men before my lord the king: yet
didst thou set thy servant among them that
did eat at thine own table. What right
therefore have I yet to cry any more unto
the king? [29]And the king said unto him,
Why speakest thou any more of thy matters? I have said, Thou and Ziba divide the
land.

ZIMRI

[zim'rī] The fifth king of Israel, who ruled for only seven days. Zimri was a powerful military leader in charge of half of the king's chariots. At a time when the troops of the king were engaged in conflict against the Philistine city of Gibbethon, Zimri assassinated King Elah and usurped the throne. He apparently had little support in this, for as soon as the absentee troops learned of the death of Elah, they appointed Omri as king. Omri quickly returned to the capital city of Tirzah to claim his throne. Recognizing the hopelessness of the situation, Zimri set fire to the palace and perished in the flames. The treachery of Zimri was long remembered; when Jehu attacked Jezebel over thirty years later, she referred to him as "Zimri, thy master's murderer" (*2 Kin. 9:31*).

See KINGS, OMRI

SCRIPTURE

1 Kin. 16 [8]In the twenty and sixth year
of Asa king of Judah began Elah the son of
Baasha to reign over Israel in Tirzah, two
years. [9]And his servant Zimri, captain of
half his chariots, conspired against him, as
he was in Tirzah, drinking himself drunk
in the house of Arza steward of his house in
Tirzah. [10]And Zimri went in and smote
him, and killed him, in the twenty and
seventh year of Asa king of Judah, and
reigned in his stead.

[11]And it came to pass, when he began to
reign, as soon as he sat on his throne, that
he slew all the house of Baasha: he left
him not one that pisseth against a wall,
neither of his kinsfolks, nor of his friends.
[12]Thus did Zimri destroy all the house of
Baasha, according to the word of the LORD,
which he spake against Baasha by Jehu the
prophet, [13]For all the sins of Baasha, and
the sins of Elah his son, by which they

sinned, and by which they made Israel to
sin, in provoking the LORD God of Israel to
anger with their vanities. [14]Now the rest
of the acts of Elah, and all that he did, are
they not written in the book of the Chronicles of the kings of Israel?

[15]In the twenty and seventh year of Asa
king of Judah did Zimri reign seven days in
Tirza. And the people were encamped
against Gibbethon, which belonged to the
Philistines. [16]And the people that were encamped heard say, Zimri hath conspired,
and hath also slain the king: wherefore all
Israel made Omri, the captain of the host,
king over Israel that day in the camp.
[17]And Omri went up from Gibbethon, and
all Israel with him, and they besieged Tirzah. [18]And it came to pass, when Zimri
saw that the city was taken, that he went
into the palace of the king's house, and
burnt the king's house over him with fire,
and died, [19]For his sins which he sinned in
doing evil in the sight of the LORD, in walking in the way of Jeroboam, and in his sin
which he did, to make Israel to sin. [20]Now
the rest of the acts of Zimri, and his treason
that he wrought, are they not written in the
book of the Chronicles of the kings of Israel?

ZIN, WILDERNESS OF

[zin] A portion of the desert tract between the Dead Sea and the Arabah, in which was located Kadesh, or Kadesh-barnea. This wilderness area took its name from the town of Zin, located in the southernmost part of Judah, on the border of Edom. For a discussion of the events which transpired in this region, see KADESH.

REFERENCE: *Num. 13:21; 34:3; 20:1; 27:14; Deut. 32:51.*

ZION

[zī'on] This name was originally applied to the fortified hill of Jerusalem, in the period before it was inhabited by the Israelites. It is first mentioned in the Bible in connection with the conquest of Jerusalem by David (*2 Sam. 5:6-10; 1 Chr. 11:4-9*), after which this fortified area, and eventually a larger area, was called the "City of David." When the ark of the covenant was transferred from the City of David to Solomon's temple, the temple area itself became known as Zion.

In books of poetry and prophecy, Zion becomes an equivalent of Jerusalem as it is thought of as the center of religion and therefore the direct object of God's honor or punishment (*Psa. 51:18; 97:8, 149:2; Isa. 1:27; 28:16*). Zion also has a central place in the descriptions of the coming of the Messiah and the formation of the Messianic community (*Isa. 10:14; Heb. 12:22; Rev. 14:1*).

In the Christian Era, a hill to the southwest of Jerusalem has been referred to as Zion, based on its being the traditional site of the house in which the disciples were gathered on the day of Pentecost. This is not to be confused with the Old Testament Zion.

SCRIPTURE

Jerusalem

2 Sam. 5 [7]Nevertheless, David took the
strong hold of Zion: the same is the city of David.

Seat of the Lord's Reign

Isa. 24 [23]Then the moon shall be confounded, and the sun ashamed, when the LORD of hosts shall reign in mount Zion, and in Jerusalem, and before his ancients gloriously.

Mic. 4 [7]And I will make her that halted a remnant, and her that was cast far off a strong nation: and the LORD shall reign over them in mount Zion from henceforth, even for ever.

Salvation Comes from Zion

Isa. 46 [13]I bring near my righteousness; it shall not be far off, and my salvation shall not tarry: and I will place salvation in Zion for Israel my glory.

Figurative of Heaven

Rev. 14 [1]And I looked, and, lo, a Lamb stood on the mount Sion, and with him a hundred forty and four thousand, having his Father's name written in their foreheads.

ZIPPORAH

[zi pō'ra] The Midianite wife of Moses and mother of his sons Gershom and Eliezer. Zipporah was given to Moses by her father Jethro (or Reuel) in return for an act of kindness which he had performed. Their marriage seems to have had some difficult moments and for a time they were separated. It is impossible to determine whether or not the Cushite woman concerning whom Aaron and Miriam criticized Moses is to be identified with Zipporah or with another wife which he may have taken.

See Num. 12:1

SCRIPTURE

Ex. 2 [16]Now the priest of Midian had seven daughters: and they came and drew water, and filled the troughs to water their father's flock. [17]And the shepherds came and drove them away: but Moses stood up and helped them, and watered their flock. [18]And when they came to Reuel their father, he said, How is it that ye are come so soon to-day? [19]And they said, An Egyptian delivered us out of the hand of the shepherds, and also drew water enough for us, and watered the flock. [20]And he said unto his daughters, And where is he? why is it that ye have left the man? call him, that he may eat bread. [21]And Moses was content to dwell with the man: and he gave Moses Zipporah his daughter. [22]And she bare him a son, and he called his name Gershom: for he said, I have been a stranger in a strange land.

Ex. 4 [25]Then Zipporah took a sharp stone, and cut off the foreskin of her son, and cast it at his feet, and said, surely a bloody husband art thou to me. [26]So he let him go: then she said, A bloody husband thou art, because of the circumcision.

Ex. 18 [2]Then Jethro, Moses' father in law, took Zipporah, Moses' wife, after he had sent her back, [3]And her two sons; of which the name of the one was Gershom; for he said, I have been an alien in a strange land: [4]And the name of the other was Eliezer; for the God of my father, said he, was mine help, and delivered me from the sword of Pharaoh: [5]And Jethro, Moses' father in law, came with his sons and his wife unto Moses into the wilderness, where he encamped at the mount of God: [6]And he said unto Moses, I thy father in law Jethro am come unto thee, and thy wife, and her two sons with her.

ZOAR

[zō'ar] An ancient city of Palestine to which Lot escaped at the destruction of Sodom (*Gen. 19:20-23, 30*).

SCRIPTURE

Gen. 19 [20]Behold now, this city is near to flee unto, and it is a little one: Oh, let me escape thither, (is it not a little one?) and my soul shall live. [21]And he said unto him, See, I have accepted thee concerning this thing also, that I will not overthrow this city, for the which thou hast spoken. [22]Haste thee, escape thither; for I cannot do any thing till thou be come thither. Therefore the name of the city was called Zoar. [23]The sun was risen upon the earth when Lot entered into Zoar.

[30]And Lot went up out of Zoar, and dwelt in the mountain, and his two daughters with him; for he feared to dwell in Zoar: and he dwelt in a cave, he and his two daughters.

REFERENCE: *Gen. 13:10; 14:2, 8; Deut. 34:3; Isa. 15:5; Jer. 48:34.*

APPENDIX

The History of the Books of the Bible

INTRODUCTION

The articles which are found in this section are designed to furnish the student with an introduction to each of the books in the Holy Bible. Among those things discussed are the authorship and date of composition of the various books, the people to whom the books were addressed and the situation which called forth the writing of each. In addition, attention is given to special characteristics or problems of the individual books. Unfortunately, few of these matters can receive anything more than a cursory treatment. In cases where a fuller discussion is desired, the reader is invited to consult standard commentaries and reference books which deal with the problems of introduction.

The use of the word "Bible" to refer to the collected books of the Old and New Testaments did not become a common practice until the fifth century AD. The word is derived from the Greek term *Biblion,* meaning book. In the first century AD there was a body of Jewish sacred literature which was regarded as authoritative and which bore the general term "scripture," but whose limits were not as yet precisely determined. In general, however, the consensus was in favor of the same books which are found in the Protestant Bible, although the Jews of Alexandria also counted as canonical those books which constitute the *Apocrypha.* The New Testament "Canon," as the collection of works which the church considers normative and authoritative is called, was, for all practical purposes, settled by the middle of the fourth century AD.

THE DIVISIONS OF THE BIBLE

The Jews divided the Old Testament writings into three groups: the Law, the Prophets and the *Hagiographa,* or Holy Writings. The first of these divisions is comprised of the five books traditionally ascribed to Moses: *Genesis, Exodus, Leviticus, Numbers* and *Deuteronomy.* Instead of dividing the prophets into the categories of "major" and "minor," they were viewed as earlier and later prophets. In the class of former prophets were *Joshua, Judges* and the books of *Samuel* and *Kings.* The later prophets include *Isaiah, Jeremiah, Ezekiel* and the twelve so-called minor prophets. The third division of the Hebrew Bible —the Holy Writings—contains the poetical books (*Psalms, Proverbs* and *Job*), five books which are designated by the term *Megilloth* or rolls (*Song of Solomon, Ruth, Lamentations, Ecclesiastes* and *Esther*), and the historical books (*Daniel, Ezra-Nehemiah* and the books of *Chronicles*). The placing of *Daniel* among the historical books instead of the prophetic writings is perhaps to be explained on the ground that although he uttered a number of predictions, he had not exercised the office of a prophet in the same manner as had the other prophets.

In the Christian church it has been customary to divide the Old Testament books into the following categories: Historical books (*Genesis* to

Esther inclusive), Wisdom literature and Poetry (*Job, Psalms, Proverbs, Ecclesiastes, Song of Solomon* and *Lamentations*), and Prophetic books (*Isaiah* to *Malachi, Lamentations* excluded). The New Testament divides naturally into the four Gospels, *Acts,* the epistles and the *Apocalypse* or *Revelation.*

The original authors of the Bible did not divide their writings into chapters and verses as we have them today; this was a much later development. The Jews had long divided their scriptures into sections for more convenient reference, but the division into chapters as we know them was the work either of Stephen Langton or Cardinal Hugo de St. Caro, both of whom lived in the first half of the thirteenth century. The subdivision of these chapters into verses was done by a fifteenth-century rabbi, Mordecai Nathan. Previous to this system of versification, which is identical to that found in our present Bibles, subdivisions of chapters were noted by placing letters of the alphabet at equal distances in the margin of each page. The division of the New Testament chapters into verses first appeared in the Greek text edited by Robert Estienne in 1551. The first use of this system in an English version was in the Geneva Bible of 1560. After that, it was transferred to the Bishop's Bible of 1568 and the King James Version of 1611. Since that time, with slight variations in detail, it has become universally recognized. It ought always to be remembered that the division of the Bible into verses was designed as a reference aid for study of the Bible and was never intended to govern the sense of a passage. A verse or chapter division may often occur in the middle of a narrative or train of thought, thus giving the impression that the discussion of the topic has ended, when such may not be the case. The serious student should be careful not to follow a program of reading which adheres strictly to the humanly devised divisions of the Bible, but concern himself with making certain that he has discerned the context in which a verse or chapter is situated.

THE PENTATEUCH

The *Pentateuch* is the Greek name given to the five books commonly called the Books of Moses. These five books form a unit which, beginning with the record of creation and a history of the primitive world, passes on to deal more particularly with the chosen nation of Israel. It gives at length the personal history of the three great patriarchs, Abraham, Isaac and Jacob; it describes how the family of Israel grew into a nation in Egypt; it tells of its oppression and deliverance, of its forty years wandering in the wilderness, of the giving of the law with its civil and religious enactments, of the construction of the Tabernacle, of the numbering of the people, of the rights and duties of the priesthood, as well as of many other important events which befell the Jews before their entrance into the land of Canaan, and finally concludes with Moses' last discourses and his death.

For some time most Biblical critics have rejected the traditional view that Moses was the author of these five books, asserting that the Pentateuch is comprised of different documents or strata of material which originated at various stages in Israel's history. The evidence cited in support of this hypothesis includes the fact that two names are used to refer to God in different sections of the Pentateuch. The contention is that this is evidence of different sources for the collection. Duplicate accounts of events, together with variations in language and style, are also appealed to in an effort to show that various strata of material were compiled to form the Pentateuch. As one might expect, a tremendous amount of literature on this subject has been produced. Conclusions vary widely. Some claim that Moses had very little, if anything, to do with the composition of the Pentateuch; others, that it was compiled or edited at a later date, but largely from genuine Mosaic literature; still others hold to the traditional theory of Mosaic authorship. Since the limits of this article do not permit an adequate discussion of this problem, the reader is referred to standard introductory works on the Old Testament.

Genesis

Genesis is the title given to the first book of the Pentateuch by its Greek translators. The word means "origin" or "beginning"; truly, *Genesis* is a book of beginnings. It describes the beginning of man and the universe which he inhabits, the beginning of sin, the consequent beginning of an effort at redemption, and the beginning of the Hebrew nation through whom this redemption was to come.

The book of *Genesis,* together with the early chapters of *Exodus,* describes the steps which led to the establishment of the theocracy. Two ideas are seen to be predominant in this book—the people of God and the promised land. *Genesis* has a character which is both special and universal. It embraces the entire world as it speaks of God as the Lord of the whole human race; yet, as an introduction to Jewish history, it makes the universal interest subordinate to the national. Its design is to show how God first revealed himself to the patriarchs of the Hebrew race in order to make of them a people who would serve as his witnesses on the earth. This is the inner principle of unity which pervades the entire book.

The contents of *Genesis* may be conveniently outlined in the following manner:

I. *The Beginnings of History* (*1–11*)

1) The creation of the universe (*1:1–2:3*).

2) Description of the garden of Eden (*2:4-17*).

3) The creation of woman (*2:18-25*).

4) The Fall of man (*ch. 3*).

5) Cain and Abel (*ch. 4*).

6) The generations from Adam to Noah (*ch. 5*). This section is characterized by the extreme longevity of the persons noted.

7) A description of the wickedness which moved God to commission Noah to build and enter the ark, together with the details concerning the ark, the flood, and the post-deluvian events of Noah's life (*6–9*).

8) The ancient families of mankind, as they descended from Noah (*ch. 10*).

II. *The Story of Abraham* (*12–25*)

1) God's call of Abram and the covenant with him in which he was promised that his descendants should inherit the land of Canaan, that they should become a great nation and that through them all nations of the earth would be blessed (*12–17*). Abram's name is changed to Abraham and Ishmael is born to Abraham and Hagar, Sarah's handmaid.

2) The destruction of Sodom and Gomorrah, with an account of Lot's deliverance (*18–19*).

3) Abraham deceives Abimelech concerning Sarah (*ch. 20*).

4) The early years of Isaac (*21–25:18*). This section contains the birth of Isaac (*21:1-8*); the departure of Hagar and Ishmael (*21:9-21*); Abraham's faith, as demonstrated by his willingness to sacrifice Isaac (*ch. 22*); the death of Sarah and the purchase of the family burial ground from the Hittites (*ch. 23*); and the betrothal of Isaac and Rebekah (*ch. 24*). At the end of this section, Abraham's death is recorded (*25:1-11*) and the generations of Ishmael are given (*25:12-18*).

III. *The Story of Isaac* (*25:19–26:35*)

The main events in connection with Isaac's life are the birth of his twin sons, Jacob and Esau (*25:19-34*) and his sojourn among the Philistines (*ch. 26*).

IV. *The Story of Jacob and Esau* (*27:1–37:1*)

1) Jacob leaves home, after receiving his father's blessing by deceit (*27:1–28:9*). It was on this journey that he experienced the vision of the ladder at Bethel (*28:10-15*).

2) Jacob's family and his return from Haran to Canaan (*29–33*). This section gives an account of Jacob's marriages, the birth of most of his children, the shrewd dealings between Laban and Jacob and the departure of Jacob from Haran. After leaving Haran and wrestling with the angel, Jacob came into contact with Esau, but without the conflict which had been feared.

3) The last years of Jacob's life (*34–36*).

V. *The Story of Joseph* (*37–50*)

1) Joseph, because of the jealousy of his brothers, is sold into Egypt where, after a series of events, he becomes a ruler of Egypt, ranking just under Pharaoh (*37–41*).

2) Joseph's brothers come to Egypt to buy food during a time of great famine. After a time, Joseph reveals his identity to his brethren (*42–45*).

3) At the insistence of Joseph, Jacob and his family settle in Egypt (*46–47*).

4) Jacob's blessing of Joseph's two sons, Manasseh and Ephraim, and his prophecy concerning the twelve tribes (*48–49*).

5) The death of Jacob and Joseph (*ch. 50*).

Exodus

The second book of the Pentateuch bears its name because of the subject matter of the first half of the book—the departure of the children of Israel from Egypt. The word, "exodus" is derived from a Greek word meaning "going out."

Hundreds of years elapsed between the time of the events described in the closing chapters of *Genesis* and those of the beginning of *Exodus.* The exact number of years between the migration of Jacob into Egypt until the exodus is given as 430 (*12:40-41*). At the close of *Genesis,* Israel was living in the fertile land of Goshen and was being fed from the granaries of the Pharaoh. In *Exodus,* the Hebrews are seen as slaves of the Egyptians, without national consciousness or apparent religious purpose.

Exodus shows the development of Israel into a real nation, as God began the first stages of fulfillment of His promise to Abraham. After the first seven verses of the book, noting the increase and prosperity of Israel, *Exodus* is seen to fall into seven rather distinct sections:

1) The sufferings of Israel (*1:8–7:7*). This section includes the birth, education and flight of Moses; his call to be deliverer of his people and his consequent return from Midian to Egypt; and his first ineffectual attempts to prevail upon Pharoah to let the Israelites go, which resulted only in an increase in their burdens.

2) A manifestation of God's providential guidance of Israel, illustrated by the ten plagues (*7:8–13:16*). This section also includes the account of the observance of the first Passover (*ch. 12*).

3) The guiding of the people of Sinai (*13:17–18:27*), which tells of the departure and the miraculous crossing of the Red Sea. This section also contains a narrative of the principal events on the journey from the Red Sea to Sinai, including the coming of the manna, the observance of the Sabbath, the supply of water from the rock at Rephidim and the advice of Jethro concerning the civil government of the great mass of people.

4) The making of the covenant at Sinai, together with the reception of the Ten Commandments (*19:1–24:18*). The laws recorded in this section regulated the religious, civil, and social life of the Israelites.

5) Directions for the building of the tabernacle (*24:18–31:18*).

6) The renewing of the covenant after the sinful actions of the Israelites in connection with the making of the golden calf (*32:1–35:3*).

7) The actual building and dedication of the tabernacle of the Lord (*35:4–40:38*), under the supervision of the two master craftsmen, Bezalel and Oholiab.

Exodus is a book of redemption in which God delivers His people out of bondage and brings them into a special relationship with Himself.

Leviticus

In the Septuagint (The Greek version of the Hebrew Old Testament), the third book of the Pentateuch bears the title "*Levitikon*" ("pertaining to the Levites"), an adjective modifying the word "book." The Levites were the tribe from which the priests and others prominent in the worship services were chosen, in lieu of the first-born sons of all the tribes (*Num. 3:45*).

Leviticus fills an integral role in the Pentateuch. Just as it is necessary to be familiar with *Exodus* in order to understand *Leviticus,* some knowledge of *Leviticus* is necessary if one is to understand the religious activities of the Jews as portrayed in *Numbers, Deuteronomy,* and the rest of the Old Testament.

The purpose of *Leviticus* may be defined as calling attention to the disparity between God's holiness and man's sinfulness and providing concrete steps whereby man might restore the fellowship which has been lost as a result of his own defilement. The laws connected with this restoration are varied. They are both general and specific; they seek, in one way or another, to govern the whole life of the people of God. In this sense, *Leviticus* is the most thoroughly legalistic book in the entire Old Testament. Throughout its laws is seen the unyielding demand: "Ye shall be holy, for I the Lord your God am holy." On the other hand, the climax of the book is clearly ch. 16, in which instructions are given for the Day of Atonement. On this day, God provided his people with a ceremony by means of which all of their sins for the previous year were counted as forgiven. The mercy which God displays in this service so foreshadows the work of Christ that the 16th chapter has been called "the most consummate flower of Messianic symbolism."

In addition to the laws, there are also some historical sections, but these, too, are closely connected with the priesthood. They include the consecration of the priests in chs. 8 and 9, the sin and punishment of Nadab and Abihu (*ch. 10*), and the stoning of a blasphemer (*24:10ff*). In this connection, it is interesting to note that only one mention is made of the Levites and that in an incidental manner (*25:32ff*).

The book may be divided as follows:

1) Laws concerning Sacrifice (*1–7*). In this section five types of offerings are discussed: burnt offerings, meal offerings, peace offerings, sin offerings and guilt offerings. This is filled out by a discussion of the sin offering as it is to be observed by various classes of individuals.

2) An historical section featuring the consecration of the priests (*8–9*) and the sin of Nadab and Abihu (*ch. 10*).

3) A section on laws of purification from ceremonial uncleanness (*11–15*). These furnish instructions as to the appropriate sacrifices and ordinances for ridding oneself of impurity.

4) The Day of Atonement (*ch. 16*).

5) Laws dealing with the conduct of God's people (*17–20*). These include various religious and ethical laws designed to accent the separation between Israel and the heathen nations.

6) Laws concerning the holiness of the priests (*21–22*).

7) A discussion of holy days and feasts (*23–24*). Included in this section are the Sabbath, Passover, the feasts of first fruits and harvest, Pentecost, the Day of Atonement and the feast of Tabernacles.

8) The Sabbatical and Jubilee Years (*ch. 25*).

9) Promises and threats connected with obedience to the laws (*ch. 26*).

10) An appendix containing the laws concerning vows (*ch. 27*).

Numbers

This book takes its name from the fact that it contains the account of the two census enumerations of the congregation of Israel in chs. 1–4 and ch. 26. The title, however, is somewhat unfortunate since most of the book has no connection with these "numberings." The original Hebrew title, "in the wilderness," is greatly to be preferred, as the book is certainly more a vital history of the events of the period of wanderings than a catalogue of lifeless statistics.

Numbers follows naturally after *Leviticus* in the sequence of the books of the Pentateuch. After receiving the laws at Sinai, the journey to which was described in *Exodus*, the Israelites were ready to continue their march to Canaan. This book tells of their preparations, their sin in failing to trust in God and the resultant thirty-seven years of wanderings through the rough wilderness. At the end of the book, they are once again at the edge of Canaan, where they receive instructions for the conquest and division of the land.

There are a number of problems connected with the chronological and historical statements made in the book, but the limits of this article do not permit a discussion of them here. For fuller treatment, the reader is referred to any one of several standard commentaries or introductions to the Old Testament.

The principle divisions of the book are as follows:

1) The preparation for the departure from Sinai (*1:1–10:10*). The events described here took place in nineteen days. In this time a census was taken of all men who were over twenty and who could serve in military efforts (*1–4*). The total obtained was 603,550 (*1:46*). This would indicate that the total population of the group was probably near three million. The census was followed by the cleansing and blessing of the congregation (*5–6*), the offering of gifts from the various tribes (*7*), the consecration of the Levites (*8*) and the observance of the Passover at Sinai (*9:1-14*).

2) The journey from Sinai to Kadesh-barnea (*10:11–14:45*). This section includes the account of the coming of the quail (*11*), the rebellion against Moses by Miriam and Aaron (*12*), and the fateful mission of the spies (*13, 14*).

3) The wanderings of the desert wilderness (*15–19*). As noted above, this covered a period of thirty-seven years, from the end of the second to the beginning of the fortieth year in the wilderness. Ch. 15 includes various laws and a record of capital punishment for Sabbath breaking. The rebellion of Korah (ch. 16) and the budding of Aaron's rod (ch. 17) are also mentioned here.

4) The history of the last year, from the second arrival of the Israelites at Kadesh till they

reach "the plains of Moab by Jordan near Jericho" (*20–36:13*). Notable sections of this are the story of Balaam (*22:2–24:25*), the zeal of Phinehas (*ch. 25*), the second census (*26:1-51*), instructions for dividing the land (*26:52–27:11*), the appointment of Joshua as Moses' successor (*27:12-23*), various laws concerning offerings and vows (*28–30*), the war with Midian (*ch. 31*), the settlement of the tribes east of the Jordan (*ch. 32*), a review of the locations at which Israel had camped during their wanderings (*33:1-49*), more instructions concerning the conquest and division of Canaan (*33:50–34:29*), the appointment of the cities of refuge (*ch. 35*) and instructions concerning the marriage of land-owning Israelite women (*ch. 36*).

Deuteronomy

The word "Deuteronomy" is taken from the Greek word for "the second law" or "the law repeated." The book is written in the form of discourses which Moses delivered to the people in the plains of Moab on the eve of their entrance into the promised land of Canaan. These discourses are addressed to every member of the congregation of Israel and not just to a small segment, such as the Levites. The discourses are not a second law in the sense of being a different law; neither are they to be taken merely as a recapitulation of those things recorded in *Exodus, Leviticus,* and *Deuteronomy.* They are rather a forceful presentation of the most essential aspects of God's revelation with an emphasis on the spiritual principle of the law and its fulfillment, as well as a development and application of the law to circumstances which would face the Israelites in their new life in Canaan. These discourses were spoken in the eleventh month of the last year of Israel's wanderings, the fortieth year after leaving Egypt.

In the first speech (*1:1–4:43*), Moses strives briefly, but earnestly, to warn the people against the sins which had kept their fathers from entering the promised land. In order to stress the necessity of obedience, he recapitulates the chief events of the last forty years in the wilderness, emphasizing the role which disobedience and lack of trust had played in the afflictions of the Israelites.

The second discourse (*4:44–26:19*) enters more fully into the precepts of the Law. It may be viewed as the body of the whole address, the former being an introduction. This section is hortatory and legal, consisting of a review of Israel's moral and civil statutes, testimonies and judgments. This discourse is broken into two main sections: 1) chs. 5–11, an exposition of the Ten Commandments and 2) chs. 12–26, a group of special statutes on various matters, containing a strong ethical and religious emphasis.

The third discourse (*27:1–31:30*) deals primarily with the blessings of obedience and the curses of disobedience. Moses now speaks in conjunction with the elders of the people and with the priests and the Levites, whose office it would be to carry out the ceremony which Moses describes in this discourse. The place selected for the ceremony was the spot in the center of the land where the first altar to God had been erected. As soon as they passed over the Jordan, the people were commanded to set up great stones on Mt. Ebal. These were to be covered with plaster and inscribed with the law of God. They were also to build an altar, which seems to have been distinct from the stones, although it is difficult to be certain about this. Then the twelve tribes were to be divided between the two hills. Simeon, Levi, Judah, Issachar, Joseph and Benjamin were to station themselves on Mt. Gerizim to recite the blessings which God promised them if they would remain faithful to him. Across on Mt. Ebal, Reuben, Gad, Asher, Zebulun and Naphtali were to speak the curses with which the Lord had threatened disobedience.

After completing these discourses, Moses encouraged the people to follow their new leader, Joshua, and to go across and take the land which had been promised to Abraham. He wrote down the Law in a book and turned it over to the priests, who were to keep it as a perpetual reminder for all the people (*31:9-13*). It was to be read every seventh year, when the people assembled for the feast of Tabernacles.

At the command of the Lord, Moses and Joshua appeared before God at the tent of meeting. There God told them of the future infidelity of Israel and instructed Moses to leave the people a song which they were to learn and which was to serve as a witness for God against them. This song of Moses is recorded in ch. 32; it recounts the blessings which God has bestowed on his people and the corrupt manner in which they have responded to his beneficence. Ch. 33 contains Moses' blessing on the people and ch. 34 records the brief account of the death of this great leader of Israel.

Joshua

This book is named for its chief character, Joshua, whose name means "Jehovah is salvation." The Greek form of this name is Jesus. The first appearance of Joshua is as the leader of the forces of Israel against Amalek (*Ex. 17:8ff*). The manner in which he is introduced into the story indicates that he was already well established as a leader. Later, he accompanied Moses to the foot of Mt. Sinai, but did not make the ascent with him (*Ex. 24*). In *Ex. 32–33* he is also found in close association with Moses. No doubt, the years which he spent with Moses greatly influenced his spiritual development. The aspect of his life for which Joshua is most often remembered is his having brought back a positive report from the land of Canaan after serving as one of twelve men sent to spy out the land (*Num. 13*). From this it can be seen that the experience and spirit which were Joshua's equipped him well for his duties and responsibilities as the leader of God's people.

Although tradition names Joshua as the author of the book which bears his name, there is nothing in the book which necessitates this view. On the contrary, he could not have written all of the book as it includes happenings which took place after his death. The book itself is anonymous.

Modern criticism assigns the writing of *Joshua* to a period late in Israel's history instead of at a time contemporaneous with the events it records. For a discussion of the probable date of the events described, see articles on CONQUEST and EXODUS.

The book may be regarded as consisting of three parts which may be analyzed as follows:

1) *The Conquest of Canaan* (*1–12*). This includes the preparation for and crossing of the Jordan (*1–4*). After the crossing, they camped at Gilgal. Here they circumcised all the males who were born in the wilderness, as circumcision had not been observed since the departure from Egypt. Gilgal was also the scene of the keeping of the passover and the cessation of the manna. 5:13–6:27 tells of the miraculous destruction of Jericho and the salvation of Rahab. The crime and punishment of Achan is discussed in ch. 7. In ch. 8, the narrative records the avenging of the defeat which Israel had suffered at the hands of Ai because of the sin of Achan. The latter portion of this chapter tells of the setting up of the stones on Mount Ebal. The stratagem of the Gibeonites is the topic of ch. 9. In ch. 10 is contained the story of the conquest of Southern Canaan, with the aid of Joshua's long day. Chs. 11–12 describe the conquest of Northern Canaan and give a list of the defeated kings.

2) *The Distribution of the Territory* (*13–22*). This provides a record of the area which was assigned to the various tribes (*13–19*), the appointment of the six cities of refuge (*ch. 20*) and the forty-eight cities of the Levites (*ch. 21*), as well as the departure of the Transjordanic tribes to their home.

3) *Joshua's farewell addresses* (*23–24*). The first of these is a speech of encouragement and warning. The second recalls the history of Israel, with emphasis on divine interventions on their behalf. At the close of this speech, Joshua issued the famous statement, "choose you this day whom you will serve . . . but as for me and my house, we will serve the Lord" (*24:15*). The book closes with an account of the renewal of the covenant and the death of Joshua and Eleazer.

Judges

The book of *Judges* continues the history of Israel from the time of Joshua to Samuel. It is connected with the book of *Joshua* by the references to the death of Joshua in the first two chapters. The subject matter is not, however, dealt with in a strict chronological manner. The book contains a collection of accounts of events which generally took place on a local rather than a national level. In most cases it is impossible to assign any date to the events other than sometime in the period between Joshua and Samuel.

After the death of Joshua and his contemporaries, "there arose another generation after them, who did not know the Lord or the work which he had done for Israel" (*Judg. 2:10*). This generation of Israelites, as well as those which succeeded it, was characterized by a lack of national unity, indifference to the commands of God, and a general moral and spiritual decay.

The problems of the Israelites during this period were threefold. From a *political* standpoint there was tribal isolation which led to the lack of national unity mentioned above. This disorganization encouraged other nations to attack Israel. The book of *Judges* records six such major invasions. The first was the Mesopotamian invasion from the northeast (*3:8-11*) from which Othniel delivered his people. The second was by the Moabites and came from the southeast (*3:12-20*). Israel was delivered from the Moabites by Ehud, the left handed assassin of the Moabite king, Eglon. The third invasion came under the Canaanite leaders Jabin and Sisera (*chs. 4, 5*). Israel was delivered from the Canaanites by Deborah, the only woman judge of which there is any record. It is interesting to note that Sisera himself was killed by a woman, Jael, the wife of Heber the Kenite. The Midianite invasion from the southeast (*chs. 6–9*) lasted seven years and was ended under the bold leadership of Gideon. The foolish vow of Jephthah, which cost him the life of his daughter, came after he delivered Israel from the fifth invasion, that by the Ammonites from the east (*10:6–11:40*). The sixth invasion was by the Philistines, from the southwest, and was apparently something of a recurrent nature rather than one particular campaign. During a period of at least 200 years, Israel was delivered from the Philistines by Shamgar, Samson, Samuel, Saul, and David.

The major *social* problem stemmed from the recurrent failure of the Israelites to drive the Canaanites out of the land, a direct violation of God's commandment. The Israelites then intermarried with the Canaanites, adopting many of their customs. This assimilation of Canaanite culture promoted the growth of idolatry which constituted the *religious* problem of the people. The three most prominent deities of Canaanite worship were Baal, Asherah, and Dagon.

Baal was usually represented by a stone pillar and was a god of fertility, usually worshipped in the groves. At various times Baal-worship included fornication (*Jer. 7:9*), self-mutilation (*1 Kin. 18:28*), and human sacrifice (*Jer. 19:5*). Baal is the deity most often mentioned in the Old Testament as being a snare for the people of God.

The symbol of Asherah was a wooden post set up in the "high places" of idolatrous worship. The Phoenecian goddess of procreation and love, she was the chief female deity and is often mentioned in connection with Baal.

Dagon was a Philistine deity having the body of a fish with human hands and a human face. It was a temple of Dagon which Samson pulled down in his final act of strength.

There is seen in the book of *Judges* a consistent pattern—Israel is oppressed by a foreign power; the people cry to God and he raises up a judge to deliver them from their predicament; after peace is established the people become complacent and relapse into idolatry.

The judges, although chosen by God to lead His people, were not always men of ideal character, yet they fulfilled God's purposes in delivering Israel. They served in a multiple role as judicial, military, and spiritual leaders. The period of the judges may be said to extend through the life of the last judge, Samuel, whose death is recorded in *1 Sam. 25*.

Ruth

The calm scenes depicted in this beautiful little book come as a welcome contrast to the turbulent accounts of slaughter and oppression recorded in *Joshua* and *Judges*. While the previous two books, especially *Judges,* deals with the rivalries and the battles which were of major historical interest, *Ruth* records for us an episode which was probably much more typical of the actual life of the people.

The events narrated took place in the period of the Judges (*1:1*), but the book gives us no clue as to the identity of its author or the date of its composition.

The value of the book is twofold. It traces the ancestry of David to Ruth, who was a Moabitess, and it presents us with a beautiful picture of filial piety and its rewards.

The events in Ruth's life may be summarized as follows:

1) Due to a severe famine in the land of Judah, Elimelech, a native of Bethlehem, emigrated to Moab with his wife and two sons, who married two Moabite women, Ruth and Orpah.

2) At the end of ten years, all three of the women were left widows and Naomi decided to return to Bethlehem. Despite Naomi's protests, Ruth determined to return to Bethlehem with her. Ruth's dedication to Naomi and to the reli-

gion of the God of Israel is stated in 1:16-17: "Intreat me not to leave thee, or to return from following after thee: for whither thou goest, I will go; and where thou lodgest, I will lodge: thy people shall be my people, and thy God my God: Where thou diest, will I die, and there will I be buried: the Lord do so to me and more also, if ought but death part thee and me."

3) They arrived in Bethlehem at the time of the barley harvest. Ruth went out to glean in the fields of Boaz, a wealthy man whose relationship with his servants eloquently attests to his character (*2:4*). According to Hebrew law, Ruth had a right to demand that a near kinsman of her late husband take her for his wife. Boaz had been related to Ruth's husband and was willing to marry her, but since there was another man of closer kinship, it was necessary to go through certain customary and legal measures before he could rightfully claim her. 4) This being done, the two were married with the blessings of their neighbors and eventually became the parents of Obed, the grandfather of David.

The Books of Samuel

In the original Hebrew texts, *1* and *2 Samuel* formed only one book. This was first divided into two books in the Septuagint, the Greek version of the Hebrew scriptures; the two were called the *First and Second Books of Kingdoms. 1* and *2 Kings* were called the *Third and Fourth Books of Kingdoms.* The titles in the King James Version of the Bible still speak of these four books in this way.

The two books under consideration are named for Samuel, not because he was the author, but because he is the principal actor in the first part of the narrative and because of his association with and influence on Saul and David, the other two leading characters. Samuel was raised up by God at a time when Israel needed him most. Disunited and at a low ebb spiritually and politically, Israel was led by Samuel into an era of great national solidarity. Since he was both a judge (*1 Sam. 7:6, 15–17*) and a prophet (*1 Sam. 3:20*), he serves as an important connecting link between the periods of the Judges and the United Kingdom. Certainly it is fitting that these two important books should bear his name.

Jewish tradition contains a statement that the books were written by Samuel himself, but this cannot have been true, at least not for the entire composition, since Samuel's death is recorded in *1 Sam. 25:1* and *28:3.* It is quite possible, however, that Samuel was largely responsible for the first portion of this book, since we are fairly certain that he kept historical records (Cf. *1 Chr. 29:29*). That the book is a compilation of records is suggested by the great similarity which many of its passages bear to sections of the books of *Chronicles.* Whether this compilation was done by one individual or several, one of whom was Samuel himself, is a matter of conjecture and one on which no decision can be reached.

The two books deal with the period from the time of Othniel through the reign of David, in the eleventh and tenth centuries BC. This was one of the most significant eras of Jewish history as the government of Israel changed from a system of tribal judges to a form of constitutional monarchy, in which the king was to rule according to the precepts of God's Law.

The date of composition of the two books can be arrived at with some degree of assurance. It must have been after the death of David since the length of his entire reign is given in *2 Sam. 5:5.* The statement in *1 Sam. 27:6* that "Ziklag pertaineth unto the kings of Judah to this day" indicates that the division of the kingdom had already occurred, since neither Saul, David nor Solomon is ever referred to simply as a king of Judah. On the other hand, there are certain elements in the references to various religious observances which indicate that it was written before the reformation of Josiah. The date of composition, therefore, would probably fall somewhere between the reign of Rehoboam, under whom the kingdom divided, and that of Josiah.

Although repetition and apparently duplicate accounts make analysis somewhat difficult, the contents of the two books may be outlined as follows:

I. *The Life of Samuel* (*1 Sam. 1–15*)

1) The prayer of Hannah for a son, the granting of the request and the subsequent dedication of the child Samuel to the service of the Lord (*1:1–2:10*).

2) The sin of the sons of Eli which resulted in their death and the loss of the priesthood to the descendants of Eli (*2:12-36*).

3) Samuel's vision concerning the house of Eli (*ch. 3*).

4) The defeat of the Israelites and capture of the Ark by the Philistines and the death of Eli (*ch. 4*).

5) The Ark in Philistine territory (*5:1–7:4*).

6) The return of the Ark and the establishment of Samuel as a judge over Israel (*ch. 7*).

7) The appointment of Saul's sons as judges and the consequent request for a king. Samuel warns the Israelites of the perils of being ruled over by a king (*ch. 8*).

8) Saul's meeting with Samuel (*ch. 9*).

9) The anointing and election of Saul as king (*10–11*).

10) Samuel's address to the people, in which he defends his own record and exhorts them to walk in the way of the Lord (*ch. 12*). From this time forward, he serves as an adviser to the king.

II. *The Reign of Saul* (*1 Sam. 13–2 Sam. 1*)

1) The offering of sacrifice by Saul in Samuel's absence. This constituted disobedience and resulted in God's disfavor toward Saul (*ch. 13*).

2) Jonathan's rout of the Philistine army and his innocent breaking of Saul's foolish vow (*ch. 14*).

3) Saul's disobedience in sparing some of the Amalekites and their cattle (*ch. 15*). Samuel's reply to Saul's feeble excuse was the familiar "to obey is better than sacrifice and to hearken than the fat of rams" (*15:22*).

4) The anointing of David to be Saul's successor (*ch. 16*).

5) David and Goliath (*ch. 17*).

6) The love of Jonathan and David and the marriage of the latter to the daughter of Saul (*ch. 18*). Also included in this chapter is the first attempt of the jealous Saul to kill David.

7) Saul's second attempt on David's life (*ch. 19*).

8) The parting of Jonathan and David (*ch. 20*).

9) David's exile (*21–24*).

10) The death of Samuel and the marriage of David to Abigail after the death of her churlish husband, Nabal (*ch. 25*).

11) The gradual eclipse of Saul's power as he futilely sought to destroy David and protect his kingdom at the same time (*26–30*).

12) The death of Saul and his sons at the hands of the Philistines (*ch. 31*).

13) David's lamentation over Saul and Jonathan (*2 Sam. 1*).

III. *The Reign of David* (*2 Sam. 2–25*)

1) The proclamation of David as king at Hebron and his reign over Judah from that place.

2) The removal of the capital to Jerusalem (*ch. 5*).

3) The bringing of the ark to Jerusalem (*ch. 6*).

4) David's victories (*chs. 7–11:1*).

5) David's sin with Bathsheba and the rebuke by Nathan the prophet (*11–12*).

6) The rape of Tamar by Amnon, the revenge of Absalom and Amnon's murder; the flight of Absalom (*ch. 13*).

7) Absalom's return, his efforts to usurp the throne of David and his death (*14–18*).

8) David's return and Sheba's revolt (*19–20*).

9) The famine and the victory over the Philistines (*ch. 21*).

10) David's thanksgiving and last words (*22–23:7*).

11) The names and exploits of David's "mighty men" (*23:8-39*).

12) The census and the resultant plague (*ch. 24*).

The Books of Kings

As was the case with *1* and *2 Samuel,* the books of *Kings* were originally only one book. When divided in the Septuagint, they were called the *Third and Fourth Books of Kingdoms,* although the Hebrew title is simply "Kings," the same as in our English Bible. These form an obvious sequel to the books of *Samuel.*

The period covered extends from the accession of Solomon (c. 975 BC) to the death of Jehoiachin sometime after his liberation from Babylonian imprisonment (561 BC). The history contained in the two books covers the entire period of the Jewish monarchy, except for the reigns of Saul and David, which are treated in *1* and *2 Samuel.* Israel is seen in the two extremes of power and weakness; under Solomon their dominion was extended from the Euphrates to the Mediterranean to the border of Egypt (*1 Kin. 4:21*); under the last kings they were reduced to a pitiful remnant, subject alternatively to Egypt and Assyria, until they were finally uprooted and taken out of their homeland. The cause of this decadence is seen to have been the division of the kingdom under Rehoboam and the religious schism and idolatrous worship which was effected by Jeroboam's political motives. This division led to wars between the two kingdoms which naturally weakened both. In a desperate effort to maintain their position, they made foreign alliances, adopting the superstitions and deities of these heathen nations, thus incurring the wrath of God and forfeiting the benefits of the divine protection which they had hitherto enjoyed.

Although there is abundant attention given to names and dates, there is still some difficulty in reconciling apparent chronological discrepancies. This is due to the reckoning of fractions of years as complete years, the instances in which a son served as co-regent, sharing as co-regent, sharing the rule with his father, and probable errors in copying numbers.

There is a Hebrew tradition which states that Jeremiah was the author of the books of *Kings*. This theory has much to commend it, but is not without its difficulties. That he could not have been the author of the entire narrative is indicated by the account of the deportation, imprisonment and subsequent release of Jehoiachin, whereas Jeremiah was carried down to Egypt with the fugitives (*Jer. 43:1-8*). If the author was not Jeremiah, however, he was in all probability a contemporary of his who held the same views as the prophet of lamentation.

Many scholars feel that the work was composed before the fall of Jerusalem (586 BC) and, during or shortly after the exile, was revised to include the account of Jehoiachin's liberation from his Babylonian prison and the ultimate complete downfall of the Judean kingdom.

There was a regular series of state annals both for the kingdom of Judah and that of Israel, which probably embraced the whole time dealt with in the books of *Kings*, or at least to the time of Jehoiakim (*2 Kin. 24:5*). The author, or authors, of *Kings* made use of these archival sources, citing them by name. In *1 Kin. 11:41*, after the record of Solomon's reign, the author refers to the "Book of the words of Solomon." Indebtedness is also acknowledged to the "Book of the Chronicles of the Kings of Judah" (*1 Kin. 14:29; 15:7, 23*, etc.) and to the "Book of the Chronicles of the Kings of Israel" (*1 Kin. 14:19; 15:31*, etc.). These were probably written down by the prophets. An example of this type of work is seen in the history of Uzziah which Isaiah compiled (*1 Chr. 26:22*). There were also extant at the time of the compilation of the books of *Kings*, separate works of the various prophets who had lived in Israel and Judah and which probably bore the same relation to those Chronicles which the historical parts of Isaiah or Jeremiah bear to those portions of the annals preserved in the books of *Kings;* that is, they were, in some instances at least, more copious accounts of the current events by the same hand that drew up the concise narrative of the annals, though in other instances they were mere duplicates. An example of this is seen in the practical identity between *2 Kin. 19* and *Isa. 37*. Also, chapter 52 of *Jeremiah*, relating to the destruction of the temple, is quite like *2 Kin. 24–25*.

The books of *Kings* may be arranged as follows for ease of study:

I. *The Reign of Solomon* (*1 Kin. 1:1–14:43*)

1) The last days of David (*1:1–2:11*). Adonijah usurps David's throne, but flees after the anointing of Solomon. David dies and is buried in Jerusalem.

2) Solomon's formal accession to the throne and the early days of his reign (*2:12-46*).

3) Solomon's request for wisdom and his sagacious decision concerning the disputed child (*ch. 3*).

4) A description of Solomon's power, wealth, and wisdom (*ch. 4*). In this section we learn that Solomon wrote over 3,000 proverbs and 105 songs. For a further discussion of this, see the introduction to *Proverbs*.

5) The erection of Solomon's temple (*5–8*).

6) A further description of the splendor of Solomon's kingdom (*9–10*). After mentioning the stables, the navy and the great riches of the kingdom, the narrative records the visit of the queen of Sheba, who was so impressed by the scene that she remarked, "Howbeit I believed not the words, until I came, and mine eyes had seen it; and, behold, the half was not told me: thy wis-

dom and prosperity exceedeth the fame which I heard" (*1 Kin. 10:7*).

7) Solomon's wives and apostasy (*ch. 11*). One cannot read this chapter seriously without being saddened. In his search for wealth and pleasure, Solomon contracted a large number of foreign wives—many, no doubt, for political reasons. These women brought their foreign deities with them and eventually Solomon's heart was turned away from the Lord—"and his heart was not perfect with the Lord his God, as was the heart of David his father" (*11:4*). Whether or not Solomon was "the preacher" of *Ecclesiastes* cannot be proved beyond doubt. If he was, however, surely the situation to which this chapter bears witness would lead him to the statement of cynicism and despair: "Vanity of vanities, all is vanity, saith the preacher" (*Eccl. 1:2*).

II. *The Divided Kingdom* (*1 Kin. 12:1–2 Kin. 17:41*)

1) The division of the kingdom (*ch. 12*). After Solomon's death, his son Rehoboam became king. Instead of lightening the heavy tax burden which Solomon's extravagances had forced on the people, Rehoboam decided to increase it. Disgruntled, the ten northern tribes chose Jeroboam as their leader and seceded from the union with the tribes of Judah and Benjamin. In order to keep his people from returning to worship in Jerusalem, where they might be influenced to stand with Rehoboam, the king of the North instituted the worship of the golden calf. This act of political expediency was the major factor in Israel's ultimate humiliation.

2) The remainder of Jeroboam's reign (*13:1-14-20*). This section includes a rebuke to Jeroboam by a man of God which contains an amazing prophecy concerning the reformation of Josiah (*v. 2*), which was not to be fulfilled for over 300 years (*2 Kin. 23:15-18*).

3) Rehoboam, Abijam and Asa, kings of Judah (*14:21–15:24*).

4) Kings of Israel from Nadab to Omri (*14:25–16:28*).

5) Ahab, Jezebel and Elijah (*16:29–22:40*). These three individuals stand out as among the more memorable in all the history of Israel, the first two for their consummate wickedness and the latter for his fiery zeal and courageous efforts in the service of God. Ch. 17 tells of the feeding of Elijah by the ravens and his boarding at the house of the widow of Zarephath during the three and a half year drought which was on the land. Ch. 18 informs us that Jezebel's wickedness prompted her to subsidize Baal worship and a cult of heathen prophets, while she strove to exterminate the prophets of God (*v. 13*). Also contained in this chapter is the magnificent story of Elijah's "duel" with the prophets of Baal atop Mt. Carmel. Ch. 19 records the anger of Jezebel at Elijah's having slain her prophets and her threat upon his life. Elijah is reduced to desperation, but is comforted by the "still, small voice" (*vv. 11, 12*). Chs. 20–22 relate other incidents concerning Ahab, including his brutal treatment of Naboth and his death at the hands of the Syrians.

6) Jehoshaphat of Judah (*22:41-50*).

7) Ahaziah of Israel (*22:51-2 Kin. 1:18*).

8) Elijah's translation and the imparting of his spirit to Elisha (*ch. 2*).

9) Jehoram of Israel (*ch. 3*).

10) The ministry of Elisha the prophet (*4–7*). Elisha's ministry was characterized by a considerable number of miracles, including the resurrection from the dead of the son of the Shunammite woman, the healing of Naaman's leprosy, and the floating axe head. Ch. 8 records the strange phenomenon of a prophet's anointing the head of a foreign king to punish the prophet's own people. Instructions to this effect had been given to Elijah (*1 Kin. 19:15*).

11) Jehoram and Ahaziah of Judah (*8:16-29*).

12) Jehu, king of Israel (*9–10*). Having been anointed by Elisha to punish the house of Ahab for its great wickedness, Jehu set about his task with a frightening zeal. Everything which is known of him can be characterized by the statement in 9:20: "he driveth furiously."

13) Miscellaneous kings of Israel and Judah (*11–16*). During his period Israel reached a period of great prosperity under Jeroboam II, regaining many of the areas which she had previously lost.

14) The captivity of Israel by Assyria in 721 BC (*ch. 17*). The last king of Israel was Hoshea. He, like the nineteen kings before him, was guilty

of idolatrous worship. Finally, after repeated efforts by the prophets to turn the people from their idols, God allowed the ten tribes of Israel to be carried out of their homeland.

III. *The Kingdom of Judah Alone* (*2 Kin. 18–25*)

This section contains an account of the last nine kings of Judah and the fall of Jerusalem. For a better historical perspective and a fuller treatment, the reader is referred to the introduction to the books of *Chronicles.*

Although the books of *Kings* contain a great deal of historical material, history is not their primary concern. In the Hebrew canon, they are classified, along with *Joshua, Judges* and the books of *Samuel*, as the "earlier prophets." A close inspection of the books will reveal that the lessons intended to be gained from them are spiritual and not political. The writers of these books have utilized an historical framework in an effort to proclaim their message of single-eyed devotion to God, the factual information being appealed to for illustration and confirmation. In this connection, it is well to suggest that a valuable aid to a proper understanding of the history of these two books and to a filling out of the outline which they provide is to be found in the study of the prophets, especially Isaiah and Jeremiah. An intimate acquaintance with these prophets is essential for a clear grasp of the concise narrative of these books.

The Books of Chronicles

In the English versions of the Bible, the two books of *Chronicles* are placed immediately after *Kings*, although in the Hebrew canon they stand at the very end of the Old Testament. It is usually assumed that, as in the case of the books of *Samuel* and *Kings*, the two books of *Chronicles* were originally one. The Hebrew title of the books is translated "the words of the days." The name *Chronicles* is largely due to a suggestion by Jerome to the effect that they ought to bear a title derived from the Greek word for time, *chronos*. Unfortunately, the title has led many to consider the books as nothing more than copies of public documents or annals, when in reality they were designed for a serious religious purpose, as will be noted below.

The date of the *Chronicles* can be no earlier than the decree of Cyrus allowing the Jews to return from Babylon (Cf. *2 Chr. 36:22*), which sets c. 537 BC as a terminal date. The general belief that these two books form a unit with *Ezra* and *Nehemiah*, however, brings the probable date much nearer 400 BC. The closing verses of *2 Chronicles* (*36:22-23*) are almost identical to the opening verses of *Ezra* (*1:1-4*). Hebrew tradition represents Ezra as the author both of *Chronicles* and the book bearing his name. This is certainly a possibility, as the books definitely appear to have been written from the same viewpoint, but there is nothing in them to necessitate the view that one man is responsible for the entire series.

To a great extent, *Chronicles* is a sifting of source materials to arrive at the exact facts which the compiler wished to record. Among the sources specifically mentioned are five books of the kings of Israel and/or Judah (*2 Chr. 16:11; 25:26; 27:7; 20:34; 33:18; 24:27;* etc.) It is possible that these are variant designations of the same work. Named in connection with the history of David are "the words of Samuel the seer, of Nathan the prophet and of Gad the seer" (*1 Chr. 29:29*). A source cited with reference to the history of Solomon is called "The words of Nathan the prophet, the prophecy of Ahijah the Shilonite, and the visions of Iddo the seer against Jeroboam the Son of Nebat" (*2 Chr. 9:29*). In all, twenty or more sources are named. Besides this, the Chronicler often seems to be quoting from public documents and letters. Taken together, this would indicate that the range of sources to which he had access is astounding, considering the time at which the books appear to have been written. A fascinating possibility in connection with this is found in a passage from the apocrypha. In *2 Maccabees 2:13-15*, reference is made to a library which Nehemiah was collecting which would include just such documents as those referred to in *Chronicles.*

One of the great difficulties connected with the captivity and return must have been the proper distribution of land, which was yet a vital point of the Jewish economy. Another difficulty, closely connected with the former, was the maintenance of the temple services at Jerusalem. Two things were necessary to make this possible. The first was seeing that the priests and Levites were in Jerusalem at the appointed time of their courses of service and fulfilled their proper function. Since the various offices in the temple service were assigned by families, proper genealogical records were imperative. Secondly, the proper support of the Levites had to be insured if the temple service was to be maintained. Since the payment of tithes, first-fruits, etc., was dependent upon each family's being established in its inheritance, it was even more necessary to provide trustworthy genealogies. *1 Chr. 1–8* contain the efforts of the author to meet this need, while ch. 9 notes that the people were thus enabled to return to their rightful inheritances.

Having provided the desired information, the author seeks to bring the people to a realization of the true glory of their nation as the original theocracy and to a recognition of the rights and importance of the kingdom of David. Nothing could serve his purpose better than a compendious history of this kingdom, with a full account of its prosperity and the sin which led to its downfall. In preparing this history, the Chronicler chose only those materials which were integral to his purpose. His major concern is with two divine institutions—the temple service and the Davidic dynasty. The northern kingdom is scarcely mentioned, and then only where it affected the fortunes of Judah. The events mentioned in connection with David are those which relate to the worship in Jerusalem and preparations for building the temple. In dealing with the life of Solomon the emphasis lies on the building and dedication of the Temple, instead of the splendor of his kingdom and the personal events of his life. Similarly, prominence is given to the formal worship of the temple and the functions of the Levites whenever possible. The kings whose reigns are stressed are those who were in opposition to the idolatry which constantly seduced the Israelites. When the purpose of these two books is properly understood, the manner in which they treat history becomes much more explicable.

The contents of the books of *Chronicles* may be analyzed as follows (a fuller discussion of a number of points may be found in the introductory article on the books of *Kings*):

1 Chronicles

I. *Genealogical Matters* (*1–9*)

These genealogies begin with Adam (*1:1*) and are brought up to the time of the writer (Cf. *ch. 9*). It is surprising to note the large number of historical incidents mentioned in connection with the individuals named in these lists. Many of these are taken from other Old Testament scripture, but some find their origin elsewhere (Cf. *4:9, 10, 38–43*).

II. *The Reign of David* (*10–29*)

1) The last days and death of Saul and the early reign of David (*10–12*).

2) The return of the ark to Jerusalem (*13–16*). Included in this section is the account of the misfortune of Uzzah, who was killed when he reached forth to save the ark from falling (*13:9ff*).

3) David purposes to build the temple but is forbidden because of the great amount of bloodshed to which he has been a party (*ch. 17*).

4) The account of David's conquests (*18–20*).

5) The census and the plague (*ch. 21*).

6) David's preparations for building the temple (*ch. 22*). Although David was himself forbidden to build a temple for God, he set about to collect the necessary materials for such a temple, that the task of his son Solomon might be easier.

7) Designation of the duties of the Levites (*ch. 23*).

8) Organization of the government (*ch. 24*).

9) David's last words and his death (*28–29*).

2 Chronicles

I. *The Reign of Solomon* (*1–9*)

This section includes the further preparation, the building and the dedication of the Temple, as well as various other activities of Solomon.

II. *The History of Judah to Its Fall* (*10–36*)

1) The revolt of the ten tribes and the reign of Rehoboam (*10–12*).

2) The reign of Abijah (*ch. 13*).

3) The reign of Asa (*14–16*). This was a period of prosperity in Judah as Asa instituted a number of moral and religious reforms, establishing himself as a servant of the Lord.

4) The reign of Jehoshaphat (*17–20*). This

king was also diligent in his efforts to serve God. He made considerable efforts to acquaint his people with the Law.

5) The reigns of Jehoram and Ahaziah (*21:1–22:9*).

6) The reign of Athaliah, the only queen of Judah (*22:10–23:21*).

7) The reign of Joash (*ch. 24*). Ascending to the throne at the age of seven, Joash, advised by the high priest Jehoida, brought about the restoration of true worship. After Jehoida's death, however, Joash himself slipped into the worship of idols.

8) Amaziah, Uzziah, Jotham and Ahaz (*25–28*).

9) The reign of Hezekiah (*29–32*). After beginning his rule with a great religious restoration, Hezekiah helped his nation to regain a measure of power and glory.

10) Manasseh and Amon (*ch. 33*).

11) The reign of Josiah (*34–35*). In the eighteenth year of a reign that began when he was only eight years old, Josiah began the most sweeping religious reforms which Judah had ever known. During the renovation of the temple, the "book of the Law" was found, encouraging the people greatly in this time of revival.

12) The last days of Judah (*ch. 36*). After a brief reign by Jehoahaz, the throne was taken by Jehoiakim, who reigned for eleven years. During this period he was a vassal alternatively to Egypt and Babylon. In an effort to revolt against the Babylonian rule, he lost his life. He was succeeded by Jehoiachin, who reigned only three months, after which he was carried to Babylon, where he lived a number of years. The last of the Judean kings was Zedekiah. Nebuchadnezzar had already plundered Jerusalem of much of its treasures and a considerable number of its most promising men. This took place in two raids, in 606 and 597 BC. In 586 BC, during the reign of Zedekiah, the Babylonians struck once again, this time leaving none but the poorest class of people to remain in Jerusalem. Five years later, the Babylonians came to collect about 750 more captives, even after a number, including Jeremiah, had fled to Egypt (Cf. *Jer. 43*).

Ezra and Nehemiah

In Hebrew tradition *Ezra* and *Nehemiah* are regarded as one book. That the books were not one originally, however, is indicated by the presentation of identical material in *Ezra 2* and *Neh. 7:6-70.* How they came to be regarded as one must remain a matter of conjecture. They are treated together here because of their close relation to one another.

Each book bears the name of its principal character. Ezra was a descendant of the priest Hilkiah, who had helped to implement the reforms of Josiah (*2 Kin. 22:8*). He returned from the Babylonian exile about 457 BC, eighty years after Zerubabbel led the first wave of exiles back to their homeland and thirteen years prior to the return of Nehemiah. He was both a priest and a scribe whose efforts to purify the religion of the Hebrews, based on strict adherence to the Law, immeasurably influenced the course of Judaism for centuries. Ezra is sometimes regarded as the second greatest hero in the history of Israel, ranking just after Moses.

Nehemiah emigrated from Babylon to Jerusalem about 445 BC. He came not as a priest or scribe but as a civil governor with authority granted by the Persian ruler, Artaxerxes, whom he had served as cupbearer (*Neh. 2:1*), to rebuild the wall and other fortifications of Jerusalem. Despite the opposition of the foreigners who had settled in Judea during the exile, the work on the wall was brought to completion in fifty-two days after it was begun.

The tradition which represents *Ezra-Nehemiah* as being one book also names Ezra as the author. That he had a hand in the writing is not unlikely, due to the presence of material in *Ezra* written in the first person. A great portion of *Nehemiah,* however, is also written in the first person, implying that part or all of it was composed by Nehemiah himself. It has been suggested by some that this is not a proof of authorship, but may indicate that a third person compiled one or both of the two accounts, with the help of the personal memoirs of Ezra and Nehemiah. Also, it may indicate that the two men wrote a part of the books which bear their name, but that we owe their final form to a later redactor. A third possibility is that Ezra and/or Nehemiah composed an historical narrative out of available sources, adding certain items of their own composition. The two books appear to have been compiled from a variety of materials, including letters, edicts, genealogies, personal memoirs and chronicles. This helps to explain the diversity in style and language which may be seen in them.

Since a date near 400 BC was tentatively assigned to the books of *Chronicles*, the closely related books of *Ezra* and *Nehemiah* would also receive this date. One objection to this is based on the mention of Jaddua in the list of priests in *Neh. 12:11, 22.* Josephus (*Antiquities* XI, viii, 4) mentions a priest by this name who lived in the time of Alexander the Great (c. 330 BC). Several possible explanations have been offered; it has been pointed out that it would have been possible for Jaddua to have served from 400 to 330 BC, although a more likely solution is either that these were two separate individuals or that we are presented with yet another example of Josephus' unreliability as an historical witness.

The purpose of the two books was to show how God fulfilled the words of his prophets concerning the restoration of his exiled people to the land of their inheritance. To implement his purposes, he used the will of the great monarchs of that era—Cyrus, Darius and Artaxerxes. In addition, he worked through such leaders as Joshua, Zerubbabel, Haggai, Zechariah, Ezra and Nehemiah in order to bring about the rebuilding of the wall and the temple and the re-establishment of the Law as the basis for individual and community conduct. These books furnish almost all of the known history of the Jews between 536 and 430 BC. *Ezra* is concerned with the period from 536 to 456 BC, while *Nehemiah* begins about 445 BC and narrates the events of approximately twelve years.

The contents of the two books may be analyzed as follows:

I. *Ezra*

1) The return of the exiles to Jerusalem at the decree of Cyrus, 546 BC (*1–2*).

2) The work of rebuilding the temple begun, brought to a standstill through the efforts of heathen neighbors, and finally completed at the urging of Haggai and Zechariah (*3–6*).

3) Ezra's return to Jerusalem for the purpose of restoring the temple service (*7–8*).

4) The problem of mixed marriages, which threatened to plunge the Jews into the same course of idolatry which had brought about their original downfall (*9–10*).

II. *Nehemiah*

1) Nehemiah's journey to Jerusalem, made possible by Artaxerxes, for the purpose of rebuilding the wall (*1–2*).

2) A list of the builders and the repairing of the gate (*ch. 3*).

3) The rebuilding of the wall in spite of opposition led by Sanballat, Tobiah and Geshem (*4:1–7:4*).

4) The register of those who returned with Zerubbabel (*ch. 7*).

5) The public reading and exposition of the book of the Law (*ch. 8*).

6) The national repentance and the covenant of obedience (*9:1–10:39*).

7) Lists of inhabitants (*11:1–12:26*).

8) Dedication of the wall and organization of the temple services (*12:27-47*).

9) Nehemiah's reforms of abuses connected with tithes, the sabbath and mixed marriages (*ch. 13*).

In order to gain a complete picture of the history of this period, these two books should be studied in conjunction with the writings of Haggai, Zechariah and Malachi.

Esther

The book of *Esther* receives its title from its chief character, whose name was the Persian word for star. A number of individuals have been suggested as the author. Among these, Mordecai's name is most prominent; however, ch. 10 seems to rule him out as a possibility since it implies that the book was written after the time of his death. In truth, there is no way of determining who was the author of the book. His use of several Persian words and his accurate description of the life and customs of the Persian court indicate that he was a resident of Persia at a time not too far removed from that of the events narrated. It is quite probable that he had access to the official chronicles of the kings (*2:23; 10:2*), as well as to the writings of Mordecai (*9:20*).

Since it is almost surely correct to identify Ahasuerus with the Persian ruler whom the Greeks called Xerxes, the events described in *Esther* probably took place between the years 485 and 470 BC. This would mean that Esther reigned about forty years after the temple was rebuilt and about thirty years before the wall of Jerusalem was rebuilt. It has been suggested by some that she may have had at least an indirect influence in the release of the Jews for the purpose of rebuilding Jerusalem.

This book is valuable to us for several reasons. In the first place, it tells of God's providential care over his people even though they were in a distant land, far away from the center of the Hebrew religion. In this connection it is interesting to note that the name of God is never mentioned in the book. Neither is there any direct reference to worship of any kind. The allusions to fasting (*5:16*) and the "cry" of the people (*9:31*), however, seem to have a religious connotation. Likewise, Mordecai's well-known statement to Esther—"who knows whether you have not come to the kingdom for such a time as this" (*4:14*)—surely indicates belief in some type of overruling providence. A possible explanation is that the book was written at a time when the mention of the name or religion of the God of Israel was either unwise or dangerous, or both.

Esther also furnishes an account of the origin of the Jewish feast of Purim. Finally, the book records a major event in the history of Israel: their escape from complete extermination at the hands of the Persians.

In the Septuagint, the book of *Esther* contains 107 verses which are not in the Hebrew text. These are preserved in the apocryphal book called *The Rest of Esther*, found in some modern Bibles.

The main events in the story of Esther are presented in the following outline:

1) The deposition of Queen Vashti, the wife of the Persian ruler Ahasuerus, for her refusal to appear before the guests of the king (*ch. 1*). It has often been suggested that the Queen refused on grounds of modesty, but the tradition which has arisen around her suggests that her refusal is just as likely to have been the result of simple spitefulness. In order to keep such an attitude from becoming general, thus upsetting the domestic balance, Ahasuerus removed her from the throne and from his presence.

2) The choice of Esther as Queen, after an involved process of elimination (*2:1-20*).

3) Mordecai discovers a plot against the life of the king (*2:21-23*).

4) Haman's plot to destroy the Jews (*3–4*). Because of the refusal of Mordecai to pay homage to Haman, a man "above all the princes" in the Persian government, the latter influenced the King to issue a decree calling for the extermination of the Jews. Mordecai persuaded Esther to intervene, at the risk of her life, on the Jews' behalf.

5) Esther's successful petition (*5–8:2*). Finding favor with Ahasuerus, Esther revealed the heinous plot of Haman. The result was that Haman was hanged and Mordecai received his long-deserved honor for having saved the king's life.

6) The deliverance of the Jews (*8:3–9:16*). Although the decree of the King concerning the Jews could not be rescinded, it was counteracted by the issuing of another decree which allowed the Jews to defend themselves.

7) The Feast of Purim (*9:17-32*). To celebrate their deliverance, the Jews instituted the feast of Purim. This feast is still observed and is a time of great joy among Jews.

8) A description of Mordecai's greatness (*ch. 10*).

Job

The book of *Job*, taking its name from its central character, is the first of the five so-called "poetical" books. It has also been referred to as "wisdom literature." Regardless of the category into which it is placed, this book is widely recognized as one of the great literary productions of all time. Except for chs. 1, 2, and 42, it is written in the formal style of Hebrew poetry, whose beauty depends not on metre or rhyme, but on the use of parallelism, repetition and contrast.

The story is set in a region identified as "the Land of Uz" (*1:1*). This is thought to have been the area southeast of Palestine, along the border it shared with Arabia. Although it is impossible to identify the area exactly, the fact that the setting is not Hebraic gives the story an international milieu which renders it applicable to all men.

Ancient tradition names Moses as the author of the book. It is conjectured that he may have learned the story while he was in the wilderness of Midian (*Ex. 2:15*), near the supposed area of Uz. Many other possible authors, however, have been suggested; none can be agreed on with any degree of certainty whatever. The tendency of modern scholarship is to give the book a date long after the time of Moses.

The picture which is given of Job is that of a patriarch distinguished for his integrity and piety, his wealth, and the great measure of domestic happiness these things have brought. In order to prove Job's fidelity, God deprived him of all these blessings. The book is in the form of a historical poem; that is, a poem which purports to be based on an actual event. This event was an apparently public debate over the nature and cause of Job's afflictions. It is a philosophic discussion of the problem of human suffering—a classic problem which has not as yet received a classic answer. The book is a witness to the fact that God's people in all times have become frustrated in their efforts to reconcile His moral law with the prosperity of the wicked and the affliction of the righteous.

The first two chapters form a prologue in prose to the debates, giving a picture of Job's prosperity, the "wager" between God and Satan, and the resultant affliction which was Job's. Chs. 3–31 contain three series of speeches between Job and his companions, in which he defends himself against their assertion that he is being punished for some secret sin which is known only to God. Elihu's speech, recorded in chs. 32–37, points out that there is a hidden purpose in God's discipline of Job. Chs. 38–41 contain the statements of God to the participants in the discussion; these witness to the futility of man's trying to comprehend the actions of God. Ch. 42 records the restoration of Job's lost blessings.

Although the book of *Job* does not furnish us with a neatly organized solution to the problem of evil, it does illustrate several common shortcomings typical of man's efforts to fathom the secrets of God. The outlook of Job's friends was limited by their conception of the direct ratio between suffering and affliction. Job, although he could give no reason for the misery which was his, denied that great personal sin was the cause. The reader, informed by the prologue, is able to see in Job's affliction an indication of God's confidence in his servant rather than his displeasure. The lesson to be gained from *Job* is that man, since he does not have access to the "prologue" of his own life, can never adequately plumb the depths of God's dealings with men; nevertheless, he is encouraged to maintain fidelity in his devotion to God, assured that God's ultimate purposes are loving and merciful.

Psalms

The Hebrew title of the book of *Psalms* is *sepher tehillim*, meaning "book of praises"; although a number of other themes are prominent, this is surely a fitting title for this collection of religious poetry. Each psalm reflects a personal relationship between its author and Jehovah. Throughout the collection a dominant mood of hope displays confidence in His Lordship of the universe.

Since other peoples in the area in and around Palestine possessed considerable religious poetry, it is not at all surprising that the Hebrews should have produced a collection of such sublimity. The backbone of the Psalter is a number of psalms which purport to come from David. These include psalms 2–41 (except 33), 51–72, 108–110, and 138–145. Some critics deny that David actually wrote any of the psalms himself, but the information which we possess concerning David would imply that he was the sort of man who might be expected to produce such literature. That he was a skillful musician is indicated by his playing the lyre for King Saul (*1 Sam. 16:23*) and by Amos' statement that he invented instruments of music (*Amos 6:5*). His lament over Saul and Jonathan (*2 Sam. 1:19-27*), usually admitted to be genuine, displays his native poetic ability. The sensitivity and feeling thought to be a requisite of lasting poetry is demonstrated in David's repeated and extreme sorrow for his sin. His varied experiences as shepherd, musician, warrior, king, parent, lover and sinner would certainly furnish him with a background favorable to literary production. Above all, David is presented to us as a true worshipper of God, a man possessing the Holy Spirit (*1 Sam. 16:13*). Perhaps not all the psalms which bear his name are actually Davidic, but they are in the same style and a majority probably belong to him.

In addition to the psalms of David, there are two collections of Levitical psalms. Psalms 42–49 are ascribed to the "sons of Korah." Psalms 73–83, as well as Psalm 50, purport to come from Asaph. These give prominence to the tribes of Joseph. Moses, Haman, Ethan and Solomon are also mentioned, while a few of the psalms are purely anonymous (Cf. *33, 84–89*). Others have a strong liturgical character, indicating the possibility that they were developed as they were used in the worship service and on special occasions and cannot easily be attributed to any one author (Cf. *91–100*).

It is not possible to say how the psalms were collected. Few can be definitely dated. If the titles are genuine (see discussion below), they were probably written in the period from about 1500 BC to 500 BC. Most seem to have come from the period of the United Kingdom. The work of Samuel had effected a great national and spiritual unity. This, coupled with the expansion of the life of Israel by David's victories, would naturally inspire men of poetic ability to seek to record their reactions.

Some of the psalms are historical, recalling God's treatment of Israel in the past, while others are prophetic, looking to the future, even to the coming of Messiah. There are psalms of affliction, lamentation and penitence, as well as hymns of thanksgiving and trust. These are divided into five books: 1–41, which witness to David's life and faith; 42–72, a group of historical writings; 73–99, ritual psalms; 90–106, reflecting precaptivity sentiment and history; and 107–150, dealing with the captivity and return to Jerusalem. These five books are often regarded as the devotional counterpart to the five books of Moses.

Some of the psalms were deemed as particularly fitting for recitation on certain days and consequently developed a liturgical use. Some were used primarily on the Sabbath while others were reserved for the Passover, the feast of tabernacles or other Jewish holy days.

Titles appear on about 100 of the psalms. These are quite old, as many were not understood even as early as the second century BC. They are of uncertain value since a psalm "of" David does not necessarily mean that it was a product of David's, but might also be taken to mean that the psalm was written for David or dedicated to him. There is, then, no way of authenticating them. On the other hand, one might ask why the titles were appended if they did not have some basis in fact? There are several general categories into which these titles fall. Some point to the source of the psalm; others indicate a special purpose for which the psalm is best suited, a special melody for the psalm, or a particular type of musical accompaniment which is deemed fitting. The book of *Psalms* is, of course, the longest book in our Bible. The 119th psalm is the longest chapter in the Bible, while the 117th is both the shortest and the middle chapter of the Bible. Over one-third of the New Testament quotations of the Old Testament are from the Psalms.

See page 969.

Proverbs

The title of this book is taken from the assertion in 1:1 that the book is a collection of "the proverbs of Solomon the Son of David, King of Israel." A proverb is a profound maxim or epigrammatic saying. In addition to this opening statement, several other verses indicate that Solomon was chiefly responsible for the material (Cf. *10:1; 25:1*). Chs. 30 and 31 are assigned to Agur and the mother of King Lemuel, respectively, although little is known of either. It ought also to be noted that certain "wise men" are credited with being responsible for some of the maxims (Cf. *1:6; 22:17; 24:23*). Some think that the designation, "proverbs of Solomon," indicate only that they are of the type which originated with Solomon, but were not themselves necessarily his product. While this hypothesis may be true, the information which we have regarding Solomon would certainly lend credence to the view that he could have produced many of the proverbs himself. As a king constantly in touch with his subjects and with other nations, he knew men and events thoroughly. He was blessed with a God-given wisdom (*1 Kin. 4:29*) accompanied by humility (*1 Kin. 3:7*). This sagacity had been tested in practical matters requiring great diplomacy (*1 Kin. 3:16-28; 5:12*) and was widely recognized in the Near East (*1 Kin. 4:30ff; 10:1-13*). It is stated that he composed over three thousand proverbs (*1 Kin. 4:32*), many more than are contained in this book.

Chs. 1-9, perhaps either from Solomon or the above-mentioned "wise men" of Israel, contain statements to the young. These are arranged in a series of discourses in praise of wisdom. A personification of Wisdom speaks as an instructor, warning against all manner of folly. The proverbs in this section are arranged with more continuity than is seen in succeeding chapters.

Chs. 10–22:16 claim to be the "proverbs of Solomon," although as noted above, they can be but a portion of the three thousand maxims which are attributed to the wise king. This section is usually thought to be the original nucleus around which the remainder of the book was constructed.

Counsel for those in responsible positions is contained in 22:17–24:22, claiming to be "the words of the wise." Chs. 24:23-29 are designated as "the proverbs of Solomon which the wise men of Hezekiah copied out." These are usually detached statements, although there are occasional signs of continuity. There has also been some effort to bring together sayings on related subjects such as rulers, sluggards and fools.

Ch. 30, the sayings of Agur, and ch. 31, the great chapter on womanhood which purports to come from the mother of King Lemuel, complete this book of Hebrew wisdom. The latter is constructed in acrostic form, the verses beginning with the successive letters of the Hebrew alphabet.

There is no way of knowing the date at which these proverbs were compiled into one unit; neither is there any hint as to the name of the editor or group of editors. It is not impious, however, to suggest that the book was never intended as a unity, since a number of clear divisions can be seen within the collection.

The maxims contained in *Proverbs* are of great practical value for modern times. They were composed in an era of great prosperity, with all its attendant weaknesses. Their message, however, is not limited to such an age. The *Proverbs* contain principles of life which are applicable to all men in every age and condition of life.

Ecclesiastes

The word "Ecclesiastes" is the Greek equivalent for the Hebrew word *Koheleth*, or "the preacher." This title is taken from the name by which the speaker repeatedly refers to himself. "The preacher" has traditionally been identified with Solomon. Nowhere, however, is Solomon's name mentioned in *Ecclesiastes*. In 1:1, reference is made to "the son of David, king in Jerusalem." This might refer to any king of the Davidic dynasty as well as to Solomon. Even if Solomon is accepted as the speaker, that is, "the preacher," this is no guarantee that he is the writer also. Some critics uphold a composite authorship of the book because of the changes in pronominal forms and unevenness in structure. This is possible, although there is nothing about the book to prohibit the idea that one man is responsible for the entire work.

As was the case with the *Song of Solomon, Ecclesiastes* encountered considerable difficulty in being accepted into the Old Testament canon. Its eventual acceptance has continued to be a source of wonder because of an agnostic quality in the book.

There has been wide disagreement as to the underlying purpose of *Ecclesiastes.* One common interpretation is that "the preacher" wrote at the end of a misspent life, repentant for the mistakes which he had made. Those who uphold this view see the book as a commentary on life by a man looking back on what many would consider the perfect life, yet being cognizant of the disorder and sorrow which still troubled him. It contains the reflections of a man who has thoroughly tried all avenues of pleasure—sensuality, wealth, honor, folly, speculative wisdom. He has sinned in giving way to every excess of life which his position made possible and comes to the realization of the uselessness of it all. He concludes that the result of his efforts have been quite ephemeral; that there is nothing new under the sun, but all is part of the endless, frustrating round. His attitude is mirrored in the recurring phrase, "vanity of vanities, all is vanity, saith the preacher." In *Ecclesiastes*, the world is convicted of its vanity by one who has drunk of every spring.

The conclusion which "the preacher" reaches is that in such an empty and unsatisfying world where disappointment, trouble and death cannot be avoided, a quiet enjoyment of God's gifts is the only real wisdom. The man who is truly wise will "fear God and keep his commandments" (*12:13-14*), making the best of things as he finds them and trusting in the providence of God. This secret of a contented life is found in the consecration of the vigor of youth to the service of God. An understanding of this latter idea keeps the book from being merely a cry of despair and leads one to see the possibility of a rich, positive existence. It profoundly illustrates the idea that a life apart from God is a life without meaning.

Song of Solomon

The first verse of this book connects it with Solomon. Because of this, it is often called the *Song of Solomon.* It is also referred to as *Canticles* or the *Song of Songs*, implying that it is the finest of all songs. Its admittance into the Old Testament canon was widely disputed; in fact, although it was accepted as a sacred book earlier, the question of canonicity was not completely settled until after the time of Christ.

Jewish tradition names Solomon as the writer, which would place the date of the book around 1012 BC. Some hold, however, that the statement in 1:1 is a later insertion and no part of the original text. These critics also maintain that the large number of foreign words which are found in the *Song* would not have appeared in the literature of Israel until after the captivity. In recent years, an increasing number of critics have taken this view.

Although the story is not as lucid as may be desired, one likely interpretation is that a beautiful girl of Shulam, engaged to a young shepherd, is sighted by a king (apparently Solomon) who falls in love with her and carries her to Jerusalem. Although the king offers her every inducement to become his bride, the young girl remains true to her country lover, whom she describes in glowing terms to the court women. After consistently rejecting the king, she is permitted to return home to her true love.

Various efforts have been made to draw a spiritual application from this song of faithful love. Jews saw it as an allegory of the love of God for the congregation of Israel. Many Christians have accepted the allegorical view, although it is usually applied to the relationship between Christ and his bride, the church.

An early Christian writer, Theodore of Mopsuestia, maintained that the book was a mere song of human love composed on the occasion of the marriage of Solomon to the daughter of Pharaoh. Although most have been reluctant to accept such a view, it must be admitted that there is nothing in the *Song* which suggests that it is an allegory. It might easily be simply an extolling of the victory of faithful love over the temptations of wealth and worldliness, upheld as an ideal for improving society.

Isaiah

The prophet Isaiah, whose name means "Jehovah is salvation," was the son of Amoz (*1:1*), not to be confused with the prophet Amos. He prophesied during the reign of Uzziah, Jotham, Ahaz, Hezekiah and possibly Manasseh. This would mean that his ministry lasted from about 740 BC till about 700 BC. The vision which served as Isaiah's call to the prophetic ministry is recorded in ch. 6. From the description which is given of this vision, it is clear that it must have exerted tremendous influence over Isaiah throughout his life. The willingness to serve which he expressed so succinctly in 6:8 remained undaunted in spite of the knowledge that he and his message would be rejected (*6:9-13*). In the years to follow, he not only spoke of things spiritual but he offered warnings and interpretations concerning the political issues of his time. Aside from the fact that he was married to a woman called the "prophetess" (*8:3*), who bore him two sons (*7:3; 8:3*), little is known of his personal history. Jewish tradition has it that he was placed in the trunk of a carob tree and sawn asunder by order of the wicked king Manasseh. Many suppose that *Heb. 11:37* refers to him.

During the span of Isaiah's ministry, Judah underwent great periods of change. His call came in the last year of King Uzziah's reign, about 740 BC. Uzziah was, generally speaking, a good king and had brought to Judah a degree of wealth and power which she had not known since the time of Solomon. With these accomplishments, however, came the attendant sins of avarice, corruption, oppression and religious formalism. While gaining materially, Judah had retrogressed spiritually. Uzziah was succeeded by his son Jotham, who also sought to encourage the worship of Jehovah but who failed, as had his father, to break down the high places of idolatrous worship. Ahaz followed Jotham and set about to replace the true worship with devotion to heathen idols. Though rebuked by Isaiah, Ahaz led the people further in a march which, in time, was to bring them to destruction. Following Ahaz as king was Hezekiah, one of the best ever to reign over the southern kingdom. Hezekiah began his reign with a religious reformation in which he "removed the high places, and broke the pillars, and cut down the Asherah" (*2 Kin. 18:4, 22*). Under Hezekiah, Isaiah enjoyed great popularity and was given wide opportunity to present his message. Judah, however, was gripped with a malignancy which could be detained, but never fully arrested. It was during the reign of Hezekiah that the Assyrians carried Israel off into captivity. Judah herself narrowly escaped destruction by promising to pay heavy tribute to the northern invaders. Eventually, Hezekiah refused to pay the tribute. Sennacharib, the Assyrian ruler at the time, decided to march on Judah and although he was never successful in destroying the southern kingdom, the toll which was taken was a heavy one. Judah had brief moments of glory thereafter, but it was simply a matter of time until the overthrow of the nation, of which Isaiah had prophesied so long, would come to pass. The seeds of destruction had already been sown; the harvest was inevitable.

The major critical problem connected with the book of *Isaiah* is that of its unity and authorship. A large number of critics maintain that chs. 1–39 and 40–66 are two separate books by entirely different men, the author of the second portion being referred to as "Deutero-Isaiah" or "Second Isaiah." Although the scope of this brief article does not admit of a proper treatment of the problem, a few major points may be noted. Those who hold that the sections are by different authors assign chs. 40–66 to a period during the Babylonian captivity. To all appearances, the audience addressed is a different one from that of the first section. The references to Cyrus (see outline below) are made in a manner to indicate that he was already on the scene and familiar to the group addressed. This school of thought also points out that nowhere is the claim of Isaianic authorship made in the second section and there is very little in the section to conflict with the theory of a later date. On the other hand, the following arguments may be adduced in support of the unity of the book. No extant manuscript gives any hint of the book's ever having been in any other form. There are certain unusual ideas and phrases which are common to both sections of *Isaiah* but which are seldom found elsewhere in the Old Testament. The local coloring in the second section would apply more aptly to Judea than to Babylon. Also, there are certain passages in the second division, such as references to the temple services, which must be pre-exilic. These, taken cumulatively, make a strong plea for the unity of the book. For a more detailed study of this problem, the reader is referred to standard commentaries and introductory works. Fortunately, the profound religious value which *Isaiah* possesses for us is not contingent on the solution of this difficult problem.

The contents of *Isaiah* may be analyzed as follows:

Section 1: Chs. 1:39

1) Prophecies centered around Judah and Jerusalem (*1:1–12:6*). Included in this section are a description of the glories of the Messianic Age (*2–4*) and the account of the call of Isaiah (*ch. 6*). In chs. 7–12, although Isaiah is dealing primarily with various invasions which threaten Judah, reference is made to the wonderful child "Immanuel" and to the glorious age when a king of the Davidic line would institute a benevolent rule over a world without discord and wars.

2) Prophecies of judgment on the foreign and hostile nations of Babylon, Philistia, Moab, Damascus, Ethiopia, Egypt, Dumah, Arabia and Tyre (*13–23*).

3) The Apocalypse of Isaiah: the judgment of God against the world's sin and the ultimate destruction of the earth (*24–27*). Despite the dreadful nature of the punishment which was to come, this section is marked by a note of triumph and trust (Cf. especially *ch. 26*).

4) Prophecies concerning the relations of Judah and Jerusalem to Egypt and Assyria (*28–33*). In this section is contained a series of six messages of woe, directed first against one and then another of the weaknesses of Judah's national life (*28:1-29; 29:1-14; 29:15-24; 30:1-17; 31:1–32:20; 33:1-24*). The character of the Messianic Age is also further described (*32:1-18*).

5) The doom of Edom and the redemption of Israel (*34–35*). Ch. 35 is a beautiful picture of the ultimate triumph of the spiritual Zion.

6) The reign of Hezekiah (*36–39*). This section is in the nature of an historical appendix recording the overthrow of the Assyrian army (*36–37*), Hezekiah's sickness and recovery (*ch. 38*), and containing a prophecy of the Babylonian captivity (*ch. 39*).

Section II: Chs. 40–66

7) God's sovereign and providential control over history, which will be manifest in his ultimate overthrow of Babylon at the hands of Cyrus (*40–48*). Two passages of especial interest in this section are the first "suffering servant" passage, apparently alluding to the office of the Messiah (*42:1-9*), and Isaiah's sarcastic appraisal of the folly of idol worship (*44:6-23*).

8) The redemption which is possible through suffering and sacrifice (*49–55*). This division centers mainly around the three "suffering servant" passages which it contains. The first is concerned with the difficulty of his task and his rejection by those to whom he is sent (*44:1-13*). The second (*50:4-9*) speaks of the obedience and trust of the "servant" and the blessings which are to follow his work. The third is the classic passage from 52:13–53:12, which describes the life, suffering and ultimate triumph of the servant.

9) The triumph of the kingdom of God and God's universal reign (*56–66*). The sins which are prevalent in Isaiah's day are discussed in chs. 56–59. A glorious song of the Messianic Age fills chs. 60–62. The book closes with a prayer for mercy and pardon (*63–64*) and God's answer to this prayer in the form of the promise of a new heaven and a new earth (*65–66*).

Jeremiah

Jeremiah lived in the reigns of Josiah, Jehoahaz (Shallum), Jehoiakim, Jehoiachin and Zedekiah. His long career as a prophet of Judah began in the thirteenth year of Josiah (627 BC) and continued till the eleventh year of Zedekiah (586 BC), when Jerusalem was taken by Nebuchadnezzar (*Jer. 1:2-3*), although he continued to prophesy even after that event. He was "the son of Hilkiah, of the priests that were in Anathoth," a town within an hour's walking distance of Jerusalem. He was called to be a prophet while still a young man (*1:6*). In this call, he learned that a northern enemy would bring about the destruction of Jerusalem (*1:11-16*).

Jeremiah's condemnation of the sins of the people aroused much hostility against him, both in his home town of Anathoth and in Jerusalem (*11:18-23*). It is even implied that his own family "dealt treacherously" with him (*12:6*). Despite these sorrows, however, this was to prove to be the happiest time of the ministry of the weeping prophet. Under the next four kings of Judah, Jeremiah spoke out fearlessly. He drew upon himself the anger of the court by predicting the capture and ultimate destruction of Jerusalem in consequence of the people's sins. He was forced into hiding by the anger of Jehoiakim, who cut his book of prophecies with a pen knife and burned them. After the preliminary captivity under Jehoiachin, Zedekiah was appointed by the Babylonians to serve as a puppet king. In time he sought to throw off the Chaldean yoke, but was warned by Jeremiah that the safest course to follow was to remain subservient (*27:12*). Finally, under Nebuchadnezzar, Jerusalem was destroyed, bringing to fruition the many predictions of Jeremiah concerning the event. After the destruction of Jerusalem he remained for a long time in the city, but was finally forced to go to Egypt, along with his companion and secretary, Baruch. There, in the city of Tahpanhes, we have the last clear glimpses of his life; after this, nothing is certain. If he wrote 52:31, which is doubtful, he lived to extreme old age. There is a Christian tradition that the Jews at Tahpanhes, irritated by his rebukes, finally stoned him to death. On the other hand, however, there is a Jewish tradition to the effect that when Nebuchadnezzar conquered Egypt, Jeremiah and Baruch escaped to Judea where the prophet was allowed to die in peace.

There is good reason to believe that Jeremiah himself was responsible for the production of the book, although the actual writing was probably done by Baruch. In 36:1-2, 4, 8, 32, we read of his collecting and writing Jeremiah's prophecies. It is quite possible that he continued to do this in Egypt, until its present form was reached.

The messages which constantly recur throughout Jeremiah's prophecies are: 1) The impending destruction of Jerusalem by Babylon; 2) the possibility of averting this destruction by repentance; 3) the submitting to Babylonian rule after it becomes apparent that domination is inevitable; 4) Babylon herself will be destroyed, never to rise again; and 5) Judah will return from captivity and eventually achieve an unsurpassed glory.

The prophecies contained in the book are not

in chronological order, a factor which makes logical analysis somewhat difficult; however, the following general divisions of the material may be seen:

1) The call of Jeremiah (*ch. 1*).

2) The depravity of Judah and the inevitability of destruction from the north (*2–6*).

3) The illusions of temple security (*7–10*). In this section Jeremiah weeps over the attitude of the people that their formal observance of the temple services will save them from destruction. He warns them that genuine repentance is their only hope.

4) Jeremiah's complaint over his own miserable estate and the infidelity of the Jews of the covenant (*11–12*).

5) Further preaching and signs of the impending doom (*13–25*). In ch. 25, Jeremiah predicted that the length of the captivity would be seventy years.

6) Prophecies and events during the reigns of the last kings of Judah (*26–39*).

7) Prophecies and events in Judah after the captivity (*40–41*).

8) Jeremiah's activity after he is forced to flee to Egypt (*42–51*). After a final exhortation to abandon idolatry (*ch. 44*), the bulk of this section consists of prophecies against foreign nations, including a prediction of the eventual fall and desolation of Babylon.

9) A summary chapter on the captivity of Judah, possibly added by someone other than Jeremiah (*ch. 52*).

Lamentations

In the Hebrew scriptures, this book is known simply as "Lamentations." The tradition ascribing these lamentations to Jeremiah first appears in its title in the Septuagint, the Greek version of the Hebrew scriptures. The book itself, however, does not claim to be the work of Jeremiah. The basis for the tradition is probably *2 Chr. 35: 25*, in which it is stated that Jeremiah composed a lamentation over the death of Josiah; it is a mistake, however, to identify our present book with this lament over Josiah. Whoever the real author was, he was undoubtedly an eyewitness of the events which provoked his sorrowful offering. Although a number of differences have been noted between the style of *Lamentations* and that of *Jeremiah*, these may possibly be accounted for by the fact that after the destruction of Jerusalem, Jeremiah was free to speak from his heart in a manner which had previously been forbidden him. It is also possible that these odes of woe were compiled by a group of Jeremiah's disciples from the utterances of the prophet himself. This would help to explain the formal manner in which the book is arranged as well as accounting for the similarities which may also be noted between the two books.

Four of the five chapters of *Lamentations*—the exception being ch. 5—are odes arranged in acrostic form. Chs. 1, 2, and 4 each contain twenty-two verses which, in the Hebrew text, begin with the successive letters of the Hebrew alphabet. In ch. 3, each letter of the alphabet is allotted three of the sixty-six verses which comprise that ode. It has been suggested that this was done to emphasize that Israel had sinned "from A to Z."

These five odes depict the desolate condition of the forsaken city of Jerusalem, especially as contrasted with its former splendor. The reasons for God's anger toward the Jews are enumerated and an appeal is made to him to remember the affliction of his people and to take vengeance upon the conquerors of Judah.

Ezekiel

Ezekiel, the great prophet of the Babylonian exile, was taken captive in the captivity of Jehoiachin, eleven years before the destruction of Jerusalem. He was a member of a community of Jewish exiles who settled on the banks of the Chebar, a "river" or stream of Babylon. It was by this river "in the land of the Chaldeans" that he received his call to the prophetic office, in the fourth month of "the fifth year of King Jehoiachin's captivity" (595 BC). We learn from an incidental allusion (*24:18*)—the only reference which he makes to his personal history—that he was married and had a house in his place of exile, and that he lost his wife by a sudden and unforeseen stroke on the very day that the siege of Jerusalem began. The last date mentioned in his prophecy is the twenty-seventh year of the captivity, so it is certain that his ministry lasted over twenty-two years. Tradition asserts that he was murdered in Babylon by some Jewish prince whom he had convicted of idolatry and was buried on the banks of the Euphrates.

The style in which the entire book is written indicates that it is the work of one man, although some critics have doubted its unity. It is characterized by the frequency of visions and symbolical acts which were witnessed or performed by Ezekiel; several of these are noted in the outline given below. His prophecy is quite unusual in that he constantly addresses the Jews in Jerusalem and describes events that are taking place in that city, although he himself is in Jerusalem.

The purpose of Ezekiel's ministry may be seen rather clearly by noting the major divisions of the book. In the first half of the book (*chs. 1–33*) Judah is convicted of violating virtually every command which God had given. Warning is given that even the Jewish theocracy will be destroyed if the people persist in their sin. After the announcement of the destruction of Jerusalem in ch. 33, the book takes on a different tone. From this point forward, Ezekiel's message is predominantly one of comfort and encouragement to the defeated Jews. The contents of the book may be analyzed further as follows:

I. *Israel's sin and impending judgment, uttered before the final captivity* (*chs. 1–24*).

1) Biographical information concerning Ezekiel, including a note as to his personal situation and a description of his call to the prophetic ministry (*1–3*).

2) The siege of Jerusalem portrayed in four symbolical acts (*4–7*). In the first of these, Ezekiel evidently drew a picture of a city under siege, indicating that this was soon to be the condition of Jerusalem. After this, Ezekiel lay on his side for a great number of days, announcing that the nation was to be punished for its sins. By eating an inferior type of food which had been cooked on animal dung, Ezekiel predicted the famine which would accompany the siege. In the final act, Ezekiel shaved his head, burning his hair, striking it with a sword and scattering it to the winds, indicating the fate of the inhabitants of Jerusalem. Chs. 6 and 7 contain additional oracles concerning Israel's sin and imminent doom.

3) Visions of idolatry in Jerusalem and the resultant judgment and destruction of that city (*8–11*).

4) Further prophecies against Jerusalem (*12–24*). This section contains a rebuke of false prophets and hypocrites (*12–14*), a repeated emphasis on the certainty and necessity of punishment (*15–17*), a discussion of retribution and responsibility and a reassertion of God's love toward sinners (*ch. 18*), a lamentation or dirge over the rulers of Judah (*ch. 19*) and final warnings before the complete destruction of Jerusalem (*20–24*).

II. *Prophecies against the nations of Ammon, Moab, Edom, Philistia, Tyre, Sidon and Egypt* (25–32).

III. *Prophecies concerning the restoration of Israel, uttered after the destruction of Jerusalem at the hands of Nebuchadnezzar.*

1) A discussion of the responsibility of the people to respond to the call of the prophet (*33:1-20*).

2) The announcement of the fall of Jerusalem (*33:21-33*).

3) A contrast between the leadership of the faithless shepherds (kings) of Judah and Israel and the true shepherd who was to come (*ch. 34*).

4) The doom of Edom (*ch. 35*).

5) The vision of the valley of dry bones, symbolizing the resurrection of the remnant of Israel (*36–37*).

6) The prophecy of Gog and Magog (*38–39*).

7) The rebuilt Temple (*40–48*).

These last two sections have been the subject of varied conflicting interpretations. To assist in understanding them, the reader is invited to consult the standard Old Testament commentaries.

Daniel

Daniel was a youth of Jerusalem, apparently of aristocratic standing (*1:3*), who had been carried to Babylon by Nebuchadnezzar when Jerusalem fell. He quickly distinguished himself in Babylon by refusing to eat the "dainties" which the king had set before him and by exercising his unusual ability to interpret dreams (*1:8-16*). In time he was brought before Nebuchadnezzar to offer an interpretation of a puzzling dream which the king had dreamt; his explanation so impressed Nebuchadnezzar that Daniel was allowed to rise to a place of great prominence in the kingdom. His famous delivery from the lion's den came after he had become the victim of a plot to cause him to lose favor in the eyes of Darius the Mede, the conqueror of Babylon who had also shown favor to Daniel.

Although the book purports to have come from Daniel, considerable opposition to his being its actual author has been advanced. The first critic of the genuineness of the book was Porphyry of Tyre, a neo-Platonic philosopher of the third century AD who asserted that it had been written by a person living in the second century BC during the reign of Antiochus Epiphanes. The main ground for his theory was his rejection of the possibility of predictive prophecy. Since the book presented such an accurate picture of events in the time of Antiochus Epiphanes, it was therefore concluded that it was written not in the sixth century BC (the time of the captivity), but at a date after the events "predicted" had already taken place, and was therefore a fraud.

In addition to the basic argument of Porphyry, later critics have assigned a late date to the book due to certain historical references claimed to be in error or anachronistic, the apocalyptic style of writing, and the language of the book, which is claimed to come from a period later than the sixth century BC.

The question of the date of writing is closely bound up with authorship. If Daniel was not the author of this book, it was written between 605 BC and 533 BC, possibly closer to the latter date. If he was not, it is probable that the book was written in the second century BC.

The text of the book has come down to us partly in Hebrew and partly in an Aramaic dialect. Attempts to explain this all contain a certain amount of conjecture and it is unlikely that a perfectly acceptable solution will be found.

Daniel is divided into two sections of six chapters each. Chs. 1–6 are largely historical, explaining how Daniel came to be in the court of Nebuchadnezzar and of his rise to power. It tells of Nebuchadnezzar's dream of the image which Daniel interpreted to refer to the current kingdom and three world powers which would arise after it and of the kingdom of God—"a kingdom which shall never be destroyed"—which would arise during the era of the last of these great empires. This section also includes the account of the deliverance of Shadrach, Meshach, and Abednego from the fiery furnace and of the handwriting on the wall which spelled out the defeat of Belshazzar at the hands of the Medes and the Persians.

The second section, chs. 8–12, describes visions which Daniel received concerning the great world powers of the future and the kingdom of God.

The Greek translation of *Daniel* contains additions not found in the Hebrew and Aramaic text. These additions are found as separate books in the Apocrypha and are called *The Song of the Three Holy Children*, the *History of Susanna*, and *Bel and the Dragon*.

The value of the book of *Daniel* may be seen in its assurance to God's people that their situation in exile was not permanent, that God would keep his promise to Abraham, and that the Jews would still be the channel through which all nations would be blessed. It is a grand tribute to the providence of God and His lordship of history and the universe.

Hosea

It is usually agreed that the prophet Hosea was a resident of the Northern Kingdom, Israel. He mentions places in Israel not prominent in other prophetic writings in such a way as to imply a personal acquaintance with them. He is also well aware of political, religious, and social developments in Israel. There are, to be sure, certain definite references to Judah, but the bulk of the prophecy is directed to Israel.

Hosea's ministry covered a long period, as indicated by developments in the story and by the list of kings included in 1:1. Although his message was primarily concerned with Israel, he lists four kings of Judah (Uzziah, Jotham, Ahaz, and Hezekiah) and only one from Israel (Jeroboam II); during the years covered by the reigns of the four kings mentioned, however, no less than six kings ruled in Israel. It has been conjectured that Hosea refrains from naming them because they ruled such a short time and because their reigns were marked by violence. Despite the fact that the exact date of Hosea's ministry cannot be established, it is probably safe to estimate that he was active from before the middle of the 8th century BC until about 720 BC.

At the beginning of Hosea's preaching, Israel was enjoying the prosperous period of the reign of Jeroboam II. The seeds of certain difficulty, however, were seen to lie in Israel's trying to preserve her position by political machinations instead of relying on God. An example of the chaos which resulted may be seen in the fact that in the twenty-one years that followed Jeroboam II, Israel was ruled by six different kings, four of whom were assassinated.

Israel's past and future troubles are attributed by Hosea to her persistent practice of idolatry. The people are offering sacrifices on heathen altars; adultery and cult prostitution are prevalent. The figure which Hosea often uses to describe the spiritual condition of the Israelites is a lack of knowledge. He is not speaking simply of intellectual knowledge, but of a real personal relationship with God.

Running throughout the book is the theme of God's enduring love in spite of the degenerate condition of Israel and her indifference to that love. In chs. 1–3, the faithless actions of Israel toward God are illustrated by the relationship between Hosea and his worthless marriage partner, Gomer. The names of his children indicate the attitude of God toward Israel. The first is named "Jezreel" after the city which was the scene of Jehu's brutality and which signified that God would punish his people. Lo-Ruhamah (Not pitied) and Lo-Ammi (Not my people) are the names given to the two other children, signifying the estrangement which was the inevitable result of the actions of Israel. God's love is illustrated in Hosea's willingness to take his wife back from the practice of harlotry—though not without some discipline.

The second division of the prophecy, found in chs. 4–14, presents a detailed picture of the depths of depravity to which Israel had gone, with alternating passages of reproof, threats of punishment, and assurances of restoration.

Joel

The name "Joel" means "Jehovah is God." This was evidently a favorite name in Old Testament times as there are twelve other men mentioned in the Bible who bear this name. Apart from his name and the fact that he was the son of Pethuel, nothing can be said of Joel with any degree of certainty. He was probably from Judah, as his many references to Jerusalem imply.

The time of the writing of the prophecy has long been a disputed matter. It has been placed in every period of prophetic activity, though most scholars agree in giving it either an early, pre-exilic date, probably in the reign of Uzziah (c. 830 BC) or Joash (c. 750 BC) or a late post-exilic date. The reasons adduced for an early date are its position as the second in the book of the Twelve Prophets in the Hebrew Canon, the lack of any mention of the nation of Israel, and the apparently active condition of religion which would fit the early years of the reign of Joash. Those who contend for a late date argue that the lack of any mention of Israel is due to the fact that it had already been destroyed. It is also maintained that the lack of any reproof for idolatry and the activity of the priesthood fits best with the period after the return from exile.

The land of Judah had evidently suffered a devastating plague of locusts followed by famine and drought. The plague is described in four stages referring either to four kinds of locusts or four stages of development in the common locust. This great hardship offered Joel a propitious opportunity to speak of a greater judgment which was to befall the nation and to call for a season of repentance, fasting and mourning (*2:12*).

In 2:28ff Joel describes the "day of the Lord." On the first Pentecost after Jesus' resurrection, Peter spoke of the events of that day as fulfilling "that which was spoken by the prophet Joel" (*Acts 2:16ff*). The remainder of the prophecy is thought by many to be a picture of the Christian Era and the triumph of the gospel with its placing of the sickle to the "fields white unto harvest" (*3:13;* Cf. *John 4:35*).

The vivid description, the intense call to action, and the careful, faultless style of this short work have made it a classic of Hebrew literature.

Amos

The prophet Amos was a native of Tekoa, a city set on a hill of 2,700 feet overlooking the bleak wilderness of Judah and visible from Bethlehem, five miles to the north. The region still bears its ancient name and is, as in the time of Amos, a pasture area filled with flocks of sheep and goats. Amos was not of the professional class of prophets nor was he a son of a prophet; he was a herdsman and a dresser of sycamore trees when he received his summons from God—"The Lord took me as I followed the flock, and the Lord said unto me, 'Go, prophesy to my people Israel' "

(*7:15*). Although this type of life was austere and simple, Amos had evidently come in contact with the commercial centers of Palestine, as he displays considerable knowledge of the habits and attitudes of the people to whom his message is directed.

The opening verse of the prophecy places the activity of Amos "in the days of Uzziah, king of Judah, and in the days of Jeroboam the son of Joash, king of Israel. . . ." Based on this statement and a description of the prosperity which arose under Jeroboam II, it is probable that Amos preached near 750-740 BC. Since the book seems to be a collection of a series of prophetic addresses delivered on different occasions, there is no way of determining how long Amos' ministry lasted.

Although Amos was a resident of the southern kingdom, his message was directed to Israel, particularly to its leading cities of Bethel and Samaria. As noted above, a high degree of prosperity had been achieved during the reign of Jeroboam (Cf. *2 Kin. 14:23-29*). Areas which had been lost were regained and the borders of the kingdom were greatly enlarged. Israel had gained control of the major trade routes and Samaria had established herself as a great commercial center. A rich merchant class had grown up and, as a result of robbery, violence and a general absence of scruples, was enjoying all manner of luxuries, as seen in the sumptuous character of their houses (*3:15*). The merchants were encouraged to follow this course by their avaricious wives whom Amos describes as "cows of Bashan" (*4:1*). The whole picture is one of a complete lack of justice, mercy and normal regard for human life.

The condition of religion in Israel was on a level which matched the low moral and social standard. Although the shrines of God were well attended, they were subjected to the grossest sort of immorality and abuse, fornication and drunkenness being practiced in the very presence of the altar. The worship which was carried on was strictly a formal affair, devoid of any spiritual content. The effect of religion on the conduct of the worshippers was negligible.

This intolerable situation could do nothing but bring the wrath of God. It was to announce this wrath that Amos came to Israel. His message, save for the last chapter, is one of pure condemnation and judgment. In the first two chapters, he announces that the whole area of Palestine is to suffer punishment for its evil, naming some of the most heinous crimes of the eight nations included in this jeremiad. The depravity of these nations is seen in the sins with which they are charged. The Ammonites are condemned "because they have ripped up women with child in Gilead that they might enlarge their border" (*1:13*); doom is promised to the Moabites because their taste for revenge was so strong that they burned to lime the bones of the king of Edom (*2:1*).

After scoring the neighboring nations, Amos turns his attention to Israel. He condemns them for the wealth they have gained at the expense of the poor (*2:6-7*) and for the other excesses noted above. In chapter 4 he recalls the punishments which God had formerly used to recall his people from sin and warns that this generation shall not escape a like trial—"therefore this will I do unto thee, O Israel: and because I will do this unto thee, prepare to meet thy God, O Israel" (*4:12*). The Israelites were warned that the only course which they can follow to avert the imminent disaster is to seek the Lord and to "let justice roll down like waters, and righteousness like an everflowing stream" (*5:24*).

The coming destruction is pictured in chapter 7 by the visions of a plague of locusts, a fire and a plumb line used for measuring the people for destruction. Israel is pictured as a basket of summer fruit (*8:1*), a graphic figure of the short span of life which is to be hers. The closing verses of Amos' prophecy sound a note of hope as he speaks of the restoration of the Davidic strain, referring undoubtedly to the Messiah.

The influence of Amos' rustic background is seen in the many agricultural metaphors which he employs and in the plain-spoken manner in which he delivers his message, heedless of the efforts which are made to silence him (*7:10-17*). Throughout the prophecy one can discern Amos' unflagging conviction that sin will not go unpunished and that the righteousness of God will ultimately triumph.

Obadiah

Obadiah is the shortest book in the Old Testament. The name "Obadiah" means "servant of the Lord" and was quite common from the time of David until the close of the Old Testament. It is found thirteen times in the Old Testament but it is impossible to determine which of these men was the author of this prophecy.

The occasion of the prophecy was a plunder of Jerusalem in which the Edomites had participated and for which they were to be punished. There were four such plunderings and it is difficult to determine to which of these the prophecy refers; many scholars assign it to a time after the destruction of Jerusalem at the hands of the Babylonians, led by Nebuchadnezzar, in 586 BC, during the reign of Zedekiah.

The Edomites were descendants of Esau and were thus related to the Jews, but there was a longstanding enmity between them. Throughout the Old Testament prophecies, there is a denunciation of Edom. The Edomites lived in the rocky range south of the Dead Sea and had built almost impregnable fortresses in the canyons and gorges of these mountains. The magnificent ruins at Petra attest to the greatness which Edom once knew.

This prophecy of Obadiah's tells of the sin of Edom and describes its approaching doom. In the closing passage of the book, the restoration of Judah is foretold. In 582 BC, only four years after the destruction of Jerusalem to which many think this prophecy refers, Edom was overcome by the Babylonians. Until the time of Christ they enjoyed several revivals of power (the Herods, for instance, were an Edomite family), but after the destruction of Jerusalem in AD 70, the Edomites disappeared from history.

Jonah

The book of *Jonah* gains its title, of course, from its chief character. The son of Amittai (*1:1*), Jonah was a native of Gath-hepher, a village of the tribe of Zebulun. Hence, he was a prophet of Israel. If he is to be identified with the Jonah of *2 Kin. 14:25*, he lived in the time of Jeroboam II (the first half of the eighth century BC) and had played some role in helping that king to regain lost territory (*2 Kin. 14:25*). He was evidently well known and probably held quite a respected place in the Northern Kingdom.

There is no way of telling who was actually the author of the book or at what time it was written.

The story itself is one of the most familiar of the Old Testament. Jonah, a prophet of God, is called to deliver a message of repentance to Nineveh, the capital city of the Assyrians. Since Nineveh was already in the process of destroying the Jews, Jonah sought to avoid discharging his commission and boarded a ship bound for Tarshish. He was cast overboard by the sailors in the midst of a storm and swallowed by a great sea monster which the Lord had provided for this purpose.

After being released from the fish, Jonah preached his message to Nineveh and was able to bring about their repentance. Because of his hostility toward this Gentile nation, Jonah began to brood God, by the lesson of the gourd, showed Jonah that he was concerned for other nations besides Israel.

There has been considerable speculation as to the motives of God in sending Jonah to the Ninevites. One generally accepted idea is that God sought to rebuke the parochial spirit of the Jews by offering his favor to the Assyrians, thus demonstrating the capacity of the Gentiles for salvation. In keeping with this suggestion, it is interesting to note that Jonah's place of embarkation was Joppa, the same city from which Peter was called to deliver the gospel to the household of Cornelius, the first Gentile Christians. It has also been suggested that the purpose of Jonah's message was to forestall the Assyrian captivity of Israel by causing the Ninevites to repent of their lust for conquest. A third interpretation which some have preferred is that the key to understanding Jonah lies in Christ's reference to him in *Matt. 12:40-41*; that is, that Jonah was an antitype of Christ and that the central event of the narrative is the escape from the belly of the great fish on the third day (*1:17; 2:10*), just as the central event in the life of Christ was his resurrection from the dead on the third day.

Micah

Micah was called the "Morasthite" because he was a native of Moresheth, sometimes called Moresheth-gath (*1:14*) due to its location in the southwestern part of Judah near the Philistine city of Gath. Little is known of Micah apart from his prophecy. He is mentioned in *Jer. 26:18* as having prophesied in the reign of Hezekiah; the opening verse of *Micah* places his activity in the time of Jotham and Ahaz as well. The period covered by the reigns of these three kings of

Judah was from 751 to 687 BC. The reference in *Jeremiah* is taken by many to be an indication that his main work was in the reign of Hezekiah and that he might therefore be partly responsible for the revival of religion under that king. Micah was a contemporary of Isaiah in Judah and of Hosea in Israel. Some have supposed him to have been a disciple of Isaiah. That there was some contact between the two seems evident from the practically identical passages in *Isa. 2:24* and *Mic. 4:1-3*.

Micah's message was directed to Samaria and Jerusalem, the respective capitals of Israel and Judah, and therefore responsible to some degree for the corruption which had overtaken these two kingdoms. Ch. 1 announces the doom that is to befall Samaria for her idolatry. Ch. 2 is a message of woe for the ruling class, because of their oppression of the poor. In this chapter Micah records the efforts of representatives of this class to suppress his preaching (*2:6, 11*). The sins of the ruling classes, as well as prophets and priests, are dealt with in ch. 3.

The tone of the prophecy shifts abruptly in the opening verses of ch. 4, as Micah pictures the future glory of Jerusalem, or Zion. In 4:9, however, he lapses back into a message of impending doom. A remarkable prophecy is contained in 4:10, as Babylon is named as the conqueror of Judah although, at this time, Assyria was the leading power and Judah by no means appeared safe from her threats. About 100 years later, however, the prophecy was fulfilled as Judah, having survived the Assyrian conquests, was overrun by the forces of Babylon. Another well-known prophecy is contained in 5:2, where it is stated that a ruler for Israel "whose goings forth have been from of old, from everlasting," will come out of Bethlehem. When Herod inquired of the scribes as to the birthplace of Jesus, this prophecy was cited as having been fulfilled (*Matt. 2:1-6*). Chs. 6 and 7 are a continuation of the picture of moral corruption and resultant punishment, but with an assurance that God will show compassion for Israel and will allow a remnant to flourish again, thus keeping the promise which he had made to Abraham (*7:20*).

Nahum

Nahum's message, falling in the last half of the 7th century BC, tells of the destruction which is to befall Nineveh for lapsing back into wickedness. In 3:8-10 Nahum refers to the destruction of Thebes (No-Amon) as an event already past. This is known to have taken place in 663 BC, at the hands of Ashurbanipal, king of Assyria, during his expedition into Egypt. The fall of Nineveh, to which the prophecy points, took place in 606-607 BC. The date of Nahum's prophecy, therefore, may be fixed somewhere within this period of about fifty years, probably nearer the latter date.

The name "Nahum" was a fairly common one and means "consolation" or "consoler," a fitting name for the prophet who brought comfort to the oppressed nation of Judah. Little is known of the personal life of Nahum. He is called the "Elkoshite" in 1:1, which would suggest that he was from a locality known as Elkosh. One theory has it that Elkosh was a city in Galilee, while others place it in Judah or Assyria. Still another tradition identifies Nahum's home with Capernaum ("village of Nahum") and makes Elkosh merely the place of his birth. It is impossible to determine which of these traditions is correct.

As noted above, the subject of Nahum's message is the impending downfall of Nineveh. In ch. 1 God is pictured as one who will triumph over his enemies, regardless of their might. In the rest of the book the reasons for Nineveh's doom are noted. Two sins in particular are singled out. The first is unmerciful military power which plunders, kills and destroys in a heedless and remorseless fashion. The second is the corrupt practice of commerce which causes all morality and integrity to be sacrificed for the sake of acquisition of wealth and lustful pleasures.

Nahum's prophecy represents the cry of the outraged conscience of the nation of Judah over the oppression which they have suffered at the hands of the Assyrians. It is marked by a feeling of satisfaction which almost approaches glee in anticipation of Nineveh's receiving the punishment which is her just due.

Habakkuk

Little can be said with any degree of certainty concerning the prophet, Habakkuk. He was probably a contemporary of Jeremiah, writing in the last half of the seventh century BC. Ch. 1:5-6 contains a threat of the Chaldean (Babylonian) nation's being raised up as an instrument to punish the disobedient Jews. This would date the book either before the rise of Babylon in 625 BC or before the immediate threat to Judah in 606 BC.

The style and approach of the book is unique among the prophets in that it contains the account of Habakkuk's complaints against God and God's answers to these complaints. Habakkuk exemplifies a great faith and a high conception of God, but he is perplexed because events have not taken the course which he had desired. The first complaint which he registers in 1:2-4 is that his preaching to the people has not resulted in repentance on their part. God's answer to this is that he is raising up the Chaldeans to punish the Jews for their disobedience (*1:5-11*). This furnishes Habakkuk with the material for his second complaint—why will God punish His people at the hand of a nation which is even more wicked and unholy than that which is punished? (*1:12–2:1*). God then assures Habakkuk that the Chaldeans are not to go without punishment and that unwavering faith on the part of the Jews will ultimately be rewarded (*2:2-4*). Ch. 2:5-20 contains a condemnation and threat of punishment for aggression, violence, and idolatry. The final chapter of the book is a song of praise of God and His judgment, exemplifying belief in the principle set out in 2:4, "the just shall live by his faith."

Zephaniah

In the opening verse of this prophecy, the lineage of Zephaniah is traced through four generations back to Hezekiah. If this individual is to be identified with King Hezekiah, it is likely that Zephaniah sought to gain authority for his words by showing himself to be of royal blood. If this is the case, it makes his criticism of the ruling classes more notable. Zephaniah probably lived in Judah and quite possibly in Jerusalem. In ch. 1:4, he speaks of Jerusalem as "this place," and in 1:10-11, he exhibits considerable knowledge of the topography of the city.

The first verse of the book places it in the reign of Josiah (c. 642-611 BC). Since the condition described is worse than what might be expected after the reforms of Josiah had been implemented, the prophecy was probably written in the early part of Josiah's reign, as he did not begin his reformation until eighteen years after he had taken the throne.

The social condition of the land was characterized by injustice and oppression (*3:1-3*) and by prosperity which had been gained by violence and fraud (*1:8-9*). The spiritual condition of the people was equally as bad. Josiah had ascended to the throne in the wake of the evil reign of Manasseh. At the time of this writing, Baal was still worshipped (*1:4*). People who claimed to worship God were really swearing by Milcom, another name for the heathen deity Moloch, who was worshipped with human sacrifice (*1:5*). Many had completely "turned back from the Lord" (*1:6*). The people had grown skeptical, feeling that God would not take any sort of action one way or the other (*1:12*). Perhaps it is this situation which made the people ready to accept the reforms of Josiah.

The key idea in Zephaniah's prophecy is the "Day of the Lord," mentioned repeatedly throughout the book. On that day the Lord will avenge Himself for the corruption of His people. The day of destruction is pictured as being imminent and terrible, a day in which few will escape. In order to fulfill His original promise to Abraham, however, God will spare a faithful remnant who will serve as a channel of blessing to the world. The glorious situation in which this remnant will find itself is pictured in ch. 3. They are to be given a pure language "that they may all call upon the name of the Lord, to serve him with one consent" (*3:9*). A beautifully comforting picture of the fortunes of the "Daughter of Zion" is contained in 3:13. "The remnant of Israel shall not do iniquity nor speak lies; neither shall a deceitful tongue be found in their mouth: for they shall feed and lie down, and none shall make them afraid."

Haggai

Haggai was probably born in Babylon during the captivity, but 2:3 indicates that he might possibly have seen the temple of Solomon, which would mean that he was born in Palestine and was an old man at the time of his ministry. He was the first prophet after the captivity and was mentioned by Ezra as having been a co-worker with Zechariah in encouraging the people to complete the building of the second temple (*Ezra 6:14*). Although it cannot be determined what span the life of Haggai covered, the prophecies contained in this book were delivered in a four-month period in 520 BC, "the second year of Darius the King" (*1:1*).

In 536 BC, after seventy years of captivity, a number of exiles returned to Judah by permission of Cyrus. They were led by Zerubbabel the governor and Jeshua the high priest. Shortly after their return, they began the task of rebuilding the temple, the foundation stone being laid in the second month of the second year after the return (*Ezra 3:8-10*). Opposition to the building program arose from the half-cast Samaritans, descendants of the foreign colonists who were introduced into Samaria in 722 BC (*2 Kin. 17:24-41*), and the work was brought to a halt. A feeling of indifference had arisen; at the time of Haggai's ministry, the people had built "ceiled houses" for themselves, but they had allowed the Lord's temple to go unfinished for sixteen years. The purpose of Haggai's ministry was to renew interest in the rebuilding of the temple.

The first of his four prophecies (*1:1-15*) was delivered on the first day of the sixth month of the second year of Darius—about August-September, 520 BC. This was addressed to the leaders, rebuking them for the spiritual lethargy which had allowed the temple to lie unfinished for such a long time. Haggai cites this lethargy as a chief cause for God's having withheld His blessings from the people (*1:6*). Haggai's words were so effective that it was only twenty-four days later that the work of rebuilding the temple was begun.

The second message (*2:1-9*), delivered about a month later (October), was designed to encourage those who were despondent over the disparity in glory between the former temple and the one which they were erecting. He assured them that a greater glory than that of the past temple was to come to the house of Israel. In this connection, he speaks of the "desire of all nations" (*2:7*), interpreted by many to refer to the Messiah.

Two months after the second message, Haggai spoke to the people for a third time. In this section (*2:10-19*), Haggai informs the people that their past indifference had kept them from accomplishing the things which they set out to do but that God would bless their future endeavors.

The last of the prophecies contained in the book was delivered the same day as the third and is found in 2:20-23. In this, the prophet speaks of the establishment of Zerubbabel, a symbol of the idea that God's people were to stand as the power of the heathen nations was broken.

Zechariah

Filled with references to the Messiah the prophecy of Zechariah is admitted by expositors to be an extremely difficult book to interpret. The prophet was the son of Berechiah and the grandson of Iddo (*1:1, 7*). Apparently, he had been born in Babylon and had returned to Jerusalem in the group led by Zerubbabel sixteen years previous to the time of his ministry (*Neh. 12:4, 16*). He was a contemporary of Haggai and began his ministry two months after Haggai had begun his, in 520 BC. The work of rebuilding the temple was already in progress. Zechariah preached at least two years after Haggai ceased to prophesy (*7:1*) and possibly even longer.

The conditions are the same as those described in the introduction to *Haggai*. The purpose of Zechariah's preaching was to join Haggai in the task of encouraging the construction of the temple and to see it through to its completion. He and Haggai deserve much credit for the rebuilt edifice. Zechariah met his task with reproof for shortcomings, encouragement and exhortations, promises of God's blessing and statements looking forward to the Messianic era. The book is divided into two parts: chs. 1–8, concerned mainly with the rebuilding of the temple, and chs. 9–14, dealing with future events, notably the coming of Messiah and the glory of His reign.

Zechariah begins his book with a reminder that the captivity had been a result of disobedience. He continues by relating a series of visions designed to show that God is in control of history and will bring a glorious blessing to the faithful remnant of His people. Jerusalem is pictured as so prosperous it is having to be enlarged to hold the people (*ch. 2*). The vision of Joshua the high priest, clothed in filthy rags (*ch. 3*) seems to be a definite prevision of the atonement of Christ. Other visions in the book point to the certainty of God's judgment and ultimate victory over sin, culminating in the coming of the Messiah.

Malachi

The time in which Malachi wrote cannot be definitely determined. From references to the temple and the priests, it may be assumed that it was after the return from captivity. The conditions described are similar to those which prompted the reforms of Ezra and Nehemiah, and the book may date from that period. Nothing is known of Malachi, but that he considered his words to have the full approval of God is seen throughout the book.

The Jews had returned from captivity a zealous and hopeful people. After a short period of indifference, Haggai and Zechariah had been able to stir them to rebuild the temple and the wall of Jerusalem had also been restored. The people, however, had become disillusioned; things simply were not as good as they had hoped. Drought and its accompanying crop failure, together with opposition from various enemies, had made life difficult. Skepticism, doubt, and general neglect of spiritual matters had crept in. They were offering imperfect sacrifices and failing to give their tithes. The priests were lax and did little to encourage them. Mixed marriages with the heathen and divorce had become common.

The heart of Malachi's message was to point out to the people that they could never expect prosperity as long as they continued in the sins described above. After assuring them of God's blessings if they would repent, he shifts to the subject of the approaching Day of the Lord. This day will be ushered in by Elijah, who will act as a forerunner of Messiah, after which Messiah will come. In the New Testament (*Matt. 3:1-12; 11:14*), this Elijah is identified with John the Baptist.

The writing of Malachi closes the period of prophetic activity. After this time, the scribes and priests came to the fore of religious leadership in the activity of expounding that which had already been written.

The Gospels

The term "synoptic" is used to refer to the first three gospels, due to the fact that they take the same essential approach in recording the life, death and resurrection of Jesus. The gospel of John, although it does not contradict the Synoptic gospels, presents the story of the Christ from a different standpoint. One of the major problems in New Testament studies is called the Synoptic problem. This is concerned with explaining the presence of material which is common to two or three of these gospels, as well as accounting for the material which is peculiar to each.

A number of theories have been put forth in an attempt at solution of this problem. In general, the approach of these hypotheses is to postulate several sources on which the authors of *Matthew, Mark* and *Luke* seem to be dependent. One of these is said to be gospel which was very much like, if not identical, with our gospel of *Mark.* This is alleged to have appeared first and to have been used by Matthew and Luke. A second source is discerned by a tabulation of materials which are common to *Matthew* and *Luke*, but which are not found in *Mark.* This source is usually referred to as "Q." In addition to these two main sources, scholars have discerned other possible documents or collections of oral tradition in the materials which are peculiar to *Matthew* or *Luke.* This basic approach has been subject to wide variation and this brief presentation is given merely to familiarize the student with the nature of the Synoptic problem. Standard critical works should be consulted if a closer acquaintance with this problem is desired.

Matthew

The first of our four gospels is anonymous, but tradition has ascribed it to the apostle Matthew. Several early historical references agree in stating that this gospel was originally written by Matthew in the Hebrew language for an audience of Hebrew Christians. There is, however, no trace of a Hebrew or Aramaic original and scholars agree that the present gospel is not a translation but was originally written in Greek; thus, the references to a gospel written in Hebrew remain something of a mystery. Some have questioned whether Matthew was the real author of the first gospel. There is, of course, no way of achieving certainty on the matter, but it is difficult to see why the name of such an obscure person as Matthew would have become associated with the gospel if he were not its author.

The sum of the information which the Bible provides on Matthew, or Levi, as he was sometimes called, is that he was a tax collector whom Jesus summoned to be an apostle and that he entertained several of his friends at a banquet at which Jesus was the guest of honor (*Mark 2:14-15*).

A major factor in determining the date of the

gospel is the discussion of the destruction of Jerusalem in ch. 24. Jerusalem was overrun in AD 70. The obvious inference is that the gospel was penned before this date; however, scholars who deny the possibility of predictive prophecy would, of course, insist that the gospel was written after the fall of Jerusalem. There is no way of determining the exact year of the writing.

It is generally conceded that this gospel was designed primarily for a Jewish audience. This is borne out by the frequent citation of prophecy and by the author's efforts to establish the relationship between Jesus and the Jews. The gospel was obviously written for the purpose of convincing men that Jesus of Nazareth was the anticipated Messiah, the sovereign Lord over a spiritual kingdom which would never be destroyed. That the idea of a kingdom is prominent in the mind of the writer is proved by his use of the phrase "kingdom of heaven" over thirty times in the gospel.

Mark

Tradition unanimously ascribes the second gospel to John Mark. In an anti-Marcionite prologue to the gospels, written between AD 160 and 180, the following statement is found: "Mark . . . was Peter's interpreter, and after Peter's decease wrote down this Gospel in the region of Italy." Irenaeus, Clement of Alexandria and Tertullian also attest to the Marcan authorship. Although the gospel itself does not name its author, the information which we have concerning Mark coincides with the picture of the writer presented by the gospel—that of a Jewish Christian familiar with Jewish life and thought as well as with the Hebrew scriptures. Mark is known to have been a Palestinian Jew who was closely associated with the teachings of Jesus and his apostles. It was to the house of Mary, the mother of Mark, that Peter went after his imprisonment (*Acts 12:12-17*). Peter speaks of "my son Mark" in *1 Pet. 5:13.* Mark was a companion of Paul and Barnabas on the early portion of the first missionary journey; he left the party at Perga in Pamphylia (*Acts 13:13*), incurring the sharp disapproval of Paul. In later years, however, we learn that Mark had regained the confidence of Paul and was singled out by the apostle as being particularly useful to him (*Col. 4:10; 2 Tim. 4:11*).

The gospel furnishes no assistance in determining the city of its origin. Rome has usually been favored due to the fact that most of the early writers who ascribe the book to Mark also name Rome as the place of writing.

Due to the vivid description of the destruction of Jerusalem in chapter 13, many critics—as in the case of *Matthew*—have assigned the gospel to a period after AD 70, the date of those events. Tradition, however, places the writing somewhere near the death of Peter, probably around AD 65. A possible motive for writing the gospel was the strengthening of Christians in a time of persecution. Since Nero's persecution took place in AD 64, the period around AD 65 would certainly fit this condition. If the belief in predictive prophecy is allowed, the most probable date for the gospel is four or five years previous to AD 70, while the great temple at Jerusalem was still standing (*Mark 13:1-2*).

It appears likely that Mark's gospel was written for the benefit of the Christians at Rome, many of whom were probably Gentiles. This latter hypothesis is supported by the absence of references to the Jewish Law and only one quotation from the Old Testament. In addition, Hebrew phrases and customs which might not be understood by Gentiles are carefully explained (Cf. *3:7; 5:41; 7:2; 10:46; 14:36; 15:34; 9:43; 14:12; 15:42*).

The gospel is written in a terse, concise style with an air of immediacy about it, as illustrated by the use of the word "straightway" or "immediately" twenty-seven times. It is not a biography in the strictest sense, as Jesus' birth, family and childhood are not mentioned. It is rather a graphic setting forth of the elements in Christ's life which might serve to bolster the courage of his disciples in a difficult period.

Luke

Although the writer of the third gospel does not identify himself, the voice of the first two centuries of the Christian Era was unanimous in ascribing it to Luke. Since this gospel and *Acts of Apostles* are generally considered to have been written by the same person, the reader is referred to the introduction to *Acts* for a further discussion of the authorship of these two books.

Since *Acts* appears to have been written around AD 61 or 62 and since it speaks of a "former treatise," usually acknowledged to be the third gospel, by the same author (*Acts 1:1*), the gospel of *Luke* was probably written at some time in the few years previous to that date.

It is impossible to determine the place at which the gospel was written. Several early writers assigned it to Achaia. The probability that *Acts* was written at Rome has caused many to suppose that this gospel also had its origin in that city. Another likely suggestion is that Luke wrote the gospel in Caesarea while Paul was in prison there in c. AD 60.

Luke is described by Paul as "the beloved physician" (*Col. 4:14*). Since Paul is known to have had some sort of physical disability, it has been conjectured that Luke may have been responsible for prolonging the life of the apostle, thus enabling him to carry out his vast missionary efforts. He was a companion of Paul on many of his travels and, in the last correspondence which we have from the apostle, is mentioned as the only one who remained with him (*2 Tim. 4:11*). That he was a Gentile is indicated in *Col. 4* in which Epaphras, Demas and Luke are grouped together in distinction from those "of the circumcision."

Irenaeus, Tertullian, Origen and Eusebius inform us that Luke wrote the third gospel under the influence of Paul. Doubtless, no Christian privileged to live in the presence of the great apostle could fail to reflect his influence. The language of the preface to the gospel (*Luke 1:1-4*), however, clearly states that Luke exercised independent scholarship in gathering the information from which he composed his life of Jesus.

Theophilus, the individual to whom both the gospel and *Acts* are addressed, was apparently a Gentile, perhaps a new convert, who wanted to learn more of the life and teachings of Jesus. It is quite possible that Theophilus was a wealthy individual who was to serve as a patron for the book, introducing it to a larger circle of readers.

The approach which Luke uses in writing his gospel leads one to believe that he had as a primary motive the setting forth of Christianity as a universal religion without racial limitations. The lineage of Jesus is traced past Abraham all the way back to Adam to show that Christ is thus related to all men and not just to the Jews. The picture of Jesus which is given is not that merely of a Jewish Messiah but the Friend and Savior of all that believe him and receive him. It is the first half of a narrative (*Acts* being the second) which traces the origin, development, and advance of Christianity from Bethlehem to Jerusalem, to Antioch, to Macedonia, to Achaia, to Ephesus, and finally to Rome, the capital of the Western world. If anyone was qualified to present such a narrative, certainly Luke was that person. He had close contact with several eyewitnesses of Jesus' life such as Mark and James, the brother of the Lord. In addition to his close companionship with Paul, he had also traveled with Silas, a member of the Jerusalem church.

During the nineteenth century, Luke's writings were assailed as being historically untrustworthy. As archaeological evidence from the first century has been uncovered, however, Luke has emerged as one of the ablest and most accurate historians of the ancient world.

Luke's rendition of "the greatest story ever told" is presented not with flourish, but with simplicity and dignity. He uses a popular, nonliterary Greek, omitting Semitic and Latin "barbarisms"; yet, he manifests a rich vocabulary and a high degree of literary artistry, as seen in his ability to sketch the character of an individual in a few graphic strokes of the pen. A noted critic of the Bible has called the third gospel "the most beautiful book ever written."

John

The fourth gospel was recognized as a sacred book early in the second century AD. Theophilus of Antioch (c. 170) was the first writer to name John as the author. Shortly thereafter, Irenaeus attributed the gospel to John, identifying him as the disciple who had leaned on Jesus' breast (Cf. *John 21:20*). Irenaeus' witness is especially valuable since he was a disciple of Polycarp, who had been personally acquainted with John. Clement of Alexandria credits John with having composed a "spiritual gospel."

Ch. 21:24 attributes the gospel to "the disciple whom Jesus loved." There are several things which can be stated rather safely about this individual. That he was a Jew is borne out by his quotations from the Hebrew Old Testament and his acquaintance with Jewish customs and habits of thought. His detailed knowledge of the topography would indicate that he was a Palestinian Jew. He was clearly a contemporary—in fact, an eyewitness—of the events which he was recording. Many of the things which he reported imply that he was an intimate associate of Jesus. By a process of elimination, the author is apparently identified with John the apostle, the son of Zebedee, who figures rather prominently in the gospel accounts.

Most tradition has pictured John as having come to Ephesus after the labors of Paul were finished there. During the reign of Domitian, he is said to have been banished to Patmos, where he received the *Revelation;* shortly thereafter, he was freed and returned to Ephesus.

Most of the difficulty over the authorship of the fourth gospel stems from a statement by Papias which seems to imply that there were two individuals named John in Ephesus at the same time—John the apostle and a man designated as John "the Elder" or "Presbyter." Many critics have assigned the fourth gospel to this latter John. As with many problems of introduction, no final solution can be reached; however, tradition and internal evidence seem to point to John the apostle as the author.

The early attestation to the book would indicate that it was written near the end of the first century, probably before the exile to Patmos, although a date after John's traditional return to Ephesus is by no means ruled out.

There are a number of differences between the over-all character of this gospel and that of the "Synoptic Gospels"—*Matthew, Mark* and *Luke. John* provides us with more information concerning Jesus' ministry in Jerusalem than to the Synoptists, whose emphasis lies on the Galilean ministry. There are also variations in the chronology of the events of the passion week. Many of the difficulties included in reconciling these two accounts might possibly be solved if it were recognized that the aim of the gospels was not to furnish an orderly biography of Jesus consisting of names, places and dates; rather, it was to present a full picture of the essential nature and personality of the Christ. Each of the gospel writers sought to achieve this in a different way. It is perhaps an error to exalt one gospel over another, since each complements the other in portraying this life and teachings of the Incarnate Word.

John's aim is set forth in 20:30, 31—"these (things) are written that ye may believe that Jesus is the Christ; and that believing ye may have life in his name." In order to lead men to eternal life, he sought first to convince them of the deity of Christ. The miracles which he records act as "signs" to confirm this deity. The figures which he uses to refer to Jesus (for example, Bread, Light, Shepherd, Truth, Life, Vine) clearly point to Jesus' extraordinary nature. In fact, it seems that every episode in Jesus' life is consciously presented in such a way as to reinforce the writer's initial assertion that Jesus of Nazareth was truly the Eternal Word of God who "became flesh and dwelt among us, full of grace and truth" (*John 1:14*).

Acts of Apostles

It is generally admitted that the author of the third gospel and of *Acts of Apostles* is the same person. Both works are dedicated to an individual named Theophilus (*Luke 1:3; Acts 1:1*). *Acts 1:1* refers to a "former treatise" which would seem to imply the third gospel. It is clearly evident that the author of *Acts* was a companion of Paul. This is borne out by passages written in the first person, usually designated as the "we" passages (*16:10–17:1; 20:5–21:17; 27:2–28:31*). These indicate that the author joined and left the missionary party on several occasions and that he accompanied Paul on his journey to Rome. Paul names Luke as a companion in *Col. 4:14, Philem. 24,* and *2 Tim. 4:11.* The medical language found in *Luke-Acts*, while insufficient proof in itself, corroborates the reference of Paul to Luke as "the beloved physician" (*Col. 4:14*). The voice of the early church, represented by such men as Tertullian, Clement of Alexandria, Tatian, and Irenaeus, was wholly in favor of Luke as the author both of the third gospel and *Acts of Apostles.* For further information concerning this benefactor of Christianity, the reader is referred to the introduction to *Luke.*

This history of the young church—and that is plainly what *Acts* is—appears to have been written in the early part of the seventh decade of the first century, probably around AD 62 or 63. Jerusalem was destroyed by the Romans in AD 70, but there is no indication in *Acts* that the writer knew anything of the event. In fact, Jerusalem is pictured as the still-thriving center of an active Judaism, with the temple service and sacrifices being carried out in a normal manner. This was never the situation after AD 70. Another reason for dating the epistle at this time is that Luke apparently brings his history up to the date at which he was writing. The last event recorded in the book is Paul's living in a hired house in Rome, awaiting trial before Caesar (*Acts 28:30*). This is usually thought to have been in AD 61 or 62. If Luke composed *Acts* after this date, it is difficult to understand why he would have omitted an account of Paul's trial and the decision which was handed down, or why he would not have mentioned the persecution of Christians by Nero which took place later in that decade. Luke's absolute silence concerning any of the important events occurring between AD 64 and 70 make it extremely likely that he composed his book before the former date.

The book of *Acts* is constructed around the activities of two main characters, Peter and Paul. Chapters 1–12 deals mainly with the "Acts" of Peter while the remainder of the book is devoted largely to Paul.

The major areas of history with which the author has dealt are: 1) the establishment and progress of the church at Jerusalem until the dispersion which arose at the time of Stephen's death (*chs. 1–7*); 2) the preaching of the gospel to the surrounding area, including its introduction to the Gentiles (*chs. 8–12*); 3) the preaching tours of Paul and the struggle to define the church's position with regard to the law of Moses (*13:1–21:16*); and 4) of Paul's imprisonment, which began in Jerusalem and was concluded in Rome (*21:17–28:30*). As has been noted in the introduction to the third gospel, the historical accuracy of Luke, once questioned widely, has now received extensive substantiation; there is little reason to suppose that the events took place in any way other than that described by Luke.

The obvious probability concerning the place of writing of *Acts* is Rome. The whole book is an account of the advance of Christianity from Jerusalem to Rome and the last events described take place in Rome. Other locations are, of course, possible, but none suggests itself so readily as Rome.

As in the case of the third gospel, *Acts of Apostles* is addressed to Theophilus, usually thought to have been a Gentile who was interested in learning more of Christianity and who may have been expected to finance the publication of the book to a larger audience.

Acts is valuable to us for a number of reasons. In the gospels, we are given the account of the life of Christ and the commission which He gave to His disciples for the purpose of redeeming mankind. *Acts* informs us of the activities of the leading apostles in carrying out that commission. It tells us of their relationship to one another and to their other co-workers as they dealt with the various problems which faced the young church. It tells of the introduction of Christianity to the Gentile world and of the resultant struggle for unity between Jew and Gentile.

Romans

The epistle to the Romans is universally recognized to be a product of the apostle Paul. Virtually every feature of the letter gives the impression of genuineness. Statements in the epistle indicate that Paul was going to Jerusalem with the collection for the poor which he had gathered (*ch. 15:25-27*). Since both *1* and *2 Corinthians* stress this collection, this would imply that the epistle was written shortly after these two letters and toward the end of Paul's third missionary journey. Most scholars date the epistle near AD 58 and name Corinth as the city of its origin.

The epistle is addressed "to all God's beloved in Rome." Although some ancient manuscripts omit the word, "Rome," it is generally agreed that the Roman church was the recipient of the letter. The line of discussion which Paul follows would indicate that the church in Rome contained considerable numbers of both Jew and Gentile members.

As the apostle to the Gentiles, Paul would naturally have a great interest in Rome, since it was the capital of the Gentile world. He sought to preach the gospel in that great city and to travel on as far as Spain in his missionary efforts. It would be the normal course of action to use the capital of the empire as a base for his further preaching activities. It is probably true that one of Paul's purposes in writing this epistle was to familiarize the Roman Christians with his teaching and to clear up any questions which they might have with regard to the relationship between the Law of Moses and the gospel of Christ. As in other letters, the apostle undoubtedly sought to prepare his readers for false teachers and trouble-makers who might come to Rome to stir up dissension in the church. In order to carry out this purpose it was necessary to give a clear statement of true doctrine that it might be used as a measure of any false teaching which might arise. In addition to these reasons for the epistle, it served as a letter of introduction for the deaconess, Phoebe, as a petition for the prayers of the Roman brethren, and as a greeting to various members of the church in the capital city. There is, however, no one purpose which is sufficient in itself to have caused the epistle to be written. All of the above-mentioned factors must be taken into consideration to account for the presence and the character of this profound writing.

The main theme of the epistle is justification by faith. Paul points out the great need for righteousness, both by the Jews who have had the Law and by Gentiles who are "a Law unto themselves." This righteousness is then shown to be attainable only apart from the Law and in Christ. God's providing of this righteousness, contingent on man's faith, is called "justification." The justified believer is enabled to die to sin and the Law and to live a holy life by the sanctifying work of the Holy Spirit. This new relationship to God brings adopted sonship and the assurance of salvation from sin.

The oft-discussed and misunderstood chapters 9–11 deal with the plight and ultimate fate of the Jews. It is pointed out that God's rejection of the Jews was a natural and just consequence of their having failed to recognize Christ as the perfect fulfillment of the Law and that to which it pointed from its inception. This rejection of Israel, however, is seen to be neither total nor final and it is clearly indicated that God will show mercy to those Jews who acknowledge Jesus as Lord. Chs. 12–15 contain exhortations regarding the practical aspects of the new life in Christ while the final chapter consists largely of personal notices.

The Corinthian Correspondence

Paul founded the church at Corinth on his second missionary tour (*Acts 18:1-8*). In Paul's absence, Apollos preached to the church there (*Acts 18:24–19:1*). Judging from Paul's statements in *1 Cor. 1:26-31*, the church had drawn most of its members from the lower, uneducated class of people. These people found it difficult to shake off the influences of their environment and to commit themselves wholly to the religion of Jesus. The letters to the Corinthians, universally acknowledged to have come from Paul, witness to the problems encountered by the Corinthian church in its adjustment to the new life in Christ.

There is good evidence that Paul wrote at least four letters to the church of God at Corinth. After leaving Corinth, Paul continued his ministry in Ephesus. On hearing various reports of the situation at Corinth from members of Chloe's household (*1 Cor. 1:11*), from Apollos (*1 Cor. 16:12*), and in answer to questions presented in a letter brought by Stephanus, Fortunatus, and Achaicus (*1 Cor. 16:17*), Paul wrote our *1 Corinthians* from Ephesus (*1 Cor. 16:8*). It is believed that Timothy carried this letter to the Corinthians. The date of this letter was some time between AD 54 and AD 57. In *1 Cor. 5:2*, Paul mentions a previous letter in which he had warned the Christians in Corinth to separate themselves from immoral people. Thus our *1 Corinthians* is really the second letter which the Corinthians received. After the writing of *1 Corinthians*, things seem to have taken a turn for the worse, prompting the apostle to make a trip to Corinth in person (*2 Cor. 2:1; 12:14; 13:1, 2*). This visit turned out to be unfruitful, even painful, for the apostle. Greatly disappointed by the reaction of the Corinthians, Paul returned to Ephesus and wrote what is usually referred to as the "severe" letter (*2 Cor. 2:3-11; 7:5-16*). It seems likely that Paul may have sent Titus with this letter, giving him instructions to return via Macedonia to meet him. This letter apparently brought the desired result, prompting Paul to write a fourth letter (all or part of our *2 Corinthians*) in which he expresses joy over their repentance and issues further exhortations to faithfulness.

1 Corinthians

As noted above, *1 Corinthians* was written for the purpose of correcting certain difficulties which had arisen in the church at Corinth and which had come to the attention of Paul and of answering questions which the church had sent to him in a letter delivered by Fortunatus, Stephanus, and Achaicus. In a large measure, the problems are dealt with individually, although principles are presented in connection with one which might easily be applied to another. By noticing what these problems were and the order in which Paul dealt with them, we can form a clear outline of *1 Corinthians*. Chs. 1–4 contain a rebuke for the parties which had arisen as a result of a divisive spirit and a failure to humble themselves before the true wisdom of God. Ch. 5 is a strong rebuke for a case of incest which existed in the church. In ch. 6, Paul deplores the practice of Christians' carrying their litigations into heathen courts. The latter part of that chapter is devoted to urging the Corinthians to "flee fornication," evidently quite a problem in licentious Corinth. Ch. 7 deals with the problems connected with marriage. The problems of Christian liberty and the behavior of Christians in a community where idolatry was the norm is discussed in chs. 8–10. Ch. 11 is concerned with the conduct of women in public worship and the abuses which the Lord's Supper was suffering. Chs. 12–14 are devoted to the proper use of spiritual gifts. Included in this section is the famous "love chapter," chapter 13. The problems connected with the resurrection of the dead is the subject of ch. 15, while ch. 16 is devoted to practical matters such as the collection for the poor at Jerusalem and the apostle's intended visit to Corinth, as well as the customary salutations, warnings, and benediction.

2 Corinthians

As with *1 Corinthians*, the author can be no one but Paul. *2 Corinthians* was written a short time—perhaps only a few months—after *1 Corinthians*, from some city in Macedonia where Paul had gone to receive Titus' report of the effect of the "severe letter." The news which Titus brought was so encouraging as to move Paul to express to the Corinthians his joy at hearing of their change of heart. Also contained in the letter is a defense of his apostleship and of his conduct among the Corinthians, both of which had evidently come under strong criticism.

Critics have often asserted that *2 Corinthians* is not one, but two separated letters which were later put together to form a single epistle. Those who hold to such a view usually identify chs. 10–13 with the "severe letter" referred to above. That there is a noticeable change in tone between chs. 1–9 and 10–13 cannot be denied; the latter section is indeed marked by severity. If this is to be identified with the "severe letter," however, part of it must have been lost, for it does not meet all the requirements of the letter as described in chs. 1–9. The strongest argument for the unity of the epistle is found in the absolute absence of any manuscript which contains the epistle in any form other than that which appears in our Bible.

Galatians

There has been remarkably little opposition to the Pauline authorship of the epistle to the Galatians. The writer calls himself Paul in two places (*1:1; 5:2*). The second reference practically rules out the notion that the first is merely an arbitrary insertion by a forger. The epistle contains numerous historical references to the life of Paul which are capable of being harmonized with *Acts of Apostles*.

The date and place of writing of the epistle is difficult to discern. It was probably written either from Syrian Antioch before the council of Jerusalem (*Acts 15*) or from Ephesus on the second or third missionary journey.

At the time of Paul the Roman province of Galatia included the old kingdom of Galatia proper to the north and also parts of Lycaonia, Pisidia, and Phrygia which adjoined it to the south. Since the letter clearly implies that the churches addressed were all founded in the same general period, Paul could not have been writing to both areas. It is now generally agreed, for various reasons, that Paul was writing to the churches in Southern Galatia, which he established on the first missionary tour.

Paul had preached the gospel to these churches and had been graciously received, even being received as a divine being (*4:14*). He had established what appeared to be strong churches. Shortly after his second visit to them, however, he received word that they were suffering from a serious defection as a result of Judaizing teachers.

Paul tries to destroy the influence of the false teachers by defending himself against the attacks they had levelled at his apostleship and by refuting the Judaistic claims of the corrections of mingling Christianity with certain Jewish laws, especially circumcision. He asserts that his authority and teaching were not derived from the older apostles but came directly from Jesus Christ. He defends the faith by pointing out, with scripture, logic, and allegory, that the true function of the Law was not to rival Christianity, but to act as a servant to guide men to Christ, who has established a religious and social unity which recognizes no difference between Jew and Greek, free man and slave, male and female.

Historically, the epistle contains a primary account of the beginnings of the Christian church and its problems of adjustment. Theologically, it is one of the chief keys to Paul's interpretation of the Christian message. Because of this interpretation of the relation of Christianity to the Law of Moses, the epistle has sometimes been referred to as the Christian Declaration of Independence.

THE PRISON EPISTLES

Ephesians, Philippians, Colossians and *Philemon* are sometimes designated by the term "Prison Epistles," since all four mention that they are being written from prison. It has traditionally been assumed that these references were to Paul's first Roman imprisonment. In the modern period of biblical criticism, however, Caesarea and Ephesus have been suggested as alternative possibilities for the place of imprisonment from which the letters were written. Caesarea has been favored mainly because of the years which Paul spent in prison there (*Acts 24:27*), thus affording the length of time demanded by conditions described in the letters. It has also been argued that Paul's plan to visit Spain (*Rom. 15:23-24*) could be more easily harmonized with his avowed intentions to visit Philippi and Colossae (*Philem. 22* and *Phil. 2:24*) if he were in Caesarea and planned to visit these cities on his way to the West than if he were in Rome. In connection with this, it ought to be noted that for Paul to have been released in Caesarea would have meant certain death at the hands of the hostile Jews. Yet, in *Philem. 22*, Paul seems to await his release eagerly. Also, in *Col. 4:11*, Paul mentions that only three men "of the circumcision" had been a comfort to him. It is inconceivable that Philip, in whose home Paul had visited, would not also have been a comfort to him if he had been in Caesarea.

A number of plausible arguments are presented favoring Ephesus as the place of origin of these epistles. It is contended that *1 Cor. 15:30-32* and *2 Cor. 1:8-10* imply an Ephesian imprisonment. Also, Paul's allusions to his companions indicate that he was surrounded by Asian Christians whose presence might be more easily explained if he were in Ephesus rather than Rome. It is not unlikely, however, that Paul would find himself in the company of old friends in practically any section of the evangelized world. In order to explain the references to the "praetorium" (*Phil. 1:13*) and "Caesar's household" (*Phil. 4:22*), it has been pointed out that the use of "praetorium" might imply the official residence of the government in any province and that "Caesar's household" might refer to all those who were attached to the personal service of Caesar whether in Rome or elsewhere. While the validity of these assertions cannot be denied, the use of the terms would appear much more natural if they referred to Rome. The presence of Onesimus, with whom *Philemon* is concerned, is cited as evidence for a non-Roman origin. It is maintained that a runaway slave would not travel all the way to Rome but would seek refuge in a neighboring city. Rome, however, was a favorite refuge for such individuals as they sought to get as far away from their masters as possible and to lose themselves in the great mass of humanity in that city. In addition to these considerations, Rome is favored by many because of Paul's discussion of his impending trial as a life and death affair. This would scarcely fit any place but Rome, since Paul could always exercise his right appeal from another city.

In view of the various arguments presented in favor of these three cities, it must be admitted that the suggestions in favor of a non-Roman milieu possess considerable merit, especially with regard to Ephesus. These are not, however, of such a nature as to render the traditional Roman view untenable or even improbable and the student probably should not concern himself too greatly with this problem, as a proper interpretation of the epistles is not dependent on a solution of the problem.

Ephesians

The Pauline authorship of *Ephesians* is supported by a strong chain of external evidence reaching back to the very beginning of the second century AD. A number of early writers apparently quote from the epistle. Such authorities as Irenaeus and Clement of Alexandria definitely state that it was a product of Paul. It was even included in the canon of Pauline epistles prepared by the heretic Marcion (AD 140). The writer identifies himself as Paul in 1:1 and 3:1. The form of the epistle follows the Pauline pattern in beginning with a greeting and expression of thanksgiving, followed by a discussion of doctrinal matters. The only major characteristic which is missing is the group of personal greetings usually found at the end of Paul's letters. This might be accounted for by the audience for whom the epistle was destined (See discussion below). Despite this considerable evidence, however, it has become common for biblical critics to deny the Pauline authorship of the book. Their contention is that the concept of the church which the writer possesses, plus several subtle differences in language and style, indicate that the actual author was an individual who was familiar with Paul's writings, especially *Colossians*, but who lived a number of years after the apostle. These objections, while worthy of consideration by the serious student, are not insurmountable obstacles to belief in the genuineness of *Ephesians*. Most scholars who recognize Paul as the author of the book assign it to a date near the end of Paul's first imprisonment in Rome (Cf. *3:1; 4:1*), around AD 61. As was the case with Colossians (*Col. 4:7-9*), the letter was delivered by Tychicus (*6:21*).

Ascertaining the original destination of this epistle is one of the major problems of introduction connected with it. Most early writers spoke of the epistle as having been addressed to the Ephesians. The titles which are found on most manuscripts agree with this view. There are, however, some notable exceptions which might indicate that the title was an early insertion and not part of the original text. It must be admitted that certain elements of the epistle, such as the lack of personal greetings to a church with whom his relations were most intimate, might imply a destination other than the traditional one. Fortunately, however, there is no doctrinal teaching of the book whose interpretation is contingent on a solution of this problem.

As Paul meditated in his place of imprisonment, he was able to grasp fully the significance of the work which had filled his years as an apostle. He recognized the church as the spiritual body of Christ and saw its role in the uniting of all things in heaven and on earth. This basic idea of unity is set forth in 1:3-10; the rest of the epistle serves to emphasize this great central truth of Christianity. Paul informs his readers that God's eternal purpose is to gather the universe into one body, that he might restore harmony between himself and his creatures. This purpose is to be realized through Christ and through "the church, which is his body, the fulness of him who filleth all in all" (*1:22-23*). The vision which Paul has is that of a great oneness of birth and faith and life in which all the saints, panoplied with the armor of God (*6:10-18*), might work together to overcome the foes of righteousness "that in the ages to come he might show the exceeding riches of his grace in his kindness toward us through Christ Jesus" (*2:7*).

Philippians

The city of Philippi, named for Philip of Macedon, was the leading city of the district of Macedonia and a Roman colony (*Acts 16:12*). Its inhabitants were Roman citizens and enjoyed all the attendant privileges. There were few Jews in the city; there was, in fact, not even a synagogue. The only place for worship was a "place for prayer" by the riverside (*Acts 16:13ff*).

The church in Philippi was the first church to be established in Europe. It was established by Paul while on his second missionary journey, shortly after receiving the "Macedonian call" while in Troas (*Acts 16:9ff*). The Philippians were noted for the manner in which they contributed to the support of benevolent and missionary work (*2 Cor. 8; Phil. 4:15-19*). Fifty years after this time, the church in Philippi was commended by Polycarp for the steadfastness which it exhibited. Despite this admirable showing in its early years, the Philippian church van-ished from history before the middle of the second century. Paul is acknowledged to be the undisputed author of the epistle. Not only does he name himself as such, but the epistle bears all the marks of the Pauline style and the material contained in the brief work contains nothing which would suggest a motive for forgery.

The time of writing is closely bound up with the place of origin of the letter. If it originated in Ephesus, its date is probably near AD 54. If it was from Rome, it must be dated from about AD 62-64.

A number of motives for writing are to be seen in the letter. An obvious one is to express his gratitude for the gift which had been sent to him by the Philippians and to inform them of the unselfish manner in which Epaphroditus had discharged his mission in ministering to Paul. He also used the epistle as an occasion of telling them of his feelings for them and of his own personal condition. In addition, he informed them of the impending visit of Timothy and of the return of Epaphroditus, thus assuring both of them a good reception (*2:19-20*). Finally, he warns them that they will suffer for the gospel (*1:29, 30*) and that they must guard themselves against those who would seek to introduce false doctrines into the church (*3:1ff*). It is best characterized as a letter of joy, emanating from a heart full of love.

Colossians

The Pauline authorship of the epistle to the Colossians was not questioned until the second quarter of the nineteenth century. Since that time certain scholars have charged that the language and thought of the epistle is too unlike the other epistles attributed to Paul to have come from the pen of the apostle. Most biblical scholars, however, seem to feel that the Christological problem with which the epistle deals is of such a nature as to warrant a change in vocabulary and style; therefore, the authenticity of the epistle is generally upheld.

This epistle is classed with the Priton Letters of the apostle Paul. For a discussion of the time and place of imprisonment, the reader is referred to the introductory notes to the epistles, given above.

Colossae was a city of Phrygia in the Lycus River Valley, on the great highway from Ephesus to the Euphrates Valley, near Hierapolis and Laodicea. Col. 4:12-15 makes it plain that the church had been established in Colossae at some prior date. Many of the Colossians apparently engaged in angel-worship. The most important of these angels and the protector of the city was Michael.

The name of the founder of the church in Colossae is uncertain. Since *Acts 16:6* and *18:23* state that Paul went through the region of Phrygia, it is often assumed that he must have reached Colossae on these visits. Paul, however, nowhere states that he had been either in Colossae or even near it. While Paul was preaching in Ephesus, it would have been easy for others to radiate to Colossae from that place. In *Col. 1:1*, Paul seems to imply that this very thing happened and that the individual most responsible for carrying the gospel to Colossae was Epaphras. This, coupled with Paul's assertion in 2:1 that he had not seen their faces, has caused tradition and scholarship to reach almost unanimous agreement in ascribing the foundation of the Colossian church to Epaphras.

The results of the early efforts of the church in Colossae had evidently been satistactory (*1:4-6*). At the time of the writing of the epistle, however, the church was in danger of being misled by certain false teachers. It is difficult to determine the exact nature of the Colossian heresy, but it is fairly safe to conclude that it reflected the widespread efforts of philosophy and cults to find the relation between man's inner life and the universe.

The teachings which were embodied in the heresy had the reputation of wisdom and Christ was considered the greatest source of wisdom. It was of an exclusive nature and encouraged some measure of asceticism, as indicated by the teachings on foods. It apparently ignored much of the true doctrine of Christ regarding the fulness of the God-head dwelling within him and the fact that he alone obtained redemption for man's sins. The heresy also promulgated a cult of angels. Much conflicting material has been written concerning the origin of this cult; however, due to lack of information, the only safe conclusion concerning angel-worship at Colossae is that it was present and evidently found its origin in paganism.

There was certainly an element of Judaism in

the heresy, as seen in the advocating of circumcision (*2:11*), the upholding of the law (*2:14-15*) and the observance of special seasons; yet, it is virtually impossible to assign the heresy to any particular group or school of thought. Whether the heresy reflects the influence of occidental philosophy, oriental cults, gnosticism, normative or extreme Judaism, it appears safe only to say that the ideas are still in a germinal form and do not indicate a full-strength movement of any of these.

The greatest danger of the heresy lay in its asserting the insufficiency of Christ in the work of redemption and supplementing the work of Jesus with the cult of angels, thereby robbing Him of His sovereign rule. The purpose of the epistle to the Colossians is to convince the readers that the problems to which they sought an answer in the heresy found their solution only in the gospel.

Paul approaches the problem by pointing out the unique relationship of the Son to the Father. He is the image of the invisible God and in Him all the fulness of the Godhead dwells (*1:15, 19*). Greek philosophical thought was familiar with the terms, "image" and "fulness," but it applied them to the Logos, or a personification of divine energy. Paul applied them to Christ in an absolute sense. He is the image of God not because He is merely like Him, or because He reflects His qualities in some ways, but because He is the full and perfect representation. If Christ bears this unique relationship to the Father, He is supreme over all creation, composed of the redeemed and reconciled, over which this same Lord is supreme and to which obedient man must submit himself.

Along more practical lines, Paul informs his readers that they are to be emancipated from mere ceremonial observance, asceticisms, and elements of pagan devotion. Against the various traditions of men he sets the only trustworthy tradition—the true doctrine of Christ.

In this epistle, Paul speaks of the new life in Christ in which the believer enjoys spiritual union with Christ in heaven (*3:1-4*), separation from his sins (*3:5-9*), and investment with a new Christlike character (*3:10-11*). Concerning the social life of the church, he urges brotherly affection and forgiveness (*3:12-14*), peace (*3:15*), mutual edification by word and song (*3:16*), consecration to Christ, and thankfulness to God in everything (*3:17*).

1 Thessalonians

The city of Thessalonica, named for the stepsister of Alexander the Great, was the leading harbor of Macedonia. It was built on a hill overlooking a beautiful fertile plain as well as the Thermaic Gulf. In both Macedonian and Roman times it was an important city, due to its harbor and to the great Egnation highway which ran through it. The church was established in that city by the apostle Paul, together with Silvanus (Silas) and Timothy, on the second missionary journey, probably in AD 50 (*Acts 17:1-9*). Both of these companions of Paul are mentioned in the introductory verses of the two Thessalonian letters. The period of time spent with the Thessalonians was sufficient for a mutual love and loyalty to develop. The church in Thessalonica was composed largely of Gentile believers who "turned from idols to serve the living and true God" (*1 Thess. 1:9*).

In all probability, these two letters, almost universally admitted to be genuine, were written by the apostle from Corinth in AD 50 or 51, shortly after his missionary activities in Thessalonica. They are thought to be the earliest of the extant Pauline epistles.

After the missionaries left Thessalonica to continue their journey on into Achaia, Paul often sought to return and visit the Christians there but was unable to fulfill this desire (*1 Thess. 2:18*). In his place, he sent Timothy to encourage and further establish them in sound doctrine and to bring a report of their current spiritual condition (*1 Thess. 3:1-2, 5*). At the time of the writing of *1 Thess.*, Timothy had brought back an encouraging report (*1 Thess. 3:6-10*). The first three chapters of this letter contain Paul's message of thanksgiving for this good report. Timothy's account of conditions at Thessalonica, however, was apparently not without its disturbing elements. From an apologetic strain which runs throughout the first three chapters in defense of the conduct of the evangelists while among the Thessalonians, it appears that an antagonistic element was trying to undermine the influence of the apostle. Paul points out that he was no burden to the disciples while in Thessalonica but had provided his own support (*2:*

9), and that his attitude toward them had been that of a nurse toward a child (*2:1-12*).

It had also come to Paul's attention, probably as a result of Timothy's report, that the Thessalonians were in need of additional teaching on the second coming of Christ. They were concerned about the disciples of their number who had died, thinking that death meant that these would have no share in the glory of the Lord's second advent. Because of this, many were neglecting the ordinary duties of life and had fallen into the sins which often accompany idleness; 4:13-18 is devoted to correcting their misconceptions. The apostle assures them "by the word of the Lord" (*4:15*) that the dead in Christ are at no disadvantage but shall fully share in the blessings of His coming.

The remaining sections of the last two chapters contain admonitions against worldliness, a serious problem in an idolatrous city such as Thessalonica, and exhortations to remain steadfast in the faith that their "whole spirit and soul and body be preserved blameless unto the coming of our Lord Jesus Christ" (*5:23*).

2 Thessalonians

2 Thessalonians appears to have been written only a few weeks, or perhaps months, after the first letter. In this period, a new situation had arisen at Thessalonica. It was now being taught that the Day of the Lord, for which Paul had urged them to be ready, had already arrived. The apostle displays some uncertainty as to the origin of this new idea (*2:1-2*) and seems perplexed that such a notion could arise in the wake of his rather extensive teaching on the matter (*2:5*). In this epistle, he reviews what he had evidently taught them concerning the signs of the Lord's coming and exhorts them to abide in those teachings, separating themselves from any who promulgate a different doctrine.

THE PASTORAL EPISTLES

1 and 2 Timothy and Titus

The two epistles to Timothy and that to Titus were first given the term, "Pastorals," by Thomas Aquinas. It has since been popularized and is almost universally used to refer to these three epistles. Although the epistles do deal, at least partially, with the duties of Church administration, the term is somewhat inappropriate to much of the material contained in them.

In each of the epistles, the writer names himself as Paul. The mannerisms used in the writings, the general situation, and the doctrine set forth are not essentially foreign to Paul and to his time. There has been, however, continued opposition to the Pauline authorship of these epistles since the second century. The leading arguments which have been advanced against the authenticity of the epistles are on linguistical, chronological, and ecclesiastical grounds. From the standpoint of linguistics, or language, it is asserted that there is a large number of words used in these epistles which are not found in the letters acknowledged to have come from Paul. The difference in vocabulary is held to be so great that the letters could have never come from the same pen. Other scholars, however, pointing to Paul's extensive rabbinical education, his varied background, and the necessity of adapting vocabulary to the needs of the audience, feel that the supposedly "un-Pauline" terms used in the Pastorals sustain a close relation to the working vocabulary of the church of the first century and could quite easily have come from Paul. The Christological argument is based on the assumption that Paul was condemned to death at the end of his first imprisonment, recorded in *Acts* and that there is therefore no room to allow for the events mentioned in the Pastorals. The evidence, however, seems to be quite strong that Paul was acquitted at the end of his first imprisonment. That he felt he was going to be released is made clear by his letters to the Philippians and to Philemon, informing them that he intended to visit them soon. The favorable treatment which he had received while in prison would certainly seem to support his optimism. In addition to this, there are several references in early Christian literature to Paul's having been released, after which he continued his missionary efforts, preaching in places as far away as Spain. If this tradition is true, there is little difficulty in finding room in Paul's life for the events referred to in these epistles.

The ecclesiastical argument assumes that the church organization of elders and deacons, which is presupposed by the Pastorals, could not have reached this stage of development in the time of Paul. The scriptures, however, indicate that the organization referred to in those epistles was common to the early church. The famine relief was handled through the elders (*Acts 11*); Paul ordained elders in every church (*Acts 14:23*); elders played an important role in the Jerusalem council (*Acts 15*); Paul spoke to the elders of Ephesus (*Acts 20:17-31*); also, church leaders are indicated in *1 Thess. 5:12-13.* Based on this information, it might well be argued that the ecclesiastical polity bears a closer resemblance to the time of Paul than it does to the second century when a hierarchy of church leadership began to develop.

Those who oppose the Pauline authorship of these epistles would make their author a deliberate forger who might possibly have included a few genuine scraps of Paul's writings in his fabrication of the epistles. It seems somewhat unlikely, however, that the numerous personal allusions are the work of sheer imagination or that the tender passages in the epistles are the products of a willful forger. It may be concluded, then, that while there are elements in the Pastoral epistles which are somewhat peculiar, these do not appear great enough to render belief in the traditional Pauline authorship unreasonable.

The letters were personal letters written to Timothy and Titus, and are concerned with the discharging of responsibilities to the churches at Ephesus and Crete. A primary interest is the preservation and propagation of the truth of the gospel and a maintaining of good conduct on the part of believers. Attention is given to the qualifications and responsibilities of the leaders of the church. Considerable space is also accorded to a type of false teaching which was troubling the churches in these places. Due to the lack of descriptive information of this doctrine, it is impossible to identify it with any recognized heresy in the early days of the church, although certain elements of Judaism may be seen, such as contentions about the Law (*Tit. 3:9*), Jewish fables (*Tit. 1:14; 1 Tim. 1:4*), and endless genealogies (*Tit. 3:9; 1 Tim. 1:4*). The writer of the epistles appears to be more interested in the moral tendency of the rival teaching than in the doctrine itself; therefore, much is kept from our understanding.

Among the special characteristics of the epistles the "sure sayings" (*1 Tim. 1:15; 4:19; Tit. 3:8; 2 Tim. 2:11*) are worthy of consideration by Christians. Throughout the epistles there is an emphasis on the essential nature, attributes, and unity of God as the sovereign creator and savior of all men and on Christ as the only mediator between God and man. Christian character also receives considerable attention as the individual disciple is urged to prepare himself for every good work and to strive to maintain a high level of work and worship within the church.

If Paul is accepted as the author of the epistles, the order in which they were written is probably: 1) *1 Timothy*, 2) *Titus*, and 3) *2 Timothy.*

1 Timothy

Due to the lack of historical information, little that is definite can be said about this epistle as far as date and place of writing are concerned. Most scholars who uphold the Pauline authorship place the date of the epistle near AD 64, naming Macedonia as the probable place of writing.

Timothy, a native of Lystra, was converted by Paul on the first missionary journey (*1 Tim. 1:2, 18; Acts 14:6-23*) and became a traveling companion of the apostle. He was with Paul during his first imprisonment in Rome. From Rome, he undoubtedly made the trip to Philippi of which Paul speaks (*Phil. 2:19-23*). Sometime after Paul's release from prison, he probably took up the work at Ephesus. It is to Timothy, as the minister at Ephesus, that Paul addresses this epistle.

Paul had warned the Ephesian elders of the dangers that faced them (*Acts 20:17-31*). It appears that these dangers had become a reality. Teachers had arisen who were not abiding by the sound doctrine of the gospel (*6:3*). Timothy was still comparatively young and needed much counsel and guidance for action in the case. Being prevented by his duties from returning to Ephesus personally, Paul penned this letter to furnish Timothy with the needed advice, to encourage him in his work with the false teachers and to exhort him to be diligent in the performance of his ministerial duties.

2 Timothy

At the time of this writing, Paul has been arrested a second time; on this occasion, he is apparently under stricter custody than before. The outlook is rather gloomy; death appears certain and the venerable old apostle longs for the companionship of his younger fellow-worker, Timothy.

Paul's second arrest, coming during the Neronic persecution, would place the date of this epistle in late AD 67 or early AD 68. The place, of course, is Rome. Timothy had evidently left Ephesus (*4:12*) and was probably on the way to Rome, possibly someplace in Macedonia. Beyond this supposition, little can be said.

The letter is motivated by Paul's desire to give further instruction concerning the battle with the false teaching, his desire for fellowship with his disciple, and his need for his cloak, his books and his parchment which he had left at Troas. In the closing chapter of the epistle, Paul utters the inspiring statement which could be spoken only by a man with boundless confidence in the Lord: "For I am now ready to be offered, and the time of my departure is at hand. I have fought a good fight, I have finished my course, I have kept the faith: Henceforth there is laid up for me a crown of righteousness, which the Lord, the righteous judge, shall give me at that day: and not to me only, but unto all them also that love his appearing" (*4:6-8*).

This epistle marks the last extant letter of the beloved apostle who, according to tradition, was shortly thereafter led out on the Ostran way where he was beheaded, thus ending the life of the figure whose influence on Christianity was second only to that of Jesus.

Titus

The place of composition of this epistle is quite uncertain. It may have been Nicopolis, Thessalonica, or Philippi, or somewhere on the road to Nicopolis. If Paul is accepted as the author (See the discussion under *Pastoral Epistles,* above), it is generally agreed that the date was shortly after *1 Timothy,* about AD 64 or 65.

By birth a heathen (*Gal. 2:3*), Titus was probably converted by Paul (*Tit. 1:4*). At Jerusalem, Paul had resisted the demands of the Jews that Titus be circumcised on the grounds that he was to be an example of the freedom from the Law which Christianity had made possible. He had made two trips to Corinth to assist in gathering the collection for the poor saints in Jerusalem and had been commended as a faithful helper (*2 Cor. 7-8*). After Paul's release from prison, Titus probably accompanied him on his preaching trips and was left in Crete to assist in the work of the church there. Cretans had been present on the day of the Pentecost after Jesus' resurrection (*Acts 2*), but the origin of Christianity on that island province cannot be positively traced. Paul had evidently visited the island and had been struck with the general immorality of the Cretans and with the imperfect organization of the church. The purpose in writing the epistle seems to have been quite similar to that of *1 Timothy.* False teaching of a similar type had crept in and Paul sought to counsel Titus concerning the action which he should take. He instructs Titus as to the qualifications which elders should possess, informs him on how to deal with various classes, encourages him to emphasize the ideal of Christian living, and warns him of the dangers of the false teaching and its proponents.

Philemon

Philemon is universally acknowledged to be a companion letter to *Colossians.* The evidence for this rests mainly on the information concerning Onesimus. Onesimus comforted Paul in prison (*v. 11*). He is mentioned in *Colossians* as "one of you." He was being sent with both letters, along with Tychichus. The epistle to Philemon is concerned with the reception of Onesimus. These facts lead to the conclusion that the epistles to the Colossians and to Philemon were written and delivered at the same general time. Based on the date and place of origin assigned to *Colossians,* this would place the letter as having been written from Rome, c. AD 58 or 64.

The recipient of the epistle, Philemon, may have been an elder in the Colossian church. He was surely a leader in the church, as it met in his home (*v. 2*). Paul was acquainted not only with Philemon but with what appears to be his family (Apphia and Archippus), and sends his greeting to them. He was probably a man of some means, known to be warm-hearted and hospitable. He appears to have been a good friend of the apostle, having been with him in some former work, and having carried on a good work in the apostle's absence.

Onesimus was a former slave of Philemon who had absconded, possibly with some money (*v.*

18). He had gone to Rome to seek refuge. While in Rome, Onesimus had come in contact with Paul in some way and had been brought to faith and repentance by the apostle. After his conversion, Onesimus had been a great source of comfort for Paul. Although Paul appreciated the aid which Onesimus had given him, he felt that the slave should be returned to his master. Knowing the case and feeling that Philemon would not be a hard master, Paul had persuaded Onesimus to return to the household of his rightful owner. Philemon had the legal right to take the life of the slave, as Onesimus had committed one of the gravest offences in ancient law. Paul, in this letter, serves as an advocate to insure the proper reception for Onesimus.

The epistle shows what Paul was in little things, demonstrating a partial cause for his great missionary success. His interest in this matter appears to be as great as it is in the concern over the heresy that troubles the entire Colossian church. In order to show the importance he attached to it, he wrote with his own hand, filling the letter with his consuming love. *Philemon* gives a beautiful picture of first-century family life; the parents are well known for their hospitality and kindness, the son is a worker in the church, and the household is the center of the local congregation.

Hebrews

This epistle, unlike the thirteen which precede it, bears no name and omits the customary apostolic salutation. As a result, there has been much discussion and speculation as to the real identity of the author of the book. The Eastern church, and particularly the church at Alexandria, regarded the work as having come from Paul, at least indirectly. In the African church, Barnabas was mentioned as a possible author of the epistle; this view, however, gave way to the Alexandrian view by the fourth century. In Rome and the Western world, the Pauline authorship of Hebrews was not generally held until the latter part of the fourth century. It was not until the council of Trent in the sixteenth century that the Roman church finally decreed it to be an epistle of Paul's. Despite the ruling of the council, it is impossible to be certain as to the actual author. The two men whose names are most often connected with the book are Paul and Apollos. Those who favor Paul appeal to the opinion of the Eastern church and the affinities in language and thought between Hebrews and the recognized Pauline epistles. In addition, the references to "our brother Timothy" (*13:23*) and "they of Italy" (*13:24*) could easily have come from Paul. It also appears that the writer was imprisoned, from his request for prayers that he might be restored to his readers. This statement could be made to fit any of the several imprisonments of the apostle. The arguments which have been advanced in opposition to the Pauline authorship are not without considerable merit. There is nothing in the epistle which suggests the necessity of anonymity, yet Paul's name is absent from the letter. The writer reveals himself as belonging to a subapostolic generation, numbering himself with those to whom the immediate hearers of the Lord had delivered the gospel; as has been pointed out in connection with other epistles, Paul was always quick to assert his independence in learning the gospel. There are several differences in style, language, and categories of thought between Paul and the writer of Hebrews. For Paul the Old Testament is Law; for Hebrews it is covenant. Paul's characteristic terms, "Our Lord Jesus Christ" and "Christ Jesus" are not found in Hebrews. Paul's doctrine of Christ revolves around the death, resurrection and living presence of Christ in the church; that of Hebrews is built around the priesthood of Christ. The apostle's doctrine of justification by faith does not appear in the epistle.

The argument favoring Apollos as the author of Hebrews is based on the fact that what is known about Apollos fits what can be determined about the author from the epistle itself. The writer uses excellent Greek and has a superb style. He appears to have had a wide philosophical knowledge. These things, as well as other aspects of the epistle, suggest that if he was a Jew, he was influenced by Hellenistic thought. His reference to the epistle as a "word of exhortation" (*13:22*) suggests that he was also a preacher. Apollos was a Jew, "an Alexandrian by race, a learned (or eloquent) man," "mighty in the scriptures," and he "powerfully confuted the Jews" (*Acts 18:24ff*). The Alexandrian type of thought, the arguments from Jewish tradition and ceremony, and the fluent style may all have come from an "eloquent Jew of

Alexandria." The main difficulty with supposing Apollos to be the author is that this notion never occurred until the time of Luther. Also, simply because the description of the writer fits Apollos does not make him the author. The only conclusion which can be reached is that which Origen expressed: "God only knows who wrote the Epistle to the Hebrews."

The phrase, "They of Italy salute you" (*13:24*), indicates that the letter was written either *from* or *to* Italy. There is no hint, except this possibility, as to the origin of the epistle. If it was not written from Rome, there is no way of determining its origin. The title, "To Hebrews," was not part of the original document but was affixed to the epistle at an early date and is found in all present Greek manuscripts and nearly all ancient versions. Although there has been some support of the theory that the letter was written to Gentiles, the writer of the epistle presents his arguments as if the recipients are well grounded in Judaism. Since the title was affixed by those who were in the best position for knowing the character of the recipients, it is probably safe to conclude that the epistle was directed to a Hebrew audience.

Because of large collections of Jews in Alexandria, Rome, and Jerusalem, all three have been suggested as the destination for the epistle. Rome and Jerusalem appear to have the strongest positions, but there is nothing definite or conclusive in either case. The locality is not, however, of primary importance if it is agreed that the epistle is addressed to Hebrew Christians.

The epistle appears to have been composed during some persecution of the church. The condition of mind of the readers made them ill-fitted for meeting severe trials. The writer characterizes them as children in religious intelligence, needing the most elementary kind of teaching (*5:12*). As a result of their weakness, they were in danger of lapsing into some kind of error which had as a part of it a return to the observance of the Law of Moses. The main purpose of the epistle is to establish Christianity as being superior to the Law. The author sets forth the superiority of Christ to angels (*1:5–2:18*), to Moses and Joshua (*3:1–4:2*), and to the Levitical high-priesthood (*chs. 5–7*). Chs. 8 and 9 contain a contrast between the tabernacle and its sacrifices and the sacrifice of Christ. Chs. 10–13 contain exhortations to remain faithful to the Christian religion and its principles and to separate from Judaism.

The date of the epistle is uncertain. The only thing that can be ascertained is that it was probably written shortly after AD 60. The latest possible date for its composition is AD 96, when it was alluded to by Clement of Rome.

James

The author of this epistle identifies himself as "James, a servant of God and of the Lord Jesus Christ." It is impossible to decide with absolute certainty as to which of the New Testament individuals bearing this name was the author of the book. Since James, the Son of Zebedee, was martyred in c. AD 44, he is usually excluded as a possibility. Usually named as the author is James the brother of the Lord (*Matt. 13:55; Gal. 1:9*) or James the son of Alphaeus. Whether these be one and not two men is a problem of difficulty which cannot be discussed fully in this space. Suffice it to say that the author is probably that James who occupied a prominent position in the Jerusalem church (*Gal. 2:9*) and who acted as president of the conference on circumcision (*Acts 15:18*Cf. also *Acts 12:17; 21:18*). Josephus speaks of him as a man of "pre-eminent justice." His personal bearing was evidently such that men immediately looked to him for spiritual leadership.

The address of the book, "to the twelve tribes which are scattered abroad," indicates that it was written from Jerusalem, as the "dispersion" —another translation of the greeting—referred to all Jews living away from Jerusalem. There is great disagreement as to the date of the epistle, suggestions ranging from AD 44 to AD 62, the latter date being the time of the martyrdom of James the Just, as the spiritual patriarch of Jerusalem has sometimes been called.

Those who favor an early date maintain that the absence of any mention of the controversies which disrupted the church after Paul began to preach is a sure indication that the epistle was written prior to these disputes. On the other hand, other scholars contend that the situation suggested by the epistle might just as easily indicate a later period. Usually mentioned in this connection is James' treatment of the relationship between faith and works. The doctrine of justification by faith, for which Paul contended, would naturally be subject to the type of abuse which this epistle presupposes—the substitution of a barren speculative faith for the true faith which works by love and purifies the life from sin.

Just as "the twelve tribes which are scattered abroad" (*1:1*) suggests Jews, the phrase, "my brethren," indicates that these were Jewish Christians. The epistle is eminently practical, dealing with the problems which faced the Christian community in that age and which yet remain a problem in the modern church. Among these are impatience under trial, hearing God's word without doing it, resting in an empty faith which does not influence the life, inordinate love of worldly possessions, lack of restraint of the tongue, failure to trust in the providence of God, partiality toward the rich and contempt of the poor, and a general lack of attention to those attitudes and actions which constitute "pure and undefiled religion."

1 Peter

The case for the Petrine authorship of the first epistle which bears the name of the Galilean fisherman is quite strong. Polycarp in his epistle to the Philippians makes numerous citations from it. Irenaeus, Clement of Alexandria, Tertullian and Origen all quote it, naming Peter as the author. The writer calls himself Peter (*1:1*) and is acquainted with the life and teachings of Christ to a degree which would seem most natural in an apostle. In addition, there are a number of phrases in the epistle which might be taken as alluding to events in Peter's life or which have counterparts in his speeches recorded elsewhere in the New Testament.

The question of the date of this epistle is closely connected with the occasion which brought it forth. A "fiery trial" seems to have been imminent in the lives of the Christians living in the areas mentioned in the opening verse of the epistle. The exact date and character of this persecution cannot be determined. A large number of scholars would identify this "fiery trial" with the persecution which arose under Nero in AD 64, in which Peter is believed to have lost his life. If this is the case, the epistle was written shortly before this, possibly in AD 63.

In 5:13 Peter implies that he is writing from Babylon. Scholarship has been divided over the question of whether this referred to the literal Babylon on the Euphrates or was used as a figurative designation for Rome. Neither position is without its merits. Those who contend for Rome maintain that the conditions were such that it was necessary to avoid any mention of Rome in such a letter, lest governmental suspicion be aroused. The use of "Babylon" as a figure for Rome in *Rev. 17* is also cited in support of this view. Finally, it is pointed out that Babylon had been destroyed long before the writing of the epistle. The advocates of the view that the place of writing was the literal Babylon on the Euphrates would maintain that although Babylon was destroyed prior to this time, there was still a sufficient population in that area to support a church and it is not unlikely that the gospel would have found its way to these people. It is also pointed out that the Christians in Rome might consider the reference to them as the "church in Babylon" as an affront to their dignity. As with other problems noted in this series of introductory articles, there is no way of ascertaining the exact truth on this matter. Fortunately, however, the interpretation of the epistle is not contingent on the solution of this problem.

The objectives of the epistle, as gathered from its contents, were: 1) To comfort and strengthen the Christians addressed in a period of rather severe persecution. To this end, he sets before them the glory of the heavenly inheritance which is reserved for the faithful as well as the blessedness which comes from suffering for the sake of Christ. 2) To reinforce the teaching which they had received with regard to the practical and spiritual duties involved in their calling as Christians. He exhorts his readers to abstain from the worldly pleasures which characterized their former existence and to discharge faithfully the obligations which were placed upon them by their various stations in life. He encourages them to be ready to provide a reasonable defense of the things for which they stand and to display a spirit of true Christian love in their association with one another. 3) To remove all doubts as to the soundness and completeness of the religion which they had received. To this end, he assures them that they were not following "cunningly devised fables" but had received true knowledge concerning the Lord Jesus

Christ, to whose glory the apostle himself had been an eyewitness (*Matt. 17*).

2 Peter

Attestation to the authenticity of the second epistle which bears Peter's name is noticeably scarce among early Christian writers, although traces of the epistle do appear in some early works. The epistle was officially admitted to the New Testament canon in the latter half of the fourth century, but not without difficulty. Eusebius lists it as among the "antilegomena" or "disputed" books. Jerome, writing in AD 350, stated that "Peter wrote two epistles . . . the second of which is denied by many to be his, because of differences in style from the former." Several explanations have been offered for the late general acceptance of this epistle. It is short and contains little material that might be styled as "quotable." Also, it may have been written to an obscure region which would render difficult the tracing down of the history of the epistle when it was being considered for canonicity.

The epistle makes an earnest attempt to establish itself as a product of the apostle Peter. The writer identifies himself in 1:1 as Simon Peter. He indicates that he was present at the transfiguration (*1:16-18*). He further suggests an awareness of the prediction which Christ made to him (Cf. *2 Pet. 1:12-14* with *John 21:13, 19*). The over-all spirit of the epistle seems to be one of sincerity; it is difficult to believe that it was written by an individual who was making an overt effort to deceive his readers.

The primary reason that scholars have doubted the genuineness of *2 Peter* is the great difference in vocabulary and style between it and *1 Peter*. Each of these epistles contains a large number of words which are not found in the other. This, of course, may be partially explained by the difference of subject matter. On the other hand, there are several words which are found in both these epistles, but seldom elsewhere in the New Testament, which would point toward a common author. The differences in style may possibly be accounted for by such a simple condition as the using of two different scribes to write down the thoughts of the same individual.

The date of the epistle, if Peter was its author, must fall sometime before his death which probably took place in AD 67 or 68. Other than this terminal date, it is difficult to reach any conclusion. Those who deny the Petrine authorship of the epistle would assign it to a time somewhere near the middle of the second century.

The epistle was occasioned by the writer's awareness of false teachers who were spreading their destructive doctrines among the churches. This prompted him to write a letter warning of their activity. He wrote also to stir his readers to growth in Christian character (*1:5-15; 3:18*) and to encourage them to be patient in their expectation of the Lord's return (*3:1-14*).

(For a discussion of the relationship between *2 Peter* and the epistle of Jude, see the introduction to *Jude*.)

1 John

Although this epistle does not bear the name of its author, early Christian writers often cited it as having come from the apostle John. Tradition was unanimous in accepting their view until the 16th century, when efforts began to be made to credit the epistle to someone other than John. Since the epistle does not name its author, no definite conclusion can be reached; however, the case for Johannine authorship is greatly enhanced by the unusually strong tradition which has grown up around this anonymous epistle.

Tradition states that John spent the last years of his life in Ephesus, using that city as a central point for his work among the churches in the area and writing from there. Most scholars place the time of composition of *1 John* after AD 80, allowing time after the flight from Jerusalem before AD 70 for John to have established the reputation which the writer of the epistle apparently enjoys.

In the fourth century the epistle was considered to be addressed to the Parthians. The title, "to the Parthians," actually occurs in several late manuscripts. There is no tradition of any relation between John and Babylon or the Parthians and it is uncertain how this title arose. Knowledge is entirely too scarce on this matter to reach any definite conclusion. Whoever the readers were, they are usually thought to be a definite church or group of churches. "My little children" would not be appropriate for the whole of Christians throughout the world. The group addressed did not consist of men newly converted. The language presupposes Christians, some of whom were "fathers" in the faith while others had enjoyed the privilege of being brought up in a Christian atmosphere, hearing the truth "from the beginning."

The purpose of the epistle was to combat various forms of error which had crept into the church. False teachers had gone out from the faithful and had begun to teach another doctrine. John refers to these teachers as "Antichrist" and "false prophets." It is not possible to pinpoint the heresy with which John dealt. It is possible only to affirm that it bore some likeness to those early heresies which denied the reality of Christ's fleshly existence.

In addition to this doctrinal error, the attitude of the "children" toward the Christian faith and life was not as it should have been. Their original enthusiasm had waned and needed to be renewed. They were in danger of yielding to the attraction of the pleasures of the world. It seems that their special need lay in a lack of recognition of the primary duty of Christians—love of the brethren. It was this combination of doctrinal, moral, and spiritual imperfection which occasioned the epistle.

John sought to meet these problems by affirming the reality of the incarnation of Christ, by exhorting all classes to separate from the world and by encouraging them to live in a relationship of love for Christ and their brethren.

The writing does not really resemble an epistle since it has no greeting or salutation and no references to acquaintances such as those which mark the writings of Paul. On the other hand, it does not present a speech which has been written down, either before or after delivery, as John repeatedly refers to the fact that he is writing. The epistle is marked by extreme simplicity of style, almost devoid of simile or metaphor. Its original purpose was to instruct and edify its readers. It still renders this service to modern Christians.

2 John

The second epistle ascribed to John experienced some difficulty in achieving canonicity, but it has been recognized generally since the fourth century. There is allusion in early Christian writing to at least one shorter epistle of John, and one writer quotes *2 John 10*, stating that it was written by John the apostle.

There seems to be a definite similarity and connection between this and the first epistle which bears John's name. The writer, however, does not give his name, but refers to himself only as "the elder." It has been stated that John the apostle would not use this lesser term of himself; Peter, however, also used the term (*1 Pet. 5:1*). It has been supposed that John the elder was a different man from John the apostle, and there is a tradition of two graves of John at Ephesus. Whether they be one or two men can probably never be decided, but the tradition is fairly strong in attributing the epistle to a man whose name was John.

The "elect lady," to whom the epistle is addressed, has been variously identified as the whole church, some local church, a church in Babylon, or an actual woman. Whichever the case may be, the matter is of little consequence. The purpose of the letter is to express the writer's appreciation of the loyalty of this "lady and her children" (*1-4*), to entreat her to walk in love and to keep the Lord's commandments (*5-6*), to warn her against deceivers (*1-11*), to inform her of his plan to visit soon (*v. 12*), and to convey the greeting of her "sister" (*v. 13*).

The epistle is usually thought to have been written near the end of John's life, probably about AD 90; it is also thought that both its origin and destination were somewhere in Asia Minor. In some respects, *2 John* is almost a miniature edition of *1 John*, for almost every phrase in it occurs in the larger work as well.

3 John

3 John was not definitely admitted to the New Testament canon until the middle of the fourth century and later still outside Greek and Latin Christianity. The points of discussion concerning the author, who refers to himself simply as "the elder," are the same as those noted above in the introduction to *2 John*. The only matter to be established is whether or not the two epistles were written by the same author. If face value is to be accepted, they are surely the work of one man. They are almost exactly of the same length, probably determined by the size of an ordinary papyrus sheet. The phraseology is so similar as to lead to the conclusion that if they are not the work of one man, one is a slavish imitation of the other. Since there is no apparent reason for such a forgery, it seems reasonable to uphold the traditional view that both are the product of one man named John.

The letter is addressed to Gaius. There are three men in the New Testament who bear this name (*1 Cor. 1:14; Acts 19:29; Acts 20:4*). As this was one of the most common names in the Greek and Roman world, there is no way of knowing if the recipient of the letter was any of these mentioned. In any case, this Gaius was evidently a prominent member of some church in which the apostle took an interest, and was especially noted for his hospitality. The statements made with regard to the time and place of composition of *2 John* apply to *3 John* as well.

The epistle was occasioned by the approaching visit of traveling missionaries to the church where Gaius was a member. These men were dependent on the hospitality of fellow-Christians for their livelihood. In the congregation was an influential man named Diotrophes. On previous occasions, he had arrogantly boycotted and excluded certain individuals from the fellowship of the church. John had previously written a letter on this matter but it had been suppressed or ignored as a result of Diotrophes' refusal to recognize the authority of the writer. John writes this letter to inform Gaius as to the proper course of action and to tell him of his plan to visit him and the church as soon as possible.

Jude

Origen characterized the book of Jude as an "epistle of but few lines, but full of powerful words of heavenly grace." The writer identifies himself as "Jude, a servant of Jesus Christ and brother of James" (*1:1*). He is commonly thought to have been the brother of Jesus as well. If this is the case, some biographical information can be pieced together concerning him. He was at one time an unbeliever (*John 7:5*), yet he appeared in the upper room with his mother and the other disciples after the ascension of Jesus (*Acts 1:14*). *1 Corinthians 9:5* would seem to imply that he was married.

Those who deny that this Jude was the author do so on grounds that the subject matter of the epistle necessitates placing it in a period long past the time that Jude would be expected to live. It is claimed that the term, "apostles of the Lord," (*vv. 17, 18*), is used in such a way as to indicate reverence for men who had lived long before. A close examination of the passage, however, will not make this conclusion inescapable. The reference is to the words which the apostles had spoken at a former time; the apostles themselves might easily be living. It is also maintained by some that the type of heresy which is described by the writer did not come into existence until after the apostolic era. A diligent examination of the letters of Paul and John, however, will reveal parallels to virtually every irregularity noted by Jude.

There is nothing in the epistle to indicate either its place of writing or the area to which it was addressed. The general phrase, "to them that are sanctified by God the Father and preserved in Jesus Christ, and called," would seem to refer to all Christians; yet, the tone of the denunciation of the heretics is such that one is prone to feel that the epistle was written to a particular community or region.

One of the major problems encountered in the study of *Jude* is its marked similarity to *2 Pet. 2:1–3:4.* Both letters tell of heretics who deny the Lord (*2 Pet. 2:1; Jude 4*), who have crept in secretly, doing their work deceptively (*2 Pet. 2: 1; Jude 4*), whose motive is covetousness (*2 Pet. 2:3; Jude 11*), who despise authority (*2 Pet. 2: 10; Jude 8*), who spoke with "swelling words of vanity" (*2 Pet. 2:18; Jude 16*), and who acted like brutes (*2 Pet. 2:12; Jude 10*). Both epistles liken these men to Balaam (*2 Pet. 2:15; Jude 11*) and characterize them as "wells without water" and "clouds carried along by winds" (*2 Pet. 2:17; Jude 12*).

The obvious inference of these remarkable similarities is that one of the writers used the other in the composition of his epistle. Those who contend that the writer of *2 Peter* used *Jude* as a source maintain that if Jude had used *2 Peter* he would not have restricted himself to material taken from the second chapter. The general view of this group is that *2 Peter* is an expansion of *Jude*. Critics who favor the view that Jude used *2 Peter* in the composition of his letter point out that the second chapter of *2 Peter* follows easily and without any apparent dislocation from the first. This would tend to negate the idea that the author of *2 Peter* composed an original letter, inserting a large portion of *Jude* in a convenient place. Also, the description of the heresy which is given in *Jude* seems to be a bit darker than that in *2 Peter,* indicating perhaps that the apostasy mentioned in *2 Peter* has had time to move into an advanced state. In this connection, it is even possible to see in *Jude 17, 18* a reference back to *2 Peter 3:2-4.* These considerations have led a large number of scholars to conclude that Jude penned his epistle sometime after *2 Peter* was written and drew heavily on the phraseology of that epistle in his stern denunciation of the troublesome error.

Revelation

The voice of the early church speaks clearly in asserting that the author of the *Revelation* was the apostle John. Justin Martyr, Irenaeus, Hippolytus, Tertullian, Clement of Alexandria and the Muritorian canon furnish strong external evidence for the authenticity of the book. It should be noted, however, that opposition to this view also began early. In the second century the notion arose that the writer of the *Revelation* could not be identified with the apostle John, especially if the latter be named as the author of the fourth gospel. The basic approach used in assailing the Johannine authorship of *Revelation* is to contrast this book with the gospel of *John.* That there are striking dissimilarities between the two books must be admitted. The letter is characterized by a much more abrupt and uneven style of Greek. There are, however, a number of similarities which should not be overlooked. Words and phrases such as "Lamb," "water of life," and the admonition "to keep the commandments" are common to both. Both contain a striking quotation from *Zechariah 2:10* (Cf. *Rev. 1:7; John 19:37*). Both feature the repetition of the Greek article and the use of parenthetical explanations for the sake of emphasis and fulness. Many of the apparent incongruities are minimized when one considers the radical difference in subject matter between the two books. The roughness of the *Revelation,* as compared to *John,* might be partially accounted for by the overwhelming character of the experience of the visions on Patmos. It has also been suggested that John may have used a scribe in the composition of the gospel, while doing the actual writing of *Revelation* himself. In view of these latter considerations, as well as the strong attestation to the Johannine authorship by the early church, the traditional view seems by no means untenable.

Most scholars date the book around AD 96, during the reign of Domitian. In this period Christianity found itself pitted against the entire Roman Empire. The early Christians had experienced some persecution, especially at the hands of Nero, but the suffering under Domitian was much more general and severe. Domitian had claimed for himself a title indicating deity and any Christian who failed to pay homage to him was subject to punishment which might include the death penalty. It was in this kind of atmosphere that the *Revelation* was received. The style in which the book is written is called "Apocalyptic." Apocalyptic literature is highly figurative, making extensive use of vivid imagery and symbolism. It is concerned mainly with things of the future, especially with regard to the end of time. This type of literature flourished in the centuries immediately preceding the time of Christ. The Old Testament itself furnishes several such examples in *Ezekiel, Daniel* and *Zechariah.*

The first three chapters of the *Revelation* provide us with a thumbnail sketch of the seven churches in Asia, describing their weaknesses and strengths, together with the problems with which the church of that era was faced. Beginning with the fourth chapter, the writer records a series of visions which he has received. These have been subject to wide and conflicting interpretations, none of which has been free of considerable difficulty. Generally speaking, however, the various interpreters of the book are in agreement that it was designed to assure the churches that God was aware of them in their time of struggle and that, as Lord of History, He would effect the eventual triumph of good over evil. Other apparent aims of the book are to call attention to the inevitable reality and nature of the judgment day and to demonstrate the beauty of divine worship and the glories of the heavenly realm.

The History of the Formation and Translation of the English Bible

THE CANON OF THE BIBLE

The word "canon" is derived from a Hebrew term meaning "cane" or "reed." Since the reed was one of the first instruments of measurement used by man, the term carries with it the idea of a norm or pattern by which other things are measured. In the Christian church it has been used to refer to that collection of writings which comprises our Bible and which has come to be regarded as the authoritative and inspired word of God. The existence of a definite list of books which were to be considered as final authority was made a necessity by several circumstances. As men began to sense that the authentic voice of God was no longer being heard in religious pronouncements it was inevitable that they should seek to preserve those writings which were acknowledged to bear the stamp of prophetic or apostolic authority. When efforts were made to destroy all extant copies of the writings which Jews and Christians held sacred, it became a matter of no small importance to determine which of these writings were to be singled out as especially precious and worthy of all efforts at protection. In addition, the appearance of fraudulent and heretical documents claiming for themselves divine inspiration called for the formulation of a list of books to which the church could appeal in matters of faith and practice.

The Old Testament Canon

In the first century AD there was a body of Jewish sacred literature which bore the general term, "scripture," which believers regarded as inspired of God, but whose limits were not as yet precisely determined. The general Jewish consensus was in favor of the list of books found in the Protestant Bible. In Alexandria, however, there was a tendency to include a larger number of books in the Old Testament canon, the additional writings being those designated by Protestants as the *Apocrypha.* The books of the Apocrypha originated in the "inter-testamental period"—the time between the writing of *Malachi* (c. 400 BC) and the coming of Christ. They include 1 and 2 Esdras, Tobit, Judith, the Rest of Esther, the Wisdom of Solomon (similar to Proverbs and Ecclesiastes); Ecclesiasticus, sometimes called the Wisdom of Jesus, the son of Sirach; Baruch, which claims to have been written by the scribe of Jeremiah; three additions to the books of Daniel—the Song of the Three Holy Children, the History of Susanna, and the History of the Destruction of Bel and the Dragon; the Prayer of Manasses, King of Judah; and the historically valuable 1 and 2 Maccabees. Since the Reformation, Protestants have rejected the apocryphal books as spurious, but the council of Trent (AD 1546), citing Augustine's support of the Alexandrian view, officially included the Apocrypha in the canon recognized by the Catholic church.

The Old Testament scriptures were early divided into the Law, the Prophets, and the Writings. The Law contained the first five books of the Old Testament; this is generally thought to have been the first group of writings to have received canonical standing. It achieved this status at least as early as the end of the third century BC and probably much earlier. The Prophets, consisting of the writings of the prophets themselves and the historical books which tell of their times, were regarded as authoritative by the second century BC. The remaining books of the Old Testament (Psalms, Proverbs, Job, Song of Solomon, Ruth, Lamentations, Ecclesiastes, Esther, Daniel, Ezra, Nehemiah, 1 and 2 Chronicles) were known to Jews as the Writings. These received recognition as inspired and authoritative probably about 100 BC.

Although we give thirty-nine the number of books in the Old Testament, the Jews consider these same books to be only twenty-two. This apparent discrepancy is explained by the fact that the following groups of books are counted as only one book each: Judges-Ruth, 1 and 2 Samuel, 1 and 2 Kings, 1 and 2 Chronicles, Ezra-Nehemiah, Jeremiah-Lamentations, and the twelve minor prophets. Hence, when the Jewish historian, Josephus, writing in the first century AD, speaks of the Hebrew canon as containing only twenty-two books, he does not reject any of those which comprise our present Old Testament canon.

The New Testament Canon

The development of the New Testament canon was somewhat more complex than that of the Old Testament. A primary reason for this was that while the entire Old Testament was produced within a small geographical area, the various New Testament books had widely divergent origins. This being true, it was only natural that there should be great difference in opinion among the churches as to which books were truly sacred, each church giving preference to those with which it was most familiar. In answer to the need for moral and spiritual support, it became commonplace for the churches to correspond with each other and to exchange the letters which they had received from the apostle or from other outstanding Christian leaders. It is, of course, impossible to trace the exact manner in which this took place, but it is safe to say that a group of writings developed which achieved a place alongside the Old Testament scriptures. Such a collection would ordinarily consist of the Gospel, several of the Pauline letters and several letters bearing the names of apostles or outstanding church leaders such as Peter, John, James, or Jude. To these would be added one or more Apocalypses, usually either that of John, which stands in our canon, or those of Peter and Hermas.

As early as AD 95, Clement of Rome wrote a letter to the church in Corinth in which he apparently uses language from Matthew, Luke and several Pauline epistles. Nowhere, however, does he cite these writings as divine. The writings of Ignatius (c. AD 115) are also seen to contain considerable Pauline material as well as quotations from the gospel of Matthew, 1 Peter, and 1 John. Papias, who wrote in the first half of the second century, quotes from the gospel of John and mentions the writings of Matthew and Mark. *The Teaching of the Twelve Apostles*, or *Didache*, written near the beginning of the second century, either quotes or alludes to Matthew, Luke, John, Acts, Romans, the letters to the Thessalonians and the first epistle of Peter. The earliest designation of a passage from the Gospels as scriptures is found in the epistle attributed to Barnabas, which has been dated near AD 135. By the time of Justin Martyr (c. AD 153), the Gospels were being read in Rome along with the Old Testament books. At about this same time Tatian compiled a harmony of the four Gospels called the *Diatessaron* which is evidence that it was generally agreed upon that only these four Gospels gave an inspired and trustworthy account of the life and teachings of Jesus.

One of the most notable of the heretics who troubled the church in this period was Marcion, a Gnostic teacher. In order to support his views and in an effort to break completely with Judaism, Marcion formed a canon consisting of an expurgation of Luke's gospel and ten of Paul's letters. This is the first clear evidence of the canonization of Pauline writings. As noted above, the struggle with heresy such as that of Marcion forced the church to a decision on which books it was to regard as authoritative and upon which it could rely in its struggle with error. After this period, it is much easier to give an accurate account of the development of the New Testament canon.

Irenaeus, the widely acquainted bishop of Lyons in the latter part of the second century, wrote much in opposition to the heresies which confronted the Christian church. It is significant that in his writings he appealed to the New Testament as scripture, citing the four Gospels, the Acts, the Pauline epistles, the general epistles, and the Apocalypse or Revelation of John. He was explicit in insisting that the number of Gospels be no more nor less than four. Tertullian of Carthage, writing between AD 197 and 223, took a position quite similar to that of Irenaeus.

The real landmark of this period is a document known as the Muratorian Fragment, so named after the Italian scholar, Muratori, who discovered it in Milan in 1740. This document dates near the end of the second century and concerns itself with listing those books which were to be considered as canonical. It includes the Gospels, the Acts, the Pauline epistles, the Apocalypse of John, 1 and 2 John and Jude. It omits Hebrews, 1 and 2 Peter, James, and 3 John. It also included the Apocalypse of Peter, but admits that it was rejected by some of the churches.

The most outstanding Christian figure of the third century was Origen. The information which he furnishes about the canon is especially valuable because of the wide scope of his learning and his communication with other centers of Christian thought. Of the disputed books, Origen was uncertain concerning James, 2 Peter, and 3 John, but he accepted the Revelation of John. In his discussion of Hebrews, Origen made the famous statement that "God alone knows who wrote the epistle to the Hebrews."

For all practical purposes, the fourth century marks the final stages of the development of the New Testament canon. The great church historian of the first quarter of this century, Eusebius of Caesarea, gave a summary of the views on the canon. Eusebius accepted the same books which constitute our New Testament, although he expressed some reservation about Revelation, and acknowledged that the canonicity of several of the books which he accepted was disputed by some.

As the church of the fourth century labored to reach a definitive statement of those things which it believed, in its struggle against heresy and in its adjustment to the support of the state, the voice which was clearest in shaping and reflecting orthodox belief was that of Athanasius, bishop of Alexandria. Each year at Easter, Athanasius sent a letter to the churches in his diocese. In the letter of AD 367, he included a list of books which were to be recognized as scripture. This list consisted of the twenty-seven books which constitute our New Testament. Athanasius invested these with finality by the statement, "Let no one add to these. Let nothing be taken away."

Just as these men reflected the views of the church as a whole rather than their own opinions, the councils which ultimately fixed the canon were doing little more than putting the official seal of approval on what had already become standard in the churches. Of several councils which spoke on the matter, perhaps the most notable was the council of Carthage of AD 397, which ratified the list of books as we now have them. This virtually settled the question of the canon of the Christian Bible, although the Revelation of John was long achieving acceptance in the Eastern churches.

The New Testament "Apocrypha"

Although the term "apocrypha" technically applies only to those books mentioned above which sought a place in the canon of the Old Testament, a number of writings appeared after the close of the period of New Testament literary activity which purported to be inspired of God and worthy of a place in the canon and which may be spoken of as constituting a New Testament "apocrypha." Generally speaking, these were patent forgeries and never received the measure of acceptance which was accorded the Old Testament Apocrypha. They were often attacks on or defenses of some doctrine or heresy, or contained fantastic miracle-stories, which often bordered on the ridiculous, about the life of Jesus. Among these are the Gospels according to Nicodemus, the Hebrews, the Ebionites, the Egyptians, Peter, Pseudo-Matthew, Thomas and Joseph the Carpenter. A good example of how these were used to promulgate private doctrines is seen in the Gospel of the Ebionites. This group, which was vegetarian, pictures John the Baptist as eating wafers instead of locusts and wild honey. In addition to the Gospels there are Acts of Pilate, Paul, Peter, John, Andrew, Philip, and Thomas, the Martyrdom of Matthew, and the Apostolic History of Abdias. In the class of epistles, we find the Letter of Lentulus, the Epistle to the Laodiceans, the Correspondence of

Paul and Seneca, and the Epistle of Apostles. Apocalyptic works, characterized by a high degree of symbolism and predictive elements, included the Apocalypses of Peter, Paul, Thomas, and Stephen. With rare exception, there is little difficulty in distinguishing between them and the truly inspired Word.

RECONSTRUCTION OF THE ORIGINAL TEXT

The story of the production and preservation of our Bible is a fascinating and often romantic one. The Old Testament books, of course, had been standardized before the time of Christ and we can be assured that we have texts practically identical to those used by the early church. The case is considerably different with regard to the New Testament. Unfortunately, there are no original manuscripts of the New Testament writings which are known to be in existence. Nevertheless, enough manuscripts of high quality have been found to furnish us with a text which must be quite close to that possessed by the early Christians.

Writing Materials

The writing material which was in current use at the time of the production of the New Testament and for several centuries thereafter was papyrus. This material was produced by taking strips of pith from the papyrus reed and gluing them together in a horizontal and vertical pattern to form a mat. This was then pounded or pressed and allowed to dry, producing a suitable surface for writing. The width of these pieces might be anywhere from five inches to a foot, depending on their quality. There were recognized grades of this material, used for different purposes, just as we have numerous grades of paper today. These pieces of papyrus were then pasted into scrolls, usually about thirty feet long and occasionally reaching over 100 feet in length. In the second century AD the papyrus "codex" came into being. The codex is that form used in our own books; that is, pages were fastened together to form a volume. These could contain a larger amount of writing than a scroll and therefore facilitated the collection of New Testament books into a group. Papyrus was not extremely durable. It rotted easily or became brittle and disintegrated with time. For this reason, there were few fragments of any significance preserved on this material until a large group of extremely valuable papyri dating to the second century AD were discovered in this century in Egypt. Before this discovery, all of our ancient manuscripts were written on vellum, which was simply a fine quality of animal skin prepared for writing on both sides.

The Manuscripts

The vellum manuscripts which have been found were made between the fourth and fifteenth centuries. There are two types of these, Uncials and Cursives. The Uncial Manuscripts were written in large capital letters without spaces between them and appeared something like this–PAULANAPOSTLETOTHEGENTILES–though written, of course, in Greek. Although these were more difficult to read than the Cursive, which are written in small connected letters, they are of far greater value because of their age.

There are literally thousands of manuscripts of the Bible or parts of it in existence. The best known of these are three Uncial codices known as the Sinaiticus, Vaticanus and Alexandrinus. The Codex Sinaiticus, so called because it was discovered in the monastery of St. Catharine on Mt. Sinai, is the only extant manuscript which contains the entire New Testament. A German scholar, Constantine Tischendorf, while visiting in the monastery in 1844, recognized the manuscript as it lay in a trash basket, waiting to be burned. The basket contained forty-three leaves of a beautiful copy of the scriptures dating back to the first half of the fourth century. Over a period of fifteen years, Tischendorf carried on an unsuccessful search for the remainder of the manuscripts. Finally, he was able to locate the remainder of the 347-page manuscript. In 1933, the major portion of this same manuscript was sold to the British museum for half a million dollars.

The Codex Vaticanus, so named because it has resided in the Vatican library since 1481, is also dated in the fourth century. This is probably the oldest and best of the Greek manuscripts. It does not, however, contain the entire New Testament, a portion of Hebrews and the Pastoral epistles (1 and 2 Timothy, Titus), Philemon and Revelation being missing. The Codex Alexandrinus was made in the fifth century in Alexandria and contains the entire Bible with some fragments of Matthew, John, and 1 Corinthians missing. This manuscript is also in the British museum, having been presented to the Royal Library in 1757.

The most noteworthy manuscript in the United States is the fourth century Codex Washingtoniensis, discovered in Egypt in 1906 and presently located in the Smithsonian Library in Washington, D.C. Two other important Uncial manuscripts are the Codex Ephraemi Rescriptus and Codex Bezae. The former of these is what is known as a palimpsest text; that is, the original manuscript was erased and written over, although it is still possible to determine the original text. In this case, the writing was done by Ephraem; hence the designation of the manuscript. A large portion of each of the New Testament books is missing from this manuscript, while two books (2 Thessalonians and 2 John) are missing altogether. Codex Bezae is named for Theodore Beza, who obtained the manuscript from the monastery of St. Irenaeus in Lyons in 1562 and presented it in 1581 to the University of Cambridge where it now resides. This is a text in both Greek and Latin, containing only the Gospels, Acts, and a small section of 3 John. The most important recent discovery in manuscripts has been the Chester Beatty Papyri, collected in the early years of the twentieth century and dating back into the second century AD.

Apart from the manuscripts themselves, scholars are able to ascertain the original text by the use of ancient translations from the Greek, from citations of the scriptures by early Christian and Jewish writers and from lectionaries or books containing daily readings for devotional purposes. Through the use of these materials biblical scholars have been able to reconstruct a text unrivalled for accuracy and integrity by any other ancient writings.

ANCIENT TRANSLATION

The Old Testament which was used by most of the early church was not in its original Hebrew but was a Greek translation of the Hebrew scriptures known as the Septuagint and often designated simply by the Roman numeral LXX. It is so named and abbreviated because of a tradition which asserts that Ptolemy Philadelphius (285-247 BC) ordered a Greek version of the scriptures to be completed by about seventy Palestinian elders for use by the Jews in Egypt. It is difficult to determine just how much of the tradition is factual, but the important thing to be noted is that the Jews of the Dispersion were allowing Hebrew to fall into disuse and were in need of a translation into their vernacular. Many of the quotations of the Old Testament which are found in the New Testament are from the Septuagint version.

The need for translations into the languages of the readers resulted in numerous versions. Among the more notable are a second century Syrian version called the Old Syriac, the fourth or fifth century Peshitta ("simple") Syriac which superseded the Old Syriac, the second century translation in Coptic, the vernacular language of Egypt, and the second century Old Latin version. The most important translation before the Reformation was the Latin version commonly referred to as the Vulgate. Just as the settling of the canon was necessitated by the widespread separation of the churches and the rise of heresy, these same factors made a single, authoritative text desirable. The absence of a uniform text to which all Christians could appeal in their encounters with heretical doctrine prompted Damascus, Bishop of Rome, to commission Jerome, the greatest Latin scholar of the latter part of the fourth century, to produce a version which would meet the needs of the church for a standard text. The first installment of this text, a translation of the Gospels, appeared in AD 383. Jerome's method in making the translation was to revise the Old Latin versions, aided by the use of Greek manuscripts. His first translation of the Old Testament was made from the Greek Septuagint; however, by AD 405, he had completed a translation of the Old Testament from the original Hebrew. It was some time before the new version was able to supersede the Old Latin, but it was destined eventually to become the common Bible of Europe for many centuries. The first English Bible, that of John Wycliffe, was based on this edition. The Vulgate is still the authoritative Bible of the Roman Catholic Church, although it has undergone many revisions.

Translation Into Other European Languages

Prior to and during the period of heaviest activity in English translation of the Bible, with which this review is primarily concerned, there was elsewhere in Europe similar enthusiasm in presenting the Bible to the common people in the vernacular. A Norman-French Bible was in use in Northern France in the middle of the thirteenth century. The fifteenth century brought an Italian and a Dutch version, in addition to various translations in Slavonic and Scandanavian tongues. Many German translations were in existence before the monumental translation of Martin Luther which appeared in the complete Bible in 1534 and which was a chief factor in the standardization of the German language.

THE TRANSLATION OF THE ENGLISH BIBLE

The story of the translation of the Bible into English is one of persecution, courage and intrigue as well as scholarship and spiritual dedication. The clergy and other learned men had always had some access to the Latin Vulgate. Since few of the common people could read and manuscripts were too expensive to buy, this was about all that was required and no complete translation of the Bible or even the New Testament is known to have come from the Anglo-Saxon period. By the middle of the eighth century, however, it is believed that all of the gospels existed in Anglo-Saxon.

John Wycliffe

The first complete English Bible which is known of is that attributed to John Wycliffe (c. 1324-1384). It is difficult to ascertain just what part Wycliffe actually played in the translation. It is often asserted that his colleague, Nicholas of Hereford, was responsible for a great portion of it, especially in the Old Testament. Since the translation was made from the Vulgate edition, it contains the Apocryphal books of the Old Testament. Regardless of his part in the actual translation, Wycliffe was at least the moving spirit behind this version, being motivated by a strong conviction that the laity needed to have an edition of the Bible made available in their common speech. After Wycliffe's death, the work of spreading the copies of his translation was carried on by his followers, known as the "poor priests" or "Lollards." In 1428, forty-four years after his death, the church expressed its disapproval of Wycliffe's labors by ordering his body disinterred, burned, and the ashes cast into the river Swift. Despite the church's efforts to suppress Wycliffe's work, about 170 manuscripts of the Wycliffe Bible are still in existence. This is made even more remarkable when one considers that the printing press had not yet been invented.

William Tyndale

The invention of the printing press loosed a tide of translations that no amount of opposition could stem. A Hebrew Bible appeared in 1488 and the Greek New Testament edited by Erasmus was published in 1516. The first edition of the New Testament to be printed in English was the work of William Tyndale. Tyndale's conviction about the significance of his labors is expressed in his statement that if his life were spared he would enable a common plowhand to know as much of the Bible as the pope. Due to opposition to his work and the lack of funds, Tyndale was forced to pursue his work on the continent, first edition appearing in 1526. In this work he was assisted by John Fryth and William Roye, both of whom later were condemned to death as heretics. In the same year in which the first printing was made, the hierarchy of the English church published a prohibition against the translation. Despite this action, copies continued to make their way into the country. To enforce the prohibitions, the Bishop of London bought up all the copies he could find and burned them. Augustine Packynton, a London merchant who supported Tyndale, raised money for his project by selling Tyndale's Bibles to the Bishop for his bonfire. Through the support of men like Packynton, Tyndale continued his work, beginning work on an English version of the Old Testament and bringing out revisions of the New Testament in 1534 and 1535. In 1530 a royal proclamation was issued, calling for total suppression of the translation of the scriptures "corrupted by William Tyndale." It was stated that the king would provide a translation in the vernacular when such action was deemed expedient. After years of eluding the authorities, Tyndale was finally apprehended and on October 6, 1536, he was strangled and burned at the stake. His dying prayer was "Lord, open the King of England's eyes." It is difficult, if not impossible, to overestimate the value of Tyndale's work in providing us with an English Bible.

Coverdale, Matthew, and Taverner

The first printed edition of the entire Bible into English was that of Miles Coverdale which appeared in 1535. Coverdale, a tactful man, dedicated his translation to King Henry VIII, thus probably sparing his work from some of the difficulties with which it might otherwise have met. The work was substantially based upon that of his friend Tyndale, although there were numerous variations; in addition to the changes in translations, it omitted Tyndale's preface and notes which had been offensive to some. Coverdale included the Apocrypha in his translation, but not without a question as to its validity. The first Bible to obtain official support was probably that published in 1537 under the name of Thomas Matthew. The Taverner Bible of 1539 holds the distinction of being the first Bible printed completely in England. This was a revision of Matthew's and Tyndale's Bible by an English scholar, Richard Taverner, with some individual translation of considerable merit.

The Great Bible

The first "authorized" version was the "Great Bible," so called because of the size of its pages which measured nine by fifteen inches. Oliver Cromwell commissioned Coverdale to serve as editor of this new version. Apart from this, many of the facts involved in the preparation of this Bible are somewhat obscure. Due to superior facilities, the printing was scheduled to have been done in Paris, but difficulties with the authorities forced the work to be completed in London. The Great Bible made its initial appearance in April, 1539. Although the purpose of the translation was to make the scriptures available to the common people, the prologues discouraged public discussion of the Bible by laymen, urging that men of higher learning be consulted on difficult points of interpretation. A second edition of this Bible appeared in 1540 with an introduction by Archbishop Cranmer. Because of this, the Great Bible is often referred to as "Cranmer's Bible."

The Geneva Bible

The next great landmark among English translations was the Geneva Bible of 1558. Such men as Calvin, Knox, and Coverdale were all in touch with this monumental work. The individuals who are usually given credit for the major portion of the actual work are William Whittingham on the New Testament and Anthony Gilby and Thomas Sampson on the Old Testament. These men relied heavily on Tyndale's work and upon the Great Bible in their translation. Due to the use of the word "breeches" in the translation of Genesis 3:7 ("they sewed fig leaves together and made themselves breeches"), this Bible has often been called the "Breeches Bible." It proved to be the most popular Bible produced in English up to that time. In addition to its translation and annotations, its popularity was enhanced by its use of Roman type and the division of the chapters into verses; this was the first time this had been done in an English Bible. Subsequent versifications of the English Bible owe much to the Geneva Bible.

The second Bible to receive the designation, "authorized," was the Bishops' Bible of 1568, so called because the committee of revisers was composed largely of bishops. A second edition of the Bishops' Bible appeared in 1572.

The Douay-Rheims Catholic Bible

The demand by English-speaking Catholic clergymen for a Bible in their native tongue was met by the efforts of William Cardinal Allen, president and founder of the English college at Douai, France, which was moved to Rheims for a short time. Because of the location of the college, the version which Allen was instrumental in having produced has come to be known as the Douay or Douay-Rheims version. The New Testament in this version was published in 1582 and the Old Testament in 1610. It was made from the Latin Vulgate, in preference to the Hebrew and Greek texts.

The King James Version

The most famous and most durable of all

English versions has been the King James Version of 1611. A remark regarding mistranslations in the existing Bibles was made at the Hampton Court Conference on religious grievances in 1604. The idea of a new translation caught the imagination of King James and he determined to have a new version made which might be established as the uniform text of the entire commonwealth. Fifty-four scholars were chosen for the task. These were to be divided into six groups, each being assigned a section of the scripture for translation and revision. Each individual in a group was to make an individual translation of the section assigned to his group. When this was completed, the members of the group were to compare their work and formulate a translation which was acceptable to all. Similarly, each group was to present its product to the entire company for final approval. In addition, all learned individuals in the churches were urged to render any aid which they might in eliminating obscurities in the text. By the time the work was finally begun in 1607, only forty-seven of the original fifty-four were available for work on the project. Ten of these met at Westminster and were assigned the Pentateuch (the first five books of the Old Testament) along with the historical books which follow from Joshua through the two books of Kings. Eight more, at Cambridge, had charge of the rest of the historical books, together with Job, Psalms, Proverbs, Song of Solomon and Ecclesiastes. At Oxford one company of seven had the prophets assigned to them and another company of eight were entrusted with the four Gospels, Acts of Apostles, and the Revelation of John. A second company at Westminster was engaged in translating the remainder of the New Testament while a second company at Cambridge was given the books of the Apocrypha.

The translators received certain general instructions from the king to regulate them in their work. They were required to abide by the translation of the "Bishops' Bible" as much as the original text would allow; to retain proper names in their original form; when several words might fit equally well, to use that which had been preferable to the best ancient writers; to use the current chapter and verse divisions; to use no marginal notes, unless to explain particular Greek or Hebrew words, and to cite references to parallel passages insofar as it seemed desirable. These forty-seven men struggled with the version for over three years, finally bringing it to publication in 1611.

As a result of its arrival on the scene at a propitious time in history, the King James or Authorized Version (although King James did not bear the expenses of the project and there is no record of an official "authorization") has long held the foremost position among English translations insofar as its popularity is concerned. The majesty and beauty of its language, not to mention the familiarity which centuries of use brings, have made this popularity not unjustified. There are, however, certain facts which the serious student should bear in mind. The Authorized Version was based upon the faulty Greek text of Erasmus which was compiled without the benefit of the better manuscripts which have since been discovered. It was never intended to be the final revision of the scriptures "once for all delivered to the saints." In fact, no one today reads the Authorized Version in the English in which it was originally written, as this is so archaic as to sound foreign to modern ears. Yet, this was the language of the common man in the 1600's. An edition was published in 1629 omitting the Apocrypha which had been included in the original version. Extensive revisions of this version appeared in 1762 and 1769. It is also interesting to note that the King James Version aroused the same sort of clamor which greeted translations of the Bible into modern speech in this century.

Modern Translations of the Bible

With the discovery of better texts and the needs for a Bible in the vernacular—the same need which produced all the great versions—scholars have continued to present the Bible to us in revised forms. The English Revised Version, usually referred to simply as the Revised Version, appeared in the New Testament in 1881 and in the complete Bible in 1885. This version differed from the King James Version in over thirty thousand places in the New Testament alone. In 1901 an American edition known as the American Revised or American Standard Version appeared. This version was similar to the Revised Version although it embodied changes which were preferable to the American Revision committee. In the twentieth century numerous other modern speech translations have occurred, usually the work of one or two individuals. Most notable among these are the versions of Weymouth, Moffatt, Goodspeed, Phillips, and the Riverside New Testament. In 1949, the complete Bible appeared in "Basic English," a simplified form of English based on a 1,000-word vocabulary.

The most widely accepted translation of the twentieth century has been the Revised Standard Version. This work was begun in 1930, the New Testament being complete in 1946 and the Old Testament in 1952. Another well-received translation has been the New English Bible which first appeared in 1961. All of these modern speech translations have met with opposition and cries of corruption of the sacred writing. None, to be sure, is perfect; yet, probably without exception, each has been made with a high regard for the Holy Word and a sincere desire to render more intelligible that which is the true will of God for every man.

Summary of the Translations

John Wycliffe's Bible (c. 1382)
William Tyndale's New Testament (1526)
Miles Coverdale's Bible (1535)
Thomas Matthew's Bible (1537)
Richard Taverner's Bible (1539)
Great Bible—The first "authorized" Bible (1539)
Geneva Bible—The "Breeches Bible" (1558)
Bishop's Bible (1568 and 1572)
Douay-Rheims Catholic Bible (1610)
King James or Authorized Version (1611)
English Revised Version (1881-1885)
American Standard Version (1901)
Revised Standard Version (1946-1952)
The New English Bible (1961)

MODERN DIVISIONS OF THE BIBLE

The original authors of the Bible did not divide their writings into chapters and verses as we have them today; this was a much later development. The Jews had long divided their scriptures into sections for more convenient reference, but the division into chapters as we know them was the work either of Stephen Langton, archbishop of Canterbury in the reigns of John and Henry III, or Cardinal Hugo de St. Caro, the first member of the Dominican order to be raised to the rank of Cardinal. Both of these men were active in the first half of the thirteenth century. It was Hugo who devised the first concordance, which would necessitate some type of versification in order to prove workable. As stated above, the division of the chapters was identical to our present divisions, but the smaller subdivisions did not correspond to our system of versification. Instead, the chapters were subdivided by placing the letters A, B, C, D, E, F, G, in the margin at an equal distance from each other, depending on the length of the chapter. This system of versification was adopted into the Latin Vulgate, which had previously had no subdivisions at all.

The sub-division of the Old Testament chapters into verses was done by Rabbi Mordecai Nathan, about 1445. This rabbi, in imitation of Hugo, drew up a concordance to the Hebrew scriptures for the use of Jews. Although he followed Hugo in his division of the books into chapters, he improved upon his subdivisions, giving us our present numerical arrangement of verses. This was found to be much more convenient and has been followed since that time. The division of the New Testament chapters into verses first appeared in the Greek text edited by Robert Estienne in 1551. Tradition has it that Estienne devised his system while traveling on horseback from Paris to Lyons.

It ought always to be remembered that the division of the Bible into verses was designed as a reference aid for study of the Bible and was never intended to govern the sense of a passage. A verse or chapter division may often occur in the middle of a narrative or train of thought, thus giving the impression that the discussion of the topic has ended, when such may not be the case. The serious student should be careful not to follow a program of reading which adheres strictly to the humanly-devised divisions of the Bible, but should concern himself with making certain that he has discerned the context in which a verse or chapter is situated.

The Kings of Israel and Judah

It is not always possible to arrive at the exact date of the reigns of the kings listed in this chart; therefore, many dates are approximate. They are, however, based on careful historical investigation and may be trusted to be reasonably accurate.

Italic figures following names indicate length of reign.

THE UNITED MONARCHY

Saul 1020-1000   David 1000-961   Solomon 961-922

THE DIVIDED MONARCHY

JUDAH

Rehoboam *8* 922-915
Foolish government caused schism.

Abijah (Abijam) *3*..915-913

Asa *41* 913-873
Reformer. Repelled Ethiopian attack.
Got Ben-hadad, king of Syria, to attack Israel.
Established court of appeals.

Jehoshaphat *25* 873-849
Reasonably faithful.
Good material wealth in Judah.

Related History

918: Shishak, king of Egypt, attacks Judah, Philistia, Edom. Destroys 150 towns.

Assyria stirring under Asshur-nasir-apli; Northern Syrian campaign, 870.

ISRAEL

Jeroboam I *22* ....c. 922-901
Instituted bull-cult to preserve his kingdom.

Nadab *2* 901-900
Killed and replaced by Baasha.

Baasha *24* 900-877
Attacked by Ben-hadad (Syria).

Elah *2* 877-876

Zimri *7 days* 876
Slew Baasha's house. Burned himself alive when Omri arose.

Omri *8* 876-869
Established strong dynasty.
Fought with Tibni for power.
Built up Samaria.
Made treaty with Tyre.
Arranges Ahab-Jezebel marriage.
Defeated Moabites (not in Bible).

JUDAH	*Related History*	ISRAEL
Helped Israel in battle against Syria.	Shalmaneser III (Assyria) attacked Aram (Syria) at Qarqar, 853 (date definite).	**Ahab** *20* ....869-850 Omride dynasty member. Husband of Jezebel. War with Syria. Ahab killed at Ramoth-Gilead. PROPHETS: *Micaiah* and *Elijah*
Jehoram *8* ....849-842 **Ahaziah** *1* ....842 **Athaliah** *7* ....842-836 Ahab's sister. Married to Jehoshaphat. Slew all descendants of David, except Joash. Killed when Jehoida the priest put Joash on the throne.	*(Both of these kings were killed in revolt of Jehu)*	**Ahaziah** *2* ....850-849 **Joram** *8* ....849-842 PROPHETS: *Elijah* and *Elisha* **Jehu** *28* ....842-814 Took throne by bloody purge. Lost Phoenecia and Judah as allies. Vassal of Assyria in 841.
Jehoash (Joash) *40* ..836-797 Instituted some reforms while the priest Jehoida was still alive. Crushed at hands of Hazael, king of Aram. (Syria)	805: Adad-nirari III rising in Assyria. Went against Syria. 802: Aram (Syria) was prostrate. This allowed Joash to recover lost territory.	**Joahaz** *16 (17)* ......814-798 Israel in pretty bad shape. **Joash** *16* ....798-782 In war with Ben-hadad, king of Aram, recovered lost territory. Defeated Amaziah, reducing Judah to vassal. Assassinated in palace revolt.
Amaziah *29* ....797-769 Defeated by Joash, king of Israel. Assassinated in palace revolt.		
Uzziah (Azariah) *36 (52)* 769-734		**Jeroboam II** *35 (41)* .783-748 Strong member of Jehu dynasty.

(In this period, both Israel and Judah regained prosperity and power.)

Reconquered Elam. Restored trade lines. Built in the deserts. Stable time for state. **Jotham (co-regent)** ..749-734 **(King)** 734	Assyria and Egypt were both weak. Tiglath-Pileser (called Pul in Bible) (745-727) went against Babylon, Assyria proper, and northern cities of Syria. 738: Pul fought coalition in central Syria (may have been led by Uzziah).	Regained Solomonic boundaries to north. PROPHETS: *Amos* ..c. 752-738 *Hosea* . c. 746-735 **Zechariah** *6 mo.* ....748 **Shallum** *1 mo.* ....748 **Menahem** *10* ....748-738 Paid for Assyrian help. **Pekahiah** *2* 738-736

JUDAH

Ahaz *20 (16)* 734-715

Refused to join coalition against Assyria. Attacked by Syria and Israel (c. 20,000 killed). Some of Ahaz' sons killed.

Against advice of *Isaiah,* sought aid from Tiglath-Pileser V in 732. Subsequently Assyria attacked Damascus.

PROPHETS: *Isaiah* ....(734*ff*)
Micah

Isaiah urged against coalition with Syria and Israel.

Related History

Tiglath-Pileser leveled Syria and took the world. Tried to break up nationalism. Left Israel with homogeneous population.

Egypt had declined to pure chaos. Hoshea sought help from them, but it failed to materialize.

In Assyria, Shalmaneser V took over. Samaria finally fell under him, or more probably, Sargon II.

Israel a fourth Assyrian province.

ISRAEL

Pekah *4 (20)*......736-732/1

Ally of Rezin of Aram (Syria), against Assyria (Judah refused to join coalition). Troops sent on Judah. Jerusalem held.

Damascus attacked by Tiglath-Pileser V.

Assyria attacked Israel, took all but Ephraim and Western Manasseh (733). Hoshea appointed to succeed him.

Hoshea 9 ......732/1-723/2

Appointed by Assyrians.

Revolted. Israel (Samaria) taken in 722, by Assyria, probably under Sargon II. 27,290 Israelites taken.

JUDAH ALONE

JUDAH

Ahaz 734-715

Judah preserved by vassalage alliance and Ahaz' worship of Assyrian gods.

Hezekiah 29 715-687

715: Cleansed temple of Assyrian cult-matter, breaking vassalage relationship. Attempted reestablishment of Davidic empire and true worship. Began revolt.

705: Revolt came to head with death of Sargon and accession of Sennacherib. Hezekiah was joined by Philistia, Ekron, Askelon, Babylonia, and Ethiopia. Arab mercenaries were hired.

Moab and Edom backed out of the alliance. Philistia and Egypt were defeated.

Hezekiah forced to come to terms with Sennacherib at Lachish. Paid enormous tribute and surrendered much territory.

689: Hezekiah ready to revolt again.

689-687: Sennacherib's second attack on Judah. Troops decimated by plague. Sennacherib returned home, where he was slain by his sons.

PROPHETS: *Isaiah* and *Micah*

Related History

720: Sargon defeated Hamath at Qarqar, and put down revolt in Egypt. No revolt left in West.

717: Sargon razed Carchemish.

705: Sennacherib succeeds Sargon as king of Assyria.

701: Sennacherib began western campaign of division and conquest. Mopped up everything but Jerusalem, including 46 walled cities, and 200,000 prisoners.

701: Sennacherib returned to put down Babylonian rebellion. This completed in 700.

691: Sennacherib defeated at Tigris by Babylon and Elamites.

689: Sennacherib defeated Babylon and was once more free to come west.

Assyria made several forays against Egypt in this period. In one of these, Esarhaddon the king was killed. Succeeded by Asshurbanipal.

663: Sack of Thebes.

661: Death of Asshurbanipal. Decline began.

JUDAH

Mannasseh *45* 687-642
Evil and notorious. Practiced child sacrifice.

Amon *2* 642-640
Murdered in uprising by anti-Assyrian party. Josiah set up in his place.

Josiah *31* 640/39-609/8
Made king at age eight by "people of the land."
Instituted religious revival in eighth year of his reign.
Took Assyrian provinces of Gilead, Megiddo, and Samaria.

622: Book of the Covenant found in temple.
Extirpation of Bull cult at Bethel.
Covenant renewed.

609: Killed while trying to stop Necho II from attacking Nebuchadnezzar.
PROPHETS: *Zephaniah* ....(c. 625-615)
Nahum . ...(c. 612)
Jeremiah . ...(c. 628-580)

Jehoahaz II (Shallum) *3 mos.* 609/8

Jehoiakim *11* 609/8-597
Placed on throne by Pharaoh Necho II.
Loyal to Nebuchadnezzar, though unwillingly.

601: Revolted, probably after Nebuchadnezzar suffered defeat from Egypt.
PROPHETS: *Jeremiah* and *Habakkuk*

Jehoiachin *3 mos.* 597
Powerless. Taken to Babylon in first deportation. Territory of Judah radically reduced.

Zedekiah (Mattanai) *11* 597-587
Appointed by Nebuchadnezzar.
Began to talk of revolt, based on hope of Egyptian aid.

587: Jerusalem fell after siege of a year and a half. Second great deportation.

Related History

Egypt: Psamtik I began to reign in 663. Weak, but ambitious ruler. Revival of Egyptian culture.

628: Death of Asshurbanipal, king of Assyria. Succeeded by Assur-etil-itani, then by Sin-shar-ishkun. A time of chaos in Assyria.
Babylon: Nabopolasser rising.
Assyria:
Indo-Aryan tribes moving. Medes coming westward.

612: Cyaxares, king of Medes, destroyed Nineveh (*See* NAHUM), killed Sin-shar-ishkun. Conquered Iran in 610-609. This completed fall of Assyria.

Egypt: Psamtik followed by Necho II (609-594). Tried to save Assyria from Babylon, then a rump nation of Assyria. Josiah tried to prevent this and was killed. May have saved Nebuchadnezzar.
Necho put Jehoiakim (Eliakim) on the throne of Judah, taking Shallum hostage.

605: Nebuchadnezzar defeated Necho at Carchemish. Returned to Babylon to establish successful dynasty.

Egypt: Psamtik II and Hophra made token effort to help Judah against Babylon, but nothing more.

Alphabetical Table of the First Lines of the Psalms

Miracles Recorded in the Scriptures

IN THE OLD TESTAMENT

In Egypt

Aaron's rod turned to serpent ....Exodus 7:10-12.
The plagues:
Water made blood.....Exodus 7:20-25.
Frogs ....Exodus 8:5-14.
Lice ....Exodus 8:16-18.
Flies ....Exodus 8:20-24.
Murrain ....Exodus 9:3-6.
Boils and Blains.......Exodus 9:8-11.
Thunder and hail......Exodus 9:22-26.
Locusts ....Exodus 10:12-19.
Darkness ....Exodus 10:21-23.
Slaying of firstborn.....Exodus 12:29-30.
Parting of Red Sea.......Exodus 14:21-31.

In the Wilderness

Curing of waters of Marah ....Exodus 15:23-25.
Sending of manna........Exodus 16:14-35.
Water from the rock.....Exodus 17:5-7.
Death of Nadab and Abihu ....Leviticus 10:1-2.
Burning of the congregation ....Numbers 11:1-3.
Death of Korah, etc.....Numbers 16:31-35.
Budding of Aaron's rod...Numbers 17:8.
Water at Meribah........Numbers 20:7-11.
The brazen serpent......Numbers 21:8, 9.
Stoppage of Jordan......Joshua 3:14-17.

In Canaan

Fall of Jericho..........Joshua 6:6-25.
Staying of sun and moon..Joshua 10:12-14.

Under the Kings

Death of Uzzah.........2 Samuel 6:7.
Withering of Jeroboam's hand ....1 Kings 13:4-6.

By Elijah

Staying of oil and meal...1 Kings 17:14-16.
Raising of widow's son...1 Kings 17:17-24.
Burning of the sacrifice at Carmel ....1 Kings 18:30-38.
Burning of the captains...2 Kings 1:10-12.
Dividing of Jordan......2 Kings 2:7, 8.

By Elisha

Dividing of Jordan.......2 Kings 2:14.
Cure of Jericho waters....2 Kings 2:21, 22.
Destruction of mocking children ....2 Kings 2:23, 24.
Supply of waters to armies ....2 Kings 3:16-20.
Increase of widow's oil...2 Kings 4:2-7.
Raising Shunammite's son.2 Kings 4:32-37.
Healing the poison pottage ....2 Kings 4:38-41.
Twenty loaves for 100 men ....2 Kings 4:42-44.
Cure of Naaman's leprosy.2 Kings 5:10-27.
Making the axe swim.....2 Kings 6:5-7.
Smiting the Syrian army..2 Kings 6:18-20.
Revival of the dead......2 Kings 13:21.

Mentioned by Isaiah

Destruction of Assyrians..2 Kings 19:35.
Return of sun on dial.....2 Kings 20:9-11.

During the Captivity

Deliverance from fiery furnace ....Daniel 3:19-27.
Deliverance from lions' den ....Daniel 6:16-23.

Miscellaneous

Smiting of Philistines....1 Samuel 5:3-12.
Deliverance of Jonah.....Jonah 2:1-10.

IN THE NEW TESTAMENT

The Miracles of Jesus

Nature of the Miracle	Matthew	Mark	Luke	John
Contained in One Gospel Only				
Two blind men restored	9:27-31			
Healing of the Dumb Demoniac	9:32, 33			
Tribute Money in the Mouth of a Fish	17:24-27			
Deaf and Dumb Man Cured		7:31-37		
Blind Man Healed		8:22-26		
Jesus Escapes Unseen from His Pursuers			4:30	
First Miraculous Draught of Fishes			5:1-11	
Widow of Nain's Son Raised			7:11-17	
Woman with an Infirmity Healed			13:10-17	
Man with Dropsy Cured			14:1-6	
Lepers Cleansed			17:11-19	
Ear of the High Priest's Servant Restored			22:50, 51	
Water Turned into Wine				2:1-11
Nobleman's Son Healed of Fever				4:46-54
Impotent Man at the Pool of Bethesda				5:1-16
Man Blind from Birth Healed				9:1-41
Raising of Lazarus				11:1-46
Second Draught of Fishes				21:1-11
In Two Gospels				
Unclean Spirit Cast Out		1:23-26	4:33-37	
Centurion's Servant Healed	8:5-13		7:1-10	
Blind and Dumb Demoniac	12:22		11:14	
Daughter of Syrophenician Woman Cured	15:21-28	7:24-30		
Four Thousand Fed	15:32-39	8:1-9		
Fig Tree Cursed	21:18-22	11:12-14		
In Three Gospels				
Cleansing a Leper	8:1-4	1:40-45	5:12-15	
Peter's Wife's Mother Cured	8:14, 15	1:30, 31	4:38, 39	
Tempest Stilled	8:23-27	4:36-41	8:22-25	
Devils Cast into Swine	8:28-34	5:1-20	8:26-40	
Palsied Man Cured	9:1-8	2:3-12	5:18-26	
Healing Woman with the Issue of Blood	9:20-22	5:25-34	8:43-48	
Jairus' Daughter Raised	9:23-25	5:22-24 5:35-43	8:41, 42 8:49-56	
Withered Hand Restored on the Sabbath	12:10-13	3:1-5	6:6-10	
Jesus Walks on the Sea	14:22-32	6:47-51		6:16-21
Lunatic Child Healed	17:14-18	9:17-29	9:37-42	
Blind Bartimeus	20:30-34	10:46-52	18:35-43	
In All Gospels				
Feeding the Five Thousand	14:15-21	6:34-44	9:12-17	6:5-13

Miracles of the Disciples of Jesus

Lame man at Temple gate healed. Acts 3:1-11
Death of Ananias.............. Acts 5:5-11
Death of Sapphira.............. Acts 5:5-11
Many sick healed.............. Acts 5:12-16
Apostles delivered from prison... Acts 5:19
Miracles of Stephen............ Acts 6:8
Miracles of Philip.............. Acts 8:6
Saul's blindness .... Acts 9:3-9
Ananias recovers Saul.......... Acts 9:17
Peter heals Aeneas............. Acts 9:33-35
Dorcas restored to life.......... Acts 9:36-40
Peter delivered from prison...... Acts 12:6-11
Elymas blinded .... Acts 13:11
Cripple healed at Lystra......... Acts 14:8-10
Damsel with spirit of divination.. Acts 16:16-19
Miracles by Paul............... Acts 19:11
Eutychus raised .... Acts 20:8-10
Viper's bite harmless.......... Acts 28:3-6
Publius' father healed.......... Acts 28:8, 9

Comprehensive SUBJECT INDEX

Index

Primary references to subjects appear in **bold face type**; secondary references are in regular type face.

A

B

C

K

L

Bibliography

THE FOLLOWING BOOKS have been of great help to the author in preparing the articles in this book and will make valuable additions to any religious library.

Bright, John. *A History of Israel.* Philadelphia: Westminster Press, 1959.

A Companion to the Bible. Edited by J. J. von Allmen. New York: Oxford University Press, 1958.

Encyclopedia of Religion and Ethics. Edited by James Hastines. 13 volumes. Edinburgh: T. and T. Clark, 1909.

Hastings' Dictionary of the Bible. Edited by James Hastings. New York: Charles Scribner's Sons, 1909.

International Standard Bible Encyclopedia. Edited by James Orr. 5 volumes. Grand Rapids, Michigan: Wm. B. Eerdmans, 1957.

The Interpreter's Dictionary of the Bible. 4 volumes. New York: Abingdon Press, 1962.

Miller, Madeleine S. and Miller, J. Lane. *Harper's Bible Dictionary.* New York: Harper and Brothers, 1952.

Nave's Topical Bible. Nashville, Tennessee: The Southwestern Company, 1960.

The New Bible Dictionary. Edited by J. D. Douglas. London: The Inter-Varsity Fellowship, 1962.

Peake's Commentary on the Bible. Edited by Matthew Black and H. H. Rowley. New York: Thomas Nelson and Sons Ltd., 1962.

Richardson, Alan. *An Introduction to the Theology of the New Testament.* New York: Harper and Brothers, 1958.

———. *A Theological Word Book of the Bible.* New York: Macmillan Company, 1960.

Wright, G. Ernest. *Biblical Archaeology.* Philadelphia: Westminster Press, 1957. Also available in paperback abridged edition.

——— and Freedman, David Noel. *The Biblical Archaeologist Reader.* Garden City, New York: Anchor Books, 1961.

Biblical Map Index

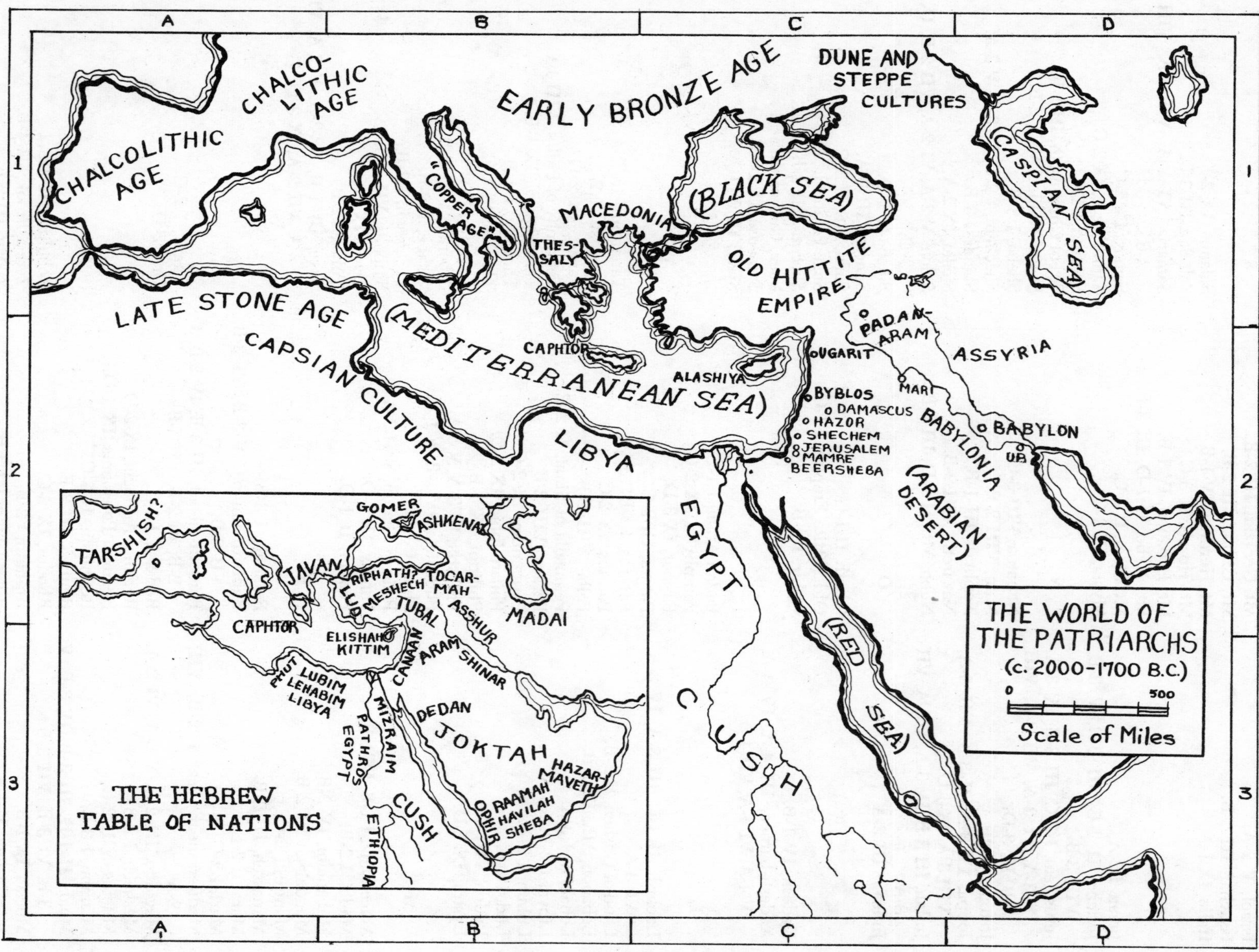
A
B
C
D
1
2
3
CHALCOLITHIC AGE
CHALCO-LITHIC AGE
EARLY BRONZE AGE
DUNE AND STEPPE CULTURES
"COPPER AGE"
MACEDONIA
(BLACK SEA)
CASPIAN SEA
THES-SALY
OLD HITTITE EMPIRE
LATE STONE AGE
CAPSIAN CULTURE
(MEDITERRANEAN SEA)
CAPHTOR
ALASHIYA
LIBYA
UGARIT
PADAN-ARAM
ASSYRIA
MARI
BYBLOS
DAMASCUS
HAZOR
SHECHEM
JERUSALEM
MAMRE
BEERSHEBA
BABYLONIA
BABYLON
UR
(ARABIAN DESERT)
EGYPT
CUSH
(RED SEA)
THE WORLD OF THE PATRIARCHS
(c. 2000-1700 B.C.)
0
500
Scale of Miles
TARSHISH?
GOMER
ASHKENAZ
JAVAN
RIPHATH?
TOGAR-MAH
LUD
MESHECH
TUBAL
ASSHUR
MADAI
CAPHTOR
ELISHAH
KITTIM
CANAAN
ARAM
SHINAR
PHUT
LUBIM
LEHABIM
LIBYA
MIZRAIM
PATHROS
EGYPT
DEDAN
JOKTAH
HAZAR-MAVETH
RAAMAH
OPHIR
HAVILAH
SHEBA
CUSH
ETHIOPIA
THE HEBREW TABLE OF NATIONS

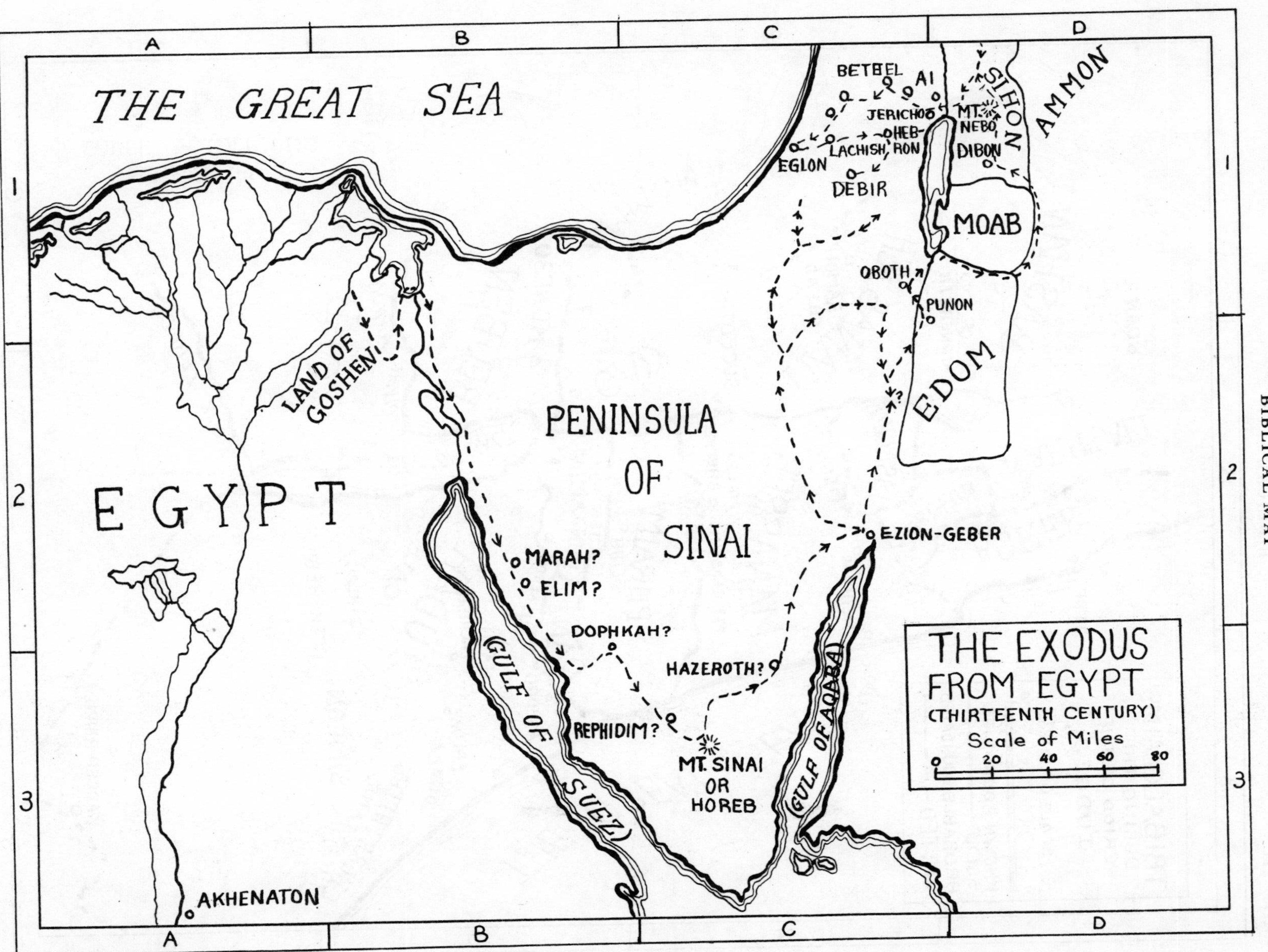
THE EXODUS
FROM EGYPT
(THIRTEENTH CENTURY)
Scale of Miles
0 20 40 60 80
THE GREAT SEA
EGYPT
PENINSULA
OF
SINAI
LAND OF
GOSHEN
AMMON
SIHON
MOAB
EDOM
MT. NEBO
DIBON
BETBEL
AI
JERICHO
HEB-RON
LACHISH
DEBIR
EGLON
OBOTH
PUNON
EZION-GEBER
HAZEROTH?
MT. SINAI
OR
HOREB
DOPHKAH?
REPHIDIM?
MARAH?
ELIM?
(GULF OF SUEZ)
(GULF OF AQABA)
AKHENATON
A
B
C
D
1
2
3

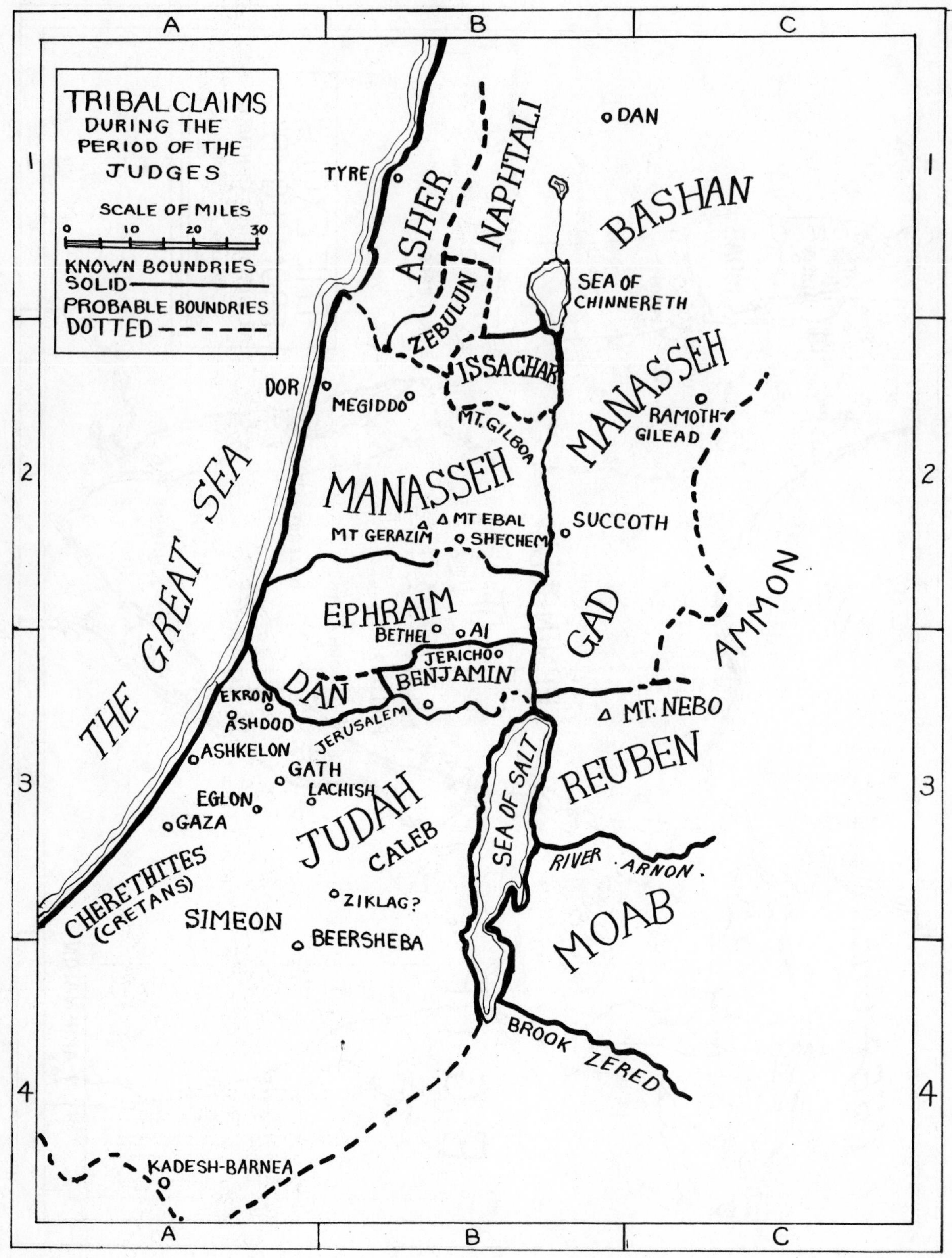
A
B
C
1
2
3
4
TRIBAL CLAIMS DURING THE PERIOD OF THE JUDGES
SCALE OF MILES
0 10 20 30
KNOWN BOUNDRIES SOLID
PROBABLE BOUNDRIES DOTTED
TYRE
ASHER
NAPHTALI
DAN
BASHAN
SEA OF CHINNERETH
ZEBULUN
ISSACHAR
DOR
MEGIDDO
MT. GILBOA
MANASSEH
RAMOTH-GILEAD
THE GREAT SEA
MANASSEH
MT EBAL
MT GERAZIM
SHECHEM
SUCCOTH
EPHRAIM
BETHEL
AI
GAD
AMMON
JERICHO
BENJAMIN
DAN
EKRON
ASHDOD
JERUSALEM
MT. NEBO
ASHKELON
GATH
LACHISH
SEA OF SALT
REUBEN
EGLON
GAZA
JUDAH
CALEB
RIVER ARNON
CHERETHITES (CRETANS)
SIMEON
ZIKLAG?
BEERSHEBA
MOAB
BROOK ZERED
KADESH-BARNEA

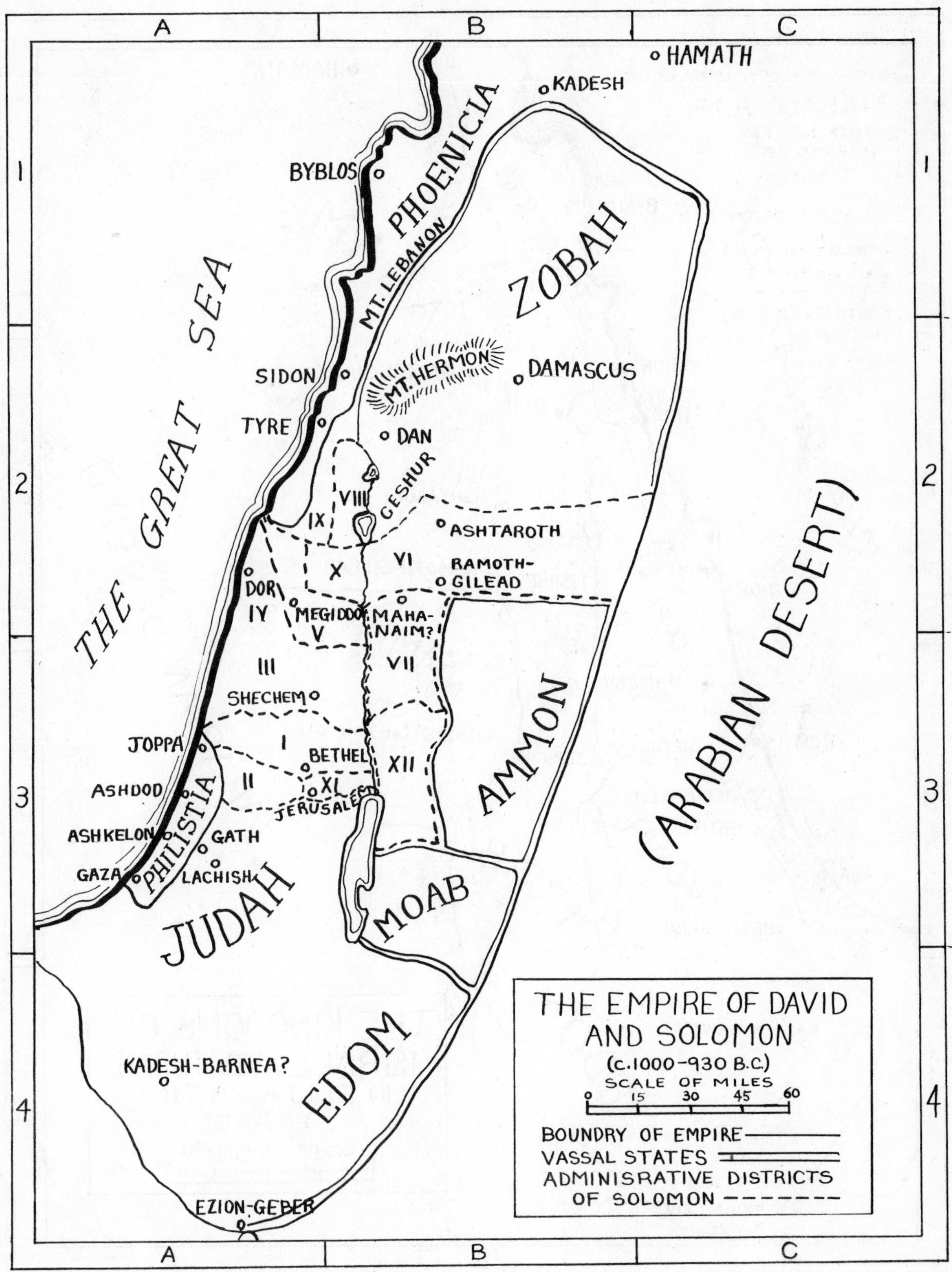
A
B
C
1
2
3
4
HAMATH
KADESH
PHOENICIA
BYBLOS
MT. LEBANON
ZOBAH
THE GREAT SEA
MT. HERMON
SIDON
DAMASCUS
TYRE
DAN
GESHUR
VIII
IX
ASHTAROTH
X
VI
RAMOTH-
GILEAD
DOR
IY
MEGIDDO
V
MAHA-
NAIM?
III
VII
(ARABIAN DESERT)
SHECHEM
AMMON
JOPPA
I
BETHEL
XII
II
XI
ASHDOD
PHILISTIA
JERUSALEM
ASHKELON
GATH
GAZA
LACHISH
JUDAH
MOAB
EDOM
KADESH-BARNEA?
EZION-GEBER
THE EMPIRE OF DAVID
AND SOLOMON
(c.1000-930 B.C.)
SCALE OF MILES
0 15 30 45 60
BOUNDRY OF EMPIRE
VASSAL STATES
ADMINISRATIVE DISTRICTS
OF SOLOMON

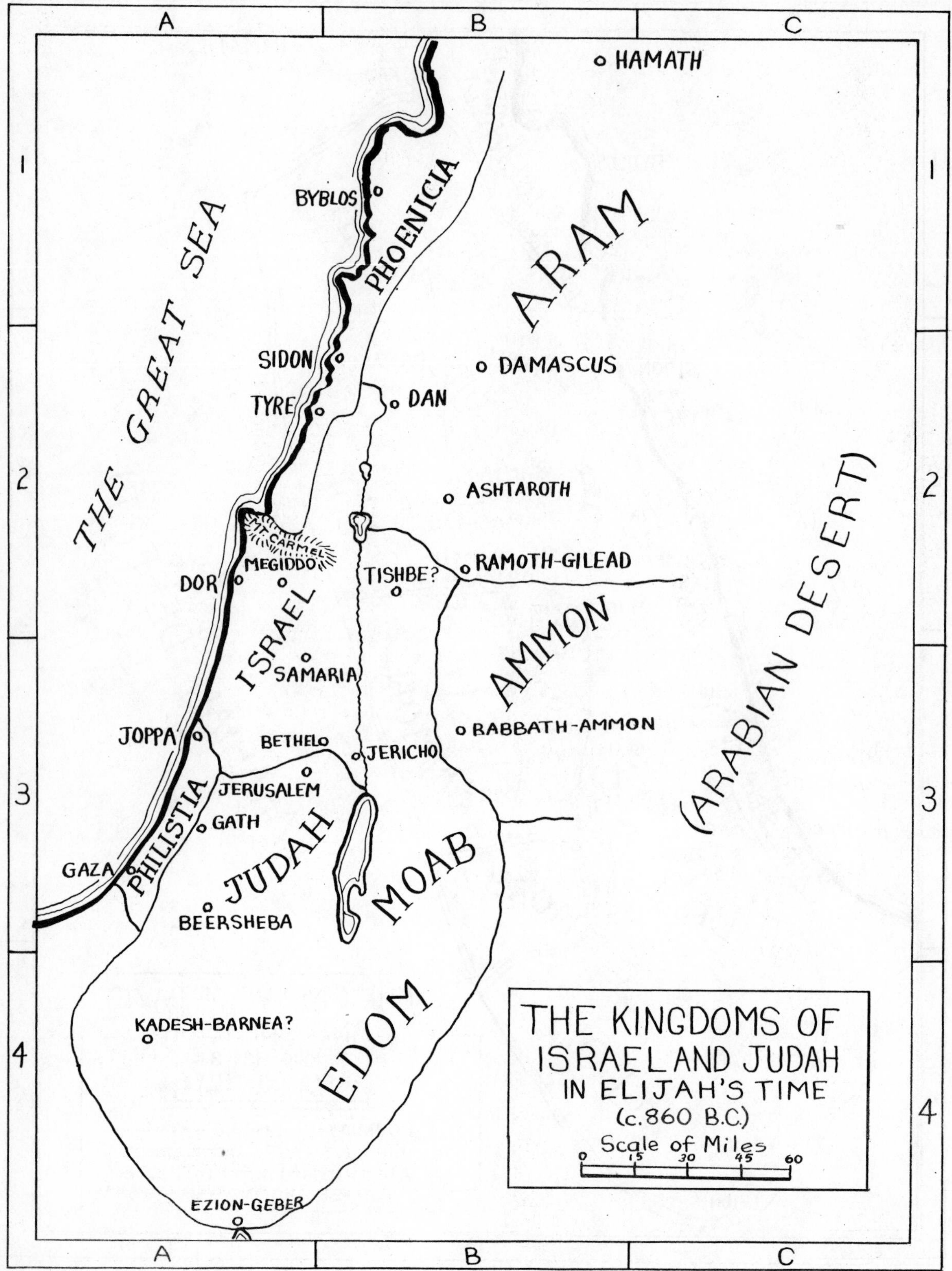

A
B
C
1
2
3
4
HAMATH
BYBLOS
PHOENICIA
THE GREAT SEA
ARAM
SIDON
DAMASCUS
TYRE
DAN
ASHTAROTH
(ARABIAN DESERT)
MT. CARMEL
MEGIDDO
RAMOTH-GILEAD
DOR
TISHBE?
ISRAEL
AMMON
SAMARIA
JOPPA
BETHEL
JERICHO
BABBATH-AMMON
JERUSALEM
PHILISTIA
GATH
GAZA
JUDAH
MOAB
BEERSHEBA
EDOM
KADESH-BARNEA?
EZION-GEBER
THE KINGDOMS OF
ISRAEL AND JUDAH
IN ELIJAH'S TIME
(c.860 B.C.)
Scale of Miles
0 15 30 45 60

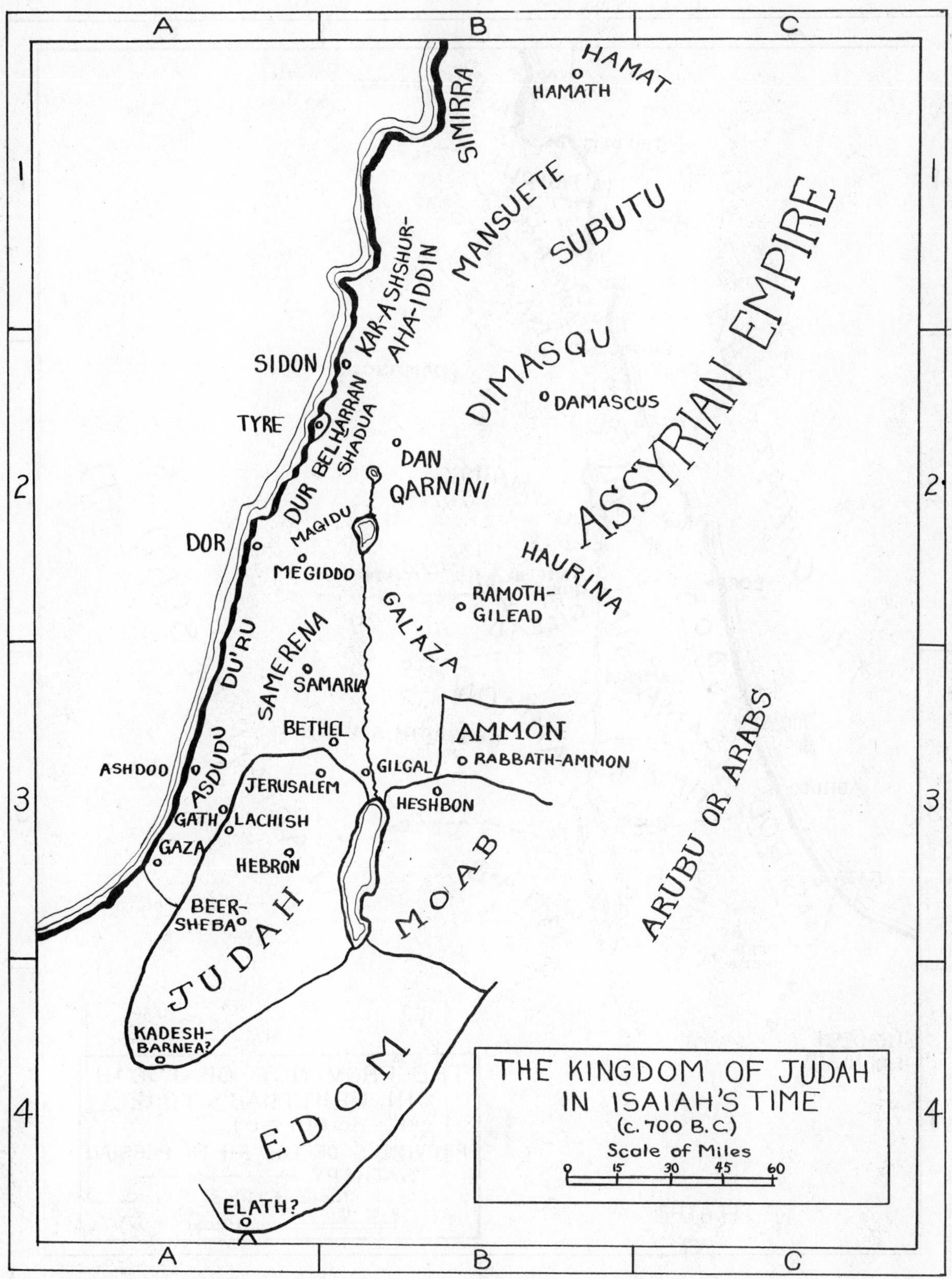
A
B
C
1
2
3
4
HAMAT
HAMATH
SIMIRRA
MANSUETE
SUBUTU
ASSYRIAN EMPIRE
KAR-ASHSHUR-
AHA-IDDIN
SIDON
DIMASQU
DAMASCUS
TYRE
DUR BELHARRAN
SHADUA
DAN
QARNINI
MAGIDU
DOR
MEGIDDO
HAURINA
RAMOTH-
GILEAD
GAL'AZA
DU'RU
SAMERENA
SAMARIA
BETHEL
AMMON
RABBATH-AMMON
ASHDOD
ASDUDU
GILGAL
JERUSALEM
HESHBON
GATH
LACHISH
GAZA
HEBRON
ARUBU OR ARABS
BEER-
SHEBA
JUDAH
MOAB
KADESH-
BARNEA?
EDOM
ELATH?
THE KINGDOM OF JUDAH
IN ISAIAH'S TIME
(C. 700 B. C.)
Scale of Miles
0 15 30 45 60

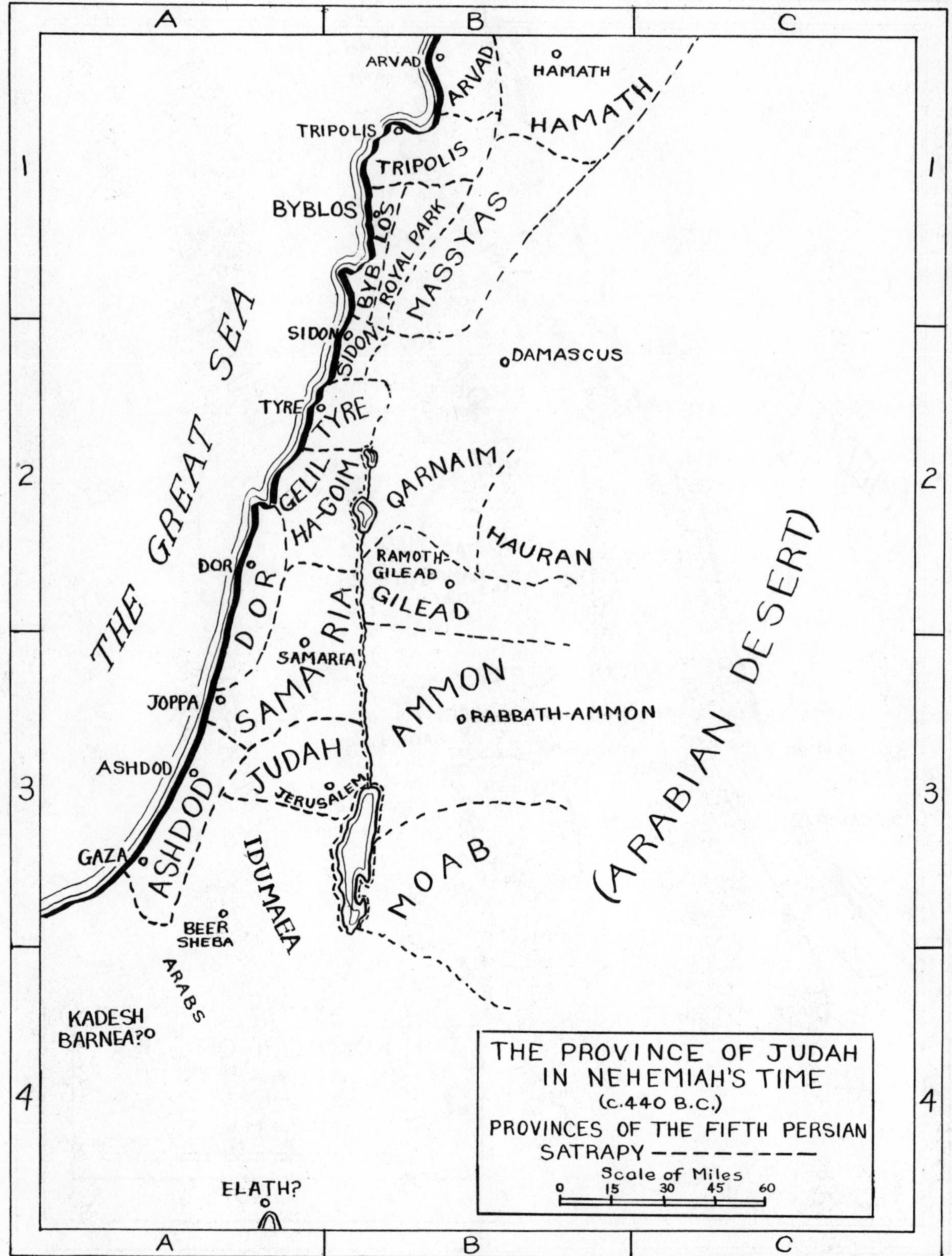
A
B
C
1
2
3
4
ARVAD
ARVAD
HAMATH
HAMATH
TRIPOLIS
TRIPOLIS
BYBLOS
BYBLOS
ROYAL PARK
MASSYAS
SIDON
SIDON
DAMASCUS
THE GREAT SEA
TYRE
TYRE
GELIL HA-GOIM
QARNAIM
HAURAN
RAMOTH-GILEAD
GILEAD
DOR
DOR
SAMARIA
SAMARIA
JOPPA
AMMON
RABBATH-AMMON
(ARABIAN DESERT)
ASHDOD
ASHDOD
JUDAH
JERUSALEM
GAZA
IDUMAEA
MOAB
BEER SHEBA
ARABS
KADESH BARNEA?
ELATH?
THE PROVINCE OF JUDAH IN NEHEMIAH'S TIME
(c.440 B.C.)
PROVINCES OF THE FIFTH PERSIAN SATRAPY --------
Scale of Miles
0 15 30 45 60

A
B
C
1
2
3
4
(MEDITERRANEAN SEA)
CAESAREA PHILIPPI
TETRARCHY OF PHILIP
CHORAZIN
CAPERNAUM
BETHSAIDA
MAGDALA
GERGESA
TIBERIAS
SEA OF GALILEE
GALILEE
NAZARETH
NAIN
DECAPOLIS
CAESAREA
PLAIN OF SHARON
PELLA
PERAEA
SAMARIA
SAMARIA
GERASA
ANTIPATRIS
JOPPA
LYDDA
EPHRAIM?
JERICHO
BETHANY BEYOND JORDAN?
EMMAUS
JERUSALEM
BETHPHAGE?
BETHANY
BETHLEHEM
ASCALON
GAZA
JUDAEA
HEBRON
DEAD SEA
IDUMAEA
NABATAEA
PALESTINE
DURING THE
MINISTRY OF JESUS
Scale of Miles
0 5 10 15 20 25 30

THE LANDS OF
PAUL'S JOURNEYS
SCALE OF MILES
0 100 200 300
(BLACK SEA)
(ADRIATIC SEA)
(MEDITERRANEAN SEA)
ITALIA
ROME
TARENTUM
SICILIA
SYRACUSE
PANNONIA
DALMATIA
DACIA
MOESIA
THRACIA
MACEDONIA
PHILIPPI
THESSALONICA
BEROEA
ACHAIA
ATHENS
CORINTH
SAMO-
THRACE
TROAS
ASSOS
MYSIA
BYTHYNIA ET PONTUS
PERGAMUM
THYATIRA
SARDIS
ASIA
PHILADELPHIA
EPHESUS
MILETUS
SAMOS
PATMOS
CNIDUS
RHODES
PATARA
CRETE
GALATIA
ANTIOCH
PISIDIA
ICONIUM
LYSTRA
DERBE
PAMPHYLIA
CAPPODOCIA
REGNUM
POLE-
MONIS
ANTIOCHI
REGNUM
CILICIA ET SYRIA
TARSUS
ANTIOCH
CYPRUS
SALAMIS
PAPHOS
SIDON
TYRE
DAMASCUS
CAESAREA
JOPPA
JERUSALEM
GAZA
ARABIA
AEGYPTUS
CYRENAICA
A
B
C
D
1
2
3